The *Virgin* Alternative Guide to British Universities

Piers Dudgeon

THE VIRGIN ALTERNATIVE GUIDE

'The best bar none... Most university guides tell you what grades are needed for entry, but fail to give any impression of what it's really like... *The Virgin Alternative Guide* bridges this gap. Amusing contributions from students already on their way to degrees detail the nitty gritty of student life at each institution, including accommodation, health, living on a shoestring, low- and high- workload courses, union life, societies, sports and – last but not least – watering holes and where to get a decent curry... The guide is based on thorough research [and] includes an official facts section, covering acceptance requirements to employment expectations.'
Times Educational Supplement

'Glistening with success – a worthy contender for the best all-purpose buy for the aspiring undergraduate.'
Yorkshire Post

'This is a very impressive piece of work... a serious and honest picture of student life at each major higher education establishment in the UK... VAG looks set to take over as the nation's favourite antidote to the occasional excesses of the higher education marketing professionals.'
Careers Adviser

'The guide offers racy but reliable profiles that focus as much on the way of life as academic considerations.'
Daily Telegraph

'The value of this book lies in the info-crammed pages on universities, starting with Aberdeen and ending with York.'
The London Evening Standard

'Lesson learned... Get studying this guide!'
Sun

'Welcome to VAG, an invaluable assessment... raw, earthy and direct.'
Wolverhampton Express & Star

'It's the warts and all approach to help students make their choices.'
Leicester Mercury

'Serious and honest'
Times Higher Educational Supplement

'Where you can believe what you read'
Cardiff Western Mail

'Just the thing to make a truly informed choice'
Dundee Sunday Post

This edition first published in 2002
by Virgin Books Ltd
Thames Wharf Studios
Rainville Road
London W6 9HA

First published in Great Britain in
2002 by Virgin Books Ltd

A catalogue record for this title is
available from the British Library.

ISBN 0 7535 0543 6

Use has been made of figures of
first-degree qualifiers entering
employment (1999/00) and population
statistics, source: HESA Individualised
Student Record 2001,
reference December 2001.
Copyright © Higher Education
Statistics Agency Limited, 2002
Reproduced by permission of
the Higher Education Statistics
Agency Limited

HESA cannot accept responsibility for
any inferences or conclusions derived
from the data by third parties.

Design & Technical Consultant
Jonathan Horner

Printed and bound by
Creative Print and Design (Wales),
Ebbw Vale

CONTENTS

CONTENTS

INTRODUCTION

For the first time since its inception in the 11th century, the university sector has become a buyer's market. For the first time you, the applicant, hold the whip hand. And don't the universities just know it! Their PR and marketing departments are in overdrive.

You have choice, but with professional marketing forces at work, that choice is becoming ever more confusing. *VAG* is about interpreting that choice. We use official statistics and special draw-downs from Government databases about everything that goes on day-to-day at each university in the country, but what makes *VAG* special is that we commission student views – views from the ground, research from students who are studying there now – and we go on campus ourselves, we sit in the bars, we talk not simply to student unions, the student-elected ex-students who organise facilities and events on campus and who may themselves be shooting an official line, but to real students, people in the swim.

CHANGE

There is much that is changing. This year, for the first time, I noticed students exercising caution. Since loans replaced grants, many simply cannot afford to go out as much as they did in the 1980s and '90s. The pattern is becoming more of a once or twice-a-week binge, and many of those hugely expensive student union nightclubs are less than full. I noticed this personally on a trawl along the south coast, from Brighton to Plymouth – greatly to be recommended, incidentally, if you want to take the application procedure really seriously, though employ a tape recorder as you'll remember little. Other VAG researchers reported more of the same elsewhere in the country.

There is, however, a more fundamental change afoot. Due to the Government's drive to get 50% of sixthformers into university by 2010, universities are greatly increasing the number of places on offer and they are dropping their offer levels, which is making it much easier (for some) to get in. In the Durham entry I have an interview with a guy called Robin Siddle, who got a place to read Archaeology with an AS level and a GNVQ. Durham is one of the choosiest universities in the country. Robin got a place because he is genuinely interested in his subject, he made an effort to advance himself despite what his teachers told him about Durham's recruitment policy, and he happens to have a toughie of a mum who supports him in everything he does. The lesson is, go for what you really want, whatever anyone says.

Given the wider choice and softer options, it is ever more crucial that you understand where value truly lies. There's no point in listening to your parents because the university pecking order has changed since their day; it is in a continuing process of change. It is now ten years since a whole raft of new universities were formed out of our polytechnics. Many have succeeded in one way or another, and just a few have made the transition to university-of-value in the fullest sense.

VALUE

So what is value in the fullest sense? What makes a university a good investment? Is it the teaching? Is it the type or level of job that a particular degree will get you on graduation?

In the university market good value is not tied to cost. We have masses of information about cost of living, what it costs to survive, accommodate yourself or go out for a night in any part of Britain. If you want to minimise cost you should consider going to a uni close to home, but also consider whether independence from home is part of what going to university is about. You would certainly not choose London, which is horrendously expensive even with the extra loan. Bradford is probably the cheapest option, and, as it happens, there are very good reasons for choosing Bradford which have nothing to do with cost of living. And that is the point. Cost is important, but nothing whatever to do with good value when it comes to choosing a university.

TEACHING

Teaching obviously comes to the fore. Student-staff ratios and views from students about the kind of teaching support and resources available are of interest. More significant are departments that show flair in curriculum design – either *vocational flair*, as at Stirling for example, where a subject is given an application that converts directly into an inspired career prospect, or *creative flair*, as at Sussex, where cross-faculty combinations remove blinkers, provoke original thought associations, make good researchers and articulate, innovative adaptable students in any field. Sussex is hailed as the inventor of this approach. We advise you at all costs to avoid those unis that combine everything with everything else in the curriculum without any guiding principle other than timetable feasibility.

Even more fundamental is teaching ability and time-to-teach. We highlight departments that achieve Excellent ratings (18+ points out of 24) in the Quality Assurance Agency inspections.

Consistent Excellence over the years suggests a teaching culture with deep-rooted character (York, for example).

Teaching may be as much a talent as a skill, at the very least it should be a preoccupation. You can spend three or four years in a cutting-edge research department and come away certain of little more than the number of warts on your professor's face. Take the London School of Economics, for example. More than half its students are postgraduates; only 37% are full-time undergrads. Is their pre-occupation with research an advantage or disadvantage to you as an undergraduate? Do good researchers make good teachers? The student/staff ratio at LSE is 17:1; at Oxford it is 13:1, at Cambridge, 12:1; at Imperial College, 9:1. Recent teaching inspection results have been high, certainly, but not amazing, and why do they scour the four corners of the earth for undergraduates and accept only the cream from UK applications, a conspicuously privileged minority (LSE's independent school intake is 42%, even though only 7% of our children go to independent schools)? The question is, how much value does LSE *add* by means of its teaching? Average A-level points at entry are 28 (340 in new parlance), Oxford's is 29, Cambridge's is 30. But the first class/upper second pass rate at LSE is 70%, as against 83% at Oxford and 89% at Cambridge. How much is it down to LSE's teaching that Fortune 500 companies flock to it to grab the best of its students? *Or would the same students have done as well elsewhere anyway?* There are some students for whom LSE is the best choice in the world; others might founder.

OPEN ACCESS

For sure, university lecturers are going to have to get much better at teaching now that access is open to all. The controversy about Oxbridge picking and choosing its undergraduates – the latest cash-for-places crisis notwithstanding – has arisen as a result of the Government's demand that every university meets certain benchmark intake figures. Each uni is now set a benchmark as to how many applicants they should take from state/independent schools, how many from social classes IIIM (skilled manual), IV (partly skilled) and V (unskilled) – what we refer to as 'non-traditional student intake' – and, finally, how many they should take from the so-called 'low participation neighbourhoods' (poor post code areas). It is the biggest exercise in social engineering since University College London set up shop as 'the Cockney College' in 1826 in response to Oxford and Cambridge's policy to take exclusively from the privileged classes.

The teaching of the choosiest of universities will have to adapt if they are to reach their new clientele. And it is already happening. Ironically, in 1999/2000 the Cockney College met none of its Government benchmarks, but it is taking measures to ease non-traditional applicants in to the UCL regime. While this revolution proceeds apace, and unless you want to be a guinea pig in the experiment, it is apposite to look at our Student Profile sections to see what kind of applicant each uni currently attracts, but also to note, for example in our Cambridge entry, just how quickly even the most unusual applicant can become swept up in (and intensely loyal to) the culture of their university when said student culture is carefully prepared to have that sort of inclusive effect.

When recently I went to speak to a sixthform at an independent school in North Yorkshire, and mentioned to the headmaster that his privileged students were not especially favoured by the Government's open access policy, he said, 'For God's sake don't say too much about that! They're uncertain enough as it is!' But I like to think, perhaps wishfully, that the Government's eye is not on making life unfair or fair for anyone, but on cranking up teaching quality and making it available to all irrespective of socio-economic background. Hence, *uni-versity*, uniting diversity through education.

For the time being, official entry grades still vary widely and applicants should be wary of assuming that the best universities are those that ask most points at entry in the face of teaching inspections and assessments which accord real value elsewhere. For this reason we now publish a subject by subject Entry Table which carries teaching inspection results.

GRADUATE EMPLOYMENT

But, I hear you say, that's all very well. What happens when I opt for a uni with low entry requirements and high inspection results and a future employer shares the popular misconception as to reputation? I'd rather go off to a job interview with a degree from Oxford or Cambridge under my arm than one from Northumberland or Bristol West of England.

The first point is that employers these days are amazingly well informed. Increasingly they actually influence or design course form and structure at degree level. Second, the facts do not support your view. Our information on graduate employability is no longer limited to numbers of graduates in employment six months after graduation – fairly meaningless, when there's only a handful of percentage points between the worst and the best university records. Today, we tap in to the Government's Higher Statistics Agency database in Cheltenham, which records where almost everybody ends up and from which uni/subject/department they come.

We now know, for example, that City University or Heriot-Watt or even Napier are more focused on getting graduates jobs in the financial sector than Oxford, which is actually the fourth most dedicated uni in this regard. So, if you want a job in the financial sector, it should interest you to look at all these and, indeed, at London Guildhall, York, Essex, Bournemouth, East Anglia and Imperial College.

Another interesting dimension is that very often a graduate employment focus comes not from a course but from some sort of extra-curricular activity in which the university excels. There is, for example, no dedicated media course at Exeter, but journalism and radio/TV are both strong graduate employment areas in Exeter's graduate employment portfolio because they have award-winning media societies in their Students' Union.

STUDENT CULTURE

This wakes us up to the fact that value is not limited to course availability or teaching. Employers have understood this for ages. Research shows that graduate recruiters seek at least two qualities above degree classification – enthusiasm and oral communication (an ability to speak clearly, to argue logically, persuasively, and to be interesting). Almost as highly rated is an ability to solve problems, to communicate effectively using the written word, to exercise so-called personal/transferable skills (presenting and marketing yourself), to work well as a team member, etc... And our core message to university applicants is that you will acquire these skills most effectively not in the lecture theatre or tutorial room, nor parrot-fashion in some workshop, but by becoming immersed in a vibrant student culture, which, in VAG, it is our purpose to rate, uni by uni.

By 'culture', people understand 'theatre, classical music, art', but that is popular usage of the word. Think of culture in the scientific sense as a nutrient substance in which micro-organisms appear and grow. For micro-organisms read 'skills graduate recruiters want'. For culture read 'the total range of activities and ideas of a group of students at a particular university'.

On one level, the importance of student culture justifies the Government open-access strategy to make particular student bodies more diverse. For demographic diversity – a student body drawn from a range of backgrounds and cultures – is bound to lead to a richer experience, as well as to enhance empathy and understanding.

It is a fact, for example, that throughout the length and breadth of this country Islamic Soc is the most popular student society, and strength in number appears not always to flow from a high Islamic student population. This fact is true from Dundee in the north to East London in the south, from Lampeter in the west to South Bank in the east. Nor was this something chased in by September 11th, though as the entries for both Exeter and Sussex show, the eye-balling by Imperial West of Fundamentalist East has served to crystallise a context in which it would show. We see it rather as a nationwide change of gear – two decades of club-loons giving way to one in which students are seriously rehearsing the idea that university might be an opportunity not only to learn facts and skills and get out of your head, but also to grow as an individual, and gain self-possession and control.

When you go to university the first thing you will have to survive is Freshers Week, a mad round of drinking and clubbing and getting to know other first-year undergraduates. Central to this first week will be the Freshers Fair, where the student societies set out their stalls and try and get you to become a member. These societies cover anything you care to imagine, from Islamic Soc to Cock Soc – that's generally something to do with cocktails. Consider how some of these could impart skills and broaden your perspective on life. Debating or Drama would obviously enhance oral communication; Rugby, teamwork; Role-play, problem-solving; the university magazine, your written communication skills... and Cock Soc possibly your stamina. Above all, get involved, and right now make your choice on this basis from among the tapestries that unfurl before you.

In VAG 2003 we have levelled criticism at some new universities for failing to see that skills demanded by employers are imbibed through ethos or the process of activity in student union societies more effectively than in tell-him fashion in seminars or skills workshops. We perceive a failure to realise that this is the significant difference between the old, vocational, polytechnic ethos and that of the university-of-value in the fullest sense.

'New uni' Northumbria has recently made enormous strides in enriching its student culture. To begin with, look at sport. Northumbria's teams came 15th nationally last year, while the older, traditional university in Newcastle, which puts much store by sport, came 19th. In the matter of student media, the radio station – N.S.R. – was nominated for Best Newcomer in the Radio 1 awards two years ago and this year The Nerve, its news programme, was nominated in the category of Best Factual Programme. At the same time,

Northumbria's new magazine, *Incite*, was nominated in the *Independent* newspaper awards in the category of Best Student Magazine. This year Northumbria found itself among the top ten providers of students to journalism in the country, yet the graduates who became journalists didn't come from a course in media studies or journalism. They came from departments like business, engineering, computer and biosciences. There can be few clearer pictures of the impact of student culture on graduate employment than this.

A strong student culture has also enabled Northumberland, possibly more than any other new uni which shares a city with an older, more traditional foundation, to hold its head up and mix well in a multi-faceted society, which you will have to do when you get out into the world: 'I think what is important about being a student in Newcastle,' said a Northumbria student, 'is that the ex-poly and the university mix very well. There is little snobbery, rather a healthy competitive rivalry, especially when it comes to sport. Sport is the only time it gets mentioned that we're an ex-poly; then we're proud to be a poly! They call us the poly kids; we call them the rahs, but very often students find themselves living in a house with both uni and poly students, which is unheard of in places such as Oxford.'

Oxford Brookes is of course as new a university as Northumbria and very good for certain things, business, languages, publishing, property/built environment, etc, but it doesn't have as rich a student culture as Northumbria, and it is rare indeed for students of the two universities in the city of Oxford to co-habit.

So let's get to the nitty gritty:

1. Ignore parents who argue on the basis of how it was in their day. Get informed about the revolution that is going on in higher education.

2. Log on to www.ucas.com. Go to *Students*. Then *Courses*. Then *Undergraduate Course Search*. Then *Courses starting in 2003*. Then *Choose by Subjects*. Suppose you choose English. Well there are 3,143 degree courses in English, but only 397 in Eng Lit. You will then be given the choice as to whether you want to study English with another subject or on its own. This cuts your choice down still further. If you opt for studying English alone you will be asked whether you have a preference of region or particular universities. Assuming that at this stage you don't, all 397 courses will be listed under about 35 university or college headings. Pick a dozen possibles and turn to *VAG*.

Compare entry requirements against teaching assessments. Consider employment rates and strengths. Look at the chances of getting a first or upper second degree – these vary from 40% to over 80%. Read our reviews and consider where you will be happy. City, town or countryside? Lively, impersonal, expensive London? Wild, exciting, affordable Newcastle? Laid-back, rural Lampeter? Beautiful, friendly Durham? Streetwise metropolitan Manchester? Secluded, tight-knit Stirling? How would you respond?

Where there's big-city action, there needs to be Student Union support – late-night bussing, pay-later taxi arrangements, info about off-limits areas, etc. Get a feel of what support's on offer. What kind of situation suits you? Will you thrive on a self-contained campus – Nottingham, Exeter, Bath, Sussex, or at a civic uni, where the buildings are dotted around the city – Bristol, Leeds, Central England, Sheffield? Do you favour strong, public-school-style college loyalties – Durham, Lancaster, Oxbridge, or the more diverse mix of Liverpool John Moores, Leeds Met? Which are the most happening university cities? Which campuses deliver a real buzz? Where's the best social life? Where are the best facilities? Which are good at sport (and how good)? Where does music, theatre, dance, film thrive? What's the student media like? London and some other cities are very expensive. What price survival? Our cost of survival estimate is a student view of cash in pocket for food, beer, local travel + two nights out a week. Accommodation costs are given separately.

Above all, consider what value a university will add to your life, not just in academic terms, but in cultural terms, not simply to enhance certain skills for employers to exploit, but for yourself. For it is time, at last, to do something for yourself.

THE EDITORIAL TEAM

We would like to thank all those students who filled in questionnaires and/or agreed to be interviewed, and those students who actually wrote copy. If you are reading this and are about to go to university, drop us a line, join the editorial team for 2004. Financial and other rewards, and the chance to get yourself in print (looks great on the CV) are the lure, so tarry not. Contact me at:

kau52@dial.pipex.com

Our thanks also to the university statistics departments and admin offices who have provided us with answers to our many questions, to the Quality Assurance Agency for England, and the Funding Councils for Scotland and Wales, who have helped provide us with the latest teaching assessments, to HESA, the Higher Education Statistics Agency, who supplied demographic facts and figures and amazingly detailed information about first degree qualifiers entering employment in 2000. This is copyright information which we have used with their permission and we are happy to print their disclaimer that HESA cannot accept responsibility for any inferences or conclusions which we have made or derived from their data. We are grateful, too, to BUSA – the British Universities Sports Association – who supplied overall team placings for both men and women last session; to the NSDF – National Student Drama Festival who supplied us with an up-to-date listing of their prestigious awards; to the *Guardian* and *Independent*, whose influential Student Media Awards brighten our lives; to BBC Radio 1 for information about the national Student Radio Awards; and to the Reward Group, which offers the only cost-of- living league table in the UK.

DISABLED STUDENTS

From September 2002, the Special Educational Needs and Disability Act 2001 (now part of the Disability Discrimination Act 1995) will start to come into force giving disabled students legal rights against discrimination. The institutions covered by the law are required to make 'reasonable' adjustments for disabled students. The law covers not only the provision of courses, but also admissions and 'student services' such as catering, accommodation finding services and field trips. If you are having any problems getting the support you need, make sure you check what your rights are under the new law.

Below, **Skill**, the National Bureau for Students with Disabilities, explains what support is available for disabled students.

What support can I get?
Every institution has a member of staff responsible for co-ordinating support for disabled students. Often known as the disability co-ordinator or disability officer, it is always worth making contact as early as possible to discuss your support needs. Skill's publication Into Higher Education 2002 provides contact details for disability co-ordinators in the UK.

If you have support needs that are linked directly to your education, then you can apply for Disabled Students' Allowances (DSAs). DSAs can pay for: non-medical helpers, for example sign language interpreters or note takers: specialist equipment, for example a computer if you have difficulty assessing the universities IT resources; and other educational support related to your disability.

Where can I get more information?
Skill produces a range of information sheets and publications including Into Higher Education 2002, which is priced at £2.50 for disabled students or available free of charge on Skill's website, www.skill.org.uk. You can contact Skill with enquiries on their freephone number, 0800 328 5050 (voice), 0800 068 2422 (text), Monday to Thursday, 1:30pm to 4:30pm, or email info@skill.org.uk or visit www.skill.org.uk.

TEACHING EXCELLENCE

The teaching assessment statistics in the Academic Excellence boxes with each university entry are the result of inspections by the QAA and Higher Education Funding Councils for Scotland and Wales. An explanation of how they work is included in the Entry Requirements section on page 14. The Joint Funding Council's Research Assessment for 2001, which gives an idea of a university's strength in depth, rated subjects on an ascending points system of quality: 1, 2, 3a, 3b, 4, 5 and 5*. We have included those courses given 5 or 5*: 5 indicates International Excellence in some sub-areas and National Excellence in virtually all others; 5* indicates International Excellence in a majority of sub-areas and attainable levels of national excellence in all others. Where a league table position in these Research Assessments is mentioned in the running text, it relates to table published by the *Times Higher Education Supplement* on December 14, 2001, which included the Institute of Cancer Research at No. 4, an Institute not included in our Guide.

GRADUATE EMPLOYMENT

Every uni entry carries an Employment file or box. Key Areas of employment constitute 5% + of the total graduate provision by each university. Niche Areas of employment constitute above-average provision. The Top Ten ratings in these Employment boxes show top graduate providers in terms of percentages of graduates placed in employment at each institution; they are, therefore, relative to size of institution.

Piers Dudgeon, April, 2002

ALTERNATIVE UNIVERSITY RANKINGS

As this guide makes plain, there's more to university than academia, even though league tables traditionally concentrate on that aspect of university life. Our categories include teaching ratings, but focus too on student culture, on extra-curricular involvements, societies, club activities, media and arts awards, and on employment prospects.

There are five categories, each worth 20% of the total figure, which determines ranking.

SCENE refers to the campus/city/town social scene and is a percentage computation of the star system included in the *What It's Really Like* box with each university entry.

UNION includes the number of clubs and societies on offer, national team sporting success and national awards for drama and media. Small universities, those with less than 6,500 undergraduates, are weighted (+25 points).

TEACH computes the Excellence percentages included in the *At A Glance* box with each university entry and the number of students that graduate with a first or upper second.

JOBS computes the most recently available graduate employment history, see the *Employment* files with each entry.

SATIS computes drop-out rates after one year, in an attempt to gauge student satisfaction.

PLACE/UNI	SCENE	UNION	TEACH	JOBS	SATIS	TOTAL
1. Nottingham	20	18.6	16.5	19.2	19.4	93.7
2. Leeds	20	19.3	15	19.2	18.8	92.3.
3. Sheffield	20	18.3	15.3	19.2	19.4	92.2
4. Edinburgh	20	16.7	16.9	19	19.2	91.8
5. Manchester	20	16.8	16.2	19.2	19	91.2
6. Oxford	14	19.6	18	19.2	19.6	90.4
7. Birmingham	20	16.3	15.3	19	18.8	89.4
8. Bristol	18	16	16.5	19.2	19.6	89.3
9. University College	20	15.4	16	18.8	18.8	89
10. Newcastle	20	15.9	14.2	19.4	19.2	88.7
11.Cambridge	14	17	18.3	19.2	19.8	88.3
12. Warwick	16	16.2	16.4	19.4	19.4	87.4
13 = Glasgow	20	13.4	15.9	19	18.6	86.9
13 = Imperial	18	14.4	16.1	19.2	19.2	86.9
15. LSE	20	11.9	16.3	19	19.6	86.8
16. Exeter	16	17	14.2	19.2	19	85.4
17. Cardiff	18	17	11.5	19.2	19.2	84.9
18. Bath	16	14.7	15.6	19	19.4	84.7
19. Leicester	20	11.5	13.9	18.8	19	83.2
20. Strathclyde	20	10.2	15.3	19	18.4	82.9
21. Durham	14	16.4	15	18.2	19.2	82.8
22 = York	14	15	15.9	18.6	18.8	82.3
22 = Hull	16	14.5	13.6	19.4	18.8	82.3
24 = King's London	18	11.6	14.5	19	18.6	81.7
24 = Southampton	14	15.5	14.8	18.2	19.2	81.7
26. Liverpool	20	10.2	13.8	18.8	18.6	81.4
27. Sussex	18	13.4	12.2	19.2	18.2	81
28. Aberdeen	16	11.7	15.2	18.8	18.2	79.9
29. Nottingham Trent	18	12.1	11.8	19.6	18	79.5
30 = Northumbria	20	9.6	12.6	18.8	18.2	79.2
30 = East Anglia (UEA)	16	10.6	14.6	18.8	19.2	79.2

PLACE/UNI	SCENE	UNION	TEACH	JOBS	SATIS	TOTAL
30 = UMIST	18	9.6	13.8	19.4	18.4	79.2
33 = St Andrews	10	13.2	17.3	19	19.2	78.7
33 = Brunel	16	13.5	11.8	19	18.4	78.7
33 = Portsmouth	16	13.2	11.9	19	18.6	78.7
36. Lancaster	14	11.9	14.9	19	18.8	78.6
37. Loughborough	12	14.3	13.9	19	19	78.2
38. Leeds Met	20	10.4	10.6	18.2	18.8	78
39. Reading	14	11.9	14.3	19.2	18.4	77.8
40. Manchester Met	20	9.2	11.4	19.2	17.4	77.2
41. Essex	14	12.3	13.6	18.6	18.4	76.9
42. Aston	18	7.5	13.3	19.2	18.6	76.6
43. De Montfort	18	9.5	13.2	18.8	17	76.5
44. Heriot-Watt	16	10.6	12.5	18.8	18.4	76.3
45. Surrey	12	12	14.2	19.2	18.4	75.8
46. West of England	16	10.5	12.2	18.8	18	75.5
47. Stirling	10	11.8	15.7	19.2	18.6	75.3
48. Queen Mary	18	7.3	12.8	19.2	17.8	75.1
49 = Sheffield Hallam	16	9.4	12.4	18.8	18	74.6
49 = Liverpool J M	20	7.5	10.9	18.6	17.6	74.6
51. Plymouth	16	9.4	12.3	18.6	18.2	74.5
52. Kent	12	12.5	12.5	19.2	18.2	74.4
53 = Swansea	14	11.3	10.3	19.2	19	73.8
53 = City	16	7.2	14.0	19	17.6	73.8
55. Bradford	14	8.9	14	18.6	18.2	73.7
56. Brighton	16	8.1	12.3	19	17.6	73
57. Keele	12	10.4	13	18.8	18.6	72.8
58. Oxford Brookes	14	8.7	13	18.8	17.8	72.3
59 = Dundee	16	6.2	12.7	19	18	71.9
59 = Central Lancashire	14	10.7	10.6	19.2	17.4	71.9
61. Royal Holloway	10	10.9	13.3	18.8	18.8	71.8
62. Greenwich	18	7.8	10.5	18.2	17.2	71.7
63. Goldsmiths	18	3.9	12.7	18.8	17.8	71.2
64 = Kingston	16	6.8	11.3	19.2	17.8	71.1
64 = Aberystwyth	12	10.8	10.3	18.8	19.2	71.1
66. Queen's Belfast	12	6.6	14.2	19.2	18.6	70.6
67. Coventry	14	7.7	12.2	18.2	17.4	69.5
68. Teesside	16	8	9.5	18.2	17.4	69.1
69. Gloucestershire	12	10.3	9.5	18	18.8	68.6
70. Bournemouth	16	3.7	11.9	18.8	18	68.4
71. Salford	16	4.1	11.3	19	17.6	68
72. Staffordshire	14	9.3	9.3	18.2	16.4	67.2
73. Bangor	12	8.4	9.7	18.6	18.4	67.1
74 = Westminster	16	2.7	12.8	18.2	17	66.7
74 = Central England	16	3.6	11.5	18.2	17.4	66.7
76. Middlesex	14	6.8	10.8	18.2	16.6	66.4
77. South Bank	16	5.2	11.4	17.6	15.6	65.8
79 = Luton	12	7.5	9.8	19.2	17	65.5
79 = Glasgow Cal	16	2.4	11.5	18.8	16.8	65.5
80. Ulster	10	6.2	13.1	18.2	17.8	65.3
81. Sunderland	12	5.8	11	18.8	17.2	64.8
82 = East London	18	2.4	11	16.2	16.6	64.2
82 = Hertfordshire	12	4.8	10.6	19	17.8	64.2

13

PLACE/UNI	SCENE	UNION	TEACH	JOBS	SATIS	TOTAL
84 = Robert Gordon	12	4.2	11.2	19.2	17.4	64
84 = North London	16	4	10.2	18.2	15.6	64
86 = Anglia	12	3.4	12.4	18.2	17.4	63.4
86 = Cranfield	8	4	14.4	19.6	17.4	63.4
88. Wolverhampton	12	4.7	11.6	17.6	17.2	63.1
89. Derby	14	2.7	10.7	18.2	17.4	63
90. Napier	14	1.8	10.3	18.6	17.8	62.5
91. London Guildhall	16	0.7	9.7	18.6	17.2	62.2
92. Abertay Dundee	14	3.6	9.4	18.4	16.2	61.6
93. Glamorgan	10	6.7	8.3	18.6	17.4	61
94. Huddersfield	12	1.7	10.8	18.6	17.4	60.5
95. Lampeter	10	4.9	8.7	17.4	18	59
96. Thames Valley	14	2.2	7.4	17.8	15.8	57.2
97. Paisley	10	0.7	11.2	17	16	54.9
98. Lincoln	8	1.8	8.8	18.2	17.6	54.4

WHICH SUBJECT?
WHICH UNI FOR BEST VALUE?

Browse our Subject table, use the UCAS course finder (www.ucas.com), then return to read the VAG profiles to find out which uni will suit you.

Column 1 shows university or college; column 2 the ball-park official offer level – always the lowest is shown, the base point level of entry; there are sometimes thousands of different courses for a subject with varying entry requirements. Column 3 shows teaching ratings by outside inspectors.

COLUMN 2: ENTRY REQUIREMENTS – 'A' LEVEL POINTS

A = 120 points
B = 100 points
C = 80 points
D = 60 points
E = 40 points

A full account of the new points tarrif is given on the UCAS website.

In Music, Drama and Art, A level points are not always significant. Look with a curious eye at these top-value universities that have scored well at inspection and ask less at A level. Equally, look with suspicion at the high-demanding unis which have not performed well on inspection.

COLUMN 3: INSPECTION RATINGS

Only Government-funded institutions are subject to inspection (Buckingham University is not). England and Wales began their programme of inspections with three ratings, **Excellent, Satisfactory, Unsatisfactory**, while Scotland marked their assessments **Excellent, Highly Satisfactory, Satisfactory, Unsatisfactory**. Later England and Scotland scored universities with *points* (maximum 4) on each of six criteria:

4 points each: maximum score = 24 points

1. Curriculum Design, Content, Organisation
2. Teaching Learning and Assessment
3. Student Progression and Achievement
4. Student Support and Guidance
5. Learning Resources
6. Quality Assurance and Enhancement

ACCOUNTANCY/FINANCE

ENTRY	UNI/COLLEGE	RATING
High	UMIST	
280 points +	Warwick	
	Edinburgh	Excellent
	LSE	
	Nottingham	
	Queen's Belfast	
	Aston	
	Birmingha	
	Swansea	
	Sheffield	
	Leeds	
	Manchester	
	Newcastle	
	Glasgow	Highly Satis
	Cardiff	Excellent
	City	
	UEA	
	Lancaster	
	Bristol	
	Reading	
	Exeter	
	Southampton	
Medium-High	Loughborough	
240-280 points	Essex	
	Kent	
	Durham	
	Hull	
	Keele	
	Liverpool	
	Aberdeen	Highly Satis
	Kingston	
	Robert Gordon	
	Brunel	
	Bangor	
	Bournemouth	
	Brighton	
	Nottingham Trent	
	Westminster	
Low-Medium	Stirling	Highly Satis
180-240 points	Aberystwyth	Excellent
	Bristol West England	
	Hertfordshire	
	Manchester Met	
	Portsmouth	
	Buckingham	
	Leeds Met	
	Ulster	
	Plymouth	
	Dundee	Excellent
	Northumbria	
	Liverpool JM	
	Wolverhampton	
	Central England	
	North London	
	Sheffield Hallam	
	Heriot-Watt	Highly Satis
	Salford	
	Napier	Satisfactory
	De Montfort	
	Glamorgan	Excellent
	South Bank	
	Staffordshire	
	Central Lancs	
	Huddersfield	
	Luton	
	Middlesex	
	Blackburn	

ENTRY	UNI/COLLEGE	RATING
Low-Medium	UWIC (Cardiff)	
180-240 points	Anglia	
	Coventry	
	Farnborough	
	Lincoln	
	Norwich City	
	Regent's	
	Royal Agric	
Low	Glasgow Cal	Highly Satis
80-180 points	Paisley	Satisfactory
	Sunderland	
	East London	
	Teesside	
	Northampton	
	Southampton Inst	
	Strathclyde	Satisfactory
	Abertay Dundee	Satisfactory
	Bolton Inst	
	Greenwich	
	Oxford Brookes	
	Swansea Inst	
	Gloucestershire	
	Bucks Chilterns	
	Thames Valley	
	Newport	
	Bradford College	
	Croydon	
	London Guildhall	
	Suffolk	
	NEWI	

AGRICULTURE, FORESTRY, AGRICULTURAL SCIENCES

ENTRY	UNI/COLLEGE	RATING
Medium-High	Birmingham	
240-280 points	Sussex	
	Leeds	20
	Kent	
	Glasgow	
Low-Medium	Aberdeen	
180-240 points	Stirling	
	Newcastle	22
	Essex	
	Bangor - Forestry	Excellent
	- Agriculture	Satisfactory
	Dundee	
	Nottingham	23
	Queen's Belfast	21
	Reading	21
	Cranfield	22
	Wye/Imperial	22
	Sheffield Hallam	
	Sunderland	
	Edinburgh	
	South Bank	
	Southampton	
	Chester	
	Brackenhurst/	
	Nottingham Trent	
	Roehampton/Surrey	
	Bournemouth	20
	Coventry	
	Bishop Burton	
	East London	
	Northumbria	
	Royal Agricultural	
Low	UEA	
80 180 points	Scot Agric	

ENTRY	UNI/COLLEGE	RATING
Low	Bolton	
80-180 points	De Montfort	16
	Plymouth	**22**
	Writtle	19
	Aberystwyth - Agric.	Satisfactory
	- Forestry	Excellent
	Anglia	
	Strathclyde	
	Sparsholt	20
	Worcester	
	Harper Adams	**23**
	Gloucestershire	
	Bristol West England	20
	Bucks Chilterns	20
	Derby	
	Northampton	
	Wolverhampton	
	Trinity Carmarthen	Satisfactory
	Central Lancs	18
	Nescot	
	Suffolk	
	Greenwich	20
	Highlands & Islands	

AMERICAN STUDIES

ENTRY	UNI/COLLEGE	RATING
High	Birmingham	22
280 points +	Edinburgh	
	Hull	23
	Nottingham	22
	Sheffield	
	Sussex	23
	Swansea	
	Warwick	
Medium-High	Aberystwyth	
240-280 points	Brunel	21
	Dundee	
	East Anglia	24
	Essex	
	Exeter	
	Keele	24
	Kent	21
	King's College (KCL)	
	Lancaster	
	Leicester	23
	Liverpool J Moores	21
	Manchester	
	UMIST	
	Queen's Belfast	
	Reading	21
	Ulster	22
Low-Medium	Central Lancashire	24
180-240 points	De Montfort	
	Glamorgan	
	King Alfred's College	18
	Lampeter	
	Middlesex	22
	Plymouth	
	Sunderland	
	Wolverhampton	21
Low	Canterbury Christ	21
80-180 points	Derby	21
	East London	
	Gloucestershire	
	Goldsmiths	
	Liverpool Hope	19
	London Guildhall	M
	Manchester Met	

ENTRY	UNI/COLLEGE	RATING
Low	Northampton	18
80-180 points	York St John	17

ARCHAEOLOGY

ENTRY	UNI/COLLEGE	RATING
High	Cambridge	23
280 points +	Oxford	**22**
	St Andrews	
	Sheffield	22
	UCL	23
	Birmingham	
	York	24
	King's College	
	UEA	
Medium-High	Manchester	23
240-280 points	Bristol	
	Reading	23
	Warwick	
	Bradford	22
	Leicester	
	Queen's Belfast	23
	SOAS	
	Kent	
	Durham	23
	Southampton	
	Edinburgh	
	Newcastle	21
	Glasgow	
	Nottingham	21
	Aberdeen	
	Cardiff	Excellent
	Liverpool	22
	Exeter	
	Bangor	
Low-Medium	Lampeter	Excellent
180-240 points	Bournemouth	22
	King Alfred's	
	Chester	
	East London	
Low	Cumbria	
80-180 points	Newport	
	Trinity Carmarthen	

ARCHITECTURE/DESIGN/ENG.

ENTRY	UNI/COLLEGE	RATING
High	Cambridge	Excellent
280 points +	Edinburgh	Highly Satis
	Newcastle	Excellent
	Liverpool	Satisfactory
	Nottingham	Excellent
	Sheffield	Excellent
	Bath	Excellent
	Cardiff	Excellent
	Strathclyde	Excellent
	UCL	Excellent
	Kingston	Satisfactory
Medium-High	Queen's Belfast	Satisfactory
240-280 points	Glasgow School Art	Excellent
	Edinburgh Coll Art	Highly Satis
	Manchester Met	Satisfactory
	Manchester	Satisfactory
	Dundee	Satisfactory
	Leeds	
	Liverpool JM	Satisfactory
	Napier	
	Robert Gordon	
	Bristol West England	

ENTRY	UNI/COLLEGE	RATING
Medium-High	Brighton	Satisfactory
240-280 points	East London	Excellent
	North London	Satisfactory
	Oxford Brookes	Satisfactory
	Portsmouth	Satisfactory
Low-Medium	Leeds Met	Satisfactory
180-240 points	Central England	20
	De Montfort	Satisfactory
	Greenwich	Excellent
	Luton	
	Wolverhampton	
	Paisley	
	Plymouth	Satisfactory
	Sheffield Hallam	20
	Lincoln	Satisfactory
	Nottingham Trent	
	South Bank	Satisfactory
	Robert Gordon	Highly Satis
	Kent Institute	Satisfactory
	Huddersfield	Satisfactory
	Anglia	
	Northumbria	21
Low	Westminster	Satisfactory
80-180 points	Glamorgan	Satisfactory
	Gloucestershire	
	Derby	19
	NEWI	Satisfactory
	Swansea Institute	
	Glasgow Caledonian	

ART: Fine Art/Illustration

Portfolio paramount in most cases.

ENTRY	UNI/COLLEGE	RATING
High	Oxford	24
280 points +	Exeter	
	Leeds	23
Medium-High	Aberystwyth	Satisfactory
240-280 points	Central England	22
	Derby	20
	Newcastle	20
	Northumbria	22
	Nottingham Trent	22
Low-Medium	Lincoln	20
180-240 points	Oxford Brookes	23
	Chester	*20*
	Liverpool J Moores	*19*
	Chichester	22
	Derby	20
	Huddersfield	21
Low	Anglia	21
80-189 points	*Canterbury Christ*	*19*
	Falmouth	24
	Wolverhampton	21
	East London	21
	Chichester	22
	Cumbria	21
	Lincoln	20
	Leeds/Bretton	23
	London Guildhall	23
	Robert Gordon	Highly satis
	Edinburgh/Coll Art	Highly Satis
	Hull/Scarborough	
	Newport	
	Oxford Sch Art & Des	
	Sunderland	21
	Goldsmiths	22

ENTRY	UNI/COLLEGE	RATING
Low	Arts Inst Bournemth	21
80-189 points	Bradford College	21
	Cardiff Inst (UWIC)	Excellent
	Glasgow School Art	Highly Satis
	Herefordshire Coll	16
	Manchester Met	22
	Northbrook	21
	Norwich	21
	Reading (Uni)	19
	Slade School (UCL)	23
	Southampton Inst	17
	Swansea Inst	Excellent
	Staffordshire	22
	Suffolk College	15

Colleges and universities for which A level grades are even less critical for selection:

UNIVERSITY	RATING
Bath Spa	22
Brighton	22
Bristol West England	22
Buckingham Chilts	20
Central Lancs	22
Cleveland	20
Coventry	
Croydon	19
Dundee	Highly Satis
Gloucestershire	21
Heriot-Watt	
Hertfordshire	22
Highlands & Islands	
Kent Institute	22
Kingston	21
Leeds Met	21
London Institute	22
Loughborough	23
Middlesex	21
NEWI	Satisfactory
North London	22
Northampton	23
Plymouth	21
Reading College	18
Sheffield Hallam	22
Southampton	22
Southport	
Surrey Institute	21
Swindon College	20
Ulster	19
Westminster	21
Wimbledon	23

BIOSCIENCES

Assessments have been made for both molecular and organismal biosciences; where the outcome was different in each case, the first of the two scores in column 3 relates to organismal biosciences.

ENTRY	UNI/COLLEGE	RATING
High	Bath	24
280 points +	Birmingham	24, 23
	Bristol	22, 24
	Cambridge	24
	Cardiff	Excellent
	Edinburgh	Excellent
	Exeter	22

ENTRY	UNI/COLLEGE	RATING
High	Hull	23
280 points +	Imperial College	22
	Kent	24
	King's College (KCL)	22
	Leeds	22, 23
	Manchester	23
	UMIST	22
	Nottingham	23
	Oxford	24
	Queen Mary	22
	Southampton	23
	Swansea	Excellent
	University College	24, 22
Medium-High	Aberdeen	Excellent
240-280 points	Aberystwyth	Excellent
	Aston	23
	Bangor	Excellent
	Durham	24
	East Anglia	22
	Keele	22, 21
	Lancaster	21
	Newcastle	22, 24
	Plymouth	22
	Queen's Belfast	21
	Reading	21
	Royal Holloway	24, 21
	St Andrews	Excellent
	Salford	24
	Sheffield	24
	Stirling	Higly satis
	Strathclyde	Highly satis
	Surrey	21, 22
	Ulster	21, 22
	York	24
Low-Medium	Bradford	20
180-240 points	Brighton	22
	Bristol West England	24
	Central Lancashire	22
	Chester College	21
	Coventry	16, 19
	De Montfort	21
	Dundee	Excellent
	Essex	23
	Glasgow	Excellent
	Glasgow Caledonian	Highly satis
	Heriot-Watt	Highly satis
	Huddersfield	22
	Kingston	24
	Leicester	22
	Liverpool Hope	21
	Northumbria	21
	Nottingham Trent	24
	Oxford Brookes	23
	Portsmouth	22
	Sheffield Hallam	22
	Surrey/Roehampton	23
	Warwick	23
	Wolverhampton	23
Low	Abertay Dundee	Highly satis
80-180 points	Anglia Polytechnic	21
	Barnsley College	
	Bath Spa UC	21
	Bell College	
	Bolton Institute	22
	Canterbury Christ	21
	Cardiff Inst (UWIC)	Excellent
	Derby	22
	East London	19
	Edge Hill College	23

ENTRY	UNI/COLLEGE	RATING
Low	Glamorgan	Satisfactory
80-180 points	Greenwich	20
	Hertfordshire	21
	Hull/Scarborough	
	Lincoln	
	Liverpool	19
	Liverpool J Moores	23, 22
	Luton	22
	Manchester Met	22
	Middlesex	
	Napier	Highly satis
	Nescot	18
	NEWI	Satisfactory
	North London	18
	Northampton	
	Paisley	Highly satis
	Queen Margaret UC	Excellent
	Robert Gordon	
	South Bank	20
	Staffordshire	22
	Sunderland	24
	Sussex	22
	Teesside	
	Westminster	21
	Worcester UC	20

BUSINESS/MANAGEMENT

ENTRY	UNI/COLLEGE	RATING
High	Bath	
280 points +	Birmingham	21
	Bristol	
	Brunel	
	Cardiff	
	City	
	Durham	
	Edinburgh	
	Imperial	
	Keele	21
	King's	
	Lancaster	
	Leeds	
	LSE	24
	Loughborough	22
	Newcastle	
	Nottingham	
	Oxford	
	Reading	21
	Royal Holloway	21
	St Andrews	
	SOAS	
	Sheffield	
	Southampton	23
	Surrey	
	University College	
	Warwick	
	York	22
Medium-High	Aberdeen	
240-280 points	Aberystwyth	
	Aston	24
	Bournemouth	
	Brighton	
	Buckingham	
	East Anglia	23
	Essex	
	Exeter	22
	Glasgow	
	Hertfordshire	

ENTRY	UNI/COLLEGE	RATING
Medium-High	Hull	
240-280 points	Imperial/Wye	
	Leicester	
	Liverpool	23
	Manchester	24
	Portsmouth	
	Queen Mary	
	Queen's Belfast	23
	Robert Gordon	
	Salford	
	Stirling	
	Strathclyde	
	Sussex	
Low-Medium	Bangor	
180-240 points	Barnsley	
	Bradford	
	Bristol West England	23
	Cardiff Institute	
	Central England	21
	Central Lancashire	
	Chester	
	Cornwall College	
	Coventry	22
	Cranfield	
	Dundee	
	East London	
	Glamorgan	
	Gloucestershire	
	Kent	21
	Lampeter	
	Liverpool Hope	
	Liverpool J Moores	22
	Luton	
	Middlesex	
	North London	24
	Northumbria	22
	Nottingham Trent	
	Oxford Brookes	24
	Plymouth	
	Royal Agricultural	
	Staffordshire	
	Sunderland	
	Surrey/Roehampton	
	Swansea	
	Trinity All Saints	
	Ulster	24
Low	Abertay Dundee	
80-180 points	Anglia Polytechnic	20
	Askham Bryan	22
	Bath Spa	20
	Bell	
	Blackburn	22
	Blackpool	21
	Bolton	
	Bradford College	
	Buckingham Chilts	
	Canterbury Christ	21
	Chichester	19
	Colchester Institute	
	Croydon	
	De Montfort	
	Derby	22
	Doncaster	22
	Edge Hill	
	European Business	
	Exeter College	22
	Farnborough	19
	Glasgow Caledonian	
	Greenwich	20

ENTRY	UNI/COLLEGE	RATING
Low	Gyosei College	
80-180 points	Harper Adams	
	Heriot-Watt	
	Huddersfield	
	Hull Scarborough	
	UHI	
	Holborn	
	King Alfred's	22
	Kingston	
	Leeds Metropolitan	24
	Lincoln	
	London Guildhall	22
	London Institute	22
	Manchester Met	23
	Napier	
	Newport	
	Nescot	
	NEWI	
	Northampton	
	Northbrook	
	Paisley	
	Queen Margaret	
	Regents	
	St Martin's	
	St Mary's College	17
	Salford	
	Scottish Agricultural	
	Sheffield Hallam	22
	Southampton Institute	
	South Bank	20
	Stockport College	22
	Stranmillis	
	Swansea Institute	
	Teesside	
	Thames Valley	
	Trinity Carmarthen	
	Westminster	
	Wolverhampton	
	Worcester	21
	Writtle College	
	York St John	21

CHEMISTRY

ENTRY	UNI/COLLEGE	RATING
High	Birmingham	Satisfactory
280 points +	Cambridge	Excellent
	Durham	Excellent
	Glasgow	Excellent
	Imperial	Excellent
	King's College	Satisfactory
	Oxford	Excellent
	Southampton	Excellent
	York	Satisfactory
Medium-High	Bath	Satisfactory
240-280 points	Bristol	Excellent
	Cardiff	Excellent
	East Anglia	Satisfactory
	Exeter	Satisfactory
	Heriot-Watt	Highly Satis
	Hull	Excellent
	Keele	Satisfactory
	Leicester	Excellent
	Manchester	Excellent
	UMIST	Satisfactory
	Newcastle	Satisfactory
	Nottingham	Excellent
	Queen Mary	Satisfactory
	Queen's Belfast	Satisfactory

ENTRY	UNI/COLLEGE	RATING
Medium-High	St Andrews	Excellent
240-280 points	Surrey	Satisfactory
	Swansea	Satisfactory
	University College	Satisfactory
	Warwick	Satisfactory
Low-Medium	Aberdeen	Highly Satis
180-240 points	Aston	Satisfactory
	Bangor	Excellent
	Bradford	Satisfactory
	Brighton	Satisfactory
	Coventry	Satisfactory
	Derby	Satisfactory
	Edinburgh	Excellent
	Glamorgan	Satisfactory
	Glasgow Caledonian	Excellent
	Herdtfordshire	
	Kent	Satisfactory
	Lancaster	Satisfactory
	Leeds	Excellent
	Loughborough	Satisfactory
	Nottingham Trent	Excellent
	Oxford Brookes	Satisfactory
	Reading	Satisfactory
	Salford	Satisfactory
	Sheffield	Satisfactory
	Stirling	
	Strathclyde	Excellent
	Sussex	Satisfactory
	Teesside	Satisfactory
Low	Anglia Polytechnic	Satisfactory
80-180 points	Bell College	
	Bristol West England	Satisfactory
	De Montfort	Satisfactory
	Dundee	Satisfactory
	Greenwich	Satisfactory
	Huddersfield	Satisfactory
	Kingston	Satisfactory
	Liverpool	Satisfactory
	Liverpool J Moores	Satisfactory
	Manchester Met	Satisfactory
	Napier	Highly Satis
	North London	Satisfactory
	Northumbria	Satisfactory
	Paisley	Highly Satis
	Plymouth	Satisfactory
	Robert Gordon	Excellent
	Sheffield Hallam	LSatisfactory
	Staffordshire	MeSatisfactory
	Sunderland	Satisfactory
	Wolverhampton	Satisfactory

COMPUTER

ENTRY	UNI/COLLEGE	RATING
High	Cambridge	Excellent
280 points +	Oxford	Excellent
	Imperial	Excellent
	Bristol	Satisfactory
	York	Excellent
	UCL	Satisfactory
	Manchester	Excellent
	Warwick	Excellent
	Southampton	Excellent
	King's Coll	Satisfactory
	Royal Holloway	Satisfactory
	Leeds	Satisfactory
	Durham	Satisfactory
Medium-High	Birmingham	Satisfactory
240-280 points	Sheffield	Satisfactory

ENTRY	UNI/COLLEGE	RATING
Medium-High	Nottingham	Satisfactory
240-280 points	Sussex	Satisfactory
	Queen Mary & West.	Satisfactory
	Essex	Satisfactory
	Kent	Excellent
	Liverpool	Satisfactory
	Bath	Satisfactory
	Cardiff	Satisfactory
	Lancaster	Satisfactory
	Loughborough	Satisfactory
	Reading	Satisfactory
	Surrey	Satisfactory
	Exeter	Excellent
	UEA	Satisfactory
	Edinburgh	Excellent
	Queen's Belfast	Satisfactory
	St Andrews	Highly Satis
	Swansea	Excellent
	Trinity All Saints	
	Newcastle	Satisfactory
	Brunel	Satisfactory
	Bradford	Satisfactory
	Leicester	Satisfactory
	UMIST	Satisfactory
	Hull	Satisfactory
	Aston	Satisfactory
Low-Medium	Glasgow	Excellent
80-180 points	Strathclyde	Highly Satis
	Aberdeen	Satisfactory
	Stirling	Satisfactory
	Keele	Satisfactory
	Kingston	Satisfactory
	Aberystwyth	Satisfactory
	Salford	Satisfactory
	Bangor	
	Ulster	Satisfactory
	Glasgow Cal	Satisfactory
	Hertfordshire	Satisfactory
	Lampeter	
	Cranfield	Satisfactory
	Heriot-Watt	Highly Satis
	Bristol West England	Satisfactory
	Nottingham Trent	Satisfactory
	Roehampton/Surrey	Satisfactory
	Teesside	Excellent
	Manchester Met	Satisfactory
	South Bank	Satisfactory
	Central England	Satisfactory
	Central Lancs	Satisfactory
	Coventry	Satisfactory
	Huddersfield	Satisfactory
	Luton	Satisfactory
	Middlesex	Satisfactory
	Buckingham	
	Chester	Satisfactory
	Leeds Met	Satisfactory
	Lincoln	Satisfactory
	Liverpool JM	Satisfactory
	Westminster	Satisfactory
	Staffordshire	Satisfactory
Low	Abertay Dundee	Satisfactory
80-180 points	Edge Hill	
	City	Satisfactory
	Brighton	Satisfactory
	Dundee	Satisfactory
	Bournemouth	Satisfactory
	Plymouth	Satisfactory
	Anglia	Satisfactory
	Northumbria	Satisfactory

ENTRY	UNI/COLLEGE	RATING
Low	UWIC (Cardiff)	Satisfactory
80-180 points	Sheffield Hallam	Satisfactory
	East London	Satisfactory
	Liverpool Hope	Satisfactory
	Bolton	Satisfactory
	Writtle	
	Oxford Brookes	Satisfactory
	Goldsmiths	
	Wolverhampton	Satisfactory
	Canterbury Christ	Satisfactory
	Worcester	
	Bell	
	Napier	Satisfactory
	Nescot	Satisfactory
	Sunderland	Satisfactory
	Portsmouth	Satisfactory
	De Montfort	Satisfactory
	Derby	Satisfactory
	Greenwich	Satisfactory
	Gloucestershire	Satisfactory
	Northampton	Satisfactory
	Bucks Chilterns	Satisfactory
	Newport	Satisfactory
	North London	Satisfactory
	Southampton Inst	Satisfactory
	Bradford College	
	Thames Valley	Satisfactory
	Robert Gordon	
	Paisley	Satisfactory
	Farnborough	Satisfactory
	Trinity Carmarthen	
	London Guildhall	Satisfactory
	Suffolk	Satisfactory
	Swansea Inst	Satisfactory
	Blackburn	Satisfactory
	Blackpool & Fylde	
	Doncaster	Satisfactory
	Highlands & Islands	
	Ravensbourne	
	Glamorgan	Satisfactory
	NEWI	Satisfactory
	St Mark & St John	Satisfactory
	Norwich	
	Barnsley	

DENTISTRY

ENTRY	UNI/COLLEGE	RATING
High	Bristol	19
280 points +	Queen's Belfast	24
	Liverpool	21
	Birmingham	22
	Dundee	
	Glasgow	
	King's College	24
	Leeds	23
	Manchester	24
	Newcastle	23
	Queen Mary	24
	Sheffield	23
	Uni Wales Col. Med.	
Low-Medium	Manchester Met	21
180-240 points	Cardiff Institute	

DRAMA/THEATRE ARTS

Note: performance talent sometimes required.

ENTRY	UNI/COLLEGE	RATING
High	Cambridge	
280 points +	Leeds	
	Birmingham	21
	UEA	21
	Manchester	21
	Royal Holloway	23
	Sussex	
	Warwick	24
	Exeter	22
	Lancaster	24
	Glasgow	Highly Satis
	Goldsmiths	22
	Queen Mary & West.	21
	Kent	24
Medium-High	Loughborough	23
240-280 points	Hull	24
	Bristol	23
	Brunel	23
	Queen's Belfast	
	Bristol West England	
	Aberystwyth	Satisfactory
	Bangor	
	Huddersfield	17
	Salford	23
	Ulster	22
	Central England	
	Liverpool JM	21
	Southampton Inst	21
	Dartington	23
	Plymouth	21
	Northumbria	22
	King Alfred's	19
	South Bank	
	De Montfort	22
	Derby	18
Low Medium	Bretton Hall	22
180-240 points	Central School Drama	23
	Cumbria	
	Edge Hill	14
	Reading	24
	Staffordshire	
	Westhill/Birmingham	17
	St Martin	19
	Coventry	
	Roehampton/Surrey	21
	North London	22
	Central Lancs	20
	Luton	
	Middlesex	22
	Warrington	19
	Anglia	
	Wolverhampton	19
	Chester	17
	East London	19
	Liverpool Hope	19
	Northampton	21
	Nottingham Trent	
	Scarborough/Hull	
Low	Worcester	
80-180 points	Bishop Grosseteste	
	St Mark & St John	
	Bolton Institute	20
	York St John	20
	Queen Margaret	Highly Satis
	Manchester Met	23
	Glamorgan	Excellent

ENTRY	UNI/COLLEGE	RATING
Low	Gloucestershire	
80-180 points	Newman	
	St Mary's	20
	Bucks Chilterns	
	Barnsley	
	Trinity Carmarthen	Satisfactory
	Guildford Sch Acting	
	Guildhall Mus/Dram	
	Northbrook	
	Nescot	

Colleges and universities for which A level grades are not critical for selection:

	UNI/COLLEGE	RATING
-	Brighton	
-	Cleveland	
-	Heriot-Watt	
-	Hertfordshire	15
-	LIPA	
-	London Inst	20
-	Rose Bruford	20

ECONOMICS

ENTRY	UNI/COLLEGE	RATING
High	Cambridge	24
280 points +	Oxford	23
	Warwick	24
	LSE	23
	Nottingham	24
	Durham	
	UCL	24
	Edinburgh	Satisfactory
	Aston	
	Bath	24
	Sussex	
	St Andrews	Excellent
	Bristol	23
	Manchester	24
	Birmingham	23
	Glasgow	Satisfactory
	Leeds	
	Sheffield	
	Southampton	24
	Essex	24
Medium-High	Lancaster	
240-280 points	York	24
	Royal Holloway	
	Cardiff	Satisfactory
	Keele	23
	Leicester	
	Surrey	23
	City	22
	UEA	23
	Hull	22
	Loughborough	23
	Queen Mary & West.	
	Queen's Belfast	
	Reading	21
	Swansea	Satisfactory
	Bradford	
	SSEES/UCL	
	Newcastle	23
	Brunel	22
	SOAS	21
	Kent	
	Goldsmiths	22
	Liverpool	22
	Exeter	

ENTRY	UNI/COLLEGE	RATING
Medium-High	Aberdeen	Excellent
240-280 points	Glasgow Cal	
	Strathclyde	Satisfactory
	Ulster	
	Bangor	Satisfactory
Low-Medium	Heriot-Watt	Satisfactory
180-240 points	Salford	20
	Stirling	Excellent
	Aberystwyth	Excellent
	Lincoln	
	Westminster	
	Plymouth	
	Bristol West England	23
	Nottingham Trent	22
	Dundee	Satisfactory
	Hertfordshire	22
	Manchester Met	
	Portsmouth	21
	Buckingham	
	Greenwich	20
	Kingston	21
	Central England	21
	Huddersfield	
	Leeds Met	24
	North London	
	Napier	Satisfactory
	South Bank	20
	Coventry	23
	De Montfort	
	Luton	
	Middlesex	21
	Anglia	
	Central Lancs	
	Derby	
	Liverpool JMoores	
	Northumbria	22
	Wolverhampton	
	Glamorgan	Satisfactory
	Staffordshire	24
Low	Abertay Dundee	Excellent
80-180 points	Bolton	
	East London	20
	Teesside	
	Northampton	
	Oxford Brookes	24
	London Guildhall	23
	Paisley	Satisfactory
	Sunderland	
	Bucks Chilterns	
	Thames Valley	
	Doncaster	
	Open	22

ENGINEERING

1. Aeronautics

ENTRY	UNI/COLLEGE	RATING
High	Southampton	21
280 points +	Bath	
	Bristol	22
	Manchester	20
	UMIST	20
	Strathclyde	
	Imperial	22
	Liverpool	20
	Sheffield	
	Queen's Belfast	21
	Loughborough	23

ENTRY	UNI/COLLEGE	RATING
Medium-High	Glasgow	
240-280 points	Brunel	20
	Cranfield	22
	City	19
	Salford	
	Lincoln	18
Low-Medium	Queen Mary	
180-240 points	Hertfordshire	22
	Staffordshire	
	Brighton	
Low	Coventry	18
80-180 points	Bristol West England	
	Farnborough	
	Kingston	24
	NEWI	
	Highlands & Islands	
	Stockport	

ENGINEERING

2. Chemical

ENTRY	UNI/COLLEGE	RATING
High	Cambridge	23
280 points +	Oxford	23
	Imperial	22
	Bath	20
	UCL	20
	UMIST	22
Medium-High	Queen's Belfast	21
240-280 points	Swansea	Excellent
	Nottingham	21
	Sheffield	21
	Strathclyde	20
	Edinburgh	19
	Birmingham	21
	Aston	19
	Newcastle	21
	Loughborough	22
	Surrey	18
Low-Medium	Bradford	20
180-240 points	Leeds	19
	Heriot-Watt	19
	Teesside	17
	Brighton	
	Northumbria	
Low	South Bank	18
80-180 points	Glamorgan	
	Paisley	

ENGINEERING

3. Civil

ENTRY	UNI/COLLEGE	RATING
High	Cambridge	23
280 points +	Oxford	23
	Imperial	21
	UMIST	22
	Bristol	22
	Durham	
	UCL	19
Medium-High	Southampton	21
240-280 points	Sheffield	21
	Queen's Belfast	22
	Strathclyde	Highly Satis
	Swansea	Excellent
	Cardiff	Excellent

ENTRY	UNI/COLLEGE	RATING
Medium-High	Nottingham	22
240-280 points	Edinburgh	Highly Satis
	Birmingham	21
	Manchester	18
	Surrey	22
	Warwick	21
	Exeter	
	Cranfield	
	Leeds	19
	Oxford Brookes	21
	Newcastle	20
	Aston	20
	Bath	22
	City	19
	Loughborough	22
Low-Medium	Glasgow	Highly Satis
180-240 points	Liverpool	22
	Wolverhampton	20
	Writtle	
	South Bank	20
	Portsmouth	
	Sheffield Hallam	18
	Heriot-Watt	Highly Satis
	Doncaster	
	Ulster	19
	Dundee	Highly Satis
	Greenwich	21
	East London	21
	Nottingham Trent	20
	Bristol West England	
	Leeds Met	21
Low	Bradford	20
80-180 points	Brighton	21
	Salford	19
	Coventry	19
	Glamorgan	Satisfactory
	Hertfordshire	18
	Northumbria	
	Plymouth	23
	Bolton Inst	20
	Aberdeen	Highly Satis
	Abertay Dundee	Highly Satis
	Paisley	Highly Satis
	Napier	Highly Satis
	Glasgow Cal	Satisfactory
	Kingston	22
	Newport	
	Liverpool JM	20
	Stockport	Not approved

ENGINEERING

4. Electrical, Electronic

ENTRY	UNI/COLLEGE	RATING
High	Cambridge	23
280 points +	Oxford	23
	Imperial	24
	UCL	22
	York	24
	Bristol	24
	Durham	
	Southampton	24
	Leeds	23
	King's Coll	20
Medium-High	Queen Mary	21
240-280 points	UMIST	22
	Sheffield	24
	Birmingham	24

ENTRY	UNI/COLLEGE	RATING
Medium-High	Queen's Belfast	24
240-280 points	Swansea	Excellent
	Kent	21
	Brunel	21
	St Andrews	
	Cardiff	Excellent
	Bath	20
	Lancaster	
	Warwick	21
	Edinburgh	Excellent
	Essex	24
	Manchester	20
	Exeter	
	Glasgow	Satisfactory
	Cranfield	
	Royal Holloway	
	Newcastle	21
	Hull	24
	Aston	21
	Leicester	
	Loughborough	22
	Reading	21
Low-Medium	Lincoln	18
180-240 points	Strathclyde	Excellent
	Surrey	23
	Liverpool	21
	Bristol West England	21
	Salford	16
	Central England	19
	Manchester Met	21
	Nottingham	22
	UEA	19
	Ulster	20
	Bradford	21
	Dundee	Satisfactory
	Hertfordshire	20
	Huddersfield	24
	De Montfort	19
	Bournemouth	19
	Doncaster	18
	London Guildhall	
	Heriot-Watt	Excellent
	Portsmouth	20
	Nottingham Trent	20
	Sunderland	19
	Luton	20
Low	Farnborough	
80-180 points	Staffordshire	20
	Bell	
	City	21
	Robert Gordon	Satisfactory
	Brighton	20
	Coventry	18
	Leeds Met	17
	Liverpool JM	18
	Northumbria	22
	Plymouth	18
	Sheffield Hallam	18
	Anglia	19
	East London	15
	Derby	19
	Greenwich	17
	Teesside	21
	Middlesex	19
	Southampton Inst	19
	Oxford Brookes	19
	Aberdeen	Satisfactory
	Bangor	Satisfactory
	Sussex	21

ENTRY	UNI/COLLEGE	RATING
Low	Central Lancs	15
80-180 points	Paisley	Satisfactory
	South Bank	19
	Napier	Satisfactory
	Glasgow Cal	Satisfactory
	North London 22	
	Wolverhampton	
	Abertay Dundee	Satisfactory
	Glamorgan	Excellent
	Bolton Inst	20
	NEWI	Satisfactory
	Blackburn	18
	Highlands & Islands	
	LIPA	
	Newport	Satisfactory
	Swansea Inst	
	Westminster	21
	UWIC (Cardiff)	Satisfactory
	Ravensbourne	
	Reading Coll	
	Stockport	Not approved
	Blackpool & Fylde	

ENGINEERING

5. General

ENTRY	UNI/COLLEGE	RATING
High	Cambridge	23
280 points +	Imperial	23
	Oxford	23
	Bristol	
	Dundee	
	Durham	22
Medium-High	UCL	
240-280 points	Aberdeen	
	Birmingham	
	Cardiff	
	Lancaster	22
	UMIST	
	Strathclyde	
	Warwick	
	Bangor	
	Edinburgh	
	Loughborough	
	Leicester	20
	Queen Mary	19
	Surrey	
	Reading	
	Aston	
	Portsmouth	
Low-Medium	Leeds	
180-240 points	City	
	Ulster	20
	Liverpool	20
	Central England	19
	Manchester Met	
	Plymouth	
	Bradford	20
	Salford	
	Heriot-Watt	
	Brunel	22
	Hertfordshire	20
	Glasgow	
	Exeter	20
	Nottingham Trent	
	Luton	
	East London	

ENTRY	UNI/COLLEGE	RATING
Low-Medium	Sunderland	
180-240 points	Teesside	
	Bristol West England	
	Staffordshire	
Low	Paisley	
80-180 points	Hull	
	Brighton	
	Huddersfield	
	Coventry	18
	Northumbria	
	Middlesex	
	Derby	
	Oxford Brookes	
	Napier	
	Robert Gordon	
	Glasgow Cal	
	Sheffield Hallam	21
	Glamorgan	
	Greenwich	17
	Wolverhampton	20
	Leeds Met	17
	Northampton	18
	Central Lancs	20
	Liverpool JM	
	South Bank	17
	UWIC (Cardiff Inst)	
	Bolton Inst	
	Southampton Inst	19
	De Montfort	19
	Highlands & Islands	
	Swansea Inst	
	Westminster	
	Barnsley	
	Blackburn	
	Doncaster	18
	Newport	
	Cornwall	
	Lincoln	

ENGINEERING

6. Mechanical, Production

REQUIRED	UNI/COLLEGE	RATING
High	Imperial	Satisfactory, 22
280 points +	Bath	Excellent
	Oxford	23
	Bristol	Excellent
	Durham	
	Leeds	Satisfactory
	Strathclyde	Excellent
	King's Coll	Satisfactory
	Southampton	Satisfactory, 21
Medium-High	Sheffield	Excellent, 24
240-280 points	UCL	Satisfactory
	UMIST	Satisfactory
	Queen's Belfast	Satisfactory, 21
	Swansea	Satisfactory
	Lancaster	Satisfactory
	Newcastle	Satisfactory
	Nottingham	Excellent, 24
	Birmingham	Satisfactory, 20
	Edinburgh	Satisfactory
	Manchester	Excellent
	Warwick	
	Exeter	
	Cardiff	Excellent
	Loughborough	Satisfactory, 23

ENTRY	UNI/COLLEGE	RATING
Medium-High	Aston	Satisfactory
240-280 points	Leicester	
	Surrey	Satisfactory
	Reading	Excellent
	Oxford Brookes	Satisfactory
Low-Medium	City	Satisfactory, 19
180-240 points	Glasgow	Highly Satis
	Queen Mary	Satisfactory
	Central Lancs	Satisfactory
	Liverpool	Satisfactory, 20
	Central England	Satisfactory, 19
	Cranfield	Excellent, 22
	Hertfordshire	22
	Brunel	Satisfactory, 20
	De Montfort	Satisfactory
	Dundee	
	Bristol West England	Satisfactory
	Heriot-Watt	Highly Satis
	Doncaster	
	Westminster	Satisfactory
	Ulster	Satisfactory
	Salford	Satisfactory
	Derby	Satisfactory
	Nottingham Trent	Satisfactory
	Luton	Satisfactory
	Bournemouth	Satisfactory, 18
	East London	18
	Northampton	Satisfactory
	Teesside	Satisfactory
	Staffordshire	Satisfactory
	Sunderland	Satisfactory, 19
Low	Hull	Satisfactory
80-180 points	Glasgow Cal	Satisfactory
	Bradford	Satisfactory
	Brighton	Satisfactory
	Coventry	Excellent, 18
	Writtle	19
	Huddersfield	Satisfactory
	Northumbria	Satisfactory
	Manchester Met	Excellent
	Anglia	Satisfactory, 19
	Farnborough	
	Leeds Met	Satisfactory, 17
	Middlesex	Satisfactory
	Newport	Satisfactory
	Robert Gordon	Highly Satis
	Aberdeen	Highly Satis
	Sussex	Satisfactory
	Napier	Satisfactory
	Paisley	Highly Satis
	Bell	
	South Bank	Satisfactory, 18
	Harper Adams	Satisfactory
	Lincoln	18
	Portsmouth	Satisfactory
	Sheffield Hallam	Satisfactory, 21
	Glamorgan	Satisfactory
	Southampton Inst	Satisfactory, 19
	Bucks Chilterns	Satisfactory
	Wolverhampton	Satisfactory
	Abertay Dundee	Highly Satis
	Kingston	Satisfactory, 24
	Greenwich	Satisfactory
	Liverpool JM	Satisfactory
	Plymouth	Satisfactory
	Bolton Inst	Satisfactory
	NEWI	Satisfactory
	Swansea Inst	Satisfactory
	Highlands & Islands	

ENTRY	UNI/COLLEGE	RATING
Low	UWIC (Cardiff Inst)	Satisfactory
80-180 points	Stockport	Satisfactory

ENGLISH

REQUIRED	UNI/COLLEGE	RATING
High	Cambridge	Excellent
280 points +	Oxford	Excellent
	UCL	Excellent
	King's College	Satisfactory
	Birmingham	Excellent
	Edinburgh	Highly Satis
	UEA	Satisfactory
	Manchester	Satisfactory
	St Andrews	Highly Satis
	Southampton	Excellent
	Sussex	Excellent
	Newcastle	Excellent
	Durham	Excellent
	Exeter	Excellent
	Bristol	Excellent
	Leeds	Excellent
	Sheffield	Excellent
	Warwick	Excellent
	Cardiff	Excellent
	Liverpool	Excellent
	York	Excellent
	Nottingham	Excellent
	Royal Holloway	Satisfactory
	Glasgow	Excellent
	Lancaster	Excellent
	Swansea	Satisfactory
	Kent	Satisfactory
Medium-High	Queen Mary	Excellent
240-280 points	Brunel	Satisfactory
	Keele	Satisfactory
	Leicester	Excellent
	Reading	Satisfactory
	Loughborough	23
	Goldsmiths	Satisfactory
	Queen's Belfast	Excellent
	Salford	Satisfactory
	Dundee	Excellent
	Essex	Satisfactory
	Aberystwyth	Excellent
	Hull	Satisfactory
	Northumbria	Excellent
	Stirling	Excellent
	Ulster	Satisfactory
	Aberdeen	Highly Satis
	Bangor	Satisfactory
	Strathclyde	Highly Satis
	Bristol West England	Excellent
	Falmouth	
Low-Medium	St Martin	Satisfactory
180-240 points	Central England	Satisfactory
	Lincoln	
	Portsmouth	Satisfactory
	Leeds/Trin/All Saints	Satisfactory
	Sheffield Hallam	Excellent
	Manchester Met	Satisfactory
	Nottingham Trent	Satisfactory
	Huddersfield	Satisfactory
	Central Lancs	Satisfactory
	Blackburn	
	Hertfordshire	Satisfactory
	King Alfred's	Satisfactory
	Kingston	Satisfactory

ENTRY	UNI/COLLEGE	RATING
Low-Medium	Lampeter	Satisfactory
180-240 points	Wolverhampton	Satisfactory
	Teesside	Satisfactory
	Ripon & York St John	Satisfactory
	Bretton Hall	Satisfactory
	Staffordshire	Satisfactory
	Edge Hill	Satisfactory
	Northampton	Satisfactory
	Scarborough/Hull	
	Westhill/Birmingham	
	Westminster	Satisfactory
	Worcester	Satisfactory
Low	London Guildhall	
80-180 points	Liverpool JM	Satisfactory
	South Bank	
	Chester	Excellent
	Luton	Satisfactory
	Middlesex	Satisfactory
	Roehampton/Surrey	Satisfactory
	St Mark & St John	Satisfactory
	East London	Excellent
	Anglia	Excellent
	Chichester	Satisfactory
	Colchester	
	Coventry*	
	Liverpool Hope	Satisfactory
	North London	Excellent
	Bath Spa	Excellent
	Canterbury Ch Ch	Satisfactory
	Bishop Grosseteste	
	Cumbria	
	Southampton (New)	
	De Montfort	Satisfactory
	Greenwich	Satisfactory
	Buckingham	
	Newport	
	Sunderland	Satisfactory
	Oxford Brookes	Excellent
	Plymouth	Satisfactory
	Gloucestershire	Satisfactory
	Glamorgan	
	Bucks Chilterns	
	Newman	
	St Mary's	Satisfactory
	Thames Valley	Satisfactory
	NEWI	
	Doncaster	Satisfactory
	Trinity Carmarthen	
	Swansea Inst	

*for non-native English speakers

GEOGRAPHY

ENTRY	UNI/COLLEGE	RATING
High	Cambridge	Excellent
280 points +	Oxford	Excellent
	Bristol	Excellent
	Durham	Excellent
	St Andrews	Excellent
	King's Coll	Excellent
	Sheffield	Excellent
	LSE	Satisfactory
	Edinburgh	Highly Satis
	Nottingham	Excellent
	UCL	Excellent
	Reading	Excellent
	Liverpool	Satisfactory
Medium-High	Leeds	Excellent

ENTRY	UNI/COLLEGE	RATING
240-280 points	Birmingham	Excellent
	Manchester	Excellent
	Exeter	Excellent
	Hull	Satisfactory
	Swansea	Excellent
	Leeds Met	
	Queen's Belfast	Satisfactory
	Queen Mary & West.	Excellent
	Southampton	Excellent
	Loughborough	Satisfactory
	SOAS	Satisfactory
	Aberystwyth	
	Brunel	Satisfactory
	Cardiff	
	Royal Holloway	Satisfactory
	Glasgow	Excellent
	Leicester	Satisfactory
	Sussex	Satisfactory
	Bradford	
	Keele	Satisfactory
	Strathclyde	Excellent
	Newcastle	Satisfactory
	Aston	
	Central England	
Low-Medium	Westminster	Satisfactory
180-240 points	Lancaster	Excellent
	Aberdeen	Excellent
	Cranfield	
	Dundee	Satisfactory
	Salford	Satisfactory
	Plymouth	Excellent
	Sheffield Hallam	
	Ulster	Satisfactory
	Northumbria	Satisfactory
	Bristol West England	Satisfactory
	Kingston	Satisfactory
	Lampeter	Satisfactory
	Portsmouth	Excellent
	Hertfordshire	
	Ripon & York St John	Satisfactory
	Manchester Met	Satisfactory
	Stirling	
	Nottingham Trent	Satisfactory
	Staffordshire	Satisfactory
	Brighton	Satisfactory
	Luton	Satisfactory
	Middlesex	Satisfactory
	Anglia	Satisfactory
	Central Lancs	Satisfactory
	Chester	Satisfactory
	Coventry	Excellent
	Chichester	Satisfactory
	Greenwich	Satisfactory
	Southampton Inst	
Low	St Martin's	Satisfactory
80-180 points	Roehampton/Surrey	Satisfactory
	East London	
	Liverpool Hope	Excellent
	Huddersfield	Satisfactory
	Newport	
	Oxford Brookes	Excellent
	South Bank	
	Edge Hill	Satisfactory
	Canterbury Ch Ch	Excellent
	London Guildhall	Satisfactory
	Sunderland	Satisfactory
	Glamorgan	Satisfactory
	Gloucestershire	Excellent
	De Montfort	Satisfactory

ENTRY	UNI/COLLEGE	RATING
Low	Derby	Satisfactory
80-180 points	Liverpool JM	Satisfactory
	Newman	
	Wolverhampton	Satisfactory
	North London	Satisfactory
	Northampton	Satisfactory
	St Mark & St John	Satisfactory
	Barnsley	
	Trinity Carmarthen	
	Worcester	Satisfactory
	Bath Spa	Satisfactory
	NEWI	
	St Mary's College	Satisfactory

HISTORY

ENTRY	UNI/COLLEGE	RATING
High	Cambridge	Excellent
280 points +	Oxford	Excellent
	LSE	Excellent
	Royal Holloway	Excellent
	Edinburgh	Excellent
	York	Excellent
	St Andrews	Excellent
	Southampton	Satisfactory
	Warwick	Excellent
	Durham	Excellent
	Manchester	Satisfactory
	Sheffield	Excellent
	Glasgow	Highly Satis
	Leeds	Satisfactory
	Sussex	Satisfactory
	Kent	Satisfactory
Medium-High	King's College	Excellent
240-280 points	Birmingham	Excellent
	Nottingham	Satisfactory
	Bristol	Satisfactory
	UEA	Satisfactory
	Lancaster	Excellent
	Liverpool	Excellent
	Swansea	Excellent
	Cardiff	Satisfactory
	Hull	Excellent
	Reading	Satisfactory
	Dundee	Highly Satis
	Leicester	Excellent
	SSEES/UCL	Satisfactory
	Newcastle	Satisfactory
	SOAS	Satisfactory
	Essex	Satisfactory
	Queen Mary	Satisfactory
	UCL	Excellent
	Keele	Satisfactory
	Salford	Satisfactory
	Brunel	Satisfactory
	Goldsmiths	Satisfactory
	Queen's Belfast	Excellent
	Stirling	Highly Satis
	Leeds Met	Satisfactory
	Bradford	Satisfactory
	Aberdeen	Highly Satis
	Strathclyde	Highly Satis
	Ulster	Satisfactory
	Exeter	Satisfactory
	Aberystwyth	Satisfactory
	Westminster	Satisfactory
Low-Medium	Bristol West England	Satisfactory
180-240 points	Bangor	Satisfactory

ENTRY	UNI/COLLEGE	RATING
Low-Medium	Lincoln	
180-240 points	Lampeter	Satisfactory
	Manchester Met	Satisfactory
	Sheffield Hallam	Satisfactory
	Plymouth	Satisfactory
	Central Lancs	Satisfactory
	Hertfordshire	Satisfactory
	Huddersfield	Satisfactory
	Kingston	Satisfactory
	King Alfred's	Satisfactory
	Leeds/Trin/All Saints	Satisfactory
	Ripon & York St John	Satisfactory
	Teesside	Satisfactory
	Wolverhampton	Satisfactory
	Staffordshire	Satisfactory
	Brighton	
	Coventry	23
	Westhill/Birmingham	
	Liverpool JMoores	Satisfactory
	Northumbria	Satisfactory
	Nottingham Trent	Satisfactory
	South Bank	
	Luton	Satisfactory
	Middlesex	Satisfactory
	Anglia	Satisfactory
	Chester	Satisfactory
	Derby	Satisfactory
	Glamorgan	Satisfactory
	Chichester	Satisfactory
	Colchester	
	East London	Satisfactory
	Liverpool Hope	Satisfactory
	North London	Satisfactory
	Norwich	
	St Mark & St John	Satisfactory
Low	Cumbria	
80-180 points	Southampton (New)	Satisfactory
	St Martins	Satisfactory
	Roehampton/Surrey	Satisfactory
	Portsmouth	Satisfactory
	Northampton	Satisfactory
	Buckingham	
	Greenwich	Satisfactory
	Newport	Satis (Comb Sts)
	Suffolk	
	Oxford Brookes	Satisfactory
	Edge Hill	Satisfactory
	Worcester	Satisfactory
	Bolton	Satisfactory
	Canterbury Christ	Excellent
	London Guildhall	
	De Montfort	Satisfactory
	Sunderland	Satisfactory
	Gloucestershire	Satisfactory
	Newman	
	Barnsley	
	Bishop Grosseteste	
	Doncaster	
	NEWI	Satisfactory
	Trinity Carmarthen	Satisfactory
	Bath Spa	Satisfactory
	Stranmillis	
	St Mary's	Satisfactory

LANGUAGES (French, German)

ENTRY	UNI/COLLEGE	RATING
High	Cambridge	22
280 points +	Oxford	21
High	British Institute	18
280 points +	Manchester	19, Fr.; 21, Ger.
	Birmingham	18, Fr.; 19, Ger.
	St Andrews	22
	Royal Holloway	21, Fr.; 19, Ger.
	Edinburgh	21
	Durham	22
	King's Coll	21, Fr.; 20, Ger.
	Glasgow	22
	Leeds	22, Fr.; 22, Ger.
	Sheffield	21, Fr.; 20, Ger.
	Heriot-Watt	21
	SSEES/UCL	
	York	22
	Southampton	18
Medium-High	Nottingham	16, Fr.; 22, Ger.
240-280 points	Bristol	20, Fr.; 21, Ger.
	UCL	21, Fr.; 23, Ger.
	Liverpool	22, Fr.; 19, Ger.
	Warwick	21, Fr.; 23, Ger.
	Cardiff	Satisfactory
	Reading	21, Fr.; 20, Ger.
	Swansea	Satis, Fr.; Ex,Ger.
	Bradford	18
	Queen's Belfast	20, Fr.; 19, Ger.
	Sussex	22, Fr.; 17, Ger.
	Bath	19
	Lancaster	20, Fr.; 19, Ger.
	Kent	19
	Newcastle	22
	Exeter	22, Fr.; 24, Ger.
	UMIST	18
	Surrey	18
	Loughborough	
	UEA	19
	Leicester	19, Fr.; 21, Ger.
	Goldsmiths	17
	Stirling	20
	Hull	21
	Keele	20, Fr.; 19, Ger.
	Aberdeen	22
	Strathclyde	22
	Ulster	20, Fr.; 19, Ger.
	Bristol West England	21
	Queen Mary & West.	23
	Aston	22
	Salford	20
	Wolverhampton	19, Fr.; 17, Ger.
Low-Medium	Bangor	Satisfactory
180-240 points		
(Fr. only)	Lampeter	Satisfactory
	Manchester Met	21
	London Guildhall	19
	Liverpool JM	19
(Fr. only)	Brighton	20
	Kingston	21
	Coventry	21
	Northumbria	23
	Robert Gordon	19
	Westminster	23, Fr.; 20, Ger.
	Oxford Brookes	22
	Staffordshire	21
	South Bank	22
	Anglia	21
	Luton	20
	Middlesex	19
	Nottingham Trent	17
	Portsmouth	23, Fr.; 21, Ger.
	Huddersfield	15

ENTRY	UNI/COLLEGE	RATING
Low-Medium		
180-240 points		
(Fr. only)	Trinity All Saints	17
(Fr. only)	Liverpool Hope	19
	North London	20
Low/120-180	Bolton	19
(Fr. only)	Roehampton/Surrey	19
	East London	18
	Northampton	
	Derby	18
(Fr. only)	Canterbury	
	Sunderland	17
	De Montfort	17
	Glamorgan	
	Bucks Chilterns	
	Thames Valley	18

LAW

ENTRY	UNI/COLLEGE	RATING
High	Cambridge	Excellent
280 points +	Bristol	Excellent
	Birmingham	Satisfactory
	Edinburgh	Highly Satis
	Leeds	Satisfactory
	Oxford	Excellent
	UCL	Excellent
	Durham	Excellent
	King's Coll	Excellent
	Manchester	Excellent
	Nottingham	Excellent
	Queen's Belfast	Excellent
	Sheffield	Excellent
	Warwick	Excellent
	Reading	Satisfactory
	Glasgow	Highly Satis
	LSE	Excellent
	Southampton	Satisfactory
	Leicester	Excellent
	Cardiff	Satisfactory
	Newcastle	Satisfactory
	Oxford Brookes	Excellent
	Queen Mary	Satisfactory
	Brunel	Satisfactory
	City	Satisfactory
	UEA	Excellent
	Sussex	Satisfactory
	SOAS	Excellent
	Liverpool	Excellent
	Swansea	Satisfactory
	Aberystwyth	Satisfactory
	Dundee	Highly Satis
	Kingston	Satisfactory
	Manchester Met	Satisfactory
	Nottingham Trent	Satisfactory
	Strathclyde	Highly Satis
	Ulster	Satisfactory
	Hull	Satisfactory
Medium-High	Keele	Satisfactory
240-280 points	Westminster	Satisfactory
	Stirling	
	Essex	Excellent
	Bournemouth	Satisfactory
	Hertfordshire	Satisfactory
	Exeter	Satisfactory
	Lancaster	Satisfactory
	Aberdeen	Highly Satis
	Leeds Met	Satisfactory
Medium-High	Napier	
240-280 points	Bangor	
	Bristol WestEngland	Excellent
	Blackburn	
	Sheffield Hallam	Satisfactory
	Brighton	
	Northumbria	Excellent
	Coventry	Satisfactory
	Kent	Satisfactory
Low-Medium	Liverpool JM	Satisfactory
180-240 points	Staffordshire	Satisfactory
	Huddersfield	Satisfactory
	Greenwich	Satisfactory
	Middlesex	Satisfactory
	Teesside	Satisfactory
	Lincoln	Satisfactory
	De Montfort	Satisfactory
	Plymouth	Satisfactory
	Derby	Satisfactory
	Central Lancs	Satisfactory
	North London	Satisfactory
	Portsmouth	
	Wolverhampton	Satisfactory
	Croydon	Satisfactory
	Buckingham	
	South Bank	Satisfactory
	Anglia	Satisfactory
	Luton	Satisfactory
	East London	Satisfactory
Low	Glasgow Cal	Satisfactory
80-180 points	Bolton Inst	
	Edge Hill	
	Robert Gordon	
	Central England	Satisfactory
	Northampton	Satisfactory
	London Guildhall	Satisfactory
	Abertay Dundee	Satisfactory
	Glamorgan	Satisfactory
	Bradford College	
	Bucks Chilterns	
	Sunderland	
	Thames Valley	Satisfactory
	Doncaster	
	Paisley	
	Southampton Inst	Satisfactory
	Bell	
	Holborn	
	NEWI	
	Swansea Inst	Satisfactory

MATHEMATICS

ENTRY	UNI/COLLEGE	RATING
High	Cambridge	23
280 points +	Oxford	
	Warwick	
	Durham	21
	Imperial	22
	Bristol	23
	LSE	22
	Birmingham	24
	Southampton	20
	Royal Holloway	22
	Edinburgh	Excellent
	Manchester	22
	Sheffield	21
	Nottingham	23
	Leeds	??
	Bath	24

ENTRY	UNI/COLLEGE	RATING
Medium-High	St Andrews	Excellent
240-280 points	UMIST	22
	Sussex	23
	Swansea	Satisfactory
	Brunel	22
	Cardiff	Satisfactory
	York	22
	Kent	21
	King's College	21
	Liverpool	23
	Portsmouth	22
	Leicester	22
	Aston	19
	Salford	21
	UCL	23
	Exeter	22
	Glasgow	Highly Satis
	Queen's Belfast	22
	Newcastle	
	Essex	20
	Surrey	21
Low-Medium	Lancaster	22
180-240 points	Loughborough	22
	Keele	22
	Aberdeen	Highly Satis
	Stirling	Highly Satis
	Aberystwyth	Satisfactory
	Huddersfield	21
	Queen Mary & West.	21
	Reading	22
	Ulster	22
	City	23
	Bangor	Satisfactory
	Plymouth	20
	Bristol West England	21
	Brighton	22
	Hertfordshire	21
	Heriot-Watt	Highly Satis
	UEA	23
	Napier	Highly Satis
	Westhill/Birmingham	
	Westminster	20
	De Montfort	20
	Manchester Met	20
	Kingston	23
	Luton	
	Nottingham Trent	21
	Teesside	
	Chester	22
	Chichester	
	Northumbria	21
Low	Hull	22
80-180 points	Glasgow Cal	Highly Satis
	Dundee	Highly Satis
	Central Lancs	19
	Anglia	
	Coventry	23
	Liverpool Hope	21
	Liverpool JM	21
	Greenwich	19
	Oxford Brookes	22
	Strathclyde	Highly Satis
	Bolton	20
	Canterbury Christ	22
	Edge Hill	20
	Goldsmiths	21
	St Martin	
	Sunderland	
	Sheffield Hallam	23

ENTRY	UNI/COLLEGE	RATING
Low	Glamorgan	Satisfactory
80-180 points	North London	21
	Derby	21
	Middlesex	20
	Northampton	
	Wolverhampton	20
	Paisley	Highly Satis
	London Guildhall	18
	Bath Spa	
	Barnsley	
	Open	20

MEDIA

ENTRY	UNI/COLLEGE	RATING
High	Warwick	23
280 points +	Leeds	22
	Sussex	23
	City	19
	Leicester	21
	Sheffield	
	Birmingham	
	Nottingham Trent	21
	Westminster	23
	Liverpool	
	Bournemouth	22
	Goldsmiths	22
	Cardiff	Satisfactory
	Royal Holloway	
	Stirling	Highly Satis
	Essex	
Medium-High	UEA	23
240-280 points	Lancaster	
	Bradford	
	Brunel	20
	Ulster	21
	Loughborough	
	Portsmouth	
	Brighton	
	Staffordshire	
Low-Medium	St Martin's	
180-240 points	Napier	Highly Satis
	Sheffield Hallam	19
	Oxford Brookes	21
	Trinity All Saints	
	Roehampton/Surrey	
	Falmouth	18
	Warrington	19
	Bangor	
	St Mark & St John	19
	Queen Margaret	
	Sunderland	22
	Central Lancs	22
	Huddersfield	18
	King Alfred's	18
	Hertfordshire	
	Manchester Met	
	Glamorgan	
	Anglia	18
	Lampeter	
	Northampton	21
	Northumbria	
	Liverpool JM	22
	London Guildhall	17
	Cumbria	19
	Edge Hill	20
	Robert Gordon	
	Bristol West England	22
	De Montfort	20

ENTRY	UNI/COLLEGE	RATING
Low-Medium 180-240 points	Lincoln	17
	South Bank	20
	Central England	21
	Wolverhampton	19
	Luton	22
	Leeds Met	19
	Middlesex	
	Surrey Inst	17
	Teesside	
	Greenwich	19
	East London	16
	North London	17
	UC Chichester 24	
	Colchester	
	Farnborough	17
Low 80-180 points	Glasgow Cal	Highly Satis
	Coventry	18
	Suffolk	
	Canterbury Christ	20
	York St John 20	
	Swansea Inst	
	Worcester	
	Southampton Inst	18
	Gloucestershire	20
	Bucks Chilterns	18
	St Mary's	
	Barnsley	
	Thames Valley	
	Paisley	
	NEWI	
	Doncaster	
	London Inst	20
	Trinity Carmarthen	Satisfactory
	Ravensbourne	
	West Herts	

ENTRY	UNI/COLLEGE	RATING
High 280 points +	Cambridge	Excellent
	King's Coll	Excellent
	Birmingham	Excellent
	Oxford	Satisfactory
	Imperial	
	Nottingham	Excellent
	Royal Academy	Excellent
	Manchester	Excellent
	Glasgow	Highly Satis
	Royal Holloway	Satisfactory
	Goldsmiths	Excellent
	Sussex	Excellent
	York	Excellent
	Southampton	Excellent
	Bristol	Satisfactory
	Liverpool	Satisfactory
	Sheffield	Excellent
Medium-High 240-280 points	Durham	Satisfactory
	Cardiff	Satisfactory
	City	Excellent
	UEA	Satisfactory
	Leeds	Excellent
	Reading	Satisfactory
	Brunel	Satisfactory
	Ulster	Excellent
	Exeter	Satisfactory
	SOAS	Excellent
	Hull	Satisfactory
	Bangor	Excellent
	Keele	Excellent
	Lancaster	Excellent
	Queen's Belfast	Excellent
	Bristol West England	
Low-Medium 180-240 points	Newcastle	Satisfactory
	De Montfort	
	Warrington	
	Edinburgh	Highly Satis
	Napier	Satisfactory
	Surrey	Excellent
	Hertfordshire	Satisfactory
	Central Lancs	
	Colchester	
	Kingston	Satisfactory
	Leeds Coll Music	
	Strathclyde	
	Westhill/Birm	
	Welsh Coll Music	Satisfactory
	Bucks Chilterns	
	Middlesex	Satisfactory
	South Bank	
	Anglia	Excellent
	Chichester	Satisfactory
	Derby	Satisfactory
	Liverpool Hope	Satisfactory
	Staffordshire	
	Bretton Hall	Satisfactory
	St Martin	Satisfactory
Low 80-180 points	Dartington Coll	
	Roehampton/Surrey	Satisfactory
	Northampton	Satisfactory
	Bolton	
	Scarborough/Hull	
	Wolverhampton	Satisfactory
	Bath Spa	Satisfactory
	Oxford Brookes	Satisfactory
	Manchester Met	
	Canterbury Ch Ch	Satisfactory
	Ripon & York St John	
	Huddersfield	Excellent

MEDICINE

ENTRY	UNI/COLLEGE	RATING
High 280 points +	Cambridge	21
	Oxford	21
	Birmingham	20
	Bristol	20
	Edinburgh	Highly satis.
	Glasgow	Excellent
	Leicester	23
	Manchester	24
	Newcastle	24
	Nottingham	
	Queen's Belfast	22
	Uni Wales Coll Med	
	St George's	23
	Dundee	Excellent
	UCL	21
	(Royal Free	18)
	Aberdeen	Excellent
	Imperial	21
	King's College	22
	Liverpool	24
	Queen Mary & West.	21
	Sheffield	19
	Southampton	24
	St Andrews	Highly satis.
	Leeds	18

MUSIC

Note: high level talent in performance (incl Grade 8 RSM) is required for entry to some of these courses.

ENTRY	UNI/COLLEGE	RATING
Low	Sunderland	
80-180 points	Barnsley	
	Coventry	
	Thames Valley	Satisfactory
	Royal Coll Music	Excellent
	NEWI	
	Salford	Excellent
	Central England	Excellent

Colleges and universities for which A level grades are not critical for selection:

- Brighton
- Glasgow Cal
- Guildhall Mus/Dram
- Highlands & Islands
- Lincoln
- LIPA
- Newcastle College
- Rose Bruford
- Westminster

PHYSICS

ENTRY	UNI/COLLEGE	RATING
High	Cambridge	23
280 points +	Oxford	23
	Imperial	22
	Bristol	23
	Warwick	24
	Durham	24
	Royal Holloway	23
	Nottingham	23
	Liverpool JM	
Medium-High	UMIST	21
240-280 points	UEA	
	UCL	23
	Sheffield	22
	Birmingham	23
	Manchester	24
	Southampton	22
	St Andrews	Excellent
	Loughborough	23
	York	24
	King's College	22
	Leeds	24
	Bath	24
	Glasgow	Excellent
	Queen's Belfast	23
	Reading	24
	Swansea	Excellent
	Bangor	
	Edinburgh	Excellent
	Queen Mary & West.	21
	Cardiff	Satisfactory
	Exeter	22
	Liverpool	24
	Newcastle	21
	Kent	21
Low-Medium	Keele	22
180-240 points	Leicester	23
	Aberdeen	
	Hull	23
	Hertfordshire	
	Aberystwyth	Satisfactory
	Lancaster	23
	Surrey	23
	Staffordshire	22
	Westhill/Birm.	
	Heriot-Watt	Highly Satis

ENTRY	UNI/COLLEGE	RATING
Low-Medium	Salford	23
180-240 points	Portsmouth	20
	Central Lancs	19
	Nottingham Trent	24
Low	Dundee	Highly Satis
80-180 points	Northumbria	23
	Strathclyde	Excellent
	Sussex	22
	Napier	Satisfactory
	Sheffield Hallam	24
	Glamorgan	
	Glasgow Cal	Highly Satis
	Robert Gordon	Highly Satis
	Paisley	Satisfactory
	Barnsley	

POLITICS

ENTRY	UNI/COLLEGE	RATING
High	Cambridge	
280 points +	Oxford	24
	St Andrews	
	LSE	22
	Newcastle	23
	Edinburgh	Highly Satis
	Nottingham	24
	Royal Holloway	
	Warwick	24
	Bristol	23
	Durham	
	Exeter	23
	Liverpool	
	Manchester	24
	Birmingham	
	Leeds	23
	Sheffield	24
	Sussex	23
	UEA	24
	Glasgow	Highly Satis
	Reading	22
	Bath	24
Medium-High	York	**24**
240-280 points	Cardiff	Satisfactory
	Hull	23
	Swansea	Satisfactory
	Lancaster	23
	Queen's Belfast	23
	Queen Mary & West.	23
	Brunel	
	Dundee	Highly Satis
	Leeds Met	
	Leicester	
	SSEES/UCL	22
	Stirling	Highly Satis
	Southampton	
	SOAS	
	Kent	
	Essex	24
	Loughborough	
	Goldsmiths	22
	Keele	24
	Bradford	24
	Ulster	
	Aberdeen	Highly Satis
	Strathclyde	Excellent
	Aberystwyth	Excellent
	Aston	
	Bangor	
	Westminster	22
Low-Medium	Salford	24
180-240 points	Manchester Met	

ENTRY	UNI/COLLEGE	RATING
Low-Medium	Plymouth	22
180-240 points	Kingston	23
	De Montfort	24
	Bristol West England	21
	Central England	21
	Hertfordshire	
	Huddersfield	23
	Sheffield Hallam	
	Staffordshire	
	Coventry	23
	Brighton	
	Lincoln	22
	Nottingham Trent	22
	South Bank	21
	Wolverhampton	
	Luton	
	Middlesex	22
	Buckingham	
	Central Lancs	22
	Liverpool JM	22
	Anglia	20
	Derby	
Low	St Martin's	
80-180 points	Greenwich	
	Southampton Inst	
	Northumbria	22
	Portsmouth	23
	Teesside	
	East London	
	Northampton	
	Oxford Brookes	22
	Robert Gordon	
	Sunderland	20
	Glamorgan	Satisfactory
	Gloucestershire	
	North London	
	Barnsley	
	Thames Valley	
	London Guildhall	22
	Open	22

PSYCHOLOGY

ENTRY	UNI/COLLEGE	RATING
High	Cambridge	24
280 points +	Oxford	24
	Durham	23
	Edinburgh	Highly Satis
	Leeds	23
	Sheffield	22
	UCL	22
	St Andrews	Excellent
	Bath	
	Nottingham	24
	Birmingham	23
	Liverpool	22
	Warwick	21
	York	24
	Bristol	23
	Cardiff	Excellent
	LSE	23
	Royal Holloway	24
	Sussex	21
	Kent	22
	Newcastle	24
	Manchester	22
	Hull	23
	Reading	24
	Swansea	Excellent

ENTRY	UNI/COLLEGE	RATING
High	City	21
280 points +	Goldsmiths	22
	Queen's Belfast	24
	Surrey	22
	Loughborough	24
	Essex	22
Medium-High	UEA	
240-280 points	Brunel	22
	Keele	23
	Leicester	24
	Southampton	21
	Stirling	Excellent
	Portsmouth	23
	Exeter	23
	Aston	22
	Hertfordshire	23
	Huddersfield	20
	Bangor	Excellent
	Glasgow	Excellent
	Ulster	23
	Bradford	
	Heriot-Watt	
	Strathclyde	Highly Satis
	Sheffield Hallam	24
	Bristol West England	22
	Lincoln	21
	Southampton Inst	19
	Staffordshire	23
Low-Medium	Bath Spa	21
180-240 points	Lancaster	24
	Leeds Met	20
	Aberdeen	Highly Satis
	Coventry	21
	Glasgow Cal	Highly Satis
	UWIC (Cardiff)	Excellent
	Wolverhampton	21
	Anglia	**22**
	Greenwich	22
	Queen Margaret	
	Dundee	Excellent
	Plymouth	23
	South Bank	20
	Central Lancs	24
	Kingston	
	Middlesex	21
	Bournemouth	
	De Montfort	22
	Teesside	20
	Buckingham	
	Central England	
	King Alfred's	21
	Trinity All Saints	
	Manchester Met	22
	Westminster	24
	Edge Hill	22
	York St John	20
	Westhill/Birmingham	
	Worcester	20
	St Martin	
	London Guildhall	22
	Liverpool JMoores	19
	Nottingham Trent	22
	Northumbria	22
	Derby	20
	Gloucestershire	21
	Luton	22
	Roehampton/Surrey	23
	Bolton	24
	Chester	20

ENTRY	UNI/COLLEGE	RATING
Low-Medium	North London	19
180-240 points	Northampton	20
Low	Abertay Dundee	Highly Satis
80-180 points	Sunderland	20
	East London	23
	Liverpool Hope	22
	Oxford Brookes	23
	Canterbury Ch Ch	20
	Paisley	Highly Satis
	Glamorgan	Satisfactory
	Bucks Chilterns	21
	Newman	19
	Thames Valley	20
	Bradford College	
	Doncaster	
	Suffolk	21
	NEWI	

SOCIAL POLICY

REQUIRED	UNI/COLLEGE	RATING
High	Edinburgh	Excellent
280 points +	LSE	Excellent
	Royal Holloway	
	Glasgow	Excellent
	Nottingham	21
	Sheffield	Excellent
	Sussex	Satisfactory
	Essex	
Medium-High	Durham	21
240-280 points	Newcastle	Excellent
	Birmingham	Satisfactory
	Leeds	20
	Manchester	Excellent
	Cardiff	Satisfactory
	Stirling	
	Swansea	Satisfactory
	Liverpool	
	Queen's Belfast	19
	Warwick	24
	York	Excellent
	Kent	Excellent
	Bath	Excellent
	Goldsmiths	Satisfactory
	Bristol	Satisfactory
	Ulster	Excellent
	Hull	Excellent
	Loughborough	23
	Southampton	21
	Aston	
	Nottingham Trent	Satisfactory
Low-Medium	Leeds Met	Satisfactory
180-240 points	Bradford	
	Bangor	Satisfactory
	Sheffield Hallam	22
	Queen Margaret	
	Plymouth	Satisfactory
	Lincoln	Satisfactory
	Brighton	Satisfactory
	Hertfordshire	17
	King Alfred's	
	Salford	
	Wolverhampton	Satisfactory
	Coventry	21
	Manchester Met	21
	Paisley	
	Staffordshire	
	London Guildhall	Satisfactory

ENTRY	UNI/COLLEGE	RATING
Low-Medium	Brunel	Excellent
180-240 points	South Bank	
	Teesside	Satisfactory
	Luton	Satisfactory
	Middlesex	19
	Roehampton/Surrey	Satisfactory
	Anglia	
	Central England	
	Central Lancashire	Satisfactory
	Glamorgan	
Low	St Martin	
80-180 points	De Montfort	Satisfactory
	Bucks Chilterns	
	Portsmouth	Satisfactory
	East London	Excellent
	North London	Satisfactory
	Edge Hill	Excellent
	Suffolk	
	Gloucestershire	
	Newport	
	NEWI	
	Somerset	

SOCIOLOGY

ENTRY	UNI/COLLEGE	RATING
High	Cambridge	
280 points +	Oxford	
	Edinburgh	Excellent
	Bristol	21
	Royal Holloway	21
	Aston	
	LSE	20
	Manchester	21
	Leeds	20
	Birmingham	24
	UEA	16
	Glasgow	Excellent
	Nottingham	21
	Sheffield	Excellent
	Surrey	21
	Sussex	24
	Essex	22
Medium-High	Durham	21
240-280 points	Newcastle	
	Cardiff	Satisfactory
	Liverpool	21
	Stirling	Excellent
	Swansea	Satisfactory
	Warwick	24
	York	23
	Brunel	22
	City	19
	Goldsmiths	21
	Leicester	19
	Queen's Belfast	19
	Reading	22
	Ulster	17
	Kent	21
	Bath	19
	Lancaster	21
	Loughborough	23
	Exeter	21
	Hull	20
	Keele	22
	Bradford	17
	Nottingham Trent	19
	Aberdeen	Excellent
	Sheffield Hallam	22

ENTRY	UNI/COLLEGE	RATING
Medium-High 240-280 points	Strathclyde	Highly Satis
	Bangor	Satisfactory
	Southampton	21
	Westminster	18
Low-Medium 180-240 points	Trinity All Saints	20
	Salford	20
	Manchester Met	21
	Plymouth	20
	Oxford Brookes	21
	Kingston	21
	Bristol West England	23
	Greenwich	23
	Hertfordshire	17
	King Alfred's	
	Coventry	21
	Central England	18
	Staffordshire	17
	Central Lancs	18
	Gloucestershire	20
	Luton	18
	Middlesex	19
	Portsmouth	20
	Roehampton/Surrey	20
	Northumbria	20
	Liverpool JM	18
	Anglia	20
	Chichester	
	Colchester	
	De Montfort	17
	Derby	18
	East London	19
	Huddersfield	
	Liverpool Hope	22
	North London	
	Norwich	
Low 80-180 points	South Bank	19
	Edge Hill	
	Abertay Dundee	
	Bolton	
	Northampton	20
	Teesside	19
	Canterbury Ch Ch	
	Worcester	21
	Bath Spa	22
	Sunderland	21
	Glamorgan	Satisfactory
	Bucks Chilterns	16
	St Mark & St John	22
	Thames Valley 22	
	Doncaster	
	London Guildhall	17
	Abertay Dundee	
	St Mary's Strawb	20

SPORT/SPORT SCIENCE

ENTRY	UNI/COLLEGE	RATING
High 280 points +	Bath	23
	Birmingham	
	Leeds	
	Stirling	
	Ulster	23
Medium-High 240-280 points	Exeter	
	Liverpool JM	
	Swansea	
	Edinburgh	
	Loughborough	23
	Bangor	

ENTRY	UNI/COLLEGE	RATING
Medium-High 240-280 points	Brunel	
	Leeds Met	22
	Durham	
	Glasgow	
	York St John	
	Northumbria	21
	Trin/All Saints	20
	Hertfordshire	
	Hull	
	Brighton	
	Essex	
	Central Lancs	
	Kingston	
	Portsmouth	21
Low-Medium 180-240 points	UWIC (Cardiff)	
	Aberdeen	
	Sunderland	20
	Chichester	21
	Manchester Met	**22**
	Edge Hill	
	Sheffield Hallam	
	Salford	
	Nottingham Trent	
	De Montfort	23
	Plymouth	
	Staffordshire	22
	Wolverhampton	
	King Alfred's	
	Northampton	
	Strathclyde	
	Southampton (New)	
	Westhill/Birmingham	
	Westminster Uni	
	Worcester	
	St Martin	22
	Gloucestershire	
	South Bank	
	Greenwich	
	Huddersfield	
	Luton	
	Middlesex	
	North London	
	Roehampton/Surrey	21
	Teesside	
	Warrington	
	Chester	23
	Southampton Inst	21
	Bristol West England	
Low 80-180 points	Bolton	21
	Liverpool Hope	
	Anglia	
	Newport	
	Oxford Brookes	
	Canterbury Christ	21
	Glamorgan	
	Bucks Chilterns	
	St Mary's	21
	Thames Valley	
	Barnsley	
	Trinity Carmarthen	
	Coventry	
	St Mark & St John	
	NEWI	
	East London	

THEOLOGY

ENTRY	UNI/COLLEGE	RATING
High	Cambridge	23

ENTRY	UNI/COLLEGE	RATING
280 points +	Oxford	
	Birmingham	23
	Edinburgh	Highly Satis
Medium-High	Durham	23
240-280 points	Bristol	
	Newcastle	22
	Sheffield	
	Cardiff	Satisfactory
	Exeter	
	Manchester	
	Leeds	23
	King's College	
	SOAS	22
	Kent	**20**
	St Andrews	Highly Satis
	Nottingham	23
	Stirling	Excellent
	Queen's Belfast	22
	Lancaster	24
	Heythrop	
Low-Medium	Hull	23
180-240 points	Bangor	Excellent
	Glasgow	Highly Satis
	Oxford Brookes	
	Lampeter	
	King Alfred's	
	Manchester Met	
	Aberdeen	Highly Satis
	Leeds/Trin/All Saints	
	Westhill/Birmingham	
	Middlesex	
	Chester	22
	Chichester	
	Derby	22

ENTRY	UNI/COLLEGE	RATING
Low-Medium	Liverpool Hope	23
180-240 points	York St John	21
Low	St Martin	19
80-180 points	Roehampton/Surrey	
	Wolverhampton	21
	Greenwich	
	Bath Spa	
	Canterbury Christ	22
	Anglia Poly Uni	23
	Sunderland	
	Newman	
	Gloucestershire	23
	Trinity Carmarthen	Satisfactory
	Franciscan St. Centre	
	London Bible College	
	Highlands & Islands	
	St Mark & St John	23
	St Mary's	
	Open	22

VETERINARY SCIENCE

ENTRY	UNI/COLLEGE	RATING
High	Cambridge	23
280 points +	Royal Vet College	24
	Edinburgh	Excellent
	Glasgow	Excellent
	Liverpool	24
240 points	Middlesex	
Low-Medium	Bristol West England	
180 +	Bristol	24
140 points	Napier	

The Virgin
**Travellers'
Handbook**

The definitive guide for students and
career gap travellers planning a gapyear

'A gapyear
will change
your life'
Richard Branson

Tom Griffiths

Virgin

gapyear.com

'Recommended reading'
The Times

The definitive guide for students and career gap travellers planning
a gapyear. It's packed to the brim with essential information and practical
advice on everything you need to consider for your time out.

- Preparation and getting started
- Budgeting and finances
- Travelling alone or with friends
- Health and safety

- The final countdown
- Working overseas
- Dealing with parents and advice for parents
- Home to reality

With advice ranging from how to pack to how to use the internet, and
including a 100-page directory of the top 50 backpacking destinations,
this guide tells you everything you need to know, plus a huge number
of things you hadn't even thought of!

**'This excellent handbook shows the loopholes,
tricks, contacts and danger spots'**
Buzz

UK UNIVERSITIES

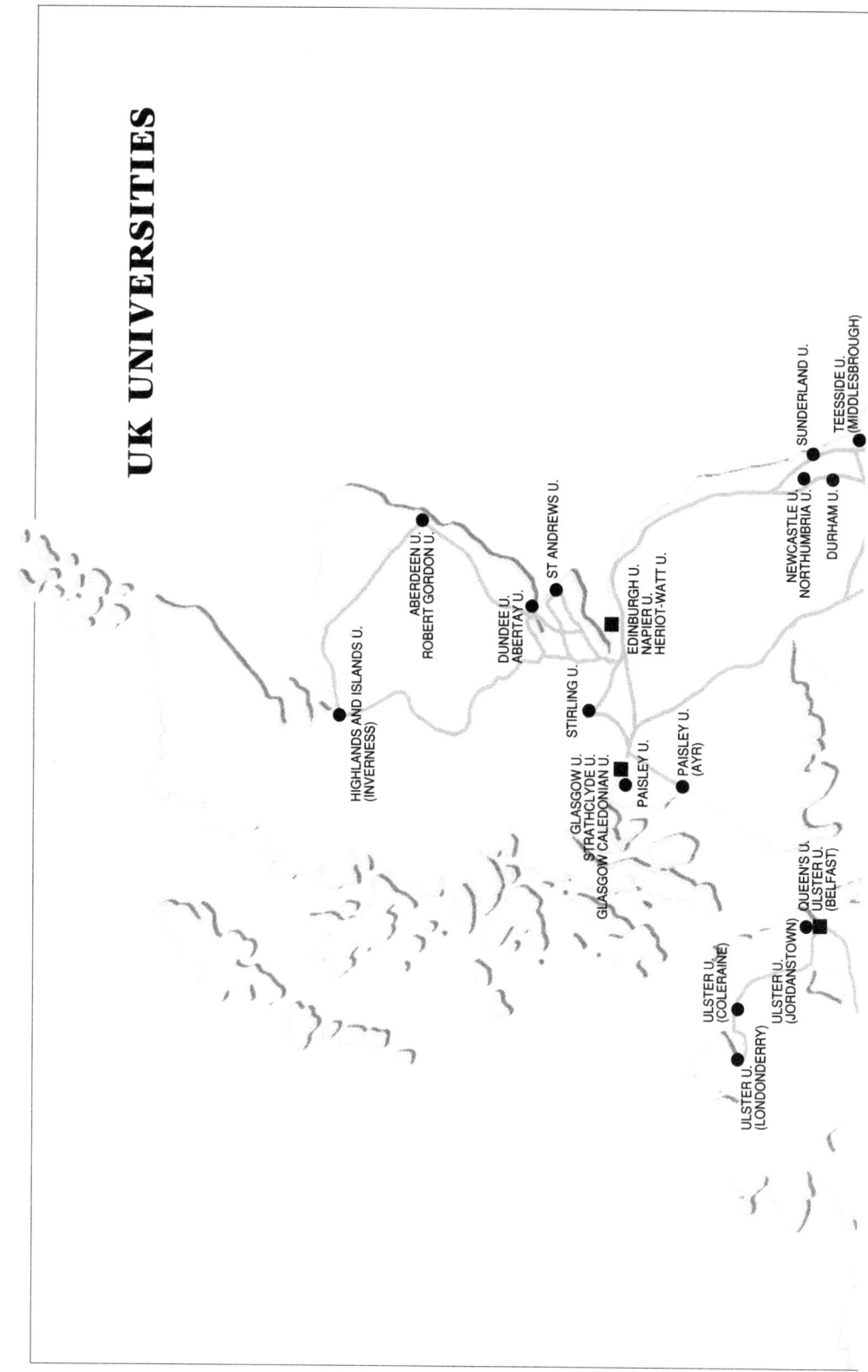

HIGHLANDS AND ISLANDS U.
(INVERNESS)

ABERDEEN U.
ROBERT GORDON U.

DUNDEE U.
ABERTAY U.

ST ANDREWS U.

STIRLING U.

GLASGOW U.
STRATHCLYDE U.
GLASGOW CALEDONIAN U.

PAISLEY U.

PAISLEY U.
(AYR)

EDINBURGH U.
NAPIER U.
HERIOT-WATT U.

NEWCASTLE U.
NORTHUMBRIA U.

SUNDERLAND U.

DURHAM U.

TEESSIDE U.
(MIDDLESBROUGH)

ULSTER U.
(COLERAINE)

ULSTER U.
(LONDONDERRY)

ULSTER U.
(JORDANSTOWN)

QUEEN'S U.
ULSTER U.
(BELFAST)

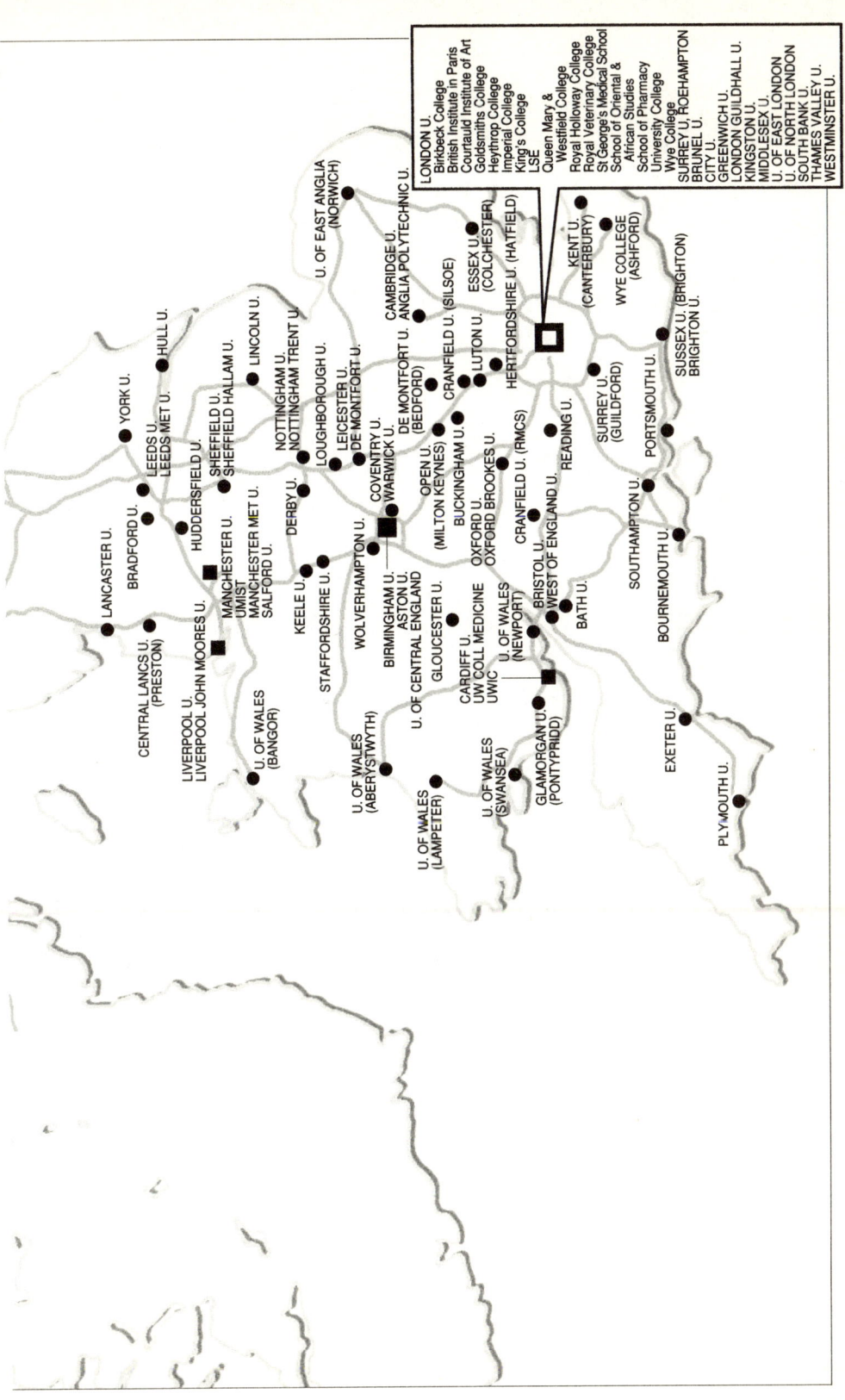

LONDON U.
Birkbeck College
British Institute in Paris
Courtauld Institute of Art
Goldsmiths College
Heythrop College
Imperial College
King's College
LSE
Queen Mary &
  Westfield College
Royal Holloway College
Royal Veterinary College
St George's Medical School
School of Oriental &
  African Studies
School of Pharmacy
University College
Wye College
SURREY U. ROEHAMPTON
BRUNEL U.
CITY U.
GREENWICH U.
LONDON GUILDHALL U.
KINGSTON U.
MIDDLESEX U.
U. OF EAST LONDON
U. OF NORTH LONDON
SOUTH BANK U.
THAMES VALLEY U.
WESTMINSTER U.

U. OF EAST ANGLIA
(NORWICH)

CAMBRIDGE U.
ANGLIA POLYTECHNIC U.

ESSEX U.
(COLCHESTER)

DE MONTFORT U.
(BEDFORD)

CRANFIELD U. (SILSOE)

LUTON U.

HERTFORDSHIRE U. (HATFIELD)

KENT U.
(CANTERBURY)

WYE COLLEGE
(ASHFORD)

SUSSEX U. (BRIGHTON)
BRIGHTON U.

HULL U.

LINCOLN U.

NOTTINGHAM U.
NOTTINGHAM TRENT U.

LEICESTER U.
DE MONTFORT U.

LOUGHBOROUGH U.

OPEN U.
(MILTON KEYNES)

BUCKINGHAM U.

OXFORD U.
OXFORD BROOKES U.

CRANFIELD U. (RMCS)

READING U.

SURREY U.
(GUILDFORD)

PORTSMOUTH U.

YORK U.

LEEDS U.
LEEDS MET U.

SHEFFIELD U.
SHEFFIELD HALLAM U.

HUDDERSFIELD U.

DERBY U.

COVENTRY U.
WARWICK U.

BIRMINGHAM U.
ASTON U.

U. OF CENTRAL ENGLAND

BRISTOL U.
WEST OF ENGLAND U.

BATH U.

SOUTHAMPTON U.

BOURNEMOUTH U.

BRADFORD U.

MANCHESTER U.
UMIST
MANCHESTER MET U.
SALFORD U.

KEELE U.

STAFFORDSHIRE U.

WOLVERHAMPTON U.

GLOUCESTER U.

CARDIFF U.
UW COLL MEDICINE
UWIC

U. OF WALES
(NEWPORT)

LANCASTER U.

CENTRAL LANCS U.
(PRESTON)

LIVERPOOL U.
LIVERPOOL JOHN MOORES U.

U. OF WALES
(BANGOR)

U. OF WALES
(ABERYSTWYTH)

U. OF WALES
(LAMPETER)

U. OF WALES
(SWANSEA)

GLAMORGAN U.
(PONTYPRIDD)

EXETER U.

PLYMOUTH U.

UNIVERSITY OF ABERDEEN

The University of Aberdeen
Regent Walk
Aberdeen AB24 3FX

TEL 01224 273504
FAX 01224 272031
EMAIL sras@abdn.ac.uk
WEB www.abdn.ac.uk/sras

Aberdeen University Students' Association
Elphinstone Road
Aberdeen AB24 3TU

TEL 01224 274200
FAX 01224 274247
EMAIL office@ausa.org.uk
WEB www.ausa.org.uk

VAG VIEW

*A*berdeen *is the oldest university institution outside Oxbridge and its Chair of Medicine was the first established in the English-speaking world. King's College Aberdeen was founded in 1495. Considering the highly traditional backdrop, it well deserves the feather in its cap awarded this year for being among the elite in extending a welcoming hand to non-traditional applicants – 13% came from poor areas – while showing no signs of beefing up its drop-out rate (the usual flip side of such an altruistic policy). These newcomers can luxuriate in an excellent record in both the teaching and research assessments and in graduate employment: 89% of its teaching is either Excellent or Highly Satisfactory, and it achieved a whole host of world-class Grade 5* and Grade 5s for its research (see* Academic Excellence *box, page 42).*

On the downside, it can be cold and grey this far north, and thanks to North Sea oil the cost of living is high (though the university's Joblink does much to re-store the student pocket).

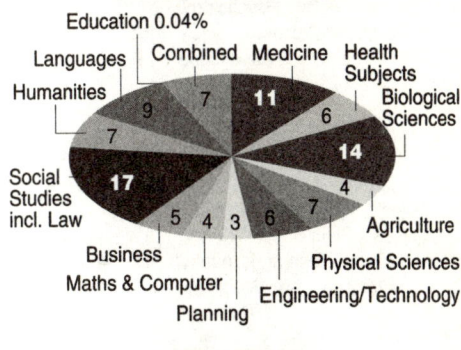

SUBJECT AREAS (%)

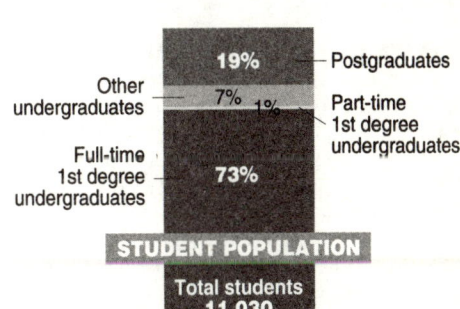

STUDENT POPULATION

Total students
11,030

UNIVERSITY/STUDENT PROFILE

University since	**1495**
Situation/style	**Civic**
Student population	**11,030**
Full-time undergraduates	**8,020**
- mature	**16%**
- overseas	**10%**
- male/female	**48/52**
- state sector intake	**81%**
- non-traditional student intake	**13%**
- drop-out rate	**9%**
- undergraduate applications	**Up 17%**

*see Introduction for key to tables

VIEW FROM THE GROUND
by Rob Littlejohn

Aberdeen is on the North East coast of Scotland, pretty much final step on the way to the Arctic (a couple of farms and the odd island notwithstanding). Easily reachable, if you've a bit of time on your hands, Aberdeen provides a safe haven for those trying to get as far away as possible from parents, and the rest of civilisation.

The Granite City, as it is accurately called (everything is grey, and I mean everything), harbours a bit of a cosmopolitan atmosphere (there's some docks) and a very long beach. The climate is raw, as are the people, but when the sun shines, everything warms up and it's actually a beautiful city.

ACADEMIC EXCELLENCE

TEACHING:
(Rated Excellent, Highly Satis. or 17+ out of 24)

Economics, Geography, Sociology, Medicine, Cellular & Molecular Biology, Organismal Biology, French Studies.	**Excellent**
Chemistry, Geology, Maths & Statistics, Civil Engineering, Mechanical +Manufacturing Engineering, Theol., Finance & Accounting, History of Art, History, Law, Philosophy, Politics, English, Psychology.	**Highly Satis.**
Euro langs. other than French	**22**
Planning & Landscape	**19**

RESEARCH:
Top grades 5/5*

French	**Grade 5***
Community-based Clinical Subjects, Physiology, Biological Sciences, Plant & Soil Science, Pure Maths, Town and Country Planning, Law, Sociology, Theology	**Grade 5**

KING'S COLLEGE CAMPUS

The city itself is framed around the ridiculously long Union Street (surely the only street in the world to have two McDonald's on it), with the main university campus about a mile (and a lung-busting hill) north of the main centre. This is the King's College campus, the oldest part of the university, located in the imaginatively entitled Old Aberdeen. There are other campuses (or should that be campii?), one in town which is not used anymore, except to keep dead bodies for first year medics to play about with, and the hospital, where they keep the live bodies for the rest of the medics to play about with.

The university loves the fact that King's is around 500 years old and makes a point of telling you this at every opportunity. Look out for marketing-gone-mad photos of King's College all over the shop (the King's College Visitors' Centre Shop, to be precise) and on postcards, T-shirts, mugs, biros, novelty condoms (if only) and other useful items.

STUDENT PROFILE

The students come in eight distinct groups: **Aberdonians,** who talk smugly about pubs in other parts of town and watch quietly as we get lost; **Country Teuchters** (pronounced *'choochters'* – there you know some local dialect already), very similar to Aberdonians, but without the urban sophistication; **Edinburgh Public Schoolers,** a feature of most Scottish unis with better English accents than most of those south of the border and more money than sense; **Other Scots** – Scotland has a greater tradition of staying at home to study and we do get some Edinburghers keen to distance themselves from a public school education, Glaswegians pining for home, sectarianism and annoying accents, and Dundonians just happy to be somewhere else. There's also the **Huge Bands of Others** – Northern Irish, random English, foreign students and Greeks, the final lot warranting their own category for sheer number!

ACADEMIA

Aberdeen is known for medicine, for biosciences, and for education – in 2001, the local base of Northern College (which also has an Excellent rating in social work) became part of the university. It is known, too, for its wide-ranging cross-faculty combined honours courses, which sometimes focus hard on areas of national domination in the employment tables – accountancy-finance, for example. In these areas, in property and agriculture too, they are among the leaders. The uni is also distinguished most famously for law, while close ties with the North Sea oil industry brought prominence to engineering and geology. Increasingly popular among applicants, it appears, are English and Psychology.

As one of four ancient universities in Scotland, the teaching is traditional, seminars, tutorials, etc, and some of the lecture rooms full of traditional character (and draughts). The flip side is that the Scottish system is more flexible than the English and that Aberdeen has a good reputation, without the stigma of being an Oxbridge wannabe, like St Andrews or Edinburgh. It, like the city, prides itself on a lack of pretension, and has had good showings in the university league tables.

Whether that means anything is up for debate, but there are those who think that it does.

> *It can be cold and grey this far north, and thanks to North Sea oil the cost of living is above average, but the bonus is a traditional university education with an inspired cross-faculty syllabus and the strong record in graduate employment which results from it.*

AT A GLANCE

ACADEMIC FILE:

Subjects assessed	**26**
Excellent/Highly Satisfactory	**89%**
Average requirements	**280 points**
Students-staff ratio	**15:1**
First/2:1 degree pass rate	**63%**

ACCOMMODATION FILE:

Guarantee to freshers	**100%**
Style	**Halls**
Approx price range pw	**£42-£75**
City rent pw	**£55-£65**

WHAT IT'S REALLY LIKE

UNIVERSITY:

Social Life	★★★★
Campus scene	**Small & friendly**
Student Union services	**Good**
Politics	**Student issues**
Sport	**Competitive**
National team position	**30th**
Sport facilities	**Improving**
Arts opportunities	**Drama, music exc.; film good; dance, art poor**
Student newspaper	**Gaudie**
Student radio	**Phase fm**
Nightclub	**Factory, Liquid Loft**
Bars	**Seasons, Snivells, Dungeon, Associates**
Union ents	**Miscalculation, Underground, Warp**
Union clubs/societies	**100**
Most popular society	**Cinema Club**
Smoking policy	**NS in Associates**
Parking	**Adequate**

CITY:

Entertainment	★★★★
Scene	**Intoxicating**
Town/gown relations	**Good**
Risk of violence	**Low**
Cost of living	**Above average**
Student concessions	**Average**
Survival + 2 nights out	**£70 pw**
Part-time work campus/town	**Average/excellent**

SOCIAL SCENE

STUDENTS' ASSOCIATION Ten minutes walk from King's College lie the bars – **Seasons**, **Sivells** (most popular), **Dungeon**, **Associates** (non-smoking) – the **Games Room** (8 full-size snooker tables, 8 pool tables, video games and quiz machines), and two nightclubs, **The Factory** and **The Liquid Loft** – *Miscalculation* (Thurs, R&B), *Underground* (Fri, big beat) and *Warp* (Sat, '60s, '70s, '80s). The clubs also play host to comedians, and weekly live bands. It's a wild old scene. An annual ball puts it all back together, attracting some 2,000 to the free bar and headline acts.

SPORT Facilities are generally good for those foolish enough to brave exposure, and the hills up the road in Deeside are glorious. In fact, all of the countryside surrounding Aberdeen is pretty stunning and, if you can pull yourself out of bed on a Saturday or Sunday morning, it's worth the time and effort. There are various uni societies whose sole aim seems to be to see how much pain they can inflict on people in the name of hiking and hillwalking, but if you wait until the summer and find a friend with a car, it's much more pleasant. The local football team (Aberdeen FC) have recently been ranked the worst in Europe, but may have turned the corner by the time you read this. They're worth a visit at least once, if only to hear as wide a range of profanities as you can in the western world (never satisfied, these Aberdonians).

TOWN Aberdeen can infuriate anyone not just wanting cheesy tunes and cheap drinks; most students love it. The pubs are numerous and range from the swanky to the wanky, with a number of solidly down to earth ones in between. There are only a few pubs near the campus, but town is overflowing. The clubs are either shiny and annoying or a dive with very sticky floors and, as long as you rotate your evenings out, there should

be enough to keep you interested throughout your four years.

For the more discerning arts lovers, besides the bus to Glasgow or Edinburgh, there's the nationally renowned **Lemon Tree** which gets decent bands and alternative theatre and, for a city its size, all the venues do remarkably well.

Safety is not a real problem – town/gown relations are generally amicable and the real enemy is the North Sea wind. Nice parks as well, though I wouldn't recommend them after dark.

The city council cleaned the main street of chewing gum recently and the city has won 'City In Bloom' titles on more than one occasion; it's a decent place to live, though expensive.

The oil industry still hikes prices around the city, but this does mean there is good quality of life. The place is small enough to be friendly, especially on campus, but never really claustrophobic.

The real problem is the grey – when the sky

WHERE GRADUATES END UP

23% Health (Medicine), Key Areas
8% Wholesale/Retail,
7% Education,
7% Finance,
6% Public Admin,
6% Manufacturing,
Property*, Accountancy, Niche Areas
Agric/Forestry*,
Film/Video, Defence,
Hotel/Restaurant, Sport

*indicates Top 10 Graduate Provider

Approximate employed **94%**

turns in November, the horizon kind of merges with the granite buildings and you lose yourself in a big grey blanket. Aberdeen, though, is a friendly place

and home to the best chip shop in Britain. What more could you want?

JOBS

With its academic strengths in medicine, law, education, there's no surprise that these areas are very popular destinations (law after further training), as indeed are finance and accountancy, which, taken together as commerce come second only to health. Agriculture and the property industry are very strong too.

GETTING THERE

☞ By road: from south, A92 and ring road where you'll pick up signs; from north, A96 or the A92.
☞ By rail: Edinburgh, 2:30; Dundee, 1:15; Newcastle, 4:50; London King's Cross, 7:00.
☞ By air: Aberdeen International Airport.
☞ By coach: London, 11.30; Birmingham, 12.35; Newcastle, 7.35.

UNIVERSITY OF ABERTAY DUNDEE

The University of Abertay Dundee
Bell Street
Dundee DD1 1HG

TEL 01382 308080
FAX 01382 308081
EMAIL iro@abertay.ac.uk
WEB www.abertay.ac.uk

Abertay Dundee Students' Association
158 Marketgait
Dundee DD1 1NJ

TEL 01382 227477
FAX 01382 206569
EMAIL [initial/name]@tay.ac.uk
WEB www.abertayunion.com

VAG VIEW

*L*ocated on a modern campus in the city centre, Abertay has four academic schools: School of Computing, the Dundee Business School, School of Science & Engineering and the School of Social & Health Sciences. Formerly, it was the Dundee Institute of Technology.

Among its research centres is the International Centre for Computing and Virtual Entertainment (IC-CAVE), the country's first dedicated research and development facility for computer games and virtual entertainment. A defining mark is that Abertay was the first university to offer Computer Games Technology as a degree, a course designed in conjunction with ex-Abertay student David Jones, the creator of Lemmings and Grand Theft Auto. Along

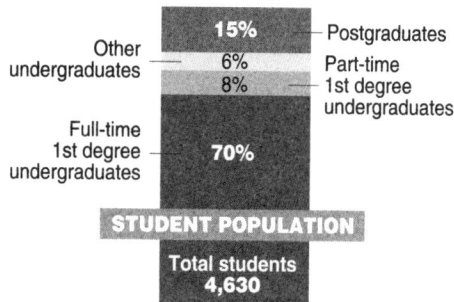

with an MSc in software engineering and a degree course in computer games writing, there is a BSc in computer games with Japanese, and up for validation, a BA in Interactive Entertainment Design, which focuses on the new media and creative industries. Small wonder that the uni can lay claim to being the fourth highest spender on networked computers among UK unis.

UNIVERSITY/STUDENT PROFILE	
University since	**1994**
Situation/style	**Civic**
Student population	**4,630**
Full-time undergraduates	**3,250**
- mature	**39%**
- overseas	**9%**
- male/female	**52/48**
- state sector intake	**98%**
- non-traditional student intake	**27%, high**
- drop-out rate	**19%, high**
- undergraduate applications	**Up 9.4%**
see Introduction for key to tables	

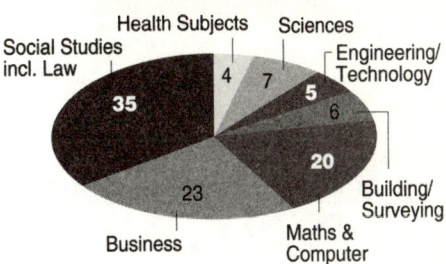

SUBJECT AREAS (%)

Health Subjects — 4
Sciences — 7
Engineering/Technology — 5
Building/Surveying — 6
Maths & Computer — 20
Business — 23
Social Studies incl. Law — 35

STUDENT PROFILE

There is a huge student community in Dundee, with two universities and three colleges. Abertay accounts for a high local intake and sizeable mature and overseas student populations. The uni gained the largest access partnership grant from the Scottish Funding Council last year for coming third in a British league table measuring intake of students from disadvantaged neighbourhoods. Sadly they have not managed to peg the concomitant drop-out rate, which last year stood at a depressing 19%, but maybe this is a necessary settling down period, as they build their student base apace.

ACADEMIA

In addition to a newish £8 million library, and a CD ROM library and several networked databases, all students have access to laser colour copying and printing. New course developments include the BA Interactive Entertainment Design, a BA in International Business Management, a BSc in Forensic Sciences, which builds on existing academic strengths, and BAs in Communication, Criminological Studies, Web Design & Development, Golf Tourism, and Media, Culture &

Society. These are backed up with various new resources, such as a computer arts design studio, a food photography studio and a sports science laboratory.

ACADEMIC EXCELLENCE	
TEACHING:	
Economics.	**Excellent**
Chemistry, Maths &	**Highly Satis.**
Statistics, Mechanical +	
Manufacturing Engineering,	
Civil Engineering, Cellular &	
Molecular Biology, Psychology.	
RESEARCH EXCELLENCE:	
Top grades 5/5*	**None**

SOCIAL SCENE

STUDENTS' ASSOCIATION As a result of the local intake, weekends didn't used to figure much in the Students' Association ents calendar, and the extra-curricular life was fairly lame. But now they have a whole raft of new clubnights: *Sugar Shack*, a current chart night – might be *Cheesy Peeps*, *Sure Thing* (traffic light disco), *Smoky Beats* (R&B, hip hop), or *School Disco*; also *Superstition*, an '80s night, and *High Voltage*, the new alternative night.

Daytime obsessions are satisfied this year by thirty-four clubs and societies. Media-wise there's a newish student magazine, rather unfortunately entitled *Writers' Block*.

SPORT Beyond the new sports science laboratory, students must look to local council facilities, though these do include Astroturf pitches and good swimming pools. Few teams do well at uni national level (BUSA), but they concentrate on specialist areas and come out champions at ju-jitsu – kick boxing, and currently at Gaelic Football. With the new BA, Golf Tourism, and Abertay student Stuart

AT A GLANCE	
ACADEMIC FILE:	
Subjects assessed	**14**
Excellent/Highly Satisfactory	**50%**
Average requirements	**180 points**
Students-staff ratio	**18:1**
First/2:1 degree pass rate	**44%**
ACCOMMODATION GUARANTEE:	
If freshers apply by Sept. 1	**100%**
Style	**Halls, flats, houses**
Price range pw	**£40-£60**
City rent pw	**£35-£50**

Wilson playing in the British Open last year, things are on the up in this area of sport too.

TOWN Pubs are the focus and the cost of living is low compared to Aberdeen, Glasgow and Edinburgh. *Dundee Uni* entry shows how, 'Recently Dundee has reinvented itself, etc...'

WHAT IT'S REALLY LIKE

UNIVERSITY:	
Social Life	★★★
Campus scene	**Local, friendly**
Student Union services	**Developing**
Politics	**Activity low**
Sport	**16 clubs. Brit. Gaelic Footie Champ. Golf good**
National teamposition	**126th**
Sport facilities	**Fitness suite**
Arts	**Dance, music, film average; art, drama poor**
Student magazine	**Writers' Block**
Media/arts awards	**None**
Live ents venue	**Liquid**
Bars	**Sports & Main**
Union ents	**Sugar Shack, Superstition, High Voltage, etc**
Union clubs/societies	**34**
Most popular society	**Role-Playing**
Smoking policy	**Union, halls OK**
Parking	**Adequate**
CITY:	
Entertainment	★★★★
Scene	**Pubs, good live**
Town/gown relations	**Average**
Risk of violence	**Average**
Cost of living	**Low**
Student concessions	**Good**
Survival + 2 nights out	**£80 pw**
Part-time work campus/town	**Poor/average**

PILLOW TALK

All freshers who return their accommodation application forms by September 1 in their year of entry are guaranteed places in self-catering halls/flats/houses, some of which are en suite. Students may apply for accommodation in subsequent years. Cost per week is £40-60.

WHERE GRADUATES END UP

17% Wholesale/Retail*,	Key Areas
11% Manufacturing,	
11% Public Admin*,	
9% Health/Social Work,	
8% Finance	
Chemical/Pharmaceutical,	Niche areas
Construction*, Defence,	
Electron/Electric*, Legal,	
Sport	

*indicates Top 10 Graduate Provider

Approximate employed **92%**

JOBS

A continual theme in Abertay's mission is to ensure a profitable transfer to the world of work. The whole ethos is attuned to it. Courses are designed in close co-operation with business, industry and the public sectors. Many are accredited by professional bodies, most include a work placement or offer a language (French, German, Spanish or Japanese) and a study abroad option. All include communication and IT skills.

GETTING THERE

☛ By road: M90, M85, A85, A972.
☛ By rail: Newcastle, 3:00; London Euston, 6:00.
☛ By air: Dundee Airport for internal flights; Edinburgh International Airport is an hour away.
☛ By coach: London, 10:05; Birmingham, 10:05; Newcastle, 6:05.

• •

UNIVERSITY OF WALES, ABERYSTWYTH

The University of Wales, Aberystwyth
Old College
King Street
Aberystwyth
Ceredigion SY23 2AX

TEL 01970 622021
FAX 01970 627410
EMAIL university-admissions@aber.ac.uk
WEB www.aber.ac.uk

Aberystwyth Guild of Students
The Union,
Penglais,
Aberystwyth
Ceredigion SY23 3DX

TEL 01970 621700
FAX 01970 621701
EMAIL sss@aber.ac.uk
WEB www.union.aber.ac.uk

VAG VIEW

*T*he value of the Aber experience can be measured on a number of fronts, though it may seem, at first, that it makes its appeal by satisfying a host of minority interests.

Aber's location, for example, might make it a top choice for many applicants, while others might find this small seaside town limiting. Its academic strengths are in niche areas: countryside management, tourism, international politics, Welsh/Celtic studies, Irish, geography and earth sciences, equine science, marine & freshwater biology, information & library studies, theatre, film and TV (a £3.5-million centre for these opened in 2001), and will, inevitably, again appeal to some and not others.

The uni certainly has its specialisms, its very Welshness can seem daunting to some, but it isn't long before you realise that what makes Aber a good bet is the way it delivers every aspect of student services right through academia and into the social side of the Students' Guild, to meet the needs of students, whatever their expectations.

The statistics speak for themselves – a high intake (12%) from places in which 'going to university' is not traditional, and a mere 4% drop-out rate, which indicates that once here, you'll want to stay.

CAMPUS

'Think Wales; think west; think coast,' write Pete Liggins and Kate Glanville. 'It is then slap bang in the middle, a lovely seaside town whose two main industries are tourists in the summer and students in the closed season.'

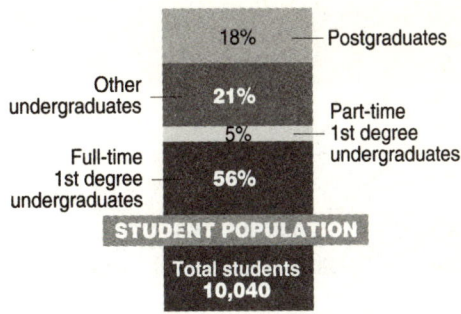

STUDENT POPULATION
Total students **10,040**

Most of the university, including the main Students' Guild building, is contained within the Penglais campus, set on a hill above beautiful Cardigan Bay. But there is another campus at Llanbadarn, less than a mile away and home to the Department of Information and Library Studies, the College of Further Education and the Institute of Rural Studies (a key element in Aber, they are, relative to size, the second largest graduate provider to land-based industries). The sites are linked by a common telephone system, and there's a good bus service (if you're too lazy to walk).

AT A GLANCE	
ACADEMIC FILE:	
Subjects assessed	**19**
Excellent	**42%**
Average requirements	**240 points**
Student-staff ratio	**15:1**
First/2:1 degree pass rate	**61%**
ACCOMMODATION FILE:	
Guarantee to freshers	**100%**
Style	**Halls + village**
Catered	**65%**
En-suite	**10%**
Price range pw	**£33-£48**
Town rent pw	**£45-£52**

STUDENT PROFILE

The student body is diverse. There are plenty of English here, though homage is paid to the Welsh hosts by their own countrymen, and the Students' Guild, or *Yr Undeb* as it translates in Welsh, plays a key role in supporting the native lingo: 'The unwritten rule is that you should accept anyone's right to speak in Welsh and not get paranoid that they are talking about you if you can't understand.'

Politics scores highly in undergraduate course assessments and research assessments, and there is a history here of Welsh Nationalist agitation: the Queen came unstuck a few years back. She had to make an early exit following a demo about the way

UNIVERSITY/STUDENT PROFILE	
University College since	**1872**
Situation/style	**Campus-by-the-sea**
Student population	**10,040**
Full-time undergraduates	**5,640**
- mature	**12%**
- overseas	**8%**
- male/female	**50/50**
- state sector intake	**93%**
- non-traditional student intake	**12%**
- drop-out rate	**4%, low**
- undergraduate applications	**Up 10%**
see Introduction for key to tables	

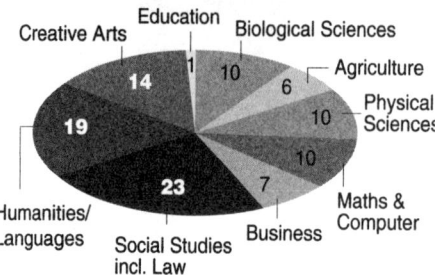

SUBJECT AREAS (%)

Creative Arts — Education — Biological Sciences — Agriculture — Physical Sciences — Maths & Computer — Business — Social Studies incl. Law — Humanities/Languages

14 · 1 · 10 · 6 · 10 · 10 · 7 · 23 · 19

the English had treated the local lingo in times past. But don't run away with the idea that Aber is politically strung up. Activity generally is no more nor less than would be expected from an environmentally aware student body. This year's main issues are student hardship, tuition fees, Nestlé and 'Don't Drink & Dive', the latter reminding us where we are.

ACADEMIA

Notwithstanding the specialist strengths, there's great flexibility right across the Arts curriculum, and small group teaching. All courses are modular and you will have access to the National Library of Wales (over six million books, maps and prints). The university's own library has over 700,000 volumes and 4,000 current periodicals in stock, as well as CD Roms, networked databases and other electronic sources. This year there is a new Sports & Exercise degree programme and department, and a new campus-wide, on-line teaching and

The uni has its own specialisms, which may or may not appeal, but what really makes Aber a good bet is the student services, and everything is so laid back here: the sun shines, things slow down; it's life without the big city stresses.

ACADEMIC EXCELLENCE

TEACHING:	
English, Info/Library Studies, Welsh, Earth Studies (incl. Enviro Science, Geography & Geology), Politics, Biological Sciences, Accounting & Finance, Economics	**Excellent**

RESEARCH: *Top grades 5/5**	
Celtic Studies, Politics	**Grade 5***
Drama/Dance/Performing Arts	**Grade 5**

learning initiative available to all students.

SOCIAL SCENE

STUDENTS' GUILD Llanbadarn has a shop and recently refurbished **Outback** bar, entertainment facilities, discos and pool room. Back at base camp, in the new Guild building (opened 2001), there's **Bar 9** and a nightclub, the **Joint**.

Cwrt Mawr Bar is the halls pub.

Unsurprisingly, this coastal resort is not a draw for big name bands, but 'live' is definitely part of the ents menu, which recently included Gorkys, Supernaturals, Cosmic Rough Riders, Rob Rouse, Chris Anderson, John Oliver, Andy Zaltman, The Hot Puppies, and the regular menu runs: Games night/PS2 (Monday); Comedy Network/Karaoke (Tuesday); *Re-load* (Wednesday) – a selection of cheese from five decades; *Live Lounge* (Thursday) – free entry band night; *Play* (Friday) – clubnight, and *Time Flies* alternating with *Beach Party* or other on Saturdays.

Besides all this there are new dance, art and drama workshop spaces, an art cinema, studio theatre and art gallery. Student media is pre-eminent with *The Courier* (*Yr Utgorn*) and Bay Radio. Oh, and the most active student society (one of about 50) is Indie Soc.

SPORT It's a big thing at Aber, American Football being the current area of excellence. Now there is to be a Sports & Exercise degree, so interest and facilities can only get better. There are fifty acres of pitches and specialist facilities for water sports, including a boat house, an indoor swimming pool, two sports halls, an all-weather floodlit sports pitch, squash courts and indoor facilities for football, badminton, basketball, hockey and tennis. Cardigan Bay and nearby Snowdonia offer windsurfing and skiing opportunities, respectively, and there is orienteering, mountain-biking, rambling, sub-aqua and hang-gliding too.

TOWN On the entertainments front in town, there's a one-screen cinema, where films tend to be shown around two to three weeks after their actual release date. The flick makes up for this by being cheap, friendly and licensed – so you can have a pint while watching the film – and the programme sports some of the cheapest and best local advertising you will ever have the pleasure to view. The cinema's ethos seems to sum up the whole town; everything is more laid back here: the sun shines and things slow down; it's life without the big city stresses.

Aber is also blessed with a number of pubs – 'beyond definition; every taste should be catered for somewhere. There is something of a worrying trend, however, towards refitting and furbishing with an emphasis on American *tack*, for each of these is a true local – one in particular won't serve a pint of Guinness in less than five minutes.'

Safety is not an issue in Aberystwyth.

WHAT IT'S REALLY LIKE

UNIVERSITY:

Social Life	★★★★
Campus scene	Contained, tight-knit & fun
Student Union services	Good
Politics	Student hardship, fees, Nestlé, 'Don't Drink/Dive'
Sport	50 clubs
National team position	70th
Sport facilities	Good
Arts opportunities	Music good; art avge; rest poor
Student magazine	The Courier
Student radio	Bay Radio
Nightclub	The Joint
Bars	Bar 9, Cwrt Mawr, Outback
Union ents	Comedy, cheese, clubnights beach parties
Union clubs/societies	100
Most popular society	Indie Soc
Smoking policy	None
Parking	Good

TOWN:

Entertainment	★★
Scene	Scenic seaside
Town/gown relations	Good
Risk of violence	Low
Cost of living	Average
Student concessions	Poor
Survival + 2 nights out	£45-£55 pw
Part-time work campus/town	Good

PILLOW TALK

For freshers, both self-catered and catered halls of residence are on offer, also flats and houses for 1,000 in the Student Village: 65% of accommodation is catered, 10% en suite, price range pw is £33 - £48 at time of writing, as against £50 in the town. Newly available are 500 places in a superb seafront complex of halls.

JOBS

Besides the usual university careers services, the Guild offers a range of NSLP skills courses, some to help develop skills through running clubs and societies, being a course-rep, getting involved in

WHERE GRADUATES END UP

12% Wholesale/Retail,	Key Areas
9% Public Admin,	
9% Education,	
8% Finance,	
8% Manufacturing,	
8% Computer,	
6% Personnel,	
6% Health/Social Work	
Defence, Agric/Forestry*,	Niche Areas
Film/Video, Telecom,	
Library/Archival*,	
Market Research	

*indicates Top 10 Graduate Provider

Approximate employed **94%**

the student media or community projects. Others are straight 'key skills' courses of the kind that employers like to see developed alongside academic achievement. They also have a drop-in careers advice and CV clinics in their Job Shop.

GETTING THERE

☛ By road: A484 from north or south; A44 from the east.
☛ By rail: London Euston, 5 hours. Chart your route carefully or you'll end up on a slow local line through the mid-Wales countryside.
☛ By coach: London, 7:00; Newcastle, 11:00.

ANGLIA POLYTECHNIC UNIVERSITY

Anglia Polytechnic University
East Road
Cambridge CB1 1PT

TEL 01223 363271
FAX 01223 352973
EMAIL angliainfo@anglia.ac.uk
WEB www.apu.ac.uk

Anglia Students' Union
East Road
Cambridge CB1 1PT

TEL 01223 460008
FAX 01223 417718
EMAIL su-president.ac.uk
WEB www.asu.apu.ac.uk

VAG VIEW

*T*he only poly-turned-uni to include *'polytechnic' in its title, despite a move to change this, Anglia still also retains its noble poly mission to serve the region, and does so more successfully than its older established Cambridge neighbour. From the Essex coast and the River Blackwater northwards to the Wash, APU is the first name on many an applicant's lip.*

The university comes out of Cambridgeshire College of Arts and Technology and the Essex Institute of Higher Education, which merged in 1989 to form Anglia Higher Education College. In 1991, this became Anglia Polytechnic, and Anglia Polytechnic University in the following year.

It was a very swift rise. The student population has increased from 7,000 in 1992 to the current level of 23,400, and was up again last year by 13%, making it one of the fastest growing universities in the UK. This may be reason enough for its high undergraduate drop-out rate (also 13%). More likely, it is that the student culture remains relatively under-developed.

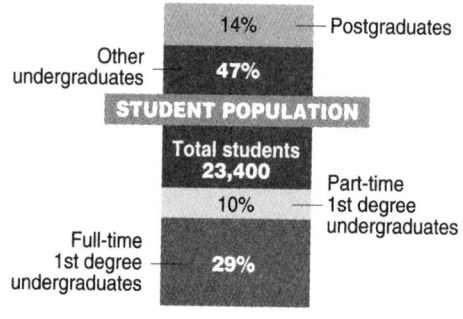

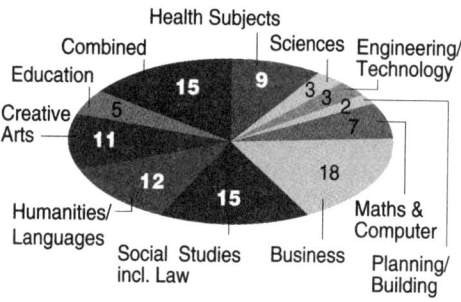

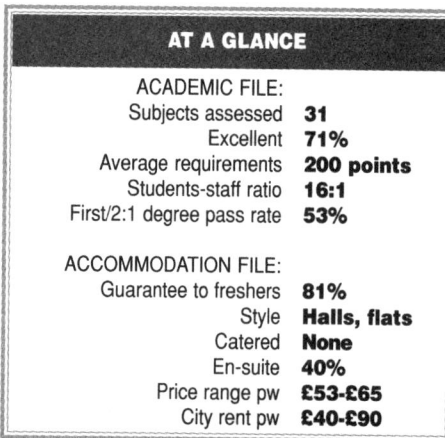

AT A GLANCE	
ACADEMIC FILE:	
Subjects assessed	**31**
Excellent	**71%**
Average requirements	**200 points**
Students-staff ratio	**16:1**
First/2:1 degree pass rate	**53%**
ACCOMMODATION FILE:	
Guarantee to freshers	**81%**
Style	**Halls, flats**
Catered	**None**
En-suite	**40%**
Price range pw	**£53-£65**
City rent pw	**£40-£90**

CAMPUSES

APU is on the move, change is a constant condition. There are currently four campuses. The two main ones are in Cambridge city centre and in Chelmsford, Essex, the latter gradually moving into the nearby Rivermead campus, also in Chelmsford, but located ten minutes' walk away, on the banks of the River Chelmer. Rivermead began as an accommodation site and home for the main library, but since Spring 2000, has also housed APU's School of Education. Now, a new building for the Ashcroft International Business School is to open here in September 2002. It is part-funded by the entrepreneur Lord Ashcroft KCMG, who was appointed chancellor of the university in

November 2001. The school is not new to APU. It has been based for some years at the university's Danbury Park site. The fourth campus is at nearby Benfleet, where access to locally franchised courses has been encouraged for some time, and which now offers a mix of further and higher education courses – BA Hons Humanities, Modern Business Applications and Behavioural Studies; HNDs in sport and tourism, and an HNC Business Information technology.

To those who criticise that the multiplicity of campuses makes for little focus or sense of belonging, it should be said that the current strategy of increasing centralisation at Rivermead and Cambridge is designed to cure that.

UNIVERSITY/STUDENT PROFILE	
University since	**1992**
Situation/style	**City/town campuses**
Student population	**23,400**
Full-time undergraduates	**6,860**
- mature	**52%**
- overseas	**13%**
- male/female	**41/59**
- state sector intake	**95%**
- non-traditional student intake	**13%**
- drop-out rate	**13%, high**
- undergraduate applications	**Up 13%**
see Introduction for key to tables	

STUDENT PROFILE

There's an eclectic mix of arty types, nurses (hence the dominant 59% female proportion), laddish engineers and teachers.

This is not a traditional university; there are many local and mature students who come here more for APU tickets into industry than anything else. Over 40% are part-time, many sponsored by employers, on employment related under-graduate and post-graduate courses.

Writes Jill Walker. 'We have lots of mature students [currently 52%] who work hard and make everyone work harder 'cos they are the only ones to do the reading. Lots of students tend to be local, though Cambridge is far more international than Chelmsford.'

ACADEMIA

Language and computer resources are good, and there are TV studio and editing facilities at Cambridge. There's the Learning Resources Centre at Rivermead, which incorporates the main library, and ULTRALAB at nearby Chelmsford, APU's famous learning technology research centre which produces educational CD-ROM and web learning materials, and is concerned with software development, research, teaching and advising government policy, their research appearing regularly on TV programmes such as *Horizon* and *Tomorrow's World*.

As can be seen from our *Academic Excellence* box, below, APU now records Excellent ratings across a wide range of subjects, though it still asks little of a student by way of grades at application. Note, too, that it is developing in the research area, achieving international standing with a Grade 5 in the recent research assessment exercise in English Language & Literature.

The whole point about degree work at APU is that it is vocationally orientated, degrees translate into jobs (see page 52), but this doesn't restrict the range to technical subjects. New courses this year appear in the areas of ecology and conservation, zoology, and tourism, as well as in computing, e-commerce and financial management, and there's an interesting HND in broadcasting.

APU is one of very few universities to offer optometry and ophthalmic dispensing at undergraduate level, but look, too, at the Art & Design degrees, which seriously bolster their employment figures, as does the Sports Science degree, which has productive links with the English Cricket Board's local Centre of Excellence, which APU founded. Look, also, at their large programme of drama degrees, which set the scene at the **Mumford Theatre** on Cambridge Campus.

ACADEMIC EXCELLENCE	
TEACHING:	
(Rated Excellent or 17+ out of 24)	
Social Work, Music, English.	**Excellent**
Philosophy	**24**
Nursing, Theology	**23**
Psychology	**22**
Modern Languages, Molecular & Organismal Biosciences, Art & Design	**21**
Sociology, Building & Civil Eng, Politics, Subjects Allied to Medicine	**20**
Land/Property Mgt, Town/ Country Planning, Electron & Electrical Eng, Mechanical/ Aeronautical & Manuf Eng	**19**
Communication/Media Studies, Tourism, History of Art	**18**
RESEARCH:	
Top grades 5/5*	
English Language & Literature	**Grade 5**

WHAT IT'S REALLY LIKE

UNIVERSITY:	
Social Life	★★★
Campus scene:	**Diverse**
Student Union services	**Poor**
Politics	**Interest low**
Sport	**12 clubs**
National team position	**107th**
Sport facilities	**Poor**
Arts opportunities	**Drama, music exc; dance good; film, art average**
Student newspaper	**Apex**
Bars	**Big Bar, Little Bar**
Union ents	**Life, Mumbo Jumbo, BOGOFF**
Union clubs/societies	**37**
Smoking policy	**Bars OK**
Parking	**Poor**
CITY	
Entertainment	★★★
Scene	**Clubs poor, atmosphere good**
Town/gown relations	**Average-poor**
Risk of violence	**Low**
Cost of living	**Average**
Student concessions	**Good**
Survival + 2 nights out	**£50 pw**
Part-time work campus/town	**Average**

SOCIAL SCENE

STUDENTS' UNION The student newspaper *Apex* appeals across the campus divide, and an even bigger divide was traversed by an APU student who was recently Production Manager on the Cambridge University student newspaper. The social side of things is still mainly Cambridge campus based and not that inspiring, beyond the highly successful Summer Ball – *Life* on Tuesday, *Mumbo Jumbo* on Friday, Comedy Network, etc, before many leave for the weekend. Recently they have also been involved in 'Battle of the Bands' and DJ competitions.

Cambridge Campus is small, but busy. The union has two bars (rather less than enterprisingly called **Big Bar** and **Little Bar**), a café called **Batman**, recently converted into a non-smoking, continental-style baguette bar and the Mumford Theatre. There is a union bar and shop at Chelmsford.

> *Chancellor Lord Ashcroft, successful businessman and enthusiastic investor in APU, may be something of a role model for the kind of student APU attracts. There's been a tight working relationship with industry for many years.*

SPORT There are tennis courts and a multigym on the Cambridge campus, and 100 metres away lies the Kelsey Kerridge Sports Centre with a large gym and nearby swimming pool. Half a mile north of the campus there are three football pitches, a rugby pitch and a cricket square. Rowing crews rack their eights at Emmanuel College Boat House. Rowing is APU's big strength and most popular sports club. There's a gym and fitness centre at Chelmsford.

TOWN In the city they have the Drama Centre and newly refurbished Arts Theatre, but most students find themselves in clubs, pubs and live music venues. Popular student clubnights are currently *Livewire* @ **Toxic 8** and *Double Dragon* @ **The Fez**.

PILLOW TALK

There are currently 1,600 places available, which means in effect that they can accommodate 81% of freshers. Current cost in Cambridge is about £65 pw; at Chelmsford £53 pw – all self-catering but including bills. APU's policy on allocation: is 30% UK students, 30% international students, 40% students with disabilities. There is now 40% accommodation available en suite.

JOBS

Chancellor and enthusiastic investor in APU, successful local businessman Lord Ashcroft, is also an APU *alumnus*, something of an entrepreneurial role model, perhaps, for the kind of student that the uni likes to attract.

APU has enjoyed a tradition of working with industry for many years. Programmes are designed in collaboration with employers in the health sector, in local government, in the legal sector, in engineering, in science-based industries, in the ICT sector, in media. APU also provides a range of commercial services to business: managed training services, professional and personal develop-ment, high level skills training, etc. The university also works in partnership with a number of companies on the development of employees, for example with Ford Motor Company, Jaguar Cars, Visteon, Anglia Water, Yorkshire Water, Superdrug, and a range of companies in the agro/pharmaceutical industry.

For undergraduates, there are work placements available with over 100 companies, including Barclays, PriceWaterhouseCoopers, BT, Lloyd's

Register, M&S, Sainsbury's, Standard Life. There are in-company award-bearing courses for Marconi, Ford, Suffolk County Council, and the university provides consultancy and research for Superdrug, M&G and Dixons.

GETTING THERE - Cambridge
☞ By road (from London): M25/J27, M11/J11, A10. From west or east: A45. From northwest: A604. From Stansted Airport: M11.
☞ By train: London's Liverpool Street, under the hour; Nottingham, 2:30; Sheffield, Birmingham New Street, 3:00.
☞ By coach: London, 1:50; Birmingham, 2:45; Leeds, 5:00; Bristol, 5:30.

GETTING THERE - Chelmsford
☞ By road: A12, A130 or A414.
☞ By rail: London Liverpool Street, 35 mins.
☞ By air: 10 miles from the M25 and access to Stansted Airport and Heathrow.

WHERE GRADUATES END UP	
17% Education,	Key Areas
16% Wholesale/Retail*,	
9% Health/Social Work,	
7% Finance,	
7% Manufacturing,	
7% Computer,	
6% Public Admin	
5% Personnel	
Agric/Forestry,	Niche Areas
Artistic/Literary*,	
Legal, Media, Sport	
*indicates Top 10 Graduate Provider	
Approximate employed	91%

☞ By coach: London, 1:40; Norwich, 5:00.

ANGLO-EUROPEAN COLLEGE OF CHIROPRACTIC

Anglo-European College of
Chiropractic
13-15 Parkwood Road
Bournemouth BH5 2DF

TEL 01202 436200
FAX 01202 436312
EMAIL aecc@aecc.ac.uk
WEB www.aecc.ac.uk

VAG VIEW

*C*hiropractic is a physically manipulative treatment of neuro-musculoskeletal disorders, principally of the spine and pelvis. The idea is that the spine controls all, and that Chiropractic releases 'the power within'.

The thing is, it works, and this is the place to be if you want to learn how to do it, and cop a BSc then MSc degree accredited by the General Chiropractic Council. Also, Bournemouth is the place to be if you want to have a good time (see Bournemouth Uni entry). In fact you could be forgiven for taking the etching in the college prospectus, which shows a turbaned figure sitting on the buttocks of his patient, pummelling his spine, as an advertisement for either.

Resources include a licensed prosection anatomy lab, specialist library and a college clinic, where students treat some 50,000 outpatients each year. No accommodation, but Bournemouth landladies welcome all.

COLLEGE PROFILE	
Founded	**1965**
Status	**HE College**
Approx fees pa	**£6,650**
Degree awarding university	**Portsmouth**
Student population	**425**
College accommodation	**None**
Town rent pw	**£45-£60**

The Students' Union organises sport; there are tennis courts and facilities for martial arts, aerobics, badminton, circuit training and basketball. Students produce their own magazine – The Column...

GETTING THERE
☞ By road from the east or north M3/M27/A31/A348. North and west, A350 (down from the A303) or A35 (coastal).
☞ By rail, it's 96 minutes from London Waterloo, Bristol under 3 hours, Birmingham or Cardiff less than 4, Manchester about 5.
☞ By coach: London, 2:15; Bristol, 3:10.

ARTS INSTITUTE AT BOURNEMOUTH

The Arts Institute at Bournemouth
Wallisdown Road
Poole
Dorset BH12 5HH

TEL 01202 533011
FAX 01202 537729
EMAIL general@arts-inst-bournemouth.ac.uk
WEB arts-inst-bournemouth.ac.uk

COLLEGE PROFILE

Founded	**1883**
Status	**Art College**
Degree awarding body	**Surrey Inst.**
Student population	**2,150**
Full-time undergraduates	**500**
College accommodation	**Halls, £65 pw**
Town rent pw	**£45-£60**

DEGREE SUBJECT AREAS:
Design (incl costume, 3-D, graphic), art, photography, film, animation, etc

VAG VIEW

*R*e-named, and with a tastefully designed new prospectus, the old Bournemouth & Poole College has found its way with ease into the third millennium. Known for such specialisms as Costume Design, and set

appropriately enough on the way to Wareham (way-to-wear-'em, geddit?), this Dorset-based institute recently branched out with Film & Animation and promptly won a Queen's Anniversary Award for media education. The Wallisdown campus is adjacent to Bournemouth University and students benefit from the broad spectrum of decadence which that institution has to offer (see appropriate entry). New for this year is accommodation for 100 freshers in West House and East House – but you don't get parking permits if you live in these halls.

GETTING THERE
☛ By road: A35 east/west; A338 south from Salisbury.
☛ By rail: Bournemouth, 12 mins; London Waterloo, 1:50 (direct); Exeter, 3:34 (via Salisbury and Southampton).
☛ By coach: London, 2:15; Bristol, 3:10.

• •

ASKHAM BRYAN COLLEGE

Askham Bryan College
Askham Bryan
York
YO2 3PR

TEL 01904 772211
FAX 01904 772288
EMAIL meltow@askham-bryan.ac.uk
WEB www.askham-bryan.ac.uk

VAG VIEW

*W*ith its three farms (174 hectares) just a few miles from York, Askham Bryan would appear to be an agricultural college, but its BTEC and HND in Agriculture (awarded 21 points out of 24 in the assessments) are the visible tip of the proverbial iceberg, for the college also plays a leading role in Leeds Uni's School of Continuing Education, which reaches out to towns and villages as far north as Teesside.

Back at Askham Bryan's beautiful campus, however, first degrees do concern animal, land management and food production, and, as notably, business. Learning resources are good and York Uni's library is available, as is the

COLLEGE PROFILE

Founded	**1938**
Status	**HE College**
Degree awarding university	**Leeds**
Student population	**545**
Degree undergraduates	**56**
College accommodation	**Halls**
Availability to freshers	**100%**
Cost pw (no food/food)	**£40-£65**
City rent pw	**£50**

DEGREE COURSES:
Business Management, Animal/Land Management and Technology

London-based British Library's one offshoot at nearby Boston Spa.

There are 244 single study-bedrooms with shared bathrooms and kitchens, and twenty-four self-catering units. There's a bar and regular discos and live bands. Askham Bryan is small, friendly, but unless you're into sport, there's little else. Sport, especially the rugby players, dominate.

GETTING THERE

☛ By road: make for the A1237 York ring road (part of which is the A64), then pick up sign to Askham Bryan where these two roads intersect.
☛ By train to York: Leeds, 30 mins; Sheffield, 1:15; Manchester, 1:30; London King's Cross, 2:00; Birmingham New Street, 3:00.
☛ By coach: London, 5:00; Bristol, 7:20.

ASTON UNIVERSITY, BIRMINGHAM

Aston University, Birmingham
Aston Triangle
Birmingham B4 7ET

TEL 0121 359 3611 ext 4812
FAX 0121 359 4664
EMAIL j.r.seymour@aston.ac.uk
WEB www.aston.ac.uk

Aston Students' Guild
The Triangle
Birmingham B4 7ES

TEL 0121 359 6531
FAX 0121 333 4218
EMAIL president@aston.ac.uk
WEB www.astonguild.org.uk

VAG VIEW

*A*ston is a small university, independent, and, following recent advances from the massive Birmingham University, they have decided they want to keep it that way. They would like to emphasise, however, that they are part of Birmingham city – hence 'Aston University, Birmingham' is their title this year.

Aston is, indeed, slap bang in the eye of the urban vortex, yet, against all odds, sheltered from its excesses in an attractive, green-field campus bowl – a surprising and tasty morsel in Birmingham's tangled spaghetti junction. As a student said, looking out, 'The dual carriageway acts as a kind of natural barrier. You go under the flyover and suddenly, wow! It's Birmingham.'

Aston is for science, engineering and business, the strength of particular areas of science being highlighted by recent teaching assessments – Pharmacy (full marks), Biological Sciences and Optometry (23/24), and the teaching of the BSc Human Psychology courses just scored 22/24 ahead of the uni's traditionally strong engineering departments (19, 20 and 21). Then last year all its business and management courses scored full marks – 24/24, and you see why they say the Business School is one of the best in Europe.

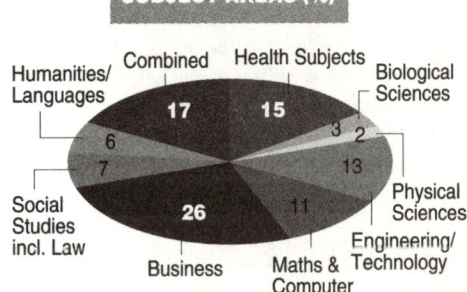

SUBJECT AREAS (%)

Combined 17 · Health Subjects 15 · Humanities/Languages 6 · Social Studies incl. Law 7 · Business 26 · Maths & Computer 11 · Engineering/Technology 13 · Physical Sciences 2 · Biological Sciences 3

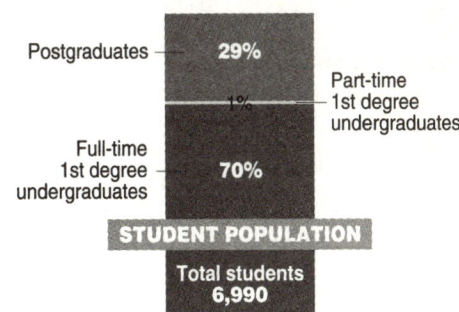

Postgraduates 29%
Part-time 1st degree undergraduates 1%
Full-time 1st degree undergraduates 70%

STUDENT POPULATION
Total students 6,990

Aston is heavy on workload, extremely well resourced and geared to top-class employment by means of industry contact, study-abroad programmes, language combinations (the QAA rate German and French at 22/24) and sandwich courses. Seventy per cent of Aston undergraduates are on sandwich courses. Last

AT A GLANCE

ACADEMIC FILE:

Subjects assessed	**17**
Excellent	**71%**
Average requirements	**280 points**
Students-staff ratio	**20:1**
First/2:1 degree pass rate	**62%**

ACCOMMODATION FILE:

Guarantee to freshers	**100%**
Style	**Flats**
Catered	**None**
En-suite	**30%**
Price range pw	**£50-£73**
City rent pw	**£35-£40**

year they placed 80% of their graduates in employment after six months, and their 4% unemployment rate (about 30 students) places them up there with the best.

Successful applicants last year scored an average 21 points at A level, almost BBC (now 280 points), and yet, at the same time, the uni manages to be ranked high for widening access to those groups historically less likely to enter higher education.

Their marketing is keen. For Open Day there is a student ambassador scheme. Twenty to thirty student guides take prospective students (and increasingly their parents) on 30-minute campus tours. 'We have 1,200 come along on Open Day,' I was told and that was for a 1,300 intake. Aston has deliberately remained small, compact. The policy has brought its own financial headaches. The strategy was to gear themselves up with staff and projects to scoop some financial rewards at last year's research assessments – the uni places strong emphasis

UNIVERSITY/STUDENT PROFILE

University since	**1966**
Situation/style	**City campus**
Student population	**6,990**
Full-time undergraduates	**4,990**
- mature	**20%**
- overseas	**7%**
- male/female	**50/50**
- state sector intake	**84%**
- non-traditional student intake	**11%**
- drop-out rate	**7%**
- undergraduate applications	**Up 1%**

*see Introduction for key to tables

not only on its links with industry, but on research-led teaching – and they were successful, with international renown in Business & Management, European Studies, Optometry and General Engineering (which includes Computing Science).

CAMPUS

Aston is very defined, very straightforward, very scientific. You get what you see at The Triangle. The clean lines of this modern, high-rise, plate-glass, green-field Birmingham city campus (complete with artificial lake) brook no idle intent. And the no-nonsense efficiency far from cripples any desire for after-work pleasure, either at the Students' Guild or a walk away in the centre of Brum itself. Do not, however, be over-sensitive to the attentions that will be heaped upon you the moment you walk through the doors, for this really is – above all else – a very close-knit community.

STUDENT PROFILE

You pick up serious suits in the business section, earnest, professional techies behind the superb lighting and sound systems in the Guild Hall, as they prepare for some serious Aston student live music evening (they know how to put a party together: Fusion – dance music – is the most popular society), and then there's the fresh-faced authenticity that binds it all together. Aston is the only university where someone like me will be met by union and university executives around the same table. There are no divides and there is an exuberance about their open, genuinely caring attitude, which some might find intrusive or a contra-current to the existential flow of undergraduate life, but it is in fact quite disarming, and seems to go down with less viscosity than syrup among the types that come here. See what you think, sign up for an Open Day.

'Each year 150 volunteers elect to become Aston aunties and welcome freshers,' said one.

Why aunties?

'Well, "Auntie knows best!" Every year we have different slogans, like "We are family!" or "The cream of Brum." Everyone wants to be an auntie. We have 300 applicants. We pioneered it about 28 years ago. For Fresher's Week we try and do everything. We've got city tours, campus tours, supermarket trips (?!), cultural crawls, canal cruises, fun things like go-karting and paintballing, an Alton Towers trip, and the departments all have other things organised, library visits and so on.

'We've all been out manning the car parks in the pouring rain, and the arrivals this year have been fantastic. I have been watching with admiration this year, as aunties go up to cars with a

ACADEMIC EXCELLENCE

TEACHING:
(Rated Excellent or 17+ out of 24)

Pharmacy, Businesss & Management	**24**
Biological Biosciences, Optometry	**23**
German, French, Psychology	**22**
Electronic Engineering	**21**
Civil Engineering	**20**
Chemical Eng, Maths	**19**

RESEARCH:
Top grades 5/5*

Optometry, General Engineering, Business & Management, European Studies	**Grade 5**

WHAT IT'S REALLY LIKE

UNIVERSITY:

Social Life	★★★★
Campus scene	**Lively, caring suits & techies**
Student Union services	**Good**
Politics	**Interest low**
Sport	**40 clubs**
National team position	**107th**
Sport facilities	**40 clubs**
Arts opportunities	**Dance, music excellent; drama good**
Student magazine	**Helios**
Nightclub	**Guild Hall**
Bars	**Einstein's, Blue Room, The Loft**
Union ents	**Flux, Insomnia, Revive, Fondue, School Daze, Ukg**
Union clubs/societies	**82**
Most popular societiy	**Fusion (dance music), Islamic**
Smoking policy	**Zonal in Guild**
Parking	**No**

CITY:

Entertainment	★★★★★
Scene	**Excellent**
Town/gown relations	**Average**
Risk of violence	**High**
Cost of living	**High**
Student concessions	**Excellent**
Survival + 2 nights out	**£60 pw**
Part-time work campus/town	**Average/excellent**

"Welcome, my name's so-and-so, I'm an auntie!" That's your first impression of Aston.'

What if you have spent all summer carefully modelling yourself on Ewan McGregor, or some such cool anti-hero, then this cream-of-Brum auntie wades in with that line?

'We had a classic quote yesterday from a student whose parents had just left: "Oh, I haven't even been here for twelve hours yet and I feel at home already!"'

If any other union bod had said this I wouldn't have believed it. It's the sort of unlikely... but at Aston what you see really *is* what you get. You can thrust, you can parry, but 'you won't hear a thing against Aston from us,' admitted one of the Guild sabbaticals. 'We're in these jobs because we adore it, not because we can't bear to leave but because we want to see it get bigger and better.'

ACADEMIA

Broadly Aston consists of three faculties: Life & Health Sciences (Pharmaceutical & Biological Sciences, Vision Sciences); Engineering and Applied Science (Civil Engineering, Chemical Eng. and Applied Chemistry, Mechanical & Electrical Eng., Electronic and Applied Physics, Computer Science and Applied Maths); and Management Languages & European Studies. The latter includes the Aston Business School and the School of Languages and European Studies. The Business School is one of the largest in Europe. Related courses tackle the behavioural side of enterprise, such as Organisational Studies,

> *Aston is mainly for science, engineering and business. It is very defined, very straightforward, very scientific. You get what you see at The Triangle, and students do seem to enjoy themselves.*

Human Psychology and Psychology with Management. See also *Jobs*, page 58.

SOCIAL SCENE

STUDENTS' GUILD The Guild offers three bars, **Einstein's** (basement with big screen and two man-size pool tables), the **Blue Room** (a café by day) and **The Loft**. Then there's the **Guild Hall**, which, together with the Blue Room, gives a max building capacity of 1,150. There are five events a week: *FLUX* (house, trance), *Revive* ('70s, '80s funk & disco), *School Daze* ('80s, early '90s), *UKG* (garage, R&B) and *Fondue* (cheese & commercial dance). Visitors included the ubiquitous Timmy Mallet, Toby Anstis, Chesney Hawkes, Artful Dodger, DJ Pied Piper.

WHERE GRADUATES END UP

17% Health/Social Work,	Key Areas
17% Manufacturing*,	
11% Finance,	
6% Public Admin,	
9% Computer*	
Accountancy,	Niche Areas
Chem/Pharmaceutical*,	
Business/Management,	
Eng/Industrial Design,	
Defence, Electron/	
Electric, Legal, Market	
Research*, Telecom*	

*indicates Top 10 Graduate Provider

Approximate employed **96%**

Ents is not the only extra-curricular focus. There are masses of sports clubs and societies on offer, with Islamic gaining ground this last year. Media-wise there's the student magazine, *Helios*; there was a Radio Society which, for whatever reason, disbanded. 'We are a small uni and the same people are involved in putting on events and entertainments would be doing the radio or TV. The Drama Club is very active; we have eighty clubs and societies altogether.'

SPORT On campus there are two sports centres – Woodcock (with swimming pool) and Gem Sports Hall (with a synthetic floodlit pitch), while out of the city the Recreation Centre spans 95 acres. There is slim evidence of national standards, it is sport for everyone; 'relaxed' is the word used, although the options are varied enough to include American Football, and one of the Aston ladies plays for Aston Villa Ladies!

TOWN See Student Birmingham, page 70.

PILLOW TALK

There are high-rise and low-rise halls on campus, all self-catering, and last September new lakeside residences opened to provide 650 en-suite rooms with telephones, around 1,450 rooms with shared bathrooms and toilets, and washbasins in each room. All students share kitchens with big fridges, cookers, microwaves, etc. Ther are two large launderettes on campus. The development brings total rooms to 2,100, which means that around 50% of all undergraduates – all first years and most final years – can now live in campus accommodation. Price range pw is £50-£73 for forty weeks, including all bills and cleaning.

JOBS

Aston is one of twenty-two unis that own and manage the TargetedGRAD.com website, a dedicated link between premier employers and high-calibre graduates. Areas of particular strength include business, management, marketing, human resources, international business, management consultancy, computing, IT, engineering, telecommunications, pharmacy and optometry. If you have your eyes tested in England there's a 15-20% likelihood that it will be an Aston graduate doing it. Readers who want to find out exactly what Aston graduates are doing should consult www.careers.aston.ac.uk and follow the link, *What do Aston Graduates do?* Their top ten employers included PriceWaterhouseCoopers, Accenture, Boots and Procter & Gamble.

GETTING THERE

☞ By road: M6/J6, A38M 3rd exit, then first exit at Lancaster Circus roundabout.
☞ By rail: Bristol Parkway, Sheffield, 1:30; London Euston, 1:40; Liverpool, Manchester, 2:00; Leeds, 3:00. New Street 12 mins' walk from campus.
☞ By air: Birmingham International Airport.
☞ By coach: London, 2:40; Bristol, 2:00.

UNIVERSITY OF WALES, BANGOR

University of Wales, Bangor
Gwynedd LL57 2DG

TEL 01248 382016
FAX 01248 370451
EMAIL admissions@bangor.ac.uk
WEB www.bangor.ac.uk

Bangor Students' Union
Gwynedd r LL57 2TH

TEL 01248 388000
FAX 01248 388020
EMAIL undeb@undeb.bango.ac.uk
WEB www.undeb.bangor.ac.uk

VAG VIEW

*B*angor started life on 18 October, 1884, in an old coaching inn – a promising beginning, particularly as half the student intake was female, which was swimming against the tide in 1884. Today Bangor is still predominantly female and, while asking relatively few points to get in, it has risen to become one of the best universities in the

UK. *Don't take it just from me, in September 2001 the* Guardian *put Bangor among the top 5 countrywide, and latest statistics show that it is moulding its reputation out of increasing numbers of entrants for whose families the option of university is new, and is doing this while retaining rigorous standards of teaching, and, indeed, without alienating their new clientele: their drop-out rate – 8% – is fine. Why, therefore, there should have been a 15% drop in applications last year (which is not the same as student population of course – Bangor is well populated) is a complete mystery.*

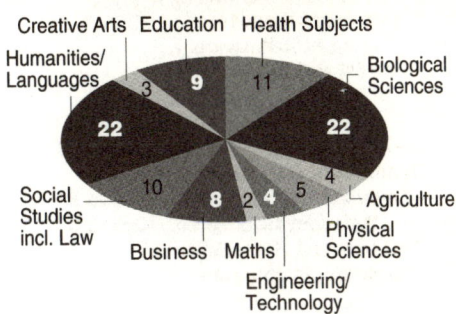

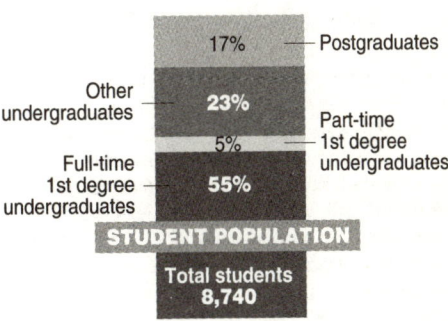

CAMPUS

Setting the whole deal in context for the semi-final of University Challenge, Jeremy Paxman described the natural environs of Bangor – just across the Menai Strait from the Isle of Anglesey – as 'one of the most beautiful locations of any British university, between the beaches of Anglesey and the mountains of Snowdonia.' Such is not to every student's taste.

North Wales is different from the rest of Wales: they're the real Welsh up here; Welsh is still the natural language over much of Gwynedd. It is a small, town-size community that manages not to protest at the regular incursion of a student population which now totals, in all, some 10,000 students, and more than doubles the local population at the start of each term. Relations with the natives couldn't be better, however. Perhaps it has something to do with living between spectacular, inspirational Snowdonia and the sea. While not exactly a campus university, all the buildings, with the exception of the School of Ocean Sciences, which is a few miles from the Menai Bridge, are within walking distance of one another.

STUDENT PROFILE

There is a large Welsh population, a predominantly female population and a sizeable mature population. But cutting-edge cool it really is not. If you come to Bangor, you'll fall in love with the surroundings...not the talent. You may be sporty, interested in outward bound perhaps, maybe a classical music lover, but 'you've gotta be designed for life,' as one student put it, for, to put it succinctly, 'you'll probably find more night life in a tramp's vest.' Fortunately for those interested in the tramp's vest department, the Students' Union is currently more active than it has ever been.

There's a healthy overseas contingent, too, and the uni goes out of its way to help them settle. The International Welfare Unit assists and advises, and orientation days are arranged to help international students get acclimatised to the country. The ELCOS (English Language Courses for Overseas Students) Unit provides instruction for those whose language skills need polishing. There's also an organisation (called 'Shekina') which offers help to wives and husbands of students and organises a range of activities, including English language courses.

UNIVERSITY/STUDENT PROFILE	
University College since	**1884**
Situation/style	**City sites**
Student population	**8,740**
Full-time undergraduates	**5,310**
- mature	**21%**
- overseas	**7%**
- male/female	**42/58**
- state sector intake	**93%**
- non-traditional student intake	**13%**
- drop-out rate	**8%, low**
- undergraduate applications	**Down 15%**
see Introduction for key to tables	

ACADEMIC EXCELLENCE

TEACHING:
Chemistry, Welsh, Music, **Excellent**
Ocean Sciences, Theology,
Psychology, Russian, Forest
Sciences, Biological Sciences.

RESEARCH:
Top grades 5/5*
Psychology, Welsh   **Grade 5***
Agric & Forest Sciences,   **Grade 5**
Business & Regional Dev,
Sport/Health/Exercise Sciences

ACADEMIA

Eight departmental scholarships, each worth £1,000, show Bangor doing their bit to balance the effect of tuition fees. Details are sent following uni application via UCAS.

With Excellent ratings in a range of subjects which seems to strike almost the perfect balance: psychology/theology, chemistry/ecology, engineering/ocean studies, Welsh/English, there is also a healthy emphasis on, well, health – from Nursing & Midwifery to Sport and PE Sciences (very heavily subscribed) – and on environmental and agricultural courses (Forest Sciences are especially strong). In the Arts, Music rates Excellent; among languages, Russian also made top marks, and their Multi-Media Language Centre is a pioneer of digital language-laboratory technology. True to the uni's roots in North Wales, where Welsh is still the mother tongue, they offer degree courses in a number of subjects through the medium of Welsh, as well as informal tuition in Welsh in various subjects.

Highlight of last year was the delivery of a £3.5-million, ocean-going research vessel, the Prince Madog, for use in teaching and research in the School of Ocean Sciences.

A notable feature is the special provision for students with disabilities – study support centres which house CCTVs, scanners and braille embossers. They also have induction loops and infra-red transmission equipment to help those with hearing difficulties, and ramps and lifts in the main buildings to help those with mobility problems. Their Dyslexia Unit is internationally renowned.

Two new honours degree courses involving the Internet have just come into being: the BA in E-commerce & Internet Systems, and the BSc in Internet Systems & E-commerce. There's also a new part-time BA Honours degree in Internet Learning & Organisations.

SOCIAL SCENE

STUDENTS' UNION The uni has made a £1-million investment in the Students' Union. There's a 1,000-capacity **Amser/Time** nightclub (nominated in seven categories in this year's Welsh music awards) and three bars: 390-capacity **Main** (**Prif Far**), the 100-capacity basement bar, **Jock's**, and fifteen minutes away in an award-winning scenic location on the banks of the Menai Straits, the 150-capacity **George Bar**. Prices are very low.

Monday is '60s, '70s, '80s @ Amser/Time; Wednesday is *Trash* @ Main (rock, metal, indie); Thursday is *Nice Choons* (cheesy charty chunes), run by the Athletic Union, or *Clwb Cymru* @ Main (a night for Welsh-speaking students); Friday is *Jukebox* @ Amser/Time (chart hits); successive Saturdays are *Future Funk* (funkin' pumpin' house), *Ba Da Boom* (discofutureretroraggabreaksoul afroskankjazzfunkbeats!), *Oblivion* (bangin'

WHAT IT'S REALLY LIKE

UNIVERSITY:	
Social Life	★★★★
Campus scene	**Beautiful, close-knit, Welsh, very female**
Student Union services	**Good**
Politics	**Internal**
Sport	**Women's rugby is big**
National team position	**73rd**
Sport facilities	**Good**
Arts opportunities	**OK**
Student magazine	**Y Ddraenen**
Student newspaper	**Seren**
Nightclub	**Amser/Time**
Bars	**Main/Prif Far, Jock's, The George**
Union ents	**Alternative, cheese, funk, hard house, retro trance, R&B**
Union clubs/societies	**63**
Most popular society	**Community Action**
Smoking policy	**Not in restaurant**
Parking	**Good**
CITY:	
Entertainment	★★★
Scene	**Scenic, fun**
Town/gown relations	**Average-poor**
Risk of violence	**Low**
Cost of living	**Average**
Student concessions	**OK**
Survival + 2 nights out	**£60 pw**
Part-time work campus/town	**Average/poor**

trance and hard house), *Elevate* (hard house & hard trance) and *Nation* (R&B, dance, disco cheese & charts) @ Amser/Time.

Recent visitors among DJs have been Mr Scruff, Scratch Perverts, DreadZone, Krafty Kuts, Bentley Rhythm Ace, Stanton Warriors, Lovely Helen, Lisa dehfufuh, Dean Wilson, and M-Zone. Live music has brought Electric Soft Parade, Cosmic Rough Riders, Mansun, My Vitriol, Queen Adreena, Seafood, Kid Galahad, TetraSplendour, Damage.

There are twenty-six student societies – Community Action is probably the most popular, but the Bangor Archaeological Society: Trowelers & Research Diggers has the best name – BASTARD, and thirty-seven sports clubs, which indicate where preferences lie. There's a Welsh-language student magazine called *Y Ddraenen* and an English newspaper, *Seren*. Political activity is high, but centred on...Welsh language recognition. The drama soc, Rostra, made it to the Edinburgh Fest with *The Midnight Lemur* last year. The uni has its own professional chamber ensemble and student symphony orchestra, chamber choir, opera group, chamber ensembles and concert band.

SPORT You will benefit from a Lottery-sourced, £4.5 million extension to the sports hall There's great emphasis on sport, thanks to the Sports Science and PE courses. Outward-bound activities, such as mountaineering, are especially popular, as are rowing, sailing and canoeing.

Women's Rugby won the UK national BUSA Shield last year, as well as being Team Of The Month in Rugby World magazine.

TOWN 'As far as towns go, we ain't no Liverpool or Birmingham,' writes Becki Thurston, 'but that doesn't mean we're pants and boring. It would be implausible to lie and say Bangor was a humungous city: you certainly can't fit too many sandwiches in it. But we've got most of your main street stores and quite a few of your individual off-beat shops as well.

'Although it's designated a city, it's diddy. The bonus is that we take over. There's nowhere doesn't feel like home. Wherever you go, wherever you are, you'll bump into someone you know.

AT A GLANCE	
ACADEMIC FILE:	
Subjects assessed	**20**
Excellent	**45%**
Average requirements	**200 points**
Student-staff ration	**16:1**
First/2:1 degree pass rate	**52%**
ACCOMMODATION FILE:	
Guarantee to freshers	**100%**
Style	**Halls**
Catered	**13%**
En-suite	**15%**
Price range pw	**£43-£78**
Town rent pw	**£35-£45**

Trouble is, it's impossible to get anywhere on time; everyone knows not only everybody, but everybody's business too. People know who you snogged last night, even before you've sobered up enough to realise!

'The rock scene is certainly a case for Mulder and Scully, but it is out there! **The Octagon** is such a dive it's classic. Yep, you're gonna stick to the floor. It has been compared to a cattle market, but where else would we students feel at home. If you're living in halls and you don't fancy a walk down a hill, Upper Bangor is student heaven, hosting enough pubs to get you absolutely ratted. Then, when suitably pissed, you can fill your belly with as many take-out types as you like, before going home to chunder. Another advantage of Bangor's size is that competition between pubs etc. is strong. So prices are low.'

For arts lovers the city offers a varied mix of classical concerts; there are regular visits from such as the BBC National Orchestra for Wales and foreign orchestras, and the new **Centre for Creative & Performing Arts** opened recently.

> *It has risen to become one of the best universities academically... but, even if you deny a student's claim that you'd find more night life in a tramp's vest, Bangor, because of its geographical position, is not everyone's choice.*

PILLOW TALK

Uni halls are offered to all freshers, 13% catered, 15% en suite; price range: £43-£78, so there's plenty from which to choose. Nice, confident touch in offering summer-vacation halls accommodation to prospective undergraduates – with or without parents – to get a taste of the place. One hall exclusively for Welsh speakers; one exclusively for women.

WHERE GRADUATES END UP

19% Education,	Key areas
14% Health/Social Work,	
12% Wholesale/Retail,	
10% Public Admin,	
6% Finance	
Agric/Forestry*, Sport*,	Niche areas
Radio/TV, Hotel/Rest,	
Legal, Archival/Cultural	

*indicates Top 10 Graduate Provider

Approximate employed   **93%**

JOBS

There's a careers service, of course, but in contrast to today's workaholic university careers services,

Bangor's seems, to say the least, gentlemanly. For example, the Students' Union tell me, 'A graduate recruitment fair is to be held in the summer term for the first time this year...looking to make it a regular annual event[!!]'. Bangor, however, is not battling for a place for its students in the electronic industries or even much in business or finance (accounts for 6%).

Education is its mainstay – nearly one fifth of graduates go into the sector, then health accounts for 14%. Agriculture/forestry and sport are also particularly well served.

GETTING THERE
☛ By road: A5, A55, A487; 90 minutes from M56.
☛ By rail: London Euston, 4:00; Birmingham New Street, 3:00; Manchester Oxford Road, 2:30; Liverpool Lime Street, 2:15.
☛ By coach: London, 8:00; Leeds, 6:15.

BARNSLEY COLLEGE

Barnsley College
Old Mill Lane Site
Church Street
Barnsley
South Yorks S70 2AX

TEL 01226 216171/2
FAX 01226 216613

EMAIL programme.enquiries@barnsley.ac.uk
WEB www.barsley.ac.uk

COLLEGE PROFILE

Founded	**1990**
Status	**HE College**
Degree awarding university	**Leeds, Leeds Met, Sheffield**
Full-time degree undergraduates	**1,234**
ACCOMMODATION:	
Availability	**10% students**
Style	**Hall**
Self-catering single/shared	**£45**
Town rent pw	**£30-£45**

DEGREE SUBJECT AREAS:
Music, art & design, business, health, humanities. Combined hons across media, performing arts, sports or social sciences

VAG VIEW

*W*ith Band Studies, Creative Music Technology and Popular Music Studies among the degree courses, don't be surprised that students have a fun time here. There are ents nightly – including a multi-

*media quiz night with computer images and karaoke – and they have the largest venue for live bands in the town (360 capacity). Concessions are rife at places like **O'Neills**, with live bands four nights a week (student band nights Monday and Tuesday) and there are over thirty other pubs. Nightclubs include **Regents Park** and **Hedonism** (Disco inferno is the night).*

Although there were problems last year with the student mag, Pants *emerged triumphant this year. There are over thirty societies – Christian Union being the most popular. Sport is also well catered for; all the usual team games are on offer, including Ladies' Rugby (rather than Women's Rugby), handbags to the ready presumably.*

Finally, it's a cheap place to live, and the market, we are told, is 'fab'.

GETTING THERE
☛ By road: M1/J38, A637, A635.
☛ By rail: London King's Cross (via Leeds), just under 4 hours; Newcastle (via Leeds), 3:00; Birmingham New Street (via Sheffield), 2:00.
☛ By coach: London, Newcastle, 4:15.

UNIVERSITY OF BATH

University of Bath
Claverton Down
Bath BA2 7AY

TEL 01225 323019
    01225 826091 (prospectus)
FAX 01225 826366
EMAIL p.a.elmer@bath.ac.uk
WEB www.bath.ac.uk

Bath Students' Union
Claverton Down
Bath
Somerset BA2 7AY

TEL 01225 826612
FAX 01225 444061
EMAIL union@union.bath.co.uk
WEB www.bath.ac.uk/busu

VAG VIEW

*B*ath is a small university bursting with
energy, and has become first choice for
thousands capable of Oxbridge, but wanting
the unique Bath experience, and, so it
maintains, wanting a better mix of students.
It is true that it greatly exceeds Oxbridge's
intake from state schools, lower income
brackets and intake of undergraduates from
neighbourhoods that don't traditionally send
their sons and daughters to university, that it
has formed a partnership with The
University for Swindon & Wiltshire Project,
designed to provide 'an accessible, flexible,*

UNIVERSITY/STUDENT PROFILE	
University since	**1966**
Situation/style	**City campus**
Student population	**10,800**
Full-time undergraduates	**5,700**
- mature	**10%**
- overseas	**13%**
- male/female	**56/44**
- state sector intake	**80%**
- non-traditional student intake	**7%, low**
- drop-out rate	**3%, low**
- undergraduate applications	**Up 7%**
*see Introduction for key to tables	

*high-quality system of education ...
responsive to local needs,' and indeed, that it
is home to a ground-breaking provision for
dyslexic students. But the figures for diversity
are hardly ground-breaking in the national
context; in fact they are not at all dramatic.
Bath exceeds its government benchmark only
in its state school intake and then only
marginally.*

*As at Oxbridge, value comes in Bath's
high teaching and research assessment
ratings (still good this year, although the uni
did actually fall from 7th to 19th position
nationally, Cambridge came first, Oxford
third). Value is also evident in its better-than-
Oxbridge sports record, facilities and
coaching expertise, and in its highly focused
graduate employment record, bolstered by its
language courses, IT facility and a 45%
sandwich course provision. But, in
particular, it beats Oxbridge in the character
of extra-curricular opportunity which its
largely scientific and technical student body
actually takes on board.*

STUDENT PROFILE

Bath's secret is that culturally it has not allowed its

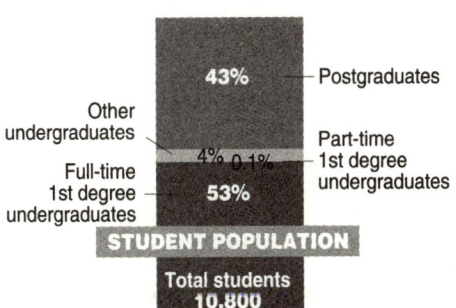

SUBJECT AREAS (%)

Languages — Combined — Health Subjects — Social Studies — Biological Sciences — 7 — 2 — 7 — 12 — 13 — Physical Science — 8 — 14 — 22 — Business — 10 — 5 — Maths & Computer — Architecture/Technology — Engineering/Technology

STUDENT POPULATION

43% — Postgraduates
Other undergraduates
Full-time 1st degree undergraduates — 4% — 0.1% — Part-time 1st degree undergraduates — 53%

Total students
10,800

scientific, technological and business base to dictate its personality.

'We may not have the sort of student traditionally likely to be involved in the arts,' a student told me, 'but that is what actually attracts students here. If we offered a drama course it would be the drama students who would be in all the plays, whereas, here, students have a lot better chance to be involved because there isn't a specific drama course, a specific music course and so on.' Where there is academic specialism there is also encouragement and opportunity to cross the traditional arts/science divide. This is the essence of modernity. There are tremendous opportunities for scientists to make a mark in the arts or in the media at Bath – journalism, radio and TV. As a result, this university is a well-balanced, stimulating and fulfilling place to spend three or four years.

Just how this impacts on student life is shown by reporter Anna Kennedy – 'Although the uni is small and not as socially diverse as some larger universities,' she writes, 'it is not claustrophobic and it feels like a community. We have loads of societies and freshers are really encouraged to get involved. It's wicked getting involved and organising events. You get to know everyone really quickly and don't feel anonymous like you might do in a bigger university.'

CAMPUS

The self-contained campus is situated two miles south-east of the city, up Bathwick hill. City and uni are linked by a special bus service – 'not always reliable, but quick, cheap and easy, and, like some people I know, it runs till 3 am most nights,' I was told. A central building houses the Library and Learning Centre (with 24-hour access), the Careers Office and Students' Union, all set around The Parade, a walkway not unlike a shopping precinct. The concrete and golden Bath stone buildings are unique, but, as I discovered, on a wet, wintry, foggy day they do not look their best.

ACADEMIA

The university concentrates on seven areas – Sciences, Social Sciences (Economics, Politics, Psychology, Social Policy, Social Work, Sociology), Engineering, Pharmacy & Pharmacology, Business, Languages, and Sport. There's a top-notch record from inspections, see *Academic Excellence* box. A Department of Computer Science opened in October 2001. Among new courses are joint degrees in communications and electronic engineering, which combine human/psychological aspects of computer/human communication with engineering.

ACADEMIC EXCELLENCE

TEACHING:
(Rated Excellent or 17+ out of 24)

Mechanical Engineering.	**Excellent**
Architecture, Business & Management Studies, Social Policy & Administration	
Physics, Maths, Biosciences	**24**
Politics, Economics	
Pharmacology, Education, Sport	**23**
Civil Engineering	**22**
Materials Technology	**21**
Chemical Engineering, Electric & Electron Eng	**20**
Modern Languages, Sociology	**19**

RESEARCH:
Top grades 5/5*

Pharmacy, Applied Maths, Mechanical/Aeronautical/ Manufacturing Eng,	**Grade 5***
Biological Sciences,	**Grade 5**
Pure Maths, Statistics, Built Environment, Social Policy, Business/Management, European Studies, Education	

'Many subjects are rated excellent,' notes Anna, 'but lecturers' interest in you/your work varies. Some go out of their way to help, but others seem more preoccupied with their own research and are harder to get hold of than Vanessa Feltz at an all-you-can-eat-buffet. However, there is always someone around to help. We are quite reliant on the Internet as most lecturers copy their lecture notes on the website. The library is excellent, but you may have to wait for a computer.

STUDENT SCENE

STUDENTS' UNION 'Freshers' week is good fun,' continues Anna. 'It makes it easier to settle down and make friends. In the sports hall, we normally have big name bands, and a massive dance night with good DJs. *Toga Night* is the highlight. You dress in a bed sheet, have a few shandies and an amazing laugh, and if you pass out you are practically already in bed! There are many events organised to help you integrate, but if homesick, we have excellent support services. An organisation called Aware offers a free counselling service, and Nightline provides an opportunity to talk to fellow students through the night.

'Bath's social scene is not for full-on clubbers, although, if you like a laugh, cheap drinks, cheesy music and easy pulling, you will love its student nights. First year social life revolves mainly around campus. There is the **Parade**, **Plug** and **Venue**. The Parade is a coffee bar by day and a convenient place to go for a few beers at night. It is quite classy, and often open until 2 am. Average campus price for a pint is £1.60. The Plug is like a small pub. They have karaoke some nights. It's next to the Venue, the nightclub. The Venue's neither **Cream** nor **Ministry**, but its cheap, friendly and a good laugh. Mondays this year, brought '70s nights, *Inferno*. Wednesdays, *Score!* Fridays, *Horny* (always packed out!) On Friday nights everyone goes to the Venue.

'There's a weekly newspaper, *Impact*, a radio station, URB 963, and a TV station, CTV, with monitors installed in the Plug Bar, a buzzing hive every evening during happy hour, and in the Venue, which is used as a café during the day.'

The centre for arts is **The Arts Barn** – drama, dance, music, studio workshop space for visual arts and crafts. BUST is the provocatively named drama society. Rainbow Over Bath is a combined jazz, classical, contemporary and electronic music concert programme with Bath Spa College (see entry). There's a musicals society, opera, a choral society – 'not quite so elitist as the chamber choir'. They also have student bands and orchestras.

SPORT Bath attracts the sporting elite. The men came 7th in the BUSA team placings last year. 'We are getting applications from a lot of very good athletes, sportsmen and women,' I was told. 'The sports science course we now offer is really competitive; there are literally thousands of applicants.'

Unlike practically any other university, all the sports facilities at Bath are free to students. Right on campus there's a generous range of team pitches and no facility is more than a stroll away. The sports village complex, partly built with Lottery money, offers a floodlit, 8-lane running track; 50-metre and 25-metre pools; a 4-court tennis hall; 16 hard tennis courts; 2 synthetic grass pitches; a shooting range; sports hall; squash courts; a performance testing lab; weight training rooms; a physio centre, etc. All this has attracted pro athletes such as champion hurdler Colin Jackson, Olympic silver-medallist swimmer Paul Palmer, butterfly-record-holder Mark Foster, amongst others, and their presence has lifted Bath to the pinnacle of achievement. 'In swimming Bath is supreme; it's just ridiculous,' an envious Bristol student had muttered to me earlier.

Nor does all this professionalism keep the keen amateur away – a statistic, much bandied, is that 80% of students make use of what's on offer (in all, fifty-two sporting clubs, including American

WHAT IT'S REALLY LIKE	
UNIVERSITY:	
Social Life	★★★★
Campus scene	**Busy, friendly**
Student Union services	**Good**
Politics	**Union active**
Sport	**52 clubs**
National team position	**4th**
Sport facilities	**Good**
Arts opportunities	**Excellent - Drama, Dance, Music, Visual Arts**
Student newspaper	**Impact**
Student radio	**URB**
Student TV	**CTV**
Nightclub	**Venue**
Bars	**Plug Bar, Parade Bar, Sports Café**
Union ents	**Inferno, Horny, Score!**
Union clubs/societies	**100**
Smoking policy	**Bars only**
Parking	**No 1st years**
CITY:	
Entertainment	★★★★
Scene	**OK clubs, pubs**
Town/gown relations	**Good**
Risk of violence	**Low**
Cost of living	**High**
Student concessions	**Good**
Survival + 2 nights out	**£70 pw**
Part-time work campus/town	**Fair/good**

Football). Bursaries and scholarships abound.

TOWN 'Bath has one of the highest ratios of pubs to people in the UK,' reports Anna. 'Our faves are the **Assembly Inn** (full of students, Bath's cheapest pub), **Flan O'Briens** (Irish pub surprisingly), **The Huntsman** and **O'Neills** (both open most nights 'til 2 am). **The Litten Tree** is also a student favourite with regular cheap deals; also try the **Boater** and the **Porter** (veggie pub, lush food and good comedy nights). For live music, go to **Moles**, probably the best club in Bath – small, but with awesome music and up-and-coming live bands.

'The most popular town nights are: Monday – **Cadillacs**, cheap to enter, cheap beer, cheap music and cheap people. Think of the Boddingtons cow on the advert, "Its like a cattle market in here.... wa-hey!" Tuesday – **The Fez Club**, the Moroccan corner of Bath, good dance nights. If house cocktails seem bargainious at a quid, there's no alcohol in them stupid! (Not that I've been caught out...ehem!). Wednesday – *Cocobanana @* **Babylon**, small, excellent music, guarantees a laugh.

AT A GLANCE	
ACADEMIC FILE:	
Subjects assessed	**21**
Excellent	**86%**
Average requirements	**300 points**
Students-staff ratio	**15:1**
First/2:1 degree pass rate	**70%**
ACCOMMODATION FILE:	
Guarantee to freshers	**Apply by 31.7**
Style	**Halls, houses**
Catered	**One hall**
En-suite	**46%**
Approx price range pw	**£44-£84**
City rent pw	**£50-£65**

Thursday – **Ts**: looks like a bomb shelter, and some sleazies have probably been there since the war trying to get lucky, but you can't help but like it...?!!

'All tastes of music are catered for, from punk, (*Discord* @ **Babylon** on Thursday) to funk (*Mr Phats Funk Emporium* @ **Moles** on Wednesday). from reggae (**Hat & Feather**, Wednesday), to R&B (*Bling Bling* @ **Delfter Krug**, Tuesday).

'Local residents are friendly and Bath is a totally non-threatening city. The average pub price is around £2.20 a pint, although some more expensive. Monitor events through *Impact* (the SU newspaper) or URB (the radio station).'

PILLOW TALK

Bath guarantees uni accommodation to all new, single, full-time first-year undergraduate degree course students who apply for it by July 31. Style of accommodation includes self-catering, standard or en-suite (46%) rooms grouped around a communal kitchen. On campus, there are generally eight to thirteen students per kitchen group, either in low-rise, terraced houses or halls, all within a ten-minute walk of the central academic complex. In the more recently built, off-site complexes, which are all very close to the central bus/train station, there are smaller cluster flats for two to six students. The nearest they get to a catered hall is one residence on campus which offers an optional meal-plan – students can have breakfast and dinner five days a week in the main restaurant. At time of writing, price per week varies between £43.97 and £84.23.

Writes Anna: 'There are three main halls on campus, Westwood, Norwood and Eastwood. Westwood is probably the highest standard, but everyone applies for a 'pod room' at Westwood. Beware, they are limited. Eastwood is pleasant, especially in summer and we loved it! Norwood is a

high-rise above the Venue, and can be noisy. Wherever you live, play loads of tricks on neighbours but don't get on the wrong side of your housekeeper. Avoid a house with a resident tutor nearby, or parties may end abruptly!

'Off campus, there's John Wood Court, Wells Road and Pulteney House. Mainly foreign students live here. Town halls tend to be of a higher standard then campus halls but you can feel isolated. Obviously, town halls also incur daily travelling costs.'

JOBS

Bath's careers service is highly focused.

'Sorted' is a Students' Union employee scheme, the programme aims to train, educate and develop students in key skills and aid Students' Union Officers and representatives in fulfilling their roles more effectively. Why get involved? 'Despite having top qualifications, employers have suggested that many graduates of today lack the

WHERE GRADUATES END UP	
20% Manufacturing*,	Key Areas
11% Finance,	
8% Computer,	
7% Public Admin	
Accountancy*,	Niche Areas
Business/Management*,	
Eng/Industrial Design*,	
Aeronautical Manuf*,	
Architecture, Chemical/	
Pharmaceutical,*	
Defence*, Electron/	
Electric*, Telecom	

*indicates Top 10 Graduate Provider

Approximate employed   **95%**

important skills needed for the world of work. "Sorted" is designed specifically to develop both you and your career prospects. It provides CV filling, life-enhancing opportunities from experts and professionals as well as experienced student trainers.'

GETTING THERE

☛ By road: M4/J18, A46.
☛ By rail: London Paddington or Southampton, 1:30; Birmingham, 2:15; Cardiff, 1:50.
☛ By air: Bristol Airport.
☛ By coach: London, Birmingham, 3:15

BATH SPA UNIVERSITY COLLEGE

Bath Spa University College
Newton St Loe
Bath BA2 9BN

TEL 01225 875875
FAX 01225 875444
EMAIL enquiries@bathspa.ac.uk
WEB www.bathsap.ac.uk

Bath Spa Students' Union
Newton St Loe
Bath BA2 9BN

TEL 01225 872603
FAX 01225 874765
EMAIL students-union@bathspa.ac.uk
WEB www.bathsap.ac.uk/su

VAG VIEW

*B*ath Spa University College came out of
the merger of Bath Academy of Art,
*Bath College of Education and Newton Park
College, the last two being originally teacher
training colleges. There are now four
faculties – Applied Sciences, Art and Music,
Education and Human Sciences, and
Humanities – on two campuses, Sion Hill
Campus, which specialises in art and design,
and the larger, but tranquil, Newton Park
Campus. It is a small, quiet and supportive
community, appealing particularly to female*

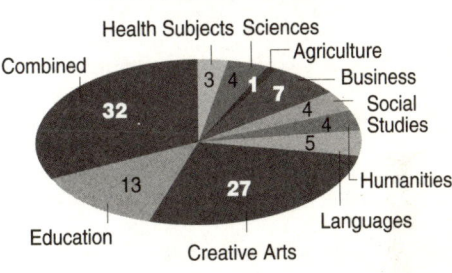

SUBJECT AREAS (%)

CAMPUSES

Newton Park is four miles west of the city in a
landscaped saucer of Duchy of Cornwall
countryside, an original Capability Brown design,
with a Georgian manor house at its administrative
hub and a cash dispenser, recently installed by the
Students' Union. There are half hourly and late-
night buses to and from town.

Sion Hill is within walking distance of the city
centre on the north side and is reserved for Art and
Design. It comprises a large modern building and
the Georgian crescent Somerset Place, set in
attractive grounds.

COLLEGE/STUDENT PROFILE

University College since	**1999**
Situation/style	**Campus**
Student population	**4,280**
Full-time undergraduates	**2,420**
- mature	**25%**
- overseas	**4%**
- male/female	**31/69**
- state sector intake	**94%**
- non-traditional student intake	**10%**
- drop-out rate	**11%**
- undergraduate applications	**Up 47%**

*see Introduction for key to tables

*(69%) and mature undergraduates (25%),
though it teaches pre-university too. One
student told of its 'friendly, warming
atmosphere.' She admitted, 'I arrived a timid,
not-sure-why-I-was-leaving-home type of
person ... if you have a shell to come out of,
you'll discard it within weeks of coming here.'*

*It is far from being some sort of specialist
dumping ground for sensitive souls, however.
Bath Spa comes out high in any league table
of new unis and university colleges, which is
why last year undergraduate applications
increased by a staggering 47%.*

ACADEMIA

They won the right to award their own degrees in
1992, and course design displays individuality and

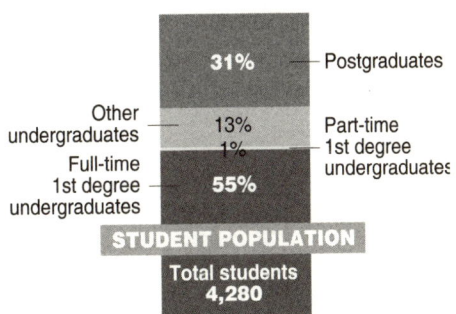

STUDENT POPULATION
Total students
4,280

AT A GLANCE

ACADEMIC FILE:

Subjects assessed	**10**
Excellent	**70%**
Typical requirements	**180 points**
Students-staff ratio	**19:1**
First/2:1 degree pass rate	**62%**

ACCOMMODATION FILE:

Guarantee to freshers	**97%**
Style	**Halls**
Approx price range pw	**£50-£70**
City rent pw	**£45-£55**

flair. BA and BSc specialised awards include Creative Music Technology, English and International Education, Music, Art & Design (including Fine Art), Creative Arts (two from Fine Art, Music, English, Textile Design), Enviro Science, Food Management, Human Ecology, Remote Sensing and Geographic Information Systems and Social Science. At Newton Park, an academic interest in music is given a performance dimension at the **Michael Tippett Centre**, recently refurbished and extended to make a 250-seater auditorium.

Commercial Music is their first two-year foundation degree (one of the Government's initiatives for widening participation in higher education), and is the first course of its kind in the UK. Performance and songwriting are key elements of the course. Students played their first live gig in January 2002. It's a very creative scene at Bath Spa. There's also an MA Creative Writing course, three of whose earliest graduates found immediate publication – Simon Kerr, Karen Sainsbury and Mimi Thebo. Can we see here, perhaps, the successor to the late Malcolm Bradbury's literary forcing ground at East Anglia Uni?

Then there are the regular BA and BSc single awards, for which a second subject must be

ACADEMIC EXCELLENCE

TEACHING:
(Rated Excellent or 17+ out of 24)

English, Environmental Studies	**Excellent**
Sociology, Art & Design	**22**
Environmental Biology, Psychology	**21**
Business/Management	**20**

RESEARCH:
Top grades 5/5* **None**

selected in the first year: arts, humanities, social science, business, religion, health, etc. Finally combined BA/BSc awards give subjects equal weight. On the teacher education front, there's a three-year BA/BSc Hons degree with a guaranteed PGCE place (primary).

WHAT IT'S REALLY LIKE

UNIVERSITY:

Social Life	★★★
Campus scene	**Quiet/mature teachers, funky artists**
Politics	**Quiet**
Sport	**Relaxed**
Arts opportunities	**Excellent**
Student newspaper	**B.S.E. - Bath Spa Experience**
Union ents	**3 pw**
Live venue capacity	**250**
Union Clubs/Societies	**20+**
Smoking policy	**Bar, some halls**
Parking	**None**

CITY:

Entertainment	★★★
Scene	**Compact, touristy**
Town/gown relations	**Good**
Risk of violence	**Low**
Cost of living	**High**
Student concessions	**Good**
Survival + 2 nights out	**£70 pw**
Part-time work campus/town	**Fair/good**

SOCIAL SCENE

There are the usual comedians, hypnotists, discos – Friday is *Frisky* – theme nights, tribute bands and all-night parties, but increasingly students are making their own entertainments. There's also a

WHERE GRADUATES END UP

26% Education*,	Key Areas
14% Wholesale/Retail,	
8% Health/Social Work,	
6% Manufacturing,	
6% Public Admin,	
6% Personnel	
Artistic/Literary*,	Niche Areas
Hotel/Restaurant*,	
Film/Video,	
Library/Archival*,	
Market Research	

*indicates Top 10 Graduate Provider

Approximate employed	90%

sports hall and tennis courts, gym, etc.
See Bath Uni entry for city scene.

GETTING THERE
☛ By road Newton Park: from London and east: M4/J18, A46, A4, A39 to Wells, turn left after 200 yards into Newton Park Estate. By road Sion Hill:

M4/J18, A46, A420, first left to Hamswell, at second give-way take a right and second right into Landsdown Crescent, over crossroads, first right to Sion Hill on your right.
☛ By rail: London Paddington or Southampton, 1:30; Birmingham, 2:15; Cardiff, 1:50.
☛ By air: Bristol Airport.

BELL COLLEGE OF TECHNOLOGY

Bell College of Technology
Almada Street
Hamilton
South Lanarkshire ML3 OJB

TEL 01698 283100
FAX 01698 282131
EMAIL enquiries@bell.ac.uk
WEB www.bell.ac.uk

VAG VIEW

*B*ell is a well-organised operation. There are four faculties (Business, Engineering, Science, Health and Social Science) and Bell Innovations Ltd, a consultancy and training company that forges links with companies that help plan their courses and where students make profitable connections. Most undergrads study to HNC, HND or Diploma; many are mature. There are part-time, career-related degree courses for nurses and police officers as well the subjects listed in the box.

Eleven miles southeast of Glasgow, Bell is geographically and conceptually close to its partner university, Strathclyde (see entry), and if its students might wish they were even closer, so as to take advantage of the Glasgow nightlife, Hamilton entertains with a few pubs and clubs, a wide range of sports facilities, and cinemas, theatres and museums are available locally. At the Students' Union there's ents throughout the year; clubs and societies range from sport to political and cultural groups. A

COLLEGE PROFILE	
Founded	**1972**
Status	**HE College**
Degree awarding university	**Strathclyde**
Student population	**1,492**
Degree undergraduates	**452**
ACCOMMODATION:	
Availability to freshers	**100%**
Style	**Hall flats**
Cost pw (no food)	**£40**
Town rent pw	**£40**
DEGREE SUBJECT AREAS:	
Business, law, leisure, social sciences, engineering, management, biological and environmental sciences, architectural technology, chemistry, etc	

fitness studio and the Sportsbarn (for indoor games) are popular.

GETTING THERE
☛ By road: M74/J6.
☛ By rail: London, 5:27; Edinburgh, 2:04.
☛ By coach: Edinburgh, 2:00.

BIRKBECK COLLEGE

Birkbeck College
University of London
Malet Street
London WC1E 7HX

TEL 020 7631 6000
FAX 020 7631 6351
EMAILadmissions@admin.bbk.ac.uk
WEB www.bbk.ac.uk

Birkbeck Students' Union
University of London
Malet Street
London WC1E 7HX

TEL 020 7631 6335
FAX 020 7631 6349
EMAIL president@bcsu.bbk.ac.uk
WEB www.bbk.ac.uk/su

VAG VIEW

*L*earn as you earn – London's Birkbeck College was founded in 1823 as the London Mechanics' Institution, and was admitted as a school of the University of London in 1920. It provides study programmes for adults engaged in earning their livelihood or looking after their families during the day. It is located in Malet Street in central London, adjacent to the University of London's Senate House and Students' Union. The College is organised in four faculties.

Students, who benefit from Birkbeck's excellent teaching reputation and an accommodating entry policy – life experience, aptitude for a particular subject and commitment are the chief requirements to get on a degree course – are mostly aged between 25 and 45 and come from a variety

COLLEGE PROFILE	
College of London Uni since	**1920**
Situation/style	**City site**
Student population	**15,390**
Undergraduates: part-time	**3,300**
full-time	**10**
Accommodation	**None**

DEGREE SUBJECT AREAS:
Science, computer, social studies (geography, law, psychology, politics, economics), business, languages, humanities

of backgrounds. Birkbeck is rarely given credit in league tables for its open access policy, but they recruit some 20% from the poorest Group IV neighbourhoods, which is 41% higher than the national average.

Students' Union facilities include a shop, a bar, a TV room. There's an unambitious JCR ents programme – an occasional disco, two in the first term – Freshers and Christmas (this year they had Jylt play). Eighteen societies currently grab students' interest (the most popular is Philosophy Soc), and one sports club (Football). A few intercollegiate fixtures are played out at the college's grounds in Hackney Marshes, which is a way away and sounds a bit soggy. There used to be a volleyball club, which met every Tuesday in the gym at ULU, and a gym club, but apparently no more. All facilities of the University of London Union are available to Birkbeck students of course.

One of the major concerns of Birkbeck union is the welfare of its part-time, mature students and there is a Students' Advice Centre open in the evening.

There is a student magazine, called Lamp & Owl.

ACADEMIC EXCELLENCE	
Subjects assessed	**19**
Excellent	**63%**
TEACHING:	
(Rated Excellent or 17+ out of 24)	
English	**Excellent**
History of Art, Organismal	**24**
Biosciences, Politics	
Molecular Biosciences	**22**
Business/Management, Maths	**21**
German	**20**
Linguistics, Spanish, French	**19**
RESEARCH:	
Top grades 5/5*	
English, Iberian/Latin American,	**Grade 5***
History	
Psychology, Crystallography,	**Grade 5**
Law, Economics,	
Earth Sciences, Politics,	
German/Dutch/Scandinavian,	
History of Art, Philosophy	

GETTING THERE

☞ Euston Square (Circle & Metropolitan lines); Warren Street (Victoria line); Goodge Street (Northern line); Russell Square (Piccadilly line).

STUDENT BIRMINGHAM - THE CITY

Birmingham has shaken off its grey image to incredible effect in the last decade. Developments right across Britain's second city total hundreds of

millions of pounds. Improved social and shopping facilities carry the bonus of better graduate job prospects and mean that whatever you're after from your student career, Birmingham can probably supply.

CLUBS

Gone are the '70s clubs of old (although postgrads can still be heard reminiscing about the 'nites' they had at **The Dome**) to be replaced by superclubs **DNA**, **Code** and **The Works**, all of which host national club events.

The student is a fickle consumer, so club favourites vary hugely from year to year, but those cropping up time and time again as firm favourites are **Zanzibar**, a funky, multi-coloured club hosting several rooms of dance and cheesy pop (and a toy train which circles the bar!), **Brannigans** for cheesily cheerful tracks that you last danced to at a school disco, weekly cover bands and the occasional appearance by such as Jason Donavan or Chesney Hawkes, and **Bobby's** for an eclectic mix of – you've guessed it – old cheese and current dance tracks.

The Works, DNA and Code also have popular student nights, although arguably their regular *God's Kitchen* all-nighters and Vodbull UK or Ryno drinkathons are most student-renowned.

There are fewer commercial student nights purely for hip hop, R&B and garage fans, but you will find clubs with rooms devoted to less than cheesy beats, and many smaller venues such as the **Rat and Parrot** with such nights.

LIVE

The newly-opened **Birmingham Academy** is the best local venue – it's one of the essential stops on any band's UK tour, its reputation boosted far and wide in 2001 by Radio 1's hosting most of its *One Live in Birmingham* events there.

The **Wolverhampton Civic**, just a short train ride away, is still seen as a main Midland live venue, and the **NEC** is equally popular with bands of U2 or S Club proportions. In the smaller venues expect massively varying music styles and quality. **Ronnie Scott's** offers more than just jazz (Dean from *Big Brother 2* even strummed on this stage) whilst the **Fiddle and Bone** is a pub with a plethora of acts for free – from tribute bands to student musos through to Beethoven. Further into the backstreets you'll find a glut of pubs with fascinating (but sometimes frightening) live acts.

COMEDY, THEATRE, ARTS

Judging by the success of venues like the **Glee Club**, the new rock 'n' roll this may be. The venue attracts the best comic newcomers and the established talents of Eddie Izzard and Harry Hill – all for under a fiver if you go on a student night.

At the newly-revamped **Hippodrome** or **Alexandra Theatre** can be seen an array of Lloydesque and other West End shows, as well as the magnificent Welsh National Opera.

In the **Symphony Hall**, the renowned City of Birmingham Symphony Orchestra resides, playing host also to hundreds of international performers and offering a huge variety of classical music all year round.

For smaller fry the **Midlands Arts Centre**, or MAC as it is known, nestles comfortably on the edge of Cannon Hill Park near the University of Birmingham. With its combination of theatre, exhibitions, cinema and a damn fine bar it offers excellent choice and value. The **Electric Cinema**, showing arthouse, world and classic cinema in a charming setting, is the place to go if you want to see something a little bit different, although if it's Hollywood blockbusters you're after the **Odeon**, **UGC** and **Starcity** complexes offer about six billion different films, allegedly on twice as many screens.

For theatre **The Rep** in town has come in for a great deal of well-deserved praise lately with their showcase for new work, **The Door**, and also show fantastic productions in their main theatre. Stratford-upon-Avon is but a short train ride away, but watch out for the RSC's value for money student trips to productions there. For community productions (usually) as good as the professionals, check out the **Crescent Theatre**, offering Shakespeare and other productions.

For art you are spoilt in Brum, **The Barber Institute** on the University of Birmingham's campus is astounding. For more modern exhibitions head for **Ikon** or **The Angle** galleries.

Crucially all these places offer heavy discounts for students. Life with a 10% discount is what being a student is all about.

SHOPPING

The shopping situation in Birmingham shows best how much the city has changed. Once overshadowed by the concrete-smothered **Bull Ring**, the monstrosity has now been reduced to a hole in the ground, ready for a brand new shopping centre in its place which should come into being by 2003. The operation has left room for the rest of Brum shopping world to flourish – the newly-opened **Mailbox** offers a chance to drool at **Harvey Nichs**. Department stores like **Rackham's** has just about every designer name you care to mention. Realistically though most students will stick to the pedestrianised areas around New Street and the Pallasades, where every high street store you could want is juxtaposed with designer off-cut stores and street markets.

Rebecca Taylor

UNIVERSITY OF BIRMINGHAM

The University of Birmingham
Edgbaston
Birmingham B15 2TT

TEL 0121 414 7170
FAX 0121 414 3850
EMAIL admissions@bham.ac.uk
WEB www.bham.ac.uk

Birmingham Guild of Students
Edgbaston Park Road
Birmingham B15 2TU

TEL 0121 472 1841
FAX 0121 471 2099
EMAIL enquiries@guild.bham.ac.uk
WEB www.bugs-bham.co.uk

VAG VIEW

*B*irmingham is the original redbrick
university, with all that that entails
beyond its masonry – none of the snobbery
attached to Oxbridge and, in the region at
least, a reputation second only to Oxbridge.
Its teaching is among the very best in the
country – 85% of assessments meet our
criteria of Excellence (only medicine was a
little disappointing recently, see Academic
Excellence box, page 73). Brum's research
record (it came 23rd in the recent
assessments) and its graduate employment

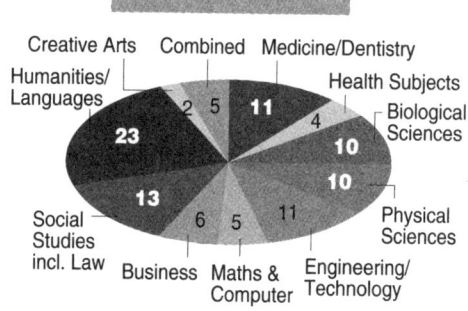

SUBJECT AREAS (%)

record, particularly in the areas of health,
engineering, finance, accountancy and
business are equally good. Together with the
city and campus scenes, they serve to make
Birmingham a sound choice.

If you don't enjoy a three-year spell here,
it is unlikely to be Birmingham's fault. Most
manage to; the drop-out rate (at 6%) is
encouragingly low.

CAMPUS

The self-contained University of Birmingham
campus lies a couple of miles south of the city in
leafy Edgbaston. Parking is not encouraged.

UNIVERSITY/STUDENT PROFILE

University since	**1900**
Situation/style	**Campus**
Student population	**27,110**
Full-time undergraduates	**13,710**
- mature	**11%**
- overseas	**10%**
- male/female	**47/53**
- state sector intake	**74%**
- non-traditional student intake	**8%, low**
- drop-out rate	**6%, low**
- undergraduate applications	**Up 3%**
see Introduction for key to tables	

VIEW FROM THE GROUND
by Rebecca Taylor

STUDENT PROFILE

Birmingham students come from all over.
Southerners think that Brum is north enough for
them. Northerners, already bored of Manchester,
see it as the next best city without London's
expense. Thanks to strong overseas links there's
also a large international community. In fact, be it
fashion, music or religion, anything goes. The gist
is that there are loads of people with interests
sympathetic to yours, and you'll meet them
through lectures, accommodation or socialising.

In an effort to ease the plight of disabled students,

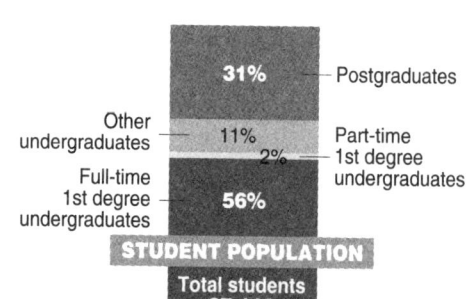

STUDENT POPULATION

Total students
27,110

the uni has recently instigated a five-year action plan to adapt and re-design facilities and access points. For international students, there's now a full-time Student Adviser and free lessons in English during term time.

ACADEMIA

Most lecturers are as concerned about undergraduate progress as about their research, tutors (one for each subject you study) are happy to help if you tell them your concerns and there are several ways to register complaints or worries (student reps, course questionnaires, tutors).

The library is well stocked, although around essay time it may be necessary to visit the city's Central Library, where books won't already have been squandered by fellow students, and computer clusters are available in each department.

Recent major academic projects include a new Teaching & Learning Resources Centre, teaching labs for Biosciences, Chemistry, Geography, Environmental Science and Physics, Computer Science buildings, and a European Research Institute, opened by the Prime Minister in November 2001, its mission to bring together key areas of European policy and strategy.

The recent takeover of nearby Westhill College brings new part-time programmes and facilitates wider access to the uni's degrees. A so-called Black Country Strategy is a project to create an extra 100 places for medical students in partnership with NHS hospital trusts in the Black Country area (Wolverhampton, Dudley, Sandwell and Walsall), the aim to retain a high number of qualified medical staff in an area where there is a shortfall at present. From 2003 there'll be a graduate entry course in medicine. Finally, the School of Education is currently piloting an Internet-based distance learning project.

You can expect to be asked for around 320 points at A level to come here. For a first degree in Medicine or Dentistry you'll need 340: preference is given to applicants with no alternative offer from elsewhere; mature applications are welcomed; particular attention is placed on what applicants have done beyond A levels to show commitment and motivation in the care of others.

SOCIAL SCENE

GUILD OF STUDENTS The main source of non-academic entertainment on campus is the union, called Birmingham Uni Guild of Students or BUGS for short. This isn't purely to baffle your non-Brummy friends – the Guild was the first union in the country and earned the right to a sophisticated name. By day they offer numerous cateries and

---

ACADEMIC EXCELLENCE

TEACHING:
(Rated Excellent or 17+ out of 24)

History, Music, Geography, English, Geology	**Excellent**
Sociology, Elect/Electron Eng	**24**
Organismal Biosciences, Maths. Physiotherapy, Classics.	
Russian, Middle Eastern/ African Studies, Biochemistry, Physics, Molecular Biosciences, Psychology, Economics, Theol.	**23**
Dentistry, Italian, Iberian Studies, American Studies, HistoryArt, Dentistry, Nursing, Sport,Tourism.	**22**
Chemical Engineering, Civil Engineering, Drama, Business, Education, Philosophy.	**21**
Manufac & Mechanical Eng Materials Technology, Medicine	**20**
German	**19**
French	**18**

RESEARCH:
Top grades 5/5*

Clinical Lab. Sciences, Anatomy, Psychology, Chemical Eng, Metallurgy & Materials, Middle East/African Studies, Russian/E. European Studies, French, German/Dutch/Scand, Italian, Music, Sport.	**Grade 5***
Hospital-based Clinical, Pre-Clinical, Bio-Sciences, Chemistry, Physics, Pure Maths, Applied Maths, Computer, Civil Eng, Eelc & Electron Eng, Law, Politics, German, English, Iberian & Latin American, Greek, History, History of Art, Theology, Educ.	**Grade 5**

---

bars, from **Joe's**, the typical trendy student bar, to the delicious hot food of **Café Connections**.

There's the chance to join one of over 100 societies, and a huge range of student services (legal advice, local info from the ARC, part-time job info at the Job Zone, etc).

But there is a catch. These services are partly paid for by bar profits, so, whilst the Guild still costs less than non-student bars, it's often cheaper to go to student nights in the city centre than to stay on campus. As a result, freshers often go to hall bars before moving on to one of the city-centre clubs and bars. Students living in neighbouring Selly Oak or Harbourne frequent the many local student pubs and balti houses in those areas, as

WHAT IT'S REALLY LIKE

UNIVERSITY:

Social Life	★★★★★
Campus scene	**Traditional, busy, cosmopolitan**
Student Union services	**Good**
Politics	**Average; student issues**
Sport	**Key**
National team position	**2nd**
Sport facilities	**Very good**
Arts opportunities	**Film excellent; drama, dance, music, art good**
Student newspaper	**Redbrick**
Student radio	**Burn FM**
Student TV	**Guild TV**
Nightclub	**Berlin's**
Bars	**Joe's, Beorma**
Union ents	**Club 99, Fab, Frenzy, FabnFresh**
Union clubs/societies	**180**
Most popular society	**Carnival**
Smoking policy	**Bars OK**
Parking	**Poor**
CITY:	
Entertainment	★★★★★
Scene	**Excellent**
Town/gown relations	**Average**
Risk of violence	**High**
Cost of living	**High**
Student concessions	**Excellent**
Survival + 2 nights out	**£50 pw**
Part-time work campus/town	**Excellent**

happening place and there is that self-same disinterested, confident air that you notice at all our best traditional universities and which makes you want to find out what is happening and get involved. Fact is Birmingham isn't just about getting rat-arsed and going for a closing-time curry.

On campus, artistic input is high. Across drama, dance, music and art, extra-curricular societies are very active. The Film Society is excellent. Musically, there's a chamber orchestra, an orchestra of 100 and a choir of 220. For art there's **The Barber Institute** – founded in 1932 it incorporates both Fine Art and Music departments and has been described as 'one of the finest small picture galleries in the world'. There's also a musical theatre group which nurtures, milks and dispenses talent that abounds among students. If you're into theatre, Birmingham is one of the places to be. There's a Guild group and a Drama Dept group in the uni's **Studio Theatre**; students perform all over the city (often before taking their productions to the Edinburgh Fringe), and there's a student humour night at the **Glee Club** in town.

If it's media you're after, Birmingham's newspaper office, radio and TV stations are to be found in the basement of BUGS. I walked in on a bubbly lunchtime session in the TV studio – a televised radio programme that was transmitting over the whole city live. Finally, sports-wise, Birmingham's teams were the second best in the country last year.

SPORT The Munrow Sports Centre's mission statement 'to enhance the sporting experience of the university by providing opportunities at all levels' sums up the sporting situation. For the casual athlete the *Active Lifestyles Programme* offers weekly courses in martial arts, swimming, aerobics and team games for under £20 a term. Clubs exist at university, inter-departmental and inter-hall levels in every imaginable sport. Interests are more than catered for by the 25m pool, two gyms, a climbing wall and full-size running track, as well as two floodlit, synthetic pitches – all on campus.

The tradition is to encourage sport for all, but make no mistake, Birmingham is second only to Loughborough in the British national team championships, year after year.

well as the most popular city club nights. The exception is Friday night when *Frenzy* at the Guild is sold out by Thursday.

Birmingham students with long memories deplore the current Guild's lack of political teeth. 'Gone are the days when the NUS had any political balls,' one said. 'They are jobbing politicians now, they have zero influence,' I was told. Despite their impressive Debating Chamber, we're talking local issues, university policy, academic issues, etc. There'll be no chaining themselves to railings here, let alone anyone working their rocks off on international issues. Nevertheless, the Guild is a big, bustling,

> *Birmingham is a big, bustling, happening place and there is that self-same disinterested, confident air that you notice at all our best universities and which makes you want to find out what is happening and get involved.*

By Lake Coniston in Cumbria, 170 miles away, they have a Centre for Outdoor Pursuits (watersports, mountaineering, mountain biking, etc). Nearer home, besides the campus synthetic pitches and tennis courts, there are seventy acres of pitches five miles from home, served by coaches and minibuses. And there's a new degree in golf.

Town Favourite clubs are **Zanzibar** for cheese and dance music, **Brannigans** for pure cheese and the occasional live-in-the-flesh blasts from the past such as Jason Donovan. Monthly excuses to get wasted on the cheap are Vodbull UK (£1 for double vodka and red bull) and Ryno (drinks included in £10 entry). See *Student Birmingham* (page 70), for the rest.

The city does have less desirable areas (name a city that doesn't) but the average student has little contact with them, and if you're sensible about sticking in groups after dark and not flashing your cash around you shouldn't have any problems. As in all student areas there are complaints from disgruntled locals about kick-out time noise and student mess, but the Guild liaises with residents and police to keep the peace.

Generally you should be able to survive on around £50 a week, giving you two nights out at £8-£15 each (depending on where you go), £25 for food and beer and a (healthy!) walk to uni each day. Don't forget one-off expenses like books and clothes!

PILLOW TALK

Most freshers live in university accommodation, which is currently being revamped. The main area is the Vale, a beautiful grassy area set around a lake which houses catered and self-catered halls and is just fifteen minutes from the main area of campus. Other self-catered halls are either adjacent to the main campus (the ultra posh Jarratt Hall), opened September 2001 and boasting 620 en-suite

bedrooms) or a bus journey away (The Beeches and Hunter Court). University House, the Oxbridge-style original residence, is ideally situated next to the Guild.

Housing quality varies – new developments are modern, with Internet access and mod cons in kitchens, but are more pricey. As for the rest, the less you pay, the less you get.

The older, catered residences may seem old-fashioned in decor and organisation (set meal times, hall tutors) but offer a stress-free introduction to university life with plenty of people to meet and no cooking hassles.

JOBS

If you do find yourself dipping into the overdraft it's easy to find a job at the Guild, where students are given decent wages for bar work, security, marketing, and other jobs. Alternatively,

---

WHERE GRADUATES END UP

19% Health	Key Areas
11% Manufacturing,	
10% Finance,	
7% Education,	
7% Public Admin,	
5% Personnel,	
5% Computer	
Accountancy*,	Niche Areas
Business/Management,	
Aeronautical Manuf,	
Eng/Industrial Design,	
Chemical/Pharmaceutical,	
Defence, Electron/Electric,	
Legal, Market Research	

*indicates Top 10 Graduate Provider

Approximate employed **95%**

---

businesses around the city always want flexible, enthusiastic part-timers. Most of them advertise in the Guild's Job Zone.

Most courses encourage skills that'll be required by employers on graduation – presentations, written work and group work are normally part of assessment, and computer skills are exercised in project work.

Information Services give actual courses on presentation, computer skills and library skills, the Careers Centre on interview and CV preparation.

Involvement with the world beyond campus is an aspect of a number of courses, and the proximity of important industries and businesses, as well as artistic nuclei, is key. The Arts School non-vocational courses give special attention not just to

---

AT A GLANCE

ACADEMIC FILE:

Subjects assessed	**46**
Excellent	**85%**
Average requirements	**320 points**
Student-staff ratio	**14:1**
First/2:1 degree pass rate	**68%**

ACCOMMODATION FILE:

Fresher guarantee only to	**1st-choice applicants**
Style	**Halls**
Catered	**29%**
En-suite	**20%**
Price range pw	**£49-£119**
Town rent pw	**£45**

---

what is studied, but *how* a subject is studied. Organisation, analysis, presentation, communication and problem-solving are skills to the fore.

GETTING THERE
☞ By road: A38. Avoid entry through suburbia from the M40; instead use M42/J1, A38.

☞ By rail: London Euston, 1:40; Bristol Parkway or Sheffield, 1:30; Liverpool Lime Street, Manchester Piccadilly,1:40; Leeds, 2:15. Frequent trains from New Street to University Station.
☞ By air: Birmingham Airport.
☞ By coach: London, 2:40; Bristol, 2:00; Manchester, 2:30.

BIRMINGHAM CENTRAL ENGLAND *see* CENTRAL ENGLAND

BIRMINGHAM COLLEGE OF FOOD TOURISM & CREATIVE STUDIES

Birmingham College of Food
Tourism & Creative Studies
Summer Row
Birmingham B3 1JB

TEL 0121 604 1000
FAX 0121 200 1376
EMAIL admissions@bcftcs.ac.uk
WEB www.bcftcs.ac.uk

VAG VIEW

*T*here's nothing quite like BCFTCS for food and tourism. Its international reputation draws students from all over the UK, Ireland, indeed the world, as does its strong international links with industry – contacts passed on to students at the big trade fairs at which the college exhibits. The college has won a Queen's Anniversary Prize for its success in working with industry. Appropriate to its international flavour, the Modern Languages Department is particularly strong and all students are encouraged to take advantage of this. Equipment and the Resource Centre (library, computer banks) are top notch and access good. Work placements, or working visits abroad, are deemed essential.

Accommodation is constantly improving – single sex halls of residence with en-suite bathroom available. Small Cambrian Hall is situated close to Broad Street, centre of the student action in this buzzing city.

Sport is good – four football teams, one

COLLEGE PROFILE	
Founded	**1961**
Status	**F/HE College**
Degree awarding university	**Birmingham**
Total student population	**4,500**
Full-time undergraduates	**2,542**
ACCOMMODATION:	
Availability to freshers	**96%**
Style	**Halls**
Cost pw (no food)	**£52-£62**
City rent pw	**£45**
DEGREE SUBJECT AREAS:	
Food, tourism, hospitality, leisure	

rugby. A student said, 'We're better than UCE and Aston, which makes us about average.' Ents centre on the **Guild Bar** in the basement of the college, and outside mega events such as club-crawls. There are also parties or get-togethers in the halls of residence.' See also Student Birmingham, *page 70.*

GETTING THERE
☞ By road: from the north, M6/A38(M) or M5/A46; from southwest, M5/A456; from London, M40/M42/A45 or M1/M6/A38(M). No parking on campus, but there's an NCP nearby.
☞ By rail: London Euston, 1:40; Bristol Parkway or Sheffield, 1:30; Liverpool Lime Street or Manchester Piccadilly,1:40; Leeds, 2.15.
☞ By air: Birmingham International Airport.
☞ By coach: London, 2:40; Bristol, 2:00; Manchester, 2:30.

BISHOP BURTON COLLEGE OF AGRICULTURE

Bishop Burton College of Agriculture
Bishop Burton
Beverley
East Yorkshire HU17 8QG

TEL 01964 553000
FAX 01964 553101
EMAIL enquiries@bishopb-college.ac.uk
WEB www.bishopb-college.ac.uk

VAG VIEW

The Yorkshire Wolds are important farming country and not too far from civilisation – 7 miles from Hull; York, 25 to the west. Two miles to the east lies Beverley, an almost Cotswoldy market town with a small but beautiful minster.

*There is an active Students' Association housed in the appropriately named **Meadows**, with a fast-food outlet, bar with disco dance area and satellite TV.*

Not surprisingly there's an outdoor sort of ethos and Bishop Burton is quite a sporty place – rugby (union and league), hockey, soccer, cricket, tennis, badminton, basketball, netball, squash, snooker, archery, clay pigeon shooting and golf are available. Accommodation on the estate includes some single en-suite rooms.

COLLEGE PROFILE	
Founded	**1954**
Status	**F/HE college**
Degree awarding university	**Lincoln Uni**
Student population	**2,211**
Full-time undergraduates	**397**
ACCOMMODATION:	
Availability to freshers	**80%**
Style	**Student village**
Cost pw (no food)	**£45-£60**
Town rent pw	**£40-£50**

DEGREE SUBJECT AREAS:
Countryside and environmental management (including ornithology), equine science and garden design

GETTING THERE

☞ By road: A1079 from York; M62/J38, B1230 from the south.
☞ By rail: Hull, 12 mins; York, 1:43.
☞ By coach: York, 1:00.

BISHOP GROSSETESTE COLLEGE

Bishop Grosseteste College
Newport
Lincoln LN1 3DY

TEL 01522 527347
FAX 01522 530243
EMAIL registry@bgc.ac.uk
WEB www.bgx.ac.uk

VAG VIEW

Small and mainly female, there's a practical emphasis here on the primary teacher training courses (working with children, schooling in motivation, self-esteem, etc.). The ethos flows from the roots of this church-based college, named after Robert Grosseteste, Bishop of Lincoln in the thirteenth century and the first Chancellor of

COLLEGE PROFILE	
Founded	**1862**
Status	**HE college**
Degree awarding university	**Hull**
Total student population	**1,030**
Full-time degree undergraduates	**780**
ACCOMMODATION:	
Availability to freshers	**100%**
Style	**College**
Cost pw (food)	**£67**
Town rent pw	**£35-£40**

DEGREE SUBJECT AREAS:
Drama, heritage, English literature; also BA/BSc Hons (QTS) – Education

Oxford Uni. But it would be wrong to see Grot, as it is affectionately known, as just that, for, in addition to the teacher and education degrees, they offer BA Hons degrees in Arts in the Community (Drama), English Literature and Heritage Studies. All Hull Uni named degress.

With the college's academic evolution came something of a social revolution. Meltdown is a society for clubbers dedicated to shameless hedonism as far away as Leeds, Liverpool, Birmingham and Manchester, the society existing alongside SSAGO, the Student Scout and Guide Organisation, and of course the Christian Union. Otherwise, the bar is focus for ents four or five times a week.

Sports include netball, hockey, football, women's football, cricket and rugby. 'Our general aim is to keep fit and play the game with a high element of fun,' they say.

See Lincoln University entry for more about the city.

GETTING THERE

☞ By road: from the north, A15; from Sheffield way (NW) via the A57 on to A46 Lincoln by-pass.
☞ By rail: London King's Cross via Newark (on the main east coast line), 2:00; Nottingham, 1:00.
☞ By coach: London, 4:10.

BLACKBURN COLLEGE

Blackburn College
Feilden Street
Blackburn
Lancs BB2 1LH

TEL 01254 55144
FAX 01254 682700
EMAIL (via website)
WEB www.blackburn.ac.uk

VAG VIEW

*T*his is a mainly further education college, twenty miles or so north of Manchester and with a small accommodation facility nearby. In 1995 it became an associate college of Lancaster Uni, three junctions up the M6. There are also tie-ups with Huddersfield, Glamorgan and Hull unis. Teaching assessments brought a Satisfactory for Computing and Business (1994), 19/24 for Design, 18 for Engineering.

Language courses are available in tandem with many subjects; there's a Sony language laboratory and partnership projects and exchanges with colleges in Belgium, Denmark, Spain, Greece, Poland and the Netherlands. Computer facilities are

COLLEGE PROFILE	
Founded	**1888**
Status	**F/HE College**
Degree awarding university	**Lancaster, Huddersfield, Glamorgan, Hull**
Total undergraduates	**725**
College accommodation	**House**
Availability	**40 places**
Cost pw (no food)	**£45**
Town rent pw	**£40**

DEGREE SUBJECT AREAS:
Accounting, business, criminology, English, leisure, design, electronics, telecommunications, computing, law

impressive – more than 1,000 stations, 700 on the college network.

GETTING THERE

☞ By road: from north, south, west, M6/J31, A677; from east, M65.
☞ By rail: Manchester Victoria, 44 mins; Lancaster, 1:03; Preston, 23 mins.
☞ By coach: London, 5:30; Manchester, 1:10.

BLACKPOOL AND THE FYLDE COLLEGE

Blackpool and The Fylde College
Ashfield Road
Bispham
Blackpool FY2 0HB

TEL 01253 352352
FAX 01253 356127
EMAIL visitors@blackpool.ac.uk
WEB www.blackpool.ac.uk

VAG VIEW

*T*he Fylde is the name given to the chin of land jutting out over the Ribble Estuary, 25 miles northwest of Manchester. Blackpool & The Fylde, like Blackburn College, is an Associate College of Lancaster Uni and is closer to it by one junction of the M6. There are four campuses. Most of the degree study goes on at Bispham, to the south of the town.

There's a sports hall at the Bispham campus and plenty of college teams – hockey, football, badminton, netball and basketball. Thanks to an HND in Performing Arts, there's also a thriving student theatre group, The English Society. Blackpool is as you find it – **The Gynn**, **Yates's**, **The Merrie England**, **Never On A Sunday**, **Brannigans** and **The Counting House** are fave haunts, **Addisons** and **The Palace** the student nightclubs.

COLLEGE PROFILE

Founded	**1948**
Status	**F/HE College**
Degree awarding university	**Lancaster**
Student population	**37,396**
Total undergraduates	**1,151**
College accommodation	**None**
Town rent pw	**£35-£40**

DEGREE SUBJECT AREAS:
Counselling, business (incl E-commerce), computing, engineering (incl Mechatronics), construction, English, food sciences, hospitality, leisure management, art & design

GETTING THERE

☞ By road: M6/J32, M65.
☞ By rail: Manchester Piccadilly, 1:15; London Euston, 2:25.
☞ By coach: London, 6-7:00; Liverpool, 2:30.

BOLTON INSTITUTE OF HIGHER EDUCATION

Bolton Institute of Higher Education
Deane Road
Bolton BL3 5AB

TEL 01204 528851/900600
FAX 01204 399074
EMAIL enquiries@bolton.ac.uk
WEB www.bolton.ac.uk

VAG VIEW

*B*olton Institute was formed out of the Bolton Institute of Technology and Bolton College of Education (Technical). Subsequently Bolton College of Art was incorporated. Three faculties – Arts, Science & Education and Business – operate out of three sites, all in Bolton. There are two halls of residence, both self-catering.

They have the distinction of being able to award their own degrees, and have been waiting more or less patiently in the wings for the next time that the government decides to create new universities. Following the rise of the University of Gloucestershire this year (see entry, page 206) they are clearing their throats loudly once more. Recent teaching assessments suggest that there is every reason for confidence. Top scorers have been

INSTITUTE PROFILE

Founded	**1982**
Status	**HE college**
Situation/style	**Town campuses**
Student population	**6,560**
Full-time undergraduates	**2,900**

ACCOMMODATION FILE:
Availability to freshers	**100%**
Style	**Halls**
Cost pw (no food)	**£45**
Town rent pw	**£30-£40**

Education, Psychology, Nursing and Health Studies – all full marks; Philosophy, Materials Science, 23/24; Biosciences, 22; Art & Design, Leisure Studies, Sport, Tourism, 21.

The academic picture apart, Bolton's proximity to Manchester and to the Pennine Moors makes for a nice balance. A couple of nights of Mancunian debauchery followed by a soul-searching chill-out on the wilderness of Tufton Moor might be just the thing if you ever manage to tear yourself away from what is becoming quite a groovy student scene. The Students' Union is now located on the main, Deane campus, leaving the other two sites with bistros, restaurants and snack bars. There are two bars – both with satellite TV – an ents venue and a café. Bolton itself offers a handful of clubs, but it's Manchester for the high life.

Sport facilities include a large multi-court sports hall, fitness centre, specialist coaches, access to playing fields, all-weather pitches,

swimming pool. Relative proximity to Lake District encourages interest in orienteering, rock-climbing, etc.

GETTING THERE
☛ By road: M61/J3, A666 for Chadwick; M61/J5, A58 for Deane. You could use either route in for Moor Street. Good map in official prospectus.
☛ By rail: connections with Manchester frequent.
☛ By air: Manchester Airport 30 mins away.
☛ By coach: London, 5-7:00; Liverpool, 2:00.

BOURNEMOUTH UNIVERSITY

Bournemouth University
Talbot Campus
Fern Barrow
Poole
Dorset BH12 5BB

TEL 01202 524111
FAX 01202 702736
EMAIL prospectus@bournemouth.ac.uk
WEB www.bournemouth.ac.uk

Bournemouth Students' Union
Talbot Campus
Fern Barrow
Poole
Dorset BH12 5BB

TEL 01202 595765
FAX 01202 535990
EMAIL subu@bournemouth.ac.uk
WEB www.subu.org.uk

VAG VIEW

A quick look at Bournemouth's Employment *box (page 83) shows serious strengths – commerce (finance, business management, accountancy) and media (advertising, film, journalism and radio/TV industries) among them. Clearly anyone wanting a job in computing gets served pretty well too; computer animation, computer-aided product design, microelectronics are all strong niche areas. There are others, a key one is tax and business law, another catering and tourism, yes and even forensic archaeology. The point*

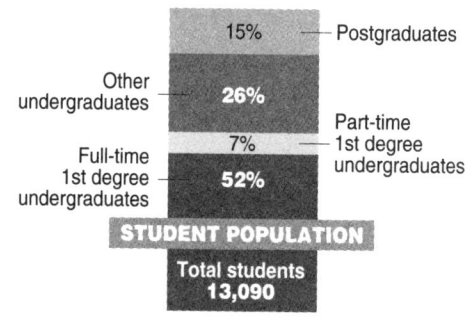

about Bournemouth is that it is niche-rich in employment terms. Another point is that the premier seaside resort, where this uni resides, surprises with a few intriguing little niches of its own.

CAMPUSES
Talbot (two miles from the town centre) is the main campus; the other, Bournemouth, or Town Campus, is more of a collection of town sites, with teaching facilities for Business, Health, Design, Engineering, Computing, Conservation. There's a no-parking rule within a mile. Students are also discouraged from bringing cars on to Talbot, though many do. There's a free bus service between campuses and halls.

UNIVERSITY/STUDENT PROFILE	
University since	**1992**
Situation/style	**Campus**
Student population	**13,090**
Full-time undergraduates	**6,875**
- mature	**24%**
- overseas	**3%**
- male/female	**52/48**
- state sector intake	**91%**
- non-traditional student intake	**7%**
- drop-out rate	**10%**
- undergraduate applications	**Down 3%**
see Introduction for key to tables	

STUDENT PROFILE
'On first entry to the place you may think you've

entered a photo shoot for a *Next* catalogue, owing to arrivistes trying to impress anyone who may be watching,' writes Aidan Goatley. 'Look more closely and you can spot those who've been there longer than a year and for whom ironing is not the most important thing in the world.'

In fact, though statistically nearly a quarter of undergrads are mature, the main campus is very studenty and unpretentious. This may be a new-uni, career-orientated student body, but there's an excellent scene both in union and in town, and a relaxed feel. People here know how to enjoy themselves.

ACADEMIA

Courses which attract the well-informed are

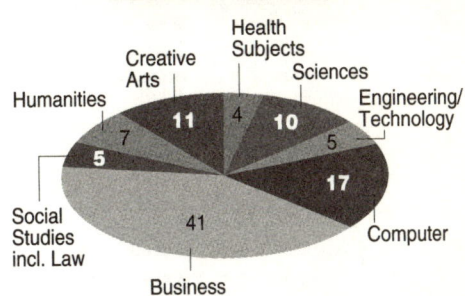

SUBJECT AREAS (%)

- Humanities 5
- Creative Arts 7
- Health Subjects 11
- Sciences 4
- Engineering/Technology 10
- Computer 5
- Business 17
- Social Studies incl. Law 41

AT A GLANCE	
ACADEMIC FILE:	
Subjects assessed	**20**
Excellent	**70%**
Average requirements	**240 points**
Students-staff ratio	**18:1**
First/2:1 degree pass rate	**49%**
ACCOMMODATION FILE:	
Guarantee to freshers	**100%**
Style	**Halls, flats, houses, hotels**
Catered	**Some hotels**
En-suite	**500 rooms**
Price range pw	**£45-£80**
City rent pw	**£45-£60**

Accounting, Financial Services, Leisure Marketing, Tourism, Computing, Applied Psychology & Computing, Microelectronics & Computing, Software Engineering, Media Production, Multimedia Journalism, TV & Video Production, Advertising Management, Public Relations, Scriptwriting Film & TV. Many of the lecturers are drawn from the world of work. PR guru Max Clifford recently made a £25,000 donation to the uni and offered his services as lecturer in the fine art of spin-doctoring, by way of saying thanks to Bournemouth for seeing his daughter, a sufferer of rheumatoid arthritis, through a communication studies degree.

Two much-vaunted specialisms are the BA Taxation & Revenue Law (they were the first in this field and have now been given the green light for the fully qualifying LLB Hons Tax Law) and Computer Visualisation & Animation (the uni is home to the National Centre for Computer

Animation). More recently, new degrees have been introduced in the areas of hospitality, tourism, environmental and coastal management, nutrition, sports development and management, nursing, media production, music, screenwriting... Note, too (*Academic Excellence* box), their first Grade 5 in research, for Art & Design – that's international stature.

A new 5-storey library is under construction, due to be opened late this year.

SOCIAL SCENE

STUDENTS' UNION **The Old Fire Station** (TOFS for short) is the uni's town club, the envy of many a student union up and down the country. It's *very* cool. *Sonic* big bad drum 'n' bass is resident, *Grooverider* was the mid-week attraction the day we went. The student special is still *Time Tunnel*, a

ACADEMIC EXCELLENCE	
TEACHING:	
(Rated Excellent or 17+ out of 24)	
Media Production & Scriptwriting	**22**
Communication & Journalism & PR, Nursing & Midwifery, Archaeology, Business, Tourism	
Land-based Enterprise (Agric), Subjects Allied to Medicine, Art & Design	**20**
Electrical & Electronic Eng. Food Qual/Service Industries	**19**
Product Design/Design Visualisation/Eng. Business Development, Modern Langs (Bus: French, Germ, Spanish)	**18**
RESEARCH:	
Top grades 5/5*	
Art & Design	**Grade 5**

WHAT IT'S REALLY LIKE	
UNIVERSITY:	
Social Life	★★★★
Campus scene	**Spin doctors & suits/up-beat ents**
Student Union services	**Good**
Politics	**Little interest**
Sport	**Relaxed**
National team position	**103rd**
Sport facilities	**Good**
Arts opportunities	**Available**
Student magazine	**Nerve**
Student radio	**Nerve FM**
Nightclub	**TOFS**
Bars	**Dylans, D2, Heat**
Union ents	**Lollypop, Time Tunnel, Liberation**
Union clubs/societies	**34**
Smoking policy	**Smoking OK**
Parking	**Poor despite many with cars**
TOWN:	
Entertainment	★★★★
Scene	**Excellent**
Town/gown relations	**Good**
Risk of violence	**Average**
Cost of living	**Above average**
Student concessions	**Good**
Survival + 2 nights out	**£60 pw**
Part-time work campus/town	**Good**

open seven days a week. The new one on Bournemouth campus is known as **Bar Heat**.

What else is it good for? Well, media of course. *Nerve* came second in the *Guardian* awards last year and Nerve TV won the NASTA (National Student Television Association) awards, sweeping the categories, five then seven in consecutive years. Music is also worth a mention. There's a good orchestra and choir. And an excellent strategy called *Go For It,* which enables freshers to have a bash at any of the society activities, take a diving test, a supervised bash at the climbing wall, whatever it is, suck it 'n' see. BUSCA, the Community Action Soc is very popular and had seven major projects on the go when we were there.

SPORT With the arrival of the new course in sports management (see *Academia* above), which specialises in golf, a brand new golf simulator has been installed in the Department of Sport and Recreation. This joins the south coast's premier climbing facility, the Hot Rocks climbing wall. Proximity to the sea encourages windsurfing, sailing, paragliding, jet skiing, etc. The uni provides full-time instructors and facilities for a wide range of other sports, but the emphasis is on sport-for-all rather than national domination. A sports hall includes squash courts and multigym. Cricketers play at the county-standard ground, Dean Park.

legendary Saturday night out, three dance floors, one for every decade, free entry before 10.30pm. Popular this year have also been the funk fancy dress parties which go under the generic *Happy Mondays* title – *Back to Skool, Rumpshaker R&B, Take That Boyband, Rocky Horror Haloween Special,* and *'70s Disco Inferno: Burn It Up Baby!* Tuesday alternates *The Comedy Factory* with *Vibe* (live gig nights) and *The Jazz Club,* Thursday is *Sonic* or *Rewind* or *Friction* (Brandon Block's big night out) or discohousin' *Superfly.*
Friday is *Lollipop,* the popstar favourite as long living as *Time Tunnel* which follow. Balls are frequent – Freshers, Christmas, Valentine's, Sport and Summer.
Meanwhile, closer to home at Talbot's **Dylans Bar**, there's a whole different menu, quizzes, music mixes, monthly live gigs drinks promo nights, magic and the national *Playstation 2 Challenge.* Dylans, like **D2**, are your campus bars,

> *Serious, specialist graduate opportunities are on offer, and it all goes on in a Brighton-style seaside resort, bursting with no fewer specialist hedonistic opportunities.*

TOWN Bournemouth is bursting with gays – population apparently triples in size in summer. Mmmm . . . Get hold of your Pink Gay Map and roam! But, in fact, whatever your taste in rumpy pumpy, this is quite a town. Dropped in the middle, where four roads meet, we found wall-to-wall pleasure zones. Scribbled on the back of an envelope in the first 50 yards was a **Slug and Lettuce**, **Smokey Bar/Restaurant**, **Gino's Italian**, **Coral's** betting shop, **Strictly Beats** specialist record store, **Blue Café Bar**, **Anaretto's** (Italian restaurant), **City Kebab & Pizza** bar, **Destiny Records** store... And so it went on, into the distance past clubs – **Extreme**, **Zoo & Cage**, pubs and more of the same. It is an extraordinary place, a born again English seaside resort. At last, eyes fall on a first floor job agency – SOS Recruitment – and you realise you're going to need a job as well, but if bar and club life proves too much, there's always the beach, which even has a no-smoking section.

PILLOW TALK

Accommodation is guaranteed for first years, but the guarantee includes hotels and guest houses, so get in quick. Places in the student village on Talbot and in Hurn House and newly built Cranborne House in central Bournemouth are limited to 250, 152 and 500, respectively. Rooms in Talbot are en suite. Prices range from £45 to £80 at time of writing. As in most seaside resorts, town accommodation is plentiful and good.

JOBS

Serious career-orientated students are appreciated at Bournemouth – 66% get the feel of work on sandwich courses and the uni is among the best in the country for getting graduates into careers within six months of graduation. Part-time work opportunities whilst studying are legion.

GETTING THERE

☞ By road: M3/M27/A31/ A338, The Wessex Way; at second r/about follow uni signs to Talbot. From west A35 then A3049 (Wallisdown Road). For Bournemouth campus, leave A338 at St Paul's r/about (Travel Interchange junction) on to St Paul's road and find a car park.
☞ By rail: London Waterloo, 1:45; Bristol, 2:30; Manchester, 5:37.
☞ By coach: London, 2:15; Bristol, 3:10.

WHERE GRADUATES END UP	
13% Manufacturing,	Key Areas
13% Finance*,	
11% Computer*,	
7% Wholesale/Retail,	
5% Personnel,	
5% Health/Social Work	
Accountancy, Advertising*,	Niche Areas
Business/Management, Architecture, Electron/ Electric, Eng/Industrial Design, Film/Video, Hotel/Restaurant, Journalism*, Publishing, Radio/TV*, Telecom	

*indicates Top 10 Graduate Provider

Approximate employed **94%**

UNIVERSITY OF BRADFORD

The University of Bradford
Richmond Road
Bradford BD7 1DP

TEL 01274 233081
FAX 01274 236260
EMAIL enquiries@bradford.ac.uk
WEB www.bradford.ac.uk

Bradford University Union
Richmond Road
Bradford BD7 1DP

TEL 01274 233300
FAX 01274 235530
EMAIL ubu-communications@beadford.ac.uk
WEB www.ubui.co.uk

VAG VIEW

It would be a terrible shame if the television images of the Bradford riots were to stem the rising tide of university applications – deservedly 2% up in 2001. Persistently, it seems, the south-of-Watford brigade in the national press – i.e. most of the national press – finds comfort in cliché when it comes to writing about this uni or indeed the town. Talking to Bradford students, the feeling is of living in another world to the one reported There is no siege mentality, the university is inextricably part of the town, but it is hardly akin to Belfast as centre of sectarian/racist strife, nor, as the

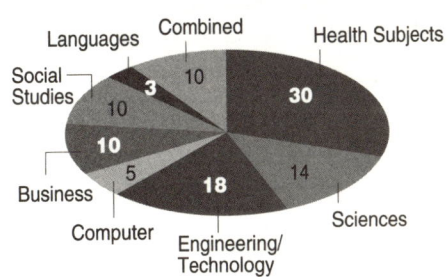
SUBJECT AREAS (%)

Independent had it, is it some kind of backwater lost in the embers of the industrial revolution – though some values, hard

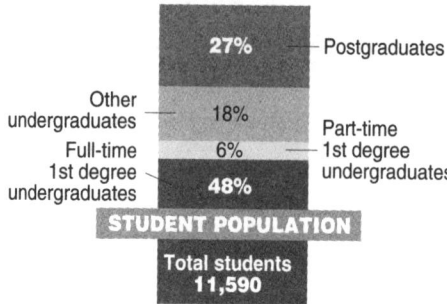

STUDENT POPULATION	
27%	Postgraduates
Other undergraduates — 18%	
Full-time 1st degree undergraduates — 6%	Part-time 1st degree undergraduates
48%	
Total students 11,590	

learned there, are still forging its future.

What's more, academically, Bradford Uni leads the way nationally and internationally in particular areas (see Academia *below), and students do actually like it here. Bradford is not London, nor is it Milton Keynes (thank God!), nor yet is it Leeds. Bradford may challenge the southern picture of where England is/should be, but what it offers undergraduates is a very studenty, close-knit, pub-based, curry-central experience, uninhibited by issues of wealth and class. To many a Bradford student, the southerner's picture of the acceptable face of the North, namely Leeds, because of its premier-league nightclubs and Harvey Nichs, appears rather expensive and, well, just a tad* outré. *Bradford students can easily partake of Leeds, as the city is just a few moments down the road, but very few do.*

CAMPUS

The main campus, a ten-minute stroll from town, is compact and bounded by roads on all four sides. All teaching, except for Business Studies, is carried out on site, and there are many halls of residence.

UNIVERSITY/STUDENT PROFILE	
University since	**1966**
Situation/style	**City campus**
Student population	**11,590**
Full-time undergraduates	**5,550**
- mature	**24%**
- overseas	**5%**
- male/female	**49/51**
- state sector intake	**91%**
- non-traditional student intake	**14%**
- drop-out rate	**9%**
- undergraduate applications	**Up 2%**
see Introduction for key to tables	

It is a relatively small uni and has a reputation for being a particularly close-knit friendly community. There's crime in the city, as in any city, but there's a safety bus at night to truck you anywhere from campus within a seven-mile radius. The union makes student safety an absolute priority.

STUDENT PROFILE

Bradford's open access policy means that a third of its entrants come from social classes IIIM, IV and V and nearly 15% from poor neighbourhoods, yet it manages so to fulfil the lives of these non-traditional students that it has a drop-out rate of only 9%, fairly average in the circumstances. There is also a large mature student population (24%).

Most undergrads are scientists and techies, but there is a humanities stratum that ensures life doesn't get too predictable.

ACADEMIC EXCELLENCE	
TEACHING:	
(Rated Excellent or 17+ out of 24)	
Philosophy, Politics	**24**
Pharmacology, Other Subjects	**23**
Allied to Medicine, Nursing	
Archaeology	**22**
Electric & Electronic Eng	**21**
Chemical Engineering, Civil Eng,	**20**
General Eng, Molecular Biosci	
Modern Langs (incl Russian)	**18**
RESEARCH:	
*Top grades 5/5**	
European Studies	**Grade 5***
Biomedical Sciences,	**Grade 5**
Mechanical/Aeronautical/	
Manufacturing Eng, Politics,	
Archaeology, Philosophy	

ACADEMIA & JOBS

A uni since 1966, it came out of Bradford Technical College, which itself grew out of the textile industry in the 1860s. Today the connection between higher education and the workplace remains key. Their slogan is 'Making Knowledge Work' and they have erected a 5-metre high, bronze sculpture celebrating it. There's a first-class Modern Languages Department, which facilitates an international dimension to much else of what's on offer academically, and they ride high in the tables for graduate provision in the manufacturing and health industries, particularly in electronic & electrical manufacturing and in the pharmaceutical industry. A quarter of intake is

WHERE GRADUATES END UP

28% Health/Social Work*, Key Areas
12% Manufacturing,
13% Wholesale/Retail,
6% Public Admin,
6%Education,
5% Finance,
5% Computer
Chem/Pharmaceutical, Niche Areas
Eng/Industrial Design,
Electron/Elec, Telecom

*indicates Top 10 Graduate Provider

Approximate employed **93%**

---

now in health/medical sciences and Bradford has the country's largest Optometry Department. You may need 280 points for that or for Pharmacy, but if it's engineering you're after you can float in on a foundation course.

Among recently introduced degrees are those in Cybernetics, in Medical Engineering, and three combinations of politics and law, vocationally designed in the Department of European Studies.

Other key strands take us further into the ethos of the place. Among recently introduced courses is a BSc South Asian Studies, a degree based in the Department of Social & Economic Studies, but nourished by a recipe of influences from Archaeological Sciences, the Development & Planning Centre, and Bradford's famed, specialist Department of Peace Studies (peace politics studied from the standpoints of ethics, psychology, sociology, history).

SOCIAL SCENE

Principal gathering place at the **Richmond** (the uni building) is the **Steve Biko** bar, famous for its appearance in the CAMRA Good Beer Guide and distinguished, too, by an L-shaped pool table and jukebox. At **Commie** (the Communal Building) it's **JB's** (150 capacity) and a small nightclub, **Escape** (100), both with big screen TVs. Also in the Commie are the main venue, **The Basement** (1,300 capacity), home to cheesy/dance Friday night disco, FND, and now **Colours** (450), actually part of the Basement, though you can't see the joins, for late-night licence, smaller gigs and club-nights. Other clubnights are currently Rock Sox (rock/indie) and Cheesy Sox (cheese/retro). Recent live acts include Craig Charles, Paul Oakenfold, Stanton Warriors, Terrorvision, Rainbow and Timmy Mallet.

There may be no arts faculty at Bradford but

they have three of the most pulsating arts venues to be found anywhere. **Theatre in the Mill** is home to BUTG (Bradford Uni Theatre Group), which puts on a show (student or pro) every week and has the cheapest bar (**Scaff Bar**) in the uni. **The Tasmin Little Music Centre** does similar stuff for a student jazz ensemble, choral society, chamber choir and three orchestras, and an amazing series of Music for Lunch at the **Alhambra Studio** in Great Horton Road. Then there's **Gallery II** for art.

Student cinema, BSC, happens three times a week – art movies and the latest blockbusters, many only a few months after general release, all for a couple of quid. Showings are in **Great Hall** (capacity, 1,300).

Media-wise there's Scrapie, the award-winning,

WHAT IT'S REALLY LIKE

UNIVERSITY:	
Social Life	★★★★
Campus scene	**Close-knit, active, fun**
Student Union services	**Good**
Politics	**Average; Bacardi banned**
Sport	**35 clubs**
National team position	**87th**
Sport facilities	**Good**
Arts opportunities	**Excellent drama dance, film, music; art avge**
Student magazine	**Scrapie**
Guardian Awards	**Scrapie web site**
Student radio	**RamAir fm**
Nightclub	**Basement, Escape**
Bars	**JB's, Steve Biko, Colours**
Union ents	**FND, Rock Sox, Cheesy Sox**
Union clubs/societies	**85**
Most popular societies	**Cult TV, Roleplay, Pharmacy socs**
Smoking policy	**Zonal throughout**
Parking	**Good**
CITY:	
Entertainment	★★★
Scene	**Curry central/ rough in parts**
Town/gown relations	**OK**
Risk of violence	**Average**
Cost of living	**Very low**
Student concessions	**Excellent**
Survival + 2 nights out	**£40 pw**
Part-time work campus/town	**Good/excellent**

AT A GLANCE

ACADEMIC FILE:	
Subjects assessed	**20**
Excellent	**60%**
Average requirements	**240 points**
Students-staff ratio	**18:1**
First/2:1 degree pass rate	**47%**
ACCOMMODATION FILE:	
Guarantee to freshers	**100%**
Style	**Halls**
Approx price range pw	**£45-£58**
City rent pw	**£25-£40**

fortnightly magazine, which really is cool. Now webbed too, it was a near miss at the *Guardian* awards recently. Meanwhile RamAir fm has been runner-up in the Radio 1 recently too. Among some fifty societies, TSA is popular with techies who fancy setting up gigs, as are Cult TV, Roleplay, and Pharmacy Soc.

Sport There are thirty-five sports clubs – womens volleyball came second in the national BUSA Shield this year and the match was voted best in the country. There's an on-campus sports centre (25m swimming pool, sauna suite, solarium, brand new Nautilus fitness suite, etc.), squash courts and two sets of playing fields, a dozen or so in all for cricket, football and rugby, plus 9,000 square metres of artificial turf sand-grass for five-a-sides, netball and including a full-size hockey pitch. One site is behind the halls of residence, the other four miles from campus, where the pavilion has a bar.

Town Bradford is curry central and the cheapest university city in the country. You'll be amazed by the cost, the quality and the sheer number of eateries. You eat it with chapatis here, not rice, and a three-year degree is barely enough time to be sure that you have found the best. Prices hover

> *Courses and work-ethos grow out of its industrial past and mingle with its richly patterned cultural present. Bradford is not simply curry central and the cheapest university city in the country, it is a real experience, which students enjoy.*

around £2.50 for a basic chicken dish with chapatis. At **Mumtaz Paan House** on Great Horton Road they charge by weight. Students have curry locals; staff and dishes become firm friends.

Bradford, a city of traditional pubs was shaken a few years ago with the advent of **Hogshead** (aka Bar Ikea), **Varsity**, the **Freestyle & Firkin** – not pubs, but bars where food is part of the deal. **Chicago Rock Café** also came to town – all on Great Horton Road, right by the uni. Still, there's atmosphere in older student haunts, however often they refurbish them – **The Peel** (Richmond Road), **Delius Lived Next Door** (Claremont) and the **Queens Hall**, though this is a bit *ex*-student: replete with MTV during the day, but suits and towny vibes at night.

Gaudi's (was **Tumbler's**) and **Club Rio** – Wednesday night (indie/'80s) are enjoyable venues almost on campus, the first tucked behind the Richmond, Club Rio practically next door to Longside halls. City clubs **Nexus** (was **Underworld**: late night cellar drinking), and **Pickwicks** (now **Bar Margaloof** but still known as Pickwicks: student DJs: pop, dance and indie) are a student institution.

PILLOW TALK

Trinity Hall, at the Laisteridge Lane site, offers en suite and is most expensive. It is overshadowed by the two tower blocks, Revis and Dennis, both catered. The halls on the main campus are cheaper and uncatered, and there is little to choose between Shearbridge Green, Longside and Kirkstone, but Bradford and University halls get the thumbs down.

GETTING THERE

☞ By road: M62 and M606 connect with national motorway network; from north, A629/A650; from northeast, A1 or A19, then A59, A658.
☞ By rail: London King's Cross, Birmingham, 3:00; Edinburgh, 4:00; Manchester, 1:00.
☞ By air: Leeds/Bradford Airport.
☞ By coach: London, 4:30; Manchester, 1-2:30.

BRADFORD COLLEGE

Bradford College
Great Horton Road
Bradford
West Yorkshire BD7 1AY

TEL 01274 753241
FAX 01274 741060
EMAIL admissions@bradfordcollege.ac.uk
WEB www.bradfordcollege.ac.uk

*B*radford College, formerly Bradford and Ilkley Community College, arose from a series of mergers involving the technical college, the regional college of art and design, and three colleges of education. Though a further education college in the main, it has an established tradition of providing higher education programmes across a wide range of subjects.

There is a formal association with Bradford University, and they are currently in talks, which may result in a full merger. Teacher Education, one of the college's mainstays, was hit hard early in 2002 by what has been described as the 'worst ever' rating by government inspectors. Overall the department scored 13 out of a possible 24, notching up two scores of 1 out of 4 in the process, which seems to have been unprecedented. Bradford University validate the college's degrees. Many university authorities have attacked the assessments and brought the present system effectively to an end, but it is events like this which show their worth – not because a college has been attacked, but because it is 99% sure that the judgement will result in the course becoming one of the best in the country by the time you apply.

The college is building rapidly in areas as diverse as ophthalmic dispensing (selling specs and associated clinical work) and process systems (engineering), both natural first degree progressions from BTEC courses in their School of Science & Technology. The School of Art, Design & Textiles is another string to its bow worth drawing out. The faculty

COLLEGE PROFILE	
Founded	**1982**
Status	**F/HE College**
Degree awarding university	**Bradford**
Student population	**28,975**
Full-time degree undergraduates	**2,133**
ACCOMMODATION:	
Availability to freshers	**60%**
Style	**Halls**
Cost pw (no food)	**£49-£70**
City rent pw	**£25-£40**

DEGREE SUBJECT AREAS:
Ophthalmic dispensing, art, design (incl textiles, crafts), law, computer, health, culture, society, primary education

has been providing courses, from GNVQ to Masters, for more than 150 years, and there's continuity with Bradford's industrial past in the placing of the well-equipped studios in former Bradford mills.

Investment at the Students' Union has brought a cybercafé, **Megabytes**, and the refurbishment of **Horton's Bar** (another bar, **SU2**, is within the halls of residence).

GETTING THERE

☞ By road: M62 and M606 connect you to the national motorway network; from the northeast, the A1 or A19, then A59 and A658; from the north it's the A629/A650.
☞ By rail: London King's Cross, 3:00; Edinburgh, 4:00; Birmingham, 3:00; Manchester, 1:00.
☞ Leeds/Bradford Airport is close at hand.
☞ By coach: London, 4:30; Manchester, 1-2:30.

BRETTON HALL *see* LEEDS UNIVERSITY

STUDENT BRIGHTON – THE CITY

Today, Brighton remains distinctive in its 'anything goes', alternative attitude, which embraces everything from the arts to sexuality. Known as the gay capital of Britain, Brighton is oozing with sexuality no matter which side you bat for, hence the numerous 'saunas' (Amistead Maupin-style) dotted around the city and strip clubs for the straight guys. Is it any wonder that such elegance, extravagance, splendour and diversity, should

discover within itself such a lively nightlife?

NIGHTLIFE
Brighton has more than thirty clubs, most of which, to keep things simple post-pre-club, are situated in one strip along the sea front, home to the famous **Zap Club** (where Damian Harris deejayed before setting up Skint), **Concorde II**, **Skint Records**, **Big Beat Boutique** (which has

regular visits from the Brightonians Fat Boy Slim and Phats & Small) and **Essential**. The popular Essential summer festival moved to Hackney Marshes this year due to FMD scares; hopefully a one-off.

Modern day clubbers journey the width of the country to come here to the cat's lair of the amazing *Pussy Cat* club, at the **Zap**. This place is a true and perfect representation of all things hedonistic and diverse within the safe environs of Brighton. It by no means ends here: There is an interesting array of hip hop nights and many 'open-mic' formats with celebrity DJs mixing with student promoters. If it is hard trance you are after, lesbian & gay nights, reggae or salsa, you won't be disappointed. With great promotions on drinks, the sound of the '70s, '80s and '90s retro never sounded so good - cheesy poptastic nights that celebrate Wham and Britney are very popular with students. Midweek madness continues with the Latino feel and many participate in the carnival-style nights. You could be forgiven for thinking that no one worked in Brighton, as weeknight events are virtually as full as the big weekend ones. Prices are moderate for a growing city, and during the week they fall as fast as any Argentinean football player. Word of warning: don't piss off the bouncers - they are some of the most aggressive in the country.

EATS

You'll find whole streets, like Preston Street, devoted to food and drink, there are late night eateries and 24-hour supermarkets, and over 400 restaurants - posh minimalist, English, French, Indian, Mexican, fish & chips, organic burgers (gorgeous!), Japanese, Thai, lesser known oriental, tapas, Greek, Italian pizza/pasta, Spanish, Lebanese, Egyptian, American, Cajun, greasy spoon, vegetarian, places with beautiful views of the sea, sushi and take-away. The best is a tiny Cajun called **Blind Lemon Alley**, on Sundays you have the extra treat of Phil Mills' live blues. Among the many drinking dens, ranging from your posh, sophisticated Friday night boozer to the independent breweries, **Alicats** is very student friendly, it shows films every night.

COST

The many language schools attract a large number of foreigners to the student equation and employment has been a problem in this area, though opportunities do seem to be improving and wages have recently become more competitive.

SHOPS

Though cost of living is rising, choice of where to spend is not a problem. There are more than 700 independent shops. The Lanes have old antique shops, designer shops and several restaurants, bars and cafés. Congregating around Pavilion Square there are often musicians and performers. North Laine is the bohemian centre of the town. With feel good veggie cafés, cocktail bars, great second-hand bargain shops and a mishmash of fabric and clothes shops there is not much you cannot get your mitts on in this district. Kemp Town boasts a superb second-hand bookshop and several record shops and Churchill Square provides for all high street needs.

STREET/BEACH LIFE

Brighton really comes to life in summer. Travellers and locals flock to the beach to enjoy the food and the bars, the fire juggling displays, the free film show on huge screens, free concerts courtesy of Fat Boy Slim, basketball and volleyball and a new very safe and clean children's play area.

ARTS

All over the city, self-expression is highly appreciated - in an abundance of galleries, and the Brighton University gallery is one of the best. Innovative, contemporary art is displayed in fine form and at very reasonable prices. There are also many live music venues, which again cater to all tastes. Since the long-awaited reopening of the **Dome Concert Hall** in February 2002, artists such as the London Philharmonic, Courtney Pine and Dame Kiri Te Kanawa have appeared.

In terms of comedy, theatre and film Brighton is incredibly spoilt. **The Dome** plays host to famous artists such as Lee Evans and Jack Dee. **Komedia** has two different productions simultaneously every night, one in the main room, the other in the cabaret bar. **The Theatre Royal** & the **Brighton Centre** get the big-name touring artists as well snooker championships and the Labour Party Conference. The **Gardner Arts Centre** on Sussex University campus plays host to art, film, theatre, comedy, music, etc. and is nationally acclaimed. Finally, there are three cinemas. The **Odeon** is the most student-friendly; the **UGC** is part of the Marina multiplex (also bowling, McDonalds and a giant ASDA) and the **Duke of York** shows all the beautiful arty films and is very special indeed.

Alice Brooks

UNIVERSITY OF BRIGHTON

University of Brighton
Mithras House
Lewes Road
Brighton BN2 4AT

TEL 01273 600900
FAX 01273 642825
EMAIL admissions@bton.ac.uk
WEB www.brighton.ac.uk

Brighton Students' Union
Moulsecoomb Campus
Lewes Road
Brighton BN2 4AG

TEL 01273 642870
FAX 01273 600694
EMAIL ubsu@bton.ac.uk
WEB www.UBSU.net

VAG VIEW

*B*righton town has recently been re-born as a city, a seemingly inevitable consequence of our long-time perception of it as London-by-the-sea (see Student Brighton, page 84). Brighton is an energetic, laid-back, imaginative, vibrant, artistic, commercial, alternative, innovative, refreshing coastal cocktail, and its very own uni evinces many of these elements too.

First of all, the creativity of Brighton students fits them perfectly into the picture. The university traces its roots back to 1877, when the School of Art opened on Grand Parade, opposite the Royal Pavilion. The Faculty of Art, Design & Humanities as it is today is very much part of this town. The cream of the art world strut their funky stuff around Brighton looking like they have just stepped out of The Face magazine, while the commercial, innovative and energetic bits find expression in the Brighton Business School, the School of IT and the Chelsea School of Sport.

For some time, even Brighton academia has been more than simply reflective of the timbre of what they now call a city; it has been an integral part of it through CPD (its Continuing Professional Development initiative) – the uni works with local councils, health authorities and industry throughout the whole region to educate and re-educate 'the workforce', as they put it like something out of Soylent Green. And now, or nearly now – in 2003 – in partnership with Sussex University up the road, they are launching the Brighton & Sussex Medical School. There'll be a centre on the Sussex University campus and a building on Brighton University's Falmer campus,

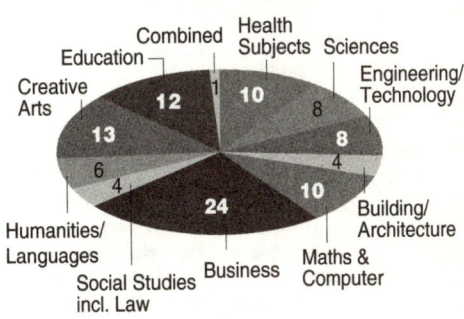

SUBJECT AREAS (%)

- Education — 1
- Combined
- Health Subjects — 10
- Sciences — 8
- Engineering/ Technology — 8
- Creative Arts — 12
- Building/ Architecture — 4
- 13
- Maths & Computer — 10
- 6
- 4
- Humanities/ Languages
- Business — 24
- Social Studies incl. Law

opposite, and there'll be a training facility at the Royal Sussex County Hospital, the whole project ensuring ever closer links between the people's University of Brighton and the local community.

CAMPUS

Brighton University spreads through central Brighton and into the surrounding areas of Moulsecoomb, Falmer and Eastbourne. North up the Lewes Road from the arts centre on Grand Parade – (rail and bus links are good, parking is not) – you get to the Moulsecoomb campus, which houses the Business School, the Faculty of Science & Engineering, which includes pharmacy, maths,

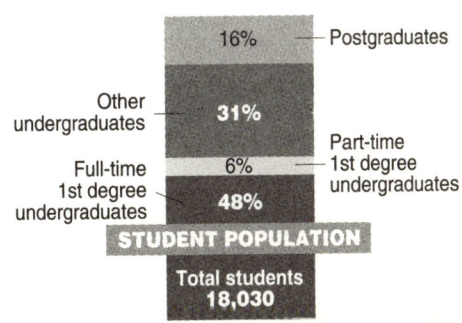

- 16% — Postgraduates
- Other undergraduates — 31%
- Part-time 1st degree undergraduates
- Full-time 1st degree undergraduates — 6%
- 48%

STUDENT POPULATION

Total students
18,030

engineering, and the Faculty of IT. Further on you find the Falmer campus, actually bang opposite the University of Sussex campus. While Grand Parade is the old art college and Moulsecoomb is the old technical college, the Falmer site was once Brighton's teacher training college and still offers teacher training today, along with health subjects.

Off to the east along the coast from Brighton, is the Eastbourne campus, the uni's nationally renowned Chelsea School of Sports Science. They opened a £3-million sports centre there in November 2000. Outdoor pitches and indoor facilities are open to the public – widening access, integrating with the community. It's what this uni is all about, in case you hadn't heard.

STUDENT PROFILE

From the foregoing it must be clear that there can

UNIVERSITY/STUDENT PROFILE	
University since	**1992**
Situation/style	**Seaside campuses**
Student population	**18,030**
Full-time undergraduates	**8,630**
- mature	**40%**
- overseas	**6%**
- male/female	**44/56**
- state sector intake	**93%**
- non-traditional student intake	**9%**
- drop-out rate	**12%**
- undergraduate applications	**Down 3%**
*see Introduction for key to tables	

be no typical Brighton student. It is all too disparate. The cutting-edge artists may be the most visible, but creative arts is not representative of the whole student body.

Most notably, perhaps, students here are mature (40% of undergraduates), which means, not that they are all wrinklies but that they come here after their 21st birthday and may well be more work-orientated than your traditional undergrad freeloader. They are here for a clear-cut purpose.

There is also a big international intake. The 6% figure we give in the *Profile* box above refers only to the full-time first degree undergraduates. Many more from abroad come among the other half of HND undergrads, etc, in the 18,030 total. Brighton has long been known internationally for its language-school history, so those same folk now flock across the Channel to the uni 'We have a big language school here, do a lot of language work with all kinds of undergraduates.'

ACADEMIC EXCELLENCE	
TEACHING	
(Rated Excellent or 17+ out of 24)	
Philosophy	**24**
Pharmacology & Pharmacy	**23**
Nursing, Maths, Art & Design,	**22**
Subjects Allied to Medicine, Organismal, Molecular Biosciences, Library/Ingo Mgt	
History of Art, Civil Eng, Educ	**21**
Modern Languages (Dutch,	**20**
French, German, Iberian Studies, Italian), Elec/Electron Engineering, Building.	
RESEARCH:	
*Top grades 5/5**	
Biomedical Sciences,	**Grade 5**
European Studies, Art & Design	

ACADEMIA & JOBS

There is a strong vocational tradition and a large number of sandwich courses. The university is divided into six faculties: **Art, Design & Humanities** is one of the best in the country, covers (among much else) art and architecture, design, dance, fashion, digital music, theatre, photography, fine art, 3D design, textiles, etc. Fashion with Business is renowned. Other courses are in sympathy with humanities, history of design, visual culture, etc. **Business, Education, Sport & Leisure**: the Business School is high on links with Europe; languages are key and the BSc European Business with Technology, which demands fluency in two languages, is serious stuff.

WHERE GRADUATES END UP	
22% Education*,	Key Areas
10% Health/Social Work,	
9% Manufacturing,	
6% Finance,	
5% Wholesale/Retail,	
5% Computer,	
5% Personnel	
Hotel/Restaurant, Sport*	Niche Areas
Eng/Industrial Design,	
Construction, Architecture,	
Advertising, Film/Video,	
Artistic/Literary, Library/	
Archival, Publishing	
*indicates Top 10 Graduate Provider	
Approximate employed	**95%**

Engineering & Environmental concerns natural and built environments, the distinctive characteristic its design orientation which so endears it to the construction industry (see our *Employment* box, page 90). **Information Technology** enjoys close links with industry and thrives on innovative post-grad research. **Health:** the Health Faculty is in cahoots with five local hospitals, embraces courses ranging from biology to occupational therapy and nursing, which just got a good rating (see *Academic Excellence* box, also page 90).

SOCIAL SCENE

STUDENTS' UNION The sad truth is that ents at Brighton have been flattened by a series of mishaps. First they had the **Basement**, a seriously good club/venue that was commandeered by the uni administration. Then they took over **Akademia,** a café bar and theatre on Manchester Street, which again was prised from them. Now all they have is **Falmer Bar** and two regular clubnights, *Essence* (jungle) and *Temptation* (garage). There is a handful of societies – a mere 15, the most popular of which is Asian Soc – and a magazine called *Backbeat*. They used to meddle with Sussex's radio station, but no longer apparently. There seems an aimlessness about the Students' Union, which the students don't deserve. The union tells me that the political focus is on student funding and housing, but when I find myself at the doors of Grand Parade, art students press flyers into my hand about the war in Afghanistan, and I am forced to the conclusion that the Students' Union is not representing the voice of its students any more in Brighton.

That there is so little happening is a surprise because Brighton is itself such a happening place. It was only six years ago that Damian Harris's Skint label made waves big enough to wash Sony money down the M23 and bathe Lo-Fidelity Allstars, Fatboy Slim and Bentley Rhythm Ace in commercial success. The Brighton (big beat) Sound, as it came to be known, didn't just happen, it grew out of a scene that had been gestating nicely down here for many a year – 'There's so many people really into their music here and doing what they want that it has deserved success for some time,' said Harris at the time. He had been an art student at the Grand Parade campus. Nor was it just music. For at least thirty years, experimental theatre has been thriving in the town, which is why Sussex

Uni's progressive **Gardner Arts Centre** exists, and you find the **Sussex Arts Club**, **Brighton Little Theatre Company**, the **Brighton Tech Theatre**, the **Marlborough Pub Theatre**, the **New Venture Theatre**, and the well-known **Albert** pub.

Perhaps the students couldn't care less what the union puts on. Perhaps it has become superfluous because there is so much happening in town – as in London students join the city as much as they join a university. But actually, the city isn't the first draw. When I ask why the uni's official prospectus no longer commences with a puff about 'exciting Brighton', I am told by a university official, 'We did some focus groups on our prospectuses and sixthformers wanted the flip of what we thought it would be. They wanted the course list at the front.

> *There is masses of creative energy and hedonistic nouse at Brighton, but don't expect much nannying by the union; this is a uni for more or less self-sufficient individuals.*

WHAT IT'S REALLY LIKE

UNIVERSITY:	
Social Life	★★★
Campus scene	**Individual**
Student Union services	**Supportive in a hands-off way**
Politics	**Average; student issues, anti-war**
Sport	**20 clubs but very competitive out at Eastbourne**
National team position	**25th**
Sport facilities	**Good**
Arts opportunities	**Drama/Dance OK**
Student magzine	**Backbeat**
Nightclub	**None**
Bars	**Falmer Bar**
Union ents	**Essence (jungle), Temptation (garage)**
Union clubs/societies	**35**
Most popular society	**Asian**
Smoking policy	**NS/zonal**
Parking	**Not good**
TOWN:	
Entertainment	★★★★★
Scene	**Exceptional**
Town/gown relations	**OK**
Risk of violence	**Low**
Cost of living	**High**
Student concessions	**Good**
Survival + 2 nights out	**£100 pw**
Part-time work campus/town	**Average/excellent**

That's the real world, the first thing you look at is the courses.' Is that now the bottom line? At Brighton University, there is time only to work? Three or four years to party, form your own opinions, work out how you can make a difference, is no longer what it is about? If so, then it really is time that the students' union got itself into gear.

SPORT Out at the sporty Eastbourne campus there's the new £3 million facility. Women's sport is particularly strong, though both sets of teams do well at inter-university level.

PILLOW TALK

Accommodation is all self-catered, mainly halls but also uni-leased houses/flats. The uni accommodation service has details of around 3,000 rentable properties in and near Brighton.

GETTING THERE

☞ By air: Gatwick and Heathrow Airports.
☞ By road: M23 (past Gatwick), A23 to Brighton, on to A27 eastbound for Falmer, taking right turn

AT A GLANCE	
ACADEMIC FILE:	
Subjects assessed	**21**
Excellent	**71%**
Average requirements	**160 points**
Students-staff ratio	**23:1**
First/2:1 degree pass rate	**52%**
ACCOMMODATION FILE:	
Guarantee to freshers	**70%**
Style	**Halls, flats, village**
Approx price range pw	**£48-£61**
City rent pw	**£45-£80**

(south on B2123) for Moulsecoomb. From east or west, A27, etc. For Eastbourne, A27 and signs south on to A22.
☞ By rail: London Victoria, 1:10. Change at Brighton for Moulsecoomb and Falmer (8 mins).
☞ By coach: London, 1:50.

STUDENT BRISTOL - THE CITY

A love of Bristol develops through attrition rather than in a road-to-Damascus flash. Like chest hair (male perspective only) this love grows in imperceptible degrees, but is not entirely unwanted once it's there.

THE GLOSS

Of city entertainments the popularity of clubs and particular club-nights waxes and wanes, but there is much variety from which to choose. Sports night at **Wedgies** is the quintessential Bristol experience, repelling and attracting people in equal measure. Go to **Steamrock** for cheese. **Creation**, **Evolution**, **Club Loco** and **Po Na Na** have more of a mix. **Lakota** is the Bristol showpiece for music for the kids, attracting big name DJs. **Blue Mountain** and **Thekla** are also around for the music purists. For the Radio 2 listeners the **Old Duke** has jazz and blues all week, and several street festivals in the summer. **Finnegans Wake** and **Mulligan's** provide the inevitable Irish theme pubs with music.
Classical concerts take place in **St George's**, a converted cathedral, the union's **Anson Rooms** hosts regular concerts from pop bands on provincial tours as do **Fiddlers** and the **Fleece and Firkin**. For theatre there is the **Hippodrome** with musicals, big shows, expensive tickets and seats in

the rafters, also the renowned **Old Vic**, the **New Vic**, the **QEH**, the union theatre and many more.
For film there are three out of town multiplexes, a few standard cinemas including the **Orpheus** and the students' favourite, **ABC**. On the waterfront are the arts cinemas, the **Watershed** and **Arnolfini**, both showing independent and foreign films. In addition there is the **Cube**, an arts cinema which everyone who considers themselves media cool has heard of, but no one has actually been to. In short there is more in Bristol than you will possibly get round to seeing.

As many a resident will point out, there is a great deal going on. Locals will claim that Bristol has all that London can offer, without the hectic pace or aggro. That's the city PR line, in fact. Urbane Kate Freeman offers a more sober spin:

To small-town boys and girls, Bristol's an easy and usually welcome way into city life, but those coming from London tend to complain about the provincial air, the lack of urgency in the pace, and the lack of a 24-hour chemist at the end of the road. Unfortunately, Bristol is still far from becoming a 24-hour city. Only a few bars on Park Street have a late licence, and almost everything shuts down firmly at 2 am at the latest. Everything, that is, except the exquisite

Courtyard Café on Park Row, open twenty-four hours serving good food and coffee and with friendly waiters. Great for a post-club stop-off or a middle of the night essay-finishing celebration.

There is sadly also a shockingly high proportion of homeless people in the central area, and traffic is a nightmare, with plans for metered parking places extending to residential areas in the near future. Only bring a car if you really need to, and think of it as a good thing: even if you never get anywhere near a gym, with all those hills, you won't even need to.

A GRITTIER SCENE

Beyond the bar and club gloss, a grittier local culture has produced acts like Massive Attack, Portishead, Tricky. The **Ashton Court Festival** is the annual showcase for these. Get *Venue Magazine* and work your way into this city. Kate invites us to her particular furrow:

'Although the days when students could boast, "I live on the same street as Roni Size," are over, the Bristol music scene is still humming. It may not be London or Manchester, but the legacy of the Bristol Soun' lingers on. What really sets the city apart are the more lowfi venues in Stokes Croft. Crowned by the recently reopened and eagerly anticipated **Lakota**, they offer more cutting edge beats and a cooler shade of retro with nights such as *Shaft @*

The Maze. And we mustn't forget little **Thekla**, the club on a boat, in the busy dockside area. With an upstairs seated bar and downstairs packed dancing to funky hip hop, breakbeats and other mixes, it doesn't get more chilled than this.

'If you want an extra-curricular activity to really write home about, there are also loads of opportunities for student DJs to show their skills in public, either at the clubs themselves, or in the laid-back atmosphere of intimate bars such as **Cosies**, a vaulted underground wine-bar in St Paul's. Or if your clubbing tastes are even more adventurous, try the infamous *Spank* night held monthly at the **Bierkeller** – a fetishist's delight, it's the perfect excuse for a trip to rubber-gear shop **Religion** or **Ann Summers** (one of a couple of their extra-X-rated branches).

'Live music can be a disappointment, with no big music venue nearer than Cardiff, but plenty of mid-size bands play the Bristol University Union [see *page 96*].

'Bristol's gay scene is small but welcoming, and students forge good links to city social and support networks. The uni has a thriving LGB society and in addition to several new gay clubs, the main artsy venues in the city are the unofficial scene.'

Kate Freeman & Daniel Sefton

UNIVERSITY OF BRISTOL

The University of Bristol
Senate House
Tyndall Avenue
Bristol BS8 1TH

TEL 0117 928 9000 X4021
    0117 925 0177
FAX 0117 925 1424
EMAIL admissions@bristol.ac.uk
WEB www.bris.ac.uk

Bristol Students' Union
Queens Road
Clifton
Bristol BS8 1LN

TEL 0117 954 5815
FAX 0117 954 5817
EMAIL president-ubu@bristol.ac.uk
WEB www.ubu.org.uk/

VAG VIEW

*B*ristol is what parents, teachers and employers consider a 'good' university, observes student Daniel Sefton. Its reputation has been formed over many years in the minds of the older generations as a 'blue chip' establishment, its place set firmly in the second rank of British universities after Oxford and Cambridge. Whatever the carps about its public school intake, there's no question as to its academic reputation or to the student culture its union creates. It is

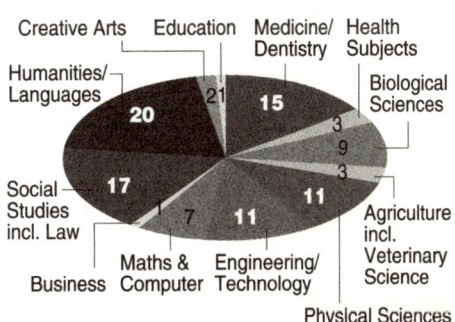

SUBJECT AREAS (%)

Creative Arts — Education — Medicine/Dentistry — Health Subjects
Humanities/Languages — 21 — 15
Biological Sciences — 3
9
20 — 3
Social Studies incl. Law — 17 — 11
7 — 11
Agriculture incl. Veterinary Science
Business — Maths & Computer — Engineering/Technology
Physical Sciences

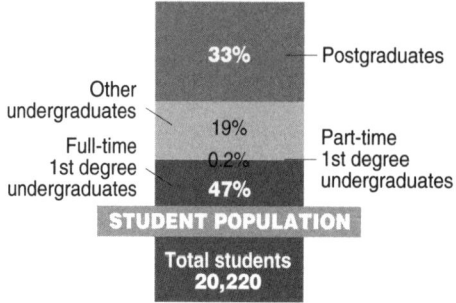

33% — Postgraduates

Other undergraduates

Full-time 1st degree undergraduates

19%

0.2%

47%

Part-time 1st degree undergraduates

STUDENT POPULATION

Total students 20,220

perhaps more bent on research, less of a hands-on university, than some, but the spirit of the place still runs in deep.

CAMPUS

The university and the city are geographically all one – it is all jumbled up together – which means there is less a sense of uni community than on a self-contained campus plot. On the other hand, there are no feelings of insularity, as at places like East Anglia, for example. It is fragmented, but the university somehow manages to keeps its hold on you in the city, the process beginning in Stoke Bishop Halls, a huddle of six fresher halls – like a mini campus just laden with pastoral care.

Here's Daniel Sefton's guide: 'The six Stoke Bishop halls, where you will begin, are about half an hour's walk from the main university precinct and at least forty-five sober minutes' walk from the city centre. Consequently, there is a strong hall culture in Bristol, especially in Stoke Bishop where even the nearest pub is ten minutes' walk away over the Downs. Thus, although the university schedule evening buses to transport students between the union, the halls and town centre, much activity is initially centred on the super-cheap hall bars.

'The halls are a mixture of catered and self-catered, and are much of a muchness. Wills Hall is worth singling out though. Reputed to be the most 'rah', Henley, Ascot, etc, the reputation is firmly deserved. Try Churchill, Durdham or Manor Hall (in Clifton) if this is not your thing.

'Between the Stoke Bishop halls and the top of Whiteladies Road are **the Downs** – a huge stretch of open land, Bristol's wonder of the world. They make Bristol one of the greenest cities in Britain, wonderful to sit out on in the summer and an ample sports ground all year round, but every day you have to traipse over them for ten minutes to the top of Whiteladies Road, where your day invariably begins.

'Leading down the hill from the Downs, Whiteladies Road is the major student strip – a

procession of brightly lit bars and fast food joints. The main university Precinct is off Whiteladies' along Woodland Road, the Arts faculty in elegant detached town houses, the Science faculty further on in a series of ugly buildings we can euphemistically call "post-war architecture". Behind the department blocks is the understocked and soporific **Arts Library**. A minute away is St Michael's Hill along which many fine pubs can be found. On the opposite side of Whiteladies Road is the Students' Union building, a hellish vision in concrete. It is positioned ten minutes walk from the main university precinct near the remaining three halls of residence, but about half an hour from the Stoke Bishop halls.'

STUDENT PROFILE

What puts some people off was neatly summarised by another student as follows: 'Bristol University has the reputation, especially among some of its more northerly competitors, as being a bit of a shandy-drinkin', southern poof's university, comprising mostly ex-Oxbridge wannabes and the like.' Today, if you provoke union bods with criticisms along these lines they are genuinely and quite endearingly hurt: 'The change has already occurred. It really isn't actively snooty any more.' The truth is that this is not a university falling over itself to widen access,

UNIVERSITY/STUDENT PROFILE	
University since	**1909**
Situation/style	**Civic**
Student population	**20,220**
Full-time undergraduates	**9,520**
- mature	**12%**
- overseas	**15%**
- male/female	**49/51**
- state sector intake	**57%, low**
- non-traditional student intake	**5%, low**
- drop-out rate	**2%, low**
- undergraduate applications	**Down 1%**
see Introduction for key to tables	

or if it is, it is not succeeding. Along with Oxbridge, Nottingham and Exeter, Bristol takes relatively few – only 57% – entrants from state schools, even though 93% of our children attend them. 'Bristol is perceived as consisting of home county, public school Oxbridge rejects,' writes Daniel, but the perception, whatever the statistics may say, is misplaced apparently: 'If this impression is not entirely undeserved, nor is it a true reflection of the reality of life at Bristol. The Sloane uniform is an in-joke among Bristol University students,

ACADEMIC EXCELLENCE

TEACHING:
(Rated Excellent or 17+ out of 24)

Law, Mechanical Engineering, Chemistry, Geography, Applied Social Work, English.	**Excellent**
Electrical & Electronic Eng, Anatomy, Education, Molecular Biosciences, Veterinary	**24**
Drama: Theatre, Film, TV, Maths, Physics, Economics, Pharmacology, Philosophy, Politics, Psychology	**23**
Iberian Studies, Civil Engineering, Aerospace Engineering, Organismal Biosciences	**22**
Sociology, Italian, German	**21**
Russian, French, History of Art, Medicine	**20**
Dentistry	**19**

RESEARCH:
Top grades 5/5*

Community-based Clinical, Clinical Dentistry, Anatomy, Psychology, Biochemistry, Chemistry, Earth Sciences, Applied Maths, Statistics, Civil Eng, Geography, Social Work, Russian/Slavonic/East European, Drama/Dance/ Porforming Arts, Education	**Grade 5***
Clinical Laboratory Sciences, Biological Sciences, Veterinary, Physics, Pure Maths, Computer, Electrical/Electronic Eng, Mechanical Eng, Law, Politics, Social Policy, Sociology, Accounting, English, French, German/Dutch/Scandinavian, Italian, Classics, Philosophy, Theology, Music	**Grade 5**

high entry requirements that admit confident, ambitious and able students.'

ACADEMIA

Bristol is one of the top handful of universities academically. More than 89% of its subjects have been rated Excellent or 19 points or more out of 24, and 320 points at A level are averagely required to get in here. Academically it offers courses which its league table equivalent in the north – Durham – does not: Medicine, Dentistry, Veterinary Science, for a start. But equally Durham has its own strengths which Bristol lacks, for example Arabic, Chinese, Japanese.

Medicine and veterinary subjects – including now a degree in Veterinary Nursing with an easier requirement at A level – guide much that is going on on the science side. Even the new £16-million Synthetic Chemistry building was promoted as leading to 'substantial improvements and refurbishments in medical laboratories.' Other new medical research buildings are planned, and there is an exciting medical bias to certain aspects of work in the Physics Department (mobile phones and power lines as health hazards); again, in Engineering Mathematics, finely tuned minds are being brought to bear on the problem of lung disease. It is interesting, though, that they came out of the teaching assessments worse in Medicine and Dentistry than most other subjects recently (see our *Academic Excellence* box on page 96).

There are occasional whimpers about lecturers being more interested in research than in teaching students, and certainly Bristol is hot on research – they came 16th nationally in last year's assessments – but look at the staff:student ratio, 13:1, which is far better than most and equal to Oxford and Cambridge.

If you got in, chances are you'll muddle through. Only 2% drop out, which is surely the acid test.

drawing a rather defensive laugh. Bristol is a relatively wealthy university with a high proportion of former public school students and a lack of ethnic, regional and financial diversity in its intake. This is a problem that the university is addressing through a policy to bring in a greater range of students. To be frank, if you consider yourself one of the green-welly brigade, you are likely to apply to Bristol, as are your friends. Do so, you'll love it. If on the other hand you are bewildered or repelled by this description, do not let Bristol's reputation put you off. Not only is the Sloanish element a minority, it barely impinges on life here, and if Bristol is exclusive, it is due to the

AT A GLANCE

ACADEMIC FILE:

Subjects assessed	**35**
Excellent	**89%**
Average requirements	**320 points +**
Studentstaff ratio	**13:1**
First/2:1 degree pass rate	**76%**

ACCOMMODATION FILE:

Guarantee to freshers	**90%**
Style	**Halls, houses**
Approx price range pw	**£35-£92**
City rent pw	**£45-£60**

WHAT IT'S REALLY LIKE

UNIVERSITY:	
Social Life	★★★★
Campus scene	**Lively, civic, well-heeled**
Student Union services	**Good**
Politics	**Student issues; activity high**
Sport	**35 clubs, mens/womens rugby, lacrosse, real tennis strong**
National team position	**10th**
Sport facilities	**Improving**
Arts opportunities	**Drama, dance, music excellent; film good; art avg**
Student magazine	**Epic**
Student newspaper	**Epigram**
Student radio	**Burst FM**
Nightclub	**Anson Rooms**
Bars	**Epi, Mandela**
Union ents	**Cheese**
Union clubs/societies	**170**
Smoking policy	**Bars OK**
Parking	**Poor**
CITY:	
Entertainment	★★★★★
Scene	**Full on**
Town/gown relations	**Good**
Risk of violence	**Average-high**
Cost of living	**High**
Student concessions	**Good**
Survival + 2 nights out	**£70 pw**
Part-time work campus/town	**Excellent**

SOCIAL SCENE

STUDENTS' UNION As I write, there is some doubt as to whether the union building will continue as is, whether facilities will move... The main SU bar is **The Epi** – trendy comfortable sofas, pool tables, a big-screen TV and a small arcade. If you're a keen sportsman (especially a rugby player) then Wednesday night, *Sportsnight*, is the one for you. A smaller, quieter bar is the **Mandela Bar** (capacity about 100/150) with student-run club nights, gigs. For food, **Café Zuma**, situated next to the Epi, serves up a basic range of meals and snacks through the afternoon and into the evening. The **Anson Rooms** on the first floor (capacity: 1,000) is the biggest live venue in Bristol. **Colston Hall** may hold more people but it's all seating; you don't get the same atmosphere. Recent live acts include Pet Shop Boys, Robert Plant, Divine Comedy, Bluetones, Mercury Rev, Zero 7, Magwai. There's also the Avon Gorge, a function room with big panoramic views.

'Union societies are prodigious,' reports Daniel – 135 at the last count, 'and used as stepping stones towards independent student companies, in for example theatre, music (the successful club-night promoters, Bubblegum), comedy (Marcus Brigstocke and Club Seals are recently graduated), or newspaper (Internet parody newspaper, *Naivete*). '

The Drama Society collects awards regularly, as does *Epigram*, the student newspaper (though neither managed it last year). Student radio _ BURST fm is back on air, rumoured to be web-broadcasting and going digital with Bath Uni this year.

SPORT Positions in the BUSA leagues are good, always on the edge of the top 10. There are around thirty-five sports clubs. Rugby was amazing last year, they have a student in the English Uni team, two women on the British lacrosse team, one of the top real tennis players in the country, and the uni is the regional headquarters for the Lawn Tennis Association. Rowing is perennially popular.

TOWN Only on Wednesdays when sports night sees the Epi transformed into a heaving mass of sweat, beer and vomit does the bar overcome the disadvantage of having nearby pubs such as the **Berkeley** and **Clifton Wine Bar** selling drinks more cheaply. See *Student Bristol* (page 92) for the gloss.

JOBS

The level of teaching is very high, the level of extra-

WHERE GRADUATES END UP

19% Health (Med, Dent),	Key Areas
12% Finance,	
8% Manufacturing,	
7% Public Admin,	
6% Personnel,	
6% Education,	
5% Computer	
Accountancy,	Niche Areas
Business/Management*,	
Advertising, Aeronautical	
Manuf, Eng/Industrial	
Design*, Defence*, Legal,	
Market Research,	
Publishing, Radio/TV	

*indicates Top 10 Graduate Provider

Approximate employed **96%**

curricular opportunity is equally rich, there's a good careers service, and a precedent which suggests that when you complete your course you'll be snapped up by an employer before your feet touch the ground. A large number of Bristol graduates go either into the health industry or into commerce (finance, accounting, business management), **but** there are alternatives – see *Employment* box, page 96.

> *Whatever the carps about public school intake, there's no question as to academic reputation or to the student culture its union can create.*

GETTING THERE

☛ By road: M4/J19, M32 or M5/J17 and follow the signs to the zoo (an elephant). Coach services 2:30 hours from London.
☛ By rail: London Paddington or Birmingham New Street, 1:30; Nottingham, 3:00.
☛ By air: Bristol Airport.
☛ By coach: Birminghan, 2:00; London, 2:20.

BRISTOL, UNIVERSITY OF THE WEST OF ENGLAND

University of the West of England
Frenchay Campus
Coldharbour Lane
Bristol BS16 1QY

TEL 0117 344 3333
FAX 0117 34 2810
EMAIL admissions@uwe.ac.uk
WEB www.uwe.ac.uk

West of England Students' Union
Frenchay Campus
Coldharbour Lane
Bristol BS16 1QY

TEL 0117 344 2577
FAX 0117 344 2986
EMAIL union@uwe.ac.uk
WEB www.uwesu.net

VAG VIEW

*A*cademically, it seems, UWE has made it, claiming sixth place in a league table of all universities, based on QAA (in full) reports. Yet still it asks relatively low points at A level. In terms of graduate employment, it is equally impressive, having just announced a mere 3.7% unemployed from its 2000 graduate outflow. Such top-line success has done a lot to convince students that they no longer deserve to be tarnished with the poly brush.

The problem has been rather that they have been short-dealed on campus, so that even their student village has been shoved aside for more academic building, and some freshers have had a rude awakening, suddenly finding themselves flailing around alone in what is increasingly a fairly punchy city.

Now, we hear, the uni has just embarked on a £.90-million spend on campus facilities, so maybe the final corner has been turned.

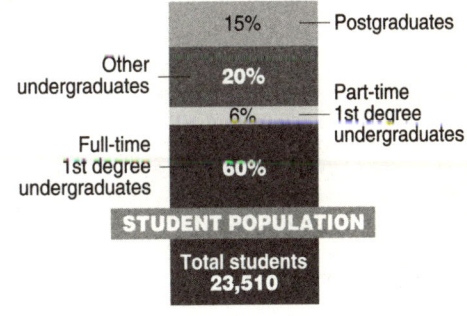

STUDENT PROFILE

Like Oxford Brookes, but unlike many other universities established in 1992, there's quite a high intake from independent schools. Says Roy Delaney, ex-editor of *Westworld*: 'I came from a Council House background, no pretensions me. When I signed up I was sitting next to a kid from Eton. We have a whole range, a real people mix.' Another student said, 'West is the cool uni; we're more streetwise than Bristol students. A lot of UWE students congregate round the Arches to the west of Montpellier, Gloucester Road, Stokes Croft, Cheltenham Road. It's more Bohemian. Bristol students live in Clifton, Redland, more

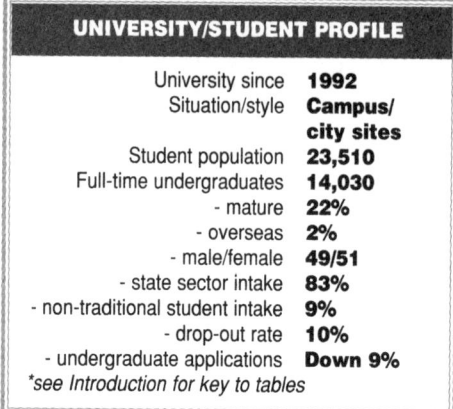

UNIVERSITY/STUDENT PROFILE	
University since	**1992**
Situation/style	**Campus/ city sites**
Student population	**23,510**
Full-time undergraduates	**14,030**
- mature	**22%**
- overseas	**2%**
- male/female	**49/51**
- state sector intake	**83%**
- non-traditional student intake	**9%**
- drop-out rate	**10%**
- undergraduate applications	**Down 9%**
see Introduction for key to tables	

SUBJECT AREAS (%)

Education 4 · Health Subjects 5 · Creative Arts 8 · Sciences · Agriculture incl. Vetinary Science 12 · Humanities/ Languages 13 · 3 · 6 · 8 · Engineering/ Technology · 14 · 17 · 10 · Planning/ Building/ Architecture · Social Studies incl. Law · Business · Maths & Computer

polished.' Truth is that the student body is as diverse as its various campuses, though the uni is committing its resources to widening participation still further, claiming fifty-seven initiatives in progress.

CAMPUSES

FRENCHAY (address above) **Location:** north of the city, near Bristol Parkway Station. **Faculties:** Applied Sciences, Business, Built Environment, Computer & Maths, Economics & Social Science, Engineering, Languages & Euro Studies, Law. Library has new £6.5 million extension.

BOWER ASHTON Kennel Lodge Road, off Clanage Road, Bower Ashton, Bristol BS3 2JU; Tel: 0117 966 0222. **Location:** south of river, west but in easy reach of city centre. **Faculties:** Art, Media & Design. **Learning resources:** specialist library, well-equipped studios and workshops. **Sport facilities:** five-a-side football pitch; eighteen-hole pitch & putt close to hand. **Ents facilities:** opening hours short in **Bower's Bar**, but good, buzzy atmosphere.

REDLAND Redland Hill, Bristol BS6 6UZ; Tel: 0117 974 1251. **Location:** northwest of city centre **Faculties:** Education. Transferring to Frenchay in 2001.

ST MATTHIAS Oldbury Court Road, Fishponds, Bristol BS16 2JP; Tel: 0117 965 5384. **Location:** sometime monastery overrun by cats, northeast of city centre, near Glenside (see below), good bus service to city action. **Faculty:** Humanities. **Accommodation:** two halls. **Learning resources:** library. **Sport facilities:** cricket square, two soccer pitches, gym. **Ents facilities:** **St Matt's** bar.

GLENSIDE Blackberry Hill, Stapleton, Bristol BS16 1DD. Tel: 0117 958 5655. **Location:** sometime asylum north-east of city centre, nearest to St Matthias, good bus service to city action. **Faculties:** Health & Social Care. **Accommodation:** purpose-built, self-catering. **Learning resources:** library. **Sport facilities:** space for aerobics, etc. **Ents facilities:** student/staff social club, good restaurant, not far from Frenchay.

ACADEMIA

The nine subjects most recently assessed scored

ACADEMIC EXCELLENCE	
TEACHING :	
(Rated Excellent or 17+ out of 24)	
Law, Business & Management, English	**Excellent**
Organismal Biosciences, Pharmacology & Pharmacy, Molecular Biosciences	**24**
Sociology, Town/Country Planning, Business, Economics	**23**
Communication & Media Studies, Land & Property Management., Art/Design, Psychology, Nursing	**22**
Modern Languages (French, German, Spanish, Linguistics), Building, Elec/Electron Eng, Politics, Maths, Subjects Allied to Medicine	**21**
Agriculture	**20**
RESEARCH:	
Top grades 5/5*	
Accounting and Finance	**Grade 5**

between 21 points out of 24 and full marks – for Education – which is exceptional. For business, health, built environment (this year sees a new 3-storey Architecture & Planning building with a 200-seater lecture theatre), computer and law the uni is strong, and they outgunned Bristol – 23 points to 21 – in the Sociology Department. Again, UWE's excellent Department of Time-Based Media (TV, video, multimedia, radio and sound production) is making waves. Media-wise all round things are looking cool, what with student mag *Westworld* winning Best Design at the *Independent* awards this year and running up Oxford Uni for Best Photography and Trinity Dublin for Best Design in the *Guardian* awards.

Finally, in the recent research assessments they scored Grade 5 – that's international renown – in Finance & Accounting, one of the key areas of employment into which their graduates pass.

SOCIAL SCENE

STUDENTS' UNION UWE has nine sites (including associate Hartpury College), five in Bristol, but even at HQ Frenchay a sense of community is lacking. 'Very few people stay after lectures,' says Laura. 'Mainly you have to sort out your own fun.'

Capacity at Frenchay's **Escape** and the **Venue** bar together is about 720. On Friday nights they do a club-night, *Fried*, the usual 'desperation disco'. *Poptastic* – '70s/'80s – was fed to freshers last year and Frenchay has this sporadically throughout the year. Then there's six-weekly *Bristol Cream* – local bands; and *Club Classics*, 'a decade of the best house tunes: '88-'98'. *Giggles Comedy Club* is another regular, as are the balls – Freshers', Snowball (just before Christmas) and the May Ball/Graduation Ball. A marquee and two floors of the SU building are opened up and the patio linked to **Traders** (a university/non-SU facility) making a 2,500 capacity. There's also the occasional dual promotion with Bristol.
'We hire a club [**Odyssey**, **Powerhouse**] or piggy back on to a regular club night together.' See also *Student Bristol, page 92.*

UWE has a particular reputation for staging musicals. **The Centre for Performing Arts** is based at the **Octagon**. When the new Educational faculty rises on Frenchay there'll be a performing arts centre attached. Among societies the Poly Players are a surprise – an 'English drawing room group, comedy': students write and perform their own plays around the sites.

WHAT IT'S REALLY LIKE

UNIVERSITY:	
Social Life	★★★
Campus scene	**Diverse mix**
Politics	**No interest**
Sport	**Competitive, but poor facilities**
National team position	**70th**
Arts	**Available**
Student magazine	**Westworld**
Independent awards	**Best Design**
Nightclub	**Venue**
Bars	**Escape, Traders**
Union ents	**5-6 pw**
Union clubs/societies	**100+**
Smoking policy	**Bars, halls only**
Parking	**Poor**
CITY:	
Entertainment	★★★★★
Scene	**Full on**
Town/gown relations	**Good**
Risk of violence	**Average-high**
Cost of living	**High**
Student concessions	**Good**
Survival + 2 nights out	**£70 pw**
Part-time work campus/town	**Excellent**

SPORT UWE's not noted for sport, though its team performance at BUSA/national level is not bad (44th this year). 'The sports centre is a few squash courts and a pretty well kitted-out gym and that's about it. Mostly we go outside.' One little gem is American Football – UWE entices deprived Bristol students to join up.

PILLOW TALK

Both Bristol and UWE are civic universities, but Bristol students have a cocoon period in halls where there's masses of pastoral care, whereas at UWE you'll quite likely have to fend for yourself from the start, particularly if you come through Clearing. The uni's guarantee to freshers is carefully, not to say legalistically worded. Basically they'll sort you out uni accommodation if you

> *Both Bristol and UWE are civic universities, both have serious academic and employment strengths, yet Bristol seems more focused and broader in appeal, perhaps because the student culture is more developed.*

accept an offer of a place, firm, and return the accommodation application form, completed in full, by 1 July and pay a holding fee up front.

Possibly the lack of accommodation at Frenchay will improve with the announcement of a £90-million campus spend.

AT A GLANCE

ACADEMIC FILE:

Subjects assessed	**30**
Excellent	**77%**
Average requirements	**200 points**
Students-staff ratio	**19:1**
First/2:1 degree pass rate	**45%**

ACCOMMODATION FILE:

Guarantee to freshers	**Apply before July 1**
Style	**Flats, houses**
Catered	**None**
En-suite	**2.5%**
Price range pw	**£43-£54**
City rent pw	**£52**

'Most students live in uni-managed accommodation around Bristol,' writes Laura Tytler. 'There are groups of flats in the centre of town – Favell House, Waverleigh House and The Rackhay, which I would recommend most. The atmosphere is good and all you need is right on the doorstep: infinite clubs, bars, etc and a 24-hour Spar shop.' This year new accommodation in the city centre – Nelson House and Drake House – will open.

JOBS

From 5.5% UWE graduates unemployed, they are down to 3.7% this year. The uni is strong in health, finance, manufacturing (with a particular genius in the area of aeronautical manufacture), computer, construction, defence, education, film/video, telecom and other areas too. See our *Employment* box for the fruits of their close participation with Aardman Animation, BAe Systems, Hewlett Packard, BBC, Lloyds TSB, Orange, Rolls Royce and Virgin.

GETTING THERE

☛ By road to Frenchay, Glenside, St Matthias: M4/J19, M32 or M5/J16, A38; Redland: M5/J17, A4018; Bower Ashton, M5/J19, A369.
☛ By rail: London Paddington, Birmingham New Street, 1:30; Nottingham, 3:00.
☛ By air: Bristol Airport.
☛ By coach: Birminghan, 2:00; London, 2:20.

WHERE GRADUATES END UP

16% Health/Social Work, Key areas
11% Finance,
11% Manufacturing,
9% Education,
6% Public Admin,
6% Wholesale/Retail,
6% Computer,
5% Personnel
Aeronautical Manufac*, Niche Areas
Construction, Defence, Electron/Electric, Film/Video, Legal, Property, Telecom

*indicates Top 10 Graduate Provider

Approximate employed **94%**

BRITISH COLLEGE OF NATUROPATHY & OSTEOPATHY

British College of Naturopathy
& Osteopathy
120-122 Finchley Road
London NW3 5HR

TEL 0207 435 6464
FAX 0207 431 3630
EMAIL bcd@bcno.ac.uk
WEB http://www.bcno.ac.uk

BCNO is a private institution; fees last year were £6,250; there is some government help. Osteopathy is a system of manipulation of joints and tissue, Naturopathy a holistic approach to the same. If you're interested, this is the place to do it.

GETTING THERE

☛ By road: opposite Finchley Road tube.
☛ By Underground: Finchley Road gives access to Metropolitan and Jubilee lines.

COLLEGE PROFILE

Founded	**1936**
Status	**HE College**
Degree awarding university	**Westminster**
Degree undergraduates	**221**
College accommodation	**None**
City rent pw	**£70**

DEGREE SUBJECT AREAS:
Osteopathic & naturopathic medicine

BRITISH INSTITUTE IN PARIS

Departement d'Etudes Francaises
Institut Britannique de Paris
9-11 Rue de Constantine 75340
Paris Cedex 07, France

TEL 00 331 44117383/4
FAX 00 331 45503155
EMAIL (see website)
WEB www.bip.lon.ac.uk

COLLEGE PROFILE

University College since	**1894**
Degree awarding university	**London**
Situation/style	**City site**
Student population	**2,080**
Full-time/sandwich undergrads	**132**
Institute accommodation	**None**

DEGREE SUBJECT:
French Studies

VAG VIEW

*T*his is part of the University of London, originally set up to teach French to English students and vice versa. British students spend their year abroad here, but there is also a fully fledged BA. The fee situation is the same as at any UK-based university. Contact Dr Elaine Williamson, who is head of French if you're interested. Be sure to make clear to your LEA that it is a University of London course.

- -

BRUNEL UNIVERSITY

Brunel University
Uxbridge
Middlesex UB8 3PH

TEL 01895 274000
FAX 01895 203102
EMAIL admissions@brunel.ac.uk
WEB www.brunel.ac.uk

Union of Brunel Students
Uxbridge
Middlesex UB8 3PH

TEL 01895 462200
FAX 01895 462300
EMAIL su.president@brunel.ac.uk
WEB www.ubsonline.net

VAG VIEW

*O*ut of a nineteenth-century, technical background, Brunel established itself in the late 1960s as a science/technology/ engineering uni, which was 'all well and good if you had long oily hair, wore AC/DC T-shirts and had the personality of a walnut,' recalls Satiyesh Manoharajah. 'But, dammit, it just wasn't sexy. However, things have been a-changing these past few years. The Social Sciences and Arts faculties have greatly expanded, bringing an influx of generally more exciting students and, indeed, women!'

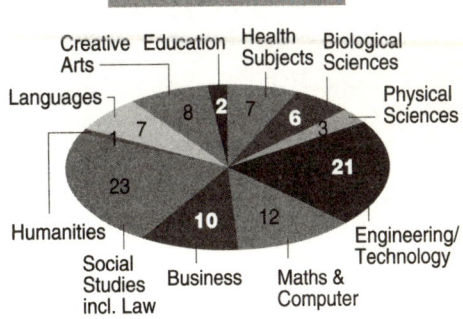

SUBJECT AREAS (%)

Creative Arts — 8
Education — 2
Health Subjects — 7
Biological Sciences — 6
Physical Sciences — 3
Engineering/ Technology — 21
Maths & Computer — 12
Business — 10
Social Studies incl. Law — 23
Humanities — 7
Languages — 1

VIEW FROM THE GROUND
by Naveed Mohammed

Brunel, the University of West London, is based northwest of the city, close to the M25, M40 and M4, Heathrow Airport is also just round the corner – fifty minutes by tube and thirty minutes by overland train to central London. Social life on campus revolves around halls and Students' Union. Freshers' Week is and will always remain a highlight. I don't remember much of mine, but I spent £250 in the bar, which is something, as bar prices are pretty decent considering that the university is on the edge of London – pints, spirits and mixer clock in at just under £2 each. Compared

UNIVERSITY/STUDENT PROFILE	
University since	**1966**
Situation/style	**Suburban campuses**
Student population	**14,670**
Full-time undergraduates	**8,800**
- mature	**21%**
- overseas	**6%**
- male/female	**54/46**
- state sector intake	**85%**
- non-traditional student intake	**9%**
- drop-out rate	**8%, low**
- undergraduate applications	**Up 13%**
see Introduction for key to tables	

to other union bars it is a little expensive, but special promos and offers make up for it.

SOCIAL SCENE

Loco's, the union bar has had a £180,000 overhaul. The union nightclub is busiest on a Wednesday for *Decades*, advance tickets usually sell out by mid-day Monday. Live bands are thin on the ground, but there are many bands constantly in London and a night bus from Trafalgar Square for all the dirty stop-outs who miss the last tube home.

A week's living costs are about £75-£100 for food, booze, going out two or three nights and travel – not including accommodation. You can spend a lot less than this, or a lot more. Try as you might to resist, an overdraft and credit card will become your best friends. Balance this by using the university part-time job shop, their jobs database can be accessed on the computer network. The union employees about 200 part-time staff a year.

TOWN The Uxbridge campus is just outside Uxbridge town, home to a nine-screen cinema, large department stores, some nice pubs and an nightclub called **Royale's** – infamous in the student community for its all-you-can-drink-for-£10 nights, almost as challenging as its glitzy

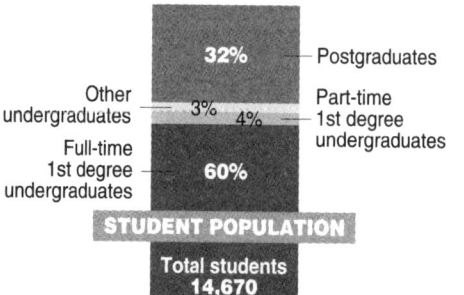

Other undergraduates **3%**
4%
Postgraduates **32%**
Part-time 1st degree undergraduates
Full-time 1st degree undergraduates **60%**

STUDENT POPULATION
Total students **14,670**

trashiness. There are a few nice places to eat, curry houses and Chinese restaurants among them. A real night out requires a trip into London, the night bus goes past the Uxbridge campus.

SPORT For training there's an impressive two-floored, air-conditioned gym that I've been meaning to join for a while, it costs about £10 a month for unlimited use. There are sports pitches, basketball and squash courts and a quite daunting climbing wall too. You can dabble, satisfy curiosity or take up fanatically more or less what you want to, even become part of a university team. (See *Uxbridge Campus*, page 103, for more developments.)

WHAT IT'S REALLY LIKE	
UNIVERSITY:	
Social Life	★★★
Campus scene	**Lively, trecky, sporty**
Student Union services	**Good**
Politics	**Average Student issues**
Sport	**Good**
National team position	**20th**
Sport facilities	**Good**
Arts opportunities	**Excellent drama, film; good art, dance, music**
Student magazine	**Route 66**
Student radio	**B-1000**
Nightclub	**Academy**
Bars	**Loco's Bar**
Union ents	**Decades - pop & cheese classics**
Union Clubs/Societies	**120**
Smoking policy	**Union OK**
Parking	**Good**
CITY:	
Entertainment	★★★★★
Scene	**Cheesy local clubs London beckons**
Town/gown relations	**Good**
Risk of violence	**Average**
Cost of living	**High**
Student concessions	**Good**
Survival + 2 nights out	**£75 pw**
Part-time work campus/town	**Good**

PILLOW TALK

You must live in halls in the first year; freshers and foreign students from ninety-one countries are given priority. Accommodation is standard or en suite, with keypad or VIN card access. All rooms are self-catered with about eight people sharing a kitchen. They are well sized, a bit weird when you first see them but once your stuff is in they become home. You will make some great friends in halls and also some bad ones!

All freshers are guaranteed accommodation on campus, though there could be a delay for late candidates coming through clearing. We're talking halls and flats, some 30% are en suite. Prices vary between £50.50 and £62.50 at time of writing. For those wanting the most modern facilities, a new 328-room hall is due for completion in early 2003.

CAMPUSES

Uxbridge is by far the biggest campus, and is packed with bizarre, grey, concrete buildings, but well laid out, with all the main facilities (bars, small shop, HSBC bank and cash points, a **Waterstones** and travel agents) located centrally. Most of the students are here. The Runnymede, Twickenham and Osterley campuses are much smaller, cosier and far more beautiful than Uxbridge, but there is less of a university atmosphere. See *Academia* for where *you* would study.

UXBRIDGE CAMPUS (address above). **Ambience:** besides being an anagram for Big Durex and the location for the filming of the late Stanley Kubrick's *Clockwork Orange*, Uxbridge is now the epicentre of arts and ents at the uni. **Accommodation:** halls or flats. Halls range from adequate to luxurious, but most freshers wind up in flats (aka Bosnia). They look pretty grim but socially they are more fun than halls. **Ents:** all day every day it's the union's **Loco's** bar for total wipe-out, arcade games, pool, jukebox, fast food, courtyard drinking. The **Academy**, the uni's principal nightclub (capacity 600), just underwent a six-month refurb and has a new £25k sound rig. Decades is the big night (Wednesday) – pop & cheese, '60s, '70s, '80s, '90s classics. Recent live acts were Asian Dub Foundation, Dodgy, Chesney Hawkes. **Arts:** Drama and film are excellent, but dance, music and art are OK/good. **The Arts Centre** is the platform for lunchtime and evening musical concerts throughout the year. Student groups include The Brunel Singers, an orchestra, guitar, brass, wind and string groups; all are professionally trained and music bursaries are awarded annually. Classes in photography and various visual art forms are given on a weekly basis by visiting professionals. There are several student drama groups. **Sport:** at Uxbridge it's sport-for-all. The real dash is at Osterley, but facilities are good here and the campus is about to take sports science

from Osterley: The Department of Sports Sciences will be moving to Uxbridge Campus. Planning permission has just been granted for major new sports facilities, including a 6-lane synthetic athletics training track with associated field event facilities, two natural turf football pitches, one full sized synthetic football pitch plus tennis and netball courts. Since last year a new weights training centre has been installed. There's a boathouse close to Runnymede, use of the Queen Mother Reservoir for sailing, and the **Sportsbar**.

RUNNYMEDE CAMPUS Englefield Green, Egham, Surrey TW20 0JZ. Tel 01784 431341. Fax 01784 472879. **Ambience**: Twelve miles from the Uxbridge campus in 65 acres of woodland, Runnymede is home to students and rabbits in unequal number. **Accommodation:** ten self-catering halls, some shared rooms. **Ents: Runnymede Bar** is the only union bar to sell a range of real ales, and has a beer garden, pool, jukebox and arcade. **Chompers** is the eaterie. **Thumpers** is the venue (capacity 200). **Sport:** see Uxbridge.

OSTERLEY CAMPUS Borough Road, Isleworth, Middlesex TW7 5DU. Tel 020 8891 0121. Fax 020 8891 8211. **Ambience:** Sports-mad Brunel University College, or BUC, or Borough Road, as the former West London Institute has been variously known, is to lose its sports science department, which will leave it a haven for nurses and the like. Eleven miles southeast of Uxbridge Campus, but only a couple of miles away from Twickenham Campus, the Borough Blazer was once the traditional song of this close-knit band of sporting brothers. **Accommodation:** single and shared study-bedrooms with kitchenette access and five main meals a week. **Ents: Lancaster Bar** – 'ideal for those who like a quiet drink with fifteen rugby players and a burning newspaper shoved up their arse' – has just been refurbished; pool, jukebox, new games and arcades in foyer. **Beehive** is the venue (200 capacity, video jukebox, big screen). **Sport:** the sports hall is excellent and at the moment they still have supreme athletics facilities.

TWICKENHAM CAMPUS 300 St Margaret's Road, Twickenham, Middlesex TW1 1PT. Tel 020 8891 0121. Fax 020 8891 8270. **Ambience:** Teachers and social workers. **Accommodation:** single and shared study-bedrooms with kitchenette access and five main meals a week. **Ents: JCR** (from common room to nightclub with 250 capacity) has had a facelift and new sound and lighting systems. **Twickenham Bar** is the watering hole, also known as **Maria Grey**. **Sport:** see neighbouring Osterley.

ACADEMIA

Brunel continues to introduce cutting-edge techno courses such as the BSc in Multimedia Technology & Design, but a few years ago it spread its wings,

quadrupled in size and took on a broader academic brief – social work, sociology, politics, law, psychology (with valuable new social science combinations, such as American Studies/Sociology, English/Psychology), health (with a new course in Medical Genetics), sports studies, sciences and arts (from English to Film/TV Studies, from American Studies to Drama). Overall, teaching assessments have not been as good as some universities that demand less points at A level, but in some of these newer courses (Drama, American Studies, Film & TV, Sport Sciences), it has performed especially well, as indeed it did recently in Education (23 points out of 24, see our *Academic Excellence* box).

Writes Naveed, 'Pressure of work builds gradually in your first year, not too bad unless you go totally wild. It gets more intense after that. Computers are available freely as is the Internet and you can get network access in quite a few rooms in halls – the university is looking to have this in all rooms. The library is big, but in high demand – don't expect to find 'that' book a few days before your big assignment deadline, though there's plenty of study room and a silent floor, lockers, and good media library.'

> *Engineering and sport – Audley Harrison and James Cracknell learned their stuff here – were once Brunel's sole territory, but things are now changing.*

Brunel welcomes applications from disabled students and those with special needs. They currently have three Disability Officers, one of whom is a Dyslexia Co-ordinator, who are available to help and advise students and potential applicants with special needs.

Distance Learning is now an established route to degrees at undergraduate and postgraduate level. In many cases the qualification can be earned without attending the university. In other cases, short periods of attendance may be required. Distance Learning awards are considered equivalent to those earned by full-time study. Contact the Admissions Office for information.

This year a new Graduate School opened, and for undergrads there's a revised faculty structure:

Faculty of Arts & Social Sciences (Uxbridge) – Politics, American Studies & History, Business & Management, Economics & Finance, English, Human Sciences, Law, Performing Arts.

Faculty of Life Sciences – Biological Sciences, Education (Twickenham), Geography & Earth Sciences (Uxbridge), Health & Social Care (Osterley), Sport Sciences (Osterley, but Uxbridge

Campus from August 2002).

Faculty of Technology & Information Systems
– Design (Runnymede), Electronic & Computer Engineering, Information Systems & Computing, Mathematical Sciences, Mechanical Engineering, Systems Engineering.

JOBS

Brunel is well known for pioneering sandwich courses and encouraging the specific skills and vocational aspects of courses that are important factors to recruiters.

See our *Employment* box opposite: the 17% health provision comes out of the Osterley campus. The Department has a long history of providing courses for nurses and health care professionals, and has been enlarged by mergers with the London School of Occupational Therapy (1980), the West Middlesex Hospital School of Physiotherapy (1986) and St Mary's Hospital School of Physiotherapy (1991). A Brunel physiotherapist went to the Winter Olympics in Salt Lake City as Chief Physiotherapist to the Great Britain Team. Most students registering for courses do so as part of a full-funded contract with the National Health Service Executive Education Commissioners.

The 11% of graduates going into computing is engineered by a range of courses specialising in modern technologies such as Internet Engineering, E-commerce, Multimedia Design & Technology and, most recently, Mobile Phone Technology & Computing.

WHERE GRADUATES END UP

17% Health/Social Work,	Key Areas
11% Computer*,	
9% Manufacturing,	
8% Finance,	
8% Education,	
7% Wholesale/Retail,	
5% Personnel,	
5% Public Admin	
Advertising, Defence,	Niche Areas
Business/Management,	
Film/Video, Journalism,	
Publishing, Radio/TV,	
Sport, Telecom,	
Eng/Industrial Design	

*indicates Top 10 Graduate Provider

Approximate employed **95%**

GETTING THERE

☛ By Underground: **Uxbridge** – Metropolitan line and Piccadilly during peak hours. Then bus, U3 or U5. **Twickenham** – Richmond (District line) then H37 bus; or Hounslow East (Piccadilly line) then H37 bus. **Osterley** – Piccadilly line.
☛ By rail: **Uxbridge** – to West Drayton. U3 to campus. **Runnymede** – to Egham, 30 mins' walk to campus. **Twickenham** – St Margaret's Station then H37 bus or Richmond Station and H37 bus. **Osterley** – Isleworth Station and 5 mins' walk.

• •

UNIVERSITY OF BUCKINGHAM

The University of Buckingham
Hunter Street
Buckingham MK18 1EG

TEL 01280 814080
FAX 01280 822245
EMAIL admissions@buckingham.ac.uk
WEB www.buckingham.ac.uk

Students' Union
The University of Buckingham
Hunter Street
Buckingham MK18 1EG

TEL 01280 822522
FAX 01280 812791
EMAIL student.union@buckingham.ac.uk
WEB www.buckingham.ac.uk/life/social/su/

VAG VIEW

*T*his is Britain's only independent university. Tuition fees are steep (approx. £2,730 per term), but most degrees are completed within two years (note, however, that there are four terms in the Buckingham year). All EU students are eligible for LEA awards, and the uni awards scholarships that can bring cost down within reasonable limits.

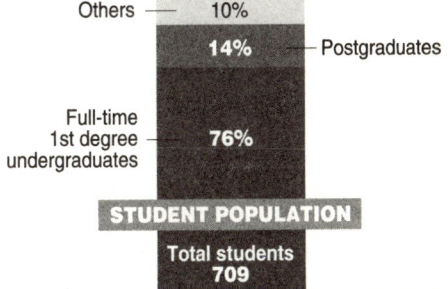

Others — 10%

14% — Postgraduates

Full-time 1st degree undergraduates — 76%

STUDENT POPULATION

Total students
709

UNIVERSITY/STUDENT PROFILE

University since	**1976**
Approx tuition fees per term	**£2,730**
Situation/style	**Town campus**
Student population	**709**
- mature	**33%**
- overseas	**72%**
- male/female	**47/53**

CAMPUS

The three sites – Hunter Street, 8-acre Verney Park and the recently developed Chandos Road complex, are walking distance apart and within the town boundaries.

STUDENT PROFILE

A popular picture of Buckingham is of a place for rich also-rans, but that isn't a view shared by all school sixthform advisers to whom we spoke. Many undergrads are mature and 72% hie from overseas; there are a few more women than men.

ACADEMIA

There is much to be said for Buckingham's quiet, Oxbridge-style tutorial system, small-class tuition and 1:10 staff-student ratio. Departments include Accounting, Business, Economics, English Language Studies (EFL), English Literature, Financial Services, History, History of Art, Information Systems, International Hotel Management, International Studies, Law, Marketing, Politics and Psychology. Law, with more than 200 undergraduates is by far the most popular. They say that for A level candidates they ask for three passes, but combinations of A and/or AS levels are also considered.

Degree courses are very concentrated, and an extra six months has been added to some to ease the pressure and enable calendrical adjustments between school academic years and the uni regime. As an independent institution Buckingham doesn't submit to the teaching assessments, but it is widely regarded for its teaching. There are libraries at each site, a language centre and a networked IT set-up (a computer suite at Verney Park is accessible 24/7). The intensity of the academic experience leaves little time for fun and games, however.

SOCIAL SCENE

STUDENTS' UNION At one-tenth of the average size of a British university, Buckingham provides a cosy enough environment. The union, located in the **Tanlaw Mill** on the Hunter Street site (refectory and **George's Bar**, pool tables, video games, lounge with Satellite TV), organises discos

WHAT IT'S REALLY LIKE

UNIVERSITY:	
Social Life	★★
Campus scene	**Small, friendly, multi-cultured, mature**
Politics	**Internal**
Sport	**Local & BUSA**
Arts opportunities	**Few**
Student newspaper	**The Millennium**
Union ents	**Functions, films, discos, balls**
Union venue	**Tanlaw Mill Refectory & George's Bar; Monastic cellars**
Union Societies	**Mainly cultural**
Smoking policy	**Refectory OK**
Parking	**Permit required**
TOWN:	
Entertainment	★★
Scene	**Trad pubs**
Student concessions	**Some**
Cost of living	**High**
Survival + 2 nights out	**£70 pw**
Part-time work campus/town	**Not required**

AT A GLANCE

ACADEMIC FILE:	
Approx. points required	**160-240**
Subject assessments	**None**
ACCOMMODATION FILE:	
Guarantee to freshers	**100%**
Style	**Halls**
Approx price range pw	**£65**
Town rent pw	**£55**

and a Graduation Ball. Last year the ball featured a Blues Brothers tribute band and the Funky Diva's band, a disco, casino, laser rifle shooting, and even a (temporary) tattoo artist. Then there's the **Franciscan Building** (Verney Park) for private-hire cellar parties. There are currently twelve societies, mainly cultural or departmental, quite a few organised trips and a series of concerts and lectures. The film society (BUFS) shows films two nights a week. For escape, there are various restaurants and traditional country pubs in Buckingham, or Milton Keynes (14 miles), Oxford (23 miles), London (58 miles). Bring a car.

SPORT Four all-weather tennis courts, one all-weather five-a-side pitch, a swimming pool, gym complex and sports field; other playing fields a mile away. There are riding schools in the vicinity. The uni teams are mainly locally competitive. Matches played against alumni and staff are also regular features. There is a campus fitness programme – aerobics classes, martial arts – and a well-equipped fitness centre.

PILLOW TALK

Guaranteed first-year, self-catered accommodation in mixed halls of residence at Hunter Street and Verney Park, or shared flats at Hunter Street.

GETTING THERE

☛ By road: make for Buckingham by-pass. M40/J9 from the south, then A41, A421. Also A422, A421, as well as A413 from the north.
☛ By rail: London Euston, 1:00; Birmingham New Street, 1:20.
☛ By air: Heathrow or Gatwick.
☛ By coach: London, 1:20.

BUCKINGHAMSHIRE CHILTERNS UNIVERSITY COLLEGE

Buckinghamshire Chilterns University College
Queen Alexandra Road
High Wycombe HP11 2JZ

TEL 01494 522141
FAX 01494 465432
EMAIL (see website)
WEB www.bcuc.ac.uk

Buckinghamshire Chilterns Students' Union
Queen Alexandra Road
High Wycombe HP11 2JZ

TEL 01494 446330
FAX 01494 558195
EMAIL students.union@bcuc.ac.uk
WEB www.bcsu.org.uk

VAG VIEW

*B*CUC *can trace its history back to a School of Science and Art founded in 1893 and into Buckinghamshire College of Higher Education, formed in1975 out of High Wycombe College of Technology and Art and Newland Park College of Education. From 1992 Brunel University validated its degrees. Then, in 1999, four years after it had been given powers to award its own degrees, the college was confirmed by the Privy Council as Buckingham Chilterns University College.*

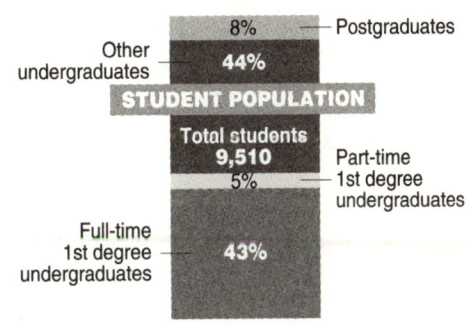

COLLEGE/STUDENT PROFILE	
University College since	**1999**
Situation/style	**3 town/rural campuses**
Student population	**9,510**
Full-time degree undergraduates	**4,080**
- mature	**28%**
- overseas	**2%**
- male/female	**42/58**
- state sector intake	**97%**
- non-traditional student intake	**12%**
- drop-out rate	**14%, high**
- undergraduate applications	**Down 2%**
see Introduction for key to tables	

LOCATION

The college is sited at three locations within a short distance from London. Two – High Wycombe and Wellesbourne campuses – are within the market town of High Wycombe itself, and one – Chalfont Campus – is some ten miles to the east, centred on an eighteenth-century mansion and set in 200 acres close to the village of Chalfont St Giles. All faculties are located in High Wycombe other than Business (the largest) and Health (nursing), which are on Chalfont Campus.

STUDENT PROFILE

There is a large mature population (28% of full-time degree undergrads), and many under-graduates are not reading for degrees. The state

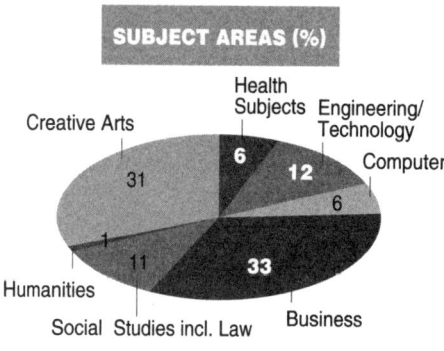

SUBJECT AREAS (%)

Creative Arts — 31
Health Subjects — 6
Engineering/Technology — 12
Computer — 6
Business — 33
Social Studies incl. Law — 11
Humanities — 1

AT A GLANCE

ACADEMIC FILE:	
Subjects assessed	**12**
Excellent	**50%**
Typical requirements	**140 points**
Students-staff ratio	**23:1**
First/2:1 degree pass rate	**42%**
ACCOMMODATION FILE:	
Guarantee to freshers	**80%**
Style	**Halls**
Cost pw (no food/food)	**£50-£68**
Town rent pw	**£55**

sector and non-traditional student intake is high and the drop-out rate, at 14%, is very high – quite bothersome even if quite clearly Bucks Chilterns is beginning to shape up in other ways like a uni.

ACADEMIA & JOBS

BCUC offer a major portfolio of degrees through six faculties: Applied Social Sciences & Humanities, Business, Art & Design, Health, Leisure & Tourism

ACADEMIC EXCELLENCE

TEACHING:
(Rated Excellent or 17+ out of 24)

Nursing	**23**
Psychology Tourism/Sport	**21**
Agriculture, Art & Design	**20**
Communications & Media	**18**

RESEARCH:
Top grades 5/5* **None**

and Technology. Much has changed since their reputation (an international one) relied solely upon furniture production and design. The town of High Wycombe has been associated with the craft for more than a century and BCUC still delivers the largest range of furniture design programmes in the world, but the areas now attracting the interest of students and employers are more diverse (see our Employment box).

Relative to size, BCUC are the largest graduate providers to advertising; students of their Graphic Design department – they are the eighth largest provider in this area – regularly win national awards. Incredibly, they are also the largest graduate providers to Sport, another area where industry links – for example between Sports Management and premier rugby club Saracens – bear fruit. Niche success, careers-wise, in Film/Video recommends us to production courses

in their Applied Social Sciences & Humanities faculty, where Drama and Creative Writing are also building reputations. In the Health faculty, Nursing has just scored 23 points out of 24 in the teaching assessments, while their Technology faculty earns national prominence for its Centre for Rapid Design & Manufacture. The Business faculty picks up on a college-wide emphasis on language acquisition and features European and international courses in collaboration with partners abroad.

SOCIAL SCENE

An active ents scene, promisingly profiled in monthly magazine, *Intercourse*, and weekly newsletter, *Foreplay*, is offered at both Chalfont and the main High Wycombe campus. Event of the year is the May Ball, 'a black-tie, 12-hour blinding party with over 2,000 members of BCSU (the union) attending. Past acts include Robbie Williams, the Divine Comedy, Louise, the Bootleg

WHERE GRADUATES END UP

15% Wholesale/Retail*,	Key Areas
15% Manufacturing,	
9% Health/Social Work,	
6% Public Admin,	
6% Finance,	
6% Computer,	
5% Personnel	
Advertising*, Sport*,	Niche Areas
Aeronautical Manufac,	
Architecture, Artistic/	
Literary*, Film/Video,	
Market Research,	
Publishing	

*indicates Top 10 Graduate Provider

Approximate employed	**92%**

Beatles and the James Taylor Quartet,' I was told. **'Bar 1: Bar 2** (650 capacity) at Chalfont has recently been refurbished with a fantastic new lighting and sound system. It and **The Venue** (800) at High Wycombe have ents seven nights a week. Currently among the regular spots are *Crash* (cheese, '70s to today), *Loaded* (indie/alternative), *Platinum* (R&B/garage), *Binary Motives* (hip hop/drum 'n' bass). Then there's the stuff at **The Final Whistle**, Wellesbourne (120 capacity).

High Wycombe itself has various pubs and nightclubs, a cinema, a theatre and a sports centre. A free minibus to the cinema is available to students, as are lifts home after ents nights.

There is an active sports scene, both at BUSA and inter-site level, as you might imagine, but strangely, considering the academic specialism, few campus facilities.

PILLOW TALK

There are two halls at High Wycombe – Brook Street and John North Halls, with self-catering accommodation for 500. At Chalfont a recent development brings the total rooms to 700 (some en suite); there's a choice of self-catering or catered accommodation here.

GETTING THERE

☛ By road to High Wycombe: M40/J4, A4010; to Newland Park, M40/J2, A355, right on to A40, left on to Potkiln Lane.

☛ By rail to High Wycombe: London Marylebone, 35 mins.
☛ By Underground to Chalfont: Chorley Wood (Metropolitan line).

WHAT IT'S REALLY LIKE	
UNIVERSITY:	
Social Life	★★★
Campus scene	**Lively local**
Politics	**Activity low**
Sport	**Sport for all**
National sporting position	**88th**
Arts opportunities	**Music, film good; drama average; art, dance poor**
Student magazine	**Intercourse**
Union ents	**7 pw**
Live venue capacities	**120, 650, 800**
Union Clubs/Societies	**42**
Most popular society	**Surf**
Smoking policy	**None**
Parking	**Non-existent**
TOWN:	
Entertainment Scene	★ **Get to London**
Risk of violence	**Average**
Cost of living	**Very high**
Student concessions	**Excellent**
Survival + 2 nights out	**£50 pw**
Part-time work campus/town	**Good/poor**

THE UNIVERSITY OF CAMBRIDGE

Cambridge Intercollegiate Applications Office
Kellet Lodge
Tennis Court Road
Cambridge CB2 1QJ

TEL 01223 333368
FAX 01223 366383
EMAIL ucam-undergraduate-admissions@lists.cam.ac.uk
WEB www.cam.ac.uk

Cambridge University Students' Union
11/12 Trumpington Street
Cambridge CB2 1QA

TEL 01223 356454/333313
FAX 01223 323244
EMAIL infor@cusu.cam.ac.uk
WEB cusu.cam.ac.uk

VAG VIEW

*C*ambridge University began life early in the 13th century, more than 100 years later than Oxford. Its colleges have always been self-governing, with their own property and income, but the university itself is no slouch as investor: currently it has over £500 million of capital projects in development.

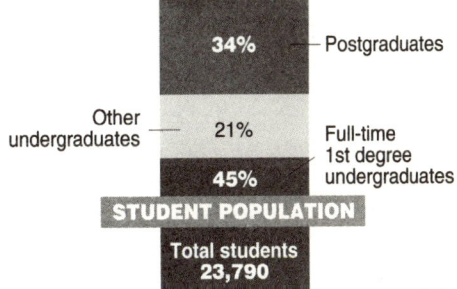

Postgraduates 34%
Other undergraduates — 21%
Full-time 1st degree undergraduates 45%
STUDENT POPULATION
Total students 23,790

UNIVERSITY/STUDENT PROFILE

University since	**1209**
Situation/style	**City collegiate**
Student population	**23,790**
Full-time undergraduates	**10,860**
- mature	**4%**
- overseas	**8%**
- male/female	**54/46**
- state sector intake	**52%, low**
- non-traditional student intake	**6%, low**
- drop-out rate	**1%, low**
- undergraduate applications	**Down 7%**

see Introduction for key to tables

STUDENT PROFILE

First, Cambridge students are bright: in the 2001 entry, 90% achieved three Grade As at A level, compared with 11% across the country.

'If you're thinking of applying to Cambridge: congratulations!' writes Caroline Muspratt, who is studying Modern & Medieval Languages at Christ's. 'Why do I say that? Because even to consider applying, you must be a straight-A student, from a private school, with a white, middle-class background and parents who earn nearly £100K a year. Right?

'Wrong!. It's a common misconception that state school students, ethnic minorities, poor people, etc, don't get in. None of this matters. It won't affect your application, it won't change the friends you make, the societies you join, or the grades you get. I'm from a state school, I have working-class parents, and I'm the first person in my family ever to go to university. And yes, there are people here who went to Eton and have spent their whole lives being groomed for Cambridge: but students are students and the public-state divide is

AT A GLANCE

ACADEMIC FILE:

Subjects assessed	**35**
Excellent	**97%**
Average requirements	**360 points**
Student-staff ratio	**12:1**
First/2:1 degree pass rate	**89%**

ACCOMMODATION FILE

Guarantee to freshers	**100%**
Style	**College rooms**
Catered	**Majority**
Price range pw	**£45-£55**
Town rent pw	**£50-£75**

little more than a media fabrication. The university is extremely welcoming to overseas students and ethnic minorities: CUSU (the students' union) recently won a national award for ethnic diversity and its publication, *The Little Black Book!*

Second, we must conclude from the foregoing that Cambridge students are intensely loyal, for the fact is that the uni *doesn't* meet its generously low application benchmarks either for state school applicants or for social class IIIM, IV or V applicants, or for applicants from so-called 'low participation neighbourhoods'.

It seems that the exclusive nature of the place rubs off pretty quickly on its students from whatever background they come. Asked what kind of relationship students have with townies and with neighbouring Anglia Polytechnic Uni (which has a 95% state school intake as against Cambridge's 52%), working-class Caroline wrote: 'The two institutions rarely mix, though certain societies are open to students from both universities; for instance, an Anglia student was recently Production Manager on the Cambridge University student newspaper. The town and gown divide is more marked, and some city pubs tend to be students-only, or locals-only. There are places where town and gown happily mix – go into almost any of the pubs on King Street, for example, and you'll meet some really friendly people.'

The reason that Caroline tends not to mix with these 'really friendly people' is that she is all bound up with the exclusive Cambridge experience, and this very exclusivity is what going to Cambridge is about. Nor can it be a bad thing if exclusivity only means, as Caroline writes, that 'Cambridge [is] one of the best universities in the world – the teaching quality is unsurpassed.' Can it?

Cambridge impresses and forms its students, it is a strong and ancient culture that few undergraduates would resist. It is exclusive not because it excludes applicants from state schools or working-class families, but because it is an exclusive environment in the sense of unique, and picks students at interview that will not be cowed by its strength, but will meet it with their own.

Now a third-year student, Katie Lydon went to school at Bolton Comprehensive. and is 'more than fulfilled,' and quite unable to identify the typical Cambridge student or dominant group, only the caricature: 'Cliques grow up around sports, drama and other activities, as well as drinking societies and simple friendship groups. Although there is the odd example of the elitist stereotype, they are in the minority. Some groups, like sports teams and drinking societies, can dominate bar areas and seem intimidating, but this only tends to happen a few times a term, or after sporting victories.'

ACADEMIA

Scouring recent records for a ripple in an otherwise glassy-smooth academic performance, we could only come up with the teaching assessment of Veterinary Science: dropped a point – a whole point from perfect! – but actually the only point dropped in assessments undertaken at the four unis so far inspected.

Cambridge were guilty of testing students' memories rather than getting them to think deeply enough, apparently.

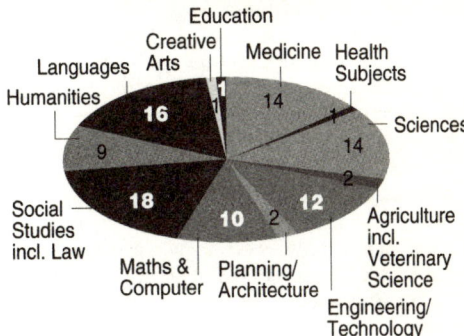

SUBJECT AREAS (%)

ACADEMIC EXCELLENCE

TEACHING:
(Rated Excellent or 17+ out of 24)

Chemistry, History, Law, Computer Science, Architecture, Music, English, Geography, Geology, Anthropology	**Excellent**
Psychology, Molecular Biosci, Organismal Biosci, Pharmacol, Economics, Classics, Philosophy	**24**
Archaeology, Educ, Celtic, Social/Pol Sciences, Theology, Anatomy, Maths, Chem Eng, Materials Science, General Eng, Oriental Studies, Physics & Astronomy, Vet Science	**23**
Modern Langs, Land Economy, History of Art	**22**
Medicine	**21**

RESEARCH:
Top grades 5/5*

Clinical Laboratory Sciences, Community-based Clinical, Hospital-based Clinical, Psychol, Biochem, Zoology, Chemistry, Physics, Earth Sci, Pure Maths, Applied Maths, Statistics, Computer, General Eng, Metallurgy, Law, Asian, Celtic, English, French, German/Dutch/Scandinavian, Italian, Iberian, Linguistics, Classics, Archaeol, History, Hist & Philosophy of Science, Philosophy, Music	**Grade 5***
Education, Theology, History of Art, Russian, Middle East & African, Business, Sociol, Economics, Anthropology, Geography, Town & Country Planning, Chemical Eng, Veterinary, Biotechnol, Plant Sciences, Genetics, Pharmacology, Anatomy	**Grade 5**

'The work ethic is very strong throughout the university,' warns Caroline. 'You'll be expected to study hard, and to achieve a lot in a short time... It can initially be intimidating, and I wasn't the only one who spent the first few weeks convinced that the interviewers had made a mistake. After a few alcohol-aided evenings out with other freshers, you realise that you are on a level pegging with most of them.

'Teaching is done through supervisions and lectures. Supervisions are given by fellows or research students to one or two students. It's a very intensive way of learning, and the short teaching term (eight weeks) means that there isn't much let up. This can take its toll, especially in the stressful summer exam term. Libraries are excellent, but...it can be difficult to get hold of books when the entire year is doing the same paper.'

SOCIAL SCENE

STUDENTS' UNION 'Fresher's Week is organised by college JCRs (Junior Common Rooms), involving pub crawls and ents,' writes Katie. 'What I found especially encouraging was the willingness of the different year groups to mingle, and the fact that you are assigned "college parents" in different years to help you settle in.'

Societies occupy the free time of a large number, and are a way to create a sympathetic circle of friends, wider than your college might allow. The Cambridge Union boasts more than 400 societies. The most active is LesBiGay. Drama Society is big on tours to America and Europe every year, and a high number of productions go to the Edinburgh Festival. Media-wise, 'The two student papers are a training ground for would-be hacks,' adds Katie, 'and positions like May Ball President, Union President and those on the JCRs are awarded after strenuous public hustings, since they develop the communication, teamwork and leadership skills sought by employers.'

There is no central nightclub, but CUSU run popular student nights at local clubs – **Life** on Wednesdays, *Big Holy Noise* @ **5th Avenue** on Tuesdays – and regular clubnight ents at many colleges, open to the whole university. (NB *Jingles*, cheese at Queens', and the infamous drum 'n' bass nights at Clare.) Recent live acts at the university include Pulp, Roni Size, Nitin Sawhney and Wheatus.

SPORT 'Sports facilities are abundant,' writes Katie, 'but vary between colleges. If sport is your thing, check out the college facilities, where exactly the

WHAT IT'S REALLY LIKE

UNIVERSITY:	
Social Life	★★★★
Campus scene	**Bright, exclusive, focused, fun**
Student Union services	**Well organised, but no venue**
Politics	**Active, diverse campaigns**
Sport	**Huge.**
National team position	**11th**
Sport facilities	**Good**
Arts opportunities	**Drama/dance excellent, rest good**
Student magazine	**Inprint, May Anthologies, etc**
Student newspaper	**Varsity, Cambridge Student**
Independent awards	**Best Photog**
Student radio	**CUR**
Radio 1 awards	**Best word prog**
Student TV	**CUTE**
Nightclub	**None**
Union ents	**Town clubs + College JCRs**
Bars	**All colleges**
Union clubs/societies	**400+**
Parking	**Buy a bike**
CITY:	
Entertainment	★★★
Scene	**Cheesy clubs, great pubs**
Town/gown relations	**Average-poor**
Risk of violence	**Low**
Cost of living	**Average**
Student concessions	**Good**
Survival + 2 nights out	**£50-£60 pw**
Part-time work campus/town	**Expellable offence**

playing fields and so on are before you apply. All have or share a boathouse and operate a novice rower training programme, which can be a really good way of getting to know people if you can hack the early mornings.

TOWN 'If you're looking for somewhere with 24-hour opportunity, forget Cambridge; take a 45-minute train ride to London.

'Club fare in town ranges from cheesy, sweaty **5th Avenue** (inexplicably known as **Cindies**) through the slightly nicer **Life** to the new **Toxic 8**. **Po Na Na** and **Fez** are smaller, more chilled and alternative. There is a student night at one or other of these every weeknight.

'What the city lacks in clubs, it makes up for in pubs. There are dozens in the town centre, ranging from cosy locals to trendy wine bars. New restaurants are springing up all the time, best fry-ups are to be had at **Belinda's** and **Martins**. **Chez Gerard** and **Café Rouge** are popular destinations for *diner a deux*, and **Midsummer House** is the favourite mega-expensive place to take your parents. Cambridge is,' says Katie, 'a very safe place to live,' but what does it all cost?

'Cambridge is a relatively cheap city,' writes Caroline. 'If you're trying to work out a budget, allow about £50-£60 per week for food, going out two nights a week, and all the other bits and pieces you'll need. I tend to get through about £500 per eight-week term, not including room rent. Books and equipment usually come free of charge: for scientists, all the scary chemicals are provided, and for arts students, the libraries are amazingly well-stocked. Travel costs should be zero: you'll soon find that everything in Cambridge is within walking distance (unless you're at Girton).

PILLOW TALK

'Room rents are subsidised by the colleges and they are increasing, but you can currently expect to pay about £60 a week on average. Every college has a normal canteen and a Formal Hall. You'll pay between £1-£2 per meal. In Formal Hall, you'll pay about £4, but for this you get a three-course meal with coffee, served by waiting staff as you sit on long, candlelit tables. Grace is said in Latin and vast quantities of wine and port are consumed.'

GETTING THERE

☞ By road: M25/J27, M11/J11, A10. From west or east, A45. From northwest, A604.
☞ By rail: London's Liverpool Street, under the hour; Nottingham, 2:30; Birmingham, 3:00.
☞ By air: Stansted Airport, M11.
☞ By coach: London, 1:50; Birmingham, 2:45; Leeds, 5:00; Bristol, 5:30.

COLLEGE CAMEOS
by Katie Lydon

CHRIST'S

Cambridge CB2 3BU

Tel 01223 334900

WEB www.christs.cam.ac.uk

Founded in 1448, Christ's is a beautiful college situated in its own extensive grounds in the centre of town. It has a strong academic reputation, regularly tops the Tompkins Table, and there's a strong atmosphere of study. Library access is 24-hour access and computer facilities, including room connections, are available. Christ's also makes 'easy offers' to around a third of its intake.

The balance of north/south and state/independent school students is relatively good, with 49% of the 2000/01 intake coming from the state sector. Women are under represented, but not drastically.

Uniquely, there are two bars, though one closes at 8.30pm. The ents committee puts on around four themed nights a term, and there is a formidable biennial May Ball. The JCR publish an alternative prospectus (see web site).

The college sporting reputation has become good and the drama society, CADS, is well known and respected across the university. The college has a squash court and boathouse – sports pitches are twenty minutes away – and use of its own theatre; there is a cinema that puts on both recent releases and classic films.

> *What I found especially encouraging was that you are assigned 'college parents' in different years to help you settle in.*

Writes Christ's Caroline Muspratt of the accommodation: 'The rooms are generally very good apart from the "typewriter", a horrible building at the back of Christ's. You may be lucky enough to get an en-suite bathroom; otherwise you can be sharing with anything from three to twelve people. The kitchens are usually very small and ill-equipped: the college wants to encourage everyone to eat in Hall. Upper Hall opens for breakfast, lunch and dinner, and the food ranges from excellent to mediocre. Formal Hall, which starts later in the evening, is particularly good: you can book in guests, and the three-course meal is served in a medieval dining hall.'

CHURCHILL

Cambridge CB3 0DS

TEL 01223 336000

WEB www.chu.cam.ac.uk

Churchill was founded in 1960. The distance (five-minute cycle) from town is more than compensated for by the extensive grounds, proximity to sports facilities and the relaxation of being off the tourist trail. Academically it is strong and improving – up six places to ninth in the *Tompkins Table* this year, dominant subjects are computing, natural sciences and engineering

The state school presence is high (around 70%), and men are the dominant sex (around 77%), though Churchill was the first all-male college to admit women (1972). While very different from and less photographed than its older, town centre counterparts, Churchill's modern architecture is Grade I listed and popular for its functionality.

College ents are regular and popular with students throughout the university, as is its huge bar. All rooms have network and phone connections, and there are extensive sports facilities on site.

CLARE

Cambridge CB2 1TL

Tel 01223 333246

WEB www.clare.cam.ac.uk

Founded in 1326, Clare is the second oldest college. It occupies extensive grounds that begin in a town-centre huddle of other colleges, and stretch to straddle the River Cam across to the University Library and arts faculties. It is friendly and academically successful – rated in the top six of this year's *Tompkins Table* – and is continually over-subscribed. Students are quite evenly divided between the arts and sciences. English and engineering applicants are encouraged to take a gap year.

Clare choir is famed in Cambridge and throughout the country, and Clare is also home to some of the best alternative ents in the university. Its hugely popular cellar based venue hosts regular live band sessions ranging from jazz to drum 'n' bass, attracting names such as the James Taylor Quartet. Its May Ball is renowned and tickets sought after.

The drama and art societies are particularly good, and Clare sports teams, especially rugby and hockey (men's and women's) and boat club are strong.

Accommodation is usually very good, with most first years living together in the same court, many in en-suite bathrooms. In later years there is the opportunity to move out to the large houses

---

WHERE GRADUATES END UP

15% Health (Medicine, Veterinary), 11% Finance, 9% Manufacturing, 8% Computer, 7% Education, 6% Public Admin — Key Areas

Accountancy, Business/Management*, Advertising, Aeronaut Manufacture, Architec, Eng/Industrial Design, Artistic/Literary, Chem/ Pharmaceutical, Defence, Film/Video, Journalism*, Legal, Publishing, Radio/TV — Niche Areas

*indicates Top 10 Graduate Provider

Approximate employed **96%**

---

that constitute Clare Colony, a short walk along the river.

CORPUS CHRISTI

Cambridge CB2 1RH
Tel 01223338056
WEB www.corpus.cam.ac.uk

Founded in 1352, Corpus is situated right in the centre of Cambridge, opposite Kings (popular myth claims that Corpus actually owns Kings' land and that the lease is soon to expire, to the amusement of the inhabitants of the smaller college). Small but friendly, Corpus' architecture is as pretty as that of its bigger neighbours, but the college is better than most at protecting its students from the constant tourist invasion that can be a liability of a central college.

Corpus places a strong emphasis on academic pursuits, and presents an incentive to achievement in the form of its controversial academic room ballot. Strengths are mainly in the arts, especially history and English, but it is also strong in engineering.

Traditionally enthusiasm is the only pre-requisite here for sport, and the college offers a wide range of facilities, including on-site squash and a strong boat club. There's an annual sports 'Challenge' with Corpus Christi, Oxford.

The JCR is active and the bar a central feature, though its opening hours are variable. The film society puts on a regular mix of classic and new titles, and the drama society (*The Fletcher Players*) is well known and has links with the intimate, adjacent venue, **The Playroom**.

DOWNING

Cambridge CB2 1DQ
Tel 01223 334800
WEB www.downing.cam.ac.uk

Downing is one of the newer town centre colleges, founded in 1800 just off Cambridge's main shopping street, close to the science, architecture and engineering faculties (the Sidgwick arts site is a little further). Once through the gates one finds an array of unusual neo-classical architecture and large, open, green spaces. It's a peaceful retreat, brilliant in summer. The atmosphere is friendly and lively, politically neutral and relaxed.

Academically, Downing is always in the Top 10; all subjects are well represented; law and medicine are particular strengths. The library is well stocked and pleasant, with an especially good law section.

The JCR organises a good Freshers' Week; bar, common room and TV room are excellent. Termly events usually attract big name DJs and are popular across the university. They are perennially successful in sports; particular strengths are rowing, rugby and athletics.

There are network connections in all rooms.

EMMANUEL (EMMA)

Cambridge CB2 3AP
TEL 01223 334200
WEB www.emma.cam.ac.uk

Emma is a relaxed, open college founded in 1584 in the centre of town, opposite the arts cinema and the largest pub in the country. Emma students come from a wide range of backgrounds. It offers scholarships and hardship funds; financial status should never be a barrier to entry.

Emma is also outstanding academically, consistently featuring among the top five colleges. Arts are a particular strength, and it is often the most popular choice for English applicants.

The bar runs weekly funk and cheese events and is the best and most popular in Cambridge. Sport is strong, especially women's rowing and football. There's a squash court and an outdoor swimming pool. The municipal (and indoor) pool is close by, as are most of the shops and both cinemas. Drama and film societies are prominent, and a May Ball happens every other year.

Most rooms have network connections; unusually, Emma offers a free, weekly laundry service.

FITZWILLIAM (FITZ)

Cambridge CB3 0DG
TEL 01223 332000
WEB www.fitz.cam.ac.uk

Founded in 1969, Fitz is one of the newest colleges

in the university, occupying modern, spacious, award-winning buildings – the oldest date from 1963, very different from the classical architecture elsewhere but regarded as functional and user-oriented in a way older colleges often aren't.

Being set a five-minute bike ride away from the town centre in open, generally quiet grounds, students have a reputation for being relaxed and sociable. The college is good academically, comes about mid-*Tompkins Table*, but is not as frenzied as some. A high proportion of its intake comes from state schools.

Tradition isn't as prominent as in other colleges, though there is just enough to remind you that you are at Cambridge. The bar is well-loved and is the centre of social activity, and what are widely thought of as some of the best ents in Cambridge are put on twice termly.

Sport, especially football, is strong, and the college has its own squash court and gym.

GIRTON
Cambridge CB3 0JG
TEL 01223 338999
WEB www.girton.cam.ac.uk
Girton was founded as a women's college in 1869, began to admit men in 1979 and now the latter slightly outnumber the former. It sits on a beautiful 50-acre site a couple of miles out of the city centre and, uniquely, has its own student car park. Architecturally impressive and undisturbed by tourist invasion, the distance encourages a close-knit community and strong collegiate atmosphere; there's a 24-hour garage across the road for bits and pieces, and Girton village isn't far.

Girton isn't the most academic of colleges, the atmosphere is unpressured and relaxed. The **Cellar Bar** is the social focus and ents venue. Girton formal hall food is famed across the university for its quality, so much that the boat clubs and drinking societies of other colleges strive to get themselves invited for dinner. Sport is popular at Girton, and facilities include an on-site indoor heated swimming pool. The boat club is popular and does well.

Students initially live in college, then move out to nearby houses or Wolfson Court – much more central, near the University Library and Sidgwick site.

GONVILLE & CAIUS
Cambridge CB2 1TA
TEL 01223 332447
WEB www.caius.cam.ac.uk
Founded as Gonville in 1348, 'Caius' (pronounced 'Keys') was added to the name in 1558. It occupies a convenient city centre site, but tourist traffic is less than might be expected as it sits between Trinity's famous Great court and King's Chapel.

Caius is academically strong, always in the top half of the *Tompkins Table*, and its particular strengths are in economics, law, history and medicine. The always accessible library is excellent, as are the computer rooms, and most student rooms are connected. Drama and music are popular, and *Caius Films* has become a prominent presenter of varied movies, drawing a cross-collegiate audience.

Sport is taken fairly seriously, with the boat club very successful. Squash, netball, football, hockey and racquet facilities are within a few minutes walk of college and served by a licensed pavilion.

Uniquely its students are compelled to buy forty-five dinner tickets per term at around £4 each. While this may seem a little expensive, the result *is* a stronger college atmosphere.

The college can accommodate all undergraduates well, though again, quite expensively.

HOMERTON
Hills Rd, Cambridge CB2 2PH
TEL 01223 411141
WEB www.homerton.cam.ac.uk
Homerton was founded in 1695 and moved to its present site in 1894. It is a college of education, where students generally complete four years, not matriculating until the second year. Recently, however, there have been reports that Homerton is to scrap the BEd and replace it with a system of first degrees and PGCEs.

Situated a bit out of the town centre, close to the railway station, Homerton tends to cultivate a fairly close community. There is a relatively high proportion of mature students, and women outnumber men. They recruit mainly from state schools, though students are drawn from all backgrounds.

Participation in university activities, such as journalism, drama and politics, is strong. Facilities are excellent – Homerton's on-site sound and dance studios are the rehearsal venue for many university productions. It also boasts its own gym, squash court and sports field. Men's rugby and women's rowing are both strong.

Students initially live in college, but there is the opportunity to move out into houses scattered around the town in later years.

JESUS
Cambridge CB5 8BL
TEL 01223 357626
WEB www.jesus.cam.ac.uk

Jesus was founded in 1496 and, 'greener' and more open than some of its neighbours, overlooks the common and river from its spacious grounds, five minutes from the city centre.

Academically Jesus is relatively strong, and takes its students from a variety of backgrounds. The JCR bar is a popular social hub, but ents are few because of lack of room. Music and drama are strong, and the college offers exhibitions to organ and choral scholars.

Sport is very strong, and the college's location means that all of its facilities, which include pitches for soccer, American football, cricket, rugby and hockey, and squash and tennis courts, are on site. The boat club is a short walk across the common.

Accommodation for all undergraduates is in college or houses across the street – some of the latter have been recently refurbished and a new on-site block of en-suite accommodation opened.

KING'S

Cambridge CB2 1ST
TEL 01223 331100
WEB www.kings.cam.ac.uk

Founded in 1441, King's and its famous chapel are most popularly representative of Cambridge. Its public perception, however, as the epitome of prestige and tradition in Cambridge, contrasts sharply with the reality. It takes over 80% of its students from the state sector and is reputedly obsessed with being politically correct. Its students aren't required to wear gowns at formal dinners or elsewhere – in fact, there are *no* formal arrangements for meals.

King's fame attracts more tourists than any other college, but most come only to visit the chapel, and careful controls ensure that this doesn't impinge on study too much.

Academically King's is average, but its students are the most diverse bunch in the university. The atmosphere is relaxed and while students work hard, they make time for other activities – university drama, politics and journalism all feature high numbers of King's students.

Ents, based in their **Cellar**, are among the best in Cambridge, with queues forming long before the tickets for their famous termly *Mingle* events go on sale. The choir is of course world famous, making several recordings a year, and choral and organ scholarships are offered. Sport isn't a King's strength, perhaps something to do with the fact that its rowers wear purple lycra?

LUCY CAVENDISH

Cambridge CB3 0BU
TEL 01223 332190
WEB www.lucy-cav.cam.ac.uk

Lucy Cavendish was founded in 1965 as a college for mature women. It is placed in a pretty *cul-de-sac* behind St John's, five minutes from the city centre.

Academically, medicine, law and veterinary science are strong. Sport isn't a particular strength, although the first Lucy Cavendish rowing crew hit the river a couple of years ago. Having had to start at the bottom, its reputation has yet to rise to the surface. The college has its own gym and access to squash and badminton courts. There's a summer ball after the festivities of May Week have died down and its own students are still around.

A recently built block of rooms with en-suite facilities has increased the on-site accommodation available to students.

MAGDALENE

Cambridge CB3 0AG
TEL 01223 332100
WEB www.magd.cam.ac.uk

Magdalene (pronounced 'Maudlin'), founded in 1542, straddles Bridge Street, alongside the river on the north side of the city. Its grounds meet those of St John's and allegedly trespass on its land, which why students of the former refer to Magdalene students as their 'villagers'.

You'll hear that there is an overwhelming public school presence, and that tradition is paramount, with a nightly, formal candlelit dinner. In fact, figures do not indicate such a leaning, and Magdalene students claim no atmosphere of elitism or arrogance. Most regard the dinner (non-compulsory) as a pleasant social occasion rather than an imposed tradition.

Academically, it is not outstanding, but its students participate widely in university activities, including sport, drama and journalism, and have recently had a heavy involvement with the Cambridge Union.

Facilities are good – the college shares playing fields with St John's – and it has its own Eton Fives court. Most impressive facility is its music room, with grand piano, two harpsichords and an organ. The bar and other social facilities are good, and well complemented by the adjacent **Pickerel Inn**.

NEW HALL

Huntingdon Rd, CB3 0DF
TEL 01223 351721
WEB www.newhall.cam.ac.uk

Ten minutes walk from the city centre, New Hall was founded in the 1950s to increase access to Cambridge for women. It is still a women-only college, but contrary to popular myth is not an introverted, convent-like place.

Indisputably, many New Hall students are

pooled here as second choice, but many others chose to be there, and the two 'groups' cohere to form a pleasant and sociable community. In a recent referendum held to decide whether to go co-ed, students voted in favour of remaining single-sex.

Academically New Hall is continually close to the bottom of the *Tompkins Table*. Particular strengths are medicine, physics and economics. The college hosts the largest contemporary exhibition of women's art in permanent residence.

Its futuristic **Dome** houses a famed rising kitchen, applauded when it appears at meal times, and is generally thought of as one of the best ent venues in the university, hosting large events with big-name DJs – including the respected termly *Vibrate* – and yes, men *are* allowed in. No May ball, but a garden party is held.

Sports facilities are good, including tennis, squash and netball courts, and the college is close to playing fields. New Hall rowers are feared by other colleges' women crews.

College accommodation is available to all undergraduates.

NEWNHAM

Cambridge CB3 1DF
TEL 01223 334700
WEB www.newn.cam.ac.uk
Newnham was founded in 1871 as an all-women college, continues to admit female students only, and, like New Hall, is anything but insular – guests of both sexes are welcome around the clock...as long as they are accompanied.

The college is situated close to the river and Sidgwick arts site, in attractive grounds with extensive gardens (where, uniquely, you may walk on the grass). Students are from a mix of backgrounds, though predominantly state school. Unspectacular academically, Newnham's strengths are in the arts.

Sport facilities include cricket, hockey, lacrosse, football and rugby pitches, a croquet lawn and tennis courts. Newnham's is the oldest women's boat club in England. Newnham students are also heavily involved in life outside college, particularly in drama and journalism.

PEMBROKE

Cambridge CB2 1RF
TEL 01223 338100
WEB www.pem.cam.ac.uk
Pembroke was founded in 1347 and enjoys the benefits of a central location without the hassles of being on the tourist trail. It has pretty gardens, hidden from the roads by high walls.

Academically strong, computer facilities are good, and student rooms are mostly connected to the network. Pembroke also has busy dramatic, musical and journalistic interests. *The Pembroke Players* and the musical society are known across the university, and the college has its own newspaper, *Pembroke Street*. They also have a popular bar and regular ents, a sports ground and boat club, and enjoy high-level participation and reasonable success in rowing, rugby, football, netball and hockey.

Accommodation is good and either in college or nearby houses; a new block has just been completed.

PETERHOUSE

Cambridge CB2 1RD
TEL 01223 338200
WEB www.pet.cam.ac.uk
Peterhouse is the oldest and smallest college in Cambridge. Founded in 1284, the buildings are attractive and close to Pembroke and the engineering and science faculties.

Reputed to be more stringent than most in its interviewing and admissions procedures, Peterhouse has particular strengths in classics, English, history, law, engineering, maths, medicine and natural sciences. Its stereotype – oft denied – is that of a staunchly right-wing, public-school environment. Men outnumber women significantly, but allegations of a sexist culture appear unfounded as girls from other colleges choose to join Peterhouse choir and other activities. (the college has its own theatre). Sports are actively pursued, particularly rugby, football and rowing. The college also has its own magazine and many of its students are involved in university newspaper journalism.

QUEENS'

Cambridge CB3 9ET
TEL 01223 335511
WEB www.quns.cam.ac.uk
Founded in 1448, in pleasant grounds straddling the river, and close to most faculties, Queens' is open, pleasant, and students say the most people-based college in Cambridge. Certainly its students come from staggeringly different backgrounds. Around the top of the academic league tables, strengths are in natural sciences, medicine, engineering, languages and law.

Facilities are fantastic, including a hall that hosts some of the biggest ents in Cambridge (such as the famed cheesy *Jingles*); it doubles as theatre or sporting venue. The entertainment schedule is the envy of the university, and there is a huge May Ball every other year. The drama society puts on some of the most innovative and controversial plays in Cambridge, there's a thriving gossip magazine, the film society provides a college cinema two nights a week, and the sporting ethos, while placing emphasis on enjoyment, embraces success at university level (there are squash courts and playing fields). Yet, Queen's still manages to remain a genuinely friendly, relaxing, unpretentious, but inspiring place to be.

College can accommodate all students, and all rooms are connected to the internet.

ROBINSON
Cambridge CB3 9AN
TEL 01223 339100
WEB www.rob.cam.ac.uk

Robinson is the newest Cambridge college, founded in 1979 and based in red-brick buildings behind the University Library and arts faculties, next to the uni rugby ground – slightly out of town (five-minute cycle), but close to sports facilities. Its 'new' status means tradition is kept to a minimum. Here, Cambridge stereotypes are despised and disproved.

Academically average, the emphasis is on personal freedoms and development. Robinson draws the majority of its intake from state schools; the atmosphere between staff and students is very open and respectful, with meetings open to everyone.

Ents are well attended and include karaoke and music nights featuring anything from cheese to jazz. The JCR publishes its own alternative prospectus – check the web site.

Accommodation is comfortable, functional and available to all undergraduates.

ST CATHERINE'S (CATZ)
Cambridge CB2 1RL
TEL 01223 338300
WEB www.caths.cam.ac.uk

Catz is a small college on the main street, along from King's, almost opposite Corpus Christi, and within ten minutes' walk of the main arts, science and engineering faculties. Founded in 1473, its relatively small size makes for an inclusive community. There's a good social mix, though women are a minority (usually around 40%).

It has a tradition of academic excellence, though it has recently dropped in the *Tompkins Table*. Strengths are in natural sciences, geography and medicine. The library is new and well stocked.

Even though its ents are generally poor, Catz has a good social tradition: Freshers' Week is legendary, recently the bar and common room have been refurbished, and its formal dinners are popular and over-subscribed.

Music and drama are strong, and Catz has its own 150-capacity theatre in the **Octagon** buildings. The literary Shirley society is the best known in Cambridge. Sport is strong, notably rugby and athletics.

The boathouse is a short cycle away, and facilities are generally good – there's an Astroturf pitch, courts for racquet sports, and pitches for field sports. Swimming is a Catz strength, and though it doesn't have its own pool, the excellent, new town facility is close.

Students live initially in college, moving out to the Octagon colony of flats near the Sidgwick site in the second year.

ST JOHN'S
Cambridge CB2 1TP
TEL 01223 338600
WEB www.joh.cam.ac.uk

St John's was founded in 1511 in the centre of Cambridge, next to its long-standing rival, Trinity. It is the second largest college in Cambridge and so is able to house all its undergraduates. Architecturally impressive, its buildings chart varied and increasingly modern styles, culminating in the listed Cripps Building, seen as ugly by some, but functional and popular accommodation for first years.

Academically, John's is very strong (fourth in the tables for the last couple of years, and generally in the top five) and boasts an impressive and very well-stocked new library. Its beautiful Old Library houses many ancient manuscripts. Computing facilities are excellent, with two main computer rooms and terminals scattered around the library and in the JCR. All student rooms in college have Internet connections. Book grants are automatic; travel grants and hardship loans are generous.

St John's choir is respected globally, the college chapel providing a beautiful setting, and the Jazz Society is famed across the university. Drama – the *Lady Margaret Players* – is a great tradition, the freshers' play a big draw, and they have their own venue in the **School of Pythagoras**, apparently the oldest university building in the country. The film society operates twice a week, and there are disco clubnights three times a term in the underground **Boiler Room**, noted for its drum 'n' bass, hip hop and cabaret. Sport is strong, especially rugby, football and the famous Lady Margaret Boat Club. There are extensive pitches at the back of college and a new boathouse just down the river. There are also squash, badminton, tennis and netball facilities. Finally, John's formal hall is arguably the best (and best value for money), and tickets for their May Ball are among the most sought after.

SELWYN
Cambridge CB3 9DQ
TEL 01223 335846
WEB www.sel.cam.ac.uk

Selwyn was founded in 1882 and sits in pleasant grounds close to the Sidgwick site of arts faculties. The college's proximity to green fields and fifteen-minutes distance from the bustle of the city centre gives it an atmosphere less claustrophobic than most.

Not noted for its academic reputation, though usually in the top half of the *Tompkins Table*, Selwyn's strengths include engineering, history and natural sciences.

There is an even mix between arts and science students and between men and women, and students come from a wide variety of backgrounds.

Facilities are good – the library is satisfactory. For arts students, faculty libraries are on the doorstep and can be equally accessible. Most student rooms are connected to the internet, and communal computer facilities are good.

Drama (*The Mitre Players*) have their own venue in the **Diamond**, and the music and film societies are also active.

Sport is not a major strength, except rowing, where in recent years Selwyn has become a force. The bar is popular, and there are several student run ents. The impressive May Ball is biennial.

All undergraduates can be accommodated either in college or in nearby houses.

SIDNEY SUSSEX
Cambridge CB2 3HU
TEL 01223 338800
WEB www.sidney.cam.ac.uk

Sidney was founded in 1596 on what is known to today's students as 'Sainsbury's Street'. The modern world beyond the gates may be extremely busy, but once inside you'll find architecture dating back 400 years and a relaxed and unpressured atmosphere.

Accommodating a balance of arts and science students, with an even ratio of women to men, Sidney isn't the most academic of colleges, although it is currently pushing its way up the *Tompkins Table*.

The bar is good and run by students, with a sound system better than that of most other college bars, pool table and table football. The frequent ents are well attended

College food has allegedly improved since it was voted second worst in Cambridge in 1993. Sport isn't strong. A sports ground, a short cycle away, is shared with Christ's; the boathouse is close.

Students are accommodated either in college or in nearby houses.

TRINITY
Cambridge CB2 1TQ
TEL 01223 338400
WEB www.trin.cam.ac.uk

Founded in 1546, Trinity is the largest college in Cambridge. Situated centrally with beautiful views onto the river and the Backs and next to St John's, Trinity is its (friendly) rival in almost everything.

The college architecture is much admired, notably the Wren Library and Great Court, whose '*run*' was made famous in *Chariots of Fire* (though actually filmed at Eton).

There is an impressive academic record – they are rarely out of the top four or five in the *Tompkins Table* (No. 3 this year) – particularly in sciences. Contrary to popular belief, it recruits a significant majority from the state sector; women are, however, poorly represented (around 40%).

As befits the richest college in Cambridge, facilities are excellent, the library well stocked and computer facilities first class. Book grants are available to all students, room rents are among the lowest in the uni (although rooms have varying facilities, due to the age of the buildings, all are comfortable).

Ents aren't particularly notable, but the bar is well used, if a bit small. Extra-curricular activities are fervently pursued, and sport is strong. The boat club has recently listed several impressive victories, facilities are superb and nearby.

TRINITY HALL (Tit Hall)
Cambridge CB2 1TJ
TEL 01223 332500
WEB www.trinhall.cam.ac.uk

Trinity Hall was founded in 1350 and nestles in pretty riverside grounds next to Trinity, its bigger and richer rival. There is a popular myth about Trinity porters phoning their Tit Hall counterparts to ask them to turn the music down at some gig – the reply came that Trinity Hall was 'there first' and so would do as it pleased. This anecdote sums up the atmosphere – it's a close, strong community that refuses to be overshadowed by its neighbours simply because of its size. There's a good mix of students and of men and women.

Tit Hall is, according to the *Tompkins Table*, academically average, but its traditional strength is law. The new library, overhanging the river, is well stocked, if a little noisy in the summer, when it's a feature on guided punt tours.

Bar and JCR are lively and ents often referred to as the best. They face tough competition from King's, but are enjoyed for their individual style, the quality that best represents Tit Hall's students.

Sport and sporting facilities are good, and drama and music societies active.

CANTERBURY CHRIST CHURCH UNIVERSITY COLLEGE

Canterbury Christ Church
University College
North Holmes Road
Canterbury
Kent CT1 1QU

TEL 01227 782490
FAX 01227 470442
EMAIL admissions@cant.ac.uk
WEB www.cant.ac.uk

VAG VIEW

*C*anterbury Christ Church University
College, founded by the Church of
England in 1962, is one of a handful of true
university colleges, in that, like a university,
it has the distinction of being allowed to
award its own named degrees. Located in
modern buildings on an historic site (part of
St Augustine's Abbey built in AD597), it was
a teacher training college until, from 1977, it
began developing degree programmes.

Education is still highly rated and 29% of
graduates find work in the industry, but now
the curriculum includes degrees in English,
History, International Business, Art, Music,
Radio, Film & TV (where there are links with
Sky), Religion, Sport Science and social sciences,
and since 1987 there has been a major
expansion in courses for the paramedical and
nursing professions, hence the dominant female-
student presence and 26% health industry take-
up of graduates. As our Academic Excellence
box (page 121) shows, recent teaching
assessments have been uniformly good, but the
real acid test was passed when subjects such as
music, radio/film/TV, art and sport began to
find popular expression in the extra-curricular
life of the college, which is growing fast.

Canterbury is a good place to be – small and

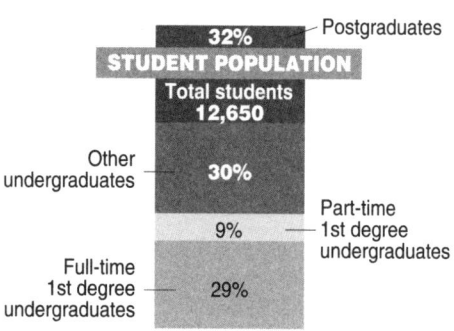

SUBJECT AREAS (%)

Combined — 52
Health Subjects — 26
Sciences 0.2%
Maths & Computer 1%
Business 1%
Humanities 2%
Creative Arts 2%
Education — 16

STUDENT POPULATION

Total students 12,650

Postgraduates 32%
Other undergraduates 30%
Part-time 1st degree undergraduates 9%
Full-time 1st degree undergraduates 29%

friendly, if not exactly jumping with action – as
our reporter, Will Vokes-Dudgeon, discovered:

STUDENT SCENE

'Canterbury is a very small city – just big enough to
hold a cathedral, some run of the mill shops and a
fair range of pubs – and on first visit you might
wonder that there's room for two degree-awarding
institutions. The more widely known of these is the
University of Kent (UKC), a traditional campus
university situated up what has become known to
the thousands of UKC students who trundle up and
down it daily as Mount Everest.

'C4's campus is situated around the other (east)
side of the city, covers relatively little space, is
reasonably hard to find, and, on initial inspection,
looks more like a sixthform college than university.
Everyone, it seems, knows one another, friendliness
being facilitated by the only bar on campus having

COLLEGE/STUDENT PROFILE

University College since	**1999**
Situation/style	**City campus**
Student population	**12,650**
First degree undergraduates	**3,730**
- mature	**43%**
- overseas	**3%**
- male/female	**30/70**
- state sector intake	**95%**
- non-traditional student intake	**7%, low**
- drop-out rate	**10%**
- undergraduate applications	**Down 6%**

*see Introduction for key to tables

AT A GLANCE

ACADEMIC FILE:

Subjects assessed	**23**
Excellent	**74%**
Typical requirements	**200 points**
Students-staff ratio	**21:1**
First/2:1 degree pass rate	**43%**

ACCOMMODATION FILE:

Guarantee to freshers	**35%**
Style	**Halls**
Approx price range pw	**£64-£83**
City rent pw	**£45-£60**

ACADEMIC EXCELLENCE

TEACHING:
(Rated Excellent or 17+ out of 24)

Geography, History	**Excellent**
Maths, Radio/Film/TV Studies, Nursing, Other Subjects Allied to Medicine, Theology	**22**
American Studies, Physics, Chemistry, Leisure/Sport, Business/ Managment, Biosciences	**21**
Psychology, Social Science, Media & Cultural Studies	**20**
Art & Design	**19**

RESEARCH:
*Top grades 5/5** **None**

the capacity of a kennel.

'On a Monday the Students' Union take over one of the local nightclubs, **Churchill's**. This C4 night is a favourite of UKC students, which can have nothing to do with C4's 35/65 male/female ratio, I am sure. Tuesday nights are either karaoke, live comedy or quiz nights at the C4 union, except that every other week students hike up Mount Everest to UKC's nightclub **The Venue**. Wednesday, as at every uni in the UK, is Sports Fed night, where all the teams get horrifically drunk in the SU. Thursday sees the

WHAT IT'S REALLY LIKE

COLLEGE:

Social Life	★★★
Campus scene	**Lively, local**
Politics	**Left of Centre**
Sport	**Competitive + sport-for-all**
National team position	**96th**
Arts opportunities	**Excellent**
Student mag/news	**Eye Eye**
Student radio	**C4 Radio**
Student TV	**CTV**
Union ents	**5 pw**
Live venue capacity	**450**
Union Clubs/Societies	**40**
Smoking policy	**NS except Union**
Parking	**Very poor**

CITY:

Entertainment	★★★
Scene	**Touristy, historic, very studenty; pubs OK**
Town/gown relations	**Good**
Risk of violence	**Low**
Cost of living	**Average**
Student concessions	**Adequate**
Survival + 2 nights out	**£60 pw**
Part-time work campus/town	**OK**

opening of **Frame 25**, the student cinema, which shows recent movies on a weekly basis. Friday night is disco night in the SU bar. There are balls all year round – Freshers', Halloween, Graduation, Christmas – the climax being the huge Summer Ball with fairground and bands such as Republica, Space and the Bluetones, all for the small sum of £35.

'Student media is big: C4 Radio was the first British student radio station to broadcast all over the world via the Internet; it does so more locally on an FM band. There is also CTV, a completely student-run TV station

'Among other societies, Paintballing appears to have taken most by storm this year since sabbaticals returned from a weekend bonding mission well smitten, and there are lots of music groups and student bands, which, unfortunately, have been banned by the Council from playing in the union due to excessive noise levels. There is also a popular Dance and Drama Society

'Sport at C4 is taken seriously, particularly with

WHERE GRADUATES END UP

29% Education*,	Key Areas
26% Health/Social Work*,	
8% Wholesale/Retail,	
6% Manufacturing,	
5% Public Admin	
Radio/TV, Advertising,	Niche Areas
Library/Archival	

*indicates Top 10 Graduate Provider

Approximate employed	**93%**

local rivals UKC, though facilities could be a lot better: the college's **St George's Fitness Centre** includes the usual weights and resistance equipment; a swimming pool lies a few minutes from campus; and strong links with UKC and the local public school, King's, help.

There are a few rooms on site, but most accommodation is beyond campus, the majority of first years (prioritised for halls) living either at Canterbury East (next to the train station) or at the Mount, Vernon Place, or at Northgate, all of which are reasonably close by.'

GETTING THERE
☛ By road: M2 and A2 connect Canterbury to London and beyond.
☛ By coach: London Victoria, 1 hour 45 mins.
☛ By rail: two or three times an hour from London Victoria, Charing Cross and Waterloo East stations. The fast service takes 1 hour 20 mins.

STUDENT CARDIFF - THE CITY

You've perfected the dialect, stocked up on laverbread and exhausted your considerable repertoire of sheep jokes. Now it's time to face reality, you're going to Cardiff. Yes, it is in Wales, but yes, it is also the up-and-coming cosmopolitan British city and a place jam-packed per square yard with the best drinking, dancing and shopping outside of London. Note also that the Welsh know how to have a good time far better than any of us tight-arsed English and rarely worry about the results of such over-indulgence. Note also that, no matter how funny you think it may be, locals will soon tire of your comedy Welsh accent.

SHOPPING
The student loan in your back pocket is going to be burning a hole right about now – interest free overdrafts and credit cards aren't much help either – and the Welsh capital is a fine place to utilise the government's personal little gift to you. All the usual High Street names are here (many with student discounts), but you're going to have to head a little off the beaten track if you really want to stand out from the crowd. First stop, before you're over you're credit limit, is the High Street Arcade. And that had better be a very high credit limit because with shops like **Pussy Galore**, **Wardrobe** and **Absolut** – and the *French Connection*, *Red or Dead*, *Versace* and other designer labels therein – you're going to have to cut down on such extravagences as food and drink for a few weeks.

Back out on Queen's Street is **TK Maxx**: student heaven with its heavily discounted brand name goods. The store keeps last seasons fashions on sale at some 25-50% cheaper than retail and stock everything from underwear to outerwear. **Topshop** is next door with NUS discount and generally reasonable prices, you'll soon find yourself gravitating towards its entrance.

Also worth checking out are **Barkers** and **Chessmen**, both in the Castle Arcade, and both (particularly the former) selling fashionable alternatives to what everybody else is wearing. For those of you of a baggy disposition, **Westworld** is situated just across the road, and with it a healthy selection of *Carhartt* and *Box Fresh* urbanwear.

FILM
Unfortunately the Queen's Street ABC is no more, lost with it the prospect of a sub-£2 cinematic night out. But the ever-popular **Odeon** is still there and a movie with a generous helping of popcorn will still bring you change from a fiver. For those of you with Daddy's car, or at least a decent grasp of the bus timetable, the **UCI** on the Bay will surely have something for you on one of its twelve screens. Looking a little further afield than Hollywood is the **Chapter Arts Centre**. Critically acclaimed left-field productions and a gallery displaying high-calibre exhibits are all there to fire the cells that lectures couldn't.

ARTS
For the more culturally aware among you, Cardiff has a lot to offer. Besides the aforementioned Chapter Arts Centre, there is the beautifully located **National Museum & Gallery** – everything from the pop-art of *David Hockney's Photoworks* to more traditional classical viewing. **The Centre for Visual Arts** also deserves a mention.

Stage-wise, the Welsh capital is blessed with both the **New Theatre** and **The Sherman**, the latter proving student friendly with its NUS concessions and reputation as a prime comedy venue (Craig Charles, Simon Fast Show Day, etc). The venue is also good for Wales' own new breed of playwrights, the current hot ticket being Manic Street Preachers-related Patrick Jones.

EATING OUT
Whilst most bars south of Cathays are not going to suit your fragile student budget, there are a few

gems to be uncovered. A self-styled Latin-American café bar and restaurant popular by word of mouth is **Las Iguanas**. Happy 'hour' (5-7.30pm, all night Sun/Mon) and the early bird menu (before 6.30pm) do not leave one disappointed – at these times, a first-rate three-course meal with two jugs of sangria will set you back no more than a crisp twenty. Choose from nachos, burritos, enchilada or any number of exotic sounding dishes and wonder why you stuck to the take-away tandoori for so long.

Unfortunately for every Iguanas there are another five deco-influenced yuppy hangouts just waiting to sneer at your Oxfam-designer chic and intimidate you with a £3 warm frothy pint and undernourished nouvelle cuisine. If, as a result, you never stray further than the student ghettos of Cathays and Roath and their reassuring array of not-too-fancy pubs, takeaways and greasy-spoons, then (and particularly if a post-tiles stomach-settler is what you're after) I would have to remind you of **Ramon's** and its hangover-easing array of fine fried food. Any student who claims not to have sampled one of Senor Ramon's infamous breakfasts is a liar.

If it's Italian you desire then the choice is varied. **Topo Gigio**, **Giovanni's** or **Waldos** all send a diner home happy. Likewise **Old Orleans**, **Jumping Jacks** and **The New York Deli** if ribs and fries are your choice. Indian and Chinese are too numerous to mention, no doubt you'll soon find a favourite of your own, a post-club hangout where, in your inebriated state, the kindly patron will serve you chips with curry sauce and gently mock your state of mind.

Vegetarians must visit Woodville Road. Never too far from most student lodgings **The Peppermint Lounge** and **Greenhouse** both offer excellent value specialist dishes. Finally, no summary of student hangouts would be complete without **The Warm as Toast Café** (or **Twat's** as your psyche will affectionately recall it). With regular DJ spots and a healthy choice of snacks and meals – most notably the mega, mega breakfast – this café-cum-bar is the perfect space to discuss that exam for which you really should be studying.

PUBS

The Woodville (or Woody for those in the know) is a student haven, running various offers leading to a sub-£1.50 pint, decent cheap food and a buoyant atmosphere. The **Firkin** pubs (of which Cardiff has two) should already be known to you – enjoy their decent own-brews, £3.50 Sunday lunch and giant jenga. There are numerous others, **The Crwys**, **Mackintosh**, **Pen & Wig** to name a few. The city centre is also awash with bars whose expensive drink prices succumb (as do nightclubs) to a student night, the conventional £1 a bottle or the more frivolous happy hour. Of the few with any real character are the – newly opened – **Cuba** and **Bar Emporium**.

CLUBS & LIVE VENUES

Clubbing is an area in which Cardiff comes into its own. What has always been a healthy and vibrant scene is now growing still further into something rivaling the likes of Bristol, Liverpool and Manchester. Through a combination of refurbishment, rethinking, new promoters and considerable cash the city is now drawing in visitors for the club culture alone. Long standing favourites like **The Hippo Club**, **Emporium** and **Zeus** are having the ranks bolstered by a new breed. What was once the slightly dodgy Forum is now self-styled superclub **Apocalypse** – big name DJs of the calibre of Sasha and Judge Jules, weekly – cheap! – student nights and a 6am curfew.

If big name house and trance isn't your thing then head further down town to **Emporium**, still overpriced but with an essential atmosphere and DJs a little left of the mainstream. LTJ Bukem and Bentley Rhythm Ace are among the big names spinning the platters. Tuesday is student night.

On any given day there's a cheap night out in all of the big clubs. For chart and cheese playlists with cheap bottled lager the best in the category has to be **Evolution**, a fair hike down to the bay, but well worth the trek. If leopardskin booths and porn movie ambience is your thing – and to be frank, it should be – **Po Na Na** is a must.

For acts as diverse as Supper Furry Animals, The Beta Band, Barry Manilow and Courteney Pine in recent times, seek out venues like **The Coal Exchange**, **St Davids Hall**, **The CIA** and **The Great Hall**. Closer to the cutting edge is **Clwb Ifor Bach**. It's membership only but with weekly *Xplosure* – new band slots, the hottest underground names at the weekend and various club nights spread over its three floors you would have to be pretty useless not to find something that appeals to you. Traditionalists will want to visit **Café Jazz** or **The Toucan Club**, where those of a jazz-funk-salsa-samba persuasion can strut their polyester-clad selves to some seriously groove-ridden DJs and live bands. They even offer samba lessons in-between.

Maybe it's devolution, maybe it's the untapped potential, hell, it may even be the Manics, Stereophonics and Catatonia – whatever, Cardiff is starting to live up to its remit as a capital city.

Adrian Read

CARDIFF UNIVERSITY

Cardiff University
46 Park Place
Cardiff CF10 3AT

TEL 029 2087 4839
FAX 029 2087 4457
EMAIL prospectus@cardiff.ac.uk
WEB www.cardiff.ac.uk

Cardiff Students' Union
Park Place
Cardiff CF1 3QN

TEL 029 2078 1400
FAX 029 2078 1407
EMAIL studentsunion@cardiff.ac.uk
WEB cardiffstudents.com

VAG VIEW

Cardiff is one of the best deals going. Tip-top uni academically, not the hardest to get into and a fantastic social scene. Yet there are many among English sixthformers who still quibble, which may be what keeps the acceptance rate at a relatively promising level of 1 in 6.

'You have applied to a number of universities,' writes Lisa Andrews, 'but the choice has come down to a place at Cardiff or a place at an English university. Which do you go for? Consider: 34% of the students studying at Cardiff come from Wales, while the majority of the rest move here from English towns. If you are worried you might be outnumbered coming here, forget it.'

CAMPUS

Cardiff is a campus in the city, a kind of academic precinct, separate and yet part of the city. A short walk from the reassuringly classical lines of the main university buildings brings you to the fastest growing capital in Europe. Yet, when you go there what you notice is its compactness and accessibility, its clean lines and the way they have maintained the airiness of a wide open space. The city is also still a cheap place to live – more than 2% below the national average – and the Students' Union conspire to make it more affordable by employing 300 students to service their facilities. Moreover, the crime rate is livable with and decreasing on campus since the introduction of CCTV in the local community and halls. See *Student Cardiff*, page 122.

STUDENT PROFILE

Writes Lisa: 'It's all rain, rugby and sheep, right? Wrong. Okay, so if you opt to study at Cardiff, chances are that nine times out of ten you'll get soaked on the way to lectures and spend the next hour dripping puddles in your pew. And on match days, it's hard to avoid the Welsh rugby spirit, if

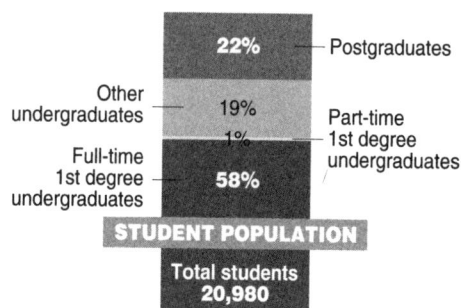

STUDENT POPULATION
Total students
20,980

only because your quiet local is heaving with red-shirted fans. But with 12,000 students of 100 nationalities, Cardiff is nothing if not culturally diverse.'

The statistics support Lisa's case: 11% of degree undergraduates come from beyond Europe, and a highish independent school intake is balanced by a 19% recruitment from the lower socio-economic groups IIIM, IV and V, and a 10% take from the non-traditional student heartlands. It's a well-balanced picture, and there is no surprise that their drop-out rate is way below the national average at 4%.

UNIVERSITY/STUDENT PROFILE	
University since	**1988**
Situation/style	**Civic**
Student population	**20,980**
Full-time undergraduates	**12,240**
- mature	**12%**
- overseas	**11%**
- male/female	**44/56**
- state sector intake	**84%**
- non-traditional student intake	**10%**
- drop-out rate	**4%, low**
- undergraduate applications	**Down 4%**
see Introduction for key to tables	

ACADEMIA

Cardiff's courses range from Photojournalism to Astrophysics, the uni swings neither towards the arts nor the sciences.

Twenty-one subject areas have been assessed as Excellent, one of the best scores in the UK, so good in fact that the uni is moved by some truly amazing results in the recent research assessment exercise – it rose fifteen places in the league table to No. 8 – to distinguish itself from the other federal universities of Wales by awarding its own degrees. It already has the power to do so, but must give the University of Wales two years notice if it intends to wield it. Even if you may sometimes feel, like Lisa, that 'the research programmes in which many Cardiff lecturers are involved take a toll on their availability to students outside of lecture times,' you have to derive some confidence from the result.

The international calibre of research can be gauged by the grades 5 and 5* listed in our *Academic Excellence* box. Now, agreements with Peking University and Tsinghua University will facilitate exchanges of senior academic staff designed to improve quality of research. Meanwhile, Cardiff has become home to the UK's first Centre for Astrobiology – it will link the study of biology with astronomy – and this year they're throwing £3.5 million at the Chemistry

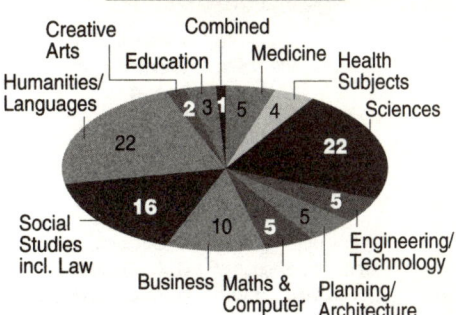

SUBJECT AREAS (%)

Creative Arts — Combined Education — Medicine — Health Subjects — Sciences 22 — Humanities/Languages 22 — 2 3 1 5 4 — Social Studies incl. Law 16 — Business 10 — Maths & Computer 5 — Planning/Architecture 5 — Engineering/Technology 5

Department, creating a new laboratory and other facilities. A further £3.2 million conjures up a 500-seater lecture theatre and resource centre, while £12 million is set aside for next year's project, a new life sciences building.

SOCIAL SCENE

STUDENTS' UNION 'Your NUS card is your passport to the best years of your life. Why? Because it gives you access to Cardiff Students' Union, independently recognised by, er, the *Independent* as the biggest and best equipped in Britain.

'The union is a top-class venue under continual enhancement. The **Tafarn** bar is a relaxed, olde worlde style pub by day and a raucous meeting place after dark, offering optimum consumption of cheap beer. Evenings in the Taf inevitably lead to nights in **Solus**, the union's 1,600-capacity, custom-built nightclub with an immense dance floor and state-of-the-art sound and lighting systems. With an eclectic music policy crossing the spectrum from big beat to cheese, few would dispute that Solus offers some of Cardiff's best nights out.'

The current menu reads Monday, *Fun Factory* (free entry to the most popular party night of the week); Tuesday, *Cheese Factory* and comedy; Wednesday, *Jive Hive* ('60s through to '80s), Thursday, '80s night and cinema; Friday, *Quids In* (Brit pop, big beats and £1-a-pint); Saturday is *Disco Stu* (the union's Saturday night blinder).

For the more discerning, the union has a major concert hall which regularly hosts top bands. The adjoining **Seren Las**, a lunchtime café-bar and intimate club by night, acts as a chill-out room for top-name gigs and is also establishing itself as an underground hotspot for cutting edge drum 'n' bass and dance acts.

The union is not just popular for its bargain booze and carefree clubbing, either. You feel at Cardiff that the union actually looks after your interests. A disastrous undergraduate semester

ACADEMIC EXCELLENCE

TEACHING:
Mechanical Engineering, **Excellent** Chemistry, Architecture, Environmental Engineering, Maritime Studies, English Language, Optometry, Philosophy, Psychology, Town & Country Planning, Pharmacy, Electrical & Electronic Engineering, Archaeology & Ancient History, Biosciences, Accounting & Finance, Anatomy & Physiology, Biochemistry, Civil Eng, Dentistry, Medicine, Education.

RESEARCH:
Top grades 5/5*
Subjects Allied to Medicine, **Grade 5*** Psychology, Civil Eng, English, Theology, Education
Pharmacy, Mammalian & **Grade 5** Medical Biology, Physics, Earth Sciences, Pure Maths, Computer, Electrical & Electronic Eng, Built Environment, Town/Country Planning, Law, Sociology, Business, European Studies, Celtic, Archaeology, History, Media Studies, Music

WHAT IT'S REALLY LIKE

UNIVERSITY:

Social Life	★★★★★
Campus scene	**Vibrant premier scene**
Student Union services	**Good**
Politics	**Activity low**
Sport	**58 clubs**
National team position	**13th**
Sport facilities	**Good**
Arts opportunities	**Excellent**
Student newspaper	**Gair Rhydd**
Guardian awards	**Best campaign**
Student radio	**XPress Radio**
Radio 1 awards	**Best newcomer**
	Best male presenter
Nightclub	**Solus**
Bars	**Tafarn, Seren Las**
Union ents	**Fun Factory, Comedy Club**
Union clubs/societies	**136**
Smoking policy	**Union OK**
Parking	**Adequate**

CITY:

Entertainment	★★★★
Scene	**Buzzing**
Town/gown relations	**Poor**
Risk of violence	**Average**
Cost of living	**Low**
Student concessions	**Excellent**
Survival + 2 nights out	**£50 pw**
Part-time work campus/town	**Good**

uni is a major contender in the BUSA leagues, as well as a consistent producer of talent at international level. The Talybont Sports Centre has a £2 million multi-purpose sports hall and there are 33 acres of pitches. Sports bursaries are available.

The uni forms part of the English Cricket Board's £300,000 Centres of Excellence scheme, which enables young cricketers to combine their talents with a higher education.

PILLOW TALK

University-owned accommodation in Cardiff has all home comforts with the added benefit of freedom from parental control.

All freshers are guaranteed a place in halls of residence, which are of a universally high standard. The bigger residences are over-subscribed, so consider one of the smaller halls – just as modern, but often with larger rooms and a more intimate atmosphere.

However, the university's biggest and newest hall, Talybont, is student paradise, with its own bar and comprehensive sports facilities. It's also next to a 24-hour Tesco: perfect for those midnight munchies and obligatory trolley snatches! The lazy should avoid University Hall, a good half-hour away from the main college: the free bus service isn't so free – Uni Hall rent is £200 extra per year to subsidise it – and all other halls are within easy walking distance.

Most second years move into private accommodation in the student village surrounding

AT A GLANCE

ACADEMIC FILE:

Subjects assessed	**40**
Excellent	**53%**
Average requirements	**300 points**
Students-staff ratio	**19:1**
First/2:1 degree pass rate	**62%**

ACCOMMODATION FILE:

Guarantee to freshers	**100%**
Style	**Halls, flats, village**
Catered	**11%**
En-suite	**75%**
Price range pw	**£39-£68**
City rent pw	**£38-£42**

timetable, introduced a few years ago to allow staff more time for research has been abandoned following a successful campaign by the excellent student newspaper, *Gair Rhydd* (which means *Free Word* and claims 14,500 readers a week). The paper won the *Guardian's* Best Campaign award last year and was runner-up for same in the *Independent* awards.

'Cardiff has one of the best Students' Unions in Britain,' writes Lisa. 'Besides the regular six-night ents programme, it is home to 58 sports clubs and 117 societies. High on the list are the Film Society, Act One, for drama, LGB, the lesbian/gay group, SHAG, sexual health awareness group, etc. Besides the campaigning *Gair Rhydd*, there's XPress Radio, winner of two gongs in the Radio 1 awards this year and now teamed up with local station Galaxy 101 to ensure round the clock broadcasting on 106.2 FM. There's no excuse to leave with just a degree listed on your CV.'

SPORT All traditional sports are catered for and the

the university, where they enjoy the proximity of shops, pubs, and – oh yes – lecture theatres.

Rent is comparatively cheap, but for a reason: Cardiff student houses are not noted for their luxury, only for mice, slugs, and damp.

JOBS

Taking financial activities with accountancy and business, you could say that commerce outdoes public administration as Cardiff's top avenue for graduate employment (see box opposite), though the latter achieves second highest concentration countrywide. There is a whole host of international courses in accounting, economics and business administration, which feed the habit. Also boosting the graduate employment picture is Cardiff's provision to the telecommunications industry and to market research and to engineering/industrial design – electronics and architectural engineering courses are key here. The 9% health provision brings to mind the link with the University of Wales School of Medicine (see entry), plus a wide range of degrees in biosciences, including Applied Biology, Genetics, Neuroscience, Zoology, Anatomical Science, Optometry, Pharmacology... and some interesting BScs in Psychology, such as the joint honours in Psychology and Criminology. Success in areas such as radio/TV and publishing bring to mind success in student media, also the fact that the country's best postgrad course in journalism is run at Cardiff, while in the undergraduate school you can tune in to such as Journalism, Film & Broadcasting in their Faculty of Humanities & Social Studies – a school wide ranging in scope and characterised by a wealth of joint honours courses.

As ever, in a university with good teaching and

> *Cardiff is surely one of the best deals going: tip-top academically, still not the hardest to get into and a fantastic social scene.*

a rich student culture of extra-curricular activity, you find a good employment record, with only 4% left out in the cold.

WHERE GRADUATES END UP	
13% Public Admin*,	Key Areas
11% Manufacturing,	
9% Health/Social Work,	
9% Finance,	
7% Wholesale/Retail,	
6% Education	
Accountancy, Telecom*,	Niche Areas
Aeronautical Manufacture,	
Chemical/Pharmaceutical,	
Eng/Industrial Design*,	
Electron/Electric, Legal,	
Library/Archival,	
Market Research*,	
Publishing, Radio/TV	

*indicates Top 10 Graduate Provider

Approximate employed **96%**

GETTING THERE

☛ By road: M4/J32, A470 signposted Cardiff or M4/J29, A48(M)/A48 and A470 signposted City Centre. Make for the Cathays area of the city.
☛ By rail: London Paddington, 2:30.
☛ By air: Cardiff airport for USA and inland.
☛ By coach: London, 3:00; Manchester, 5:40.

UNIVERSITY OF WALES INSTITUTE, CARDIFF

University of Wales Institute, Cardiff
PO Box 377 Western Avenue
Cardiff CF5 2SG

TEL 029 2041 6070
FAX 029 2041 6286
EMAIL admissions@uwic.ac.uk
WEB www.uwic.ac.uk

UWIC Students' Union
Cyncoed Road
Cardiff CF2 6XD

TEL 029 2041 6190
FAX 029 2076 5569
EMAIL studentunion@uwic.ac.uk
WEB www.uwicsu.co.uk

VAG VIEW

*U*WIC is where it's at for sport. They came in 3rd place overall among BUSA teams last year. This is a small college, tiny compared to Loughborough and Birmingham who pipped it, but the college's commitment, demonstrated recently in the opening of a new running track and National Indoor Athletics Centre, is as complete as the students' commitment to the culture that goes

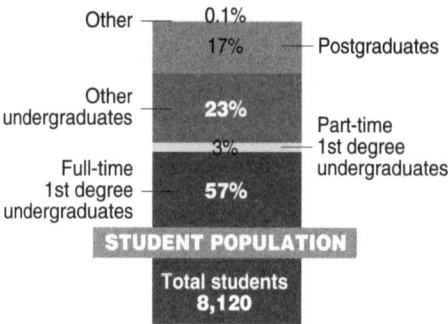

Other — 0.1%
17% — Postgraduates
Other undergraduates — 23%
Part-time 1st degree undergraduates — 3%
Full-time 1st degree undergraduates — 57%

STUDENT POPULATION

Total students
8,120

with it, 'When a Cyncoed student hits the bar, anything goes,' recalls Rob Blunt, musing on 'one of life's unanswered questions: why the essay that was researched, drafted, redrafted and put in a week early always got a lower mark than the one scribbled at four in the morning, assisted by six pints of Caffreys?'

Academically, UWIC's assessment results are hardly much to shout about, and 16 points or less will see you in, but the new Principal is making a real effort to sort things out academically and the restructuring of both academic and administrative staffing is pulling things round.

Two huge achievements by the union have been to buy two established venues in Cardiff city centre – **Reds** nightclub and **Stamps Bar** – an unprecedented deal that makes Wednesday and Thursday student nights: booze is £1 a glass if you pay with the SU's second achievement, namely the Stashcard, a debit card that can be charged up to the tune of £250 and spent at all union outlets and various retailers in the city.

SUBJECT AREAS (%)

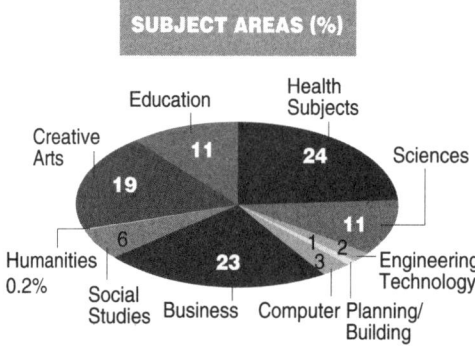

Education — 11
Health Subjects — 24
Creative Arts — 19
Sciences
Engineering Technology — 11
Humanities — 6
0.2%
Social Studies — 23
Business — 3
Computer Planning/ Building — 2

CAMPUS LIFE

CYNCOED CAMPUS Cyncoed Road, Cardiff CF2 6XD. **Faculties:** Education and Sport. **Ents & Ambience:** Teachers and wannabe sports stars, and the highest concentration of first years. **Taffy's Bar** (capacity raised to 500 since recent refurb) is the main UWIC ents venue, and has had a major upgrade with a £15,000 sound and light system. Wednesday and Friday are regular club nights, *Sportsnight* and *Loveshack* respectively. **Sport:** this is where the new, multi-million pound athletics track and Sportlot-funded **National Indoor Athletic Stadium** are to be found alongside rugby, football and cricket pitches, indoor and outdoor tennis courts, gym, indoor cricket nets, swimming pool, volleyball, netball, basketball, badminton and squash courts, and a dance studio. As the **Wales Sports Centre for the Disabled** is also here, they've got some of the best resistance-training equipment available anywhere.

COLCHESTER AVENUE CAMPUS Colchester Avenue, Cardiff CF3 7XR. **Faculties:** Business, Leisure and Food. **Ents & Ambience:** Workaday, daytime scene – Sky TV, darts and PlayStation, but no

AT A GLANCE	
ACADEMIC FILE:	
Subjects assessed	**18**
Excellent	**39%**
Average A level requirements	**16 points**
Students-staff ratio	**20:1**
First/2:1 degree pass rate	**55%**
ACCOMMODATION FILE:	
Guarantee to freshers	**90%**
Style	**Halls**
Approx price range pw	**£48-£67**
City rent pw	**£38-£42**

WHAT IT'S REALLY LIKE	
COLLEGE:	
Social Life	★★★★
Campus scene	**From sports crazy to arts cool**
Politics	**Student issues, interest low**
Sport	**Key**
National team position	**3rd**
Sport facilities	**Excellent**
Arts	**Art, dance excellent; drama, music, film good**
Student magazine	**Retro**
Nightclub	**Reds**
Bars	**Taffy's, Tommy's, TIME^2**
Union ents	**Cheesy, boozy**
Union clubs/societies	**40**
Most popular society	**Christian Union**
Smoking policy	**Bars & halls OK**
Parking	**Just adequate**
CITY:	
Entertainment	★★★★
Scene	**Brilliant**
Town/gown relations	**OK to poor**
Risk of violence	**Average**
Cost of living	**Low**
Student concessions	**Excellent**
Survival + 2 nights out	**£50 pw**
Part-time work campus/town	**Average/excellent**

evening ents or bar at Colly Ave, as it's known. So it's off to Taffy's up the hill at Cyncoed, where you're likely to be housed, too, or across the road to the **Three Brewers**.

HOWARD GARDENS Howard Gardens, Cardiff CF2 1SP. **Faculty:** Fine Art. **Ents & Ambience:** Couldn't be more different from, more alternative to, the sporting scene that dominates the personality of UWIC. **Tommy's Bar** is the focus, recently redesigned by two students who gave it a massive, spray-painted graffiti wall. Eclectic ents on Tuesdays and Fridays.

LLANDAFF CAMPUS Western Avenue, Cardiff CF5

WHERE GRADUATES END UP	
21% Education*,	Key Areas
15% Public Admin*,	
12% Health/Social Work,	
9% Manufacturing,	
8% Wholesale/Retail,	
8% Manufacturing,	
5% Finance	
Hotel/Restaurant, Sport*,	Niche Areas
Defence, Advertising,	
Library/Archival, Telecom	

*Indicates Top 10 Graduate Provider

Approximate employed **91%**

2YB. **Faculties:** Art, Design & Engineering and Community Health Sciences. **Ents & Ambience:** Complete makeover just complete, including – a first for UWIC – an Advice & Representation Centre

(**ARC**) with an educational & welfare officer and full-time welfare adviser. Also here the new **TIME^2** bar and gymnasium. Thursday and Saturday are disco nights here. See *Student Cardiff*, page 122.

PILLOW TALK

UWIC guarantees 90% of first years accommodation. They have 527 single study-bedrooms on Cyncoed, of which 165 are self-catered and en suite, and 50 are self-catered with shared bathroom facilities. The remaining 312 rooms are catered (meals provided centrally). At Plas Gwyn there are 391 rooms – all self-catered, en suite. The Fairwater Halls consist of 100 rooms – all catered for centrally.

GETTING THERE

☛ By road: M4/J29, A48(M)/A48.
☛ By rail: London Paddington, 2:30.
☛ By air: USA and inland destinations.
☛ By coach: London, 3:00; Manchester, 5:40.

UNIVERSITY OF CENTRAL ENGLAND

University of Central England in Birmingham
Franchise Street
Perry Barr
Birmingham B42 2SU

TEL/FAX 0121 331 5595
EMAIL postmaster@uce.ac.uk
WEB www.uce.ac.uk

UCE Students' Union
Franchise Street
Perry Barr
Birmingham B42 2SU

TEL 0121 331 6801
FAX 0121 331 6802
EMAIL union.president@uce.ac.uk
WEB www.unionofstudents.com

VAG VIEW

The University of Central England is a huge, urban conglomeration of a dozen or so sites, incorporating business, engineering & technology, built environment, law & social sciences, computing, health, the enormous Birmingham Institute of Art & Design, and two little gems – the Jewellery School, set in the old Jewellery Quarter, and the Birmingham Conservatoire.

It must be difficult at times for students to see the shape of the whole, although, for most, the uni begins and ends at the main campus, Perry Barr.

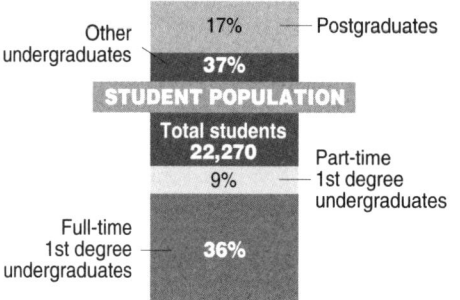

SUBJECT AREAS (%)

- Education
- Health Subjects
- Creative Arts — 20
- 5
- 20
- Engineering/Technology
- 3
- 10
- Languages
- 12
- 15
- 10
- 5
- Social Studies incl. Law
- Business
- Computer
- Planning/Building/Architecture

STUDENT POPULATION

- Other undergraduates — 17% Postgraduates
- 37%
- Total students 22,270
- 9% — Part-time 1st degree undergraduates
- Full-time 1st degree undergraduates — 36%

CAMPUS SITES

PERRY BARR Main UCE campus and Students' Union HQ. **Location:** north of city; approach via M6/M5 Junction 7 and A34 Walsall Road. **Access to city:** 15 minutes by bus plus rail link to Birmingham New Street. **Faculties:** Built Environment, Computing & Information Studies, Engineering & Computer Technology, Health & Community Care, UCE Business School, Law & Social Sciences. **Accommodation:** two halls for 850 students – the Coppice and newly completed Oscott Gardens (en suite); both self-catering. **Bars:** **The Planet**, clubnight (party & dance anthems), discos, Comedy Network, quiz, film, Balti nights, karaoke, hypnotists, etc. plus games & pool room, TV screens.

EDGBASTON CAMPUS Westbourne Road base for the other union centre and bar, **The Edge**. **Location:** Edgbaston, south city suburb; accessed via M5/J3, A456 or M5/J4, AA38. **Access to city:** regular, cheap and late-night bus service. **Faculties:** Education and the newly built Health & Community Care building. **Accommodation:** one hall – 245 single study-bedrooms and 34 shared (two bedrooms and joint study); self-catering. **Bars:** One, modern and expensive. Edge club night (disco, party & club anthems), live acoustic, Balti, theme nights, sports, video racing, hypnotists, etc.

GOSTA GREEN Big bonus access to Aston Guild

UNIVERSITY/STUDENT PROFILE

University since	**1992**
Situation/style	**Civic**
Student population	**22,270**
Full-time degree undergraduates	**8,100**
- mature	**35%**
- overseas	**10%**
- male/female	**40/60**
- state sector intake	**96%**
- non-traditional student intake	**18%, high**
- drop-out rate	**13%, high**
- undergraduate applications	**Up 1%**
see Introduction for key to tables	

facilities. **Location:** adjacent to Aston Uni campus, edge of city centre; accessed via M6/J6, A38M. Ignoring the signs to Aston, leave the A38M at the third exit and take the first exit at Lancaster Circus r/about. **Departments:** Fashion, Textiles & 3-D Design and Visual Communication. **Bars:** See *Aston Uni* entry: 'UCE is a friendly rival,' say the Aston Students' Guild. 'They use our facilities. It's a nice balance to our scientists and business students; about half the people who use our coffee shop are the UCE Arts lot.'

VITTORIA STREET Recent refurbishment makes this the smartest, coolest site within UCE; also state-of-the-art workshops and technology. **Location:** city centre – the famous old Jewellery Quarter – a walk from Birmingham New Street. **Faculty:** UCE's Jewellery School, first to be purpose-built anywhere: Watchmaking and Silversmithing courses included too.

PARADISE CIRCUS This is the purpose-built Conservatoire with small practice rooms and large performance areas. There is a union office and bar.

MARGARET STREET Grade I listed Venetian Gothic property houses the Art Department and is centrally sited.

STUDENT PROFILE
As diverse as its campus sites, but with the emphasis clearly on work-purpose. Many are mature, many local and many from overseas. It's an eclectic mix, but somehow they keep it all together and move their students along with effective commitment.

ACADEMIA
Ex-Birmingham Poly, multi-faceted, proud to maintain its links with its past through the vocational nature of its courses, work placement ideology, strong links with industry, enlightened entry arrangements (GNVQ and Access courses – largely through its network of eighteen associated colleges) and part-timer education, UCE marches into 2002 with an exciting clutch of new courses: BA Human Rights, LLB Law with Legal Practice/American Legal Practice/Criminology, BSc Music Technology, BSc Business Information Technology with Artificial Intelligence, BSc Computing with Artificial Intelligence, BSc Information Systems with Artificial Intelligence, BSc Software Engineering with Artificial Intelligence, BSc Community Health Nursing.

Facilities are good – ten libraries sited at different uni locations (300,000 volumes at Perry Barr alone) – and students can count on in-depth

ACADEMIC EXCELLENCE	
TEACHING:	
(Rated Excellent or 17+ out of 24)	
Music	**Excellent**
Art & Design, Education, Radiog/	**22**
Podiatry/Health Studies	
Communication & Media Studies,	**21**
Economics/Bus/Mgt, Politics	
Town & Country Planning,	**20**
History of Art, Nursing,	
Information Studies	
Electrical & Electronic Eng,	**19**
General Engineering,	
Automative & Manufacturing	
Engineering	
Sociology, Building & Land	**18**
& Property Mgt	
RESEARCH:	
Top grades 5/5*	**None**

source material whatever their specialism.

The Birmingham Conservatoire is a little gem, a lively, creative environment, one of our leading music colleges. It has been going in one form or another since 1859. Into its 525-seat **Adrian Boult Hall** comes an eclectic assortment of the best concert fare that the city has to offer, including its own student musicians of course, for this is largely a performance-based set-up with workshop sessions an important part of the curriculum. The Conservatoire stages some 250 concerts, recitals and masterclasses a year and makes a crucial cultural contribution to the shape of the university.

Overall, recent teaching assessments have been good enough to enable a jump from 60%

AT A GLANCE	
ACADEMIC FILE:	
Subjects assessed	**22**
Excellent	**73%**
Average requirements	**180 points**
Student-staff ratio	**21:1**
First/2:1 degree pass rate	**42%**
ACCOMMODATION FILE	
Guarantee to freshers	**If non-local & apply by 31.5**
Style	**Halls**
Catered	**5%**
En-suite	**19%**
Price range pw	**£44-£70.50**
Town rent pw	**£45**

Excellent or 17points or more out of 24, to 73%, with health, art & design and the all-important education all hitting 22 points.

Last year saw the launch of the long-awaited £110-million Technology Innovation Centre at Millennium Point – a state of the art technology transfer centre to which the uni's engineering and technology degree programmes have now transferred.

> *Diverse and multi-faceted, Central England is proud to maintain its links with its poly past through its course and work-placement ideology, strong links with industry, and enlightened entry arrangements.*

SOCIAL SCENE

STUDENTS' UNION There are three main bars; the largest of them is **Bar 42** at Perry Barr, which holds events all through the week. The main union night of the week is Fridays, *Toons*. Different DJs and acts frequently appear to show off their stuff, and drinks are at crazy student prices. The other two union bars (**The Edge** and the **Village Inn**, once part of Aston Uni's student village at Hansworth Wood, now UCE's so-called Hamstead Campus) are regular drinking spots, providing weekly events such as karaoke, quizzes...yup and cheap drinks all week. The *Dazed and Confused* tour visited this year, and the union holds internal competitions to find UCE's Greatest DJ talent. They're still looking. See also *Student Birmingham*, page 70.

Student newspaper is *Spaghetti Junction*; so far plans to launch a student radio station have not materialised. There are some thirty different societies, the most active being RAG, the charity fund-raiser.

SPORT A new sports facility has been purchased and two of UCE's rugby league players were selected for international duties in the Euro Championships this year.

GETTING THERE

☛ By road: M1, M5, M6 and M40 all give ready access to the city. See also campus notes.
☛ By rail: Bristol Parkway or Sheffield, 1:30; London Euston, 1:40; Liverpool, 2:00; Leeds, 3:00.
☛ By air: regular internal and international flights to Birmingham International Airport, 15 mins' journey time by train to New Street.
☛ By coach: London, 2:40; Bristol, 2:00; Manchester, 2:30.

WHAT IT'S REALLY LIKE

UNIVERSITY:	
Social Life	★★★
Campus scene	**Civic campus, deeply diverse**
Student Union services	**Good**
Politics	**No interest**
Sport	**30 clubs; rugby league strong**
National team position	**127th**
Sport facilities	**Average**
Arts opportunities	**Faculty based**
Student mag/news	**Spaghetti Junction**
Nightclub	**Bar 42, Perry Barr**
Bars	**The Edge, Village Inn**
Union ents	**Friday club night Toons**
Union clubs/societies	**60+**
Most popular society	**RAG**
Smoking policy	**Bars & halls only**
Parking	**OK**
CITY:	
Entertainment	★★★★★
Scene	**Frenzied**
Town/gown relations	**Average**
Risk of violence	**High**
Cost of living	**High**
Student concessions	**Abundant**
Survival + 2 nights out	**£75 pw**
Part-time work campus/town	**Excellent**

WHERE GRADUATES END UP

23% Health/Social Work,	Key Areas
11% Education,	
11% Wholesale/Retail,	
9% Manufacturing,	
6% Finance,	
5% Public Admin	
Architecture, Radio/TV,	Niche Areas
Artistic/Literary,	
Property*, Legal	

*indicates Top 10 Graduate Provider

Approximate employed **92%**

UNIVERSITY OF CENTRAL LANCASHIRE

University of Central Lancashire
Preston
Lancs PR1 2HE

TEL 01772 892400
FAX 01772 894954
EMAIL cenquiries@uclan.ac.uk
WEB www.uclan.ac.uk

Central Lancashire Students' Union
Fylde Road
Preston PR1 2TQ

TEL 01772 513200
FAX 01772 908553
EMAIL supresident@uclan.ac.uk
WEB www.yourunion.co.uk

VAG VIEW

*C*entral Lancashire is expanding fast. The university traces its origins back to 1828, when Preston Institution for the Diffusion of Knowledge was founded. Applications were up 6% last year, thousands attend partner colleges in the north-west of England, and there are around 2,500 postgraduate students. Indeed growth in student numbers now makes them the eighth largest university and the graph is set to continue over the next ten years with the development of electronic and distance learning. All students will experience some elements of this in their study, and some will study this way entirely. The computer infrastructure is in place and students have access to more than 300 software pacakges.

Central Lancs is also known as a caring university. A fourth-year health student, confined in a wheelchair since infancy, went out of her way to praise its accessibility to the disabled, the helpfulness of staff, and for the chance they gave her of the 'few wild years' she had enjoyed there.

Wild indeed, and not only on its beautiful Cumbria Campus at Newton Rigg, Penrith, but also in its approach to entertainment in Preston, for which it has an ents-industry reputation.

Central Lancs is ultimately about getting its graduates jobs, however, and it hunts high and low in recruitment. One unfortunate, if perhaps inevitable, result of its open access and expansionist policy is a current, high drop-out rate of 13%.

CAMPUSES
Besides Preston, they have the aforesaid campus at the head of the Eden Valley, where the Faculty of Land-based Studies is based.

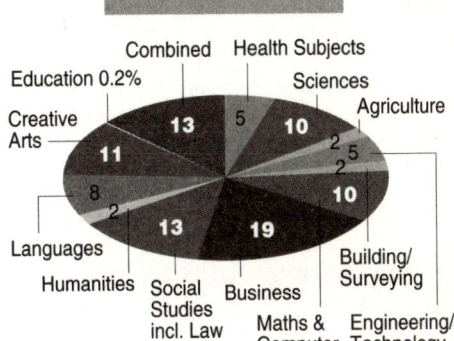

SUBJECT AREAS (%)

Combined 13, Education 0.2%, Creative Arts 11, Languages 8, Humanities 2, Social Studies incl. Law 13, Business 19, Maths & Computer, Health Subjects 5, Sciences 10, Agriculture 2, 2, 5, Engineering/Technology 10, Building/Surveying

STUDENT PROFILE
Central Lancashire is recruiting a large number of undergraduates from the state sector and students from social groups who haven't traditionally benefited from a university education. Mature students make up almost half of undergraduates and a large number of exchange students mingle with an otherwise broadly local student population.

ACADEMIA
In the curriculum they have taken their

UNIVERSITY/STUDENT PROFILE	
University since	**1992**
Situation/style	**Town campus**
Student population	**24,000**
Full-time undergraduates	**9,950**
- mature	**49%**
- overseas	**3%**
- male/female	**44/56**
- state sector intake	**96%**
- non-traditional student intake	**18%, high**
- drop-out rate	**13%**
- undergraduate applications	**Up 6%**
*see Introduction for key to tables	

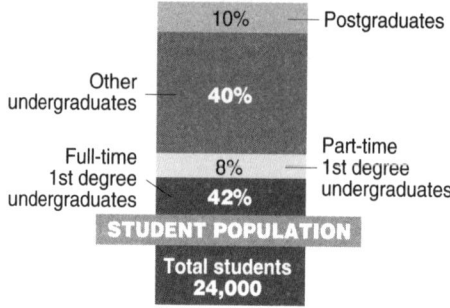

traditional, poly, vocational strengths and given them an international dimension. The European and American exchange programmes are among the most impressive anywhere in the UK and they co-ordinate their partnership policy as far afield as Romania and Russia. As a result, the 'local', city-centre campus is now a very cosmopolitan place; cultural awareness is to the fore; and it is no surprise to learn that the International Society is the most popular with students. All students have the opportunity to spend some study time abroad.

Obviously work-directed is the Faculty of Land-based Studies, which incorporates the academic work of the Cumbria Campus and Myerscough College, and covers forestry, horticulture, equine studies, countryside subjects, tourism and leisure. The campus estate comprises 245 hectares and is made up of the Newton Rigg and Sewborwens farms.

It is when you get into the more singular vocational courses that you begin to wonder whether vocational and university always go hand in hand – the comprehensive degree in Policing, for example, which not only provides specialist study

ACADEMIC EXCELLENCE

TEACHING:
(Rated Excellent or 17+ out of 24)

American Studies, Psychology, Education, Nursing	**24**
Linguistics, Journalism & PR, Subjects Allied to Medicine, Art/Design Biological Sciences, Business, Politics Modern Languages	**22**
	21
Building, General Engineering	**20**
History of Art/Architec/Design, Physics, Astronomy & Maths	**19**
Sociology, Agric & Forestry	**18**

RESEARCH :
Top grades 5/5* **None**

in forensic science, but also in day-to-day beat work. There's also a degree in Motor Sport!

One feels more secure with their much-praised degrees in Journalism and the communications industry, in the nursing and midwifery provision, which, along with Education & Deaf Studies, picked up full marks (24 points) in recent assessments. All in all, the academic picture is increasingly convincing, with Psychology and American Studies also scoring full marks, and the overall Excellence rating rising in three years from 38% to 63%

SOCIAL SCENE

STUDENTS' UNION There are three bars. The

AT A GLANCE

ACADEMIC FILE:

Subjects assessed	**30**
Excellent	**63%**
Average requirements	**200 points**
Students-staff ratio	**18:1**
First/2:1 degree pass rate	**43%**

ACCOMMODATION FILE:

Guarantee to freshers	**95%**
Style	**Halls, flats, hostel**
Catered	**None**
En-suite	**25%**
Price range pw	**£47-£62**
City rent pw	**£35-£45**

Polygon is the main one, open all day (11 am – 11pm) and incorporating a bistro (till 6 pm), pool tables, video games and gaming machines.

The **Venue Bar** (2 am licence from Thursday through Saturday) is open for gigs and events held in the **Venue Hall**, and there's **Union Square** (2 am, Tuesday and Thursday through Saturday), which also operates as a venue. Both Venue Bar and Union Square have recently had money lavished on them. Ents occur on five nights.

Student clubnights organised by *Feel* continue to get excellent reviews, with *Mixmag* referring to the **Venue** as 'one of the best venues in clubland and one of the best house clubs in Britain.'

Talking about performance, it is often forgotten that they also have a serious crack at the arts too. For the last decade they've taken productions to the Edinburgh Fringe, and this year they've got a performing-arts degree module on offer.

Theatre, music, dance and art all go on in **St Peter's Church** and the **Grenfell Baines Gallery**, the uni's arts centre in town.

Journalism was given a further fillip last year

WHAT IT'S REALLY LIKE

UNIVERSITY:

Social Life	★★★★
Campus scene	**Local, mature, but lively**
Student Union services	**Good**
Politics	**Student issues; interest low**
Sport	**Competitive**
National team position	**66th**
Sport facilities	**Good**
Arts	**Drama, dance, film, music excellent; art good**
Student newspaper	**Pluto**
Independent awards	**Sports journalist**
Guardian awards	**Website of Year**
Student radio station	**Yo! fm**
Nightclub	**The Venue**
Bars	**Polygon, Union Square**
Union ents	**Feel, Free2Dance, Stand & Deliver, Bootylicious**
Union clubs/societies	**100**
Most popular society	**International**
Smoking policy	**Union, halls OK**
Parking	**Adequate**

CITY:

Entertainment	★★★
Scene	**Small city scene**
Town/gown relations	**Good**
Risk of violence	**Average**
Cost of living	**Very low**
Student concessions	**Abundant**
Survival + 2 nights out	**£50 pw**
Part-time work campus/town	**Good**

writes Neil Doughty, 'there's always somewhere to hide away out of the rain. Some might contest that with so many pubs you'd need to be careful to avoid the "locals only" places where the only use for sawdust is mopping up the blood after a fight. Not so! With 20,000 students making up a sixth of the in-term residents of Preston, the locals are well aware of the benefit of students to the local economy, and are very accommodating – loads of student discounts, tons of shops, a range of restaurants and two large-screen cinemas mean that there's always something to do when the workload lessens. Staff in venues all over town are always friendly. Even the nightclubs are relaxed both in terms of atmosphere and prices. With no dress code in the week, and drinks prices fair, the town is ideally suited to students. Twice a month the Students' Union is taken over by the wannabe super-club behemoth that is *Feel*, Preston's premier club night. *Feel* is recognised nationally, and, best of all, it'll probably cost you less than a tenner.'

PILLOW TALK

The Student Accommodation Service cannot guarantee all freshers uni accommodation. There are self-catered halls, cluster flats (some en suite), houses and a hostel. New private-sector student flats are being built close to campus.

JOBS

The nursing and midwifery provision accounts for the strong showing in Health (box, below); Land-based Studies the Agriculture/Forestry showing; media the journalism/publishing/radio/TV, and graphic design the artistic strength. Fashion and, unusually, astronomy, also find their graduates certain employment from this uni, so I am told.

when student newspaper *Pluto* picked up Best Journalist in the *Independent* awards, while the student website won the *Guardian* award. Student journalism goes regularly awarded, and three years ago they delivered a student radio station – Yo! fm.

SPORT A £12-million outdoor multisport complex two miles from campus is now open. Nationally, they are about mid-table in the uni leagues. Good facilities are available at Newton Rigg for rugby, football, hockey, netball, basketball, tennis, badminton, and there's a purpose-built weights room. Cumbrian clubs include Climbing Club, Conservation Volunteers and Clay Pigeon.

TOWN And Preston? 'With something like 40–50 pubs within five minutes' walk of the university,'

WHERE GRADUATES END UP

16% Wholesale/Retail*, Key Areas
15% Health/Social Work,
13% Manufacturing,
7% Public Admin,
7% Finance,
6% Education
Agric/Forestry*, Niche Areas
Aeronautical Manufacture,
Artistic/Literary, Sport
Electron/Electric,
Journalism*, Legal,
Publishing, Radio/TV

*indicates Top 10 Graduate Provider

Approximate employed **96%**

GETTING THERE
☛ By road: travelling south, M6 (J32/M55), exit 1 (A6); travelling north, M6/J31, A59.

☛ By rail: London, 3:00; Manchester Oxford Road, 50 mins; Lancaster, 23 mins.
☛ By coach: London, 5:15; Liverpool, 1:00.

CENTRAL SCHOOL OF SPEECH & DRAMA

Central School of Speech & Drama
64 Eaton Avenue
London NW3 3HY

TEL 020 7722 8183
FAX 020 7722 4132
WEB www.cssd.ac.uk

VAG VIEW

*T*his is a drama school with a long and fine reputation, located on two sites, the main one at Swiss Cottage (Finchley Road), the other at 1-5 St Pancras Way, Camden, London NW1 0PB; both are within easy reach of central London. The big drum was beaten recently for new circus skills course – the first degree of its kind – in conjunction with The Circus Space, the outfit once commissioned to train 100 aerialists for the central show in the Millennium Dome. The course is proving very popular.

No residential accommodation, but they'll help you find it. A Students' Union provides a

COLLEGE PROFILE	
Founded	**1906**
Status	**Drama School**
Degree awarding university	**Open Uni**
Situation/style	**2 city sites**
Student population	**726**
Degree undergraduates	**405**
College accommodation	**None**
City rent pw	**£65-£90**

DEGREE COURSES:
Acting, Drama and Education, Theatre Practice, Theatre Practice

range of sporting activities (including netball, squash, yoga, basketball), although sport is generally not high on the list of priorities. Fees are £1,025 per year.

GETTING THERE
☛ Jubilee line to Swiss Cottage or Metropolitan to Finchley Road or Northern line to Camden Town.
☛ No car parking at the school.

CHESTER COLLEGE

Chester College
Parkgate Road
Chester CH1 4BJ

TEL 01244 375444
FAX 01244 373379
EMAIL enquiries@chester.ac.uk
WEB www.chester.ac.uk

VAG VIEW

*F*ounded in 1839 by the Church of England and now an accredited college of the University of Liverpool, the curriculum of this largely local college majors on Education, the industry for which around half of its mainly female graduates are bound.

There are good teaching assessment results, particularly in the most prominent of all its departments, Physical Education/ Sports Science, which daily colours the campus lary green with sportswear and scored 23 points out of 24 at inspection,

pipping Theology, the subject truest to its foundation, which managed a mere 22. Also popular are Drama, English and Psychology, which scored 20. Amongst students of science, maths and computer, there's a particular attraction in a partnership forged with 400 + employers, who are involved in the design of courses, work placements, etc – all part of the career-based learning recipe which characterises their cross-faculty BA/BSc degree programme and facilitates a solid graduate employment rate.

Sport is of obsessive extra-curricular interest and there are constantly evolving facilities to *support it: recently, a refurbished all-weather hockey pitch, a 25m pool, a fitness suite and aerobics arena. The Students' Union organises ents with clubs in town. There's a wide range of accommodation, including ten halls on campus. If you don't get a college-owned room or house in your first year (not everyone does), they'll help you find a place in town.*

GETTING THERE
☛ By road: the college is situated at the junction of the A540 and Cheyney Road.
☛ By rail: London Euston, 2:45; Sheffield, 2:25; Birmingham New Street, 1:45; Liverpool Lime Street, 40 mins; Manchester Oxford Road, 1:00.
☛ By coach: London, 6:00; Sheffield, 3:00.

COLLEGE PROFILE	
Founded	**1839**
Status	**HE College**
Degree awarding university	**Liverpool**
Situation/style	**City campus**
Student population	**6,960**
First degree undergraduates	**2,820**
ACCOMMODATION FILE:	
Availability to freshers	**70%**
Style	**Houses, flats, halls, student village**
Cost pw (no food/food)	**£34-£77**
Town rent pw	**£35-£45**

UNIVERSITY COLLEGE CHICHESTER

University College Chichester
Bishop Otter Campus
College Lane
Chichester PO19 4PE

TEL 01243 816002
FAX 01243 816078
EMAIL admissions@ucc.ac.uk
WEB www.ucc.ac.uk

UC Chichester Students' Union
Bishop Otter Campus
College Lane
Chichester PO19 4PE

TEL 01243 816392
FAX 01243 816391
EMAIL student_union@ucc.ac.uk
WEB www.uccsu.org.uk

VAG VIEW

*T*he college, situated between the South Downs and the sea at Chichester and at nearby Bognor Regis, was earlier known as the West Sussex Institute of Higher Education, then as Chichester College of Higher Education until 1999, when it became University College Chichester and gained the

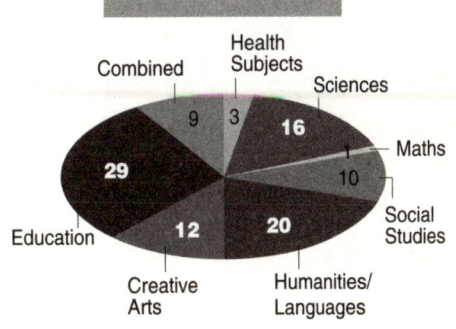

SUBJECT AREAS (%)

Combined — 9
Health Subjects — 3
Sciences — 16
Maths — 1
Social Studies — 10
Humanities/Languages — 20
Creative Arts — 12
Education — 29

power to award its own degrees. Forty-nine per cent of its graduates go into Education.

CAMPUSES
The Bishop Otter Campus, in name at least, takes us back to 1839 when Bishop Otter College was founded by the Church of England as a teacher training establishment; there is, today, a striking modern chapel in the grounds of campus, which itself lies within this walled cathedral city, widely known for its annual Festival of Music and Arts.

The less imaginatively named Bognor Regis

COLLEGE/STUDENT PROFILE	
University College since	**1999**
Situation/style	**Coastal sites**
Student population	**4,530**
Degree undergraduates	**2,510**
- mature	**26%**
- overseas	**4%**
- male/female	**30/70**
- state sector intake	**94%**
- non-traditional student intake	**11%**
- drop-out rate	**7%**
- undergraduate applications	**Up 2%**
see Introduction for key to tables	

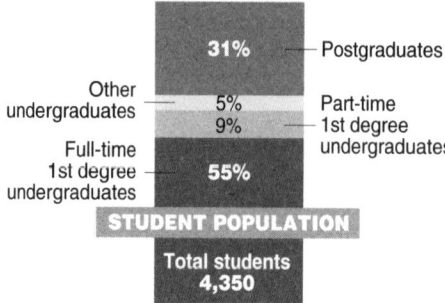

STUDENT POPULATION

31%	Postgraduates
Other undergraduates 5%	Part-time
9%	1st degree undergraduates
Full-time 1st degree undergraduates 55%	

Total students 4,350

Campus lies five miles hence. Bognor is, as it sounds, a rather passé seaside resort.

Bishop Otter is the bigger of the two, though Bognor has most of the teacher training. The campuses are far enough apart to cause something of a psychological split, so currently the Students' Union is preoccupied with getting the bus service between the two improved.

STUDENT PROFILE

Lots of students are local and mature. There is a strong female presence and great sporting prowess.

ACADEMIA

The college delivers a straightforward, well-balanced modular course programme with a focus on religion, sport and the arts. Undergraduates may study for single honours, joint or major/minor programmes, or BA (QTS).

The religious degrees reflect the college's past, of course, while Sport Science brings to mind the more pervasive modern interest of staff and student interests, and sustains a well-equipped Sports Centre. The School of Arts offers modules in Music, Dance, Art, and offers a unique course in Related Arts. There is a strong tradition in jazz and classical music and regular student music society performances and workshops (college and cathedral are regular venues). Dance (ballet, jazz and tap) is supported by a Studio, and, like music and art, involves public performance/exhibition at both student and professional level. The Related

ACADEMIC EXCELLENCE

TEACHING:
(Rated Excellent or 17+ out of 24)

Media	**24**
Art & Design	**22**
Drama/Dance/Cinematics, Sport	**21**
Health Science/Studies	**20**
Business	**19**

Arts course allows specialism in either of the three disiplines, but also looks for useful relationships between them.

There's a Learning Resources Centre at Bishop Otter – a library (200,000 items), a media and computer facility, and art gallery. A similar centre at Bognor Regis has recently been refurbished.

SOCIAL SCENE

The majority of students are local, so weekends are not that big. The union is not fazed by this unduly, being inspired more by the sporting strain (which happens midweek) than the religious or artistic elements, who in any case tend to be the more

WHAT IT'S REALLY LIKE

COLLEGE:	
Social Life	★★★
Campus scene	**Female, sporty, lively ents**
Politics	**Average**
Sport	**Nationally competitive**
National team position	**61st**
Arts opportunities	**Music, dance excellent; drama, art good; film poor**
Venue	**Murray Hall**
Bars	**Bishop's, Macklin**
Union ents	**Discos, etc**
Union clubs/societies	**35**
Most popular csocieties	**Music Theatre, Multi-cultural**
Smoking policy	**Bars, halls OK**
Parking	**Poor**
TOWN:	
Entertainment	★★
Scene	**Arts good**
Risk of violence	**Low**
Cost of living	**High**
Student concessions	**Average**
Survival + 2 nights out	**£50 pw**
Part-time work campus/town	**Good**

'mature' undergraduates.

Wednesday is the Athletic Union"s *Fever Pitch*, and is the usual vomitorium. With more than a quarter first degree undergraduates mature, what, I wonder, does the union give them?

'Lots of coffee,' fires the reply.

'Monday nights we do an Open Mic night in the **Bishops** bar here. We have a stage now, we gutted it out over the summer. A lot of money has gone into this and the **Mac** (the **Macklin**) at Bognor. Fire regs allow 200 at any one time here in Bishops.

AT A GLANCE

ACADEMIC FILE:

Subjects assessed	**11**
Excellent	**64%**
Typical requirements	**180 points**
Students-staff ratio	**22:1**
First/2:1 degree pass rate	**44%**

ACCOMMODATION FILE:

Availability to freshers	**60%**
Style	**Halls, hostels**
Approx price range pw	**£78**
Town rent pw	**£40-£60**

We're strict on ID-ing people because the townies tend to come in under age. Tuesday is a DJ or karaoke, Thursday a pre-clubbers party; what was *Shagadelic* is now called *Bubblegum*. Then we do a deal with **Club Vision** in Bognor. The club puts on coaches. Then Friday night is a DJ chill-out. Saturdays we do events, a film night, same in Bognor. Sunday we do the national *Playstation2* competition. Sometimes, there's low-cost live acts, we do a big market on tribute bands: Robbie Williams and Tom Jones tribute bands, they were stunning…for the money. We have balls, too – Freshers, Graduation – they're our biggest nights.'

Besides the sport clubs, there are alternative music societies, arts societies, role-playing games, even an English Literature Appreciation Society. Oh, and an LGB (gay) Society flourishes, regularly holding events on campus and in a gay pub in the town, though not apparently as brazenly as in some larger institutions. 'There's been a big growth,' says a bod at the union. I presumed that he was referring to student take-up at the Fresher Fayre.

PILLOW TALK
There is catered accommodation available in halls at both sites, and higher capacity and en suite at Bognor.

JOBS
Most graduates go into the education or health industries. The college came 6th nationally in its provision of graduates to the sports industry.

WHERE GRADUATES END UP

49% Education*,	Key Areas
9% Health/Social Work,	
9% Wholesale/Retail,	
6% Public Admin	
Property, Sport*	Niche Area

*indicates Top 10 Graduate Provider

Approximate employed	**93%**

GETTING THERE
☛ By road: to Bishop Otter campus, A286 from the north. From east and west it's the A27. The road between Chichester and Bognor is the A259.
☛ By rail: London Victoria, 0:45; Birmingham, 4:00.
☛ Frequent trains from Gatwick Airport.
☛ By coach: London, 4:40; Birmingham, 6:00.

CITY UNIVERSITY

City University
Northampton Square
London EC1V OHB

TEL 020 7040 5060
FAX 020 7040 8995
EMAIL admissions@city.ac.uk
WEB www.city.ac.uk

City University Students' Union
Northampton Square
London EC1V 0HB

TEL 020 7505 5600
FAX 020 7505 5601
EMAIL massive@city.ac.uk
WEB www.cusuonline,org

VAG VIEW

City University received its Royal Charter granting it full university status in 1966. The university is, as its name suggests, very much at the hub of City life and occupies a singular place in the world of higher education.

CAMPUS
City Uni inhabits the famed City of London, but is only fifteen minutes from the West End, a dawdle from Islington, with its theatres, cinemas, fashionable restaurants, trendy bars, clubs and traditional pubs, and a short way (in the opposite direction) from Clerkenwell, once-artisan London and now a fashionable area for cool, young, City-mile workers. The main university buildings form

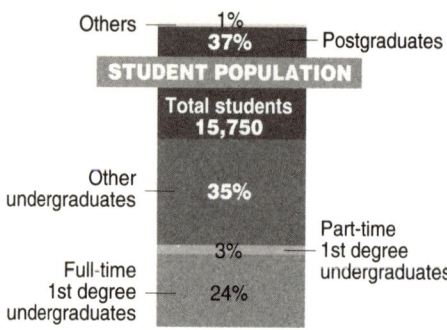

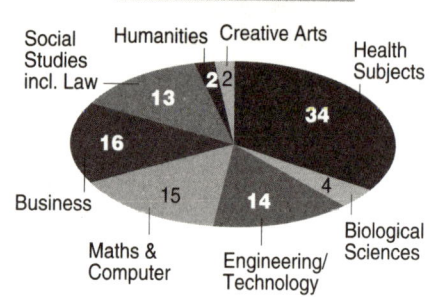

part of Northampton Square. Main library, lecture theatres and Students' Union are here. The Department of Arts Policy and Management are nearby in the Barbican Centre. The Dept. of Radiography and halls of residence are also within walking distance. The St Bartholomew School of Nursing is some way away in West Smithfield and Whitechapel in the East End. The Business School is on the move to new premises in the heart of the city.

'City University is located within walking distance of no less than four tube stations (Barbican, Angel, Farringdon, Old Street), but strangely very few people can ever find it!' writes Catherine Teare. 'Tasteful, grassy Northampton Square, which supports a sizeable bandstand and water trough, has been the site for many an adventure for students – a place to chill in summer and the bandstand a place to shelter when raining. The men's rugby team used to use it for their initiation ceremonies – something about running round it in the buff!'

STUDENT PROFILE

Full-time, first-degree undergraduates, many of whom are mature and from overseas, make up an unusually small percentage of the student body. Many more students are part-timers and there is a large number of postgraduate students. Says Catherine Teare: 'City University is like nowhere else. The mixture of cultures and personalities makes it one of the most diverse universities in London.'

ACADEMIC EXCELLENCE

TEACHING:
(Rated Excellent or 17+ out of 24)

Business & Management, Music	**Excellent**
Art & Design, Maths, Subjects Allied to Medicine	**23**
Electrical & Electronic Eng, Psychology, Library/Info Mgt	**21**
Nursing	**20**
Sociology, Land & Property Mgt, Mechanical & Aeronautical Engineering, Communication & Media Studies, Civil Eng.	**19**

RESEARCH:
Top grades 5/5*

Music	**Grade 5***
Optometry, Law, Business/ Management, Library/Info Management, Art &Design	**Grade 5**

ACADEMIA & JOBS

Formerly the Northampton Institute, the uni places great emphasis on links with industry (in particular engineering, and computing, where many of its graduates end up) and with the professions – journalism, law, banking (a quarter of graduates go into commerce – the Business School is moving teaching to a brand new building in the heart of the City this year, providing, so they say, 'a state-of-the-art resource for management education in the 21st Century). And then there's the health provision – 15% go into the sector; St Bart's School of Nursing and Midwifery is now part of the uni, and there are links with London teaching hospitals.

UNIVERSITY/STUDENT PROFILE

University since	**1966**
Situation/style	**City sites**
Student population	**15,750**
Full-time undergraduates	**3,860**
- mature	**24%**
- overseas	**14%**
- male/female	**48/52**
- state sector intake	**78%**
- non-traditional student intake	**8%**
- drop-out rate	**12%**
- undergraduate applications	**Down 3%**

*see Introduction for key to tables

WHERE GRADUATES END UP

18% Finance*,	Key Areas
18% Wholesale/Retail*,	
14% Health/Social Work,	
8% Manufacturing	
Accountancy, Legal,	Niche Areas
Business/Management*,	
Market Research,	
Property, Publishing*	

*indicates Top 10 Graduate Provider

Approximate employed **95%**

Many courses are taught by lecturers working professionally in the subject area, which is one reason why City scores so well on the careers front. Almost half the staff in the Actuarial Science & Statistics Department, for example, are Fellows of the Institute of Actuaries. There are strong links with the College of Law, where City law graduates (who tend to be particularly well schooled in performance skills) are guaranteed a place to complete their legal practice training. The Journalism degree is also worth special mention as it is widely recognised as one of the leading courses in the country. Delivered in the heart of the capital city's media industry, it too benefits from lecturers with impressive career credentials. Overall the uni's academic record – 83% excellent (see our *Academic Excellence box, page 140*) – is impressive indeed.

SOCIAL SCENE

STUDENTS' UNION The internationally renowned Journalism course (famed for launching our First Lady of Conflict, Kate Adie) provides welcome support to the extra-mural media side of life. The monthly glossy *Massive* keeps students well informed of forthcoming events and current hot topics.

The Students' Union has done well to try to give a stable base for the disparate and scattered student body, but frankly, other than the union-centred weekday entertainments and the sound community life in one of the halls, student life at City is London- rather than university-central. Not all do warm to this, which may well help to explain the high drop- out rate – 12%. Applications fell 3% last year.

'Does City have a campus life? Yes and No,' writes Catherine. 'Students use a number of sites dotted around London, which makes it hard for us to feel like we belong.

'Meeting places include the **University Refectory** (*interesting* food!), the Square and the Students' Union. The Students' Union makes sure it puts on evening entertainment at least three times a week and obviously everybody is welcome.

'There are two bars, a shop and an eaterie as well as a Student Advice Centre and over 60 clubs and societies.

'**Saddler's Bar** is open five days a week from 9am, but closes at 11pm. It has a Western theme (check out the saddles!) and offers a few more extras than the usual pub – pool tables, latest arcade titles, quizzes and a chill-out room on major party nights. The **Wonderbar** venue uses cutting edge design and a phat sound system at night, while in the day it acts a bit more mild mannered as **Poncho's**, a popular Tex Mex-style eaterie, MTV playing in the background to encourage rhythmic chewing.

'At night the Wonderbar can adopt many a guise – gyrating club, band venue, cabaret theatre, football terrace (for live matches), cinema and cocktail bar. Lighting on the variety of club events and gigs is psychedelic, while the stage-mounted DJs are surrounded by pumping dancers. The most popular night is Wednesday when all the 'sporties' come in to celebrate or commiserate over wins and losses.

WHAT IT'S REALLY LIKE

UNIVERSITY:

Social Life	★★★
Campus scene	**Closed weekends**
Student Union services	**Average**
Politics	**Little interest**
Sport	**Striving**
National team position	**90th**
Sport facilities	**Average**
Arts opportunities	**Film excellent; drama avg; art, dance, music poor**
Student magazine	**Massive**
Student newspaper	**Massive Voice**
Nightclub	**Wonderbar**
Bars	**Saddlers**
Union ents	**Cheesy**
Union clubs/societies	**60**
Most popular society	**Film**
Smoking policy	**Bars, halls OK**
Parking	**Non-existent**

CITY:

Entertainment	★★★★★
Scene	**Excellent local pubs, clubs, arts**
Town/gown relations	**Good**
Risk of violence	**Average**
Cost of living	**Very high**
Student concessions	**Good**
Survival + 2 nights out	**£80 pw**
Part-time work campus/town	**Good/excellent**

TOWN 'As City University is located in central London it affords a wild social life. If you walk north towards Angel you come to Upper Street, which must have the most bars and restaurants in one area after the West End. There is something for everyone, cheap and expensive. It has a friendly, safe atmosphere and a 24-hour Sainsbury's on Thursday to Saturday, so you can food-shop at 3am in the morning!

'If you walk west down Roseberry Avenue, you come to **Exmouth Market** and its surrounding area. This offers pretty much the same as Upper Street, but on a smaller scale. Exmouth Market has some of the best sandwich shops in London and, especially in the summer, a really welcoming atmosphere.

'Camden is a mere ten-minute tube ride away, while the West End is twenty minutes on the bus. Many clubs offer discounts to students with an NUS card, but you must make sure you go on the right night. The nearest places to shop are Holloway Road, Oxford Street and Camden.'

> *Strong lines into the professions – business, finance, law, health – and very much a London experience; but don't expect to be nannied.*

SPORT Interest may be high but levels and facilities are not impressive. There are pitches in Walthamstow; a small rowing club is based, of course, on the Thames. There's the Saddler's Sports Centre, with badminton, football, netball, tennis, aerobics and yoga and a good martial arts programme, a couple of squash courts, and some Islington facilities are popular nearby.

PILLOW TALK

There are two halls of residence, both within walking distance of the main site. The first, Finsbury & Heyworth Halls, are linked by a bar/common room; fees include an evening meal and late breakfast on Saturdays and Sundays. Walter Sickert Hall, which overlooks the Regents Canal, is more plush, with en-suite, single study-bedrooms. Next to Finsbury/Heyworth is a block of purpose-built self-catering flats, which comprise three to six single study-bedrooms, living room/kitchen and showers. Newly available to first years are self-contained flats (single study-bedrooms with shared facilities) at Francis Rowley Court, about ten minutes' walk from the uni.

'City University has a number of rooms in halls,' Catherine reports, 'but not enough to accommodate every first year who needs one. I cannot lie, living in London *is* expensive. You can end up paying £90 for a hovel with no heating, if you're not careful.

'The halls are a mixture of flats and single study-bedrooms. Some are en suite and some require you to share facilities with ten other people. Finsbury & Heyworth Halls have a bar, which creates more of a community than is present in other halls. It is run by the Students' Union and, unlike the union, is open at weekends.

'Halls offer safety in your first year, so book early. If you are not lucky enough to get in, then try to share with a large number of people. It is cheaper and more fun than living by yourself. Popular student areas include Hackney, Stoke Newington and Shoreditch.'

GETTING THERE

☞ All sites are well served by buses.
☞ Parking is difficult and expensive.
☞ Nearest Underground stations to main sites: Angel (Northern line), Farringdon and Barbican (Hammersmith & City, Metropolitan and Circle). Moorgate (Hammersmith & City, Metropolitan, Circle and Northern) is close to the Business School.
☞ For the School of Nursing, it's either Whitechapel (District and Metropolitan), Aldgate (Metropolitan), Aldgate East (Metropolitan and District), or Tower Hill (District).

AT A GLANCE

ACADEMIC FILE:

Subjects assessed	**18**
Excellent	**83%**
Average requirements	**260 points**
Students-staff ratio	**14:1**
First/2:1 degree pass rate	**57%**

ACCOMMODATION FILE:

Guarantee to freshers	**65%**
Style	**Halls**
Approx price range pw	**£77-£90**
City rent pw	**£70**

CLEVELAND COLLEGE *see* TEESSIDE UNIVERSITY

COLCHESTER INSTITUTE

Colchester Institute
Sheepen Road
Colchester
Essex CO3 3LL

TEL 01206 518000
FAX 01206 763041
EMAIL info@colch-inst.ac.uk
WEB www.colch-inst.ac.uk

INSTITUTE PROFILE

Founded	**1886**
Status	**F/HE College**
Degree awarding university	**Anglia**
Situation/style	**Town campus**
	Seaside sites
Full-time undergraduates	**578**
Accommodation	**None**
Town rent pw	**£45-£55**

DEGREE SUBJECT AREAS:
Art & design, business, hospitality and leisure management, media, music

There are campuses at Colchester and at Clacton, twelve miles to the south-east. In addition there is The Essex School of

Occupational Therapy (HNDs), based at Witham, ten miles south-west of Colchester. Institute learning resources are good – 100,000 books, tapes, etc, a Media Centre with editing and production equipment, 600 computer workstations. Art and Design scored 22 points out of 24 in the assessments. With an eye to its mature student population, the institute has a nursery with qualified staff.

GETTING THERE

☛ By rail: London Liverpool Street, 47 mins; Norwich, 58 mins; Clacton – Colchester, 27 mins.
☛ By road: A12; from Colchester to Clacton it's the A133; a free bus service runs twice a day between the two campuses.
☛ By coach: London, 2:10; Birmingham, 6:00; Norwich, 6:15.

CORNWALL COLLEGE WITH DUCHY COLLEGE

Cornwall College with Duchy College
Pool
Redruth
Cornwall TR15 3RD

TEL 01209 611611
FAX 01209 611612
EMAIL enquiries@cornwall.ac.uk
WEB www.cornwall.ac.uk

VAG VIEW

Cornwall College encourages local students way down in the depths of Cornwall to get on to all sorts of HND foundation-type courses – from Surf Science to Journalism – often passing them on to Plymouth University to finish them off, as it were. No doubt they'll become an integral part of the mooted University of Cornwall. Actual degrees are Business Admin., Science, and a raft of environmental resource management and health & social care management BScs. There are campuses at Pool – surfing and water sports are a major attraction near here – and at Falmouth, the Marine School, where sailing and fishing are

the thing. Out at Duchy College – Stoke Climsland, Rosewarne and Wadebridge – they offer horse riding and golf courses.

GETTING THERE

☛ By road: A30. By coach: Plymouth, 2:00.
☛ By rail: Plymouth, 1:30

COLLEGE PROFILE

Founded	**1928**
Status	**F/HE College**
Degree awarding university	**Plymouth**
Degree undergraduates	**162**
College accommodation	**Halls**
Availability	**250 places**
Cost pw (no food)	**£50**
Town rent pw	**£50**

COURTAULD INSTITUTE OF ART

The Courtauld Institute of Art
Somerset House
The Strand
London WC2R ORN

TEL 020 7848 2645
FAX 020 7848 2410
EMAIL ugadmissions@courtauld.ac.uk
WEB www.courtauld.ac.uk

VAG VIEW

The Courtauld is the international centre for the study of Art History, for which it scored 23 out of 24 points in the teaching assessments. Its library, together with the institute galleries, the quality of its scholarship, and proximity to centres of artistic interest, such as The National Gallery, The National Portrait Gallery, The Royal Academy and The Hayward Gallery, to name but a few, make it a magnet for students from all over the world.

Belonging to the federal University of London, Courtauld students may avail themselves of its Students' Union in Malet Street and LU intercollegiate halls of residence. The Courtauld sports few ents of its own – one or two parties each term 'with free drink,' and one ball per year. There is no union bar, but the Lyceum, a pub nearby, is it in all but name. As for sport, 'anyone who wishes can play football – very informal, relaxed events.' There are a few societies, a Christian Union, History of Art Reading Group, the Football Club and Postgraduate Society (theatre trips).

Undergraduates are taught in small groups of around eight and there is a one-to-one relationship between each student and his or her personal tutor. European Art and Culture is the focus, which naturally includes European languages. In the main, students go on to teach or work in museums, galleries, auction houses or in publishing.

GETTING THERE

☞ Aldwych (Piccadilly line), Temple (Circle, District), Holborn (Central, Piccadilly), Covent Garden (Piccadilly) are all close by.

COVENTRY UNIVERSITY

Coventry University
Priory Street
Coventry CV1 5FB

TEL 024 7688 7688
FAX 024 7688 8311
EMAIL genenq.ad@coventry.ac.uk
WEB www.coventry.ac.uk

Coventry University Students' Union
Priory Street
Coventry CV1 5FJ

TEL 024 7657 1200
FAX 024 7655 1239
EMAIL suexec@coventry.ac.uk
WEB www.coventry.ac.uk

VAG VIEW

After devastating bombing during the Second World War, Coventry rose from the ashes to become a major industrial force. Elements of what later became the university evolved during this time, and in 1970 the Coventry College of Art merged with Lanchester College of Technology and Rugby College of Engineering Technology to form Lanchester Polytechnic, named after a leading industrialist. In 1987 the name was changed to Coventry Polytechnic. Then, in 1992, the poly became Coventry University.

UNIVERSITY/STUDENT PROFILE

University since	**1992**
Situation/style	**City campus**
Student population	**16,940**
Full-time undergraduates	**9,570**
- mature	**39%**
- overseas	**5%**
- male/female	**56/44**
- state sector intake	**94%**
- non-traditional student intake	**16%**
- drop-out rate	**13%, high**
- undergraduate applications	**Up 0.2%**

*see Introduction for key to tables

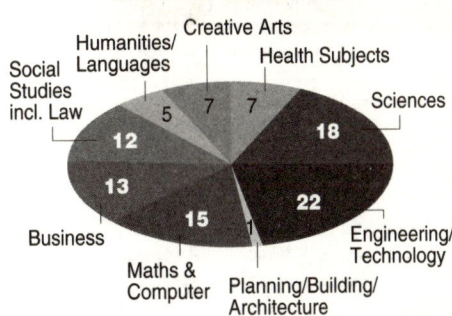

SUBJECT AREAS (%)

Humanities/Languages 7, Creative Arts, Social Studies incl. Law 5, Health Subjects 7, Sciences 18, Business 12, 13, 15, 22 Engineering/Technology, Maths & Computer, Planning/Building/Architecture

CAMPUS

The modern precinct campus is directly opposite the bombed-out ruins of the original cathedral. Looking around the ecclesiastical shell is a thoughtful experience. Students from Cov were sketching it at the time we visited. Especially memorable is a sculpture of reconciliation (two figures embrace to express forgiveness for the Luftwaffe's devastation of Coventry) created by Josefina de Vasconcellos and, as it happens, given by Richard Branson. An identical sculpture stands in the Peace Garden at Hiroshima, Japan.

STUDENT PROFILE

There is a large mature student population, bent on vocational training. Many undergrads come via the state sector from the locality, but also a lot from overseas. A sizeable section of first degree undergrads are part-timers. You will not find it difficult to get in. The uni has been diligent in its open access policy, giving many families their first taste of a university education. Perhaps inevitably, there is a big drop-out rate of 13%.

ACADEMIA

One school's careers master said, 'They have deliberately gone for the vocational – that was their background. We have students for whom Coventry is exactly right.'

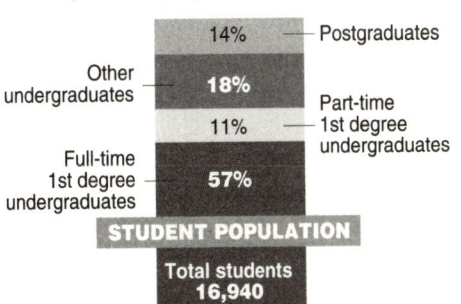

14% — Postgraduates
Other undergraduates 18%
11% — Part-time 1st degree undergraduates
Full-time 1st degree undergraduates 57%

STUDENT POPULATION

Total students 16,940

The continuing connection with industry helps mould its courses and keeps its employment record good and inward investment healthy, while a programme of expansion continues. Last April

ACADEMIC EXCELLENCE

TEACHING:
(Rated Excellent or 17+ out of 24)

Mechanical Engineering, Geography.	**Excellent**
Subjects Allied to Medicine, Economics, History, Maths Politics	**23**
Building, Art/Design, Business & Management, Nursing	**22**
Sociology, Modern Languages, Psychology	**21**
Town & Country Planning, Civil Eng, Biosciences	**19**
Communication & Media Studies, General Engineering, Mech/Aero/Manuf Eng, Electric & Electronic Engineering	**18**

RESEARCH:
*Top grades 5/5** **None**

they acquired the Odeon cinema on Jordan Well, soon to become home to the Performing Arts and Communications, Culture & Media departments. A new £20-million library, claimed to be a model of energy efficiency, is to open this summer. Major investment has been made in WebCT, an electronic learning environment for students. David Grantham, a law lecturer, predicted, 'Eventually we will replace a lot of traditional lecturing because the benefits are so overwhelming.'

The uni has just set in motion £1.5-million plans for an Advanced Digitisation and Modelling

WHAT IT'S REALLY LIKE

UNIVERSITY:	
Social Life	★★★★
Campus scene	**Culturally mixed, city scene**
Student Union services	**Poor**
Politics	**Activity and interest low**
Sport	**Nationally competitive**
National team position	**58th**
Sport facilities	**Average**
Arts opportunities	**Film, art exc.; dance, music popular; drama improving**
Student magazine	**Elephant & Castle**
Student radio	**Phoenix**
Nightclub	**The Planet**
Bars	**Oasis**
Union ents	**Eclectic**
Union clubs/societies	**60**
Smoking policy	**Zonal**
Parking	**Poor**
CITY:	
Entertainment	★★★
Scene	**A few choice clubs 'n pubs**
Town/gown relations	**Poor**
Risk of violence	**Variable**
Cost of living	**Low**
Student concessions	**OK**
Survival + 2 nights out	**£60 pw**
Part-time work campus/town	**Good**

Laboratory to enhance their research into automative design. Traditional emphases are shifting, however. Social sciences and health sciences are increasingly popular, as are courses in communications, and courses in dance and arts practice now lend distinct and very different influences to a symphony of courses no longer dominated by the characteristic Coventry timbre of technology, science and engineering.

> *The continuing connection with industry helps mould its courses and keeps its employment record good and inward investment healthy, but it's no longer all science and engineering at Cov.*

SOCIAL SCENE

The campus is a hive of activity revolving around the sports-themed **Oasis**, the bar on the top floor of the union building. It serves food from breakfast through to late-night munchies and screens all the top sporting fixtures.

Artie and indie types will be found in the **Golden Cross** and **Fads** cafeteria in the art block. Language and engineering students will be found in the library. Sporting people will be found at the union bar or slumped in the corner somewhere. Overseas students spring up everywhere.

Much of uni social life is dominated by societies, particularly sports. Of more unusual societies, Role Play, many different self-defence clubs and the Friends of Palestine group might be of interest. Most have their own local haunts: for example, the **Hope and Anchor** is frequented by 'The Lanch' Rugby Union team. Sporting societies often organise fund-raising events – Man 'O' Man, The Full Monty, the Slave Trade, etc. – and such events are high on the social calendar (and have to be seen to be believed!).

The Planet on the corner of Cox Street and Lower Ford Street, a short walk from campus, describes itself as 'an NUS entertainment venue open to cardholders and up to two guests'. Four levels, the **Millennium Bar**, **Platform 1** (intimate area, futuristic theme), the **Main Area**, and finally the **Mezzanine**, which looks out over the main dancefloor and stage and houses a VIP bar. The nightclub is open from 10pm to 3am, Planet pre-club from 8, where you get all the student fare – karaoke, *Stock Market* drink promos, vodka and tequila nights, live bands. Friday is 'The Unofficial Start to the Weekend' (that's *Phase*, mainline dance and cheesy). When we were there, Saturday night was *Luv Bug*, a '70s night, retro disco spun by Murray Mint and Disco Dick... The previous Friday had seen Judge Jules. Two events were billed – *Flowerz* (to alternate with *Luv Bug*) and *Soul Control*, both showcase house and soul nights.

SPORT The uni made 58th in the overall BUSA ratings for team sports last year, and generally that's about the level. It's had its Olympic swimmers; now there are sports scholarships worth £4,000 to tease out talent in other spheres. Thirty-seven acres of uni playing fields, four miles from the city centre, cater for rugby, soccer, hockey and cricket, and there's a 9-hole golf course. There's also a uni sports complex, the Alma Sports Centre, with facilities for five-a-side football, martial arts, table tennis and weightlifting.

Indoor sports are provided at the Coventry Sports Centre.

Town Cost of living is quite low, and since the university dominates a large part of it, there are lots of student discounts in shops, cinemas and restaurants.

Andrew Losowsky admits the city's lawless reputation: 'Cov has a reputation for being dangerous., which is a shame, as underneath the concrete nightmare is a friendly enough place. Reasons to brave it practically quadrupled with the opening of **Skydome**, a huge multiplex with a sizeable gig venue, nine-screen cinema, bars, restaurants and two outstanding clubs. It'll never quite beat the NEC, but a valiant effort nonetheless, and much closer to home. Most pubs in Cov are of the Rat, Parrot and Firkin ilk, but **The Golden Cross** and **The Hand and Heart** are worth a look for something different.'

PILLOW TALK

'Priory Hall is the largest of the student residences over 600 rooms,' writes Jennifer Johnston. 'It is dominated by lads who haven't yet discovered how to open a tin of beans – yes, you've guessed it – Priory is catered accommodation. Singer Hall is organised into flats and is self-catered. Caradoc Hall is a tower block of self-contained flats and is just out of the city centre. There are lots of suitable student houses in the Stoke, Earlsdon and Radford areas of the city, with good low rents.'

JOBS

Students are encouraged to be career orientated and are given work-experience opportunities. The uni has its own employment agency, CUBE, which finds anything from part-time jobs to graduate careers. In addition, you are encouraged to take on roles of authority and responsibility, to become president of a society or an executive member on the Students' Union committee. The union's magazine, *Elephant and Castle*, encourages budding journalists, and the city's focus on engineering and media should encourage anybody wishing to pursue such a course to come to Coventry.

WHERE GRADUATES END UP	
19% Health/Social Work.	Key Areas
13%Manufacturing,	
8% Public Admin,	
7% Wholesale/Retail,	
7% Personnel*,	
7% Finance,	
5% Education	
Sport, Agric/Forestry,	Niche Areas
Advertising*, Telecom,	
Construction, Journalism	

*indicates Top 10 Graduate Provider

Approximate employed **92%**

GETTING THERE

☛ By road: from London M1/J17, M45, A45, signs for City Centre. From the south, M40/J15, A46, signs for City Centre. From the southwest, M5, M42/J6, A45. From Northwest, M6/J2, City Centre signs. From the north, M1/J21, end of M69, signs to City Centre.
☛ By rail: London Euston, 80 mins; Manchester Piccadilly, 2:30; Nottingham, 1:45; Bristol, 2:30.
☛ By air: Birmingham Airport.
☛ By coach: London, 1:20; Leeds, 4:00.

CRANFIELD UNIVERSITY

Cranfield University
RMCS Shrivenham
Swindon SN6 8LA

TEL 01234 785400
FAX 01234 785768
EMAIL info@cranfield.ac.uk
WEB www.cranfield.ac.uk

Cranfield Association of Students
Shrivenham
Swindon SN6 8LA

TEL 01793 785704
FAX 01793 782551
EMAIL/WEB (via uni site)

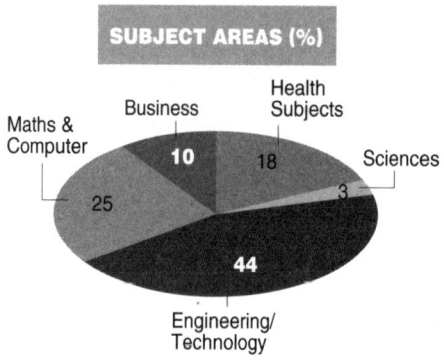

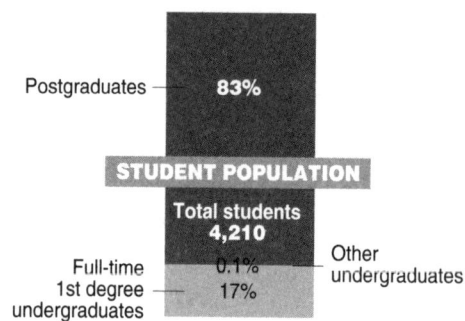

VAG VIEW

A College of Aeronautics was founded at Cranfield, Bedfordshire, in 1946, the idea to harness defence technology for civil purposes. Twenty-three years later the college became Cranfield University, which today is one of Western Europe's largest academic centres for strategic and applied research, development and design. It is unique in its almost entirely postgraduate focus, though there is an undergraduate facility at its Royal Military College of Science, which owes its existence to a contract signed in 1984 with the Ministry of Defence.

From the start the plan was to admit civilians to the RMCS courses as well as military personnel, even though the the college would be situated within a secure military base at Shrivenham in Wiltshire.

CAMPUS

Shrivenham is a spot in the Vale of the White Horse, Oxfordshire, about eight miles northeast of Swindon. The college, set in more than 650 acres, is surrounded by a high security fence. The military ethos is, as one would expect, pervasive and the student experience quite unlike that of a traditional university, particularly as the number of undergraduates is so small.

STUDENT PROFILE

Many of Shrivenham's undergrads are mature, have had experience of work, have careers as officers in the forces, or have come straight from school with University Cadetship commissions. If you come here as an 18-year-old out of civvy street, you can expect to encounter quite an exclusive scene. Bear in mind, in particular, that your military colleagues are likely to have a bit more money to

> *Behind the wire at RMCS Shrivenham a few civvy undergrads can enjoy the rigours of Europe's largest academic centre for strategic and applied research, development and design.*

UNIVERSITY/STUDENT PROFILE

University since	**1969**
Situation/style	**Rural campuses**
Student population	**4,210**
Full-time undergraduates	**700**
- mature	**10%**
- overseas	**8%**
- male/female	**70/30**
- state sector intake	**84%**
- non-traditional student intake	**13%**
- drop-out rate	**13%**
- undergraduate applications	**Not recorded**
see Introduction for key to tables	

AT A GLANCE

ACADEMIC FILE:	
Subjects assessed	**8**
Excellent	**88%**
Average requirements	**220 points**
Students/staff ratio	**2:1**
ACCOMMODATION FILE:	
Guarantee to freshers	**100%**
Style	**Halls, houses**
Approx price range pw	**£45-£70**
Town rent pw	**£50**

spend. One student said, 'The military have loads more money than us civilians and you notice it when you all go out.'

ACADEMIA

Faculties include Engineering (Aero-mechanical

ACADEMIC EXCELLENCE	
TEACHING:	
(Rated Excellent or 17+ out of 24)	
Mechanical Engineering, Management & Business.	**Excellent**
Agriculture, Aeronautical & Manufacturing Engineering, Materials Technology	**22**
Radiography	**21**
General Engineering	**20**
RESEARCH:	
Top grades 5/5	**None**

Systems, Civil, Command & Control, Mechanical, Software, Electrical, Electronic, and Info Technology), Computing & Management, and Radiography. A 'flexible and sympathetic approach to applications' is promised, but they are not about to open the floodgates to applicants, as 'the number of places are few'. This is not necessarily a contradictory proposition if it suggests an awareness that not all candidates are suited to Shrivenham for other reasons.

Once in, there are clear advantages. The uni claims a 2:1 student/staff ratio overall; there are excellent academic facilities (laboratories and workshops) and equipment with technical staff as support, an extensive network of computers, 24-hour access to the Computer Centre (by means of a swipe card outside normal hours), free use of the Internet, a library (100,000+ vols and many thousands of journals, audiovisual aids and specialist reports), text books on loan, a stationery allowance, and scholarships (appropriate to qualifications initially and, once at the uni, to performance in the end-of-year exams).

The Language Unit provides courses in French, German, Spanish, Italian, Russian and Chinese, and there are listening cassettes to help you get a grounding in Arabic, Russian and Japanese, as well as all sorts of other language learning resources. Finally, at the end of a course, your CV carries Cranfield's industry-recognised profile of excellence, described by the uni as 'a virtual guarantee of employment'.

SOCIAL SCENE

There are three bars on campus. On Wednesday night, as a rule, it's a drink in the **Pavilion** and then the local and then there's a party at the **College Club** (known as **The Old Forge** and the subject of a recent major makeover). There's also

WHAT IT'S REALLY LIKE	
UNIVERSITY:	
Social Life	★★
Campus scenes	**Military ethos**
Student Union services	**Basic**
Politics	**Restricted**
Sport	**Locally competitive**
National team position	**127th**
Sport facilities	**OK**
Arts	**Drama, music film OK**
Student news	**Student Matters**
Union ents	**2-3 pw**
Live venue capacity	**200**
Union clubs/societies	**42**
Most popular society	**Car Club**
Smoking policy	**Bars & halls OK**
Parking	**Good**
TOWN:	
Entertainment	★★
Scene	**Pubs, town clubs**
Town/gown relations	**Good**
Risk of violence	**Average**
Cost of living	**Average**
Student concessions	**Not a lot**
Survival + 2 nights out	**£40 pw**
Part-time work campus/town	**Average**

some sort of event on a Friday, live acts about once a month, a Winter Ball and a Military Ball in the summer (disco, ballroom dancing and a casino).

Choral Soc and Orchestral Soc meet regularly, and there's a Drama Society in a theatre, recently refurbed to include tiered seating. The biggest and best supported club is the Car Club with over 250 members and a fully-equipped workshop.

SPORT The tri-service background ensures a keen sporting scene – there are forty-two sports clubs. On-campus facilities include a golf course, swimming pool, even a beagle pack and riding stables; club activities include canoeing, mountaineering, parachuting, gliding, sub-aqua, potholing and sailing.

TOWN On the civvy street side of the fence, Shrivenham village has a couple of pubs – the

Barrington Arms and the Eagle – and you'll find Swindon isn't a bad place for clubs and pubs.

PILLOW TALK

All freshers are offered on-site accommodation in Princes House, which is self-catering. Study bedrooms are graded as small, standard, en-suite and twin and are priced accordingly. You may take meals in the officers' messes.

JOBS

Employment is pretty much guranateed on graduation. See *Employment* box.

GETTING THERE

☛ By road to Shrivenham: M4/J15, then A419, A420. Drive through the village and the college is on the right past the Golf Club.

☛ By rail to Swindon: London Paddington, 52 mins; Birmingham, 1:57; Bristol Temple Meads, 2:39.

☛ By coach to Swindon: London, 2:00.

WHERE GRADUATES END UP	
52% Defence*,	Key Areas
16% Health,	
8% Manufacturing,	
6% Computer	
Aeronautical Manufac,	Niche Areas
Property	
*indicates Top 10 Graduate Provider	
Approximate employed	**98%**

CROYDON COLLEGE

Croydon College
Fairfield
Croydon CR9 1DX

TEL 020 8686 5700
FAX 020 8760 5880
EMAIL info@croydon.ac.uk
WEB www.croydon.ac.uk

VAG VIEW

You could study any of six Sussex BA Business courses at Croydon – with Accounting, Human Resource Management, IT Legal Studies, Marketing, or on its own. There's also a Law degree on offer, and in the School of Art & Design, BA degrees in Photomedia (that's basically photography /editing), Theatre Practice (sets, costume and lighting), Film & Video, Graphic Design, Fashion with Business, Media Design Management and Fine Art.

There are bars, a Students' Association and

COLLEGE PROFILE	
Founded	**1888**
Status	**F/HE College**
Degree awarding universities	**Sussex,**
	Open Uni
Degree undergraduates	**810**
College accommodation	**None**
Town rent pw	**£50**
DEGREE SUBJECT AREAS:	
Fashion, art, design, law, business, accounting, marketing, resource mgt	

ents programme, active music and drama societies and a variety of sports clubs. Croydon lies twenty minutes south of London.

GETTING THERE

☛ By road: A23 south of London.
☛ By rail: London Victoria, 16 mins.

CUMBRIA COLLEGE OF ART & DESIGN

Cumbria College of Art & Design
Brampton Road
Carlisle
Cumbria CA3 9AY

TEL 01228 400300
FAX 01228 514491
EMAIL admissions@cumbriacad.ac.uk
WEB www.cumbriacad.ac.uk

VAG VIEW

*L*ocated on three sites in Carlisle, the main green-field campus overlooking Rickerby Park and the River Eden – paradise indeed – Cumbria is also a cracking college academically, with scores of 21 out of 24 for Art & Design and 19 for Communication & Media in the teaching assessments. It is also exceptionally well kitted out with Apple Macs and PC systems and all the software you could hope for to throw graphics, images and words round the screen to your heart's content, but where it really scores is in its media production facilities – video acquisition and editing technology, from VHS and S-VHS to two Beta-SP edit suites and a range of video-editing and audio-recording systems, including Soft Image animation software. Recently they announced a £4.5 million development incorporating a new library, theatre and dance studio, and improved teaching accommodation. So what's it all for?

The HND and degree course programmes are handled by three Schools: **Communication & Media** – BAs in Graphic Design, Media, Multimedia Design & Digital Animation; **Critical & Contextual Studies** – BAs in Heritage Management, Visual Arts & Culture (art, design & craft from a historical and other contextual points of view), Creative Arts (performance, fine art, literature, music, electronic & lens-based media), and the BA Joint Honours studies: History, Archaeology,

Heritage, Art History, Environmental Studies, Literature, Film, etc.; and the **School of Fine & Applied Arts** – BAs in Design Crafts and Fine Art.

A Students' Union provides all the usual support and ents. While Carlisle itself is not exactly a-buzz with nightlife, with the rise of Northumbria Uni in the town – students use their bar – there's a new attitude brewing.

GETTING THERE

☛ By road: M6/J43, A69 west.
☛ By rail: Preston, 22 mins; Manchester Oxford Road, 2:18; York, 2:46; Newcastle, 1:30.
☛ By coach: Manchester, 2:30; York, 6:45.

COLLEGE PROFILE

Founded	**1822**
Status	**Art College**
Degree awarding university	**Central Lancashire**
Student population	**1,000**
Full-time degree undergraduates	**685**

ACCOMMODATION:

Availability to freshers	**43%**
Style	**Halls**
Cost pw (no food)	**£47.50-£55**
Town rent pw	**£35-£45**

DEGREES:
Archaeology, Contemporary Culture, Creative Writing, Film Studies, History, Journalism, Performance Studies, pop Music, Heritage Management, and various Art & Design faculty courses.

DARTINGTON COLLEGE OF ARTS

Dartington College of Arts
Totnes
Devon TQ9 6EJ

TEL 01803 862224
FAX 01803 863569
EMAIL registry@dartington.ac.uk
WEB www.dartington.ac.uk

VAG VIEW

*D*artington – a village in the shadow of Dartmoor, nestling in the valley of the River Dart, lies just southeast of Buckfast Abbey and a couple of miles northwest of alternative lifestyle haven Totnes. It is an ideal setting to enjoy the intense, artistic Dartington experience and what the QAA

inspectorate recently described as their 'charismatic and innovative teaching'.

There are carefully worked out combined honours programmes involving all the subjects listed in our box on page 152. Resource budgets are spent on performance technology as well as the recently overhauled Library and Resources Centre. Links with professional companies and projects with

COLLEGE PROFILE

Founded	**1961**
Status	**HE College**
Degree awarding university	**Plymouth**
Situation/style	**Rural campus**
Full-time undergraduates	**419**

ACCOMMODATION:

Availability to freshers	**95%**
Style	**Halls**
Cost pw (no food)	**£43-£46**
Town rent pw	**£40-£50**

DEGREE SUBJECT AREAS:
Art & design, writing, arts management, theatre arts, music, performance

clients, both local and European, are part of the deal. They are not hung up on academic qualifications for entry. They'll want to meet you and see what you have to offer personally and artistically.

The student bar is the hub. There's a pool table, games arcade and juke box, and hot food is served from 2-5pm. Ents include poetry slams, bands, jazz nights, competitions, quizzes and theme nights. Much entertainment is made by the students themselves, and at nearby Dartington Arts, an organisation that puts on all kinds of concerts, exhibitions, films and theatre. There's also a five-week Arts Fest at Dartington College in the summer. Local pubs are very good (you'll get a list, well-analysed, when you arrive) and many have student nights, quizzes against the locals, etc. Artistic Totnes is within walking distance, while Torbay, Exeter and Plymouth are nearest for the club scene, etc. For stuff about Exeter and Plymouth, see uni entries.

First years are given priority for hall residence, but on-site accommodation is not guaranteed. Some halls are ten to fifteen minutes' walk away.

Sport is not strong.

GETTING THERE
☞ By road: A38, A384 or A385.
☞ By rail: London Paddington, 2:30 (Exeter); from Birmingham, 3:00. Sometimes trains go through to Totnes, sometimes change.
☞ By coach: London, 5:30; Birmingham, 6:30.

DE MONTFORT UNIVERSITY

De Montfort University
The Gateway
Leicester LE1 9BH

TEL 08459 45 46 47
FAX 0116 2577515
EMAIL enquiry@dmu.ac.uk
WEB www.dmu.ac.uk

De Montfort Students' Union
4 Newarke Close
Leicester LE2 7BJ

TEL 0116 255 5576
FAX 0116 257 6309
EMAIL (see website)
WEB www.dsu.dmu.ac.uk

VAG VIEW

*D*e Montfort has two centres of education, Leicester and Bedford. The recent loss of their Milton Keynes and Lincoln operations coincides with figures that suggest something of a blip in DMU's fortunes: a drop-out rate of 15% and a 7% drop in undergraduate applications. However, the old set-up was always a bitty structure and maybe now they can concentrate on their strengths, which are many and various.

On the bright side, the university came top in the recent research assessments among

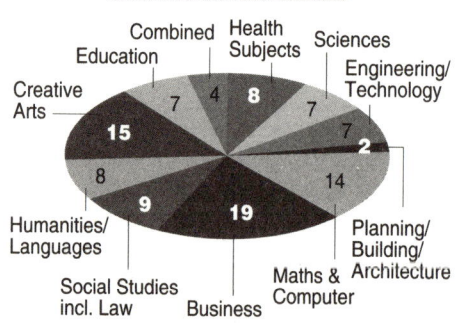

SUBJECT AREAS (%)

Combined Education — 7
Health Subjects — 4
Sciences — 8
Engineering/Technology — 7
Creative Arts — 15
— 7
— 2
Humanities/Languages — 8
— 9
— 19
— 14
Social Studies incl. Law
Business
Maths & Computer
Planning/Building/Architecture

new universities, tying with Sheffield Hallam and gaining two Grade 5s – Politics and English – which indicates international standing.

STUDENT PROFILE

There's a large mature undergraduate population and an open-access policy that brings in many who might not have gone to uni a few years ago. But they're such a fun-loving crew that neighbouring Leicester Uni students are wont to crash in on the excellent ents. Down south, on the Bedford campus, the sportsmen and women drum up their own campus morale, as they do in sports clubs up and down the country.

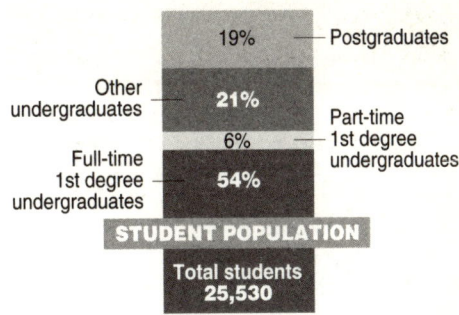

STUDENT POPULATION	
Total students	25,530

UNIVERSITY/STUDENT PROFILE	
University since	**1992**
Situation/style	**City/town campuses**
Student population	**23,530**
Full-time 1st degree undergrads	**12,720**
- mature	**25%**
- overseas	**2%**
- male/female	**47/53**
- state sector intake	**94%**
- non-traditional student intake	**14%**
- drop-out rate	**15%, high**
- undergraduate applications	**Down 7%**
see Introduction for key to tables	

ACADEMIA

Leicester faculties include Applied Sciences, Arts and Multi-disciplinary Studies, Built Environment, Business, Computing Sciences, Design & Manufacture, Engineering and Manufacture, Health and Community Studies, Humanities, Law. The Bedford faculty includes the School of Education which offers teacher training courses and the School of Contemporary Studies comprising humanities and sports science courses.

'I'd recommend DMU for someone who wanted to do something competitive like Pharmacy but didn't have the grades, say, for the School of Pharmacy in London.'

'It's very, very popular, and we have a high regard for it for Business Studies. We are talking here about vocational training – they have an impressive record on employment.'

These are quotes from schools career officers. Our *Academic Excellence* box opposite demonstrates that DMU's priority is being met, and that it isn't all science and business.

Recently, the teaching of the BA Performing Arts and BA/BSC Dance & Drama in Contemporary

Culture was rated 22 out of 24, and last year Politics, with full marks at inspection (and its grade 5 for research), joined a growing list of successes which have taken DMU's 'Excellent' quota from 63% to 73% in two years.

These results are more than ticks on a page. Take the score by the Media Department of 20 out of 24, which has fed interest into extra-curricular journalistic activities. The student radio station, Demon fm, is one of the finest in the country and rarely out of the Radio 1 awards, this year being judged Best Station against university radio stations throughout the land.

SOCIAL SCENE

STUDENTS' UNION/LEICESTER 'De Montfort Students' Union is known for the **Arena** (capacity 1,200, voted 4th best University venue recently) which

ACADEMIC EXCELLENCE	
TEACHING:	
(Rated Excellent or 17+ out of 24)	
Business & Management	**Excellent**
Politics	**24**
Land & Property Management,	**23**
Leisure Industry & Sport	
Drama/Dance/Cinematics,	**22**
Art & Design, Nursing, Psychol	
History of Art, Archit & Design,	**21**
Town & Country Planning,	
Molecular Biosciences,	
Pharmacology	
Communication & Media Studies	**20**
Speech & Language Therapy,	
Maths, Building, Education	
European Studies (Bedford),	**19**
Electric/Electron Engineering,	
Materials Technology,	
General Engineering.	
RESEARCH:	
Top grades 5/5*	
Politics, English	**Grade 5**

regularly has high-calibre bands playing – recently Artful Dodger, Coldplay, Mansun, Craig David, and Atomic Kitten. John Peel calls it his favourite student venue. Thursdays and Saturdays host *Kinky Afro* and *The Big Cheese* respectively, where 1,200 students get extremely drunk together. **The Lava Lounge** is the downstairs bar at the union where cheap drinks are served from 11.30 am till about 11pm, or later if there's a special event. **Toxic** is the upstairs bar in the union with sofa style seating and a mini dancefloor with DJ block.

The Scraptoft Halls have band nights and discos, and hold the annual Grand Summer Ball on their lawns - The

> *DMU is English, media, performing arts, politics, sport, not just science and business, and here, more than at most, the union gets you involved.*

Lightning Seeds and Terrorvision have headlined recently.

TOWN See *Student Leicester – The City*, page 270.

SPORT Bedford are the sporty boys, not Leicester (see *Sport*, below). At Leicester there's an emphasis on fun rather than serious competition. There's the John Sandford Sports Centre, a fitness studio, solarium, weight training and gym. The centre also hosts the ever popular 4-a-side league. Extensive playing fields can be found at Scraptoft. Council-owned facilities for swimming, athletics and cycling are close to the city.'

STUDENTS' UNION/BEDFORD Although Bedford's students are spread between two sites, there is an exceptional sense of community. Bedford students spend a lot of their time at the union bars. Wednesday nights at Polhill are the stuff of legend. Bedford is also the only campus that has balls: Freshers', Christmas and the Summer Ball are always a big success.

SPORT DMU's Bedford campus used to be Bedford's Sports College and features regularly in the BUSA finals. They've been finalists in Women's Rugby at Twickenham and in Men's Football at Walsall FC, and were the first student Men's Hockey finalists in the HA Trophy. Gongs in BUSA Mountain Biking Championships and White Water Kayak Championships give the spread. The annual Rugby Sevens is as famous as it is notorious. The town is also home to the international standard Bedford Athletic Stadium and has three swimming pools.

TOWN Popular off-campus clubnights include Thursday at **Enigma** (excellent prices, countless drinks promotions) and Mondays at **The Club**. There's also **The Plaza** (a bit poor), and **The Limehaus** (cosy but cramped). Bedford's pubs range from the **The Foresters** (traditional), to theme **Porter Blacks** (Irish bar, top Guinness). **The Pilgrims Progress** is excellent value with decent food. For something a bit more classy, try **The Bull Nosed Bat**, **Chicago Rock Café** or **Yates**.

For cinema, theatre and comedy, Lansdowne has the **Bowen West Theatre**, which stages both national and university productions and runs dance studios. In the town centre there is the **Corn Exchange**, which has seen the likes of Eddie Izzard grace its stage. The **Aspects** complex is five

WHAT IT'S REALLY LIKE

UNIVERSITY:	
Social Life	★★★★
Campus scene	**Unpretentious, fun-loving, studenty**
Student Union services	**Good**
Politics	**Recent major successes**
Sport	**Competitive**
National team position	**37th (Bedford)**
Sport facilities	**Good**
Arts opportunities	**Average, music & film good**
Student newspaper	**Fusion**
Student radio	**Demon FM**
Radio 1 awards	**Station of 2001**
Nightclub	**Arena**
Bars	**Toxic, Lava Lounge**
Union ents	**Massive**
Union clubs/societies	**60+**
Most popular society	**Demon FM, Football**
Smoking policy	**Union, bars OK**
Parking	**Poor-adequate**
CITY/TOWN:	
Leicester Nightlife	★★★★★
City scene	**Top town - clubs, pubs, curries**
Town/gown relations	**OK**
Risk of violence	**Average-high**
Cost of living	**Average**
Student concessions	**Good**
Survival + 2 nights out	**£60 pw**
Part-time work campus/town	**Leicester, good**

minutes' walk from Polhill and home of Enigma and the six-screen **Virgin** multiplex. Opposite is **Slots and Zap Zone**, which gives you the opportunity to shoot your mates to your hearts content.

PILLOW TALK

Writes Rob Malyan. 'Although the university has recently opened two new halls for first years, places are not guaranteed, so make sure you register asap. Many first years live in Scraptoft Halls and travel into the city site for lectures. The bus ride can take up to three quarters of an hour if the traffic is busy and a cab will be at least £6. Scraptoft campus itself is a beautiful, green field location, the halls are basic but nice, and the site does have its own **Sports Hall** and **SU bar** with occasional ents. Virtually everyone who has lived at Scraptoft has excellent memories of their time there – reunions are held every year. A number of privately owned, self-catered halls close to City campus are also available but are pricey.'

About 60% of freshers get into halls. Students over the age of 23 or who live locally will not normally be offered a place. The uni currently has around 3,200 places in a mix of owned and leased properties. About 30% of accommodation in Leicester is catered, 94% in Bedford. There is none en suite. Price range pw in Bedford is £38.85 to £57.45 pw, in Leicester, £48.45 to £61.00pw. They are planning to add an extra 500 places by the academic year 2003/4, many of which will be en suite.

JOBS

94% of DMU's year 2000 graduates were in employment or further study within six months of completing their course. Alongside their chosen subjects, students are taught transferable skills beloved of employers, such as communication, team working and problem solving. A feature of many of DMU's programmes is paid work placements. All sandwich courses have placement tutors with extensive employer contacts. The uni runs joint research projects with industry and business in which students are involved. Employers help plan relevant student projects as well as providing our students with work experience and graduate jobs. There are professional qualification programmes with the Chartered Institute of Marketing and the Association of Chartered Certified Accountants,

and partnerships with such as British Aerospace, Boots, Pharmacia Ltd, Unisys, Unipart, Guinness, the Ministry of Defence, Walkers Snack Goods and the Leicester Mercury.

AT A GLANCE	
ACADEMIC FILE:	
Subject assessments	**30**
Excellent	**73%**
Average requirements	**180 points**
Students-staff ratio	**22:1**
First Class/2:1 degree pass rate	**59%**
ACCOMMODATION FILE:	
Guarantee to freshers	**60%**
Style	**Halls, flats, houses**
Student satisfaction	**55%**
Approx price range pw	**£45-£60**
Average city rent pw	**£40**

WHERE GRADUATES END UP	
18% Education,	Key Areas
12% Wholesale/Retail,	
10% Manufacturing,	
8% Health/Social Work,	
7% Computer,	
7% Finance,	
6% Public Admin,	
5% Personnel	
Agric/Forestry,	Niche Areas
Eng/Industrial Design,	
Advertising, Journalism,	
Market Research, Sport	
Approximate employed	**94%**

GETTING THERE

☞ Leicester by road: M1/J21 or M6 then M69.
☞ By rail: London St Pancras, 75 mins.
☞ By air: Birmingham International Airport or East Midlands International Airport.
☞ Bedford by road: 50 miles north of London, A6.
☞ By rail: London King's Cross, 50 mins.

UNIVERSITY OF DERBY

University of Derby
Kedleston Road
Derby DE22 1GB

TEL 07801 202330
FAX 01332 294861
EMAIL admissions@derby.ac.uk
WEB www.derby.ac.uk

Derby University Students' Union
Kedleston Road
Derby DE22 1GB

TEL 01332 591507
FAX 01332 348846
EMAIL udsu@derby.ac.uk
WEB www.udsu-online.co.uk

VAG VIEW

Since it became a university in 1992 Derby has expanded fast and operates now from seven sites. With three times as many students as it had in 1992, a host of new departments have sprung up, and Derby's drive to translate degrees into jobs has put them comfortably in the top twenty of universities for getting most students into careers within six months of graduation. This has not been achieved without the odd hiccup.

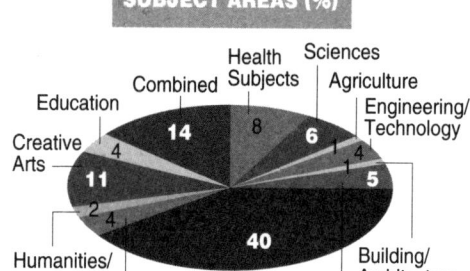

SUBJECT AREAS (%)

Education 14 · Combined Subjects 8 · Health Sciences · Agriculture 6 · Engineering/Technology 4 · 5 · Building/Architecture · Maths & Computer · Business 40 · Social Studies incl. Law 4 · 2 · Humanities/Languages 11 · Creative Arts 4

CAMPUS

Derby's campus sites range in size and facilities from the Ritz to B&B. The main site is **Kedleston Road**, ten minutes walk from the city centre, where all the heavy stuff like law, business and science go on. There are many regular buses to it, it's the home of the Students' Union, and the place where most things happen.

The other sites are scattered around, but are

UNIVERSITY/STUDENT PROFILE	
University since	**1992**
Situation/style	**City campus**
Student population	**11,980**
Full-time undergraduates	**7,550**
- mature	**41%**
- overseas	**2%**
- male/female	**46/54**
- state sector intake	**97%**
- non-traditional student intake	**15%**
- drop-out rate	**13%, high**
- undergraduate applications	**Up 4%**
see Introduction for key to tables	

also generally well served in terms of transport.

Writes Mario Cacciottolo: **'Green Lane Campus** is a beautiful old Gothic structure near the town centre that is good to look at, but as it's listed there is absolutely no chance of having that much-needed extension.

'**Mickleover Campus** is allegedly made of cardboard, so a dry winter is crucial. It has two drama studios where regular student productions are held. The quality of performance is often high, so a visit is recommended, but the heating is pre-Noah, so bring a coat.

'**Cedars** is where stuff like occupational therapy gets done, though eventually all courses based here will move to the Kingsway Hospital site. Some of the facilities are in need of updating, especially the canteen.

'**Britannia Mill** is another attractive but larger building where art and design students glue and scribble. Not far from Kedleston Road, easily accessible, it's even next to a football pitch. What more do you want?

'**Jackson's Mill** is where the textile people get together to weave, and **High Peak** is the uni's latest site, situated in the north of the county and catering for courses like, well, catering and health and beauty.'

High Peak was the further and higher education college that Derby took over in 1998. It gave them effectively a 'one stop shop' for education post-16. This year they have acquired the former Devonshire Royal Hospital in Buxton and students will transfer from High Peak between Autumn this year and 2003.

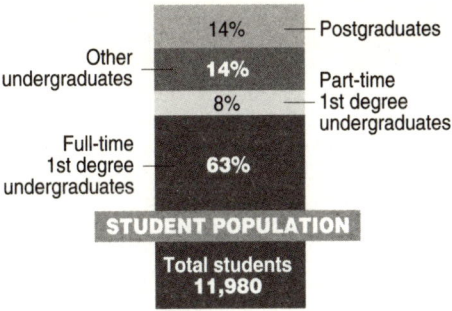

14% — Postgraduates

Other undergraduates 14%

8% — Part-time 1st degree undergraduates

Full-time 1st degree undergraduates 63%

STUDENT POPULATION

Total students 11,980

STUDENT PROFILE

The uni is committed to the ideal of higher education for all and keeps its entry requirements low to that end. This open access policy has attracted a large mature and part-time student population and many from so-called 'low-participation neighbourhoods', students from families to whom university is a new experience. Though this has also resulted in a high drop-out rate (13%), many who come here are focused on what they are about, perhaps more keenly sometimes than your average traditional undergraduate, who is still jumping through academic hoops because that is what he has been trained to do.

> *Derby's operation is about open access and the kind of educational intervention that will translate degrees into careers. The union, meanwhile, provides the anaesthetic. It's a workable collaboration.*

ACADEMIA

The academic bedrock is Engineering, the School of

ACADEMIC EXCELLENCE
TEACHING:
(Rated Excellent or 17+ out of 24)

Geology	**Excellent**
Pharmacy	**24**
Educ, Biology, Subjects Allied to Medicine, Business, Theology	**22**
American Studies, Tourism, Maths/Computing	**21**
Art & Design, Psychology	**20**
Constr Mgt/Architec Tech,	**19**
History of Art, Electrical & Electronic Eng, Nursing	
Modern Languages, Sociology, Drama, Dance & Cinematics.	**18**

RESEARCH:	
*Top grades 5/5**	**None**

Environmental and Applied Sciences, the Business School, Art & Design, Education, Human Sciences & Law – all this before Education and their School of Health & Community Studies, which together find nearly a third of their graduates jobs. Looking down graduate employment areas in the box on page 159, one is driven to single out, too, their courses in tourism and hospitality management, which prove a strong niche.

There have been growing pains in all this – nearly a decade ago, law and computing, subjects introduced after Derby was awarded university status, had required second visits by the assessors, as did pharmacy more recently. Today their School of Computing & Technology is one of their most innovative, with hybrid courses such as Electronics with Music Technology, Biological Imaging, Live Performance Technology, Visual Product Design. To these, a couple of years ago, was added the first-ever degree in E-commerce. Meanwhile, their social or human sciences course designers responded to setback with equal drive, eyeing the multi-racial society in which they live in the Midlands to bring new strategies, such as the pastoral and mediation aspects, to their courses. And, when recently the inspectors returned to re-examine Pharmacy, after it had scored 16 out of 24, they gave it full marks, a result which outstripped all Derby's other marks. It's an impressive response record, and recent assessments – Education, Biology, Theology, American Studies, Civil Engineering, History of Art, Psychology, Art & Design, Electronic & Electrical Engineering and Nursing – leave no doubt as to teaching quality (see box, opposite).

They have underpinned growth with investment in a hi-tech Learning Centre – from books (over 250,000 in stock) to periodicals (1,500 UK and overseas magazines subscribed to), from microfiches to CD-ROM, from audio-visual aids to the Internet. The centre provides 250 workstations, the electronic hub of a network that is connected to the other uni sites and halls of residence.

SOCIAL SCENE

STUDENTS' UNION The union's problem is the scattered diversity of the student populace, and UDSU, as they like to be known, have met it with a policy of owning bars on campus, on accommodation sites, and altogether off-site in the town, bringing the university into the town, in fact. They own, manage and run three nightclubs and

WHAT IT'S REALLY LIKE	
UNIVERSITY:	
Social Life	★★★★
Campus scene	**Friendly mix, good ents**
Student Union services	**Good**
Politics	**Average Grants not fees**
Sport	**27 clubs. BUSA Cricket Shield**
National team position	**125th**
Sport facilities	**Good**
Arts opportunities	**OK drama, art, film, dance**
Student newspaper	**DUSTED**
Student radio	**Bedlam FM**
Nightclub	**Union 1, Union 2**
Bars	**Union Arms, Lonsdale, Riverside, Late Bar**
Union ents	**SPANK, Dirty Dozen, Time Travel, Solid State**
Union clubs/societies	**43**
Most populr societies	**Christian Union, Afro-Caribbean**
Smoking policy	**Bars & clubs OK**
Parking	**Poor**
CITY:	
Entertainment	★★★
Scene	**Small, friendly, pub rock/indie**
Town/gown relations	**Good**
Risk of violence	**Average**
Cost of living	**Average**
Student concessions	**Good**
Survival + 2 nights out	**£60-£70 pw**
Part-time work campus/town	**Good/average**

But, hey! the year before they copped the BUSA Cricket Shield, so it can't be all bad.

Discounted membership packages are available at the **Riverside Health Club**, run by the union. There's a gym and a wet area – sauna, spa, steam room and cold plunge pool. On-site facilities provide for football, rugby, badminton, etc. Clubs accommodate American football, martial arts, snowboarding as well as the more usual sports. For outdoor pursuits, the Peak District lies less than twenty miles to the northwest.

TOWN Derby is nicely poised between 'friendly town' and 'sprawling metropolis'. There are plenty of shops that sell all necessities for the modern undergraduate (HMV, Sainsbury's, Waterstone's, Next, McDonald's), all within a neat and tidy shopping precinct. An increasing number offer student discounts. There is very little litter on the streets, as teams of council workers with picky-up-sticks regularly snap at your heels while you walk. The architecture is pleasant without being spectacular.

Derby can also offer several nightclubs, which do student nights. They can be a bit of a meat market, though, so bring yer cattle prodder. There is also a large variety of pubs, all of which are worth at least one visit. There are three cinemas, two of which are multiplexes and require a short trip by taxi. The third is at the Green Lane campus (the **Metro**) and dispenses arthouse fare, so there's plenty to keep film lovers happy. All provide discounts for students.

PILLOW TALK

Available are halls with flats, halls with lodges, and some houses. They are of a good standard at

AT A GLANCE	
ACADEMIC FILE:	
Subjects assessed	**31**
Excellent	**61%**
Average requirements	**160 points**
Student-staff ratio	**20:1**
First/2:1 degree pass rate	**46%**
ACCOMMODATION FILE:	
Guarantee to freshers	**Applications before 31.8**
Style	**Halls with flats, lodges, some houses**
Catered	**None**
En-suite	**17%**
Approx price pw	**£50-£65**
Town rent pw	**£35-£50**

six bars, like the multi-level **Union Arms Bar** and the **Late Bar**, and **Lonsdale Bar** and **Riverside Bar**. Live bands appear at **Union 1**, the larger of two in-house clubs (**Union 2** is the other) – recently Shola Ama, Kele Le Roc, K-Klass, Reef, JJ72, Timmi Magic and Chicane visited. Regular clubnights shuttle between the two. Union 1: *SPANK* (Wednesday) and *The Dirty Dozen* (Saturday); Union 2: *Time Travel* (Saturday) and *Solid State* (Tuesday). The city's **Pink Coconut** provides an exclusive student indie clubnight, *Uncut*. Balls May and Graduation – are huge.

SPORT They are not a serious contender in the national uni league – they came 125th last year.

various locations around the city; none is catered; 17% are en suite (all rooms at Peak Court are en suite). Freshers are guaranteed accommodation if their applications are received by August 31.

JOBS

The Quality Standards Kitemark has been awarded to the Career Development Centre and the School of Access and Further Education for guidance provision. The Students' Union also run an Employability training programme.

GETTING THERE

☛ By road: Kedleston Road campus is just off the A38, the main southwest/northeast thoroughfare which goes south to Exeter and meets the M1 at Junction 28. M1/J25 for access from the east, A6 from the southeast (Loughborough way).

WHERE GRADUATES END UP	
15% Education,	Key Areas
15% Health/Social Work,	
11% Wholesale/Retail,	
9% Manufacturing,	
7% Finance	
6% Personnel	
Hotel/Restaurant,	Niche Areas
Agric/Forestry,	
Film/Video, Publishing	
Approximate employed	91%

☛ By rail: rail links with Derby are easy. London is two hours away.
☛ By coach: London, 3:15.

DONCASTER COLLEGE

Doncaster College
Waterdale
Doncaster DN1 3EX

TEL 01302 553718
FAX 01302 553559
EMAIL he@don.ac.uk
WEB www.don.ac.uk

VAG VIEW

*T*he college teaches degrees as richly *diverse as Business & Football Management and Quarry & Road Surface Engineering – a combo imaginative enough to make their Screenwriting degree superfluous? They are based at four sites in and around this South Yorkshire town. College accommodation is provided on a site six miles to the west at High Melton, where there is a shop and a bar. Ents occur once a week – quizzes, games nights, discos, etc. At HQ there is a games room (pool, table tennis, etc.) and common room. A £22-million* **Dome** *complex is the leisure focus in the town, which also boasts one of the largest open-air markets in the country. There is a handful of nightclubs, a range of ethnic restaurants, a* **Warner** *multiplex cinema and the racecourse for which Doncaster is widely known.*

COLLEGE PROFILE	
Founded	**1974**
Status	**F/HE College**
Degree awarding universities	**Hull, Open, Nottingham, Sheff Hallam**
Situation/style	**Town site**
Student population	**34,000**
Full-time undergraduate population	**361**
ACCOMMODATION:	
Availability to freshers	**100%**
Style	**Halls**
Cost pw (no food)	**£47**
Town rent pw	**£50**
DEGREE SUBJECTS:	
Business (incl Football Management), advertising, fashion, music, theatre, screenwriting, engineering, computing, social sciences, humanities, etc	

GETTING THERE

☛ By road: A1(M), A630; M18/J3 or 4.

☛ By rail: Sheffield, 24 mins; Barnsley, 1.02; Wakefield, 17 mins.
☛ By coach: Birmingham, Leicester, 3:00.

UNIVERSITY OF DUNDEE

The University of Dundee
2 Airlie Place
Dundee DD1 4HN

TEL 01382 344160
FAX 01382 348150
EMAIL srs@dundee.ac.uk
WEB www.dundee.ac.uk

Dundee Students' Association
Airlie Place
Dundee DD1 4HP

TEL 01382 221841
FAX 01382 227124
EMAIL dusa@dundee.ac.uk
WEB www.dusa.dundee.ac.uk

VAG VIEW

*F*ounded in 1883 as University College Dundee, seven years later it became part of the University of St Andrews and remained so until it gained independence in 1967.

Today, Dundee is a traditional, premier-league university, but unusually relaxed and friendly. It has a history, but isn't steeped in it. Nor does it feel bound by tradition to repeat itself constantly.

CAMPUS

'Dundee lies on the East Coast of Northern Scotland, a couple of hours away from Glasgow, Edinburgh and Aberdeen,' writes Sameen Farouk. 'Next door is St. Andrews. Dundee is one of a handful of genuine get-away-from-it-all universities. The scenery up here is breathtaking, a relief from the concrete jungles of other city universities. Weather-wise, Dundee isn't the Med but it's warm and mild for most of the year, just windy, and not much colder than the rest of the UK, even during the winter months.

'The main campus, with compact teaching facilities, a new IT centre, the main libraries, the art college, sports facilities, the union, the dental hospital, John Smith Bookshop, Bonar Hall, the famous Wellcome Trust building (all within five

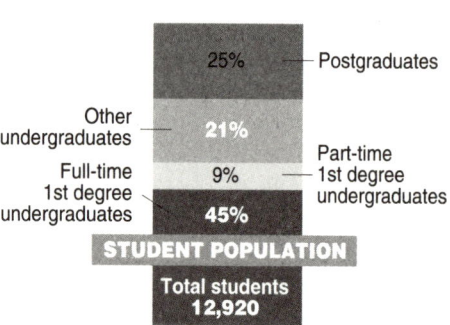

minutes walk of each other), is located on the edge of the town centre. It is safe, clean and increasingly accessible to the disabled community.

'The medical campus is located in the town's main hospital, Ninewells. Other sites, the nursing college and Northern College, the recently merged teacher training facility, are a little further out.'

STUDENT PROFILE

'Without being steeped in outmoded tradition,' writes Hannah Hamilton, 'the university retains a strong self-image, and the students form a very real community around the central core of campus.'

Dundee attracts students from all walks of life and from all areas. The inevitable scattering of public school types joins a healthy dose of students

UNIVERSITY/STUDENT PROFILE

University since	**1967**
Situation/style	**City campus**
Student population	**12,920**
Full-time undergraduates	**5,820**
- mature	**17%**
- overseas	**4%**
- male/female	**40/60**
- state sector intake	**90%**
- non-traditional student intake	**18%, high**
- drop-out rate	**10%**
- undergraduate applications	**Up 6%**
see Introduction for key to tables	

from Ireland and a very strong international community.

'Dundee could never be criticised for being a quaint English retreat,' agrees Sameen. 'The university recruits internationally and has strong Arab, Chinese, Malaysian, Korean and Hispanic communities. There is also a substantial South-Asian population. The local communities are also targeted keenly, and there is a growing population of mature students.'

The 18% intake from poor areas last year, which is high, put together with its top-rated teaching assessments and research record (see box, opposite) and its 10% drop-out rate, which is relatively OK, makes Dundee one of the elite in the context of our Government's aspirations in the higher education sector.

ACADEMIA

Characteristically, Dundee is a university for the professions, for medicine, for architecture, for finance (see our *Graduate Employment* box, page 163), and for law – it's the only uni to offer both Scots and English Law, and gained a Grade 5 (that's international expertise) at the recent research assessments.

'I suppose, if you are a Scot, and you want to study medicine,' said a sixth-form careers mistress, 'Edinburgh would have to be high on the list, but people have had very good experiences of Dundee.'

In fact, in the assessments, Dundee achieved an Excellent rating in Medicine, where Edinburgh achieved only a Highly Satisfactory, and in 1998 they won the prestigious Queen's Anniversary Prize for their pioneering use of keyhole surgery, a success which directs interest to the extraordinary levels of research going on here. Known the world over for cancer research, a radical new approach to cancer treatment has resulted from the merger of the research teams of pioneering keyhole surgeon Professor Sir Alfred Cuschieri and

> *Traditionally a uni for the professions. And now, Dundee-chic!? Are we to believe it? From Medicine to Art, it seems, Dundee operates within some sort of surprise global dimension.*

Professor David Lane, who discovered 'the guardian angel of the cell', the p53 gene. The idea is to deliver gene therapy direct to tumours via keyhole surgery, using a specially developed 'poison umbrella' needle.

If you're squeamish, like me, you'll be glad that someone else spends their days so profitably. What grabs the visitor is the real sense of excitement around here – they leapt eleven places nationally in the research assessments recently published, with

---

---

medical and biological research achieving the highest accolades (see box, above). 'You have this underlying feeling that important things are going to happen,' said Roland Wolf, director of biomedical research – and the feeling is not confined to Medicine.

The Art & Design faculty demands attention, too: Textile Design took an Excellent in the undergraduate assessments; companies like Nike and Calvin Kline die for Dundee graduates; the uni leads Britain in supplying graduates to Architecture; and although the faculty fell from Grade 5 to 4 in the research assessments, there is a sense, day-to-day, that the art/design students add vigour and momentum to what is going on in the city. For the city of Dundee is reinventing itself, and the uni is, geographically and culturally, at the very heart of that new identity. Bang in the middle of the city's new cultural quarter with its pubs, clubs and gallery shops, the Art/Design Faculty, through its reputation in the fashion and design industries, provides a global dimension to 'Dundee-chic'. Suddenly it's cool to be in Dundee, a *Sunday Times* article recently declared, and 'it does offer one hell of a night out.'

A £9-million, Lottery-funded collaboration between uni and city has resulted in **Dundee**

Contemporary Arts, a centre for visual arts with the university's Visual Research Centre at its hub, an art laboratory equipped with cutting edge facilities for producing design prototypes, videos, prints, artists' books, etc. Now the uni has copped £300,000 to preserve Scotland's historic architectural drawings in digital form, and just recently we hear that they have the world's most powerful electron microscope, capable of observing particles 10,000 times smaller than the width of a hair! Let's hope that with all its research prowess, the uni never neglects to keep its students' needs clearly in focus.

Says Sameen, 'The departments with particularly good reputations usually deserve them. However, much of it is up to you. Self-study is usually held to account through tutorial systems, but the personal tutor system seems still to be "in development". The campus IT facilities have been upgraded but there is still no general 24-hour access unlike all Dundee's neighbouring universities.'

WHAT IT'S REALLY LIKE

UNIVERSITY:	
Social Life	★★★★★
Campus scene	**Diverse**
Student Union services	**Average**
Politics	**Self-serving**
Sport	**Sport-for-all**
National team position	**83rd**
Sport facilities	**Good**
Arts opportunities	**Music, film, art excellent; drama good; dance avg**
Student newspaper	**Student Times**
Nightclub	**Mono**
Bars	**Liar, Pete's, Tav**
Union ents	**PopTart, Fusion, Coalese, DoThis DoThat, Mad For It School Daze, Dallas Big, Club Tropicana**
Union clubs/societies	**60**
Most popular	**Faculty based**
Smoking policy	**Bars, halls OK**
Parking	**Poor**
CITY:	
Entertainment	★★★
Scene	**Pubs, good live**
Town/gown relations	**Average**
Risk of violence	**Low**
Cost of living	**Low**
Student concessions	**Good**
Survival + 2 nights out	**£50 pw**
Part-time work campus/town	**Excellent/ poor**

SOCIAL SCENE

STUDENTS' ASSOCIATION Décor ranges from the scruffy intimacy of **Pete's Bar**, to the pseudo-swank of **Mono**, with the **Liar** and **Tav** bars affording comfortable, if not exactly spectacular, drinking surroundings. Regular club nights cover most styles of music, with the four bars serving some of the cheapest drinks in Dundee. Currently clubnights include *Pop Tart*, an amazing, eclectic mix of classic pop styles from the '60s to today; *Fusion*, dance music – R&B and two-step garage: 'Aiya Napa gives Ibiza a run for its money'. *Coalesce* – metal, punk and alternative; the well-tried *DoThisDoThat* (dance) – the SA notes the club's recent selection as one of *DJ Magazine*'s Top 5 clubnights, as well as featuring regularly as a ´recommended club´ in *Mixmag, Muzik* and *Ministry* magazines; *School Daze* – 'all dressed up like Britney Spears in that video;' *Dallas* – classic cheese from the '70s and '80s; Friday night's *Big* – spicey chart; Saturday, *Club Tropicana* ('80s – 'the music that made the Thatcher generation').

The SA, which is disassociated from the NUS, the national body, is frequently rated as one of the best in the country, on account of such ents being provided seven nights a week through term time.

More recently, however, we have heard voices of criticism that DUSA is prone to shoring up its own power base and being a tad control-freakish. Who knows, but it is interesting that Dundee is not the only uni that came to us this year with a take on ents which suggests that there may be more to life, however hypnotic or Pied Piperish may be DUSA's programme in **Mono** and **Pete's Bar**.

VIEW FROM THE GROUND

by Sameen Farouk

Socially, it would appear that the mainstream Dundee student is a clubber – nightclubs are, after all, saturated with them and the Students' Union seems to do all in its power to satisfy them – but there are substantial sections of the student body, especially within the international community, for which this is not true.

The campus union is the hub of most activities. The **Liar Bar** helps students who need to get plastered on the cheap (some by afternoon!). The union holds many events, and the success of the well-attended *DoThisDoThat* is surely a testament to the hard work of the ents staff. Everyone seems to have a tale to tell from the **Mono** (particularly after *Skool Daze* nights). The secondary union venue is (grotty) **Pete's Bar**, which tends to hold less mainstream stuff, like the odd Bhangra night, salsa night, even a *Vietnam War* night! Much socialising is also organised by societies.

Those wanting quieter breaks retreat to the **Chaplaincy Café**. Although religion can hardly be said to dominate campus life, Dundee has a growing religious diversity and the chaplaincy has become a popular venue, the hub of the Christian Students Society. The Islamic Society is also re-establishing itself, with support from the local community and the opening of prayer facilities. A new temple has also opened up here.

The uni has one of the best arts colleges in the UK, and also the excellent **Dundee Contemporary Arts** venue (mentioned above), but Dundee can't really compete with big city arts. The two classy theatres feature good touring acts, particularly the **Rep**. There's a bit of a live comedy resurgence, too. Music-wise, the **Caird Hall** does occasionally attract big/rising names (like Travis, Gabrielle and Ocean Colour Scene recently), but its real strength is its jazz tradition: there is a strong following here, frequent shows and an annual festival.

The main cinemas are a bit out of the way for most students, but the DCA does show excellent indy films and holds foreign film events.

Budding fresher journalists are going to be hugely disappointed with what the *Student Times* has become. It's fall from the starry heights attained by the past editor led one regular journalist to comment that it had become an 'inside joke', as DUSA acted quickly to prevent it from touching radicalism again. Its only real strength seems to be that it's free and literally littered all over the campus.

SPORT The particularly popular activities are mainstream team sports like hockey, rugby, football (not cricket), boxing and the watersports, but most sports have strong societies.

Around Dundee there is also a well-established martial arts scene. The uni sporting facilities are excellent and well managed, as is the on-campus swimming pool.

TOWN Recently Dundee city centre has reinvented itself with the multi-million-pound Dundee Contemporary Arts Theatre (DCA) and the Overgate Shopping Centre; both ideally situated near campus. Most major retailers have branches in the city centre and main high streets, but shopaholics would probably prefer to tackle the surrounding cities.

Within a competitive clubbing scene, two establishments come out on top – **Fat Sam's** and **Mardi Gras** (featured on *UK Uncovered* no less!). There are no superclubs (phew!).

Most tastes are catered for, but thankfully drum 'n' bass is not one of them.

Among loads of bars, ones worth mentioning include **Popl Nero's**, **Yates**, **Westport**, **Droughty Neebors**, **Raffles**, and the fabulous **Doghouse** (super)bar. The last four vie to compete with live entertainment. Most bars near the campus compete with the Students' Union, the DogHouse in particular with the **Midnight Café**; live music is daily establishing a stronger hold.

Dundee isn't vulnerable to big city problems, aside from homelessness. There are low crime rates, clean environments and decent public transport. Ethnic minorities will find very close-knit communities. Tayside police take a hard-line stance towards reported crime, notably assaults on students. However, some student areas are vulnerable to burglaries, and hall residents should beware of children with kleptomaniac tendencies.

Dundee is also one of the cheapest cities in the UK.

PILLOW TALK

Most people seem to have enjoyed themselves in hall. Be warned that Belmont food is notoriously bad. Personally, I found hall a bit of an expensive option. With one well-known exception, landlords have good reputations. Private housing near the campus or in the town centre is usually spacious, of very good quality and shouldn't cost more than £160 per month. Insurance rates are also low and students are exempt from paying for water, perhaps because they are not generally known to use much.

JOBS

The university gives many opportunities for CV-hungry students. Reps are required for faculties and classes and to represent the uni, to liaise with careers, and even in the halls. The union is also handy for finding work, in security, in the bars, etc, for around the minimum wage. Hours are more flexible than in town bars, pubs and cafés, which also hire students. Also, it is more reliable than call centre work.

GETTING THERE

☞ By road: M90, M85, A85, A972.
☞ By rail: Newcastle, 3:00; London Euston, 6:00.
☞ By air: Dundee Airport for internal flights; Edinburgh International Airport is an hour away.
☞ By coach: London, 10:05; Birmingham, 10:05; Newcastle, 6:05.

UNIVERSITY OF DURHAM

The University of Durham
Old Shire Hall
Old Elvet
Durham DH1 3HP

TEL 0191 374 2000
FAX 0191 374 7520
EMAIL admissions@durham.ac.uk
WEB www.dur.ac.uk

Durham Students' Union
Dunelm House
New Elvet
Durham DH1 3AN

TEL 0191 374 3310
FAX 0191 374 3328
EMAIL dsu.president@durham.ac.uk
WEB www.dsu.org.uk

VAG VIEW

*F*ounded in 1832, Durham is, like Oxford and Cambridge, a collegiate university, although University College Stockton, the satellite campus on Teesside, is alone in being a teaching facility like the Oxbridge colleges. The other Durham colleges are purely residential.

The Stockton project is interesting because it evinces Durham's commitment to widening participation among non-traditional uni-goers, and there are signs that it is part of a more general strategy to appeal beyond Durham's conservative student base.

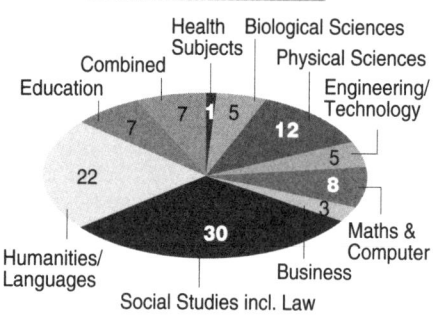

SUBJECT AREAS (%)

CAMPUS

Durham is a small, stunningly beautiful city, situated 16 miles south of Newcastle. The nucleus of the medieval city, where the five Bailey colleges and the Arts and Social Sciences Departments are located, is formed by a bend of the River Wear around a rocky peninsular, dominated by the 11th-century cathedral and castle. It is, as recent Durham graduate, Sophie Vokes-Dudgeon, recalls, a place to spark memories of unending bliss: 'Lying on the banks of the River Wear after exams, sipping Pimms and watching the rowing boats (and lycra clad rowers) weaving their way through the arches. Wandering through the cobbled streets, wrapped up warm in hat and scarf, passing hundreds of familiar faces as the snow falls around you. Going round to tea with one of your course mates in their room at the Castle, overlooking the courtyard, with the cathedral in the background. Going out for a good old boogie in a small naff club, being certain of knowing about seventy per cent of your fellow boppers, and certainly recognising the others. Dressing up in black-tie gear for formal dinners and balls, in some of the most beautiful buildings in the country. And most of all, feeling all that hard work was worthwhile as you go about your daily life in some of the most spectacular surroundings of any university city, in blissful ignorance of all the stresses and strains of big cities just a few minutes train journey away in Newcastle. If this sounds like the ideal student life, then, I promise you, Durham is the place for you.'

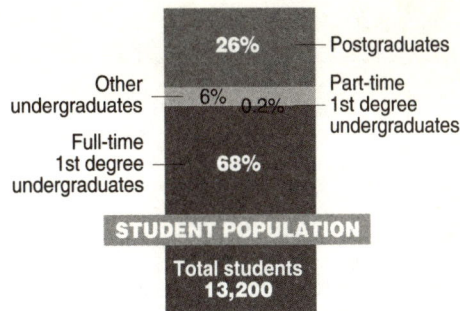

26% — Postgraduates

Other undergraduates — 6% 0.2% Part-time 1st degree undergraduates

Full-time 1st degree undergraduates — 68%

STUDENT POPULATION

Total students **13,200**

STUDENT PROFILE

'Hi, I'm Alex Pharaoh and I came to Durham from a grammar school in North Yorkshire, aware that it had a reputation of being a haven for public schoolers and Oxbridge rejects, and, yes, a lot of people here do fall into one of these categories.'

'Hi, I am a state-school educated, second-year history student from the Midlands,' writes Eleanor Neal. 'I too arrived at Durham with apprehension. I had heard the rumours that it was populated with snobby, southern Rahs, and was hoping they would be false.'

'Hi, my name's Robin Siddle and I come from sixthform college in Scarborough. I thought there'd be a lot of yuppy people there, but there are only two colleges like that – Hatfield and Castle – the other ones are, like, normal... though I have noticed there are a lot of southerners. *They* say there's a lot of northerners, but there's not.'

ACADEMIA

Physics, psychology, biosciences, maths, philosophy, archaeology, theology, English, history, chemistry, law – these are the subjects which have topped the teaching and research assessments. Academically, the uni is up there with the best, 84% of its assessments are Excellent, and in the recent research exercise, Durham leapt from 18th to 12th place nationwide. They also offer useful strengths in Arabic, Chinese, Japanese, and though they lost their medical faculty when Newcastle gained its independence in 1962 and became a university a year later in its own right, the two unis have now teamed up to launch a med school project primarily aimed at mature students. The two-year course, has a foundation year at Stockton before transfer to a regional clinical base unit.

Another recent development turns us to their

powerful Physics & Astronomy degrees – a £1.4-million supercomputer, capable of making ten billion calculations a second and 'recreating the entire evolution of the universe', has been introduced to the uni's Institute of Computational Cosmology.

If all this seems of a high order, official entry requirements are commensurately high. At interview they look for enthusiasm, motivation and work experience. But, as fresher Robin discovered, they are now open to an approach if you are coming from behind academically, but are really determined to get a place:

> *Intensely companionable, academic and sporty – the student culture at Durham is rich, and, with widening access, may be entering a new stage of evolution.*

'I didn't think I would have a chance to get in. I am probably the first in my family to go to university. When I was at Sixthform one of my teachers told me not to bother applying because Durham only ever accept people with really, really high grades. I got an AS and a GNVQ.

'I decided early on at school to do archaeology. It was something I was interested in. Quite a lot of

UNIVERSITY/STUDENT PROFILE	
University since	**1832**
Situation/style	**City collegiate**
Student population	**13,200**
Full-time undergraduates	**8,990**
- mature	**9%**
- overseas	**6%**
- male/female	**48/52**
- state sector intake	**62%, low**
- non-traditional student intake	**7%**
- drop-out rate	**4%, low**
- undergraduate applications	**Down 1%**
see Introduction for key to tables	

the other subjects, they just bored me really. And I thought I best get a degree because you kind of need one nowadays. So I did a bit of reading, joined the local Archaeological Society and the Council of British Archaeology and read a few books and decided that was what I liked.

'There are probably 150 in my year. The department is really big. There are lots of computers... it's really good. I was given essays to write as soon as I got there, on the first couple of days. They expect you to have done a bit of reading on the subject. And they expect you to read in your free time, a book every couple of weeks during the term. When I was at Scarborough Sixthform College, it was totally different. You could get away with not doing anything, it was kind of easy in a way. When you get to do your degree, you really have to work hard. You don't *know* the things in your head, so you've got to go and read them, or your lecturers will tell you.

'The library at Durham – the big one – it's massive, and it is split into sections of certain subjects, loads of books. There's a little computer system that helps you find what you want, it gives you a number and then you have to go and look for them, it's hah...! It's just such a task! I had to get a librarian to help me, there are so many rows! I mean, if there was just one row on archaeology that would be all right, but you get lost. Most books are allowed out on three-week loans. Then you can request them to come back in early. And then there's an overnight book or a three-hour book, and they are all in the Reserve Collection. So they are the books that the lecturers have put on the reading list, so that everybody has a chance of actually getting a book. If you can manage to get these three-hour ones on a Saturday night you can keep them till Monday morning, so that's another good thing. I read more in my first term than I did in my whole time at Sixthform. I have got quicker at reading, you have to. And taking notes at lectures – to start off with you write everything down, then gradually you start to develop skills, you learn what you need to write down and what you can remember. I am slipping into it now, but to start off it was mad!

'I have found a subject I am interested in and maybe that is more important than doing well in subjects at A level that I am not interested in.'

COLLEGES

Writes Alex Pharaoh: 'The smaller collegiate system promotes involvement. Each college is different, however, and seemingly contrary to the Government's strategy to expand higher education for all, college bills are planned to increase by about £1,000 in the next five years.'

There are fifteen colleges, including the Graduate Society for postgrads, Ushaw Theological College and University College Stockton.

UNIVERSITY COLLEGE STOCKTON lies south down the A1(M), on the outskirts of Middlesbrough. Official entry requirements are rather lower than at HQ, though you still get a Durham degree. Subjects on offer include the medical degree foundation, applied psychology, biomedical sciences, business finance, human sciences, environmental management/technology/development, childhood and science in society, euro studies, sport. Recently, they built 200 additional en-suite student rooms, a new library and IT resource centre, lecture rooms, laboratories and student recreational facilities.

The Durham college stereotype is described in the rivalry between the so-called **Bailey** colleges (John's, Chad's, Cuth's, University and Hatfield), situated in the Bailey area of the medieval city, and the **Hill** colleges (Trev's, Van Mildert, Mary's, Collingwood, Grey's and Aiden's), situated southwest of the Bailey. Sophie reports: 'Pick your college carefully. Within a couple of days you'll have learned your college songs and rituals, and feel a strange affiliation with this set of buildings, which will manifest itself loudly on many a river bank or touch line throughout your life as a Durham student. The stereotypical image we have is of Rahs on the Bailey and Plebs on the Hill. And then there's St Hild & St Bede, the biggest college, a minute or two further out, perhaps with a more diverse mix than some of the others. Don't go entirely by the stereotypes though; be sure to visit. I wouldn't suggest an open application either, as you're more than likely to end up in Mary's – the all-girls college. Obviously that's more likely to happen if you're female, though rumour has it Hillary someone was designated there until Freshers' Week when they realised she was a he!

'Since practically all your socialising is done in college, the bar is a vital consideration. The Hill colleges are more like a campus, all a drunken stagger from one another. Next to the Science site, computers and library too, but what you gain in convenience you certainly lack in history and surroundings. The Bailey colleges are also near enough for a bar crawl, and the cobbled streets and cathedral backdrop make it far more aesthetically pleasing. Chad's and John's bars are barely big enough to swing a cat, however, and you may be more likely to stumble upon Evensong than a pint of lager in St John's. Hild Bede bar resembles an airport lounge, but the tow path leads to nightclub **Klute** and the beer's cheap, so who complains? Colleges also differ in facilities. Hild Bede has a newish multigym, an abundance of tennis courts, squash courts, gyms, and beautiful if basic accommodation. Castle, on the other hand, offers third years the chance to live in a castle, while Collingwood gives you en-suite shower rooms and kettles. The choice is yours!'

'Trevs is very representative of the whole student body,' writes Eleanor. 'It is also friendly and has strong college spirit. There are loads of social events, two balls a year and one of the larger, and

more tasteful bars. We are fairly standard when compared to other colleges. Our accommodation is decent, not as nice as Collingwood, however. Bailey accommodation tends to be the worst, as it is the oldest and they also room some students far from the main building, Cuth's is worst for this. Hill Colleges have purpose built accommodation blocks. John's is very religious, Van Mildert is good for music opportunities, Cuth's is famed for having a bar with proper opening hours!'

Says Alex: 'My college, Collingwood, is known as one of the best. We have the most modern accommodation, more en-suite rooms, more IT networked rooms, less room sharing, better central facilities, such as bar and gym, and allegedly, better food than others. We are the newest college, and have less tradition than those on the Bailey, which can be seen as a good or bad thing. We have a great social calendar – bar theme nights, "megaformal" dinners, bops, trips, sporting events and the legendary Summer Ball.'

After Collingwood, Alex's typically intense loyalty allows endorsement of Van Mildert and Castle, but the union bar, **Kingsgate**, is rated a poor fourth – 'The college bars are better: a dozen colleges means a dozen college bars, which range from great (Collingwood) to grim (Mary's). They're run by students and you'll know everyone in your own.'

SOCIAL SCENE

STUDENTS' UNION No raves, relatively few drugs; booze is the thing, college bops and black-tie formal dinners. Less formal are the discos and gigs at **Dunelm House**, the Students' Union building. 'The union puts on a range of ents with big name DJs common, but there is a noticeable lack of big bands,' writes Alex. 'Durham can't seem to attract them, but we can see many at Newcastle and Northumbria unions.'

Kingsgate is the union bar with balcony overlooking the river; it's open every day, and there are snacks. Food is served in the nearby **Riverside Café** until 11 pm and there's waitress service. Then there's the **Margot Fonteyn Room** – known as the ballroom – with 700 capacity, a stage, a PA. Space, Jools Holland, Freestylers, Judge Jules have visited recently.

The **Vane Tempest** is a bar adjacent to the ballroom – with inflatable chairs. It serves until 1 am.

TOWN When term begins, students herd in and outnumber locals. In the past it has proved to be a recipe for disaster. 'We don't really venture out that often,' Robin remarks. 'You kind of, like, stick to colleges. You don't go out on a weekend because

WHAT IT'S REALLY LIKE

UNIVERSITY:

Social Life	★★★★
Campus scene	Lively, focused, memorable fun
Student Union services	Good
Politics	Average interest, whole spectrum
Sport	Key
National team position	9th
Sport facilities	Good
Arts opportunities	Good
Student magazine	Sense
Student newspaper	Palatinate
Student radio	Purple FM
Independent awards	Best newspaper Best website
Nightclub	The Ballroom
Bars	Kingsgate, Vane Tempest, Riverside Café
Union ents	Planet of Sound
Union clubs/societies	138
Smoking policy	Sep. coll. policies
Parking	Poor

CITY:

Entertainment	★★★
Scene	Cheesy clubs, good pubs
Town/gown relations	Poor
Risk of violence	Yes
Cost of living	Average
Student concessions	Good
Survival + 2 nights out	£40 pw
Part-time work campus/town	Excellent/good

drunk, in the middle of the road, wearing a DJ.'

The uni encourage students 'to develop good relations with their neighbours and other residents in the city'. Volunteers from Student Community Action work with locals to that end. Guidelines have been drawn up by staff and students to discourage harassment. The union president sits on residents associations, which is helping. He also has a phone line which he publicises to the residents. If there are any disturbances caused by students on late licence nights then the residents can phone him and he can sort that out. They have a university security patrol that goes round the city every night. Residents can call the patrol and direct them to a problem. They also have a night-bus which picks up all around town and drops off at all the colleges.

So what's likely to tempt you to run the gauntlet? 'There are three nightclubs in town,' writes Alex. '**DH1**, **Klute** and **Café Rock**. DH1, aka Rixies, attempts and fails to be a serious dance club. However, it's cheap and you'll know everyone in there. You either love or hate Klute - a Mecca of pop, it's crowded, hot and sweaty but fun. Café Rock is an enigma – it has a good indie night, but otherwise should be avoided.

'In the city there are a few good bars, a lot of okay pubs, and plenty of restaurants and cafés. Though most do seem to be Italian in some way, Mexico, Thailand, China and Japan have representation too. Really, you're best off heading to Newcastle (a convenient fifteen-minute train ride) for drinking and clubbing.

Student media (magazine, newspaper, radio and web) is first class, with *Palatinate* taking Best Newspaper at the national *Independent* awards last year and the website picking up the top award too. The union is also active on welfare (Advice Centre, Nightline, etc) and politics extend beyond student issues. Campaign flyers for People & Planet (previously Third World First), for Amnesty International and other groups proliferate. There's a campaigns committee which meets every week, and there are people responsible for gay issues, women's issues, environment, race, etc.

SPORT Durham is very sporty, they came 9th overall in the national team championships last year, and the beautiful river is a temptress to hundreds of novice rowers.

Academic concessions for sporty types are apparent, though not admitted.

High standards are encouraged by inter-college rivalry, Castle vrs Hatfield (rugby), Castle vrs Hild Bede (rowing). Currently, Hatfield is strong and Hild Bede is like a sports academy! College rowing crews are often better than other university crews.

that's when all the locals are out. We haven't had any trouble really, it's just that the Londoners feel a bit nervous if they go out on a Friday and Saturday, they think they are going to get picked on because of the way they talk. But I don't think they do.'

Writes Eleanor: 'Locals are generally friendly, and students are normally safe. Weekends are more dangerous, however, as county locals invade and they are more inclined to indulge in the favourite sport of student bashing. This has got worse recently. There is a large police presence if you have to go out.'

Says Alex, 'There is some tension. The students who float into town for six months a year living off a combination of their student loan, large overdraft, or mummy and daddy, do cause irritation. Trouble is easily avoidable if you shun the pink shirt/bodywarmer/scarf, and don't talk in a loud southern accent on your mobile phone at 3 am,

Sixty acres of playing fields are maintained to first-class standard.

Writes Eleanor: 'There is huge opportunity to get involved, sport happens at all levels and includes all types. Cost varies but university is around £40 a year. College is cheaper, around £10, but you have to buy kit and it is less serious.'

JOBS

'There's plenty of work available in Durham for students,' writes Alex. 'Colleges have bars and shops which need to be staffed, and a variety of shops, pubs and bars in town often have students part-timing. The union is quite good at helping you find work.

'Later, you can attend workshops, seminars, societies and clubs all dedicated to making you more employable... From what I've heard, and from what I've seen when my friends have left here, graduating from this university gives a big head start in the fight for a career.'

GETTING THERE

☛ By road: A1/J6. Well served by coaches.
☛ By rail: King's Cross, 3:00; Edinburgh, 1:00.
☛ By air: Newcastle, Teesside Airports (25m).
☛ By coach: London, 5:30; Birmingham, 4:00.

WHERE GRADUATES END UP

14% Education,	Key Areas
11% Finance,	
9% Manufacturing,	
8% Public Admin,	
6% Computer,	
5% Wholesale/Retail,	
5% Health/Social Work	
Accountancy*,	Niche Areas
Business/Management,	
Advertising, Defence*,	
Chem/Pharmaceutical,	
Eng/Industrial Design,	
Journalism, Property,	
Market Research*, Legal,	
Publishing, Radio/TV	

*indicates Top 10 Graduate Provider

Approximate employed **91%**

UNIVERSITY OF EAST ANGLIA

The University of East Anglia
Earlham Road
Norwich NR4 7TJ

TEL 01603 592216
FAX 01603 458596
EMAIL admissions@uea.ac.uk
WEB www.uea.ac.uk

Union of University of East Anglia Students
Union House
Norwich
Norfolk NR4 7TJ

TEL 01603 593272
FAX 01603 250144
EMAIL comms@stu.uea.ac.uk
WEB www.stu.uea.ac.uk

VAG VIEW

*S*et apart in rural Norfolk, this excellent university was founded in the 1960s and reaches out to the world with innovation and flair. It is among the best on virtually any grounds you care to mention, but don't expect a major city scene.

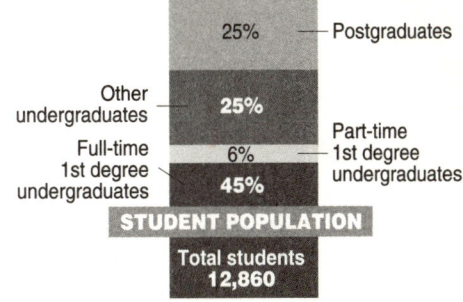

25% — Postgraduates
Other undergraduates **25%**
Full-time 1st degree undergraduates **6%**
Part-time 1st degree undergraduates **45%**

STUDENT POPULATION

Total students **12,860**

CAMPUS

UEA campus is fifteen minutes by road from the centre of Norwich, a city less than fifteen miles away from the Norfolk Broads, an area of outstanding beauty and tranquillity. The campus, built on a 320-acre, sometime golf course, has won awards for its architecture – Denys Lasdun's

UNIVERSITY/STUDENT PROFILE	
University since	**1964**
Situation/style	**Edge of city campus**
Student population	**12,860**
Full-time undergraduates	**5,750**
- mature	**25%**
- overseas	**6%**
- male/female	**36/64**
- state sector intake	**88%**
- non-traditional student intake	**7%**
- drop-out rate	**4%, low**
- undergraduate applications	**Down 1%**
see Introduction for key to tables	

computing, maths, music, linguistics, such as Music with Mathematics, for example, and even Maths with a year in Australia! There is also a new blend of Art History & Philosophy, which sounds interesting. Teaching assessments have been uniformly good, and world-class research ratings attach to subjects involved in these new courses.

The move of the **Jackson Institute** to UEA, with the largest environmental research programme in the UK, points up the international standing in research in this area (a 5* rating – its climatic research unit is a world authority, and the uni is also home to the Tyndall Centre for Climate Change Research), and there is to be a new Institute for Connective Environmental Research

ziggurats (glass-fronted buildings, tiered upwards like garden terraces after the ancient tiered mounds of Babylonia) continue to amaze, but, as student Daniel Trelfer declares, self-containment on campus isn't to everyone's taste: 'Everything you need is on campus, but while some people are happy to live for twelve weeks inside a square quarter mile, others go insane and have to run to town to feel free again.'

STUDENT PROFILE

UEA has a well-balanced student population for a pukka uni, with 88% from state schools. It does not, however, appear to be leaning over backwards to recruit from poorer neighbourhoods. There is a large mature intake (25%) – a deliberate policy (see *Academia*, below) and a preponderance of females (64%), possibly down to the nursing degrees (adult, child, learning disability, mental health). The uni is constantly beset with rumours of campus isolation and the dire effects of this upon its student clientele, but we see a pretty sharp focus on the business in hand, whether it's academic or extra-curricular, and a happy and fulfilled student body. Its drop-out rate is a mere 4%.

ACADEMIA

The big news this year is the new medical school. UEA has shown good inspection results in physiotherapy, occupational therapy and psychotherapy, in nursing and in biological sciences. It is also, as it happens, home to the Wellcome Unit for the History of Medicine. Now, this new School of Medicine will welcome its first 110 students in September 2002. As with all new med. schools, the curriculum will involve hands-on experience from the first year of study, which may be not the best news local patients will hear.

New courses elsewhere in the uni include imaginative variations on themes involving

ACADEMIC EXCELLENCE	
TEACHING:	
(Rated Excellent or 17+ out of 24)	
Law, Applied Social Work, Environmental Sciences, Developmental Studies.	**Excellent**
Politics, American Studies	**24**
Philosophy	
Economics, Media Studies	**23**
Maths, Business, Subjects Allied to Medicine	
History of Art, Architecture & Design, Molecular Biosciences, Organismal Biosciences	**22**
Drama, Dance & Cinematics	**21**
Sociology	**20**
Modern Langs & Linguistics, Electric & Electronic Engineering	**19**
Nursing	**18**
RESEARCH:	
*Top grades 5/5**	
Environmental Sciences, History, Media Studies	**Grade 5***
Biol. Sciences, Chemistry, Pure Maths, Law, Social Work, English, History of Art, Philosophy	**Grade 5**

going up over the next year – an attempt to bring together science, industry, politics, business to make real steps forward in the area of environmentalism. See also degrees in conservation, ecology, and the Development Studies degree combined with Overseas Study or Natural Resources, and many environmental science courses.

Degree programmes are modular; entry requirements testing, except that they have a policy to attract mature students, who, they feel, enrich the place, and for them entry to some courses depends on interests and experience. Generally though, UEA can call the tune, for example three A grades in the Law Department because of the American and Euro Law specialisms.

There are twice-yearly literary festivals; they have a professional writer in residence. It is here that Sir Malcolm Bradbury (author of the classic university novel, *The History Man*) set the literary firmament alight with his creative writing school, out of which came Ian McEwan and Kazuo Ishiguro among others.

There is also a fine reputation for American Studies, which scored full marks in the teaching assessments. Campus is home to the Arthur Miller Centre for American Studies.

SOCIAL SCENE

STUDENTS' UNION The SU is active on the Internet as a meeting place for websites from unions throughout the country (see www.stu.uea.ac.uk /info.uksu.html, and, more intriguing, the new site: www.tsw.org.uk). They also have a lively reputation for journalism – their TV station is Nexus TV, their radio station, Livewire. *Concrete* is the newspaper, which incorporates *The Event* entertainment magazine and was runner-up as Best Newspaper in the recent national *Independent* awards. There is a track record for graduate careers in radio/TV and publishing (see our *Employment* box, page 172), and top ratings for teaching and research in media/communications (see *Academic Excellence*, page 170).

> *UEA is a top uni with an independent streak and a host of interesting specialisms. Self-containment on the old golf course is choice for some, others feel driven to to run to town to feel free again, but a mere 4% drop out.*

There are fifty societies and forty sports clubs. Gays get a good deal here: LBG is among the most active societies (and political campaigns were heavy on the Section 28 issue), along with *Concrete*, Games Soc and Livewire. **The Studio** is the UEA theatre, drama is another top-scoring course rating.

LCR (Lower Common Room) has been voted the best student venue in the country by the music industry's *Live!* magazine. Each year more than fifty live bands grace its stage, recently Ash, Scratch, Perverts, Super Furry Animals, Embrace, Wheatus, Andrew WK, Fun Lovin' Criminals, Atomic Kitten, Boy George, Nicky Blackmarket, Ed Harcourt, Turin Brakes, Ugly Duckling, Afroman, Nigel Rouse. So now you know. Its weekly sell-out disco – cheese pop with specialist music on rotation in another room – is legendary and the 3-weekly *Retro* is massively popular.

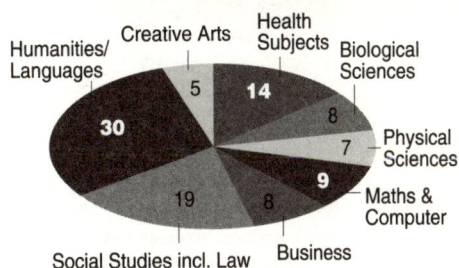

SUBJECT AREAS (%)

Humanities/Languages 30
Creative Arts 5
Health Subjects 14
Biological Sciences 8
Physical Sciences 7
Maths & Computer 9
Business 8
Social Studies incl. Law 19

Union Bars feature **The Pub** – all-day opening, pool tables, table footie, arcade machines, jukebox and large screen TV. A quieter, non-smoking alternative is **The Back Bar** – music-free and comfortable. Then there's the **Lunchbox** and **The Hive** with food and late licence on Tuesdays and Thursdays for private parties. *Live in the Hive* includes (free) local bands, as well as karaoke, quizzes, games and comedy shows.

Besides the LCR, the uni has had its own venue in Norwich – **The Waterfront**.There are three bars and two rooms of music – '80s/'90s, *Chill 'Em Out Jazz Café* (beat poetry, jazz and student contributions), *Latin Party*, *Meltdown* (indie).

SPORT Good, though not top notch for sport (halfway up/down the national team table); good facilities. A £17.6-million, integrated indoor and outdoor facility, including an Olympic-size swimming pool and a human performance laboratory opened recently. Women's hockey is very strong. Other big deals are football, tennis, trampolining, rugby, athletics, kerfball and American footie.

TOWN Apparently, Norwich has a pub for every day of the year. It also has the **Theatre Royal** (touring companies, RSC, National), **The Maddermarket**, a smaller, amateur but vibrant venue. The bohemian **King of Hearts** rules for music, art, jazz, literature readings, and **The Norwich Arts Centre** for live music, from rock and jazz to chamber music, exhibitions, dance workshops and comedy – David Baddiel, Frank Skinner, Lee & Herring and The Fast Show's Simon Day all played here last year. There are three cinemas – the **ABC** and the **Odeon** (in the heart of the excellent Magdalen Street curry scene

WHAT IT'S REALLY LIKE	
UNIVERSITY:	
Social Life	★★★★★
Campus scene	**Lively**
Student Union services	**Good**
Politics	**Active**
Sport	**40 clubs, but not obsessional**
National team position	**69th**
Sport facilities	**Good**
Arts opportunities	**Excellent**
Student newspaper	**Concrete**
Ents magazine	**Event**
Student radio	**Livewire**
Student TV	**Nexus**
Independent awards	**TSW web site**
Nightclub	**The Waterfront**
Bars	**Union bars (2) + The Hive, The Lunchbox, LCR**
Union ents	**Cheese Pop, Retro, Jazz Café, Latin Party, Meltdown**
Union clubs/societies	**90**
Most popular societies	**LGB, Concrete, Games, Livewire**
Smoking policy	**One NS bar**
Parking	**Poor**
CITY:	
Entertainment	★★★
Scene	**OK pubs, clubs**
Town/gown relations	**Average**
Risk of violence	**Low**
Cost of living	**Average**
Student concessions	**Abundant**
Survival + 2 nights out	**£60-£80 pw**
Part-time work campus/town	**Good/excellent**

AT A GLANCE	
ACADEMIC FILE:	
Assessments	**24**
Excellent	**83%**
Average requirements	**280 points**
Students-staff ratio	**23:1**
First/2:1 degree pass rate	**65%**
ACCOMMODATION FILE:	
Guarantee to freshers	**100% non-locals**
Style	**Halls/ terraces, village/flats**
Catered	**None**
En-suite	**48%**
Price range pw	**£43-£63.61**
City rent pw	**£40-£50**

JOBS

A recent survey of graduates in 2000 showed that 4.9% only were unemployed after six months. Points of interest from our Employment box include their strength (9th position nationally) as a graduate provider to the financial sector, the health provision mentioned above, and the media, especially advertising, radio/TV and publishing (4th in the national Top Ten).

GETTING THERE
☛ By road: A11(M), A47.
☛ By rail: London Liverpool Street, 2:00; Birmingham New Street, 4:00; Sheffield, 3:50.
☛ By air: Norwich Airport.
☛ By coach: London, 2:50; Birmingham, 6:00; Sheffield, 7:00.

– **Nazma**, **Norwich Tandoori**, **Bombay**, **Passage to India**); and there's **Cinema City** for arthouse.

PILLOW TALK

All first years who normally live outside a 12-mile radius of UEA are guaranteed study bedrooms in halls and flats, provided they meet a given deadline. Norfolk, Suffolk and Waveney Terraces, Orwell Close and Wolfson Close provide self-catering accommodation in groups of up to fifteen study-bedrooms; Nelson Court and Constable Terrace – 'the closest thing to the Ritz' – in slightly smaller groups with plush, en-suite facilities. Since 1994 accommodation has also been offered in a student village: ten buildings with apartments for six to eight students.

WHERE GRADUATES END UP	
13% Finance*,	Key Areas
12% Manufacturing,	
11% Health/Social Work,	
8% Public Admin,	
7% Education,	
7% Wholesale/Retail	
7% Personnel,	
A ccountancy, Advertise,	Niche Areas
Legal, Library/Archival,	
Publishing*, Radio/TV	
*indicates Top 10 Graduate Provider	
Approximate employed	**94%**

UNIVERSITY OF EAST LONDON

The University of East London
Longbridge Road,
Dagenham RM8 2AS

TEL 020 8223 3000
FAX 020 8590 7799
EMAIL admiss@uel.ac.uk
WEB www.uel.ac.uk

UEL Students' Union
Block C
Longbridge Road
Dagenham RM8 2AS

TEL 020 8590 6017
FAX 020 8597 6987
EMAIL barkings@hotmail.com
WEB uelsu.org.uk

VAG VIEW

In UEL we have the former East London Poly. Its stated mission is 'to provide the highest possible quality of education in order to meet' – not the needs of the country or Europe or the world, but – 'the needs of individuals and of the communities and enterprises in our region.' The mission is, as we discovered, no less ambitious for its narrower geographical focus.

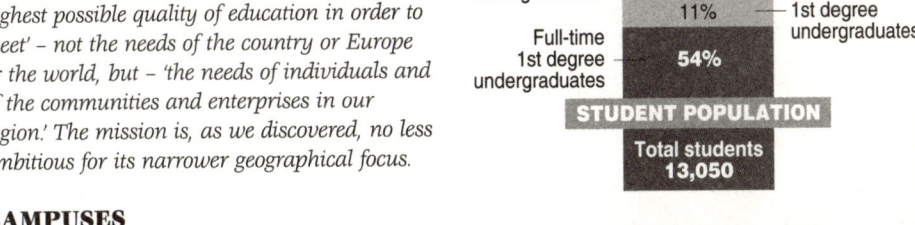

CAMPUSES

BARKING CAMPUS (address above) **Departments:** Accountancy, Anthropology, Applied Sports Science, Business, Civil Eng., Communication (PR, advert., journalism) Computing, Criminology, Economics, Education, Euro Studies, Languages, Law, Linguistics, Politics, Social Sciences. **Accommodation:** halls of residence – groups of flats for six with shared kitchen/diner, shower, bathrooms and toilets.

STRATFORD CAMPUS Romford Road, London E15 4LZ. Tel 020 8223 3000. **Departments:** Applied Sports Science, Archaeology, Architecture, Biosciences (incl. biochem., biology, microbiology & parasitology), Enviro. Studies, Health (incl. physiotherapy, nursing, physiol. & physiotherapy), Maths & Computing. **Accommodation:** university house or flat-share at Park Village nearby. Landscaped last year and a number of new buildings planned. Facilities include Fitness on the Green (fitness and training centre), restaurant and Students' Union Bar (Maryland House).

DOCKLANDS CAMPUS 4-6 University Way, London E16 2RD. Tel 020 8223 3000. **Departments:** Cultural & Media Studies, Design (Fashion, Textiles, Graphics, Product Design), Electrical & Manufacturing Engineering, Innovation Studies. There is a Library & Learning Resource Centre and a Multimedia Production Centre. At the hub is The Thames Gateway Technology Centre (TGTC), its purpose to further graduate employability, business start-up, and the development of the

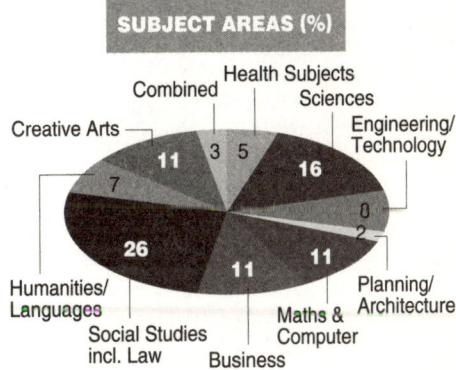

campus as a learning centre for business. **Accommodation:** five new halls of residence for 384 students. Study bedrooms, arranged as three- or five- person flats sharing a kitchen, each with en-suite shower/toilet, many with stunning waterside view of Royal Albert Dock.

STUDENT PROFILE

There is a large ethnic population and a very large mature student population. It has one of the worst student drop-out rates of any English university (17%). One student, who claimed only to have finished her course 'by biting back rancour about absent tutors, sub-standard facilities, a whole course offered but never delivered,' provoked a professor to reply: 'It is ironic that a university that has made such efforts to widen participation and

UNIVERSITY/STUDENT PROFILE	
University since	**1992**
Situation/style	**City sites**
Student population	**13,050**
Full-time undergraduates	**7,070**
- mature	**50%**
- overseas	**10%**
- male/female	**47/53**
- state sector intake	**97%**
- non-traditional student intake	**15%**
- drop-out rate	**17%, high**
- undergraduate applications	**Down 13%**
see Introduction for key to tables	

thinkers, painters and even the odd serial killer as you blast through the past and into the future. This is [UEL's] Cultural Studies. Doing this course gave me the cutting edge perspective that you need as a thriller writer today. Because of it I now spend my days with psychos who read Baudrillard, sleuths who are addicted to crime fiction and two cats who get psychoanalysed when I'm between books.'

Cultural Studies is a department that was rated Excellent in the English faculty inspection and world class Grade 5 in last year's research assessments. And there is a woman behind all this called Dr Patel.

A team of clinical psychologists at UEL, led by Dr Nimisha Patel, has just won an award from the British Medical Association for a manual called *Clinical Psychology, 'Race' and Culture*, which challenges assumptions and practices of clinical psychology and shows supervisors, tutors and practitioners to integrate issues of 'race' and culture into their training programme. Dr Patel's book has arisen directly from 'work with black and minority ethnic groups' under the auspices of UEL – 'The university is becoming widely recognised as a pioneer in this area,' she said. 'My own clinical experience of working with refugees has taught me that it is impossible to divorce psychology from the cultural context. In an increasingly multi-cultural society, health practitioners in all fields will need the skills to understand and deal with these issues.'

include students from both under-represented social groups and mature backgrounds should find itself coming under such heavy criticism from someone who has benefited directly from the very policy.' Which sort of begs the whole question, doesn't it?

ACADEMIA

With a 21:1 student-staff ratio, an Excellence rating of only 61%, and an official requirement of 160 points at A level, you could be forgiven for lacking confidence. There appears, however, to be at least one good reason why you should give UEL a chance. 'Imagine a rollercoaster that begins in the 17th century and ends somewhere around now,' said Scarlett Thomas. 'Along the way you can wave at revolutionaries, artists, philosophers, writers,

> *An authentic culture, some good specialist academic lines into employment, but you'll need strong commitment and keen insight to make it really work.*

Is this not precisely what the university was set up to do?

JOBS

UEL's relatively poor graduate employment record is another league-table criticism. It is tempting to say that league tables weren't made for a uni where 40% of non-mature entrants come from social classes III, IV or V, and 15% from so-called 'low-participation neighbourhoods'. But there are moves to enhance their reputation, such as The Thames Gateway Technology Centre for the new-media, culture and design students (see *Docklands Campus* above), and there are masses of applied language courses to enhance employment possibilities.

The 20% health provision (see box, page 175) directs us not only to the health promotion and management degrees, but to immunology, human biology, a couple of specialist degrees concerning

ACADEMIC EXCELLENCE	
TEACHING:	
(Rated Excellent or 17+ out of 24)	
Architecture, English	**Excellent**
Psychology	**23**
Art & Design, Civil Eng,	**21**
Economics, Subjects Allied to Medicine	**20**
Sociology, Pharmacology, Education, Biosciences	**19**
Linguistics & Modern Languages, Mechanical, Manufacturing Eng.	**18**
RESEARCH:	
Top grades 5/5*	
Communication/Cultural/Media	**Grade 5**

WHERE GRADUATES END UP

20% Health/Social Work, 10% Public Admin*, 10% Wholesale/Retail, 9% Education, 8% Finance, 5% Manufacturing 5% Personnal Eng/Industrial Design, Architecture, Film/Video, Legal, Library/Archival*, Artistic/Literary*, Market Research, Publishing, Sport	Key Areas
	Niche Areas

*indicates Top 10 Graduate Provider

Approximate employed **81%**

WHAT IT'S REALLY LIKE

UNIVERSITY:	
Social Life	★★★★
Campus scene	**Beleaguered, authentic, urban culture**
Student Union services	**Average**
Politics	**Anti-racism & free education**
Sport	**Relaxed/20 teams**
National team position	**None**
Sport facilities	**Average**
Arts opportunities	**Some**
Student mag/news	**FUEL**
Student radio	**Hubbub**
Nightclub/Bars	**Duel 1, 2 and 3 - each campus**
Union ents	**Reggae, Smooth Grooves, Club Commercial, Frolic, Melting Pot**
Union clubs/societies	**40**
Most popular society	**Islamic**
Smoking policy	**NS except bars**
Parking	**Poor**
CITY:	
Entertainment	★★★★★
Scene	**Local clubs 'n uptown flavours**
Town/gown relations	**Poor**
Risk of violence	**Random**
Cost of living	**High**
Student concessions	**OK**
Survival + 2 nights out	**£60 pw**
Part-time work campus/town	**Good, must travel**

infectious diseases, various medical and biomedical sciences courses, Pharmacology, Physiotherapy and the social areas – Social Research with Professional Studies as well as social work type courses.

The artistic strength comes out in a raft of textile and surface decoration courses, and the uni has always been strong in the info-techno archival sector, taking 8th position this year in the national league table.

SOCIAL SCENE

Political awareness is the most notable aspect at student level, and a culturally rich ents programme, including dedicated and *Mixed Flavour* discos – indie, soul, swing, '70s/'80s, jungle, hip hop, ragga – comedy nights, cabaret, live bands, video nights and the odd society 'do' (including plays on the **Venue** stage). One-offs include Spring Ball, Valentine Bash, Diwali Rave, Hallowe'en Night, Christmas Rave.

Recent scheduled live acts include DJ Skully – UK DMC Technics Winner, Starski, other student bands and Sonya Fariq. A lot of bar activity/events are laid on by students through cultural societies. Recently, there's been an attempt to simplify the basics by calling the bars at the three campuses (Stratford, Barking and Docklands respectively) **DUEL 1**, **DUEL 2**, **DUEL 3**, which released the following menu: DUEL 1: *Abomination*, every Wednesday – cheese and pop filth. DUEL 2: 100% Raggae/Smooth Grooves (R&B, garage etc), rotating Tuesdays, *Club Commercial*, Thursday – commercial dance. DUEL 3: *Happy Mondays* – indie and alt. flavours, *Frolic* every Friday. Students vote the previous week for the music policy. *The Melting Pot*

is Wednesday's 'a bit of it all'. DUEL 2/3 gets regular comedy (*Mirth Control*) on various nights.

About thirty societies are up and running. Hard to tell which is the most active, but the Islamic society generally has the largest membership.

Student media includes a magazine, *Fuel*, and radio station (new venture), Hubbub. *Fuel* was shortlisted for a *Guardian* award in '99, and won the Commission for Racial Equality award for best student publication dealing with issues of race.

In the political arena, they are one of a handful of universities capable of organising a decent sit-in and they got together with Goldsmiths recently to do a *Rough Guide to Occupation*. Currently, they describe the level of activity as 'average, meaning less people compensate with great awareness and enthusiasm!'

SPORT Relaxed attitude, twenty teams, not

nationally competitive, but won their rugby league last year. Teams make use mainly of council pitches and halls that offer student discounts. A swimming pool is used for water polo, sub-aqua and canoeing; there are two gyms, facilities for aerobics, dance, badminton, table tennis, karate, circuit training, volleyball, basketball, indoor football, a squash court, four tennis courts, a fitness centre. Playing fields are a few miles away,

at Little Heath. Badminton is available near the Stratford campus and there are other recreational activities on offer – golf, sailing, windsurfing, skiing, sub-aqua, riding, and weekend and vacation courses are arranged.

TOWN 'Well it's London, so all bets are off,' said my informant. 'Cost of living is high, general things (food etc) are fairly priced compared to other places. It's the social side of things that costs so much. Start saving now. Risk of violence is, surprisingly random. Arguably, people would say London is prone to greater violence. But really it's all quite random. You'll need about £50 to live on if you want to go out at least two nights. Chance of employment is high. Both within the Students' Union and wider a-field.'

GETTING THERE
☛ **Stratford** by Underground, Central Line; closest overland rail station is Maryland (connect London Liverpool Street).
☛ **Barking** by Underground, City & Hammersmith and District lines; Goodmayes overland station.
☛ **Docklands** via the Docklands Light Railway.

EDGE HILL COLLEGE

Edge Hill College
St Helens Road
Ormskirk
Lancashire L39 4QP

TEL 01695 584274
FAX 01695 584355
EMAIL enquiries@edgehill.ac.uk
WEB www.edgehill.ac.uk

VAG VIEW

*E*dge Hill is a higher education college offering degrees awarded by the University of Lancaster to a largely local, and 24% mature, undergraduate body. The preponderance of female students (66%) is down to the Health Faculty (midwifery and nursing) in Fazakerley, Liverpool. Of graduates, nearly half go into the Education sector – primary and secondary preparation is available – and a number go into business or financial activities or sport (where there is a large number of course possibilities and a £3.4-million campus Centre), but there are some interesting courses to tempt you elsewhere. In media, for instance, Science Journalism looks inviting, and in amongst the joint honours, such as the criminology combos look to have unusual propensities, as do some involving film, writing or drama. The campus **Rose Theatre** is used by the student Footlights Society and by visiting companies.

With so many students mature and from the locality, and with Ormskirk not being exactly a global centre of entertainment, don't expect too wild a time. Although, it appears they make do. When Edge Hill was taken to court by a neighbour for the regular early hours clamour, a judge was reported as commenting, 'It's like Brideshead Revisited meets St Trinian's isn't it?', as the prosecution itemised the complainant's five-year 'noise diary'. Should such merry japes as singing Don't Cry For Me Argentina as your mates climb a tree shouting football chants not be your idea of a good time, however, Preston, Manchester and Liverpool are close.

GETTING THERE
☛ By road: M6/J26, M58/J3, A570 to Southport. The uni is 2 miles along on the right.
☛ By rail: Northern Line Merseyrail train connections from Liverpool Central and Preston Stations. Alight at Ormskirk, not Edge Hill.

STUDENT EDINBURGH – THE CITY

Despite its ancient past, Edinburgh is a modern city. It may have a dominant castle overlooking historic gardens and the Royal Mile, inebriated with touristy whisky and kilt shops, but the new Scottish Parliament and re-vamped National Museum of Scotland have conspired to give Edinburgh something of a new start. What's more, it's a city for the young. A fresh, dynamic energy makes Scotland's capital – cultural, cosmopolitan, stylish and very much at the forefront of European life – one of the best places to spend your student days in the new millennium.

CAFÉ BAR SCENE
If you can handle the hills, Edinburgh is also a walking city, with nowhere being too far away. Should you tire, there's more than enough café bars to suit every taste and satisfy the weary wanderer's appetite. The **Human Be-In** is typical of the capital's smart new establishments, with a chic modernist décor and the best salads in town. For the less weight-conscious is **Favorit**, where drinks and snacks are served until 3am. Forget kebabs, their bacon butties are the only way to satisfy the late-night munchies.

The **Elephant House** on George IV Bridge offers great coffee and a first class view of the castle, and as long as you can handle the ubiquitous elephant memorabilia and Harry Potter bores (J K Rowling apparently wrote her books here), it's always a safe study break bet. Buy a book at the popular **Book Stop Café** near Bristo Square and get a free coffee to sip while enjoying your purchase. For those flash with the cash, head to **Plaisir du Chocolat** on the Royal Mile, where an entire loan could be blown on the best hot chocolate money can buy. Regular caffeine haunts for that rare breed of early-rising students are the George Square **Negociants** and its more distinguished next-door neighbour **Iguana**, both of which change image as the coffee drinkers change beverage.

WIDE SCREEN
The city excels in cinemas, thanks mainly to the **Cameo** in Tollcross, where there's thematic music before the credits roll and the pleasure of enjoying a pint in its enticingly comfortable seats. The Cameo features only the best films - those too good to be seen at your local Odeon, ignoring the worst experimental stuff that the more arty cinemas play. The best of these is the **Filmhouse**, which is especially recommended for foreign films. Hollywood Blockbusters are left to the **UGC Multiplex** at Fountainpark or the new **Ster Century Cinema** at the Ocean Terminal on the docks in Leith. The city's annual International Film Festival in August features UK premieres of films that'll be the talk of the country within a few months. For those with less cash to splash, joining the University of Edinburgh's Film Society is a bargain bet, with £15 allowing free entry to all showings throughout the academic year.

DRAMA KINGS
The intimate environment of the Lyceum consistently offers much loved productions, be they straight-up Shakespeare or post-modern avant-garde. The world famous **Traverse**, nestling nearby amongst high-class eateries, dishes up excellent experimental Scottish drama as well as having one of the hippest bars in Edinburgh. If you're into more mainstream theatre or opera, head to the **King's Theatre** or **Festival Theatre**, while if comedy or musicals are your thing, then the **Playhouse** is likely to appeal. Stars of tomorrow feature at the student-run **Bedlam Theatre**, Bristo Place.

NOT THE USUAL

Edinburgh's 2,000 or so pubs stay open until at least midnight throughout the week, with many not shutting up shop until 1am or 3am at the weekends. On arrival, you might hear about the Rose Street Crawl and the stretch of pubs on the Grassmarket. Don't shoot there. For 100% proof, check out the **Living Room** on the Cowgate. With bargain prices, cosy sofas and chilled atmosphere, it's the perfect pre-club pub. The **Pear Tree** is a major student haunt, particularly in the summer, when not spilling your drink in the packed beer patio becomes the main objective of the night's drinking. Vodka fiends love **Bar Kohl**, but if ice cream's your poison, then **Mr Boni's** in Toll Cross might prove to be heaven.

For those who like their drinks horizontal, **Medina** is a must, although with its Moroccan cave interior of rugs and beanbags, you'll end up feeling readier for bed than for clubbing. New to the scene is **Brass Monkey** on Drummond Street, where you can not only lie down on comfy cushions to enjoy your beer, but also watch DVD's whilst you're doing it: pure genius. For something a little different, check out **The Forest** on the West Port, a non-profit making café that specialises in giving artists a space to show new work. Although not licensed to sell alcohol, you can bring your own, so it's perfect for when the funds run dry. Drunk in the city after hours and not ready for bed? Best not to make a habit of it, but the notorious **Penny Black** behind the Burger King on Princes Street East End opens for business at 5am, as does the **Scotsman's Lounge** on Cockburn Street. When the hangover kicks in, head to the **City Café**, where the funky leather booths prove ideal for post-binge gossip and recovery sessions.

IN THE CLUB

Edinburgh's club scene is growing but still trails behind other British cities, including Glasgow. For underground music check out the arty **Bongo Club**, which despite having the worst toilets in Edinburgh, offers the best hip hop and reggae sounds in town. Their *El Segundo* and *Headspin* nights come particularly recommended. If drum 'n' bass or house is your line, head to **La Belle Angele**, where *Manga* and *Ultragroove* sell out every month. Despite being hailed as the saviour of the Edinburgh club scene upon its opening in 2001, the **Honeycomb** has so far failed to deliver the goods. *Motherfunk* on Tuesdays is nevertheless always chocker, with free entry and cheap drinks proving especially popular with students. Let down only by its sub-standard sound system, **Ego** on Picardy Place caters for a more glammed-up crowd and is especially popular amongst the gay community. Goths, hairy rockers and technoheads will enjoy moshing/raving at **Studio 24**, whilst nu-metallers will find kindred spirits at **The Citrus Club** on Grindlay Street. The city's best-loved indie night is *The Egg* every Saturday at the **Art College**, but for something less trendy, try the **Liquid Room**'s Friday *Evol* night. If terrible music and ugly punters are what you're after, head on to **Revolution**, **Subway** or the **Cavendish**, where even the Elephant Man could get a snog. R&B groovers can get jiggy at **Gaia** on Friday nights. Venues chop and change their nights each week, so for complete up-to-date listings pick up a copy of *The List* or the Edinburgh *Student*.

RETAIL RELIEF

Although playing second fiddle to Glasgow in terms of highstreet shops, Edinburgh excels in the vintage market. If retro is the requirement, **Armstrongs** and **The Rusty Zip** always deliver the goods, while **Flip** on South Bridge is particularly good for flares, cords and comedy seventies gear. For the ultimate in budget retailing, check out the numerous charity shops on Nicholson Street. Skaterkids are well-serviced in Edinburgh, with both **Cult Clothing** and **Odd One Out** especially popular with the baggy-trousered contingent. Antiquarians wile away the hours at the myriad secondhand book shops on the West Port, while the gorgeous Victoria Street is the best place for buying gifts. For music, head to Cockburn Street, home to the capital's number 1 music shops, **Fopp** and **Avalanche**, both of which are infinitely better value than their mainstream Princes Street rivals. Living up to its name, **Whiplash Trash** is a few doors down, offering a bizarre selection of things, and **Crew 2000**, the drugs and sex advice shop, aptly enough lies opposite. The city's supreme poster outlet, **Kick Ass**, helps to make Cockburn Street what it is, while refined photography emporium **Beyond Words** gives the street the touch of class that its name sorely lacks.

ADDRESSES

Café Bars: Favorit, 19/20 Teviot Place, 220 6880 and 30-32 Leven Street, 221 1800. Iguana, 41 Lothian Street, 220 4288. Negociants, 45-47 Lothian Street, 225 6313. Plaisir Du Chocolat, 251-253, Canongate, 556 9524. The Book Stop CafÈ, 4 Teviot Place, 226 6929. The Elephant House, 21 George IV Bridge, 220 5355. The Human Be-In, 2/8 West Crosscauseway, 662 8860

Cinemas: Cameo, 38 Home Street, 228 4141.Filmhouse, 88 Lothian Road, 228 2688. Ster Century Cinema, Ocean Terminal, Ocean Drive, Leith, 553 0700. UGC Fountain Park, Fountainpark,

Dundee Street, 0870 9020417. University of Edinburgh Film Society, 60 The Pleasance, 557 0436

Theatre: Bedlam, 11b Bristo Place, 225 9873. Festival Theatre, 13-29 Nicolson Street, 529 6000. King's Theatre, 2 Leven Street, 529 6000. Playhouse, 18-22 Greenside Place, 0870 606 3424 Royal Lyceum, Grindlay Street, 248 4848. Traverse Theatre, 10 Cambridge Street, 228 1404

Pubs and Stuff: Bar Kohl, 54, George IV Bridge, 225 6936. Brass Monkey, 14, Drummond Street, 556 1961. City Cafe, Blair Street, 220 0125. The Forest, 9, West Port, 221 0237. Living Room, 235-237, Cowgate, 225 4628. Medina's (downstairs at Negociants), Lothian Road, 2225 6313. Mr Boni's Ice Cream Parlour, 4 Lochrin Buildings, 229 5319. Pear Tree House, 8 West Nicolson Street, 667 7533. The Penny Black, 17 West Register Street, 556 1106 Scotsmans Lounge, 73 Cockburn St, 225 7726

Clubs: Bongo Club, 14 New Street, 556 5204. Cavendish, West Tollcross, 228 3252. Citrus Club,

40-42 Grindlay Street, 622 7086. Ego, 14 Picardy Place, 478 7434. Honeycomb, 15-17 Niddry Street, 530 5540. La Belle Angele, 11 Hasties Close, 225 7536. Gaia, 28 Kings Stables Road, 229 9438. Revolution, 31 Lothian Road, 229 7670. Studio 24, 24 Calton Road, 558 3758. Subway, Cowgate, 225 6766 and Lothian Road, 229 9197. Wee Red Bar, Edinburgh College of Art, Lauriston Place, 229 1442

Shops: Armstrongs, 83 Grassmarket, 220 5557; 66 Clerk St, 667 3056. Avalanche, 17 West Nicolson Street, 668 2374; 63 Cockburn Street, 225 3939; 28 Lady Lawson Street, 668 2374; 2-3 Teviot Place, 226 7666. Beyond Words, 42-44 Cockburn Street, 226 6636. Crew 2000, 32 Cockburn Street, 220 3404. Cult Clothing, 7 North Bridge, 556 5003. Flip, 59-61 South Bridge, 556 4966. Fopp, 55 Cockburn Street, 220 0133. Kick Ass, 34 Cockburn Street, 662 7318 Odd One Out, (girls) 18 Victoria Street, 220 6400, (boys) 62/64 Candlemaker Row, 220 0477 The Rusty Zip, 14 Teviot Place, 226 4634. Whiplash Trash, 53 Cockburn Street, 226 1005

UNIVERSITY OF EDINBURGH

The University of Edinburgh
57 George Square
Edinburgh EH8 9JU

TEL 0131 650 4360
FAX 0131 651 1236
EMAIL enquiries.scls@cd.ac.uk
WEB www.ed.ac.uk

Edinburgh University Student Association
Student Centre House
5/2 Bristo Square
Edinburgh EH8 9AL

TEL 0131 650 2656
FAX 0131 668 4177
EMAIL president@eusa.ed.ac.uk
WEB www.eusa.ed.ac.uk

VAG VIEW

If you are looking at the employers' surveys or parents' perceptions, it's Oxbridge then Durham and Bristol, and Edinburgh is the Scottish equivalent of these. Edinburgh, they know, is the place to be. An Edinburgh degree is a very good degree to have. It is still considered to be part of a Scottish person's birthright. They do not admit to offering a Scottish quota.

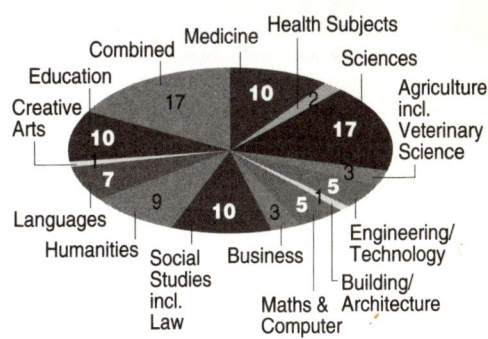

SUBJECT AREAS (%)

CAMPUS

'The University is primarily divided into two main campuses, two miles apart,' writes James Lumsden. 'George Square (with its central city location) for Arts & Social Science, and KB (King's Buildings) for Science and Engineering. Recently, the university has spent wads of cash reinventing KB into somewhere that you no longer want to

leave before you arrive. The result reminds some of a cross-channel ferry. George Square, meanwhile, has its own brand of ugliness, in the shape of Appleton and David Hume towers. For a beautiful city that's known as the "Athens of the

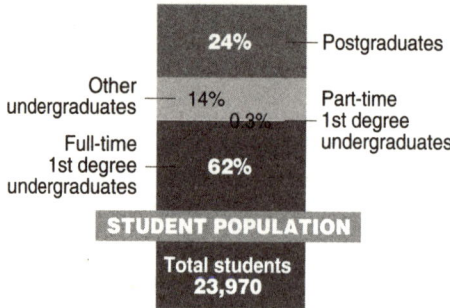

STUDENT POPULATION

24% Postgraduates

Other undergraduates — 14%

0.3% — Part-time 1st degree undergraduates

Full-time 1st degree undergraduates — 62%

Total students 23,970

North", Edinburgh University seems to have done its damnedest to flout convention.'

STUDENT PROFILE

'Often represented by a myopic media as a toffs' university,' James continues, 'the true diversity of

UNIVERSITY/STUDENT PROFILE	
University since	**1583**
Situation/style	**Civic**
Student population	**23,970**
Full-time undergraduates	**14,790**
- mature	**14%**
- overseas	**11%**
- male/female	**46/54**
- state sector intake	**63%, low**
- non-traditional student intake	**8%**
- drop-out rate	**4%, low**
- undergraduate applications	**Up 5%**
see Introduction for key to tables	

student and university life at Edinburgh goes misrepresented; there are nearly 20,000 students from a wide variety of backgrounds and circumstances. In recent history a large number of English students have chosen to study at Edinburgh, but, with the introduction of tuition fees and a four-year degree programme, English applications have fallen lately.'

A couple of years ago the *Sunday Times* Style section advised 'anyone looking for a university education where they can live like Sebastian Flyte, hang out with viscounts and guzzle Champagne for breakfast,' should look no further than Edinburgh. The uni certainly has its share of rahs and the public school girls come here in abundance. Even if the community is so huge that the young grandees are never really *IT*, we're looking at only 63% from the state sector, and a very low take (8%) from the poorer neighbourhoods.

The uni knows it's got to do something about this, especially as many of its Scottish compatriots

– Stirling, Dundee, Glasgow, Aberdeen – have shown that they can make an open access policy work. So, look forward to change, and consider whether Edinburgh's genetic makeover, which *as a matter of fact* is on the way, could benefit *you*...

They are looking to target state school sixthformers interested in studying law or medicine; they're offering seventy-five bursaries worth £1,000 per year of the degree programme; they are actively involved in LEAPS (the Lothian Equal Access Programme for Schools).

ACADEMIA

Moray House Institute of Education is the Uni's new Faculty of Education. Founded in 1835, there are two campuses, Holyrood in the heart of the Old Town, adjacent to the university's central premises and, six miles to the west, on the northwest edge of the city, a campus hitherto known as the Scottish

ACADEMIC EXCELLENCE	
TEACHING:	
(Rated Excellent, Highly Satis. or 17+ out of 24)	
Computer Studies, Physics, Chemistry, Electrical & Electronic Engineering, Geology, Maths & Statistics, History, Finance & Accounting, Sociology, Social Work, Cellular & Molecular Biology, Organismal Biology, Veterinary Medicine.	**Excellent**
Business & Management, Civil Engineering, Music, Architecture, Geography, History of Art, Law, Philosophy, Politics, Theology, French Studies, Medicine, Nursing, English, Psychology.	**Highly Satis.**
Chemical Engineering	**19**
European Languages	**21**
RESEARCH:	
Top grades 5/5*	
Hospital-based Clinical, Pure Maths, Computer, Electrical & Electronic Eng, Geography, Middle Eastern & African, English, German/Dutch/ Scandinavian, Philosophy	**Grade 5***
Psychology, Bio Sciences, Veterinary, Chemistry, Physics, Earth Sciences, Applied Maths, Civil Eng, Law, Anthropology, Sociology, Asian, Accounting, Celtic, French, Iberian/Latin American, Linguistics, History, Theology	**Grade 5**

Centre for Physical Education, which is home to PE, Leisure Studies and Applied Sports Science.

Overall, teaching assessments have been top of the range, and there must have been the odd shock wave when Edinburgh's celebrated Faculty of Medicine achieved but a Highly Satisfactory rather than an Excellent rating. No doubt they have now instituted the improvements recommended by SHEFC: earlier clinical contact and teaching in the community. Subsequently, the uni announced a £38-million spend on a new medical facility for 450 undergraduates and 400 staff to open this year.

There is an incredible 2,275,000-vol library, and excellent computer facilities and language laboratories. Yet there can be a problem in getting to use some of these resources. 'Queues for the Crisis Loans are lengthening ... study resources are being stretched to the limit,' said one student. It's a story repeated the length and breadth of the country. One nice touch at Edinburgh is that students are assigned a Director of Studies, a guardian angel trained to guide you through your course.

A whole raft of new courses come in this year for engineers, computer whizzes and mathematicians: Artificial Intelligence and Maths, Chemical Engineering with Environmental Engineering, Chemical Engineering with Management Techniques, Economic History and Business Studies, Electronic Business, Electronics and Computer Science, Electronics and Software Engineering, Embedded Electronics System Engineering, Medicinal Chemistry, Mobile Communications and Multimedia Engineering. There's also an intriguing introduction to another plane altogether – Psycholinguistics.

SOCIAL SCENE

'I know everyone is supposed to fall in love with their university, but Edinburgh just makes it so easy,' writes Holly Crane without a hint of gush. 'It's the ideal advert for higher education: a place where you learn not only facts and formulae from your academic studies, but also about what you can do, what you want to do – and what you don't want to do – with the rest of your life.'

Holly is sensitive to 'a discernible buzz about the university, a condensed feeling of potential, and energy. This is partly due to the city itself: there's just enough of the "ivory tower" atmosphere

It's the ideal advert for higher education: a place where you learn not only facts and formulae from your academic studies, but also about what you can do, what you want to do – and what you don't want to do – with the rest of your life.

to leave you inspired but not oppressed by your impending academia. But it's also to do with the type of students. With many doing four-year (or longer) degrees, there is, if not more time, then more reason, to get up off your arse and do something a bit different.'

There is opportunity aplenty to do just this – loads of clubs and societies, 170 of the latter alone, centred on **The Pleasance**, the most popular being Film Soc, The *Edinburgh Student* (newspaper, there's also a mag called *Hype* and a radio station, Fresh Air fm) and Nightline (welfare). *Edinburgh Student* is Britain's third biggest student newspaper, with a weekly circulation of 12,000 copies distributed to all the universities and higher education colleges around Edinburgh. It is also Britain's oldest student newspaper – Robert Louis Stevenson founded it in 1887. Meanwhile the University Theatre Company draws crowds for its many productions at **Bedlam Theatre**, the site of Bristo Bedlam, where 'the mad, manic and mental' were once locked away. All these often win national awards, this year they took the technical gong at the NUS Drama Fest. Then of course there's the politics. This year they've been beavering away at a Wall of Debt campaign, Quality Assurance, Semesterisation, Education policy with Scottish Parliament, Setting up CHESS (the Coalition of Higher Education Students in Scotland).

A recent development for night-time pleasure is **The Potterow** – 'the previous union premises had dry rot and needed to be replaced and the university offered to build us this. So we did,' I was told. There's a 1,200 capacity, but every Friday they stick it together with **Teviot**, the old venue, to make the real gravy: 2,500 students cough up for the *Bristo Square Experience* – student party tunes, house and dance music, hip hop, live bands, comedy, cabaret and karaoke, chill out areas and more. Saturday nights are big theme nights like the *Skool Disko*, *Funk Train* monthly and *Big Cheese* fortnightly.

Down at King's Buildings, there's a new £3.4 million student facility for the 7,000 science and engineering campus – catering and bar facilities, a games room, squash courts, a multi-gym, a sports hall and advisory and welfare services.

KB get quizzes, pool comps and film nights by way of ents.

WHAT IT'S REALLY LIKE

UNIVERSITY:

Social Life	★★★★★
Campus scene	**Diverse, active, self-assured**
Student Union services	**Good**
Politics	**Union focused**
Sport	**Key**
National team position	**6th**
Sport facilities	**Good**
Arts opportunities	**Good**
National drama awards	**Technical**
Student magazine	**Hype**
Student newspaper	**Student**
Student radio	**Fresh Air FM**
Nightclub	**Potterow**
Other venues	**Teviot, The Pleasance**
Union ents	**Bisto Square Experience - huge**
Union societies	**170+**
Most popular societies	**Film Soc**
Smoking policy	**Union OK**
Parking	**Poor**

CITY:

Entertainment	★★★★★
Scene	**Seething**
Town/gown relations	**Good**
Risk of violence	**Average**
Cost of living	**High**
Student concessions	**Excellent**
Survival + 2 nights out	**£60-£70 pw**
Part-time work campus/town	**Good/excellent**

SPORT The university is pre-eminent in sport, came 6th in the UK last year. Besides its twenty-five acres of playing fields and a residential centre on the shore of Loch Tay, there's a sports centre with conditioning gymnasia, a fitness and sports injury centre, and a wide range of team and individual activities. Sports bursaries are offered through the PE Department.

TOWN 'When you do step out, the city offers everything,' writes James Lumsden. 'There are enough bars and pubs to see you from this life into the next, and plenty of theatres, cinemas, clubs, and 'cultural stuff' to stop at, en-route. The city centre is geographically compact, so getting around can usually be accomplished on foot. Although there are plenty of cost-friendly student hangouts (as well as various student discount schemes) Edinburgh is still an expensive city. Metropolitan rates apply to taxis, restaurants and the better bars. See Student Edinburgh (page 177).

'Perhaps Edinburgh's biggest downside is the weather, which too often is dark, wet and cold. Those with Seasonal Affective Disorder should seriously think about going elsewhere. For the brief period that summer shines forth however, the city is fantastic; the beer gardens do a roaring trade and the parks are full of sunbathers and sizzling barbecues.'

PILLOW TALK

Freshers from outside Edinburgh are guaranteed a place in uni accommodation provided they apply by September 1, and that UCAS has guaranteed their place at Edinburgh by that date. There's a mix of traditional full board halls, student houses, and flats – 44% catered, 18% en suite, the price ranges from £56 (self-catering) to £101 (full board en-suite) Look out for new Chancellors Court this year, which will be all mod cons.

Main accommodation for first years is Pollock Halls, a complex of houses, together with a bar, shop and dining rooms, which take around 2,000 first years. All rooms are single, but, if you pay extra, you can upgrade to a double bed and en-suite shower. Most people go for full board; breakfast and supper in the week and three meals at the weekend. However, each house has a kitchen area where you can test out your culinary talents (toast). Another residential area is Robertson's Close which consists of self-catering flats. There are also student houses run by the university.

JOBS

As our *Employment* box shows (page 183), more than a third of graduates make it into the health and education sectors, while finance, accountancy and business/management soak up a good deal of

AT A GLANCE

ACADEMIC FILE:

Subjects assessed	**32**
Excellent/Highly Satisfactory	**94%**
Average A level requirements	**320 points**
Student-staff ratio	**14:1**
First/2:1 degree pass rate	**75%**

ACCOMMODATION FILE:

Guarantee to freshers	**If non-local & accepted by September 1**
Style	**Halls, flats, houses**
Catered	**44%**
En-suite	**18%**
Price range pw	**£56-£101**
Approx. city rent pw	**£55**

what's left. All of that, however, is before you begin to consider what happens to the engineers and technologists, and indeed the arts graduates, who find a whole host of interesting niches.

Latest figures available show 65.1% of first degree graduates going directly into employment, with 21.2% moving into further full-time study or training. A further 7.2% take time out travelling, while only 3.6% were recorded as still seeking employment or training at December 31 following graduation.

Edinburgh is one of six universities most targeted by major UK and international companies apparently, but they've also developed contacts with small firms in the region through a local initiative 'Graduates for Growth' – slick route to jobs in the fastest growing sector of the economy.

Oh, and a group of students have put together ESoc, the Edinburgh Entrepreneurial Society to encourage undergrads to think about setting up their own businesses. The scheme is already active within the Bases group at Stanford University in California.

GETTING THERE
☞ By road: M90 or M9 or A1 or M8.

WHERE GRADUATES END UP	
21% Health **(Medicine, Veterinary),** **14% Education,** **9% Finance,** **7% Manufacturing,** **5% Wholesale/Retail**	Key Areas
Accountancy, **Business/Management,** **Agric/Forestry,** **Advertising, Aeronautical** **Manufacture, Architec,** **Eng/Industrial Design,** **Artistic/Literary, Defence,** **Film/Video, Journalism,** **Library/Archival**	Niche Areas
Approximate employed **95%**	

☞ By rail: London King's Cross, 4:30; Glasgow Central, 50 mins; Newcastle, 1:30.
☞ By air: Edinburgh Airport for inland and international flights.
☞ By coach: Glasgow, 1:10; London, 9:10; Birmingham, 8:10; Newcastle, 3:10.

EDINBURGH COLLEGE OF ART

Edinburgh College of Art
Lauriston Place
Edinburgh EH3 9DF

TEL 0131 221 6000
FAX 0131 221 6001
EMAIL registration@eca.ac.uk
WEB www.eca.ac.uk

VAG VIEW

The origins of this college lie in the Drawing Academy, founded by the Trustees of the Edinburgh Board of Manufacturers in 1760. From 1821 an Edinburgh School of Arts was established and thirty years later, as a tribute to the great Scottish engineer James Watt, it changed its title to the Watt Institution and School of Arts, a moment in its history remembered today in the validation of its degrees by Heriot-Watt University. Currently there are talks in progress with the university for a merger by the summer of 2001.

The college today is spread over two campuses within five minutes walk of each other at the very heart of the Old Town. Although there is institutional accommodation

COLLEGE PROFILE	
Founded	**1908**
Status	**Art College**
Degree awarding university	**Heriot-Watt**
Total student population	**1,640**
Full-time undergraduates	**1,300**
ACCOMMODATION:	
Availability	**Overseas priority**
Style	**Town flats**
Cost pw (no food)	**£45**
City rent pw	**£50**
DEGREE SUBJECT AREAS:	
Art/Design (Fine Art with Edinburgh Uni), architecture, planning	

for only forty-three, students coming from outside the Edinburgh and Lothian area may apply for college-managed accommodation in the city centre.

*There is an active Students' Union, two bars – **The Wee Red Bar** (capacity 200) and **The Wee Red Lounge** (250). There is also a student newspaper,* The Wee Red Herring. *All college students have full use of the range of facilities at Heriot-Watt (see entry, page 218).*

GETTING THERE

☛ By road: from the north M90 across the Forth Bridge or the M9 down from Stirling. The A1 up from Newcastle. The M8 from Glasgow.
☛ By rail: London King's Cross, 4:30; Glasgow Central, 50 mins; Newcastle, 1:30.
☛ By air: Edinburgh Airport is a few miles to the West and offers inland and international flights.
☛ By coach: Glasgow, 1:10; London, 9:10; Birmingham, 8:10; Newcastle, 3:10.

UNIVERSITY OF ESSEX

The University of Essex
Wivenhoe Park
Colchester
Essex CO4 3SQ

Essex Students' Union
Wivenhoe Park
Colchester
Essex CO4 3SQ

TEL 01206 873778
FAX 01206 873423
admit@essex.ac.uk

TEL 01206 863211
FAX 01206 870915

VAG VIEW

*I*t is all too easy to underestimate Essex, a uni launched around the same time as York, Sussex, Warwick in the mid-'60s, but which, after it had marked its card as main '60s seat of revolution, never quite found its way back into careers masters' hearts. Yet, in teaching inspections recently, Electronic Systems Engineering, Sports Science, Philosophy, Economics, Politics, Tourism, Molecular Biosciences, Sociology, Psychology and Art History, only dropped six marks overall. And last year in the research assessments, they came 10th – way ahead of the likes of Durham and Nottingham; York came 18th, Sussex 31st, and Warwick just pipped Essex into 6th.

The University of Essex is considered to be one of the best Social Science universities in the country, especially for law, politics and sociology. There are other good reasons for opting for Essex – sport and student media among them. It is also convenient for London.

So, why has it had to rely so heavily on Clearing to encourage applicants in?

CAMPUS

Essex will never win any prizes for aesthetic beauty. It is a grey, drab institution, made almost

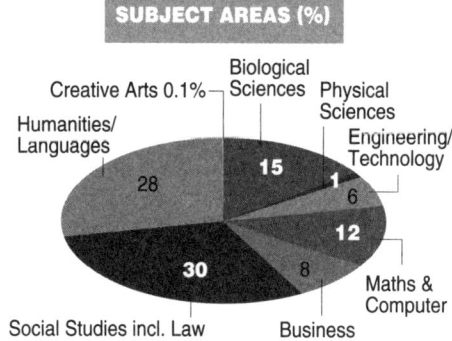

SUBJECT AREAS (%)

Creative Arts 0.1%
Biological Sciences
Physical Sciences
Humanities/Languages 28
Engineering/Technology 1
15
6
12
30
8
Maths & Computer
Social Studies incl. Law
Business

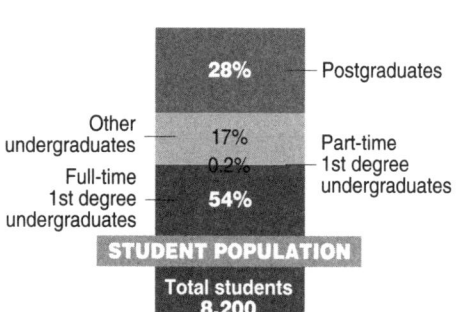

Postgraduates 28%
Other undergraduates 17%
Part-time 1st degree undergraduates 0.2%
Full-time 1st degree undergraduates 54%

STUDENT POPULATION
Total students
8,200

entirely of concrete. The brick, high-rise towers that house students are a blot on the Colchester skyline, which is not particularly nice to look at anyway. The campus comprises 200 acres of

UNIVERSITY/STUDENT PROFILE

University since	**1965**
Situation/style	**Town campus**
Student population	**8,200**
Full-time undergraduates	**4,460**
- mature	**20%**
- overseas	**32%**
- male/female	**52/48**
- state sector intake	**91%**
- non-traditional student intake	**11%**
- drop-out rate	**8%**
- undergraduate applications	**Up 12%**

see Introduction for key to tables

ACADEMIC EXCELLENCE

TEACHING:
(Rated Excellent or 17+ out of 24)

Law	**Excellent**
Electronic Systems Eng,	**24**
Sports Science, Philosophy, Economics, Politics, Tourism	
Molecular Biosciences	**23**
Sociology, Psychology, Art History	**22**
Linguistics	**21**
Maths, Nursing	**20**

RESEARCH:
Top grades 5/5*

Economics, Politics, Sociology	**Grade 5***
Psychology, Electrical & Electronic Eng, Law, Accounting, Linguistics, History, History of Art, Philosophy	**Grade 5**

landscaped parkland, two miles from the centre. Colchester, capital of Roman Britain and now commuter and garrison town and base camp for Essex uni, is today a regional centre of commerce, light industry and high technology (population 150,000). It is also a dormitory city for commuters to London, an hour away by train.

STUDENT PROFILE

Nick Margerrison notes the mixed student profile as 'one of the best features – it is a small, friendly university; you will enjoy your time here, along with Sharon, Tracey and Wayne. Actually, the university has a large overseas contingent too, especially Greek.' Mixed socially, economically and nationally – more than a third of students come from overseas; people come to Essex University from almost every conceivable part of the known world. 'This provides you with a unique chance to get to know a wide variety of different cultures.'

ACADEMIA

There are five Schools – Comparative Studies (Humanities, but with a cross-cultural, international approach), Social Sciences, Law, Maths & Computer Sciences, Science & Engineering – and consistently good teaching assessments recently – full marks for Electronic Systems Engineering and 22 out of 24 for Psychology, Sociology and Art History. While we're on the subject, a new History of Modern Art degree includes a ten-day subsidised visit to New York. Traditionally, Essex is strong in its links with Europe (ties with 50+ Euro Unis) – Socrates/Erasmus exchange schemes proliferate, as

> *Essex is seriously underrated. Tenth best in the country for research, consider it for social sciences – law, politics, economics, sociology; for biosciences; for sport; and much else; but close your eyes to its architecture.*

do Tempus (East/West). Notably, Law continues to dispense a number of graduates to the profession, and their unemployed rate overall compares well with the best among universities.

At Essex the first year is thrown open to a study of four or five courses to enable you to investigate your chosen subject from a variety of points of view. This might involve studying Sociology from an Economics point of view, History from a Psychology pov. Then in the second year you move forward to a single or joint honours degree with deeper understanding.

New undergraduate courses this year are in business and management, health science and psychology, drama, languages, criminology, and there's a new course on human rights. The Human Rights Centre on campus is a leader in its field.

SOCIAL SCENE

STUDENTS' UNION Being close to London has a negative effect on the uni scene at weekends when many depart for the metropolis, but there's no reason to leave, as far as Stephen J Peters can see: 'The SU is well run and campaigns hard on student issues. The bar is relatively big, with decent numbers of one-armed bandits and pool tables. Beer is reasonable, though prices do keep sneaking up quietly. The university magazine isn't bad, nor is the radio station.' *Parklife* is the mag, *The Rabbit* is

WHAT IT'S REALLY LIKE

UNIVERSITY:

Social Life	★★★★
Campus scene	**Diverse, fast developing**
Student Union services	**Good**
Politics	**Activity high Student issues**
Sport	**34 clubs**
National team position	**56th**
Sport facilities	**Good**
Arts opportunities	**Excellent**
Student magazine	**Parklife**
Student newspaper	**The Rabbit**
Student radio	**RED**
Nightclub	**Underground**
Bars	**SU, Level 2, Café Mondo**
Union ents	**Tonic, Score, Boogie Nights, Garage Heaven, Big Cheese, Rapture**
Union clubs/societies	**111**
Most popular society	**Silly Society**
Smoking policy	**NS food areas**
Parking	**No parking if you live on campus**

CITY:

Entertainment	★★★
Scene	**Clubs 'n pubs**
Town/gown relations	**Average**
Risk of violence	**Low**
Cost of living	**Average**
Student concessions	**Adequate**
Survival + 2 nights out	**£50 pw**
Part-time work campus/town	**Excellent/good**

the newspaper – campus is running with them, apparently; RED is the radio station.

The Students' Union has just completed a £1-million refurbishment of its facilities; a new bar opened in October 2001, and new nightclub and live performance facilities are under construction. The biggest single bar is the **SU Bar** and there's a new all-day alternative, **Café Mondo**; and then there's **Level 2**, a small venue (275 capacity) with late bar extensions, comedy nights, society nights, local bands, discos, drink promotions, etc.

The Underground is the main venue (850 cap). Beware Wednesday evenings if you're allergic to rugger buggers – it's Sports Fed night: *Score*. There's *Tonic* on Friday, plus *Boogie Nights*, *Garage Heaven*, *Big Cheese*, *Rapture*, the usual karaokes, society nights (Monday) and live acts – recently, Judge Jools, So Solid Crew, Craig Charles. Tuesday night is student night in town.

TOWN 'Colchester suffers from its relative proximity to other major venues in attracting big names in entertainment,' writes Stephen. 'Some occasionally grace us with their presence, but for the real stars get on the train to Cambridge or London. New talent can be seen at the local **Arts Centre**. But if you like a drink, Colchester and its environs can provide. Most tolerate students as long as you don't share your dinner with their toilet floor. The Wivenhoe Run is infamous, and has to be experienced if you reckon you can down a few. Colchester is a garrison town. Students, squaddies and alcohol are a volatile mix. Most of the time, though, you wouldn't know they are there. Find out where not to go in town when you get here (most notably the squaddie pubs).

'The nightclubs are pretty useless with the **Hippodrome** winning the award for naffest dive in history. Stick to the university nightclub, and only venture to the Slapperdrome on student nights. The music played on campus comes from all genres, from heavy metal to cheesy choons.

'Local transport links are average. Buses are frequent and not too expensive. Have the right change though, or the bus drivers, notoriously miserable, get a bit shirty. Trains to London are quick and reasonably reliable. And if you have a bit of money to spend, **Lakeside** and **Bluewater** are just down the road. But stay down the university bar – it is the best place to spend three years of your life.'

At the union, besides ents, there's an excellent secondhand bookshop (student buy 'n' sell), and a good Job Shop for part-time work.

SPORT 'Sporting facilities are good, apart from the non-existent swimming pool, a perennial campaigning issue,' Stephen writes. 'Performance

AT A GLANCE

ACADEMIC FILE:

Subjects assessed	**18**
Excellent	**78%**
Average requirements	**200 points**
Students-staff ratio	**16:1**
First/2:1 degree pass rate	**58%**

ACCOMMODATION FILE:

Guarantee to freshers	**100%**
Style	**Halls, flats, houses**
Catered	**None**
En-suite	**49%**
Price range pw	**£39-£65**
Town rent pw	**£50-£60**

in traditional sports suffers due to the small student numbers and large non-playing population, with football a notable exception. Rugby and hockey are the most sociable sports for both sexes. If you like a quiet drink, don't go down the bar on Wednesday evenings.'

There's a recently extended sports hall with six badminton courts, fitness room, sauna, sun-bed, squash courts, table tennis, climbing wall, plus a sportsturf pitch, floodlit tennis courts, three cricket pitches (one artificial wicket) plus nets, Squirrel Run circuit, eighteen-hole disc/frisbee-golf. A relatively new Master's degree in Sports Science (Fitness and Health) is a sign of the commitment. City sports clubs offer sailing, windsurfing, canoeing. Uni swimming club uses the pool at Colchester Leisure World. A new sports bursary scheme has just been unveiled; contact the university for more details.

PILLOW TALK

More new rooms have recently been built on campus for first years. As with most other places, the private sector varies in standard and cost. More than half of students live in uni accommodation, the majority of which is on campus. Tesco is within walking distance of campus, so shopping is easy. Accommodation ranges from flats for fourteen to sixteen in the famous Towers to smaller, en-suite flats for six people. Rent levels are among the lowest in the country, £39-£65 per week.

JOBS

Within six months of graduation in 2000, 47% of Essex first degree students were in employment, with a further 25% pursuing further study. Degree subject areas with a particularly strong employability record include Accounting Finance

WHERE GRADUATES END UP	
13% Finance*,	Key Areas
11% Wholesale/Retail,	
10% Public Admin,	
9% Manufacturing,	
9% Health/Social Work,	
7% Education	
8% Computer,	
6% Personnel	
Publishing*, Legal,	Niche Areas
Library/Archival*,	
Construction, Advertising,	
Defence, Accountancy	
*indicates Top 10 Graduate Provider	
Approximate employed **93%**	

and Management, Computer Science, Economics, Electronic Systems Engineering and Law. Key industries/professions for Essex graduates include: IT, telecommunications, law, financial services, market/social research. The students' union provides NSLP training sessions which provide skills such as Assertive Communication, CV enhancement, Time management, etc

GETTING THERE

☛ By road: A12. Well served by coach services.
☛ By rail: London Liverpool Street, 1:00; every half-hour; Birmingham New Street, 3:30; Sheffield, 4:00. Ten-minute taxi run to campus.
☛ By coach: London, 2:10; Birmingham, 6:00; Norwich, 6:15.

• •

EUROPEAN BUSINESS SCHOOL

ACADEMIC EXCELLENCE	
Founded	**1979**
Situation/style	**Campus**
Status	**Private**
	School
Tuition fees pa (approx)	**£8,000**
Degree awarding university	**Open**
Degree undergraduates	**750**
ACCOMMODATION:	
Availability to freshers	**50%**
Style	**Halls, flats**
Cost pw (incl food)	**£200**
City rent pw	**£75-£120**

European Business School
Regent's College
Regent's Park
London NW1 4NS

TEL 020 7487 7654
FAX 020 7487 7425
EMAIL exrel@regents.ac.uk
WEB www.ebsLondon.ac.uk

VAG VIEW

B ased in London's Regent's Park, the school offers five business degrees. Languages are an important element. Strong links with the business world, both through those who teach and manage the school and through students, many of whose parents have businesses of their own. On-site accommodation is available to some but not all undergraduates.

GETTING THERE

☞ By road: via York Gate off Marylebone Road.
☞ By Underground: between Baker Street and Regent's Park tubes, giving access to Metropolitan, Hammersmith & City, Circle, District and Bakerloo lines.

EUROPEAN SCHOOL OF OSTEOPATHY

European School of Osteopathy
Boxley House
The Street
Boxley
Kent ME14 3DZ

TEL 01622 671558
FAX 01622 662165
EMAIL kellyrose@eso.ac.uk
WEB www.eso.ac.uk

COLLEGE PROFILE

Founded	**1951**
Status	**HE College**
Tuition fees pa (approx)	**£6,000**
Degree awarding university	**Uni Wales**
Degree undergraduates	**185**
College accommodation	**None**
Local rent pw	**£50**

VAG VIEW

A clinic is based at Maidstone in Kent, and the school is at the village of Boxley nearby. It's a four-year course, 50/50 pre-clinical and clinical. Fees are between £6,000 and £7,000 pa. The BSc is validated by the University of Wales.

GETTING THERE

☞ By road: M20/J6, sign to Boxley.
☞ By rail: London Victoria, 1:00.

UNIVERSITY OF EXETER

The University of Exeter
Northcote House
The Queen's Drive
Exeter EX4 4QJ

TEL 01392 263035
    01392 263030 (prospectus)
FAX 01392 263857
EMAIL admissions@exeter.ac.uk
WEB www.exeter.ac.uk

Exeter Guild of Students
Devonshire House
Stocker Road
Exeter EX4 4PZ

TEL 01392 263540
FAX 01392 263546
EMAIL M.F.Rosewarne@ex.ac.uk
WEB www.guild.ex.ac.uk

VAG VIEW

E xeter became a university in 1955, and in the 1970s, they took St Luke's College of Education into the fold.

'The university is very easy to fall in love with,' writes Jo Moorhouse. 'It has one of the most beautiful campuses in the country, in one of the most beautiful counties in Britain.'

The uni stands at the M5 gateway to the West Country, and is about to enhance its dominion over the region, in partnership

SUBJECT AREAS (%)

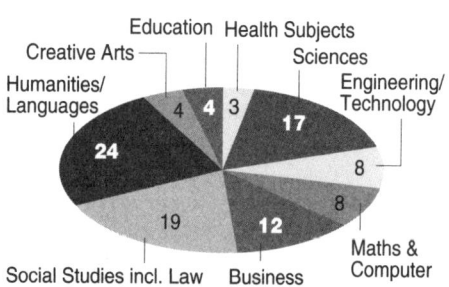

Education Health Subjects
Creative Arts
Humanities/Languages — Sciences
Engineering/Technology
4 4 3
17
24
8
19 12 8
Social Studies incl. Law   Business   Maths & Computer

with Plymouth, in the matter of the new University of Cornwall.

Exeter has had an interest in Cornwall for some time through its School of Mines in Camborne, and the Institute of Cornish Studies (postgraduate and lifelong learning). Now the uni will become a very significant force in the West Country economy right down to Land's End. Arguably the spend could not be in safer hands, for Exeter already disseminates some £100 million in the locality, has recently successfully handled £15 million from an anonymous donor to set up a Finance & Investment Centre on campus, and acted as custodian of many millions donated by alumnus Sheik Sultan Bin Mohammed Al Qasimi, whose Institute of Arabic and Islamic Studies opened in July 2001. Indeed, Exeter has had an MA in finance and investment for twenty-five years and spends much of its time imbuing its undergraduates with the Midas touch – a quarter of whom go into commerce, 10% becoming accountants.

CAMPUS

The Streatham campus, which has the reputation of having one of the best social scenes in the country, is indeed beautifully set on a hill, fifteen minutes walk from the centre of the cathedral city, which itself lies close to the sea on one side and the moors on the other. The School of Education at St Luke's College is a mile away, but the Students' Guild operates a frequent minibus service between the two. The engineering base – the aforesaid Camborne School of Mines – is two hours away, between Redruth and Camborne in West Cornwall, though shortly it will join Falmouth College of Arts in its palm-strewn acres at the hub of the new Cornish university.

STUDENT PROFILE

The uni has a reputation as a haven for the green wellie brigade, hooray Henrys career down from London by the Golf-full, future City slickers out for a last taste of freedom in the idyllic West Country before being tethered to their work stations in the Square Mile. 'We have lots of Sloanes, the car park is full of Volkeswagens,' the union president told me. Certainly the uni's performance in the accountancy, finance & banking fields seems to support this, and the guild's web site address used to be gosh.exeter.ac.uk.

The widening participation strategy gets plugged here, and there's a support network in

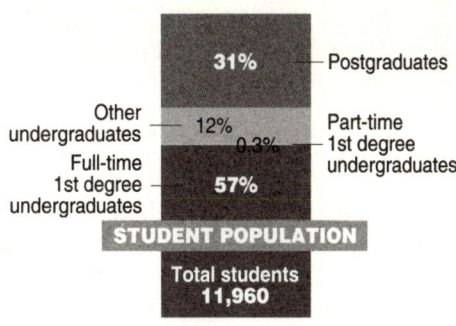

31%	Postgraduates
Other undergraduates 12%	Part-time 1st degree undergraduates
0.3%	
Full-time 1st degree undergraduates 57%	

STUDENT POPULATION

Total students
11,960

place for those students who meet with financial hardship – uni hardship funds and Students' Guild loans, but the facts are that only 69% of entrants to Exeter are from the state sector, and the uni draws almost solely from traditional uni-going socio-economic groups.

But it's not as if they choose them at interview, and hey, applications were 7% up last year!

UNIVERSITY/STUDENT PROFILE	
University since	**1955**
Situation/style	**Campus**
Student population	**11,960**
Full-time undergraduates	**6,820**
- mature	**10%**
- overseas	**5%**
- male/female	**49/51**
- state sector intake	**69%, low**
- non-traditional student intake	**5%**
- drop-out rate	**5%**
- undergraduate applications	**Up 7%**
see Introduction for key to tables	

ACADEMIA

Academically, Exeter is one of our premier-league establishments, and recent teaching assessments have been very good (both Education and Archaeology got full marks), although overall results are not as good as Durham, Bristol or Nottingham, which have a similar student clientele.

The big news this year is the Peninsula Medical School, another joint venture of the universities of Exeter and Plymouth. Contact: medadmissions @pms.ac.uk (see also: www.pms.ac.uk). First undergraduate intake will occur in October 2002, half in Exeter (at St Luke's), half in Plymouth. Staff are in place. Both unis already have successful postgraduate medical schools (see our *Academic Excellence* box, page 190, the world-class research rating for Hospital/Clinical Studies). One of the key points about the new school, from the uni's pov, is

ACADEMIC EXCELLENCE

TEACHING:
(Rated Excellent or 17+ out of 24)

English, Geography	**Excellent**
German, Education,	**24**
Archaeology	
Psychology, Politics, Theology	**23**
Drama, Dance & Cinematics,	**22**
French, Italian, Maths, Physics,	
Classics, Business, Biosciences	
Sociology, Materials Technology,	**21**
Sport Sciences	
Russian, Iberian Studies,	**20**
Middle Eastern & African,	
Studies, General Engineering	

RESEARCH:
Top grades 5/5*

German/Dutch/candinavian	**Grade 5***
Hospital/Clinical, Applied	**Grade 5**
Maths, Psychology, Physics, Law,	
Economics, Politics, Sociology,	
Accounting, Middle Eastern &	
African Studies, English,	
Russian/Slavonic/East	
European, Classics,	
Archaeology, History, Theology,	
Education, Sports	

that it binds them tighter into the regional community, which will be ever bigger come the University of Cornwall. Students will work initially with patients in Plymouth and Exeter, then into Truro in Cornwall, finally up amongst the hillbillies in North Devon.

Another string is a telling modern specialism in things Arabic. 'It has had a lot of inward investment from that direction,' we were told. 'It is very good on Middle Eastern languages, there's a large teaching/library facility on that side.' The inward investment came from Sheik Sultan Bin Mohammed Al Qasimi, ruler of Sharjah and sometime History PhD student here. He gave millions to fund new accommodation at Exeter and two professorships in a new Institute of Arabic and Islamic Studies. A further consequence of the connection is that Exeter has copped a grant to set up engineering, English, business and management courses at the University of Sharjah.

This year there are new courses in Arabic and Islam in a wide spectrum which also includes education, English, film, classics, a couple of Internet courses and Physics with Astrophysics. Among a number of new politics and language courses in the School of Social Sciences is a BA in International Relations, which became a theme in

conversation with diverse people on campus while we were there, shortly after the Twin Towers tragedy.

We began with a chat with the union president, who noted that, 'Equal Opportunity societies are doing particularly well among students – such as LGB, International Society, Racial Ethnic Rights, and the societies that deal with particular nationalities – Singapore Society is quite big, Hong Kong, Thai. But International Society is probably the most active, organising two trips out a week to places all over the country.

'I did politics and there was quite a cross-over with Arab/Islamic, history of the Middle East, Middle East politics, etc, and the resource [the Institute of Arabic & Islamic Studies] is really good: letters, firsthand evidence... A lot of people don't realise that you don't have to know Arabic to study there. With the building of the institute – fantastic building! – we have got the largest Arabic Library and Middle East resource outside the Middle East and America. That may seem a bit random, here in Exeter, but the fact is that we are in the forefront on this thing, and it has a knock-on effect. Even the Vice-Chancellor is working with a Free Burmah Coalition between Exeter and LSE. There have also been stop-the-war-in-Afghanistan campaigns recently, and since September 11th, with the Arabic/Islamic presence, they have had some fantastic debates – one a week at the moment, and they have been so well attended that they have had to move them out of the seminar rooms into the Arab Centre. They started off just informing people about Islam, but they have built on that with debates about Western civilisation vrs Islamic civilisation, about the merits of war, will war spread anywhere else?'

Ending our visit on a literary note, I was told by

AT A GLANCE

ACADEMIC FILE:

Subjects assessed	**32**
Excellent	**78%**
Average requirements	**300 points**
Students-staff ratio	**18:1**
First/2:1 degree pass rate	**64%**

ACCOMMODATION FILE:

Guarantee to freshers	**100%**
Style	**Halls for freshers**
Catered	**48%**
En-suite	**30%**
Price range pw	**£83-£99.80**
City rent pw	**£40-£45**

another: 'We've just set up a new creative writing and arts programme with a screenwriter in residence, and there's a plan to offer it as a module to undergraduates – short courses, weekend workshops. J K Rowling is a graduate of Exeter, you know, though she did French with Greek and Roman Studies, what we call Classical Studies. Film Studies is also up and coming. Single honours, it is run jointly by English and Modern Languages. We have a public museum, a collection of cinema and pre-cinema memorabilia, the suit that Charlie Chaplin wore in *The Tramp,* and so on.'

And wasn't that nice young man from *Pop Idol* also here? I muse, wondering what new course we might find on our next trip.

STUDENT SCENE

STUDENTS' GUILD The **Ram** in Devonshire House is the main bar, always busy in the evenings, video juke box. Then there's the **Ewe** in Cornwall House, also home to the **Lemon Grove** nightclub, coffee bar during the day, Lemon Grove in the evening and the **Lemmy** – a nightclub – Friday and Saturday nights. 'It's the biggest nightclub in Exeter with a capacity of 1,350,' my guide told me. 'A fantastic evening out, a *Double Lemmy* is a must, Friday and Saturday nights, which is why I am looking a bit rough today.

'Last week we had the Orange tour (DJs), the week before we had Slinky come and play. The Lemmy also doubles as a concert venue, so on Wednesday nights we put on all the campus bands – there's a tradition of that here, goes back ages, five or six bands each night. Then, afterwards, it's down to a club in town called **Timepiece**, which we work with on Athletic Union nights, the money raised going back into coaching and training, which is why we do so well in the BUSA League.' Big acts play the **Great Hall** (1,700 capacity), 'We've got Wheatus playing next week, we had Orbital there last week. Generally we have five big name concerts a term and little ones every now and then in the Lemmy. Then we have the university orchestra, choral society, in the Great Hall at this time of year. Christmas Carols is a must, free mince pies! There's also a tradition of musicals in **Northcote** [the part-'pro' campus theatre, very good acoustics, high-banked auditorium for maximum visibility]. This year Footlights are doing *Singing In the Rain,* which is brilliant because the stage has got a rain deck on it so it can actually rain on stage. Then Gilbert & Sulivan are doing another production, and there's a university dance theatre production. Three altogether.'

There's a tradition for musicals at Exeter, *Guys & Dolls* and *Sweet Charity* in recent years. Later I wondered whether the choice this year of *Singin' In*

WHAT IT'S REALLY LIKE	
UNIVERSITY:	
Social Life	★★★★★
Campus scene	**Out-going, well-heeled, lively**
Student Union services	**Good**
Politics	**Student issues**
Sport	**Key**
National team position	**5th**
Sport facilities	**Good**
Arts opportunities	**Excellent**
National drama awards	**Writing**
Student newspaper	**Exposé**
Student radio	**URE**
Student TV	**XTV**
Nightclub	**Lemon Grove**
Bars	**Ram, Ewe**
Union ents	**Double Lemmy**
Union clubs/societies	**190+**
Parking	**Good; permit**
CITY:	
Entertainment	★★★
Scene	**Good pubs; small, safe city**
Town/gown relations	**Average**
Risk of violence	**Average**
Cost of living	**Average**
Student concessions	**Good**
Survival + 2 nights out	**£70 pw**
Part-time work campus/town	**Good**

The Rain had anything to do with a major new meteorological research centre going up on campus, 'unusual because it is designed to rain indoors'. Campus life *is* thoroughly integrated after all, as the matter of student media demonstrates.

There is massive interest in media, and although the uni doesn't offer Media Studies, they have a surprising number of graduates going into media (see *Employment* box, page 193). Someone lists, 'Nick Baker, the wildlife presenter, Emma B from Radio 1, Isobel Lang, the weather presenter, people on the production side, like Paul Jackson who produced Red Dwarf - he came back to do a creative writing thing with the students in English, Stewart Purvis, chief exec of ITN.' Some 400 freshers attended a *Welcome to the Media* event in freshers week last year. Those who stuck with it were subjected to a period of training by the *Exposé* team – the student newspaper was runner-up in the travel section of the *Guardian* awards this year and is often represented. 'As well as *Exposé* we have Expression fm,' I was told – 'just moved from the medium wave. In the evenings there's an on-air welfare session.' People at Exeter University have problems? I mouth in astonishment. 'Oh, they do!' I was assured. 'That's really successful, narrowly pipped at best marketing awards at the weekend. And we've got XTV when the camera's are working properly. We are moving from analog to digital. Then we have the web, and the radio is on the Internet as well, many of the students on a year-out listen to that.'

SPORT All major team games are well represented, also martial arts, watersports (rowing, canoeing, sailing – six Lark dinghies on the Exe Estuary) and even ultimate frisbee. On-campus facilities include sports hall (basketball, netball, volleyball, tennis, badminton, indoor cricket net), a climbing wall and traversing wall, rooms for fencing, martial arts, weights, etc. Pitches include two all-weather pitches, large grass pitch with nets area, and there are sixty off-campus acres of playing fields nearby. 'A lot of work has been done on all-weather pitches, floodlights for hockey and football, new cricket pitches, and the sports hall is being made half as big again,' I was told. 'Sports science students are over at St Luke's as are PGCE. We have this sports scholarship which pays for accommodation. We want to attract top people. Richard Dawson is one of our scholars.' Dawson had that week been propelled into the England touring XI of India.

TOWN 'There are certain pubs that you shouldn't really go into,' warns Juliet Oaks, 'and during Freshers Week the Guild does advise you which to avoid. Most pubs don't mind a small group of students sitting having a quiet drink, but if there is a large group or you plan to drink a lot, stick to student haunts. The safest bets are **The Imperial** ('Impy'), **The Thirsty Camel**, **The Black Horse** ('Blackie'), **The Victoria Inn** ('Vic'), **Henry's Bar** and **Chumleys**. First years spend most of their life on campus, with the regular Thursday night venture to **Warehouse**. Although Exeter is a city, it is in the West Country. Clubbing is not exactly the best. However, there is at least one student night at a club every night of the week - Mondays is **Rococo's**, Tuesdays is **Arena**, Wednesdays is **Timepiece**, Thursdays is **Volts** or **Warehouse** and Fridays and Saturdays are the Lemmy. Entry before 10:30 is usually free or very cheap. Some of the clubs distribute tickets beforehand and these are definitely worth getting. A night out can cost

from £2 (only drinking water while clubbing and walking home) to £40 (drinking in town pubs and at the clubs, getting pissed and getting a taxi home)! For shopping there's enough diversity for anyone, from skaters to Goths.'

PILLOW TALK

All Freshers' are guaranteed university accommodation, mostly in catered halls (three meals a day, seven days a week). Single sex accommodation is available in self-catering residences. Most student rooms have their own phone and IT data points for email and Internet access, though there is an annual connection charge. The en-suite figure in the At A Glance box of 30% apparently covers 'enhanced rooms', rooms fitted to a higher standard but actually without private showers or toilets. This figure will increase to 50% in 2004. £32 million is being invested over the next three years to replace halls (Duryard and Birks) built in the 1960s. The project caused something of a problem with Exeter Council last year over interim housing for 1,100 freshers who would ordinarily be allocated to the sixties' monstrosities. There were prolonged stints in temporary accommodation. We are assured that it won't happen this year.

Price range per week is £82.50 (shared twin room - standard) to £99.80 (single en suite room). Writes Juliet Oaks. 'The halls are all OK. Duryard and Birks are located at the bottom of 'cardiac hill', so don't opt for these if you have any type of heart problem or if '60s tower blocks are not your thing! Actually, bit by bit they are being replaced, and the atmosphere in these halls is the best on campus, even the food is pretty good. Exeter halls, on the other side of campus, are in general better equipped, but they can be a bit snobbish, and, although the Christmas and Summer balls are great, the socials tend not to be so good. Mardon Hall has a bit of a reputation. Closest to campus, it is also probably the poshest. The richer students (known as Sloanes) seem to live there, as well as some second and third years. Lukies – education or sports science students – get first refusal for St Lukes halls, twenty minutes away. They have a reputation for partying hard.

'If you don't want to live in halls, there's always Lafrowda – self-catering flats (seventies tower blocks - the enhanced ones are the best bet), and

The success of Exeter in putting graduates into the City masks other specialities – student cultural activities beyond the curriculum, which are similarly successful in launching graduate careers, especially in the media.

there are other self-catering blocks, both on campus and spread around the city. These tend to be popular with foreign students, but they are really for second, third and fourth years.'

JOBS

'Exeter is known as a university that produces students with a wide range of skills, not merely academically sound,' writes Juliet. 'The uni helps you with applying for jobs through career fairs and by helping you create a CV and fill in application forms.'

They produce a booklet for employment, outlining what you will require besides a degree to get a job at a worthwhile level in a competitive industry. There's a team of trainers to enable you to take those skills and training on board. There are two recruitment fairs a year in Great Hall, plus a Law Fair because of strength in that area. An Innovation Centre on campus provides start-up homes for small businesses, usually hi-tech. Funding is available in the region.

GETTING THERE

☛ By road: M5/J30.

WHERE GRADUATES END UP	
17% Education,	Key Areas
11% Finance,	
8% Personnel,*	
7% Computer,	
6% Wholesale/Retail,	
6% Public Admin,	
6% Manufacturing	
Accountancy, Advertising,	Niche Areas
Business/Management,	
Defence*, Sport,	
Journalism, Radio/TV	
*indicates Top 10 Graduate Provider	
Approximate employed **96%**	

☛ By rail: London Paddington, 2:30; Birmingham, 3:00; Plymouth, 1:15.
☛ By air: Exeter Airport for inland, European and some trans-Atlantic flights. Fifteen mins from campus by taxi.
☛ By coach: London, 4:00; Birmingham, 4:30.

● ●

FALMOUTH COLLEGE OF ARTS

Falmouth College of Arts
Woodlane
Falmouth
Cornwall TR11 4RA

TEL 01326 211077
FAX 01326 212261
EMAIL (via website)
WEB www.falmouth.ac.uk

VAG VIEW

*D*egrees are offered in Fine Art, *Broadcasting Studies, English with Media Studies (there is a new Media Centre nearing completion), Graphic Communication, Illustration, Journalism Studies, Photographic Communication, Studio Ceramics, and Visual Culture, and now History of Modern Art & Design and Spatial Design: Interior & Landscape. Academic standards are high.*

Falmouth is a seaside town below Wendron Moors in West Cornwall, about ten miles south of Truro. The college is close to some of the most lovely scenery that this country has to offer, and it is itself set in eight

COLLEGE PROFILE	
Founded	**1938**
Status	**F/HE College**
Degree awarding university	**Plymouth**
Situation/style	**Campus**
Student population	**1,620**
Degree undergraduates	**1,146**
ACCOMMODATION:	
Availability to freshers	**156 students**
Style	**Flats**
Cost pw (no food)	**£59**
Town rent pw	**£40-£50**

DEGREE SUBJECT AREAS:
Broadcasting, English, fine art, design (graphic, textile, interior/landscape, ceramics, 3D), history of art, illustration, journalism, photography, film, etc

palm-tree strewn acres between the town, the harbour and the beach.

Teaching assessments are good, and there are all kinds of developments going on in the postgrad area, including a diploma in Professional Writing carrying a bursary known as the Springboard Award, donated by the Jane and David Cornwell Charitable Trust. David Cornwell, a local man, is better known as ex spy writer, the novelist John le Carré.

There are new student residences – clusters of five en-suite rooms around shared dining rooms. Sadly – or is it an exciting proposition – Falmouth is about to lose its independence and become the hub of a new University of Cornwall being masterminded by the big boys east of the border in Devon: Exeter and Plymouth universities. There's a

development plan for the new campus, the start of which seems to be to move Exeter Uni's Camborne School of Mines there in 2004. 'It will give Falmouth more critical mass,' I was told a tad euphemistically.

GETTING THERE
☛ By road: A30, A3076, A39.
☛ By rail: Truro, 4 hours + from London Paddington; change there for Falmouth.
☛ By air: Newquay Airport to Heathrow in an hour.
☛ By coach: Exeter, 3:30.

FARNBOROUGH COLLEGE OF TECHNOLOGY

Farnborough College of Technology
Boundary Road
Farnborough
Hampshire GU14 6SB

TEL 01252 407028
FAX 01252 407007
EMAIL (see website)
WEB www.farn-ct.ac.uk

VAG VIEW

*F*arnborough is about 35 miles from the centre of London, and famous for its Air Show, so we shouldn't be surprised that a college which prides itself on its links with industry and business offers a BEng (Hons) degree in Aerospace Engineering. The Engineering Faculty is, however, but one arrow in Farnborough's quiver. Environmental Management is another – two first degrees (BSc Hons), in Conservation Management and in Pollution Control. The School of Business, the largest outside the university sector, offers BA (Hons) validated by Surrey Uni in Business Administration, Accounting, Marketing, the Science & Management of Exercise, Health, and Leisure Management (the latter awarded by Portsmouth Uni). The college also offers BSc degrees in Computing and in Media Technology.

Proximity to London has obvious advantages and there's an active students' union, Tuesday and Friday discos, Christmas and Halloween balls, a mag, Substandard, and a radio station (FCTFM). There's beer at the **Sub Bar** for £1-£1.50, a 550 capacity in the live music venue that holds 400, and half board

COLLEGE PROFILE	
Founded	**1957**
Status	**HE College**
Degree awarding universities	**Surrey, Southamhpton, Portsmouth**
Total student population	**5,795**
Full-time undergraduates	**528**
ACCOMMODATION:	
Availability to freshers	**70%**
Style	**Halls**
Cost pw (no food/food)	**£55-£80**
Town rent pw	**£45-£55**

DEGREE SUBJECT AREAS:
Accounting, business admin, leisure management, marketing, aerospace engineering, computing, environment, media technology, exercise & health

accommodation in six halls of residence less than a mile from campus. Trips are arranged to London nightclubs.

GETTING THERE
☛ By road: M3/J4.
☛ By rail: London Waterloo, 32 mins.
☛ By coach: London, 1:00.

UNIVERSITY OF GLAMORGAN

The University of Glamorgan
Pontypridd
Mid Glamorgan CF37 1DL

TEL 01443 483348
FAX 01443 482925
EMAIL enquiries@glam.ac.uk
WEB www.glam.ac.uk

Glamorgan Students' Union
Treforest
Pontypridd CF37 1UF

TEL 01443 483500
FAX 01443 483501
EMAIL pres-of-glam@hotmail.com
WEB www.glam.ac.uk

VAG VIEW

Friendly atmosphere, pleasant setting, accessible, sporty and with a decent employment record.

CAMPUS

The campus lies at Treforest in the Taff Valley, an ex-coal mining village, so not pretty, but the surrounding countryside is beautiful, and there are stunning views over the valley. It stands a couple of miles from the market town of Pontypridd and (you may be relieved to hear) a mere quarter of an hour away from Cardiff by cheap trains which run every twenty minutes from just outside the university.

'Living up here isn't a drag,' writes Fiona Owen, 'it's nice to belong to a close-knit community, and the college is nearly all on one campus, apart from the Law School, which is across the road. The area is scenic and there are lots of places to go for lovely walks with your friends or your new squeeze. Pontypridd Park is open every day and it's a really nice place to chill on a sunny day.'

STUDENT PROFILE

There's a high Welsh state school intake and a very high number (25%) from poor neighbourhoods. Once on board, there's a friendly atmosphere and pleasant setting – 'Glamorgan University is small

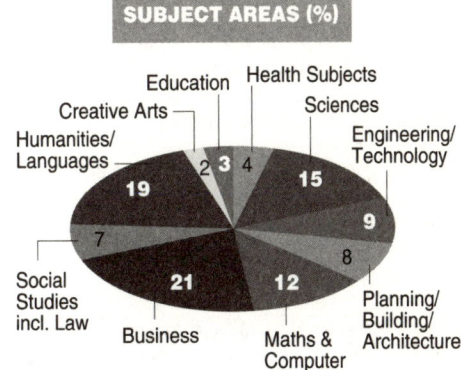

SUBJECT AREAS (%)

- Education
- Health Subjects
- Creative Arts
- Sciences
- Humanities/Languages — 19
- Engineering/Technology — 15
- 2 3 4
- 9
- 7
- 8
- Social Studies incl. Law
- 21 Business
- 12 Maths & Computer
- Planning/Building/Architecture

enough to generate real warmth and a sense of close-knit community, but large enough for you to be inconspicuous when that's what you want/need,' writes Beth Smith. Perhaps it is the fact that the notion of university is so novel for many of the kids who come here that there is a high drop-out rate at undergraduate level of 13%.

ACADEMIA

More than 200 courses are on offer – Arts & Humanities; Social Sciences; Business; Law; Design; Engineering & Construction; Computing & Technology; Sciences & Maths, Nursing, and a

UNIVERSITY/STUDENT PROFILE	
University since.	**1992**
Situation/style	**Rural campus**
Student population	**17,530**
Full-time 1st degree undergrads	**6,570**
- mature	**9%**
- overseas	**5%**
- male/female	**55/45**
- state sector intake	**97%**
- non-traditional student intake	**25%, high**
- drop-out rate	**13%, high**
- undergraduate applications	**Down 12%**
see Introduction for key to tables	

AT A GLANCE	
ACADEMIC FILE:	
Subjects assessed	**17**
Excellent	**41%**
Average requirements	**180 points**
Students-staff ratio	**22:1**
First/2:1 degree pass rate	**42%**
ACCOMMODATION FILE:	
Guarantee to freshers	**75%**
Style	**Halls, flats**
Approx price range pw	**£38-£75**
Local rent pw	**£35-£45**

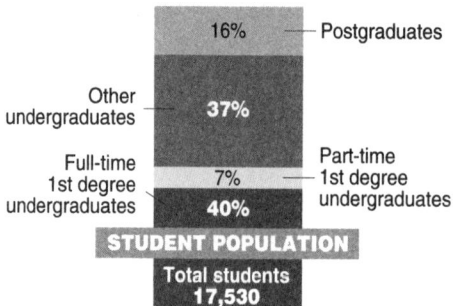

STUDENT POPULATION
Total students
17,530

- 16% — Postgraduates
- Other undergraduates — 37%
- Full-time 1st degree undergraduates — 7%
- Part-time 1st degree undergraduates — 40%

whole raft of joint and combined possibilities. There is an unexciting record in the teaching assessment results (41% Excellent), though students will tell you that the teaching is good, and certainly their employment record is sound (see *Employment* box, page 197). Getting accepted at Glamorgan is not too testing, and there are very useful foundation courses as facilitator. A large proportion of its undergraduates is studying not to degree level, but to HND.

ACADEMIC EXCELLENCE

TEACHING:
Business Studies **Excellent**
Mining Surveying, Creative
Writing/Theatre & Media Drama,
Electrical & Electronic Eng,
Accounting & Finance,
Public Sector Schemes, Welsh

RESEARCH:
Top grades 5/5* **None**

SOCIAL SCENE

STUDENTS' UNION 'If you're a disco queen and demand that you put your spangly dancing trousers on at least a couple of times a week, the union has a formidable entertainment schedule to tease and tantalise you,' Fiona reassures.

There's **Smiths** bar/café, which serves food, snacks and drinks, accompanied by MTV, pool and arcade machines, and the gorgeously aromatic, freshly baked cookie and baguette bar. Alternatively, there are cafés in G and B blocks and a large main refectory. Then there's the bar – **Baa Bar**, and **Shafts** nightclub, where there's something on every night of the week. Regular clubnights are *Nocturnal* (house & trance), *Crunchies* (party), *Chartbusters* (chart & party) and *Touchdown* (club classics). Recent live acts include Robby Williams, Artful Dodger, Tall Paul, Lost Prophets, Reef and The Tiny Twins.

There's an active student media set-up. The web site copped a *Guardian* award recently, and the mag, *Leek*, and radio station, Fusion fm, offer plenty of challenge and opportunity. Among the other twenty-eight societies this year, the most popular were Chiropractic (ask not, lest I bend more than your ear) and Amnesty International, which shows there's humanity besides manipulation afoot.

'There are three things that dominate every student's life: money, alcohol and sex,' warns Stephen Harley. 'But if you come to Glamorgan there is a fourth thing, the mountain on which they built the university. Whenever you go down the hill from the halls of residence you should do as much as possible while you're at the bottom. The first time you go out for the evening and forget your wallet will, I promise you, be the last.

'The second point, important to note, is that the

nightlife in Treforest is... well it isn't. There is a handful of good pubs which have the expected student buzz and the ents at Shafts make up for the short hours. Generally, life in Treforest is peaceful enough.' (See also *Student Cardiff, page 122.*)

SPORT is a major part of university life, in particular rugby, though this term it was womens basketball that took the Welsh national honours and the uni are perennially champions at golf somewhere or other. There's a Sports Centre with six badminton courts, climbing wall, all indoor sports, but no swimming pool. There's a smaller hall for keep-fit, table tennis, martial arts, fencing, plus four squash courts (one glass-backed), two conditioning rooms, sauna/solarium suite, and thirty acres of floodlit pitches – football, rugby and hockey, plus trim trail, cricket pitch, archery. Coaching and a sports scholarship scheme is available for students competing at national/international level. Nearby you'll find swimming pools, golf courses, running tracks, and Brecon Beacons for horse riding, canoeing, mountaineering, hang gliding, walking. Also sailing and windsurfing.

PILLOW TALK

Campus accommodation is available to some 1,300 students, half in en-suite residences, some fully catered, some self-catered. Many students live in private rented accommodation locally; others in Cardiff.

JOBS

There's a good showing in the graduate employment tables. The nursing degrees feed through to the 8% health provision, the built environment and architecture degrees to the construction industry (where they came 3rd nationwide), and the various computing and engineering degrees making their mark in telecommunications (where they came 5th), aero

WHERE GRADUATES END UP
12% Public Admin*, Key Areas
12% Wholesale/Retail,
9% Manufacturing,
9% Finance,
8% Health/Social Work,
6% Education,
6% Computer
Agric/Forestry, Niche Areas
Aeronautical Manufacture,
Construction*, Electron/
Electric, Legal, Market
Research, Radio/TV,
Telecom*
*indicates Top 10 Graduate Provider
Approximate employed **93%**

manufacture, etc. But what is interesting about Glamorgan is that very often it is a collaboration between the curriculum and the student extracurricular activities which makes a mark on the employment tables – as, for example, in radio (where Fusion fm is a function of academia) and the award-winning website and the popular Chiropractic Soc. The Theatre & Media Drama department is also instrumental, which is a healthy sign.

GETTING THERE

☛ By road: M4/J32, A470. Exit Llantrisant, A473.
☛ By rail: London Paddington, 2:45; Birmingham, 2:15; York, 5:00.
☛ By air: Cardiff Airport.
☛ By coach: London, 4:00;
Birmingham, 3:40; Bournemouth, 6:00.

STUDENT GLASGOW – THE CITY

Glasgow, is a cracking city, and it's changing at an incredible rate as well. What's going on at the moment, cleaning up all the older areas, it's phenomenal. A very, very cultured place and not a violent city at all. There are pockets, of course, but central Glasgow is peaceful. No problems with students being mugged or beaten up – one incident this year. The police have got the place tied up. You can't walk for more than thirty seconds without being on camera.

'Why Glasgow?' you'll be asked. Well, as I tried to reassure all my anxious relatives and friends that

the whole of Scotland was not like *Trainspotting*, I came to realise that my new home for the next four years did have a certain stigma. I seriously think my overly worried mother believed I would be delivered back home in a body bag with a needle sticking out of my arm. To my amazement and my parents' relief, the traditional image of Glasgow as being rough and industrial is a pile of cack; in truth, it is a completely cosmopolitan place. Basically, if Glasgow has not got it then I doubt you really need or want it.

Glasgow is a very real city, with real people,

and real issues. The lack of pretension and snobbery and the general friendliness is why I love it. Although my home is 300 miles down the road, I have never felt more at home than in Glasgow.

The city itself is a sprawling mass of offices, excellent shops, fabulous bars and has by far and away the coolest clubbing in Scotland, but if this is not enough, stick yourself on a train and less than half an hour away you're in Loch Lomond or another equally beautiful rural district.

From art galleries and high brow theatre to big name DJ's and underground clubs, Glasgow has it all. There's more entertainment and stuff going on than you could shake a stick at, and never to my knowledge is there a dull day. Actually that's a big lie, one problem with Glasgow is that the weather tends to take the proverbial. Make sure you pack your wellies and that attractive Mac that's been lurking in your wardrobe all these years, as you will experience four if not forty seasons in one day.

CITY SCENE

Even when the weather is pants there is an exciting atmosphere in Glasgow, especially now, since the major renovations that have been going on in the city centre. What has evolved is a trendy, fashionable and cultural city. Every week major new bars, restaurants, shops and clubs are opening.

The city's eclectic mix of clubbing and music leaves other cities on their knees. Whether it's drum 'n' bass, Latin or mainstream house, there is a scene out there for you. Glasgow is home to some of the best venues and clubs in Britain. The legendary **SubClub** for all your underground, hard house and techno needs, **The Tunnel** for mainstream house, with *Cream* taking residence once a month, and **The Arches** for big name DJ's like Judge Jules and Tall Paul.

Arts-wise, Glasgow has a fine selection of galleries and museums, theatres and concert halls. As one of the major cities north of the border it attracts most concerts and tours, from Pulp to The National Ballet. The theatre scene is electric eclectic – no one big theatre but a host (fourteen at least) offering rep (cheapest: Gorbals-based **Citizens' Theatre**), cutting edge drama (**Tramway**, **Tron**), opera – the **Royal Scottish Opera** is brilliant and not just for upper class Toscas – ballet (at the **Royal**), nightclub-cum-theatre (**Arches** beneath Central Station), comedy and lightest entertainment at **Pavilion**; pantos and hypnotists at **King's**.

Art Galleries are in abundance. The

Kelvingrove Art Gallery & Museum is superb and a delightfully peaceful place to wander. The **People's Palace** (telling Glasgow's history) and **St Mungo's Museum** (which houses Dali's masterpiece, *The Crucifixion*) and the **Botanic Gardens** are others among the gems in a treasure trove of lazy Sunday occupations.

Among interesting cinemas, the **Grosvenor** near campus presents off-beat fare at weekends; the **Glasgow Film Theatre** for sheer variety – foreign to Hollywood gloss; plus the usual multi-screens.

If sport is more your bag, Glasgow has more than enough going on. Not only can you see two of Scotland's best football teams in action, there are also loads of lower league clubs which welcome students with open arms. Partick Thistle, for example, based in Maryhill, offers cheap tickets and a student membership card for wannabe Jag fans. If rugby is your game, then you'll have to head out to Edinburgh for international action, but University squads play frequently and are an excellent substitute. For other sports all the universities run clubs for athletics, netball, tennis, even ultimate frisbee, whatever that is!

Ultimately though, Glasgow is a *student* city. There is probably nowhere better than Glasgow for pubs, but with some of the cheapest drink prices in Britain, even the clubs and bars make themselves ridiculously accessible to the student pocket. How can you refuse vodka and mixer at 70p on a Tuesday night in **Los Borrachos** and **Underworld**? If you can make it to a club after that, **Trash** will take £2 off you and let you get even more spannered until you have forgotten where you live and your name. Repeat this for the rest of the week, or for as long as you can sweet talk your bank manager into extending your overdraft!

Although Glasgow city centre offers itself to students with open arms, student heaven is a mile or so out of town. There are probably more Glaswegians in the West End of Madrid than there are in Glasgow's own West End student capital. The Byres Road area is the ultimate student village, with Safeway, banks, underground station and pubs all within walking distance. It is only a few minutes from town and is an excellent base for students who can choose the madness of the city or the relaxed vibe here (see *Campus Glasgow*, page 199).

Rachel Richardson,
Sharon Gaines and Peter Mann

UNIVERSITY OF GLASGOW

The University of Glasgow
University Avenue
Glasgow G12 8QQ

TEL 0141 330 4575
FAX 0141 330 4413
EMAIL admissions@gla.ac.uk
WEB www.gla.ac.uk

Glasgow University SRC
University Avenue
Glasgow G12 8QQ

TEL 0141 339 8541
FAX 0141 337 3557
EMAIL enquiries@src.gla.ac.uk
WEB www.src.gla.ac.uk

VAG VIEW

*G*lasgow is to Edinburgh what New York
is to Paris. It is exciting, diverse, you
can have a riotous time, but there is also a
creative precariousness, something of an
edge which sets it apart from Edinburgh and
certainly from all those middle England cities
of bop. If you're up to it, Glasgow is more
likely to bring the innovative artist out in
you.

*This particular university – one of three
in the city – speaks of the city's traditions,
gives an objective sense of its long history,
and is appropriately set three miles west of
the city centre.*

*What you get is a twofold opportunity –
excellent teaching in a well-respected and
traditional university, and, within reach, a
modern exciting urban culture which may
surprise the unexpected in you, if into it you
dare fall.*

CAMPUS GLASGOW

'Glasgow itself has some wonderful sites,' writes
Sharon Gaines – 'Georgian and Gothic

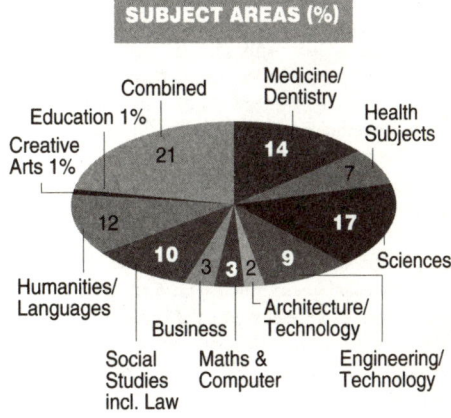

SUBJECT AREAS (%)

Combined 21
Education 1%
Creative Arts 1%
Medicine/Dentistry 14
Health Subjects 7
Sciences 17
Architecture/Technology 9
Business 2
Maths & Computer 3
Social Studies incl. Law 3
Humanities/Languages 10
12
Engineering/Technology

architecture stand majestically on stalwart hills.
Steeples tower over the city in every direction,
their blackened bricks engulfing years of
laborious history. Alleyways and open washing
areas hold an air of early Glasgow before
tracksuits, orange buses and broken bottles of
Buckfast. This is Mackintosh's home town. His
Willow Tea Rooms and the **Tea Rooms of Miss
Cranston** capture the later period of
architectural development and continental
flavour in Glasgow. The School of Art is another
of Charles Rennie's awesome buildings.

'But the West End, by the university, has its

AT A GLANCE	
ACADEMIC FILE:	
Subjects assessed	**33**
Excellent/Highly Satisfactory	**91%**
Average requirements	**300 points**
Students-staff ratio	**16:1**
First/2:1 degree pass rate	**68%**
ACCOMMODATION FILE:	
Guarantee to freshers	**100%**
Style	**Halls, flats**
Catered	**20%**
En-suite	**15%**
Price range pw	**£49.77-£91.77**
City rent pw	**£45-£60**

UNIVERSITY/STUDENT PROFILE	
University since	**1451**
Situation/style	**City Campus**
Student population	**23,100**
Full-time undergraduates	**14,250**
- mature	**35%**
- overseas	**5%**
- male/female	**45/55**
- state sector intake	**85%**
- non-traditional student intake	**16%**
- drop-out rate	**7%**
- undergraduate applications	**Up 4%**
see Introduction for key to tables	

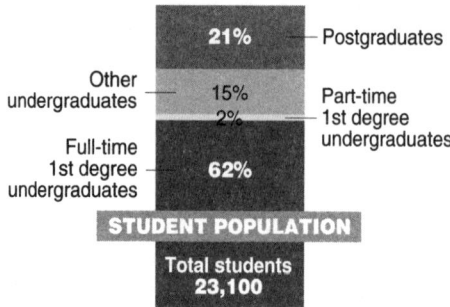

Postgraduates — 21%

Other undergraduates — 15%

Part-time 1st degree undergraduates — 2%

Full-time 1st degree undergraduates — 62%

STUDENT POPULATION

Total students
23,100

own unique atmosphere. Ashton Lane winds round cobbled paths leading to the trendiest pubs in this friendly part of town, while Byres Road facilitates the most extensive pub crawl – each within spitting distance. If the opulent Merchant City is the heart of the city, Great Western Road is its lungs. An old church looms over small quaint shops while half a mile of animal-like headlights shuffle slowly towards the flyover and three colossal tower blocks stand triumphantly in the distance. An awesome sight.

'If the more tranquil appeals to you – imagine gliding through a collage of a thousand colours of trees winding down a path passing two city heroes, dodging squirrels and birds until you land on a nineteenth-century bridge where the rain crashes down into the River Clyde, gushing downstream. This is the university's Kelvingrove Park – glorious in the autumn, brimming with smiling faces in the summer as everyone collates from across Glasgow on the hills.'

Campus overlooks Kelvingrove Park. Is it always so idyllic? 'Okay, it's not all roses,' Sharon concedes – 'The park is notoriously dangerous at night as are various parts of the city, but this is true of most big cities.'

There is another, less well-known Glasgow Uni campus to the south, in Dumfries. Crichton Campus, as it is known, offers innovative study programmes to a mixture of full-time and part-time students. Its population has more than doubled in the last year, and by 2005 they reckon they'll have 1,500 participants. It is situated beside the Crichton Business Park in eighty-five acres of parkland and gardens (see *Crichton Campus*, page 201).

STUDENT PROFILE

Glasgow's state sector intake is 85%, Edinburgh's is 63%; Glasgow's take from poor areas is 16%, Edinburgh's is 8%. In other words, Edinburgh is a long way behind Glasgow in attaining a realistic cross-section of the population on campus and in spreading the traditional privilege of higher education further into the social morass.

To encourage take-up, the uni is running summer schools with bursaries on offer from the Royal Bank of Scotland aimed specifically at those whose personal or financial circumstances might otherwise discourage application. The first intake of students to benefit from the schemes have arrived this year, so we can expect to see even more optimistic statistics in next year's Guide.

What we may also be saying is that if you're a Sassenach it could follow that at Glasgow, more than at Edinburgh, you'll want to befriend the Scots fairly quickly or set up your own more isolated social life... Having said that, one student commented that 'there is a sense of community – you cannot fail to walk down University Avenue without bumping into someone who wants to nick your lecture notes.'

ACADEMIA

Thirty-three assessments and a 91% Excellent or Highly Satisfactory result speaks for itself. One

ACADEMIC EXCELLENCE

TEACHING:

(Rated Excellent, Highly Satis. or 17+ out of 24)

Computer Studies, Physics, Chemistry, Geography, Geology, Philosophy, Sociology, Cellular & Molec Biology, Organismal Biology, English, French, Medicine, Veterinary Medicine, Psychology, Social Policy.	**Excellent**
Civil Engineering, Music, Maths & Statistics, Mechanical + Manufacturing, Engineering, History of Art, History, Finance & Accounting, Law, Politics, Social Work, Theology, Dentistry, Nursing, Drama.	**Highly Satis.**
European Languages	**22**

RESEARCH:

Top grades 5/5*

Psychology, European Studies, English, Sports	**Grade 5***
Clinical Laboratory Sciences, Hospital-based Clinical, Biological Sciences, Veterinary, Physics, Pure Maths, Applied Maths, Statistics, Computer, Electrical & Electronic Eng, Mechanical Eng, Town & Country Planning, Law, Politics, Accounting, French, History, History of Art, Theology	**Grade 5**

characteristic of the syllabus is a huge programme of joint honours degrees – arts and social sciences.

This year there are new degrees in archaeology, theology, Slavonic, mechanical and electrical engineering, environmental design, maths, economics and aeronautical engineering with industrial placement.

The merger with **St Andrew's College** a couple of years ago gave them a Faculty of Education at a stroke, and now the uni is opening a new building to provide a main-campus location for the faculty. Shortly afterwards came the new School of Modern Languages & Cultures, which attaches at all levels to give an international dimension to many degrees through six departments – Celtic, French, German, Hispanic, Italian, Slavonic.

In the world-class, Grade 5* research-rated School of English and Scottish Language and Literature (see box opposite), the uni has appointed three writers of international stature to a Chair of Creative Writing. Alasdair Gray, James Kelman and Tom Leonard together cover all of the major genres and forms – biography, drama, including radio, screen, and theatre, essays, poetry, novels, novellas, and short stories.

Research-wise, Glasgow ascended six places overall to 29th in Britain last year, quadrupling its Grade 5* ratings (world excellence). Ninety-five per cent of research staff are in subject areas rated 4, 5 or 5*, and in the area of technology they have just opened an 'embassy' in Silicon Valley – the first UK university so to promote technology transfer deals. Yet, Glasgow's reputation is for being better focused on teaching their students than most. They make a deliberate effort to get more young staff in, and special needs advisers are on hand for students with disabilities and learning disadvantages.

THE CRICHTON CAMPUS Within a stone's throw of Paisley University's business, management and computing set-up, Bell College's School of Health Studies, and the Dumfries & Galloway College's business and social science centre, Glasgow are offering five broadly-based BAs, taught through 'virtual' and 'residential' lecturing. Glasgow-based expertise is on hand through video link-ups, while the benefits of one-to-one small group teaching is also maintained. Students have the same entitlement to Glasgow Uni facilities as those based at the main campus in the city.

Course enquiries to Wendy Anderson, Crichton University Campus, Rutherford and McCowan Buildings, Crichton Estate, Bankend Road, Dumfries DG1 4ZL. Tel: 01387 702001; Fax: 01387 702005; E-mail: W.Anderson@crichton.g

SOCIAL SCENE

Glasgow, like UMIST, Imperial College, St Andrews, Edinburgh and Dundee, have cut themselves off from the National Union of Students at a saving of many thousands of pounds each year. It's a moot point, however, whether Glasgow's own bureaucracy is better organised. 'Glasgow Uni is probably the most divided university in Glasgow,' writes Rachel Richardson with reference to the 'different bodies operating different aspects of university life. This leads to certain divisions.'

There are four union-type bodies – the Students Representative Council, Glasgow University Union and Queen Margaret Union. SRC is the political arm and administers the student societies, which are legion, supports volunteers and class representatives and is the official voice of the

WHAT IT'S REALLY LIKE

UNIVERSITY:	
Social Life	★★★★★
Campus scene	**Lively, diverse**
Student Union services	**Good**
Politics	**Activity average**
	Student issues
Sport	**45 clubs**
National team position	**22nd**
Sport facilities	**Good**
Arts opportunities	**Drama, music, art exc; dance good; film average**
Student newspaper	**GU Guardian**
Herald Press Awards	**All categories**
Student magazine	**GUM (oldest in Scotland)**
Student radio	**SubCity Radio**
Student TV	**G.U.S.T.**
Nightclubs	**Qudos, Hive**
Bars	**Jim's Bar, Beer Bar, Deep-6, Altitude**
Union ents	**Cheesy Pop rules + rock & indie**
Union clubs/societies	**120**
Most popular societies	**Role-play, Debating**
Smoking policy	**Union OK**
Parking	**Poor**
CITY:	
Entertainment	★★★★★
Scene	**Very cool**
Town/gown relations	**Good**
Risk of violence	**Average**
Cost of living	**High**
Student concessions	**Good**
Survival + 2 nights out	**£70 pw**
Part-time work campus/town	**Average/good**

students on campus. Then there is GUSA, the sports association founded in 1881 that administers the sporting clubs. Adding to the confusion, postgrads have an organisation called the Research Club and there are boat clubs for both men and women, neither of which is affiliated to GUSA.

GUU operate from an impressively scary looking building at the foot of Gilmorehill. They have their own nightclub, **The Hive** (*Lollipop* on Thursdays – free entry, more of the same on Saturdays and often something a little different on Fridays) plus the **Beer Bar** (traditional, with the names of the campus's fastest drinkers immortalised round the bar), the **Deep 6** basement bar (pseudo-trendy music bar – live bands, karaoke, juke box – open till 2am Fridays, £1-a-pint, half price cocktails, etc.), and finally the style-bar, **Altitude**.

> *Glasgow is exciting, diverse, there is a creative precariousness, something of an edge which sets it apart from Edinburgh. Glasgow is more likely to bring the innovative artist out in you, though this is the most traditional of the three Glasgow unis.*

QM's ents programme operates out of **Jim's Bar**, radically refurbished in the summer of 2001 and now open till 2 am every day of the week, and **Qudos Bar,** 1,100 capacity, and both nightclub and concert venue. The QM's main event is the long-running *Cheesy Pop*, which takes place on Friday night, but there is also a rock night on Tuesdays and an indie night on Thursdays, plus a little bit of everything on Saturday. Recent live acts (2001) include The White Stripes, Starsailor, Belle and Sebastian, The Divine Comedy, Groove Armada, Ryan Adams, Alkabama Three, Cosmic Rough Riders (and many others).

Mention must be made of the lively journalistic scene at the uni: SubCity Radio, the *Glasgow University Guardian* (newspaper), the *Glasgow University Magazine* (oldest student magazine in Scotland) and GUST (oldest student TV station in the UK). These are perennially in and out of national awards. Last year, writers for the *Guardian* won all the categories at *The Herald* Scottish Student Press Awards, including Student Journalist of the Year. GUST won Best Station for the sixth consecutive time at the National Association of Student Television Awards.

SPORT Excellent facilities, including a 25m pool, steam room and sauna, two activity halls with sprung flooring, basketball, volleyball, five-a-side soccer; a fitness and conditioning area, fully equipped. £1,500 pa bursaries offered in squash, athletics, rowing; £1,000 pa, golf: some forty courses in the area.

PILLOW TALK

Catered or self-catered halls of residence and a number of self-catered student apartments are available, 20% catered, 15% en suite. Price ranges from £49.77 (lowest self-catered) to £91.77 (highest catered). Look out for new accommodation this year: Queen Margaret Residences will have 400 places available, all en suite.

JOBS

As our Employment box shows, and the university confirms, Glasgow graduates flock into medicine, dentistry, veterinary medicine, nursing, social work, teaching, accountancy and engineering, often into the cutting-edge electronic technology industries.

WHERE GRADUATES END UP	
25% Health Medicine/Dent/Veterinary), **15% Education, 8% Manufacturing, 8% Wholesale/Retail, 7% Finance, 5% Public Admin Accountancy,**	Key Areas
Aeronautical Manufac, Architecture, Defence, Electron/Electric, Eng/Industrial Design, Journalism, Library/Archival, Sport, Telecom	Niche Areas
Approximate employed **95%**	

Law, via further study, is also a popular choice. The uni records only 5% of graduates of the year 2000 still seeking employment seven months later.

GETTING THERE

☛ By road: M8/J19 or J18. Good coach services.
☛ By rail: Edinburgh, 50 mins; London King's Cross, 5:00. Main campus Underground Station is Hillhead.
☛ By air: Glasgow Airport.
☛ By coach: London, 8:20; Birmingham, 6:20; Newcastle, 4:20.

GLASGOW CALEDONIAN UNIVERSITY

Glasgow Caledonian University
City Campus
70 Cowcaddens Road
Glasgow G4 0BA

TEL 0141 331 3000
FAX 0141 331 3449
EMAIL d.black@gcal.ac.uk
WEB www.caledonian.ac.uk

Glasgow Caledonian Students' Association
70 Cowcaddens Road
Glasgow G4 0BA

TEL 0141 332 0681
FAX 0141 353 0029
EMAIL s.a.brady@gcal.ac.uk
WEB www.sa.gcal.ac.uk

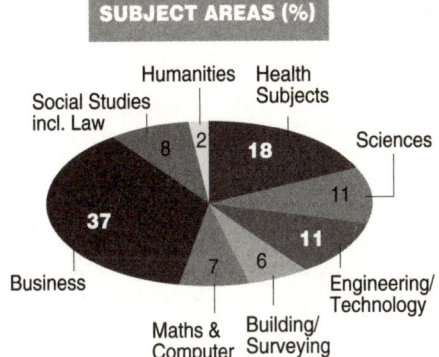

SUBJECT AREAS (%)

Humanities 2
Social Studies incl. Law 8
Health Subjects 18
Sciences 11
Engineering/Technology 11
Building/Surveying 6
Maths & Computer 7
Business 37

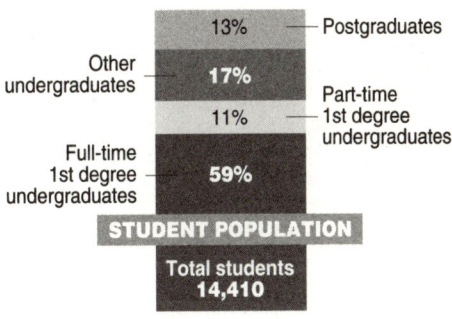

STUDENT POPULATION

- Postgraduates 13%
- Other undergraduates 17%
- Part-time 1st degree undergraduates 11%
- Full-time 1st degree undergraduates 59%

Total students 14,410

VAG VIEW

Having now centralised operations on two sites instead of five, undertaken a hugely ambitious, £38-million building programme, which has seen new accommodation (Caledonian Court – 320 self-catering flats), a Sports Centre, a £17-million Health building and a stylish new design for **Asylum**, *the pleasure-zone on City campus, the uni has settled down to develop its on-going mission to extend access to higher education to as wide a section of the populace as it can. To that end, Cally, as this uni is endearingly known, runs one of the largest summer schools in the country and sends so-called 'link students' into schools to show potential recruits what higher education is all about.*

CAMPUSES

City campus is on Cowcaddens Road, opposite Buchanan Bus Station in the city centre. This is the main university site. **Park campus** is on Park Drive, where the West End starts, the more salubrious area where Glasgow Uni may be found.

STUDENT PROFILE

'Most of Cally's recruits,' writes Rachel Richardson, 'are home-based students looking for a more vocational course in the faculties of Business, Health and Science and Technology, but talking about Caledonian as one group of students is difficult as they are not lumped together in one campus. One good aspect of the smaller campuses, like Park in the West End, is that they have a brilliant community spirit, and provide you with an instant set of a couple of hundred friends.'

Statistically, Cally has jumped in at the deep end, with some 28% of its entrants from groups which do not traditionally supply the university sector, and it has not been easy to get a cohesive student culture going. *The drop-out rate is high – 16%, which is 2% more than it was two years ago*

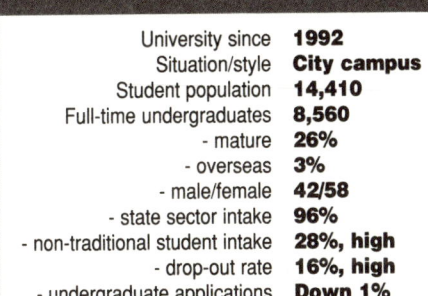

UNIVERSITY/STUDENT PROFILE	
University since	**1992**
Situation/style	**City campus**
Student population	**14,410**
Full-time undergraduates	**8,560**
- mature	**26%**
- overseas	**3%**
- male/female	**42/58**
- state sector intake	**96%**
- non-traditional student intake	**28%, high**
- drop-out rate	**16%, high**
- undergraduate applications	**Down 1%**

*see Introduction for key to tables

ACADEMIA

The uni offers courses across six areas – Business, Engineering & the Environment (including Architectural Technology and various building and surveying courses, Music Technology with Electronics, and a host of other engineering and technology courses), Entrepreneurial & Service Sector (all kinds of management/ retail/consumer courses), Health (including masses of nursing), Mathematical & Physical Sciences, and Social & Behavioural Sciences (they have recently been accredited by the Law Society of Scotland to run an LlB degree).

Entry-wise, they want students who are motivated with enthusiasm and drive rather than A grades. Learning resources include libraries on both sites, the William Hartley Building at City being the largest, with 150,000 volumes and study space for almost 1,000. Much student learning is computer based and subject specialist facilities are available.

ACADEMIC EXCELLENCE

TEACHING:	
Chemistry, Physiotherapy	**Excellent**
Physics, Consumer Studies,	**Highly Satis.**
Maths & Statistics,	
Finance & Accounting, Mass	
Communications, Sociology,	
Social Work, Dietetics &	
Nutrition, Occupational Therapy,	
Psychology, Radiography,	
Biology, Nursing	
RESEARCH:	
Top grades 5/5*	**None**

SOCIAL SCENE

Asylum, Cally's fun palace at City, fronts onto the uni **Refectory** and union shop. It was designed by Graven Images, responsible apparently for many of the trendier café bars in Glasgow. It houses **Refuge**, the main disco bar, and an upstairs **Haven** with DJ booth and pool tables during the day. There's also a bottle bar and a newly designed **Lounge Bar** at the back. At Park campus there's **The Bedsit** for club nights and tribute bands.

The large mature, local and part-time population is suggested as the reason for the recent lack of interest in entertainments at Asylum. Also, there was a fire in 1998: 'Students got out of the habit of Asylum; many off-loaded onto Strathclyde uni [just round the corner], whereas earlier people came because their friends did. It was what you did. Asylum was the place to go.'

The full-time, non-student ents manager, busy

AT A GLANCE

ACADEMIC FILE:	
Subjects assessed	**23**
Excellent/Highly Satisfactory	**65%**
Average requirements	**180 points**
Students-staff ratio	**18:1**
First/2:1 degree pass rate	**50%**
ACCOMMODATION FILE:	
Guarantee to freshers	**40%**
Style	**Halls, student village**
Approx price range pw	**£59-£70**
City rent pw	**£45-£60**

WHAT IT'S REALLY LIKE

UNIVERSITY:	
Social Life	★★★
Campus scene	**Friendly poly**
Student Union services	**Average**
Politics	**Student issues, Activity low**
Sport	**Some**
National team position	**101st**
Sport facilities	**Good**
Arts opportunities	**Music, film average; drama, dance, art poor**
Student magazine	**Re:Union**
Student TV	**Campus TV**
Nightclub	**Asylum, Bedsit**
Bars	**Refuge, Haven, Lounge**
Union ents	**3 pw**
Union clubs/societies	**10-15**
Most popular society	**Muslim Students**
Smoking policy	**Union OK**
Parking	**Poor**
CITY:	
Entertainment	★★★★★
Scene	**Cool**
Town/gown relations	**Good**
Risk of violence	**Average**
Cost of living	**High**
Student concessions	**Good**
Survival + 2 nights out	**£70 pw**
Part-time work campus/town	**Good.**

rationalising why only Karaoke seems to draw a crowd these days, while round the corner at Strathclyde they have upwards of 2,000 student party-goers, had even considered strippers to win their clientele back – 'but the university would be down on us for that.'

Not deemed an incentive apparently. How had Howard Marks – recently made Honorary President – gone down? I wondered. 'First time he was a success, the place was full of devotees, but when he came last time people were complaining that they'd actually paid to see him,' I was told by the editor of Cally magazine, *Re:Union*, recently shortlisted for the *Independent* newspaper's award for small budget student publications. St Andrew's won, as usual, but *Re:Union* had only been going for a few issues when it was judged worthy.

The challenge at Cally is that after nightfall it is deserted. In the day, the bars are full to overflowing. But doesn't that suggest that Asylum is simply not competing with the city in the way that nearby Strathclyde manage? Perhaps it's time to give the show back to the students and let them get on with making mistakes and learning from them.

Elsewhere, too, the union has recently under-performed. 'It was always strong for societies,' said Kenny Hannah, 'but in the last year and a half the emphasis is for students to spend whatever little time they've got in the library or working to pay the rent at the end of the week. All we've got now is maybe eight, ten politically motivated or course-related really. So the concentration on culturally interesting societies has been diluted.'

See also *Student Glasgow, page 197.*

> *Cally has jumped in at the deep end, with 28% of its entrants from groups which do not traditionally supply to university, and it has not been easy to get a cohesive student culture going. The challenge is that after nightfall the uni can be deserted.*

WHERE GRADUATES END UP	
27% **Health/Social Work***,	Key Areas
13% **Wholesale/Retail**,	
11% **Finance**,	
8% **Public Admin**	
8% **Manufacturing**	
Business/Management,	Niche Areas
Architecture,	
Construction, Electron/	
Electric, Telecom,	
Eng/Industrial Design	
*indicates Top 10 Graduate Provider	
Approximate employed **94%**	

catering – four rooms, kitchen and bathroom.

JOBS

The 27% health industry provision reveals the most measurable success story of Cally in nursing, optometry, podiatry, occupational therapy, radiation science, ophthalmic dispensing and the like. There are also nutrition degrees and even Medical Illustration, as well as the applied bioscience courses. Following the new law degree, we can expect to see graduate employment taking off in a new direction. Meanwhile, bedrock business and finance courses continue to leave their mark on the graduate employment picture, as do the engineering degrees and architectural technology and built environment courses.

GETTING THERE

☛ By road: M8/J19 or J18. Good coach services.
☛ By rail: 50 minutes Edinburgh, 5 hours London.
☛ By Underground: Cowcaddens and Buchanan Street Stations are near City campus; nearest Underground to Park is Kelvinbridge.
☛ By air: Glasgow Airport.
☛ By coach: Edinburgh, 1:10; London, 8:20; Birmingham, 6:20; Newcastle, 4:20.

SPORT Facilities are good at both campuses and there are loads of sports clubs: rugby, soccer (male and female), hockey, athletics catered for alongside such as snowboarding, hillwalking and table tennis. It's the Bearsden dry ski slopes for GCU Club Ski and the real white stuff for weekends in semester two. The Hillwalking and Mountaineering Club is the largest – weekends away in Glen Coe.

PILLOW TALK

All accommodation lies within a four-mile radius of the city. Caledonian Court consists of self-catering flats, six to eight bedrooms. Gibson Hall is a traditional catered hall, convenient for Park. David Naismith Court and Red Road Court offer self-catered accommodation north of City campus. Shelley Court and Yorkhill Court are again self-

GLASGOW SCHOOL OF ART

Glasgow School of Art
167 Renfrew Street
Glasgow G3 6RQ

TEL 0141 353 4500
FAX 0141 353 4746
EMAIL info@gsa.ac.uk
WEB www.gsa.ac.uk

VAG VIEW

*T*his is one of the oldest and largest
independent art schools in the country.
*It is centred on the Mackintosh Building,
generally considered to be the masterwork of
former student Charles Rennie Mackintosh.*

*There are three curricular schools: Design
& Craft, Fine Art and Architecture. Teaching
assessments have been Excellent for
Architecture and Highly Satisfactory for Fine
Art and Design & Craft.*

*Resources include a library, substantial art
archives of international significance, two
galleries and various other in-house exhibition
areas. Becoming a student entails participation
in the flourishing artistic community of the city
of Glasgow.* Tramway, *one of the largest and
most innovative art spaces in the UK, and* The
Centre for Contemporary Art *(CCA), just next
door to the school, provide the platform for this.
An active Students' Association promotes
educational and cultural activities. Limited
accommodation nearby in Margaret Macdonald
House (self-catering flats).*

GETTING THERE

☛ By road: from west, M8/J19; from east, J15.
☛ Good coach services nationally end up at
Buchanan Street Bus Station.
☛ By rail: Edinburgh, 50 mins; London, 5 hours.
☛ By air: major destination, airport bus service to
city centre.
☛ By coach: Edinburgh, 1:10; London, 8:20;
Birmingham, 6:20; Newcastle, 4:20.

UNIVERSITY OF GLOUCESTERSHIRE

The University of Gloucestershire
The Park
Cheltenham
Gloucestershire GL50 2QF

TEL 01242 532825
FAX 01242 543334
EMAIL gthatcher@chelt.ac.uk
WEB www.chelt.ac.uk

Gloucestershire Uni Students' Union
PO Box 220
The Park (Elwes Building)
Cheltenham GL50 2QF

TEL 01242 532848
FAX 01242 261381
EMAIL pksu@chelt.ac.uk
WEB www.chelt.ac.uk/su

VAG VIEW

*T*he sometime Cheltenham & Gloucester
College of Higher Education was
*established in 1990, following a merger
between the College of St Paul and St Mary
and the higher education section of
Gloucestershire College of Arts and
Technology.*

*In October last year the college was
awarded university status after a
confidential Quality Assurance Agency
(QAA) report on its standards, and many
years trying.*

CAMPUS

There are three sites, all in Cheltenham, though a Gloucester presence is planned – Park campus is the main site, then there's Francis Close Hall (FCH) and Pittville. When you turn up at Park, don't confuse it with the nearby Gloscat, monstrous further education establishment in crying need of a facelift. No, this is the one up the road that copped the dosh. The main campus is leafy, white, everything – halls, bars, lecture theatres – close to hand and spanking new it seems, though many of the buildings must have been here for some time.

A brand new, £15-million campus, with its own Students' Union and bar, will open soon a few miles away in the cathedral city of Gloucester.

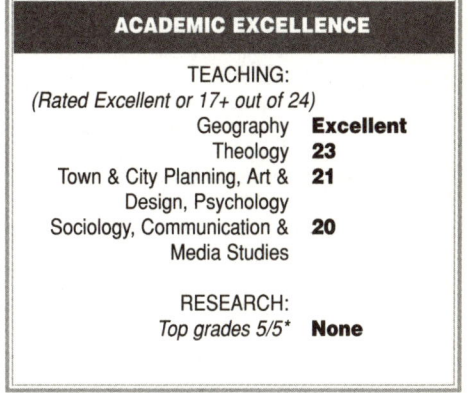

SUBJECT AREAS (%)

Education 11 — Health Subjects 2 — Sciences 17 — Planning/Architecture — Creative Arts 15 — 5 — 9 — Humanities 10 — 5 — 26 Business — Computer — Social Studies

UNIVERSITY/STUDENT PROFILE	
University since	**2001**
Situation/style	**Town sites**
Student population	**9,100**
Degree undergraduates	**5,220**
- mature	**40%**
- overseas	**2%**
- male/female	**40/60**
- state sector intake	**80%**
- non-traditional student intake	**10%**
- drop-out rate	**6%**
- undergraduate applications	**Down 3%**
see Introduction for key to tables	

STUDENT PROFILE

Broadly, Pittville attracts interesting/arty-types, Park besuited-&-booted business management-types, and FCH sporty-types. But on sight there's not a lot to tell between them. Like Oxford Brookes, and unusual in a new-uni demography, there's a lean to independent school types and a very low drop-out rate – only 6% last year. Students talk of the 'really great sense of community – unusual for an institute split into various campuses', 'loads of like-minded fruitcake friends', 'the time of your life in a really friendly, close-knit (not quite incestuous) lovely little spa town in Gloucestershire – Ooo-Arrrhhh!'

'One of its darkest secrets,' another girlie confided, 'is the wealth of gorgeous men – I've certainly met a few, and am still with one of them!'

Make of that what you will.

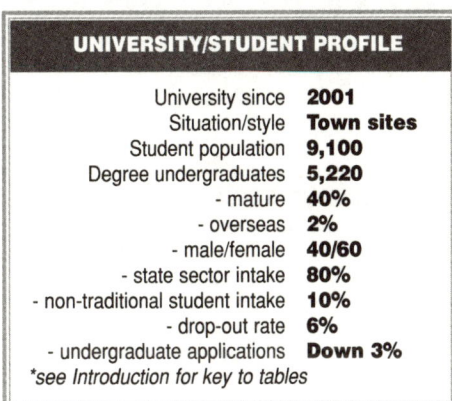

14% — Postgraduates
Other undergraduates 22%
Part-time 6% — 1st degree undergraduates
Full-time 1st degree undergraduates — 57%

STUDENT POPULATION
Total students 9,100

ACADEMIA

First degree subjects fall into three faculties: Arts & Education (split between Park and Pittville), Business & Social Studies (Park), Environment & Leisure (FCH). The programmes (BA/BSc Hons) are modular and very broad based. There is a choice of single, joint or major/minor courses, each of them composed of more than twenty modules with often less than clear synergy between subjects.

Hundreds of main subject combinations are offered, from which you will build your course.

SOCIAL SCENE

'Cheltenham & Gloucester is a fab, mad, lovely

WHAT IT'S REALLY LIKE

UNIVERSITY:	
Social Life	★★★
Campus scene	**Middle of the road and local**
Politics	**Interest low**
Sport	**Very competitive**
National team position	**29th**
Arts opportunities	**OK, film good**
Student newspaper	**Space**
Nightclub	**Park Bar & town**
Bars	**On each campus**
Union ents	**Cheesy + huge Balls**
Union clubs/societies	**50**
Most popular societies	**Pittville Degree Show, Film Soc**
Smoking policy	**Union bars OK**
Parking	**Poor**
TOWN:	
Entertainment	★★★
Scene	**OK clubs, pubs, good shopping**
Risk of violence	**Low**
Cost of living	**High**
Student concessions	**Excellent**
Survival + 2 nights out	**£55 pw**
Part-time work campus/town	**Average/excellent**

AT A GLANCE

ACADEMIC FILE:	
Subjects assessed	**15**
Excellent	**47%**
Typical requirements	**180 points**
First/2:1 degree pass rate	**48%**
ACCOMMODATION FILE:	
Guarantee to freshers	**68%**
Style	**Halls**
Approx price range pw	**£49-£85**
Town rent pw	**£45**

international interest in the Business School and an ever-increasing stream of Chinese, and Norwegians for some reason. Two, it has always prided itself on its big balls rather than its weekday ents. Last year's Summer Ball sold 7,300 tickets, which, the union claims, makes it the biggest in the country, and I would not doubt it. They took over the entire Grandstand at Cheltenham Racecourse, offered an 80-foot bungee jump, a 20-table prize casino, two 12-seater simulator rides, five giant fairground rides, five DJ venues, nineteen bars, and featured Atomic Kitten, Hear'Say, Chicane, Dum Dums and Boom! They also have Christmas Ball, Freshers Ball, Graduation Ball...

place,' I was told and didn't find much to contradict it. Currently there are three bars, one on each campus – the imaginatively named **Park** and **Pittville** bars and **Stumpy's Bar** at Francis Close Hall. A workmanlike ents programme makes good use of the large, airy Park Bar with stage and seriously provocative sound and lighting systems.

Mondays alternate fancy dress parties with *Drink Around The World* events, a different country represented at each of the three bars. There's karaoke Tuesday; fun and games type *Open-the-Box* drink promo nights on Wednesdays; Pittville Bar *Bingo* on Thursdays, a new soul night – *Soul Train* – alternating with live band nights on Fridays; and various balls and the odd *Doctors & Nurses* night on Saturdays.

> *There's a middle-of-the-road feel about this new uni, which may be no bad thing. The huge inter-scheme modular programme continues to baffle, but the union is spot on, and the clean white lines of Park promise students the luxury to which many may well already be accustomed.*

This reveals two facts about Glos. One, that it is largely a local uni – 60% of last year's intake was home-based – and so tends to be a bit deserted at weekends, though this *is* changing, thanks to

And it is fair to point out, too, that the emphasis now is on clubnights in town with the local SU bar simply providing a kind of pre-club, warm-up session. The **Embassy** pulls them in for *Manic Mondays* and *Loaded* (on Wednesday). Thursdays it's *Big Holy Noise at* **Time**, and Fridays it's *Disco Inferno* at **Enigma**.

There is a sense of the society scene maturing. *Space* is the excellent fortnightly newspaper. The Film Society is very active. PDS (The Pittville Degree Show Society) puts on charity fund raisers throughout the year. The Art Society puts on fine shows at the end of each year in Pittville. If this is to be but the beginning of something bigger, it will take organisation and investment. What university status means immediately to the sports clubs apparently is a £50,000 spend to change logo and crest.

SPORT They do well in the BUSA leagues – their

teams came 29th overall last year – and have hosted some of the national finals. There is a swimming pool, sports hall, pitches (known as *The Folley*), a fitness suite and a sports science lab.

Town Cheltenham itself has fantastic shops (classy, unique and your high street shops too), some good pubs, the **Arts Centre** and a few clubs, the most popular being sporties club **Enigma**. Then there's **Time** (trendies, ravers), **Fez Club** (charty, trendy), **Sub Tone** (jazzy, funky hip place), **Mondos** (silly, townies, charty, short skirts, gelled hair), **The Attic** (grungy), **Embassy & Knights** (London scene, some good student nights).

'Gold Cup Week brings the Irish to town and loadsa money,' a student confides, 'a great week for all the girls to go out. You get plied with drink after drink. This week is RAG week, just the best week of the academic calendar!! Tons of fun and misbehaviour, being on a float, driven in front of crowds of people, drunk in charge of a water pistol by 9am, expecting a lot of "cheek" from the rugby boys. And all for charity!' Is it *always* so...baby doll? I venture. 'Well, Christmas carols in FCH chapel are always a laugh...specially with all that *mulled* wine in you.' Now come *on*!

PILLOW TALK

Apply early for one of the 600 beds in the luxurious-looking, mixed, self-catering or half-board halls. Priority goes to first years and overseas students; the college will help you find private accommodation in the town.

WHERE GRADUATES END UP	
17% Education,	Key Areas
11% Wholesale/Retail,	
9% Health/Social Work,	
8% Computer,	
8% Finance,	
7% Manufacturing,	
7% Public Admin,	
5% Personnel	
Sport, Publishing,	Niche Areas
Property, Film/Video,	
Artistic/Literary,	
Agric/Forestry	
Approximate employed	**90%**

JOBS

Most graduates find employment in Education or in the wholesale/retail industry, but there is also a strong lean to placement in artistic, media and sporting industries, so look at their theatre, film, video, advertising, professional media, multimedia, fine art and the sport & exercise science courses, an interest rooted in one of the uni's original constituent parts, a sports college.

GETTING THERE

☞ By road: M5/J11 or M40/A40 or M4/J15, A419. Good coach service.
☞ By rail: Bristol Parkway, 45 mins; Birmingham, 1.00, London Paddington, 2.30.
☞ By coach: London, 2:35; Birmingham, 1:10.

GOLDSMITHS COLLEGE

Goldsmiths College
Lewisham Way
New Cross
London SE14 6NW

TEL 020 7919 7537 (prospectus)
    020 7919 7171
FAX 020 7919 7975
EMAIL admissions@gold.ac.uk
WEB www.goldsmiths.ac.uk

Goldsmiths Students' Union
Dixon Road
London SE14 6NW

TEL 020 8692 1406
FAX 020 8694 9789
EMAIL gcsu@gold.ac.uk
WEB (see above)

VAG VIEW

*G*oldsmiths *is a college of the University of London, famous for its postmodern art department, ents programme, and for the active commitment of its students to fairness and justice. It is located in Southeast London.*

'Ours is one of the most exciting colleges in the country,' I was told. 'It's unpretentious [Oh, right], set in London and neatly poised between a bad-ass ents programme and radical action. We have one of the most politically active Students' Unions in the country.' This was a student leader and he was right, and it all sounds intriguing, if a bit lost between 'commercial' and 'radical real'.

CAMPUS

'So, you want to know about Goldsmiths?' exclaimed Siobhan Daly. 'Well, don't come here looking for the architectural splendours of Oxbridge or the serenity of Durham. This is south-east London: bold, brash and full of embodiments of Delboy Trotter. One of my friends cried when she arrived, saying that it looked more like Grange Hill than a university.'

But isn't Deptford supposed to be the new Hoxton, or is it the new Montmartre?

UNIVERSITY/STUDENT PROFILE	
College of London Uni since	**1990**
Situation/style	**Campus**
Student population	**7,330**
Full-time undergraduates	**3,650**
- mature	**55%**
- overseas	**12%**
- male/female	**35/65**
- state sector intake	**68%**
- non-traditional student intake	**8%**
- drop-out rate	**11%**
- undergraduate applications	**Down 13%**
see Introduction for key to tables	

STUDENT PROFILE

You don't need me to say this. The student type here is best described as 'arty'. There are no natural sciences taught at Goldsmiths and Damian 'pickled-cows' Hirst, Placebo, Julian Clary and Blur all strutted their stuff here in glorious Goldies, so you can see where the scene is at. 'This doesn't, however, mean that you have to conform to the general "I'm-finding-myself" principle of dressing,' I am reassured. 'Just do whatever you want; be yourself.'

'If you are a heterosexual man, you'll love it here. If you are a homosexual woman, you'll also love it here. Goldsmiths is 65% women and the competition is hot! This is probably why *Club Sandwich* is so popular. If you are homosexual, the

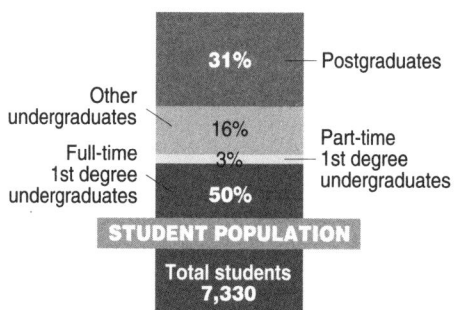

31% — Postgraduates
Other undergraduates
16% — Part-time 1st degree undergraduates
Full-time 1st degree undergraduates — 3%
50%

STUDENT POPULATION
Total students 7,330

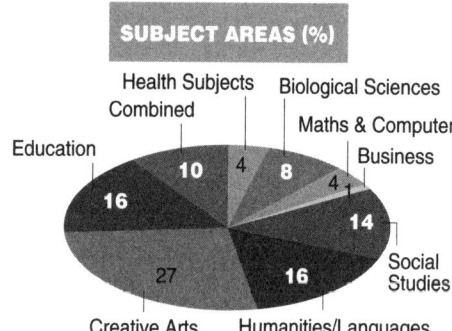

SUBJECT AREAS (%)

Health Subjects Combined — Biological Sciences
Education — Maths & Computer
— Business
10, 4, 8, 4
16
27 — 16
— Social Studies
Creative Arts — Humanities/Languages

LGB relations here are brilliant, and there's usually a *Coming Out Night* once a term.'

ACADEMIA

The standard of teaching of Goldsmiths is variable, if one is to go by the official teaching assessments. The Psychology Department is very good, whereas the English Department didn't do so well. Sport-based degrees here have virtually no facilities and the college is in the process of trying to change the last remaining gym into art space.

However, there is a Goldsmiths way of teaching which may not always coincide with the inspectorate's. They are vigorously non-

ACADEMIC EXCELLENCE	
TEACHING:	
(Rated Excellent or 17+ out of 24)	
Music	**Excellent**
Sociology	**23**
Media & Communications,	**22**
Drama, Psychology, Art &	
Maths	**21**
Design, Economics, Politics	
History of Art	**19**
RESEARCH:	
*Top grades 5/5**	
Communication/Cultural/Media,	**Grade 5***
Sociology	
Anthropology, English,	**Grade 5**
Art & Design, Music	

judgemental and the subject combinations are very much their own, interdisciplinary, encouraging innovative ideas: visual and performing arts exerting a liberating influence among mathematical and social scientists, for example.

The Media & Communications course is extremely popular with students. Fine Arts has the lowest work load – never arrange to meet art students in the library – they'll never find it. If they did, they'd discover some 230,000 vols, 9,500 music scores, a computer centre (200 Macs and PCs) and language facility, all in the Rutherford Information Services Building. Investment has recently been directed to new music practice rooms for solo and ensemble work.

If the proof that it all works is not to be found in their teaching assessment record, which is hardly earth shattering – 67% puts it on a par with Glasgow Caledonian – against the odds, perhaps, it may be glimpsed in their sound graduate employment statistics. Look at our *Employment* box (page 212) for the areas – education, the arts, media, for example – that attract Goldsmiths' students in number.

If you choose to study here you will be in London, and that gives you as many choices and opportunities as you are willing to take. You will be in a better position than media-fixated Exeter students, for example, when it comes to trying to get a placement on a London-based national paper.

However, at the risk of inducing paranoia, undergrads should be aware that your uni is about to review its overall significance. Goldsmiths aims to adjust its post-grad/undergrad populations to 50/50 by the year 2006. Currently it's a mere 30/50. (Might this have something to do with the college dropping from 26th to 42nd place nationally in the recent research assessment table?)

SOCIAL SCENE

STUDENTS UNION Some say that the union's gone more social than political these days, but at least their building is still called **Tiananmen**. **G-Club**'s the club, **Bar Revolution**'s the bar. Among many societies, especially active, besides LGB, are the African Dispora, Stage & Musical Society, the Student Assembly Against Racism and the Asian Cultural.

Famed student magazine *Smiths* regularly

WHAT IT'S REALLY LIKE

COLLEGE:	
Social Life	★★★★
Campus scene	**Trendy, radical**
Student Union services	**Average**
Politics	**Campaigning**
Sport	**Relaxed**
National team position	**117th**
Sport facilities	**Average-poor**
Arts opportunities	**Excellent**
Student newspaper	**Smiths**
Student radio	**Wired**
Nightclub	**G-Club**
Bars	**Bar Revolution**
Union ents	**The Soup, Spreadlove, London Calling**
Union clubs/societies	**30**
Most popular societies	**LGB, African Diaspora, Stage/ Musical, Footie**
Smoking policy	**Union & halls OK**
Parking	**Non-existent**
CITY:	
Entertainment	★★★★★
Scene	**Wild, expensive & locally cool(?)**
Town/gown relations	**OK**
Risk of violence	**High**
Cost of living	**Very high**
Student concessions	**Average**
Survival + 2 nights out	**£70 pw**
Part-time work campus/town	**Locally poor**

features in the student media awards, but owing to a recent bust-up with authority it's been out of print this term; student radio is Wired.

'Our Students' Union may be a concrete monstrosity, but there's a fab nightlife hidden inside and rather outstanding alcohol prices,' writes Siobhan. 'May I also recommend Wednesday night's *Club Sandwich* – fabulous for cheesy music, a good boogie and a great night out?' Weekly fare also includes *Luurve Machine* and the comedy club, *Comedy Gold*, and *Contraflow* – breakbeat, drum 'n' bass, future funk electro madness with DJs Dax, Aphrodite, Boomer, Spin Doctor and and DJ Hooch. *The Soup*'s a weekly journey into retro: '60s, '70s...

'There is a lot of political activity at Goldsmiths with parties such as the Young Conservatives, Young Labour and Young Socialist Workers all vying for your attention,' Siobhan continues. 'There are also NUS and union initiated campaigns, such as the National Demo against tuition fees. So, if that's your thing, get involved.

'If you're worried about not finding religious

AT A GLANCE

ACADEMIC FILE:	
Subjects assessed	**15**
Excellent	**67%**
Average requirements	**240 points**
Students-staff ratio	**16:1**
First/2:1 degree pass rate	**60%**
ACCOMMODATION FILE:	
Guarantee to freshers	**75%**
Style	**Halls**
Approx price range pw	**£60-£80**
City rent pw	**£60**

'If you're coming from an obscure little village where everybody knows each other and they all leave their cars and houses unlocked, wise up, lock up, tie everything down, walk in well-lit areas and carry that safety alarm your Mum bought you.'

SPORT The playing fields are at least half an hour's drive away in Kent. Few seem to make it; they came 117th in the national team listings last year.

PILLOW TALK

'Halls here are quite reasonable for London [£60-£80 per week]; my flat is £60 before bills so make of that what you will,' reveals Siobhan. Decent en-suite hall development sees Loring now satisfying 400 students and Dean House 95. 'The on-site Loring Hall is the best on offer in my opinion,' Siobhan confirms, 'every room has an en-suite bathroom, personal telephone (you will be grateful for it!) and you can get cable television. Rachel Macmillan Halls have a good reputation for friendliness but are about a thirty minute walk from college. They're also bleak and old. Raymont is well esteemed, but St James's (all-girls) had cockroaches a couple of years ago and Surrey House smells. I do however, recommend staying in halls during your first year, even if you already live in London, as you get to meet so many people.'

JOBS

Their provision came first in two of our tables – Library/Archival Information Services (which might be anything from museums to libraries to art galleries, etc; and in Radio/TV. Education grabs most, nearly a quarter of graduates; but their provision to the publishing and advertising industries was 3rd and 4th best in the country.

support groups, don't be, as there are a lot of good societies such as the Christian Union and Muslim Society, as well as local chaplains and a multi-denominational prayer room.

'Apart from the wonders of the hallowed union, there are some good pubs in New Cross. I'd particularly like to point out the **Hobgoblin** on New Cross Road which has just been refurbished and is fab – there's also 20% off drinks between 3 pm and 8 pm, Monday to Friday – perfect drinking time! There's also the **Goldsmiths Tavern** (no relation), licensed until 2 am, the **Marquis of Granby** and the **New Cross Inn**, all within crawling distance of each other. The one club in New Cross is entitled **The Venue** but, personally, the all-black façade and the "A Tribute to..." nights rather put me off. Luckily, central London is only about a twenty minute journey from both New Cross and New Cross Gate stations.

'The cost of living in London is high. Travel is expensive; eating out is expensive; even food shopping is expensive.

> *Goldsmiths has a reputation for good live music and a dance club, for cutting-edge ideas and revolution, but remember this is South London, not first choice perhaps for those weaned on less 'authentic' beauty.*

GETTING THERE
☛ By road: at the junction of A2 and A20.
☛ By rail: New Cross Gate or New Cross Underground and overland.

UNIVERSITY OF GREENWICH

The University of Greenwich
Maritime Greenwich Campus
Old Royal Naval College
Greenwich
London SE10 9LS

TEL 0800 005 006
020 8331 8000
FAX 020 8331 8145
EMAIL courseinfo@greenwich.ac.uk
WEB www.greenwich.ac.uk

Greenwich Students' Union
Cooper Building
King William Walk
Greenwich
London SE10 9JH

TEL 020 8331 7629
FAX 020 8331 7628
EMAIL studentsunion@gre.ac.uk
WEB www.greenwich.ac.uk

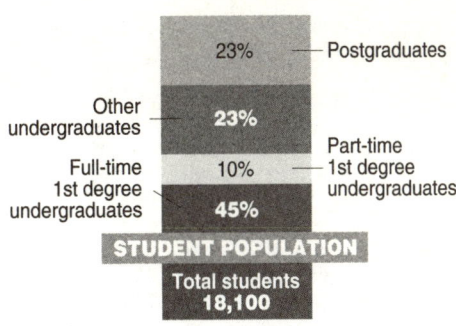

STUDENT POPULATION
Total students
18,100

VAG VIEW

Greenwich Uni is rooted disparately in Woolwich Poly, Avery Hill College of HE, Dartford College of Education and Garnett College. Certainly it is difficult to get a handle on the whole thing. However, this year there have been concerted moves towards a more holistic view. They have restructured their Schools of study and distributed them across four sites – Avery Hill, Maritime Greenwich, Dartford and Medway, with the main emphasis on Maritime Greenwich, opened in 1999 and now increasingly the centre of operations.

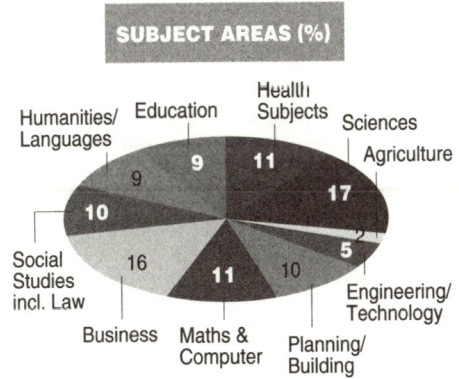

SUBJECT AREAS (%)

CAMPUSES

MARITIME GREENWICH (address page 212), the £8-million development of the Sir Chris Wren designed, former Royal Naval College in Greenwich is the uni flagship campus. There's a library, computing facilities of course, some postgrad accommodation, a conference centre and the Greenwich Maritime Institute (a research/postgrad teaching facility). Now, this year, there's also **Bar Latitude**, a brand new bar where you can indulge

in karaoke and *Text Message Night*. Excellent party atmosphere, by all accounts.

AVERY HILL Bexley Road, Eltham, London SE9 2PQ, and Every Hill Road, Eltham, London SE9 2HB. Particularly good student atmosphere here, on 86 acres of parkland. There's a magnificent library, the **Dome** nightclub and accompanying **Jesters Bar**, two gyms, soccer, rugby, lacrosse and hockey and cricket pitches, a running track and tennis courts. The **Sparrows Farm Centre**, a short walk away, has squash courts, fitness suite, sauna and solarium and the **Sports Bar**. Regular ents on Wednesdays and Fridays.

DARTFORD Oakfield Lane, Dartford, Kent DA1 2SZ. There's a swimming pool here too, a sports hall, netball and tennis courts, soccer and cricket pitches. The greenfield campus is of course close to **Bluewater** and home to a recently refurbished cosy bar and **The Zone**, which hosts nights such as *Superheroes* and *Dairylea*, the ultimate cheesy experience.

MEDWAY Pembroke, Chatham Maritime, Kent ME4 4AW. Incorporates the Natural Resources Institute, a sports hall with badminton and basketball courts and a weights room. There's a friendly bar and club, **The Sub**, with resident DJs and regular ents.

WOOLWICH Wellington Street, Woolwich, London SE18 6PF. There's a sports hall, fitness room, two squash courts, a recently refurbished bar aptly named **Poolside** because it was a swimming pool. **The Deepend** is the place where the biggest events are held, a 1,000-capacity venue and a regular spot for Tim Westwood and Goldfinger.

STUDENT PROFILE

Many come from overseas and receive sterling support. The university provides immigration info concerning visas, working and health, and academic assistance: English classes, study skills, personal tutors and social events geared to

UNIVERSITY/STUDENT PROFILE

University since	**1992**
Situation/style	**City sites**
Student population	**18,100**
Full-time undergraduates	**8,100**
- mature	**62%**
- overseas	**6%**
- male/female	**49/51**
- state sector intake	**95%**
- non-traditional student intake	**13%**
- drop-out rate	**14%, high**
- undergraduate applications	**Down 0.4%**

see Introduction for key to tables

integrate into the British and uni communities. There are also many mature students (62%) (and good childcare facilities) and a number of part-timers. Of full-time undergrads, 95% come from the state sector and 13% from neighbourhoods new to the idea of university; 14% drop out after a year (which is a lot).

ACADEMIA

The new schools, created for academic session 2002/2003, are: Architecture & Construction; Business; Chemical & Life Sciences; Computing & Mathematical Sciences; Education & Training; Engineering; Health; Humanities; NRI (Earth & Environmental Sciences); Social Sciences & Law (Social Science subjects).

Recent strong performers in the teaching assessments are Pharmacology & Pharmacy, Nursing & Midwifery, Town & Country Planning.

ACADEMIC EXCELLENCE

TEACHING:
(Rated Excellent or 17+ out of 24)

Environmental Studies, Architecture.	**Excellent**
Town & Country Planning	**24**
Sociology, Pharmacology, Nursing	**23**
Psychology	**22**
Building, Land/Property Mgt, Civil Engineering	**21**
Molecular Biosciences, Organismal Biosciences, Educ, Economics, Agriculture, Business	**20**
Communication/Media, Maths	**19**
Subjects Allied to Medicine	**18**

RESEARCH:
Top grades 5/5* **None**

There are new BA courses in construction business management, real estate, digital design, and two courses – Rehabilitation Science and Forensic Science awaiting validation at time of writing.

Disabled and dyslexic students benefit from a dedicated Resource Centre.

SOCIAL SCENE

STUDENTS' UNION 'The main objective at Greenwich (apart from studying of course!) is to have fun,' writes Tammy Howland. 'Our Students' Union provides an extensive range of opportunities and Greenwich cards, free to all students living in the borough, which offer free or reduced entry to many

WHAT IT'S REALLY LIKE

UNIVERSITY:	
Social Life	★★★★
Campus scene	**Ents-focused**
Student Union services	**Good**
Politics	**Interest low**
Sport	**30 clubs; rugby big**
National team position	**76th**
Sport facilities	**Good**
Arts opportunities	**Interest low**
Student magazine	**Sarky Cutt**
Nightclubs	**Dome, Sub, Deepend**
Bars	**Bar Latitude, Sport's Bar, Jesters, The Zone, Poolside**
Union ents	**It's a dream, Loaded, Dairlea (cheese), Fruity (R&B, garage), Dizzy**
Union clubs/societies	**80**
Most popular society	**Gaelic**
Smoking policy	**Union & halls OK**
Parking	**Mostly good**
CITY:	
Entertainment	★★★★★
City scene	**London**
Town/gown relations	**Average-good**
Risk of violence	**Woolwich worst**
Cost of living	**Variably high**
Student concessions	**Locally not much**
Survival + 2 nights out	**£75 pw**
Part-time work campus/town	**Good**

places in London. The union ents' cards are also an excellent way to save money. Your days spent at Greenwich will be memorable, exhausting, fun, hard work and exciting, so join us for the Meanest Time of your life!'

AT A GLANCE	
ACADEMIC FILE:	
Subjects assessed	**30**
Excellent	**63%**
Average requirements	**160 points**
Students-staff ratio	**20:1**
First/2:1 degree pass rate	**42%**
ACCOMMODATION FILE:	
Guarantee to freshers	**100%**
Style	**Halls, flats, houses**
Catered	**11%**
En-suite	**45%**
Price range pw	**£47-£86.52**
City rent pw	**£50-£80**

WHERE GRADUATES END UP	
17% Education,	Key Areas
11% Health/Social Work,	
9% Wholesale/Retail,	
8% Public Admin,	
6% Manufacturing,	
6% Finance,	
6% Computer,	
6% Personnel	
Architecture, Property,	Niche Areas
Construction, Defence,	
Sport, Film/Video, Legal,	
Library/Archival,	
Market Research*,	
Advertising, Radio/TV,	
Eng/Industrial Design	
*indicates Top 10 Graduate Provider	
Approximate employed	**91%**

The SU manages to lay on some twenty events each week, circulating news of them in *Get Out*, a 'what's on' listing and utilitarian partner of the excellent student monthly magazine *Sarky Cutt*. Typical disco menu is, Monday – *It's a Dream*, all bars. Tuesday – Karaoke @ **Sparrows Farm**; *Dairylea* @ **The Zone** (cheesy). Wednesday – *Loaded* @ **The Dome**; Bar Footsie @ **Bar Latitude**. Thursday – Karaoke @ **Bar Latitude**, *Fruity* @ **The Deepend** (R&B, garage). Friday – *Dizzy* @ **The Dome** (classic party tunes). Recent live acts include The Gorillaz at Freshers Ball, Westwood and Gold-finger, and Dream Team at the Christmas Ball.

Annual events include the Fresher's Ball, Fresher's Fair, Football Dinner and Dance, Christmas Dizzy and Valentine's Ball. The biggest event of the year is the May Ball. The **Café Royal** in London and **Alexandra Palace** have provided glamorous settings for this black tie evening. Past guests include Radio One DJ Mark Goodier, Alison Limerick, Ultra Nate, Dannii Minogue and Sash.

There are fifty societies, the most popular being Gaelic Soc, and thirty clubs, most popular being Rugby. There's no politics and no arts to speak of. Sport makes up a large part of life at Greenwich.

Teams participate in thirty-six of the forty-nine national BUSA (British University Sports Association) leagues, and came 76th last year.

> *There's an access policy so open that it is difficult not to get in. Nearly a third of graduates will end up educating our children and healing the sick, so we trust they are doing a good job teaching them. With the move to Maritime Greenwich a strategy is, at last, in place.*

JOBS

Our *Employment* box above shows the areas of strength: health, teaching, business, management and information technology are paramount. Media, literary, design and sports are important niche areas. The Students' Union run a leadership programme.

GETTING THERE

☛ By road from M25, join A2 (J2) and follow signs to Woolwich Ferry, thence Greenwich.
☛ By rail to main Greenwich site: trains to Greenwich or Maze Hill overland stations, or Docklands Light Railway from Bank.
☛ By coach: Bristol, 2:20; Birmingham, 2:40; Newcastle, 6:05; Manchester, 4:35.

GUILDFORD SCHOOL OF ACTING *see* SURREY UNIVERSITY

GUILDHALL SCHOOL OF MUSIC & DRAMA

Guildhall School of Music & Drama
Silk Street
Barbican
London EC2Y 8DT

TEL 020 7382 7192
FAX 020 7256 9438
EMAIL butler@gsmd.ac.uk
WEV www.gsmd.ac.uk

COLLEGE PROFILE

Founded	**1880**
Status	**Conservatoire**
Situation	**City site**
Degree awarding universities	**City (Drama), Kent (Music)**
Student population	**919**
Full-time degree undergraduates	**455**
College accommodation	**Flats in hall**
Availability	**178 places**
Cost pw (no food)	**£69**
Town rent pw	**£65-£80**

DEGREE SUBJECT AREAS:
Acting, stage management, music

Situated in the Barbican Centre, close to City Uni, this is the school which actors Ewan McGregor, Joseph Fiennes, Art Malik and Neil Morrissey attended. Graduates from the BA (Hons) Acting and Stage Management & Technical Theatre courses obtain City Uni degrees; BMus graduates a Kent degree. Accommodation is available in a hall of residence: 178 bedrooms divided into 40 flats. A Students' Union organises various clubs and societies, and links with City University enable all GSMD students to use their facilities.

GETTING THERE
☞ By Underground: Barbican, St Paul's and Liverpool Street stations offer access to Central, Circle, Metropolitan, Hammersmith & City lines

GYOSEI INTERNATIONAL COLLEGE

Gyosei International College
London Road
Reading RG1 5AQ

TEL 0118 931 0152
FAX 0118 931 0137
EMAIL luk@gyosei.ac.uk
WEB www.gyosei.ac.uk

COLLEGE PROFILE

Founded	**1988**
Status	**Business School**
Fees pa (approx)	**£6,500**
Degree awarding university	**City Uni**
Situation/style	**Town campus**
Full-time undergraduates	**370**
College accommodation	**Halls**
Availability to freshers	**100%**
Cost pw (no food/food)	**£55-£80**
City rent pw	**£50**

DEGREE SUBJECT AREAS: :
Business, culture and language

VAG VIEW

Gyosei offers first degree business students what they call a 'bi-cultural education'. The college has a Japanese base and offers 'first-hand knowledge and experience of Japanese business and culture...' As a student at Gyosei you will get 'invaluable links with Japan, with Japanese people, with Japanese companies...' and, in particular, with the Nozu Group of Japanese companies. It's an impressive route to success. Three- to four-year degree courses lead to BA degrees awarded by City University. There are also close links with nearby Reading University. Gyosei actually operates out of the uni's original site on London Road, their two halls of residence accommodate Reading students as well, and some of Gyosei's students live in one of the uni's halls. Students of Gyosei have access to Reading Students' Union.

GETTING THERE
☞ By road: M4/J11.
☞ By rail: London Paddington, 30 mins; Bristol Parkway, 1:00; Birmingham New Street, 2:15.
☞ By air: direct bus/train services from Heathrow and Gatwick.
☞ By coach: London, 1:20; Brighton, 3:45.

HARPER ADAMS AGRICULTURAL COLLEGE

Harper Adams Agricultural College
Edgmond
Newport
Shropshire TF10 8NB

TEL 01952 815000
FAX 01952 814783
EMAIL admissions@harper-adams.ac.uk
WEB www.harper-adams.ac.uk

VAG VIEW

*H*arper Adams is a first-class agricultural college on the borders of Shropshire and Staffordshire. They have the distinction of being able to award their own degrees. The college scored 23 out of 24 points for the undergraduate provision. Learning resources include the college's 175-hectare farm, a library (38,000 volumes, 800 journals), a computer centre and the largest covered field demonstration area in the UK.

All first-year students are accommodated and catered for in college. This is a very sporty place – rugby, clay pigeon shooting and mountain biking bring them national, even international gongs. There's a well-equipped sports hall with weights room, indoor swimming pool, snooker table, tennis and squash courts, and students organise outward-bound activities – mountaineering, orienteering and abseiling. Union facilities include a couple of bars.

COLLEGE PROFILE

Founded	**1901**
Status	**Agric College**
Situation/style	**Rural campus**
Student population	**1,797**
Degree undergraduates	**985**
College accommodation	**Halls**
Availability to freshers	**100%**
Cost pw (incl food)	**£66-£90**
Town rent pw	**£40**

DEGREE SUBJECT AREAS:
Agriculture & land-based industries

GETTING THERE
☛ By road: M6 (J 13 or J14), A518, A41, B5062.
☛ By rail to Shrewsbury: Birmingham New Street, 1:10; from London to Stafford, 1:40.

HEREFORDSHIRE COLLEGE OF ART & DESIGN

Herefordshire College of Art & Design
Folly Lane
Hereford HR1 1LS

TEL 01432 273359
FAX 01432 341099
EMAIL hcad@hereford-art-col.ac.uk
WEB www.hereford-art-col.ac.uk

*T*he college offers Illustration and Design Crafts at degree level, the latter focusing on ceramics, metalwork (jewellery and ironwork) and textiles (including printing). Product marketing is a key element; drawing skills are essential for acceptance. The Illustration degree involves work experience and a broad sampling of courses such as Book Arts, Typography, Computer Imaging and Photography.

COLLEGE PROFILE

Founded	**1949**
Status	**Art College**
Degree awarding university	**Central England & Uni Wales**
Degree undergraduates	**96**
College accommodation	**None**
City rent pw	**£45**

GETTING THERE
☛ By road: north/south, A49; west along the A438; A465 from southwest.
☛ By rail: Shrewsbury, 39 mins; Birmingham, 2:22.

HERIOT-WATT UNIVERSITY

Heriot-Watt University
Riccarton Campus
Edinburgh EH14 4AS

Heriot-Watt Students' Association
Riccarton Campus
Edinburgh EH14 4AS

TEL 0131 451 3376
FAX 0131 451 3630
EMAIL admissions@hw.ac.uk
WEB www.hw.ac.uk

TEL 0131 451 5333
FAX 0131 451 5344
EMAIL admissions@hw.ac.uk
WEB www.hwusa.org

VAG VIEW

Heriot-Watt is a research-led, technological university, high on academic-industrial and business collaboration. Sited on the edge of Edinburgh, it is small but achieves big results: 73% of its teaching assessments have scored Excellent or Highly Satisfactory, it has a very sound graduate employment record, yet it is not too demanding of high grades to get in.

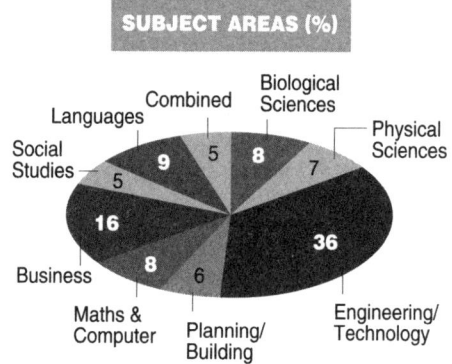

SUBJECT AREAS (%)

CAMPUSES

The main campus at Riccarton, 6.5 miles south-west of Edinburgh city centre, accommodates the faculties of Science, Engineering and Economic & Social Sciences. It is an attractive 380-acre campus in a huddle with a number of independent research companies. There's a modern, almost space-age, feel to it: smart, modern buildings are set in pleasant grounds with trees, green playing fields, an attractive artificial loch, squirrels, ducks and swans.

'The sense of seclusion at leafy Riccarton campus definitely aids study,' writes Richard Biggs, 'and has given rise to a community spirit that doesn't exist at inner city universities. However, the LRT buses that run to and from campus tend to be erratic – not fun in winter.'

Since the merger with **The Scottish College of Textiles in '99**, H-W also has a Scottish Borders campus. Situated in Galashiels – hence Gala, as the campus is known – a small town in the Scottish Borders, SCoT is only 33 miles/90 minutes by bus from Edinburgh, but unfortunately (if you are in a hurry) some two and a half hours by train, which detours via Berwick-upon-Tweed.

STUDENT PROFILE

'The University,' we read, 'is committed to equal opportunities for all, irrespective of age, colour, disability, ethnic origin, gender, marital status, religious or political beliefs, sexual orientation or other irrelevant distinction.' Sounds good, and in H-W's case it *is* good. They go out of their way to pull in a diverse mix of student, being one of the elite universities who show that open access can be made to work by concentrating their efforts on relative merits and on abilities and potential. So, they can gather 18% of the uni's student body from among groups which don't normally think of university, hang on to them for the duration (only 8% drop out, which is below average) and find 95% of them jobs within six months of graduation. You can't ask much more than that.

The concentration of technical courses accounts for the very high male to female ratio – a third more men than women. So what does Heriot-

UNIVERSITY/STUDENT PROFILE	
University since	**1966**
Situation/style	**City campus**
Student population	**7,440**
Full-time undergraduates	**4,460**
- mature	**47%**
- overseas	**19%**
- male/female	**66/33**
- state sector intake	**90%**
- non-traditional student intake	**18%, high**
- drop-out rate	**8%**
- undergraduate applications	**Up 8%**
see Introduction for key to tables	

Watt do about it? Equally impresssively, they start up 'Women into Science and Engineering', a scheme offering taster courses, with attendant scholarships, to female pupils. It's a scheme that flows from the university's absolute commitment to equal opportunity, which lies at the heart of their 'open access' strategy. This is a caring university in the best sense, the student is the principal focus.

There is also a big foreign exchange programme – so, you'll find a rich mix of cultures, on campus. All students can choose to study abroad at some point during their course.

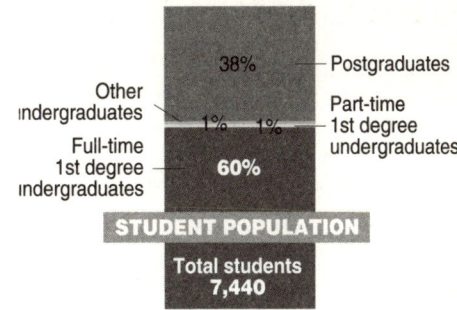

STUDENT POPULATION

Total students
7,440

AT A GLANCE

ACADEMIC FILE:

Subjects assessed	**15**
Excellent/Highly Satisfactory	**73%**
Average requirements	**220 points**
Students-staff ratio	**18:1**
First/2:1 degree pass rate	**52%**

ACCOMMODATION FILE:

Guarantee to freshers	**Must apply by 1.9**
Style	**Flats and halls**
Price range pw	**£32-£64**
City rent pw	**£55**

ACADEMIA

They specialise in science, engineering, technology, business and management, and have particular niches in photonics, actuarial maths and statistics, languages (translating and interpreting) and petroleum engineering. 'Modern languages are an outstanding strength,' one sixthform adviser confirmed. 'You can walk straight out of Heriot-Watt into a job in the EC.' School careers staff also point to their cross-faculty courses, for example Environmental Management & Technology or Food Science, Technology & Management, and to their courses aimed at boom areas, such as Microelectronics. Pharmaceutical Chemistry appeals directly to the Pharmaceutical industry which is equal to 27% of the UK's manufacturing industry. Their unique BSc in Brewing and Distilling is rarely short of applicants possibly for different reasons.

They have just concentrated all academic departments into six schools and two postgraduate research institutes. There are schools of Built Environment; Engineering & Physical Sciences; Management & Languages; Mathematical & Computer Sciences, Textiles & Design, and Life Sciences. There are three ten-week terms, four modules a term, twelve each year, and there's an emphasis on combining e-learning with traditional, face to face teaching methods, very often utilising the latest educational technology, which they have developed.

The two postgrad institutes are the Edinburgh Business School and the PG Institute of Petroleum Engineering

In research, they surprised last year by falling from 36th to 54th place in the recent assessments, but they are quick to point out that they came top in the UK for petroleum engineering and for actuarial mathematics and statistics (for which they are the only provider outside London), top in Scotland for built environment, applied mathematics and for food science and technology. Our *Academic Excellence* box, below, list the subjects that made the world-class ratings (grades 5* and 5). All research areas in engineering and physical sciences, management and languages were rated at least Grade 4.

Not so long ago, Heriot-Watt was a very sporty uni with, for its size, exceptional showings in the national teams sports league, then suddenly they

---

ACADEMIC EXCELLENCE

TEACHING:
(Rated Excellent, Highly Satis. or 17+ out of 24)

Electrical & Electronic Eng.	**Excellent**
Civil Engineering, Computer Studies, Physics, Chemistry, Maths & Statistics, Mechanical + Manufacturing Eng, Finance & Accounting, Cellular & Molecular Biology.	**Highly Satis.**
Chemical Engineering	**19**
European Languages	**21**

RESEARCH:
Top grades 5/5*

Mineral & Mining Engineering.	**Grade 5***
Applied Maths, Statistics, Built Environment	**Grade 5**

fell from grace and it became clear that the sporting expertise had come largely from the Moray House Institute of Education, a teacher training college and Scottish Centre for Physical Education, which had upped and left them to become the Faculty of Education at the University of Edinburgh.

> *Heriot-Watt is a scientific university, which, with clear principles and scientific efficiency, ensures a companionable set-up and hugely successful conversion from academia to graduate employment.*

Perhaps this rankled more than we knew – certainly the sport was missed, for they have just welcomed the first group of students onto a new Sport and Exercise Science core degree within the School of Life Sciences, a discipline which, with their watchful eye for employment potential, can also combine with psychology or management. A BSc in Biology with Sport and Exercise Science has now also been introduced.

WHAT IT'S REALLY LIKE	
UNIVERSITY:	
Social Life	★★★
Campus scene	**Like clockwork**
Student Union services	**Good**
Politics	**Low level**
	Student debt
Sport	**31 clubs, hockey strong**
National team position	**40th**
Sport facilities	**Good**
Arts opportunities	**Music, film good; dance, art average, drama poor**
Student newspaper	**Watts On**
Nightclub	**Zero Degrees**
Bars	**Jinglin' Geordies, Liberty's**
Union ents	**JAM (cheese), live bands + indie**
Union Clubs/Societies	**66**
Most popular societies	**International and activity socs**
Smoking policy	**Union OK**
Parking	**Poor**
CITY:	
Entertainment	★★★★★
Scene	**Seething**
Town/gown relations	**Good**
Risk of violence	**Average**
Cost of living	**High**
Student concessions	**Excellent**
Survival + 2 nights out	**£80-£100 pw**
Part-time work campus/city	**Average/good**

SOCIAL SCENE

STUDENTS' ASSOCIATION

On-campus entertainment facilities consist of three bars – café bar **Liberties**, traditional type boozer, **Jinglin' Geordies,** and disco, **Zero Degrees**. They have been accused of falling down a bit on the social side, with no union night on Saturday suggesting no desire to compete with the city and the main body of students (a high number of whom own their own cars) tending to head towards the city centre after classes, leaving the campus largely deserted. But cheesy *JAM Friday* at the nightclub, and live music followed by an indie club the night before, are now very popular, and recent live acts have included Ministry of Sound, the Orange Music tour – the Stanton Warriors, and live music from local bands.

Edinburgh, of course, has plenty on offer at the weekend, indeed at any time (see *Student Edinburgh*, page 177).

Down at Gala, they are also getting some sort of scene together. There are new union premises and a full ents programme. There's even a musician-in-residence and lashings of sponsorship from North Sea oil, which has led to COMA – not a state of unconsciousness due to inebriation, but the name for a network of groups available for gigs.

SPORT Facilities at Riccarton include three sports halls, floodlit rugby pitches and synthetic tennis courts, eight squash courts – on campus is the national training centre for squash, weight rooms, conditioning and sports science facilities, and there's a 6-lane swimming pool due by the time you get there, as well as a Sports Medicine Centre and a £5 million Football Academy to be run in association with Heart of Midlothian FC.

Last year the hockey team was the only Scottish team to have been in a British final. The performance of uni teams overall left them at 40th, which for their student population is good, and certainly a good deal better than the 75th they managed when Moray House deserted them.

PILLOW TALK

Get your application for accommodation in by September 1 and you can choose between catered and self catered study bedrooms and self-catering flats, all a short stroll away from everything else. Of the 1,800 study bedrooms, more than 1,000 have their own shower and toilet, and there are never more than five sharing a kitchen, which comes with fridge freezer, cooker, kettle etc. Bring your own crockery, cutlery, pots and pans. Catered students have access to a pantry for snacks and hot drinks. For a small subscription, you can have access to a phone, the Internet and the Heriot-Watt Intranet. There is, in any case, free room-to-room and incoming calls, and voicemail.

The cost per week ranges from £32 (twin room, self-catered flat) to £64 (large single catered study bedroom in hall).

JOBS

There are courses directly relevant to particular careers, as already mentioned. The box above shows how the engineering, pharmaceutical, built environment and financial courses inform the employment picture. The language provision (remember particularly the interpreter element) make their more hidden impact. The most recent statistics show that 95% of Heriot-Watt graduates were in employment, or had settled into postgrad study, within six months of graduation.

Their strength is a close relationship with industry, business and national support networks, which enables them to build entrepreneurial skills into many of the degree courses.

They are a member of the Scottish Institute for Enterprise, a five-university consortium that teaches entrepreneurial skills to undergrads and postgrads. Students are helped to identify where their opportunities might lie; there's a student

WHERE GRADUATES END UP	
19% Manufacturing*,	Key Areas
15% Finance*,	
11% Wholesale/Retail,	
7% Computer,	
5% Public Admin	
Accountancy,	Niche Areas
Chem/Pharmaceutical,	
Eng/Industrial Design*,	
Construction*, Property*,	
Electron/Electric*	

*indicates Top 10 Graduate Provider

Approximate employed **94%**

business plan competition, seminars, workshops, etc.

GETTING THERE

☞ By road: A71 or A70; if the latter, turn off at Currie on to Riccarton Mains Road.
☞ By rail: London King's Cross, 4:30; Glasgow Central, 50 mins; Newcastle, 1:30.
☞ By air: nearby Edinburgh Airport for inland and international flights.
☞ By coach: Glasgow, 1:10; London, 9:10; Birmingham, 8:10; Newcastle, 3:10.
☞ To Gala, A7 south from Edinburgh.

UNIVERSITY OF HERTFORDSHIRE

University of Hertfordshire
College Lane
Hatfield
Hertfordshire AL10 9AB

TEL 01707 284800
FAX 01707 284870
EMAIL admissions@herts.ac.uk
WEB www.herts.ac.uk

Hertfordshire Students' Union
College Lane
Hatfield
Hertfordshire AL10 9AB

TEL 01707 285000
FAX 01707 286150
EMAIL uhsu@herts.ac.uk
WEB uhsu.herts.ac.uk

VAG VIEW

Herts Uni is among the most impressive of the new universities in rate of growth, enhancement of learning resources and graduate employment, and one reason for this is the contact with industry and the capital city which their strategically advantageous location has enabled them to maintain.

Headquartes are in Hatfield, a New Town, but it grew out of an historic Old Town, ancient home of the Cecil family who found the

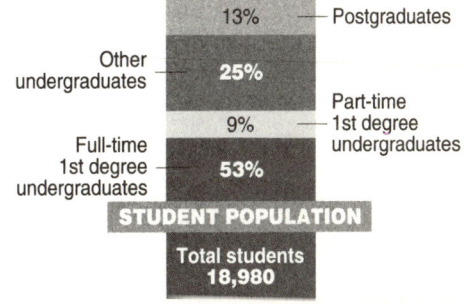

Postgraduates	13%
Other undergraduates	25%
Part-time 1st degree undergraduates	9%
Full-time 1st degree undergraduates	53%

STUDENT POPULATION

Total students
18,980

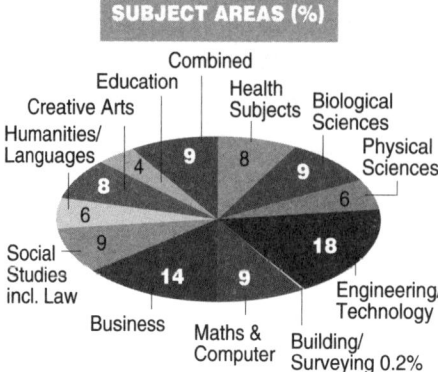

SUBJECT AREAS (%)

Combined — Education — Creative Arts — Humanities/Languages — Health Subjects — Biological Sciences — Physical Sciences — 9 — 8 — 9 — 4 — 8 — 6 — Social Studies incl. Law — 9 — 18 — 14 — 9 — 6 — Business — Maths & Computer — Building/Surveying 0.2% — Engineering/Technology

operate virtually as a single campus community.

The two Hatfield campuses will be made one by cycleways, by footpaths and shuttle buses. It is a huge undertaking. There will be a new Learning Resources Centre, a 500-seater auditorium, 1,600 new bed spaces, and acres of sports fields to gee up their unexceptional national league positions.

Herts isn't known for sport at the moment (although they were American Football national champs from 1997-2000 apparently, 106th was last year's national position), but provision at the new campus will be high quality and change all that. There'll be a sports hall with twelve badminton courts/volleyball, basketball and indoor hockey, a 25-metre, 8-lane swimming pool, a large health and

position, seven miles or so northwest of London, well suited to the political stratagems that made them the 'Kingmakers' of English politics. Today this same location finds this international science, engineering and hi-tech, business-orientated uni equally well set – on the north-south A1, minutes from the M25 and M1, and within striking distance of four airports – Luton, Stansted, Heathrow and Gatwick.

CAMPUSES

Yet because the uni is scattered – there are campuses in an arc described by Hatfield, Hertford, St Albans and Watford – it hasn't been easy for students to get a fix on the whole thing. Now that is to be overcome with a £105-million new campus – the de Havilland Campus, no less – half a mile from the present Hatfield site. In September 2003, this will draw into it the uni's Business School and Faculty of Humanities and Education. The Hertford and Watford campuses will close, and the University of Hertfordshire will

ACADEMIC EXCELLENCE	
TEACHING:	
(Rated Excellent or 17+ out of 24)	
Environmental Studies	**Excellent**
Philosophy	**24**
Psychology, Business	**23**
Mechanical, Aero & Manuf Eng,	**22**
Art & Design, Subjects Allied to Medicine, Education	
Maths, Molecular Biosciences, Physics	**21**
Linguistics, Elec/Electro Eng, General Eng, Nursing	**20**
Building Services Engineering	**19**
Civil Engineering	**18**
RESEARCH:	
Top grades 5/5*	
History	**Grade 5**

fitness suite, a four lane indoor cricket centre, a 12-metre high climbing wall, as well as the new grass and artificial pitches. We will have to see whether all this will in fact tempt the pale-faced Hatfield spods away from their work stations.

Until September 2003, however, the campus situation remains as follows:

HATFIELD CAMPUS (see address, page 221) **Faculties:** Art & Design, Combined & Continuing Studies, Engineering, Health & Human Sciences, Information Sciences, Natural Sciences, and the Business School's Social Sciences Dept.

HERTFORD CAMPUS Mangrove Road, Hertford, Herts SG13 8QF. Tel: 01707 285406. **Faculty:** The Business School.

ST ALBANS CAMPUS 7 Hatfield Road, St Albans, Herts AL1 3RS. Tel: 01707 286210. **Faculty:** Law.

UNIVERSITY PROFILE	
University since	**1992**
Situation/style	**Suburban campuses**
Student population	**18,980**
Full-time undergraduates	**10,040**
- mature	**27%**
- overseas	**14%**
- male/female	**53/47**
- state sector intake	**96%**
- non-traditional student intake	**13%**
- drop-out rate	**11%**
- undergraduate applications	**Down 9%**
*see Introduction for key to tables	

WATFORD CAMPUS Wall Hall Aldenham, Watford, Herts WD2 8AT. Tel: 01707 285606. **Faculties:** Humanities, Languages & Education.

ACADEMIA

Historically, Herts is noted for aero-engineering, computer science, areas into which they still pour graduates. They have progressed rapidly, too, in environmental sciences, in law and in health, and business – Business & Management, Economics, and Tourism picked up 23 points out of 24 in the teaching assessments recently (as indeed did Nursing).

Meanwhile, they slipped quietly out of subjects like drama, sociology and traditionlal forms of engineering, investing heavily instead in Pharmacology, benefiting from being located in the most heavily concentrated area of pharmaceutical R&D in the country.

It is interesting to note, however, that in the recent research assessments they slid down the league table from 65th to 93rd place, achieving international recognition only in…history.

New courses this year look to be more in tune with their core strengths, such as BSc – Computer Aided Product Development, Media Technology & Digital Broadcast, Multimedia Technology, Motorsport Engineering, Music Composition & Technology, and others similar. Suddenly that traditional Drama, Dance & Cinematics looks hopelessly out of place.

At de Havilland, the new Learning Resources Centre will make full use of latest technological developments, in particular their very own computer system, Studynet, what they call their 'Managed Learning Environment', a simple personalised academic workspace for every student on which will appear profiled information relevant to each individual's programme of study, as well as a range of personal information management tools linking students to course databases.

JOBS

Six months after graduation in 2000, 74.3% of graduates were in employment, 13.2% in further study, 8.9% unemployed; while 3.5% were not available for employment. See our *Employment* box, above. The uni sees its strongest areas as IT & telecoms, education, health and engineering.

For part-time work the Students' Union has an employment office with opportunities for 600.

WHERE GRADUATES END UP	
16% Health/Social Work,	Key Areas
14% Manufacture,	
11% Education,	
9% Wholesale/Retail,	
7% Computer,	
6% Finance,	
5% Public Admin,	
5% Personnel	
Telcommunications,	Niche Areas
Electron/Electric Manuf,	
Aeronautical Manuf,	
Agric/Forestry, Property,	
Publishing, Film/Video,	
Journalism, Legal,	
Chem/Pharmaceutical,	
Construction, Defence	
Approximate employed	**95%**

VIEW FROM THE GROUND
by Katherine Cooley

HATFIELD

The main campus is Hatfield, where the [original] **Learning Resources Centre** is based. With hundreds of computers, your very own e-mail and the facility to look up the George Clooney Web page, a café downstairs serving cheese toasties and banana milkshakes to eager students throughout the day and night, and copies of all the text books you need to research for those lectures you accidentally slept through, you can't complain.

The Students' Union HQ is also based at Hatfield, where the Ents Department organises exciting acts and fun evenings for all students, at all the campuses.

Hatfield entertainment facilities include the **Elehouse** pub, which offers a wonderfully healthy food bar during the day, making a change from Pot Noodles and oven chips, and a pleasant pub atmosphere in the evenings. Downstairs there is a shop, open daily from Monday to Friday, where you can satisfy your cravings for Pringles and cream eggs, as well as allowing you to stock up on paper and pens in preparation for your lectures (you know,

> *Herts Uni is among the more impressive new universities in its ruthlessly pursued academic strategy and streamlining of graduates for employment. Now, perhaps the new campus will give a real student culture a chance to develop.*

WHAT IT'S REALLY LIKE

UNIVERSITY:	
Social Life	★★★
Campus scene	**Bit spoddy**
Student Union services	**Average**
Politics	**No interest**
Sport	**43 clubs**
National team position	**106th**
Sport facilities	**Good**
Arts opportunities	**Drama excellent; rest good**
Student newspaper	**Universe**
Student radio	**Crush**
Nightclub	**The Font**
Bars	**Elehouse, Wall Hall Bar, Boatie**
Union ents	**Big (cheese), Fever, Pop Tart, Roobarb & Custard, It's All Good (house), Funky (garage)**
Union clubs/societies	**60**
Most popular societies	**Drama, Christian, Alternative Music**
Smoking	**Bars only**
Parking	**Poor**
CITY:	
Entertainment	★★ – ★★★
Scene	**London beckons**
Town/gown relations	**Average**
Risk of violence	**Low**
Cost of living	**High**
Student concessions locally	**OK**
Survival + 2 nights out	**£45-£55 pw**
Part-time work campus/town	**Excellent/good except Hatfield town**

run by students for students and can be received by the majority of halls. There's also the *Universe* newspaper to keep you informed of the good and the bad goings-on. The most active societies are Christian Union, Drama and Alternative Music. The only downside to this campus is the lack of shops and entertainments within the town centre. **The Galleria**, a local outlet centre, offers cut-price clothes, but the town centre itself offers little variety of shops and the nightlife is poor.

WATFORD & HERTFORD

The next two campuses are Wall Hall, near Watford, and Balls Park in Hertford. Both are set in beautiful surroundings in the countryside and offer very much the same facilities as Hatfield – learning resource centres and union bars. They also have a wide variety of acts and entertainments, catering for all musical tastes. Only a short bus ride from the Wall Hall campus is Watford, a bustling town with great shopping facilities, pubs and nightclubs for those who fancy a wild night out. The Hertford campus is also within easy access of Hertford town centre, which offers good shops and pubs.

ST ALBANS

The fourth campus is St Albans, a small campus for those studying Law. It is based in the lovely city of St Albans. It is easily accessible from Hatfield, where most first years are normally housed, and close to the town centre, which boasts many high-street chain stores, as well as a variety of specialist shops catering for the individual. There is a refectory and a Students' Union area, which although small provide good daytime facilities, such as a TV and a pool table. Oh, and the town has the oldest pub in the UK apparently, **Ye Old Fighting Cocks**.

PILLOW TALK

Freshers are guaranteed accommodation if they send in their accommodation application forms before 'A' level results are published and have accepted an unconditional offer of a course place by August 31.

Campus accommodation means, first and foremost, halls: self-catering with single study bedrooms and shared bathrooms/showers (only 3% of housing is en suite). In addition, at Hatfield and Hertford, shared rooms are available, and on the Hatfield and Watford campuses you get a choice, too, of newer flats and houses. Note that the guarantee doesn't oblige them to put you in uni *campus* accommodation. You could end up in off-campus lodgings and private, rented houses. Prices per week range from £49 (cheapest self-catering) to £69 (full board in lodgings); shared houses between

those things in between sleep and alcohol).

Across the courtyard is the main venue for big events, the **Font** [due for £450,000 redevelopment in the summer of this year, 2002]. Weekly clubnights include *Big* (perfect pop and cheesy chart), *Roobarb & Custard* ('80s), *Pop Tart* ('90s), *It's All Good* (house), *Funky Styles* (garage), *Large Innit?* (party dance) and *Fever* ('70s). Numerous live acts and big name DJs visit, due to being close to London – recently Timmy Mallet, Chesney Hawkes, Orange Music, Ministry of Sound, Lisa Pin Up, Chicane, Damage, Blue... Twice a year the Students' Union holds a ball with fantastic line-ups. The Summer Ball also offers an interesting combination of food, drink and a selection of fairground rides, only for those with iron stomachs!

Hatfield has the radio station, CRUSH, which is

£55 and £59 per week plus bills

From September 2003, you might be wise to opt for one of the new rooms up for grabs at the de Havilland campus. All will be self-catered, specified to the highest standards, with network points and the most modern facilities. New sports and catering facilities will be adjacent.

GETTING THERE

☛ **Hatfield** by road: A1(M)/J3. By rail: London King's Cross, 22 mins. ☛ By coach: London, 1:00. ☛ **Hertford** by road: Mangrove Road runs off the A414. By rail: London King's Cross, 25 mins. ☛ **Watford** by road: M1/J5. By rail: London Euston, 20 mins. ☛ **St Albans** by road: M25/J22, A1081. By rail: London (Thameslink), 25 mins.

AT A GLANCE	
ACADEMIC FILE:	
Subjects assessed	**30**
Excellent	**53%**
Average requirements	**200 points**
Students-staff ratio	**18:1**
First/2:1 degree pass rate	**53%**
ACCOMMODATION FILE:	
Guarantee to freshers	**Apply by 31.8**
Style	**Halls, flats, houses**
Catered	**None**
En-suite	**3%**
Price range pw	**£49-£66.50**
Town rent pw	**£55-£59**

HEYTHROP COLLEGE

Heythrop College
Kensington Square
London W8 5HQ

TEL 020 7795 6600
FAX 020 7795 4200
EMAIL r.bolland@heythrop.ac.uk
WEB www.heythrop.ac.uk

VAG VIEW

*H*eythrop is an independent college within the University of London specialising in theology and philosophy and with a refreshingly evolutionary concept of higher education. For their inspiration they turn to the Swiss psychologist Jean Piaget, noted for his revolutionary work on the cognitive functions of children. Piaget wrote that 'the principal goal of education is to create people who are capable of doing new things, not simply of repeating what other generations have done... The second goal of education is to form minds which can be critical, can verify, and not accept everything they are offered.' Trawling through all that the higher educational establishments of this country can offer, such a breathtakingly simple statement seems almost unutterably bold. Their teaching is the traditional university method of tutorials and small-group seminars. They possess one of the finest collections of theological and philosophical literature anywhere to be found, their 250,000 volumes available to

COLLEGE PROFILE	
College of London Uni since	**1971**
Full-time undergraduates	**147**
- mature	**40%**
- overseas	**10%**
- male/female	**65/35**
ACCOMMODATION:	
Availability to freshers	**100%**
Style	**Halls**
Approx cost pw (catered)	**£75-£90 pw**
City rent pw	**£65-£90**

every one of their students without queue.

STUDENT SCENE

'Ideally situated in the centre of Kensington, Heythrop projects an atmosphere of elegance and solemnity, but this really is the most friendly of colleges,' writes Clare Barker, 'quite impressive given the great diversity among Heythrop students. A huge number are either mature undergraduates or postgrads; then there's the diversity of religions and interests, and the proximity of **Lamda** – its drama students share one of our common rooms and make more unorthodox the already bizarre crowd milling around the corridors... And then there are the nuns. Campus is owned by nuns – and they keep rabbits. The nuns (and their rabbits) are very amiable and don't seem at all fazed at having leery students sharing their home. However, their presence leads to Heythrop having a prevailing feeling of a religious institution – strange, considering the vast number of philosophy students who are not diplomatic in the expression of their beliefs.'

GETTING THERE

☞ The college is tucked behind High Street Kensington, a short walk from Kensington Palace. High Street Ken station gives access to Piccadilly, Circle and District lines.

UNIVERSITY OF THE HIGHLANDS & ISLANDS

UHI Millennium Institute
Caledonia House
63 Academy Street
Inverness IV1 1BB

TEL 01463 27900
FAX 01463 236736
EMAIL eo@fc.uhi.ac.uk
WEB www.uhi.ac.uk

VAG VIEW

Some 350 years after Sir Thomas Urquhart first proposed the idea of a university equipped to overcome the difficulties in living in the more farflung reaches of Britain, it has met with the technology to make it work. UHI Millennium Institute, now its legal title, is a federal network of colleges that makes use of information and communication technologies to overcome geographical distance. As a student you will have a regional reference point of at least one participating college. These are further education colleges whose higher education provision was just beginning to develop when the UHI project grew with them. Already UHI have 5,821 students and degree validation from the Open University. Subjects range from a BA

UNIVERSITY PROFILE	
Federal university since	**1998**
Student population	**5,821**
Full-time undergraduates	**2,824**
- mature	**45%**
- overseas	**1%**
- male/female	**48/52**

DEGREE SUBJECT AREAS:
Gaelic, cultural studies, fine art, music, theology, business, tourism, hospitality management, outdoor pursuit, sciences (incl enviro, marine, etc), social sciences, rural studies, computing, construction, aero/mechanical/electrical/ machatronic engineering

in Gaelic at Lews Castle College and Sabhal Mor Ostaig, the Gaelic college on Skye, to a BSc in Engineering at Inverness or Moray. It is an exciting project; one to watch.

HOLBORN COLLEGE

Holborn College
200 Greyhound Road
London W14 9RY

TEL/FAX 020 7385 3377
EMAIL hlt@holborncollege.ac.uk
WEB www.holborncollege.ac.uk

London University, Wolverhampton and the University of Wales validate the four degrees on offer. London's law degree is an

COLLEGE PROFILE	
Founded	**1983**
Status	**Private HE College**
Fees pa (approx)	**£2,100-£4,000**
Degree undergraduates	**500**
College accommodation	**None**

DEGREE SUBJECT AREAS:
Law, Business, Accountancy

external programme – full-time, part-time or distance learning courses are available. The law degree awarded by Wolverhampton is again full-time, part-time or distance learning Now, too, there is a BA (Hons) in Business Administration and another in Accountancy awarded by the University of Wales.

The main advantage of this college has to be the correspondence route. You can take up to seven years to complete your course, professional bodies complying, and if you fancy spending a year in college, and a few at home, you're more than welcome.

GETTING THERE
☛ Hammersmith Underground (Piccadilly, District, Hammersmith & City lines) or Barons Court (Piccadilly, District).

UNIVERSITY OF HUDDERSFIELD

University of Huddersfield
Queensgate
Huddersfield HD1 3DH

TEL 0870 901 5555
    01484 422288
FAX 01484 516151
EMAIL prospectus@hud.ac.uk
WEB www.hud.ac.uk

Huddersfield Students' Union
Milton Hall
Queensgate
Huddersfield HD1 3DH

TEL 01484 538156
FAX 01484 432333
EMAIL su-president@hud.ac.uk
WEB ayup.hud.ac.uk

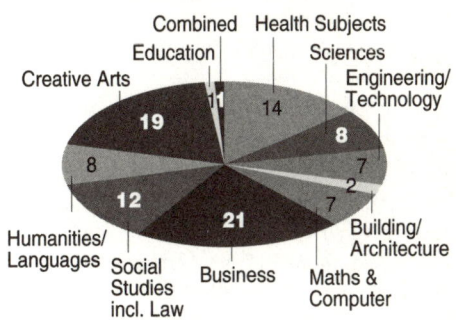

SUBJECT AREAS (%)

Combined — 11, Education, Health Subjects, Sciences 14, Creative Arts, Engineering/Technology 8, 19, Humanities/Languages 8, 12, Social Studies incl. Law 21, Business, Maths & Computer 7, 2, 7, Building/Architecture

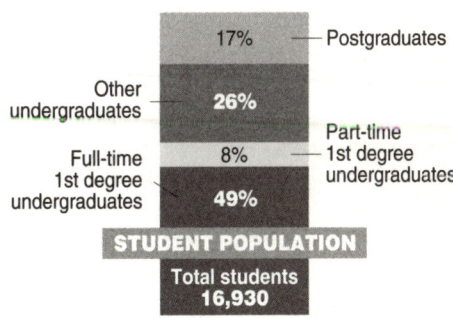

- Postgraduates 17%
- Other undergraduates 26%
- Part-time 1st degree undergraduates
- Full-time 1st degree undergraduates 8%
- 49%

STUDENT POPULATION
Total students
16,930

VAG VIEW

*T*he uni traces its history back to the Young Men's Mental Improvement Society, founded in 1841. It was awarded university status in 1992 after passing through two other incarnations, first as a technical college then as a polytechnic. Today it has a city-centre campus (Queensgate – the central focus), Holly Bank campus, two miles to the north, and Storthes Hall, four miles to the south-east.

Huddersfield town is a strange mix. Its roots in the industrial revolution are not in doubt. It is also known far and wide for its annual poetry festival, with famously the **Albert** pub as artistic font; folk and jazz are equally present. Yet they can pull down their arts centre to make way for a shopping precinct!

Student Dave Colley writes: 'Ex-Heritage minister Stephen Dorrell once famously remarked that Huddersfield was the Paris of the North. Now I can't pretend this didn't raise a few eyebrows, but he did have a point of sorts.'

The uni and the town are of a similar weave. There is this traditional, industrial, people-culture – major strengths are electronic engineering, IT and social work, and in health areas such as nursing and midwifery. But then you hear that they have the largest music department of any UK university, which combines an academic focus with opportunities for musical performance. In the recent research assessment exercise they won a coveted – world renown – Grade 5 – for music. (See box, below.)

The indigenous Yorkshireman is unlikely to shout much about the uni, he doesn't even look at it objectively and certainly won't waste his breath convincing a soft southerner of things he is unlikely to understand. Yet, southerners can be the very best ambassadors, should they take time to discover the soul of Huddersfield Uni... 'I can't remember a more depressing view,' wrote student Tim Wild, a film-maker who came up from Brighton, possibly the most exciting and sunny blue city in Britain. 'In the forefront, the twin towers of the council blocks, ably supported by the dual carriageway and the gas

works. Most people only have the vaguest idea where the bloody place is, so I'll attempt to clear up the confusion. Smack bang in the middle – three hours away from London by car, and about three thousand light years away in attitude. That's why this place is special – they really couldn't give a toss whether you're from Taunton or Timbuktu as long as you can hold your ale and laugh at yourself. If it's glamour and sophistication you're after, then stay away, because you'll only spoil it for the rest of us. I won't pretend it's paradise, but that's part of the appeal, in an odd way. Because it's the middle of nowhere, there are no cliques, no élite to try and be part of. It's just cold and grey and everyone here's in it together.

'Like the blitz, without the Germans.'

CAMPUS

The university has recently given the city-centre Queensgate campus a makeover, replacing some of the 1960s' tower blocks with the new Harold Wilson Building (natch) – HQ for the School of Human & Health Sciences. Holly Bank, two miles north is for teacher training, not a huge element in the graduate workplace – David Blunkett studied here – (now you're getting warm). Storthes Hall campus is set in 350 acres of parkland four miles away from the main campus and connected to it by a subsidised bus service.

STUDENT PROFILE

Huddersfield is real; the union website address is ayup.hud.ac.uk; social climbers need not apply.

ACADEMIA

The eight academic schools are: Applied Sciences (Transport and Logistics, Chemical and Biological Sciences, Geographical and Environmental Sciences), Computing and Mathematics, Design Technology (Textiles, Architecture), Education, Engineering, Business, Human and Health Sciences, (Nursing, Podiatry, Behavioural Science, Social Work, Health Studies, Careers Guidance), Music and Humanities. It is particularly good on sandwich courses. The School of Engineering recently attracted some £1.85 million towards its Centre for Precision Technologies – a major research centre for nano-technology, precision engineering to almost atomic levels.

Recent successes in the teaching assessments (max points 24) have been Nursing and Midwifery (22 points), Design Technology (21), Hospitality Management (22), Transport & Logistics (22), Education April (22), Politics (23). 'I went there,' a sixthform careers master from a public school said

AT A GLANCE	
ACADEMIC FILE:	
Subjects assessed	**29**
Excellent	**57%**
Average requirements	**180 points**
Students-staff ratio	**20:1**
First/2:1 degree pass rate	**51%**
ACCOMMODATION FILE:	
Guarantee to freshers	**First choice applicants**
Style	**Halls**
Catered	**None**
En-suite	**83.6%**
Price range pw	**£48.70-£63**
City rent pw	**£25-£70**

WHAT IT'S REALLY LIKE	
UNIVERSITY:	
Social Life	★★★
Campus scene	**Laid-back, authentic**
Student Union services	**Good**
Politics	**Interest low**
Sport	**Regional, not national force**
National sporting position	**119th**
Sport facilities	**Average**
Arts opportunities	**Music, film good; art avg; drama dance poor**
Student newspaper	**Ayup**
Student radio	**Ayup Radio in dev**
Nightclub	**Eden**
Bars	**Milton Hall, Underground**
Union ents	**Masses**
Union clubs/societies	**20**
Smoking policy	**Union OK**
Parking	**Non-existent**
TOWN:	
Entertainment	★★★
Scene	**Music, poetry, drama, pubs**
Town/gown relations	**Good**
Risk of violence	**Average**
Cost of living	**Low**
Student concessions	**Good**
Survival + 2 nights out	**£40 pw**
Part-time work campus/town	**Average**

to me, 'and spent a couple of days with the Dept of Distribution. Yup, they've looked at the market very carefully and where there's a gap they have gone. In this case transportation – transport & logistics – and they've gone hard for it.' Did he see my eyes glaze over? 'I have to say,' he continues, 'I have seen more enthusiasm among the staff at Huddersfield – both in this department and in Hotel & Catering – than at any other university in the land. I had thought, Oh, Huddersfield, can I really afford the time to go? And I was surprised, *very* surprised.'

There's 24-hour computer access, good support for students with disabilities and a whole raft of intriguing new courses this year, including some in radio journalism, creative writing, TV production, PR, advertising & design management, architecture (good uni for this), computer games programming, green science...

SOCIAL SCENE

STUDENTS' UNION The nightclub, **Eden** (950 capacity), takes the honours in an otherwise weak club scene in town, with appearances by chart acts and club tours. There's little that Eden hasn't seen, including a drugs bust as late as the mid-nineties.

From music to film, from nursing to software engineering, from automotive design to entrepreneurship and business, Huddersfield has its markets covered, but if it's glamour you're after, stay away, because you'll only spoil it for the rest of us.

At **Milton Hall** bars (including the famed **Underground** bar) there's a whole lotta other ents going on – party nights, karaoke, discos and happy hours. If you're up for a sprightly pub crawl, six quality pubs can be found outside the main gates of the university campus. Add a kebab shop,

Sainsbury's and the **Tudor Cinema** within a few hundred yards and you can begin to understand why most first-year students can't even find their way back to the train station on a weekend.

SPORT Facilities are not extensive. There's a sports hall on campus, with a newish fitness centre and playing areas elsewhere, which provide for football, rugby (league and union), hockey, cricket and tennis. There is also a new Astroturf pitch and two new top-quality soccer pitches. Students have a discount at an Olympic standard sports centre with swimming pool in town.

PILLOW TALK

There is first-class accommodation at Storthes Hall,

WHERE GRADUATES END UP

14% Manufacture, Key Areas
14% Wholesale/Retail,
12% Health/Social Work,
9% Finance,
6% Public Admin,
6% Education
Architecture, Niche Areas
Electron/Electric Manuf.

Approximate employed **93%**

house about 95% in halls or houses, or lodgings and flats in the private sector – they tell me there's 83.6% en-suite in university accommodation, so someone's been counting. Price range is £48.70 to £63 per week in halls, an amazing £25 to £70 in town.

JOBS

As the man said, 'They've looked at the market very carefully and where there's a gap they have gone.' The *Employment* box shows where that will lead.

GETTING THERE

☛ By road: M62/J24, M1/J38-40.
☛ By rail: London via Wakefield, 3:30; Liverpool Lime Street, 1:45
☛ By air: Leeds/Bradford or Manchester Airports.
☛ By coach: London, 5:00; Manchester, 6:30; Leeds, 1:10.

the **Rendezvous Bar** (pool comps, quiz nights, karaoke etc.) and various other facilities. Otherwise, there are halls available in and around the town centre. You're guaranteed a place in halls if Huddersfield makes you a firm offer. They can

UNIVERSITY OF HULL

The University of Hull
Cottingham Road
Kingston upon Hull HU6 7RX

TEL 01482 466100
FAX 01482 442290
EMAIL admissions@admin.hull.ac.uk
WEB www.hull.ac.uk
Hull University Union

University House
Cottingham Road
Hull HU6 7RX

TEL 01482 445361
FAX 01482 466280
EMAIL ust@union.hull.ac.uk
WEB www.hull.ac.uk/su

VAG VIEW

The city's most famous literary son, the late poet and librarian Philip Larkin, described Hull as 'in the world, yet sufficiently on the edge of it to have a different resonance.'

For centuries it was cut off from the rest of the country to the south by the Humber, to the north by the glorious, wide open Yorkshire Wolds (unknown to the tourist even now, thank God), and to the west by a large expanse of nothing. Then all the way from Liverpool on the opposite coast came the M62 (which connects, north and south, with the A1(M)) and suddenly Hull became part of the rest of the world, though as student Adam Ford told me, 'You'd be surprised at the number of people in Liverpool who still think that the M62 stops in Leeds.'

The essence of Hull is that it is distinct, not just because it has its own telephone system

SUBJECT AREAS (%)

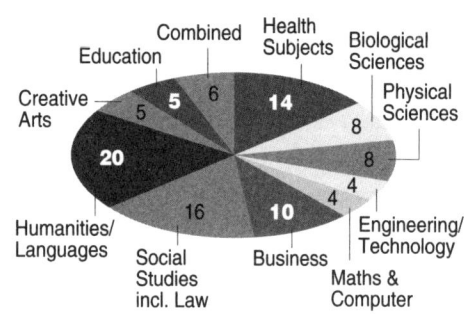

and white phone boxes, which once urged a student to paint the town red. 'It is separate culturally,' a sixthform college careers master said to me in hushed tones. He teaches just an hour away and still he can't find his way into it; he sends pupils to Newcastle (two hours to the north), to York (an hour to the west), to Sunderland, to Teesside, but rarely, if ever apparently, to Hull.

The point, then, is that in its insularity, Hull has developed this 'unique [cultural] resonance.' For the same reason, it is a cheap place to live, more than 2% below the national average: you can buy a three-bedroom house there for £25,000; parents do and sell it when their darling leaves. But perhaps more important than all this is that academically the University of Hull is very strong, with high

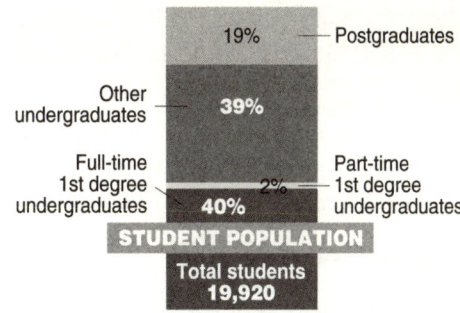

STUDENT POPULATION

Total students
19,920

UNIVERSITY/STUDENT PROFILE	
University since	**1954**
Situation/style	**Campus**
Student population	**19,920**
Full-time undergraduates	**7,980**
- mature	**37%**
- overseas	**9%**
- male/female	**42/58**
- state sector intake	**89%**
- non-traditional student intake	**13%**
- drop-out rate	**6%**
- undergraduate applications	**Up 5%**
see Introduction for key to tables	

scores in teaching assessments, the Queen's Anniversary Prize for Social Work and Social Policy, a first class reputation for arts & social sciences – politics and languages especially – for health (they are starting up a medical school with York in 2003), for science and for business. What's more, the campus is a friendly, lively and creative place to be.

CAMPUS

'The university is situated on Cottingham Road, about half an hour's walk, or a fifteen minute bus ride, from the city centre,' writes Albertina Lloyd. 'Cottingham Road connects Beverly Road and Newland Avenue, and you will come to know these three roads very well – Newland Avenue for shops (one claimed to sell "everything but the girl" and gave the band their name) and cafés, Cottingham Road for take-aways and Beverly Road for pubs. So, all that a student needs is situated within a short distance of the campus itself.'

Now I am also told that with the recent move

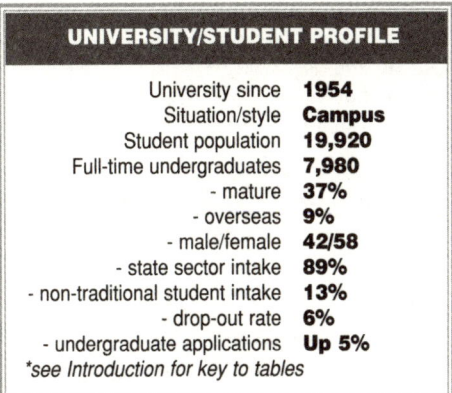

> *This uni is very strong indeed, with high scores in the teaching assessments, the Queen's Anniversary Prize for Social Work and Social Policy, a first-class reputation for politics and languages, and a buzzing student population.*

south of the University of Lincoln (née Lincoln & Humberside), Hull is involved in the purchase of the old and neighbouring L&H campus, and intends to locate its Health Education provision there, including Nursing and Medical Education. Other plans for the site are 'still under discussion.'

There is, too, Hull's Scarborough campus, a few miles north up the coast, which is known for drama, and indeed carried off two awards at this year's NUS Drama Festival held in Scarborough, its patron Sir Alan Ayckbourn, whose plays are always premiered in the town's **Stephen Joseph Theatre**, which he runs.

STUDENT PROFILE

Perhaps because it has been so hidden away, Hull has had to develop its student clientele more deliberately than other universities. Certainly, now, it is one of this country's 'access elite' in that it enjoys a pukka academic and research reputation, but has a student body well-balanced relative to the population as a whole. With the rahs streaming past it on the A1 up to Durham, Hull has been able to bring in some 13% of its undergraduates from areas of this fair isle which do not normally send their children into higher education. Unashamedly, too, it has filled all but 11% of its undergraduate ranks with pupils from...*state* schools.

Once ensconced on campus, Hull students become stereotypical (beer, beer and more beer) or sign up as members of one of the healthy sub-groups – clubbers, metallers, crusties and skaters. At any rate, all intermingle without any trouble. 'Hull prides itself on being one of the friendliest campuses in the country,' notes Danny Blackburn. 'It is a genuinely warm and welcoming environment, in which everyone feels as if they

ACADEMIC EXCELLENCE

TEACHING:
(Rated Excellent or 17+ out of 24)

Chemistry, History, Social Policy, Social Work	**Excellent**
Hispanic Studies; Drama, Electron Engineering	**24**
Theology, American Studies, Physics, Psychology, Biosciences	**23**
Italian, SE Asian Studies, Maths, Economics, Philosophy	**22**
French, German	**21**
Sociology, Dutch, Education	**20**
Scandinavian Studies	**19**

RESEARCH:
Top grades 5/5*

Geography, Law, Politics , Asian Studies, English, History, Music	**Grade 5**

belong. The bars, corridors and lecture theatres all emanate a tremendous feeling of one-ness; it is apparent from day one. Hull's campus is, on a human scale, large enough always to be fun and exciting, but small enough to be personal, comfortable and unimposing.'

So it is that, unlike many newer unis who attempt such a strategy without the same academic and cultural grit, Hull hangs onto its motley crew – the drop-out rate is a mere 6% – educates them, and then finds all but 3% of them good jobs at the end. You can't ask much more than that.

ACADEMIA

Besides Hull's very good record of teaching excellence, there are enviable resources. The **Brynmor Jones Library**, named after a former Vice-Chancellor, has 850,000 volumes, subscribes to more than 3,500 periodicals and contains a window-blind on which is written a poem by Stevie Smith. There are also all the usual electronics services and a 24-hour access, networked computer system reaching out from the **Computer Centre** to academic buildings and residences. The hub of language teaching is the **Language Institute**, incorporating the **Open Learning Centre**, where you can have a language assessment and teaching programme individually designed for you.

Says Albertina of her own experience, 'Each student is assigned a personal tutor to help with work and personal problems. Departmental deadline policies vary, but help, extensions and mitigating circumstances are considered if you contact your tutor in good time. All departments are considerate and helpful if dealt with correctly.'

SOCIAL SCENE

Hull is a centre for the arts, particularly for music, poetry and theatre. The Hull Truck Company, based at **Spring Street Theatre**, is one of this country's most highly renowned creative seedbeds, and also stages one-night fringe, comedy, poetry readings and jazz productions, and galvanises the city's annual festival. The **Hull New Theatre** looks after the more conventional drama, and **May Street Theatre** is the place for dance and mime. For films, the pioneering **Take Two**, with its classic cinema fare, and the arthouse/cult cinema, **Hull Screen**, balance the more commercial ten-screen **Odeon** and eight-screen **UCI**. All these offer student discounts.

On campus the **Gulbenkian Theatre** is the

WHAT IT'S REALLY LIKE

UNIVERSITY:

Social Life	★★★★
Campus scene	**Very friendly, lively, creative**
Student Union services	**Good**
Politics	**Average interest; wide issues**
Sport	**Competitive**
National team position	**53rd**
Sport facilities	**Good**
Arts opportunities	**Drama excellent; music good; dance, film avg; art poor**
National drama awards	**Style/Impact Producer's Award**
Student newspaper	**Hullfire**
Student radio	**Jam 1575**
Nightclub	**Union**
Bars	**Resnikov, John McCarthy, Chico Mendes, Continental**
Union ents	**Twisted (cheese), Future Methods (drum 'n' bass)**
Union clubs/societies	**150**
Most popular societies	**Drama, Hempology**
Smoking policy	**Zonal**
Parking	**Poor**
CITY:	
Entertainment	★★★★
Scene	**Good clubs**
Town/gown relations	**Poor**
Risk of violence	**Average**
Cost of living	**Below average**
Student concessions	**Average**
Survival + 2 nights out	**£50 pw**
Part-time work campus/town	**Good/average**

focus of a drama course which scored full marks in the teaching assessments. There is a newspaper, *Hullfire*, and a student radio station, Jam 1575,. The Tech. Comm. is a parallel organisation into sound and lighting systems and gets its performance kicks at the Friday and Saturday discos.

STUDENTS' UNION Upstairs at the union is the **Resnikov**, which is the place to hang out after lectures (or before, depending on how dire they are). The **John McCarthy Bar** (he's a Hull graduate) has recently been refurbished, but someone forgot to put any windows in, so light and airy it is not. It is renowned for its Wednesday nights of drunken debauchery, when it opens its doors to the fifty plus sports clubs, and there's some wicked comedy on a Sunday night. The **Chico Mendes** is open for societies' parties, while the new **Continental Bar**, despite resembling an airport lounge, provides excellent food and quiet relief from the Resnikov.

'They organise live gigs – bands such as Star Sailor and Wheatus – and provide a range of evening entertainment,' writes Albertina. 'There is a *Comedy Club* every fortnight, featuring touring stand-ups, and Friday/Saturday nights are dedicated to *Twisted*, the union's cheesy disco. *Twisted* specials are organised for Christmas, Halloween etc, and the clubnight has featured live performances from the likes of Jason Donovon and Chesney Hawks.

'The union building contains several bars, cafés, a shop, a counselling service, an advice centre, a travel shop, a bookshop and many other convenient services. There is a huge range of societies, from drama to sports to drinking societies. It is also very easy to get funding to start your own.'

Politically the union is active. 'The union council is largely left wing and campaigns are well supported,' says Peter Bainbridge. Campaigns have supported Third World First, Animal Rights and Amnesty International, and there's a particularly active Women's Committee and Lesbian and Gay Society. 'Though the locals aren't the most tolerant of folk,' says Peter, 'there are gay-friendly places, such as **Polar Bear** pub and **Silhouettes**.' At the union there's also the usual advice centre and job service and an active Student Community Action (HUSSO) with more than 1,000 student volunteers working with homeless, the elderly and people with special needs. Altogether, Hull Uni is a place which attracts students who like to get involved.

TOWN Writes Albertina, 'Most things are, like housing, very cheap in Hull. A pint of lager averages £1.40 and spirits £1 a shot, as most clubs,

pubs, shops and restaurants offer student discounts and promotions. Hull city centre is very good for squandering the student loan as it has two shopping centres, two departments stores, an indoor market and plenty of chain stores and boutiques.

'Entertainment-wise the city has an ice rink, swimming baths, a bowling alley, several multiplex cinemas... There are plenty of places to eat – chain restaurants, Indian, Thai and several vegetarian restaurants.

'The city also has a large number of nightclubs, all of which have student nights on different days in the week, with cheap or free entry to students and many promotional drink offers.

'Most of the larger clubs cater for a wide range of musical tastes, such as indie, drum 'n' bass, hip hop and R&B. **The Room**, **The Waterfront** and **Lexington Avenue** (LA's) also feature popular guest DJs and performers on a fairly regular basis.

'The scene is particularly good for alternative music fans. **Spiders** (www.spiders-nightclub.co.uk) opens Fridays and Saturdays as an exclusively alternative music club. **The Adelphi Club** shows live performances from up and coming alternative music bands, as well as poetry readings and stand-up comedy. If you are into punk, rock or metal then Hull is definitely the place to come.'

SPORT 'The campus sports and fitness centre is very well equipped,' continues Albertina. 'Membership for the gym is reasonable and includes the services of a personal trainer, who will organise a specialist routine. You then pay per session.' There are two large halls for indoor sports, six squash courts, a solarium, a gym, and, adjacent to the centre, pitches for football, rugby, hockey, cricket, nine tennis courts, and a floodlit all-weather surface. The boat, canoe and sub-aqua

AT A GLANCE	
ACADEMIC FILE:	
Subjects assessed	**33**
Excellent	**76%**
Average requirements	**240 points**
Students-staff ratio	**17:1**
First/2:1 degree pass rate	**60%**
ACCOMMODATION FILE:	
Guarantee to freshers	**Apply by 1.9**
Style	**Houses, flats, halls**
Catered	**51%**
En-suite	**10%**
Price range pw	**£48-£86**
City rent pw	**£35-£40**

WHERE GRADUATES END UP

15% Health/Social Work, Key Areas
13% Manufacturing,
10% Finance,
9% Education,
9% Wholesale/Retail,
7% Public Admin
Accountancy, Niche Areas
Business/Management,
Aeronautical Manufac,
Chem/Pharmaceutical*,
Defence, Journalism,
Electron/Electric, Legal,
Library/Archival, Market
Research, Property,
Publishing, Sport

*indicates Top 10 Graduate Provider

Approximate employed **97%**

clubs have a boathouse on the Hull. Bursaries are available, some specifically for disabled athletes.

PILLOW TALK

'Purchase of the old Lincoln and Humberside University campus will mean more accommodation and facilities available to students,' reports Albertina. 'As I write, uni accommodation includes student houses situated on streets off Cottingham Road, the Taylor Court group of apartment buildings on campus, and halls of residence situated in Cottingham, fifteen minutes from Campus by bus. Cottingham is a suburban village on the edge of the city with its own supermarkets, shops and pubs. Free internet access to the university network is available in all halls and university-leased houses, as is a cleaner.

'Traditional catered halls are being phased out, Thwaite Hall being the only one in use at the moment. There's a close-knit community at Thwaite and it's good socially, though some might find it a little claustrophobic. The Lawns complex on the edge of Cottingham is the university's main accommodation facility. It has several halls (some completely self-catered, some close to a dining hall that provides an evening meal), self-catered flats and bungalows, and a bar, shop and cafeteria.

'Traditional Halls and the Taylor Court Flats (for which overseas students are given priority) are the most expensive, followed by the Lawns, with rented houses being the cheapest. There is also a huge range of privately owned student accommodation, much of it situated around Cottingham Road, Beverly Road and Newland Avenue.

'Housing is plentiful, and it is very cheap. Average weekly rent on a privately leased four-bedroom student house is £35 per person.'

The uni guarantees accommodation to all applicants whose residence application is received by September 1: 51% of its accommodation is catered, 10% en-suite, price per week (lowest/highest) is £48-£86.

JOBS

They have one of the best graduate employment records in the country – 97% of students graduating in 2000 were employed six months later. The law department in particular has exceptional ties to industry. See box, above.

GETTING THERE

☛ By road: M62, A63, A1079, B1233.
☛ By rail: Leeds, 1:00; Manchester, 2:15; London King's Cross, 4:30; Birmingham New Street, 3:00.
☛ By air: Humberside, Leeds/Bradford Airports.
☛ By coach: London, 5:10; Manchester, 3-4:00; Newcastle, 4-5:00.

IMPERIAL COLLEGE

Imperial College
 of Science, Technology & Medicine
Exhibition Road
South Kensington
London SW7 2AZ

Imperial College Union
Beit Quad
Prince Consort Road
London SW7 2BB

TEL 020 7594 8014
FAX 020 7594 8004
EMAIL admissions@ic.ac.uk
WEB www.ic.ac.uk

TEL 020 7594 8060
FAX 020 7594 8065
EMAIl (see website)
WEB www.su.ic.uk

VAG VIEW

*P*art of the federal University of London, but enjoying more independence than most, Imperial College is a world beater in the areas of medicine, engineering, technology, maths and science. Its research record is similarly amazing, the second best in the entire country. Make no mistake about it, if you get a place at Imperial you should be made.

On the ground, however, the college has a reputation for being a haven for 'boring computer spods who think it's okay to wear sandals with socks,' as one distraught girlie student put it, adding with a stamp of her little foot, 'The male:female ratio here is about 100:1, but blokes have practically no chance of getting a woman, ever, and consequently Imperial is the sexual frustration capital of Britain!'

Extraordinary, really, when you consider that they have the biggest student venue in London, the cheapest bar prices in the city, the most clubs and societies in the country and an enviable ents programme of some six clubnights a week and regular top-line live acts and comedy.

> *The male:female ratio is about 100:1 but, although that makes it very easy for most women to pull, what they pull is not guaranteed to be human.*

CAMPUSES

'The main campus is situated in South Kensington, Zone 1, Central London,' writes Saurabh Pandya. 'We are right next to the Victoria & Albert, Science and Natural History museums (and are granted free access to them). Travel is easy, the nearest tube is a ten-minute walk away. Generally, it is a low crime area, well lit and pretty safe for students, especially as the uni, the union and most uni accommodation are all within five minutes of each other.'

Says Sarah Playforth, 'This has got to be the best situated college in London, probably in England and perhaps even in the world. If you come from a small town like I do, you'll be blown away by it. Now, the negative. If daddy doesn't own half the oil fields in Texas you are likely to hit a major financial crisis if you eat out at anywhere other than McDonalds. Yes, central London is an extremely expensive place. By the time you graduate you'll probably have acquired an overdraft equivalent to the annual budget of a small country.'

There is an important satellite campus, too,

SUBJECT AREAS (%)

Maths & Computer **17**
Business **5**
Medicine **24**
Biological Sciences **10**
Physical Sciences **16**
Engineering/Technology **28**

Wye College, Wye Village, Ashford, Kent TN25 5AH; Tel 01233 812401. 'Quiet village surroundings and 15th-century buildings give the college a surface air of quietude and tradition,' writes Kieran Alger. It's probably as far removed from your image of London University as it could get. See also *Academia*, page 236.

STUDENT PROFILE

'On behalf of the male population of Imperial, I am making a plea for all female applicants reading this,' writes Saurabh, *'please* to consider the college for one of your UCAS choices. Why? Because we don't do no girly/arty subjects such as English, theology, psychology, etc, and as a result we have possibly the worst male to female ratio of any university in the country. Officially this is 36:64, but it feels like 10:90. No exaggeration! Walk in to the union bars. There's (almost) nothing but men.'

Worse still, on the scale suggested by our correspondent at St Andrews, where you have a one in three chance of marrying an undergrad colleague, Imperial would appear to come last:

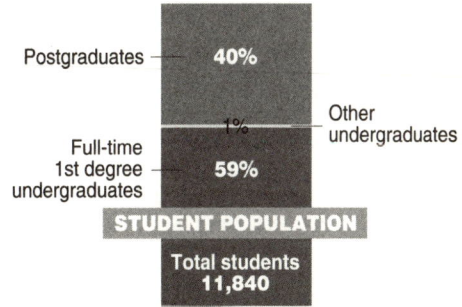

Postgraduates **40%**
Other undergraduates **1%**
Full-time 1st degree undergraduates **59%**
STUDENT POPULATION
Total students **11,840**

UNIVERSITY/STUDENT PROFILE	
School of London Uni since	**1908**
Situation/style	**City campus**
Student population	**11,840**
Full-time undergraduates	**6,980**
- mature	**1%**
- overseas	**27%**
- male/female	**64/36**
- state sector intake	**60%, low**
- non-traditional student intake	**6%, low**
- drop-out rate	**4%, low**
- undergraduate applications	**Down 13%**
*see Introduction for key to tables	

'Although the preponderance of males makes it very easy to pull,' writes Sarah Playforth, 'what they pull is not guaranteed to be human.

'The good thing about the student body, however, is that the college's international reputation leads to a large cultural diversity and you can make friends from all over the world.'

There is, indeed, a large overseas contingent, but a disproportionately small state school intake, and few undergrads from poor neighbourhoods. Realising this, Imperial, like UMIST, Cambridge, Oxford, Bristol, and some sixty other universities have participated in the government's £4-million project to round up kids from inner city areas and put them in summer schools to get a taste of university. The idea is that they will come from social groups excluded from fees, so there'll be no problem in not being able to afford tuition (though what they'll make of the living costs in Kensington is a moot point). The real point surely is to ensure that no-one will be cowed by the idea of applying to such an august institution. All will certainly need ability at Imperial.

ACADEMIA

'The work is hard, let's get that straight from the outset,' writes Saurabh. 'Most successful applicants have AAB or higher at A-level, and so a high standard will be expected of you. But help is always at hand should you fall behind. There are plenty of tutorials, one-to-one time with the lecturer; lecture notes are always on the web, and if you e-mail a particular lecturer they will always meet with you and explain anything that you don't understand. Most subjects have a representative, a student in your year, chosen by your vote, whose responsibility it is to ensure that you know what's going on, that the web notes are of a satisfactory standard, and so on.

'The library occupies five floors and is shared with the Science Museum. It is pretty comprehensive, and as you would expect at a science and technology uni, the computing facilities are also first rate. There are plenty of PCs, and these are upgraded every eighteen months. Staff tend to be leading figures in their field, and regardless of subject you will get a world class education by coming here.'

Ninety-three per cent of Imperial's teaching assessments have been Excellent or scored 21 or more points out of 24. Its research record in last year's assessment is second only to Cambridge. Thirteen departments were graded 5* (that's world class), and seven scored 5 (mostly world class), and all have either shown improvement or maintained their position, which, as they will tell you, is a unique achievement among the top four universities in the UK.

Recently, they have reorganised into four faculties: Engineering, Life Sciences, Medicine, and Physical Sciences. Following the merger with the Charing Cross and Westminster Medical School, they have the largest medical school in the country. Distinctive features of ICSM's course are that it lasts for six years and it will carry particular emphases

ACADEMIC EXCELLENCE	
TEACHING:	
(Rated Excellent or 17+ out of 24)	
Chemistry, Business & Management, Computing, Geology.	**Excellent**
Electrical & Electronic Eng, Materials Technology	**24**
General Engineering	**23**
Chemical Eng, Mech, Aero & Manufacturing Eng, Molecular Biosciences, Organismal Biosciences, Physics	**22**
Civil Engineering, Medicine	**21**
RESEARCH:	
Top grades 5/5*	
Clinical Laboratory Sciences, Hospital-based Clinical, Bio Sciences, Chemistry, Physics, Pure Maths, Applied Maths, Computer, General Eng, Chemical Eng, Civil Eng, Mechanical/ Aeronautical/ Manufacturing Eng, Mineral/ Mining Engineering	**Grade 5***
Community-based Clinical, Pre-Clinical, Statistics, Electrical/Electronic Eng, Metallurgy, Business, History	**Grade 5**

on ethics, law, communication skills and information technology.

Mergers have formed the academic character of the college since the beginning, where, in 1907, it arose out of the marriage of the prestigious Royal College of Science, the Royal School of Mines and the City & Guilds College. The RCS gave Imperial Pure Science, the RSM gave it Mining (and related fields, such as Geology) and the CGC, Engineering. Today there are other influences. Imperial has now signed with Wye College. Wye brings the food industry, agriculture, the environment and business management into the Imperial equation, and a lot more besides. It is known now as the college's Department of Agricultural Sciences.

Says the university, 'The future of our rural environment and how we use it to produce safe and healthy food is of critical importance in this new millennium. The Department, already widely known for its interdisciplinary approach (integrating science and management) to new technologies, strategies and policies affecting rural development worldwide, has modern laboratories and facilities, including an award-winning learning resources centre and working farm on a 350-hectare estate.'

SOCIAL SCENE

STUDENTS' UNION In March 2002, Imperial students voted again to maintain their independence from the National Union of Students. The Students' Union, like UMIST, St Andrews, Edinburgh, Glasgow and Dundee, manage their own affairs. 'Don't worry about your student discounts,' Ed Sexton assures, 'ICU cards are accepted at most places in London, and you can also get a University of London Union (ULU) card, which is widely recognised.'

'There are four main bars around campus, three on the union ground floor, and **Southside Bar** (Southside Halls, Princes Gardens). The recently merged medical campuses, which form the Imperial College School of Medicine and are situated around West London, have their own very lively bars, social events and clubs.' The astonishing prices (especially for London and even before promotion) give away a pint for £1.20.

Union facilities feature **Da Vinci's**, a modern-style café bar – trivia nights, cocktail nights and live jazz, big screen sport, Wednesday club-nights for the sports crowd (with recent additional barbecue facilities), pre-club Saturday nights (guest DJs) and a non-stop succession of Friday clubnights. Catering includes curries served in a *chill-out room* with cocktail bar. The wood-panelled **Union Bar** is a more typical pub – Wednesday night's sports night.

In addition, a **Concert Hall** is used for bigger

WHAT IT'S REALLY LIKE	
UNIVERSITY:	
Social Life	★★★★
Campus scene	**Heavily techno-male, but enter-prising core**
Student Union services	**Good**
Politics	**Low interest**
	Student issues
Sport	**Excellent**
National team position	**35th**
Sport facilities	**Good**
Arts opportunities	**Drama, dance, film excellent; art avg; music good**
Student newspaper	**Felix**
Student radio	**IC Radio**
Student TV	**IC TV**
Nightclub venues	**Da Vinci's, dBs**
Bars	**South Side Bar**
Union ents	**Friday club/disco**
Union clubs/Ssocieties	**248**
Most popular club	**Rugby**
Smoking policy	**Bars, halls OK**
Parking	**Non-existent**
CITY:	
Entertainment	★★★★★
City scene	**Wild, expensive**
Town/gown relations	**Average**
Risk of violence	**Average**
Cost of living	**Very high**
Student concessions	**Good**
Survival + 2 nights out	**£80 pw**
Part-time work campus/town	**Good/average**

events and there's a smaller venue, **dBs** (increasingly known by its full name **Decibels**). Another attraction of the union is the cinema – 'the biggest student cinema in the country and the sixth biggest screen in London. It shows films much later than elsewhere but only go if you think the film is worth getting a sore bum for,' says our reporter.

'At Imperial what they call Freshers Week is four days,' writes Saurabh, 'that is four days free of lectures. You will arrive on a Saturday, and by the Wednesday you will have your first proper lectures. On the first day, most people move their stuff into halls, there's a lot of going around speaking to random people, finding out their names and what courses they do and then forgetting almost instantaneously. There may be a free barbecue and some drinks, followed by a mass exit to the union, everyone drinking themselves silly and then dancing to some high quality cheese. As a result, Sunday is fairly quiet. Monday consists of departmental welcome lectures. Tuesday is the freshers fair. Then, the next two weeks are a mix of

AT A GLANCE

ACADEMIC FILE:

Subjects assessed	**15**
Excellent	**93%**
Average requirements	**320 points**
Students-staff ratio	**9:1**
First/2:1 degree pass rate	**68%**

ACCOMMODATION FILE:

Guarantee to freshers	**If offer accepted by 13.9**
Style	**Halls**
Catered	**Linstead only**
En-suite	**A few**
Price range pw	**£40-£95**
City rent pw	**£60-£80**

hall and union events: boat trips, halls dinners, comedy nights, pub crawls and Freshers Ball. This year the theme was "bad taste villains".

'The number of clubs at Imperial is pretty overwhelming – not far short of 300 from which to to choose, everything from Chess, to E-commerce, to Rugby to Juggling. And just because we are a science and technology based uni, it doesn't mean we don't have any arty clubs – Opera, Drama, Art, Dance, etc are all very active. The quiz team has done particularly well recently – Imperial has won *University Challenge* two years running!'

Students arts are indeed good, and film is rated excellent by students. Media, too, is very active both from a techno and literary pov. There's the award-winning newspaper, *Felix*, and IC Radio and IC TV. Politics, however, are no big deal.

Above all, and despite the sexual frustrations of some, Imperial is a friendly place, even Sarah agrees: 'To be fair, the people here aren't as bad as I've made out. I have managed to make a good many excellent friends here who I would not trade for anyone.'

Down at rural Wye, there's a distinctly different breed, and not what you might think. Owing to Wye's interdisciplinary approach, or is it the state of farming (?), almost a third opt for a business course, so that your average Wye-guy can be found not driving a tractor but done up in a penguin suit on his way to a ball, or to one of their eccentric clubs. Thursday nights see the Beaus, the Garters, the Jock-Strap Farmers and the mysterious Druids take over the union in a whirl of practical jokes, initiation ceremonies and over-consumption of alcohol. Membership of these peculiar clubs is by invitation only.

SPORT Besides national competition in the uni leagues, where Imperial came 35th last year, they excel in the London University league. But in rowing – the big thing at ICS – you're talking international levels. Writes Saurabh, 'The boathouse at Putney Bridge received a lottery grant last year, and has brand new facilities, including a fully equipped gym. The football teams share their facilities with Chelsea Football Club, and it isn't uncommon to see some of their Premier stars coming off the training ground as you get off the team coach. If you are just interested in general fitness, there's an underground gym next to the main campus, though it is quite small, and more focused on cardio stuff rather than weights.'

The Sports Centre at Prince's Gardens (Exhibition Road) includes a 25m swimming pool, four squash courts, a gym, a 25m rifle range, a training studio, sauna, steam room and poolside spa bath. Nearby there are tennis and netball courts, and a weights room. The 60-acre grounds lent to Chelsea for training are at Harlington, near Heathrow. Facilities include a floodlit multi-purpose surface and a pavilion with bar. There are a further 15 acres at Teddington (four pitches and a cricket square), 22 acres at Cobham, the boathouse at Putney and a sailing club at Welsh Harp Reservoir in North West London. In addition, its hospital sites at Paddington and Fulham Palace Road have 25m swimming pools and squash courts.

PILLOW TALK

You are guaranteed either Imperial College or London University if you accepted an unconditional academic offer by a certain date in September (13th this year). 'If you are lucky,' writes Saurabh, 'you'll get into one of the halls right next to campus, and you can spend all year perfecting your "get up at 8:55 and be in time for 9:00 lecture" technique. These are the Southside, Northside and Beit halls. If you are especially lucky, you will be placed in Beit Hall, which was opened last year and has brand new rooms with Ikea-style kitchens and every amenity you could possibly want. The other halls next to the uni aren't too bad, if a bit '70s in style – there are plans to refurbish these in 2003. Rooms are adequately sized, although the kitchens are a tad small and will be shared by a scrum of between six and twenty people. The other halls are situated either in Evelyn Gardens (fifteen minutes from campus) or Pembridge Gardens (forty minutes, or twenty by tube).

'Regardless of what hall you are in, there is a great community atmosphere. There are several hall events over the year, the hall Christmas dinner is one in particular to look forward to. Compare this to UCL [University College], where students are assigned rooms and there are no hall events whatsoever. Imperial halls are a great way to meet people, and you really do make a load of friends by the end of the first year.

'As for non-freshers, uni accommodation isn't really an option as there is such a massive demand for such a small amount of places. This is one of the major disadvantages of going to a London uni.'

JOBS

'Imperial students tend to do quite well in the real world,' Saurabh writes in understatement. 'There is a dedicated careers service, and regular talks from companies (usually on Tuesday evenings).' Sixty-one per cent of students who graduated in 2000 were in employment six months later, 30% in further study. See www.careers.ic.ac.uk/fds/index.htm for more detail.

WHERE GRADUATES END UP

39% Health (Medicine)*,	Key Areas
12% Finance*,	
9% Computer*,	
8% Manufacturing	
Accountancy,	Niche Areas
Business/Management*,	
Aeronautical Manufacture,	
Chemical/Pharmaceutical,	
Eng/Industrial Design*,	
Defence*, **Electron/**	
Electric, Telecom	

*indicates Top 10 Graduate Provider

Approximate employed **96%**

GETTING THERE

☞ By Underground: South Kensington (Circle, District and Piccadilly lines).

• •

UNIVERSITY OF KEELE

The University of Keele	Keele Students' Union
Keele	Keele
Staffordshire ST5 5BG	Staffs ST5 5BJ
TEL 01782 584003/4/5	TEL 01782 583700
FAX 01782 632343	FAX 01782 712671
EMAIL undergraduate@keele.ac.uk	EMAIL sta15@kusu.keele.ac.uk
WEB www.keele.ac.uk	WEB www.kusu.net

VAG VIEW

*K*eele was recently named as one of our elite universities, one of a handful which manage to attract a well-balanced student body from a diverse range of socio-economic levels while maintaining a top-class teaching capability, a low drop-out rate and excellent employment prospects. Unsurprisingly, applications are up 5%.

Its academic strategy made it unique from the start, the emphasis on a broad education, seen at its best in the dual honours degree, which they pioneered and which offers a rare opportunity to study from both science and arts points of view. Ninety per cent of Keele's students opt for this type of degree.

There is also a concentration of student freedoms at its isolated campus. The whole

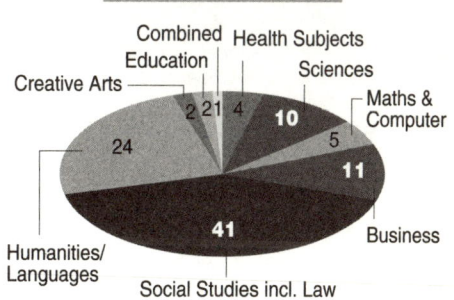

SUBJECT AREAS (%)

Combined Education 2 · Creative Arts 2 · 1 · Health Subjects 4 · Sciences 10 · Maths & Computer 5 · Business 11 · Social Studies incl. Law 41 · Humanities/Languages 24

'60s experiment which is Keele would seem to have found its form forty years on.

CAMPUS

'It's the centre of England and the middle of nowhere,' write Mark Holtz and Gareth Belfield. 'Keele University's self-contained campus is a

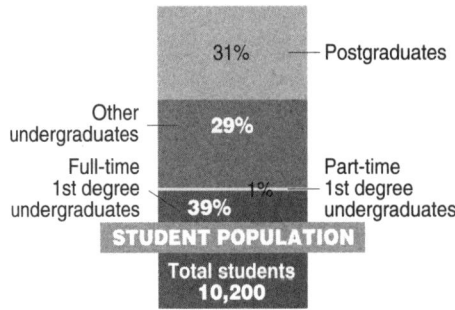

	31% — Postgraduates
Other undergraduates	29%
Full-time 1st degree undergraduates	Part-time 1st degree undergraduates
	1%
	39%

STUDENT POPULATION

Total students 10,200

ACADEMIA

Big news is Keele's new joint Medical Faculty with Manchester University. A free standing medical school is to be established on campus. There's also a new clinical skills lab at the Dept of Nursing & Midwifery, which simulates a ward environment.

ACADEMIC EXCELLENCE
TEACHING:
(Rated Excellent or 17+ out of 24)
Applied Social Work, Music **Excellent**
American Studies, Politics, **24**
Philosophy, Education
Economics, Psychology **23**
Sociology, Maths, Organismal **22**
Biosciences, Physics
Nursing, Molecular Biosciences, **21**
Management
French, Russian, **20**
Subjects Allied to Medicine
German **19**
RESEARCH:
Top grades 5/5*
Law **Grade 5***
Applied Maths, General Eng, **Grade 5**
English, Politics, Social Policy,
American Studies, History

stone's throw from Stoke-on-Trent, a constant worry for those students without protective headgear. In theory, the university is set within tiny Keele village, but the campus has grown over such a large area that saying it is part of Keele village is akin to saying that London is part of Westminster. The campus is on a hilltop and is so exposed you expect a policeman to come along and arrest it for indecency. Nearby Newcastle-under-Lyme, Hanley (Stoke) and Crewe can be reached by the bus service called (joyfully) PMT. Train-wise, Manchester is only thirty minutes away, as is Birmingham. London direct can be done in around two hours. The M6 is within earshot of the campus, and sounds like the sea if you are drunk enough.

UNIVERSITY/STUDENT PROFILE	
University since	**1962**
Situation/style	**Rural campus**
Student population	**10,200**
Full-time undergraduates	**4,010**
- mature	**13%**
- overseas	**17%**
- male/female	**49/51**
- state sector intake	**89%**
- non-traditional student intake	**14%**
- drop-out rate	**7%**
- undergraduate applications	**Up 5%**
see Introduction for key to tables	

STUDENT PROFILE

'Take a generous measure of "traditional" students, two heaped tablespoons of mature, nursing, international and local students, heavily season with postgraduates, add a dash of complete weirdoes and you have the recipe for the most diverse and interesting concoction of a university anywhere in the world.

'It's impossible not to fit in at Keele, with over half the students living together on campus, you're never really in danger of running out of people to borrow sugar from.'

And in Physics, we hear that there is to be a new North Staffs Centre on campus, and a multinational project is setting everyone alight building a ginormous telescope in southern Africa.

Back on the ground, Keele is out-performing most in the business of educating undergraduates, with full-mark scores in the teaching assessments for Politics, International Relations, Philosophy and Education recently, and with Economics and Psychology only dropping one mark apiece. Note, too, there was a Grade 5* rating for Law in the research assessments. Other strengths worth consideraing are American Studies, Professional & Applied Ethics and Primary Care Sciences.

Besides medicine, there are new courses in the areas of visual arts, information systems, global politics, astrophysics, nuclear & particle physics, music technology, English and American literature, new minors in Japanese, Russian and Spanish, and a science foundation year.

STUDENT SCENE

STUDENTS' UNION 'There's a shop, diner, travel centre, printer, advice unit, and more bars than a very big jail,' write Mark & Gareth. 'There's also a bookshop, newsagents, and a supermarket (essentially an off-licence small snack selection).

'The social life is awesome. At any given moment in time, there is a party going on somewhere. Although the **Ballroom** (with daily market) is a compact venue, with **Sam's Bar** capacity reaches 1,200, and recent acts include Cast, Space, Republica, Lightening Seeds, Shed Seven, Liberty, the famous five that didn't make it on POPSTARS, DJs Paul Jackson and Yousef.

The nightclub, **The Club** (500), frequently buzzes to the sounds of big name DJ's and their accompanying tours. Bars also include no-smoking **BJ's** (50), the **Gallery Bar** (300) and elsewhere a pub, owned and run by the union, the **Golfer's Arms**.'

Current clubnights include *Manic Mondays* (cheese), the stock market drinking game, *Bar Footsie*, *Loaded* (pop and chart), *House Nation*, mid-week *Retro Rooms*, *Outlaw* (nu-metal, rock, indie, ska/punk and alternative, with occasional funky and chemical beat). Then there's the weekly *Liquid Jazz* with Just Friends resident, and Monday's *Junglist Movement* (drum 'n' bass with extra funky hip-hop & breaks thrown in), *Get Funked!* (funked up hip hop, breaks, funk and soul), and *Bling!* (finest US/UK R&B and hip-hop scenes).

For film, something special is **Moviedrome** – billed as 'the ONLY theatre in Stoke-on-Trent where you can drink and smoke!' – big hits and classics from the UK & US box office shown on the giant screen with 'surround' sound.

> *A well-balanced and diverse student body, a top-class teaching capability, a low drop-out rate and excellent employment prospects. Applications are up 5%.*

Keele has a history of political turbulenc: 'In the '70s,' write Mark and Gareth, 'Keele pre-empted Wales and Scotland by attempting to gain independence from Britain. Passports were issued, border patrols were set up, a national anthem created, and an unsuccessful attempt to enter the Eurovision Song Contest was made. More recently, Keele was the first university to reject the Government's tuition fees proposals.' Right now, they've boycotted Union Square because of a disagreement with the uni over the union's ownership.

SPORT Facilities include a gym, sports hall, floodlit synthetic pitch, fifty acres of grass pitches 'so green they'd make Kermit blush', tennis courts, fitness centre, squash coursts, etc. Form is good.

TOWN 'Aaarghh! Keele is in the Potteries, where the main industry is not so much in decline, as plummeting down a precipice of bankruptcy. Locals refer to you as "duck" if they like you. If they don't like you they'll just try to run over you.'

WHAT IT'S REALLY LIKE

UNIVERSITY:	
Social Life	★★★★
Campus scene	**Isolated, active**
Student Union services	**Good**
Politics	**Very active**
Sport	**Competitive**
National teamposition	**57th**
Sport facilities	**Average**
Arts opportunities	**Excellent**
Student mag/news	**Kinetic**
Student radio	**KUBE**
Nightclub	**The Club**
Bars	**Sam's Bar, BJ's, Gallery, Golfer's Arms**
Union ents	**Frenetic**
Union clubs/societies	**80**
Most popular society	**Drama**
Smoking policy	**Union, halls OK**
Parking	**Good**
TOWN:	
Entertainment	★★
Local (Stoke) scene	**Pubs/clubs**
Town/gown relations	**OK**
Risk of violence	**Average**
Cost of living	**Below average**
Student concessions	**Average**
Survival + 2 nights out	**£50 pw**
Part-time work campus/town	**OK/poor**

AT A GLANCE

ACADEMIC FILE:	
Subjects assessed	**28**
Excellent	**68%**
Average requirements	**240 points**
Students-staff ratio	**18:1**
First/2:1 degree pass rate	**62%**
ACCOMMODATION FILE:	
Guarantee to freshers	**First choice applicants**
Style	**Single study bedrooms**
Catered	**None**
En-suite	**20%**
Approx price range pw	**£42-£70**
Town rent pw	**£30-£40**

PILLOW TALK

Freshers with Keele as first choice have uni accommodation guaranteed – self-catered single study-bedrooms, 20% en suite; prices from £42-£70, as against £35 in town. 'There is something inexplicably nice about campus accommodation,' sigh Mark & Gareth in unison, 'even if the cleaning ladies have mastered the art of knocking, unlocking your door, opening it, coming in, and saying, "Ooh, I'll come back when you've had time to put some clothes on," all in two seconds.'

JOBS

Graduate rates of employment are good, typically showing only 6% unemployed.

GETTING THERE

☛ By road: from the north M6/J16, A500, A531, right on to A525, right through Keele village; from south, M6/J15, A5182, left on to A53, right at Whitmore following signs.

WHERE GRADUATES END UP	
15% Health/Social Work,	Key Areas
12% Manufacturing,	
11% Finance,	
9% Personnel*,	
9% Public Admin,	
8% Education,	
6% Wholesale/Retail	
Business/Management,	Niche Area
Electron/Electric, Telecom,	
Chem/Pharmaceutical,	
Agric/Forestry, Property*,	
Publishing	

*indicates Top 10 Graduate Provider

Approximate employed **94%**

☛ By rail: good service more or less everywhere, London 1:30 to Stoke-on-Trent station, then taxi.
☛ By coach: London, 4:00

UNIVERSITY OF KENT AT CANTERBURY

The University of Kent at Canterbury
The Registry
Canterbury CT2 7NZ

TEL 01227 827272
FAX 01227 827077
EMAIL recruitment@ukc.ac.uk
WEB www.ukc.ac.uk

Kent University Students' Union
The University
Canterbury CT2 7NW

TEL 01227 765224
FAX 01227 464625
EMAIL union-sabbs@ukc.ac.uk
WEB www.su.ukc.ac.uk

VAG VIEW

There is something of a southeast, middle-of-the-road feel about Kent. Writes Catherine Robertson, a student there: 'UKC is, in a nutshell, a friendly, politically correct campus where it is easy to work hard, play hard, or do a little of both.'

The teaching and research are good, there are some notable niche areas – languages, English, drama, sociology, law, space science, for instance – and plenty goes on, yet for some reason its reputation still doesn't quite shine through. It's a bit like Essex in this regard. Both are also progeny of the 1960s, situated in the south east, excel at social sciences, tireless at getting their graduates jobs, and both, being located so temptingly close to London, can be a tad dull at weekends.

CAMPUS

'UKC campus is situated on top of an alarmingly steep hill about a mile out of the main city,' continues Catherine. What is also true is that in the time you can walk from the city centre to the UKC campus, you could have driven in a car to Dover,

SUBJECT AREAS (%)

Combined 16
Biological Sciences 15
Engineering/Technology 5
Creative Arts 4
7
Humanities/Languages 22
Social Studies incl. Law 21
Business 10
Maths & Computer

gateway to Europe, which fact is only interesting in its pointing to the cosmopolitan nature of the place: 'The campus location is great for town, and the town is great for Europe,' as Catherine puts it succinctly. It is a frame of mind that prevents undergraduates from feeling claustrophobic, for, as graduate Will Vokes-Dudgeon points out, 'You can be more or less self-sufficient on campus, you could spend your entire first year without visiting the city, though you'd probably go mad.'

STUDENT PROFILE

UKC' is not a place for Oxbridge rejects, but it takes quite a chunk of entrants from independent schools and only 9% from the poorer neigbourhoods, so there is a fairly middle-class feel to the student body, whence emanates strong mature and overseas flavours, too.

Indeed, Will has formed the opinion that 'if you are at all xenophobic, UKC is most definitely not for you, for overall it has the highest international student population in the country. Last year more than 200 Chinese executives from the Chin Financial Services Training Scheme joined up at UKC's Chaucer College to train at the Business School.'

Catherine goes so far as to maintain that the reason why 'many British people haven't even heard of UKC [is] the uni's dedication to attracting overseas students,' but concludes that however multifarious is its makeup, 'what you will find is a friendly student body, and lecturers and tutors who pursue their own work as energetically as they do yours.' (I am not sure that I caught the significance of this last remark.)

ACADEMIA

While 73% of teaching assessments meet our definition of Excellent, two that recently scored full marks (Drama and Biosciences) help define the breadth of this university's academic

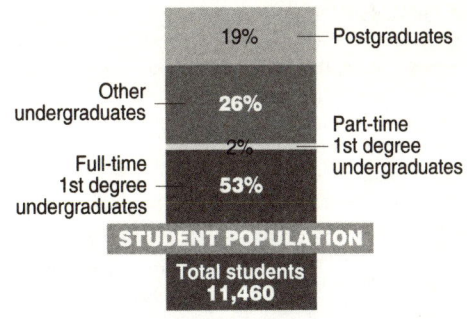

STUDENT POPULATION
Total students 11,460

Postgraduates 19%
Other undergraduates 26%
Part-time 1st degree undergraduates 2%
Full-time 1st degree undergraduates 53%

ACADEMIC EXCELLENCE

TEACHING:
(Rated Excellent or 17+ out of 24)

Computing, Anthropology, Social Policy & Administration	**Excellent**
Drama & Theatre Studies, Molecular Biosciences, Organismal Biosciences, Philosophy	24
History of Art, Classics, Archaeology, Psychology	22
Sociology, Electrical/Electron Engineering, American Studies, Subjects Allied to Medicine, Business/Management, Maths, Physics	21
Theology, Film Studies	20
Modern Languages (French, German, Italian, Euro Studies, Linguistics)	19

RESEARCH:
Top grades 5/5*

Social Policy, Statistics	**Grade 5***
English, Applied Maths, Law, Anthropology, Drama/Dance/ Performing Arts	**Grade 5**

UNIVERSITY/STUDENT PROFILE

University since	**1965**
Situation/style	**City campus**
Student population	**11,460**
Full-time undergraduates	**6,120**
- mature	**15%**
- overseas	**22%**
- male/female	**48/52**
- state sector intake	**87%**
- non-traditional student intake	**9%**
- drop-out rate	**9%**
- undergraduate applications	**Up 3%**

see Introduction for key to tables

reputation, although the greatest number still find places in the internationally renowned Social Sciences faculty, a field in which UKC is pre-eminent, as both its teaching and research assessments show (see box above).

UKC is also one of a few unis to offer American Studies with a year in the USA. They are also committed to encouraging the assimilation of European culture far and wide in the curriculum by study in Europe, by taking on a European language, or by combining one of their top-rated artistic or media packages with advanced work in a foreign language, as in the European Arts course.

'Academically the university has a strong reputation for modern languages,' Catherine acknowledges, 'thanks to it's proximity to Europe and the encouragement to students to study abroad for a year, but the School of English is also strong, especially the Centre for Post-Colonial Studies, which has an outstanding reputation.' (Note the Grade 5 – world renown – which English achieved in the recent research assessments.)

Look, too, at the drama and film degrees in the humanities faculty. They now have a stand-up comedy element in Drama, a department which not only scored full marks at the teaching assessments, but also achieved Grade 5 at the research assessments. Focus for both student and professional theatre companies (and a student film society when not showing at **Cinema 3**) is the campus-based **Gulbenkian Theatre**.

> *Kent is pre-eminent in social sciences, including languages, and has many other strengths – drama, biosciences, physics...and a hot graduate employment set-up. It's just a bit PC/middle-of-the-road student-wise. But you may like that.*

In autumn 2000, UKC went fully modular with proper semesters – two twelve-week semesters and a final one of six weeks duration. Of the teaching, Catherine writes, 'Lecturers are generally lively and you are encouraged to work alone, but seek help as needed.

PILLOW TALK

'Although living in town as a fresher is an option, it is not a very popular one. After all, who are you going to live with? Most first years opt for halls in one of the four colleges or their posher extensions, or in Parkwood student village.

'The colleges tend to be the easiest way to make friends as there are usually seven people randomly thrown together in a corridor and you all just mix and match. The four colleges where the majority of first years end up: are called Eliot, Darwin, Rutherford and Keynes, although you can get a place in Tyler Court or Becket Court, both new sets of accommodation. A problem with the colleges (or possibly an advantage, depending on your disposition) is that they are semi-self-catered, i.e you get breakfast included in the rent, though only until 9.30 am!

'Parkwood is just off the main campus and made up of groups of houses for four-to-six students. It is generally favoured by third years and foreign students, and they seem to get priority. The houses tend to allow more freedom than halls, but can feel detached, as everything other than **Woody's** bar is on the main campus.

SOCIAL SCENE

'First years tend to stay on campus to socialise, simply because it is cheaper and more convenient. There are five main bars: **Origins** is in Darwin (trendy-type bar, good fajitas), **Rutherford Bar** – guess where that is (a drinker's bar, good juke box). **Mungo's** is in Eliot (should be better than it is, no atmosphere) and then there's **Keynes Bar** (concrete garden, popular in summer). Parkwood has the aforesaid Woody's, which is more of a pub than a bar and is haunted by the more cliquey sports clubs (you'll see what I mean). For those of you who don't want to spend all your time drinking alcohol, there is also the **Gulbenkian Theatre** coffee bar.

'Now, what to do with your new-found friends once the bars have thrown you out into the cold, cold, night? Generally, people head onto **The Venue**, the campus club with a capacity of 1,200

WHAT IT'S REALLY LIKE

UNIVERSITY:	
Social Life	★★★
Campus scene	**Friendly, southern**
Student Union services	**Good**
Politics	**Student issues**
Sport	**Competitive**
National sporting position	**36th**
Sport facilities	**Good**
Arts opportunities	**Film, drama exc, music art good; dance avg**
Student newspaper	**Kred**
Student radio	**UKCR**
Nightclub	**The Venue**
Bars	**Lighthouse, Mungoes, Origins, Woodies**
Union ents	**All the stuff**
Union clubs/societies	**120**
Most popular society	**Music**
Smoking policy	**Bars OK**
Parking	**Poor**
CITY:	
Entertainment	★★★
Scene	**Touristy, historic, very studenty**
Town/gown relations	**Good**
Risk of violence	**Low**
Cost of living	**Average**
Student concessions	**Adequate**
Survival + 2 nights out	**£60 pw**
Part-time work campus/town	**Good**

and a café bar, **The Lighthouse** (200). It is closed on Tuesdays and Sundays but that's not a problem. Regular nights are Mondays, Sports Fed night, where each sports club takes a turn as host. Thursdays are retro nights, when disco classics are played alongside '80s anthems, so I'm told. The weekends are easily the most successful nights, with Fridays being *Redemption* and Saturdays hosting *Stardust*, each a regular and popular feature of contemporary dance and classic anthems. One problem with Canterbury is the lack of big name live music. There are no real venues on campus or in the local area. So, if you want to see a band, chances are you'll have to go to London, which is only an hour and a half away.

'In Fresher's Week you will be bombarded with offers to join societies. The biggest tend to be the sports clubs. Others include working with the student radio station (UKCR) and the student newspaper (*KRED*). Most academic subjects have a society so you'll have plenty to choose from.'

SPORT Sports-wise there are thirty clubs, all the usual stuff plus Choi Kwang Do, Taekwondo and Kendo (one of only five unis to offer this) and American Football (UKC Falcons). It's been strong recently in fencing, badminton and basketball. Various sports offer bursaries, some in cahoots with UKC alumni. UKC does well nationally at all the team sports, coming 36th in the national team league last year.

TOWN 'If you're feeling particularly adventurous then go to town for a change of scenery,' continues Catherine. 'It is a city because it has a famous cathedral (to which you will no doubt take your parents when they come to visit), but its size is no more than that of a large town, and if you are coming from a large, lively city you may at first be disappointed. However, Canterbury is deceiving in the sense that it appears quieter than it actually is. One thing it does not lack is pubs, and many of my friends have spent a happy drunken evening in the enchantingly named **Bishop's Finger** (the nun's delight apparently!) If you're feeling sophisticated, there's **Oranges** wine bar; or if you fancy some impromptu jazz, go to **Simple Simon's**. There really is something for everyone. After the pubs shut, things get a bit tricky, as Canterbury is not renowned for it's club scene. **Alberry's** is recommended, but go with a group as it's pretty cliquey. **The Works** is another favourite but don't be fooled **The Works**, **The Bizz** and **Baa-Bars** are all just different levels of the same building and not three different clubs!'

The city is certainly small, but nevertheless

AT A GLANCE	
ACADEMIC FILE:	
Subjects assessed	**29**
Excellent	**72%**
Average requirements	**260 points**
Students-staff ratio	**17:1**
First/2:1 degree pass rate	**53%**
ACCOMMODATION FILE:	
Guarantee to freshers	**90%**
Style	**Halls, village**
Approx price range pw	**£50.26-£60.48**
City rent pw	**£45-£60**

manages to support two train stations, two higher education institutions (see Canterbury Christ Church) and an arts school, ensuring that its population largely consists of students... alongside the French: the town centre is heaving with tourists.

Besides the pubs and smattering of clubs there are masses of restaurants, a cinema, a theatre (the **Marlow**) and a laser quest, though that is about it. The **Penny Theatre** had a bit of a reputation for new and alternative bands. It has now been taken over by the *It's A Scream* crew and dishes out Yellow Cards to students for a cheaper deal, but it's mainly peopled by Canterbury Christ Church students.

All-in-all we can't be too surprised that there's a campus evacuation to London over the weekend.

JOBS

Perennially, UKC comes up with the goods when it comes to getting graduates jobs, regularly finding

WHERE GRADUATES END UP	
11% Finance,	Key Areas
10% Manufacturing,	
10% Education,	
9% Computer,	
9% Public Admin,	
9% Wholesale/Retail,	
9% Health/Social Work	
Accountancy,	Niche Areas
Advertising, Defence*,	
Telecom, Electron/	
Electric, Film/Video,	
Legal, Library/Archival,	
Market Research,	
Publishing, Radio/TV*	
*indicates Top 10 Graduate Provider	
Approximate employed	**96%**

all but 3 or 4% employment within six months.

KRED and UKCR nurture an interest which propels a large percentage of graduates into TV, radio and publishing, as well as film, as can be seen from our Employment box on page 245.

GETTING THERE

☛ By road: from west, M2, A2; south, A28 or A2; east, A257; northeast, the A28; northwest, A290.
☛ By rail: London Victoria, 85 mins; London Charing Cross or Waterloo East, 90 mins.
☛ By air: Heathrow and Gatwick.
☛ By coach: London Victoria, 1 hour 45 mins.

KENT INSTITUTE OF ART & DESIGN

Kent Institute of Art & Design
Oakwood Park
Maidstone
Kent ME16 8AG

TEL 01622 757286
FAX 01622 621100
EMAIL info@kiad.ac.uk
WEB //kiad.ac.uk

VAG VIEW

In 1987 three Kentish art colleges merged – Canterbury, Maidstone and Medway – and the result, known as KIAD, is now the third largest higher education Art & Design college in the UK. Alone among such colleges, they have a School of Architecture. Proximity to Europe, a large overseas student population (13% undergrads) and strong links abroad give an international flavour. There is accommodation, but the college is small, and when the work is done, the scene is not exactly overpowering.

Maidstone (address above) is for graphic design, illustration, photography, time-based media; Canterbury (New Dover Road, Canterbury CT1 3AN Tel: 01227 769371) is for fine art and architecture; Rochester (Fort Pitt, Rochester ME1 1DZ Tel: 01634 830022) is for fashion, interior architecture, and design, silversmithing etc, 3D design, editorial & advertising photography.

INSTITUTE PROFILE

Founded	**1987**
Status	**Art College**
Degree awarding university	**Kent**
Student population	**1,970**
Full-time undergraduates	**1,560**
ACCOMMODATION:	
Availability to freshers	**100%**
Style	**Halls, flats, houses**
Cost pw (no food/food)	**£40-£65**
City/town rent pw	**£45**

GETTING THERE

☛ By road: Rochester: M20/J4, A228. Maidstone: M20/J6, A229. Canterbury: from the west, M2, A2; from the south, A28 or A2; from the east, A257; from the northeast, A28; from the northwest, the A290.
☛ By rail: London to Canterbury, 90 mins; to Maidstone, under the hour; Rochester, 40 mins.

KING ALFRED'S COLLEGE

King Alfred's College
Winchester
Hampshire SO22 4NR

TEL 01962 827534
FAX 01962 827406
EMAIL admissions@wkac.ac.uk
WEB www.wkac.ac.uk

VAG VIEW

Founded as a Diocesan teacher training establishment, it is now a university sector college with a range of Southampton University degrees on offer. There is a high proportion of mature undergrads (47%) and about a quarter of all students are part-timers, although there is plenty of accommodation for those from afar.

Almost half its graduates go into the

education sector and on inspection Education scored full marks. In fact, inspections all round have been good recently: Theology, 23 out of 24, Business, 22, Sport, 21.

The college is also making a reputation in Drama, Theatre and Television Studies (19/24). They have their own theatre, the **John Stripe**, as well as a dance studio for a Performing Arts degree. The student-led theatre company, KASPA (King Alfred's Society for the Performing Arts) is very active.

Elsewhere, in East Asian and Business Studies and in combos which include Japanese, there are interesting opportunities. Japanese was rated 20 points out of 24 in the assessments after a Japanese Language & Business Culture course came on line.

They have also built an interesting course in Biopsychology on the back of research into the benefits of an interdisciplinary approach to Psychology, which scored 21 in the assessments. The Basingstoke and Winchester School of Nursing and Midwifery became part of King Alfred's in '94, and it is developing all sorts of multi-disciplinary courses in Health Care. There's also an Archaeology course, which attracts. Resource-wise they are backing all this with a substantial library extension, open since the end of last year.

If there's a problem it's that Winchester is an expensive sort of place – 'steeped in history, home of wine bars, cobwebbed inns and olde

COLLEGE PROFILE	
Founded	**1840**
Status	**HE College**
Degree awarding university	**Southampton**
Situation/style	**Campus**
Student population	**5,150**
Full-time undergraduates	**2,850**
ACCOMMODATION:	
Availability to freshers	**100%**
Style	**Halls**
Cost pw (no food/food)	**£61-£83**
City rent pw	**£55**

worlde antique shops,' said a student. 'It is a city not because of size, but because of its cathedral. It is quiet, picturesque and affluent. The better off you are financially, the better you will survive. Most of the college's accommodation is at a large student village, West Downs, which won a design award, or at Chilbolton Court about half a mile from campus.

GETTING THERE

☛ By road: M3/J10; northwest, A272, B3041; southwest, A3090.
☛ By rail: London Waterloo, 1:00; Bristol Parkway, 2:15; Birmingham, 3:15; Southampton, 20 mins.
☛ By air: Gatwick, Heathrow, Southampton.
☛ By coach: London, 2:00; Birmingham, 5:30.

KING'S COLLEGE, LONDON

King's College, London
Waterloo Bridge House
Waterloo Road
London SE1 8WA

TEL 020 7836 5454
FAX 020 7836 1799
EMAIL enquiries@kcl.ac.uk
WEB www.kcl.ac.uk

King's College Students' Union
3rd Floor Macadam Building
Surrey Street
London WC2R 2NS

TEL 020 7836 7132
FAX 020 7379 9833
EMAIL president@kclsu.org
WEB www.kclsu.org

VAG VIEW

*K*ing's College London is one of London University's oldest and most prestigious colleges, founded by George IV in 1829 and one of the federal university's original colleges in 1836. Undergraduates feel part of this strong tradition, but until recently the scattered nature of the college did little to foster a sense of identity. In the course of its history it has developed through many mergers, most recently, in the summer of 1998, with United Medical & Dental Schools of Guy's Hospital (where medical teaching began in the 1720s) & St Thomas's (where

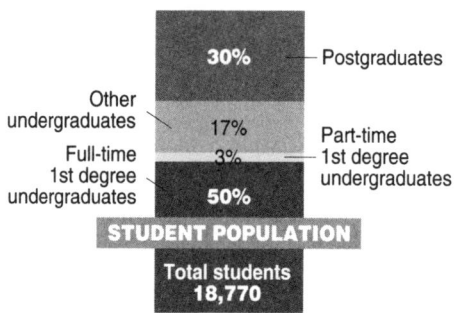

SUBJECT AREAS (%)

Humanities — Creative Arts
Languages — Education 0.3%
Social Studies incl. Law
Medicine/Dentistry — 26
10
6
13
15 — Health Subjects
2
7
Business — 4 — 7 — 9
Maths & Computer — Physical Sciences — Biological Sciences
Engineering/Technology

30% — Postgraduates
Other undergraduates — 17%
Part-time 1st degree undergraduates
Full-time 1st degree undergraduates — 3%
50%

STUDENT POPULATION

Total students 18,770

Medicine has been taught since the 16th century). Since then, King's have sold off their Kensington and Chelsea campuses and, at a cost of some £200 million, completely re-drawn the campus map.

CAMPUSES

There are now five campuses, four of which cluster around the Thames, close to the centre of town. With the Students' Union **Macadam** building at its core is the Strand Campus, on the north bank,

just south of Covent Garden. Here, too, are the schools of Humanities, Law and Physical Sciences. Just across the river via Waterloo Bridge is the new Waterloo campus, incorporating Education, Management, Health & Life Sciences, Nursing & Midwifery and the Stamford Street apartments with the basement gym, K4, which appeared on TV's *Watchdog* as an exemplary fitness club.

Three bridges to the east lies Guy's Campus. Students of Medicine and Dentistry entering King's in 1999 were the first to study at this purpose-built centre close to London Bridge. The campus incorporates a new SU building with bar, swimming pool, ballroom, shop and welfare centre, as well as accommodation.

And then there's St Thomas' Campus (Continuing Medical & Dental teaching), which overlooks the Houses of Parliament north across the river at Westminster Bridge, and Denmark Hill Campus, south of the Oval. The only site a little out on its own, Denmark Hill is base for clinical teaching at King's College Hospital and the Dental Institute, and home to the Institute of Psychiatry.

All residences – halls (catered or self-catered), apartments or student houses (mainly for mature students) – are within London Travel Zones 1 or 2, and close to one or more of the campuses.

Word on the ground is that KCL succeeds not in spite of, but because of its location: 'Want to live and work smack in the centre of London? You got it,' write Ben Jones and Chris Wilding. 'Want high frequency bus and tube links with a 30% discount? You got it. Clubs? Pubs? Venues? Theatres? Museums? Galleries? Shops? Yeah, got them too. In fact, by nestling snugly and unassumingly within the heart of the capital, King's College London appears to students as a seventh heaven.' But at a price.

STUDENT PROFILE

Both King's and University College, London, the

COLLEGE/STUDENT PROFILE	
College of London Uni since	**1836**
Situation/style	**Civic**
Student population	**18,770**
Full-time undergraduates	**9,450**
- mature	**18%**
- overseas	**9%**
- male/female	**48/52**
- state sector intake	**66%, low**
- non-traditional student intake	**8%**
- drop-out rate	**7%**
- undergraduate applications	**Down 6%**
see Introduction for key to tables	

AT A GLANCE	
ACADEMIC FILE:	
Subjects assessed	**27**
Excellent	**82%**
Average requirements	**300 points**
Students-staff ratio	**12:1**
First/2:1 degree pass rate	**63%**
ACCOMMODATION FILE:	
Guarantee to freshers	**100%**
Style	**Hall, flats**
Approx price range pw	**£44-£98.21**
City rent pw	**£80**

ACADEMIC EXCELLENCE

TEACHING :
(Rated Excellent or 17+ out of 24)

Law, Geography, History, Music.	**Excellent**
Classics, Dentistry	**24**
Portuguese, Subjects Allied to Medicine, Education	**23**
Spanish, Pharmacology	**22**
Anatomy, Physics, Environmental, Medicine, Molecular and Organismal Biosciences	
French, Nursing, Maths	**21**
German, Electronic & Elec Eng	**20**

RESEARCH:
Top grades 5/5*

Community/Clinical (Psychiatry), Clinical Dentistry, Anatomy, War Studies, German/Dutch/ Scandinavian, Portuguese, Spanish, Classics, History, Philosophy	**Grade 5***
Clinical Laboratory Sciences, Pre-Clinical Studies, Pharmacy, Nutrition & Dietetics, Biophysics, Pure Maths, Applied Maths, Electrical & Electronic Eng, Mechanical/Aeronautical/ Manufacturing Eng, Law, Theology, Music, Education	**Grade 5**

mother of all London University colleges, have a high public school intake, UCL's being higher than King's by about 8%. There is, at King's, what one student described as a 'friendly competitiveness' with students from UCL. I have heard a KCL student refer to UCL students as 'godless scum', while UCL routinely call KCL the Strand Poly.

ACADEMIA

Teaching assessments in Classics, Dentistry, Education, Maths, Nursing & Midwifery, Pharmacology & Pharmacy have recently helped to increase KCL's Excellence rating substantially to 82%, but then they were hit by an audit which called into question the college's 'ability to maintain quality and standards in the future.' KCL hit back suggesting that the quality people were simply fostering their own preference for a centralised 'corporate'

King's is a smart option if you're up to a London scene. Nearly half graduates go into into the health industry, 10% into finance, business & accountancy, and a sizeable wedge into media and the communications industry.

quality assurance system, and that the uni's own system had proved adequate in many top-rated departments, but the QAA insisted that evidence was sparse of 'an effective degree of monitoring, or of executive action at college level.'

Traditional, small tutorial and seminar teaching methods are one source of the high first and upper second graduation results at KCL. Modular course structures with semester assessments permit extensive interdisciplinary course programming (e.g. chemistry and philosophy). Music is as strong as medicine and can be found in harmony with applied computing; war studies combines with theology, amongst other subjects, and there's an international centre for prison studies within the Law School. Recently, the college acquired the former Public Record Office building in Chancery Lane and is converting it to a library and information centre for Law, Humanities and Engineering.

With the rise in academic excellence figures comes a rise in graduate employment statistics. Two years ago, an amazing 99% of King's graduates found employment a year after graduation. Regularly, the figures are good, almost half enter the health industry.

STUDENT SCENE

In keeping with many unions' apparent assumption that they can educate the masses by naming bars after prominent politicians, the showpiece attraction of King's Strand campus is its airy venue, **Tutu's**. Blessed with a stage, bar, café, dancefloor and spectacular views of the South Bank, this offers an in-house retreat for the college's loose-livered and free of fancy. A bust of the venue's namesake presides with piously disapproving glare over a feast of comedy nights, discos, live acts and all the other student malarkey.

Fave nights currently are *Phase* (cheese/dance), Saturday's indie club night, *Collide-a-scope*, listed in *Time Out* and attended by many a non-student, *Score*, which, you may guess, is the sports night, *The Hop* (more cheese), *Fuse* (entertaining and eclectic mix: R&B, house, Bhungra) and *Comedy Basement*, Thursday's comedy night. Recent live acts include Green Day, Beth Orton, Pulp, Linkin Park, Haven, South.

Macadam's third floor contains the traditional student watering hole **The Waterfront**, which acts as a perfectly pleasant preamble to its

WHAT IT'S REALLY LIKE

UNIVERSITY:

Social Life	★★★★
Campus scene	**Cosmopolitan, conservative**
Student Union services	**Average**
Politics	**Average: student issues**
Sport	**44 clubs**
National team position	**50th**
Sport facilities	**Poor**
Arts opportunities	**Good**
Student mag/news	**Roar**
Nightclub	**Tutu's**
Bars	**The Waterfront, Guy's Bar, Inverse, Tommy's Bar**
Union ents	**Phase, The Hop, Collide-a-Scope, Fuse, Score**
Union clubs/societies	**94**
Most popular societies	**Salsa**
Smoking policy	**No policy**
Parking	**None**

CITY:

Entertainment	★★★★★
City scene	**Wild, expensive**
Town/gown relations	**OK**
Risk of violence	**Average**
Cost of living	**Very high**
Student concessions	**Abundant**
Survival + 2 nights out	**£70 pw**
Part-time work campus/town	**Excellent**

coming from), accommodation rents, etc – but with the bright lights of the West End topping the list of countless distractions, it will only ever deter a relatively small proportion of its students from finding ways to get deeper in debt.

SPORT There are four sports grounds in Surrey and South London, rifle ranges at the Strand, the aforesaid K4 fitness club, a swimming pool and gym at Guy's, and highly successful boat and sub-aqua clubs. Nationally, KCL's teams came 50th last year in the BUSA (uni) team leagues.

JOBS

KCL is always up there with the best in graduate

WHERE GRADUATES END UP

40% Health (Med, Dent)*, 8% Finance, 6% Wholesale/Retail, 6% Manufacturing, 5% Education, 5% Public Admin	Key Areas
Accountancy, Telecom, Business/Management, Advertising, Publishing, Radio/TV, Legal, Library/Archival, Market Research, Defence	Niche Areas

*indicates Top 10 Graduate Provider

Approximate employed **95%**

big brother, Tutu, upstairs. With beer nearly half the price of the non-student establishments a stumble away, it's not hard to see why it entertains a cheery crowd.

Clubs and societies are legion, with Salsa, Debating and the King's Players (theatre), popular choices. A further popular activity (although one without its own noticeboard) was reported by irreverent and controversial student tabloid *Roar*. '*Basement Boys Use Bogs for Buggering*' ran the headline. *Roar*, incidentally, won the prestigious *Guardian* **Impact Award** a couple of years ago and is regularly nominated for its reporting.

All in all, the union keeps its flock busy – politically it confines itself to such as student hardship (a reality in London wherever you're

employment, 40% going into the health industry and large numbers into commerce and, after pupilage, into law. There are other interesting specialisms, however, notable media. See our *Employment* box, above.

GETTING THERE

☞ **Strand campus**: Temple (District Line, Circle), Aldwych (Piccadilly), Holborn (Piccadilly, Central). **Waterloo campus**: Waterloo/Waterloo East overland; Waterloo Underground (Bakerloo, Northern). **Guy's campus:** (Northern) and overland. **St Thomas' campus**: as Waterloo or Westminster (Circle, District, Northern, Bakerloo). **Denmark Hill campus**: Denmark Hill overland.

KINGSTON UNIVERSITY

Kingston University
Cooper House
40-46 Surbiton Road
Kingston upon Thames KT1 2HX

TEL 020 8547 2000
FAX 020 8547 7080
EMAIL admissions-info@kingston.ac.uk
WEB www.kingston.ac.uk

Kingston Students' Union
Main Site
Penrhyn Road
Kingston upon Thames: KT1 2EE

TEL 020 8547 8868
FAX 020 8547 8862
EMAIL president@kingston.ac.uk
WEB www.kingston.ac.uk/guild

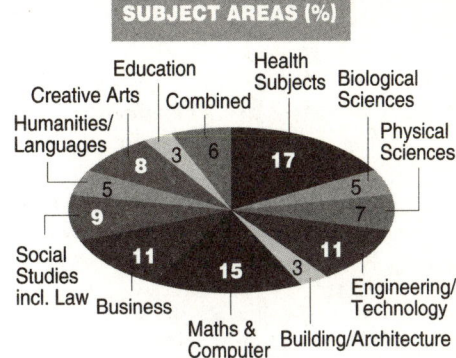

SUBJECT AREAS (%)

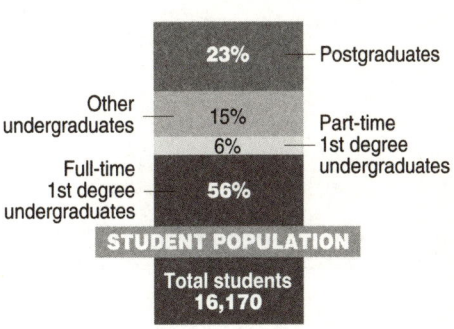

STUDENT POPULATION
Total students 16,170

VAG VIEW

*W*hatever they tell you about Kingston being the oldest royal borough, the place where Saxon kings were crowned (the Coronation stone lies in the Guildhall – King's Stone, geddit?), it is, in the cold light of reality, a monstrous suburban shopping centre and housewife's paradise. The Bentalls Centre rules. Shoppers come from miles to the mall, the market and the endless chain-shops, while its pubs and clubs attract streams of youthful revellers and the sometime Kingston Poly delivers higher education to sixteen thousand students.

We're talking vocational at Kingston, 'even those courses that don't on the surface appear to be vocational,' says the marketing department. 'The transferable skills that students gain while they're here make them very employable.' Students say that London being only fifteen minutes away facilitates the career process further.

CAMPUS SITES

The uni is based at four campuses near the A3, London's south-west outflow – Penrhyn Road, Kingston Hill, Knights Park and Roehampton Vale.

PENRHYN ROAD Kingston upon Thames, KT1 2EE. Tel (all sites): 020 8547 2000. **Faculties:** Science and some Technology.

KINGSTON HILL Kingston upon Thames, KT2 7LB.

Faculties: Business, Education, Music, Law, Social Work, and Healthcare Sciences.

Knights Park Kingston upon Thames, KT1 2QJ. **Faculties:** Art & Design, Architecture, Quantity Surveying, Estate Mgt.

Roehampton Vale Kingston upon Thames, KT1 2EE. **Faculties:** Mechanical, Aeronautical and Production Engineering.

UNIVERSITY/STUDENT PROFILE	
University since	**1992**
Situation/style	**London sites**
Student population	**16,170**
Full-time undergraduates	**9,120**
- mature	**49%**
- overseas	**12%**
- male/female	**48/52**
- state sector intake	**90%**
- non-traditional student intake	**10%**
- drop-out rate	**11%**
- undergraduate applications	**Up 16%**
*see Introduction for key to tables	

STUDENT PROFILE

They attract a mix of customer, from engineers to trendy artists, from nurses to would-be lawyers and City types, most notably a mature undergraduate body (49%!). A large slice of entrants come from socio-economic groups traditionally least likely to consider university. One effect may be their highish drop-out rate of 11%. No dip is in sight.

> *We're talking vocational – engineering, construction, computer, architecture, industry, health, education, etc. That aside, the mature population and opening hours at the Guild do not suggest a pulsating, 24/7 student scene.*

ACADEMIA

Subjects which have scored well recently in the teaching assessments are Building, Land & Property Management, Town & Country Planning, Mechanical, Aeronautical & Manufacturing Engineering, Radiography, Maths and Politics. No subjects made it to world class level in the research assessments, though overall they rose eight places to 81st position in the national league.

Each of the four campuses has its own faculties library. On top of a large main collection, Penrhyn Road, open seven days a week, has a language studio and the Mineralogical Society's library. At Kingston Hill a new learning resources centre has been built on to the old library. Knights Park has a collection of over 150,000 slides covering design, art, graphics and performing arts. Roehampton Vale supplies the engineers with science data sheets on aerodynamics and a collection of British standards on CD-Rom.

SOCIAL SCENE

STUDENTS' UNION Blue polo-shirted Freshers' Angels ease you into uni life, answer questions, be the voice of experience, and that first week culminates in *Freshers Hangover Party* – live bands,

ACADEMIC EXCELLENCE	
TEACHING :	
(Rated Excellent or 17+ out of 24)	
Business & Management, English, Geology.	**Excellent**
Building, Land & Prop Mgt,	**24**
Town & Country Planning, Mech, Aeronaut & Manuf Eng.	
Radiography, Maths, Politics	**23**
Civil Engineering	**22**
Modern Languages, Sociology, Electrical & Electronic Eng., Art & Design, Economics	**21**
Hist. Art/Architec./Design	**20**
RESEARCH :	
Top grades 5/5*	**None**

Degrees are modular. Sandwich courses are available in science and science/business subjects, also in science/French programmes. There's an optional, employment-enhancing language scheme for non-language undergraduates in Mandarin, Russian, Japanese, Italian, Spanish, German and French. Also, a Teaching & Learning Support scheme supplies individually or group-designed study skills programmes, EFL courses for overseas students and a 'peer assisted' learning scheme for first years with advice sessions from second years. Entry is not testing.

WHAT IT'S REALLY LIKE	
UNIVERSITY:	
Social Life	★★★
Campus scene	**London**
Student Union services	**Average**
Politics	**Student issues**
Sport	**Competitive**
National team position	**62nd**
Sport facilities	**Could do better**
Arts opportunities	**Drama, music, film, art good; dance poor**
Student newspaper	**Rhubarb**
Nightclub	**K1**
Bars	**Hannafords, Knights Park**
Union ents	**Eclectic**
Union clubs/societies	**50**
Most popular society	**Rugby**
Smoking policy	**Gannets, Hannafords OK**
Parking	**Adequate**
CITY:	
Entertainment	★★★★★
Local scene	**Cheesy**
Town/gown relations	**Average**
Risk of violence	**Low**
Cost of living	**High**
Student concessions	**Average**
Survival + 2 nights out	**£70 pw**
Part-time work campus/town	**Excellent,/good**

PAs, DJs, staged at **The Works** nightclub locally.

Of four bars, the biggest is at the main site on Penrhyn Road. **K1** is situated on the ground floor of so-called **Town House** between the union shop and the offices. Ents comprise pre-club nights – 'from cheesy pop to Bhangra via R&B, hip hop and garage – karaoke, theme nights, quiz nights, big screen sports, free PS2, regular drinks promotions.' As Kieran Alger reports, 'Ents at Kingston do little to break the mould. The mix of cheap drinks, DJs and widescreen football can be found anywhere in the country. History tells of visits of All Saints and DJ Paul Oakenfold, but restrictive pub licensing hours hamper the union and generally annoy the students.' Opening hours, Monday to Friday, are 11-23.00, Saturday 12-23.00, Sunday 12-22.30.

Cannots, the eaterie at Penryn Road, has gone health conscious with the menus, but still allows you to smoke. New style **Hannafords** at Kingston Hill, also a smoke zone, now has food and a decent coffee machine, more your 'café bar than bomb shelter', as they put it. Ents again fairly humdrum, but there's a hall of residence next door, so it's more of a community bar than K1. Opening hours are no freer, however.

Knights Park Bar is the arty bar, small (150 capacity) but with more of a bohemian ambience – the only bar at Kingston to sell absinthe – telling influence of the fashion, art and graphic design students. There's a varied music policy and the added bonus of a canal-side patio which makes it a popular summer venue. Again, restrictive opening hours.

'Living in Kingston can be expensive,' warns Kieran. 'Students still face the London housing extortion despite missing out on some of the city benefits. Rented accommodation can cost anything from £65-90. Even at these prices, quality is not guaranteed. First years have the comfort of halls.' Kingston Hill campus has on-site, en-suite facilities. There are four other residential sites including

Middle Mill Hall, self-catering flats opposite Knights Park Campus.

SPORT From football, rugby and hockey to Gaelic football and snowboarding, some thirty sports clubs fulfil most needs. Much of the activity takes place at the uni's sports facility at nearby Tolworth Court. There are also fitness facilities at Penrhyn Road. Kingston runs an Elite Athlete scheme to encourage students to compete at top levels in their sport. There's rowing on the Thames.

JOBS

Employment prospects are very good indeed, with Architecture and Construction especially solid. Only 4% generally are unemployed after six months. With an eye to the CV, there's been a skills development and certification scheme since last year, run jointly by union and uni, the aim to develop skills such as communication, IT, teamwork and literacy. There was even a special Champagne awards ceremony when twenty-seven

WHERE GRADUATES END UP

12% Education,	Key areas
11% Manufacturing, 10% Wholesale/Retail, 10% Finance, 7% Health/Social Work, 5% Personnel	
Business/Management, Architec, Construction, Chem/Pharmaceutical, Electron/Electric, Legal, Eng/Industrial Design, Library/Archival, Market Research, Property, Publishing, Sport, Telecom	Niche Areas
Approximate employed **96%**	

students were awarded Skillscert certificates by the vice-chancellor. Sounds a little bit of a ritualistic bureaucratic boost to union wallahs, but the thinking is on the right lines.

GETTING THERE

☞ By road: M1/J6a, M25/J13, A30, signs to A308 (Kingston). From London: A3 to Robin Hood Roundabout, then A308.
☞ By rail: frequent trains from London Waterloo to Kingston. No Underground this far out, but well served by buses.
☞ By air: Heathrow.

UNIVERSITY OF WALES, LAMPETER

University of Wales, Lampeter
Lampeter
Ceredigion SA48 7ED

TEL 01570 422351
FAX/TEL 01570 423530
EMAIL recruit@lampeter.ac.uk
WEB www.lamp.ac.uk

Lampeter Students' Union
Ty Ceredig
Ceredigion SA48 7ED

TEL 01570 422619
FAX 01570 422480
EMAIL union@lampeter.ac.uk
WEB www.lamp.ac.uk/su/activeframe.htm

VAG VIEW

*L*ampeter is a small, close-knit community with a strong rootstock in higher education. On March 1 (St David's Day) 2002, they celebrated 175 years as an institute of learning/teaching. They have been awarding degrees here for longer than any institution in England and Wales other than Oxbridge.

Although, today, first degree undergraduates number less than 1,000, and the entire syllabus focuses on arts and humanities, Rachel Extance recommends opting for Lampeter 'if your idea of the perfect university looks like an Oxbridge college, is peaceful, friendly, tucked away in the country, and a little bit out of the ordinary, then the University of Wales Lampeter is the place for you.

CAMPUS

'Don't be surprised if you have only just heard of the place, it is set in the heart of mid-west Wales and its train station was removed by Beeching in the 1960s. Clearly its isolation will be a consideration. Looking at a map, you may note the

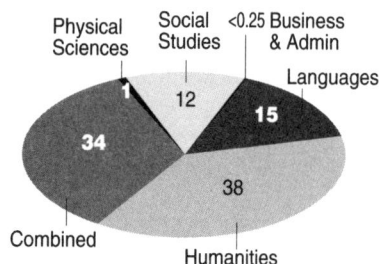

SUBJECT AREAS (%) UNDERGRAD INTAKE

Physical Sciences 1; Social Studies 12; <0.25 Business & Admin; Languages 15; Humanities 38; Combined 34

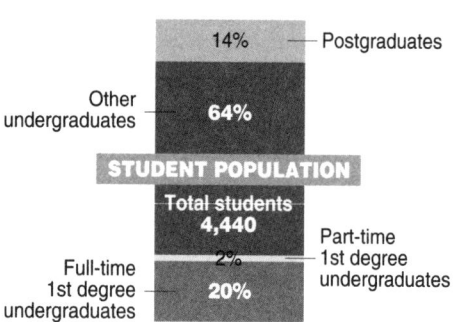

STUDENT POPULATION
Total students 4,440

Postgraduates 14%; Other undergraduates 64%; Part-time 1st degree undergraduates 2%; Full-time 1st degree undergraduates 20%

UNIVERSITY/STUDENT PROFILE	
University College since	**1971**
Situation/style	**Rural campus**
Student population	**4,400**
Full-time undergraduates	**890**
- mature	**40%**
- overseas	**1%**
- male/female	**44/56**
- state sector intake	**88%**
- non-traditional student intake	**16%**
- drop-out rate	**10%**
- undergraduate applications	**Up 7%**
see Introduction for key to tables	

distance between Lampeter and the nearest towns with more than ten houses, a post office and possibly a branch of Spar, but be advised that it is quite easy to get out of Lampeter if you know exactly when the two-hourly bus service runs.

'The theoretical advantage of being away from the shops is that your money will last longer. In practice you may spend as much money as your friends in the city because Lampeter contains fourteen pubs within a mile radius, with a cash point next to practically all of them.'

The campus is situated in a beautiful and inspirational place, not far from the Preseli Mountains, where the gigantic stones of the innermost sacred circle of Stonehenge, once Britain's national necropolis, are supposed to have been cut. This is mythic Wales, celebrated in the oldest story in *The Mabinogion*, a magical collection of eleven stories sustained orally since earliest times and written down in the fourteenth century. The story which comes from this particular area ('Pwyll, Lord of Dyfed') is probably the oldest, maybe as old as the second millennium BC.

ACADEMIA

There is much in Lampeter's programme that reflects this backdrop. Its spiritual aspirations for a start. 'Lampeter was founded by Bishop Burgess in 1822 as a theological college for the Church in Wales,' Rachel observes. 'The Theology & Religious Studies Department continues to be strong, with Islamic Studies and Religion, Society & Ethics and Jewish Studies just some of the courses run. A mosque sits at the back of the department.'

AT A GLANCE	
ACADEMIC FILE:	
Subjects assessed	**11**
Excellent	**36%**
Average requirements	**160 points**
Students-staff ratio	**18:1**
First/2:1 degree pass rate	**51%**
ACCOMMODATION FILE:	
Guarantee to freshers	**100%**
Style	**Halls, flats, houses**
Approx price range pw	**£37-£67**
Town rent pw	**£35-£40**

ACADEMIC EXCELLENCE	
TEACHING: Archaeology, Environmental Archaeology, Classics, Ancient History	**Excellent**
RESEARCH: *Top grades 5/5** English Language & Literature Theology	**Grade 5**

The unique course in Religion, Ethics & Society traces the development of our multi-faith, multi-cultural society and is taught as often by lecturers in English, History and Philosophy as by lecturers in Theology. The Students' Union religious societies ('older than the hills') have developed along similar lines. Also relevant to Lampeter's mythic backdrop is the emphasis on Ancient History and Archaeology. The region is littered with burial mounds and cromlechs redolent of civilisations long past.

Now, in Lampeter's quest for relevance in the modern world, there are also degrees in Business Management, Information Technology, Media Studies, British Studies, French with Arabic and even Voluntary Sector Studies. The latter is a development from an innovative distance learning course for care workers, which won them a Queen's Anniversary Prize in 1998. Media Studies makes use of the new **Media Centre**, which includes a TV studio, editing suite, video-conferencing facilities, satellite link-up and range of video equipment. British Studies is perhaps a response to European Union and may attract more students from abroad. As elsewhere, falling numbers focus the strategy. This year the German Department disappeared.

All courses are modular in scheme and taught in small groups. A fully equipped IT facility joins a library (170,000 vols), developed over 150 years and the Founders' Library (20,000 vols printed between 1470 and 1850).

STUDENT PROFILE

'The student population is incredibly diverse,' writes Rachel. 'A high percentage are mature students; there is also a sizeable band of foreign students (Greeks, Italians, French, Americans, to name just some of many nationalities you will encounter). There's a wide variety of religious groups, too. The place is simply too small for people not to get on with each other. Being in a small community, miles from anywhere is a great way of bonding people.'

Lampeter is in fact one of the government's elite access universities, with an 88% take from the state sector, 16% from among families to whom going to uni is a novel idea, while still maintaining an average sort of drop-out rate of 10%. Low entry requirements may have played a part in attracting students in the first place, but ethos, curriculum and teaching standards, and the peculiarly friendly and active away-from-it-all scene have kept them here. Applications climbed 7% last year.

> *Lampeter specialises in arts and humanities, and represents a particular away-from-it-all experience. The student body is small, but undergraduates here have a very good time.*

STUDENT SCENE

STUDENTS' UNION At the hub, **Old Bar** is the small, warm and friendly watering hole and host to *Band in the Bar* on Tuesdays and occasionally to karaoke nights. **The Extension** is the club venue, holds the latest licence in Ceredigion on a Saturday night, and is scene of discos on Wednesdays, Fridays and Saturdays, also big bands, comedy, games and more. Recent live acts include Relish, Jylt, Ukelele Kings, Whisky Before Breakfast, Familiar, Cheryl Beer, Dr and the Medics. The alcohol is cheap and plentiful, but interestingly the union is looking very seriously at meeting what it detects to be a need for an alcohol-free environment for students in the evenings. 'The union also houses a catering outlet called **Dewi's**,' adds Rachel, 'a TV room, pool tables, a games room, and, all importantly, the pigeon holes for post.'

There are twenty-four societies, ranging from animal rights to arts and crafts, probably the most

WHERE GRADUATES END UP

19% Wholesale/Retail*,	Key Areas
12% Education,	
8% Health/Social Work,	
8% Finance,	
8% Public Admin	
Agric/Forestry, Legal,	Niche Areas
Library/Archival*	

*indicates Top 10 Graduate Provider

Approximate employed **87%**

popular are Archaeology and Battle Society. There's also a very active Film Society (commercial and arthouse). They are not overly political, but equal rights is something they take very seriously. A student newspaper, *Luna*, carries basic union news, and there's a satirical magazine, *1822* – 'very popular, always causes a stir,' I am told. Both are always on the look-out for writers.

With an eye to the sizeable mature student population (40%), the union has set up a nursery. There is even a Welsh language playgroup. All round there's a strong welfare service, including Nightline and two 'pro' counsellors.

SPORT There are eighteen clubs, ranging from surfing to Tae Kwon Do. The national student sports organisation, BUSA, gave it a special 'most improved' award recently. 'Being small, there are brilliant opportunities for everyone to have a go,' said a student, 'and if you're half good at anything, chances are you'll get in a team. Cricket and football are particularly successful.'

TOWN 'Lampeter town itself is compact,' writes Rachel, 'with two supermarkets, a Boots, and a couple of New Age clothing shops. The crime rate is practically non-existent! But unlike in the big cities, entertainment is not handed to you on a plate. Of the fourteen pubs, some are famed for their lock-ins, the **Ram Tavern** is noted for its food, the **Cwmann** for its bar quiz and live music, the **Quarry** for its disco, and the **Kings Head** as the main haunt of the football team.'

WHAT IT'S REALLY LIKE

UNIVERSITY:	
Social Life	★★★
Campus scene	**Small, friendly, relaxed, rural**
Student Union services	**Average**
Politics	**Average: main issue equal rights**
Sport	**18 clubs: surfing to tae kwon do**
National team position	**111th**
Sport facilities	**Improving**
Arts opportunities	**Drama, music, film good; art, dance average**
Student magazine	**1822 (satire)**
Student newspaper	**LUNA**
Nightclub	**The Extension**
Bars	**Old Bar**
Union ents	**3 discos a week**
Union clubs/societies	**42**
Most popular society	**Archaeology, Battle socs**
Smoking policy	**Union, some halls OK**
Parking	**Good**
TOWN:	
Entertainment	★★
Scene	**Scenic, boozey**
Town/gown relations	**OK**
Risk of violence	**Low**
Cost of living	**Low**
Student concessions	**Average**
Survival + 2 nights out	**£50-£70 pw**
Part-time work campus/town	**Average**

PILLOW TALK

Two mainly first-year halls are full board; returning third and fourth years are more likely to self-cater. Some newer halls are en suite and more expensive. Living out in the second year and third year, you can get a nice place for around £40 a week, and you don't have to pay for the summer holidays. The size of the town means you're never living too far away.

JOBS

For part-time work, the union is the main source. There are jobs available in the bar and Extension, the union shop, security and with Union Entertainments. Working for Ents can mean anything from setting up the Extension for a gig, taking money on the door, or deejaying.

For serious employment, there's an annual Careers Fair in the second term, and a dedicated employability unit. Students are encouraged to join IT/Management courses and other modules that boost employability.

GETTING THERE

☛ By road: A485; the M4 is about 45 mins away.
☛ By rail: London Euston, 5:00; Cardiff Central, 1:30; Birmingham New Street, 4:10.
☛ By coach: London, 5:55; Birmingham, 7:25.

UNIVERSITY OF LANCASTER

University of Lancaster
University House
Lancaster LA1 4YW

TEL 01524 592015
FAX 01524 846243
EMAIL ugadmissions@lancaster.ac.uk
WEB www.lancs.ac.uk

Lancaster Students' Union
Slaidburn House
Lancaster LA1 4YA

TEL 01524 593765
FAX 01524 846732
EMAIL (see website)
WEB www.lusu.co.uk

VAG VIEW

A well-thought-out curriculum, a 63% chance of ending up with a first or upper second, consistently good teaching assessments, a recent £50 million capital expenditure on resources (art gallery, libraries, union, music buildings, halls, etc.), a popular college structure, good student ents (they own their own nightclub in town), an active media, drama scene and sporting tradition, and a beautiful 250-acre, landscaped campus within sight of the Lakes – all this contributes to Lancaster remaining a special kind of choice.

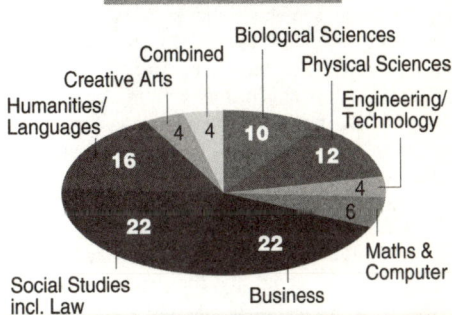

CAMPUS

The uni is far away from the industrial towns of popular imagination. It sits up to the north of the county, sandwiched between the sea and the Forest of Bowland, a huge open fell space giving life to myriad becks. Lancaster itself, which is nearby, is a city, certainly, but it is small and has cobbled streets and its buildings are historic, well-maintained, indeed many are probably protected. Really the setting is almost too perfect, and it is at once clear that the streetwise club-loon who has pencilled in Manchester, Leeds or Birmingham would not be a happy bunny up here on the fells, however longingly (or loyally) writes Lisa Maree about the place from her poolside home-from-home during an exchange year in California.

'The university has a beautiful countryside

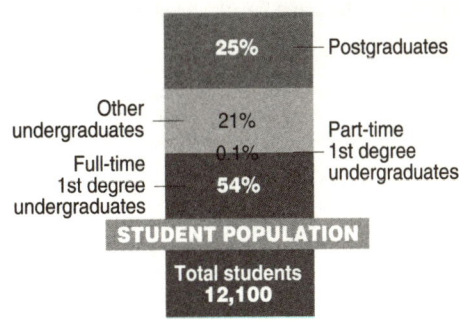

location at Bailrigg, on the outskirts of Lancaster,' she states. 'It is three miles from Lancaster city centre and set in acres of landscaped woods and parkland. On a clear day the view can extend as far as the Lakeland fells. In the centre of campus is Alexandra Square – the focus, the administrative

UNIVERSITY/STUDENT PROFILE	
University since	**1964**
Situation/style	**Rural collegiate campus**
Student population	**12,100**
Full-time undergraduates	**6,570**
- mature	**16%**
- overseas	**13%**
- male/female	**45/55**
- state sector intake	**89%**
- non-traditional student intake	**11%**
- drop-out rate	**6%, low**
- undergraduate applications	**Down 3%**
see Introduction for key to tables	

then so long as you get the required marks in your first year exams, transfer between departments is easy. This flexible programme in Part One is very popular.

They also have secret weapons in their educational armoury, like the Active Learning Unit, to which everyone is encouraged to submit. Special modules can be worked into your course-mix which will develop skills that employers want. And there's a first-class exchange scheme with nearly one tenth of Lancaster students exchanging with European and US institutions at some point during their degree.

Our *Academic Excellence* box, below, shows the breadth of subject area in which the uni excels. Research-wise it stands at 14th in the national league table, but this is certainly not at the expense of teaching, and the special needs office for students with disabilities is exemplary.

COLLEGE LIFE
The essential element of the Lancaster experience is the collegiate system. Virtually everything is done with or for your college

Writes Lisa: 'The nine colleges of the university – Bowland, Cartmel, County, Furness, Fylde, Grizedale, Lonsdale, Pendle and Graduate – are a very distinctive feature of campus life. Even staff are members, many of them active in collegiate

hub, where also the Students' Union offices, the extensive and well-quipped library and shops can be found. Cultural and recreational facilities on campus include a theatre studio, art gallery, concert hall, multi-denominational chaplaincy centre and large and well-equipped sports complex.

'Some of the university buildings were erected in the 1960s and the architecture is now looking decidedly outdated, but if character is what you want, don't let that dishearten you unduly. Historic Lancaster is just ten minutes away by bus, a friendly, bustling place which has all the amenities of a larger city, while retaining the unique charm of its antiquity.

STUDENT PROFILE
'The best thing about the uni is the warm, friendly atmosphere created by the students in their somewhat wind-chilled and rainy environment. The student body comprises a wide cross-section of people, including large percentages of privately educated and overseas students.'

Wide cross-section, indeed. As it happens, Lancaster is one of the UK's 'access elite', managing somehow to combine an ability to entice its students from a wide socio-economic spectrum with a low drop-out rate of 6%.

ACADEMIA
The system is that your first year is a kind of taster year. They've woken up to the fact that a number of students study subjects at degree level that they haven't studied at school. In Part One (your first year) you take three subjects. One of these has to be what you intend to major in, but the other two can be completely off the wall. If you registered to do Politics, but, after a first year studying Politics, Law and Computing (for instance), you decide that you really should have applied to do Law all along,

ACADEMIC EXCELLENCE	
TEACHING: *(Rated Excellent or 17+ out of 24)*	
History, Applied Social Work, Business & Management Studies, English, Environmental Sciences, Geography, Social Policy & Admin, Music.	**Excellent**
Theatre Studies, Psychology, Philosophy, Theology	**24**
Linguistics, Art & Design, Physics, Politics	**23**
Engineering, Maths & Stats	**22**
Sociology, Molecular Sciences, Organismal Biosciences	**21**
French, Italian with Iberian	**20**
German	**19**
RESEARCH: *Top grades 5/5**	
Physics, Statistics, Sociology, Business	**Grade 5***
Psychology, Earth Sciences, Computer, Law, Social Work, European Studies, English, Linguistics, Theology, Education	**Grade 5**

life. The colleges vary considerably in atmosphere and size, but each is a busy centre of social, recreational and educational activity. All on-campus accommodation is located within college, which makes it easy to get to know people and quickly to gain a sense of belonging in this kind of supportive community.'

You might think, with campus being a small, all-encompassing 'city' miles from anywhere, and there being no need to get off it for anything, that college life among 500 or so (or less) student colleagues could get a bit claustrophobic in time, but that is not the experience of students. As it is, any feelings of break-out are effectively displaced by a two-tier eco-system. By your second year you will probably be ready to break out, but the urge is satisfied by leaving your college residence rather than the uni as a whole. For in your second year renting accommodation in town is actively encouraged, while continuing allegiance to your college is ensured by both sporting and course activities. The result of this very successful organic experiment is that when you ask students what it's like at Lancaster University, the words that crop up time and again are 'friendly', 'relaxed', 'unintimidating'. In fact, I can't imagine that Lancaster's system of 'personal advisers' – a 1:5 staff to student welfare and educational advice service, ever has much to do.

SOCIAL SCENE

'Each of the colleges also has its own JCR (Junior Common Room), complete with bar and pool table,' reports Lisa. 'Many universities have only one union bar and the nine we have on campus provide perfect venues for bar crawls that last all night long. At the end of the academic year each college also has its own entertainment event, affectionately named the *Extrav*, which usually results in farcically ridiculous antics and the presence of Chesney Hawkes or Abba and Elvis tribute bands.'

A poll puts **Pendle Bar** in first place in a college league of bars, followed closely by **Grizedale** (*Shite* disco on Friday) and **Lonsdale**. Most colleges organise subsidised fortnightly trips to clubs – Liverpool and Manchester are just over an hour away.

The high-scoring Drama Department (full marks on inspection) empowers a studio theatre and the on-campus **Nuffield Theatre**, used for both student and 'pro' touring companies.

'There is a huge variety of societies,' writes Lisa. 'including alternative music, Taekwando, photography, kickboxing, floorball, debating and juggling. If politics is your passion, the union is one of the most pro-active at the moment, campaigning

WHAT IT'S REALLY LIKE	
UNIVERSITY:	
Social Life	★★★★
Campus scene	**Healthy, lively, college-based**
Student Union services	**Good**
Politics	**Increasingly active**
Sport	**Competitive nationally + big Inter-coll League**
National team position	**42nd**
Sport facilities	**Good**
Arts opportunities	**Art excellent; drama, music, film good; dance poor**
Student newspaper	**Scan**
Student radio	**Bailrigg FM**
Nightclub	**Sugarhouse**
Bars	**College bars**
Union ents	**Frisky, Shite, Popscene**
Union clubs/societies	**90**
Most popular society	**Hiking**
Smoking policy	**Bars & halls OK**
Parking	**No first years**
TOWN:	
Entertainment	★★★
Scene	**Excellent pubs, OK clubs**
Town/gown relations	**Good**
Risk of violence	**Low**
Cost of living	**Average**
Student concessions	**Average**
Survival + 2 nights out	**£60 pw**
Part-time work campus/town	**Poor/average**

for just about everything from abortions to AIDS. The Film Society is the largest society, and very popular are the radio station, Bailrigg fm, and *Scan*, the bi-monthly newspaper.

SPORT Inter-college rivalries mean that if you enjoy sport, but aren't good enough to play at inter-university level, you will certainly be good enough to play at college level. A very high proportion of students enjoy competitive team sport, even those that aren't that good.

Lancaster are national champions at Taekwando and do tolerably well in the national uni team sports (42nd nationally last year), but the place really comes alive at Roses – Lancaster vrs York Uni, a huge weekend of sport and socials.

TOWN 'The social life at Lancaster should not be

AT A GLANCE	
ACADEMIC FILE:	
Assessments	**28**
Excellent	**86%**
Average requirements	**260 points**
Students-staff ratio	**19:1**
First/2:1 degree pass rate	**63%**
ACCOMMODATION FILE:	
Guarantee to freshers	**100%**
Style	**College**
Approx price range pw	**£41-£55**
Town rent pw	**£45**

PILLOW TALK

'University accommodation costs are low [approx £41-£55 per week]. All rooms are self-catering, equipped with the basics and have telephone and internet access, though quality does vary between colleges. In your second year, you will need to find off-campus accommodation with the help of the university housing office and in your third year you can choose whether to return to halls. Average local rent is around £45 per week.'

JOBS

The Careers Service provides seminars and of course fairs for graduate recruitment. There is a

WHERE GRADUATES END UP	
13% Manufacturing,	Key areas
10% Wholesale/Retail,	
10% Public Admin*,	
9% Finance,	
9% Health/Social Work,	
7% Education	
6% Personnel	
Accountancy, Advertising,	Niche Areas
Business/Management,	
Publishing, Journalism,	
Defence, Library/Archival,	
Legal, Market Research*,	
Chem/Pharmaceutical,	
Aeronautical Manufac	
*indicates Top 10 Graduate Provider	
Approximate employed	**95%**

underestimated,' writes Guy McEvoy. 'Lancaster town itself has been transformed over the past five years by massive investment from the major brewers. Trendy pubs are now displacing the traditional Northern watering hole in the centre of town (though these can still be found on the edges if that is your thing). The union-run **Sugarhouse** remains the most popular club.'

Writes Lisa: 'If you are on a very tight budget I would suggest drinking in the college bars before going out into Lancaster and then clubbing dry. The price of a pint of beer in the city is around £1.80 and in the college bars, about £1.60 (an average weekly budget including food, beer, travel and two nights out will set you back between £60 and £70).

'Student friendly pubs include **The Merchants**, **The Firkin**, **The Walkabout**, **Paddy Mulligan's**, **The Waterwitch** and **Blob Shop**. Recommended nightclubs are Sugarhouse, of course, Wheatus appeared here recently, and **Liquid**, **The Carleton** (host to Chesney Hawkes in the past), **Elemental**, and **Tokyo Joe's** in Preston. The Sugarhouse has a variety of different club nights, including *Popscene*, which showcases indie rock, the popular *Frisky Friday* night of big cheese, as well as '80s night, *Relax*.

'Restaurants in Lancaster that cater to student pockets include **Paulo Gianni's**, **Bella Pasta**, **The Golden Dragon** and **Marco's**. You can also find several venues for movie watching and theatre-going in the city centre.

good record with usually only 4% or 5% failing to find something to do after six months. Finance, accountancy and business/management taken together as 'commerce' are probably most popular, but there are any number of interesting niche areas (see box above).

GETTING THERE

☛ By road: M6/J34, A683 or M6/J33, A6.
☛ By rail: London Euston, 3:30; Newcastle, 3:00; Sheffield, 2:30; Leeds, 2:30; Manchester, 1:30.
☛ By coach: London, 5:50; Leeds, 3:55.

STUDENT LEEDS – THE CITY

'There are many phrases bandied about to describe Leeds but 'University City' is not one of them. Nevertheless, 'the Jewel of the North' is dominated by its 50-odd thousand students to the extent that it really does seem to die when they go in the vacations. The city has been totally transformed in recent years by a massive regeneration programme and so it is no wonder that students apply in droves to study here.

CULTURE

'Cultural highlife' and Yorkshire may not sit in the same sentence too often, but a quick look around confirms that there is much to tear you away from the numerous pubs and bars. **The West Yorkshire Playhouse** is a highly regarded theatre that stages the best productions in the North, many straight from London. Sir Ian McKellan, Ben Elton and Irvine Welsh have all premiered productions here and it's very student friendly, with discounts available.

For art truly on the cheap, there are many free galleries, some of which showcase student work. The best of these are **The Henry Moore Institute** and **The Leeds Art Gallery,** which stand next to each other in town. A quick mention must be given to **The Royal Armouries** which was given to Leeds ahead of London and contains 8,000 exhibits for under a fiver.

FILM

In the age of the futuristic multiplex the best thing about film in Leeds is that the cosy independent cinema has survived. Like most places everything is student friendly price-wise, but real value and satisfaction can be found in the cinemas, which are dotted around studentland and cost around £2.50 a pop.

The Hyde Park Picture House is eighty-five years old and the height of cool. Cult and independent films, as well as the occasional blockbuster, can be found here, and its location slap bang in the in the middle of Hyde Park ensures that it's a student favourite. Headingley has two lovely cinemas – **The Cottage Road** and **Lounge** – both quite plush and with a lovely retro feel to them. Finally **ABC** in town plays the latest that Hollywood has to offer for prices that seem to be stuck in 1987.

PUBS

A must in these parts is completing the fabled Otley Run, involving a drink in every establishment from **Boddington Hall**, four miles north of campus, to Leeds Met's **Met Bar** on the outskirts of the city centre – four miles, twenty-odd pubs and a lot of drinking. All these pubs are geared towards students and the best remain the same year in, year out. **The Original Oak** and **The Skyrack** in central Headingley are pretty much the busiest pubs in the world. No space to move, but forever popular – go on your own and you'll soon bump into someone you know. Also cheap and cheerful

24/7 are the union bars: at Leeds Uni, it's **The Old Bar** (rumoured to be the longest in Europe) and now **Stylus** (see page 264), and down the road, the aforementioned Met Bar, which hosts legendary student events.

CLUBS

A massive explosion. That's the only way to describe the growth in Leeds clubland in the last few years. Wherever you turn in the city centre there seems to be a new club springing up. Whatever you're looking for is here. For a guaranteed good night out, **Liquid** is a big favourite. Intimate, it has a reasonable pricing system and varied music policy, centring on its top midweek big beat night, *Dust*. If you're into largin' it at every opportunity then **The Afterdark** in Morley is without doubt the best techno club north of London, with a galaxy of stars playing. Deeply fashionable and just off Leeds University campus is **The Faversham**, a pub in the week but a club on Thursday to Saturday with a crowd that is there to be seen. Situated in Call Lane, the redlight district, **The Fruit Cupboard** hosts the best R&B night in the city and is great for chilling out. Finally, no sampling of Leeds clubland can go by without mentioning the renowned hard house night *Speed Queen* at **The Warehouse**. Attracting an up for it gay/straight/TV crowd this is the jewel in Leeds' clubland crown. Yet there are many, many gems, many, many facets to explore before you'll find your favourites. Events details can be found in the weekly edition of *Leeds Student*, the newspaper for all students in Leeds.

SHOPPING ON A GRANT

The diversity of the new Leeds is not more clearly demonstrated than in the variety of places to shop. From the many charity shops to **Harvey Nichols** your budget can be catered for. The main areas are in town and the best is **The Victoria Quarter**. Under a stained glass arcade many independent and designer labels compete for your loan, but be prepared to spend. **The Corn Exchange** is another big hall much along the same lines. If strapped for cash go to Hyde Park Corner and Headingley. Both have smaller independents and charity shops at the cheapest prices possible.

STUDENTLAND

While most students in most cities tend to live in the same areas, nowhere takes this to the extreme that Leeds does. There is a stretch of Leeds north of the centre which has a high percentage of students. It is a bit of culture shock to some, though, to see windows barred up – a result of a high crime rate.

Furthest away but very popular is Headingley.

Famous for the cricket ground, this is still within walking distance of the university, albeit a long one. Closer in is Hyde Park, shabbier than Headingley but with more atmosphere; Burley, cheap but grim; Woodhouse, cobbled streets straight from the Hovis ad; and there are plusher places just off the city centre. Rents are cheap, as supply way outstrips demand, so the golden rule is to relax – there's enough to go round.

IN CONCLUSION
It's an old cliché but this place is so big that everyone fits in, and there is so much for everyone. People spend the best years of their lives here.

ADDRESSES
Culture West Yorkshire Playhouse, Quarry Hill Mount, LS1; 0113 213 7700. Henry Moore Institute, The Headrow, LS1; 0113 246 9469. Leeds Art Gallery, The Headrow, LS!; 0113 247 8248. Royal Armouries, Armouries Drive, LS1; 0990 106 666.
Film The Hyde Park Picture House, Brudenell Road, Hyde Park; 0113 275 2045. The Cottage road Cinema, Cottage road, Headingley; 0113 230 2562; The Lounge Cinema, North Lane, Headingley; 0113 230 2562. ABC, Vicar Lane, LS1; 0113 245 1013.

Pubs The Original Oak, Otley Road, Headingley; 0113 245 8842. The Skyrack, Otley Road, Headingley; 0113 275 2133. The Old Bar/Stylus, Leeds University Union; 0113 231 4294. The Met Bar, Leeds Metropolitan University Students Union; 0113 209 8401.

Clubs Liquid, Central Road, LS1; 0113 242 7253. AfterDark, South Queen Street, Morley; 0113 252 3542. The Faversham, Springfield Mount; 0113 245 8817. The Fruit Cupboard, Call Lane, LS1; 0113 243 8666. Warehouse, Somers Street, LS1; 0113 246 8287.

Shops Harvey Nichols, Briggate, LS1; 0113 204 8888. The Victoria Quarter, Briggate, LS1; 245 5333. The Corn Exchange, Call Lane, LS1; 0113 234 0363.

Naveed Raja

UNIVERSITY OF LEEDS

The University of Leeds
Leeds LS2 9JT

TEL 0113 243 1751
FAX 0113 244 3923
EMAIL admissions@leeds.ac.uk
WEB www.leeds.ac.uk

Leeds University Union
Leeds LS1 1UH

TEL 0113 243 9071
FAX 0113 244 8786
EMAIL comms@luu.leeds.ac.uk
WEB www.luuonline.com

VAG VIEW

In the North, the traditional top choice is between Leeds, Manchester, Sheffield and Newcastle, and there is nowt but a couple of blips in the assessments – less than perfect initial judgements on the BBC-approved broadcasting course and the Leeds flagship course, Medicine – to suggest that Leeds is not still up there with the front runners.

'What Leeds Uni has to offer, which I doubt anywhere else could match,' observed a recent graduate, 'is the students themselves. There's a real atmosphere about the place. You can do whatever you want without being criticised for it. You can really get involved. And at Leeds, students do. You don't come to a place like Leeds if you're an introvert.'

SUBJECT AREAS (%)

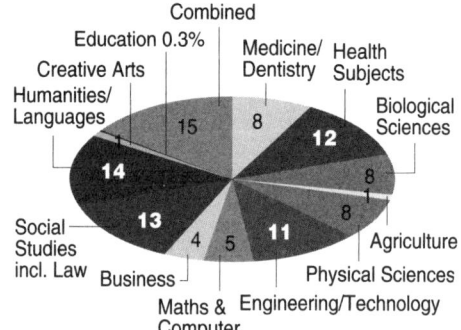

CAMPUS
'The university campus is conveniently situated between the town centre and the bulk of student housing areas, everything's within easy walking distance,' writes Londoner Amy Shuckburgh.

'Transport is very cheap, easy to use and pretty reliable. It's relatively safe – burglary can be a problem, most student houses have window bars, door grates or burglar alarms as deterrents, but on the whole, it doesn't have an intimidating feel to it. The same precautions should be taken as in any city: it is inadvisable to walk around late at night on your own; use taxis if possible; union night bus services are provided for girls along all routes, both girls and boys are strongly advised not to walk through Hyde Park at night.'

The union has an arrangement with Amber Cars – any student can travel free on production of their union card, which is then presented by the driver to the union for payment. The union settles with the student later.

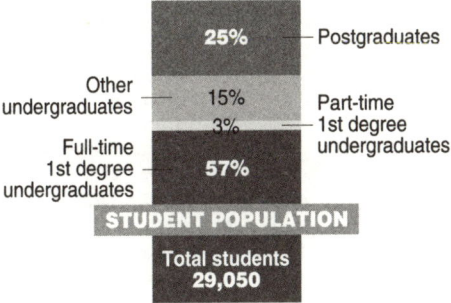

STUDENT PROFILE

You can in fact expect to meet a wide range of people at Leeds. There is a huge students population. But in broad terms you will find more caught up and involved than elsewhere. There is a clear distinction at the broadest level with Leeds Met down the road: 72% from state schools as against their 93%; 8% from non-traditional student recruitment areas as against Leeds Met's 14%... 'There is sometimes a lot of snobbery from Leeds University students towards Leeds Met,' admitted a student, 'but a lot of that is created by the Met students. We go to things there and they come to gigs here, and the newspaper [*Student Direct*] is joint with the Met, as are LSR [radio] and Community Action, Rag and Nightline.' All of which is true, but Leeds Met is mainly involved in distribution of *Student Direct*, never would Leeds let it loose on editorial policy.

ACADEMIA

Academically Leeds has a good reputation across the board. Joint Honours Arts Faculty courses are among those that distinguish the curriculum. The range of programmes is wide, challenging, with intriguing cross-faculty schemes; employers take a

ACADEMIC EXCELLENCE

TEACHING :
(Rated Excellent or 17+ out of 24)

Chemistry, English, Geography, Music, Geology.	**Excellent**
Subjects Allied to Medicine, Philosophy, Physics	**24**
East & South Asian Studies, Pharmacology, Dentistry, Fine Art, Electrical & Electronic Eng, Molecular Biosciences, Politics, Psychology, Theology	**23**
Maths, Iberian, French, German, Communication/Media, Anatomy, Organismal Biosciences	**22**
Arabic	**21**
Sociology, Russian, Agriculture, Nursing, Materials Technology, Food Science	**20**
Italian, Chemical Eng, Classics, Civil Engineering	**19**
Medicine	**18**

RESEARCH :
Top grades 5/5*

Food Science, Electrical and Electronic Eng, Mechanical/Aeronautical/ Manufacturing Eng, Town & Country Planning, English, Italian	**Grade 5***
Clinical Laboratory Sciences, Physiology, Other Subjects Allied to Medicine, Psychology, Biological Sciences, Chemistry, Physics, Earth Sciences, Environmental Sciences, Pure Maths, Applied Maths, Statistics, Computer, General Eng, Civil Eng, Geography, Law, Social Policy, Business & Management, Asian Studies, History, Philosophy	**Grade 5**

keen interest in graduates with two named subjects from Leeds. The Leeds College of Health is now the uni's School of Healthcare Studies, which gives fresh vigour to its Medical and Dentistry School and to other courses related to medicine (courses, like Radiography), which scored full marks in the teaching assessments. Now, two new research colleges, focusing on post-genome science and the understanding of human diseases on a molecular level, are set to stimulate collaboration and create closer links between the university and the city's teaching hospitals.

Particularly mentioned by sixthform careers teachers are languages – 'One reason we recommend Leeds is that you can do exotic languages, Arabic,' said one. More recent high scores in the teaching assessments are for Psychology, Philosophy (full marks), Politics, Theology and Education. In the recent research assessment the uni came 26th nationally.

The big news is the merger with arts/education college, Bretton Hall (close to Wakefield), which took place last year, supported by a £9 million investment, which is currently rejuvenating the already highly regarded schools in Performing & Visual Arts, Music, Cultural Studies, Education, Textiles and Fashion. A new School of Performance & Cultural Industries offers Acting, Arts Management, Creative Writing and Dance, and there is a new performance space planned.

SOCIAL SCENE

The long-awaited overhaul of Leeds union has happened. A £4.8m extension has effectively added 40% more shopping and meeting space for students and given the city a new music venue. The new nightclub is called **Stylus** (capacity 1,000), which is adjacent to **Bar Coda** (capacity 290). There are then two bars jointly known as **The Terrace** (complete with sun-terrace and disabled access). Then there's the **Old Bar**, a traditional pub really, down in the basement. That leaves the **Riley Smith Hall** (capacity 600) to host productions from the students' performing societies and **The Refectory** (capacity 2,000) as the biggest venue in Leeds. In addition, the union now has six shops, including Leeds' second largest newsagent, an off-licence, a card and ticket shop, a copy shop, one selling past exam papers and the last union-run bookshop in the country.

Traditionally, LUSU (the union) has been

WHAT IT'S REALLY LIKE	
UNIVERSITY:	
Social Life	★★★★★
Campus scene	**Seriously good**
Student Union services	**Good**
Politics	**Active: student & international**
Sport	**52 clubs**
National team position	**12th**
Sport facilities	**Good**
Arts opportunities	**Drama, dance, music, film, art excellent**
National drama awards	**Best drama critic**
Student newspaper	**Leeds Student**
Independent awards	**Best arts journalist**
	Best campaign
Student radio	**LSR fm**
Radio 1 awards	**Marketing/Promo**
	Best factual prog
Nightclub	**Stylus**
Bars	**Bar Coda, The Terrace, Old Bar**
Union ents	**Fruity, Loaded**
Union clubs/societies	**212**
Most popular societies	**Music Theatre, Christian Union**
Smoking policy	**Zonal**
Parking	**Poor**
CITY:	
Entertainment	★★★★★
Scene	**Wild**
Town/gown relations	**Average**
Risk of violence	**Average**
Cost of living	**Low**
Student concessions	**Abundant**
Survival + 2 nights out	**£60-£80 pw**
Part-time work campus/town	**Average/good**

known for heavier stuff than ents. 'There is a left-wing, anti-Capitalist stance at Leeds. It is very prevalent here,' I was told. I say that there is also a reputation for being a bit self-consciously PC. I recall a few years ago that the *Sun* was banned from the union for advertising a Knickerbox brassiere doing what it was designed to do. 'The *Sun* was banned, but that was voted in at an OGM by the students, then the ban was lifted... I think you've got to be politically correct, but you can take it over

> *There's a real atmosphere about the place. You can do whatever you want, you can really get involved. And at Leeds, students do. You don't come here if you're an introvert.*

been on tour, had a CD out, played gigs in the city.

'The Film Society is very big, and the Film Making Society has really taken off. For art we've got all the resources in the city – Henry Moore Institute and the galleries and the gallery exhibition in the Parkinson Court.'

I venture to ask whether there is a personal cost, what with all this intense activity and pressure from work. 'Nightline is very high in demand... very heavily subscribed. It isn't any one thing that drives people to use it. You've got financial pressures, academic pressures, and then you've got the social pressures – to conform, to party, to pull in the grades, and then you've got other problems like housing. You don't come to a place like Leeds if you're an introvert. There's pressure from all sides.'

Ents regularly consist of *Fruity* every Friday

the boundaries...' They describe their political activity now as 'average, the main issues this year are student funding, ethical and environmental issues and international issues. We've got the campaign against the arms trade; the environmental group People and Planet, and things like Amnesty International and Jubilee 2000 to rid us of Third World debt. There's a huge scattering of political groups.

'At Leeds we are very, very strongly two separate institutions, the university and the union. Everybody knows that. But there's mutual respect. Community issues, drug and alcohol policy, things like that we work together on, but politically we like to be independent.'

Besides getting involved in politics, they have a track record in media. The radio station, LSR, took two gongs in the Radio 1 awards last year. *Leeds Student*, the weekly student newspaper that was described as 'streets ahead' of its competitors by the *Guardian* recently, took Best Arts Journalist and Best Campaign in the *Independent* student media awards. Then there are the arts, and fund-raising, sport and Community Action (over 600 students are involved in this). 'There are many groups within the union that work really hard. For drama, we've got **The Raven Theatre**. It seats a couple of hundred. The Theatre Group does three or four plays a term. The really big shows, musicals – *Grease, The Whizz, Hair* – are produced in The Riley Smith Hall.

'There's modern dance (they run jazz, tap, contemporary lessons), there's ballroom and salsa every Wednesday in the **Refectory**, which is packed out. You can barely move in there.

'The Symphony Orchestra and Symphonia and the chorals are all involved in the Leeds concert season, and then there's dance big bands – they've

– classic, cheesy, student toons – and *Loaded* every Thursday – '90s night. Recent live acts include Faithless, Ian Brown, Groove Armada, Super Furry Animals, the Charlatans, Eels, OPM, Soft Cell, Wheatus, Ash, Sum 41, Embrace, So Solid Crew, Damage, and many more.

SPORT The teams came 12th in the national uni team league last year. Women's Rugby deserve a special mention. They got four in the England Student squad and one in the England Academy. There are facilities to match attainment at this level – two sports halls, one large enough to take 1,500 spectators. Playing fields are five miles from campus; there are also cricket squares, a floodlit synthetic pitch and six floodlit tennis courts. There's rowing both in Leeds and York, sailing on nearby lakes and reservoirs, hiking, climbing, canoeing and caving in the Yorkshire Dales. Students may use the city's international swimming pool, and golf courses in the area.

PILLOW TALK

Every first-year undergraduate student who applies for accommodation by June 1 is provided with uni accommodation. There are halls of residence (meals provided), shared houses, self-catering flats - some en suite. The price range – £35 to £70 per week – is reasonable, even in comparison to the extraordinarily low levels of rent in the city: £30-70 per week. The uni option varies from basic/cheap to plush/expensive. Some is on campus; the rest within easy walking or busing distance.

JOBS

Most of its graduates end up in the health industry or in financial activities, accountancy or business/management. But there are a number of intriguing niche areas (see box, page 265). What is for sure is that Leeds does offer 'the full thing', which is why it succeeds so often in competition with other universities and why graduates from Leeds are so popular with employers.

GETTING THERE

☛ By road: M62/J39, M1; or M62/J27, M621; or A1, A58; or A65, A650.
☛ By rail: Newcastle, 1:45; London Euston, 2:30; Birmingham New Street, 2:20.
☛ By air: Leeds/Bradford Airport.
☛ By coach: London, 4:00; Edinburgh, 6:00.

LEEDS COLLEGE OF ART & DESIGN

Leeds College of Art & Design
Jacob Kramer Building
Blenheim Walk
Leeds LS2 9AQ

TEL 0113 202 8000
FAX 0113 202 8001
EMAIL info@leeds-art.ac.uk
WEB www.leeds-art.ac.uk

VAG VIEW

There's an international dimension to the fore. Students are advised and encouraged to take a European language option in their first year, and funding from the EU Socrates and Leonardo da Vinci programmes allows regular exchanges with art and design colleges in Europe.

Among the first-year mandatory modules on the Visual Communications course are Typography, Calligraphy, Computer-aided Design and Media Studies. Workshops and learning resources include industry-standard equipment. Entry decisions focus on students' portfolios.

A Students' Union exists. There's no accommodation, but the college will fix you up.

COLLEGE PROFILE

Founded	**1846**
Status	**Art College**
Degree awarding university	**Leeds**
Student population	**2,500**
Full-time undergraduates	**316**
College accommodation	**None**
City rent pw	**£36-£39**

DEGREE SUBJECT AREAS:
Fashion, interior design, photography, visual communications, textile design

GETTING THERE

☛ By road: from the south, M1; from north, A1; east and west, M62.
☛ By rail: London King's Cross, 2:30; Liverpool Lime Street, 2:00; Manchester Piccadilly, 1:15; Newcastle, 1:45; Sheffield, 1:15.
☛ By coach: London, 4:00; Edinburgh, 6:00.

LEEDS COLLEGE OF MUSIC

Leeds College of Music
3 Quarry Hill
Leeds LS2 7PD

TEL 0113 222 3400
FAX 0113 243 8798
EMAIL enquiries@lcm.ac.uk
WEB www.lcm.ac.uk

COLLEGE PROFILE

Founded	**1965**
Status	**Conservatoire**
Degree awarding university	**Leeds**
Situation/style	**City site**
Student population	**2,600**
Full-time undergraduates	**191**
College accommodation	**None**
City rent pw	**£36-£40**

DEGREE COURSES:
Jazz Studies, Performing Arts

VAG VIEW

*T*he largest music college in Britain is part of an exciting £4.5 million purpose-built development on Quarry Hill, in the centre of Leeds, beside the famous **West Yorkshire Playhouse** and **Yorkshire Dance Company**. The Jazz degree at LCM is second to none. Both it and the college's other degree, Performing Arts, are performance orientated. There's a fully equipped 24-track recording studio, digital recording and editing facilities, computers, aural laboratory, electro-acoustic equipment, a song-writing studio, a library and music archive, a Yamaha keyboard studio, etc.

GETTING THERE

☞ By road: from the south, M1; from north, A1; east and west, M62.
☞ By rail: London King's Cross, 2:30; Liverpool Lime Street, 2:00; Manchester Piccadilly, 1:15; Newcastle, 1:45; Sheffield, 1:15.
☞ By coach: London, 4:00; Edinburgh, 6:00.

LEEDS METROPOLITAN UNIVERSITY

Leeds Metropolitan University
Calverley Street
Leeds LS1 3HE

TEL 0113 283 2600
FAX 0113 283 3114
EMAIL course-enquiries@lmu.ac.uk
WEB www.lmu.ac.uk

Leeds Met Students' Union
Calverley Street
Leeds LS1 3HE

TEL 0113 209 8400
FAX 0113 234 2976
EMAIL [name]@lmu.ac.uk
WEB www.lmsu.org.uk

VAG VIEW

*L*eeds Met is a centre of applied learning, a relatively new university with full marks or near full marks in vocational subjects like business management, economics, education, health, drama, sport. It has the low drop-out rate and the high employment rate of a top-of-the-league traditional university, and it reflects the character of the city: an active union ensures that it is a fun place to be.

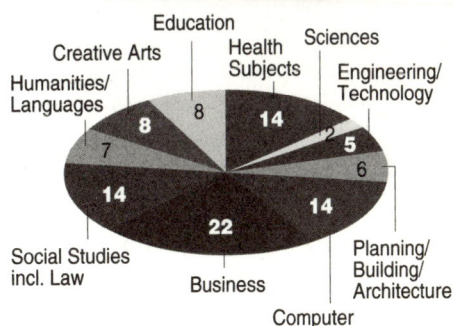

SUBJECT AREAS (%)

CAMPUS

City Campus, close to Leeds Uni campus, includes Union HQ, the **Studio Theatre** and **University Art Gallery** (both open to the public). There are teaching facilities both here at Calverley Street and at nearby Queen Square. Beckett Park Campus is three miles away in 100 acres of parkland in Headingley. The cultures of the two sites differ as to the type of student. Sports, business and computing students colour Beckett Park, while City has a lot more arts, health sciences and engineering. 'Students who play sport go out there;' said a student. 'Students who want the library and the big ents come down here.'

City campus is located in a quite extraordinary area of Leeds. Woodhouse Lane and Calverley

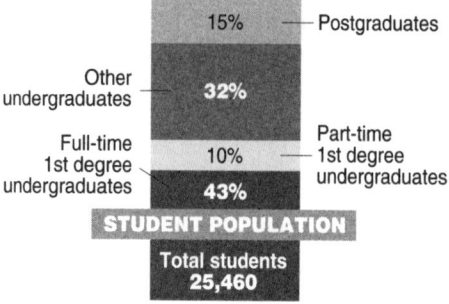

STUDENT POPULATION

Postgraduates 15%

Other undergraduates 32%

Full-time 1st degree undergraduates 43%

Part-time 1st degree undergraduates 10%

Total students 25,460

more the mature type of student. People who have been out in the world. There are also lots of international students, many of whom come on exchange. It's a much more cosmpolitan atmosphere than in Leeds University.'

ACADEMIA

Consistent with the emphasis on work experience, a number of courses involve a language dimension and some a participating European university, like International Business Finance or European Marketing (run in cahoots with Hochschule Bremen, Germany, or the Groupe ESC Normandie at Caen, France). Again, most students acquire

ACADEMIC EXCELLENCE
TEACHING :
(Rated Excellent or 17+ out of 24)
Business/Mgt, Economics **24**
Education, Subjectas Allied to **23** Medicine
Drama/Dance/Cinematics, **22** Sport
Civil Engineering, Building, **21** Land & Property Mgt, Art & Design, Nursing
Psychology **20**
Modern Languages, **19** Communication & Media Studies
RESEARCH:
Top grades 5/5* **None**

Street, besides incorporating both universities, take in BBC North (TV and Radio) and **The Dry Dock**, a pub in a converted barge anchored to a grassy knoll. Just before we arrived it had been attacked by robbers; a security man had been coshed with the inevitable blunt instrument. Now there we were, bombarded aurally by ambulance sirens tearing to and from the nearby Leeds Infirmary, left in no doubt that this is the centre of something.

Next door to Union HQ is a massive, new £20-million development, the new 6-floor, 9,000 sq metre LMU Learning Centre. Alongside welcome areas, shops, information points and LMU's **Gallery & Studio Theatre**, the centre, we hear, has been designed in eco-friendly style. In this urban vortex, will it make much difference?

Temporally there is confusion here on a Friday, when the world turns its back on modernity and visits 1970 again. Kids arrive from miles around to *Love Train @* **Town & Country Club** in nearby Cookridge Street.

STUDENT PROFILE

'The demographics are quite different to Leeds University. A large proportion of students at our Leeds site are part-time. They'll come from the Yorkshire area, maybe do evening courses. The full-timers, who come from all over, tend to be

skills in computing during the duration. Other courses aimed at specific careers include Public Relations, Tourism Management, Landscape Architecture, Urban Development. Then there's a range of civil engineering and built environment courses; another of health studies courses, including Mental Health Nursing, Physiotherapy, Environmental Health, Dietetics; and an interesting raft of electronics courses – including Electronics, Media & Technology. It is all thoroughly vocational; the ethos is 'putting students to work'.

In pursuit of this, Leeds Met is involved with Teaching Company schemes, putting recent top graduates into local companies with uni resource back-up, creating all kinds of partnerships and technology transfer schemes. Up the road, Leeds University is also concerned with the employment destinations of its graduates, but the Met is, by choice, offering access to a different kind of student: 'we want as wide a variety of people as possible to benefit from the opportunities provided by the university,' they say.

UNIVERSITY/STUDENT PROFILE	
University since	**1992**
Situation/style	**City sites**
Student population	**25,460**
Full-time undergraduates	**10,840**
- mature	**40%**
- overseas	**2%**
- male/female	**48/52**
- state sector intake	**93%**
- non-traditional student intake	**14%**
- drop-out rate	**6%**
- undergraduate applications	**Down 1%**
see Introduction for key to tables	

WHAT IT'S REALLY LIKE	
UNIVERSITY:	
Social Life	★★★★★
Campus scene	**Sporty, spicy, action focused**
Student Union services	**Average**
Politics	**Student issues, interest low**
Sport	**Competitive & sport-for-all**
National team position	**21st**
Sport facilities	**Good**
Arts opportunities	**Drama par, rest below par**
Student newspaper	**Leeds Student**
Student radio	**LSR fm**
Radio 1 awards	**Marketing/Promo Best factual prog**
Nightclub	**The Met**
Bars	**Met Bar, Kirkstall Brewery, Becketts Sports**
Union ents	**Blast!, Event Horizon, Under The Influence, Star, Electric Head, The Bop, Cheese**
Union clubs/societies	**49**
Smoking policy	**Union OK**
Parking	**Poor**
CITY:	
Entertainment	★★★★★
Scene	**Wild**
Town/gown relations	**Average**
Risk of violence	**Average**
Cost of living	**Low**
Student concessions	**Abundant**
Survival + 2 nights out	**£60-£80 pw**
Part-time work campus/town	**Good/excellent**

SOCIAL SCENE

Live! magazine voted them Best Gig Venue in the country, and as Leeds student Naveed Raja admits, 'LMU's Met Bar hosts legendary student events.' It is a huge area, a whole floor of the building which includes an enormous bar, café and the concert hall itself, which has a stage, decent dressing rooms and a built-in DJ studio block, besides formidable sound and lighting equipment. The whole thing is fully sound proofed, floating in plastic so that the

> *There are completely different cultures in the two universities in Leeds. This is a centre for applied learning and the place with the reputation for nightlife. You'll find no middle-class socialism at Leeds Met.*

Learning Centre next door remains oblivious.

Currently, LMU sweeps the board in this city for ents. 'Anyone who's anyone plays Leeds Met. Leeds Uni are better at things political,' is the considered student opinion. 'Ents is a totally professional area,' Kate Denby tells me. 'Everyone who works there is a paid professional, although we do have two students who work part-time for us in an events capacity, qualified to do lighting for example. We generally do nine events a week across all three venues, so there's a lot to organise. Our main venue holds 1,500 people; it's the whole of the floor below us.

'On Wednesday it's *OTT*. No gimmicks, no pretensions...just *OTT* – basically an '80s night; all the sports teams play on Wednesday and end up going to *OTT*. It's cheesy, a tradition, and mainly LMU, though some do come down from LU.'

On Friday it's *Star* (a club-night of high-profile DJs 'taking indie clubs to another dimension'); and on Saturday (appropriately enough) it's *Saturday Night*, a cheesy night. Nothing has changed since last year – and why should it? – *Saturday Night* has been a fixture since it was the Leeds Poly bop. The clubnights, the recent live acts – Divine Comedy, Mark & Lard, Republica, Jungle Bros, Billy Bragg, the comedy and movie nights, big-screen footie and private parties add up to an ents programme rarely surpassed elsewhere.

SPORT At Beckett Park you'll find the Regional Gymnastics Centre, two sports halls, gyms, swimming pool, athletics track, floodlit games areas, tennis courts, etc. A successful Lottery bid has secured £1 million for floodlit synthetic turf pitches and an upgrade of the athletics stadium to international standard. Competition takes place in all sports, at all levels. 'There's also a students union out at Beckett Park,' informs Kate Denby, 'with a bar, 450-500 capacity (sports theme), some accommodation (it used to be wholly accommodation but over the past few years it's become lecture theatres, offices, course buildings).'

TOWN Leeds is an exciting city. It is compact and there is something in it for everyone, but how you handle it will depend on whence you come. 'If you look at any city there are areas which you say, "Don't walk through there at night or in the day with your wallet showing and your earphones

AT A GLANCE	
ACADEMIC FILE:	
Subjects assessed	**25**
Excellent	**56%**
Average requirements	**200 points**
Students-staff ratio	**19:1**
First/2:1 degree pass rate	**50%**
ACCOMMODATION FILE:	
Guarantee to freshers	**60%**
Style	**Halls, flats**
Approx price range pw	**£53-£70**
City rent pw	**£30-£65**

JOBS

The point about LMU is that the uni is designed to get its students employed. 'There are completely different cultures in the two universities in Leeds,' began Kate when I pressed her for a student profile. 'This is a centre for applied learning. I'm doing a degree in Public Relations. It's hands on. What you generally find is a lot of students go on placement. They might have a year's placement or a day each week placement. I have no lectures on a Thursday and go into a company and work one day a week. You can do that sort of thing off your own bat or you can get placements via the placements office. People who come here have a

in,"' says Kate. 'Hyde Park is not great. Headingley is probably the better area for students. It's the Woodhouse area on the other side of Hyde Park, with Little London and Chapeltown nearby, that are quite dodgy areas. You wouldn't advise people to walk through. We have instances. On the back of the union cards we have the number of a taxi firm that is endorsed by us and by Leeds University. They are a reputable company and we work quite closely with them. If you call that number and you don't have any money on you, you just hand that card over as your fare; they get that card to us and when you come to pick up your card you pay us for the fare. We advise avoiding private hire taxi companies; there have been instances... We also run a women's minibus service from Beckett Park campus, where the bus service isn't quite so good as in the city.'

PILLOW TALK

Uni-owned/managed halls or flats, self-catered student houses, private lodgings. They can't guarantee all first years accommodation, but along with Leeds Uni they belong to UNIPOL, Student Homes, an accommodation bureau at 8-12 Fenton Street, Leeds LS1 3EA, which will help students find their own (Tel: 01426 981 107). LMU are working hard on enhancing their own accommodation. The £17-million residential development, Kirkstall Brewery, has two squash courts, a weight training and fitness centre, a two-floor bar complex (capacity around 1,000), regular weekly and one-off events, laundry and shop.

WHERE GRADUATES END UP	
14% Health/Social Work,	Key Areas
11% Education,	
8% Finance,	
8% Wholesale/Retail,	
6% Manufacture,	
6% Public Admin	
Hotel/Restaurant, Sport*,	Niche Areas
Business/Management,	
Telecom*, Property,	
Legal, Library/Archival,	
Construction, Architecture	
*indicates Top 10 Graduate Provider	
Approximate employed	**91%**

goal! They know what they want to do. We've got an Events Management course, for example, very popular, been going for about five years. And Tourism Management and people going into leisure studies. It's across the board – we've got sport, business, computing.'

GETTING THERE

☞ By road: M1, A1 or M62. Good coach services.
☞ By rail: Newcastle, 1:45; London Euston, 2:30; Birmingham New Street, 2:20.
☞ By air: Leeds/Bradford Airport.
☞ By coach: London, 4:00; Edinburgh, 6:00; Bristol, 5:45.

STUDENT LEICESTER – THE CITY

One of the most fab things about Leicester is its location right in the centre of the country, which means nowhere seems too far away. No matter how

much you want to get away from home, it is mentally and financially beneficial, especially in the first year, if home is not hundreds of miles away. Again, whether from the north or south, you will feel comfortable in Leicester because there is an excellent mix of people, more than 30,000 of them students.

Leicester is still sometimes unfairly seen as having little more to it than Walkers Crisps and Gary Linekar, but the city's profile is always on the up, be it through its football and rugby teams, Comedy Festival (nationally acclaimed comedians attract a 20,000+ audience), curries or nightclubs. Leicester is compact enough to retain a strong community atmosphere and modern enough to combine this with all you could want from a major city.

There is always something going on. It hosts the largest Caribbean Carnival outside of London and the biggest Hindu Festival outside of India. If you stay over the summer, the Abbey Park Festival is a fantastic occasion to get drunk in the sun, and that's before you look at theatre, cinema and so on.

LIVE VENUES

De Montfort University's **Arena** was voted 4th best University venue recently and regularly attracts high calibre bands to what John Peel calls his 'favourite student venue.' Thursdays and Saturdays host *Kinky Afro* and the *Big Cheese* respectively where 1,200 students get extremely drunk together.

Other gig venues include the very swish **De Montfort Hall** (named after the 13th-century Earl of Leicester, not the uni), popular with the bigger acts (Stereophonics, Ash, The Charlatans, Elvis Costello), and Leicester University's **The Venue** has seen Ben Folds Five and Ooberman recently. It, too, has its popular club nights (*Mega*, *Reagans*, *Brighton Beach*). The world famous **Princess Charlotte** has hosted Sebadoh, Gay Dad, Add n to (x), E-Z Rollers, Badly Drawn Boy and Arab Strap and features numerous club nights. **The Factory** and **The Shed** book small and local acts and are supportive of student bands, so get your tapes in!

PUBS & CLUBS

Leicester has a diverse range of clubs and pubs. Everybody has their own favourite and new pubs are opening all the time, but mention might be made of the **Swan & Rushes** close to DMU Uni, and the local haunt for Leicester Uni students – the **Wyvern** in Granby Street. Go to Market Square for traditional pubs (**The Globe**, **The Bank**, **Yates's Wine Lodge**) and for Irish – **O'Neill's** and **Molly O'Grady's**. It's a case of take your pick. Leicester's two late bars are **Bar Gaudi** and **Poo na na** for chilled out drinks when the pubs have closed.

The club scene is currently nights such as *All Points North* and *Get It On*. **Flaming Colossus** (host of *All Points North*) regularly features DJs such as

Boy George, Brandon Block, Pete Heller and Phats and Small. **Junction 21** is quite similar on Saturdays, but on Fridays has a more beats-style night (the aforementioned *Get It On*, where Midfield General, Bentley Rhythm Ace, and David Holmes have played). **Streetlife** is Leicester's main gay nightclub and has the soundest door policy in the city. You can lose the plot at various all-nighters but it's best to check flyers for one-off events. These normally take place at **Club City**, **The Playground** and **Starlight 2001**.

Fans of the less specialist, more mainstream clubs should try **Kudos, Creation** or **Life** (Leicester Uni do promotions here), **Brannigans**, **The Rhythm Room** or **Zanzibar**. The ever popular **Mosquito Coast** is the most student friendly of these. If you're a bit of an indie/guitar hero than Abbey Street houses **The Fan Club** and **Oxygen**, where nights alternate indie, rock, retro.

CINEMA, THEATRE, COMEDY

Leicester has three main theatres: **The Haymarket** often previews London productions and **The Phoenix** swaps between performance and cinema in an absolutely jammed weekly programme that features dance, film festivals, operas and comedy. **The Y Theatre** also has a diverse programme that is always worth checking out and occasionally has nicely relaxed music nights. A gem. All the theatres are on the major comedy circuits where you can see the likes of Dylan Moran and Stewart Lee perform. Granby Street has a **Jongleurs** comedy club and the Arena hosts *The Gug Club* every other Wednesday.

There are two multiplexes in Leicester. **Warners** at the **Meridian** leisure complex is twenty minutes drive away and next door to a Fatty Arbuckles, McDonalds if you want to make a night of it. A very similar arrangement can be found at Freemans Common where there are two pubs, a restaurant and a twelve screen **Odeon**.

SHOPPING AROUND

You can't talk about Leicester and shopping without mention of Europe's largest covered market. From clothes to food, some days are better than others and you'll have to be prepared to get to know when to go there for what, but this is where Leicester's real roots are, and their vegetables aren't bad either. Ask the Linekars, Gary used to work here and the family still maintains a stall.

Alternative shopping may be had in St Martin's Square, just behind the market and in Silver Street (hippy and studenty things and The Silver Arcade for secondhand /designer clothes).

Rob Malyan and Amanda Dodson

UNIVERSITY OF LEICESTER

The University of Leicester
Mayors Walk
University Road
Leicester LE1 7RH

TEL 0116 252 5281
FAX 0116 252 2447
EMAIL admissions@le.ac.uk
WEB www.le.ac.uk

Leicester Students' Union
Percy Gee Building
University Road
Leicester LE1 7RH

TEL 0116 223 1111
FAX 0116 223 1112
EMAIL lusu@le.ac.uk
WEB www.le.ac.uk

VAG VIEW

*L*eicester University is flanked by twenty acres of parkland a short walk from the city centre. It sees itself as the more pukka of the city's two unis, the student attitude being, 'De Montfort's the Poly,' and the De Montfort attitude being, 'There is still something of an air of institutional superiority, them being Leicester's redbrick.' However, there's no snobbery involved, for Leicester is in fact one of the government's elite access universities – one of the few which manage to attract students from a wide range of cultural backgrounds while at the same time maintaining the highest teaching and research standards, a low drop-out rate (a mere 5%) and excellent graduate employment figures. What students immediately appreciate is that Leicester has one of the best unions in the country, and not just for the excellent ents laid on – though that, most definitely, too.

CAMPUS

'The main university campus is situated conveniently close to the city centre and within

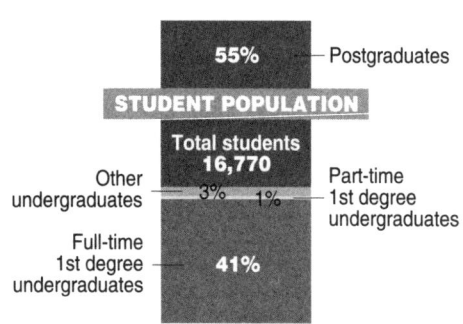

SUBJECT AREAS (%)

Humanities/Languages 23
Combined 4
Medicine 14
Sciences 25
Engineering/Technology 4
Maths & Computer 5
Social Studies incl. Law 25

STUDENT POPULATION
Total students 16,770
Postgraduates 55%
Other undergraduates 3%
Part-time 1st degree undergraduates 1%
Full-time 1st degree undergraduates 41%

UNIVERSITY/STUDENT PROFILE	
University since	**1957**
Situation/style	**City campus**
Student population	**16,770**
Full-time undergraduates	**6,930**
- mature	**8%**
- overseas	**7%**
- male/female	**49/51**
- state sector intake	**85%**
- non-traditional student intake	**11%**
- drop-out rate	**5%**
- undergraduate applications	**Down 2%**
see Introduction for key to tables	

walking distance of all university halls of residence,' writes Christina McGear. 'Unlike many inner city universities, everything you need is situated on campus including banks, restaurants, cafés, shops, the university library and union. This means that you never have far to walk between lectures.'

STUDENT PROFILE

Student type? They'll tell you many are from the Southeast – which is true, with a number from independent schools, good, white middle-class kids – and then they'll admit that there's a huge contingent from Wales. Why Wales? Because Leicester is far enough from Wales to make you feel like you are away and yet not too far for discomfort. And maybe that's as much of the truth as you are likely to get. For Leicester is the choice of students from more than 100 countries and has always been convenient to a wide cross-section of UK journeymen, being sited along that zippy M1 corridor and not too far north even for the softest southerner.

ACADEMIA

With 81% of its teaching assessments either Excellent or scoring 18+ out of 24, Leicester's teaching record is first class and backed by an annual £3 million spend in the university library, an excellent Student Learning Centre with workshops and self-learning materials designed to develop study skills and a well-equipped Language Centre supporting the uni's policy of 'languages for all'.

There are five faculties – Arts, Law, Medicine, Science, Social Sciences. Top teaching assessments are in Economics, Sport, Psychology, Physics, Politics, History of Art, Maths, and Biosciences. The most recent assessment in Social Sciences, for Communication & Media gives credibility to the Communications & Society BSc established out of the uni's Centre for Mass Communication Research. The research centre also produces MAs in Mass Communications, both residential and distance learning (a Leicester postgrad speciality).

Its Faculty of Medicine, which with Physics and American Studies recently clocked 23 out of a maximum 24 points on inspection, would be a jewel in anyone's crown, and was one of three medical schools that have just been given the go-ahead to form new joint schools with other universities. Leicester's partner is Warwick. Part of the deal is a fast track medical degree for Biological Science graduates.

Their research record in Pharmacology gained a Grade 5 (international renown) in the assessments and shows up in our *Employment* box, page 275, as a significant niche area. The uni also has a reputation in the fields of physics and astronomy, claiming the largest uni-based space research centre in Europe and playing a leading role in the creation of the National Space Science Centre (the major Millennium landmark project for East Midlands). The Challenger Learning Centre opened in 1999,

> *What students immediately appreciate is that Leicester University has one of the best unions in the country, and not just for the excellent ents they lay on – though that, most definitely, too.*

ACADEMIC EXCELLENCE

TEACHING :
(Rated Excellent or 17+ out of 24)

History, Law, Chemistry, English.	**Excellent**
Economics, Leisure & Sport, Psychology	24
Physics, Politics, Medicine, American Studies	23
History of Art, Maths, Biosciences	22
German, Communications/Media	21
Italian, General Engineering	20
Sociology, French	19

RESEARCH:

Genetics,	**Grade 5***
Pharmacology, Biochemistry,	**Grade 5**
Biology, Physics, Pure Maths, Applied Maths, General Eng, Law, Economics, English, Archaeology, History	

the rest in 2001. There are three degrees in physics, space science and technology, the department gaining a Queen's Award in 1994 for its 'world class teaching, research and consultancy programme ... practical results from advanced thinking.'

The uni is now the third largest provider of postgraduate teaching in Britain, a reputation marked historically by the fact that genetic fingerprinting was developed here. It is also home to the Richard Attenborough Centre for Disability and the Arts.

SOCIAL SCENE

Unlike at self-contained Nottingham or Lough-borough, entertainment-wise, competition here is with the city. When we appeared, the union was taking the challenge of a couple of new pubs seriously, but with a confident gleam in its eye, for when it comes to home-grown ents Leicester SU has a pedigree.

When the house scene was in its infancy their *High Spirits* club night travelled to **Es Paradis** in Ibiza, to the **Queen Club** in Paris and the **Venue** in Jersey. There must have been some energy around in those days. Even today, Leicester maintains a full-time, non-student ents manager with two

UNIVERSITY:	
Social Life	★★★★★
Campus scene	**Lively, traditional, excellent vibes**
Student Union services	**Good**
Politics	**Involved**
Sport	**Competitive**
National team position	**54th**
Sport facilities	**Good**
Arts opportunities	**All excellent**
Student newspaper	**Ripple**
Student radio	**LUSH FM**
Student TV	**LUST**
Nightclub	**Element**
Bars	**Redfearn, Oasis, Mirage**
Union ents	**Urban Music, Reagans, Brighton Beach**
Union clubs/societies	**120**
Most popular society	**Law**
Smoking policy	**Union OK**
Parking	**Poor**
CITY:	
Entertainment	★★★★
City scene	**Top town - clubs, pubs, curries**
Town/gown relations	**OK**
Risk of violence	**Average-high**
Cost of living	**Average**
Student concessions	**Good**
Survival + 2 nights out	**£60 pw**
Part-time work campus/town	**Good**

assistants, though, along with student taste, the focus has shifted – to the *Mega*, with theme nights and giveaways, and *Reagans*, an '80s sell-out night.

'Union ents happen at the **Venue**, at **Element** (newly refurbished) and the **Redfearn** pub,' writes Christine. 'There's also a Monday contract with one of the clubs in town, **Creation** – student-only nights offering cheap drinks and often a theme party. Tuesday nights are well spent in the **Life** nightclub in town, and there's a good pub quiz at the Redfearn. The most popular union night is Wednesday's night, *Reagans*, it takes place in the Venue. Thursday night takes place in Element: *Lollipop* is '70s, soul and disco music. *Urban Music* is the new Saturday soul, swing, hip hop, R&B and garage night. *Soulsocial*'s on Monday. *Enemy* is part of Mega – a huge event at the on a Friday night. The music varies from chart and dance to house and garage with drinks on cheap promotion. In the past, *Mega* has welcomed special guests including Radio One DJs, Timmy Malet and Thomas from *Big Brother*. There may be a theme night too. For the

weekend, *Locomotion* ('60s/'70s) in **Elements** is the big night.'

In addition to all of this there are special events throughout the year, such as *Brighton Beach* – 'mods, rockers, pills and '60s sun, sea and sand...a chance for Leicester's perpetually drunk undergrads to escape the endless hell of '80s cheese and '90s pop,' as student newspaper *Ripple* puts it.

'There are also endless clubs and societies to join,' writes Christine, 'ranging from Dance and Drama to religious societies to completely obscure, imaginative ones.'

As befits the seriousness with which the union goes about its business, there is also a good campaigning arm. Campaigns this year include *Think Global* – getting students to appreciate the cultural context at Leicester and think internationally; *Be Heard* – campaign involvement; *Money Matters* – managing money and 'Grants not Fees'; *No Quality Without Equality* – prejudice and equal opportunity; *Welfare and Well Being* – student safety, drugs.

Student safety has been a problem: bottle-wielding thugs at their Mega night a couple of years ago and now seven students attacked in one week in Victoria Park after dark, one stabbed in the arm after refusing to hand over his mobile phone.

SPORT is big, though local competition is with Nottingham rather than international-level Loughborough, and developments are now afoot to lock horns more meaningfully with De Montfort University. A *Varsity Day* is planned. There's a sports hall, Greenhouse 1, in the Charles Wilson Building on campus, and new rugby, lacrosse and football pitches at Stoughton Road, east of campus, close to Manor Road Sports Centre (Greenhouse 2) and the accommodation halls.

TOWN Continues Christina: 'There's an impressive blend of cultural diversity, a diverse arts scene as well as an electric nightlife. The city centre is not as vast or as imposing as say Manchester, but it's big enough and crucially varied enough to provide something for everyone.

Take a trip around the ancient Roman Jewry wall or to the **New Walk** museum, its Egyptian and Dinosaur exhibits really are something to see. For the compulsive shopper, Leicester offers a mix of most traditional high street stores and the more interesting curio shops and bazaars.

'For food and drink, Leicester has it all. Endless Italian, Indian and Mexican establishments as well as some highly recommended English restaurants too. Alternatively, why not try Thai, Cantonese or Nepalese? It's all here in superabundance.

'De Montfort Uni have their favourite town

AT A GLANCE

ACADEMIC FILE:

Subjects assessed	**26**
Excellent	**81%**
Average requirements	**280 points**
Students-staff ratio	**14:1**
First/2:1 degree pass rate	**58%**

ACCOMMODATION FILE:

Guarantee to freshers	**100%**
Style	**Halls, houses**
Approx price range pw	**£37-£88.90**
City rent pw	**£35-£50**

week for a room in a shared house.'

JOBS

Leicester graduates are popular with employers. Most go into the health industry or into commerce (financial activities, accountancy), but the uni's sound record in a number of niche areas – media among them (Ripple, LUSH and LUST – newspaper, radio and TV stations) – ensure a number of other interesting options.

GETTING THERE
☛ By road: M1/J21 or J22. Good coach services.
☛ By rail: London St Pancras, 1:20; Manchester

clubs and we have ours – we're affiliated with **Kudos**, sell tickets for them, split the profits. Then there's **Mosquito Coast** and bars like **Last Plantagenet**, the **Rhythm Rooms**. If you want to see where Leicester students drink, take a trip down Granby Street.'

See also *Student Leicester*, page 270.

PILLOW TALK

A record number of 4,000 freshers joined up this year causing consternation among the accommodation managers, Beaumont hall apparently having its music room, common room and games room turned into dormitories. We are assured this was a mere blip in an otherwise serene scene. Housing is plentiful and various, the range reflected in that of cost – £37 per week for plain, self-catered rooms in a house, to £88.90 per week for catered, single rooms with en-suite facilities. 'All halls are within walking distance of the campus,' writes Christine, 'and are served regularly by the number 80 bus. Beaumont Hall in Oadby is one of the most attractive, set amongst beautiful botanical gardens. Cost of rented private accommodation varies between £35 to £50 per

WHERE GRADUATES END UP

17% Health (incl Medicine), Key Areas
11% Finance,
10% Wholesale/Retail,
9% Manufacturing,
9% Public Admin,
6% Education,
6% Personnel,
5% Computer
Accountancy, Defence, Niche Areas
Legal, Advertising,
Chem/Pharmaceutical,
Telecom, Library/Archival,
Market Research,
Publishing, Radio/TV

Approximate employed **94%**

Piccadilly, 1:30; Sheffield, 1:30; Birmingham New Street, 1:00; Nottingham, 0:30.
☛ By air: Bus from Birmingham International and East Midlands International Airports.
☛ By coach: London, 2:30; Leeds, 3:00; Cardiff, 4:10.

UNIVERSITY OF LINCOLN

The University of Lincoln
Brayford Pool
Lincoln LN6 7TS

TEL 01522 882000
FAX 01522 882088
EMAIL admissions@humber.ac.uk
WEB www.lincoln.ac.uk

Lincoln Students' Union
Brayford Pool
Lincoln LN6 7TS

TEL 01522 882000
FAX 01522 882088
EMAIL (see website)
WEB www.ulstudentco-op.com

SUBJECT AREAS (%)

Health Subjects
Biological Sciences
Medicine 0.2%
Combined
Agriculture
Physical Sciences
Engineering/
Technology
Creative Arts — 24
1 3 2 1 2 2
19
10
1
12 23
Building/
Architecture
Humanities
Social Studies Business Computer
incl. Law

VAG VIEW

*T*his year sees a change of name (from Lincoln & Humberside), the scrapping of plans for a £50-million campus development in Hull, the sale of the old Humberside campus to Hull Uni, and a move down south to Lincoln, scooping up De Montfort's Lincoln-based faculties of Art & Design and Agriculture on the way. Says

UNIVERSITY/STUDENT PROFILE	
University since	**1992**
Situation/style	**City campus**
Student population	**14,330**
Full-time undergraduates	**6,590**
- mature	**47%**
- overseas	**6%**
- male/female	**46/54**
- state sector intake	**97%**
- non-traditional student intake	**17%**
- drop-out rate	**12%**
- undergraduate applications	**Up 15%**
*see Introduction for key to tables	

Vice-Chancellor Professor David Chiddick, the move 'will sweep away all the confusion in one go.'

One can see what he means. The Humberside campus in Hull and the Lincoln campus were miles apart not only geographically but in every sense. The University of Lincolnshire and Humberside was a disjointed concept at best. And what a move! Think of the city of Lincoln, doesn't it remind you of Canterbury or York, both highly successful olde worlde cathedral seats

of learning? To fresher Caroline Stocks when she first set eyes on it, the place seemed promising if rather sedate: 'It's easy to see why so many pensioners flock to Lincoln during the summer, or why the annual Derby-and-Joan Christmas outing is to the town's festive market. There's the majestic cathedral and ancient castle, which sit on a hill overlooking the town, with its tiny old shops on cobbled streets. There are the visitors who stroll along the castle ramparts before taking a look at the 19th-century prison museum. There's the Brayford Pool, where swans paddle lazily, pausing only to let pleasure boats or brightly painted barges pass. And overlooking this pool... there are the university buildings...£32 million worth, and very modern.'

Alas, even five years after the first university building went up, this city has still not made the transition to university seat. However cobbled and cloistered Lincoln may seem, the large, modern, glass-fronted, conference-centre style university building refuses not only to draw the city to itself in spirit, but even physically to fit in.

And another thing, why, one wonders, if the move from Hull was supposed to be a total uproot, were 1,500 students left stranded in the centre of Hull city, with masses of money being pumped into facilities for them up there?

CAMPUS

'The campus in Lincoln, situated on the riverside in this picturesque cathedral city cost £32 million, so it's pretty impressive,' reports Paula McManus, 'although sometimes it feels more like an airport or shopping centre than a university: security guards are constantly on patrol to stop any damage being

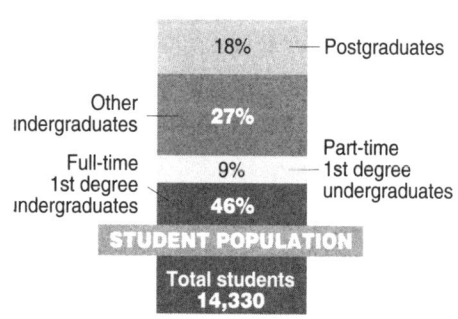

18% — Postgraduates
Other undergraduates — 27%
Part-time
Full-time 1st degree undergraduates — 9% — 1st degree undergraduates
46%
STUDENT POPULATION
Total students
14,330

done to this sparkling new building."

STUDENT PROFILE

Recruitment has been successful among social groups that do not traditionally consider university, around a third of non-mature entrants coming from the middle to lower end of the spectrum and a high 17% from so-called 'low-participation neighbourhoods'. Most applicants are, however mature. Applications were up 15% last year – fourth highest increase, in fact.

ACADEMIA

Faculties now offered are Health & Life Sciences;

ACADEMIC EXCELLENCE

TEACHING :
(Rated Excellent or 17+ out of 24)

Education	**24**
Politics	**22**
Tourism, Health Studies, Psychology	**21**
Food Science, Art & Design	**20**
Agric/Agricultural Sciences	**19**
Engineering	**18**

RESEARCH :
Top grades 5/5* **None**

AT A GLANCE

ACADEMIC FILE:

Assessments	**20**
Excellent	**45%**
Average requirements	**180 points**
Students-staff ratio	**15:1**
First/2:1 degree pass rate	**43%**

ACCOMMODATION FILE:

Guarantee to freshers	**100%, on or off campus**
Style	**Halls, flats**
Catered	**None**
En-suite	**85%**
Price range pw	**£54-£60**
City rent pw	**£35-£40**

Social Sciences & Law; Business & Management; Art, Architecture & Design; Computing Sciences; Media & Communication. Business and computing are the biggest draw at this stage, but see also *Jobs,* page 278.

'Lectures are small, intimate,' writes Caroline just prior to the influx from Hull. 'It's hard to imagine how the anticipated extra students – at present there are 3,500 undergraduates, a number expected soon to double – will fit into the two lecture halls. A good aspect is that you invariably have seminars with the lecturer rather than a PhD student, so if you don't understand something in the lecture you can discuss it in seminar. Students also have a seminar on essay writing, presentation, and basic computer skills. These seem dull and

> *Recruitment has been successful among social groups that do not traditionally consider university. There are seminars on how to student. Lectures are small, intimate. But how far are uni and city up and running as a student scene?*

extra work, but they are actually helpful.

' The library is adequate. At present, student numbers mean you can usually find a computer to work on. [The uni in fact claims a student to computer ratio of 8:1.] Practical courses such as Media Production and Computing are reliant on computers, and there are separate teaching rooms with more PCs. The only problem with computer provision is that there is not 24-hour access.'

Language and cultural experience is an integral part of the recipe. Study abroad arrangements are made in Europe and Australia; formal exchange arrangements are made with sixty-two EU universities or colleges; 25% of first degree students take a language as part of their course and 15% spend six months or more abroad.

SOCIAL SCENE

Reports Caroline: 'Freshers Week for me was pretty forgettable. The £30 price tag for 'Freshers Week wristbands' seemed pretty steep, particularly as most of the organised events took place in city pubs, and disgruntled, dissatisfied we supped watered-down shots of tequila. The pub crawl down Steep Hill (do not let anyone tell you that Lincoln is completely flat – this hill seems almost vertical, it even has rest stops half way up!) was an experience, particularly as it began with an open-topped bus ride in the pouring rain. Things will get better for future generations, I expect. The Students' Union building was only opened last year. I am sure the university will improve organisation as it ages.

WHAT IT'S REALLY LIKE	
UNIVERSITY:	
Social Life	★★
Campus scene	**Still shaping up**
Student Union services	**Embryonic**
Politics	**Student issues**
Sport	**Establishing**
National team position	**127th**
Sport facilities	**Good sports hall**
Arts opportunities	**Film OK**
Student magazine	**Bullet Surprise**
Student radio	**Siren FM**
Venue & bar	**Delph Bar**
Union ents	**Developing**
Union clubs/societies	**30**
Smoking policy	**Bars, halls OK**
Parking	**Poor**
CITY:	
Entertainment	★★
Scene	**OK pubs, clubs**
Town/gown relations	**Average**
Risk of violence	**Low**
Cost of living	**Average**
Student concessions	**Average**
Survival + 2 nights out	**£40 pw**
Part-time work campus/town	**Average**

STUDENTS' UNION 'The union bar is in the same building as the Sports Centre. The bar is reminiscent of a school hall. The Sports Centre is good, it has football and hockey pitches and a gym, but it is open to the public, students are only really welcomed at off-peak times. Why so, if the centre is supposed to be a facility for those at university?

SPORT 'Lincoln isn't the best place if you are keen on competitive sport. There are hockey, football, and rugby teams, but purely because of the 'newness' of the uni, these teams aren't yet established. We are not major contenders yet against other universities.

TOWN 'So we got into town. At the moment students have made a limited impact: businesses are only just beginning to cater for them, and the university is itself so new that organising social events seems to be a difficult task. Basically, Lincoln is a safe, quiet town; perfect if you don't want to be in the centre of the action. It has many pubs, the best are the **Varsity** (which always has student offers), **Yates** (somewhere to take your parents for dinner when they visit), **Walkabout** (a great place to watch sport), and the **Vaults** (an underground establishment where you can't use your mobile phone without a bearded biker-type shouting at you, though their Czech Republic beer

is cheap). The union bar offers pints at £1.50, and one day it should be a decent concert venue as it has the capacity to hold 300 people.

'The best of the clubs (of which there are few) is **Pulse & Ritzy**, which plays pop. **The Avenue** also plays pop music and has R&B nights, but the décor can be off-putting. **Po-na-na** has '80s, indie and rock nights, and for *Gatecrasher* wannabes there's dark and dingy **Sugar Cubes**.

'Although there's **Pizza Hut** and **McDonalds**, eating out is aimed at day-trippers rather than students. For cheap, edible food, the best place is the refectory inside the **Atrium**.

'Visiting Nottingham for a night out only costs £7 return, and although Lincoln has no motorways to let you travel anywhere quickly, it is easy enough to follow the country roads to Newark, Sheffield, or Skegness for a day beside the sea.

'The cost if living is not especially high: I am able to survive on about £30 a week. It's not necessary to budget for transport, as everything is so small and compact.'

PILLOW TALK

There are already 1,000 self-catering places available. The university guarantees to arrange accommodation on and off campus to all first year students, generally in halls of residence and apartments. All campus accommodation is self-catered – subsidised restaurants are only five minutes away – 85% is en suite. Price per week ranges from £54 to £60.

'Freshers live in self-catered apartments in a student village,' Caroline tells us. 'You are put with a wide cross section of people, which can mean that your flatmates are so different from you that you have nothing in common. The buildings are in good condition, although the flats don't get visited by a cleaner. Remember to complain if you're not happy about your accommodation. As part of a flat of girls on the ground floor, we didn't feel safe as drunken people hammered on our windows at night. After complaining to the Accommodation Services, security guards made more regular patrols. Private accommodation is reasonably priced (about £35-£40).'

JOBS

Part-time work: 'If money is a bit short, then you'll probably look for a job. Most people work in the local pubs or restaurants, though finding work can often be a struggle. The new multiplex cinema will certainly offer more jobs to students.'

Graduate jobs: the uni's degrees in Animation, Architecture, Architectural Technology, Fine Art, Graphic Design (including design for TV and film), Illustration, Interactive Design, Interior Design,

Museum/Exhibition Design and Phonic Art (a sound-based fine art course) take many of Lincoln's graduates into the niche areas shown in our *Employment* box – the TV and film industries, into radio, architecture, advertising and industrial design (see box opposite).

The success in the personnel line reminds us of their Human Resources degree and the 6% health provision of the Health Studies, Physiotherapy line and, indeed, that little nugget of a BSc (Hons) Neuroscience, the only strictly medical provision.

GETTING THERE

☛ By road: from north, A15; northwest, A57, A46 Lincoln by-pass.
☛ By rail: King's Cross, 2:00; Nottingham, 1:00.
☛ By coach: London, 4:10.

WHERE GRADUATES END UP	
13% Wholesale/Retail,	Key Areas
13% Public Admin*,	
11% Manufacturing,	
8% Finance,	
6% Health/Social Work,	
5% Education,	
5% Personnel	
Agric/Forestry, Legal,	Niche Areas
Advertising, Architecture,	
Publishing, Radio/TV,	
Eng/Industrial Design	

*indicates Top 10 Graduate Provider

Approximate employed **92%**

STUDENT LIVERPOOL – THE CITY

Liverpool is a city with a thriving alternative student scene, clustered around three main epicentres: the city centre, Lark Lane and Penny Lane/Smithdown Road. Here's a whistle-stop guide to the hidden gems.

STAR PUB

Despite being part of the tired Firkin chain of pubs, the **Finch & Firkin** (Smithdown Road) is one of Liverpool's most popular student pubs, due to its proximity to the centre of student population. **The Pilgrim** is a basement pub in Pilgrim Street offering cheap beer and passable Sunday lunch fare. It's quiet, safe and pleasant – a good place to chill the morning after the night before. Lark Lane's **Albert Hotel** is a busy, smoky student local with a friendly atmosphere and good draught beers. **The Dovedale Towers** on Penny Lane is a distinctive castle-like pub that should be avoided on Friday and Saturday nights. During the day it's a comfortable haven for skiving students.

STAR BAR

Fleet Street's **Rocomodo's** (Modo's) is suave and modern. It serves posh cocktails at decent prices, is often filled with beautiful people and opens until 2. Next best in town, also in Fleet Street, is **Baa Bar**, which serves £1 cocktails called 'shooters' and is a common first stop on nights out in the city centre. The **Penny Lane Wine Bar** is friendly and small, with a good summer beer garden.

STAR EATERY

Best take-away in Liverpool is Smithdown Road's little-known **Pizza Parlour** – authentic pizzas at decent prices, with wine or Italian beer to drink at the counter while your order is prepared. The **Everyman Bistro** on Hope Street is attached to the famous theatre set up by graduates of the Liverpool Uni in the 1960s. At moderate prices the food is healthy, well-presented and often veggie friendly. The adjacent bar was one of the first places in Liverpool to stock the legendary spirit Absinthe – scourge of the Romantics and very trendy. The **Tavern Company** on Smithdown Road is a superb Mexican restaurant loved by students and parents alike. **Maranto's** (Lark Lane) is a large restaurant with a huge bar serving good, moderately priced international cuisine. More expensive is nearby **Viva**, but well worth it as a treat (or when the parents are in town).

CLUBS

Cream at **Nation** (Walstenholme Square) is mainstream, but intensely popular. It's a world-renowned night and attracts the biggest DJs around. Every Wednesday the club targets students with *Medication*. The city's biggest techno nights are *Voodoo @* **RedZone** in Duke Street and *Bugged Out* at **Cream**. For drum 'n' bass check out *Chrome* and *Soundbombing*. Another outstanding club is the gay friendly **Garlands** (Eberle Street).

SHOPS

Hardman Street's **Bulletproof** is a good retailer of pretty much passé seventies clothing; it sells clothes by weight. Slater Street's **Liverpool Palace** and School Lane's **Quiggins** are *pot pourris* of student goods and services – from tatooists to African art. The University of Liverpool's **Monday Market** taps the same market for books, wall hangings and plants, but some stallholders provide products as diverse as PCs and collector's items.

THEATRE & MOUTH ART

The **Everyman**, Hope Street, is one of the most student-friendly venues around, is known for giving local writers a break, and has started the careers of several big-name Liverpudlian actors, like Pete Postlethwaite and Julie Walters. The more 'street level' **Unity Theatre** nearby does workshops and alternative theatre experiences. The **Mask Theatre** is soon to be set up on Dale Street and will also feature poetry and comedy. Currently, Hanover Street's **Neptune** is a cosy venue favoured by touring shows and comedy acts.

The **Egg Café** (Newington, top floor) has bags of atmosphere and features open floor slots for local poets. The Everyman Bistro hosts the *Dead Good Poets Society*, a collective of performance poets, twice a month. The **Hub Café** (Berry Street) is setting up a regular event to meet growing demand.

FILM, MUSIC & COMEDY

There are a few good chain cinemas on London Road, Switch Island and Edge Lane. Alternative film venues are receding – the **Plaza** in Crosby is under threat. The **Philharmonic**, Hope Street, shows a series of classic films on its unique raising screen, with its traditional cinema organist.

Probably the two best venues for live music are Hotham Street's **L2** and **The Picket** (Hardman Street). The former is a 1,000-capacity theatre with an indie slant – in the past the likes of the Charlatans and Primal Scream have played there. The Picket is famed for showcasing loads of local bands. The Up Front comedy club and *Rawhide* at **Life** (Bold Street) specialise in the field. With the Everyman theatre they stage mainly established comedians. **Uncle Pieheads Comedy Parlour** at the Guild of Students hosts national competitions and some decent comedians.

VISUAL ART

The Tate Gallery on Albert Dock has three floors featuring major touring exhibitions. **The Walker Gallery** (William Brown Street) offers traditional fare. Liverpool Uni has a small gallery by Abercromby Square. The **Open Eye** (Wood Street) exhibits touring photographic shows. Seek out also a plethora of little-known galleries, like the **Bluecoat Chambers** (School Lane).

Lee Hall

• •

UNIVERSITY OF LIVERPOOL

The University of Liverpool
Student Services Centre
150 Mount Pleasant
Liverpool L69 3GD

TEL 0151 794 5928
FAX 0151 794 2060
EMAIL ugrecruitment@liv.ac.uk
WEB www.liv.ac.uk

Liverpool Guild of Students
PO Box 187
160 Mount Pleasant
Liverpool L69 7BR

TEL 0151 794 6868
FAX 0151 794 4174
EMAIL guild@liv.ac.uk
WEB www.guildofstudents.com

VAG VIEW

*E*stablished in 1881, Liverpool is the original redbrick university. It is a great big bustling traditional university, which far from feeling a need to keep up with the times seems somehow to absorb government exigencies and move at its own pace and in its own space. Liverpool is a well-balanced university and what you might call a safe bet, if you're up for a uni among those at the very top.

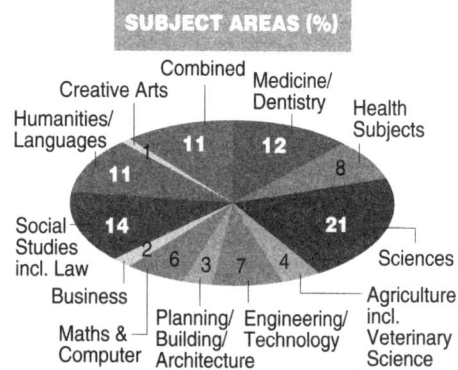

SUBJECT AREAS (%)

Combined
Creative Arts 1
Humanities/Languages 11
Medicine/Dentistry 11
Health Subjects 12
8
Social Studies incl. Law 14
21 Sciences
Business 2 6 3 7 4
Maths & Computer
Planning/Building/Architecture
Engineering/Technology
Agriculture incl. Veterinary Science

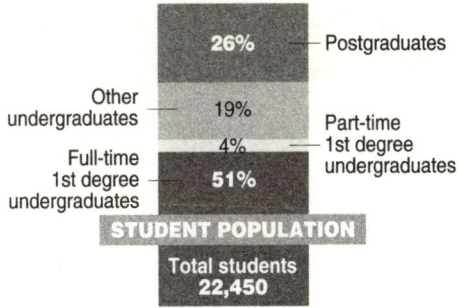

Postgraduates	26%
Other undergraduates	19%
Part-time 1st degree undergraduates	4%
Full-time 1st degree undergraduates	51%

STUDENT POPULATION

Total students **22,450**

CAMPUS

The campus **Precinct** is a few minutes' walk from the centre of this city, famous for football, the Beatles and the Mersey ferry. With Liverpool Uni, John Moores, Liverpool Hope and Sir Paul McCartney's Lipa, Liverpool is now, also, one of the major centres of higher education in Britain.

STUDENT PROFILE

Liverpool Uni is popular with state and public school kids and students from a whole range of backgrounds. The low drop-out rate (7%) shows that the uni knows how to hang on to them.

UNIVERSITY/STUDENT PROFILE

University since	**1881**
Situation/style	**Civic**
Student population	**22,450**
Full-time undergraduates	**11,380**
- mature	**13%**
- overseas	**6%**
- male/female	**49/51**
- state sector intake	**83%**
- non-traditional student intake	**13%**
- drop-out rate	**7%**
- undergraduate applications	**Up 2%**
see Introduction for key to tables	

ACADEMIA

Some 84% of the assessment ratings have been Excellent or scored 19 points or more out of 24 (see *Academic Excellence* box). Faculties include Arts, Engineering, Law, Medicine & Dentistry, Science, Social & Environmental Studies, and Veterinary Science. Liverpool pulled out of teacher training a couple of years ago, but this year there is a new Management School, which will focus on e-business, e-learning and entrepreneurship, and promote links with global business. The new school opens in the autumn of this year. Established programmes such as Accounting, Economics and Business Studies will be taught alongside a suite of exciting new undergraduate programmes, for 2002

ACADEMIC EXCELLENCE

TEACHING:
(Rated Excellent or 17+ out of 24)

History, Law, English, Geology & Environmental Sciences.	**Excellent**
Medicine, Philosophy, Physics, Veterinary	**24**
Town/Country Planning, Maths	**23**
Anatomy, Politics & Media, Management	
French, Civil Eng, Psychology, Economics, Pharmacol, Nursing, Arachaeology, Classics	**22**
Iberian Studies, Sociology	**21**
Materials Technology, Dentistry, Electron & Electric Eng	
General, Manufacturing & Aerospace Eng, Subjects Allied to Medicine	**20**
German, Organismal Biosciences, Molecular Biosciences	**19**

RESEARCH:
Top grades 5/5*

Physiology, Mechanical/ Aeronautical/Manufacturing Eng	**Grade 5***
Clinical Laboratory Sciences, Pharmacology, Biological Sciences, Veterinary, Chemistry, Physics, Earth Sciences, Pure Maths, Applied Maths, Computer, Electrical & Electronic Eng, Metallurgy, American Studies, English, French, German/Dutch/Scandinavian, Archaeology, History	**Grade 5**

entry, including E-Business, Marketing, Human Resources Management and International Business. The E-business degree is designed for operations at the forefront of the digital economy.

On a more traditional note, there are interesting inter-disciplinary combined honours BAs – a group of languages, humanities and arts subjects have integrated with another of sciences, maths and social studies – and there is an arts, social and environmental studies joint honours programme offering further intriguing combinations, such as French & Pure Maths or Maths & Philosophy.

Just announced is a £23-million project to create a Biosciences Centre and Biotechnology Business Incubator, with world-class facilities for research, teaching and new biotech businesses – this is an area which scored a mighty Grade 5 at the recent research assessments. Like Newcastle,

Liverpool copped full marks on inspection recently for the teaching in its Faculty of Medicine, dwarfing the efforts of Leeds, Sheffield, Birmingham, and we can report that a new £4-million educational centre opened in January of this year, a facility which includes two lecture theatres, with 600 and 240 seats, two seminar rooms, and conferencing facilities. Sadly, however, before the cheers of celebration had died down, a QAA inspection of the four-year Nursing degree revealed that student nurses were spending too few hours on clinical placements and knuckles were rapped. (On

> *Liverpool is a great big bustling traditional university with some of the best teaching in the country, not least in Medicine. But mythic status may be accorded it when you start talking about the town.*

re-assessment the department scored a mighty 22 points – two short of full marks.) Perhaps the nurses were enjoying the city's nightlife too much – something parents of Liverpool students may prefer not to read about.

SOCIAL SCENE

STUDENTS' GUILD They have the largest students' union building in the country (the second largest in Europe apparently) – ten bars, two main venues, many smaller ones, two games rooms, five food outlets, a large shop, coffee shop, opticians, USIT Campus Travel, seven conference rooms, a table tennis room, pool room, theatre/cinema, barbers, hairdressers, and media centre. Two years ago they launched a publication for all Liverpool students and called it *Liverpool Student*. To create it, four other publications were scrapped, including the 63-year-old *Liverpool Gazette* and *Sphinx* magazine which, after 103 years had become an integral part of Liverpool University. Now established, *Liverpool Student*, like other top student city newspapers, *Leeds Student*, Manchester's *Student Direct* and *London Student*, has become a virtual passage into the media. If that's your thing, get involved. The paper produced Best Reporter at the national *Independent* awards last year and runner-up *Guardian* Student Journalist of the year. A year earlier it was *Independent* Newspaper of the Year.

As elsewhere, there are all kinds of societies with which to get involved – seventy at the last count and fifty-five sports clubs. Among the former, the most popular are Drama, RockSoc, Islamic and LUST – that's Liverpool Uni Show Troupe.

For most freshers, to begin with, the focus for entertainment will be on the Guild. Recalling the days of yore when Liverpool students (Channel Four's Jon Snow among them) made waves politically and drank a lot, the bar names have political nuances (or at least some do). There's **Mandela, Saro Wiwa, Liver, James E Brown, Ang Sang Su Ki, Gilmour, Stanley, Mountford,** and probably the least political – **Courtyard** and **Balcony**. The 2,000-capacity venue is the **Mountford Hall**. There are five weekly ents plus concerts. The two regular clubnights are *Double Vision* (Mondays). Billed as 'the biggest student night on Merseyside', it regularly exceeds capacity. Saturday is *Time Tunnel* (retro night), when capacity is regularly met. Recent live acts include David Gray, Bluetones, Orbital, Reef, Toploader, Feeder, Shed Seven, Ash, Groove Armada,

WHAT IT'S REALLY LIKE	
UNIVERSITY:	
Social Life	★★★★★
Campus scene	**Great time, unpretentious**
Student Union services	**Good**
Politics	**Activity high**
Student Issues	**55 clubs**
Sport	**55 clubs**
National team position	**31st**
Sport facilities	**Good**
Arts opportunities	**Excellent**
Student newspaper	**Liverpool Student**
Independent awards	**Best reporter**
Student radio	**XS Live**
Nightclub	**Mountford Hall**
Bars	**Saro Wiwa, James E Brown, Ang Sang Su Ki, Mandela, Gilmour, Liver, Stanley, Courtyard, Balcony**
Union ents	**Time Tunnel, Double Vision**
Union clubs/societies	**70**
Most popular societies	**Drama, RockSoc, Islamic, LUST**
Smoking policy	**Union OK**
Parking	**Adequate**
CITY:	
Entertainment	★★★★★
City scene	**Fab**
Town/gown relations	**Good**
Risk of violence	**Average**
Cost of living	**Low**
Student concessions	**Excellent**
Survival + 2 nights out	**£60 pw**
Part-time work campus/town	**Average/good**

Terrorvision, Faithless, Spiritualized, Artful Dodger), Proclaimers, They Might Be Giants, Human League, JJ72, Starsailor. Coming up, as I write: NME Awards Tour featuring Andrew WK, 100 Reasons plus Cap Down, The Hives plus many more. They are one of the top music venues in the city and one of the busiest student venues in the country.

Sport They are nationally strong. The **Sports Centre** includes swimming pool, four squash courts, weight training, indoor cricket nets, climbing wall, sunbeds, facilities for aerobics, dance, trampolining. There's a hall at the gym for judo, fencing, archery, four additional squash courts, rifle and pistol range and a weights room. The main sports ground, near the halls, includes two floodlit artificial turf pitches for hockey, field sports, five rugby and six soccer pitches, four tennis courts, a lacrosse pitch, two cricket squares and two artificial wickets, bar and cafeteria. Two other grounds add a further six soccer pitches, and there's a base for climbing, walking, canoeing and field studies in Snowdonia, which accommodates eighteen.

Town Most first years dwell in massive catered halls (Greenbank or Carnatic) three miles out, and maybe more should heed Lee Hall's advice and get out: 'If you're looking for a quiet life with a cup of cocoa before bedtime there's not much point in coming to Liverpool.' If you don't go out of your way to upset the natives, Liverpool's a fairly safe place to be. See Lee's article, page 279.

PILLOW TALK
All freshers who apply by August 31 are guaranteed a place in halls, of which 57% are catered, and a mere 3% en suite. Prices per week range from £51.45 to £82.74. A 4-bedroom house typically costs £37.43 per person, per week.

If you're expecting luxury accommodation you'll be sorely disappointed, though the community spirit which grows up in halls like Rankin on the Carnatic site stand you in great stead. They have bars and ents, and are linked to uni and city centre by a regular bus service.

JOBS
PULSE is a new job-centre service that has been set up by the uni to help students find part-time jobs with local employers during term and more full-time during the vacations.

Close on a third of graduates end up in the health industry. As well as providing individual advice and information on careers, the uni runs skills sessions to help students present themselves well at job fairs, seminars, interviews. The service was ranked in the Top 10 most efficient Careers Services in the UK by recruiters in a survey by the

WHERE GRADUATES END UP	
28% Health (Medicine, Dentistry, Veterinary)*,	Key Areas
10% Manufacturing,	
9% Finance,	
7% Public Admin,	
6% Wholesale/Retail	
Construction, Defence,	Niche Areas
Chem/Pharmaceutical,	
Eng/Industrial Design,	
Aeronautical Manufac,	
Architec, Accountancy	
*indicates Top 10 Graduate Provider	
Approximate employed **94%**	

Performance Indicators Project (2001).

The Guild also runs LUSTI (Liverpool Uni Student Training Initiative) to train students in key transferable skills such as communication, assertiveness, time and stress management, meeting skills etc.

GETTING THERE
☛ By road: M6/J21a, M62, A5080, A5047. Well served by National Express coaches.
☛ By rail: Manchester, 40 mins; Sheffield, 1:45; Leeds, Birmingham, 2:00; London King's Cross, 3:00.
☛ Liverpool airports for inland/Ireland flights.
☛ By coach: London, 5:00; Manchester, 50 mins.

AT A GLANCE	
ACADEMIC FILE:	
Subjects assessed	**37**
Excellent	**84%**
Average requirements	**280 points**
Students-staff ratio	**15:1**
First/2:1 degree pass rate	**56%**
ACCOMMODATION FILE:	
Guarantee to freshers	**All who apply by 31.8**
Style	**Halls**
Catered	**57%**
En-suite	**3%**
Approx price range pw	**£53**
City rent pw	**£37-£65**

LIVERPOOL HOPE COLLEGE

Liverpool Hope College
Hope Park
Liverpool L16 9JD

TEL 0151 291 3295
FAX 0151 291 2050
EMAIL admission@hope.ac.uk
WEB www.hope.ac.uk

VAG VIEW

*L*iverpool Hope has a reputation in teacher
training and increasingly in science,
humanities and social science degrees
(Psychology and Sociology both scored 22 out
of 24 points on assessment), all validated by
Liverpool Uni. Entrance qualifications are
low, compared with the university.

Roots lie in an ecumenical amalgamation of
two colleges for women (St Katherine's, an
Anglican foundation, and Notre Dame, its
Roman Catholic neighbour), championed years
ago by the city's Anglican Bishop David
Sheppard and the late Roman Catholic Bishop
Derek Worlock. The recently built, £5.3-million
Sheppard–Worlock Library celebrates the
ecumenical union with 250,000 books, sixty PCs
and 500 study places. Even now, 72% of
undergraduates are female and the college
moves forward with Christian values to the fore.
Theology & Religious Studies are still a feature
of their Single and Combined Honours BA and
BEd programmes, and just scored 23 points on
assessment.

At Everton, a £15.5-million development is
home to Hope's community-education strategy,
to new self-catering accommodation, to the
Faculty of Fine Art & Design (20 points on
assessment) and to a performing arts centre for
use both by students and local people. There is
also accommodation at Hope Park and four
miles away at Aigburth.

Ents tend to be traditional fare, bands of the
tribute variety, comedians, karaoke, jazz nights
and society thrashes in the **Pavilion Bar** (500

COLLEGE PROFILE	
Founded	**1980**
Status	**HE College**
Degree awarding university	**Liverpool**
Situation/style	**City campus**
Student population	**6,410**
Full-time undergraduates	**3,550**
ACCOMMODATION FILE:	
Availability to freshers	**95%**
Style	**Halls**
Cost pw (food)	**£61**
City rent pw	**£37-£65**

capacity). Another bar (the **Derwent**) holds 200.
There is now, too, **Hope on the Waterfront**, a
modern cyber café with videowall at reclaimed
Albert Docks, open to all seven days a week.

For sport, they have recently installed a
floodlit, all-weather Astroturf pitch; and there's
a gym. A Mountaineering club does its thing at
Plas Caerdeon, Hope's Outdoor Education
Centre. This old manor house in 18 acres of
woodland overlooking the glorious Mawddach
Estuary (Snowdonia) hosts field and study trips,
but it's also a bolt hole for music students on
composition weekends, drama students for
rehearsals and anybody needing regeneration.

GETTING THERE
☛ By road: M62, M6/J21a. Well served by coach.
☛ By rail: Manchester, 40 mins; Sheffield, 1:45;
Leeds, Birmingham, 2:00; London King's Cross, 3:00.
☛ Speke Airport five miles away.
☛ By coach: London, 5:00; Manchester, 50 mins.

LIVERPOOL INSTITUTE FOR PERFORMING ARTS

Liverpool Institute for Performing Arts
Mount Street
Liverpool L1 9HF

TEL 0151 330 3232
FAX 0151 330 3131
EMAIL reception@lipa.ac.uk
WEB www.lipa.ac.uk

VAG VIEW

Sir Paul McCartney, Dame Judi Dench, Mark Knopfler, Richard Branson, Carly Simon, Sir George Martin are names with which to conjure, and all are patrons of Lipa, Liverpool's so-called Fame School. Performing Arts degrees, awarded by Liverpool John Moores University, are available in Acting, Community Arts, Dance, Enterprise management and Music, and a degree in Sound Technology. They are top performers in the annual National Student Drama Festival. Last year they took five awards.

*All students follow the same core programme: IT (including light, sound and video), Professional Development and Contextual Studies, plus specialist classes in their chosen subject. All students must take part in performance projects, workshops and electives. A learning resources centre has three midi suites, a CAD suite, the 500-seat **Paul McCartney Auditorium** and the **Studio Theatre**; the **Lipa Bar** and canteen are also available for performances. There are five large rehearsal rooms, many small practice rooms with pianos, small guitar amps and drum kits, and it is also possible to gain access to rehearsal spaces for dance and theatre with sound and lighting equipment,*

two SVHS video editing suites, dedicated computers for hard disk recording and practice rooms with technics turntables for DJs.

*Students have ready access to the uni's **Cooler** and **Scholar's** bars, and the **Base** (the gym). The ISPB provides entertainment in the bar or canteen most nights.*

GETTING THERE
☛ By road: M62 (east/west), which connects with M6 (north/south) at Junction 21a.
☛ By rail: Manchester, 40 mins; Sheffield, 1:45; Leeds or Birmingham, 2:00; King's Cross, 3:00.
☛ Liverpool airports for flights inland and to/from Ireland.
☛ By coach: London, 5:00; Manchester, 50 mins.

INSTITUTE PROFILE

Founded	**1996**
Status	**HE College**
Degree awarding university	**Liverpool JM**
Full-time undergraduates	**515**

ACCOMMODATION:
Availability to freshers	**100%**
Style	**Halls**
Cost pw (no food)	**£47**
City rent pw	**£37-£65**

DEGREE COURSEs:
Performing Arts, Sound Technology

LIVERPOOL JOHN MOORES UNIVERSITY

Liverpool John Moores University
Roscoe Court
4 Rodney Street
Liverpool L1 2TZ

TEL 0151 231 5090/1
FAX 0151 231 3194
EMAIL recruitment@livjm.ac.uk
WEB www.livjm.ac.uk

Liverpool John Moores Students' Union
The Haigh Building
Maryland Street
Liverpool L1 9DE

TEL 0151 231 4900
FAX 0151 231 4931
EMAIL isuvhann@livjm.ac.uk
WEB www.livjm.ac.uk/lsu/

VAG VIEW

*Liverpool John Moores, known as JMU, is more city orientated than the older Liverpool-based university. To begin with, JMU's many buildings are strewn all over the city, and the Students' Union building, **The Haigh**, is an integral part of the Liverpool scene. Through the uni's affiliation with Sir*

Paul McCartney's Liverpool Institute for Performing Arts (see above), JMU have a proud association with the city's most influential artists of all time. Then again, they draw many students from the region, and roots run deep into the city's industrial history.

JMU's origins go back to 1823 as the Liverpool Mechanics' and Apprentices' Library. As poly, the institution brought together the

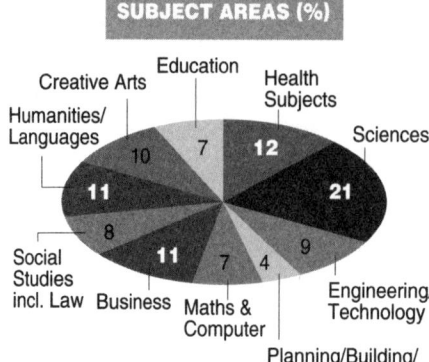

SUBJECT AREAS (%)

Creative Arts · Education · Health Subjects · Humanities/Languages · Sciences · Social Studies incl. Law · Business · Maths & Computer · Planning/Building/Architecture · Engineering/Technology

is learned and imbued here can be applied on graduation in the world of work.

CAMPUS

Writes Emma Hardy: 'JMU buildings are scattered across the city, many are impressive. The School of Media, Critical and Creative Arts, where I study, is one of the most impressive buildings in Liverpool. Located next to the Anglican Cathedral, the views from it are spectacular and the facilities are exemplary. The main library is a great glass structure of imposing stature and, like much of the rest of the university, likely to take your breath away when you first see it. But there are some grim high rise blocks too. Prospective students do well to bear in mind that what they see on Open Day are the best bits and that there is good reason why attention is diverted away into the attractions of the city.'

STUDENT PROFILE

When JMU decided to promote itself via the delights of the city's nightlife – the vice-chancellor appeared on the back of bucking bronco in one of the most famous Liverpool nightclubs, and the prospectus came out looking like a glossy, youth culture, leisure magazine – it met with raised eyebrows and blustering copy in the press. Whatever JMU applicants actually thought about it – and Brighton Uni was surprised when their cool, laid-back art students said recently that they would have preferred to see a course list up front, rather than a puff about swinging Brighton – there is no doubting that undergraduates at JMU are up for a bit of bronco.

City Colleges of Art and Design and Building, Commerce, and the Regional College of Technology, the City of Liverpool College of Higher Education, the IM Marsh College of Physical Education, the FL Calder College of Home Economics and the Liverpool College of Nursing and Midwifery – all of which give a good clue to the uni's academic profile today.

Finally, JMU owes its name and ethos to one of the city's most famous entrepreneurs. Sir John Moores CBE (1896-1993) built Littlewoods – the football pools organisation – from scratch. 'Sir John's business success was built upon his philosophy of the equality of opportunity for all,' the uni says. 'This fundamental belief... is a reflection of the university's commitment to higher education, to access, to flexibility and to participation.' Most of all, perhaps, it gives the clue to the underlying ethos – applied learning – they are very hot, across the board, on how what

Asked to give us a profile, Emma concluded, 'Despite the huge diversity in matters of taste and style, your JMU student is a mellow person, out to enjoy their time at university. The general atmosphere is far from snobbish, and with such a wide range of people studying here, friends are not hard to find, no matter what your age, or what your interests.'

The statistics show that 94% of applicants come from the state sector and a staggering 21%

UNIVERSITY/STUDENT PROFILE

University since	**1992**
Situation/style	**Civic**
Student population	**20,670**
Full-time undergraduates	**11,250**
- mature	**27%**
- overseas	**10%**
- male/female	**47/53**
- state sector intake	**94%**
- non-traditional student intake	**21%, high**
- drop-out rate	**12%**
- undergraduate applications	**Down 3%**
see Introduction for key to tables	

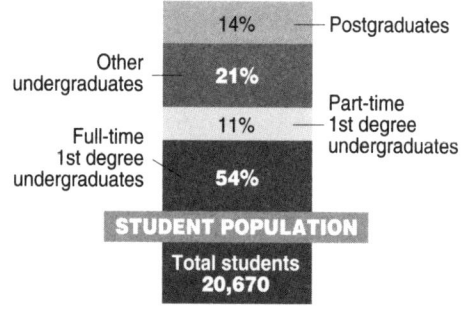

14% — Postgraduates
Other undergraduates — 21%
Full-time 1st degree undergraduates — 54%
Part-time 1st degree undergraduates — 11%

STUDENT POPULATION

Total students
20,670

from neighbourhoods in which going to university is hardly habitual. There is also a large mature population and a significant overseas presence. JMU's problem is not getting students so much as hanging on to them, their drop-out rate is running at 12% – a comment on recruitment strategy? Interestingly, JMU have this year opened up a campus centre where students have better access to any help they need of a social or academic kind. Long overdue.

ACADEMIA

Vocational bias, strong on sandwich courses, good contacts with industry – professional associations offer direct employment routes, for example, in Pharmacy, Surveying and some Engineering programmes. Faculties include: Built Environment; Law, Social Work, Social Policy; Art; Business; Modern Languages; Media, Critical & Creative Arts; Education and Community Studies; Health; Human Sciences; Social Science; Biological and Earth Sciences; Biomolecular Sciences; Computing and Maths Sciences; Electrical Engineering, Electronics & Physics; Engineering & Technology; Pharmacy and Chemistry; and the European Institute for Urban Affairs.

Subjects that did well in the teaching assessments recently are Health Studies; Pharmacology, Biosciences, Communication & Media; Building, Land & Property Management, Nursing; Politics, Business & Management. Sport got a Grade 5* rating in the research assessments last year, which indicates world renown, and General Engineering's Grade 5 demonstrates national and international excellence.

Writes Emma: 'JMU are big on student feedback. Every member of every course has the opportunity to put their views to those with power, through a network of student representatives. Tutors are approachable and changes do get made. Questionnaires regarding each and every module taught are distributed to students and the university does listen to complaints. The emphasis is on making the student experience as enjoyable as possible.

SOCIAL SCENE

STUDENTS' UNION 'As a prospective student, bear in mind that it is up to you to make the most of your time at JMU. This means finding out about what is going on at your university and getting involved in what interests you. Radio

JMU casts a wide net and delivers a vocational discipline. It also researches student opinion tirelessly in an effort to enrich their time here and stem the worryingly persistent drop-out rate.

ACADEMIC EXCELLENCE

TEACHING :
(Rated Excellent or 17+ out of 24)

Health Studies	**24**
Pharmacology, Organismal Biosciences	**23**
Communication & Media, Building, Land & Property Management, Nursing, Politics, Molecular Biosciences, Business & Management	**22**
Drama & Dance, American Studies, Maths, Education	**21**
Civil Engineering	**20**
Modern Languages (French, German, Russian, Spanish), Psychology, Art & Design	**19**
Sociology, Town & Country Planning, Electric & Electron Eng, General Eng	**18**

RESEARCH :
Top grades 5/5*

Sport	**Grade 5***
General Engineering	**Grade 5**

stations, newspapers, clubs, societies and events need student support to make them work and many students do not get as involved with them as they could.

'Possibly of more immediate interest is that the union building, the Haigh, has a bar (**Scholars**) and a club (**The Cooler** – a 500-capacity nightclub with state-of-the-art technology and new air-conditioning system, hence its name) offering cheap alcohol. Entry is free. Every night of the week there is a different music theme in The Cooler, and there are screenings of recent movies and big screen football.'

Saturday's *Loveshack* has long been rated the best retro night in town. Recent live acts include Amsterdam and Jylt.

Another popular meeting place is **Sanctuary**, a café bar, chill-out zone with sofas, speciality coffees, etc. There are also bars at the IM Marsh (Education) and Byron Street sites.

Among the most successful student societies (there are sixty-two in all this year, plus twenty sports clubs) is the radio station, Shout fm, and now there's a student magazine, *Air*, which in its previous incarnation

WHAT IT'S REALLY LIKE

UNIVERSITY:

Social Life	★★★★
Campus scene	**Local, top scene**
Student Union services	**Good**
Politics	**Not much**
Sport	**22 clubs**
National team position	**83rd**
Sport facilities	**Good**
Arts opportunities	**Music excellent; drama, dance, film, art good**
Student magazine	**Air**
Student newspaper	**Liverpool Student**
Student radio	**Shout fm**
Nightclub	**The Cooler**
Bars	**Scholars, Sanctuary**
Union ents	**Loveshack (retro)**
Union clubs/societies	**82**
Most popular societies	**Shout fm**
Smoking policy	**Union OK**
Parking	**Poor**

CITY:

Entertainment	★★★★★
City scene	**Fab**
Town/gown relations	**Good**
Risk of violence	**Average**
Cost of living	**Low**
Student concessions	**Excellent**
Survival + 2 nights out	**£60 pw**
Part-time work campus/town	**Average/good**

as *Shout* figured in the *Guardian* student awards, but disappeared with the founding of multi-uni newspaper *Liverpool Student* (see Liverpool Uni entry).

Sport Good facilities for uni team sports, most are three miles from the city centre at the Education & Community base – gym, dance studios, sports halls, indoor swimming pool, pitches, all-weather athletics track – and at the St Nicholas Centre by the cathedral – sports hall, gym, weight training room. JMU's proudest boast is its Base Fitness Centre, well equipped and professionally staffed. There's a student sports pass for free/reduced price access to facilities – badminton courts, swimming pools, squash courts, athletics tracks. Big celebration in recent memory is when their Michelle Rogers won the Olympic gold medal at judo.

Town Writes Emma: 'The nightlife in Liverpool is fantastic. There are simply more drinking establishments than it is healthy for one student to visit during their years of study. It's not all pubs

and clubs however, Liverpool is a city of heritage and culture, which has recently seen a lot of artistic and creative investment and development.

'Safety is one of the first considerations for a student, but despite the bad press it receives, Liverpool is no more dangerous than any other city. JMU continue the work of worried parents by constantly reminding students of the common sense rules of personal safety, and have an excellent welfare service, situated in the student union, the Haigh.'

PILLOW TALK

'Pretty much all university halls and JMU residences are fine except Crete and Candia Towers, which should be avoided at all costs,' said a

AT A GLANCE

ACADEMIC FILE:

Subjects assessed	**33**
Excellent	**64%**
Average requirements	**200 points**
Students-staff ratio	**19:1**
First/2:1 degree pass rate	**45%**

ACCOMMODATION FILE:

Availability to freshers	**40%**
Style	**Student village**
Approx price range pw	**£42-£63**
City rent pw	**£37-£65**

student. 'You have been warned.'

JMU students seem to congregate around the city centre, which is a good idea since the place has spruced itself up remarkably of late, and more buildings are being renovated for student use.

WHERE GRADUATES END UP

20% Education, Key Areas
12% Manufacturing,
10% Health/Social Work,
10% Wholesale/Retail,
8% Finance,
6% Public Admin
Aeronautical Manufacture, Niche Areas
Artistic/Literary, Radio/TV,
Chemical/Pharmaceutical*,
Construction, Electron/
Electric, Sport

*indicates Top 10 Graduate Provider

Approximate employed **93%**

JOBS

Employment opportunities are good, both during and after study. Situated in the Haigh is UNITEMP, JMU's own employment agency. It does offer some exclusive Unitemp related jobs, but doesn't beat getting the local newspaper, visiting the job centre, or simply asking around for vacancies.

For graduate employment there's Workbank, who assist recruitment with courses on transferable skills, CV writing, interview technique, etc.

GETTING THERE

☞ By road: M62, M6/J21a. Well served by coach.
☞ By rail: Manchester, 40 mins; Sheffield, 1:45; Leeds, Birmingham, 2:00; London King's Cross, 3:00.
☞ Liverpool airports for inland/Ireland flights.
☞ By coach: London, 5:00; Manchester, 50 mins.

LONDON GUILDHALL UNIVERSITY

London Guildhall University
Course Enquiries
133 Whitechapel High Street
London E1 7QA

TEL 020 7320 1616
FAX 020 7320 1163
EMAIL enqs@lgu.ac.uk
WEB www.lgu.ac.uk

London Guildhall University
Students' Union
2 Goulston Street
London E1 7TP

TEL 020 7247 1441
FAX 020 7247 0618
EMAIL studentunion@lgu.ac.uk
WEB www.lgu.ac.uk/facilities/su.html

VAG VIEW

A century and a half after London Guildhall (the old City of London Polytechnic) started out by offering 'evening classes for young men', there is still a significant student population on part-time courses. The uni is one of the largest providers of part-time business courses in the country. It's this part-time population that boosts the mature student percentage, and you will in fact meet many youthful full-time undergrads, as well as many students studying other than business.

It is an unusual set-up for a university nevertheless, with its sites strewn around London's Square Mile financial district, a diversity united, a student suggested, by the resilience of its more streetwise youthful student clientele, devoid of opulent silver spoons and armed with a left-wing, if somewhat lethargic, political bias.

It may well be, as they hope, that London Guildhall's merger with North London University this year, which they say will make them into the third largest uni in the UK, heralds a sounder base – improved resources (larger libraries, greater access to IT), increased subject choice, wider range of sports and entertainment facilities, strengthened links with employers, etc, but it

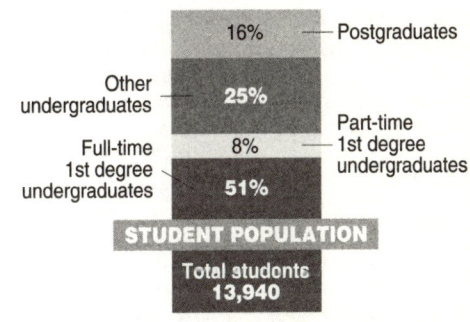

16% — Postgraduates
Other undergraduates 25%
Full-time 1st degree undergraduates 8% — Part-time 1st degree undergraduates
51%

STUDENT POPULATION
Total students
13,940

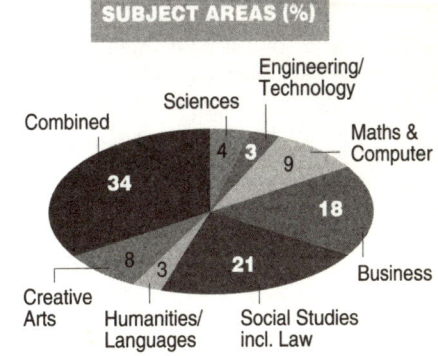

SUBJECT AREAS (%)

Combined 34
Sciences 4
Engineering/Technology 3
Maths & Computer 9
Business 18
Social Studies incl. Law 21
Humanities/Languages 3
Creative Arts 8

cannot immediately bring things into sharper focus. At a vote, 88% of students were against it. This is unlikely to count much, however. The merger will probably happen and result in a name change to London Metropolitan University.

UNIVERSITY/STUDENT PROFILE	
University since	**1992**
Situation/style	**Civic**
Student population	**13,940**
Full-time undergraduates	**7,100**
- mature	**45%**
- overseas	**14%**
- male/female	**44/56**
- state sector intake	**93%**
- non-traditional student intake	**12%**
- drop-out rate	**14%, high**
- undergraduate applications	**Down 12%**
see Introduction for key to tables	

CAMPUS

Eight sites, Calcutta and Central Houses, Jewry Street, Moorgate, Goulston Street, Whitechapel, Tower Hill and Commercial Road. The university's main Moorgate site is built on what used to be one of the most (in)famous insane asylums in England. The Bethlem Royal Hospital (originally based at nearby Liverpool Street Station) moved to the site in the late 1670s. The East End is a racially diverse area with, in particular, a thriving Bangladeshi community giving the cultural flavour to the eating and shopping delights of Brick Lane.

STUDENT PROFILE

Barings broker, and breaker, Nick Leeson, and multi-millionaire Mark Thatcher, the former Tory PM's son, both did time here. So did singer Alison Moyet, Sonya from Echobelly and pant-stroking comedy maestro Vic Reeves, so don't expect to find it easy to denote a typical student.

'It's the Jarvis Cocker school of learning,' says Stuart Harkness, 'with a diverse array of mis-shapes and misfits. Nearly half of the students are part-time, with many being professionals from the City. A large amount are therefore mature. Don't fear, however, as many have mental ages seemingly half this figure.

'A high proportion originate from London and the surrounding Southeast, but the melting pot is further fuelled by those from farther afield, to the tune of 110 countries. the cosmopolitan flavour makes LGU a truly multi-culural university. Multiple faiths are therefore evident and well catered for with prayer rooms at

> *Students come with a clear purpose, and from art to business the uni does what it's asked by a whole spectrum of jokers, from pant-stroking Vic Reeves to Kate Hoey, from Nick Leeson to Alison Moyet... It's more down to earth here than a rattle-snake's belly in a wagon wheel rut.*

various university sites, a chaplaincy and numerous students' union-funded cultural societies, including Christian, Islamic, Muslim, Afro-Caribbean, to name but a few. All seem to respect each others' practices under the umbrella of LGU brotherhood.'

The university provides a three-day orientation course for international students each September. There is also a successful peer support scheme, involving language support, a buddy system and subject area support. All international students at London Guildhall University are enrolled as members of International Students House, an international students centre and club in the centre of London.

ACADEMIC EXCELLENCE	
TEACHING:	
(Rated Excellent or 17+ out of 24)	
Social Policy & Admin	**Excellent**
Art & Design, Economics	**23**
Business/Management, Politics, Psychology	**22**
Materials Technology	**20**
Modern Languages (French, German, Spanish)	**19**
Maths	**18**
RESEARCH:	
*Top grades 5/5**	**None**

ACADEMIA

The uni operates a counselling and advice facility to support students during their studies.

There are excellent courses other than in finance and business, particularly in the areas of communications, art and design, psychology, social sciences (notably law) and music technology. Note too our *Employment* file, page 296, the graduate record in advertising and radio/TV beyond the dominant bias of finance. Also, note the near perfect score in the teaching assessments for Art & Design, which highlights the uni's traditional strength of the degrees in the art and craft areas (Fine Art, Design, and Silversmithing, Jewellery & Allied Crafts).

Writes Sam Hall: 'The university is gaining a reputation for artistic excellence, with well-respected jewellery-making and furniture departments, and many student-led initiatives leading to national awards. Most recently, the Film-making Society was awarded top prize in the prestigious Fuji Film scholarship competition.'

Finally, the uni's Women's Library is the UK's oldest and most extensive library on women's history, documenting the changing role of women in society from 1600 to the present day.

SOCIAL SCENE

The fragmented nature of LGU means that not a lot of mixing goes on between students based at different sites, and obviously the union is competing with the wider attractions of London life. There is no one campus scene, and students at the main bunch of sites in Aldgate tend to hang out in their own favourite places among the many bars and cafés based in the area. Being at the edge of the City gives rise to another socialising problem – everything tends to close down when the City workers go home at night, and nothing is open at the weekend. Sadly, as a result, students tend to go home straight after their lectures.

STUDENTS' UNION The union is based in Goulston Street, where one of Jack the Ripper's victims was found. There are two bars and a diner with a variety of hot and cold food. At other sites there are three union shops, a recently refurbished bar and a snack bar. The union produces a popular monthly magazine, *G:Echo*, and holds a weekly programme of events in its ground floor **Sub Bar**. It is also one of the largest employers of LGU students, with a current student staff of 150.

'There is a huge variety of diversions on offer,' writes Sam. 'Most popular union night is on Wednesday, the boozy *Sports Clubs Disco*, and on Friday at *Sub Club*, where all pints are £1 from 5-11pm; but the fragmented nature of the sites makes student participation unpredictable.'

SPORT A new and enthusiastic sports sabbatical officer led to a resurgence in this area, so that Wednesday afternoons are kept free of lectures when the sporting fraternity is coached. There's a fitness centre at 133 Whitechapel High Street, with weights and cardiovascular gym, and another gym at the Tower Hill site. The union run a range of clubs. Last year these included football, rugby, hockey, cricket, basketball, netball, karate, climbing, sub aqua and boxing.

PILLOW TALK

No guarantee is given to freshers, but priority is given to their needs, and students from outside London, including of course non-European Union

WHAT IT'S REALLY LIKE	
UNIVERSITY:	
Social Life	★★★
Campus scene	**Mature, easy going**
Student Union services	**Average-good**
Politics	**Active**
Sport	**Low key**
National team position	**None**
Sport facilities	**Poor-average**
Arts	**Available**
Student mag/news	**G:Echo**
Union ents	**5 pw**
Live venue capacity	**None**
Union clubs/societies	**Handful**
Smoking policy	**Zonal**
Parking	**Non-existent**
CITY:	
Entertainment	★★★★★
Scene	**Wild, expensive**
Town/gown relations	**Average-good**
Risk of violence	**Average**
Cost of living	**High**
Student concessions	**Locally adequate**
Survival + 2 nights out	**£70 pw**
Part-time work campus/town	**Good**

international students, get first call.

There are three halls of residence: John Bell House, set in sunny Shadwell, which is about twenty minutes walk from the uni – 94 places, self-catering halls with shared kitchen/diners, showers and toilets. Residents have use of a large common room with table tennis, pool table and television. Claredale House in Bethnal Green, which is about two miles from university - 265 places in 68 self-catering flats with kitchen, shower room, toilet and telephone (there's also a communal laundry and stacks of parties for budding insomniacs apparently). Sir John Cass Hall, down the road in

AT A GLANCE	
ACADEMIC FILE:	
Subjects assessed	**16**
Excellent	**63%**
Average requirements	**140 points**
Students-staff ratio	**22:1**
First/2:1 degree pass rate	**34%**
ACCOMMODATION FILE:	
Guarantee to freshers	**None**
Style	**Halls**
Approx price range pw	**£63-£78**
City rent pw	**£65-£100**

WHERE GRADUATES END UP

13% Finance*,	Key Areas
11% Wholesale/Retail,	
9% Manufacturing,	
8% Personnel*,	
7% Computer,	
6% Public Admin,	
6% Health/Social Work	
Telecom, Market	Niche Areas
Research, Advertising*,	
Radio/TV*, Film/Video,	
Legal	

*indicates Top 10 Graduate Provider

Approximate employed **93%**

Hackney and a bitter rival – 131 places, self-catering halls with shared bathrooms, lounge with satellite television, table tennis and video games, an upbeat atmosphere, regular social events. Again there's a communal laundry. Price ranges between £63 and £78 per week. Private accommodation costs between £65 and £100.

JOBS

London Guildhall is engaged in an impressive number of employment initiatives, such as *Graduate Link*, a database of past-graduates giving insight into how their own careers have developed; *Trading Up*, scholarship provision to enable students to gain professional expertise in blue-chip firms and the voluntary sector; *Earn and Learn*, legal work experience – often representing solicitors in court.

There's also a mentoring scheme with City lawyers, Simmons & Simmons: Level 2 law students from backgrounds under-represented in the City are mentored in an ongoing partnership. Further, there's a law graduate employability network, and workshops on planning a career run by the Society of Black Lawyers and the Association of Muslim Lawyers.

GETTING THERE

☛ By Underground: Aldgate (Metropolitan and Circle lines), Aldgate East (District and Hammersmith & City).

LONDON INSTITUTE

London Institute
65 Davies Street
London W1Y 5DA

TEL 020 7514 6000 ext 6197
FAX 020 7514 6198
EMAIL c.anderson@linst.ac.uk
WEB www.linst.ac.uk

VAG VIEW

*T*he London Institute brings together five colleges at the forefront of learning, creativity and practice in the arts: Camberwell College of Arts, Central St Martin's (recently joined by the Drama Centre London), Chelsea, the London College of Fashion and the London College of Printing. Names such as Mike Leigh, John Galliano, Stella McCartney, Neville Brody, Jarvis Cocker and Chris Ofili are indicative of their international success. Newsweek described the institute as the 'epicentre of London style'.

There is precious little to suggest that the

INSTITUTE PROFILE

Founded	**1986**
Status	**Art Institute**
Situation/style	**City sites**
Student population	**10,280**
Full-time undergraduates	**6,630**
ACCOMMODATION:	
Availability to freshers	**11%**
Style	**Halls**
Cost pw (no food)	**£53-£106**
City rent pw	**£65-£90**
DEGREE SUBJECT AREAS:	
Drama, art, design, fashion, media, printing	

institute exists at all over and above its five constituent parts. According to a Mori poll, 10% of students were unaware that they belonged to it and a third didn't know who or what their Students' Union was.

There are student bars, of course – the **Fashion Bar** (at London College of Fashion), the **Art Bar** (at Camberwell College of Design), the **Shed** (at Furzedown Halls of Residence), and **The Boiler Room** (at London College of Printing), and a mag, Blue.

COLLEGE SITES

CAMBERWELL COLLEGE OF ARTS Peckham Road, London SE5 8UF. Tel: 020 7514 6303 Visual Arts – Silversmithing & Metalwork, Sculpture, Painting, Drawing, Ceramics; Graphic Design; Conservation.

CENTRAL ST MARTIN'S COLLEGE OF ART & DESIGN Southampton Row, London WC1B 4AP. Tel: 020 7514 7022 Ceramic Design; Fashion Design and Print; Fine Art; Graphic Design; Jewellery Design; Product Design; Textile Design; Theatre Design.

CHELSEA COLLEGE OF ART & DESIGN Manresa Road, London SW3 6LS. Tel: 020 7514 7754 Fine Art (Media, Painting, Sculpture); Design: Textiles, Interior Design, Public Art & Design.

DRAMA CENTRE LONDON 176 Prince of Wales Road, Chalk Farm, London NW5 3PT. Tel: 020 7267 1177 Acting

LONDON COLLEGE OF FASHION 20 John Princes Street, London W1M 9HE. Tel: 020 7514 7565 Costume and Make-up for the Performing Arts; Design Technology – Menswear, Women's Wear and Accessories; Fashion Promotion (Journalism, Public Relations and Broadcast); Product Development for the fashion industries.

LONDON COLLEGE OF PRINTING Elephant & Castle, London SE1 6SB. Tel: 020 7514 6538 *Film & Video; Journalism; Photography; Media & Cultural Studies; Print Media (2 degrees); Retailing (3 degrees); Visual Merchandising; Business. Communication; Graphic & Media Design; Int Travel & Tourism Mgt; Marketing and Advertising; Print Management; Publishing.*

GETTING THERE

☛ **Camberwell:** Peckham Rye or Denmark Hill overland. **Central:** Holborn tube (Central, Piccadilly lines). **Chelsea:** Sloane Square tube (Circle, District) + 22 bus down King's Road. **Drama Centre:** Queenstown Road, Battersea Park or Clapham Junction stations. **College of Fashion:** Oxford Circus tube (Central, Victoria, Bakerloo). **College of Printing:** Elephant & Castle overland or tube (Bakerloo, Northern).

LONDON SCHOOL OF ECONOMICS & POLITICAL SCIENCE

The London School of Economics & Political Science
Houghton Street
London WC2A 2AE

TEL 020 7955 7124
FAX 020 7955 6001
EMAIL ug-admissions@lse.ac.uk
WEB www.lse.ac.uk

LSE Students' Union
East Building
Houghton Street
London WC2A 2AE

TEL 020 7955 7158
FAX 020 7955 6789
EMAIL su.gensec@lse.ac.uk
WEB www.lse.ac.uk/union

VAG VIEW

*L*SE is part of the federal University of London. It is famous the world over for research. It may have been pipped into fourth place after Oxbridge and Imperial in the recent assessments, but by any standards that is good, particularly when you consider that the proportion of staff selected for assessment was higher than at any other establishment. Notwithstanding, is its reputation as a university justified?

More than half its students are

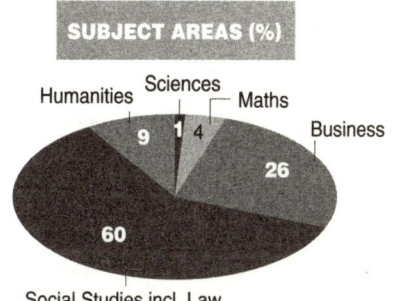

SUBJECT AREAS (%)

Humanities 9 — Sciences 1 — Maths 4 — Business 26 — Social Studies incl. Law 60

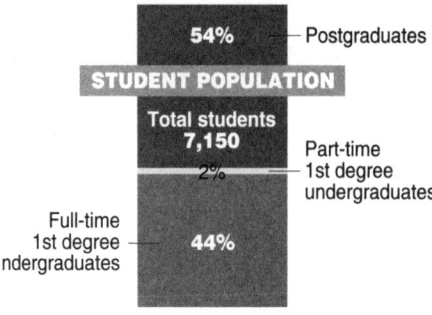

STUDENT POPULATION

54% — Postgraduates

Total students
7,150

Part-time
1st degree
undergraduates
2%

Full-time
1st degree
ndergraduates
44%

postgraduate; only 37% are full-time undergrads. Is the emphasis on research an advantage or disadvantage to undergraduates? Do good researchers make good teachers? The student/staff ratio at LSE is a disappointing 17:1; at Oxford it is 13:1, at Cambridge, 12:1; at Imperial, 9:1. Recent teaching inspection results have been high, but not amazing, and a fresher beset by overcrowded lecture halls reports that 'the administration at the LSE is, to say the least, a shambles.' And why does it need to scour the four corners of the earth for its undergraduates and accept only the cream from its UK applications, a conspicuously privileged minority (LSE's state sector take is a mere 58%)? The question is, how much value does the LSE add in its teaching? Average A level points at entry are 28 – that's 340 points in new parlance (Oxford 29, Cambridge 30). First Class/Upper Second pass rate is 70%, as against 83% at Oxford and 89% at Cambridge. How much is it down to LSE's teaching that Fortune 500 companies flock to it to grab the best of its students? Or would the same students have done as well elsewhere anyway?

What's certain is that such questions are

UNIVERSITY/SCHOOL PROFILE

School of London Uni since	**1900**
Situation/style	**City campus**
Student population	**7,150**
Full-time undergraduates	**3,110**
- mature	**8%**
- overseas	**50%**
- male/female	**54/46**
- state sector intake	**58%, low**
- non-traditional student intake	**5%, low**
- drop-out rate	**2%, low**
- undergraduate applications	**Down 1%**

see Introduction for key to tables

like water off the proverbial quacker's back because the LSE is as secure as the British Establishment, with which, despite the school's history of student revolt – Mick Jagger, Grosvenor Square and the Vietnam War and all – it is, indeed, synonymous. It goes hand in hand with Westminster, with Whitehall, with the City and with the legal and the media substrata too. In fact, its geographical position ensures it closer contact with all departments of the Establishment than either Oxford or Cambridge, and its specialist areas – Economics, International Relations, Government, Law, Finance – are what you might call the active ingredients of life in the Establishment. That is why many of its academic gurus are recognisable faces or bylines in the media. If analysis is required, it's the LSE they call up.

It is difficult to see what better finishing school you could find than that. Concludes our student mole: 'The LSE is no Utopia, but it is definitely one-up with its individual culture, school of thought, and world of opportunities.'

CAMPUS

'The LSE is the filling in a sandwich,' writes Dominique Fyfe, a student from America. 'On one side (the capital's financial and legal district) the air is serious and the suits Armani, and the FT-reading societal stress-set is on the go until long after the sun is down. On the other, west of Kingsway (the dividing line, a road where all those who cannot drive test their inabilities), lie the expensive, funky, multi-purpose Covent Garden and London's theatreland and Soho, haven for sex addicts and non-traditionalists, and the book lovers' paradise of Charing Cross Road.'

In translation, LSE is situated between Kingsway and the Strand, at the heart of London culture and the legal establishment, and not far from the City or Westminster either. It is a campus crowded with buildings, the so-called Old Building being on the site of the small hall, where it all began and from which it has steadily expanded into buildings close by – the East Building, Clare Market, St Clement, St Philips, Clement House, all built on land which is among the most expensive per square foot in the world.

STUDENT PROFILE

They come from all over the world, about a quarter from North America, over a third from Europe, another quarter from Asia... This is the cream of students anxious to acquire the LSE cachet. Last year it took less from non-traditional uni recruitment areas even than Oxford and Cambridge.

'Interesting conversation is one thing you will not find a lack of at the LSE,' writes Dominique. 'The students here think critically in the classroom but also have a point of view in friendly discussion outside. Many are highly driven, always ready for an intellectual challenge and very competitive. However, not all are so intense; some don't even find the library until summer exams!

'Naturally, most of the students you will meet here are reading for a degree in Economics, but what makes the school a fascinating place is that there are so many studying other subjects, like anthropology, finance, social psychology and philosophy, and you learn from everybody.

'The LSE is a breeding ground for global nomads. In between lectures, the Houghton Street hub of LSE activity overflows with student representatives of all races of our world. Languages you will begin to learn in this global microcosm are Indian, French, Italian, Spanish, Russian, German, not to mention English of course. Not only do these students of all cultures bring their traditions but they also bring the trendy, money-sucking, modern fashions, but don't worry if your wardrobe didn't appear in the latest issue of *Cosmo* or *GQ*; nobody really cares whether its Oxfam or Armani.'

ACADEMIA

Recent teaching assessments have been good – Industrial Relations scored full marks, Economics (23 out of 24 points), Politics (International Relations), Philosophy and Maths scored 22. Its library, the British Library of Political and Economic Science contains one million volumes, 28,000 journals (10,000 on current sub.), numerous specialist manuscripts – all totalling some three million items. Founded in 1896, it has just enjoyed a multi-million pound redevelopment by architects Foster and Partners.

Writes Dominique, 'Despite glitches in the system the lectures and classes are well enough taught. In fact I find myself wanting to go to them – a truly novel experience for me! Don't be surprised if the reading list for a class is more like a library's inventory record! The lectures are monologues, but the classes are interactive and "cosy" in size (maximum fifteen students). Essays are written for classes but not

LSE wants top scholars and looks for them all over the world. It is an international university like no other, but its forté is research; you will rub shoulders with some of the best in your field, but you won't be nannied.

ACADEMIC EXCELLENCE	
TEACHING:	
(Rated Excellent or 17+ out of 24)	
History, Anthropology, Applied Social Work, Business, Law, Social Policy & Admin.	**Excellent**
Industrial Relations	**24**
Psychology, Economics	**23**
Politics, Philosophy, Maths, Media	**22**
Sociology	**20**
RESEARCH:	
Top grades 5/5*	
Economics, Law, Anthropology, Social Policy, Accounting, International History, Philosophy	**Grade 5***
Politics, Sociology, Geography, Management, Economic History	**Grade 5**

formally assessed or given a definitive deadline, which can make procrastination seem dangerously attractive.

'Let me forewarn you, too, that the ratio of student to computer is something like 20:1, and for e-mail accessible computers, 50:1. In addition, printing a document is a rigamarole, so leave plenty of time for computer failure or long lines. LSE's library (BLEPS) is overwhelming and quite frankly I would not go there if I didn't have to. The process is as follows: when you reach the library half of the books you are looking for are not there and if they are, there is only one copy of the main text for about twenty to forty-plus students and are titled as set texts, which means that they can only be borrowed for twenty-four hours. Return it twenty-four hours too late and the librarians grow the devil's tail and horns and collect £24 of your own precious money! If that seems a tough sentence, it is and is meant to be.

SOCIAL SCENE

STUDENTS' UNION 'Many students drift in the direction of its pub, **The Three Tuns**, which has a "cool" atmosphere. The drinks are cheap, the company is friendly and the music plays at a level that doesn't reach eardrum-damaging decibels.

'The Students' Union offers a wide range of societies at the Freshers' Fair! The Socialism Society and other political groups will attack in a desperate attempt to sway you, but other societies adopt a less

WHAT IT'S REALLY LIKE

UNIVERSITY:

Social Life	★★★★★
Campus scene	**Trendy, driven, global nomads**
Student Union services	**Good**
Politics	**NUS issues**
Sport	**Competitive**
National team position	**51st**
Sport facilities	**Average**
Arts opportunities	**Limited**
Student newspaper	**The Beaver**
Student radio	**PuLSE**
Nightclub	**Three Tuns**
Bars	**Underground, Quad**
Union ents	**Crush, Comedy Club, Indie & Salsa events**
Union clubs/societies	**100+**
Smoking policy	**NS zones**
Parking	**Non-existent**

CITY:

Entertainment	★★★★★
City scene	**Wild, expensive**
Town/gown relations	**Average-good**
Risk of violence	**Average**
Cost of living	**Very high**
Student concessions	**Good**
Survival + 2 nights out	**£70 pw**
Part-time work campus/town	**Good/excellent**

obtrusive approach. There are plenty of opportunities to get involved, be it through the arts, politics, radio, religion (most religions and denominations are observed), business, or cultural groups. Sports teams exist, but I can give you little information about them, as I am motivationally challenged as regards physical activity.'

AT A GLANCE

ACADEMIC FILE:

Subjects assessed	**15**
Excellent	**93%**
Average requirements	**340 points**
Students-staff ratio	**17:1**
First/2:1 degree pass rate	**70%**

ACCOMMODATION FILE:

Guarantee to freshers	**100%**
Style	**Halls, flats**
Catered	**All save flats**
En-suite	**Some**
Price range pw	**£48-£110**
City rent pw	**£75**

These days LSE has its own dedicated ents manager and the Friday night clubnight, *Crush*, is one of the most popular student nights in London. They can get in 1,000 bodies to the three-room club, which is made up of the **Tuns**, the **Quad**, with its sofa-strewn mezzanine, and the smaller venue, the **Underground** – licence extension till 1am. There are also students nights at selected sites in London's clubland, such as **Turnmills**, **Sound**, **Hanover Grand**, **Emporium**, **The End**. Saturday night is known the city over for the long-running *Chuckle Club @* **the Tuns**, which has hosted Eddie Izzard, Phil Jupitus, Rich Hall, Stewart Lee, Rhona Cameron, Alistair McGowan and Al Murray recently. There's also a Quad clubnight on Saturday, something like *After Skool Club* (indie), or an Underground clubnight, like *Exilio*, the gay salsa night.

TOWN Top tip from Dominique: 'On arrival in London, buy the *London A-Z* (to avoid looking like a tourist only whip it out in times of emergency) and the student's bible, *Time Out*, essential to anybody's social survival kit. Manage limited finances by drinking your fill at the cheapest union bar before a night out.'

SPORT In the basement of the Old Building there's a training room and multigym. The school also has its own sports grounds in South London. There are also netball, tennis courts and four large swimming pools within two miles of Houghton Street. The University of London Union has facilities for squash, basketball, rowing and swimming. LSE cricketers may use the indoor facilities at Lords. LSE sports teams came 51st nationally last year in the national team league.

PILLOW TALK

All first year students are guaranteed a place in LSE or London University accommodation – basically halls and one block of self-catering flats. All halls provide meals. Around 18% of LSE accommodation is en suite; none of the University of London accommodation is. Estimated weekly prices for 2002/3 are £77-£110 for a single room £48-£76 for a twin room.

'Residence halls are cheap and easy,' writes Dominique, 'but in my opinion the London University intercollegiate option is preferable. You will find the quality of food to be not much better than that of pig slop, but living next door to two vets, across the hall from a nurse, next door to a musician, down the hall from an opera singer, and one floor above a physiotherapist could only happen in an intercollegiate hall. This option definitely widens your social circle. Rooms are basic with a small single bed (not much room for two if you have big plans), a desk and a wardrobe. Your room is your home and you make it your own.'

JOBS

Graduates of LSE make their careers in finance, consultancy, industrial and commercial management, and in teaching, or they undertake academic research and find expert posts as economists, lawyers or statisticians, with central and local government, or as journalists.

GETTING THERE

☛ Holborn (Piccadilly, Central lines), Temple (District, Circle lines), Charing Cross (Jubilee, Northern, Bakerloo lines).

WHERE GRADUATES END UP	
32% Finance,	Key Areas
7% Public Admin,	
5% Education	
Accountancy*,	Niche Areas
Business/Management*,	
Property, Market	
Research, Library/	
Archival*, Film/Video,	
Publishing, Advertising	

*indicates Top 10 Graduate Provider

Approximate employed **95%**

LOUGHBOROUGH UNIVERSITY

Loughborough University
Ashby Road
Loughborough
Leicestershire LE11 3TU

TEL 01509 263171
FAX 01509 223905
EMAIL admissions@lboro.ac.uk
WEB www.lboro.ac.uk

Loughborough Students' Union
Ashby Road
Loughborough
Leicestershire LE11 3TT

TEL 01509 217766
FAX 01509 235593
EMAIL president@lborosu.org.uk
WEB www.lufbra.net

VAG VIEW

*W*hen people think of Loughborough, which has been a university since 1966, they think of its engineering capability – it came out of Loughborough Technical Institute – and they think of sport, for today it is the best UK university at sport by such a long way that some of its teams can't find decent opposition on the university circuit and turn to professional clubs to sharpen their teeth yet further.

Surprise then that the weekly student magazine, Label, received a letter from a reader complaining that coverage favoured the arts at the expense of sport. Surprise, too, that alongside aeronautical and electronic and electrical manufacturing, and sport, and defence, and the construction industry, we find artistic/literary, film/video, market research and publishing as categories of graduate employment in which Lboro

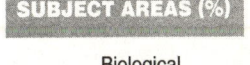

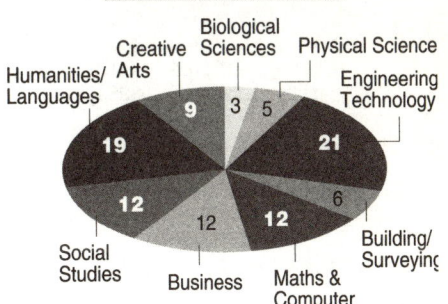

Humanities/Languages 19 · Creative Arts 9 · Biological Sciences 3 · Physical Science 5 · Engineering Technology 21 · Building/Surveying 6 · Maths & Computer 12 · Business 12 · Social Studies 12

students excel (see box, page 300).

The uni is now pre-eminent in social science, in English, in library & information management – these are all areas in which it has just been adjudged a research institution of world renown. Meanwhile, Psychology,

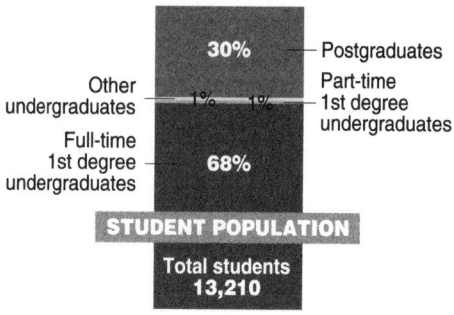

Other undergraduates
Full-time 1st degree undergraduates **68%**
30% — Postgraduates
Part-time 1st degree undergraduates
1% 1%

STUDENT POPULATION
Total students
13,210

Drama and Art & Design are among its top teaching subjects at inspection.

CAMPUS

Loughborough is a campus university situated just off the M1. 'It is one of the largest campuses in Europe,' writes Vicky Cook, 'and conforms to the stereotype of a leafy, green, self-contained campus. This has its advantages, everything is located within walking distance from halls (though the free campus bus is worth remembering on rainy days). There are bars, restaurants (although nothing gourmet) and three food shops to buy overpriced essentials when a walk into town is too great an effort. And, should campus and small market town become too claustrophobic, Leicester and Nottingham are mercifully close.

UNIVERSITY/STUDENT PROFILE	
University since	**1966**
Situation/style	**Town campus**
Student population	**13,210**
Full-time undergraduates	**8,910**
- mature	**7%**
- overseas	**4%**
- male/female	**61/39**
- state sector intake	**83%**
- non-traditional student intake	**10%**
- drop-out rate	**5%**
- undergraduate applications	**Down 7%**
see Introduction for key to tables	

STUDENT PROFILE

'A typical Lboro student,' Vicky continues, 'is one who enthuses about sport and thrives on competition, and appears to be a walking advert for sportswear companies. There are students who are not like this, but they make less noise and therefore attract less attention. Sport at Lboro is impossible to ignore. This enthusiasm is not a bad thing, but if you don't share a love of sport it can become a tad irritating. Whilst there is an increase in the number

of non-sports societies, they are still in the minority, making it more difficult to find like-minded souls.'

When, in 1998, the uni merged with the adjacent Loughborough College of Arts & Design, which is a world force in textile design, Ayshea Corrigan bewailed, 'People at the uni are really friendly, but...the sports students have a complete lack of imagination and charisma.'

The answer is that you will be in a minority if you come here and don't like sport, and you'll be in a two-thirds minority if you are female.

ACADEMIC EXCELLENCE	
TEACHING:	
(Rated Excellent or 17+ out of 24)	
Business & Management	**Excellent**
Anatomy & Physiology, Other Subjects Allied to Medicine, Psychology	**24**
Art & Design, Sociology, Drama, Mechanical, Aeronautical, Manufacturing Eng, Physics, Economics, Tourism, Physics	**23**
Maths, Chemical Eng, Electron/Electric Eng, Civil Eng, Business & Management.	**22**
Materials Technology	**21**
RESEARCH:	
*Top grades 5/5**	
Built Environment, Sociology, Sports	**Grade 5***
Electrical and Electronic Eng, Mechanical/Aeronautical/ Manufacturing Eng, Geography, European Studies, English, Library & Info Management	**Grade 5**

ACADEMIA

Though known for engineering, business and built environment, the uni is pre-eminent in Art & Design, in Social Sciences, in Health and in Drama, these faculties or departments achieving either full marks or 23 out of 24 points in recent inspections by the QAA (see box, above) or featuring at world class level in the recent research assessments, which put the uni up in the top third of the national league table.

Writes Vicky: 'Lboro is now one of the top universities, and the lecturers do generally make time for your queries and are easy to contact by e-mail. Access to the learn-server, where the module and lecture details can be found, is essential. The university has many computers, but they are scattered around campus, and there are too few in the library. All hall rooms have a network point though.'

SOCIAL SCENE

STUDENTS' UNION Writes Vicky: 'The biggest union in the country houses five bars and two nightclub areas. Nightlife tends to be campus based for

> *A typical Lboro student enthuses about sport, thrives on competition, and appears to be a walking advert for a sportswear company. But many others do survive and take advantage of expertise in quite different areas.*

freshers. These are the most popular events: *Hey-Ewe* is the Athletic Union night on a Wednesday, *FND* on a Friday, which with entry at £3.50 makes it more expensive than most places in town. Saturday is *Comedy Club*, live stand-up, usually worth a look, followed by *Platform.*'

'Ents provide variety in the form of clubnights, the odd Big Brother celeb, Zippy and George (of *Rainbow* fame) and Four Star Mary (of *Buffy the Vampire Slayer* theme tune fame). Louise was the headline act at the Freshers' ball.'

Smallish clubnights are held at **Junction** and there's also a cocktail night 8-till-late on Tuesdays called *Vibe*. Then, elsewhere, there's the regular Saturday selection of dance disco: *Platform '70s* and *Temptation '80s*, coupled with the live Comedy Club line-up. And, as Vicky notes, the big stuff on Wednesdays, *Hey Ewe* (AU – Athletics Union – geddit?): *Rodeo Bull, Bungee Fun, Gladiator Joust, Electric Chair, Karaoke, Coconut Shy, Pole Joust, Bungee Run, Striker, Snowboard.* 'There are certain rituals and traditions which we here in Loughborough have developed and institution-alised over the years,' I was told: 'The rugby shirt worn with jeans, AV's, collars up, *Hey Ewe* mayhem on a Wednesday evening followed by Echos, drinking games and of course Nasty...the Lufbra drink...' This latter, though increasingly at risk to the almighty Red Bull/voddie alternative (decried by purists as expensive and injurious to health), remains, at £1.50 a pint, the people's choice. Licence is till 2 am.

Bocca, the new food & drink balcony, is open on all event nights. Below, **The Auditorium** (and bar) is for live stuff, though it also has a projection room (the weekly cinema club – *Flix* – shows current films and costs only £20 to join). Hard by is **The Boardwalk** selling Chinese food, and during the day there are posters for sale and wherever/whenever you go, student radio LCR pumps out its choons. Occasionally the Stage Society or Drama Dept might use the Auditorium for productions, but generally stuff like that'll be revealed at **The Robert Martin Theatre**.

The Big Curvy Bar (or **BCB**) is a large drinking room with pool and games machines and incorporates **Greasy Joe's** (greasy spoon breakfasts, burgers). It has just been renovated – the whole place has been – and the SU guarantees to do up at least one bar each year. **JC's** – traditionally the most popular bar – has also recently been totally done out. Then there's **Que Pasa**, a Mexican restaurant/café bar, which becomes Junction nightclub. I also passed a can bar, supplementary drinking area just in case you have to wait around to be served on a big event night. When all shuts at the union you'll still find **Purple Onion** open at the student village for pizza, coffee and so on.

The union owns the land on which its centre stands and claims independence of the university

WHAT IT'S REALLY LIKE	
UNIVERSITY:	
Social Life	★★★★
Campus scene	**Well resourced, sports crazy**
Student Union services	**Excellent**
Politics	**Non-existent**
Sport	**Simply the best**
National team position	**1st by far**
Sport facilities	**Excellent and improving**
Arts opportunities	**Very good**
Student weekly magazine	**Label**
Student radio	**LCR**
Radio 1 awards	**Specialist Music**
Nightclub	**The Auditorium**
Bars	**JC's, Bocca, Big Curvey Bar, Junction**
Union ents	**FND, Platform**
Union clubs/societies	**105**
Most popular society	**International**
Smoking policy	**Zonal**
Parking	**No 1st years**
TOWN:	
Entertainment	★★
Scene	**Market town**
Town/gown relations	**Good**
Risk of violence	**Average**
Cost of living	**Average**
Student concessions	**Good**
Survival + 2 nights out	**£60pw**
Part-time work campus/town	**Excellent/average**

```
AT A GLANCE

ACADEMIC FILE:
Subjects assessed          19
Excellent                  83%
Average A level requirements  22 points
Students-staff ratio       18:1
First/2:1 degree pass rate 56%

ACCOMMODATION FILE:
Guarantee to freshers      99%
Style                      Halls
Student satisfaction       75%
Cost pw (no food/food)     £45-£100
Town rent pw               £45-£60
```

in what it is up to. Recent expansion revealed a new Media Centre, various franchise shops, banks, etc. There are still six bars and a nice atmosphere when you first breeze into the market/piazza-style scene on the ground floor. The centre houses the 24-hours-a-day student radio station (LCR), the student magazine offices (*Label*) and a TV/video editing suite. The 'talk' studio and production studio (drum booth, guitar booth) beyond leave you in no doubt that these students have not been overcharged at £1.4 million. Sound, vision, print, web, all of it together on a single floor and serviced by student engineers who know their stuff. The uni looks after its engineers, who make up the largest single group of undergrads in this university: a £13-million complex has just brought the six engineering departments under one faculty roof. They took the Specialist Music gong last year in the Radio 1 Awards.

SPORT Last year Lboro teams beat Birmingham into 2nd place by more than double Birmingham's number of points. Which other uni could entertain an annual competition with the Amateur Athletics Association of Great Britain? Recently, £25 million was earmarked for a new 50m swimming pool, an indoor athletics straight, a new 12-court sports hall, a sports science, sports medicine and conditioning facility (including a gymnastics analysis centre) and a water-based astro turf. Wrote Vicky: 'Lboro has an excellent sporting record, and some of the best facilities in the country. More are being built as I write – an Olympic swimming pool and two water-based hockey pitches. A student fitness suite with membership available for about £170 a year is to follow. And so it goes on. I want to make it known that there is more to Lboro than just sport!' When she filled in a form for me, Vicky marked the facilities 'excellent', opportunities 'average'. Lboro may not be a place to play sport simply for fun.

TOWN 'Town is always an alternative to the union,' she writes. 'Town-gown relations aren't too bad, it's safe. It has four clubs, including **Echos** and **Pulse**, which have student nights, and **Vice Versa**, a smart bar by day, a club by night, and as classy as Lboro gets. Don't expect to find anything ground breaking.

'The cost of a good night out in Lboro varies between £15 and £20. It's only £1.50 a pint in the union, and in town it is possible to drink spirits cheaply, and to absorb a different atmosphere in **Weatherspoons** (cheap food), **Orange Tree** (amazingly reasonable and drinkable cocktails) and **Matt's Bar** (dancing on the pool table). Loughborough also has a cinema, but that's about the only easily assessable/affordable alternative to pubs.

'Cost of living is neither one extreme nor the other, food for the week will cost anything from £20 upwards, although you learn to loathe pasta. Transport, taxis aside, is relatively cheap, the campus bus into town is 45p, the train to Leicester is £2.05 with a rail card.'

See *Student Leicester* and *Student Nottingham* (pages 270 and 342).

PILLOW TALK

'With the exception of Clearing students,' Vicky continues, 'all freshers are guaranteed hall accommodation, and it is usually possible to remain in hall throughout your time at Lboro, although a lot of people choose to spend a year in town. The halls are very varied, and as many are then divided into blocks, much depends on the eight or so people with whom you are sharing. Hazlerigg/Rutland is the only traditional hall –

```
WHERE GRADUATES END UP

26% Manufacturing*,     Key Areas
9% Computer,
9% Finance,
8% Wholesale/Retail,
5% Public Admin
Accountancy, Sport*,    Niche Areas
Aeronautical Manufac*,
Eng/Industrial Design,
Construction*,
Cheml/Pharmaceutical,
Defence*, Electron/
Electric*, Artistic,
Film/Video, Market
Research, Publishing

*indicates Top 10 Graduate Provider

Approximate employed    95%
```

corridors as opposed to blocks. Falkner/Eggington is the bargain basement, around £45 a week self catering, whilst David Collett is top of the range at around £100 a week, to mention just three of the fifteen halls available. Don't set your heart on a particular one, the allocation process appears random. Accommodation in town is more expensive, because of the utility bills, but it is quieter, less claustrophobic and less intrusive as you choose who you live with.'

All hall rooms are computer networked and carry phone sockets. There's something to suit every pocket. 'Loughborough is very hall-based,' declared another student, 'and the sense of loyalty and community spirit in these halls is of an intensity usually reserved for centuries-old universities.'

JOBS

'How much help is given and key skills taught appears to depend greatly on the department you are in,' says Vicky. 'The university does run seminars on such issues, though they are few and far between and take some tracking down. Should you need to top up your loan, the union runs an effective job exchange. However, you'll have more success if you apply at the very beginning of term.'

GETTING THERE

☞ By road: M1/J23, A512.
☞ By rail: London St Pancras, 1:45; Birmingham New Street, 1:30; Sheffield, 1:30; Nottingham, 0:20; Leicester, 0:15.
☞ By air: East Midlands Airport close by.
☞ By coach: London, 2:45; Exeter, 6:50; Newcastle, 8:10; Manchester, 4:30.

UNIVERSITY OF LUTON

The University of Luton
Park Square
Luton LU1 3JU

TEL 01582 489286
FAX 01582 489323
EMAIL admissions@luton.ac.uk
WEB www.luton.ac.uk

Luton University Students' Union
Vicarage Street
Luton LU1 3HZ

TEL 01582 489366
FAX 01582 457187
EMAIL (see website)
WEB www.luton.ac.uk

VAG VIEW

*T*hree years ago The Sunday Times *tore into Luton calling it 'the lowest form of university life'. Since then the uni has climbed many places in the media's league tables, was shown as top for graduate employment in April 2001 by the* Times *newspaper and was described recently by the* Guardian *as one of 'the most improved institutions'. We would like to say, 'Well done, and told you so,' because two years ago we said it would make it.*

The Sunday Times reporters, out for sock-it-to-'em column inches, had been unaware that Luton was on the painful curve of all new universities who are open house to the government's proposal that 50% of all sixthformers should go for a degree. They have had to dig deep, but they are getting there on a number of fronts, adding value to the lives of many who a few years ago might not have dreamed of going to university.

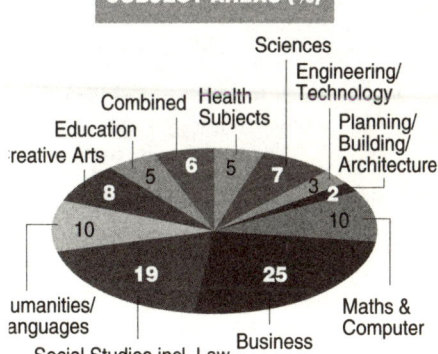

SUBJECT AREAS (%)

Widening access across socio-economic divides implies low entry requirements and lowish graduation marks for a while. When 39% of its non-mature entrants come from social groups IIIM, IV, and V, and 15% from so-called low-participation neighbourhoods, only 31% got firsts and upper seconds. Two years later, during which their teaching

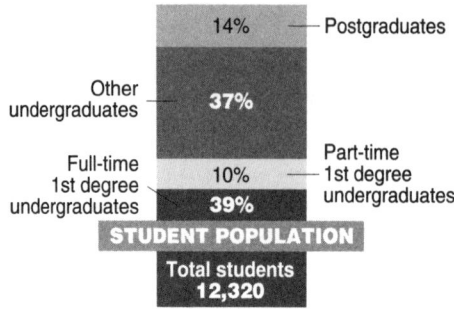

STUDENT POPULATION

Total students
12,320

assessments have been exemplary, the intake from poor areas has stayed the same and, while the non-traditional uni intake has climbed to 17%, the percentage of first class and upper second degrees has risen from 31% to 44%. What's more, their employment record has gone through the roof.

CAMPUS

Park Square is the main campus in the centre of town. There's a rural mansion a few miles away (Putteridge Bury), a conference centre and home to the Faculty of Management. Then there's a site in Castle Street in town for Humanities.

STUDENT PROFILE

Luton has one of the most diverse student populations in the country – 45% of students are over 24, 30% are from ethnic minority groups, nearly one-fifth of the student body is from

UNIVERSITY/STUDENT PROFILE

University since	**1993**
Situation/style	**Town sites**
Student population	**12,320**
Full-time undergraduates	**4,780**
- mature	**22%**
- overseas	**11%**
- male/female	**46/54**
- state sector intake	**99%**
- non-traditional student intake	**17%**
- drop-out rate	**15%, high**
- undergraduate applications	**Down 0.8%**
see Introduction for key to tables	

overseas – almost double the national average for international recruitment to a British uni. There are also plenty of locals.

Perhaps the main point in all this is that everybody who comes to Luton, comes for a purpose. They are not living out someone else's blueprint for life. They have concluded that these

days, to get on, you are going to have to get a degree. University may be a bit of a novelty thought for many of them, but very likely it is part of their own plan, often after they have been out in the workplace and seen what's missing. Someone once joked that all you needed to get into Luton in 1993 was two Es, but now you need two Es and a bag of amphetamine… Just to keep up.

ACADEMIA

Luton operates through six faculties: Business, Design & Technology, Health care & Social

ACADEMIC EXCELLENCE

TEACHING:
(Rated Excellent or 17+ out of 24)

Nursing, Health Science	**23**
Anatomy, Art & Design,	**22**
Pharmacology, Psychology, Organismal Biosciences, Molecular Biosciences, Media Studies, Building Surveying/Construction Mgt Linguistics	**21**
Modern Languages, Electrical & Electronic Engineering.	**20**
Sociology	**18**

RESEARCH :
Top grades 5/5* **None**

Studies, Humanities, Management, Science & Computing. Luton was one of the earliest purveyors of the modular course structure.

In the old days, you thought of Luton and you thought of Vauxhall Motors. Luton has always been heavily into links with commerce and industry, and it is ideally placed, between junctions 10 and 11 on the M1, twenty or so miles north-west of London, and in the vicinity of Vauxhall Motors. But while good relations with the business and industrial sectors remains at the heart of its education strategy (not complete until the graduate has a job), four or five years ago it began expanding in other important areas – £2 million on an art design studio, £5 million on a computer centre, £500,000 on a research centre, and £250,000 on a media centre.

And now we see the benefits – in percentage terms they are now the sixth among graduate providers to the radio/TV industry, and we see them operating big in other areas, such as journalism, market research, publishing, and sport – 'Media and sport are the big attractions,' one student said to me. 'Besides that broadcasting

WHAT IT'S REALLY LIKE

UNIVERSITY:

Social Life	★★★
Campus scene	Urban, prone to a good time
Student Union services	Average
Politics	Student issues; interest low
Sport	18 clubs
National team position	59th
Sport facilities	Good
Arts opportunities	Good drama; average art
Student magazine	Streaker
Student newspaper	Re:Present
Student radio	Luton FM
Nightclub	Sub Club
Bars	Main Bar, Bar None
Union ents	S.I.N., Club Crunchie, WAQ (We Are Queer)
Union clubs/societies	33
Most popular society	African Caribbean
Smoking	Union, halls OK
Parking	Adequate

TOWN:

Entertainment	★★★
Scene	Pubs, clubs
Town/gown relations	Poor
Risk of violence	High
Cost of living	High
Student concessions	Good
Survival + 2 nights out	£70 pw
Part-time work campus/town	Average/good

graduate recruitment. Worry not that Luton's overall academic Excellence score is relatively low (54%) because fifteen of its assessments were carried out between 1993 and 1995, when the uni was barely up and running. It is a sobering thought that Luton was not even a polytechnic when it was awarded university status in 1993.

SOCIAL SCENE

STUDENTS' UNION **Main Bar** is the focal point, replete with all the usual trappings – arcade machines, a juke box, tellies and the like vie for attention. An adjacent, courtyard, beer garden defeats all comers in the more clement months. Above the Main Bar lies **Bar None** and **The Coffee Shop**. The venue for most of the organised hedonism is **Sub Club**, in the basement of the building. Providing Thursday's hangover is Wednesday's *S.I.N. (cheese/chart)*, while Friday's *Club Crunchie* blasts nothing after 1996. On Saturday once a month Dot Cottens bring in *WAQ* (we are queer). The brain-damaging effects of such revelry can be put to the test at the regular *Quiz Nights*, and students with bright ideas can also put the facilities to their own use if they can convince the powers that be that enough people will attend.

Undisputed highlight of the year is the May Ball, which attracts thousands of the Luton faithful. The gowned and tuxedoed masses arrive in such numbers that the event is one of the country's largest student balls, and reckoned to be the best. For just over £30, the likes of Prodigy, Tim Westwood, Jeremy Healy, Dodgy, Space and the Bootleg Beatles rock your world, while casinos, funfairs and top nosh add to the experience.

Societies, of which there are 30-odd, include the huge Cocsoc, which aims to get punters drunk in style once a term on a variety of brightly coloured booze. Media-wise, there's magazine *Streaker* (student life laid bare), newspaper *Re:present*, and radio station, Luton fm.

studio, we've got a massive fitness suite and new scientific body fitness analysis equipment. It was only two or three years ago that the BSc Sports Therapy appeared on the course list, yet media and sport just scored big in the research assessments.

Again, they got a high research Grade 4 (max 5) in their newest subject, Tourism, which has already fed through as an important niche area in their employment statistics – see box, page 304.

Recent teaching assessments have been top class – 22 or 23 out of 24 points – in the areas of nursing, health science, anatomy, art & design, pharmacology, psychology, biosciences, media studies, surveying and construction management, the latter again a visible force in

> *Luton have one of the most diverse student populations in the country, and they have struggled through to prominence with the strategy that their job is not complete until each graduate has found a job.*

SPORT Besides access to pitches, there's the fitness centre, sauna, steam room and solarium. Sport is competitive here, not only an important academic subject – they came 59th in the national league. Womens rugby made it to top of their league and men's rugby climbed some sort of peak for the third time in four years. There are eighteen sports clubs from which to choose.

TOWN If you can tear yourself from the SU haven,

AT A GLANCE

ACADEMIC FILE:

Subjects assessed	**26**
Excellent	**54%**
Average requirements	**140 points**
Students-staff ratio	**16:1**
First/2:1 degree pass rate	**44%**

ACCOMMODATION FILE:

Guarantee to freshers	**100%**
Style	**Flats**
Catered	**30%**
En-suite	**None**
Approx price range pw	**£55**
Town rent pw	**£55**

Luton offers a varied alternative. **Charlie Brown's** continues to be a favourite in the area, and **Zone**, **Legends**, **The Edge** and **The Beach** also draw a crowd. Among bars and pubs the likes of **Brannigan's** have offers for those wielding the trusty NUS card. Cuisine is diverse, everything under the sun, but Wellington Street is popular for its numerous curry houses, including the bizarrely green-lit **Balti Nights**, which practically gives food away.

Initial NIMBYism has been replaced by arms opened to the spending power of 12,000 students, and the hostile reputation of the town is fading rapidly. As a preventive measure, however, the SU offers a 10% reduction on personal alarms and recommends their use as part of a nine-point safety routine. Minicab phones operate from the SU and the local police have provided a community bobby with direct responsibility for the uni.

PILLOW TALK

All freshers enjoy the literal melting pot of greenhouse-temperature modern halls, to which the fledgling uni treated itself as part of the first big £30-million spend. They're within staggering distance of the union, town centre and lecture halls. Three people to one bathroom. With around 25% of students living in uni-managed accommodation close by, the town centre feel almost like a campus.

JOBS

See our *Employment* box. Rarely more than 3% or 4% go without full-time employment after a year.

GETTING THERE

☛ By road: M1/J10t.
☛ By rail: London King's Cross Thameslink, 40 mins; Nottingham, 1:45; Oxford, 2:15; Birmingham New Street, 2:30.
☛ By air: London Luton Airport.
☛ By coach: London, 1:15; Manchester, 5-6:00.

WHERE GRADUATES END UP

13% Wholesale/Retail, Key Areas
12% Health/Social Work,
8% Manufacturing,
8% Public Admin,
7% Finance,
6% Education,
Hotel/Restaurant, Niche Areas
Advertising, Architecture,
Construction, Film/Video,
Journalism, Market
Research, Property, Sport,
Radio/TV*, Publishing,
Telecom

*indicates Top 10 Graduate Provider

Approximate employed **96%**

STUDENT MANCHESTER – THE CITY

Since the **Hacienda** closed in 1997 a number of clubs have tried to replace it. **Sankey's Soap** seemed to be the best contender, then closed, and has now reopened – quite a bit different to how it used to be, but *The Tribal Sessions* are quite the place to be for any true Mancunian hipster. **Planet K**, located in the trendy part of the Northern Quarter is Sankey's main rival and not quite as far off the beaten track. Although considered to be a bit passé by most students, Planet K boasts an interesting selection of DJs (recently including DJ Shadow). Another popular club, both with students and locals is **The Music Box**, which hosts a variety of regular and one-off nights, and is the current host of Mr Scruff's ever-popular *Keep It Unreal* sessions.

Right beside this is **Jilly's**, which is the club for alterna-kids and aged hard rockers. Although a tad on the gloomy side, Jilly's boasts three rooms which each play different veins of rock and metal (all equally heavy). Most challenging is perhaps the Friday night all-nighter. Also worth a mention here would be Richard O'Brien's recently opened nightclub, **Satan's Hollow**, which plays a variety of music on different nights, though mainly concentrating on the slightly gothic and theatrical! Although the entrance fee is quite high (£8.50), the Hollow boasts free drinks all night, and is definitely worth the experience!

Student favourites are still the **Ritz**, **5th Avenue** and **The Zumbar** (the latter also serves nice lunches). The stainless steel and white-walled **Elemental** is an up & coming club with a good atmosphere. All play a blend of indie and rock. 5th Avenue does tend to get a bit rough at weekends. Despite being quite a small venue, **The Brickhouse** is definitely worth a visit if you're chasing the Madchester vibe. Set in one of the arches beneath the railway-track, it has that classic industrial Northern feel. The posters of Manc classics such as Oasis, The Verve and The Happy Mondays which adorn the walls would keep the hardest fan happy. There's music to suit. The Aladdin's cave that is **Po Na Na** offers a nice alternative to indie-studenty nights, claiming to be (in their own words) a 'funky & exotic souk bar'.

Arguably the city's nightlife has been hard-hit by the new licensing hours that allow bars to stay open until 2 am. Popular late-night bars are the sci-fi themed **Fab Café** (with real daleks!), the fascinatingly-shaped **Contact Theatre** and the host of bars on Canal Street, the central point of Manchester's renowned Gay Village. The **Academy** also runs weekly nights which, being part of Manchester University, attracts a big student crowd. It is also one of the main live venues for touring bands. The city's other concert venues are **The Apollo**, **The Manchester Evening News Arena** and The **G-Mex**. For jazz fans, **Matt and Phred's Jazz Club**, **Band on the Wall** and **Jumpin' Jack's Piano Bar** are all worth a mention.

THEATRE

The Royal Exchange Theatre offers two stages (one in the round) and a combination of modern and traditional plays (all at student discounts). Situated in a rather nice area right in the city centre, it's also a good place to pop in for a cuppa during the day. Another of Manchester's major venues is **The Palace** theatre in Oxford Road. Although designed for more family-friendly showings, they offer a good mix of shows (currently showing the musical *Miss Saigon*) and fairly big names.

The Contact Theatre, with bizarre brick antenna sculpture on top, caters more to the student market and has occasional art exhibits as well as writing, DJ and drama workshops. Resplendent with vibrant orange décor, the Contact also features the **Café Deluxe**, which makes 'arty' sandwiches and a mean cup of coffee. **The Green Room** is another *avant-garde* venue which, like The Contact, boasts its own nightclub nights and a small café-bar. **The Lowry** is also

worth a mention here. Although a little more out-of-the-way than its rivals, it offers the largest stage outside of London, with Ferrari-designed seating! On a more low-key note, **The Library Theatre** offers a range of events from jazz to comedy, and traditional plays.

CINEMAS

Going to the cinema in Manchester costs about £4 pretty much everywhere. **The Filmworks** is by far the most popular, and despite seeming a little like an airport, boasts a ridiculous number of screens, some of which show IMAX 3D movies as well as arthouse and mainstream films. The **Odeon** is the city centre's only mainstream cinema, a quieter venue. In his days as Manchester United's captain, Eric Cantona used to get his French film 'fix' at the **Cornerhouse**, the best place for arthouse, foreign and small budget films. It also features a small but interesting art gallery and what is arguably the first modern-style bar in Manchester. Opened in 1985 it has an arty clientele and Belgium beers.

Although quite a way to travel out of the city and relatively expensive, **The UCI** at The Trafford Centre is also a nice little cinema complex (the outer facia has Islamic pillars beside the centre's themed foodcourt). But why not join the Manchester University Films Society? For £10 a year you get over forty films. Oh, and the **Cinecity** in Withington will appeal to those who live nearby. It has three, not particularly big screens, but it's cheap...

COMEDY

Manchester knows how to have a laugh. **The Comedy Club** is probably the best venue, especially on its infamous *Whose Line Is It Anyway* style nights. **The Frog and Bucket** is another popular comedy venue, although different in style, less slick and more traditional in its humour. They offer open mic nights on Mondays. **The Buzz** is possibly the longest running venue and has featured many a great, such as Jack Dee. Although not a very studenty venue, it's worth exploring. **The Dancehouse Theatre** is also known to host occasional comedy nights, as is **The Contact**, known for its up-and-coming, very modern acts).

SPORT

Manchester United memorabilia is everywhere and the ticket price is extortionate! Manchester City offers a more accessible option, their Maine Road grounds being far closer to the University and their blue-shirted fans loyally attending regular matches. Man City also offer discounts for students and, to be truthful, attract more Mancunian fans. Manchester Storm ice hockey is another favourite, and the Manchester Giants basketball team offer a student deal of £4 for a game.

Anyone starting at university in the next couple of years is most likely to be struck by the preparations for the 2002 Commonwealth Games. **The Aquatics Centre** is one such purpose-built swimming pool & leisure complex, partly university owned, which means cheaper rates for students. The downside is that the university is trying to jump on the bandwagon, sacrificing several halls of residence for athletes to occupy during the games.

University-owned sports complexes are the **Armitage** and **McDougall Centres**. They offer a variety of sports, cricket and football grounds as wells as gyms and tennis courts.

SHOPPING ON A GRANT

Affleck's Palace alone features more interesting little stalls than you can shake an oversized stick at, and is quite a Manc institution. A maze of a place it offers piercings, tattoos, t-shirts, CDs, vintage clothing, condoms, fancy dress, fetish wear and the ever popular rainbow-coloured hair extensions. **The Coliseum** is similar, situated behind Affleck's, on a smaller scale and with more of a gothic twist. **The Arndale Market** is handy for picking up cheap, fresh food as well as clothes, shoes and practical jokes – all fairly cheap.

The Student Market in the **Academy** sells bikes, clothes, hippie items, discount CDs and a variety of other stuff and is a favourite haunt on a Tuesday lunchtime. **The Trafford Centre** is the second biggest shopping centre in England and has literally miles of shops, but it's so big that your funky new purchases will probably have gone out of fashion by the time you leave. Most chain shops can be found in the city centre. Student discounts are ubiquitous.

ADDRESSES

Club & Live Venues: Sankey's Soap, Jersey Street, Ancotes. Tel:0161 228 0863 http://www.tribal sessions.co.uk. Planet K, 46-50 Oldham Street. Tel: 0161 839 9941. The Music Box, 65 Oxford Road, M1. Tel: 0775 914 117. Jilly's Rockworld, 65 Oxford Road. Tel: 0161 236 9971. Satan's Hollow, Princess Street. Tel: 0161 236 2019. The Ritz, Whitworth Street West. Tel: 0161 236 4355. 5th Avenue, 121 Princess Street. Tel: 0161 236 2754. Zumbar, 14 Oxford Road. Tel: 0161 236 8438. Elemental, Top of Oxford Road, Tel: 0161 236 7227. The Brickhouse, Arch 66, Whitworth Street West, M1. Tel: 0161 236 4418. Po Na Na, Charles Street. Tel: 0161 272 6044 The Fab Café, Portland Street. Tel: 0161 236 2019. The Contact Theatre, Oxford Road (next to the Students' Union) Tel: 0161 274 0600. University of

Manchester Union, Oxford Road. Tel: 0161 275 2930. The Apollo, Stockport Road, Ardwick Green. Tel: 0161 273 6921. G-Mex, Windmill Street, M2. Tel: 0161 834 2700. Manchester Evening News Arena, Victoria Station, Great Ducie Street. Tel: 0161 930 8000. Matt and Phred's Jazz Club, Oldham Street. Tel: 0161 661 7494 Jumpin' Jacks' Piano Bar, Portland Street. Band On The Wall, 25 Swan Street. Tel: 0161 834 1786 / 832 6625

Theatre: The Royal Exchange Theatre, St. Anne's Square, M2. Tel: 0161 833 9833. The Palace Theatre, Oxford Street, M1. Tel: 0161 242 2503. The Contact Theatre, Oxford Road, M15. Tel: 0161 274 3434. The Green Room, 54-56 Whitworth Street West, M1. Tel: 0161 950 5900/5777. The Lowry, Pier 8, Salford Quays. Tel: 0161 876 2000. The Library Theatre, St. Peters Square, M2. Tel: 0161 236 7110

Cinema: The Filmworks at The Printworks, 6-8 Dantzic Street Tel: 08705 888 999. Odeon, Oxford Street, M1. Tel: 0161 236 8890. The Trafford Centre, M17. Tel: 0161 746 7777. Cornerhouse, 70 Oxford Street, M1. Tel: 0161 236 8890.Manchester University Film Society, http://www.mufs.man.ac.uk. Cinecity, Wilmslow Road, Withington, M20. Tel: 0161 445 9888.

Comedy: The Comedy Store, Deansgate Locks. Tel: 08705 932 932. The Frog & Bucket Comedy Club, 102 Oldham Street. Tel: 0161 228 6335. The Buzz, The Southern, Nell Lane, Chorlton. Tel: 0161 440 8662. The Dancehouse Theatre, Top of Oxford Road. Tel: 0161 237 9753. The Contact Theatre, Oxford Road, M15. Tel: 0161 274 3434

Sport: Manchester United FC, Sir Matt Busby Way, Old Trafford, M16. Tel: 0161 872 0199. Manchester City FC, Maine Road, M14. Tel: 0161 226 2224. Manchester Storm & Manchester Giants, Manchester Evening News Arena, Tel: 0161 930 8000.The Armitage Centre, Fallowfield Campus. Tel: 0161 225 2911.The McDougall Centre, Manchester University Campus. Tel: 0161 275 5986

Shopping: Affleck's Palace, 52 Church Street. Tel: 0161 834 2039. The Coliseum, 24 Church Street. Tel: 0161 907 3935. Arndale Market in The Arndale Centre, Market Street. Tel: 0161 833 9851.Student Market, Manchester Academy, University of Manchester Union, M13 9PR. Tel: 0161 275 2930. The Trafford Centre, Dumplington (off M60). Tel: 0161 746 7777

Leonie Kenyon

UNIVERSITY OF MANCHESTER

The University of Manchester
Oxford Road
Manchester M13 9PL

TEL 0161 275 2077
FAX 0161 275 2106
EMAIL ug.admissions@man.ac.uk
WEB www.man.ac.uk

Manchester Students' Union
Oxford Road
Manchester M13 9PR

TEL 0161 275 2930
FAX 0161 275 2936
EMAIL union@umu.man.ac.uk
WEB wwwumu.man.ac.uk

VAG VIEW

*W*ith three universities – Manchester, Manchester Met and the science and technology uni, UMIST (not to mention Salford University, a 15-minute bus ride away) – whole areas of this elegant, busy city are, to all intents and purposes, university campus. With the Royal Northern School of Music and Manchester Business School also here, you have the largest conglomeration of students anywhere in the world.

Unable at first to take it all in, the effect is to make you focus on your own thing, which is precisely why there is no one Manchester University experience. If you're into sport or media or whatever, you'll find it a veritable playground, but whatever you get into, others' scenes rarely impinge, whereas they would in a smaller context – sport dominates everything at Loughborough, for example. The world here is that much bigger than at other unis, roughly three or four times the size in fact, and it focuses the mind wonderfully.

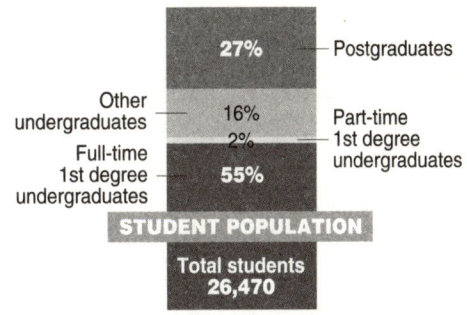

STUDENT POPULATION

Total students
26,470

SUBJECT AREAS (%)

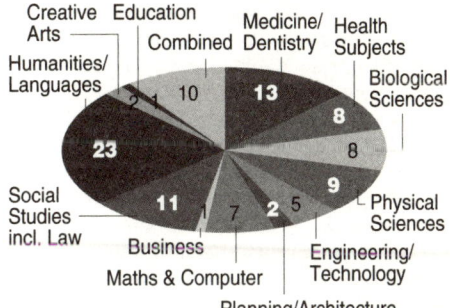

CAMPUS

Manchester Uni has grown up with the city. The Wilmslow/Oxford Road runs right through the centre of campus, linking it at the top end with Manchester Met, Whitfield Street (gateway to the city's legendary Gay Village) and UMIST, and at the bottom end with the most populous areas of student residences – Rusholme, Fallowfield, etc.

The whole street is campus, but it is also city. Manchester University has a theatre (**Contact**) and a premier gig venue (**The Academy**) and a museum (**Manchester Museum**, currently undergoing a £20-million facelift) and an art gallery (**Whitworth**) which are all key sites of this city (see Student Manchester, page 304).

City and university are absolutely inseparable, not least because they share the same vibe. It is an

UNIVERSITY/STUDENT/PROFILE	
University since	**1903**
Situation/style	**Civic**
Student population	**26,470**
Full-time undergraduate	**14,560**
- mature	**11%**
- overseas	**8%**
- male/female	**48/52**
- state sector intake	**74%**
- non-traditional student intake	**10%**
- drop-out rate	**5%**
- undergraduate applications	**Down 3%**
see Introduction for key to tables	

active, buzzing scene, a place some parents dread their children choosing.

STUDENT PROFILE

There is a socially well-balanced population with a sizeable portion now coming from non-traditional areas of supply, and a bigger state school intake than at Durham, Bristol, Exeter or Oxbridge.

In general, Manchester is a university for kids who like to make things happen – they're an intelligent, resourceful, lively crew, not afraid or too lazy to lay themselves on the line and apply themselves, and not averse to letting their hair down either. In a survey by the Adam Smith Institute (*The Next Leaders?*) they came out top for sex and drugs, leaving Cambridge to take the honours on booze.

ACADEMIA

There is no limit to the number of top-rated course assessments – 96% make our criteria of Academic Excellence (see box), and research here has a pedigree of its own – this is where Ernest, First Baron Rutherford did the work which led to the splitting of the atom, and where the computer was invented. The uni came 9th in the recent national research assessments and claims the top grade 5 or 5* ratings in 37 out of 46 subjects.

On-campus resources include the John Rylands Library, the third largest uni library in the country with more than 3.5 million books. There is no shortage of computer technology – there are now 6,000 PCs in public clusters on campus.

Work has begun on £400-million plans to create Europe's premier Biomedical campus – a series of linked scientific and hospital facilities on Oxford Road – in partnership with the Health service. Construction has begun, too, on the £39.5-million Integrative Centre for Molecular Cell Biology (ICMCB) for post-Genome research.

Rumour is rife that Manchester and UMIST are to merge – the idea is being tested on students and staff as I write. See UMIST entry, page 311

SOCIAL SCENE

STUDENTS' UNION It is an unadventurous soul who appears at the foot of MUSU's steps any day in term time and resists propulsion inside – bodies hurry purposefully like ants, while as alien visitors we were drawn irredeemably by the sights and sounds of the new **Solem Bar**. The sound inside is the city and has the power during the day to reconfigure the cranium back into last night's form. The bar's design – 'Swedish sauna meets trendy metal,' sour-pussed someone in earshot – actually makes for a cosy place to hang out, and perhaps shoot some pool on the new tables. It's a vast improvement on

ACADEMIC EXCELLENCE	
TEACHING: *(Rated Excellent or 17+ out of 24)*	
Chemistry, Law, Mechanical Engineering, Anthropology, Business & Management, Computer Studies, Music, Geography, Social Policy & Administration, Earth Sciences	**Excellent**
Physics, Management, Politics, Economics, Philosophy, Dentistry, Medicine, Pharmacology	**24**
Anatomy, Archaeology, Biosciences, Nursing	**23**
Psychology, Maths, Leisure, Subjects Allied to Medicine	**22**
German, Linguistics, Sociology, Materials Technology, Drama, History of Art	**21**
Iberian Studies, Electrical & Electronic Eng, Aerospace Eng, Town & Country Planning, Middle Eastern Studies	**20**
French, Italian	**19**
Civil Engineering	**18**
RESEARCH: *Top grades 5/5**	
Pharmacy, Pre-Clinical Studies, Biological Sciences, Computer, Metallurgy , Sociology, Accounting, French, German, Dutch/Scandinavian, Iberian/ Latin American, Theology, Music	**Grade 5***
Community & hospital-based Clinical Subjects, Nursing, Subjects Allied to Medicine, Psychology, Chemistry, Physics, Earth Sciences, Pure Maths, Applied Maths, Civil Eng, Mechanical/Aeronautical, Manufacturing Eng, Law, Anthropology, Politics, Social Policy, Management, Middle Eastern and African Studies, English, Italian, Linguistics, Classics, History, History of Art, Drama/Dance/Performing Arts	**Grade 5**

the old Serpent Bar.

'Next door to the union is the **Academy**, a 1,200-capacity live band venue,' Leonie Kenyon tells us, 'and, on the top floor of the union, is the **Hop & Grape**, not actually a pub despite it's name, but a small bar and occasional venue for live bands.

These venues have recently been visited by Placebo, Pitchshifter, Eels, and Ash, and the Academy has the infamous *Club Tropicana* cheese nights on Tuesdays, pulling itself round in time for the Student Market during the day. It's a prime spot for posters, bikes, CDs, clothes and hippy items, a favourite haunt of students especially at lunchtime when the homemade chocolate cakes are rather popular! Another union nightclub is the **Cellar**, which features *Horny* on Friday, and plays a mixture of pop and cheese. On weekday afternoons it is also used as a café.'

Twice a year comes *Club Trop All Nighter*,

> *Manchester is a university where you can experience the thrill of making things happen big-style. It is not just one university, but three gigantic ones, all clustered around Oxford Road. You do stuff together, even share halls.*

In the area of drama, the uni is a major force, the annual springtime student festival still reigns supreme. And politically, the union's campaigning reputation still goes unquestioned.

SPORT The teams came 14th in the national uni team ratings last year. Facilities include a boat house on the Bridgewater Canal, Yacht Club at Pennington Flash, Leigh, 18 miles west of the city. Pitches (31 acres) for rugby, soccer, hockey, lacrosse, cricket, netball, are close to the student village at Fallowfield, also tennis courts, all-weather, artificial grass areas and pavilion. In Fallowfield, too, is the **Armitage Centre** with sports hall and squash

AT A GLANCE	
ACADEMIC FILE:	
Subjects assessed	**44**
Excellent	**96%**
Average A level requirements	**24 points**
Students-staff ratio	**15:1**
First/2:1 degree pass rate	**66%**
ACCOMMODATION FILE:	
Guarantee to freshers	**100%**
Style	**Halls, flats**
Catered	**28%**
En-suite	**27%**
Price range pw	**£40-£93**
City rent pw	**£43**

WHAT IT'S REALLY LIKE	
UNIVERSITY:	
Social Life	★★★★★
Campus scene	**Big, busy, self-assured**
Student Union services	**Average**
Politics	**Active**
Sport	**Key**
National team position	**14th**
Sport facilities	**Good**
Arts opportunities	**Excellent; high profile drama, dance, film**
Student newspaper	**Student Direct**
Independent awards	**For diversity**
Guardian awards	**Critic of the Year**
Student radio	**Fuse FM**
Student TV	**MSTV**
Nightclub	**Cellar**
Bars	**Solem Bar, Lunar Café**
Union ents	**Horny and much much more**
Union clubs/societies	**150**
Smoking policy	**Union OK**
Parking	**Poor**
CITY:	
Entertainment	★★★★★
City scene	**Legendary**
Town/gown relations	**Average-poor**
Risk of violence	**High**
Cost of living	**High**
Student concessions	**By the ton**
Survival + 2 nights out	**£70 pw**
Part-time work campus/town	**Good/excellent**

which takes over the entire union, including the Academy next door, in a multi-faceted romp with casino and dodgems and all the rest. Early this year the gig guide to the Academy – the veritable summit of achievement of full-time ents manager Sean Morgan and his sidekick, Sarah – saw twenty-two acts between October and December.

Meanwhile, students galvanise themselves into national prominence with their media. Manchester has had a long history of student radio – Storm fm won Best Student Radio Station in 1998, but unaccountably fell away, leaving a major gap. Then in the summer of 2000, Zoe Abrams and Penny Hollings set up Fuse fm, which, with MSTV, is going from strength to strength. Meanwhile *Student Direct* – the student newspaper with a 60,000 readership, won gongs in both *Independent* and *Guardian* awards last year.

courts close by. A further 90 acres lie ten miles south, below the M63, at Wythenshawe sports ground. On campus itself is the **McDougal Centre**, which has a swimming pool, indoor games hall, gym, squash and fives courts, an outside five-a-side court, rifle range, climbing wall, bowls carpets, sauna and solarium.

This year the new Commonwealth Games swimming pool, where the swimming and diving competitions will take place (just opposite the SU) is already open to students. The old pool is being converted into more gym/fitness areas.

There are bursaries, two offered by the exclusive XXI, an elite sports club founded in 1932.

Town 'A quiet city it is not,' writes Leonie. 'It's easy to work out what's going on, though. Just grab the many student publications and well-connected *City Life* magazine. Highlights include **Jilly's Rockworld** (headbanging for crusty metallers - the 7am all-nighter is a favourite), **Sankey's Soap** (freshly reopened with some very decent DJs and great atmosphere), **The Fab Café** (if it's real Daleks you're after) and **Satan's Hollow** (which is owned and designed by *Rocky Horror* nut Richard O'Brien). The legendary Canal Street (also known as the Gay Village) is home to some of the funkiest nights out in the city, as is neighbouring Princess Street, where there are many student clubs (like the **Mutt's Nutz** – on Friday nights all the drinks are only 50p!) Student nights don't usually cost more than £8 with a few drinks, and if you use your common sense and stick with friends you'll be fine.' See Leonie's *Student Manchester*, page 304.

PILLOW TALK

All freshers are guaranteed a place in halls and flats: 28% are catered, 27% en suite; price range per week £40 - £93. The most populous areas of student residences – Rusholme, Fallowfield, etc – are at the bottom end of the Oxford Road corridor. Writes Leonie: 'From the main Manchester Library (white, colonnaded and extremely impressive), you go under the railway line and through Rusholme's Curry Mile - which, as the name would suggest, is full of curry houses and interesting Eastern-style shops. Although located next to the infamously undesirable Moss Side, it is quite safe. Getting to everything is never a problem since Oxford Road is the busiest bus route in Europe (one bus every two minutes on average), so it's always easy to get around (bus passes are a very cheap £3 a week).

'Fallowfield is the ideal place to live as it is secure, lively, and features some very nice little houses. The student halls range from very nice to eyesore (The Oak House Tower - eek!), and are backed by the university-owned Armitage Sports Centre, which offers student discounts on a range of sporty activities. The road here is lined with bars and pubs (including the oft-frequented vodka bar, **Revolution**) and has buzzing, student-orientated nightlife. Withington is a little quieter, a little more expensive, and that little bit further away from the universities and the town centre, but has a good variety of pubs, shops and coffee shops. Similarly Didsbury (home of the "Disbury Dozen" series of pubs – a pub crawl classic) has a good deal to offer, but is more expensive than the wholly studenty Fallowfield area.

'Victoria Park is seen as the posh alternative, probably because most of its halls are large, leafy, Victorian buildings. It's an area between Fallowfield and the main University campus – approximately fifteen minutes' walk from the main university buildings. The Students' Union is located at the top of the Victoria Park area, as is Whitworth Park Hall, affectionately known as the Toblerone building and the perfect choice for Arts students, since you can stagger out of bed and be right outside the Faculty of Arts. These halls tend to be a tad more expensive, partly because the rooms are nicer, partly most are catered.

'There are also private halls of residence in the Student Village in the city centre, popular with students at Manchester Metropolitan since it is right on their doorstep. Victoria Hall is another privately owned student residence, conveniently situated near the city centre. Possibly the best way to find accommodation is through Manchester Student Homes, a commission-free agency run by the universities. "Homes 4 U" on Oxford Road is also worth exploring, which has recently turned into a bizarre (if a little pretentious) mix of Internet café, "lifestyle lounge" and Estate Agent, and frequently offers some high quality, reasonably priced houses for rent. The Student Village, Lancaster House, 80 Princess Street, M1 6NF. Tel: 0161 236 1776. Victoria Hall (several locations) http://www.victoriahall.com. Manchester Student Homes, The University Precinct Centre, Oxford Road, M13 9NR. Tel: 0161 275 7680. Homes 4U, 12 Oxford Road, M1 5QA. Tel: 0161 236 0202.'

JOBS

In a national survey of companies which recruit graduates ('Signposts to Employability'), Manchester has been voted number one for graduate employability. As our *Employment* box shows (page 310), the single largest section of graduates go into the health industry, medicine and dentistry, but if you were to add financial

activities, accountancy and business management together, they would run the health area a close second. Engineering and construction are also strong and there are a number of media niches which welcome Manchester graduates each year.

The union runs what's known as the CPD (Certificate in Personal Development), a course to train you in skills your course doesn't cover (though many a student club or society might) – team building, assertiveness, meeting skills, presentation skills, time & stress management, etc.

GETTING THERE

☛ By road: M63/J10, A34.
☛ By rail: London Euston, 2:30; Leeds, 1:45; Liverpool Lime Street, 0:50.
☛ By air: Manchester Airport for international and inland flights.
☛ By coach: London, 4:35; Bristol, 5:00; Newcastle, 5:00.

UNIVERSITY OF MANCHESTER INSTITUTE OF SCIENCE & TECHNOLOGY

UMIST
PO Box 88
Sackville Street
Manchester M60 1QD

TEL 0161 236 3311
FAX 0161 200 4337
EMAIL ug.prospectus@umist.ac.uk
WEB www.umist.ac.uk

UMIST Students' Association
PO Box 88
Sackville Street
Manchester M60 1QD

TEL 0161 200 3270
FAX 0161 200 3268
EMAIL council@umiststudents.com
WEB www.umiststudents.com

VAG VIEW

*A*s far as head-hunting is concerned this is one of the best. Employers look to UMIST on a par with Oxbridge, particularly for Engineering, IT, often with a French or a German connection. Science in general is well covered there. They have specialised, and they are the best at what they do. They are in the midst of one of the biggest, if not the biggest centre of higher education in Europe, and maybe they have had to develop their identity in a way that not many other universities have. So they have looked at their strengths and developed them. Pity, then, that there is talk of a merger with Manchester University.

CAMPUS

Campus is situated just north of the Mancunian Way A57(M), at the top of the Oxford Road corridor,

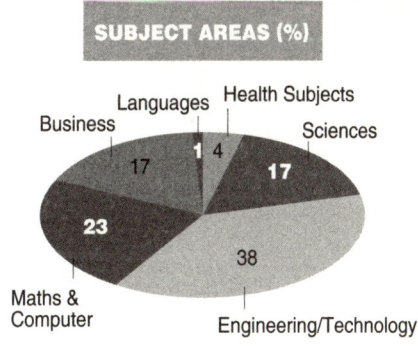

SUBJECT AREAS (%)

Languages — 1
Health Subjects — 4
Business — 17
Sciences — 17
Maths & Computer — 23
Engineering/Technology — 38

which harbours Manchester and Manchester Metropolitan universities and is close to Whitfield Street (gateway to Manchester's legendary Gay Village). It is a lively, colourful scene, a fantastic conglomeration of higher education, and though tucked away safely, its purpose-built campus a

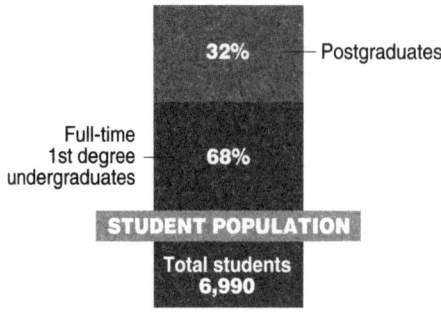

32% — Postgraduates

Full-time
1st degree — 68%
undergraduates

STUDENT POPULATION

Total students
6,990

little more out of sight than Manchester Uni, UMIST is very much part of the scene, with its own particular personality.

STUDENT PROFILE

Now, I can just hear you say, Yeah, yeah, but they're just a load of spods doing what they're told to do aren't they? How is it, then, I reply, that the UMIST Union has taken its life into its own hands in a way the other unis have not, they have adopted an entirely new constitution, broken with the National Union of Students, saved thereby £100k and put it into a building refurb and increased grants for its student societies?

INSTITUTE/STUDENT PROFILE	
Independent university since	**1993**
Situation/style	**Campus**
Student population	**6,990**
Full-time undergraduates	**4,760**
- mature	**10%**
- overseas	**15%**
- male/female	**69/31**
- state sector intake	**80%**
- non-traditional student intake	**12%**
- drop-out rate	**8%**
- undergraduate applications	**Down 0.4%**
see Introduction for key to tables	

UMIST recruits widely in the state sector (80% of its undergraduates) and from areas which have not traditionally sent to university (12% come this way, which is high for a uni of this calibre). It is one of the government's elite access universities, showing that their academic prowess can do more than preen, it can add value to a student's intellectual portfolio. UMIST is in this sense a real university, uniting diversity into a well-balanced personality, a more balanced set-up than, say, Imperial College in London. Both suffer the problem of all scientific/technological institutions – a lack of women, but there is a considered, independent streak about UMIST's student body.

ACADEMIA

UMIST offers degrees through the following departments: Biochemistry & Applied Molecular Biology; Building Engineering; Chemical Engineering; Chemistry; Civil and Structural Engineering; Computation; Electrical Engineering & Electronics; INTENGO (an engineering course for students without Physics & Maths at A level); Language & Linguistics (including Computational Linguistics, surely unique, which looks at how to write computer programs that translate language); Management; Materials Science; Mathematics; Mechanical Eng.; Optometry & Vision Sciences; Paper Science; Physics; Textiles.

ACADEMIC EXCELLENCE	
TEACHING:	
(Rated Excellent or 17+ out of 24)	
Business & Management	**Excellent**
Optometry	**23**
Chemical Engineering, Civil Eng,	**22**
Elec & Electron Engineering,	
Maths, Building, Land &	
Property Management,	
Molecular Biosciences	
Materials Technology,	**21**
Physics	
Aeronautical Engineering	**20**
Modern Languages (French,	**18**
German, Spanish, Linguistics)	
RESEARCH	
*Top grades 5/5**	
Studies/Professions Allied to	**Grade 5***
Medicine, Metallurgy	
Pure Maths,	**Grade 5**
Chemical Eng., Civil Eng,	
Electrical/Electronic Eng	
Mechanical/Aeronautical/	
Manufacturing Eng,	
Business/Management	

The curriculum has always been pioneering, drawing inspiration from its strong lines in research, offering useful combinations such as engineering with languages, science with management and opportunities in specialist, highly employable areas, such as Paper Science, Materials Science or Textiles. Recent expansion is evident on the Life/Biological side, as in Neuroscience and Bioinformatics.

Resources include the Joule Library (261,000 vols, 1,200 periodicals, masses of info-access technology and PCs) and an IT centre equipped with some of the most powerful computers in the world. Advice, as well as equipment, is available via the UMIST Information Systems Support Service. Laboratory equipment in the Pilot Plant, a laboratory for industrial-scale experiments, is constantly being up-dated; investments run into millions of pounds and, as they say, it is doubtful whether any other university in the country has the range of equipment and facilities which you will find here.

SOCIAL SCENE

As if this wasn't enough they've gone and done *Sub Tub* at **The Underground**, 'bravely taking on the Electric Chair with their unique serving of live skating, breaking and graffiti set to an appropriate soundtrack of hip hop and jungle.' *Sub Tub* is one of UMIST's three regular clubnights (also *Frenzy* and *Prohibition*) and described by Manchester Met's well-informed *Pulp* magazine as 'one of last year's best newcomers,' so if you find yourself a student at one of this great city's universities and it isn't UMIST, swallow your preconceptions and wind round to the 650-capacity club in the **Barnes Wallis Building**, part of the core quadrangle beyond the railway viaduct, the zone that also carries, **Harry's Bar** and the **Rock/Cyber Café**. Someone there – viz an assorted ents team of DJs, technicians, promoters and blagsters – is getting it together.

There is very close communion with the other unis in the area over many things, such as sports facilities (use is made of the new **Commonwealth Games Pool** in Oxford Road opposite Manchester union (MUSU), but actually on UMIST land, as they are happy to point out), and drama – there's a joint MUGSS (Manch Unis' Gilbert & Sulivan Society), producing two or three very high standard, sell-out shows a year. The UMIST Rag (charity extrav) runs the largest British uni beer fest and longest sponsored walk, the 55-mile Bogle Stroll. Other dynamic groups at UMIST include Chinese, Malaysian, Greek and Islam societies, as well as the infamous Cocktail Society. At least they don't call it CockSoc, like so many.

For the bits beyond, see Leonie Kenyon's article, Student *Manchester*, page 304. Highlights include the **Gay Village** (within Princess, Sackville, Portland, Whitworth Streets – **Follies**, **New York New York**). Canal Street is here – full of stylish bars and cafés, welcoming gays and straights. If that's your thing big-time you might like to try Manchester Met's celebrated Thursday night *G-Aytoun* (now Gay2, page 316) first. It's just across the road from UMIST. Cosy ain't it?

They also run Manutech Computers, selling top-rate, custom-built PCs to students for under £400, and Manutech Copyshop for budget binding, T-shirt printing as well as photocopying. You can begin to see why UMIST only has a less than 2% unemployment rate (presumably those Sub-Tubbed to extinction).

> *They have specialised. They are in the midst of one of the biggest, centre of higher education in Europe. They are the best at what they do.*

SPORT UMIST has five acres of pitches and shares Manchester Uni's extensive facilities. 1998 saw the opening of the new Sugden Sports Centre, with sports hall, outdoor five-a-side pitches, outdoor courts for netball and tennis and a fitness suite. There is a boathouse on the Bridgewater Canal and the Sailing Club uses Sale Water Park in Trafford.

PILLOW TALK

Traditional (catered) and self-catering residential

WHAT IT'S REALLY LIKE

UNIVERSITY:	
Social Life	★★★★
Campus scene	**Bright spods, good at a groove**
Student Union services	**First class**
Politics	**Student issues; unfevered activity**
Sport	**Competitive**
National team position	**60th**
Sport facilities	**Good**
Arts opportunities	**Drama excellent; music good; art, dance, film avg**
Student magazine	**Grip**
Student radio	**UMISTradio**
Nightclub	**Club Underground**
Bars	**Harry's Bar, Paddy's Lounge**
Union ents	**SUB TUB**
Union clubs/societies	**70**
Most popular society	**Islamic**
Smoking policy	**Union & halls OK**
Parking	**Poor**
CITY:	
Entertainment	★★★★★
City scene	**Legendary**
Town/gown relations	**Poor**
Risk of violence	**High**
Cost of living	**High**
Student concessions	**By the ton**
Survival + 2 nights out	**£60 pw**
Part-time work campus/town	**Good/excellent**

```
               AT A GLANCE

        ACADEMIC FILE:
        Subjects assessed    15
               Excellent     80%
   Average A level requirements  23 points
        Students-staff ratio  11:1
   First/2:1 degree pass rate  58%

        ACCOMMODATION FILE:
        Guarantee to freshers  100%
                   Style      Halls
        Approx price range pw  £57-£74
               City rent pw    £43
```

or guarantees of eventual employment, but sponsored places at the university. UMIST is a key artery in the academic arm of industry. Full-time staff are in place to organise sponsorship for students on a one-to-one basis. It works because industry endorses the courses here and because UMIST is in constant touch with industry about new directions in Engineering, Science, Management and related subjects, each year introducing new courses to reflect industry changes.

accommodation is provided for all first years, some also used by Manchester Uni. Sites are either on campus or southward in the direction of MUSU and on into the student areas of Rusholme, Fallowfield and Levenshulme. Each hall has a life of its own, bars, sports teams, ents, etc. None is more than a few miles from campus. A new accommodation bureau – Manchester Student Homes – has been launched jointly with neighbouring unis.

GETTING THERE
☛ By road: M63/J10, A34.
☛ By rail: London Euston, 2:30; Leeds, 1:45; Liverpool Lime Street, 0:50.
☛ By air: Manchester Airport for international and inland flights.
☛ By coach: London, 4:35; Bristol, 5:00.

JOBS
UMIST may not be providing graduates in the same quantity as some, owing to the size of the institute, but their 97% employment rate is top notch. No surprise they won a Queen's Anniversary Prize for the international standards and all-round qualities of their engineering graduates. They run what is probably the most extensive student-sponsorship scheme with industry anywhere in the UK. We are not just talking about work placements, sandwich courses

```
           WHERE GRADUATES END UP

   17% Manufacturing*,   Key Areas
   14% Wholesale/Retail*,
        13% Computer*,
        10% Finance
        Accountancy,     Niche Areas
   Business/Management*,
   Aeronautical Manufacture,
   Chemical/Pharmaceutical*,
   Eng/Industrial Design*,
   Property, Electron/
   Electric, Telecom*

   *indicates Top 10 Graduate Provider

   Approximate employed   97%
```

MANCHESTER METROPOLITAN UNIVERSITY

The Manchester Metropolitan University
All Saints
Manchester M15 6BH

TEL 0161 247 2000
TEL 0161 247 1055 (prospectus)
FAX 0171 247 6871
EMAIL prospectus@mmu.ac.uk
WEB www.mmu.ac.uk

Manchester Met Students' Union
99 Oxford Road
Manchester M1 7EL

TEL 0161 273 1162
FAX 0161 273 7237
EMAIL mmsu@mmu.ac.uk
WEB www.mmsu.com

VAG VIEW

*M*anchester Met, formerly Manchester Poly, is situated on various sites in

Manchester and in Crewe and Alsager, two towns either side of the M6 between junctions 16 and 17.

People pick MMU for its reputation as a

party-till-you-die university. When you visit, they do not disappoint: 'Everyone gets very focused on what's going here, which is massive,' confessed a student.

CAMPUS

The Manchester base, which forms the largest higher education 'campus' in the UK, is centred at the All Saints site on Oxford Road, very close to Manchester Uni, making, with UMIST and a couple of colleges, a quite extraordinary concentration of students (around 100,000) within the square mile.

Crewe & Alsager are towns about six miles apart, some thirty-five miles south of Manchester, their semi-rural campus environments a million miles away in spirit from heaving Oxford Road. 'There's not a lot of contact with Crewe & Alsager,' my guide admitted. 'They always say there is, but in practice there's not. They have their own set-up down there. They're very sports and drama orientated. I think you still get some who enrol for C&A and are quite surprised that it's not just down the road and you can't always get up here on a Saturday night! I understand quite a few drop out over that.'

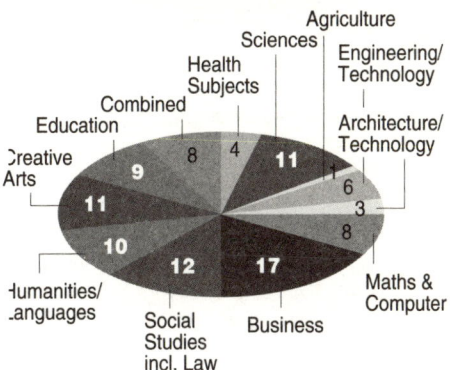

SUBJECT AREAS (%)

and there's not a lot of difference between the two departments. When students are actually here, I don't think they perceive much difference between the two establishments.'

ACADEMIA

The modular courses have a practical emphasis, tracing a clear vocational line to jobs in industry, where their employment rate is good (see our *Employ-*

> *MMU is not as staid as Manchester University. For example, we have a very strong gay scene. Of all the guidebooks in MMU, Différance is the first to sell out.*

STUDENT PROFILE

At MMU there is a high percentage of mature and part-time students. 'MMU is perceived to be the younger more dynamic university because it is not as staid as Manchester University,' said Bruce McVean, in the position of having been an engineering student at Manchester Uni and, seeking a course change to Geography, being turned down and then accepted by MMU. 'But I now know people doing Geography at Manchester

ment box, page 317).

More than 400 courses are offered from within the following faculties: Art and Design; Community Studies, Law and Education; Food, Clothing & Hospitality Management; Humanities & Social Science; Management & Business; Science & Engineering. What is notable is their approach to teaching, which has received top-class ratings in the QAA assessments: small seminar groups with considerable personal contact with tutors.

At Alsager there's a whole range of sports science subjects available, plus the departments of Humanities & Applied Social Studies (Sociology

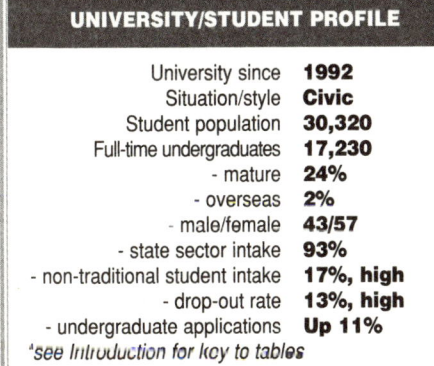

UNIVERSITY/STUDENT PROFILE

University since	**1992**
Situation/style	**Civic**
Student population	**30,320**
Full-time undergraduates	**17,230**
- mature	**24%**
- overseas	**2%**
- male/female	**43/57**
- state sector intake	**93%**
- non-traditional student intake	**17%, high**
- drop-out rate	**13%, high**
- undergraduate applications	**Up 11%**

see Introduction for key to tables

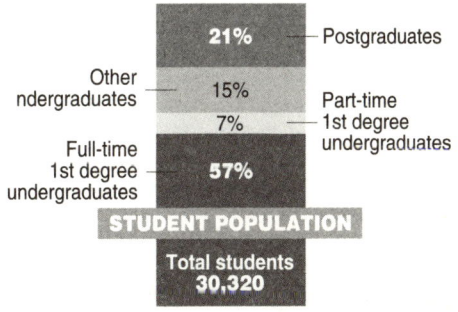

STUDENT POPULATION

Total students
30,320

ACADEMIC EXCELLENCE

TEACHING:
(Rated Excellent or 17+ out of 24)

Mechanical Engineering	**Excellent**
Drama, Business & Mgt	**23**
History of Art & Design,	**22**
Materials Technol, Psychology, Subjects Allied to Medicine, Anatomy, Art & Design, Tourism, Molecular & Organismal Biosciences	
Sociology, Modern Languages,	**21**
Electron & Elect Eng, Dental Technology, Nursing	
Maths, Town/Country Planning	**20**
Food Science	**19**

RESEARCH:
Top grades 5/5*

Sports-related Subjects	**Grade 5***

scored an excellent 21 on inspection) and the Modular Office, which looks after all inter-departmental modular mixes. At Crewe, the Business & Management Department sits alongside the Department of Environmental & Leisure Studies with its own stream, woodland and conservation habitats. Other than that, there is the School of Education (PGCEs and Primary and Secondary degrees)

SOCIAL SCENE

STUDENTS' UNION There are of course many collaborations between Manchester Uni and city central Manchester Met, the unions being but a walk apart on Oxford Road, the most visible of which is *Student Direct*, the paper which last year won both *Guardian* and *Independent* awards. *Student Direct* and Manchester Met's *Pulp* magazine now get distributed to all four unis (UMIST and Salford included). *Pulp* is now a kind of lifestyle supplement to the newspaper.

There are, nevertheless, marked differences between the two unis. There is great activity within student societies at Manchester Met – seventy all told, but, as one student said to me, 'Politics is a dirty word... We don't have a very political union. We have political groups – Socialist Workers and so on, but that whole scene is more active at Manchester University. It's a lot more that our union here provides a service, it's more of a social and representational thing.

'But we still have a really strong gay scene within the union, and what was *G-Aytoun* is now Gay2 on Tuesdays. Being close to Manchester's

famed **Gay Village** (within Princess, Sackville, Portland, Whitworth Streets), the city's gay scene is pretty influential anyway.' Gays won't need to be told about Manchester's *Mardi Gras*, an unforgettable weekend of parades and parties, and every two years **Queer Up North** bring their own influential brand of culture to the city. But the hub – day in, day out – is the Village: late licensing, all-night cafés and a huge choice of venues, all within walking distance of one another and MU and MMU and UMIST.

Watering holes at union headquarters on Oxford Road include **Blue Café**, open from 8.30 am Monday to Friday for breakfast, lunch. Then, there's **MancUnion Bar** with big screen TV and bar promotions. **K-Two** is the 900-capacity nightclub. They say that when K-Two is open till 2, MancUnion's is also open till 2, but then MancUnion has a licence till 2 every day except Sunday. Almost every major DJ has graced the K2 decks.

Besides club tours and MancMet's balls, regular fare currently includes *Booney Tunes* @ **K2** on Monday, with *2 Funky* (soul and house) upstairs,

WHAT IT'S REALLY LIKE

UNIVERSITY:
Social Life	★★★★★
Campus scene	**Huge, diverse happening place**
Student Union services	**Average**
Politics	**Low interest**
Sport	**Competitive**
National team position	**27th**
Sport facilities	**Good**
Arts opportunities	**Music, film excellent; rest good**
Student magazine	**Student Pages**
Student newspaper	**Student Direct**
Nightclub	**K-Two**
Bars	**ManUnion**
Union ents	**Booney Tunes, Gay2, Revival, Double Vision**
Union clubs/societies	**70**
Smoking policy	**Union OK**
Parking	**Poor**

CITY:
Entertainment	★★★★★
City scene	**Legendary**
Town/gown relations	**Poor**
Risk of violence	**High**
Cost of living	**High**
Student concessions	**Excellent**
Survival + 2 nights out	**£60 pw**
Part-time work campus/town	**Good/excellent**

```
AT A GLANCE

ACADEMIC FILE:
Subjects assessed          29
Excellent                  69%
Average A level requirements  14 points
Students-staff ratio       20:1
First/2:1 degree pass rate 45%

ACCOMMODATION FILE:
Guarantee to freshers      70%
Style                      Halls, houses
Approx price range pw      £45-£73
City rent pw               £43
```

Gay2 @ **K2** on Tuesday, *Revival* (dance) on Wednesday, *Double Vision* (party toons) on Friday.

Down in Crewe+Alsager there is a union presence, and bars, shops, clubs and societies at both campuses, and even a nightclub at Crewe. Currently they're running a competition to name their bars, and advertising for students to come help run ents. It is not Manchester, so don't come here if that's what you're after, but there are bus nights to city clubs and among a handful of societies may be found four – Live Music, Alternative Music, Music and Film – which suggest a commendable do-it-yourself artistry to life.

Alsager has an **Arts Centre** with a resident theatre company and a packed programme of performance and literary arts. There are two theatres (the **Axis Theatre** seating 500), a dance studio and an art gallery, and it is here that is run a Drama course so good that it was awarded 23 points out of 24 after a recent inspection. The mind/body balance is made at Alsager by a sports outfit which is one of the best in the country. There are 32 acres of playing fields, an athletics track, swimming pool, indoor facilities galore and a 1,000 square metre laboratory complex, which features a 33 x 6m track for performance data collection, regularly visited by top athletes.

PILLOW TALK

The university halls are good for first years wanting to meet people, but are not cheap and it is fairly difficult to get your first choice. The halls at All Saints have the best location; those at Didsbury require a considerable bus journey. See *Manchester Uni* entry, Pillow Talk, page 310 for city accommodation. A new bureau – **Manchester Student Homes** – has been launched jointly.

JOBS

There's a good reputation for graduate employment, and an ethos of work-related skills in their modular programmes. But there is less gained in work skills from extra-curricular student activity than at neighbouring Manchester University. See box, below, for strengths.

```
WHERE GRADUATES END UP

          17% Education,        Key Areas
    11% Wholesale/Retail,
   10% Health/Social Work,
       9% Manufacturing,
          8% Finance,
         7% Personnel*,
       5% Public Admin
   Telecom, Property,          Niche Areas
   Chem/Pharmaceutical,
     Library/Archival,
     Artistic/Literary

*indicates Top 10 Graduate Provider

Approximate employed    96%
```

GETTING THERE

☞ By road: Manchester, M63/J10, A34. Coach services good. Crewe/Alsager, M6/J16.
☞ By rail to Manchester: London Euston, 2:30; Leeds, 1:45; Liverpool Lime Street, 0:50. Crewe, connections from Manchester Piccadilly.
☞ By air: Manchester Airport for international and inland flights.
☞ By coach: London, 4:35; Bristol, 5:00; Newcastle, 5:00.

MIDDLESEX UNIVERSITY

Middlesex University
Trent Park
London N14 4YZ

TEL 020 8411 5898
FAX 020 8362 5649
EMAIL admissions@mdx.ac.uk
WEB www.mdx.ac.uk

Middlesex Students' Union
Trent Park
London N14 4YZ

TEL 020 8362 6450
FAX 020 8440 5944
EMAIL (see website)
WEB www.musu.mdx.ac.uk

VAG VIEW

*M*iddlesex is the government's way forward, making its target of half the population benefiting from higher education before 30 more than a dream. There are many impressive elements in Middlesex's strategy, not least the parallel development of their Able Centre, a disability support centre with recording studios turning out audio texts for blind students, a dyslexia support co-ordinator and a sign language bureau, which has appealed to thousands beyond campus too. But it would be a mistake to believe that Middlesex picks you up and takes you out of life in quite the same way as a traditional campus university like Nottingham, Kent or Sussex.

Most people who come to Middlesex are not that bothered that the extra-curricular scene on offer at the union is second rate, but it may be that this aspect of a traditional university education is precisely what will be seen to be important to the individual. Specifically, that skills demanded by employers – oral communication skills, enthusiasm, team work, assertiveness, problem solving, meeting and presentation skills, time & stress management, etc – but not provided in coursework, may be imbibed

> **Middlesex is doing more than its bit towards giving half our sixthform population the benefit of a higher education by 2010. But how involved is the student scene?**

practicably, sometimes subliminally, through ethos or the process of union society involvement, better than in deliberate tell-him fashion in lecture or seminar workshop, which is, of necessity, the way in so disparate a place as this. Perhaps that, indeed, was one purpose in mind when they made all these polytechnics into universities.

CAMPUS

Getting to grips with this university, is like wrestling with a family of octopuses, so many tentacles are there reaching out across North London and beyond. However, the struggle is arguably unnecessary. Once ensconced you can forget most of its bits and concentrate on the few that matter to you. There are some eighteen sites and campuses, but six main ones:

TOTTENHAM White Hart Lane, London N17 8HR Tel (for all sites): 020 8362 5000. Wood Green tube (Piccadilly line), then W3 bus. Departments include Humanities, Business Studies, Law.

BOUNDS GREEN Bounds Green Road, London N11 2NQ. Bounds Green tube (Piccadilly line). Departments include Engineering, Maths, Computer.

CAT HILL Barnet, Herts EN4 8HT. Cockfosters (Piccadilly line). Department is Art & Design.

ENFIELD Queensway, Enfield EN3 4SF. Overland to Southbury Station. Departments is Social Sciences.

HENDON The Burroughs, London NW4 4BT. Hendon Central (Northern line). Departments include Business Studies, Management, Accounting & Finance, Economics, Law.

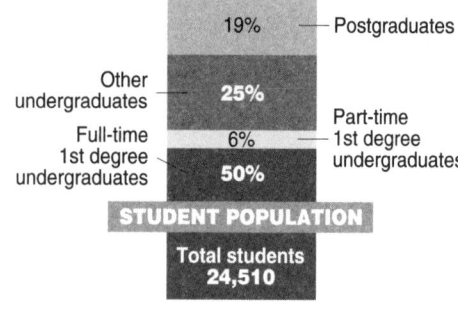

STUDENT POPULATION	
Postgraduates	19%
Other undergraduates	25%
Part-time 1st degree undergraduates	6%
Full-time 1st degree undergraduates	50%

Total students 24,510

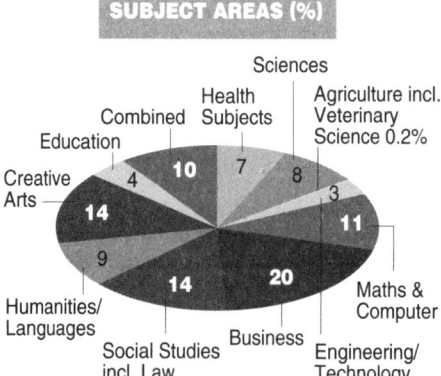

SUBJECT AREAS (%)

Sciences 7
Health Subjects 8
Agriculture incl. Veterinary Science 0.2%
Combined 10
Education 4
Creative Arts 14
Humanities/Languages 9
Social Studies incl. Law 14
Business 20
Engineering/Technology 3
Maths & Computer 11

TRENT PARK Bramley Road, London N14 4YZ. Set in 900 acres of woodlands and meadows. Cockfosters or Oakwood tubes (Piccadilly line). Departments include Performing Arts, IT, Cultural Studies, Teacher Education.

STUDENT PROFILE

Middlesex is a large university, over 20,000 students. Half of all entrants and more than a third of undergraduates are mature, many are local and many come from social groups that don't traditionally opt for university. There is a large number of part-timers among non-degree undergraduates.

ACADEMIA

The university schools are Art, Design & Performance Arts (Drama, Dance & Music); Computing Science, Engineering Systems, Health, Biological and Environmental Science; Humanities & Cultural Studies; Life Long Learning & Education; Media & Communication Studies; Business; and Social Sciences.

Top-scoring at teaching assessments have been Philosophy; Drama, Dance & Cinematics; History

UNIVERSITY/STUDENT PROFILE	
University since	**1992**
Situation/style	**Campus/ city sites**
Student population	**24,510**
Full-time undergraduates	**12,360**
- mature	**35%**
- overseas	**20%**
- male/female	**40/60**
- state sector intake	**96%**
- non-traditional student intake	**13%**
- drop-out rate	**17%, high**
- undergraduate applications	**Down 9%**
see Introduction for key to tables	

success of which can be seen in our Graduate *Employment* box data on page 320.

Among the university's attractions to mature students is the substitution of 'life skills and motivation' for traditional entry requirements. One-year access courses can also lead to a place on degree courses.

ACADEMIC EXCELLENCE	
TEACHING:	
(Rated Excellent or 17+ out of 24)	
Philosophy	**23**
Drama, Dance, Cinematics,	**22**
History of Art, Architec & Design,	
American Studies, Education,	
Nursing, Subjects Allied to	
Medicine, Politics	
Art & Design, Economics,	**21**
Psychology	
Maths	**20**
Sociology, Modern Langs,	**19**
Electric & Electron Eng	
RESEARCH:	
Top grades 5/5*	
History of Art, Architecture &	**Grade 5**
Design, Philosophy	

of Art, Architecture & Design, American Studies, Education, Nursing, other subjects allied to Medicine and Politics (see box, above). Among the subjects allied to Medicine is their ground-breaking course in Phytotherapy (Herbal Medicine) and in traditional Chinese medicine. One's attention is drawn, too, to the veterinary nursing degree, and to a raft of degrees in journalism and publishing, the

WHAT IT'S REALLY LIKE	
UNIVERSITY:	
Social Life	★★
Campus scene	**Friendly, mature, colourful, not campus focused**
Student Union services	**Average**
Politics	**Student issues**
Sport	**Competitive**
National team position	**43rd**
Sport facilities	**Good**
Arts opportunities	**Excellent**
Student magazine	**MUD**
Nightclub	**Enfield forum**
Bars	**1 on each campus**
Union ents	**DOM1, Half Time, Crown Jewels**
Union clubs/societies	**30**
Smoking policy	**Zonal**
Parking	**Poor**
CITY:	
Entertainment	★★★★★
City scene	**Wild, expensive**
Town/gown relations	**Average-good**
Risk of violence	**Average**
Cost of living	**Very high**
Student concessions	**Good**
Survival + 2 nights out	**£70 pw**
Part-time work locally	**Fair**

AT A GLANCE

ACADEMIC FILE:

Subjects assessed	**26**
Excellent	**58%**
Average requirements	**200 points**
Students-staff ratio	**21:1**
First/2:1 degree pass rate	**50%**

ACCOMMODATION FILE:

Guarantee to freshers	**Two thirds of applicants**
Style	**Halls, flats**
Catered	**None**
Approx price range pw	**£55-£70**
Local rent pw	**£60**

SOCIAL SCENE

STUDENTS' UNION The union's range of services and support networks is available across all main campuses. The four bars – at Enfield, Tottenham, Trent Park and Cat Hill – provide drinks promos and ents during the week. *DOM1* is a party night (Tuesday) at **Trent Park Bar**; *Half Time* is a chart night at **Enfield Forum** (Wednesday), *Crown Jewels* is a night of anthems at **Tottenham Bar** – all are licensed until 1 am. Enfield Forum is the largest bar; capacity is 850. The bars close at weekends. There's a Freshers' Ball, of course, and some tell of a Middlesex extravaganza, a 36-hour festival in summer at Trent Park.

A free monthly magazine is called *MUD* (Middlesex Union Direct).

SPORT Gym facilities exist on all campuses. Sport is an area of continual investment. Recent large projects include a £2.5m state-of-the-art gym, the Real Tennis Centre at Hendon, and two artificial hockey pitches at Trent Park. Students have access to university swimming pools, one indoor and one outdoor, football and rugby pitches and a golf club.

Teams do OK nationally; came 43rd last year.

PILLOW TALK

There are 2,400 places in halls, all of which are self-catering. The vast majority have been built over the past five years; all are within easy reach of their respective campuses. Private accommodation varies greatly according to where you are based,

WHERE GRADUATES END UP

15% Health/Social Work,	Key Areas
15% Education,	
12% Wholesale/Retail,	
8% Manufacturing,	
7% Computer,	
7% Public Admin,	
5% Finance	
Telecom, Publishing,	Niche Areas
Radio/TV,	
Library/Archival,	
Market Research*,	
Eng/Industrial Design	

*indicates Top 10 Graduate Provider

Approximate employed	**92%**

though generally you're into £60 per week for a house share.

JOBS

Health and education look after nearly a third of graduates. Arts and media (including publishing, which has always been a strong suit) are niche areas in which the uni is clearly succeeding, and there are others. Among their many strategies to facilitate employment is The National Centre for Work Based Learning Partnership, which was awarded the Queen's Anniversary Prize in 1996. Its clients include Ford and The Metropolitan Police.

NAPIER UNIVERSITY

Napier University
Craiglockhart Campus
219 Colinton Road
Edinburgh EH14 1DJ

TEL 0500 35 35 70
FAX 0131 455 6261
EMAIL info@napier.ac.uk
WEB www.napier.ac.uk

Napier Students' Association
12 Merchiston Place
Edinburgh EH10 4NR

TEL 0131 229 8791
FAX 0131 228 3462
EMAIL (see website)
WEB napierstudents.com

VAG VIEW

*N*apier has a strong reputation for getting its graduates jobs; indeed it figures in no fewer than six of our graduate employment *Top Tens*, which suggests a high concentration on certain work areas, and one certain reason why the Financial Times ranked Napier as the top modern university in Scotland last year.

Its difficulty has always been that it is a bit of a local uni, with a weekday frame of mind. As that begins to change, students are cheered in the process – Napier's drop-out rate has fallen by a third in just two years.

CAMPUS

Napier is a conglomeration of so many Edinburgh sites (some twelve at the last count) that the Students' Union is stretched and there hasn't been much sense of belonging. 'Napier is not a campus university,' writes Gareth L Mackie. 'Instead it has four major sites [whose faculties are currently in flux] – **Merchiston** [engineering, arts, social sciences], **Sighthill** [business and languages], **Craiglockhart** [computer, electrical & electronic engineering and maths] and **Craighouse** [management, tourism, music, media, communications, etc.] – and eight minor ones, spread out through the south and west of Edinburgh. This can be a pain if you have lectures at more than one site, though generally you'll be based in one place.

'Each site has an atmosphere of its own: Merchiston is probably the busiest and liveliest, as it is the nearest to the city centre. Craighouse only received a student bar in November 1998.

'There is no one place where Napierites congregate.'

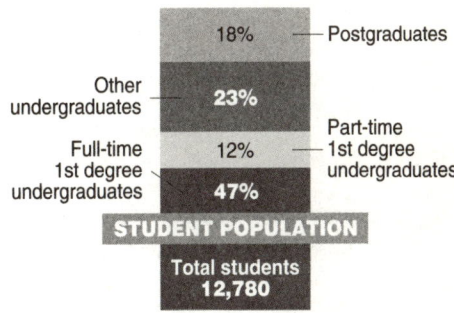

SUBJECT AREAS (%)

STUDENT POPULATION
Total students
12,780

UNIVERSITY/STUDENT PROFILE

University since	**1992**
Situation/style	**Civic**
Student population	**12,780**
Full-time undergraduates	**6,070**
- mature	**14%**
- overseas	**2%**
- male/female	**54/46**
- state sector intake	**80%**
- non-traditional student intake	**20%, high**
- drop-out rate	**11%**
- undergraduate applications	**Down 4%**

see Introduction for key to tables

STUDENT PROFILE

The student profile shows a fair mix of state and public school for a new uni, and given the number of independent school entrants there is a healthy balance in 20% of the undergraduate population coming from neighbourhoods new to the notion of sending their kids to university. This fact, were it combined with a still lower drop-out rate, would surely make it one of the government's elite 'access universities'. There is also a sizeable mature population, a number of HND students and a smattering of part-timers, the local element perhaps tending to limit the university to something of a day-time college, another feature of Napier which has vied against student focus.

ACADEMIA

Its roots are in science and engineering – the broad-based BEng in Energy and Environmental Engineering is one of many courses typically well conceived for a job in industry. The uni is known for business, too – a £24-million business school will shortly amend the faculty mix at Craiglockhart – and for built environment. Their graduate placement record in engineering and industrial design, in manufacturing (particularly in electronic & electrical manufacturing), in finance and in the construction industry, reflect these preoccupations. See, too, their hospitality, marketing and tourism management degrees, which are having a great impact on the job market (see *Employment* box, page 323).

But increasingly, too, they have begun to surprise in the Faculty of Arts & Social Sciences – Graphic Communications, Journalism, Law,

Librarianship & Info Studies and Publishing, and in their Art & Design BA/BSc courses, with Photography, TV and Film. These are very popular areas for applicants, and you will likely be interviewed. Just recently, they have been accredited by the Law Society of Scotland to run an LlB degree, and underway is a £22-million Scottish Centre for Creative Industries, which will pull together all the faculty elements and bring a studio and recording space into the picture.

Note, too, low-requirement entry (CD) to a degree in Veterinary Nursing, plus an intriguing niche degree in Ecotourism. Other new courses this year are BDes Design Futures, BSc Sport and Exercise Science, and BMus Popular Music. Let's hope the latter will benefit the ents scene, too.

For overseas students, there's a free orientation programme, including English language classes, a collection service from Edinburgh airport/train station, a welcome pack in all university accommodation including bedding and cooking utensils, tuition fees fixed for the duration of their programme, and the option to pay monthly by instalment.

At Merchiston, there's a new purpose-built, 500-PC computer lab with 24-hour access. Finally, there is a dedicated student support services department for the disabled or any student who might benefit from counselling.

SOCIAL SCENE

There are student bars at the four main sites – Merchiston, Sighthill, Craiglockhart and Craighouse – but short opening hours and limited capacities inhibit what can be done ents-wise. **Twelve** (at 12 Merchiston Place) is a café bar during the day and a pre-club (DJs, theme nights, live music) from late afternoon – latest licence is on Friday at 1 am.

There are three pool tables and games machines. At Merchiston, too, the **Apex** café recently opened to complement the **Triangle** restaurant, which opened in October 2000.

The **Craighouse Bar** (aka the **Asylum**) has summer appeal with a patio and back garden, and one area of it is a cyber café with five Internet-linked computers, which is a very nice touch. This also has pool tables, and darts and a jukebox, but appears to be open only Mondays to Fridays, from 10am to 5pm.

Writes Gareth: 'Drinking aside, there are several clubs and societies worth joining, the most popular the Gaelic Society, and it's relatively easy to form your own, so long as you can find enough like-minded people. Through the NSA, there are teams and clubs for just about every sport imaginable; from sub-aqua to mountaineering. Napier used to have the best student football team in Scotland, but it's not too hot right now. Our netball team is doing rather well, though!'

WHERE GRADUATES END UP

15% Manufacturing*,	Key Areas
14% Finance*,	
9% Wholesale/Retail,	
6% Health/Social Work,	
6% Computer,	
5% Public Admin	
Hotel/Restaurant*,	Niche Areas
Publishing*, Advertising,	
Business/Management,	
Library/Archival,	
Radio/TV, Architecture,	
Construction, Defence,	
Electron/Electric*,	
Eng/Industrial Design*	

*indicates Top 10 Graduate Provider

Approximate employed **93%**

PILLOW TALK

Uni accommodation in apartment developments in the city centre is guaranteed to freshers coming 'outwith a thirty-mile radius of Edinburgh'. There is no catered accommodation. Four-person flats have one shared bathroom; five-person flats have two shared bathrooms. The price range per person per week is around £56/£57.

Says Gareth: 'Napier provides housing for over 1,000 students, it's quite expensive but is quickly snapped up. Edinburgh has an abundance of reasonably priced flats, so it should be easy to find one in an area that suits you and your pocket. Areas to consider include Tollcross, Gorgie/Dalry, Marchmont and Bruntsfield. You may see cheaper areas, but they may not be student-friendly.'

JOBS

Many lecturers have hands-on experience, many courses have a sandwich element, and the uni guarantees to find work experience for every student who wants it. It makes six of our employment Top Tens – Finance (3rd), Engineering & Industrial Design (2nd), Manufacturing (10th), Electronic & Electrical Manufacturing (3rd), Publishing (7th) and Hotel & Restaurant (2nd).

> *Napier has a strong reputation for getting its graduates jobs. Its limitation as a university has to do with it being something of a day-time college.*

GETTING THERE

☛ By road: from north, M90; from Stirling, M9; from Newcastle, A1; from Glasgow, M8.
☛ By rail: London King's Cross, 4:30. Glasgow Central, 50 mins; Newcastle, 1:30.
☛ By coach: Glasgow, 1:10; London, 9:10.

NESCOT

NESCOT
Reigate Road
Ewell
Surrey KT17 3DS

TEL 020 8394 3038
FAX 020 8394 3030
E-MAIL (see website)
WEB www.nescot.ac.uk

VAG VIEW

*N*escot stands for North East Surrey College of Technology. Ewell, where the college is based, is near Epsom in Surrey. Some of their degree courses – Business Information Technology, Digital Imaging,

Photography & Imaging – are one-year HND top-ups. The college is especially strong in biosciences, and has close contacts with pharmaceutical companies and hospitals. There are also business and drama degrees. Learning resources are good. They have a library approaching 60,000 volumes and a bank of some 600 computers. College accommodation is scarce. For sport, there's the Swinden Sports Hall and four pitches. There's an active theatre scene; they have their own 200-seat Adrian Mann Theatre *(with computer lighting and sound system) and a new Visual & Performance Arts Centre. A Students' Union organises live bands, discos, karaoke and quiz nights.*

COLLEGE PROFILE	
Founded	**1954**
Status	**F/HE College**
Degree awarding universities	**Open, Surrey**
Student population	**6,204**
Full-time degree undergraduates	**325**

ACCOMMODATION:

Availability to freshers	**1%**
Cost pw (no food/food)	**£85**
Town rent pw	**£50**

DEGREE SUBJECT AREAS:
Biosciences, health sciences, business, computing, building, animal science, theatre, photography, etc

GETTING THERE

☞ By road: A24 out of London.　　　　☞ By rail: London Waterloo or Victoria, 30 mins.

STUDENT NEWCASTLE – THE CITY

Newcastle 2002 is another jewel of the North, a compact, cosmopolitan, lively, diverse, booming and progressive city. Ranked as the seventh best party city in the world, the Toon is also one of its leading culture centres. Along with Gateshead, its neighbour on the far, south bank of the Tyne, it is up for naming as European City of Culture in 2008. Newcastle is, in short, an ideal place to hang out as a student.

NIGHTLIFE

Geordie attitude turns on the old adage, 'work hard, play hard', and be it the legendary **Bigg Market**, the swanky watering holes of the **Quayside** or the cosmopolitan bars of Jesmond's Osborne Road, there is opportunity for everyone to play as hard as they like, very often at a price most students can afford.

When it comes to clubbing and live acts, both universities have highly commendable ents programmes. Coldplay, Faithless, Orbital, Starsailor, The Charlatans, Stereo MCs and Roni Size are just a few of the big name acts to have played in the last twelve months.

The **Telewest Arena** attracts all the major national tours, from Hear'Say to Destiny's Child and S Club 7 to Craig David, while the **City Hall** played host to the likes of Pulp and Gabrielle in 2001. The only downside is that the northerly location means a lot of smaller tours do not visit, so do not expect to see everyone.

The city's club scene has diversified in the past five years, but highly acclaimed house night *Shindig* @ **Foundation** still flies the flag. *Shindig*, which celebrates its tenth birthday in 2002 attracts a huge variety of big name DJs with Roger Sanchez, Steve Lawler, Danny Rampling, X-Press 2, Darren Emerson and Erick Morillo among those to have graced their decks. It was voted *Muzik Magazine*'s Underground Club Night of the Year in 2001.

Promise on Friday @ **Foundation** does a similar job for the harder and progressive house scene, while other notable nights include *Sugar @* **Choice**, *Reverb @* **Scotland Yard**, *Sundissential @* **Ikon** and *Traveller @* Northumbria University Student's Union. Also look out for Newcastle University's once termly *Arcane,* which has a reputation among students and locals alike.

The most notorious student-only nights are held at **Baja Beach Club** and the **Tuxedo Princess**, both on Gateshead's Quayside. The gay scene is well served in the city's pink triangle (behind the International Centre for Life), with **Powerhouse** the most popular night club.

SPORT

The whole city revolves around the fortunes of Newcastle United, so get informed. St James's Park is the most imposing landmark on the city skyline and the second largest stadium in the Premiership. Getting tickets can be a problem, however, despite the 52,000 capacity, but well worth trying for. Elsewhere, Rob Andrew's Newcastle Falcons offer a student friendly environment for Rugby fans, while the Newcastle Eagles do the same for Basketball followers. Wherever you go, don't mention any allegiance to North-East rivals Sunderland or Manchester United or you are liable to lose your facial features.

CINEMA

The **Odeon** is the most central and a brand new multiplex is due to open in the autumn of 2002. Also in the city centre is a 12-screen Warner Village, while a short drive will take you to **UCI Silverlink** or **MetroCentre**. For the more artistic, the **Tyneside Cinema** is one of the best independent cinemas in the country.

THEATRE AND COMEDY

Newcastle is one of the Royal Shakespeare Company's second homes. In the autumn, it doth take over most of the city's stages for a month of high-brow entertainment. The major venue is the **Theatre Royal**, the poshest of Newcastle's theatres. For a smaller, cheaper alternative, try the **Tyne Theatre**. If it's a more relaxed, studenty atmosphere you're after then the **Playhouse** and **Gulbenkian Studio**, in-the-round, may fill the bill. Both theatres are housed in the same building at the edge of Newcastle University's campus, and are home to the more cutting-edge Northern Stage company. Yet more experimental is the **Live Theatre**, informal champion of new talent at the heart of the bustling Quayside. For comedy look no further than the fantastic **Hyena Café**, open twelve months of the year, and the annual Newcastle Comedy Festival, which plays a number of venues across the city for a two-week spell.

SHOPPING

The only major studenty shop is **Period Clothing**,

with some fantastic stuff in store. Otherwise Newcastle blends high street stores with smaller designer boutiques well. Northumberland Street and Grainger Town are the two main shopping areas in the City Centre. A short journey will take you to the Gateshead MetroCentre and the major stores/labels. For music, **Steel Wheels**, **RPM** and **Flying Records** offer good independent options.

ADDRESSES

Clubs: Foundation, Melbourne Street, Quayside 261-8985; Powerhouse, George Street 272-3621; World Club Headquarters, Marlborough St 261-8648; Scotland Yard, Waterloo St 232-9648, Newcastle University, Kings Walk 239-3900; Northumbria University, University Campus, 227-4757, Baja Beach Club, Gateshead Quayside 477-6205, Tuxedo Princess, Gateshead Quayside 477-8899. Venues Telewest Arena and Newcastle City Hall 260-5000.

Theatre and Comedy: Theatre Royal, Grey's St, 232-2061; Tyne Theatre, Westgate Road, 232-0899; Playhouse, Barras Bridge 230-5151; Live Theatre, Broad Chare 232-8289; Hyena Cafe, Leazes Park Road, 232-6030

Cinema: Odeon, Pilgrim St, 232-6718; Warner Village, New Bridge St, 221-0202; UCI MetroCentre, 493-2022; Tyneside Cinema, Pilgrim St, 232-8289

Sport: Newcastle United, St James's Park, Gallowgate, 261-1571, Newcastle Falcons, Kingston Park, 496-1166.

Luke Edwards

●●

UNIVERSITY OF NEWCASTLE UPON TYNE

The University of Newcastle upon Tyne
6 Kensington Terrace
Newcastle upon Tyne NE1 7RU

TEL 0191 222 5594
FAX 0191 222 6139
EMAIL admissions-enquiries@ncl.ac.uk
WEB www.ncl.ac.uk

The Newcastle University Union Society
Kings Walk
Newcastle upon Tyne NE1 8QB

TEL 0191 239 3900
FAX 0191 222 1876
EMAIL comm.union@ncl.ac.uk
WEB www.unionsociety.ac.uk

VAG VIEW

*A*cademically, Newcastle is good right across the board. "Those who live in the North

perhaps understand how good it is better than those from the South,' said one Yorkshire-based school careers teacher, adding with weight, 'It is very popular among students who go there.'

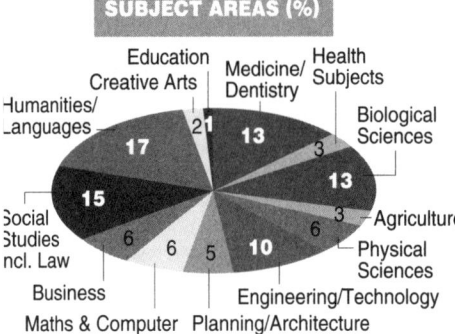

SUBJECT AREAS (%)

Education, Creative Arts, Medicine/Dentistry, Health Subjects, Humanities/Languages 17, 2, 1, 13, Biological Sciences 3, 13, Social Studies incl. Law 15, 6, 6, 5, 10, 3, 6, Agriculture 3, Physical Sciences, Business, Maths & Computer, Engineering/Technology, Planning/Architecture

Good across the board, certainly, but at the very height of academic excellence sit Medicine, Physiological Sciences, Psychology, Molecular Biosciences, Pharmacology and subjects allied to Medicine. These are the departments that scored full marks in the assessments. True, nothing has scored less than 20 points out of 24, but these did not drop a point. The subjects allied to Medicine are speech language sciences. All the top ratings are sciences with a medical tinge. Now, they have taken a new vice-chancellor, Professor Christopher Edwards, who himself has a medical tinge – he was Principal of Imperial College School of Medicine in London. Eleven months after he arrived, the national research assessments were announced, and Newcastle had improved its position by eight places over four years ago. High among the departments adjudged world class (Grade 5*) were Clinical Laboratory Sciences, Psychology, Biological Sciences... and Music, the latter seeming to remind us that there are dimensions to the Newcastle experience beyond clinical laboratories.

Where Newcastle scores over London and, yes, over Manchester, is in its packing an incredible array of cultural, artistic and hedonistic power centres into a very small space (and at relatively low cost). So much is going on, and all of it so concentrated, that the buzz on the street at night is ten times what you will feel in the greater, but more dispersed metropolis. Newcastle's undergraduates have a real and vibrant city to discover, which is why the Yorkshire teacher added the acid test slogan which seemed to question the truth of

undergraduate loyalty in any uni other than Newcastle.

Go there and see. What you notice on campus is people doing, things happening, students in control... of themselves and what they are about. 'We actually own the whole set-up,' they say. They do, union building and all.

CAMPUS

Newcastle is a campus university situated right in the heart of this compact and compelling city, within walking distance of theatres, cinemas, shops, bars, pubs, restaurants, but equally only a short way from the eye-catching north-east coast.

UNIVERSITY/STUDENT PROFILE	
Independent university since	**1963**
Situation/style	**City campus**
Student population	**18,180**
Full-time undergraduates	**9,870**
- mature	**11%**
- overseas	**4%**
- male/female	**50/50**
- state sector intake	**67%, low**
- non-traditional student intake	**10%**
- drop-out rate	**4%, low**
- undergraduate applications	**Up 4%**
see Introduction for key to tables	

STUDENT PROFILE

The student profile reveals a low proportion of state school entrants. Its government benchmark is 79%; last year its state school intake was only 67%. Its government benchmark for intake from social classes IIIM, IV and V, the poorer end of the community, is 20%; Newcastle's take last year was 16%. In other words, 'The pink pashmina and boat shoe brigade do seem to claim the majority,' as a student put it, 'but people tend to separate into their own different groups according to individual taste. There is enough to do to keep all parties

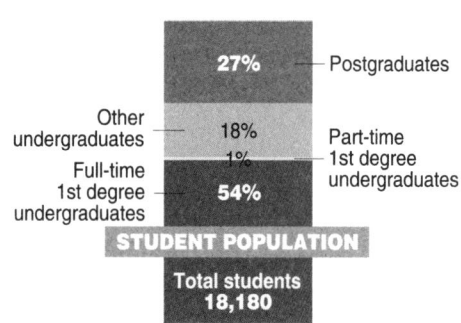

27% — Postgraduates

Other undergraduates — 18% — Part-time

Full-time 1st degree undergraduates — 1% — 1st degree undergraduates

54%

STUDENT POPULATION

Total students 18,180

happy. Freshers Week tends to be the only time when you have to put up with people who aren't necessarily "your kind of people", to quote Michael Barymore.'

On one point of open access policy they are making good ground. Among neighbourhoods in which participation in higher education is traditionally low they are now meeting their benchmark of 10%.

Statistics apart, after it has been well and truly done by Freshers Week this student body soon gets focused on making things happen, a lot of it through the union's 160 clubs and societies, but not only through them; the typical Newcastle student likes to make it happen, it is part of the culture of Newcastle University, an organic thing perhaps. Last year the uni was approached by London-based Winning Moves, the makers of Monopoly, who wanted them to pilot a game of monopoly for purchase by Newcastle students and alumni. The game went on sale in June. When asked why, out of all the universities in the UK, Winning Moves chose Newcastle, they replied: 'Students have the time of their lives at Newcastle, so its graduates have fond memories. We knew we were onto a winner.'

ACADEMIA

'The general ethos seems to be work hard, play hard,' writes Geraldine England. 'The standard of teaching obviously varies, but is generally high, some lecturers being able to communicate with their students better than others. Workloads differ, but as a rule, students doing a science degree have a whole lot more lectures than do arts students. However, when it comes to coursework and exams, the pressure seems to equalise, as all courses are based on a similar modular system.

'There are two main libraries, the **Robinson Library** and **Medical Library**, both are well resourced, well staffed and fully computerised, but be prepared for a massive demand on books when it comes to exam time. Don't think that you will be able to pop into the library a day before the holidays and find all the books you need, because you won't. The geeks will have got there first.

'Computing facilities at Newcastle are excellent, each department having a number of its own computer clusters, all linked to the net, in addition to those available in the libraries. There is even a large 24-hour access cluster, a godsend because, though you might find it difficult to imagine now, you may well have to work through the night.'

> *On campus, what you notice is people doing, things happening, students in control, which indeed they are to a greater degree than elsewhere.*

The University's Library has in fact just gained the Charter Mark – the UK's top award for excellent customer services – for the third time in a row, as a result of user-led development of its services, particularly for students with disabilities, and those new to the whole idea of academic library useage – a need in line with a policy of widening access. Last June, the Bedson Centre was added to teaching resources – lecture theatre/seminar facilities, six rooms, each fitted with interactive audiovisual equipment and available to all

ACADEMIC EXCELLENCE	
TEACHING:	
(Rated Excellent or 17+ out of 24)	
Architecture, English, Geology, Social Policy & Administration	**Excellent**
Medicine, Physiological Sciences, Psychology, Molecular Biosciences & Pharmacology, Subjects Allied to Medicine	**24**
Dentistry, Maths, Economics, Politics	**23**
Modern Languages, Linguistics	**22**
Agric, Forest & Agric Sciences, Organismal Biosciences, Classics, Education, Theol	
Chemical Engineering, Electrical & Electronic Eng, Town & Country Planning, Physics, Archaeology	**21**
Civil Engineering/Geomatics, Marine Technol, Art & Design	**20**
RESEARCH :	
Top grades 5/5*	
Clinical Laboratory Sciences,. Psychology, Biological Sciences, Music,	**Grade 5***
Community-based Clinical, Hospital-based Clinical, Clinical Dentistry, Physiology, Nursing, Earth Sciences, Pure Maths, Statistics, Computer, Chemical Eng, Civil Eng, Electrical/ Electronic Eng, Town /Country Planning, Geography, Law, Politics, Accounting, English, Iberian and Latin American, Linguistics, Theology	**Grade 5**

UNIVERSITY:

Social Life	★★★★★
Campus scene	Lively, aware, middle-class
Student Union services	Good
Politics	World issues
Sport	60 clubs
National team position	19th
Sport facilities	Good
Arts opportunities	Drama excellent; rest good
Student newspaper	The Courier
Student radio	NSR
Nightclub	The Bassment
Bars	Mens, Global Café, Subterranean, Subversions, Twisters, Cochrane, Irish
Union ents	Positive, Turbulence Eclectic, Force, Brighton Beach
Union clubs/societies	160+
Most popular society	NUTS (theatre)
Smoking policy	Union & halls OK
Parking	Adequate
CITY:	
Entertainment	★★★★★
Scene	Intoxicating
Town/gown relations	OK
Risk of violence	Average
Cost of living	Average
Student concessions	Good
Survival + 2 nights out	£60-£70 pw
Part-time work campus/town	Average/good

SOCIAL SCENE

STUDENT'S UNION 'It's the central point of social life here,' Geraldine reports, 'with seven bars and its own club, **The Bassment**. It plays host regularly to big name bands and DJs, such as Coldplay, Travis, Primal Scream, Faithless, Goldie, James Lavelle. There are also monthly music events, *Turbulence*, which has been rated the best drum 'n' bass night in the North, *Brighton Beach* (indie), *Force* (hip hop), *Eclectic* (breaks and beats), and every Friday's *Positive* is the cheese lover's dream come true. With all bars open and some really great offers, *Positive* is always a sell-out and definitely one of the best student nights in Newcastle.'

The Bassment takes about 1,000 and then they've got the 300-capacity **Global Café**. Once a term they have *Arcane* – all the proceeds fund a student from some underprivileged area of the dark continent. *Arcane* lasts from about 8pm until 6am. They bring in good DJs – Cream, Ministry of Sound, etc. As well as the two main dancefloors (Bassment, Global), there are specialist drum 'n' bass areas and chill out rooms.

Whatever's on, they open all the bars in the building (total capacity 2,200) and when one shuts down – the **Men's Bar** and the **Cochrane Lounge** seem first to go, everyone goes on to wherever the action is. Other bars are called **Subterranean**, **Subversions**, **Twisters** and **The Irish Bar**. Student and local bands do gigs, and there's an annual battle of the bands when they invite A&R men to seed record deals.

'With all these great nights out, some extra cash is bound to come in handy,' writes Geraldine in practical mode. 'The SU provides a job shop, advertising all kinds of part-time vacancies with accredited employers. It also offers welfare and advisory services in addition to supporting over100 different societies and more than sixty sports clubs.'

Ents are, indeed, but the beginning. Much is done in the context of the real world outside. Student drama producers, for example, have to survive in real terms, are dependent on public audiences, arrange sponsorship and all the rest. Two or three student-produced plays appear each year at **The Gulbenkian**, a small, vigorously experimental studio-type place. There might be a production at **Live**, the theatre on the Quayside.

Student Community Action Newcastle SCAN – 'is very big,' I was told. 'At the moment we're working on a children's outdoor experience area and a community gym-type area in the city. Our policy is that students are not just here to go to lectures but to develop skills. Volunteer work is one area for that. We find SCAN just about the easiest thing to get students involved in, and the SCAN ball is one of the best. Nightline is popular as well –

academic departments.

New academic courses this year focus on areas such as accounting, agriculture (e.g. Organic Food Production), biochemistry, business management (combinations with Japanese or Chinese), chemistry, computing (a foundation course to meet particular employer demands), modern languages, statistics, applied communication, etc.

On the accounting front, they've teamed up with PricewaterhouseCoopers to produce Business Accounting and Finance, which integrates degree level study with paid work placements in a programme designed to accelerate chartered accountancy qualification.

On food production, the Tesco Centre for Organic Agriculture is tapping uni strengths in agriculture and economics to establish a research centre dedicated to making/marketing organic food.

telephone counselling by student volunteers.'

The SU Debating Chamber, looked to us uncannily like the House of Commons, when we visited, but the campaigning seems pretty much non-party: 'The main issue this term was of course Stop the War in Afghanistan – it really got people going, so much that the union managed to hold it's first 2-quorate General Meeting in four years (quoracy is 100 people).'

The *Courier* office is a crammed galley of a room, space enough for the award-winning student weekly to be committed to Quark. The student radio station, N.S.R. (Newcastle Student Radio), was nominated for Best Newcomer in the Radio 1 awards two years ago and this time, The Nerve, its news programme was nominated Best Factual.

SPORT There are sixty sports clubs on offer and the uni came 19th nationally last year out of all universities. They are up there with the best, particularly where rugby is concerned. The much-respected American Football team is called Newcastle Mariners or Crazy Blue. On campus, the **Claremont** and **King's Walk Sports Centres** provide for aerobics, badminton, basketball, indoor hockey, soccer, netball, squash, tennis, trampolining, volleyball, fitness training, martial arts, dance, gymnastics. Swimming pools are hired by the uni for water sports. Track and field athletes use the **Gateshead International Stadium**. There are pitches and courts at Cochrane Park, Heaton (Medicals), Longbenton (with its new all-weather pitch), and at Close House, the uni estate ten miles to the west. Rowing is also popular and successful.

TOWN Heart of the action is the **Bigg Market** of *Viz* legend and its assortment of fun pubs, clubs and bars. And now there's the **Quayside** too, 'currently looking very cosmopolitan,' Geraldine reminds us, 'with the new millennium "eye-opener" bridge and its line of swish bars and restaurants. Since March, the **Baltic Art Gallery** has been open too, and the West End of the city welcomed the new **International Centre for Life** and the **Discovery Museum**, both host great exhibitions.

'Town/gown relations have improved recently, but if you go looking for trouble on Friday night down the Bigg Market, shouting, 'Daddy bought me a pony for Christmas, you'll probably find it.'

See Student Newcastle for clubs, etc (page 323)

PILLOW TALK

All first year undergraduate students are guaranteed a place in university-managed accommodation if they accept an offer and return the application form 'in time'. A mere 12% is en suite. Prices range from £64.40 to £88.13; self-

AT A GLANCE	
ACADEMIC FILE:	
Subjects assessed	**36**
Excellent	**78%**
Average A level requirements	**23 points**
Students-staff ratio	**15:1**
First/2:1 degree pass rate	**64%**
ACCOMMODATION FILE:	
Guarantee to freshers	**Non-specific Apply early**
Style	**Halls, flats**
Catered	**42%**
En-suite	**12%**
Price range pw	**£40.74-£88.13**
City rent pw	**£35-£70**

catering flats from £40.74 to £69.94. You can rent in the city from £30 to £55.

JOBS

Last year the careers service won the award for excellence in the universities and colleges category of the National Careers Awards 2001, organised by the Institute of Career Guidance. They use a web site that automatically matches students to 'ideal' vacancies. The Students' Union has the Student

WHERE GRADUATES END UP	
16% Health (Med, Dent)	Key Areas
11% Manufacturing,	
9% Finance,	
7% Public Admin,	
7% Wholesale/Retail,	
6% Personnel	
Defence, Accountancy,	Niche Areas
Agric/Forestry, Property,	
Eng/Industrial Design,	
Architecture, Chemical/	
Pharmaceutical, Radio/TV	
Approximate employed	**97%**

Development Network to enhance graduate employability through extra-curricular activities.

GETTING THERE

☛ By road: A1, A167/A696; A167 exit.
☛ By rail: Edinburgh, 1:30; Leeds, 1:45; London King's Cross, 3:00; Manchester Piccadilly, 3:00; Birmingham New Street, 4:00.
☛ By air: Newcastle International Airport.
☛ By coach: London, 6:05, Birmingham, 4:25.

NEWI

NEWI
Plas Coch
Mold Road
Wrexham LL11 2AW

TEL 01978 290666
FAX 01978 290008
EMAIL (see website)
WEB www.newi.ac.uk

VAG VIEW

*N*EWI, *as the North East Wales Institute likes to be known, is a small college of the University of Wales, but very much part of the local community. Other than the teacher/education base, NEWI offers degree courses through Humanities (some interesting media mixes with history, geography, English), business management & computing (including elements of leisure & tourism, estate management, and multimedia computing), Engineering, Built Environment (from Aarchitecture to surveying), Science (some interesting environmental courses plus Biology, Chemistry, Sport Science).*

Almost all first years are guaranteed accommodation, in their Student Village – apartments of en-suite study-bedrooms.

*Ents – discos, quizzes, live bands – are frequent (**Baldric's** and **Centenary** bars). Sport is competitive and there is a new multi-complex sports centre on campus.*

GETTING THERE

☛ By road: A483.
☛ By rail: Birmingham, 2:12; Cardiff, 3:40; Manchester, 1:30.
☛ By coach: Birmingham, 3:20.

NEWMAN COLLEGE

Newman College
Genners Lane
Bartley Green
Birmingham B32 3NT

TEL 0121 476 1181
FAX 0121 476 1196
EMAIL c.m.wilkinson@newman.ac.uk
WEB www.newman.ac.uk

VAG VIEW

*N*ewman College is a Roman Catholic foundation named after Cardinal John Henry Newman, a prominent figure in the Oxford Movement before he converted to Catholicism and wrote his Apologia on the nature of belief. You do not have to be a Roman Catholic to be accepted. Originally dedicated to teacher training, the*

teacher/education aspect still remains (BEd and BA/BSc QTS), but Newman also offers some joint and single honours courses, science, arts and humanities.

Sport is a big feature of life – there are PE and Sports Studies courses and they figure in national uni competitions. Ents are focused on **Hangovers Bar** *– band nights, comedy clubs, discos and formal balls.*

GETTING THERE
☛ By road: north/south, M5/J3, A456.
☛ By rail: London Euston, 1:40; Sheffield, 1:30; Manchester Piccadilly, 1:40; Leeds, 2.15.
☛ By coach: London, 2:40; Bristol, 2:00; Manchester, 2:30.

UNIVERSITY OF WALES COLLEGE, NEWPORT

University of Wales College, Newport
Caerleon Campus
PO Box 179
Newport NP6 1YG

TEL 01633 432432
FAX 01633 432850
EMAIL ulc@newport.ac.uk
WEB www.newport.ac.uk

Newport College Students' Union
College Crescent
Caerleon
Newport NP6 1YG

TEL 01633 432076
FAX 01633 432688
EMAIL students.union@newport.ac.uk
WEB www.newport.ac.uk/sunion/

VAG VIEW

*A*ctivities are split between two campus sites: **Newport**, *the first town of any size you come to travelling west along the M4 from England, and, just to its north,* **Caerleon** *– 'City of Legions and Court of King Arthur,' according to Geoffrey of Monmouth.*

It is on this Caerleon campus that innovative things are happening. Here have been built some of the best art and design facilities in Europe, and out of them are coming students who are taking the world of film animation by storm. Nine students have made a film, Famous Fred, *which was recently nominated for a Hollywood Oscar. Nor was this a one-off success. Recently two other students of*

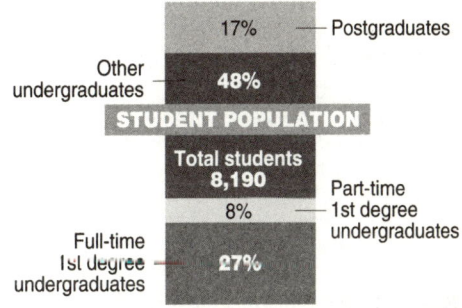

the department – Deiniol Morris and Michael Mort – have won BAFTA awards for their film, The Gogs.

There are also courses in Film and Video. If this is your bent, go for it, not least because they are 3rd in the Top 10 graduate

COLLEGE/STUDENT PROFILE	
University College since	**1996**
Situation/style	**Campus**
Student population	**8,190**
Full-time undergraduates	**1,840**
- mature	**41%**
- overseas	**2%**
- male/female	**46/54**
- state sector intake	**99%**
- non-traditional student intake	**24%, high**
- drop-out rate	**15%, high**
- undergraduate applications	**Up 11%**
see Introduction for key to tables	

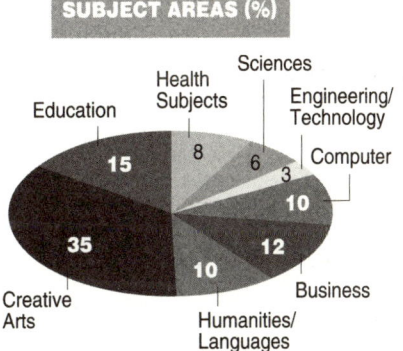

AT A GLANCE

ACADEMIC FILE:

Subjects assessed	**8**
Excellent	**None, but all Satisfactory**
Art and Design	**Grade 5 Research**
Typical A level requirements	**10 points**
Students-staff ratio	**31:1**
First/2:1 degree pass rate	**49%**

ACCOMMODATION FILE:

Guarantee to freshers	**100%**
Style	**Halls, student village**
Cost pw (no food)	**£42.75-£50**

WHERE GRADUATES END UP

32% Education*, Key Areas
12% Manufacturing,
8% Wholesale/Retail,
6% Finance,
6% Health/Social Work,
5% Public Admin
Film/Video*, Publishing*, Niche Areas
Defence

*indicates Top 10 Graduate Provider

Approximate employed **91%**

providers to the industry in the UK. What comes across in both this faculty and that of Design (Design Futures, Fashion & Textiles, Graphics) is that Newport College provides an imaginative environment. Subtlety, humour and creative thinking are to the fore.

WHAT IT'S REALLY LIKE

UNIVERSITY:

Social Life	★★
Campus scene	**Largely local**
Student Union services	**Average**
Politics	**Interest low**
Sport	**Relaxed**
National team position	**117th**
Sport facilities	**Good**
Arts opportunities	**Film excellent; music, art good; drama average; dance poor**
Student magazine	**Gos (web mag)**
Nightclub/bars	**University owned**
Union ents	**2 pw**
Live venue capacity	**500**
Union clubs/societies	**30**
Most popular society	**Rugby/IPS**
Smoking policy	**Union OK**
Parking	**Adequate**

TOWN:

Entertainment	★★
Scene	**Pubs + Cardiff**
Town/gown relations	**OK**
Risk of violence	**Low**
Cost of living	**Average**
Student concessions	**Good**
Survival + 2 nights out	**£50 pw**
Part-time work campus/town	**Good**

Accommodation is laid on with a choice of 'traditional' or en-suite rooms. For ents there's a 500-capacity venue in the **Main Hall** plus the university-owned **Clarence** bar. The most popular society is Rugby, so Wednesday's post-match disco is the focus, as are Sky big screen nights. Then there's karaoke, Chris Tarrant-inspired 'Who wants to win a crate of beer?' and other quizzes. Visitors recently included Alan Bates, a comedy hypnotist, and Booze Brothers (Blues Bros trib band). If you don't manage to stagger down the road into Cardiff, there are two clubs in Newport (**The Cotton Club** and **TJ's**).

Sport has just been boosted on Caerleon with a major new sports centre providing international-standard facilities; floodlit outdoor courts follow. They get involved with the Welsh Rugby Union and Cricket Association, as well as with BUSA and local groups.

The union is particularly active on student and awareness campaigns, which recently included breast cancer, access & equality, anonymous marking, sexual health and drug awareness.

It is all a surprisingly eclectic and energetic mix, with regular art exhibitions vying with sporting nights, e-culture (there's a new cyber café) and student concern (a new student development officer is in place).

GETTING THERE

☛ By road: M4/J25/26.
☛ By rail: London Paddington, 1:50; Birmingham New Street, 2:00; Cardiff, 40 mins; Bristol Parkway, 25 mins.
☛ By coach: London, 2:45; Manchester, 5:15.

UNIVERSITY OF NORTH LONDON

The University of North London
166-220 Holloway Road
London N7 8DB

North London Students' Union
166-220 Holloway Road
London N7 8DB

TEL 020 7753 3355
FAX 020 7753 3272
EMAIL admissions@unl.ac.uk
WEB www.uni.ac.uk

TEL 020 7753 3200
FAX 020 7753 3361
EMAIL supresident@uni.ac.uk
WEB www.su.unl.ac.uk

VAG VIEW

*N*orth London Uni became a university
in 1992. It was once the North London
Poly and will become London Metropolitan
University if the mooted merger with London
Guildhall University goes ahead and the
necessary permissions are granted. 88% of
LG students have apparently voted against
the merger. In our opinion this was not only
an unfriendly thing to do, but rather
shortsighted. North London is no ordinary
university. It is as far away from the punts
and gowns of Oxbridge as you can get. It is
a people's university, as much a part of the
local scene as the Arsenal up the road.
Eighteen-year-olds who come here to study
do so because they live in North London and
it's the obvious thing to do. Mature students
may arrive with a particular course in mind
because they can see an opening for a better
job if they study at UNL part time. But as
often they'll come because the opportunity
arose, like Angela Cameron, who gave up
work to have a baby and after two years at
home with her child decided she would take
the degree she'd passed over to get that job
after school which had led nowhere in
particular.*

*UNL is a great place, good relations
between lecturers and students – everyone
part of the same scene, and they've got a
flashy learning centre. They are, as they put
it at time of opening, 'equipped for study'.*

CAMPUS

The uni comprises a collection of sites around the
Holloway Road. Writes Maureen Okolo: 'UNL is in
the right place for a great, big, delicious slice of
London's night life. Step outside and find yourself
in the infamous Holloway Road. Packed with
takeaways, cafés, restaurants and shops. Totally
student friendly in prices. At one end [south] is

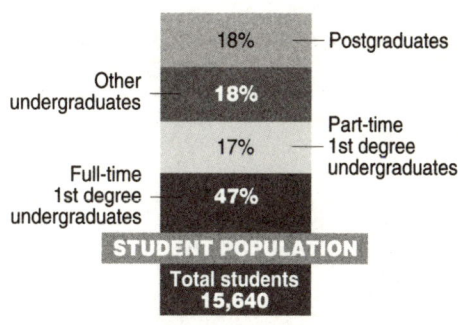

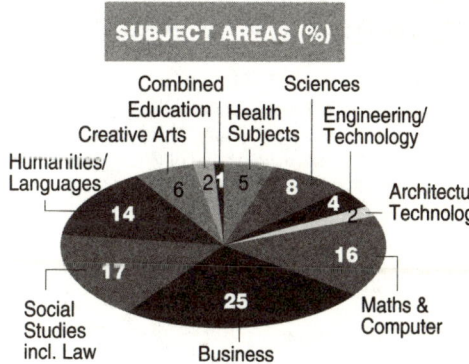

Highbury and Islington; at the other, Archway
(very long road, this, but with day and night bus
routes galore, tube and train stations close to uni
and halls, you'll be able to get around)...'

STUDENT PROFILE

Two-thirds of its undergraduate body is mature and
to a large extent drawn from the local, notably
ethnic population. UNL doesn't just preach wider
access to higher education, it ensures it.

'Uni life is great. If you like that sort of thing.
At UNL you get everyone who's into everything,'
promises Maureen. 'Just expect constant rounds of
socialising with chic, retro, funky, cool, funny
individuals from all walks of life.'

UNIVERSITY/STUDENT PROFILE

University since	**1992**
Situation/style	**Civic**
Student population	**15,640**
Full-time undergraduates	**7,300**
- mature	**63%**
- overseas	**5%**
- male/female	**45/55**
- state sector intake	**97%**
- non-traditional student intake	**13%**
- drop-out rate	**22%, high**
- undergraduate applications	**Down 10%**
see Introduction for key to tables	

ACADEMIA

Undergrads study Business, Environmental & Social Studies, and Humanities, as well as Education, Science, Computing and Engineering. Teaching assessment results are good, recently very good, with Film Studies and Art & Design dropping only two marks apiece. Throughout the uni relations between lecturers and students are very good.

ACADEMIC EXCELLENCE

TEACHING:
(Rated Excellent or 17+ out of 24)

English	**Excellent**
Business/Management	**24**
Film Studies, Art & Design, Electric /Electron Eng, Philosophy	**22**
Modern Langs (Dutch, French, German, Iberian Studies), Education	**20**
Maths, Nursing, Other subjects Allied to Medicine	**21**
Materials Technology, Food Sciences, Psychology	**19**
Library/Info, Biosciences,	**18**

RESEARCH :
*Top grades 5/5**	**None**

A few years ago they opened an eight-floor IT and language learning resources building with open-access IT, printing and scanning facilities, access to web-based learning materials developed by uni staff, a language centre with computer-assisted and satellite sources, TV and audio equipment, as well as a good old-fashioned lecture auditorium.

SOCIAL SCENE

Recently, too, the SU building was transformed. There are three bars (one non-smoking) and still plenty of space for club nights, live bands, meetings, a shop, welfare facilities... **The Rocket**, as the venue is known, has been around as long as the poly (100 years). It holds the entire history within its walls. In 1896 it was a venue for concerts, some of them conducted by proms patron Sir Henry Wood. By 1929 it had become a theatre, its centrepiece for half a century an organ played by William Lloyd Webber, father of Julian and Andrew, until it was sold to St Joseph's RC church on Highgate Hill. Now, with sophisticated sound and lighting system and changing rooms, it has come alive again as a major London club venue, recently landing the accolade from industry mag *Live!*, Best Student Venue in London. 'Notorious for its fab indie, rock, pop or R&B nights and parties, various DJs frequent this lavish venue, which has undergone a sensational transformation from typical student bar to stylish, open-plan student

WHAT IT'S REALLY LIKE

UNIVERSITY:
Social Life	★★★
Campus scene	**Mature urban warriors**
Student Union services	**Poor**
Politics	**Interest low**
Sport	**Competitive**
National team position	**77th**
Sport facilities	**Improving**
Arts opportunities	**Drama, film good; dance, musiv avg; art poor**
Student mag/news	**Big Fish**
Nightclub	**The Rocket**
Bars	**3 union bars**
Union ents	**Big Fish, Mish Mash, Club Ri Ra**
Union clubs/societies	**17**
Most popular society	**Islamic/African Caribbean**
Smoking policy	**Bars OK**
Parking	**Non-existent**

CITY:
Entertainment	★★★★★
Scene	**Wild**
Town/gown relations	**OK**
Risk of violence	**High**
Cost of living	**High**
Student concessions	**Excellent**
Survival + 2 nights out	**£50 pw**
Part-time work campus/town	**Average/excellent**

AT A GLANCE

ACADEMIC FILE:

Subjects assessed	**28**
Excellent	**61%**
Average A level requirements	**11 points**
Students-staff ratio	**26:1**
First/2:1 degree pass rate	**41%**

ACCOMMODATION FILE:

Guarantee to freshers	**65%**
Style	**Halls, flats**
Approx price range pw	**£65-£77**
City rent pw	**£70**

bar,' writes Maureen Okolo. 'Very kitsch. Complete with MTV music screen and its own café which serves wine and food. Not to mention a handy games and pool room.' Currently, Wednesday is Big Fish night and free to students. Fortnightly there's Mish Mash, a total mix (funk, hip hop, drum 'n' bass). Regularly there are DJs, live bands, 'learn-to-DJ' (or juggle!), then Thursday is Club Ri Ra – Irish night and live bands or Soca, a Caribbean night with live bands.

TOWN 'The **Tappit** bar is next door to Holloway tube station,' Maureen tells us. 'Its cool, wooden-tiled interior is the place to relax or consign yourself to oblivion. Five minutes away is the **Cornet**, a huge traditional pub that from the outside resembles a cinema. The **Hobgoblin** and the **Litten Tree** are opposite each other. Easy access.

'Head up to Upper Holloway and you will be dazzled by the bright lights... of the **Odeon** cinema. Before you reach it, pop into **O'Neills** and sample the Caffrey's.

'UNL has easy access to London's West End, but if you want to rave, it's Upper Holloway,

> *It is as far away from the punts and gowns of Oxbridge as you can get. It is a people's university, as much a part of the local scene as the Arsenal up the road.*

up the Seven Sisters to a venue known as the **Powerhaus**. Here one can club as an ambition. Or try out **The Stiff** (what's in a name?). Quite close to Finsbury Park station (train and tube).

'As for bar dropping, visit Highbury & Islington, about ten minutes from the uni sites. As I recall, from my last visit, the area has many classic bars, but names somehow fail me. I found myself tipsy on a bus on the way to Highbury. I needed food. Too many choices, pizza, curries, African, Italian, kebabs, burgers, fish 'n' chips.

Even clusters of late-night grocers and off-licences (they do sell food). I got off at Highbury & Islington. It's at the other end of Holloway Road towards the Angel. **The Garage** nightclub on Highbury Corner. DJs whip up some fast beats to make you crave to rave. **The Blue Note**, a great big club with four floors for all tastes: soul, swing, ragga, hip hop, garage. The chill out room upstairs is impeccable and very, very intimate, playing cool beats to make you ooze in your groove. Which I did. Quite well. I, um, found myself... the following morning... waking up... outside a hall of residence, sprawled on Holloway Road. With a bunch of flyers and a pub ashtray in my pocket.

WHERE GRADUATES END UP

13% Education, Key Areas
11% Health/Social Work,
10% Wholesale/Retail,
7% Finance,
6% Manufacturing,
5% Personnel,
5% Public Admin
Eng/Industrial Design, Niche Areas
Advertising, Architecture,
Artistic/Literary, Legal,
Library/Archival, Market
Research*, Sport*

*indicates Top 10 Graduate Provider

Approximate employed **91%**

'Which came as a big shock, as I don't actually live in halls.'

PILLOW TALK

The uni has four halls. All, except one, are a short distance from the five uni sites (perfect for the compulsory, late lecture starts). Tufnell Park Hall is on the Northern Line (Tube) or you can take a bus. Arcade Hall and Carl Eaton Grange are close to the uni sites. All three have self-catering facilities. James Leicester Hall (also quite close) provides an evening meal for those missing mum or dad's home cooking.

Please note: North London is considered to be trendy; rents vary from reasonable to absurd.

GETTING THERE

☛ Holloway Road Underground (Piccadilly Line).

UNIVERSITY COLLEGE NORTHAMPTON

University College Northampton
Boughton Green Road
Moulton Park
Northampton NN2 7AL

TEL 0800 3582232
FAX 01604 735500
EMAIL admissions@northampton.ac.uk
WEB northampton.ac.uk

UC Northampton Students' Union
Boughton Green Road
Moulton Park
Northampton NN2 7AL

TEL 01604 734567 X2818
FAX 01604 719454
EMAIL [firstname.surname]@ucnu.org
WEB www.ucnu.org

VAG VIEW

*K*nown until recently as Nene (pronounced
Nen if you're local, but with a long 'e' if
you are from the Peterborough end of the
river) University College Northampton, or
UCN has been basking in the glory of being
in the UK top ten for growth in applications
and being one of only seven higher education
institutions to be awarded University College
status by the Privy Council. in the latest
round It is not difficult to see why.

CAMPUS

The main Park campus, an 80-acre estate on the
edge of town, has been well designed. What strikes
the visitor immediately is the careful architectural
integration of facilities and services, none of which
limit or indeed offend the eye. Halls are in among
lecture theatres, sports centre by the nightclub,
eaterie and bar; a rugby pitch in the centre of
things gives a welcome sense of space and a
reminder that rugby is a religion both here and in
town, which has one of the best teams in the
Premier League.

Everything on campus is in seemly proportion;
nothing dominates. Close to the intriguing Leather
Conservation Centre – (Northampton is the centre
of the shoe industry; the football ground is called
The Cobblers) – is another bar, **The Pavilion**,

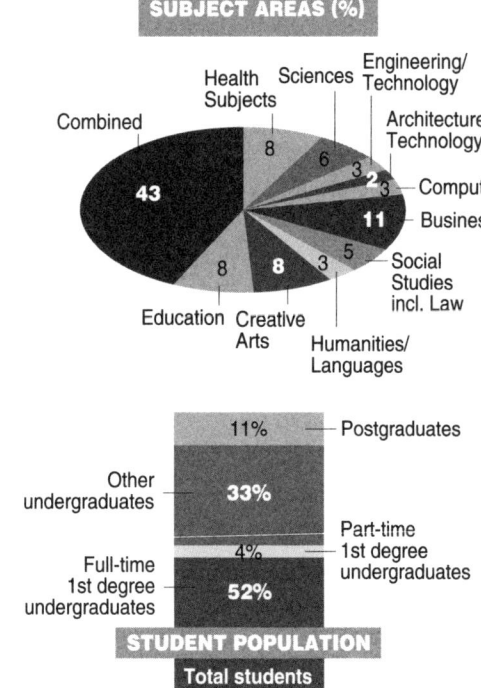

SUBJECT AREAS (%)

STUDENT POPULATION

Total students
10,740

COLLEGE/STUDENT PROFILE

University College since	**1999**
Situation/style	**Town campus**
Student population	**10,740**
Full-time degree undergraduates	**5,540**
- mature	**29%**
- overseas	**3%**
- male/female	**58/42**
- state sector intake	**97%**
- non-traditional student intake	**15%**
- drop-out rate	**13%, high**
- undergraduate applications	**Up 2%**
see Introduction for key to tables	

which looks out over picnic tables across a green
sward of more pitches to a well-established
boundary of Scots pine. Some buildings, you notice,
are named after villages in the county, the halls of
residence after notable people of the area,
including the tragic Northamptonshire poet John
Clare, whose parents were illiterate, but who
achieved national renown in his day by imbibing
the spirit of this place before going insane.

Artistically, the focus is at UCN's Avenue
campus in town, however. This 24-acre site –
twenty minutes away from Park and linked by a
free bus service – houses Art, Design, Technology
and Performance Arts. In particular there's quite a
theatre tradition. A few years ago they won the
Playwright Bursary at the NUS Drama Festival.

ACADEMIA

There are three faculties, through which are offered more than 100 degree and HND courses in addition to single and combined honours degrees. **The Faculty of Applied Sciences** includes schools of Leather Technology, Built Environment, Engineering & Technology, Environmental Science, Health & Life Sciences, and Nursing & Midwifery. Medical sciences have links with the General Hospital in Northampton and with Milton Keynes, 'Nursing courses are always over-subscribed,' I was told.

ACADEMIC EXCELLENCE

TEACHING:
(Rated Excellent or 17+ out of 24)

Art & Design	**23**
Anatomy, Nursing & Other Subjects Related to Medicine, Materials Technology	**22**
Communication & Media Drama, Dance, Cinematics	**21**
Psychology, Sociology	**20**
Building & Civil Engineering	**19**
American Studies, General Eng & Electric/Electron Eng	**18**

RESEARCH:
Top grades 5/5* **None**

The **Faculty of Arts & Social Sciences** includes Art & Design, Behavioural Studies (including a BSc in Psychology), Cultural Studies (such as a cross-cultural degree in Performance Studies – Drama, Dance, Music), Education (BA Hons QTS Primary), and Social Studies (American Studies, History, Sociology).

The **Faculty of Management & Business** includes the schools of Business, Information Systems, Law & International Business, Professional Studies (Finance and Accounting) and Management (post-grad MMB, MSc Management Studies).

Resource-wise there's a recently extended library, IT Centre and Audio-Visual Centre.

SOCIAL SCENE

Pleasure-seeking students have moulded town and college alike. 'In the last two years no end of new pubs have opened, and the student presence is acknowledged by *It's a Scream*,' a student told me. Lots of clubs offer student nights. The union has a deal with *Time* and *Envy*, which sounds almost deep. There are free buses from Park.

On campus, there's the nightclub, the

WHAT IT'S REALLY LIKE

UNIVERSITY:

Social Life	★★★
Campus scene	**Local & lively**
Politics	**Student issues**
Sport	**20 clubs, 50 teams**
National team position	**85th**
Sport facilities	**Good**
Arts opportunities	**Excellent**
Student newspaper	**Wave**
Nightclub	**The Venue**
Bars	**Central Park, Georges, Pavilion**
Union ents	**Fun Factory, R.S.V.P., Krunchie**
Union clubs/societies	**36**
Smoking policy	**Union OK**
Parking	**1,600**

TOWN:

Entertainment	★★★
Scene	**Pubs, clubs OK**
Cost of living	**High**
Student concessions	**Good**
Risk of violence	**Low**
Survival + 2 nights out	**£65 pw**
Part-time work campus/town	**Excellent/good**

Venue, with *Fun Factory* (cheesy music night) and *R.S.V.P.* (big name DJ night). At **Georges**, one of the bars (there's also **Central Park** and **Pavilion** bars) they have *Krunchie* (more cheese) and *Nailed* (live bands/indie rock). Each night there are at least two deals on, so there are always drinks on promotion, drinks for £1. Recent live acts include Judge Jules, Emma B, Nemone, Gods Kitchen, Dave Pearce, Seb Fontane, Jackie Charlton, Boy George, and comedians and live bands.

AT A GLANCE

ACADEMIC FILE:

Subjects assessed	**21**
Excellent	**48%**
Typical requirements	**160 points**
Students-staff ratio	**21:1**
First/2:1 degree pass rate	**40%**

ACCOMMODATION FILE:

Guarantee to freshers	**First & firm choices only**
Style	**Halls, flats**
Catered	**None**
En-suite	**67%**
Approx price range pw	**£30.45-£59.08**
Town rent pw	**£43**

While I was there they had Martin Taylor, a hypnotist and comedian and *Bar Footsie* (the usual Stock Exchange drinks promo).

The student nespaper is *Wave* and altogether some sixteen societies, the most active being Christian Union, kickboxing and Islam, and there are twenty sports clubs and some fifty teams. They claim the British Heavyweight Combat Ju-jitsu champion, 'some rugby lad picked to play for Ireland', and the World Karate Champion. Who are we to argue?

PILLOW TALK

College accommodation is guaranteed to 'first and firm choices' in halls or flats (some 67% are en suite. Price per week ranges from £30.45 to £59.08, while average town rent is £43 per week.

JOBS

Recent statistics show 75% of year 2000 graduates were in employment after six months and 20% in further education. There are masses of tie-ups with local businesses.

WHERE GRADUATES END UP

19% Education,	Key Areas
13% Health/Social Work,	
12% Wholesale/Retail,	
10% Manufacturing,	
7% Finance,	
6% Public Admin,	
5% Personnel	
Hotel/Restaurant,	Niche Area
Advertising, Publishing,	
Electron/Electric, Legal,	
Property, Sport	
Approximate employed	**94%**

GETTING THERE

☛ By road: M1/J15/15a/16; easy access to M5/6/25/40, A1 and A45.
☛ By rail: London and Birmingham, 1:00.
☛ By coach: London, 2:00; Birmingham, 1:35; Leicester, 1:00.

• •

UNIVERSITY OF NORTHUMBRIA

University of Northumbria
Ellison Place
Newcastle upon Tyne NE1 8ST

TEL 0191 227 4064
FAX 0191 227 3009
EMAIL (see website)
WEB www.unn.ac.uk

Northumbria Students' Union
2 Sandyford Road
Newcastle Upon Tyne NE1 8SB

TEL 0191 227 4757
FAX 0191 227 3760
EMAIL (see website)
WEB www.unionsociety.ac.uk

VAG VIEW

*T*he two universities in this city –
Newcastle and Northumbria – are
*situated within walking distance. At
Northumbria, there is a very much higher
intake from state school, from the lower
economic groups and non-traditional uni-goers
– 90%, 30% and 20% respectively, as against
67%, 16% and 10% at Newcastle.*

*Given these statistics, it looks as if the
newer university is offering these students, who
entered on far lower numbers of points than at
Newcastle, superb value, and may be
enhancing opportunity to a greater degree than
Newcastle. For, while not measuring up to its
neighbour in research terms – they came 99th
in last year's assessments, Newcastle came
32nd – overall Northumbria are level pegging in
terms of teaching excellence. They have scored
76% Excellent, while Newcastle' scored 78%.*

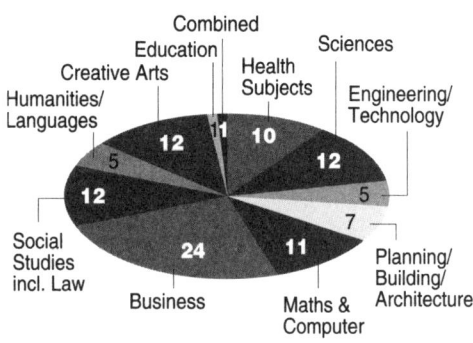

SUBJECT AREAS (%)

Combined
Education
Creative Arts
Humanities/Languages
Health Subjects
Sciences
Engineering/Technology
Social Studies incl. Law
Business
Maths & Computer
Planning/Building/Architecture

12 · 1 · 10 · 12 · 5 · 5 · 12 · 24 · 11 · 7

*On the graduate employment ticket, there is
similar optimism. Some new universities have
not taken on board the significance of the
student culture of the traditional university*

in landing their students worthwhile jobs, as opposed to any jobs. Northumbria has, and has recently made enormous strides in enriching its student culture. To begin with, look at sport. Northumbria's teams came 15th nationally last year, while the older university, which puts much store by sport, came 19th. Meanwhile, in the matter of student media, the student-run radio station – N.S.R. – was nominated for Best Newcomer in the Radio 1 awards two years ago and this year The Nerve, its news programme, was nominated in the category of best factual programme. At the same time, Northumbria's new magazine, Incite, was nominated in the Independent newspaper awards for Best Student Magazine. This year, as we show in our Employment box (page 341), Northumbria found itself among the top ten providers of students to journalism in the country, yet the graduates who became journalists didn't come from one department, from a course in journalism or even media studies. They came from departments like business, engineering, computer and biosciences. There can be no clearer picture of the impact of extracurricular student culture on undergraduate performance than this.

These sporting and media successes give the union such momentum that Northumbria can report that this year, due to fresher enthusiasm, they were able actually to double the number of student societies available due to increased interest.

A strong student culture has also enabled Northumberland, possibly more than any other new uni which shares a city with an older, more traditional foundation, to hold its head high and mix well: 'I think what is

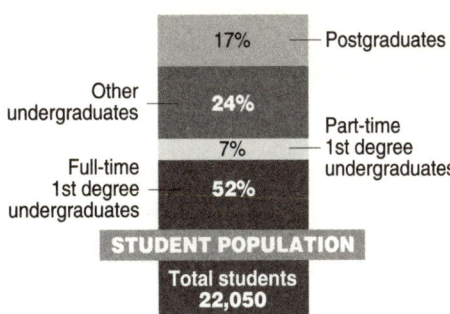

important about being a student in Newcastle,' said Susannah Bell reading History of Art at Northumbria, 'is that the ex-poly and the university mix very well. There is little snobbery, rather a healthy competitive rivalry, especially when it comes to sport. Sport is the only time it gets mentioned that we're an ex-poly; then we're proud to be a poly! They call us the poly kids; we call them the rahs, but very often students find themselves living in a house with both uni and poly students, which is unheard of in places such as Oxford.'

CAMPUSES

CITY CAMPUS (address above) Student Union, library, sports centre, language laboratories, art gallery, computer services are all here, as are the Faculties of **Arts & Design** (all Humanities, Languages, Fine Art, Design, Fashion), **Social Sciences** (Geography, Psychology, Sports Studies, Law, Politics, Sociology, Economics), **Business**, and **Science & Technology**.

COACH LANE CAMPUS Coach Lane, Benton, Newcastle upon Tyne NE7 7XA. Tel: 0191 215 6000. Recent beneficiary of a £40-million development. The Faculty of **Health, Social Work & Education**, and Departments of Chemical and Life Sciences of the Faculty of **Engineering, Science & Technology**, are 3 miles from the centre, out towards the coast. Coach Lane also has a union, library and computing facilities, a sports hall, fitness suite, activity studio and all-weather hockey pitch.

LONGHIRST CAMPUS Longhirst Hall, Morpeth, Northumberland NE61 3LL. Tel: 01670 795 000. Management students from the **Business** Faculty are 15 miles north up the A1. Longhirst is a joint project with the NTEC and provides a residential conference centre.

UNIVERSITY/STUDENT PROFILE	
University since	**1992**
Situation/style	**Civic**
Student population	**22,050**
Full-time undergraduates	**11,420**
- mature	**29%**
- overseas	**6%**
- male/female	**48/52**
- state sector intake	**90%**
- non-traditional student intake	**20%, high**
- drop-out rate	**9%**
- undergraduate applications	**Down 8%**
see Introduction for key to tables	

CARLISLE CAMPUS 4-5 Paternoster Row, Carlisle, Cumbria CA3 8TB. Tel: 0191 227 4550. There's Business and a combined honours degree at Carlisle, the latter run in conjunction with Carlisle College, an associate college of Northumbria University. The subject combinations fall broadly into the areas of humanities and social sciences.

Carlisle is even cheaper to live in than Newcastle, though entertainments are less enticing.

> *In less than a decade Northumbria has made it up the university rankings to compete with Newcastle. Given the more challenging student base, it may now be outgunning its older neighbour in terms of adding real value.*

STUDENT PROFILE

Besides the large number of entrants from the state sector and from neighbourhoods who haven't traditionally pushed their kids into higher education, there are a number of mature students and part-timers at Northumbria, part of their Lifelong Learning policy. Basically, the mix works; everyone has a cool time in a very cool place.

ACADEMIA

Northumbria's health provision is on the nursing, midwifery, physiotherapy, occupational therapy side, and finds some 15% of its graduates jobs. A fifth of the uni's intake go into business and there are some interesting Ee-business technology and commerce degrees at both City and Carlisle

campuses. They also have one of the best law schools in the country. When we spoke to a leading Chambers in Leeds, it was made clear that Northumbria was high on the list for graduate employability. Northumbria offer various routes, characterised by a particular sort of emphasis on skills, authentic courtroom simulations, etc. Then again, its fashion department excels, its engineering degrees may get a boost from the appointment of new vice-chancellor Kel Fidler, who was Professor of Electronics at York and earlier held the Chair of Electrical Engineering Science at Essex. The pharmaceutical chemistry degrees give Northumbria an employment niche in that area, their human resource management degrees lead some 5% of graduates into personnel. Top-rated subjects recently were education, nursing, modern languages, health subjects, physics. The assessors praised Northumbria's teaching of modern languages as 'imaginative', 'high quality', producing 'a high employment rate'. Sports sciences are strong. Drama scored 22 out of 24 at the assessments, is a performance-related course with a community focus, and is an active student interest off the curricular too.

SOCIAL SCENE

At City Campus the **Venue Bar**, on the first floor, is the place for live music (capacity now 3,000), while **Reds** (circular bar, 550 capacity), on the second floor, is for discos. There's also the **Northumbria Bar,** on the ground floor, and a cool meeting place, the **Purple Lounge**. Coach Lane campus has a big hall, one bar and one major clubnight on a Thursday – *Session* ('70s to '90s). At Carlisle campus, Friday sees two floors featuring resident DJs.

Reds has *Get Ya Skates On* (rock, hip hop, rap, funk) on Monday; Wednesday is *Footloose* ('70s/'80s nigh), a sell-out every week; on a Friday they have *Traveller* (dance) and on Saturday, *Wiggle* survives (the biggest night of the week – 'pulling not posing') both upstairs in Reds and downstairs in the Venue. 'Last year we had it upstairs only and we'd sell out in the first fifteen minutes,' we were told.

They boast live gigs from Stereo MCs, Embrace, Levellers, Gabrielle, Shed Seven, Goldie, James Brown, Low Fidelity All Stars, and the usual run of hypnotists and ceilidhs. 'We promote our own DJs in Reds. Last year we had a thing on Wednesday

ACADEMIC EXCELLENCE	
TEACHING:	
(Rated Excellent or 17+ out of 24)	
Business & Management,	**Excellent**
English, Law.	
Nursing, Education	**24**
Languages (French, German,	**23**
Russian, Spanish), Physics,	
Subjects Allied to Medicine	
Drama/Dance /Cinematics,	**22**
Built Environment, Electrical	
& Electronic Eng, Art, Economics,	
Library/Info Mgt, Politics	
& Design, Business, Psychology	
History Art/Design & Film,	**21**
Town/Country Planning, Maths,	
Sport, Molecular Biosciences	
Sociology	**20**
RESEARCH :	
*Top grades 5/5**	**None**

WHAT IT'S REALLY LIKE

UNIVERSITY:

Social Life	★★★★★
Campus scene	**The lively, less self-conscious one**
Student Union services	**Average**
Politics	**Average**
Sport	**Key**
National team position	**15th**
Sport facilities	**Good**
Arts opportunities	**Drama, music, film good; dance, art average**
Student magazine	**Incite**
Student radio	**NSR**
Nightclub	**Venue**
Bars	**Northumbria, Reds**
Union ents	**Get Ya Skates On, Footloose, Traveller, Wiggle**
Union clubs/societies	**60**
Most popular society	**Christian, GLOBE**
Smoking policy	**Union OK**
Parking	**Poor**

CITY:

Entertainment	★★★★★
Scene	**Intoxicating**
Town/gown relations	**OK**
Risk of violence	**Average**
Cost of living	**Average**
Student concessions	**Good**
Survival + 2 nights out	**£60-£70 pw**
Part-time work campus/town	**Average/good**

AT A GLANCE

ACADEMIC FILE:

Subjects assessed	**30**
Excellent	**77%**
Average requirements	**200 points**
Students-staff ratio	**18:1**
First/2:1 degree pass rate	**49%**

ACCOMMODATION FILE:

Guarantee to freshers	**95% of non-local freshers**
Style	**Halls, flats**
Catered	**18%**
En-suite	**13%**
Price range pw	**£50-£74**
City rent pw	**£35-£75**

PILLOW TALK

They guarantee approximately 95% freshers uni accommodation, with priority given to non-local first-years. Local students can apply for rooms only after the start of term. First-year accommodation consists of halls and flats. Claude Gibb is the most popular hall, being in crawling distance of town and lectures – 'more of a public school crowd here,' said one. The Larches is the one to avoid (rough area). Lovaine, also on campus, is handy but poky. Of flats a student said that Glenamara and Stevenson both have the advantage of a very central location. Only 18% of accommodation is catered and 13% en suite. Price per week ranges from £50 to £74 (catered, fourteen meals). City ranges from £35 to £75. New residences (345 rooms) will be opening in September 2002, adjacent to City Campus, the first at Northumbria to

afternoon so that people who didn't play sport but wanted to DJ could come in and use our decks.' There are also good opportunities for DJs to make the transition to city clubs. 'One of our DJs, who does Saturday night *Wiggle*, was a student here. He started the Wednesday night (*Footloose*) too, and now he's working six nights a week in bars and nightclubs in town.'

There's also a decent drama society – three or four productions a year, the newspaper and radio station. Probably the most active of the thirty societies is Community Student Action. GLOBE – Gay, Lesbian & Bisexual (being polite, I didn't ask about the 'o') get involved in national campaigns.

SPORT Lots to offer, a well-equipped sports hall, gym and indoor tennis courts, options to do anything from scuba diving to rugby, which has some very high-class teams and regularly trounces Newcastle Uni, good hockey, football and tennis.

WHERE GRADUATES END UP

15% Health/Social Work, Key Areas
9% Manufacturing,
9% Wholesale/Retail,
8% Education,
7% Public Admin,
6% Finance,
5% Personnel
Property, Advertising, Niche Areas
Journalism*, Legal,
Chem/Pharmaceutical,
Telecom, Construction,
Eng/Industrial Design

*indicates Top 10 Graduate Provider

Approximate employed	**94%**

341

offer en-suite facilities in all study rooms. Facilities in the four and five bedroom flats include telephone and Internet access points in all rooms, fully fitted kitchens and 24-hour security systems. Coach Lane, Longhirst and Carlisle also have halls.

JOBS

Seriously good reputation on graduate employment – see box, page 341. Contact with firms in the North East region is facilitated by all sorts of strategies, not least Northumbria's e.Business Centre, which dispenses advice and support to small and medium sized businesses, utilising uni expertise in law, technology, marketing and business.

GETTING THERE

☞ By road to Newcastle: A1(M) from the south and north; A19 from York; A69 from the west; M6 from the southwest.

☞ By road to Carlisle: A7 from the north; M6 from the south; A69 from Newcastle (the east).

☞ By rail to Newcastle: Edinburgh, 1:30; Leeds, 1:45; London King's Cross, 3:00; Manchester Piccadilly, 3:00; Birmingham New Street, 4:00.

☞ By rail to Carlisle: Edinburgh, 1.25; Leeds, 3.15; London King's Cross, 4.45; Manchester Piccadilly, 2.20; Birmingham New Street, 2.57.

☞ By air: Newcastle International airport.

☞ By coach: London, 6:05; Birmingham, 4:25.

NORWICH CITY COLLEGE

Norwich City College	TEL 01603 773136
Ipswich Road	FAX 01603 773301
Norwich	EMAIL info@ccn.ac.uk
Norfolk NR2 2LJ	WEB www.ccn.ac.uk

VAG VIEW

City College, ten minutes walk from the centre of Norwich, is a a 'one stop shop' for education post-16, offering a whole host of courses from A levels, access and foundation, NVQ and HND, right through to first degree, awarded by Anglia Polytechnic University. They have an excellent relationship with industry. Many of the first degrees are unitised so that, for example, in the Combined Arts BA (Hons) – English, History and Sociology (a Psychology course option is also in the offing) – you can stop at Year 1 and accept a CertHE, Year 2 for a DipHE, or complete the degree at the end of Year 3.

The Students' Union co-ordinates social and sporting activities, and the college has a sports hall and tennis courts. Southwell Hall of Residence offers 270 beds on campus.

COLLEGE PROFILE

Founded	**1891**
Status	**F/HE College**
Degree awarding university	**Anglia Poly**
Student population	**16,515**
Degree undergraduates	**548**

ACCOMMODATION:

Availability to freshers	**100%**
Style	**Halls**
Cost pw (no food)	**£41**
City rent pw	**£40-£50**

DEGREE SUBJECT AREAS:
Humanities, social sciences, accounting, business, marketing, tourism, science, environment

☞ By rail: less than 2 hours from London (Liverpool Street); Intercity link via Peterborough with the Midlands (Birmingham New Street, 4:00), the North (Sheffield, 3:50) and Scotland.

☞ By coach: London, 2:50; Birmingham, 6:00; Sheffield, 7:00.

GETTING THERE

☞ By road: from London it's the A11(M), A47. From the north or the Midlands, A47 King's Lynn or the A14 as far as Newmarket, then the A11.

STUDENT NOTTINGHAM – THE CITY

Nottingham is a city of big spenders. The second biggest shopping city in the UK with an annual expenditure of £3 billion, it's known as the Milan of the Midlands.

But it's also a city of students, with two large universities and eight further education institutes. Young guns pour into the city every autumn and in the holidays it's almost a ghost town.

And we're not talking the stereotyped Doc-Marten-booted, down-to-my-last-coppers students. In Nottingham they're slick, classy, and definitely big spenders.

Most of the local entertainments industry relies on students for its income, especially the pubs and bars. And of course the people of Notts don't just drink in style, their dress sense, eating habits and social life are all equally demanding.

This makes for a vibrant, exciting city, which is above all young. The graduate recruitment market's so healthy you may find yourself staying for longer than you think.

GIGGING

Rock City, Talbot Street The only big live venue in Nottingham. Despite the name it's not got a particularly rawk reputation. It hosts medium and big name bands on a weekly basis; recent highlights are Ash, Ian Brown and Air. It's dark, it's dim, and it also has a range of clubnights from '70s to student indie to heavier rock and grunge.

CLUBBING

The Bomb, Bridlesmith Gate. *The* club in Nottingham; with a national reputation, music ranging from drum 'n' bass to funk to techno, and a wicked interior, if you're on The Bomb's guest list, you're truly Nottingham royalty.

The Ballroom, Radford Boulevard, Lenton. Still known as 'the Garvey' by underground die-hards, this remains Nottingham's last tribute to the free party spirit. Its no-frills interior and non-existent door policy have made it a favourite for techno and drum 'n' bass promoters, who bring in the big names (Bolland, Clarke, Bukem, Goldie) as well as putting on free parties for all and sundry.

Media, Queen Street. A fairly new venue, and Nottingham's first attempt at a superclub. Fairly typical commercial clubbing venue, with a rather snooty attitude. Set on several levels, it's well thought out, if not a bit confusing after a few beverages. Watch out for those Trent *Schoolgirl* nights though lads. Britney-tastic!

The Works is the new kid on the block and has become a favourite with students and locals alike. Set over several dancefloors and levels, the Works is stylish and well thought out and provides good music to cater for all tastes. With a tasty, if slightly pricey, selection of cocktails at the cocktail bar, and free entry before 10 on a Friday, there are plenty of reasons to give it a try.

If you prefer Abba and Steps to garage and hip hop, there's **Ocean** on Greyfriar Street, it's the students' choice for cheese and cheap(ish) booze. Rumours on the grapevine suggest that it's due to close, though, because of the new tram system!?

Truly a loss to us all. **The Palais** on Upper Parliament Street is the classic cattlemarket and as cheesy as it comes. **The Zone**, downstairs, a student favourite on the weekend, provides Alco-Pop and Chesney Hawkes heaven to the masses. **Isis** on Redfield Way in Dunkirk looks like a deserted warehouse by day but turns into student heaven on a Wednesday, Athletics Union night, when it's packed with drunken, lycra-clad birds and Ted Baker-shirted lads, all looking for a snog. If you can't pull in here, give up trying.

DRINKING

Market Bar, Goosegate. A veteran of the Nottingham scene, the Market Bar has a stylish but intimate atmosphere. Another regular haunt of the local style posse.

Via Fossa, Canal Street. This place is massive – seven bars over two floors and a huge outdoor terrace looking onto the restored canal area, it's no wonder you can't escape it. The décor's a little schizophrenic, but that's part of its charm.

Revolution, Broad Street, is becoming massively popular among student-types and the style posse alike. As the Russian theme suggests, there are hundreds of vodka-related concoctions to tease your tastebuds. So, whether you like it shaken, not stirred or straight up with a hint of Dime Bar, it's there for you. Pumping drum 'n' bass with resident DJs on a weekend makes up for the difficulty in getting to the bar.

Other stylish bars worth trying are the **Pitcher And Piano** on High Pavement, and **Altar Ego** by the Weekday Cross in the Lace Market. **Café Barrio** off Bridlesmith Gate is one of the few places in the city which opens late every night of the week, and plays a range of music, from jazz to funk to Asian breakbeats. For more of a student atmosphere, **The Ropewalk** and **The Horn**

In Hand, both run by student pub company *It's A Scream*, are popular with Nottingham and Trent students respectively. **The Bag Of Nails** on Lenton Boulevard is almost an off-campus common room, it's so packed with second and third years from Nottingham University. And both unions have cheap and cheerful bars with good drinks offers.

There are also a number of over-decorated bars and chains in the city centre, most of which stick to the novelty-theme-and-big-screen-TV concept.

EATING

Skinny Sumo, Goosegate. A sushi bar with a nice sideline in other Asian dishes, this is perfect if you're not into fancy eating. The dishes trundle round the room on a conveyor belt, giving new meaning to the phrase 'fast food'. Hot dishes and specials are made to order.

TGI Fridays, Forman Street, part of the new **Cornerhouse** development, combines great American grill-type food with friendly staff and typically meaty American-size portions, while their wide selection of cocktails washes it all down nicely. If hunger strikes and you like your meat then TGI's is a great place for a feed.

Casa, Friar Lane. Better known as a pretty classy bar, Casa also has a restaurant section. On a raised dais looking over the rest of the room, it's still sociable, and the prices aren't bad. It's posh but not too intimidating, and if you're treating yourself to a night on the town, it's a good place to start.

V1 on Houndsgate is the only veggie fast food place in Nottingham. They do burgers and fries for die-hard greasies, but also lovely salads and sandwiches for health-conscious office workers, as well as fruit smoothies and cakes. But their classic is spicy potato wedges, with a range of dips. And it's pretty cheap too.

The C Bar on Goosegate and **Atlas Deli** on Long Row are also good for daytime snacks.

Nottingham also has a wide range of chip shops, kebab shops, burger chains and takeaways if you're a grease connoisseur, and most of the bars and pubs do pretty good food.

SHOPPING

Wild Clothing, 4 - 6 Broad Street, is good for mid-price vintage clothing, while **Red or Dead** on St Peters Gate caters for label freaks who can't afford the pricier places. **Lillywhites** on Clumber Street is the only branch of the sports shop outside London, and the **Paul Smith** shop on Byard Lane was the British designer's first outlet and workshop. Worth a visit to see the Japanese tourists reverently fondling the shirts. For menswear there is a wide range of shops – **Hope And Glory** on Pelham Street, **HSC** on Goosegate. Unisex shops include **Ark Clothing** on St Peters Gate, with labels like Hooch, Carhartt, Mambo, Quiksilver, Casio and Vans, and **Nammo** on Pelham Street, stocking Miss Sixty for the ladies and Boxfresh for the lads. **Sole Shoes** on Bridlesmith Gate is famous for its trainers – imported from New York!

Lush Cosmetics on Clumber Street has an amazing range of organic bath and body products made from natural ingredients, and a very original deli counter of fresh products, 'packaged' inside fruit and veg – not just in a different league to your usual bar of Imperial Leather, it's a different world. **Selectadisc** on Market Street is Nottingham's most comprehensive independent record shop, actually three separate shops on the same street – one for singles, one for their loosely defined dance section, and one for albums and new singles.

If you're ever at a loss for Christmas and birthday presents, you'll find what you need in **Atomic** at 34b Heathcote Street and King John's Arcade, off Bridlesmith Gate. As well as their ultra-modern lava lamps, pricey jewellery and faux-50s furniture, it stocks all manner of sleek, silver-plated accessories. And like so many shops in Nottingham they've got a lovely range of greetings cards.

PREENING

Public Hair off St Peter's Gate and **Surreal** on Byard Lane are both good mid-priced salons. **Jazz Hairdressing** on Goosegate has the usual Hockley air of effortless cool, and there are several other good independent salons and beauty parlours in the city. (Hockley is an area in the east of the city centre packed with independent restaurants, bars and shops. It epitomises the youthful atmosphere of Nottingham – money is less important than style, but if you can't afford to buy something nice, don't buy at all!

VIEWING

Warner Village Cinema complex, Forman Street (945 4052), is another part of the new Cornerhouse development. The twelve cinema screens accommodate around 3,000 people, which show not only mainstream cinema but also Bollywood, arthouse and classic movies. Standard Warner Brothers complex - nacho's and Bugs Bunny a plenty.

Broadway Cinema, 14 Broad Street (952 6600). With only two screens this is a small but stylish venue. Although it shows some Hollywood hits, it focuses more on obscure, foreign and arthouse films. Definitely the choice for anyone who likes their cinema intelligent.

Showcase Cinemas on Redfield Way (896 6766) is the luxury ocean liner of cinemas, while the Odeon on Angel Row (947 3288) is smaller but often shows the hits for longer.

The Magic Machine, Texaco Garage, Derby Road, Lenton This Blockbuster machine is a shrine to 24-hour consumerism; you can choose from 300 videos all day and night and you don't even have to be a member. It's extremely popular, dispensing over 30,000 videos every year. Every student area should have one.

Kate Allen & Mark Tew

UNIVERSITY OF NOTTINGHAM

The University of Nottingham
University Park
Nottingham NG7 2RD

TEL 0115 951 6565
FAX 0115 951 6566
EMAIL undergraduate-enquiries@nottingham.ac.uk
WEB www.nottingham.ac.uk

Nottingham Students' Union
University Park
Nottingham NG7 2RD

TEL 0115 935 1100
FAX 0115 935 1101
EMAIL StudentsUnion@nottingham.ac.uk
WEB www.students-union.nottingham.ac.uk

VAG VIEW

Nottingham is a top university, with a 91% Excellence rating, and last year Nottingham students had a 74% chance of graduating with a first or upper second. More than this, it is one of the most employer-friendly universities in the world, and students are happy here: its drop-out rate, at 3%, is very low.

CAMPUSES

'When I first visited the university, all fresh-faced and eager,' recalls second-year e-commerce and digital business student Mark Tew, 'I couldn't help but be struck by the sheer size of the place. It's BIG. Put it this way, when embarking on the almost weekly drinking binge known as "Campus 14" (a foolish display of drinking prowess in which several people of varying levels of commitment attempt all fourteen bars on campus), it's not so much guzzling the gallons of snakebite-and-black that poses a problem as the trudging round several miles of semi-mountainous campus in the driving rain. It's a tough life!'

The 300-acre University Park is the main campus – huge lake, views over Trent valley, rolling Downs that sweep away into the distance, all a neat ten

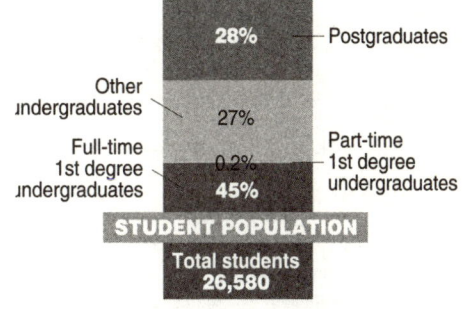

STUDENT POPULATION
Total students
26,580

Postgraduates 28%
Other undergraduates 27%
Full-time 1st degree undergraduates 45%
Part-time 1st degree undergraduates 0.2%

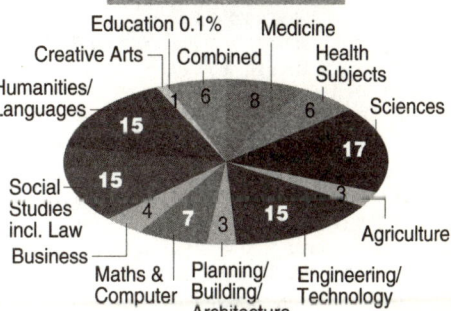

SUBJECT AREAS (%)

Education 0.1%
Creative Arts — 1
Combined 6
Medicine 8
Health Subjects 6
Sciences 17
Agriculture 3
Engineering/Technology 15
Planning/Building/Architecture 3
Maths & Computer 7
Business 4
Social Studies incl. Law 15
Humanities/Languages 15

minutes by bus from town. There is a satellite campus at Sutton Bonington, ten miles distant, for the Agric element of the School of Biological Sciences, and the recently opened £50-million Jubilee Campus on a site close to University Park, spacious, with a degree of self-containment (library, computing facilities and a Students' Union presence), home to 750 studying in the Business School, the Dept. of Computer Science and the Schools of Education and Continuing Education.

There is further development afoot at Jubilee and a mooted £8.5-million extension of the Portland Building, student centre of University Park.

STUDENT PROFILE

'I was told to expect a lot of bitter and twisted Oxbridge rejects with a big fat chip on the shoulder, but this hasn't been the case,' Mark reassures. 'The "rah-rah, sooo drunk!" toff brigade, however, is

UNIVERSITY/STUDENT PROFILE	
University since	**1948**
Situation/style	**Edge of city campuses**
Student population	**26,580**
Full-time undergraduates	**12,050**
- mature	**6%**
- overseas	**10%**
- male/female	**44/56**
- state sector intake	**71%**
- non-traditional student intake	**7%, low**
- drop-out rate	**3%, low**
- undergraduate applications	**Up 6%**
see Introduction for key to tables	

ACADEMIC EXCELLENCE

TEACHING:
(Rated Excellent or 17+ out of 24)

Chemistry, Law, Mechanical Engineering, Architecture, Business & Management, English, Geography, Music. German,	**Excellent**
Manufacturing Engineering & Operations Mgt, Classics, Psychology, Econmics, Politics	**24**
Agriculture & Food Sciences, Art History, Urban Planning, Pharmacology, Biosciences, Physics, Maths, Theology	**23**
Civil Eng, Nursing, Anatomy Electrical & Electronic Eng, American Studies, Philosophy, Education	**22**
Sociology, Chemica Eng,l Materials Technology, Subjects Allied to Medicine, Archaeol	**21**
Russian & East Euro Langs	**19**

.RESEARCH:
Top grades 5/5*

American Studies, German/ Dutch/Scandinavian, Iberian/ Latin American, Theology, Music	**Grade 5***
Pharmacy, Psychology, Genetics, Agriculture, Food Science, Chemistry, Physics, Pure Math, Applied Math, Statistics, Computer, Civil Eng, Mechanical/Aeronautical/ Manufacturing Eng, Geography, Law, Economics, Management, English, French, Russian/Slavonic/ East European, Philosophy	**Grade 5**

wider-based student body, but for the moment they remain below their government benchmarks on all counts in the matter of widening participation (2001 figures). There is richer diversity in the matter of overseas students. They have a Malaysian-based campus, which facilitates student exchange, and already they attract 2,500 students from 125 different countries.

ACADEMIA

Nottingham is best known for medicine and engineering, but many departments have excellent ratings. Most recently the departments of Economics, Politics, Classics scored full marks in the assessments, and Organismal Biosciences, Physics, Maths, Genetics and Theology dropped just one point each. There was, however, a kerfuffle over Medicine.

Nottingham is a noisy member – possibly the noisiest – of the Russell Group of universities, who reckon they're the bee's knees and don't want us to have information about their quality of teaching (at least as assessed by the 24 points method). You can't blame them – however you pull your socks up after a poor showing, it'll be years before you can publicise it through another inspection, unless you failed badly, when you are re-inspected after a year.

Medicine is Nottingham's jewel, but recently the school was given a report by the QAA not to the uni's liking, the point at issue being 'the evidence on which they [the QAA] based their judgement'. The outcome is a re-visit this year. By the time you read this, the result should be accessible on www.qaa.ac.uk/

Erasmus schemes figure in most degrees, which means if you want to study a year abroad you can – there's a trip to the States in American Studies.

Courses are taught in modules. Each years comprises two semesters over three terms; exams in january and June.

SOCIAL SCENE

STUDENTS' UNION The main students' union is based at the Portland Building, which overlooks the lake. On Friday and Saturday nights the **Buttery** bar in the bowels is open till 2 am for discos. There's also the **The DH Lawrence Bar** – he graduated from here – and there are more than twenty other bars dotted around the halls of residence. First year social life spins off halls, off societies, off departments and off sport, rather more than the union:

'It still amazes me how such fine, upstanding, intelligent people, who clearly had the "right stuff" to get into Nottingham University, all seem

definitely out in full force! Being from up t' North, it was a culture shock to say the least. But it's well worth being here if just to take the piss. "Another bottle of champers Roger?"'

'The nature of this university is to attract students from fairly wealthy, middle-class backgrounds,' said a Students' Union wallah. 'I didn't go to public school, I came from a sixthform college, and I was consigned to Lenton, a take-it-as-you-find-it hall, no pretensions whatsoever. I seemed to be in a block with Comprehensive people; we didn't have any corridors; we seemed to be a bit isolated.'

Nottingham provide summer schools to attract a

mystically drawn to the union on a Friday night,' writes Mark. 'Why? It's a *dive*! Maybe that's harsh. It's actually really nice during the day, its only real crime may be overcrowding on the weekend.

'For us connoisseurs of wining and dining though, it's well worth forging out into the real world and heading to the city centre. Top nights out can be had on most nights of the week, whatever your musical tastes. Seriously hard doses of cheese are available at **Ocean** and the **Palais**, while **Media** guarantees a quality night, especially on *Renaissance* nights (they didn't pay me to say that... honest!).'

Currently union clubnights in town are *Old Skool Dayz* @ **The Palais** and *Lurve Machine* @ **The Ark**. They've also had Blues Brothers Experience and Chesney Hawkes at The Ark, and the Comedy Society often does a stand-up open mic session there.

Nottingham has also long had an enterprising drama society. **The New Theatre**, which once exuded all the spit-and-sawdust appeal of true fringe theatre, now more suits its name. They write, produce and direct up to twenty plays a year and invariably take a production or two to Edinburgh. Theatre has always been big in this city, the **Playhouse**'s deep-rooted reputation to the fore, and **Malt Cross Music Hall** offers an eerie alternative with drama, music hall, comedy, jazz and folk, with poltergeists in attendance and spooky goings-on that no one seems able to explain. Then there's the **Theatre Royal** of course (Gilbert & Sulivan, Rocky Horror, Arthur Miller, My Fair Lady, etc.), and music and dance at the **Palace Theatre**, Mansfield.

On campus, music societies proliferate, such as Blow Soc (wind, to be sure), and for music and art there's the **Arts Centre** – a superb art gallery (with artist in residence) a recital hall next door, a bookshop and airy **Café Lautrec**.

Student reputation in media is truly stunning. Last year *Impact* was Magazine of the Year in the *Guardian* awards and Best Magazine in the *Independent* awards, as well as runner-up in the Best Arts Journalist, Best Design and Diversity sections of the *Independent* awards. URN, the student radio station, has, in the history of student radio, won more Radio 1 awards than any other. Last year it took the Innovation award. URN broadcasts throughout the year on AM, and on FM for two months.

WHAT IT'S REALLY LIKE	
UNIVERSITY:	
Social Life	★★★★★
Campus scene	**Well-heeled, bright, sporty, creative**
Student Union services	**Good-average**
Politics	**Student issues Activity high**
Sport	**Key nationally & v. active inter-hall**
National team position	**8th**
Sport facilities	**Good**
Arts opportunities	**Drama excellent; music, art good; dance, film avg**
Student magazine	**Impact**
Independent awards	**Best magazine**
Guardian awards	**Magazine of Year**
Student radio	**URN**
Radio 1 awards	**Innovation award**
Nightclub	**None**
Bars	**Buttery, D H Lawrence**
Union ents	**College & town club based, Palais, The Ark**
Union clubs/societies	**167**
Most popular society	**Cock Soc**
Smoking policy	**Mostly NS**
Parking	**Adequate**
CITY:	
Entertainment	★★★★★
Scene	**Clubby, pubby, good arts**
Town/gown relations	**OK**
Risk of violence	**Average**
Cost of living	**Average**
Student concessions	**Good**
Survival + 2 nights out	**£60 pw**
Part-time work campus/town	**Good/excellent**

Students may come from comfortable backgrounds and rarely set the firmament alight with radical political action, but Nottingham students have a caring nature, expressed in the extraordinary agenda of Community Action, some 2,000 student volunteers getting involved in arts projects (drama, music), welfare projects (including prison visiting), health, education, housing, sport, environmental projects.

> *Get into Nottingham and you have a 74% chance of leaving with a first or upper second from one of the most employer-friendly universities in the world.*

AT A GLANCE

ACADEMIC FILE:

Subjects assessed	**42**
Excellent	**91%**
Average A level requirements	**26 points**
Students-staff ratio	**14:1**
First/2:1 degree pass rate	**74%**

ACCOMMODATION FILE:

Guarantee to freshers	**Apply by 1.8**
Style	**Halls, flats**
Catered	**65%**
En-suite	**24%**
Price range pw	**£44-£103**
City rent pw	**£40-£60**

SPORT Notttingham teams came 8th nationally last year, but they also claim the largest and most comprehensive inter-hall league. There is opportunity at all levels to participate in as many as sixty-seven sports. Facilities include two sports halls, rooms for martial arts, aerobics, etc., climbing wall, fitness/weights room, **Champions** bar and restaurant, six squash courts, and at long last they have their own swimming pool (25 x 18m). Outside, there's a floodlit, artificial turf hockey pitch and athletics track. Boating (with boathouse) on the tidal Trent. Sutton Bonington has its own sports centre, squash and tennis courts, rugby, football and cricket pitches. Bursaries are available.

PILLOW TALK

Freshers are guaranteed a place in halls if they receive your 'Accommodation Preference Form' by August 1. You're talking fully catered halls & self-catering flats, 24% en suite. Price per week ranges from £44 to £103; rent in the city from £40 to £60. There are two new hall extensions on line for September 2002, with an additional ninety-six rooms, all en suite.

Writes Mark: 'There's nothing a snotty-nosed toff loves more than a spot of hall rivalry. "We are the Lincoln Infantry", "Hugh Stu take it up the arse!" and such like. It's all good harmless fun, I suppose. To be fair, all the halls are pretty nice and I don't think they really do take it up the arse. Being a former Lincolnite, my totally unbiased opinion is that it is by far the best hall in the world. Small, yet cosy bar, good food, big rooms, our very own library and even cheese and wine nights in the SCR! What more could you want? OK, so Hugh Stu has the best bar, Derby has the best women and Sherwood has a slide shaped as a dragon. So what!'

JOBS

The privileged intake and top level teaching is consistent with a fifth of its graduates making it into the professional echelon of the health industry (often as doctors) and another fifth into City professions (many as accountants). Durham (for accountants) and Newcastle (for doctors and dentists) carry a similar profile. There are, however, many other niches; see box.

WHERE GRADUATES END UP

18% Health (Medicine), Key Areas
12% Manufacturing,
10% Finance,
7% Computer,
7% Public Admin,
6% Education
Accountancy*, Niche Areas
Agric/Forestry,
Advertising, Aeronautical
Manufacture, Chemical/
Pharmaceutical*,
Eng/Industrial Design*,
Defence*, Market
Research, Telecom,
Business/Management

*indicates Top 10 Graduate Provider

Approximate employed **96%**

GETTING THERE

☞ By road: Nottingham, M1/J 25, A52. Sutton Bonington, M1/J24, A6, then left turn.
☞ By rail: London St Pancras, 1:50; Edinburgh, 4:30; Exeter, 4:00; Birmingham New Street, 1:30.
☞ By air: East Midlands Airport.
☞ By coach: London, 2:55; Birmingham, 1:30; Newcastle, 5:00; Excter, 6:30.

NOTTINGHAM TRENT UNIVERSITY

The Nottingham Trent
 University
Burton Street
Nottingham NG1 4BU

TEL 0115 941 8418
TEL 0115 848 6868 (prospectus)
FAX 0115 848 6503

EMAIL marketing@ntu.ac.uk
WEB www.ntu.ac.uk

Nottingham Trent Union of Students
Byron House
Shakespeare Street
Nottingham NG1 4GH

TEL 0115 848 6220
FAX 0115 848 6201
EMAIL firstname.surname@su.ntu.ac.uk
WEB www.su.ntu.ac.uk

VAG VIEW

*C*entred on the building in Shakespeare
Street where, in 1887, the foundation
stone was laid by Gladstone for University
College Nottingham, later to become
Nottingham University, this institution was
began life as Trent Poly in 1970, but today has
arrived on the scene as one of the most
impressive of our new universities.

CAMPUS SITES

CITY CAMPUS (address, page 349) – Burton Street is
the location of the central admin building, 'front'
for a whole load of buildings in neighbouring
streets. The Students' Union headquarters (Byron
House) is here, along with the new Boots Library,
student residences and six of the uni's nine
faculties: Art & Design, Business, Environmental
Studies, Law, Economics & Social Sciences,
Engineering & Computing.

CLIFTON CAMPUS Clifton Lane, Nottingham NG11
8NS. This is a spacious, green field campus some
four miles southwest of the city centre along the
A453. It is wholly self-contained with its own SU,
sports grounds and student residences, and is
home to the Humanities and Science &
Mathematics faculties.

'Clifton is the smaller of the two campuses

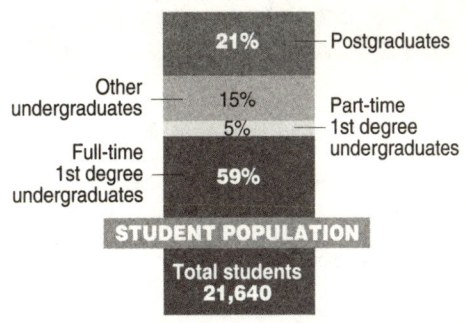

STUDENT POPULATION

Postgraduates 21%
Other undergraduates 15%
Part-time 1st degree undergraduates 5%
Full-time 1st degree undergraduates 59%

Total students
21,640

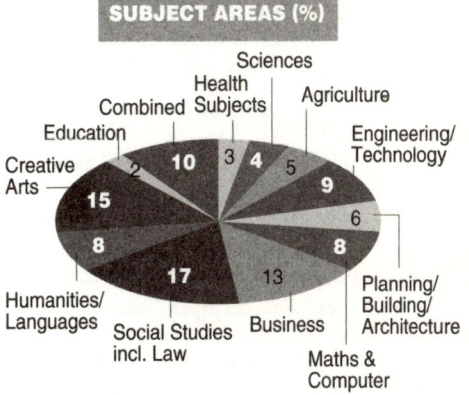

SUBJECT AREAS (%)

Sciences
Health Subjects
Combined
Education
Creative Arts — 2
Agriculture
Engineering/ Technology
10
15
3 4 5
9
6
8
8
Humanities/ Languages
17
13
Planning/ Building/ Architecture
Social Studies incl. Law
Business
Maths & Computer

with around 5,000 students,' writes Daniel Ashley,
'and still thrives on the community atmosphere. A
new student village and all weather Astroturf
allows the Clifton student to become almost self-
sufficient within the campus. Probably not a bad
thing, as the Clifton locals are not famed for their
tolerance of us.'

Clifton Hall Clifton Village, Nottingham NG11
8NJ. This is a Georgian manor house a few
minutes walk from Clifton campus and includes
lecture halls for use by the faculty of Education, a
resource centre, dance studio and refectory.

STUDENT PROFILE

The student body is unlike that of Nottingham
Uni. State school intake is 92%, as against 71% at
Nottingham; the take from the lower socio-
economic brackets is 13%, as against 7% at
Nottingham. There's also a much larger mature
undergraduate population at Trent.

At the city site there is enthusiasm and a high
focus. We had the impression that students make
the most of their three or four years here.

ACADEMIA

The uni is good at law, modern languages and

UNIVERSITY/STUDENT PROFILE	
University since	**1992**
Situation/style	**Campus & city site**
Student population	**21,640**
Full-time undergraduates	**12,710**
- mature	**19%**
- overseas	**3%**
- male/female	**50/50**
- state sector intake	**92%**
- non-traditional student intake	**13%**
- drop-out rate	**10%**
- undergraduate applications	**Up 7%**
see Introduction for key to tables	

ACADEMIC EXCELLENCE

TEACHING:
(Rated Excellent or 17+ out of 24)

Chemistry, Business & Management	**Excellent**
Physics, Molecular Biosciences, Organismal Biosciences	**24**
Subjects Allied to Medicine	**23**
Education, Politics, Sport Building, Psychology, Art & Design, Economics	**22**
Communication/Media, Maths	**21**
Electric/Electron Engineering, Civil Eng, Land & Property Mgt Materials Technology	**20**
Sociology	**19**

RESEARCH :
Top grades 5/5*

Subjects Allied to Medicine , English, Media Studies, Drama/ Dance/Performing Arts	**Grade 5**

European studies, among other things. The lecturers are often practitioners, practising lawyers, etc The law department has a very good European course, grounded in English law but requiring an expertise, too, in French or German law, as well of course as fluency in the language.

High in the teaching assessments recently have been Building (see *Jobs*, pages 351/2 – everything is a preparation for the job to come), Art & Design, Physics, Biosciences, Psychology, Health, Economics, Media.

A while ago the Centre for Broadcasting &

AT A GLANCE

ACADEMIC FILE:

Assessments	**25**
Excellent	**68%**
Average requirements	**240 points**
Students-staff ratio	**18:1**
First/2:1 degree pass rate	**50%**

ACCOMMODATION FILE:

Guarantee to freshers	**70%, apply early**
Style	**Halls + flats, or houses in private sector**
Catered	**None**
En-suite	**69%**
Price range pw	**£56.07-£58.94**
Average city rent pw	**£40-£60**

Journalism took over the old BBC studios in the city, making it the only training centre in the UK to have access to authentic broadcasting facilities, so we should not have been surprised to find Media again figure in last year's research assessments at Grade 5 (that's national/international renown), along with Health, English and Drama/Dance/ Performing Arts.

Their Art & Design department is particularly dynamic, the courses widely varying – from fashion to print media, from furniture to photography, from contemporary arts (including the performance arts that did so well at assessment) to knitware and fine art.

New courses are currently appearing in the areas of accounting, computing, business in the construction industry, criminology, engineering, floriculture, nutrition, heritage, media, mechatronics, maths, physics (which recently scored maximum points in the assessments), sociology, sport, languages and international politics.

Recently, the uni acquired their Land-based Studies department following a merger with Brackenhurst, a college with a 200-hectare farm near the historic town of Southwell, ten miles north east of Nottingham.

Resources remain a priority. Shortly to join the new library that doubled study space at Clifton Campus a few years ago is a £13-million, 450-seat lecture theatre block.

SOCIAL SCENE

The Students' Union is in the throes of proving that what it has long been doing for student entertainment it can do equally well for more serious pursuits: a Community Action Group was set up, an Employment Store has grown from one small office to two massive departments that together will deal with upwards of 9,000 placements in part-time employment this year, and the SU employment skills training programme, Stride, has broken all expectations, with every programme either full or over-subscribed.

The Students' Union bar at City has recently undergone a £300,000 facelift, giving a new continental café bar and late-night (2 am at weekends) drinking spot, **Glo Bar**, instead of last year's SUB, otherwise nomenclature is un-changed. 'Its style and ambience competes,' says Daniel, 'with all the up-market bars around town, and the drinks at student prices make a refreshing change.' With **Le Metro**, weekend, whole-building event capacity is now 2,000. At Clifton, **Brubecks** and **Arena** make a possible 700 happy. Regular nights at City include Thursday's laid-back fandangery, an open mic session and flavoured vodkas at **Acoustic Café** in Le Metro; at Glo, they have Friday's *Tease* (dance and party anthems) and Saturday's *Trolleyed* (the best and worst of the '70s, '80s and '90s). At Clifton, Monday is *Juicy* at town club **Isis** (warm-up at Arena) and Thursday is still *Shipwrecked* (all types of music) at **Brubeck's** bar. The big new association is with the Moroccan-style **Lost Weekend** nightclub in town, when both campuses unite in *Clubbered* on Wednesday's *Club & Societies* night.

The city is enormously popular with students – see *Student Nottingham*, page 342.

Platform is the weekly paper, which the *Nottingham Evening Post* prints for them. 'They have nothing to do with editorial, well ... they sort of peruse it, nick some of our stories.' It was the overall winner in the *Guardian* awards this year, won the feature writing award in both *Guardian* and *Independent* awards, and was runner up in the *Guardian*'s Critic of the Year award.

The Trent student radio station has changed its name from Kick to Fly FM and just picked up the Best Show in the Radio 1 awards. That Trent media department needs serious consideration.

SPORT Sports Science is a big course here; their teams came overall 38th in the nation last year. A new, £2 million sports hall plus all-weather pitch opened in 2001 at Clifton. There are fifty clubs, offering everything from circus skills to rugby league, traditionally the most successful club in the university.

Part of a joint venture policy with Beeston Tec, as Nottingham University is known, is a Varsity sports day. Finally, there's a lively inter-mural league at Trent for both students and staff.

PILLOW TALK

Uni accommodation is available to 70% of first years in the form of halls of residence, all self-catered, 69% of rooms en suite. current price per week ranges between £56.07 and £58.94. City rent, £40-£60.

'City site freshers are likely to find themselves in one of the many halls scattered within a mile or so,' writes Daniel, 'so it is possible to get to college both on foot or by bike. Early enthusiasm for this does tend to wane as it gets a bit colder. However, the parking facilities in City are not brilliant, and a permit must be applied for. Do this as soon as you

WHAT IT'S REALLY LIKE	
UNIVERSITY:	
Social Life	★★★★
Campus scene	**Streetwise, fun**
Student Union services	**Average**
Politics	**Interest low**
Sport	**24 clubs**
National team position	**38th**
Sport facilities	**Average**
Arts opportunities	**Drama,art, music, good; dance avg; film poor**
Student newspaper	**Platform**
Independent awards	**Feature writer**
Guardian awards	**Feature writer Overall Winner**
Student radio	**Fly FM**
Radio 1 awards	**Best show**
Nightclub	**No club, whole union, Sat night**
Bars	**Glo Bar, Clifton**
Union ents	**Trollied, Frisky, Glamourpus, Pur R&B, Old School**
Union clubs/societies	**70+**
Smoking policy	**Union OK**
Parking	**Clifton good, City campus poor**
CITY:	
Entertainment	★★★★★
Scene	**Clubby, pubby, good arts**
Town/gown relations	**OK**
Risk of violence	**Average**
Cost of living	**Above average**
Student concessions	**Good**
Survival + 2 nights out	**£80 pw**
Part-time work campus/town	**Good/excellent**

arrive. At Clifton nearly all first-year students are accommodated in the on-site, en-suite Peverell halls of residence. Halls may not be the cheapest form of accommodation, but they are certainly the best. As well as meeting all sorts of people, that £60 includes all your bills. Three warm showers a day are rarely a possibility in a shared student house!

> *Graduate employment success continues, achieved by an inspired strategy that puts back into industry what it receives from it for its academic and workplace programmes.*

JOBS

The university claims the highest number of students on (work-placement) sandwich courses anywhere in the country, students

WHERE GRADUATES END UP

13% Manufacturing,	Key Areas
10% Wholesale/Retail,	
10% Finance,	
9% Public Admin	
7% Personnel*,	
6% Computer	
Aeronautical Manufac*,	Niche Areas
Business/Management,	
Architecture, Artistic/	
Literary, Journalism,	
Publishing, Radio/TV,	
Chem/Pharmaceutical,	
Construction*, Property*	

*indicates Top 10 Graduate Provider

Approximate employed **98%**

experiencing the real world of work and gaining skills relevant to their future careers. This, along with the university's strong links with employers locally, nationally and internationally, has meant that in terms of graduate employment Nottingham Trent is one of the leaders.

In particular, graduates from the School of Property and Construction attract some of the highest graduate starting salaries in the country.

Trent is also a place for budding entrepreneurs thanks to its new enterprise centre, The Hive, a germination centre to encourage the development of ideas into sustainable businesses.

The broad strategy is to put back into industry what it receives from it for its academic and workplace programmes. For example, the £13 million City library, sponsored by Boots, gives over one floor to a Management Centre promoting new technologies and modern management techniques.

Speculation over the purpose of a new building at Clifton just ended with the news that the car manufacturer, Toyota, has joined forces with the uni to create a dealer-training centre.

GETTING THERE
☞ By road: M1/J25/6. Good coach service.
☞ By rail: London St Pancras, 1:50; Edinburgh, 4:30; Exeter, 4:00; Birmingham New Street, 1:30.
☞ By air: East Midlands Airport 12 miles away.
☞ By coach: London, 2:55; Birmingham, 1:30.

OPEN UNIVERSITY

The Open University
Walton Hall
Milton Keynes MK7 6AA

TEL 01908 274066
   01908 653231 (course query)
FAX 01908 654806
EMAIL ces-gen@open.ac.uk
WEB www.open.ac.uk

UNIVERSITY/STUDENT PROFILE

Founded	**1971**
Status	**University**
Total student population	**145,990**
Degree undergraduates	**126,810**
- mature	**95%**
- male/female	**47/53**
- overseas students	**24,348**

VAG VIEW

*T*he Open University is what it says it is – Open; open to all, regardless of academic qualifications; you don't need ANY, yet its standards are as high as any other university with a 82% Excellence rating.

In the spirit of the government's widening participation programme, they are offering free places on their own Openings programme to lone parents, disabled people and people from ethnic minority backgrounds in England and Wales to return to study. The short courses, which are available in five subjects, teach a range of study skills designed to prepare potential students for an OU undergraduate course. In any event the OU recommends most students to begin their degree with a Level 1 Foundation course.

The university is a distance learning set-up, as if you didn't know. Distance learning won't suit everyone; self-motivation and the ability to work alone while juggling work/family commitments are essential.

STUDENT PROFILE
There is no typical OU student. You might imagine that they are all mature students, people at a crossroads in their lives, but in fact, over the last few years, the OU has seen a surge in the number

of school leavers enrolling. The thing all have in common is the desire to learn.

ACADEMIA

Recent high-scoring departments at assessment are Classical Studies, Philosophy (both full marks) and Molecular and Organismal Biosciences, but, as our *Academic Excellence* box shows, these are not alone among the top scorers and in last year's research exercise, OU achieved a world-class Grade 5* in Geography. In a similar area, they have developed a course directly linked to the acclaimed *Blue Planet* TV series, which can be studied on its own or as a module of a degree.

This year will see two new undergraduate courses: Understanding Business Functions and The Rise of Scientific Europe.

Last year the second Virtual Degree Ceremony was held and Education students graduated online. This option is being extended to all OU graduates from 2002, no matter what degree they achieve.

A hi-tech mobile assessment unit travelling on a £100,000 Access Bus has been launched to visit disabled students and assess what specialist equipment and support they need to enable them to study.

Finally, 2002 will see the first students graduating from the OU with a Law Degree (LLB).

JOBS

More than 80% of OU students are in full-time employment, but a recent survey of MBA

graduates shows that 90% received promotion either during or on completion of their course apparently.

ACADEMIC EXCELLENCE

TEACHING ASSESSMENTS:
Subjects assessed **27**
Excellent **82%**

CENTRES OF EXCELLENCE:
(Rated Excellent or 17+ out of 24)
Business & Management, **Excellent**
Chemistry, Geography, Music,
Earth Sciences (Geology),
Social Policy & Admin.
Sociology, General Eng, **24**
Classics, Philosophy
Biosciences, Physics **23**
Politics, Religious Studies, **22**
Economics, Education,
Subjects Allied to Medicine,
Psychology
History of Art **21**
Maths **20**

RESEARCH EXCELLENCE:
Top grades 5/5*
Geography **Grade 5***
Art/Design, Earth Sciences, **Grade 5**
History of Art/Architecture/Design

UNIVERSITY OF OXFORD

The University of Oxford
Wellington Square
Oxford OX1 2JD

TEL 01865 270207
FAX 01865 270708
EMAIL undergraduate.admissions@admin.ox.ac.uk
WEB www.ox.ac.uk

OUSU
28 Little Clarendon Street
Oxford OX1 2HU

TEL 01865 270777
FAX 01865 270776
EMAIL info@ousu.org.uk
WEB www.ousu.org

VAG VIEW

*D*iscrimination is what the whole furore is about, but those who knock Oxford for their selection process on class grounds should give the university credit for the Department of Continuing Education, which is anything but snooty. It offers short and part-time courses leading to university - even

Master's - awards. Many of the courses are geared to the professions and industry, and there are some for personal and social development too. The department is located at Rewley House, 1 Wellington Square, Oxford OX1 2JA (Tel: 01865 270360).

As a sixthformer, the great thing is not to be fazed by the clichéd reputation. If you fancy the trademark, one-to-one tutor system, simply apply. So few do apply that

UNIVERSITY/STUDENT PROFILE	
University since	**1096**
Situation/style	**City collegiate**
Student population	**22,150**
Full-time undergraduates	**11,380**
- mature	**5%**
- overseas	**10%**
- male/female	**55/45**
- state sector intake	**51%, low**
- non-traditional student intake	**6%, low**
- drop-out rate	**2%, low**
- undergraduate applications	**Up 5%**
see Introduction for key to tables	

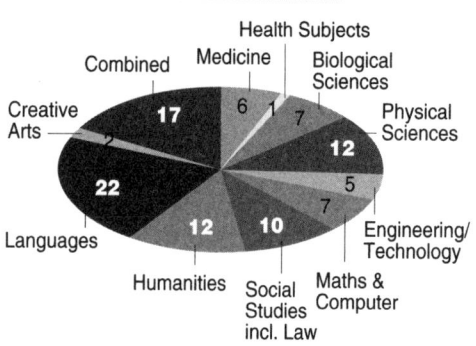

SUBJECT AREAS (%)

there's straightway a one-in-three chance you'll get in, which is way better than any other university... other than Cambridge. And as a student said to me, 'In a university of this many undergraduates, you are bound to find people you get on with.'

STUDENT PROFILE

'Oxford as a vanguard of elitism and discrimination has made the headlines countless times in the past few years. Personally, I haven't experienced any discrimination,' writes history undergraduate Rachel Cocker, 'but as a white, middle-class girl from an independent school in the North West I am not exactly a member of a minority group here.'

Rachel will tell us more, but perhaps Christabel Ashby, from a different background, may have a different story: 'I'm Christabel Ashby, I'm from London. I went to a state school, and I'm a final-year student at Keble, studying Theology. I'm not going to lie; my first few days in Oxford were terrifying. In Freshers Week we were inundated with information and events. There were both the university and the college fresher fairs [presentations to freshers by sports clubs and societies], and we were forced into going out and getting drunk by well meaning second-year students. Despite this it was really easy to make friends, and after two weeks I felt as at-home and confident as if I'd been there for years.

'The nice thing about the Oxford student scene is that it is so inclusive. Whatever you're into, you are bound to find people to hang out with. You will probably meet a few people who are a bit elitist or arrogant, but I suspect that is true of any university.'

ACADEMIA

'The myth that Oxford students have no time for a social life is false, but that we have a very heavy workload is, however, perfectly true,' continues Rachel. 'Eight weeks is a short period for a term and a lot of work is packed into it. Scientists, medics and lawyers have by far the most to do. Historians get off relatively lightly. Still, it's hard when you hear your mates at other unis talk of two-month deadlines when you're going through

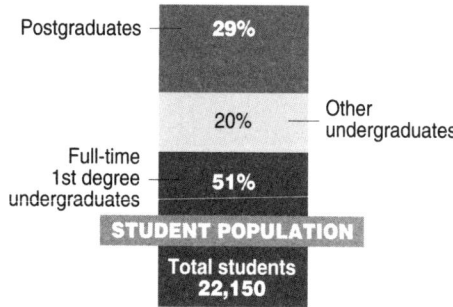

the weekly essay grind. It *is* stressful, but none of my friends have, as yet, launched themselves off Magdalen Bridge. Tutors are generally willing to give more guidance and leeway than you might imagine. At the end of every term you will be given a feedback form, and although for some this may be simply a faculty-proscribed exercise, for others students' comments have shifted the focus and structure of the course they teach.

'All colleges have computer facilities where you can type up your work or check your e-mail, an Oxford e-mail address is provided for everyone upon arrival. Oxford has some of the best libraries in the world, the state of your college library depends on its personal wealth but as the Bodleian has a copy of every book ever written, or something like it, you don't have much of an excuse for not reading that "essential" item on the reading list.'

The uni is developing a rich diversity of online resources and course materials – full details can be found at http://www.online.ox.ac.uk/. There are also little known welfare resources – a disability service, for example, even grants available from such as the Dyslexia Fund. Again, the Oxford University Resources for the Blind provide tape recordings for students with a print impairment, including dyslexia sufferers. Note-takers or readers are also available.

SOCIAL SCENE

STUDENTS' UNION 'Once you've made your newfound friends, there is a reasonable social life to be had with them. A lot of it is college based; most have weekly bops. One thing Oxford seriously lacks is a central student venue, but once you venture outside the walls of your cosy college environment there are plenty of university-wide activities in which to get involved. Theatre, journalism, music, student politics and Anglo Saxon re-enactment (apparently) are all strong. *The Oxford Student* won the *Guardian*'s award for best student newspaper this year and every year the Oxford University drama festival, 'Cuppers', sees around thirty productions performed, directed and often written by freshers. Hacks tend to gravitate towards the famed Oxford Union, where they can fine tune their debating and back-stabbing skills, and it is possible either to infiltrate or avoid their number at will.

SPORT 'This is also a big deal, from football to ultimate frisbee. There are college leagues for every sport you can think of; even pool. Most colleges have their own sports ground and of course there are the university facilities down Iffley Road, where it costs £35 for annual membership to the gym. Most people try their hand at rowing at some point during their university career and many, many join the ranks of "boaties", consigning themselves to years of early morning outings and gruelling weights sessions. All very rewarding, especially for all who get to cheer them to victory during Eights Week, while getting pissed on Pimms.

TOWN 'There are some great pubs; the most studenty of which are the **Kings Arms** and **The Turf**, both rammed to the rafters after exams. The city is also a haven for cocktail bars, and the **Duke of Cambridge** is immensely popular for its very happy "happy hour", which lasts from 5 till 8.30pm every single day of the week. Oxford also boasts some fantastic restaurants, although some of these are so fantastically priced you might have to wait

until your real Mummy and Daddy come to take you home before sampling them.

'The word that best describes Oxford clublife is "tacky", but as long as you are prepared to leave any musical pretensions at the door you can have a lot of fun. **Park End** is traditionally the pinnacle of Oxford nightlife, but despite its oft-boasted £1 million refurbishment it can get a little too cramped for comfort. **The Studio** (known as **Filth**) is a club above a supermarket, and just as classy as it sounds. If you are a bit more serious about your music there is **The Bullingdon Arms' Backroom** or **The Zodiac** on Cowley Road, which is the closest Oxford comes to a proper music venue, having played host to the likes of Carl Cox, Ronnie Size, Seb Fontaine and Judge Jules. **Oxford Brookes'** Union hosts live touring bands and probably the best student nights on Fridays and Saturdays. College balls also feature largely in Oxford life and for an average non-dining ticket you are looking at around £50. The larger balls, such as Merton in the winter and Magdalen, New, Trinity and Worcester in the summer can set you back up to £110 per person. Luckily, these only take place once every three years so a lot of people attend but one during their time here. Once you get in there, of course, everything is free.

'*Cost of living*: if you take into account that the average student here goes out at least twice a week (most people's workloads make it hard to manage more) then I would say someone with stronger self-discipline than myself might survive on £50.'

Note, if you're a home/EU publicly-funded first-year who has been granted full fee remission by your LEA, you are eligible for a bursary worth £1,000 in the first year, £500 in each subsequent year. Go to www.admissions.ox.ac.uk/finance/bursaries/index.shtml

'*Safety*: everything being just down the road encourages a feeling of safety, but there have been several attacks on students since I've been here. You do still need to be on your guard. Town/gown relations don't seem to be anywhere near as bad as in Durham, but there are a few unofficially designated townie pubs and clubs, which students avoid, though not through fear for their lives.

COLLEGE CAMEOS
by Caroline Rowe & Sacha Delmotte

BALLIOL
Broad Street, Oxford OX1 3BJ
TEL 01865 277777
WEB www.balliol.ac.uk
Founded in 1263, Balliol has a claim to be the oldest

ACADEMIC EXCELLENCE

TEACHING :
(Rated Excellent or 17+ out of 24)

Chemistry, History, Law, Anthropology, Social Work, Computing Science, English, Geography, Geology.	**Excellent**
Organismal Biosciences, Forestry & Agric Sciences, Classics, Philosophy, Politics, Psychology, Biochemistry, Fine Art	**24**
Engineering, Materials Tech. Economics, Physics	**23**
Asian/Mid-East/African Studies, Archaeology, Oriental Studies, Maths	**22**
Modern Languages, Medicine, Anatomy	**21**

RESEARCH :
Top grades 5/5*

Pharmacology, Pathology, Community & hospital-based Clinical Subjects, Psychology, Chemistry, Physics, Earth Sciences, Pure Math, Statistics, General Eng, Metallurgy, Law, Politics, Asian Studies, English, French, Italian, Russian/Slavonic/ East European, Linguistics, Classics, Archaeology, Philosophy, Theology, Music	**Grade 5***
Clinical Lab. Sciences, Anatomy, Physiology, Zoology, Biochemistry, Applied Math, Computer, Anthropology, Economics, Sociology, Management, Middle Eastern/ African Studies, Celtic Studies, German/Dutch/Scandinavian, Iberian/Latin American, History, Education	**Grade 5**

Oxford college and is situated right in the centre of town, so access and convenience are optimum. Balliol has very high academic standards, and is proud to boast its 'effortless superiority'. Today its main strengths lie in Classics, PPE, Physics and Philosophy. The college used to be very left-wing, which is still evident today in one of the most active JCRs in the university, and the bar being entirely student-run (only Hertford does this as well). There is also a notable absence of Balls or even formal hall.

Balliol has, however, always been very liberal, and was the first college to admit international students (today it has the highest percentage of overseas students of all colleges), and the first to allow women into Oxford academia. There is a fairly high proportion of state-school students, and social elitism is not rife, despite the existence of the Annandale Society (a pretentious, all public school gentlemen's club of sorts).

Balliol provides a JCR Pantry, which is open all day, serving breakfast until 11:30, and provides colossal portions. College ents are of high standard, rent is second lowest in Oxford and the bar is small but relaxed. There is a long-standing feud between Balliol and Trinity, orchestrated by a (rather rude) song, the 'Gordouli'. College gossip is assured instantaneous propagation via the *John de Balliol* bogsheet.

BRASENOSE
Radcliff Square, Oxford OX1 4AJ
TEL 01865 277510
WEB www.bnc.ox.ac.uk
Founded in 1509, BNC, as it is known, is renowned for its tourist-friendly location and its sporting exploits rather than for academic excellence. Rugby is very big and indeed sports in general tend to be edified, though to be fair it does have a good reputation for PPE and Law. The main social focus of the college is the infamous Gertie's Tea Bar, and it has a medium-size May Ball every summer term. BNC has a fairly low profile within the university, but is interestingly named after the brass doorknocker in hall.

CHRIST CHURCH ('The House')
St Allgates, Oxford OX1 1DP
TEL 01865 276150
WEB www.chch.ox.ac.uk
Founded in 1546, Christ Church is the biggest college (both in number of undergrads and in area), and still to this day has an (entirely undeserved) reputation of being a haven for rich Etonians and other public-school types. Typically, Christ Church students are fairly good at sport,and have the best kept and most central sportsground. The college does well academically and has a strong reputation for law with a specially dedicated library. Christ Church is also the second richest college after St John's and thus welfare and accommodation provisions are excellent, with rooms available for all your time in Oxford. The college is extremely beautiful, with extensive meadows, Oxford's mediaeval cathedral and an art gallery containing works by Leonardo da Vinci and Michelangelo. It holds a yearly impressive ball. Pembroke as its rival, not surprising as it technically owns the college. Film wise, while Magdalen has *Shadowlands*, Ch Ch can boast being

the location for much of the new Harry Potter film!

CORPUS CHRISTI

Merton Street, Oxford OX1 4JF
TEL 01865 276693
WEB www.ccc.ox.ac.uk

Founded 1517, Corpus is tiny, really tiny, both in land area and in student number. This feature gives it a sense of intimacy that other colleges cannot claim, and accommodation is guaranteed for all students. Corpus excels academically and is quiet as a result of all the hard work. Recently it has introduced a new tradition, the Tortoise Race, where the Corpus reptile races against the demon speed-machine from Balliol. Corpus puts on a small-scale Summer Event (advertised as the cheapest Oxford Ball) at the beginning of every Trinity term, but on the whole it has a low profile in the university.

EXETER

Turl Street, Oxford OX1 3DP
TEL 01865 279660
WEB www.exeter.ox.ac.uk

Founded 1314, Exeter is a compact college and is so close to the Bodleian Library it may as well be part of it. Public perception is that it contains rowdy, sport-playing types. This certainly appears to be the case as the bar is very active, with lots of cool, outgoing people, and intimate ents – the JCR is famously apathetic, and one rarely hears of political activism from within Exeter's walls. The college has a long-standing rivalry with its neighbour, Jesus, also on Turl Street.

HARRIS-MANCHESTER

Mansfield Road, Oxford OX1 3TD
TEL 01865 271009
WEB www.hmc.ox.ac.uk

Founded in 1786, there is very little to be said about this college since it only admits mature students, mostly to read an Arts degree. The college was founded in the eighteenth century in Manchester so as to provide education for non-Anglican students, who at the time were not allowed into Oxbridge. Following a move to Oxford, it was granted Permanent Private Hall status, and has just recently (1996) become a full college. Pleasant Gothic Revival buildings.

HERTFORD

Catte Street, Oxford OX1 3BW
TEL 01865 279400
WEB www.hertford.ox.ac.uk

Founded in 1740, Hertford has had a tumultuous past with various changes of name, owner and status over its 250-year history; it used to be a

WHAT IT'S REALLY LIKE	
UNIVERSITY:	
Social Life	★★★★
Campus scene	**Intense, challenging, satisfying**
Student Union services	**Well organised, but no venue**
Politics	**Active**
Sport	**Key**
National team position	**7th**
Sport facilities	**Good**
Arts opportunities	**Excellent**
National drama awards	**Playwriting**
Student mag/news	**Cherwell, Isis, Oxford Student, The Word**
Guardian awards	**Best newspaper, photographer, & sports journalist**
Student radio	**Oxygen 107**
Nightclub	**None**
Bars	**College bars**
Union ents	**College-based**
Union clubs/societies	**200+**
Smoking policy	**Zonal**
Parking	**Buy a bike**
CITY:	
Entertainment	★★★
Scene	**Small, good pubs, OK clubs**
Town/gown relations	**Average**
Risk of violence	**Average**
Cost of living	**High**
Student concessions	**Good**
Survival + 2 nights out	**£60 pw**
Part-time work campus/town	**Good**

subdivision of Magdalen. Hertford is very central and opposite the ever-popular **King's Arms** pub. Hertford students really know how to party (their bar is rumoured to have the highest fiscal turnover in the university). Whether this is explained by its large population of state-school students, and the distinct Northern flavour of the undergrad body in particular, would not be PC to enquire. Altogether it is a progressive establishment and was one of the first all-male colleges to admit women and the first to make the entrance exam optional. Students enjoy full accommodation, an excellent atmospheric JCR bar, which is entirely student run and concocts brilliant, toxic cocktails.

JESUS

Turl Street, Oxford OX1 3DW
TEL 01865 279720

WEB www.jesus.ox.ac.uk

Founded in 1571, Jesus is small, beautiful and wealthy, and has a reputation for being the 'Welsh College', which is perfectly fair since a not insignificant proportion of students come from Wales. The college bogsheet is *The Sheepshagger*. The college is quite insular and politically unmotivated. Jesubites have it easy: accommodation is excellent and hall food is cheap. Recently Jesus is feared in rugby circles, and does well in other sports too. It has a feud with Exeter.

AT A GLANCE

ACADEMIC FILE:

Subjects assessed	**29**
Excellent	**97%**
Average A level requirements	**29 points**
Students-staff ratio	**13:1**
First/2:1 degree pass rate	**83%**

ACCOMMODATION FILE:

Availability to freshers	**100%**
Style	**College rooms**
Catered	**100%**
En-suite	**Some**
Average price pw	**£90**
City rent pw	**£70**

KEBLE

Parks Road, Oxford OX1 3PG
TEL 01865 272711
WEB www.keble.ox.ac.uk

Founded 1870. Writes Christabel Ashby: 'Keble College is notable for being the only redbrick, Victorian college. It is ideally placed for town and most university facilities, and is right opposite the University parks. College facilities are good; we have phone and internet lines in every room, and all the rooms are nicely furnished. The college guarantees you two years accommodation.

'Keble is also rather traditional, there is formal hall every night, which means you wear your gown to dinner, which has waiter service. On the social side, there's a mixed bag. It has one of the largest undergraduate populations of Oxford colleges, which means there are lots of people with whom to make friends, but also means you will never know everyone, and seeing people you don't recognise all over the place can be a little disconcerting.

'Keble is sporty, there are lots of teams and clubs, and the bar is also fairly popular. Ents are predictable however, usually consisting of a live band or karaoke nights. These events happen once or twice a term. The JCR is well stocked with electronic games, pinball, table-footy and pool, and also has sky TV. Unlike some of the other colleges, however, there is no JCR shop.

'There is a strong sense of equality at Keble, both in terms of women's and men's rights and in gay/lesbian rights. The environment is welcoming and friendly to anyone and everyone, but at the same time its size means you are able to retain a degree of anonymity not possible in many of the other colleges.'

LADY MARGARET HALL

Norham Gdns, Oxford OX2 6QA
TEL 01865 274300
WEB www.lmh.ox.ac.uk

Founded 1878. LMH was the first college founded solely for women in the university. Since there was no vacant land in the centre of town, LMH is fairly far out of town, but this has resulted in the luxury of extensive gardens. The college began admitting men in the '70s, and since that day and age LMH has achieved an unparalleled male/female ratio of 1:1 at levels of college hierarchy. LMH is socially self-sufficient and has a low profile in the university. It is neither renowned for scholastic or sporting brilliance, and has no great political aspirations. Its sole reputation is for producing Thespians, who tend to hang out in cliques with other college actors (read 'actoars'). Otherwise unpretentious and unintimidating.

LINCOLN

Turl Street, Oxford OX1 3DR
TEL 01865 279800
WEB www.linc.ox.ac.uk

Founded in 1427, Lincoln is the smallest of the three colleges on Turl Street, but beautiful. The college is a rather wealthy one, which is evident from the extensive facilities provided to students: good accommodation, excellent sporting facilities, and allegedly the best hall food in the university. This comfort of college life means that very few Lincolnites emerge from their cushy environment to participate in university-wide activities, and thus charges of insularity are fair and merited. Overall, the college is a rather 'shy' one on the university scene, and is not really noted for spectacular achievement in any academic, political or sporting field. Tradition has it that on Ascension Day, Lincoln undergrads stroll around town in subfusc (formal wear) with the vicar of St Michael's in the Northgate and a gang of choristers 'beating the bounds', or thrashing at the town limits with canes. Then the students drink lots of ivy beer and toss hot pennies at the choirboys.

MAGDALEN

High Street, Oxford OX1 4AU

TEL 01865 276063
WEB www.magd.ox.ac.uk

Founded in 1458, Magdalen (read 'Maudlin') is a gorgeous college in every respect. It is one of the oldest, richest and most beautiful. Its buildings, extensive grounds (including the famous Deer Park), beautiful cloisters, and Magdalen Tower, and location on the banks of the River Cherwell are stunning, breathtaking. On May Day the choir sings from the top of Magdalen Tower and the tradition is to jump off the bridge into the river, although the police keep deciding to cordon it off. The film *Shadowlands* was shot there, and the money earned was spent on renovating certain college rooms. Accommodation facilities are second to none (everyone can live in throughout their whole student career), and some of the sets offered are simply amazing (bedroom, living room, and bathroom!). The college has a huge and lively bar, and puts on very good ents events, but is pretty insular (the **Lower Oscar Wilde Room** is often the site of debauched and drunken student carnage). Magdalen, like Christ Church, owns its own punt. It is academically successful and socially intense, but rather uninterested in political and JCR issues.

MANSFIELD

Mansfield Road, Oxford OX1 3TF
TEL 01865 270970
WEB www.mansfield.ox.ac.uk

Founded in 1886, Mansfield only obtained its college status in 1995; prior to that it was a Permanent Private Hall. It is among the smallest of colleges, only admitting about sixty undergrads every year. This leads to a very close-knit yet appreciably claustrophobic community. Due to the small size of the college many students explore extra-curricular opportunities in the university, and the college is famous for drama. The college is very poor and thus room rents are relatively high. Mansfield has a reputation for tolerance and is sometimes known as the LGB (Lesbian Gay Bisexual) college. Ents are diverse, with bops, karaokes, trips to the theatre, Laserquesting, and there is a triennial Venetian Masked Ball held in the seventh week of Michaelmas term.

MERTON

Merton Street, Oxford OX1 4JD
TEL 01865 276329
WEB www.merton.ox.ac.uk

Founded in 1264, Merton, along with Balliol and University, has a claim to be the oldest Oxford college, and is very rich and beautiful, containing the oldest surviving Oxford quad (Mob quad). The college has an undisputed reputation for being a centre of academic excellence, fuelled by SCR encouragement and a competitive spirit among the student population. Socially Merton appears to be fairly insular, and one rarely meets Mertonites around the university; in fact it would seem that Mertonites are quite dull. Nonetheless every year Merton puts on the only Christmas Ball in Oxford, on the last day of Michaelmas term, which is usually a roaring success. It is particularly popular with Freshers who are able to finish their first term at Oxford with style and panache (and a random snog perhaps!). Merton's tradition, the Time Ceremony, has existed for barely fifteen years, but is now firmly implanted in the college calendar, and for a day lifts the veil of seriousness which rests upon the college. It involves students walking backwards around Merton's Mob Quad while continuously downing port, on a particular day of each year.

NEW COLLEGE

Holywell Street, Oxford OX1 3BN
TEL 01865 279590
WEB www.new.ox.ac.uk

Founded in 1379, here's another beautiful college, and very inappropriately named too! New is one of the oldest, largest and most impressive colleges in Oxford and takes in part of the city walls, as well as a few ancient plague-heaps. Widely accepted as having the best and most beautiful student bar, New puts on great ents: the bops are legendary, and the Long Room is as much a site of drunken mayhem as the Lower Oscar Wilde Room at Magdalen, with many different societies hiring the room to throw crazy parties. New also puts on a gargantuan Commemoration Ball every three summers, described by many as the best ball in Oxford. Scenes from the Bond film *Tomorrow Never Dies* were filmed at New College, and the college has a fair share of Bond-girl lookalikes. New is particularly accomplished in musical matters: the college choir is one of the best in Oxford. New has been described as 'one of Oxford's least stressful places to live'.

ORIEL

Oriel Square, Oxford OX1 4EW
TEL 01865 276555
WEB www.oriel.ox.ac.uk

Founded in 1326, Oriel is mostly famous for its monotonous and undeniable domination of the river: it's a boatie's college. Apparently Oriel brings in students from America especially for their rowing prowess, regardless of their academic (in)abilities, and provides them with the best en-suite rooms in college and lavish free meals. Every extra year that sees Oriel come out victorious of the Summer Eights rowing race, another of its old boats is religiously burnt in the middle of their quad (that's Oxford tradition for you!). Architecturally the college is something of a rabbit warren. The distinctive front quad sees a Shakespeare production every summer, and the college is strong musically, with its own orchestra and choir. Academically very relaxed, the college reveres sport: those who can participate, do, and those who can't, support from one of the best boat houses on the river.

PEMBROKE

St Aldates, Oxford OX1 1DW
TEL 01865 276412
WEB www.pmb.ox.ac.uk
Founded in 1624, Pembroke is one of the poorest colleges in Oxford, and allegedly the college Boat Club Trust Fund is richer than the rest of the college put together! This astonishing fact holds its currency in donations from rich alumni rowers. Thus Pembroke is very strong at rowing, and the only plausible pretender to Oriel's rowing crown. In fact in the fifteen or so years of Oriel dominance on the river, Pembroke has been the only college capable of beating them once, several years ago; now the college is regularly second behind Oriel. Socially Pembroke is rather insular, has a low profile in the university, and academically it is laid back. A college rivalry exists with Christ Church.

QUEEN'S

High Street, Oxford OX1 4AW
TEL 01865 279167
WEB www.queens.ox.ac.uk
Founded 1624. Despite having a very high-profile

WHERE GRADUATES END UP

14% Finance*,	Key Areas
12% Health (incl Medicine),	
8% Manufacturing,	
8% Education,	
5% Personnel	
Accountancy*,	Niche Areas
Business/Management*,	
Film/Video, Journalism,	
Legal, Library/Archival,	
Advertising,	
Market Research,	
Publishing, Radio/TV,	
Eng/Industrial Design	

*indicates Top 10 Graduate Provider

Approximate employed **96%**

---

location, right in the middle of the High, the college has a very low profile in the University; one rarely meets students from Queen's. It has some of the most obviously dramatic architecture in Oxford, ranging from the classical cupola to the UFO-like Florey building off St Clement's. Queen's is very rich and is one of the cheapest colleges to attend, offering full accommodation for all your Oxford years. There is also a particularly good library. Excluded are undergrads wanting to read Single Hons English, however, a fact unconnected with the college being a home from home to Northerners. Quirkily, Queen's has an annual dinner to celebrate the survival of an undergraduate who in 1935 was viciously attacked by a boar and defended himself by driving a tome of Aristotle into the boar's mouth.

ST ANNE'S

Woodstock Rd, Oxford OX2 6HS
TEL 01865 274825
WEB www.stannes.ox.ac.uk
Founded 1879. St Anne's, very far away from the city centre, is atypical – laid back and unpretentious and lacking in the pomp and archaic traditions of older colleges. Isolation breeds self-sufficiency, and the college has a low profile in the university. A large proportion of the undergraduate community come from a state-school background, and the college is now one of the largest in terms of undergraduate numbers. Despite being a poor college, the library has around 100,000 volumes for current use, and is one of the two largest undergraduate college libraries in Oxford. The architecture is modern and unusual for Oxford, and the gardens are pleasant in the summer.

ST CATHERINE'S (St Catz)

Manor Road, Oxford OX1 3UJ
TEL 01865 271703
WEB www.stcatz.ox.ac.uk
Founded in 1963, St Catz possesses some breathtaking architecture, much of which is Grade 1 listed. Designed by Arne Jacobsen, the famous Danish architect, a spirit of openness infuses the place, with quads having no enclosing ends. It is located just outside the tourist-infested city centre, lending it some peace and tranquillity, but is still within a convenient distance of all central facilities. St Catz has exceptional resources, including the largest student theatre in Oxford, an extensive JCR building, and a moat. It is the youngest college, and, though obviously lacking traditions, has a very friendly atmosphere. Every summer St Catz has a Summer Ball which is a big success, and good bops are laid on regularly.

ST EDMUND HALL (Teddy Hall)
Queen's Lane, Oxford OX1 4AR
TEL 01865 279008
WEB www.seh.ox.ac.uk
Founded 1278. Teddy Hall, as it is informally known, is a very poor college, and rumours abound that it has been financially helped by its close neighbour Queen's. Its main reputation across the university is for being very good at sports: men excel at rugby in particular. Despite not being one of the highest profile colleges, Teddy Hall students still manage to get involved at most levels of university life, and are particularly good at drama and music. Teddy Hall is known for being the party college, where academia is not taken too seriously, and it puts on good ents.

ST HILDA'S
Cowley Place, Oxford OX4 1DY
TEL 01865 276816
WEB www.sthildas.ox.ac.uk
Founded in 1893, St Hilda's is an all-women college, not only at the JCR level, but also across the OCR and SCR. The college is home to the notorious, roaming 'Hildabeasts', which are among the most active members of the university, getting involved in many sports, societies and other extra-curricular pursuits. The college buildings are bland but pleasant, and the site is on the banks of the Cherwell, with beautiful gardens adding a colourful touch to the landscape. The college is fairly poor, and facilities are limited. St Hilda's is strong at rowing. Lots of ents events are put on, with something to keep the lasses happy every weekend. The bar is very poor, despite being the cheapest in Oxford. Being next to the river, the college owns its own punts, which are free for use by St Hilda's students and their guests. The college is seldom visited by tourists, which is a good thing.

ST HUGH'S
St Margaret's Rd, Oxford OX2 6LE
TEL 01865 274910
WEB www.st-hughs.ox.ac.uk
Founded in 1886 St Hugh's is so far out (geographically) it may as well be part of another university, and the walk into the centre of town can be long and laborious, although buses are very frequent. This is both an affliction and an attraction: St Hugh's has huge grounds (including croquet lawns and tennis courts) and there is (unfortunately small and ugly) on-site space to accommodate all students. College facilities are good and social life is tumultuous and intense. Ents are good, with a large-scale bop including a bouncy castle and barbecue organised during the summer. Despite being so far out of town, St

Hugh's students are reasonably involved across the university activities, especially in art and drama.

ST JOHN'S
St Giles, Oxford OX1 3JP
TEL 01865 277317
WEB www.sjc.ox.ac.uk
Founded 1555. This is the richest college in Oxford. St John's provides excellent facilities: there are financial rewards for the academically strong (1st, Norrington Table 1999): on-site accommodation (including luxurious sets and the strange honey-comb structures for Freshers) is guaranteed for everyone, there is a modern conference centre, and beautiful gardens adorn the quads. St John's is academically very strong and there is considerable pressure on students to work hard. The college performs well in sports as well, at rugby and rowing in particular. On the social front St John's doesn't deliver quite as well though: students tend to be quite dull, a fact reflected by the college bar which is very nice and spacious, but rarely alive and kickin'.

ST PETER'S
New Inn Hall Street, OX1 2DL
TEL 01865 278892
WEB www.spc.ox.ac.uk
Founded in 1929, St Peter's is a relatively new college in Oxford history, and covers very small grounds in the centre of town. Priorities here are much higher on social issues than on academic matters, and St Peter's doesn't excel at sports either. Nevertheless students seem fairly involved around the university, and the JCR is very active. St Peter's is very poor, which is obvious from the blatant lack or inadequacy of certain facilities. The college has a reasonable bar and puts on good ents events. Every year a middle-size Summer Ball is organised.

SOMERVILLE
Woodstock Road, Oxford OX2 6HD
TEL 01865 270629
WEB www.some.ox.ac.uk
Founded in 1929, Somerville is the most recent of colleges to have gone mixed (1994) and is located just beyond the reach of annoying tourists, yet close enough to the city centre for convenience. The generally left-wing college [with some notable exceptions – this was Margaret Thatcher's college] has always been politically very active and JCR members voice their opinions loudly. Indeed, Somervillians are active in every respect of university life, and the college has a fairly high profile amongst university students. College atmosphere is easygoing though the number of

political hacks and activists can sometimes be distressing. Somerville has good ents although the college bar is dull and bare.

TRINITY
Broad Street, Oxford OX1 3BH
Tel 01865 279910
web www.trinity.ox.ac.uk
Founded in 1554, Trinity is centrally located, next door to its arch-rival Balliol. The college has spacious and attractive grounds (which it leases from Balliol!) and elegant buildings. The undergraduate body is fairly small which lends to an intimate college atmosphere. Trinity used to be dominated by public-school types, but this has now changed. Accommodation provisions are good, and the college flats on Woodstock Road are regarded as among the best and poshest in Oxford. Trinity students have a high profile in the university, and are popular and involved in many activities. A Commemoration Ball is organised every three years in the summer and, on a more day-to-day basis, ents is good with fun bops, and Trinity men and women enjoy a lively and atmospheric bar.

UNIVERSITY
High Street, Oxford OX1 4BH
TEL 01865 276602
WEB www.univ.ox.ac.uk
Founded 1249. University is one of the colleges Oxford students hear the least about: it has an extremely low profile and is very quiet. This is despite the fact it is one of the oldest colleges (holding a claim, with Balliol and Merton, to being the oldest, although there is evidence that the college forged some deeds in 1381 to prove that it was founded in advance of Merton). The college is undeniably ancient, however, and very beautiful. Like St John's, it has a reputation for being full of bookworms who take life far too seriously and are

unaware of the existence of the words 'fun' and 'enjoyment'. College life is said to be a little slow, although the alleged existence of bops and a good bar do redeem it a little.

WADHAM
Parks Road, Oxford OX1 3PN
TEL 01865 277946
WEB www.wadham.ox.ac.uk
Founded in 1610, Wadham is a bastion of the left, with an even greater lefty image than Balliol. Getting involved in JCR and student affairs is a great springboard into the political limelight. It has always been liberal, and is very involved in LGB affairs: it hosts Queer Week, which culminates in an S&M and Fetishes Bop (where you get to see some quite outlandish costumes...). The college is also strong in music and drama (helped by the fact that Wadham has one of the university's only reasonably sized theatres), and the Saturday night bops are legendary.

WORCESTER
Worcester Street, Oxford OX1 2HB
TEL 01865 278391
WEB www.worcester.ox.ac.uk
Founded 1714. Worcester possesses huge and beautiful grounds, including tennis courts, sports grounds and a lake. Beautiful gardens decorate the college and provide a suitable backdrop to the medieval cottages and classic colonnade. All students are accommodated on the main college site. The college is presently enjoying some success at rowing and rugby, but is not known for any academic excellence. Lord Sainsbury was a Worcester student, and thus hall food is very cheap and also very good. Every three years the college hosts a huge Commemoration Ball in the summer. Worcester is lively, fairly rich and somewhat self-contained.

OXFORD BROOKES UNIVERSITY

Oxford Brookes University
Gipsy Lane Campus
Headington
Oxford OX3 0BP

TEL 01865 483040
FAX 01865 483983
EMAIL admissions@brookes.ac.uk
WEB www.brookes.ac.uk

Oxford Brookes Students' Union
Helena Kennedy Student Centre
London Road
Headington
Oxford OX3 0BP

TEL 01865 484750
FAX 01865 484799
EMAIL obsu.gensec@brookes.ac.uk
WEB www.theSU.com

VAG VIEW

If you are looking for a university not too demanding at entry, which offers a host of well-conceived modular courses in some interesting niche areas, and which enjoys the atmosphere of one of the world's true student cities, then Brookes might well be for you.

CAMPUS

Brookes is based over three main campuses; two in Headington (approx 1.5 miles from city centre) and one at Wheatley (5 miles away). A free inter-site bus service runs every half hour during the day. The Helena Kennedy Student Centre (HKSC), the main Students' Union, is housed with teaching facilities and accommodation across the road from Gypsy Lane on the Headington Hill site, formerly the house of tycoon Robert Maxwell, who called it the largest council house in England, which indeed it was. He never owned it.

STUDENT PROFILE

Oxford Brookes is uncharacteristic of most of the universities celebrating their tenth anniversary this year because of its high independent school intake. There is altogether a statistical lurch towards the middle class which serves to prompt the stereotypical image of the uni as a hang-out for air-head Sloanes who couldn't get a place at Bristol or Exeter. However, there is, too, a large overseas body of students – one fifth of degree undergraduates – and Giles Balleny insists that whatever the statistics indicate, on the ground the perception is of a rich tapestry of life.

'Brookes has an unusually varied cross section of students, which gives it a cosmopolitan outlook in everything it does,' writes Giles. 'Among the more prominent groups, public-school student types are not as dominant as people suggest,

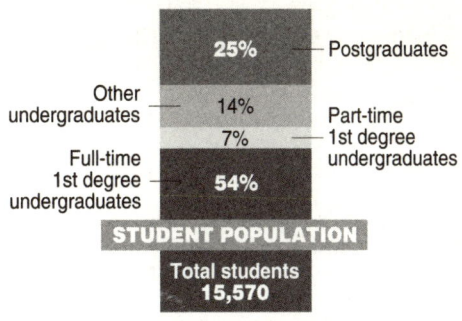

STUDENT POPULATION

- 25% Postgraduates
- Other undergraduates 14%
- 7% Part-time 1st degree undergraduates
- Full-time 1st degree undergraduates 54%

Total students **15,570**

SUBJECT AREAS (%)

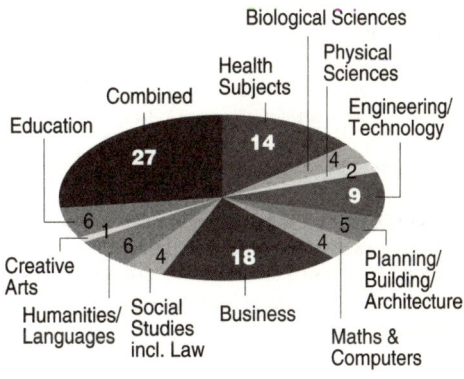

- Education 27
- Combined
- Health Subjects 14
- Biological Sciences
- Physical Sciences
- Engineering/Technology 4
- 2
- 9
- 5
- 4
- Planning/Building/Architecture
- Maths & Computers
- Business 18
- Social Studies incl. Law 4
- Humanities/Languages 6
- Creative Arts 1
- 6

although there probably is a larger public school contingent than at any other of the new universities. Most ignore their fraternising and get on with doing their own thing. Whether you are from an independent school or from a state school you will undoubtedly find "your type".

'There is also a large proportion of foreign students from a huge range of countries. Ethnic minorities from the UK are also very well

UNIVERSITY/STUDENT PROFILE	
University since	**1992**
Situation/style	**Campus**
Student population	**15,570**
Full-time undergraduates	**8,370**
- mature	**46%**
- overseas	**20%**
- male/female	**43/57**
- state sector intake	**73%**
- non-traditional student intake	**6%**
- drop-out rate	**11%**
- undergraduate applications	**Down 1%**
see Introduction for key to tables	

AT A GLANCE	
ACADEMIC FILE:	
Subjects assessed	**34**
Excellent	**74%**
Average requirements	**220 points**
Students-staff ratio	**14:1**
First/2:1 degree pass rate	**56%**
ACCOMMODATION FILE:	
Guarantee to freshers	**75%**
Style	**Halls, houses**
Approx price range pw	**£57-£76**
City rent pw	**£70**

ACADEMIC EXCELLENCE

TEACHING:
(Rated Excellent or 17+ out of 24)

Law, Anthropology, English, Geography.	**Excellent**
Planning, Business, Economics	**24**
History of Art, Real Estate Mgt,	**23**
Building, Psychology, Biology & Enviro Science, Art & Design	
Italian & Spanish, French, Maths, Politics	**22**
Sociology, Publishing, Civil Eng	**21**
Food Science, Nursing, Subjects Allied to Medicine	**20**
German, Electronic Eng	**19**

RESEARCH:
Top grades 5/5*

History	**Grade 5***
English, French	**Grade 5**

represented and play a large part in the overall feel of the place.

'In addition, statistics show that Brookes has a whopping great mature student population [actually 46% of the undergraduate population at the last count], a fact that surprises as this isn't a group of which I had been especially aware. I suppose that the great attraction of mature students to Brookes is the fact that the courses are modular, and so can be studied part-time.'

ACADEMIA

Oxford Brookes' modular programme, on which it built its reputation, has been in the making for a quarter of a century. Among a host of vocational courses that lead the way, Law raised plaudits from many school careers teachers to whom we spoke. Also, Brookes was the first to offer a Publishing degree and it is one of the few to command respect in the industry. Note, too, the European Business Studies degree, which culminates in a dual award – a British degree and German or French equivalent from the European end. Again, its Languages for Business course marries a linguistic, cultural approach with work placement, an introduction to the principles of business and microcomputing for European business and a final specialism in Marketing or Human Resource Management,

If you are looking for a uni not too demanding at entry, which offers a host of modular courses in useful niche areas, and which enjoys the atmosphere of one of the world's true student cities, it might be for you.

which must surely rate as one of the most useful vocational/business courses around. On a winning health ticket (21% find employment in the sector), their Nursing and Midwifery degrees, together with the Health Care Studies courses, make up another popular area of study following a common foundation programme. Brookes also has the first School of Osteopathy ever to be incorporated into a university.

Top-scoring departments at the teaching assessments are Planning, Business, Economics (all full marks), History of Art, Real Estate Management, Building, Psychology, Biology & Enviro Science, Art & Design. It is easy to see why property and the construction industry are important niche areas in our graduate *Employment* box on page 365.

Brookes has worked hard not only in drawing up a flexible modular programme, but in using the interdisciplinary nature of its ground-breaking modular system to maximise employment prospects, student interest and subject exploration.

Says Emily Waller: 'Individuals can pretty much design their own courses, although all the rules and regulations can be confusing, so get help if you need it. The work load is manageable, but depends on the course that you are taking. Work placements both abroad and in Britain are common. Teaching staff are generally very helpful (if you can find them). Each student is assigned a personal tutor for their years of study.

'There are three libraries, well stocked with up-to-date and ancient texts and an easy-to-use computerised catalogue; friendly individual subject librarians are always willing to help. The main library has over 1,000 private study desks and some group study rooms (great for catching up on gossip, if not for study!). It is open until 10.00 pm weekdays. Every student has free Internet and e-mail access, and computers are accessible 24/7. Computer Services – in particular the help desk – are invaluable, as the network has an annoying habit of crashing (normally about five minutes before an assignment is due in!).

SOCIAL SCENE

STUDENTS' UNION 'There's an active ents programme with regular clubnights, film nights, comedy nights and termly balls. The main SU venue [**The Venue**] has a capacity of over 1,200. It is home to Friday's *Pleasure Dome* (9 pm-2 am) – a mixture of styles. There are four union bars based around the university, the **Harts** lounge bar and **Morals** café bar, where Saturday's '70s/'80s/'90s night, *Glam*, is staged, and **Eights and Mez Bar**, and three shops supplying stationery, groceries, gifts, cards, confectionery and many other products.

'A free and confidential advice and counselling service is also on offer, as is representation for all students on academic, personal and financial issues. Over sixty clubs and societies ensure that there really is something for everyone. Currently the most popular society is Cocktail.'

SPORT Facilities are excellent and include Astroturf, squash courts, health suite, heavy weights gym, tennis courts, rugby, football, cricket and hockey pitches, fitness trails, two boat houses and a multi-purpose sports hall for aerobics, martial arts, women's boxing, circuit training, etc. The Centre for Sport is open from 7.30 am to 11.00 pm. The university teams came 41st nationally last year.

TOWN 'The night life in Oxford, always busy and full of tourists and students, is varied but expensive, even with the student discount that most clubs, pubs, bars and restaurants offer.

There is a great music and theatre scene with lots of theatres, gig venues and cinemas, but the clubbing scene is definitely mediocre (unless you are a big cheesy '60s to '80s fan). Travel around the city is regular and simple, and for women the Students' Union runs a special Safety Bus from

WHAT IT'S REALLY LIKE

UNIVERSITY:

Social Life	★★★★
Campus scene	**The middle-class 'new uni'**
Student Union services	**Good**
Politics	**Average**
Sport	**Competitive**
National team position	**41st**
Sport facilities	**Good**
Arts opportunities	**Drama, music, art excellent; film good; dance avg**
Student newspaper	**O.B. Scene**
Nightclub	**The Venue**
Bars	**Harts, Mez, Eights, Morals**
Union ents	**Pleasure Dome, Glam**
Union clubs/societies	**60**
Most popular society	**Cocktail**
Smoking policy	**Union, halls OK**
Parking	**Poor**

CITY:

Entertainment	★★★
Scene	**Small, good pubs, OK clubs**
Town/gown relations	**Poor**
Risk of violence	**Average**
Cost of living	**High**
Student concessions	**Good**
Survival + 2 nights out	**£60 pw**
Part-time work campus/town	**Good**

campus to doorstep. As long as 'home' is within the Oxford Ring Road, this is a free service. Coaches run every ten minutes to London, Gatwick, Heathrow and Cambridge. Student discounts are available.

PILLOW TALK

There are thirteen halls of residence (catering and non-catering), all with easy access to the university. Most first year students live in.

JOBS

'About 65% of Brookes' students have part-time jobs; these are very easy to get hold of through the unions' Job Shop.

Both university and Students' Union employ a lot of student staff, and Brookes' tutors tend to be very supportive of students with part-time jobs.'

The uni is very popular with employers and is always close to the top of the graduate employment league tables.

WHERE GRADUATES END UP

21% Health/Social Work, Key Areas
10% Manufacturing,
8% Education,
6%Computer,
6% Personnel,
5% Finance,
5% Wholesale/Retail,
5% Public Admin
Business/Management,
Hotel/Restaurant*, Niche Areas
Agric/Forestry, Property*,
Architecture, Construction,
Electron/Electric,
Eng/Industrial Design,
Advertising,
Market Research

*indicates Top 10 Graduate Provider

Approximate employed **94%**

GETTING THERE

☞ By road: from north, A423 or A34 or A43; London, M40; south, M4/J13, A34. Wheatley campus, M40/J8, A418. Good coach service.
☞ By rail: London Paddington, 1:00; Birmingham, 1:30; Bristol, 1:45; Sheffield, 3:30.
☞ By air: Heathrow/Gatwick; coaches/buses will stop outside Gypsy Lane campus on request.
☞ By coach: London, 1:40; Birmingham, 1:30; Leeds, 5:30; Bristol, 4:30.

- -

UNIVERSITY OF PAISLEY

The University of Paisley
High Street
Paisley PA1 2BE

TEL 0141 848 3727
FAX 0141 848 3623
EMAIL alison.copeland@paisley.ac.uk
WEB www.paisley.ac.uk

Paisley Students' Association
17 Hunter Street
Paisley PA1 1DN

TEL 0141 889 9940
FAX 0141 848 9693
EMAIL president@upsa.org.uk
WEB ces.paisley.ac.uk/life_paisley/union.htm

VAG VIEW

*P*aisley University came out of Paisley Technical College, founded in 1897. In the same year as it became a fully fledged university (1995) it began its development into nursing and midwifery, a faculty largely to be found at its campus to the south, in Robbie Burns country. The main university campus is in Paisley itself, the largest town in Scotland and just a mile or so from Glasgow Airport. Only a couple of years old is a third campus, a joint venture with Glasgow Uni and Dumfries & Galloway College on an 80-acre parkland site half a mile from the centre of a town that is many miles to the south, close to the Solway Firth (and Carlisle).

CAMPUS

PAISLEY CAMPUS takes getting to know: 'It would be

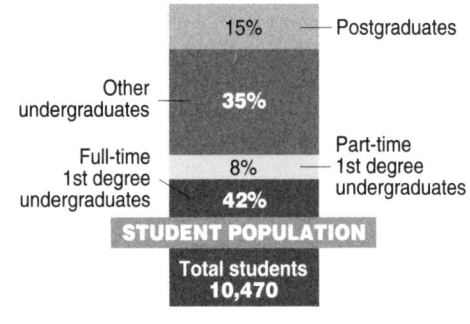

STUDENT POPULATION

Total students
10,470

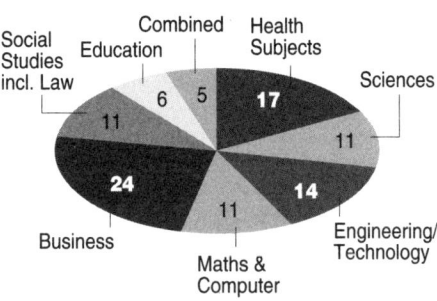

SUBJECT AREAS (%)

UNIVERSITY/STUDENT PROFILE	
University since	**1995**
Situation/style	**Town campuses**
Student population	**10,470**
Full-time undergraduates	**4,350**
- mature	**42%**
- overseas	**1%**
- male/female	**50/50**
- state sector intake	**97%**
- non-traditional student intake	**36%, high**
- drop-out rate	**20%, high**
- undergraduate applications	**Down 6%**
see Introduction for key to tables	

really easy for a fresher, such as yourself, to mistake the main campus for a hospital wing in need of a cosmetic facelift,' writes Nausheen Rai. 'The "traditional" building has a blend of lino-type tiled floors, a supposed up-to-date glass "hamster" tunnel walkway (for fashion purposes *darling*), a surgical hospital smell that leaves one feeling oddly confused, and a brand new, £6-million, out-of-sync library with glass lift, plush pink carpets, novelty chairs and lots of space.'

AYR CAMPUS (known as 'Craigie') Tel 01292 886000. Opines Nausheen: 'This is definitely the more friendly campus (if that were to make the choice). Being smaller, it's more cosy. Males may count themselves fortunate to study in this sister campus tucked away on the west coast. There's an estimated ten women to every one of them.'

DUMFRIES CAMPUS Tel 01387 702060. It is situated beside the Crichton Business Park in eighty-five acres of parkland and gardens. A £1.8-million grant from the Scottish Funding Council is underwriting the development, which builds on franchise links which Paisley has had with Dumfries & Galloway College since 1994. The campus is an element in their open-access strategy, an attempt 'to widen the provision of higher education in the south west of Scotland.'

STUDENT PROFILE

Many students are local, mature and/or part-timers and almost exclusively come to Paisley from the state sector, flooding in from neighbourhoods which haven't traditionally supplied universities, a fact possibly going some way to explain the very high drop out rate (20% among non-mature first years).

> It may be largely local, but Paisley courses are designed by industry and commerce, and there's an employment avenue from the start. Now, after 30 years campaigning, Paisley students are at last going to get facilities for a social life too.

ACADEMIA

Faculties at Paisley include Engineering, Information Sciences, Science & Technology, Social and Management Sciences (and some

---

ACADEMIC EXCELLENCE

TEACHING :
(Rated Excellent, Highly Satis. or 17+ out of 24)

Civil Engineering, **Highly Satis.**
Chemistry, Maths & Statistics,
Mechanical (incl Manufacturing)
Engineering, Teacher Education
Sociology, Social Work, Cellular
& Molecular Biology,
Organismal Biol, Psychology.
European Languages **19**

RESEARCH:
Top grades 5/5*
Accounting & Finance, **Grade 5**

---

midwifery and nursing). Faculties at Ayr are Education, Media Studies, Business, Nursing & Midwifery. Subjects at Dumfries include IT, Computing, Business & Management Studies, along with health-related courses.

A major feather in the proverbial cap this year (see box, above) is the Grade 5 in Accounting & Finance in the research assessments. It's their first and indicates international expertise. See, too (box, page 368) the nationally strong employment performances in such areas as Hotel/Restaurant, Industrial Design, Property, Electronic & Electrical Manufacture and Journalism. There are some powerful courses in the areas of media (for example, the BScs in Media Technology and Multimedia Systems), in computing (such as Business Information Technology & Accounting, Software Engineering, Computer Games Technology), in electronics (for example, Computer-aided Design, Product Design & Development), and in construction engineering, and real estate management. Feeding employment in the Catering – Hotel/Restaurant – area is the business school, which is Paisley's main emphasis.

SOCIAL SCENE

STUDENTS' ASSOCIATION The Paisley SU is a fifteen-minute walk away from campus. UPSA have been campaigning for a proper building since 1971, when they were given the present site as a temporary measure. Now, following a new union at Ayr – café-style, chrome tables,

---

AT A GLANCE

ACADEMIC FILE:
Subjects assessed	**17**
Excellent/Highly Satisfactory	**65%**
Average A level requirements	**13 points**
Scottish Highers	**CC-BBBCC**
Students-staff ratio	**20:1**
First/2:1 degree pass rate	**47%**

ACCOMMODATION FILE:
Guarantee to freshers	**90%**
Style	**Halls, flats**
Student satisfaction	**53%**
Cost pw (no food)	**£28-£38**
Town	**£35-£40**

<table>
<tr><td colspan="2">**WHAT IT'S REALLY LIKE**</td></tr>
<tr><td colspan="2">UNIVERSITY:</td></tr>
<tr><td>Social Life</td><td>★★★</td></tr>
<tr><td>Campus scene</td><td>**Friendly, local, urban cowboys**</td></tr>
<tr><td>Student Union services</td><td>**OK. New Union for 2003**</td></tr>
<tr><td>Politics</td><td>**NUS issues**</td></tr>
<tr><td>Sport</td><td>**Relaxed**</td></tr>
<tr><td>National team position</td><td>**127th**</td></tr>
<tr><td>Sport facilities</td><td>**Average**</td></tr>
<tr><td>Arts opportunities</td><td>**Few**</td></tr>
<tr><td>Student mag/news</td><td>**AM, Downbeat**</td></tr>
<tr><td>Nightclub</td><td>**Subway**</td></tr>
<tr><td>Bars</td><td>**Buroo**</td></tr>
<tr><td>Union ents</td><td>**Comedy, theme nights**</td></tr>
<tr><td>Union clubs/societies</td><td>**12**</td></tr>
<tr><td>Smoking policy</td><td>**1 room only**</td></tr>
<tr><td>Parking</td><td>**Poor**</td></tr>
<tr><td colspan="2">TOWN:</td></tr>
<tr><td>Entertainment</td><td>★★</td></tr>
<tr><td>Local scene</td><td>**Clubs, pubs**</td></tr>
<tr><td>Town/gown relations</td><td>**Poor**</td></tr>
<tr><td>Risk of violence</td><td>**Average**</td></tr>
<tr><td>Student concessions</td><td>**Adequate**</td></tr>
<tr><td>Survival + 2 nights out</td><td>**£60 pw**</td></tr>
<tr><td>Part-time work campus/town</td><td>**Fair/good**</td></tr>
</table>

PILLOW TALK

Apply early for accommodation; it's in short supply, though at Paisley unbelievably cheap. Most students bed down in flats or 'villas' in the student village at Thornly Park, two miles from campus, hard by the uni's sports facilities. Other residences are more central; all are self-catering.

Accommodation at Craigie comprises catered single or shared study-bedrooms. No accommodation at Dumfries.

<table>
<tr><td colspan="2">**WHERE GRADUATES END UP**</td></tr>
<tr><td>**13% Manufacturing,**</td><td>Key Areas</td></tr>
<tr><td>**12% Education,**</td><td></td></tr>
<tr><td>**12% Wholesale/Retail,**</td><td></td></tr>
<tr><td>**7% Health/Social Work,**</td><td></td></tr>
<tr><td>**6% Public Admin,**</td><td></td></tr>
<tr><td>**5% Finance**</td><td></td></tr>
<tr><td>**Hotel/Restaurant*,**</td><td>Niche Areas</td></tr>
<tr><td>**Aeronautical Manufacture,**</td><td></td></tr>
<tr><td>**Eng/Industrial Design*,**</td><td></td></tr>
<tr><td>**Construction, Property*,**</td><td></td></tr>
<tr><td>**Electron/Electric*,**</td><td></td></tr>
<tr><td>**Telecom, Journalism***</td><td></td></tr>
<tr><td>*indicates Top 10 Graduate Provider</td><td></td></tr>
<tr><td>Approximate employed</td><td>**85%**</td></tr>
</table>

Chesterfield sofas, very slick – they are to get one. The Paisley union is scheduled to open in September 2002. Hitherto they have held comedy and home-grown theme nights, karaoke, quizzes and talent contests. A trip the six miles into the centre of Glasgow is a regular alternative.

At Craigie there are two or three discos, a Saturday party, quizzes, karaoke, etc. In town there's the **Wulf & Whistle** and **O'Briens**, virtually union property by adoption, and three cheesy nightclubs with weekly student nights.

SPORT The Robertson Trust Sports Centre is located in the student village in Paisley. Some 1,500 students are members.

Recent improvements include turf pitches for rugby and soccer and floodlit synthetic pitches. There are also facilities for squash, multigym workouts, badminton, hockey, netball, tennis, basketball, volleyball and table tennis.

There's not much sport in Ayr.

JOBS

Paisley degree courses are designed with input from industry and commerce. Languages, IT training and work placements are key. IBM, M&S, BBC, Volkswagen, Standard Life and BAe all take Paisley undergrads on annual placements; salaries average £10,000. They have some very successful graduate employment areas – four in the national Top Tens.

GETTING THERE

☞ By road to Paisley: M8 – M74, A726, A737. For Ayr, M77/A77. For Dumfries, A76 or A701 from the north; A75 from the south.
☞ By coach to Glasgow: London, 8:20; Birmingham, 6:20; Newcastle, 4:20.
☞ By rail to Paisley: Ayr, 45 mins; Glasgow Central, 15 mins. Glasgow to London, 6:00; Liverpool, Manchester, Birmingham, 5:30; Edinburgh, 50 mins; Aberdeen, 2:45. For Dumfries: Glasgow, 2:00; Ayr, 1:50.
☞ By air: Glasgow International Airport.

UNIVERSITY OF PLYMOUTH

The University of Plymouth
Drake Circus
Plymouth
Devon PL4 8AA

TEL 01752 232 232
FAX 01752 232 141
EMAIL admission@plymouth.ac.uk
WEB www.plymouth.ac.uk

Plymouth Students' Union
Main Site
Drake Circus
Plymouth PL4 8AA

TEL 01752 663337
FAX 01752 251669
EMAIL pres_upsue@hotmail.com
WEB www.upsu.plym.ac.uk

VAG VIEW

*P*lymouth has made a vigorous rise since gaining university status – teaching assessments are consistently good, if not amazing.

The uni majors in marine and maritime courses, water sports and Australians – there's even a Surf Science & Technology degree – believe it, dudes, this really does exist; indeed, it is three times over-subscribed. Sand, sea, surf is what Plymouth is about – 'Wherever we go,' said one student, 'people say, "You look so well!"'

This preoccupation with off-coastal matters has landed Plymouth a new vice-chancellor. Roland Levinsky, ex-Vice-provost of University College, London, no less, has leapt at the chance of this senior post. Can it be coincidence that he holds a yachtmaster's off-shore certificate and has logged 15,000 sea miles in his 42-foot Meridian of Beaulieu?

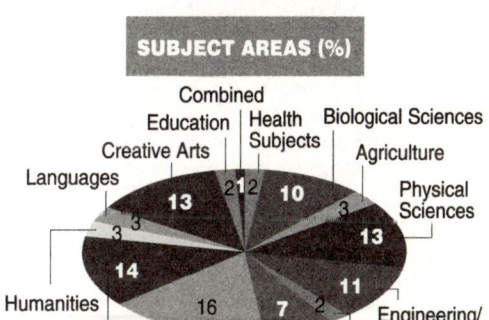

STUDENT POPULATION

- 13% — Postgraduates
- Other undergraduates 23%
- Full-time 1st degree undergraduates 47%
- 17% — Part-time 1st degree undergraduates

Total students **23,810**

SUBJECT AREAS (%)

Combined Subjects 2 · Education 1 · Health Subjects 2 · Biological Sciences 10 · Creative Arts 13 · Agriculture 3 · Languages 3 · Physical Sciences 13 · Humanities 14 · Engineering/Technology 11 · Social Studies incl. Law 16 · Business 7 · Maths & Computer 2 · Building/Architecture

STUDENT PROFILE

There's a big mature and international student draw from 100 countries and an active international office and International Students' Society. Applicants from the UK tend to be drawn from below a line drawn south of the Midlands through Wales, Bristol and London. It is almost wholly a state sector take.

UNIVERSITY/STUDENT PROFILE	
University since	**1992**
Situation/style	**City/town campuses**
Student population	**23,810**
Full-time undergraduates	**11,100**
- mature	**24%**
- overseas	**9%**
- male/female	**51/49**
- state sector intake	**92%**
- non-traditional student intake	**10%**
- drop-out rate	**9%**
- undergraduate applications	**Down 1%**
see Introduction for key to tables	

CAMPUSES

Just when you think you're getting hold of Plymouth you learn that there are four campuses, miles apart, but all in Devon. Let's start with what we know:

PLYMOUTH CAMPUS (address as above) **Faculties:** Science, Technology, Human Sciences, Business. So, what was that about a degree in surfing? 'This is the first academically rigorous surf science course

ACADEMIC EXCELLENCE

TEACHING:
(Rated Excellent or 17+ out of 24)

Environmental Science, Geography, Geology, Oceanography.	**Excellent**
Psychology, Civil Eng, Building, Nursing	**23**
Food/Agriculture, Biosciences, Politics, Sport, Tourism, Education	**22**
Art & Design, Media, Drama, History of Art	**21**
Sociology, Subjects Allied to Medicine, Maths	**20**
Materials Technology	**19**
Electronic & Electrical Eng	**18**

RESEARCH :
Top grades 5/5*

Psychology, Computer, History Art/Architecture/Design	**Grade 5**

in the world,' boasts Dr Malcolm Findlay of the Institute of Marine Studies. The first year dwells on oceanography, surfing materials and business studies. The second moves uncontroversially into areas like human biology and human performance, but in the third year you develop your own specialism. Head for the beach presumably.

EXMOUTH Douglas Avenue, Exmouth EX8 2AT. Tel: 01395 25509. **Faculty:** Arts & Education. **Ents facilities:** S.U.B. Station – two bars. **Ents, campus & city:** second biggest campus (approx 1,000 students), but if you're expecting the bright lights

AT A GLANCE

ACADEMIC FILE:

Subjects assessed	**24**
Excellent	**75%**
Average A level requirements	**15 points**
Students-staff ratio	**15:1**
First/2:1 degree pass rate	**48%**

ACCOMMODATION FILE:

Guarantee to freshers	**Non-locals before 9.7**
Style	**Halls, flats, houses**
Catered	**All halls**
En-suite	**47%**
Approx price range pw	**£42-£95**
City rent pw	**£37-£45**

and big sailors of Plymouth, you'll be disappointed. Exmouth is the relaxed, seaside campus. The **S.U.B. Station** bars provide theme nights, discos, live bands, hypnotists, club trips to Plymouth, etc.; LGB to **Boxes** or **The Loft** in Exeter. Popular local nightclub is **Samantha's**; there's a strong local live music culture. **Sport:** playing fields with pavilion close to campus. Rolle Rovers (soccer), men's and women's rugby teams, netball, basketball and cricket all perform well within their respective leagues. Diving, sailing and windsurfing facilities locally. **Media:** *Rolle-Up* is the student magazine 'because our full title is University of Plymouth: Rolle College Faculty of Arts & Education.'

EXETER Earl Richards Road North, Exeter EX2 6AS. Tel: 01392 475004/9. **Faculty:** Arts & Education. **Ents facilities:** bar, 266 ents capacity. **Ents, campus & city:** regular ents – Wednesday Film Club, Thursday pool competition, Friday theme nights – tarts & trannies, '70s, etc. A busy arts schedule includes trips to London, Birmingham, Cardiff and Cornwall art galleries and theatres. See *Exeter Uni* entry for lively student city nightlife. **Media:** *Illuminate* magazine. **Sport:** local sports facilities only; uni teams include football, hockey, rugby.

SEALE-HAYNE Newton Abbot TQ12 6NQ. Tel: 01626 325606. **Faculty:** Agriculture, Food & Land Use. Besides the strong ocean science presence there is also the wholly land-based agricultural college with perhaps a finer, certainly longer, reputation, a 22/24 teaching assessment and a Dartmoor Vineyard for production of a Pinot Blanc 'for university use'. There are also two degree courses offered in Tourism. College facilities include almost 200 hectares of land, of which 160 acres are farmed. **Ents facilities:** bar. **Ents, campus & city:** Two ents a week and plenty of boozing. There's one nightclub only in the town, **Rafters**, but Newton Abbot is a good setting-off point for the delights of the South Hams (cosy pubs, good eateries). **Sport:** sports hall, squash court, fitness room, on-campus pitches.

ACADEMIA

Plymouth are hot on study skills support programmes. There are disability services, support for dyslexia., specialist assessment for students applying for the Disabled Student Allowance, and training in the use of specialist technical equipment.

The marine bias takes the uni deep into biological sciences and the big news this year is the human Peninsula Medical School, a partnership with Exeter Uni and the NHS in Devon and

Cornwall to form a new medical school. It opens in October. The undergraduate programme will prepare students through a community-based education – contact: medadmissions@pms. ac.uk (see also: www. pms.ac.uk). Opening formally this year, too, is Plymouth's Institute of Neuroscience.

Out at Exmouth, one of the locations of the Faculty of Arts and Education, where a mass of music and theatre programmes and all kinds of pop culture can be pursued, a new £2.1 million centre with performance space, lecture theatre and seminar rooms has just opened.

Back at Plymouth, there's a whole raft of new courses which consolidate our preconceptions about the place: Coastal Environmental Science, Fisheries & Aquaculture, Marine Biology & Oceanography, Marine & Composites Technology and Nautical Studies. But here is also Computer-Oriented Mathematics, Digital Arts and Design, and their computing and engineering students have recently copped a £100,000 computer networking laboratory from Cisco Systems, one of the world's largest computing networking companies. Science doesn't have to be so serious, however. How about three years studying Plymouth's new degree in Aroma and Formulation Science, while your Ossie Masseeve is doing his beach thing with the surf?

SOCIAL SCENE

STUDENTS' UNION They have a dynamic ents manager, digging out new local bands, and as a result Plymouth is featured in many a uni tour - Orange, Ministry of Sound, etc. The May Ball, we are told, 'attracted 3,500 to a field', actually Newnham Park, the classical Georgian manor between the outskirts of Plymouth and the foothills of Dartmoor National Park. Reef played, also LTJ Bukem and Lightning Seeds.

Friday night's *Oblivion* sets the scene for the weekend on the main campus – two dance rooms, 1,450 capacity, two main bars and a bottle bar. Saturday is serious fare – drum 'n' bass, hip hop, reggae, beatz 'n' breakz and Jelly Jazz. Comedy nights are especially popular. Three venues in town team up with the union for *Happy Mondays @* **Millennium** on Union Street, Wednesday @ **Candy Store**, a superclub just five minutes from the union, and Tuesday @ **Heroes**, a club bar in the Warner complex near the famed Barbican.

When not clubbing and surfing, there are society activities, notably *Fly* magazine and SCAP,

Community Action, which has BIG ideas, last year an international project in Thika, a small town in Kenya no less.

The approach to graduate employment is highly focused; there's a rich choice of courses and a great social life. Now, teaming up with Exeter Uni will propel it further into the higher education stratosphere.

SPORT There's national/ world-class water-sport – sailing, diving, surfing, windsurfing, power-boating, wakeboarding, canoeing and waterski. A fleet of dinghies and yachts provide sailing opportunities. Plymouth is the only UK uni to have its own diving and sailing centre. Students can learn to dive professionally as part of their course (selected disciplines only) or take a recreational diving course, which is open to all students.

There's also the usual land-based team stuff. They came 46th nationally last year – most popular club is Football.

WHAT IT'S REALLY LIKE	
UNIVERSITY:	
Social Life	★★★★
Campus scene	**Lively ents, water sporty**
Student Union services	**OK**
Politics	**Interest low**
Sport	**47 clubs**
National team position	**46th**
Sport facilities	**Average**
Arts opportunities	**Drama, dance, music, art avg; film poor**
Student magazine	**Fly!**
Nightclub	**UPSU, 2 dance rooms**
Bars	**2 main bars + bottle bar**
Union ents	**Party, drum 'n' bass, hip hop, Jelly Jazz**
Union clubs/societies	**78**
Most popular society	**Football**
Smoking policy	**Union, halls OK**
Parking	**Non-existent**
CITY:	
Entertainment	★★★★
Scene	**Clubs, pubs OK**
Town/gown relations	**Poor**
Risk of violence	**Average**
Cost of living	**Below average**
Student concessions	**Average**
Survival + 2 nights out	**£50 pw**
Part-time work campus/town	**OK**

Town Plymouth – destroyed during the war and rebuilt at a low point in British architecture – has been designated second poorest ward in Europe, but you wouldn't know it since it has won huge EU investment. There's a surfeit of accommodation which costs between £37 and £45 per week, you can walk anywhere, it is a safe, friendly, smiley place. When the sun shines it is unbeatable, the beach is ten minutes away, and when it doesn't shine, maybe the snow on the nearby moors is not so bad an option.

Like nearby Exeter, Plymouth has recently become more cosmopolitan. Think huge shopping centre and **Barbican**. The Barbican is, of course, waterside, the olde worlde bit of town – boats, fish and tourists, but more to the point, pubs, clubs and restaurants. There are cafés all over the place and a Grecco-Romanesque superclub, **Candy Store**, where each room sorts different music styles and different atmospheres.

Arts-wise, there's the **Theatre Royal**, which had the Royal Shakespeare Company in residence when we were there, and the alternative **Drum Theatre** for more progressive fare. If you're seriously into painting, why not cross the border into Cornwall – many do so as to chase the surf in Newquay (current international surf and clubland Mecca) – but continue west, down to St Ives, the 'Tate of the South West', as it is known.

Back in Plymouth, the **Jazz Café** is a popular haunt – there are live acts every night. At the union there are musical theatre productions every year, and among the most popular group activity currently is a salsa class.

Then, as everyone will tell you, there's always the Eden Project. It's virtually next door, and now the uni has signed an official agreement with that nice Tim fella. Collaboration includes student placements. Future developments are likely to include new courses.

Doesn't it all begin to sound like 'Plymouth, the University of Fun'?

PILLOW TALK

Freshers are guaranteed a room in halls if they live more than twenty-five miles from the campus at which they will be studying, if Plymouth is your first choice uni, if the academic criteria of your original offer are met, and if your application for a halls place is received before July 9. So they don't ask much then! In fact, there are even more ifs and buts, so you'd better speak to them, or their lawyers, personally…and get in quick! Note, all medical students will be guaranteed an offer of a place in halls for their first year of study.

There are mixed-sex halls, flats and houses, all self-catering, 47% en suite, price per week ranging from £42 to £95. Two new halls and a new café on the way at Plymouth, and a £28-million development of new study bedrooms at Exeter.

JOBS

70% of students work part-time during term and a good Job Shop helps them, as does an Earn & Learn scheme.

The most recent figures show just 6% graduates from 2,001 unemployed after six months. The uni is a partner in Gradsouthwest, a region-wide service helping graduates to secure employment in the South West via a website and on-line CV-matching service, launched in 2002.

GETTING THERE

☛ By road: M5, A38 Exeter, Plymouth; Newton Abbot, A38, A383; Exmouth M5/J30, A376. Good coach services to Exeter and Plymouth.
☛ By coach to Plymouth: London, 4:40; Bristol, 2:30; Exeter, 1:05. To Exeter: London, 4:00; Birmingham, 4:30.
☛ By rail to Plymouth: London Paddington, 3:30; Bristol Parkway, 3:00; Southampton, 4:00; Birmingham New Street, 4:00. Exeter from London Paddington, 2:30; Bristol Parkway, 1:30; Birmingham New Street, 3:00.
☛ By air: Exeter or Plymouth City Airports.

WHERE GRADUATES END UP	
14% Manufacturing,	Key Areas
12% Public Admin*,	
9% Wholesale/Retail,	
8% Education,	
7% Finance,	
6% Health/Social Work,	
5% Computer,	
5% Personnel	
Electron/Electric,	Niche Areas
Agric/Forestry*, Property,	
Advertising, Aeronautical	
Manufacture, Architecture,	
Artistic/Literary, Chemical/	
Pharmaceutical*,	
Construction, Defence,	
Market Research,	
Publishing, Telecom*,	
Eng/Industrial Design	
*indicates Top 10 Graduate Provider	
Approximate employed **93%**	

PLYMOUTH COLLEGE OF ART & DESIGN

Plymouth College of Art & Design
Tavistock Place
Plymouth PL4 8AT

TEL 01752 203434
FAX 01752 203444
EMAIL enquiries@pcad.plym.ac.uk
WEB www.pcad.plym.ac.uk

VAG VIEW

*O*ffering Art and Design at both further and higher education levels, the college is situated in the city centre, opposite the university that validates its degrees. A good reputation is most notable in Photomedia, an HND top up, which has attracted many awards. The college is the main vocational art and design centre on the Devon and Cornwall peninsular, and there are good relationships with potential employers through The Corporation, an organisation of representatives from local industry. There is an active Students' Union, help on line to find accommodation and a fair old riot to be had in the city and university union. See Plymouth Uni *above for city/travel info.*

COLLEGE PROFILE

Founded	**1937**
Status	**Art College**
Degree awarding university	**Plymouth**
Student population	**1.320**
Full-time undergraduates	**75**
College accommodation	**None**
City rent pw	**£37-£45**

DEGREE COURSES:
Applied Arts (Ceramics, Glass, Metals) and PhotoMedia

UNIVERSITY OF PORTSMOUTH

The University of Portsmouth
University House
Winston Churchill Avenue
Portsmouth PO1 2UP

TEL 02392 848484
FAX 02392 843082
EMAIL admissions@port.ac.uk
WEB www.port.ac.uk

Portsmouth Students' Union
Alexandra House
Museum Road
Portsmouth PO1 2QH

TEL 023 9284 3635
FAX 023 9284 3667
EMAIL student-union@port.ac.uk
WEB www.upsu.net

VAG VIEW

*P*ortsea is almost an island, it has its own microclimate, slightly warmer than nearby Brighton or Bournemouth, as it sits snugly behind the Isle of Wight. For centuries, because of its strategic position, it was an important naval base, but now the focus is moving away from the military, the old naval dockyard giving itself to a pleasure zone of shops, nightclubs, bars, called Gun Wharf.

What once we detected as a military ethic in the university's 'Code of Student Discipline' seems also to have slipped away – though there remains an active OTC (Officer Training Corps), and a high input of graduates into the defence arena from a variety of departments. Today, however, military style disciplines seem to have been

SUBJECT AREAS (%)

- Humanities/Languages — 13
- Creative Arts — 8
- Health Subjects — 4
- Sciences — 21
- Engineering/Technology — 12
- Building/Architecture — 6
- Maths & Computer — 11
- Business — 18
- Social Studies incl. Law — 6

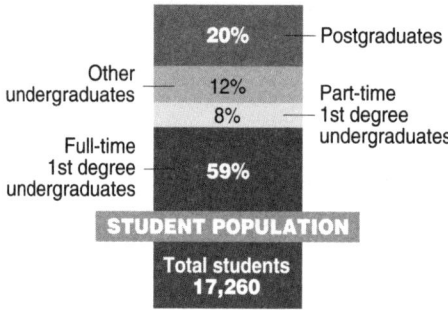

	20% — Postgraduates
Other undergraduates	12% — Part-time
	8% — 1st degree undergraduates
Full-time 1st degree undergraduates	59%

STUDENT POPULATION

Total students 17,260

sublimated in a caring ethos, modern, civilian, and maybe a slip laden with PR. They describe themselves as 'a hands-on student university: we care that our students turn up at lectures.' There is no clock-watching, but they want to find out why a student's interest is dropping away, if it is.

The uni serves up business, engineering, science, and media, art & design – vocational fare, true to its roots that lead us back to 1869, foundation year of Portsmouth & Gosport School of Science & Art. It was 100 years later that the college became Portsmouth Polytechnic, before receiving its Royal Charter as a university in 1992.

CAMPUS

Guildhall campus is the name they give to a collection of sites in the centre of town, which has a European, café-style feel to it, and there are so many students marauding about that it seems not so much town as university precinct. When students go down in the summer they are replaced by as many tourists.

The Milton and Langstone campuses are two and three miles away respectively, but the aim is to rationalise more into the central campus. The

UNIVERSITY/STUDENT PROFILE

University since	**1992**
Situation/style	**Campus**
Student population	**17,260**
First degree undergraduates	**10,260**
- mature	**24%**
- overseas	**7%**
- male/female	**57/43**
- state sector intake	**93%**
- non-traditional student intake	**11%**
- drop-out rate	**7%**
- undergraduate applications	**Down 5%**
*see Introduction for key to tables	

Business School, currently at Milton, will move to purpose-built premises closer to Guildhall in 2003.

STUDENT PROFILE

It is a predominantly male student body. A lot of mature students come here too. They tend to recruit from the south of England. For many, Portsmouth is the local university beyond which they don't look. There is a high state-school intake, and 11% of the population come from non-traditional uni heartlands. Given the unpractised element, their drop-out rate of a mere 7% should hearten applicants – there's something to stay for.

Support for the new uni intake is as good as they claim. 'There's a full-time counselling service,' a student tells me. Why? 'Students find it hard at this…at university, money problems, pressures. People think being at university is easy. It is not. I am the only child of five in my family to have gone to university. It wasn't part of the culture of my family. I have struggled here, had to get jobs. People have this concept of university, students getting drunk all the time, having a good time…I have heard about that, but never experienced it.'

ACADEMIC EXCELLENCE

TEACHING :
(Rated Excellent or 17+ out of 24)

Geography	**Excellent**
Pharmacology	**24**
French, Psychology, Politics, Subjects Allied to Medicine	**23**
Maths, Biosciences, Nursing	**22**
German, Economics, Leisure/Sport	**21**
Sociology, Italian, Civil Eng, Electric & Electron Eng, Building, Land & Property Mgt, Physics, Art & Design	**20**
Russian, Iberian Studies	**18**

RESEARCH:
Top grades 5/5*

Studies/Professions Allied to Medicine, Applied Maths, European Studies, Russian/ Slavonic/East European	**Grade 5**

ACADEMIA

There is a strong work ethic in the courses: students' aspirations are reflected in what they are going to be doing in the workplace. Teaching assessments have been good, and there is an exceptional performance in graduate employment – just look at all the Top 10 positions in our

Employment box (page 376). Alongside a 20 points out of 24 score for the teaching of Electronic & Electrical Engineering, for example, there is a 2nd place for Portsmouth in our Top 10 graduate employment table for the industry. Computing is also strong, as are business and accounting and a series of International Trade and European Studies degrees, all tagged with Euro languages. The School of Languages performed well in the assessments and was deemed world class in the recent research assessments: every student has the opportunity to learn a language at Portsmouth. The School of Pharmacy & Biomedical Sciences is also recommended by both *Academic Excellence* and *Employment* box data. The faculty of Humanities & Social Sciences just won some money with Southampton University to train health care professionals to work together: trainee nurses alongside trainee pharmacists and trainee radiographers, and so on. Health subjects, such as nursing, radiography were also top scoring at the teaching and research assessments.

> *Students' aspirations are reflected in what they are going to be doing in the workplace. Wisely, uni investment is broadening their focus with an £8-million extra-curricular project.*

And there is the expanding School of Sport & Exercise Science, whose graduates of various science and technology degrees are clearly impacting on the industry.

Their Art & Design department, which includes Media Arts (Moving Image, Photography), is finding graduates careers in film. There's a Media Development Centre with broadcast TV facilities and a digital development laboratory.

Architecture and Geography drive the Faculty of Environment, as does the Institute of Maritime Heritage Studies, based in an old boathouse in the naval dockyards area. There is some collaboration with the Navy on the latter. Portsmouth is of course famous for the Mary Rose, which no doubt disposed the uni to let this vein.

One final little gem is the Institute of Criminal Justice Studies, whose work on counter-fraud, Benefits fraud and so on, has brought it links with TV's *Crimewatch*.

STUDENT SCENE

The new Students' Union building, due to open in June, was still a building site when we visited. The investment is some £8 million, a complete student village is planned. Top of the ents menu are their mammoth balls – a new Presentation Ball for Purples (full/half colour awards – sport is big here), various societies' balls, Graduation Ball (Republica played last year) and so on. Regular clubnights are *Pop* (Friday), *Horny* (Saturday). Wednesday is *Final Whistle*, Thursday a theme night, Sunday a quiz night. Recent visitors have been club DJs – Judge Jules, DJ Luck & MC Neat, Orange Tour. There's a big student DJ competition and comedy nights every Monday. Media-wise, students are active with monthly mag *Pugwash*, often in the awards but not last year. There's also a weekly sports paper (*Purple Wednesday*) and a radio station, Pure fm.

SPORT Men's sports teams are consistently high in the national team league (24th this year overall), but Sports Science courses notwithstanding, their rating of facilities is merely 'improving'. The gym was refurbished recently 'for a ridiculous amount of money,' I am told.

WHAT IT'S REALLY LIKE	
UNIVERSITY:	
Social Life	★★★★
Campus scene	**Good mix**
Student Union services	**Good**
Politics	**Student issues, interest low**
Sport	**Strong**
National team position	**24th**
Sport facilities	**Good**
Arts opportunities	**Music excellent, film good, art, drama avg, dance poor**
Student magazine	**Pugwash**
Student sportspaper	**Purple Wednesdays**
Student radio	**PURE FM**
Nightclub	**Lighthouse**
Bars	**Ranch House**
Union ents	**Pop, Horny**
Union clubs/societies	**120+**
Most popular society	**Football**
Smoking policy	**Bars, halls OK**
Parking	**Poor**
TOWN:	
Entertainment	★★★
Scene	**Good: pubs, clubs**
Town/gown relations	**Good**
Risk of violence	**Average**
Cost of living	**Average**
Student concessions	**Excellent**
Survival + 2 nights out	**£60 pw**
Part-time work campus/town	**Excellent + jobshop**

AT A GLANCE

ACADEMIC FILE:

Subjects assessed	**31**
Excellent	**71%**
Average requirements	**200 points**
Students-staff ratio	**22:1**
First/2:1 degree pass rate	**48%**

ACCOMMODATION FILE:

Guarantee to freshers	**55%**
Style	**Halls, flats**
Cost pw (no food/food)	**£44-£82**
Town rent pw	**£47**

Geographical position gives them special potential – sailing (larks and lasers), windsurfing and canoeing. Applications for scholarships in hockey, rugby, swimming, water sports, gymnastics and netball are encouraged.

Town Portsmouth is a huge area of growth, not just for students. 'If you work in London and don't want to live there... Hence the excellent night life, large number of cafés...' Student and singer Genna Hellier was enthusing about the place over a coffee at the **Lighthouse**, the 1,100-capacity SU bar and venue. 'It is part of the reason I came here to be quite honest. It was a really nice summer's day and I saw the cafés lining the streets. It looked beautiful. I love it here. I came here really shy and now I am going into PR! I never did any sport and now I work out every day. This union here provides amazing sporting opportunities. We have over 120 sports clubs and societies.'

Further south of the campus is the new

WHERE GRADUATES END UP

16% Manufacturing*, Key Areas
9% Wholesale/Retail,
9% Finance,
8% Computer,
7% Personnel*,
7% Health/Social Work,
6% Public Admin
Aeronautical Manufacture*, Niche Areas
Chemical/Pharmaceutical,
Architecture, Construction,
Defence, Electron/Electric*,
Film/Video, Sport, Telecom

*indicates Top 10 Graduate Provider

Approximate employed **95%**

development of **Gun Wharf**, reclaimed from the MoD, and the talk of the town – 'Really nice, **Jongleurs**, **Tiger Tiger**, **Bar 38**, **Santa Fé**,' Genna went on, 'all the London-based clubs are here. There is no rivalry between locals and students. It is a very safe place to live, music is especially good here. More locally we have the **Wedgwood Rooms** and **The Pyramid**. There's a place called **Havana** for student bands, and we organise open mic nights at the union and so on. The local theatre is the **Theatre Royal**, nice little theatre in the **Guildhall**, often used for student productions. The uni also built **Wiltshire Studios**, where a lot of student productions are done.'

There's a bountiful supply of clubs, cafés and wine bars in the Guildhall area. Among pubs, the **India Arms** (Great Southsea Street) is the main student bar; pound-a-pint sessions, good tucker and pool. Other student hang-outs, such as the aforementioned Havana Café Bar and the **Frog on the Front**, are within walking distance.

The club scene ranges from cheesy handbag to razor-tuned, techno beats. The Wedgwood Rooms in Albert Road offer a fine selection of dance music and bands, making it one of the premier music venues in the city. With its restaurants, cafés and bizarre shops, Albert Road is fast becoming the Soho of this city. Commercial Road, with its huge shopping mall is perhaps better suited to those drawn in by the consumer tractor beam, while **One Legged Jockey**, which resides in this area of the city, can only be described as the Style HQ of Portsmouth.

PILLOW TALK

The new Margaret Rule Hall has just opened and there's another new hall planned for the White Swan car park site, after which, they boast, they will be in a position pretty much to offer every first year student a room in hall: 3,000 places will be available. If you don't get a place then the uni will sort you out: 'It is our philosophy to care all the way through.'

JOBS

The newly refurbished Nuffield Centre houses the careers centre and it is much used. There is a big emphasis on graduate employment: four areas in our *Employment* box made a national Top 10.

GETTING THERE

☛ By road: A3(M), 2 hours from London.
☛ By rail: London Waterloo, 1:30; Bristol Parkway, 2:15; Birmingham New Street, 3:30; Sheffield, 4:45.
☛ By coach: London, 2:30; Exeter, 6:45.
☛ By air: Southampton Airport.

QUEEN MARGARET UNIVERSITY COLLEGE

Queen Margaret University College
Clerwood Terrace
Edinburgh EH12 8TS

TEL 0131 317 3247
FAX 0131 317 3248
EMAIL admissions@qmuc.ac.uk
WEB www.qmuc.ac.uk

VAG VIEW

Queen Margaret University College began in 1875 as the Edinburgh School of Cookery and was re-named in 1930 as The Edinburgh College of Domestic Science. In 1971, following the introduction of a range of new courses, came the big break and it changed its name again.

CAMPUSES

Today it is located at three sites: the main Corstorphine campus, near Edinburgh Airport but in the grounds of a former stately home; at a campus in one of the most characterful parts of the city of Edinburgh, to the northeast of the centre, just off Leith Walk; and at the **Gateway Theatre** on Leith Walk, once a repertory theatre and more recently the Edinburgh base for Scottish Television.

CORSTORPHINE CAMPUS address above.
LEITH CAMPUS 89 Duke Street, Edinburgh EH6 8HF. Tel 0131 317 3355. Fax 0131 317 3308.
GATEWAY THEATRE 42 Elm Row, Edinburgh EH7 4AH. Tel 0131 317 3900. Fax 0131 317 3092.

ACADEMIA

There are four faculties: Arts, Business & Consumer Affairs, Social Sciences & Health Care, and Health Sciences.

At Corstorphine are the departments of Business & Consumer Studies, Communication & Information Studies, Hospitality & Tourism Management, Management & Social Sciences, Dietetics & Nutrition, Health & Nursing and Speech & Language Sciences.

Leith Campus is home to the departments of Occupational Therapy, Physiotherapy, Podiatry and Radiography.

The Gateway Theatre is naturally the base for Drama. The theatre will also become a major venue for the Edinburgh Festival and a better shop window for QMC would be hard to find. As for teaching strategy, the uni makes its position quite plain – 'People who choose Queen Margaret's mostly do so with a specific career in mind.'

PILLOW TALK

Accommodation at Corstorphine is in three halls of residence, some catered, some self-catered. They have a swimming pool, a gym, squash courts and an all-weather surface for tennis, football, hockey and netball.

SOCIAL SCENE

The Students' Association has a bar and provides ents throughout the week. Two clubnights – *Wild Wednesdays*, *Happy Fridays* – are apparently highly popular. Other highs include Trendy Wendy, Keith & Orville; otherwise it's student DJs, club reps, karaoke, quizzes, films, etc. There is of course all of Edinburgh to get to know. A special bus takes students between the city centre and Corstorphine in the early hours. See city article, page 177.

JOBS

As our *Employment* box shows overleaf, the health provision dominates the spectrum of graduate jobs. It is the highest percentage concentration of health industry employment at any institution of higher education last year. They had the fourth highest, too, in the field of artistic creativity.

GETTING THERE
☛ By road to Corstorphine: M8/J2, A8.
☛ By rail: London King's Cross, 4:30; Birmingham New Street, 5:30. Glasgow Central, 50 mins.
☛ By air: Edinburgh Airport is nearby.
☛ By coach: Glasgow, 1:10; London, 9:10; Birmingham, 8:10; Newcastle, 3:10.

WHERE GRADUATES END UP

50% Health/Social Work*, Key Areas
9% Wholesale/Retail,
8% Finance
Artistic/Literary*, Niche Areas
Library/Archival, Radio/TV

*indicates Top 10 Graduate Provider

Approximate employed **91%**

QUEEN MARY, UNIVERSITY OF LONDON

Queen Mary College
University of London
Mile End Road
London E1 4NS

TEL 020 7882 5511
FAX 020 7975 5588
EMAIL admissions@qmw.ac.uk
WEB www.qmw.ac.uk

Queen Mary College
Students' Union
432 Bancroft Road
London E1 4DH

TEL 020 7975 5390
FAX 020 8981 0802
EMAIL su-genoff@qmw.ac.uk
WEB www.qmwsu.org

VAG VIEW

A constituent college of the federal University of London and the only residential campus-university in central London, QMW arose out of the merger (in 1989) of two colleges: Queen Mary College, founded in 1885 to educate the East End poor and based at the People's Palace, now the uni's base in Mile End Road, and Westfield College, also a 19th-century institution, and a pioneer in higher education for women (men were not admitted until 1964).

A later, medical foundation arises out of a merger in 1995 between the Royal London School of Medicine & Dentistry and St Bartholomew's Hospital Medical School, and their transformation into QMW's medical school. Medical students begin their study at the People's Palace, but undergo their clinical training at the Royal London in Whitechapel and Barts in West Smithfield.

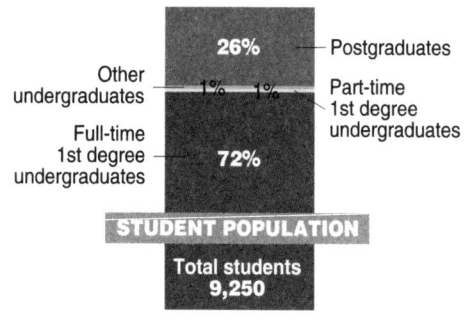

26% — Postgraduates
Other undergraduates 1% — 1% — Part-time 1st degree undergraduates
Full-time 1st degree undergraduates — 72%

STUDENT POPULATION

Total students
9,250

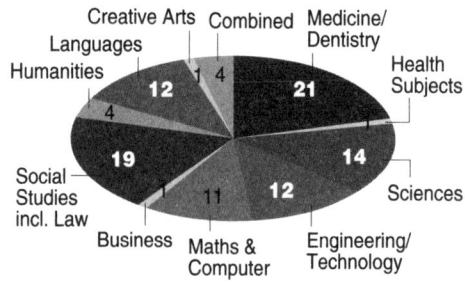

SUBJECT AREAS (%)

Creative Arts — Combined — Medicine/Dentistry
Languages
Humanities — 12 — 1 — 4 — 21 — Health Subjects
4
19 — 14 — Sciences
Social Studies incl. Law — 11 — 12
Business — Maths & Computer — Engineering/Technology

STUDENT PROFILE

'Integration between medical students and the rest of the college leaves a lot to be desired,' writes Kieran Alger, 'the two groups preferring to indulge in separate activities, the medical students enjoying their own bar, for example, and playing for separate sports teams while the main body of students mixes well, regardless of subject.'

As at other medical schools, the medical students sharply increase the public school quota and give QMW a state/public school ratio akin to Reading's or Southampton's, Warwick's or York's. The Mile End Road student population is another story. 'Queen Mary proper is a cultural melting pot,' agrees Kieran – 'a fascinating blend of overseas students, a large ethnic contingent and UK residents,' and a 28% draw last year from the lower socio-economic groups IIIM, IV and V. There are also larger than average local and mature populations, which serve to distinguish the clientele from what Kieran describes as 'the stereotypical beer and beans, lazy student'.

CAMPUS

'QMW, with its modern architecture, is one of the few universities to combine the class of the well established with the youth, vigour and dynamism of an ex-polytechnic,' continues Kieran. 'In many ways this college is the orange Kit-Kat of academia – all the chocolatey, biscuity re-assurance of our nation's biggest selling snack, but with a little twist of fruity diversity.

'Set in the heart of the multi-cultural hotch-potch which forms the East End, the student population reflects its intriguing surroundings. The East End, home of imports, the cloth trade, Phil, Grant and the Kray twins, has an illustrious history of intermingling races. From jellied eels at Spitalfield's Market to chicken balti in one of Brick Lane's curry houses, this area caters for a huge range of tastes. Just now it is also asserting its own brand of sophistication in the stunning and ever-encroaching Docklands development. The combination of Canary Wharf Tower dominating on one side and the trendification of the E1, E2, and E3 postal areas is causing a surge in social and cultural activity. The East End, with its fashionable gangster land history and eerie Jack the Ripper connections, is becoming the place London's affluent young professionals want to live. In Bethnal Green, comedian Lee Hurst has opened a comedy club. Neighbouring areas, such as Bow and Aldgate, are being inundated with new eateries, coffee houses, galleries and nightclubs.'

Clinical students head for Bart's on the Smithfield site, a square deep in the heart of the City, close to the Barbican. It is the oldest member of the college. The hospital was founded in 1123 by a jester turned monk by name of Rahere. Halls of residence cluster around it. On-site is a clinical library, research and computer facilities, a theatre, sports facilities, and a bar. The Royal London, at Whitechapel in the East End, is one of the busiest and largest hospitals in the capital. There is a £33.5-million plan to re-house Barts and the London Medical School.

ACADEMIA

Languages are to the fore throughout QMW's curriculum, there's even a

UNIVERSITY/STUDENT PROFILE	
School of London Uni since	**1915**
Situation/style	**Campus**
Student population	**9,250**
Full-time undergraduates	**6,670**
- mature	**16%**
- overseas	**17%**
- male/female	**51/49**
- state sector intake	**79%**
- non-traditional student intake	**10%**
- drop-out rate	**11%**
- undergraduate applications	**Down 3%**
*see Introduction for key to tables	

> *The college embraces two very different student bodies. There is some of the best of academia and some of the most colourful social life; if you're lucky, you'll partake of both at QMC.*

ACADEMIC EXCELLENCE

TEACHING:
(Rated Excellent or 17+ out of 24)

English, Geography	**Excellent**
Dentistry	**24**
Politics, Modern Languages	**23**
Biosciences, Subjects Allied to Medicine	**22**
Medicine, Electric/Electron Eng, Maths, Physics, Drama	**21**
Materials Technology	**20**
General Engineering	**19**

RESEARCH:
Top grades 5/5*

Law, Linguistics, Iberian/LatinAmerican	**Grade 5***
Clinical Dentistry, Physics, Pure Maths, Statistics, Mechanical/Aeronautical/ Manufacturing Eng, Metallurgy, Geography, Law, English, French, German/Dutch/ Scandinavian, Russian/ Slavonic & E. European Languages., History	**Grade 5**

special EFL Unit for the large overseas contingent.

The Department of Dentistry scored full marks in the assessments (Medicine, 21) and Modern Languages came in at 23, along with Politics. The 'Subjects Allied to Medicine' mentioned in the *Academic Excellence* box (page 379) refer in fact to a postgraduate diploma in Occupational Therapy. In the research assessments, the college came in at 48th place, with Law, Linguistics and Latin American the three world-class Grade 5* subjects.

The Engineering departments are now offering undergrad and postgrad courses in Medical Engineering and Internet Computing.

SOCIAL SCENE

The medics have their own union – SoMaD Students' Association. There are two bars: the **Clubs Union Bar** at the Royal London Hospital (Whitechapel), and **Bart's Bar**, close to Bart's Hospital in Charterhouse Square (where there is also a swimming pool, squash, tennis and badminton courts). There's also a glass-fronted bistro bar, **BarMed**, in the Medical Science building looking out on to Library Square. Regular high jinks are the Association Dinner, the Christmas

AT A GLANCE	
ACADEMIC FILE:	
Subjects assessed	**21**
Excellent	**71%**
Average A level requirements	**19 points**
Students-staff ratio	**11:1**
First/2:1 degree pass rate	**57%**
ACCOMMODATION FILE:	
Guarantee to freshers	**90%**
Style	**Halls, houses, flats**
Approx price range pw	**£67-£70**
City rent pw	**£70**

Show, Burn's Night and the sporting cup finals. There's a flourishing drama society – plays, a Christmas Show, a production for the Edinburgh Fringe – a Gilbert & Sulivan Society, a choir and orchestra, and of course Rag. Otherwise they bounce around at *Toga Nights*, *Star Wars Night*, *Austin Powers Night*, and *Mummies and Daddies Night*. I guess *Doctors & Nurses Night* is simply 'too day-time' to compete.

In Mile End Road, the more dissipated wind up rather than down at 'the best student nightclub in London' (their boast) at **Club e1**. Complete with 12K JBL sound system and state of the art computer-controlled lighting rig it is open till 2 am from Thursday through Saturday. Now fully completed, refurbished and re-designed, **e1** has a 750-capacity, top sound and lighting systems. There's dance music on Thursdays and Fridays and the ever popular *Time Out*-supported *Time Tunnel* ('60s to '90s) on Saturdays and various nights of hip-hop, swing, R&B and indie. A regular Saturday pop ('70s to the present day) extravaganza – 9 pm-2 am – is ROAR.

To catch their breath, students traditionally staggered to **The Drapers Arms** for a game of Daytona pool and table footie, a tune from the CD jukebox and a few pints of course. But a huge redevelopment at the union has increased e1 capacity from 450 to 800 and seen a refurbishment of Drapers Arms, not to the taste of all: 'The new look club has a distinctly industrial feel with open ceiling and red brick wall effects,' reports Kieran. 'The image conversion from ailing cheesiness to cutting-edge trendiness many die-hards refuse to come round to.'

There's a clubs and societies resource centre. No stranger to student media awards, the student newspaper, *CUB*, founded in 1947, is one of the oldest student papers in London.

WHAT IT'S REALLY LIKE	
UNIVERSITY:	
Social Life	★★★★
Campus scene	**Colourful, lively**
Student Union services	**Average**
Politics	**NUS issues**
Sport	**18 clubs**
National team position	**68th**
Sport facilities	**Average**
Arts opportunities	**Drama excellent**
Student newspaper	**Cub**
Nightclub	**Club e1**
Bars	**The Drapers Arms, 0181**
Union ents	**Time Tunnel, St Trinian's, Gagging For It**
Union clubs/societies	**64**
Smoking policy	**Zonal**
Parking	**Poor**
CITY:	
Entertainment	★★★★★
Scene	**Local treats; London choices**
Town/gown relations	**Average**
Risk of violence	**Average**
Cost of living	**High**
Student concessions	**Good**
Survival + 2 nights out	**£70 pw**
Part-time work campus/town	**Excellent**

SPORT Sports fields have been consolidated from small scattered sites into one major site at Chislehurst. 'Sports and society activities are abundant,' Kieran writes, 'from the bemusing tussles of the War Soc, through rock climbing, netball and fencing, to the somewhat more comfortable pastimes of rowing and rugby. The football club is of a particularly high standard, as is the women's football team. The healthy rivalry of collegiate London Uni delivers many an opportunity for battle.' Performance nationally through is not so successful, however. QMC teams came 68th last year.

PILLOW TALK
Most first years lodge in part-catered halls at South Woodford, a full thirty minutes east on the Central line. **Club 0181** provides a bar there. Newer canal-side self-catering residences closer to home in Mile End are mainly for third years, postgrads etc., but there are some places for freshers, especially if mature. There's talk of a new union café or store nearby, where Mile End Park is being given the once over with cash from a Millennium fund.

JOBS
Obviously the health industry dominates the graduate employment graph, but our *Employment* box shows that the uni appeals on a number of interesting areas for the Mile End crew.

WHERE GRADUATES END UP	
35% Health (Medicine, Dentistry)*,	Key Areas
7% Finance,	
6% Wholesale/Retail,	
6% Computer,	
6% Public Admin,	
5% Manufacturing,	
5% Personnel	
Accountancy, Advertising,	Niche Area
Business/Management,	
Defence, Legal,	
Library/Archival, Market	
Research, Telecom,	
Eng/Industrial Design	

*indicates Top 10 Graduate Provider

Approximate employed **96%**

GETTING THERE
☛ By Underground: QMW, Stepney Green (District, Hammersmith & City) or Mile End (+ Central line). The Royal London, Whitechapel tube (East London, District, Hammersmith & City lines); nearest tube to Bart's is Barbican. St Paul's (Central).

THE QUEEN'S UNIVERSITY OF BELFAST

The Queen's University of Belfast
University Road
Belfast BT7 1NN

TEL 028 9033 5081
FAX 028 9024 7895
EMAIL admissions@qub.ac.uk
WEB www.qub.ac.uk

Queen's University Students' Union
University Road
Belfast BT7 1PE

TEL 028 9032 4803
FAX 028 9023 6900
EMAIL info@qubsu.org
WEB www.qubsu.org

VAG VIEW

*N*orthern Ireland's leading educational institution has its origins in the

UNIVERSITY/STUDENT PROFILE	
University since	**1908**
Situation/style	**Civic**
Student population	**22,130**
Full-time undergraduates	**10,180**
- mature	**11%**
overseas	**8%**
- male/female	**49/51**
- state sector intake	**100%**
- non-traditional student intake	**9%**
- drop-out rate	**7%**
- undergraduate applications	**Down 0.8%**
*see Introduction for key to tables	

Queen's College, Belfast, founded in 1845. There is a traditional Oxbridge-style reputation, with good lines into the professions, medicine, dentistry, the City and law...and no small political awareness.

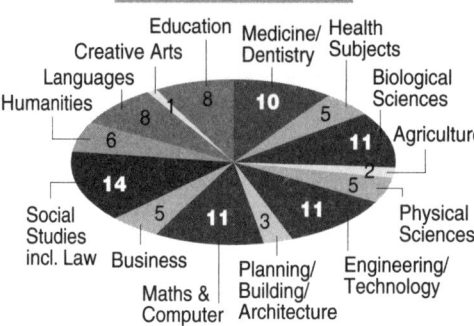

SUBJECT AREAS (%)

Education, Medicine/Dentistry, Health Subjects, Creative Arts, Languages, Humanities, Biological Sciences, Agriculture, Physical Sciences, Engineering/Technology, Planning/Building/Architecture, Maths & Computer, Business, Social Studies incl. Law

TEACHING:
(Rated Excellent or 17+ out of 24)

Applied Social Work, History, Law, English, Geology, Music.	**Excellent**
Elec & Electron Engineering, Dentistry, Psychology	**24**
Management , Archaeology, Education, Physics, Politics, Classics	**23**
Civil Eng, Enviro Planning, Medicine, Anatomy, Maths, Nursing, Theology	**22**
Iberian Studies; Chemical Engineering; Mechanical, Aeronautical & Manufacturing Engineering, Food Sci, Agric, Podiatry, Biosciences	**21**
French	**20**
Sociology, Modern Languages (German, Italian, Russian & E. Euro languages).	**19**

RESEARCH:
Top grades 5/5*

Mechanical/Aeronautical/ Manufacturing Engineering.	**Grade 5***
Community-based Clinical Subjects, Physics, Civil Eng, Electrica & Electronic Eng , Law, Anthropology, Politics, Sociology, European Studies, Irish Studies, Celtic Studies, English, Archaeology, History, Music	**Grade 5**

CAMPUS

Set a few kilometres from the city centre in a so-called 'safe' area of Belfast, the campus encompasses the Botanic Gardens and Ulster Museum. Areas around Queen's University, Stranmillis and Botanic Avenue are now busier than ever and spilling over into the once isolated city centre.

ACADEMIA

Queen's is sound academically, with good teaching assessment results, though not top, top flight, Oxbridge-style. Big scoring are Electrical & Electronic Engineering, Dentistry and Psychology (all full marks); Archaeology, Classics, Education, Physics and Politics (23 points out of 24); Medicine, a core subject, scored 22. In the recent research exercise they came 45th, sandwiched between Strathclyde and Kent.

'In some subjects – particularly medicine and engineering – Queen's has a world class reputation,' writes Cormac Bakewell, 'and its School of English can boast the Nobel Prize winning poet, Seamus Heaney, as a former student.'

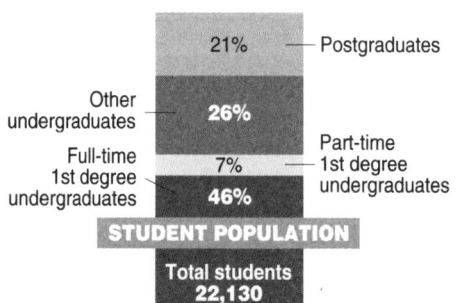

- 21% — Postgraduates
- Other undergraduates — **26%**
- Full-time 1st degree undergraduates — **46%**
- Part-time 1st degree undergraduates — **7%**

STUDENT POPULATION

Total students 22,130

SOCIAL SCENE

There are three SU pleasure zones – the **Speakeasy Bar**, the **Bunatee,** and **Mandela Hall** (capacity: 1,000) which has just enjoyed a £500,000 facelift. Altogether the union building can take 2,500 for entertainments. Regular ents include comedy and quiz nights, live bands, theme nights, etc. The big club night is *Shine*, hugely popular with townies and students alike. It's every Friday and some Saturdays. Names like Carl Cox, David Holmes and Andy Weatherall are residents or regular visitors. Also Friday or Saturday is *Hybrid* and there are Monday and Thursday discos.

Naturally students are highly politicised, with a strong focus on Northern Ireland politics, but also on student issues. A third year Queen's student of politics and prominent member of the Socialist Worker group was reported by the student newspaper, *Gown,* to have been suspended by the university following his involvement in the occupation of the administration building and the United for Free Education campaign. The union is generally characterised as nationalist and left of centre.

Queen's clubs and societies are legion, but 'many of the non-sporting societies are not as active as they once were' and 'most of the Irish students at Queen's clear off home at the weekend to get their washing done and to raid the family fridge.'

> *Northern Ireland's leading educational institution has good lines into the professions, medicine, dentistry, the City and law, and naturally enough there's no small political awareness on campus.*

SPORT They have two swimming pools (diving, subaqua, water polo and canoeing facilities), conditioning rooms, squash courts, badminton, basketball, tennis courts, volleyball, handball, hockey, netball courts, two judo squares, cricket nets, a purpose-built mountain wall and facilities for gymnastics, athletics, fencing, golf, karate, bowls, yoga and archery, seventeen pitches for rugby, soccer, gaelic, hockey, hurling, camogie

and cricket, netball and tennis courts, a floodlit training area and an athletics arena where the Mary Peters Track is situated. Opportunities for golf at **Malone Golf Club** (three miles away), sailing at Belfast Lough and Lough Neagh, waterskiing at Craigavon, gliding and parachuting at Magilligan, mountaineering in the Mourne mountains, caving in Fermanagh and rowing on the nearby River Lagan. Fifteen sports bursaries are available, sponsored by Guinness.

TOWN 'Club-wise in the city,' writes Colette Norwood, 'there's funk, soul and jazz at **The Duke of York**, Commercial Court every Friday. **The Front Page** on Saturdays boasts an impressive hip hop menu – MoWax artists regularly pack out the venue on Donegall Street. A couple of the best underground venues are **The Brunswick Club** and **The Soul & Jazz Café** on Brunswick Street. If you're short of cash seek out **Giros** off Donegall Street – it's a BYO

WHAT IT'S REALLY LIKE	
UNIVERSITY:	
Social Life	★★★
Campus scene	**Traditional, Oxbridge-style, with political punch**
Student Union services	**Average**
Politics	**Preoccupied, Northern Ireland**
Sport	**Locally competitive**
National team position	**116th**
Sport facilities	**Good**
Arts opportunities	**Strong**
Student newspaper	**The Gown**
Student newsletter	**Banter**
Union ents	**Nightly**
Live venue capacity	**1,000**
Union clubs/societies	**100**
Smoking policy	**Zonal**
Parking	**Adequate**
CITY:	
Entertainment	★★★
City scene	**Clubs, pubs, arts**
Town/gown relations	**Generally OK**
Risk of violence	**Generally OK**
Cost of living	**Average +**
Student concessions	**Adequate**
Survival + 2 nights out	**£60 pw**
Part-time work campus/town	**Good**

AT A GLANCE	
ACADEMIC FILE:	
Subjects assessed	**41**
Excellent	**83%**
Average requirements	**280 points**
Subjects assessed	**16:1**
First/2:1 degree pass rate	**59%**
ACCOMMODATION FILE:	
Guarantee to freshers	**88%**
Style	**Halls**
Approx price range pw	**£45-£62**
City rent pw	**£30-£38**

venue with hip hop, drum 'n' bass & techno sets from the *Bedlam* DJs and visitors that include Glasgow's *Test* DJs and the *Liberators* from London. Bigger venues like Queen's and Uni Ulster's Art College are also hugely popular. Always bring ID.'

The university area contains a number of theatres, such as the **Lyric**, galleries, the aforesaid museum and an excellent university-run arthouse cinema, **Queen's Film Theatre**. Down at the docks, writes Colette, '**The Waterfront Hall** has a busy itinerary with something for everyone. More traditional music shows, ballets and classic plays can be seen at the splendid **Grand Opera House**.

The Lyric, **The Arts Theatre** and **The Old Museum Arts Centre** all offer something a little more at the cutting edge. Tuesday is comedy night at **The Empire Music Hall** on Botanic Avenue.'

Every November the Belfast Festival comes to Queen's, an arts festival with an international reputation, only exceeded in size by Edinburgh's.

PILLOW TALK

'The university residences vary from big brutal '60s tower blocks in Queen's Elms to recently refurbished Victorian townhouses. If you have the option,' Cormac advises, 'go for the latter, although if you still want to come home to a cooked meal you'll have to put up with orange curtains and brown carpets in the Elms. Student accommodation is almost all within a half-mile of campus.'

JOBS

Nearly a quarter of graduates go into the health industry, a large number also into finance and accounting. Some interesting niche areas: the aeronautical industry is the sixth highest concentration of provision, telecommunications the fourth highest. Law is eventually an important professional avenue, too, with degrees in common and civil law with French or Spanish and through the eye of accounting or politics.

WHERE GRADUATES END UP	
24% Health (Med, Dent),	Key Areas
11% Manufacturing,	
9% Wholesale/Retail,	
7% Finance,	
6% Education,	
6% Public Admin,	
5% Computer	
Accountancy,	Niche Areas
Agric/Forestry,	
Architecture,	
Construction,	
Chemical/Pharmaceutical,	
Aeronautical Manufacture*,	
Electron/Electric, Telecom*,	
Eng/Industrial Design	

*indicates Top 10 Graduate Provider

Approximate employed **96%**

GETTING THERE

☛ An hour by air from London, with at least 24 flights a day each way.

RAVENSBOURNE COLLEGE OF DESIGN & COMMUNICATION

Ravensbourne College
Walden Road
Chislehurst
Kent BR7 5SN

TEL 020 8289 4900
FAX 020 8325 8320
EMAIL info@rave.ac.uk
WEB www.ravensbourne.ac.uk

VAG VIEW

Ravensbourne's two-year degree courses in Professional Broadcasting and Communication & Technology are industry standard.

There are three faculties: Broadcasting, Design (various degrees in fashion, product, interior, furniture or visual information design), and Digital Futures – where design and broadcasting meet

GETTING THERE

☛ By road: Elmstead Lane off the A208.
☛ By rail to Elmstead Road: London Bridge, 17 mins.

COLLEGE PROFILE	
Founded	**1962**
Status	**HE College**
Degree awarding university	**Sussex**
Student population	**900**
Degree undergraduate	**600**
ACCOMMODATION:	
Availability to freshers	**30%**
Style	**Houses**
Cost pw (no food)	**£67**
Town rent pw	**£40-£60**

DEGREE SUBJECTS:
Broadcasting, Communications & Technology, Art & Design

UNIVERSITY OF READING

The University of Reading
Whiteknights
Reading RG6 6AH

TEL 0118 931 8618/9
FAX 0118 931 8924
EMAIL schools.liaison@rdg.ac.uk
WEB www.reading.ac.uk

Reading University Students' Union
PO Box 230
Reading RG6 2AZ

TEL 0118 986 0222
FAX 0118 975 0337
EMAIL (see website)
WEB www.rusu.co.uk

VAG VIEW

*R*eading's areas of academic strength
cover a wider spectrum than many
imagine – cybernetics, classics,
environmental sciences, agriculture,
meteorology, film & theatre. New BAs this
year include Film, Theatre & TV Studies,
English & TV Studies. Reading's student
body is far from being limited to the
marauding agrics of popular legend. For the
last few years, the scene here has been
changing for the better and becoming more
student-focused. Suddenly there's a dedicated
special needs officer available. Suddenly they
lavish £500,000 on the union pleasure dome.

So we should not be surprised to hear
from students that campus is no longer
deserted at weekends by students attracted to
brighter lights in nearby London.

Reading, we are told, is now 24/7.

VIEW FROM THE GROUND
by Laura Cattell

The main leafy Whiteknights campus is where
most first years are accommodated, though some
are housed in halls nearby or on the old London
Road site or a mile away on Bulmershe Campus.

Whiteknights features the beautiful Whiteknights lake and is just a fifteen-minute bus ride
from town. It has to be one of the most picturesque
campuses in England, and is far enough from
Reading to be a peaceful work environment,
without being isolated. There are at least four
different buses you can catch into the centre, and
new 'Night-track' buses now run every night of the
week until 3 am.

STUDENT PROFILE

There's no denying the middle-class, white, home
counties feel at Reading, and the 'agrics' and
'rugger-buggers' with their rugby shirt collars

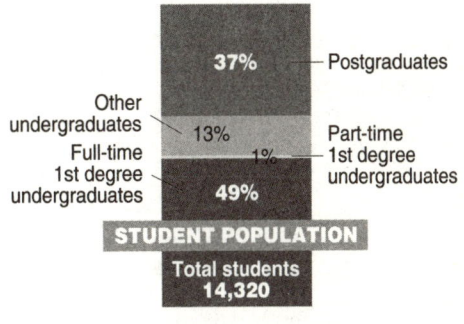

STUDENT POPULATION
Total students
14,320

- 37% — Postgraduates
- Other undergraduates 13%
- Full-time 1st degree undergraduates 49%
- Part-time 1st degree undergraduates 1%

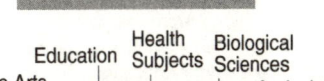

SUBJECT AREAS (%)

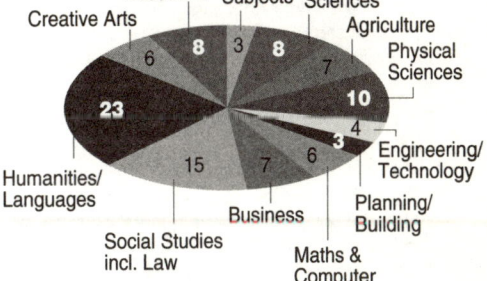

- Creative Arts 6
- Education 8
- Health Subjects 3
- Biological Sciences 8
- Agriculture 7
- Physical Sciences 10
- Engineering/Technology 4
- Planning/Building 3
- Maths & Computer 6
- Business 7
- Social Studies incl. Law 15
- Humanities/Languages 23

UNIVERSITY/STUDENT PROFILE	
University since	**1926**
Situation/style	**Campus**
Student population	**14,320**
Full-time undergraduates	**6,920**
- mature	**37%**
- overseas	**6%**
- male/female	**45/55**
- state sector intake	**78%**
- non-traditional student intake	**8%**
- drop-out rate	**8%**
- undergraduate applications	**Down 0.4%**
see Introduction for key to tables	

ACADEMIC EXCELLENCE

TEACHING:
(Rated Excellent or 17+ out of 24)

Geography, Mechanical Engineering, Environmental Sciences, Geology.	**Excellent**
Drama, Dance & Cinematics, Physics, Philosophy, Nursing, Psychology	**24**
History of Art, Typography, Archaeology	**23**
Sociology, Land & Property Mgt, Town/Country Planning, Food Science, Maths, Politics, Classics	**22**
Economcs, French, Building, Forestry & Agric Sciences, Anatomy, American Studies, Business, Biosciences, Elec/Electron Eng.	**21**
Italian, German	**20**
Linguistics, Art & Design	**19**

RESEARCH:
Top grades 5/5*

Psychology, Environmental Sciences, English, Italian, Archaeology	**Grade 5***
Agriculture, Plant Sciences, Food Science, Applied Maths, Electrical and Electronic Eng, Built Environment, Town/Country Planning, Law, Politics, Business, French, Philosophy, Typography, Drama/Dance/Performing Arts	**Grade 5**

of living is approaching that of London, so if you want a wider economic spectrum of students, why not give Reading a special loan rating?

ACADEMIA

Reading's reputation may be for agriculture, land management, cybernetics, food and soil sciences, but there's a huge range of arts, humanities, education, languages, and social studies courses. Sadly the balance between arts and science is still not even, however, the sparkling, brand new exterior of the ISMA building (Investment Banking, International Security, and Finance) and the hi-tech Agri Department making a stark contrast with the shabby Faculty of Letters and Social Sciences building.

Vice-Chancellor Roger Williams is not joking when he says, 'We do ask that you come motivated and committed.' You are expected to find your own way, it's a case of 'sink or swim'. However, every student is assigned a personal tutor, which works well if you meet with him/her when you're meant to and don't miss too many lectures.

The abolition of the Part 1 scheme, where students studied three subjects in the first year, is definitely a good thing, and the feeling is that all the courses are improving by becoming more modular. The first year is relatively relaxed until exams (Part 1). Departments take these results very seriously, though the integration of continual assessment will ease the stress.

Library and computer resources are superb.

AT A GLANCE

ACADEMIC FILE:

Subjects assessed	**41**
Excellent	**81%**
Average requirements	**240 points**
Students-staff ratio	**13:1**
First/2:1 degree pass rate	**62%**

ACCOMMODATION FILE:

Guarantee to freshers	**95%**
Style	**Halls, flats**
Catered	**75%**
En-suite	**29%**
Price range pw	**£51.20-£117.80**
City rent pw	**£50-£80**

turned up are never far away. But they are not in the majority. In fact, over 20% of students are from outside the UK altogether, from 131 different countries at the last count, many on Erasmus exchanges. These and a high percentage of mature and postgraduate students make for an almost cosmopolitan feel. I say 'almost' because of the deliberate segregation of different nationalities. Greeks are accommodated with Greeks, most Japanese students are placed together in Sibly or Mansfield Hall, and many others are on the Bulmershe campus. It is, therefore, hard to get a full sense of the Reading community.

Along with others, the university was targeted in the Government's access scheme to broaden the social status of its undergraduate base, and is beginning to make this effort. The introduction of more self-catering, and therefore more affordable, halls would help, but I believe it will take more than a government initiative to have a serious effect. Reading is not a student town. Housing/cost

There's 24-hour computer access and the library is open till around 10 pm and at weekends till 5 pm. The demand for essay books is served by a short-loan system. Popular texts are on 4hr/7day loan, and hefty fines are levied to ensure prompt return. As elsewhere, Internet access is free, and there are free IT courses or drop-in-&-learn sessions twice a week for inexperienced users.

SOCIAL SCENE

If you get a place in halls, you'll have no problem meeting lots of people. Freshers Week activities vary from hall to hall (a lot of pub crawls & toga parties), but my best memories are definitely of the Union Ball and the live LTJ Bukem gig till 4 am.

> *You may discover some top combinations in Reading's Faculty of Letters & Social Sciences and in the uni's well-known science base, but once in, self-motivation is key: you'll be expected to find your own way.*

Everyone goes to the union in the first week, and as a fresher you'll probably find the uni nightlife enough.

Just opened is the grand extension of the union. With three bars, two dance floors, and a balcony area, it's a fine addition to what is already the well-equipped offering of **Mojos**, **Café Mondial**, **Nelsons**, and the **Athletics Pavilion**. To this can now be added a brand new nightclub – **360**. There's also the refurbished union bar, **Breeze**, at Bulmershe campus. The cheapest place on campus to eat is the **Cedar Room** – £1.99 for a fry-up , or they do some healthier alternatives.

Wednesday is *Extra Time* (cheesy music-filled night, with regular PAs from chart acts), Saturday is *Candy Club*, often with guest DJs and PAs – they tend to be the big nights (£3 entry though). Thursday's *Comedy Club* has brought some top class acts, such as Junior Simpson (£3 entry, good compared to the comedy club in town – £7!). There's also *Rocket Live* on Tuesday (indie night, DJs or live bands) and new in 2002, *Urbanvibes* on Thursday when no comedy. Recent live acts include Travis, Muse, Faithless, Shed Seven, Pitchshifter, Mercury Rev. DJs include Stanton Warriors, Jon Carter, Timmi Magic (Dreem Teem), James Lavelle, Lisa Pin-Up.

Thanks to a lively music department there are plenty of choir recitals or concerts on. RUMS (Reading University Music Society) has a Choral Society, Gospel Choir and the relaxed University Singers. There is also a fantastic orchestra, concert band, and jazz band. The town is home to the famous Reading Rock Festival, of course, and the WOMAD world music festival, which means there's always a live band playing on campus.

Reading University Drama Society (RUDS) produces high quality plays and musicals, including recently *Macbeth*, *The Crucible*, and *Guys and Dolls*. Anyone is welcome to attend auditions, although a lot of talent comes from the renowned Drama and Performance studies courses at Bulmershe.

For budding journalists, DJs, broadcasters there's the award winning student newspaper, *The Spark,* and the radio station, Junction 11. Last year *Spark* managed to uncover secret information about the accommodation crisis – [200 rooms earmarked for development had to be rushed back into service to cope with the overflow of freshers] – very embarrassing for the vice-chancellor, but highly informative for student readers!

SPORT is an integral part of life. The Wolfenden sports centre offers just about any sport you want to try. An induction at the gym costs £4; £1.75 every time you use it. Uni team standards are very

WHAT IT'S REALLY LIKE	
UNIVERSITY:	
Social Life	★★★★
Campus scene	**Middle class, southern, sporty.**
Student Union services	**Average**
Politics	**Student issues**
Sport	**50 clubs**
National team position	**26th**
Sport facilities	**Good**
Arts opportunities	**Excellent drama, music, film, art; dance good**
Student newspaper	**Spark**
Student radio	**Junction 11**
Nightclub	**360**
Bars	**Mojo's, Café Mondial, Breeze**
Union ents	**Rocket Live, Extra Time, Urbanvibes, Candy Club**
Union clubs/societies	**100**
Most popular society	**Drama**
Smoking policy	**Bars OK**
Parking	**Adequate**
TOWN:	
Entertainment	★★★
Scene	**Pubs, clubs**
Town/gown relations	**Average**
Risk of violence	**Average**
Cost of living	**High**
Student concessions	**Good**
Survival + 2 nights out	**£60 pw**
Part-time work campus/town	**Good**

high, women's netball and hockey teams being particularly tough to get into if you haven't played at county level. However, there's always the Intramural (halls) programme in which anyone can play. To join a club you have to buy a Sports Federation card for £7.50 and then pay for match fees, team outfits etc.

TOWN Up until a few years ago students cleared out of Reading at the weekends to go to London, but there's no need for that anymore. The proximity is enviable (35 mins to Paddington), but Reading has enough on offer to satisfy most. The new **Oracle** shopping complex (tons of bars, clubs and restaurants) by the river have brought a lot of life to the town. **Yellow River Café** is a must or **Mr Ben's** Thai restaurant on the river. The **Hexagon**, **Rising Sun**, **21 South St**. 'Arts Centre' conglomerate has every kind of act available from The Nutcracker to Jools Holland. An excellent, but pricey club nightlife is also on offer, but check out **The Jazz Club** or **The Matrix** – most weeks they have the best special nights and live music. **Utopia** or **RG1s** provide the cattle markets (Thursdays, £1 a bottle), but if you want a chilled-out atmosphere, make for **Global Café** near the Matrix .

There are four cinemas: the **Showcase** or **Warner Brothers** for all blockbusters or the university's **Film Theatre** for interesting arthouse pictures. **Buzz Video** on Wokingham Road is *the* place to rent videos for lazy hangover days. Then there's the Museum and art exhibitions housed in the Town Hall.

PILLOW TALK

Halls are mainly fully catered with the exception of Sherfield, Bulmershe, and the self-catered blocks reserved for finalists. If you want to make any lectures in your first year, apply for a hall on campus. The best has to be Whiteknights, but equally fun and popular halls are: Wantage, an Oxbridge-style building just off campus, but very close, St Patricks, and, for friendliness (not luxuriousness!), Bridges.

If you're studying Education or Film & Drama you will most likely be placed in Bulmershe halls, where there's a closer, friendlier, if quieter, atmosphere. The bonus is that they are really modern.

Last year's accommodation crisis meant that hundreds of freshers found themselves in B&B or private accommodation for the first few weeks. A huge number of applicants got through on Clearing, and there just wasn't enough hall accommodation for everyone. If Reading is your first choice and you confirm your hall application by June, then you are guaranteed a place, but otherwise, who knows, you could find yourself in Reading for house-hunting day, just before term starts. Not ideal.

It's quite a struggle to find a decent private house near the uni that costs much less than £60 a week. The best are found by word of mouth, or occasionally through the uni accommodation services. Those around Wokingham Road, Palmer Park, and Cemetery Junction are the best bet. Steer clear of the London Road/Oxford Road area.

JOBS

Top graduate employers regularly do presentations around campus. Many courses offer work placements within the degree structure, and career modules are compulsory for every degree. The Community Service Volunteer Scheme (CSV) is very active, a great addition to your CV and highly rewarding. Within the IWLP (Institution-wide Language Programme) is the option to take free language classes in French, German, Italian, Japanese, and even Norwegian!

WHERE GRADUATES END UP	
14% Education,	Key Areas
12% Manufacturing,	
9% Finance,	
8% Wholesale/Retail,	
7% Health/Social Work,	
6% Computer	
Accountancy,	Niche Areas
Business/Management,	
Agric/Forestry*, Defence,	
Film/Video, Library/	
Archival*, Market	
Research, Publishing*,	
Radio/TV, Telecom,	
Property*	

*indicates Top 10 Graduate Provider

Approximate employed **96%**

GETTING THERE

☞ By road: M4/J11, A33. An express bus service to London leaves from outside the university.

☞ By rail: London Paddington, 0:30; Birmingham, 2:15; Oxford, 0:40; Bristol Parkway, 1:00.

☞ By air: Heathrow and Gatwick are served by bus and train.

☞ By coach: London, 1:20; Brighton, 3:45; Exeter, 3-5:00; Leicester, 5:00.

READING COLLEGE AND SCHOOL OF ARTS & DESIGN

Reading College and School of
Arts & Design
Crescent Road
Reading
Berkshire RG1 5RQ

TEL 0800 371 434
FAX 0118 967 5344
EMAIL enquiries@reading-college.ac.uk
WEB www.reading.college.ac.uk

VAG VIEW

The special deals here are HNDs which convert with an extra year into degrees. There are computing and all kinds of engineering courses, in-house and distance learning business courses, an Art & Design route that features Fine Art, Graphic Design, Photography, 3D Design, etc. And now there's also The Digital Academy, a joint venture inspired by the college's proximity to Berkshire's Silicon Valley and good relations with a series of blue-chip industrial/commercial partners.

GETTING THERE

☛ By road: M4 at J10/11.
☛ By coach: London, 1:20; Brighton, 3:45; Exeter, 3-5:00.
☛ By rail: Paddington, 30 mins; Oxford, 40 mins.

COLLEGE PROFILE

Founded	**1997**
Status	**F/HE College**
Degree awarding universities	**Oxford Brookes, Lincoln, Thames Valley**
Student population	**14,046**
Degree undergraduates	**213**
ACCOMMODATION	
Availability to freshers	**60%**
Halls (no food)	**£65**
City rent pw	**£50-£80**

DEGREE SUBJECT AREAS:
Engineering, computing, multimedia systems & design, business, fine art, fashion & textiles, design, photography

---

REGENT'S COLLEGE

Regent's College
Regent's Park
London NW1 4NS

TEL 020 7487 7654
FAX 020 7487 7425
EMAIL RBSK@regents.ac.uk
WEB www.RBSLondon.ac.uk

VAG VIEW

This is one of a federation of business schools that occupy a site in London's Regent's Park. The college offers International Business, International Marketing and International Finance & Accounting – degrees awarded by the Open University. A distinctive feature is that many students are related to present captains of industry – 'It's a fantastic networking foundation,' as one put it. A Student Centre galvanises social and sporting activities.

COLLEGE PROFILE

Founded	**1996**
Situation/style	**Campus**
Status	**Private College**
Tuition fees pa (approx)	**£8,950**
Degree awarding university	**Open Uni**
Degree undergraduates	**200**
College accommodation	**Halls, flats**
Cost pw (incl food)	**£165-£220**
City rent pw	**£70**

DEGREE COURSES :
International Business, International Marketing, International Finance & Accounting

GETTING THERE

☛ By road: via York Gate off Marylebone Road.
☛ By Underground: between Baker Street and Regent's Park tubes, giving access to Metropolitan, Hammersmith & City, Circle, District and Bakerloo lines.

THE ROBERT GORDON UNIVERSITY

The Robert Gordon University
Schoolhill
Aberdeen AB10 1FR

TEL 01224 262105
FAX 01224 262147
EMAIL admissions@rgu.ac.uk
WEB www.rgu.ac.uk

Robert Gordon Students' Association
60 Schoolhill
Aberdeen AB10 1JQ

TEL 01224 262262
FAX 01224 262268
EMAIL rgusa@rgu.ac.uk
WEB www.rgunion.com

VAG VIEW

R GU is a quite different university to nearby Aberdeen, but it knows what it is about and appears to do it well, even if, in the process, it loses some 13% of its non-mature entrants after the first year.

The uni owes its foundation to philanthropist Robert Gordon, from whose estate the Robert Gordon's Hospital was created in 1750, and which developed into a college half a century later. The uni is also the beneficiary of another Aberdeen entrepreneur, an architect by name of Tom Scott Sutherland, who presented them with the grounds and mansion at which the Scott Sutherland School of Architecture is based, a beautiful site overlooking the River Dee. Another of RGU's constituent parts is the Gray's School of Art. It too bears the name of an Aberdeen entrepreneur, engineer John Gray; it was founded in 1885.

CAMPUS

RGU is composed of a scattered conglomeration of sites in the city of Aberdeen.

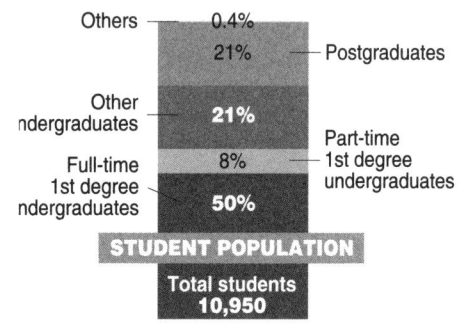

STUDENT POPULATION

Total students
10,950

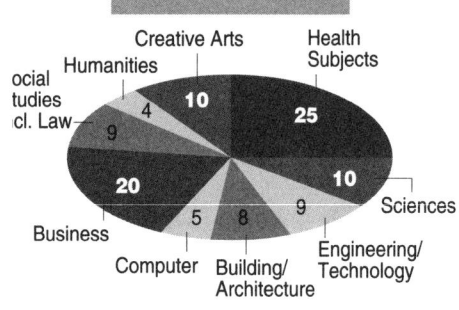

SUBJECT AREAS (%)

AT A GLANCE	
ACADEMIC FILE:	
Subjects assessed	**21**
Excellent	**57%**
Average A level requirements	**180 points**
Students-staff ratio	**18:1**
First/2:1 degree pass rate	**55%**
ACCOMMODATION FILE:	
Guarantee to freshers	**100%**
Style	**Flats**
Catered	**None**
En-suite	**10%**
Price range pw	**£49-£66**
City rent pw	**£55-£65**

UNIVERSITY/STUDENT PROFILE	
University since	**1992**
Situation/style	**Civic**
Student population	**10,950**
Full-time undergraduates	**5,500**
- mature	**20%**
- overseas	**5%**
- male/female	**40/60**
- state sector intake	**92%**
- non-traditional student intake	**17%, high**
- drop-out rate	**13%, high**
- undergraduate applications	**Down 1%**

see Introduction for key to tables

STUDENT PROFILE

There is a large state sector intake, many local, and a relatively high proportion of students (17%) from so-called low participation neighbourhoods. There are also a number of participants in RGU's Virtual Campus courses (for info, visit www.campus.rgu.com).

> *Robert Gordon enjoys the best employment record of any Scottish uni, and one of the best in the UK*

and Architecture Technology, too, the teaching of which was lauded in a recent visit by the QAA. It's another area that shows up as a significant graduate employment niche (see box).

RGU's specialism in legal management is being joined by a fully fledged LlB this year. And shortly there is to be a Sports Science degree, backed up by a multi-million pound sports centre, which has just received planning permission.

ACADEMIA

The university has undergone a substantial re-structuring of schools and faculties, as follows: Faculty of Design and Technology (Gray's School of Art, School of Computing, School of Engineering, Scott Sutherland School); Faculty of Health and Social Care (Schools of Applied Social Studies, Health Sciences, Life Sciences, Nursing & Midwifery, Pharmacy); Faculty of Management (Business School, Schools of Hotel, Tourism & Retail Management, Information & Media; Public Administration & Law).

The BEng in Mechanical & Offshore Engineering is testament to a long association with the North Sea oil industry. The tourism and hospitality degrees make the uni No. 1 in Britain as graduate suppliers to the catering industry. The nursing, nutrition, occupational therapy and physiotherapy degrees are among those health courses which preoccupy a quarter of all undergraduates and lead to 17% of them entering the health industry (see *Employment* box, page 392). The uni's new purpose-built Faculty of Health & Social Care building will be ready for students in September this year.

There are interesting degrees in Architecture

SOCIAL SCENE

STUDENTS' UNION Refurbished a few years ago at a cost of £500,000, there's a games bar and a café bar. Ents hitherto have been low profile – theme nights, events and discos. There is a new student newspaper, *Catalyst*, an interesting choice of name in a place where one senses that a wholesale change in lifestyle wouldn't go amiss.

ACADEMIC EXCELLENCE

TEACHING:
(Rated Excellent, Highly Satis. or 17+ out of 24)

Chemistry, Dietetics & Nutrition	**Excellent**
Physics, Business & Management, Graphic/Textile Design, Maths & Statistics, Mechanical & Manufacturing Eng, Architecture, Social Work, Pharmacy, Physiotherapy	**Highly Satis.**
European Languages	**19**

RESEARCH:
Top grades 5/5*	**None**

WHAT IT'S REALLY LIKE

UNIVERSITY:	
Social Life	★★
Campus scene	**Scattered, work-focused**
Student Union services	**Poor**
Politics	**Interest low**
Sport	**Relaxed**
National team position	**123rd**
Sport facilities	**Average-poor**
Arts opportunities	**Drama, dance, music good; film, art average**
Student newspaper	**Catalyst**
Nightclub	**Venue**
Bars	**Games bar, Café bar**
Union ents	**Discos, theme nights**
Union clubs/societies	**41**
Most popular society	**Gaelic Football, Christian Union**
Smoking policy	**Bars OK**
Parking	**Adequate**
CITY:	
Entertainment	★★★★
City scene	**Intoxicating**
Town/gown relations	**OK**
Risk of violence	**Average**
Cost of living	**Above average**
Student concessions	**Adequate**
Survival + 2 nights out	**£70 pw**
Part-time work campus/town	**Average/good**

SPORT Facilities are not generous yet, though the new Sports Centre will revolutionise things. There's athletics, rugby, rowing, football, archery, badminton, basketball, and of course all those outward bound activities – skiing, hillwalking, etc, which are naturally available in this area.

PILLOW TALK

Accommodation is thin on the ground, and students' advice is to get in quick. There is a commendable lack of fuss, however, at the uni: 'Everyone who applies for accommodation,' they say, 'is usually allocated accommodation.' It consists of self contained, self-catering flats, six to eight sharing, all with own bedroom, 10% en suite. Price per week ranges from £49 to £66; private rentlas in Aberdeen, £55 to £65.

JOBS

The uni enjoys the best employment record of any Scottish university and one of the best in the UK. The Graduate Employment Reference Indicator quotes RGU as having 98% of the latest crop of graduates in employment. They are strong in engineering (mechanical, offshore, electrical and electronic), robotics, pharmacy, paramedics (radiography, nutrition, dietetics, occupational therapy, physiotherapy), design, accounts/finance, computing, nursing, architecture/construction.

WHERE GRADUATES END UP	
17% Health/Social Work,	Key Areas
14% Wholesale/Retail.	
9% Manufacturing,	
6% Finance	
Hotel/Restaurant*,	Niche Area
Accountancy,	
Architecture,	
Eng/Industrial Design,	
Electron/Electric, Legal	
*indicates Top 10 Graduate Provider	
Approximate employed	**96%**

GETTING THERE

☛ By road: from south, A92, thence ring road for signs; from north, A96 or A92.
☛ By coach: London, 11.30; Newcastle, 7.35.
☛ By rail: London King's Cross, 7:00; Glasgow, 2:45; Edinburgh, 2:30; Newcastle, 4:30.
☛ By air: Aberdeen International Airport.

ROSE BRUFORD COLLEGE

Rose Bruford College
Lamorbey Park
Burnt Oak Lane
Sidcup
Kent DA15 9DF

TEL 020 83003024
FAX 020 8308 0542
EMAIL admiss@bruford.ac.uk
WEB www.bruford.ac.uk

VAG VIEW

*R*ose Bruford was the first drama school to award degrees to its students. There are two campuses, one in Greenwich, with recording studios, lighting workshops and performance studios, and one in Sidcup – an 18th-century Kentish park called Lamorbey, which has two theatres. First years spend most of their time at the Sidcup campus, travelling to Greenwich when required. Accommodation in London is extended to halls of residence owned by Greenwich Uni and Goldsmiths College.

GETTING THERE

☛ By road: A2, A210, B2214 to Lamorbey Park.
☛ By rail: New Cross station to Sidcup, 16 mins; London Bridge, 21 mins.

COLLEGE PROFILE	
Founded	**1950**
Status	**HE College**
Degree awarding university	**Manchester**
Situation/style	**Rural campus & city site**
Degree undergraduates	**549**
ACCOMMODATION:	
Style	**Halls**
Availability to freshers	**4%**
Cost pw (no food)	**£65**
City rent pw	**£65-£90**
DEGREE COURSES:	

Acting, Actor Musician, Directing, Euro Theatre Arts, Lighting Design, Music Techno, Scenic Construction & Props, Sound & Image Design, Stage Management

ROYAL ACADEMY OF MUSIC

The Royal Academy of Music
Marylebone Road
London NW1 5HT

TEL 020 7873 7373
FAX 020 7873 7374
EMAIL registry@ram.ac.uk
WEB www.ram.ac.uk

VAG VIEW

The collaboration between the Royal Academy, just south of Regent's Park, and the Strand-based King's College, both colleges of London University, is what distinguishes the BMus degree. The theory is that Academy musicians benefit academically by attending lectures at KCL, King's undergraduates from learning how to perform at the Royal Academy. Students also have a professional counsellor who is a member of the counselling team at KCL. The BMus is the only first degree course offered by the Academy.

There is a diverse student culture, with over forty countries represented. All students are found accommodation by a welfare officer; accommodation for overseas students is facilitated by the Royal Academy being next

COLLEGE PROFILE	
Founded	**1822**
Status	**Conservatoire**
Degree awarding university	**London**
Situation/style	**City site**
Student population	**588**
Degree undergraduates	**313**
College accommodation	**None**
City rent pw	**£65-£90**

DEGREE:
BMus (Perf)

door to International Student House.

GETTING THERE

☛ By Underground: Baker Street or Regent's Park tube stations, give access to Circle, Metropolitan, rloo, Hammersmith & City lines.

ROYAL AGRICULTURAL COLLEGE

The Royal Agricultural College
Cirencester
Gloucestershire GL7 6JS

TEL 01285 652912
FAX 01285 650219
EMAIL admissions@royagcol.ac.uk
WEB www.royagcol.ac.uk

VAG VIEW

The college, with its 770-hectare landholding, is involved at the forefront of research with the Long Ashton Research Station and other research centres in the EU. They also run the largest agri-student European exchange programme in the country, and it's the principal's boast that there's 'hardly a major farming/business or land-management employer in the UK and beyond that who doesn't have a former RAC student in a decision-making position.'

Accommodation is guaranteed for first years in twin or single study-rooms. There is a bar and the union organises ents.

Sport is big news, especially hockey and rugby. There's also clay pigeon shooting, karate, squash, riding, etc. It makes you feel tired thinking about it.

COLLEGE PROFILE	
Founded	**1845**
Status	**Agric College**
Situation/style	**Campus**
Student population	**520**
Degree undergraduates	**384**
ACCOMMODATION:	
Availability to freshers	**100%**
Style	**Halls**
Cost pw (catered)	**£113**
Town rent pw	**£40-£60**

DEGREE SUBJECTS:
Agriculture, Business Management, Equine & Agric Management, Farm Mechanisation with Euro Langs, Horticulture, Rural Land Management

Since October 2001, study at the RAC has

been subject only to regular uni tutorial fees.

GETTING THERE
☞ By road: within easy reach of motorway links,

M5, M42, M6, M4.
☞ By coach: London, 2:05.
☞ By rail: Oxford, 2:00; London Paddington or Birmingham New Street, 3:30.

ROYAL COLLEGE OF MUSIC

The Royal College of Music
Prince Consort Road
London SW7 2BS

TEL 020 7589 3640
FAX 020 7589 7740
EMAIL info@rcm.ac.uk
WEB www.rcm.ac.uk

VAG VIEW

*T*he RCM is in the immediate vicinity of Imperial College, the Natural History Museum, the Science Museum, the Victoria & Albert Museum, the Royal College of Art, the Royal Geographical Society and the Royal Albert Hall. Its BMus seeks to ensure the highest standards through one-to-one tuition, concerts, competitions, workshops, etc. With Imperial College they also offer a four-year BSc (Hons): Physics with Studies in Musical Performance, the joint venture the result of observation that physics brains often

COLLEGE PROFILE	
Founded	**1882**
Status	**Conservatoire**
Situation/style	**City site**
Student population	**514**
Full-time undergraduate	**370**
ACCOMMODATION:	
Style	**Halls**
Availability to freshers	**100%**
Cost pw	**£50-£75**
City rent pw	**£65-£90**
DEGREES:	
BMus, BSc Physics & Music	

demonstrate keen musical ability.

Accommodation is in a hall of residence in Hammersmith. Students may use Imperial's sports centre at Prince's Gardens. The RCM Students' Association promotes regular ents, mostly on a Friday.

GETTING THERE
☞ By Underground: South Kensington, Piccadilly, District and Circle lines.

ROYAL HOLLOWAY COLLEGE

Royal Holloway College
Egham
Surrey TW20 0EX

TEL 01784 434455
FAX 01784 473662
EMAIL liaison-office@rhbnc.ac.uk
WEB www.rhul.ac.uk

Royal Holloway Students' Union
Egham Hill
Egham TW20 0EX

TEL 01784 486300
FAX 01784 486312
EMAIL reception@su.rhul.ac.uk
WEB www.surhul.org.uk

VAG VIEW

*R*oyal Holloway, a college of London University, is situated on a 120-acre campus at Egham in Surrey, far enough to the southwest of London's bright lights to favour a concentrated regime. Students almost uniformly mention the workload, although there is a lively campus social scene

too. Whatever, the regime is very productive: 59% of students obtain firsts or upper seconds, and extra-curricular activities are of a very high standard indeed.

CAMPUS
'Holloway, isn't that a women's prison?' iterates Sarah Toms with a sigh which suggests she has heard the jibe many times before. 'It is of course,

but not here, it's in South London! You'll get used to that question. This is *Royal* Holloway, University of London – yes, the one with THAT building (Founders Hall). Located a train ride from central London – forty minutes on a good day, barring leaves on the line or the wrong kind of snow.'

It has been called 'London's Country Campus', and it is certainly a beautiful spot, made distinctive by Founder's Building, a copy of the Chateau de Chambourd in the Loire built by Thomas Holloway, who in 1886 founded a college for women there. Nearly a century later it merged with another all-female foundation, Bedford College, creating Royal Holloway and Bedford New College. You may be interested to know that there is still a preponderance of females here today.

STUDENT PROFILE

The female-dominated student body is small, little more than a third the size of the University of London's King's College or University College. Public school intake is high, as it is from overseas (the relatively new African-Caribbean society is among the strongest in the union).

UNIVERSITY/STUDENT PROFILE	
School of London Uni since	**1800**
Situation/style	**Campus**
Total student population	**6,000**
Full-time undergraduates	**4,080**
- mature	**11%**
- overseas	**32%**
- male/female	**45/55**
- state sector intake	**75%**
- non-traditional student intake	**7%**
- drop-out rate	**6%**
- undergraduate applications	**Down 13%**
see Introduction for key to tables	

ACADEMIA

Royal Holloway came through very strongly in last year's research assessment exercise, maintaining 21st place overall. The excellence of its Drama & Media Arts provision (23/24 in the teaching assessments and a Grade 5, world-class rating, in research) finds particular fulfilment for graduates in niche areas such as publishing, radio, TV, film, advertising and market research (see box, page 397).

It is clear from the *Academic Excellence* box, above, that languages are also a strength. The International Building incorporates the English, French, German, Hispanic and Italian departments, a language centre, a dedicated Japanese Studies section (including the Noh theatre

ACADEMIC EXCELLENCE	
TEACHING:	
(Rated Excellent or 17+ out of 24)	
History, Geology, Psychology, Organismal Biosciences	**Excellent 24**
Drama, Theatre & Media Arts, Physics, Classics	**23**
Maths	**22**
French, Italian, Sociology, Molecular Biosciences, Business	**21**
German	**19**
RESEARCH:	
Top grades 5/5*	
Geography, French, Music German/Dutch/Scandinavian	**Grade 5***
Drama/Dance/Performing Arts, History, Classics, English, Computer, Pure Maths, Earth Sciences, Biology, Physics, Psychology	**Grade 5**

– donated by the Japanese government), and a stylish café.

Interesting developments in biological science (a degree in Molecular Biology & Genetics recently took hold), a 23/24 rating last year for Physics teaching, and some unusually imaginative subject groupings (e.g. Maths and Psychology) further commend the college academically.

SOCIAL SCENE

STUDENTS' UNION The college is largely self-sufficient and most students spend their social hours on site, rather than succumbing to the distant twinkling lights of London. Frankly, the hour-long hike to the capital is seen as a hassle by most, as the last train back is at 11:30 pm, with no more links until 6 am the next day.

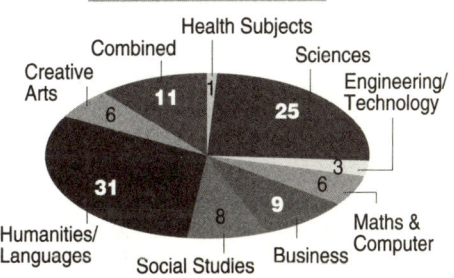

SUBJECT AREAS (%)

- Health Subjects 1
- Combined 11
- Creative Arts 6
- Sciences 25
- Engineering/Technology 3
- Maths & Computer 6
- Business 9
- Social Studies 8
- Humanities/Languages 31

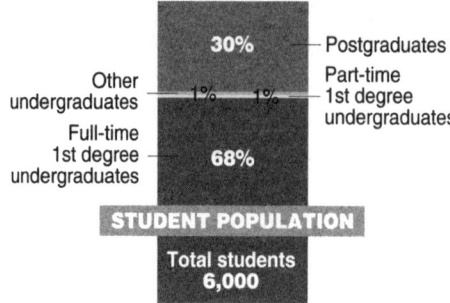

Student Population	
Postgraduates	30%
Part-time 1st degree undergraduates	1%
Other undergraduates	1%
Full-time 1st degree undergraduates	68%
Total students	**6,000**

In contrast to the friendly, welcoming campus, the nearest town, Egham, remains aloof, a cultural and social pit of suburban blandness.

To compensate for the paucity of local entertainment, the SU serves up a social calendar

WHAT IT'S REALLY LIKE

UNIVERSITY:	
Social Life	★★★★
Campus scene	**Active, friendly, artistic, female**
Student Union services	**Good**
Politics	**Big right now**
Sport	**36 clubs**
National team position	**67th**
Sport facilities	**Good**
Arts opportunities	**Drama excellent; music, film good; dance, art avg**
Student magazine	**The Orbital**
Student radio	**Insanity**
Radio 1 awards	**Best Female**
Nightclub	**Union +Tommy's**
Bars	**Union, Tommy's, Stumble Inn, Holloway's, Dive**
Union ents	**Cheese, Spaced, Orgasmatron, etc**
Union clubs/societies	**99**
Most popular society	**James Bond Appreciation Soc**
Smoking policy	**No smoking**
Parking	**Adequate**
CITY:	
Entertainment	★
Scene	**Good pubs, but London beckons**
Town/gown relations	**Good**
Risk of violence	**Low**
Cost of living	**High**
Student concessions	**Average**
Survival + 2 nights out	**£40 pw**
Part-time work campus/town	**Good/poor**

of unprecedented fullness for an establishment of this size. Every night is an ents night of some description, ranging from the usual pub quizzes on quiet Sundays to the late bars and DJs which dominate weekends and have a significant foothold in the working week as well. There's a late licence five nights a week, main hall functions two to three times a week, bar ents every other night. How many unions boast two resident DJs poached from the brighter lights of London? Both Brandon Block and DJ Swing are employed to keep the body student moving, and the latter has been known to hurl the crispest of currency into the crowd too, enhancing popularity and drinks consumption in equal measure. Recently imported additions include Ministry of Sound, Billie Piper, A1, Trevor Nelson, Apollo 440.

Tommy's is the newest bar in the union, and the most popular haunt of the socialites. Only Tuesday and Sunday see it shut before midnight, so the quiet beer with a friend at nine has a sneaky habit of turning into eight loud beers with a roomful of pissheads by kicking out time. The **Dive Bar**, attached to Tommy's, isn't as seedy as it sounds, and offers a cosier venue. The **Union Bar** is a pretty standard affair, and it is these three which combine to hold 1,200 for the big function nights – it has its own in-house technical crew. Also on campus is the strangely named **Stumble Inn** ('Stumble Out' would surely have been more appropriate), a pub to all intents and a popular one at that, ideal for those nights when aggravating your tinnitus shies you from Tommy's. **Holloway's Bar** houses sixteen pool tables, dart boards and a host of ever-changing video games, a free Playstation for the deprived, and live sports courtesy of the ubiquitous Sky TV. There is also the coffee bar, **TW20's**, a food and caffeine establishment that, according to some, is lamentable, but being dirt cheap and on campus attracts students like flies around the proverbial.

Every June they run a Summer Ball in the quads of Founders: 2,000 tickets are sold in exchange for big name acts, cocktail bar, Champagne bar, Glastonbury stage, dance tent, fairground rides, hog roast – it runs from 7 until 7 all through the night.

Media, drama and entertainments in general, are of a high standard. The Musical Theatre Society – *Sweeney Todd, Kiss of the Spiderwoman, Mystery of Edwin Drood* – has been to the Edinburgh Fringe for the last four years to great reviews. Notably this year the student radio station, Insanity, won Best Female Presenter at the Radio 1 awards, while last year the student mag, *Orbital*, was runner up in the *Guardian* awards as Best Magazine. Politics are generally not so popular, but this year saw Royal Holloway with the biggest turn out of University of London colleges at the anti-fees rally in Trafalgar Square.

The level of activity so dominates the local scene that students from Brunel University's nearby Runnymede campus have been known to mosey along to join the fray, particularly after dark.

SPORT The college has a reputation as the best sporting college in London University, and it does well in inter-LU leagues, though it languished at 67th position nationally last year.

> *The regime is very productive; more than two-thirds of students obtain firsts or upper seconds, and extra-curricular activities are of a very high standard indeed.*

A new sports complex has lifted it above its neighbours, although the current lack of a swimming pool would seem to mock its ambitions. Cricket's 1st XI has won four of the last six ULU cups, reaching the final in one of the others. Women's football has bossed the London indoor leagues for three years, and men's rugby supplies players to senior sides, such as Harlequins, Richmond and London Welsh.

TOWN 'Sadly, the surrounding area, quaint little Egham, with as many useful shops as you are likely to see students at a nine o'clock lecture, fails to happen,' Sarah reports, 'though it does have three supermarkets, a covey of takeaways, a bevy of student-friendly pubs, and **The Staines Massive**, which boasts not only a cinema, but wait for it... a *nightclub*! Those for whom the excitement proves too much, worry not. Royal Holloway is positioned a train ride away from the capital – deliberately, strategically even, to enable you to enjoy London life without paying a high price.

'Sure, the prices locally are higher than average, but not too damaging, and there is the advantage of the London loan rate and that both campus and surrounding area are fairly safe.

PILLOW TALK

'On the one hand, there is Founders Hall,' writes Sarah. 'Its rooms are fairly large and filled with an odd assortment of furniture from across the centuries. On the other, we have New Halls, built in the 1950s by an architect who won a prize for designing a Swedish prison! Affectionately known as 'Cell Block H', the rooms are, let us say, cosy...'

New Halls – Athlone, Cameron and Williamson – are catered and come with common rooms, bar, snack bar (**Times Square**), and a good community spirit. Founder's comes with common rooms, TV rooms, bar/snack bar (**Crossland Suite**); it's hard to get a room here. Reid Hall, near New Halls, is catered with en-suite rooms. Runnymede is self-catered, flat-style around a central kitchen/social area, en-suite. Three halls – Beeches, Chestnuts, Elm Lodge – are converted Victorian houses, catered but with small kitchen/pantries and laundries. Kingswood is catered, off campus (but less than a mile away and with a free bus service to campus during the day) and has rooms and flatlets on a hillside overlooking the Thames at Runnymede with squash and tennis courts, TV/common room, tapas bar and dining room.

WHERE GRADUATES END UP	
9% Manufacturing,	Key Areas
9% Finance,	
9% Computer*,	
9% Wholesale/Retail,	
8% Education,	
7% Personnel,	
5% Public Admin	
Accountancy, Artistic/	Niche Areas
Literary, Advertising*,	
Business/Management*,	
Chemical/Pharmaceutical,	
Library/Archival,	
Market Research*, Sport,	
Property, Publishing,	
Radio/TV*, Film/Video	

*indicates Top 10 Graduate Provider

Approximate employed **94%**

JOBS

The union is pioneering its own student development and volunteering scheme ('Quanta') drawn up this year. Weekly tutorials are held, teaching key skills such as feedback and communication, presentation skills, event planning and so on. Students can pass six or more of the twenty available units to gain a certificate.

For temp jobs, a weekly up-dated job file is available in the union, who themselves employ 300 student staff, working in one of the canteens, behind a bar, in union security. There are also opportunities of work in Egham or Staines.

GETTING THERE

☛ By road: M25/J13, A30.
☛ By rail: London Waterloo, 35 mins; Woking, 45; Reading, 40.

ROYAL VETERINARY COLLEGE

The Royal Veterinary College
Royal College Street
London NW1 0TU

TEL 020 7468 5200
FAX 020 7388 2342
EMAIL registry@rvc.ac.uk
WEB www.rvc.ac.uk

VAG VIEW

The RVC is a specialist college of London University. Don't expect the social facilities that exist at the other five vet unis – Edinburgh, Glasgow, Bristol, Cambridge and Liverpool – but the small LU colleges have a life of their own, and when it comes to sport, this female-dominated college does very well indeed. Rowing and hockey are strong, the new Women's Rugby club excels, and Netball won the ULU premier league last year. There are opportunities, too, for football, riding, shooting, badminton, cricket, skiing, sailing and windsurfing.

Your first two years are based in Camden, a fun place with its outdoor market, some very good pubs and well placed for city nightlife. Accommodation is in London University intercollegiate halls. In Year 3 it's off to 230-hectare Hawkshead campus, Potters Baaa.

COLLEGE PROFILE	
School of London Uni since	**1949**
Situation/style	**City & rural campuses**
Student population	**910**
Full-time degree undergraduates	**660**
ACCOMMODATION:	
Availability to freshers	**70%**
Style	**Halls**
Approx cost pw (no food/food)	**£53-£99**
Off-campus rent pw: London	**£65-£90**
Hawkshead	**£60**

GETTING THERE

☛ By road to Hawkshead campus: A1/M25 (J23).
☛ By rail: half hourly to Potters Bar from London King's Cross. There's a College minibus, or taxis from station. Camden campus: ten minutes' walk from King's Cross Station.

UNIVERSITY OF ST ANDREWS

The University of St Andrews
Admissions Application Centre
Old Union Building
St Andrews
Fife KY16 9AJ

TEL 01334 462150
FAX 01334 463388
EMAIL admissions@st-andrews.ac.uk
WEB st-andrews.ac.uk

St Andrews Students' Association
St Mary's Place
St Andrews
Fife KY16 9UZ

TEL 01334 462700/1
FAX 01334 462740
EMAIL (see website)
WEB www.yourunion.net

VAG VIEW

*S*t Andrews has a very old foundation (1410) and appeals almost as much to English students as to Scots as an alternative to Oxbridge. It is a small, very traditional university, set in an out-of-the-way seaside place known for its golf. Jargon is as prevalent here as in the great Imperial days of the public school system whence many of its students come. Some of its practices earmarked as traditions are in fact only a few years old, so the tradition of being traditional is not about to change.

The appearance of a future King of England on last year's list of undergraduates was, therefore, no great surprise. The media has been successfully kept at bay (at time of writing) even at the expense of the professional reputation of Prince William's royal film-producing uncle, and the university must be congratulated for handling that well, particularly as an attendant 45% increase in undergraduate applications was preoccupying them. However, the word is that William is not enjoying the rather academic ethos, and that he rarely spends weekends in the place.

This huge increase in applications was not in fact the largest in the sector, Bath Spa University College managed 47%, but the impact on St Andrews was for a time critical. Reportedly one first-year course had as many as 350 students registered on a module, more than 100 more than usual. The university ironed out the wrinkles and a few months later retained its reputation among the very top unis

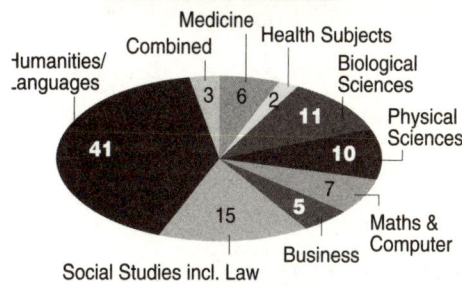

SUBJECT AREAS (%)

- Humanities/Languages — 41
- Combined — 3
- Medicine — 6
- Health Subjects — 2
- Biological Sciences — 11
- Physical Sciences — 10
- Maths & Computer — 7
- Business — 5
- Social Studies incl. Law — 15

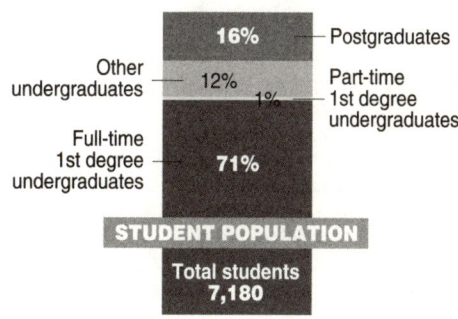

- Postgraduates — 16%
- Other undergraduates — 12%
- Part-time 1st degree undergraduates — 1%
- Full-time 1st degree undergraduates — 71%

STUDENT POPULATION

Total students
7,180

academically, coming 19th in the research assessment exercise.

Within its rather tight academic straightjacket, one of St Andrews' great attractions is the student/staff ratio – 12: 1, one of the best in Britain.

CAMPUS

St Andrews is out on its own, a small seaside town in the northeast of Scotland, surrounded by open countryside and sea, twelve miles from Dundee and around fifty from Edinburgh.

STUDENT PROFILE

The student body is dominated by public school types, but the town is relatively quiet and conducive to study, and the uni tends to attract a slightly more conservative stream of these. For a Scottish university there is a surprisingly large percentage of English students (around 40%), and, having a fine, traditional reputation, it attracts those who failed to get into Oxbridge, though quite a few do make St Andrews their first choice.

Above all, it is a friendly community. 'You can almost guarantee that every time you leave your front door, you'll see someone you know,' writes Melanie Hartley. 'When you've just crawled out of bed for a 9 am tutorial and you've only had four

UNIVERSITY/STUDENT PROFILE

University since	**1410**
Situation/style	**Town campus & sites**
Student population	**7,180**
Full-time undergraduates	**5,090**
- mature	**9%**
- overseas	**10%**
- male/female	**47/53**
- state sector intake	**59%, low**
- non-traditional student intake	**8%**
- drop-out rate	**4%, low**
- undergraduate applications	**Up 45%**

see Introduction for key to tables

ACADEMIC EXCELLENCE

TEACHING:
(Rated Excellent, Highly Satis. or 17+ out of 24)

Physics, Chemistry, Economics, Geography, Maths & Statistics, History, Cellular & Molecular Biology, Organismal Biology Psychology.	**Excellent**
Computer Studies, Business & Management, Geology, History of Art, Philosophy, Theology, English, Medicine.	**Highly Satis.**
European Languages	**22**

RESEARCH :
Top grades 5/5*

Psychology, English	**Grade 5***
Chemistry. Biological Sciences, Physics, Pure Maths, Applied Maths, Statistics, Computer, Anthropology, Politics, Iberian/ Latin American, Classics, History, History of Art, Philosophy, Theology	**Grade 5**

hours sleep, it's debatable whether that's a good thing or not! But St Andrews is a pretty close-knit society. Indeed, once people get here they don't tend to leave. They'll even tell you that one in three graduates end up marrying other St Andrews graduates!'

ACADEMIA

Teaching assessments have been top line – all are rated either Excellent or Highly Satisfactory. Interestingly, there is a part-time as well as a full-time course study option.

Traditionally, courses at St Andrews have been

AT A GLANCE

ACADEMIC FILE:

Subjects assessed	**18**
Excellent	**100%**
Average requirements	**300 points**
Students-staff ratio	**12:1**
First/2:1 degree pass rate	**73%**

ACCOMMODATION FILE:

Guarantee to freshers	**Apply by 31.5**
Style	**Halls**
Catered	**60%**
En-suite	**19%**
Price range pw	**£33.88-£92.61**
City rent pw	**£55**

academic rather than vocationally led – their more vocational type degrees were based in Dundee (now Dundee Uni) prior to the split in the 1960s which gave both unis their independence. This year, however, the two have moved closer together again with the launch of a joint degree in specialist engineering – Microelectronics & Photonics (there had already been a parlay through their pairing of Art History with Dundee's excellent School of Art & Design).

Now, too, there is a vocational element creeping into their arts programme, arts subjects mingling with information technology. There is also an increasing range of sciences with language degrees and an intriguing (possibly the ultimate!) faculty mesh with Integrated Information Technology and Theological Studies.

The whole cross-faculty strategy is evidence that this very traditional university is moving forward with insight.

A Learning and Teaching Support Unit (LTSU) works closely with the academic schools to co-ordinate and advise. Perhaps they should have gone into action on their University Challenge Team last year: students achieved the worst ever score on the television show – 40 points against Churchill College, Cambridge's 215.

SOCIAL SCENE

STUDENTS' ASSOCIATION Partly because the student population makes up such a large proportion of the town, much of the social life is created by students, the centralised location of the Students' Union making it a focal point for a large proportion of the entertainment. Location makes it unlikely, however, that the average student will get to see many big bands at the union.

Reports Melanie: 'There is no club as such; the union doubles up as a venue, hosting events all through the week. Every Friday is the *bop* – a cheesy night [*Red Not Bed*], very reminiscent of your old school discos, but a particularly revered part of student life. **Venue 2** hosts a range of different nights; *Rock-soc*, *Bulletproof* (alternative music) and *Jazz-soc* are regulars.' Saturday clubnights include *Squeeze* ('80s), *Explosion* (R&B), *Ebenezer* ('90s) or *Retro*.

'Pre-Sessional week – known as Freshers Week everywhere else – is non-stop events, including some biggish acts: recent weeks have hosted Space, Toploader and Euphoria. There are lots of 2nd, 3rd and 4th years willing to make friends – (some a bit too willing!) – and to show you around. Some will become your academic parents, a tradition that involves a weekend of parties with them, some time in November, before you get dressed up – many wittily/ridiculously as as bottles of wine,

Care Bears or condoms – and are frogmarched to the Quad on the Monday morning for a huge shaving foam fight. So fondly do many look back on their *Raisin* experience that they try to recreate it every year. [It can in fact degenerate into a mass piss-up and/or an excuse to pull: "Remember not to be forced into anything ..." warns the SA's *Alternative Prospectus*.]

'Student life is very much centred around the pubs. There are reputed to be more pubs per square

> *It is a small, very traditional university. Jargon is as prevalent as in the great Imperial days of the public school system whence many of its students come. It's very academic, and there's a 1 in 3 danger of getting married to a fellow St Andrews' student apparently.*

mile than in any other university town, which means you're never stuck for choice: **Broons** or **Bridges** if you want to hang with the yahs, **Ogstons** or **The Raisin** if you want large and loud, **Drouthy Neebors** or **The Cellar** if you're into Real Ale. Such is the pace of life that by the time you've been here a fortnight, you should have an encyclopaedic knowledge of what's available, and your weekly "happy hour'" schedule will be sorted!

'There are lots of ways in which this is a relatively cheap place to live, not least because it's small, though in fact taxis do a healthy business with flat fares of £2-£2.50 anywhere in the town.

'Going out isn't that expensive. Union nights never seem to cost more than £3, and entrance to the bar is free with your matriculation card. Pints are around £2, vodka and Coke, £1.50 in the Union, £2 elsewhere. The **Vic** happy hour (every night) has spirits + mixers for £1 and pints for £1.50.

'For entertainment other than pubs, most students look to student societies. Everybody is a member of at least one, and most people more. Options range from academic to music to political. The International Politics society recently had Michael Douglas to talk on behalf of the United Nations. You might prefer the Tunnocks Caramel Wafer Appreciation society or Quaich (whisky appreciation). You could also get involved with *The Saint* (student newspaper), which won the best budget student newspaper [Independent awards] and second best student newspaper in last year's *Guardian* awards.'

The union also one of the oldest debating societies in the world. Drama is an active aspect of student life. Each year Mermaids, a sub-committee of the Students' Association, gives financial assistance to several productions, some of which go to the Edinburgh Festival.

SPORT Golfers' paradise – the student team is one of the best in Britain. 'If this isn't your thing,' says Melanie, 'you still get to see the likes of Hugh Grant and Samuel L. Jackson strutting their stuff around town at the Dunhill Cup every October.'

In the national team championships they came 44th last year. There's a sports centre with sports hall, gym, activities room, weight training room, squash courts, solarium. Extensive playing fields, jogging and trim tracks. Golf bursaries are funded by the Royal and Ancient Golf Club.

WHAT'S ITS REALLY LIKE

UNIVERSITY:	
Social Life	★★★
Campus scene	**Conservative, traditional, little & by the sea**
Student Union services	**Good**
Politics	**Student issues; activity high**
Sport	**Competitive**
National team position	**44th**
Sport facilities	**Good**
Arts opportunities	**Drama excellent; dance, music, art good; film avge**
Student magazine	**Unreal**
Student newspaper	**The Saint**
Guardian awards	**Shoestring Award**
Nightclub	**Venue 1 & 2**
Bars	**Main Bar, Cloud 9**
Union ents	**Red Not Bed, Squeeze, Explosion, Ebeneezer, Retro**
Union clubs/societies	**100**
Most popular society	**James Bond Soc**
Smoking policy	**Union OK**
Parking	**Adequate**
TOWN:	
Entertainment	★★
Scene	**Pubs, coffee houses**
Town/gown relations	**Average**
Risk of violence	**Low**
Cost of living	**Costs high, living cheap**
Student concessions	**Average**
Survival + 2 nights out	**£60 pw**
Part-time work campus/town	**Not much**

PILLOW TALK

'Most of the halls are in the centre of town, and are steeped in traditions,' writes Melanie. 'Most first years procure an undergraduate gown soon after arrival – a tasteful red fleece type-thing and a bit pricey. Although it varies from hall to hall, there will be occasions throughout the year when you can wear these – hall dinners, photographs, chapel. Most of the halls are catered, and the food is pretty reasonable, although you'd be well advised to avoid the universally acclaimed lemon "toilet duck" mousse. Self-catering accommodation can be found in Albany Park and in Fife Park, which provide some of the most economical student accommodation in the country. "Simplistic" isn't the word for these flats, but they're cheap.'

Around half St Andrews students live in halls or other uni-owned accommodation – 60% of it catered, 19% of it en suite, £33.88 per week for single standard self-catering including heat, light & power, £92.61 per week for single en suite, catered, including heat light & power. Freshers are almost automatically given a place, but you must apply for it by May 31 in the year of entry. From then on there is no guarantee and the hunt for flats, particularly near the centre of town, can begin around the middle of January. Accommodation is quite expensive for such a small town – £55 per week – largely because students make up a high proportion of the population.

JOBS

'If you're looking for a bit of extra cash, the Dunhill Cup creates the possibility of a job washing up or directing traffic for the weekend,' Melanie reports. 'Other than this, part time work is hard to come by. The attitude of most students is that term time isn't for working, but there are occasional jobs behind bars. Most of the shops, however, seem to favour 16-year-old Madras College kids over us students when it comes to weekend work.'

Graduate employment prospects are excellent – around one fifth of graduates opt for the City, many as accountants; a number into medicine, law (after further training), education and industry, while a smattering go for more literary, artistic and literary/media pursuits. For those who graduated in 1999/2000 there are now 95.7% in employment or further training. Language strengths take many graduates to international employers. 'We have very strong contacts in the US, old Soviet republics, central Asia, China and Japan,' they tell me.

WHERE GRADUATES END UP

12% Education, Key Areas
12% Finance,
10% Public Admin,
8% Manufacturing,
7% Health (incl Medicine),
6% Wholesale/Retail
Accountancy*, Niche Areas
Business/Management,
Agric/Forestry,
Advertising, Publishing,
Artistic/Literary*, Library
/Archival, Chemical/
Pharmaceutical, Defence

*indicates Top 10 Graduate Provider

Approximate employed **95%**

GETTING THERE

☛ By road: Forth Road Bridge, M90/J3, A92 to Kirkcaldy, A915 to St Andrews; or M90/J8, A91.
☛ By rail: Nearest station on main line London (King's Cross) – Edinburgh – Aberdeen line is Leuchars (5 miles). A few trains have bus connection for St Andrews station; service bus runs from Leuchars every 20 minutes between 9am and 6pm; otherwise taxi.
☛ By air: Edinburgh Airport, airport bus to Edinburgh, thence by rail.

ST GEORGE'S HOSPITAL MEDICAL SCHOOL

St George's Hospital
Medical School
Cranmer Terrace
Tooting
London SW17 0RE

TEL 020 8725 5201
FAX 020 8725 5419
EMAIL adm-med@sghms.ac.uk
WEB www.sgms.ac.uk

VAG GUIDE

*S*t George's Hospital Medical School may no longer be the only free-standing medical school in the UK, but having the entire pre-clinical and clinical infrastructure required to teach medical students on a single campus remains a clear advantage over many.

Their entry policy is one of the more enlightened. They insist only on one science A level; it can be Chemistry or Biology; if Biology then AS Chemistry is required; but if Chemistry the other two A levels can be a modern Euro language and a Social Science.

Leisure-wise there's a Friday disco at the **Med School Bar** (650 capacity) and forty-two clubs and societies, Rowing and Film socs being the most popular.

Rootin' Tootin' itself has a colourful culture, plenty of curry houses, and – incomprehensibly to anyone coming from beyond the Southeast – has recently become the latest gentrification target. A students' handbook provides a helpful analysis of the top fifty pubs in the area.

SCHOOL PROFILE

Founded	**1751**
Status	**Associate of London Uni**
Situation/style	**City site**
Student population	**3,410**
Full-time undergraduates	**1,300**
ACCOMMODATION:	
Availability to freshers	**100%**
Style	**Halls**
Cost pw (no food/food)	**£57-£80**
City rent pw	**£65-£80**

The sports grounds are down in Cobham, Surrey – nine winter pitches and two cricket squares in summer, plus grass and hard court tennis. They also keep an eight and a four in the London Uni boathouse on the Thames and have facilities for sailing. Back at the hospital there's the Lowe Sports Centre, six squash courts, gym and areas to play badminton, basketball, etc.

GETTING THERE

☛ Tooting Broadway Underground station (Northern Line), Tooting overland.

ST LOYE'S SCHOOL OF HEALTH STUDIES

St Loye's School of Health Studies
Millbrook House
Millbrook Lane
Topsham Road
Exeter EX2 6ES

TEL 01392 219774
FAX 01392 435357
EMAIL stloyes@exeter.ac.uk
WEB www.ex.ac.uk/affiliate/stloyes

VAG VIEW

*T*he Occupational Therapy degree includes State Registration. The Health Sciences degree focuses on Applied Social and Biological Sciences, and prepares you for a career in anything from the pharmaceutical industry to hospital admin.

On-campus sports facilities provide for tennis, badminton, circuit training, pool, cricket and aerobics. There's a licensed bar. Membership of Exeter Uni's Guild of Students is automatic. See uni entry for city/travel, etc.

SCHOOL PROFILE

Founded	**1948**
Status	**HE College**
Degree awarding university	**Exeter**
Student population	**283**
Availability college accomm	**50%**
Cost pw (catered)	**£60**
City rent pw	**£40-£45**

DEGREE COURSES
Occupational Therapy, Health Sciences

COLLEGE OF ST MARK & ST JOHN

College of St Mark & St John
Derriford Road
Plymouth PL6 8BH

TEL 01752 636890
FAX 01752 636819
EMAIL admission@marjon.ac.uk
WEB www.marjon.ac.uk

VAG VIEW

*M*arjon is situated on the outskirts of Plymouth, a teacher training college offering a modular (arts/humanities based) honours degree, awarded by the University of Exeter. It began as two colleges, St Mark and St John, both founded 150 years ago in London by the Church of England.

The first thing you notice on campus is the high female presence; more than two-thirds of undergraduate students are female. The second thing you might notice is their keen attitude towards sport. They came 32nd in the national uni team tables last year, an amazing feat for such a small college. Pivotal to the sporting performance are the courses in PE & Sports Sciences. Facilities in the Sports Centre (which, though on campus is a community centre, open to the public) now include a 25m swimming pool, a fitness suite, two squash courts, fully equipped gym, three sports halls, each with four badminton courts and one with climbing wall, a dedicated computer centre and recently extended outdoor pursuits centre. Besides playing fields there is an all-weather floodlit Astro-pitch for hockey and a floodlit Astro training area. Sailing dinghies are moored in

COLLEGE PROFILE	
Founded	**1840**
Status	**HE College**
Degree awarding university	**Exeter**
Situation/style	**City campus**
Student population	**3,800**
Full-time undergraduates	**2,273**
ACCOMMODATION FILE:	
Availability to freshers	**100%**
Style	**Halls, houses**
Cost pw (no food/food)	**£50-£66**
City rent pw	**£37-£45**

Plymouth Sound; there's a fleet of plastic canoes, and a trim trail, which seems to encompass the entire campus. Mention should also be made of **The Lion & Lamb**, a bar, disco and snack bar in the sports centre. Finally, there's a sports scholarship system.

Accommodation for first years is in village houses on campus. Ents-wise there are three discos a week in the **Sub** (700 capacity), the **President's Lounge** and the **Café del Rosa**. Big dates are Christmas/Graduation and May balls. Subscribe is the student magazine and there's a radio station, Sub Culture.

See Plymouth entry for city directions.

COLLEGE OF ST MARTIN

College of St Martin
Bowerham Road
Lancaster
Lancashire LA1 3JD

TEL 01524 384444
FAX 01524 384567
EMAIL admissions@ucsm.ac.uk
WEB www.ucsm.ac.uk

VAG VIEW

*S*t Martin's is a teacher training college with a Church of England foundation, but it also teaches a number of subjects relevant to employment in the health/caring professions – nursing, midwifery, occupational therapy, radiography – in the Church, in the worlds of art, design and imaging science, in drama, dance, music, in media, in business and in the sport and leisure industries. Degrees are awarded by nearby Lancaster Uni.

The main St Martin's campus is a mile or so from the central shopping area of Lancaster. In the teacher training option there is a language expertise now spreading via voluntary language 'modules' to non-linguist courses. The sports courses are backed by on-site resources which are about to be boosted by a new £1.4 million Sports Complex. The Drama course makes use of an on-site studio, but students also get involved in major productions at Lancaster's **Dukes Theatre**. The BA (Hons) in Christian Ministry is an interesting option because it aims uniquely at employment in overseas aid work. Some students will be ordained.

The **JCR Bar** is open seven nights a week (two pool tables, games machines and 'the world's biggest TV screen'). There are six halls of residence, all but one on campus.

GETTING THERE
☛ By road: M6 (Junctions 33, 34).

COLLEGE PROFILE	
Founded	**1963**
Status	**HE College**
Degree awarding university	**Lancaster**
Situation/style	**City campus/ Town sites**
Student population	**8,875**
Full-time undergraduates	**3,330**
ACCOMMODATION FILE:	
Availability to freshers	**99%**
Style	**Halls**
Cost pw (no food/food)	**£48-£71**
Town/city rent pw	**£35-£45**

☛ By rail: Manchester Oxford Road, 1:30; Leeds, 2:30; Newcastle, 3:00; London Euston, 3:30.
☛ By coach: London, 5:50; Leeds, 3:55.

ST MARY'S COLLEGE, STRAWBERRY HILL

St Mary's College
Waldegrave Road
Strawberry Hill
Twickenham TW1 4SX

TEL 020 8240 4000
FAX 020 8240 4255
EMAIL (see website)
WEB www.smuc.ac.uk

VAG VIEW

*S*t Mary's, or SIMMS, as they prefer to call it, is a self-contained campus situated south of the England rugby ground between Richmond and Kingston. Many undergraduates are destined to become teachers, but there is a wide range of subjects on offer – drama, English, theology, Irish culture, sport (including Sport Rehabilitation), biology, health, environment, sociology, classical studies, media, geography, history.

Like Newman College it is a Roman Catholic foundation and good at sport – they came 29th in the national uni team ratings last year, a fantastic result for the college's size.

Two halls (Cashin and Cronin) offer en-suite facilities. Students' Union bars include **SU Bar** (600-800 capacity) and **Tartan Bar** (100-

COLLEGE PROFILE	
Founded	**1850**
Status	**HE College**
Degree awarding university	**Surrey**
Situation/style	**City campus**
Total student population	**2,990**
Full-time undergraduates	**2,140**
ACCOMMODATION FILE:	
Availability to freshers	**85%**
Style	**Halls**
Cost pw (no food/food)	**£62-£90**
City rent pw	**£60**

150). Two weekly discos, theme nights or live gigs. Highlights are Freshers', Christmas and intriguingly named Going Down balls.

GETTING THERE
☛ By rail: Waterloo Station to Strawberry Hill station, which is close to the college; takes thirty minutes.
☛ By Underground, it's the District line to Richmond, then overland to Strawberry Hill, or by Nos. 33 or R68 buses. No. 33 travels directly from Richmond Bus Station to the college.

UNIVERSITY OF SALFORD

TheUniversity of Salford
Greater Manchester M5 4WT

TEL 0161 295 4545
FAX 0161 295 4646
EMAIL course-enquiries@salford.ac.uk
WEB www.salford.ac.uk

Salford Students' Union
University House
The Crescent
Salford M5 4WT

TEL 0161 736 7811
FAX 0161 737 1633
EMAIL pres@students-union.salford.ac.uk
WEB www.ussu.org.uk

VAG VIEW

*T*he 2001 research assessment results
recognised Salford's departments of Built
Environment and Information Management
as world class, the best in the country.
Everyone knows that Salford is good at built
environment, at science, engineering,
computer and business, but a closer look
reveals a developing picture – in particular
into the arts, languages (also feted in the
research assessments) and media – now
eminently worth considering.

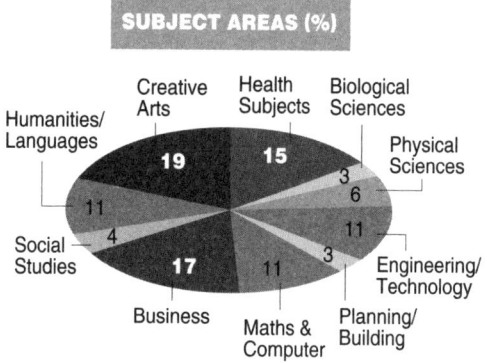

SUBJECT AREAS (%)

Creative Arts 19
Health Subjects 15
Humanities/ Languages 11
Biological Sciences
Physical Sciences 3
6
Social Studies 4
11
Business 17
Maths & Computer 11
Planning/ Building 3
Engineering/ Technology

CAMPUS

'The main campus, Peel Park, is two miles from

ACADEMIC EXCELLENCE	
University since	**1967**
Situation/style	**Campus**
Student population	**21,610**
Full-time undergraduates	**2,140**
- mature	**31%**
- overseas	**13%**
- male/female	**54/46**
- state sector intake	**95%**
- non-traditional student intake	**18%, high**
- drop-out rate	**12%, high**
- undergraduate applications	**Up 10%**
see Introduction for key to tables	

Manchester City Centre,' reports Shauna Corr.
'There are three main campuses: Adelphi,
Frederick Road and the main campus: which is
known as Peel Park.'

'So what do you know about Salford? Well, have
you ever seen the opening credits of *Coronation
Street*? That's Salford,' informs Lindsay Oakes. 'It's
where *Corrie* is set and filmed. You may also have
heard that it's a rough area with a high car crime
rate. Sadly, Salford is known more by its bad
reputation than for any of its good points. Of

course I'd be lying if I told you that there aren't
any negative aspects to living here; it's like any
suburban city area: if you're not sensible then it
could be dangerous. But where better to spend
three or four years of your student life than in the
student capital of Britain – Manchester? Salford
University actually lies closer to the centre of
Manchester than Manchester University itself. It
is only a fifteen-minute bus ride away, or five
minutes in a taxi, the way they drive round here!

STUDENT PROFILE

' There are students from all walks of life here, and
from practically every continent. There is a real
international feel to Salford because of all the
links we have with universities abroad [see

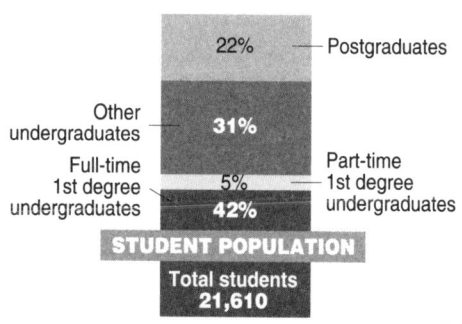

22% — Postgraduates
Other undergraduates — 31%
Full-time 1st degree undergraduates — 5%
Part-time 1st degree undergraduates
42%

STUDENT POPULATION
Total students
21,610

Academia, below]. And it may be true of many universities, but there is a real community among Salford students,' notes Lindsay, in particular among freshers in the student village.

There is also a high percentage of mature students. Since the charging of fees the uni has launched a bursary scheme – scholarships worth £3,000 each are available for undergraduate study, two reserved for local students.

ACADEMIA

Many courses have an international dimension, most offer the chance to study abroad. Excellent relationships with countries in Europe and farther afield have produced interesting Science/Arts curriculum groupings, such as Information Technology with Studies in Japan. Languages are an important department; Hispanic and Arabic are especially strong.

Everyone knows that Salford is good at built environment, at science, engineering, computer and business, but a closer look reveals a developing picture – into the arts, languages and media – all now eminently worth considering.

The 'subjects allied to medicine' which earned 22 points out of 24 at inspection relate to the School of Health Care Professions and include podiatry, radiography, occupational therapy, physiotherapy and sports rehabilitation. See also their complementary medicine degrees in the School of Community, Health Sciences & Social Care. The bioscience degrees that scored full marks (24) include Biochemistry, Physiology and Environmental Biosciences.

It is easy to go on about Salford's best known strengths. Look, for example at the *Employment* box, page 409, which shows Built Environment as a Top 10 graduate provider. But, while subjects such as built environment, science, engineering, computer and business continue to be major influences on graduate employment, there's a great deal more going on.

Interest is increasingly directed now at their Faculty of Arts, Media & Social Sciences. Politics took full marks at the assessments (see the *Academic Excellence* box, below), sociology some was accorded 20 points, and now there are some interesting mixes – with journalism or criminology, besides the more usual social policy. The faculty's School of Languages is huge: contemporary Euro culture degrees with a language, linguistics with a language, three language mixes, languages with marketing, translation and interpreting studies – these speak of assured graduate employment. A new campus-based Language Resource Centre offers advanced multimedia and language facilities, and includes a conference interpreting suite with five interpreting booths and workstations running the latest translation and linguistic software.

As for the faculty's School of Media, Music & Performance it is clear from their employment success in radio/TV, journalism, film/TV – again, see these niche areas in our *Employment* box, page

AT A GLANCE

ACADEMIC FILE:

Subjects assessed	**26**
Excellent	**69%**
Average requirements	**220 points**
Students-staff ratio	**20:1**
First/2:1 degree pass rate	**44%**

ACCOMMODATION FILE:

Guarantee to freshers	**Apply before September 1**
Style	**Student village, houses, flats**
Catered	**6%**
Price range pw	**£39.31-£80.80**
City rent pw	**£30-£60**

ACADEMIC EXCELLENCE

TEACHING:
(Rated Excellent or 17+ out of 24)

Music	**Excellent**
Organismal Biosciences, Politics, Molecular Biosciences	**24**
Drama/Dance/Cinematics, Physics	**23**
Housing, Subjects Allied to Medicine, Nursing	**22**
Art & Design, Maths	**21**
Economics, Sociology, Media, Modern Languages & Arabic	**20**
Civil Engineering, Tourism	**19**
Building & Land/Property Mgt	**18**

RESEARCH:
Top grades 5/5*

Built Environment, Library & Information Management	**Grade 5***
Statistics, European Studies	**Grade 5**

409 – are justifying the many combinations being offered with Journalism. The new degree, Journalism & Broadcast, looks especially interesting, and others, like Television & Radio. Now, the International Media Centre have put together a web site (www.Freeflowuk.com) to showcase uni bands and artistes – sound clips, biogs, news, listings and video clips all come from the School of Media, Music & Performance.

SOCIAL SCENE

STUDENTS' UNION 'The union runs four bars (one being a nightclub/bar),' writes Shauna. 'The Pav (at Castle Irwell student village) has two main nights: *Flair* on Tuesday and *3-2-1 It's Friday*, both nights are very successful. *Flair* is '60s, '70s and '80's music; *3-2-1 It's Friday* is more modern music. The Lowry Bar on Peel Park is situated in University House, it's a good day-bar. So far this year we have had a Ministry of Sound night, at which Youseff played, and we've had Jason Donovon, Timmy Mallet and Tymes Four as well

as student bands and DJs. We also have the Wallness Tavern, recently refurbished, open all day. The Sub Club, Frederick Road, is a good day bar for students on site. All bars have games' machines and pool tables. Local pubs are a bit rough and not always safe for students.

'One thing I should point out,' writes Lindsay, 'is that unlike most unis, beer and food at Salford are *not* subsidised.'

Especially active among numerous sports clubs and societies is the LGB group – lesbian/gay. '*Student Direct* is our weekly publication,' Shauna continues, 'shared with both Bolton Institute, Manchester University and UMIST.' The union rates most active societies as Plastic Surgery/Shock fm, both music socieities: 'Plastic Surgery is the DJ soc, and Shock fm deals with the student radio station.' The campus-based (TV) Channel M broadcasts to half a million people in the Manchester region with programmes developed and made at Salford's media facilities. Channel M recently beat BBC and Sky One to a Royal Television Award.

Reflecting the growth in arts degrees – note the 23 points out of 24 for Drama at the teaching assessments – students describe extra-curricular arts opportunities as excellent too. The Robert Powell Theatre was opened in October by namesake Salfordian actor, Robert Powell.

The central, Peel Park Campus contains the Lowry Museum and Art Gallery, home to the largest Lowry collection in the world. L S Lowry was born in the town.

Salford Community Action Project (SSCAP) is also very active, involved with for example Christmas parties for children and senior citizens, English lessons for overseas students' partners, work with the disabled and ex-offenders.

SPORT 'The union runs a very cheap Leisure Centre which provides a swimming pool, climbing wall (best in the northwest), weights room, badminton, tennis and squash courts, five-a-side football pitches, sun beds, sauna and jacuzzi. There is a large sports hall with just about every indoor pitch marked down, facilities for trampoline, and sports pitches at Castle Irwell for rugby, football, hockey and cricket.'

Team sport performance nationally is anything but awesome, however – the uni came 104th last year, but two student swimmers are taking a year out to compete in the Commonwealth Games, and there is healthy competition between the Manchester universities, best reflected in the Manchester/Salford boat race in the summer. Step aside Oxford and Cambridge; this is what boat races are really all about.

WHAT IT'S REALLY LIKE	
UNIVERSITY:	
Social Life	★★★
Campus scene	**Friendly, boozy**
Student Union services	**Good**
Politics	**Interest low, but SWSS & Anti-Nazi League**
Sport	**25 clubs**
National team position	**104th**
Sport facilities	**Good**
Arts opportunities	**Excellent**
Student newspaper	**Student Direct**
Student radio	**Shock fm**
Student TV	**Channel M**
Nightclub	**The Pav**
Bars	**Lowry, Sub Club, Wallness Tavern**
Union ents	**Themed, requests, tours**
Union clubs/societies	**47**
Most popular societies	**Plastic Surgery**
Smoking policy	**OK bars, halls**
Parking	**Adequate**
CITY:	
Entertainment	★★★★★
City scene	**The best**
Town/gown relations	**Average-poor**
Risk of violence	**High**
Cost of living	**Locally low**
Student concessions	**OK**
Survival + 2 nights out	**£60 pw**
Part-time work campus/town	**Average/excellent**

TOWN 'Manchester is very close by,' Shauna continues. 'There's good variety of cinemas, restaurants, pubs, clubs, theatres, concerts and comedy clubs, and a very large student population. Be careful with locals and stay safe as with all big cities. Always be careful with taxis, there are illegal and unmarked taxis that will try and reel you in. Manchester is buzzing all the time, both during the week and at weekends. Students usually stick to student nights during the week and these are very cheap, then at the weekend they mingle with the more sophisticated at more expensive places. You can find clubs that are as cheap as 50p a drink on a student night. See *Student Manchester*, page 304.

Cost-wise, as Suzanne Ashton points out, 'Salford has all the advantages of a town – cheap rent, everything close by, a friendly atmosphere – and yet still with the facilities of a city nearby.'

PILLOW TALK

They guarantee a place in one of the 4,000 study bedrooms to all freshers who have an unconditional offer and whose accommodation application form has been received by 12 noon on the September 1 in the year of admission.

The three main campuses (Peel Park, Frederick Road, Adelphi) are within walking distance of the residences. 'There is a good selection of accommodation ranging from Castle Irwell Student Village to blocks of flats and on-campus catered accommodation,' Shauna reports. 'Castle Irwell has 1,612 rooms and is 25 minutes walk from Peel Park campus. It boasts numerous playing fields, an astro-turf pitch, and **The Pav**. There is also a laundrette, taxi rank and a house with disabled access. You can also live in private housing. The Students' Union has links with Manchester Student Homes, and holds a list of safe landlords.'

Accommodation is reasonably priced, although some of the uni-leased flats are expensive (bills are included, however, and they are secure). Price range per week: catered, £71.45 - £80.80; self catered, £39.31 - £51.04.

Writes Lindsay: 'One of the best places to experience the community feel of Salford is Castle Irwell Student Village. It has a really friendly atmosphere, and you get to meet so many people, not just the ones you live with. In the summer, the entire village turns out on to the playing fields to play sports, sunbathe or even have barbecues. In the winter, you'll find yourself having a snowball

fight with someone you've never met before.'

JOBS

'There's part-time work in union bars, in ents, in the library and in Manchester,' notes Shauna, 'and a Job Shop to help you find reliable and safe, part-time or holiday work. There are loads of part-time jobs to be had.

In the context of graduate employment, see *Academia*, above (how the courses are aimed at the career market place) and our *Employment* box, below. Salford is a pioneer of sandwich courses, work placement schemes, and its links with local firms are legendary.

'There are certainly strong links with industry,' says Shauna, 'and opportunity on many courses for industrial sandwich years, home and abroad. Ninety per cent of Salford graduates find

WHERE GRADUATES END UP	
14% Health/Social Work,	Key areas
13% Manufacturing,	
10% Wholesale/Retail,	
8% Finance,	
8% Computer,	
7% Public Admin	
Aeronautical Manufacture,	Niche Areas
Chemical/Pharmaceutical,	
Construction*, Electron/	
Electric, Film/Video,	
Journalism, Market	
Research, Radio/TV*,	
Sport, Telecom	
*indicates Top 10 Graduate Provider	
Approximate employed **95%**	

employment or further in education within six months of graduation.'

GETTING THERE

☛ By road: M62 (which connects with the M6, M63)/M602. Coach services good.
☛ By rail: Salford Crescent station is on-campus; Manchester Oxford Road is a few minutes away; Liverpool, 1:20; Sheffield, 1:30; Birmingham New Street, 2:30; London Euston, 3:30.
☛ By air: Manchester Airport, international and inland.
☛ By coach: London, 4:35; Bristol, 5:00.

SCARBOROUGH COLLEGE *see* HULL UNIVERSITY

SCHOOL OF ORIENTAL AND AFRICAN STUDIES

School of Oriental & African Studies
Thornhaugh Street
Russell Square
London WC1H 0XG

TEL 020 7637 2388
FAX 020 7436 3844
EMAIL registrar@soas.ac.uk
WEB www.soas.ac.uk

School of Oriental & African Studies
Thornhaugh Street
Russell Square
London WC1H 0XG

TEL 020 7580 0916
FAX 020 7636 8376
EMAIL soasunion@tropicalstorm.co
WEB www.soasunion.org.uk

VAG VIEW

*S*OAS, part of of the federal University of London, is situated in Bloomsbury and has a close working relationship with branches of the Civil Service, especially the Foreign Office (SOAS actually teach their staff). Teaching assessments are first class. Connections with overseas governments, industry and commerce facilitate, among other things, the college's study-abroad programmes.

The Bar, capacity 200, is renowned the world over (by a discerning few). Student accommodation is provided as 500 single, en-suite study-bedrooms in cluster flats fifteen minutes' walk away on the Pentonville Road. Alternatively, students may use London Uni's intercollegiate halls. There are two squash courts on site and a sports ground at Greenford. SOAS have their own football and netball teams; women's football became local champions in their first season. London

SCHOOL/STUDENT PROFILE

School of London Uni since	**1916**
Situation/style	**City site**
Student population	**3,650**
Full-time undergraduates	**1,490**
- mature	**33%**
- overseas	**26%**
- male/female	**40/60**
- state sector intake	**66%**
- non-traditional student intake	**18%, high**
- drop-out rate	**17%, high**
- undergraduate applications	**Up 2%**

*see Introduction for key to tables

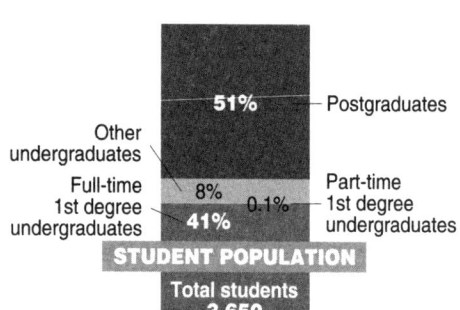

STUDENT POPULATION
Total students
3,650

51% — Postgraduates
Other undergraduates
Full-time 1st degree undergraduates — 8% 0.1% — Part-time 1st degree undergraduates
41%

ACADEMIC EXCELLENCE

TEACHING:
(Rated Excellent or 17+ out of 24)

Law, Music, Anthropology	**Excellent**
History of Art	**24**
East & SE Asian Studies	**23**
Mid Eastern & African Studies, Theology	**22**
Economics	**21**
Linguistics	**20**

RESEARCH:
Top grades 5/5*

History	**Grade 5***
Anthropology, Law, Middle Eastern/African Studies, Asian Studies, Theology, Music	**Grade 5**

Students' Union facilities are nearby, including a swimming pool and gym.

NOTES FROM A TOPICAL ISLAND
by Peter Beveridge & Catherine Wynne

SOAS is one of the smaller, specialist colleges of London University. Its size and the type of student it attracts make it radically different. Its students come from a wide range of age and ethnic groups, and coming here affords the opportunity to meet people from all over the world.

But generally students are highly motivated and courses are demanding. Beware, language courses are very intense. Teachers say that languages should become your life. Be prepared to decorate your bathroom with Vietnamese verbs!

Most activities are organised by SOAS's many societies. Every shade of political opinion and liberation struggle is represented. Many are worth getting involved in as they have interesting debates and guest speakers. You could well find yourself chatting over wine and nibbles with some chap who could get you a flash job in the UN or the World Bank.

Do not think of coming if you haven't dragged a backpack through either (a) Thailand or (b) India, or can claim to have gained a unique insight into unspoilt and indigenous cultures. If you haven't – lie! A typical conversation in the bar concerning summer activities might run: 'I'm just back from three months in South East Asia, saving villagers from acid rain.' Oh, how did you get that? 'Dad got me the job.'

Academically speaking, SOAS does all the usual disciplines, but with specific reference to Africa and Asia. This means that in Geography you're more likely to be looking at the 'Bio-geography of Savannahs in Sub-Saharan Africa' than the spatial planning of Birmingham town centre. It's strong on languages, from Chinese and Japanese to a whole shitload that you probably won't have heard of. Colloquial Cambodian, for example, looks great on your CV, and unless you're in Phnom Penh the interviewer is unlikely to challenge you on it. Forget Oxbridge, this is the place to come for experts on Africa and Asia. Law students whinge that they're the only people who ever do any work.

GETTING THERE
☞ Underground: Russell Square (Piccadilly line).

SCHOOL OF PHARMACY

School of Pharmacy
29-39 Brunswick Square
London WC1N 1AX

TEL 020 7753 5831
FAX 020 7753 5829
EMAIL registry @cua.ulsop.ac.uk
WEB www.ulsop.ac.uk

VAG VIEW

*T*he School of Pharmacy is a specialist school of the University of London. A Grade 5 in the research assessments confirms its national and international reputation.

The school, situated centrally, within walking distance of the British Museum, attracts a large overseas student population, who, along with other freshers, appreciate that it has its welcome down to a fine art. From day one everything runs smoothly and is managed in an intelligent and close sort of way. It has a small amount of its own accommodation – Coram, a hall next door to the school, twelve single rooms for those with special needs or not a lot of money, but *otherwise it's London Uni's intercollegiate halls or living out. For sport, the school shares grounds out at Enfield with the Royal Free Hospital Medical School (now part of University College London); closer to home you'll find facilities for squash, badminton, swimming, etc., and the London University Union in Malet Street is close at hand. Students at the school have their own union, bar, ents programme (there's a theme night on Friday) and JCR facilities for table tennis, pool, etc.*

GETTING THERE
☛ By tube: Russell Square (Piccadilly line); overland stations (King's Cross, St Pancras and Euston) are all within a short walk.

SCHOOL PROFILE	
Founded	**1842**
Status	**School of London Uni**
Situation/style	**City site**
Total student population	**1,140**
Full-time degree undergraduates	**540**
ACCOMMODATION FILE:	
Availability to freshers	**90%**
Style	**Halls**
Approx cost pw (catered)	**£85**
City rent pw	**£65-£90**

SCOTTISH AGRICULTURAL COLLEGE

Scottish Agricultural College
Auchincruive
Ayr KA6 5HW
TEL 0131 535 4185
FAX 0131 535 4332
EMAIL etsu@au.sac.ac.uk
WEB www.sac.ac.uk

VAG VIEW

S AC is a small college based at three sites, in Aberdeen, Edinburgh and Ayr, the largest being at Ayr. Though Agriculture as such is not available at first degree level, BTechnol Agriculture is. Technical and management skills required to manage livestock or crop enterprise are to the fore; it's a three-year course, four for an honours degree. Degrees in related specialisms are also available.

SAC ABERDEEN Craibstone Estate, Bucksburn, Aberdeen AB21 9YA. Tel: 01224 711000 BTechnol Agriculture; BTechnol Countryside Management; BTechnol Business Management.

SAC AUCHINCRUIVE Ayr KA6 5HW. Tel: 01292 520331 BTechnol Agriculture; BSc Horticulture or Horticulture with Horticulture Mgt (first 2 years at Strathclyde Uni); BSc Landscape Management, BTechnol Environmental Protection & Management (years 3 & 4 in Edinburgh); BTechnol Countryside Management; BTechnol Leisure & Recreation Management; BSc Applied Plant & Animal Science; BTechnol Food Technology.

COLLEGE PROFILE	
Founded	**1899**
Status	**HE College**
Degree awarding universities	**Glasgow, Edinburgh, Aberdeen, Strathclyde**
Situation/style	**City & town campuses**
Student population	**830**
Full-time undergraduates	**370**
ACCOMMODATION	
Availability to freshers	**50%**
Style	**Halls**
Cost pw (no food/food)	**£45-£82**

SAC EDINBURGH West Mains Road, Edinburgh EH9 3JG. Tel: 0131 667 1041 BTechnol Agriculture, BTechnol Rural Resources Management; BTechnol Environment Protection & Mgt (first 2 years at Ayr).

GETTING THERE
☛ By road: **Aberdeen** from south, A90; from north, A92. **Ayr:** B743 Ayr-Mauchline road. **Edinburgh**, 3 miles south of city centre: A720 city by-pass, Straiton Junction with the A701.
☛ By rail: **Aberdeen:** Edinburgh, 2:30; Glasgow, 2:40. **Ayr:** Glasgow, 54 mins. **Edinburgh:** London King's Cross, 4:30; Glasgow, 50 mins; Newcastle, 1:30.
☛ By air: **Aberdeen**, **Edinburgh** airports.

STUDENT SHEFFIELD – THE CITY

In recent years Sheffield has undergone a renaissance. An unemployment blackspot after the closure of the steelworks, it has since been reborn as a city of culture and clubbing. It will never match the beauty of Rome, with which it shares the distinction of being built on seven hills, but it does have its own inimitable charm, and in no city have I felt less threatened and more able to wander around in the early hours in an advanced state of inebriation.

'The Peoples Republic Of South Yorkshire' has a tradition of extending a welcome to refugees from countries around the globe: residents from Chile, Vietnam and Sudan, to name but three, have settled in this oasis of grime and peace. Now you, like them, and the 30% or so of students who choose to remain in the city after graduation, can come to live, not merely exist, in this vibrant cosmopolitan city, on one condition: if you are male, do not quail with fear if you are addressed by an ex-steelworker built like a brick outhouse as 'love' or 'duck', as these terms relate roughly to 'mate' or 'pal' and are not (usually) a come-on.

CLUBS

Sheffield found itself on the clubbers map in the early '90s with the rise of *Love To Be* at the **Arches**. Then for a little while nothing very much happened until…the birth of the mighty *Gatecrasher*.

Gatecrasher @ **The Republic** continues to punch it out with Liverpool's *Cream* for the title of the North's number one club. You'll pay through the nose for the privilege but you'll be able to boast at dinner parties during middle class-middle age, that of course you were at 'crasher every weekend, dahling'.

Sheffield also hosts another club of nation-wide repute - *NY Sushi*. Their exquisitely Japanoid style flyers only but hint at the Bladerunneresque-drum 'n' base style shenanigans that have the young people cutting a rug at **The Unit** every Friday.

The Arches, meanwhile, having recovered from their ecstatic *Love To Be* incarnation, are building a big rep for underground drum 'n' base. It's dope man.

The Students' Union also hosts its own range of nights at its three clubs/bars, occasionally overtaking the **Octagon** (a building next door with, oddly, eight walls and a vast capacity) for larger events. The most popular of these is the cheese-tastic *Pop Tarts* on Saturdays - always buy your ticket in advance; it's that bad, it's fantastic.

Be assured that's not all the clubbing in Sheffield, but all the space we have for it...

GALLERIES & THEATRES

Sheffield has more culture than a pot of organic yoghurt. The city rose to prominence on the back of steelworkers so hard that no-one dared to call them 'puffy' for an interest in art and culture. This has left Sheffield with a legacy of galleries and theatre. **The Crucible**, Norfolk Street, is the city's main venue and the smaller **Lyceum** is next door; both offer discounts for students. The students' union's drama society also stages regular performances at the **Drama Studio** on Glossop Road.

For all you arty types the city has three major galleries: the **Graves**, Surrey Street, which owns a Monet amongst other works; the **Ruskin**, Norfolk Street, which specialises in William Ruskin, and the **Mappin**, Weston Park, which stages a permanent exhibition of Victorian paintings as well as temporary exhibitions of contemporary works.

SCREENS

For film the city offers several venues. **The Showroom**, Paternoster Row, is an arthouse cinema in a complex that forms the city's media quartier, which also has a classy bar attached. The city centre also has a ten-screen **Odeon** and out at **Meadowhall** is a fifteen-screen multiplex. **The Virgin Megaplex** at Don Valley boasts 'The Full Monty' – which is a very big screen along with twenty other smaller screens. The Students' Union also has a large cinema where you can request what you want shown – *Withnail and I*, perchance?

THIS SPORTING LIFE

Sheffield is home to two football teams (though some would argue this is being generous), an ice hockey team and a basketball team. Sheffield Wednesday play at Hillsborough; United at Bramall Lane. Getting these mixed up could cause serious problems – the city is extremely partisan. Sheffield Steelers glide across the ice at **The Arena** and Westfield Sharks shoot the hoop there – I assume they get rid of the ice first.

Also, we have some fantastic facilities left over from the World Student Games, among them two world-class swimming pools, at Ponds Forge and Hillsborough. The city also hosts the *Embassy World Snooker Championship*, for which, each year, dedicated smokers from around the world make Sheffield their destination. Should yours be more esoteric tastes, you might have a flutter on the mutts at Owlerton Greyhound Stadium on Penistone Road.

MMMMMM...BEER

After all that exercise you're going to need a drink, right? New bars are sprouting up in Sheffield like mushrooms on a damp day. Start on Division Street – a good dozen pubs and bars, from **The Rat and Parrot** (real ale) to **The Halcyon** (cold bottles and cool people). Outside the city centre there are loads of vast pubs, many of which sport full and three-quarter size snooker tables. If you like booze you'll like Sheffield – a recently published guide lists over 2,000 licensed premises in the area.

CONSUMERISM

For the impoverished student Sheffield has a couple of lifelines in the form of Castle Market and Sheaf Market. Castle is brilliant for cheap veg, fish and meat; Sheaf is for your usual market tat: cheap clothes, plastic toys that break, household goods and shouty traders.

If you're a bit more flush then Division Street – of the bars fame – also has loads of chic boutiques. Chapel Walk is full of small shops with large price tags. If you're shopping for Agas, Smeg fridges, Bang & Olufsen electrical appliances then Ecclesall Road is for you, it's Sheffield's own Knightsbridge.

And then there is Meadowhall, built on the site of a former steelworks next to the M1; it's a little piece of hell on earth; like Heironymus Bosch's *The Garden of Delights*, it is absolutely nightmarish. Shop after shop after shop selling their wares at above high street prices (you pay for the convenience of everything under one roof) in an eerie joyless maze of confusing cul-de-sacs never

touched by daylight. Then again, if you like shopping and don't like getting wet you'll love it.

WASHING AND SLEEPING

As with most cities, in Sheffield students seem to find safety in numbers. The main ghetto for Sheffield University students is Broomhill: a paradise of pubs, takeaways and a supermarket. There's not a lot else because students need nothing more, and it seems only students live there. It's convenient for the campus (around ten minutes on foot), reasonably cheap and pretty safe.

Crookes, despite its name, is the next most popular area Slightly further out, it has less facilities than Broomhill, but has the compensation of a number of good pubs. Even further than this is the eponymous Walkley, which is less popular but has the advantage of the lowest rents of all the student areas. On the other side of the university is the underrated Broomhall, which has suffered in the past from a bit of a dodgy rep. It's virtually on the university's doorstep and is very cosmopolitan.

A long way further out is Ecclesall Road and Hunters Bar. Both are popular with students from both universities and the area is about the poshest in central Sheffield. The main drawback is the mile or so uphill slog to uni.

Adam Bennett

UNIVERSITY OF SHEFFIELD

The University of Sheffield
14 Favell Road
Sheffield S10 2TN

TEL 0114 222 2000
FAX 0114 222 8032
EMAIL ug.admissions@sheffield.ac.uk
WEB www.sheffield.ac.uk

Sheffield Union of Students
Western Bank
Sheffield S10 2TG

TEL 0114 222 8605
FAX 0114 275 2506
EMAIL www.sheffield.union.com
WEB sheffieldunion.com

VAG VIEW

*S*heffield is a top university across the board, but contrary to Rose Wild's view, parents of a certain generation or southerly location may yet raise an eyebrow at the thought of their little darling choosing it.

'When I announced that I was going to Sheffield University my mother shrieked "Sheffield! But I've never heard of Sheffield!",' writes Rose Wild. 'This is not something that could be said today. The city of Sheffield has, in the last few years, become such an

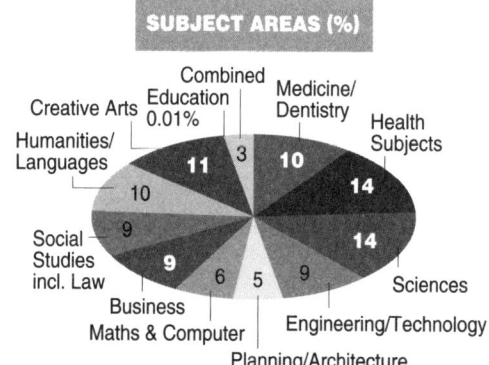

SUBJECT AREAS (%)

Combined Education 0.01%
Creative Arts
Humanities/ Languages
Medicine/ Dentistry
Health Subjects
Social Studies incl. Law
Business
Maths & Computer
Engineering/Technology
Planning/Architecture
Sciences
11 · 3 · 10 · 14 · 14 · 10 · 9 · 9 · 6 · 5 · 9

attraction that many choose to become students here on the city's merits alone.

'Obviously the promise of a place throbbing with the nation's best clubs, packed with men who'll drop their draws and strut their stuff at the mere mention of a factory closure, bursting with 40,000 partying students, and selling beer so cheap it'll make your liver wince, is enticing. But in today's cut-throat world, where new students have to pay a thousand quid just to enter this carnival of hedonistic abandon, and thereafter graduate to a future in which security is not guaranteed, it is probably worth choosing a university which gives you best value for your dosh and which has a reputation that will outshine the competition. That university is Sheffield.'

Whichever one of our statistical boxes you care to consult – 'Where Graduates End Up', 'Academic Excellence', 'What It's Really Like' – Sheffield excels. The uni is full of bright undergraduates, most of them capable of 320 points at A level, eager to become part of and contribute to a

> ***Whether it's hard learnin', heavy partying or just a friendly place to hang out, you'll find it here, and chances are you will never want to leave.***

first-class, lively scene. It is premier league for entertainment (annual union turnover exceeds £3 million), for city life (Sheffield rivals Leeds and Manchester as a serious club scene), for ways to make a difference (the uni is a cauldron for political action; there's even a Students Charter setting out your rights as a student), for developing outside interests (150 + clubs and societies), for sport (they're always in the Top 20 of the national BUSA team tables), for arts (nine theatrical productions a year, five dance societies, a gallery with rolling exhibitions of student art, a film-making society with a major production each term) and for student media – SURE (radio station), ShEP (Internet magazine) and Steel Press (newspaper); all have won prestigious awards.

CAMPUS

The city of Sheffield is roughly in the centre of England. The uni and student ghettoes are all on

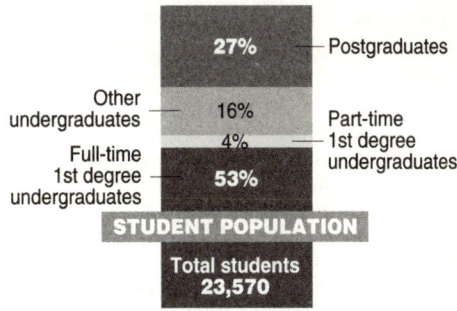

STUDENT POPULATION

Postgraduates 27%
Other undergraduates 16%
Part-time 1st degree undergraduates 4%
Full-time 1st degree undergraduates 53%

Total students 23,570

one side of it and there's a friendly community-feel to the place, although Sheffield is most definitely not a campus university. The central concourse is about fifteen minutes walk from the main city shops, with departments scattered through the surrounding area.

One word describes Sheffield, and that's 'hilly'. Most students walk everywhere, but public transport is reliable and cheap, and there's also Supertram, which runs from the centre to numerous places, including Meadowhall, the famous, out-of-town shopping centre. Having your own transport enables you to enjoy weekends, though. When you come here you'll be on the edge of the Peak District, one of the last great, beautiful wilderness areas of England.

STUDENT PROFILE

The student population is a good balance, so good in fact that this is one of the government's elite 'access' universities, a credit limited to those who take on students from low income neighbourhoods new to the notion of university, yet still able to maintain fine teaching levels – 65% get firsts and upper seconds, and low drop-out rates (3% *is* low).

State sector intake (81%) is high compared to nearby Leeds, as is the mature population. So, students come from a variety of backgrounds and areas and you can expect to meet people whose parents support them well and those trying to make a loan stretch to its limits. 'There isn't an average student at Sheffield,' says Emily McGarr, 'but this is not the place to come if your idea of a good time is Saturday night in watching TV alone.'

Writes Rose: 'One of the most striking and pleasing things about the cosy little cocoon of life, which makes this university a very pleasant place to be, is that you will rarely – if ever – come across prejudice of any sort. The union's absolute

ACADEMIC EXCELLENCE

TEACHING:
(Rated Excellent or 17+ out of 24)

History, Mechanical Engineering, Law, Sociology, Social Work, Architecture, English, Geography, Music, Social Policy, Initial Teacher Training.	**Excellent**
Russian, Automatic Control & Systems Engineering, Electron/Electric Eng, Anatomy, Biosciences, Philosophy, Politics	**24**
Landscape/Town & Regional Planning	**23**
Linguistics, East Asian Studies, Materials Technology, Physics, Archaeology, Library/Info, Psychology	**22**
Hispanic Studies, Chemical Engineering, Civil Eng, French, Maths, Pharmacology, Other Subjects Allied to Medicine, Nursing	**21**
German	**20**
Medicine	**19**

RESEARCH:
Top grades 5/5*

Pre-Clinical Studies, Animal & Plant Sciences, Molecular & Cellular Biology, Automatic Control/Systems Eng, Electronic /Electrical Eng, Metallurgy, Politics, Russian/Slavonic/East European, Library/Info Mgt	**Grade 5***
Hospital-based Clinical Subjects, Clinical Dentistry, Nursing, Psychology, Chemistry, Physics, Medical Physics & Clinical Eng, Pure Maths, Statistics, Computer, Civil Eng, Mechanical/Aeronautical/ Manufacturing Eng, Built Environment, Town/Country Planning, Geography, Law, Social Policy, English, French, Iberian/Latin American, Archaeology, History, Philosophy, Theology, Music, Education	**Grade 5**

UNIVERSITY/STUDENT PROFILE

University since	**1905**
Situation/style	**Civic**
Student population	**23,570**
Full-time undergraduates	**12,590**
- mature	**17%**
- overseas	**7%**
- male/female	**45/55**
- state sector intake	**81%**
- non-traditional student intake	**11%**
- drop-out rate	**3%, low**
- undergraduate applications	**Down 8%**

*see Introduction for key to tables

SOCIAL SCENE

STUDENTS' UNION If you arrive by train or bus you'll be met by Student Reception; volunteer students will beard you in the bars, in halls – every fresher will get a visit, even those in private accommodation.

The next impressive feature is the union concourse with large open-plan sports and activities Workspace, which includes the Viglen Computer Suite with sixteen high-spec PCs for publishing promotional material.

Then there's **The Auditorium** with 380 seats and state-of-the-art audio/visual system, it's a venue for four films a week selected by student ballot, for live jazz and comedy, and for a rolling programme of guest speakers. Fulcrum of the ents scene is **Bar 1**, which recently had a £500,000 makeover. It serves over thirty varieties of beer and takes more in a night than most pubs do in a week.

It also has **Griddles,** meat and veggie fast food emporium, and the **Pizza Bar**. **Interval** (600 capacity) is the continental style café bar – pasta, baguettes, pastries and cabaret acts.

AT A GLANCE

ACADEMIC FILE:

Subjects assessed	**43**
Excellent	**88%**
Average requirements	**320**
Students-staff ratio	**18:1**
First/2:1 degree pass rate	**65%**

ACCOMMODATION FILE:

Guarantee to freshers	**97%**
Style	**Halls, flats, houses**
Approx price range pw	**£40-£94**
City rent pw	**£35-£50**

tolerance of the sizeable gay community is but one reflection of this. Another striking feature is the high visibility of the university's religious community. A small but significant proportion of Sheffield's students, embarking upon their journey of self-discovery, stray off more well-trod paths and instead find God.'

Fusion (600 capacity) is the intimate venue for live bands and clubnights. Recently Ash, Orbital, Placebo, David Gray, Starsailor, Elbow, Pulp, Basement Jaxx, Wheatus.

Then there's **The Foundry** (1,000), which, with Fusion, is host to an amazing series of clubnights. *Tuesday Club* is drum 'n' bass/hip hop, Wednesday's *The Big One*, with top line DJs, Grooverider and LTJ Bookem, Thursday's *The Fuzz Club* (indie/metal in two rooms). Then there's *Loveshack*'s traditional roof-raising eclectic mix on Friday, and *Pop Tarts, Saturday*, the ultimate '60s/'70s retro party – which now employs two dancefloors. The monthly *Climax* is LGB night, now a widely known favourite on the gay scene. The **Octagon Centre** is the major, national-circuit venue (1,600 capacity), just recently feted *Club Mirror* 'Venue of the Year'.

Societies cover almost everything, as Rose discovered: 'The university has an amazing capacity to be all things to all people. Whether you're one of the rare few who actually come here to learn, or you're one of the many who come to play rugby, edit a newspaper, watch bands, worship God, fight injustice, walk up big hills, practise politics, become an actor or do any number of diverse and often bizarre activities – (I'm talking about *you*, Dungeons and Dragons Society!) – you can not only do them here, but you can meet a load of other people who'll do them with you. Sheffield is an incredibly *inclusive* place – everyone is made welcome; sooner or later everyone feels at home.'

A new initiative this year is Sheffield's *Give It A Go* programme. The idea is to encourage you to dip in to a whole host of activities – suck it and see before making a long-term commitment.

In the political arena, this year's fight has been against racism, and against privatisation of the halls (residential properties at the uni are to be run by a public-private partnership, Unite), and against educational funding, but you could just as well have joined societies like Amnesty International and follow their brief. There are societies for particular departments – in fact, the Edward Bramley Law Soc is probably the most active in the union. There are societies for all religions and cultures and general interest societies including Debating, Guinness Appreciation and Shiatsu Massage. The Radio Society, SURE fm, started as an individual's idea three years ago and they're now broadcasting around the union from their own studio, and there is a TV station in preparation. The student newspaper, *Steel Press*, won Newspaper of the Year in 2000, and this year won four awards: Best Reporter, Travel Writer, the Diversity award, and was Overall Winner in the *Guardian* awards. It was also runner up in the Sports Journalist category

WHAT IT'S REALLY LIKE	
UNIVERSITY:	
Social Life	★★★★★
Campus scene	**Diverse, lively, sporty, happening**
Student Union services	**Excellent**
Politics	**Anti-racism + student issues**
Sport	**Key, 50+ clubs**
National team position	**18th**
Sport facilities	**Good**
Arts opportunities	**Film excellent, drama, dance music, art good**
Student newspaper	**The Steel Press**
Guardian awards	**Best Reporter, Travel Writer, Diversity, & Overall Winner**
Student radio	**SURE fm**
Student TV	**In process**
Nightclub	**Fusion, Foundry, The Octagon**
Bars	**Bar One, Interval**
Union ents	**The Big One, The FU22 Club, Love Shack, Pop Tarts**
Union clubs/societies	**150+**
Smoking policy	**Bars only**
Parking	**Poor**
CITY:	
Entertainment	★★★★★
Scene	**Seriously good**
Town/gown relations	**Good**
Risk of violence	**Low**
Cost of living	**Low**
Student concessions	**Good**
Survival + 2 nights out	**£52 pw**
Part-time work campus/town	**Excellent**

and, in the *Independent* awards, in the Best Student Reporter category. Look at the box on page 418 to see how this impacts on graduate destinations – Sheffield came joint second to Oxford with Northumbria in the Journalism category.

The Workspace is the heart of sports clubs and societies and consists of meeting rooms and work areas with telephones and computing facilities that members can use to contact each other, meet and organise events. The manned information desk here is the place to find out about any club, society or working committee.

The Theatre Company uses the **Drama Studio** for productions ranging from Shakespearean tragedy to student-written plays on pornography to musicals. A 400-seat auditorium, extension to the

WHERE GRADUATES END UP

18% Health (Med, Dent), Key Areas
11% Manufacture,
8% Finance,
7% Education,
7% Public Admin,
6% Wholesale/Retail,
Aeronautical Manufacture*, Niche Areas
Accountancy*,
Business/Management,
Architecture, Chemical/
Pharmaceutical, Defence,
Electron/Electric,
Eng/Industrial Design,
Journalism*,
Library/Archival

*indicates Top 10 Graduate Provider

Approximate employed **96%**

union, is used by the Film Unit as a cinema four times a week, showing films well before they are released on video.

Sport Last year the union formed a new partnership with the uni, called Usport, to promote sport throughout the student body. The Goodwin Sports Centre, which includes a first-class (but cold) swimming pool, gym and numerous astro-turf pitches, is undergoing major improvements to its facilities at a cost of £14 million. There are currently some sixty sports clubs with the policy 'sport for all', covering traditional sports like rugby, hockey and cricket and newer sports like frisbee, step and skiing. You can be as involved as you like, many aerobics classes work a 'pay as you go' system for example.

Town 'Roughly a third of all Sheffield University students stay in the city after they graduate,' notes Rose, 'which indicates either a staggering lack of imagination or a real affection for the place. As someone who has been having difficulty cutting the university apron strings herself, I can assure you it is for the latter reason; I feel more at home in Sheffield than I do in the city where I grew up. After about six months of being a student here a strange transformation begins to take place and you slowly start to feel that this is where you belong. Soon you will exhibit all the signs of a Sheffield addict. Flat ground will feel strange and disorientating; you will cry out, "Awright duck," to random strangers and be surprised when they don't

smile back at you; and you will throw tantrums when pubs charge over two pounds for a pint and sandwich shops claim they've never heard of breadcakes. The terminal stages of Sheffphilia are evident when you hear yourself furiously defending Sheffield's reputation as one of the most beautiful cities in Europe.

PILLOW TALK

'Everyone who firmly accepts a place and gets their forms back on time (strongly advised) gets in university-managed accommodation. This makes life easier as you automatically meet at least 300 housemates, pay lower rent and get a cleaner. University accommodation has improved recently offering a greater range, from a cheap two-person room with shared facilities to an individual en-suite room for those who like privacy (and are rich).

'Ranmoor is the biggest and has a bar to rival no other, although smaller halls like Stevenson or Halifax are friendlier. Self-catering accommodation is popular with those who appreciate their independence and enjoy cooking. Some, like Crewe Flats, offer entertainment like a hall, others like Riverdale Flats are cheaper and quieter.

'After a year though, it can get claustrophobic and a student house without oddbods knocking on your door at 3 am for a coffee, may seem an attractive option. The student houses in Broomhill are very popular and therefore very expensive, so you may end up in Crookes or Hunters Bar, both major student living areas. Check the insurance premium before you sign a contract.'

JOBS

Employers favour Sheffield graduates not only because they have been taught well and were probably bright before they got in, but because there is a student culture here which becomes part of every student's life and subliminally Sheffield students pick up the kind of positive, no-shit mind set that employers know will mean you'll get on. By far the greatest number go into medicine, dentistry, commerce (that's financial activities of some kind, including accountancy) and further training for a career in law.

GETTING THERE
☛ By road: M1/J33, A630, A57.
☛ By rail: London, 2:30; Liverpool Lime Street, 1:45; Manchester Piccadilly, 1:00; Nottingham 1:00; Leeds, 30 mins.
☛ By air: Manchester Airport.
☛ By coach: London, 3:45; Newcastle, 4:45; Exeter, 6:30-7:30; Manchester, 3:00.

SHEFFIELD HALLAM UNIVERSITY

Sheffield Hallam University
Howards Street
Sheffield S1 1WB

TEL 0114 225 5555
FAX 0114 253 4023
EMAIL undergraduate-
admissions@shu.ac.uk
WEB www.shu.ac.uk

Sheffield Hallam Union of Students
Nelson Mandela Building
Pond Street
Sheffield S1 2BW

TEL 0114 225 4111
FAX 0114 225 4140
EMAIL [initial.name]@shu.ac.uk
WEB www.hallamunion.com

VAG VIEW

*H*allam *is big business. With more than 23,000 students it is among the largest of the new universities, and its work-orientated courses suggest that it is a teaching establishment bent on stoking the nation's economy, but there is much more to it than that. Hallam came top in last year's research assessments among new universities, tying with de Montfort and gaining three Grade 5s – Art & Design, History and Metallurgy – which indicates international standing. There is a great deal going on at Hallam, and a healthy entrepreneurial ethos underlying everything they do there.*

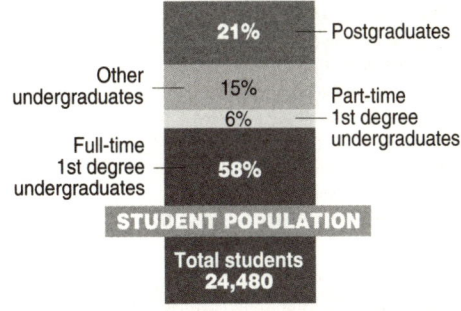

STUDENT POPULATION

Total students
24,480

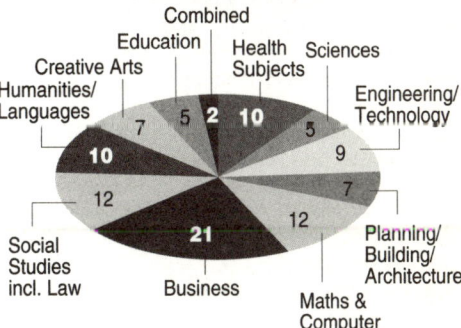

SUBJECT AREAS (%)

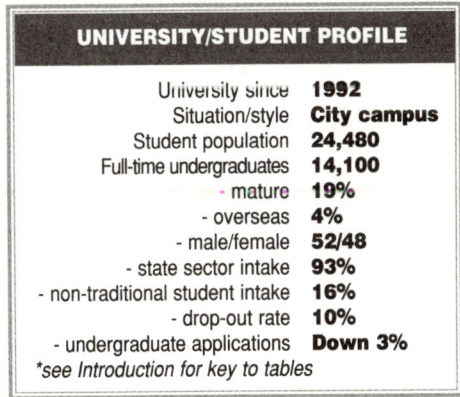

UNIVERSITY/STUDENT PROFILE

University since	**1992**
Situation/style	**City campus**
Student population	**24,480**
Full-time undergraduates	**14,100**
- mature	**19%**
- overseas	**4%**
- male/female	**52/48**
- state sector intake	**93%**
- non-traditional student intake	**16%**
- drop-out rate	**10%**
- undergraduate applications	**Down 3%**

see Introduction for key to tables

CAMPUSES

'One of the best things about Sheffield,' writes Chris Gissing, 'is that it is accessible from anywhere in the country, and (as the prospectus crows) it's right on the doorstep of the Peak District, a great place to go to chill out after those deadline blues. It is also a friendly, cheap place to live with an amazing nightlife and sporting scene

'SHU is based around three sites. City, Collegiate Crescent, and Psalter Lane, the latter being the runt of the litter, with it's school-like corridors, and grim exterior. They're aiming to

move out of there within the next two years.

'Collegiate campus is really quite good, it's a traditional, leafy campus environment, ideally placed on the *revelation* that is Ecclesall Road. Sheffield's Eccy Road is the hub of all student entertainment, with about 830 bars and 6,000 coffee houses (well, maybe not as many as that, but after the first five pubs, who cares?).

'City Campus is excellent too, centrally located and based around four or five disparate buildings, all connected by the stunningly designed **Atrium**. This glass/steel construction has masses of open space, and is like a cosmopolitan street café with tables and chairs and...well...a café. The Adsetts Centre is based here and offers 24-hour access to computers, Internet, books, photocopying etc.

Fortunately, the library staff who seemed to fine me on a weekly basis don't work twenty-four hours.'

ACADEMIC EXCELLENCE

TEACHING:
(Rated Excellent or 17+ out of 24)

English	**Excellent**
Psychology, Physics, Tourism	**24**
Maths, Education, Subjects Allied to Medicine	**23**
Sociology, Materials Technology Art & Design, Molecular Biosci.	**22**
General Engineering; Mech, Aeronautical & Manufacturing Engineering, Nursing	**21**
History of Art, Design & Film	**20**
Modern Languages (French, German, Italian, Spanish) Communication Studies.	**19**
Civil Eng, Elec & Electron Eng.	**18**

RESEARCH:
Top grades 5/5*

Metallurgy, History, Art & Design	**Grade 5**

STUDENT PROFILE

'We have the whole range,' Chris continues, 'from working-class-kid-scraped-through-on-a-BTEC/ through-Clearing sort, to Mummy-and-Daddy-paid-for-my-flat-and-course-fees-darling sort. They're all here in this city – 12% of the city's population are students. Sheffield Hallam has more working-class students than Sheffield University does, but we all seem to get along fairly well, and we are of course allowed to use each others' union bars/women/

AT A GLANCE

ACADEMIC FILE:

Subjects assessed	**25**
Excellent	**76%**
Average requirements	**220 points**
Students-staff ratio	**22:1**
First/2:1 degree pass rate	**48%**

ACCOMMODATION FILE:

Guarantee to freshers	**Will house all somewhere**
Style	**Uni & private sector rooms, flats, bedsits**
Catered	**15%**
En-suite	**25-30%**
Price range per annum	**£1,800-£3,000**
City rent per week	**£35-£50**

blokes (delete as appropriate).'

'Hallam is a place of two halves,' writes Mark Cordell. 'Around half the student body is mature. There aren't exactly grey-haired men with sticks scooting around, but Hallam does have a calmer, more serious environment than other institutions.' High mature and non-traditional uni applicants often go together with high drop-out rates. Hallam is no exception. There is a 10% drop-out rate at undergraduate level, which maybe suggests a bit of dissatisfaction. Its teaching and research assessment ratings are so good, however, that it makes it into the government's group of elite 'access' universities.

Enrich the extra-curricular student culture a bit, make the place a bit more involving, more inclusive, and maybe there would be fewer leaving before their time. Its biggest extra-curricular success is sport, and that is energised by an academic interest.

ACADEMIA

Business & Management is the biggest of its schools. Contact with the world of business and industry is close – many courses are designed in cahoots with outside sources. But now the uni has launched its Enterprise Centre, designed to imbue an enterprise culture throughout academia, encouraging students to be imaginative, innovative and bold in setting about achieving whatever their bent is. This ethos is even becoming clear in the name of courses, such as Physics with Entrepreneurship, new this year.

Currently there is exciting growth in its IT facility. Hallam has been selected, along with York and Cambridge to seed Britain's new international e-University project. An on-line version of their MSc in Information Technology & Management is the first they have agreed to commission.

Students on 400 courses at Hallam can now access their own web-based learning portals, with course details about assignments, course materials, online discussion groups, news announcements, etc.

Finally in this area of electronics, global computer giant Cisco Systems just donated equipment worth $100,000 for a laboratory for Internet working. The lab is to be used by the School of Computing & Management Science for courses covering Internet, wide area (WAN) and local area (LAN) networks.

Top scoring departments at the undergrad teaching assessments were Psychology, Physics, Tourism (all scored full marks), and Maths, Education and subjects allied to Medicine, which only dropped one point. The tourism strength gets graduates jobs in the Hotel/Restaurant category of of our *Employment* box, of course (see page 422), and the health subjects at Hallam also clearly have a huge impact in terms of graduate employment: look for Occupational Therapy, Physiotherapy, Radiotherapy & Oncology, and the degrees in Nursing – adult care, child care, mental care.

Note, too, the impact of sports degrees on the employment picture. A new Centre for Sport & Exercise Science was launched last year to provide facilities and workplace for a team of physiologists, psychologists, biomechanics and physiotherapists. Now, this year, a new fitness suite opens at City Campus.

> *Hallam came top in the research assessments among new universities. There is a great deal going on and a driving, entrepreneurial ethos underlying everything they do.*

Your degree will find you a job, but 'you will need to be self-motivated. If you're after close-knit tutorials with tutors that take a thorough interest in you, you'd be better off working hard and getting into Sheffield University,' Tom Bilton wrote to me.

Back-up resources are increasingly good, however, and Chris Gissing concludes: 'The teaching within my school (Computing & Management Science) was on the whole very good. Although there are the occasional bad tutorials, I cannot fault the department for what they offer in terms of specialist knowledge and resources. On the IT courses there is a strong bias towards industrial placements and business skills, invaluable when going into the real world of work.'

SOCIAL SCENE

STUDENTS' UNION Hallam is getting itself together well enough, but with half the intake mature, it is not the same beast as its longer established neighbour.

The Works is the venue (capacity 1,000), the main bar is **The HUB**. There's a film night in The HUB on Tuesday. Wednesday at The Works is *Voltage* (rock, skate, alt, nu metal). Friday sees *Stardust* ('60s through '90s); Saturday, *Sheff 1* (chart and dance, and a favourite choice for many a year). Recent live acts include Space and Cut le Roc.

Writes Chris: 'There's plenty of fun and games in general, and a variety of nights. The jewel in the union crown is *Stardust*. It has become so popular that there is a constant battle with ticket touts reselling tickets bought at cheaper advance prices.

'**The Wham Bar** is based at the Psalter Lane arts campus. The Collegiate Crescent bar is called **Forgers**, and is rather small, but gets rather busy thanks to the nearby halls of residence: a good place to go after exams, often held at this campus.'

There are twenty five student societies, a magazine (*S Press*), a bit of political campaigning about education funding. The most active is Rock Soc, reminding us yet again that in Sheffield we are on the edge of the beautiful and challenging Peak District – worth coming here for on its own.

SPORT The new fitness suite opening on City Campus spans 600 square metres and has more than seventy fitness stations, an array of the latest equipment, and an advanced weights and training area. The changing facilities are fully equipped for the disabled apparently, and there's also 'a sunbed, assessment rooms and full audio and satellite TV system' – they call that exercise? There'll be another suite opening on Collegiate Campus later this year.

There are thirty-four clubs and the scene is highly competitive – they came 28th nationwide in the BUSA team ratings last year. There's an annual Varsity competition with Sheffield Uni and a ball.

WHAT IT'S REALLY LIKE	
UNIVERSITY:	
Social Life	★★★
Campus scene	**Mature, diverse**
Student Union services	**Good**
Politics	**Average interest**
	Education funding
Sport	**34 clubs**
	Competitive
National team position	**28th**
Sport facilities	**Good**
Arts opportunities	**Few**
Student magazine	**S-Press**
Nightclub	**The Works**
Bars	**The HUB**
Union ents	**Voltage, Stardust, Sheff 1**
Union clubs/societies	**59**
Most popular society	**Rock Society**
Smoking policy	**Bars only**
Parking	**Poor**
CITY:	
Entertainment	★★★★★
Scene	**Seriously good**
Town/gown relations	**Good**
Risk of violence	**Low**
Cost of living	**Average**
Student concessions	**Good**
Survival + 2 nights out	**£60+ pw**
Part-time work campus/town	**Average/good**

Town 'Beyond university, there's a huge number of places to go drinking' reports Chris. 'Special mentions must go to the **Bankers Draft**, and **Weatherspoons**, which offer some great deals on food and drink.

'Sheffield University makes up for the lack of guitar-led music nights with **Fuzz Club**. Alongside top bands appearing at the **Leadmill** and the **Octagon**, there are some smaller, yet worthwhile, venues such as the **Boardwalk**. Of course, there are the obvious *Gatecrasher* nights at **Republic**, too, and sister venue **Bed** to entertain the masses and their glow-sticks.

'Wherever you go of an evening, you're pretty safe, as Sheffield has been voted the UK's safest city at night recently. There are usually enough people around to feel safe, and the city centre is well lit and well serviced by late public transport. See www.firstmainline.co.uk.'

See also *Student Sheffield*, page 413.

PILLOW TALK

They guarantee freshers accommodation only 'of a reasonable standard,' which is at least honest.

This guarantee, however basic it may sound, 'is a definite parent-friendly point to note,' says Chris, 'as finding a house, and living with smelly fridge-raiding strangers is not the most endearing start to student life. Finding housing is easier when house hunting teams are formed in co-operation with the university housing team, and groups of like-minded individualscan find somewhere to admire the various mould cultures that student housing can offer.'

Catered halls and self-catered purpose-built complexes are available. 'Housing varies from excellent (Victoria Halls, Nether Edge) to pretty nasty (City Road, Shoreham Street),' writes Chris. Ian Montgomery agrees: 'Some of the halls of residence are not very nice. I stayed in halls in Totley – six miles outside the town and not particularly pleasant.'

Besides halls, there are partnership schemes in the private sector – converted houses, single or double study bedrooms with communal or en-suite bathroom facilities and shared kitchens; private-sector house shares, flats and bedsits; and lodgings or accommodation with a family (single rooms within a home environment). Most students live in private, rented accommodation.

JOBS

See *Academia*, page 420, for those areas of the syllabus which feed through to the health industry upon graduation. Health and education account for more than a quarter of Hallam graduates, the IT areas feeding manufacturing and computing industries; tourism and sport being clearly

WHERE GRADUATES END UP

15% Health/Social Work, 12% Education, 12% Manufacturing, 9% Finance, 8% Wholesale/Retail, 7% Computer, 5% Hotel/Restaurant, 5% Public Admin	Key areas
Chemical/Pharmaceutical, Construction, Advertising, Aeronautical Manufacture, Sport, Library/Archival, Property, Telecom	Niche areas
Approximate employed	**94%**

identifiable, direct sources to their industry niches, too. Business, mechanical engineering – there are two new degrees in Automotive Engineering this year – remain Hallam's bedrock, as do the various direct degree routes into the pharmaceutical and construction industries.

GETTING THERE

☛ By road: M1 (J33), A630, A57.
☛ By coach: London, 3:45; Newcastle, 4:45; Exeter, 6:30-7:30; Manchester, 3:00.
☛ By rail: London, 2:30; Liverpool Lime Street, 1:45; Manchester Piccadilly, 1:00; Nottingham, 1:00; Leeds, 0:30.
☛ By air: Manchester Airport.

SOMERSET COLLEGE

Somerset College of Arts & Technology
Wellington Road
Taunton
Somerset TA1 5AX

TEL 01823 366331
FAX 01823 366418
EMAIL enquiries@somerset.ac.uk
WEB www.somerset.ac.uk

VAG VIEW

*S*CAT is anything but content to see itself
as a local college: it runs a Roadshow
Bus, which travels the country in a drive for
recruitment. What you get when you arrive
is a college of sufficient quality to have been
awarded the Queen's Anniversary Prize for
Further and Higher Education, a tutorial-
centred method of teaching and an
impressive Learning/Media Resources Centre
– a 45,000-volume library and full media
facilities, including a TV studio and
production and editing equipment.

Particularly popular with students are
five fashion design degrees (Fashion, Fashion
Textiles, Surface Pattern, Textiles, Textiles &
Surface Pattern), a BSc in Building and a BA
(Hons) in Packaging (design, printing, etc.).

Sports facilities include a large hall, gym
and sports pitches. The Students' Union stock
a bar and stage the usual ents.

COLLEGE PROFILE

Founded	**1975**
Status	**F/HE College**
Degree awarding universities	**Plymouth , Nottingham Trent**
Degree undergraduates	**266**

ACCOMMODATION:

Availability to freshers	**100%**
Style	**Halls, flats,**
Cost pw (no food)	**£50**
Town rent pw	**£40**

DEGREE SUBJECTS:
**Design, Business Admin, Welfare
Studies, Engineering (incl Automotive),
Social Care & Public Mgt, Arts (modular)**

GETTING THERE

- By road: M5/J25.
- By coach: London, 3:45.
- By rail: London, 2:30; Birmingham, 2:15; Plymouth, 1:23; Swindon, 1:22; Southampton, 2:34.

SOUTH BANK UNIVERSITY

South Bank University
103 Borough Road
London SE1 0AA

TEL 020 7815 7815
FAX 020 7815 8273
EMAIL (go via website)
WEB www.sbu.ac.uk

South Bank Students' Union
Keyworth Street
London SE1 6NG

TEL 020 7815 6060
FAX 020 7815 6061
EMAIL vpsocs@sbu.ac.uk
WEB

VAG VIEW

*S*outh Bank projects you into the big
city, where the streets are paved with
whatever you want them to be paved with.
You come to South Bank University, you
come to London...for a bit of gritty realism.

CAMPUS

Much of it is clustered around a triangle
demarcated by Borough Road, London Road and
Southwark Bridge Road, just south of the Thames at
Elephant and Castle. There is also the aforesaid site
at Wandsworth Road. and yet two other sites even
further away – the Faculty of Health & Social Care
at Harold Wood Hospital (Romford) and Whipps
Cross Hospital (Leytonstone) – a situation rather

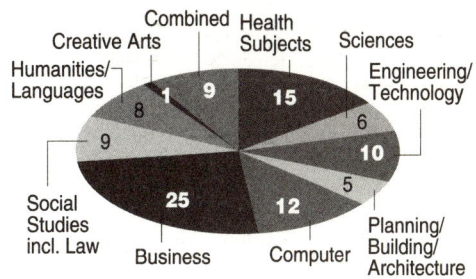

SUBJECT AREAS (%)

Combined Health
Creative Arts
Humanities/
Languages
Social Studies incl. Law
Business
Computer
Planning/Building/Architecture
Sciences
Engineering/Technology
Health Subjects

1, 9, 15, 8, 9, 6, 10, 5, 25, 12

optimistically 'solved' by calling these two distinct
sites the Redwood Campus.

'Don't come to South Bank if you are expecting a

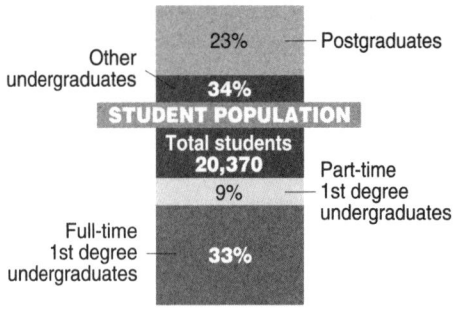

Other undergraduates — **34%**

23% — Postgraduates

STUDENT POPULATION

Total students **20,370**

9% — Part-time 1st degree undergraduates

Full-time 1st degree undergraduates — **33%**

ACADEMIC EXCELLENCE	
TEACHING:	
(Rated Excellent or 17+ out of 24)	
Education	**23**
Modern Languages, Town & Country Planning	**22**
Subjects Allied to Medicine, Politics	**21**
Communication & Media, Civil Eng, Anatomy, Biosciences, Business/Management, Economics, Nursing, Psychology	**20**
Sociology, Electrical & Electronic Engineering.	**19**
Chemical Engineering, Land & Property Mgt, Mechanical & Manufacturing Engineering, Building, Food Sciences.	**18**
RESEARCH:	
Top grades 5/5*	**None**

campus lifestyle, come to South Bank if you want the excitement of studying in London. Location – prime,' reports Lola Brown. 'Situated in Zones 1/2, the main campuses of South Bank are ideally located on the uber trendy South Bank, in walking distance of London Bridge and Waterloo stations. Elephant & Castle itself is a bit of a hole but is improving rapidly with some major urban regeneration happening. It has its own tube station (Bakerloo & Northern lines), a new bowling alley and a Tesco Metro.

'South Bank is good for gritty realism. Many of the university buildings are quite grim and old, the Students' Union is situated next to the DHSS, there are plenty of colourful local characters shouting at students, and there are no real open spaces unless you are based at Redwood Campus (some Faculty of Health courses), which is in the middle of nowhere and can feel isolated.'

UNIVERSITY/STUDENT PROFILE	
University since	**1992**
Situation/style	**City sites**
Student population	**20,370**
Full-time undergraduates	**6,730**
- mature	**40%**
- overseas	**13%**
- male/female	**50/50**
- state sector intake	**94%**
- non-traditional student intake	**12%**
- drop-out rate	**22%, high**
- undergraduate applications	**Down 7%**
see Introduction for key to tables	

STUDENT PROFILE

The majority of students come from the locality, which includes a colourful tapestry of ethnicity; most undergraduates are mature, 94% come from the state sector, more than a third come from social groups not traditionally known for going to university (IIIM, IV, V), and 12% from so-called low-participation neighbourhoods. A huge section

(22%) of young entrants drop out after a year; drop-out rates don't come much higher among young entrants.

'A real cross section,' says Lola. 'South Bank has many mature students and a diverse ethnic mix. Freshers here are not generally middle-class white kids, though there are a fair few of those too.

'We have several famous students, high numbers of sporting achievers (including members of the British Commonwealth Team) and of course Louise Woodward – but you probably won't see her, as she never hits the union for a night out.'

ACADEMIA

The portfolio of degrees is markedly vocational. There's a feel of Salford Uni about it – the health – nursing (child, adult, mental care), the nutrition,

AT A GLANCE	
ACADEMIC FILE:	
Subjects assessed	**28**
Excellent	**75%**
Average requirements	**160 points**
Students-staff ratio	**20:1**
First/2:1 degree pass rate	**39%**
ACCOMMODATION FILE:	
Guarantee to freshers	**75%**
Style	**Halls**
Approx price range pw	**£66-£80**
City rent pw	**£70**

occupational health & safety, sociology, engineering, media, computing, business, sport, built environment – South Bank is No 5 and Salford is at No 6 nationally in our Employment Top 10 for the construction industry. Again, as at Salford, many undergraduates are on sandwich courses. There's a taste of the workplace about much on offer, though the course list is not as well developed as Salford's: there's not such a priority language pro-vision, for example – Salford's is first class and

> *The teaching picture is very good. Assessments have been uniformly excellent. But the student culture is challenging, and one wonders how an ingenue, coming from afar, would take it.*

all-pervasive – and the media is more general and bland. There are some good BA/BSc combinations of the subjects that are on offer, and our advice is to pick subjects where skills content is high.

Besides Built Environment, faculties include Business & Management (by far the largest), Engineering, Computing, Design & Technology, Science, Humanities & Social Science and Health & Social Care. The course programme is modular in structure. There are decent learning resources, a centre has 400 Pentium PCs with Internet facility and allows access to a CD-ROM network. In addition, there are four libraries, one at each of the four sites, with a total of 300,000 books.

The teaching picture is very good. Assessments have been uniformly excellent, with 75% of them scoring 18 or more points out of 24, the health subjects, Education, Modern Languages (European Studies, French, German), Town & Country Planning, and Politics hitting very good scores indeed (see *Academic Excellence* box, page 424). Students of Built Environment, a bit out on a limb at a site on the Wandsworth Road quite a way from the main campus, can bask in the glory of being among the Top 10 providers to the construction industry.

SOCIAL LIFE

'It's London, innit,' explains Lola. 'Anything, anytime, whatever you like to do. The South Bank itself has a buzzing vibe every night and there are some fantastic restaurants in the Elephant – **Pizza Castella** (John Major's favourite apparently), Ivory Arch (Indian cuisine) and Tai Won Mein (super cheap scrummy noodle bar). We're close to both the **Old Vic** and Shakespeare's **Globe** theatres which'll inject you with culture. Lower Marsh, a five minute walk from uni, is extremely hip with lots of cool galleries, bars, eateries and shops. It takes only about five minutes on the tube to get to Oxford Circus so the whole of London is your oyster.

'Elephant is not, however, the nicest of areas, but keep your wits about you and everything will be cool.

'On campus the **Isobar** is used for clubnights and parties, whilst the **Arc** (which is huge) hosts bigger do's. Most club-nights are free – [the regular one is Wednesday night's Oblivion, and there are monthly comedy nights] – and several big name acts (Fabio & Grooverider, Kelle le Roc and Bentley Rhythm Ace to name a few) have played.

'Just around the back of the students' union is the over-rated, over-priced **Ministry of Sound**, an experience everyone has to try once so they can see London's entire tourist population crammed into one small space. Ministry are starting a student

WHAT IT'S REALLY LIKE	
UNIVERSITY:	
Social Life	★★★
Campus scene	**More of a London than a uni scene**
Student Union services	**OK**
Politics	**Student issues, activity low**
Sport	**Improving. 20 clubs**
National team position	**74th**
Sport facilities	**Improving**
Arts opportunities	**Music excellent, drama, dance, film good; art poor**
Student newspaper	**Scratch**
Student radio	**Radio X-cape**
Nightclub	**Isobar**
Bars	**Tavern**
Union ents	**Oblivion**
Union clubs/societies	**35**
Most popular societies	**Afrikan, Islamic, Forensic Science**
Smoking policy	**Union, halls OK**
Parking	**Poor**
CITY:	
Entertainment	★★★★★
Scene	**Excellent**
Town/gown relations	**Average**
Risk of violence	**Average**
Cost of living	**Very high**
Student concessions	**Excellent**
Survival + 2 nights out	**£80 pw**
Part-time work campus/town	**Average/excellent**

night soon, though if past experience is anything to go by the drinks will still cost a high percentage of your student loan.

'In the main Students' Union building there are three bars, the **Tavern** (traditional pub type, TV screens for sport, pool table), the **Snug** (a cosy no smoking zone) and the **Isobar**, with a café area and pool tables by day then turning into a club by night. These are always fairly busy and there is usually plenty of free entertainment. Alcohol is relatively cheap compared to drinking in the rest of London, from £1.50 a pint. There is also a union bar at the Wandsworth Road campus, but it sucks and is barely worth mentioning.

'Coming to study at South Bank will not be cheap, but it depends how you want to spend your time. There is plenty of opportunity to find a job however, so you can earn to support whatever habits you acquire living in the city.'

A social life can also be lived through one of the clubs & societies – not a great number, twenty of the former and 15 societies only – but there are some very successful cultural societies at South Bank, such as the Afrikaan society with its hugely successful club night, *Black Pepper*. Islamic is also big – there are prayer rooms for Islamic students, a Chaplaincy service and several religious societies – oh, and Forensic Science, I kid you not (and this is a good degree course to get on if you can). There is also plenty of scope for students to get involved with the student magazine, *Scratch*, or the new radio station, A-cape, or indeed to organise your own thing – as elsewhere, if you get a quorum, the union will fund it.

'Politically,' writes Lola, 'we're verging on the left wing, but the most political thing to happen is an occasional guest speaker or a meeting.'

SPORT They were finalists in the national BUSA Cricket Plate last year and cracked stick in the southern league Hockey Plate, coming out victors. They picked up a European Masters gold medal in judo last year and took first place in the MUSA marathon. Generally, team sportspersons at South Bank play hard and party harder.

PILLOW TALK
There are several halls of residence available to first years; Dante Road or New Kent are by far preferable to McLaren House, which is famed for its Nazi-like wardens and strict regimes. Accommodation is expensive, McLaren charges £72 a week, but you could probably find a flat-share not too far away for around £50.

WHERE GRADUATES END UP	
21% Health/SocialWork,	Key Areas
8% Wholesale/Retail,	
8% Computer,	
7% Finance,	
7% Education,	
6% Public Admin,	
5% Hotel/Restaurant	
Advertising, Telecom	Niche Areas
Construction*, Legal,	
Library/Archival, Market	
Research, Property,	
Legal, Library/Archival,	
Market Research,	
Property, Radio/TV	

*indicates Top 10 Graduate Provider

Approximate employed **88%**

JOBS
Everything is geared to getting a job academically, and many come here job hungry, though the student culture is hardly cohesive in comparison to some, and one wonders how a student would feel coming from afar to South Bank. The construction industry, health, finance, computing head off an interesting list of real-life opportunity in our *Employment* box.

GETTING THERE
☛ By Underground: Elephant and Castle (Bakerloo and Northern Lines) or mainline Waterloo station. Wandsworth Road site: Stockwell (Victoria and Northern lines).

UNIVERSITY OF SOUTHAMPTON

The University of Southampton
Highfield
Southampton SO17 1BH

TEL 023 8059 5000
FAX 023 8059 3037
EMAIL prospenq@soton.ac.uk
WEB www.soton.ac.uk

Southampton Students' Union
Highfield
Southampton SO17 1BJ

TEL 023 8059 5200
FAX 023 8059 5252
EMAIL susu@soton.ac.uk
WEB www.soton.ac.uk/~susu/

VAG VIEW

Southampton has one of the best academic records in the country, but has suffered a poor reputation for student satisfaction beyond academia – historically the social side of things has been a bit limp. A new union bar and gig venue has been rumoured for years, but never materialised. Campus life has been described to us as pretty dull, even though the number of student societies has always been high. Now, all that may be about to change.

CAMPUS

From east or west you rattle along the M27 until you hit Junction 5, whereupon you dive down south, following the uni signs, and suddenly, two miles from the centre of the city, there you are in it. You don't *enter* the main Highfield campus as you might Sussex campus or Nottingham. It is a campus split by University Road, a public road with uni buildings off to the left and right, so that you're not sure whether the city has wandered onto the campus or the campus has not yet quite commandeered its piece of the city (there is

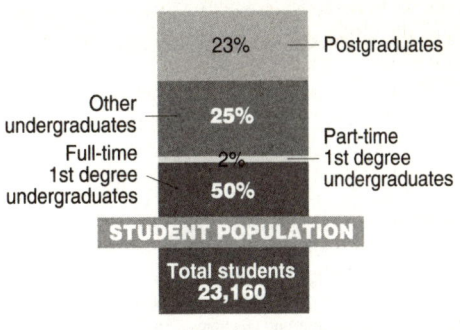

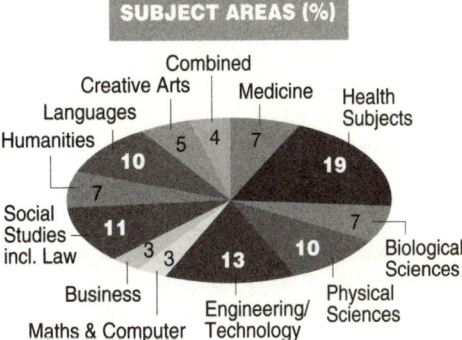

UNIVERSITY/STUDENT PROFILE	
University since	**1952**
Situation/style	**Campus**
Student population	**23,160**
Full-time undergraduates	**11,610**
- mature	**14%**
- overseas	**7%**
- male/female	**45/55**
- state sector intake	**77%**
- non-traditional student intake	**7%, low**
- drop-out rate	**4%, low**
- undergraduate applications	**Down 4%**
see Introduction for key to tables	

nothing of the excitement of Manchester's Oxford Road, where such questions would never occur).

There's a chemically, sciency feel about campus, which does not surprise, and then you're transported into some carefully landscaped botanical gardens, and on, across The Avenue, eventually to be released onto the huge, open acreage of Southampton Common, where you can...breathe! It's all rather laboratorial, claustrophobic, bursting at the seams, for such an eminent university.

You must travel a little further south for New College (see *Satellite Campuses*, below), and finally

you arrive at Southampton's Dockside Campus/ Oceanography Centre.

STUDENT PROFILE

The tradition is that, apart from a small scattering of minority groups and locals, Southampton students are middle-class understudies who like pullovers and Radio 2, and that they ended up at Southampton because Exeter didn't want them. The official statistics do not do much to contradict this view. The state school intake is 77%, the take from the lower social groups IIIM, IV, V is 17% (national average is 26%), and from traditionally low-participation neighbourhoods, 7% – all of which are below their benchmarks, set by the Government, by 4 or 5%. The public school kid intake is similar to that of Reading or Warwick. The Students' Union has, in recent years, had a Conservative pedigree: revolutionary Southampton students are not, which is perhaps why it has taken so long for the uni to be persuaded to shell out for a decent pleasure zone. However, parents note, at least it's a safe place to be: in a survey by the Adam Smith Institute of student drug-taking, Southampton came out 'most abstemious'.

ACADEMIA

As a centre of academic excellence, they take some beating – 91% of the teaching assessments

ACADEMIC EXCELLENCE

TEACHING:
(Rated Excellent or 17+ out of 24)

Chemistry, Applied Social Work, Computer Studies, Geography, English, Oceanography, Geology, Music.	**Excellent**
Philosophy, Electric/Electron Eng	**24**
Economics, Education, Medicine General Eng, Management	**23**
Ships Science, Biosciences Art & Design, Nursing, Physics	**22**
Psychology, Sociology, Civil Eng, Mech, Aeronaut & Manuf Eng	**21**
History of Art, Maths	**20**
Modern Languages (French, German, Iberian Studies).	**18**

RESEARCH:
Top grades 5/5*

Physics, Computer, Civil Eng, Electrical/Electronic Eng, Mechanical/Aeronautical/ Manufacturing Eng, Law, European Studies, Music	**Grade 5***
Clinical Laboratory Sciences, Hospital-based Clinical, Psychology, Biological Sciences, Chemistry, Environmental Sciences, Pure Maths, Applied Maths, Statistics, Operational Research, Geography, Economics, Social Policy, English, Archaeology, History	**Grade 5**

are Excellent, or 18+ out of 24, and it just came in 11th nationally for research, their world class grades increasing from two to eight and including all subject areas in the defining faculty – Engineering & Applied Science – and in the Faculty of Law.

In the Medical Faculty, rated full marks in the teaching assessments and picking up national and international plaudits for research, they are looking for the committed, well-rounded applicant; he or she may only have one science A level among the stipulated AAB: it will have to be Chemistry, but the remaining two could be Arts. They want students capable of approaching problems with a certain flair, not confined by specialism. Coursework is geared towards problem-

> *Southampton has one of the best academic records in the country, but historically the student scene has been a bit limp. Now, that may be about to change.*

solving; patient contact is made in the first term in order to develop communication skills. If you look at another area in which the uni is renowned – Geography – you see a similar sort of picture. Analytical skills, problem-solving and written and oral expression are to the fore – it's an approach to which employers relate.

In the Oceanography Centre at Southampton's Dockside, Marine Science students also have access to exceptional analytical and research facilities. The faculty produces partnership degrees with Biology, Geology, Geography, Maths, Physics, which have led to Excellent ratings in the assessments. Ellen MacArthur's stunning performance in Kingfisher, in the Vendee Global Challenge, carried with it tank and wind-tunnel research work done by the university. The yachtswoman was closely involved on campus in the design and testing processes.

Many Southampton graduates bound for the Defence industry (see *Employment* box, page 430) come from the Faculty of Engineering & Applied Science. The faculty houses Electronics and Computing, which gained world-class ratings in the research assessments, and Electronics scored full marks in the teaching assessments. Southampton is one of eight regional centres for development of the Grid, a second generation internet that will be far easier to use and more powerful than today's version.

Most interesting is their so-called Assistive Technology Centre, based in the Hartley Library, an open access workstation facility for use by students with dyslexia.

SOCIAL SCENE

STUDENTS' UNION It's a £5.33 million refurb we're talking about (after a £300k budget increase) and it's all for you, from September 2002. The original building was designed in 1966, and for the last twenty years or more it has clearly been inadequate – long has the great investment been rumoured; long has it been overdue. Even now, the university talks of 'the whole point' of the refurbishment being 'to try and improve the circulation around the building', subliminally aware perhaps of the claustrophobia that beset me, but blind, it would seem, to the project's most pertinent potential. For years students here have had to suffer the debilitating cultural effects of one of the worst union focal points in the country: 'Campus doesn't so much have a buzz as a dull whimper, which is drowned out if somebody starts mowing the lawns in the botanical gardens,' wrote Warwick Payne of life here. 'The main bar is poky and underfunded, and, as the 1967 union building was built for 3,500 students and now serves around five times the number, social events are always squashed. Go downtown.'

But now all this is behind them. No longer will students have to rely on the refectory as nightclub (*Poundstretcher* on Friday, aptly named *Medication* on Saturday). When you arrive, you will find a cinema, ents venue and two bars, where once was the debating chamber. I dare say there'll be a tantalising new ents menu to go with. Certainly the architects have done an extraordinarily good job, facilitating the new services by opening up 'dead' areas in the original design, utilising what's there in imaginative fashion.

Nor are building plans stopping there. Soon, under the auspices of the uni's Department of Sport & Recreation, there'll be a new sports facility with swimming pool and sports hall right next door to the union. Goodness knows where they'll fit it all in. Completion date for that is September 2003.

Societies have always been strong at Southampton. *Wessex Scene*, the student paper, and Surge Radio remain a feature. On religion, all major beliefs have societies. For Drama, there's the highly rated **Nuffield Theatre**, and there's a thriving Film Society. There's also a tradition of student bands. Most recently, Mark Hill, who formed Artful

WHAT IT'S REALLY LIKE	
UNIVERSITY:	
Social Life	★★★★
Campus scene	**Friendly, middle class, sporty**
Student Union services	**Average**
Politics	**Tory heartland**
Sport	**76 clubs**
National team position	**16th**
Sport facilities	**Good**
Arts opportunities	**Excellent**
Student newspaper	**Wessex Scene**
Student radio	**Surge Radio**
Nightclub	**The DC**
Bars	**Two new bars as yet un-named**
Union ents	**Poundstretcher, Medication**
Union clubs/societies	**182**
Smoking policy	**NS Uni buildings**
Parking	**No first years**
CITY:	
Entertainment	★★★
Scene	**Pubs, clubs, water**
Town/gown relations	**Average-poor**
Risk of violence	**Average**
Cost of living	**Low**
Student concessions	**OK**
Survival + 2 nights out	**£50 pw**
Part-time work campus/town	**Good**

AT A GLANCE	
ACADEMIC FILE:	
Subjects assessed	**32**
Excellent	**91%**
Average requirements	**280 points**
Students-staff ratio	**17:1**
First/2:1 degree pass rate	**57%**
ACCOMMODATION FILE:	
Guarantee to freshers	**If uni first firm choice**
Style	**Halls, flats**
Catered	**25%**
En-suite	**45%**
Price range pw	**£51-£115**
City rent pw	**£50-£70**

Dodger and stormed up the UK charts, came out of here.

SPORT The uni excels. They came 16th in last year's national BUSA team ratings. The sports grounds are just the other side of the M27; on-campus

facilities include sports hall, fitness studio, squash courts, martial arts area (Zen Shorin Do karate is the thing), and there's a rifle range. New developments include a water-based artificial turf pitch and plans for a new complex and swimming pool. Swimmers meanwhile use New College's indoor pool. There's a boatyard for watersporters.

The sailors have won the BUSA championship more times than Portsmouth care to recall. Recently, six Southampton students scooped top honours in the student class of the prestigious Tour Voile yacht race around France. They were part of a 14-strong crew representing the British Universities sailing team, and finished 9th overall, 1st in the student rankings.

Meanwhile, Social Psychologist Dr Mark Van Vugt's groundbreaking research has found that cheaper football teams, with a low level turnover of players, performed consistently better than teams with endless cash and a high player turnover. Can he have visited the Saints?

TOWN While Southampton itself has neither the size nor vigour of Manchester or its football team, nor yet the groovy cuts of Brighton or even

WHERE GRADUATES END UP	
19% Health (incl Medicine), **11% Finance,** **10% Manufacturing,** **8% Public Admin,** **7% Wholesale/Retail** **7% Computer, 5% Personnel**	Key Areas
Accountancy, Defence*, **Aeronautical Manufacture,** **Electron/Electric,** **Eng/Industrial Design,** **Journalism, Library/** **Archival, Market** **Research, Property**	Niche Areas
*indicates Top 10 Graduate Provider	
Approximate employed **92%**	

Bournemouth, it's a lively enough place to live. Having been a Regency holiday resort, the city centre has a large number of spacious parks and waterfront attractions.

'If Southampton were a person, it would be a dedicated alcoholic,' said a student. 'The city centre and waterfront have a network of colossal alcohol palaces (including Britain's largest pub, the **Square Balloon**), yet the city lacks a twilight zone, for, owing to a local statute, even nightclubs are not allowed to open later than 2.'

Ents very often go into the city – student nights, for example, to **Ikon** and **Diva**; **Academy** or **Jesters** for the weekly sports night.

There are three cinemas and the **Mayflower Theatre**, which plays host to several major West End shows. Musically, Southampton lacks a major venue and is often ignored by the larger acts: consult your Bournemouth train timetable.

PILLOW TALK

University accommodation (halls and flats) is guaranteed to all first year undergraduates who meet the terms of their offers, and name Southampton as their firm choice: 40% of fresher accommodation is catered, 45% en suite; cost per week varies from £51 to £115.

City rent costs about £50 in Southampton (£60 in Winchester for the School of Art (see page 431)). There are new and notably enlightened residences now for couples, too: Shaftesbury Avenue and Edwina House.

Avoid Bencraft and Stoneham halls. Bencraft is miles from anywhere and Stoneham is Southampton's answer to the walled city of Kowloon apparently.

JOBS

A computer-aided guidance system, Prospects Planner, trains soon-to-be-graduates in interview techniques, CV writing and management competencies. There are employer-led skills workshops, and uni support in finding a job through their own on-line vacancy service (E-jobs), and through TargetedGrad, a service linking premier employers and students from a few targeted universities.

After health, the City claims most of Southampton's graduates. So we should scarcely be surprised that the top accolade in the Institute of Chartered Accountants in England and Wales professional exams just went to a Southampton graduate, now working for PriceWaterhouse Coopers.

There are some telling niche areas, too (see box). Defence is clearly a priority. Like Portsmouth along the coast, Southampton has a very active OTC. There's a University Air Squadron and Royal Naval Unit. In 1994 they were chosen to run the Royal Navy's Engineering Sponsorship Scheme, and are now running similar programmes with the British Army and Royal Airforce. All Aerospace students attend a one-week flight test course during the summer term of their second year. The course is conducted by staff at Cranfield University (see entry).

Law is also a big draw, following further training.

Finally, as if to prompt our perception of the uni into entrepreneurial mode, we hear that they are responsible for the world's first self-heating coffee can – Nestlé's new 'hot when you want' instant coffee for consumers on the move. Shame that students only have to tip out of bed into the new union café for their caffeine burst.

SATELLITE CAMPUSES

UNIVERSITY OF SOUTHAMPTON NEW COLLEGE The Avenue, Southampton SO17 1BG. Tel 023 8059 7317. Largely appealing to the locality, New College asks less by way of entry but offers pukka Southampton BA and BSc degrees in the areas of humanities, applied social sciences, sport, life sciences, ecology, geography, human sciences. Now, this year, there's an innovative foundation degree in Health Care, which crosses traditional professional boundaries and includes nursing, physiotherapy, occupational therapy, podiatry, and health and social care administration skills.

There is an active Students' Union with a 600-capacity college bar, weekly ents and four balls a year with live bands, casino tables and inflatable bar games.

The uni is to commit a recent multi-million

pound award from the Higher Education Funding Council for England, to marketing new courses to groups currently under-represented in Higher Education.

WINCHESTER SCHOOL OF ART Park Avenue, Winchester SO23 8DL. Tel 01962 842500. This is Southampton's Art & Design faculty and has been part of the uni since 1996. They are only about twelve miles apart, but really quite separate. There has been considerable investment – £3 million bought new studios, a library (20-25,000 volumes, 100,000 slides, 4,000 videos), a lecture theatre, photo and digital workshops, seminar rooms and a Students' Union. Degrees are offered in History of Art & Design, Fashion, Fine Art, Textile Art, Textiles/ Fashion. A Fine Art Painting graduate, Katie Pratt, recently scooped the UK's most

valuable art prize, the Jerwood Prize of £30,000.

In 1995, they opened a purpose-built student village (Erasmus Park), with high quality self-catering accommodation, making plain their appeal to a more than local student clientele. A Students' Union organises film clubs, live bands, theatre groups and a summer ball.

GETTING THERE

☞ By road to Southampton: M3/J 14, A33. To Winchester: M3/J10 or A34.
☞ By coach to Southampton: London, 2:30; Bristol, 2:45; Birmingham, 3:40. To Winchester: London, 2:00; Birmingham, 5:30.
☞ By rail to Southampton: London Waterloo, 1:40; Bristol Parkway, 2:15; Birmingham, 3:30; Sheffield, 4:45; Winchester, 20 mins.
☞ By air: Southampton International Airport.

SOUTHAMPTON INSTITUTE

Southampton Institute
East Park Terrace
Southampton
Hampshire SO14 0YN

TEL 023 8031 9039
FAX 023 8033 4161
EMAIL admissions@solent.ac.uk
WEB www.solent.ac.uk

VAG VIEW

Southampton Institute, out of Southampton College of Art, the College of Higher Education and the College of Nautical Studies at Warwash, looks an attractive thoroughbred in its own right. There is an innovative vocational portfolio, an enviable record of excellence in the teaching assessments, a lively student scene and it is not too demanding at entry (140 points should see you in). What's more, its investment in student residences (almost 2,000 can now be accommodated) indicates an appeal already not restricted to a local clientele. So we should not be surprised that the institute is on the verge of being awarded University College status.

INSTITUTE PROFILE

Founded	**1984**
Status	**HE College**
Degree awarding university	**Nottingham Trent**
Situation/style	**City campus**
Student population	**10,820**
Degree undergraduates	**6,930**
ACCOMMODATION FILE:	
Guarantee to freshers	**95%**
Style	**Halls**
Approx price pw (no food)	**£70-£77**
City rent pw	**£50-£70**

and pretty soon you will go drinking with them every night until you run out of money or are barred from every club, pub or bar in the city.

STUDENT PROFILE

'A lot of the students here fall into one category: fugitives from pop,' writes Tanver Hussain. 'The blokes all look like fugitives from just about any boy band and the girls could form All Saints 100 times over. This excludes Art students and the rugby team, as you will find that they are in worlds of their own! Don't be frightened! You'll find a group of people you will naturally slot into

ACADEMIA

Right now degrees are awarded by Nottingham Trent, but soon it seems they will be their own masters in this regard. Recently they opened a £9-million centre with information technology suite, lecture theatres and admin offices. Besides Maritime (including yacht and powercraft design), faculties of the institute include Design (Fashion, Fine Art, Graphic Design, etc, plus plans for a

ACADEMIC EXCELLENCE

TEACHING :
(Rated Excellent or 17+ out of 24)

Civil Eng, Building, Land & Property Management	**22**
Drama, Dance & Cinematics, Leisure/Sport	**21**
Psychology, Sociology, Electric & Electron Engineering, General Eng, Mechanical & Manuf Eng, Materials Tech.	**19**
Town & Country Planning, Communication & Media	**18**
Art & Design	**17**

number of multimedia design and digital imaging courses); Built Environment (including a unique set of Fine Arts Valuation and antiques courses linked to national auction houses); Business (all the usual plus sport and language and law tie-ups); Law; Media Arts (including the Film Studies course that scored so highly under QAA's 'Drama, Dance, Cinematics' banner – see box, above – as well as Journalism and Advertising); Social Science (Community Studies, Psychology, Criminology, Politics, plus now Journalism & Politics); Systems Engineering (masses of computer courses and a tasty specialist degree in Media Technology for the broadcast, film & entertainment industries). The curriculum is exciting, innovative, expanding fast.

SOCIAL SCENE

STUDENTS' UNION By far the largest slice of the union budget goes to sport, and news that they might soon include 'university' in their name seems to be generating just the right sort of morale-boosting vibes in the sporty environs of the union: 'Apart from the fact that we could, at some point, be able to call ourselves a university,' said Danny Coyle, 'wouldn't it be nice if the V-necks and the Pompey scrummers could no longer ram down our throats chants like "Thickstitute" and "Destitute"!'

The union has three bars, renovated within the not so distant past, the downstairs **Base Bar** with retro nights and regular happy hours, the bar upstairs, known as the **Top Bar**, which is more your authentic pub-style venue, and the **Budweiser Sports Bar**, quiet during the day but on Wednesday nights not the place for a romantic heart-to-heart – karaoke and serious drinking with '4 for the price of 3' alcopop deals is the prelim to **Ikon** in town (with an Express Pass which will beat the inevitable queue at Southampton's biggest nightclub). This union/town tie-up is typical of the

weekly ents menu. On Monday, *Sounds of the Underground* (hip hop, break beat, drum 'n' bass) precedes entry to the town's **Rhino Club** with a £1-off voucher, and the same deal is open to students on Thursdays, following a funky house and US garage warm-up (*Unleashed*) at the union. There's a **Chicago Rock Café** link-up on Tuesdays and *Supersonic* (funk 'n' soul to rock 'n' roll) on Thursdays. Saturdays, the place is up for private hire; often private promoters come in for an all-ticket event, such as the recent sell-out promotion by Debauchery. It was rated the No. 1 place to club in the South on no less than three occasions by Ministry.

Media-wise there's the impressive *Havit* magazine.

SPORT As expected in a college dedicated to maritime subjects, water plays a key part. They have one of the premiere Maritime Schools, the sailing team being current Southampton varsity champions and coming third recently in the world yachting championships. There are, in addition, all the usual ground-based sports. Facilities include a sports hall and fitness suite, with sauna and solarium. Playing fields are four miles from the city. There's a licensed pavilion.

WHERE GRADUATES END UP

14% Finance,	Key Areas
13% Manufacturing,	
11% Wholesale/Retail,	
8% Computer,	
7% Public Admin	
Electron/Electric,	Niche Areas
Advertising, Aeronautical	
Manufacture, Film/Video,	
Business/Management,	
Architecture, Journalism,	
Legal, Property,	
Publishing, Radio/TV,	
Sport, Telecom	
Approximate employed	**93%**

PILLOW TALK

Cream of the halls crop would have to be Lucia Foster Welch, not only is it the biggest, but it has the advantage of having Ocean Village on its doorstep. The downside is that you are fifteen minutes away from the main campus and there is no common room. The other halls all have their plus points, Kimber and its spangly new kitchens or Deanery, one of the newest. All have their own laundry. You can't choose where you live, but you can choose to have an en-suite bathroom or not.

GETTING THERE
☞ By road: M3/J 14, A33. Warsash: M27/J8, A27.
☞ By coach to Southampton: London, 2:30;

Bristol, 2:45; Birmingham, 3:40.
☞ By rail: London Waterloo, 1:40; Bristol Parkway, 2:15; Birmingham, 3:30; Sheffield, 4:45.
☞ By air: Southampton International Airport.

STAFFORDSHIRE UNIVERSITY

Staffordshire University
College Road
Stoke-on-Trent ST4 2DE

TEL 01782 294000
FAX 01782 292740
EMAIL admissions@staffs.ac.uk
WEB www.staffs.ac.uk

Staffordshire Students' Union
College Road
Stoke-on-Trent
Staffs ST4 2DE

TEL 01782 294629
FAX 01782 295736
EMAIL theunion@staffs.ac.uk
WEB www.staffs.ac.uk/studentsunion

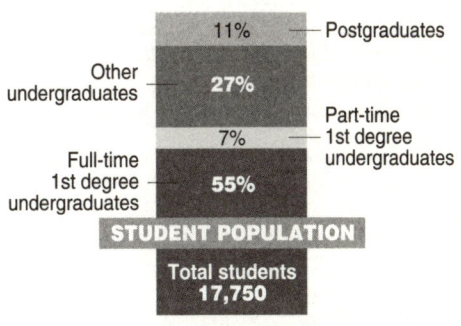

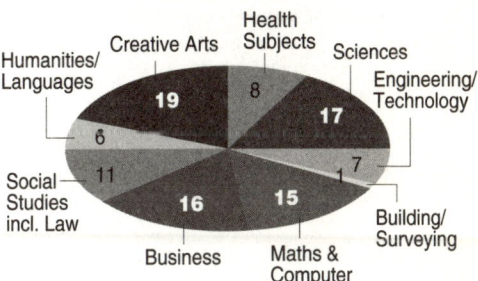

VAG VIEW

S taffordshire has expanded enormously since its days as Staffordshire Poly, and has the necessary contacts with industry to sustain a strong vocational curriculum. Aim at particular areas (see Academia, *below) and you can't go wrong: there is clear alignment between their academic strengths and their nationally excellent employment record.*

There's also good sport, a strong local ents scene and plenty of student activities to widen your perspective on life.

Yet, be aware, Staffordshire is very different from neighbouring Keele

CAMPUSES

There are sites in Stoke and Stafford, twelve miles to the south, opposite the railway station. This is an area known as the Potteries, a borough incorporated in 1907 to include Stoke-on-Trent, Hanley, Burslem, Tinstall, Longton and Fenton. Its most famous son, Arnold Bennett (author of *Clayhanger, Anne of the Five Towns* – he preferred the sound of five, so left out Fenton) couldn't get away fast enough, but that had nothing to do with the university, which only gained its status in 1992.

STUDENT PROFILE

The student profile is as you would expect. There's a sizable mature population and a sizable local intake. Most entrants are from state schools, and a third of non-mature entrants from social groups represented least at university. The uni appeals to the region with a priority application scheme.

ACADEMIA

At Stoke there's Art & Design, Business, Law, Humanities & Social Sciences and Sciences. At Stafford, Computing, Engineering & Advanced Technology and Health.

There are top teaching assessments in Economics (full marks), Psychology, Philosophy, Art & Design, Physics, Sport, Biosciences, Nursing and other subjects allied to Medicine – the latter

UNIVERSITY/STUDENT PROFILE

University since	**1992**
Situation/style	**Campus/ town sites**
Student population	**17,750**
Full-time undergraduates	**9,730**
- mature	**34%**
- overseas	**3%**
- male/female	**57/43**
- state sector intake	**97%**
- non-traditional student intake	**18%, high**
- undergraduate applications	**Down 5%**
see Introduction for key to tables	

WHAT IT'S REALLY LIKE

UNIVERSITY:	
Social Life	★★★★
Campus scene	**Lively, sporty, unpretentious**
Student Union services	**Good**
Politics	**Activity low**
Sport	**41 busy clubs**
National team position	**45th**
Sport facilities	**Good**
Arts opportunities	**Drama, music excellent; dance, film, art good**
Student newspaper	**Get Knotted**
Student radio	**GK Radio**
Nightclub	**Legends, Odyssey**
Bars	**Sleepers, LRV**
Union ents	**Underground, BSE, Mash, Gobble, Nation, Dusted**
Union clubs/societies	**74**
Most popular society	**Drama**
Smoking policy	**No policy**
Parking	**Adequate**
TOWN:	
Entertainment	★★★
Town scene	**Pubs, clubs**
Town/gown relations	**Average**
Risk of violence	**Average**
Cost of living	**Average**
Student concessions	**Good**
Survival + 2 nights out	**£50 pw**
Part-time work campus/town	**Excellent/good**

featuring midwifery and the nursing (adult, child and mental health).

Art & Design is particularly strong – they have their own art gallery in New York; why, I am not sure.

Graduate employment performance (box, page 435) highlights the computing courses, which are legion, and sport, which is a very big emphasis now, and media (in which BSc techno courses sit alongside BA courses, such as Broadcast Journalism & Politics and Digital Production Journalism). Resources in computing are especially good – two IT centres, the £5-million **Octagon Centre** in Stafford being a central focus with some 800 workstations. Recently they came up with a particularly attractive degree, BSc Interactive Entertainment Technology, a course which, like five others, helps form their School of Media & Entertainment Technology.

SOCIAL SCENE

STUDENTS' UNION There are four bars – two at the

ACADEMIC EXCELLENCE

TEACHING: *(Rated Excellent or 17+ out of 24)*	
Economics	**24**
Psychology, Philosophy	**23**
Art & Design, Physics,	**22**
Leisure/Sport, Biosciences, Nursing, Other Subjects Allied to Medicine	
Modern Languages (French, German, Iberian Studies), History of Art.	**21**
Electronic & Electrical Eng.	**20**
RESEARCH :	
Top grades 5/5*	**None**

Stoke campus, Leek Road's **Venue** (**LRV** – 1,800 capacity) and College Road's **Odyssey** (500) and two at Stafford, **Legends** and **Sleepers**. LRV stages some of the biggest student nights in the Midlands: *BSE* – disco/range of styles; *Underground* – rock, indie, alternative; *Mash* – R&B, old skool, dance, pop; *Gobble* – disco, Nation – R&B; *Dusted* – dance. There are two resident DJs and guest appearances by *Brandon Block, Trevor Nelson, Alex P, DJ Spoony* and Judge Jules. Recent visiting bands include Liberty, Top Loader, Chicane, Straw, Ash, Honey2, Atomic Kitten. There's also *Comedy Club* on Saturday. It's a busy, well-worked scene. 'We're not on the main gig circuit,' they admit, 'the DJs and their agents now ring us!' There are also three balls a year, May in March, Summer in June and Graduation in November. May Ball's the biggest.

It isn't all music. There are in fact twenty-three societies at Stoke, and the most active is Drama – there's a good Drama & Theatre Arts degree; at Stafford there are a further ten. The uni newspaper is *GK* (*Get Knotted*) and the student radio station,

GK Radio. The paper has received awards from the *Guardian* and the *Daily Telegraph*. Politics are low on the agenda, though they joined the national march on the tuition fees issue.

SPORT Academic influence brings good facilities for all and fame for some. They have forty-one clubs and came 46th nationally in the team ratings, men's hockey doing particularly well (Shield winners) – they have two members in the British university team. Their athletes performed outstandingly in the world university games. Cross country and badminton teams are strong (three internationals in the former) and four swimmers are ranked in the University Top 20. Facilities include a new sports centre, sports halls, squash courts, floodlit synthetic and grass pitches for football or rugby, fitness suites, gym with multi-gym, weights and fitness machines. There's also a dance and aerobics studio at the Sir Stanley Matthews Sports Centre in Leek Road.

TOWN Contrary to expectation Hanley, not Stoke, is the main man down among the potteries. Top venue is **The Stage**; **The Place** is the most popular club – three levels. Cavernous **Valentino's**, with rock room *Moonshine*, is also popular; trendy **Void** in Glass Street delivers a dancier theme; while for something coolly different, it's **The Locker Room**, an American-style diner with pool tables and a TV on every table. **The Club** is the No. 1 gay joint (camp, pop, dance and chart).

Just outside Hanley is **Festival Park** – multi-

There are strong ents and clear alignment between their academic strengths and their nationally excellent employment record. Staffs is a very different animal from neighbouring Keele, however.

AT A GLANCE	
ACADEMIC FILE:	
Subjects assessed	**27**
Excellent	**48%**
Average requirements	**180 points**
Students-staff ratio	**24:1**
First/2:1 degree pass rate	**45%**
ACCOMMODATION FILE:	
Guarantee to freshers	**85%**
Style	**Halls**
Student satisfaction	**76%**
Cost pw (no food/food)	**£27-£56**
Town rent pw	**£35**

screen cinema, Quasar, Water World, Super Bowl, etc. Stoke has a dry ski slope.

Theatres include the **New Victoria** at nearby Newcastle-under-Lyme, the **Rep Theatre** (Stoke) and **Theatre Royal** (Hanley). Sundays and Wednesdays are film nights at Legends in Stafford; the Drama Soc. is forty strong and puts on four plays a year, including panto.

PILLOW TALK

Stoke: six on-campus halls of residence, eight off campus. Student houses: thirty six-bedroom houses on Leek Road. Student Flats: blocks of flats, two thirds sharing, within two miles of Leek Road. **Stafford:** Stafford Court includes 249 en-suite rooms; an additional 307 rooms will be open by the time you get there and Yarlet House with fifty-one.

JOBS

Clearly the whole ethos and syllabus is career-orientated and they perform well in the graduate employment stakes, as our *Employment* box shows. In our national employment Top 10s, they came 5th in Computing, 3rd in Art & Design, 4th in Journalism and 8th in Sport, 9th in Tele-communications.

GETTING THERE

* By road: Stafford – M6/J14, A513. Stoke – M6 (J15 from south; J16 from north), A500.
* By coach: London, 4:00.
* By rail: Birmingham New Street, 40 mins; Manchester Piccadilly, 1:20; London Euston, 1:45; Nottingham, 2:00; Sheffield, 2:15

WHERE GRADUATES END UP	
13% Manufacturing,	Key Areas
12% Wholesale/Retail,	
10% Computer*,	
9% Health/Social Work,	
9% Finance,	
6% Public Admin	
Aeronautical Manufacture,	Niche Areas
Artistic/Literary*, Film/	
Video, Journalism*, Legal,	
Property, Sport*, Telecom*	
*indicates Top 10 Graduate Provider	
Approximate employed	**92%**

UNIVERSITY OF STIRLING

The University of Stirling
Stirling FK9 4LA

TEL 01786 467044
FAX 01786 466800
EMAIL admission@stir.ac.uk
WEB www.stir.ac.uk

Stirling Students' Association
University of Stirling
Stirling FK9 4LA

TEL 01786 467166
FAX 01786 467190
EMAIL susa-president@stir.ac.uk
WEB www.susa-online.co.uk

VAG VIEW

Stirling is a premier-league university with a reputation for leading the way. It was the first traditional uni to grasp the nettle of modularisation and reap the benefits of doing it in proper semesters – two blocks of fifteen weeks. Now it is leading the way in showing the government how its access policy can be made to work in preparation for its plans to have 50% of all sixthformers into university by the year 2010.

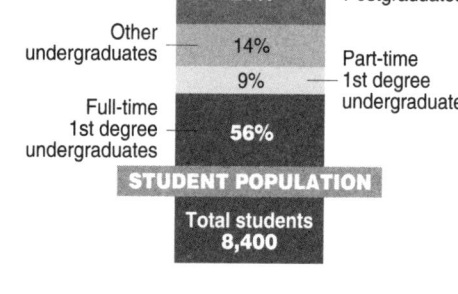

Postgraduates 21%
Other undergraduates 14%
Part-time 9%
1st degree undergraduates
Full-time 1st degree undergraduates 56%

STUDENT POPULATION

Total students 8,400

CAMPUS

The 360-acre campus is set in beautiful surroundings – a loch, Airthrey Castle, even a golf course – well away from big city life. The student community is small, relaxed and very friendly. Chances are that you will already know from this description whether you are the kind of student that will suit Stirling. It has suited various writers (Iain Banks among them) and many golfers too. Some find it pleasantly secure, others slightly claustrophobic, but the spirit of the place espouses a student-centred ethos. One told me that he felt that Stirling had given him the kind of individual teaching and personal treatment that he imagined he might have enjoyed as a sixthformer had he gone to a public school. He didn't and many don't – some 91% of entrants are from the state sector

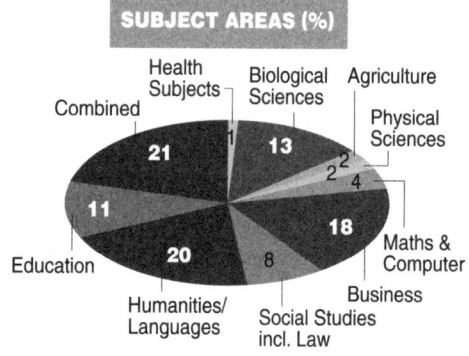

SUBJECT AREAS (%)

Combined 21
Health Subjects 1
Biological Sciences 13
Agriculture
Physical Sciences 2
2
4
Education 11
20 8
18 Maths & Computer
Humanities/ Languages
Social Studies incl. Law
Business

and many represent social groups which haven't traditionally gone to university.

STUDENT PROFILE

There are many foreign students, mature students, sporty types and stereotypical broke studenty types. Around half are Scottish, and Stirling attracts a lot of students from Ireland and from Greece. A nursing and midwifery course shifts the gender balance in favour of girls. So guys, if the thought of girls in nurses' uniforms appeals...

Stirling has met its benchmarks in the matter of attracting non-traditional applicants to its courses more or less right across the board. Besides the 91% state school kids (2% over benchmark) in the 1999/2000 academic year, they took 23% from so-called low-participation

UNIVERSITY/STUDENT PROFILE	
University since	**1967**
Situation/style	**Town campus**
Student population	**8,400**
Full-time undergraduates	**4,700**
- mature	**19%**
- overseas	**7%**
- male/female	**44/56**
- state sector intake	**91%**
- non-traditional student intake	**23%, high**
- drop-out rate	**7%**
- undergraduate applications	**Up 11%**
see Introduction for key to tables	

neighbourhoods (post codes that don't deliver many to university) – a figure that is 8% above Stirling's government benchmark, and 27% from the lower social classes IIIM, IV and V, and still managed to maintain a 62% rate of first and upper seconds.

What is truly extraordinary is that unlike most universities for whom this kind of student body is typical, Stirling do not suffer a large drop-out rate. It is a mere 7%. How they manage this may have something to do with the individual teaching and personal treatment you get here, but it may also be to do with the fact that students for whom university has not been part of the family game plan appreciate an institution that clearly knows how to shape up a curriculum.

Either that, or perhaps Stirling campus – gateway to the Highlands – is so tucked away that no-one can find their way out.

ACADEMIA

They make interesting combinations out of their chosen range of course subjects, all the time putting taught skills or knowledge-bases to work in particular disciplines. So that, for example, the 12% of Stirling graduates who went into the finance sector last year came not only from the business department, but from social sciences, even from biological sciences and humanities, i.e. from disparate courses that had been given a financial context. A subject, whatever it may be, is given an application. And even if the application doesn't draw you finally into a career in that area, you will have applied your knowledge-base, rehearsed it for real.

> *The strategy is to give your knowledge of a subject a career application through an adroit syllabus combination. A diverse student body responds well to the formula: 62% get firsts or upper seconds, and all but 4% are employed within six months.*

The first semester in the year is fitted in before Christmas. Then follows a seven-week Christmas holiday before the second fifteen-week semester, which finishes at the end of May. Students study three courses per semester and for most of these the coursework content is high. Grades are awarded for each course and these determine whether you may study honours, and later what degree you get.

Stirling has scored high in the teaching assessments, partly due to their student-centred ethos which touches all faculties. Top of the tree are Economics, Environmental Science, Theology, Sociology, Psychology, English, Business &

Management. See, too, the results of the recent research assessment in the box above – ten subjects at Grade 5, in which national and world-class excellence is implicit. Look at Stirling for social sciences, languages, media, biological sciences, accounting, marketing, management, as well as subjects like religious studies (the combo with politics suddenly looks very modern), psychology (both as social science and as science), tourism and environmental/conservation. Thirteen percent of graduates go into the health industry after toying with Nursing, Midwifery, Sociology, Social Policy Social Work, and the biosciences – Biochemistry, Biology and combinations.

SOCIAL SCENE

STUDENTS' ASSOCIATION To sustain life far from the city, SUSA puts on a fairly uninspired show from its base in the **Robbins Centre**, but no-one seems to mind.

There are five bars: **Long Bar** (the heart of campus life and the longest room in the union), **Shankies** (bar/club, capacity 400, home to discos and band nights), **Maisies** (café bar, recently renovated), and **The Alehouse** (authentic decor,

ACADEMIC EXCELLENCE

TEACHING::

(Rated Excellent, Highly Satis. or 17+ out of 24)

Economics, Environmental Science, Theology, Sociology, English, Psychology.	**Excellent**
Business & Mgt	**Highly Satis.**
Teacher Education, Maths & Stats, Finance & Accounting, Mass Communics, Philosophy, Politics, Social Work, History, Cellular & Molecular Biology, Organismal Biology, French.	
European Languages	**20**

RESEARCH:
Top grades 5/5*

Psychology, Agriculture, Social Work, Accounting, English, French, History, Philosophy, Theology, Media	**Grade 5**

WHAT IT'S REALLY LIKE

UNIVERSITY:

Social Life	★★★
Campus scene	**Small, friendly, beautiful scene**
Student Union services	**Average**
Politics	**Student issues**
Sport	**Competitive**
National team position	**23rd**
Sport facilities	**Good**
Arts opportunities	**Excellent**
Student newspaper	**BRIG**
Student radio	**Air 3**
Nightclub	**Shankies**
Bars	**Long Bar, Maisie's, Alehouse**
Union ents	**SLAM, Club Tropicana, Funkie Disposition, Cut The Rug**
Union clubs/societies	**65-70**
Smoking policy	**Halls & bars OK**
Parking	**Expensive permits**

CITY:

Entertainment	★★
Scene	**Pubs, 2 clubs**
Town/gown relations	**Average**
Risk of violence	**Low**
Cost of living	**Low**
Student concessions	**Some**
Survival + 2 nights out	**£40**
Part-time work campus/town	**Fair**

AT A GLANCE

ACADEMIC FILE:

Subjects assessed	**20**
Excellent	**95%**
Average requirements	**260 points**
Students-staff ratio	**18:1**
First/2:1 degree pass rate	**62%**

ACCOMMODATION FILE:

Guarantee to freshers	**Apply by 1.9**
Style	**Halls**
Catered	**None**
En-suite	**10%**
Price range pw	**£44.46-£62.03**
Town rent pw	**£45-£60**

Music Society sessions. 'Besides SUSA's ents, the halls of residence hold parties each semester, an excellent opportunity to get pissed and finally profess your undying love to the guy/girl across the corridor whom you've fancied all semester,' writes Suzanne Bush. 'Some academic departments also have parties at the end of the year. But the best ones are those put on by assorted sports clubs every Thursday night in the meatmarkets, sorry, clubs in town.'

There are the usual clubs and societies – 'SUDS, the Drama Society, aims to put on at least a couple of productions each semester,' Suzanne continues, 'and there's a ready supply of theatre, cinema and music in the form of the **MacRobert Arts Centre**, situated in the middle of the campus and subject to a major refurbishment right now. The Musical Society works towards one big production every year. The University Choir brings together students and people from the community and puts on a big concert every semester in Dunblane Cathedral. Also, the university has an orchestra and there's a thriving Live Music Society with student performances on a Sunday night.

'Also, Stirling has a thriving media, a student newspaper, *BRIG*, and a campus radio station, Radio Airthrey, offering music, and news programmes.' Politics is not a big issues until a big issues finds its way into this far-off campus, namely Car Parking!! Some time ago the barriers went up and £60 parking permits were required in what sounds like a hostile move on the uni's vulnerable, captive audience.

Real Ale). There isn't a large enough venue to attract many big name groups, but there are regular discos – *Funkie Disposition 3* (midway between a school disco and a rave apparently), *Cut The Rug*, *Club Tropicana*, and *SLAM* – and Live

SPORT There are excellent sports facilities, and the teams came 23rd overall last year, which is good. Particular strengths are tennis, swimming and of course golf. The uni pool has just been replaced by a six-lane, 50-metre Olympic-size pool, for, backed by £2.75 million from the Lottery, Stirling now houses the National Swimming Academy, which will sit alongside the biggest indoor tennis centre in Scotland. Bursaries are available. High performance sportsmen/women are catered for well, though there is plenty of provision for all levels.

PILLOW TALK

Freshers are guaranteed uni accommodation, provided they apply before September 1, mostly in halls. There is no catered accommodation but meal packages are available for use in campus restaurants.

Approximately 10% of accommodation is en suite; price per week varies as to halls - £50.67 to £59.46; flats - £44.46 to £62.03. Most university residences include heating and lighting costs. Town rents vary from £45 to £60, depending on service levels.

In halls you may be as many as eighteen to a kitchen, in the uni-owned Bridgehaugh flats in town you can enjoy en-suite facilities. In the fourth year, you could go for a Swiss-style chalet on the less than enticing Spittal Hill.

JOBS

Most recent statistical evidence shows 97% in employment after six months. Their record is always good. In our national employment tables, they came 4th in the Hotel/Restaurant category and 10th in the Agric/Forestry category. Commerce (financial activities and accountancy), the health industry and education sweep the board.

GETTING THERE

☛ By road: M9/J11, A9 or A91, A907, A9.

WHERE GRADUATES END UP	
13% Health/Social Work,	Key Areas
12% Finance,	
10% Education,	
10% Wholesale/Retail,	
7% Public Admin,	
6% Manufacturing,	
6% Computer	
Hotel/Restaurant*,	Niche Areas
Accountancy,	
Agric/Forestry*,	
Advertising, Film/Video,	
Radio/TV, Sport	

*indicates Top 10 Graduate Provider

Approximate employed   **96%**

☛ By coach: London, 9:00; Edinburgh, 2:20.
☛ By rail: Glasgow/Edinburgh, 55 mins ;Aberdeen, 2:30; London King's Cross, 6:00.

STOCKPORT COLLEGE

Stockport College
Wellington Road South
Stockport
Cheshire SK1 2UQ

TEL 0161 958 3417
FAX 0161 958 3305
EMAIL stockcoll@cs.stockport.ac.uk
WEB www.stockport.ac.uk

VAG VIEW

S tockport is a further and higher education college affiliated to Manchester Uni, although not all its degrees are awarded by them. Of some 400 courses on offer, the college offers degrees in Business (Manchester and Huddersfield Unis) and Professional Studies (Manchester degrees in Learning Difficulties, Social Care, Social Work). Engineering degrees include Aeronautical (Salford Uni and UMIST), Civil (Salford), Electrical & Electronic (Manchester), Manufacturing and Mechanical (Salford). There are also degrees in Biochemistry and Chemistry (Leeds, Manchester, Salford or UMIST), Biology (Manchester or Salford), and in Documentary Photography.

*Academic resources include an IT centre and a library (75,000 vols). There are two union bars – **Trantor** and **Ensleigh**. Ents include discos on Friday and Saturday, occasional live bands and a Freshers' Ball.*

COLLEGE PROFILE	
Founded	**1889**
Status	**F/HE College**
Degree awarding university	**Manchester, Liverpool JM Huddersfield**
Student population	**14,926**
Full-time undergraduates	**377**
College accommodation	**None**
Town rent pw	**£40**

DEGREE SUBJECT AREAS:
Business, childhood studies/learning difficulties, engineering (mechanical, manufacturing, aeronautical), art/design

There is a student newspaper, a radio and TV station.

GETTING THERE

☛ By road: M63/J12, A6.
☛ By rail: Stockport station is 5 mins away; it's 9 mins by rail to Manchester.

UNIVERSITY OF STRATHCLYDE

The University of Strathclyde
Graham Hills Building
50 George Street
Glasgow G1 1XQ

TEL 0141 552 4400
FAX 0141 552 5860
EMAIL (use web)
WEB www.strath.ac.uk

Strathclyde Students' Association
90 John Street
Glasgow G1 1JH

TEL 0141 567 5000
FAX 0141 567 5050
EMAIL theunion@strath.ac.uk
WEB www.theunion.strath.ac.uk

VAG VIEW

Strathclyde had its beginnings in 1796 with Anderson's Institution, an equal-opportunity, science and technology college. John Anderson had been Professor of Natural Philosophy at Glasgow University and the institution that bore his name was founded under the terms of his will. University status came in 1964 following the merger of the Royal College of Science and the Scottish College of Commerce, which fact alerts us to Strathclyde's second largest faculty after Engineering, the Strathclyde Business School. In 1993, Glasgow's Jordanhill College joined the fold and became Strath's third largest faculty, Education.

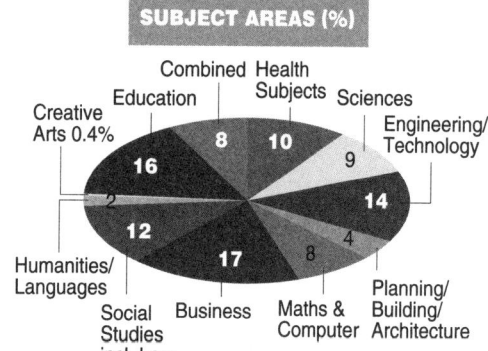

SUBJECT AREAS (%)

Creative Arts 0.4%, Education, Combined Subjects, Health Sciences, Engineering/Technology, Humanities/Languages, Social Studies incl. Law, Business, Maths & Computer, Planning/Building/Architecture

16, 8, 10, 9, 2, 12, 17, 8, 4, 14

CAMPUS

Today Strathclyde University occupies the same site as Anderson's Institution in the heart of Glasgow, though the original buildings have long gone. The inevitable **It's a Scream** pub round the corner from the union betrays the concentration of students in the immediate vicinity – Strathclyde and Caledonian universities, the College of Building and Printing, the College of Food & Technology, and the College of Commerce. The Jordanhill campus is in the West End of the city, close to Glasgow University.

STUDENT PROFILE

Strathclyde is one of three unis in the city. 'Vibe wise, it has a more relaxed atmosphere in comparison with Glasgow University, which tends to have a more academic outlook,' said a student of Glasgow Uni. Peter Mann, a student at Strathclyde, suggested differences run deeper: 'Caledonian and Strathclyde have a similar kind of population. Glasgow is quite different and generally disliked because it is full of English people. There is not a tremendous amount of mixing.' A student of Caledonian offered this Pythonesque picture of the pecking order: 'Glasgow University looks down on Strathclyde as being John Street Poly, although it's been a university since 1964. And Strathclyde looks down on us as being the old Glasgow Technical College, the lowest of the low.'

There's a 92% state school population and a huge, 21% take from the so-called low-participation neighbourhoods (largely in the Glasgow area). It's not that different from the Cally profile (96% and 28% respectively), but Strathclyde carries none of the poly cultural baggage. It was the *Royal* College; Cally was the Poly. Nevertheless, a lot of the students are local. 'There's one guy in Fusion

UNIVERSITY/STUDENT PROFILE	
University since	**1964**
Situation/style	**City campus**
Student population	**21,050**
Full-time undergraduates	**11,140**
- mature	**13%**
- overseas	**4%**
- male/female	**48/52**
- state sector intake	**92%**
- non-traditional student intake	**21%, high**
- drop-out rate	**8%**
- undergraduate applications	**Up 5%**
see Introduction for key to tables	

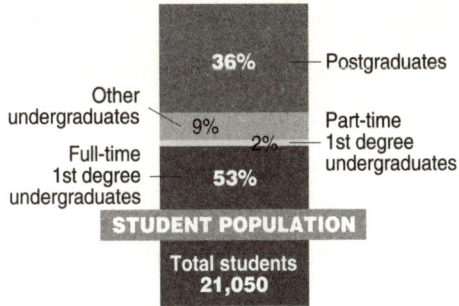

	36% — Postgraduates
Other undergraduates	9%
	2% Part-time 1st degree undergraduates
Full-time 1st degree undergraduates	53%

STUDENT POPULATION

Total students 21,050

[student radio],' said Peter, 'who's from Surrey, and he sticks out like a sore thumb.'

ACADEMIA

There is a fine academic reputation. Strathclyde's 92% Excellent and Highly Satisfactory rating in the teaching assessments actually puts it a nose ahead of Glasgow University. The uni came 44th in the recent research assessments – with Queens Belfast, Stirling, London Goldsmiths, Kent and Leicester for close company – and the edge which returned them a Grade 5* (that's world class) was neither engineering nor business, the two subjects to which one's mind turns when talking of Strathclyde, but Biomolecular & Medicinal Chemistry. The key thing is the way they teach: audio-visual, video, visual materials, computer-assisted learning programmes are all to the fore. Very close links with industry and commerce ensure a real-world, highly practical emphasis. They have a Learning Resources Base which, among other things, is there to help you in adjusting to study methods, curriculum design etc. Every student is assigned a personal tutor, and there's a built-in early-warning system to prevent any first year getting lost along the way.

SOCIAL SCENE

Strathclyde is Glaswegian not only because of the

ACADEMIC EXCELLENCE

TEACHING:
(points out of 24)

Physics, Business & Management, Architecture, Electrical & Electronic Engineering, Geography, Mechanical (incl Manufacturing) Engineering, Pharmacy, Chemistry, Politics.	**Excellent**
Civil Engineering, Computer, Psychol, Hospitality Studies, Maths & Statistics, Teacher Education, History, Law, Sociology, Social Work, Cellular & Molecular Biology, English.	**Highly Satis.**
Chemical Engineering	**19**
Planning & Landscape	**20**
European Languages	**22**

RESEARCH:
Top grades 5/5*

Subjects Allied to Medicine.	**Grade 5***
Pharmacy, Studies/Professions Allied to Medicine, Applied Maths, General Eng, Electrical/ Electronic Eng, Mechanical Eng, Law, Politics, Accounting/ Finance, English	**Grade 5**

AT A GLANCE

ACADEMIC FILE:

Subjects assessed	**26**
Excellent/Highly Satisfactory	**92%**
Average requirements	**260 points**
Students-staff ratio	**20:1**
First/2:1 degree pass rate	**61%**

ACCOMMODATION FILE:

Availability to freshers	**100%**
Style	**Halls, flats**
Approx price range pw	**£49-£68**
City rent pw	**£45-£60**

---

number of Glaswegians who attend, but in the very Glaswegian way students here go about having a good time. 'Their ents are marvelled at by other unions for their ability to bring in droves of students from rival unis, and give them just what they want – an excellent hangover for those on a budget!' reports Rachel Richardson. In fact, it is hard to assimilate the energy that is devoted to exciting pleasure in the students at Strathclyde. Whatever the legal capacity for the big night, it is not uncommon to find between 2,000 and 2,500 students here totally out of their heads. The legendary pleasure zone itself is ten floors high, yet it is not the skyscraper you expect because in some extraordinary Alice-in-Wonderland fashion they have conspired to fit its ten floors, mezzanine-style, into the space of six or seven, leading this first-time visitor into utter confusion.

'The union building never shuts before 3 am,' Peter explained. There's the **Barony Bar** on level 2, the **Games Room** (3), the **Dark Room** (4), the **Bubble Lounge** (5), and **Vertigo** is level 8. Everything's open all the time except Vertigo, the biggest venue for club nights and bands, and open three times a week at best. The Bubble Lounge has

WHAT IT'S REALLY LIKE

UNIVERSITY:

Social Life	★★★★★
Campus scene	**Excellent, best ents in Glasgow**
Student Union services	**Good**
Politics	**Student & national issues**
Sport	**49 clubs**
National team position	**55th**
Sport facilities	**Good**
Arts opportunities	**Drama, music, film, art good; dance poor**
Student newspaper	**The Telegraph**
Student radio	**Fusion fm**
Nightclub	**Vertigo**
Bars	**Barony, Darkroom, Bubble Lounge, Priory**
Union ents	**The Big Cheese, Rage, TFI Friday, Pump Up The Jam, Traffic Lights**
Union clubs/societies	**100**
Smoking policy	**Union OK**
Parking	**Poor/non-existent**

CITY:

Entertainment	★★★★★
Scene	**Very cool**
Town/gown relations	**Good**
Risk of violence	**Low**
Cost of living	**Average**
Student concessions	**Good**
Survival + 2 nights out	**£70 pw**
Part-time work campus/town	**Good**

broadcast the following semester due to licensing conflicts with other stations. In that time we have been working to get funding for our own equipment and working a lot on sorting out webcasting – broadcasting on the Internet. Now we have got the necessaries for the basic studio equipment and an Internet deal with Yahoo. The idea is that from January we will broadcast full-time. We have more DJ talent than we could possibly use. We get DJs from all over, we don't restrict ourselves to students.

'Then we've got the *Strathclyde Telegraph*. There's a real professionalism around and that shows. There's no TV yet, but there will be. Basically, I started up Fusion last year and then took this sabbatical year to get it off the ground. TV will come later. I did a degree in marketing. I've learned the bits and pieces as I've gone along, electrocuted myself a few times. When I leave here I am going for a job connected with the Internet.'

You'd better believe it.

For drama, they have two theatres – the **Ramshorn** at John Anderson, the **Crawfurd** at Jordanhill; both offer courses in all aspects of theatre and there's plenty of opportunity, too, just to be involved in student productions. The Strathclyde Theatre Group puts on ten major productions a year. The **Collins Gallery**, also on campus, runs year-round exhibitions and workshops, and there's also a concert hall for the many musical productions. Choirs, bands, a symphony orchestra, ensembles, etc go to make up the Music Society, which presents weekly lunchtime recitals by visiting artists as well as by students in the National Trust for Scotland's **Hutchesons' Hall**.

See also *Student Glasgow, page 197.*

live bands six nights a week. The Dark Room is the real dance club of the place – *Cheese* (dubbed the biggest clubnight in Scotland), *Club 99* and *Havin' It*. The **Todd Bar** is also on campus, a couple of hundred yards up the street and **Toby's** is the bar in the union area at Jordanhill.

Nor is it all booze and sweat at Strath. There are more than 100 clubs and societies. Sport is excellent (see below) and media-wise they have a cracking set-up. 'A year ago Fusion fm had its first restricted licence,' Peter Mann told me. 'It was funded from our *alumni* fund but we couldn't afford to buy our own equipment at that stage. Nor could we

> *Strathclyde is quintessentially a Glaswegian operation and it has the best union clubnights in Scotland. The bottom line may be that it has a better long-term record for graduate employment than most of Britain.*

SPORT At John Anderson campus, there are indoor facilities for basketball, netball, archery, volleyball, tennis, badminton, handball, martial arts, fencing, table tennis, gymnastics, circuit training, yoga, indoor training facilities for track & field, cricket, golf and hockey, a weight training & conditioning room, squash courts and swimming pool. Outside campus there are grass pitches, artificial floodlit pitches, and a pavilion – team games include hockey, rugby, American football and soccer. Jordanhill has a similar range of indoor and outdoor facilities on campus. Proximity to river, sea and mountains enables a whole range of other sports – from mountaineering to sailing, from rowing to skiing. There are eight bursaries available for low handicap golfers from The Royal and Ancient, each worth £1,250 a year.

PILLOW TALK

In the city, most uni accommodation is single or shared rooms in self-catering flats, some of it at a student village on JA campus, some of it a walk away. At Jordanhill it's on-campus, catered halls.

JOBS

The uni's Careers Service has twice received the National Charter Mark for excellence in customer service. Less than 3% were classified unemployed last year, which was a significantly better result than at the University of Glasgow.

GETTING THERE

☛ By road: The John Anderson campus – M74, M8/J15 or A82, M8/J15 or M8/J15. Jordanhill – M74, M8/J19 or A82, M8/J19 or M8/J19.
☛ By rail: Edinburgh, 0:50; Newcastle, 2:30; Aberdeen, 2:45; Birmingham New Street, 5:30; London King's Cross, 6:00.

☛ By air: Glasgow Airport, 15-20 minutes' drive.
☛ By coach: Edinburgh, 1:10; London, 8:20; Birmingham, 6:20; Newcastle, 4:20.

WHERE GRADUATES END UP	
15% Manufacturing*,	Key Areas
13% Education,	
10% Wholesale/Retail,	
10% Health/Social Work,	
9% Finance,	
6% Public Admin	
Accountancy,	Niche Areas
Architecture,	
Aeronautical Manufacture*,	
Chemical/Pharmaceutical*,	
Construction, Telecom,	
Eng/Industrial Design,	
Electron/Electric*,	
Hotel/Restaurant, Sport	

*indicates Top 10 Graduate Provider

Approximate employed **95%**

• •

SUFFOLK COLLEGE

Suffolk College
Rope Walk
Ipswich IP4 1LT

TEL 01473 296369
FAX 01473 230054
EMAIL infor@suffolk.ac.uk
WEB www.suffolk.ac.uk

VAG VIEW

Situated on a 12-acre campus on the outskirts of Ipswich, Suffolk College is what they call a 'mixed economy' institution – further, higher and adult education, and the mass of students are aged between 16 and 19. It's all very much a regional base – around two-thirds of students are from East Anglia, more than half from Suffolk.

A large-choice modular degree programme is on offer, and while some combos are not immediately fathomable – I mean, Early Childhood Studies with Garden Design? However, Nursing scored 20 points out of 24 at the assessments (the department offers a BSc as well as various diplomas). Look, too, at the Diagnostic and Therapeutic Radiography

COLLEGE PROFILE	
Founded	**1957**
Status	**F/HE College**
Degree awarding university	**East Anglia**
Situation/style	**Town campus**
Student population	**12,911**
Full-time undergraduates	**1,521**
College accommodation	**None**
Town rent pw	**£40**

DEGREE SUBJECT AREAS:
Art & Design, Business, Childhood Studies, Engineering, History, Literature, Media, Hospitality, Computing, Garden Design, Leisure & Tourism, Nursing, Performing Arts, Radiography, Science, Social Studies

degrees, and in the Science faculty at their employer-friendly Animal Science combinations in partnership with Otley College. Art & Design fared rather badly in the assessments at 15 points, but that hasn't deterred them from giving Fine Art a practical, business or electronic twist.

*There's a union bar, **Digby's**, and non-alcoholic toastie bar plus a TV, pool and table tennis tables, games machines, various clubs and societies, a gym, squash courts and a polygym, but no accommodation.*

GETTING THERE
☛ By road: A12 or A14.
☛ By coach: London, 2:40.
☛ By rail: London Liverpool Street, 70 mins; Norwich, 40 mins.

UNIVERSITY OF SUNDERLAND

The University of Sunderland
Student Recruitment
Edinburgh Building
Chester Road
Sunderland SR1 3SD

TEL 0191 515 3000
FAX 0191 515 3805
EMAIL student-helpline@sunderland.ac.uk
WEB www.sunderland.ac.uk

Sunderland Students' Union
Wearmouth Hall
Chester Road
Sunderland SR1 3SD

TEL 0191 514 5512
FAX 0191 515 2441
EMAIL su.president@sunderland.ac.uk
WEB www.sunderland.ac.uk

VAG VIEW

*S*underland was an area robbed of its core industries a few decades ago, but has since been reborn and its uni with it. The poly became a university in 1992, the very year that Sunderland became a city. Since then they have both been engaged in expansion.

There's a 47% mature undergraduate population, and when you read in the student magazine that 'barely half the intake have A levels,' you realise that this is no ordinary university. If you think the whole wider-access idea self-defeating – that bringing in from the highways and byways will simply lower standards – consider that when married to excellent teaching in such as Biological Sciences (which gained Sunderland full marks at a recent

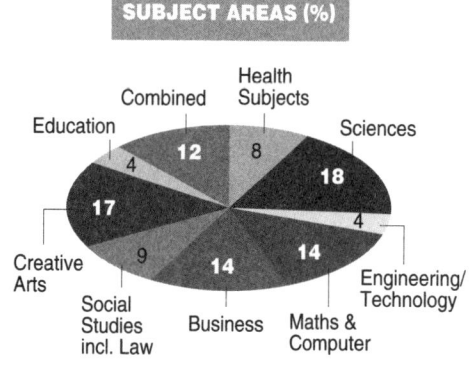

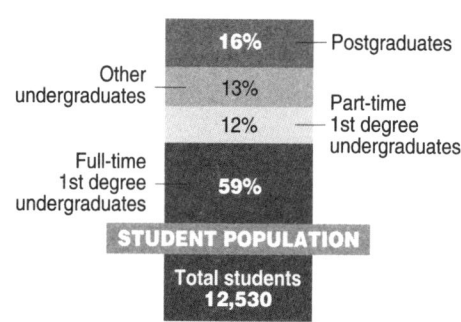

UNIVERSITY/STUDENT PROFILE	
University since	**1892**
Situation/style	**City campus**
Student population	**12,530**
Full-time ndergraduates	**7,390**
- mature	**47%**
- overseas	**4%**
- male/female	**47/53**
- state sector intake	**97%**
- non-traditional student intake	**29%, high**
- drop-out rate	**14%, high**
- undergraduate applications	**Down 12%**
see Introduction for key to tables	

inspection), Physiology and Nursing (both scored 23 out of 24 points), Pharmacy (22), Media (22) and Sociology, History and Art & Design (all 21), there is real, value-added opportunity to be had here.

CAMPUS SITES

The uni's rather beaten-up Chester Road campus is in easy reach of the town centre and the newer, award-winning St Peter's campus is but a stone's throw out at the mouth of the River Wear. The plan is to get everything over to St Peter's before too long.

Glass was one of the 19th-century industries on which the wealth of Sunderland was created (along with shipbuilding, coal mining and pottery), and in partnership with the National Glass Company, Sunderland's School of Computing levied £6 million from the National Lottery. The school is housed with the Business School at St Peter's, where they also opened a £15-million National Glass Centre. Now, money is being raised for a £20 million Arts, Design & Media Centre to be built there. There are also specialist research centres – the Industry Centre, the Ecology Centre, and the Centre for Japanese Studies. Japanese? Well, the mighty Nissan's in town!

You can see why the awards were won. St Peter's fits unobtrusively into the landscape, obediently following nature's contours as they fall down to the river. Wearmouth's iron bridge arches splendidly across the water like a young relation of Stephenson's famous iron bridge at nearby Newcastle; cranes complete the backdrop of the area's industrial past, against which the campus is heralded as an expression of the re-born character of the area. The Informatics building and Business School acquiesce in that, and there are clear practical benefits in their design, too. The jutting roofs and walkways (a modern version of Oxbridge cloisters) keep students dry as they criss-cross University Square, to and from the Prospect Building, or stand outside this no-smoking, catering and library resource while pulling on a fag (often in defiance of horizontal rain and a biting North Sea easterly). Rainwater plunges dramatically down huge chrome pipes from roofs topped with strange deckchair-shaped receivers, scanning the northern skies (for light?). Impressive, though the design never quite recovers from the creams and browns that have made St Peter's old before its time.

STUDENT PROFILE

Open access is married to excellent teaching... In some areas, there is real, value-added opportunity to be had at Sunderland.

Sunderland is one of the few campuses on which our senior reporter, who is of a certain age, can pass unnoticed in the SU bar. Besides a large local intake (and serious concentration by the uni to hang on to its students at graduation, so to boost the regional economy), international students are attracted here in increasing number, applications doubling in the last year. The Centre for International Education provides support services and activities. Such statistics help enrich the uni's reputation as high achiever in this government's race to widen access. Sunderland exceeds its benchmarks comfortably: 97% of young full-time undergrads are from the state sector (benchmark is 92%); 35% are from the lower social classes IIIM, IV, V (3% over benchmark), and a massive 29% hie from so-called low-participation (poor post code) neighbourhoods (14% over benchmark).

ACADEMIA

Recent excellent assessment results give confidence, as does their employment record. Teaching is described as 'quite relaxed, depending on your course. However, many schools have implemented a policy of compulsory attendance with penalties if you fail to attend a lecture. Gone are the days of spending all day every day in the pub!'

Work on the first phase of the promised £20-million Centre for Art, Design & Media has begun on land adjacent to St Peter's Campus. Meanwhile, the new Sony Media Centre is used by more than 800 students of radio, video and new media production, print and radio journalism, public relations and film, media and cultural studies.

The media and communications degrees are very popular, and the department well equipped –

AT A GLANCE

ACADEMIC FILE:

Subjects assessed	**28**
Excellent	**61%**
Average requirements	**160 points**
Students-staff ratio	**19:1**
First/2:1 degree pass rate	**49%**

ACCOMMODATION FILE:

Guarantee to freshers	**100%**
Style	**Halls, flats, houses**
Catered	**None**
En-suite	**10%**
Approx price range pw	**£46.50-£60**
City rent pw	**£32-£52**

ACADEMIC EXCELLENCE

TEACHING:
(Rated Excellent or 17+ out of 24)

Organismal Biosciences,	**24**
Molecular Biosciences	
Physiology, Nursing	**23**
Media, Pharmacy	**22**
Sociology, Art & Design, History	**21**
of Art, Music, Education	
Sport, Politics, Psychology	**20**
Electric & Electron Engineering,	**19**
Mechanical & Manuf Eng	
Iberian Studies	**18**

RESEARCH EXCELLENCE:
Top grades 5/5* **None**

student-run radio station Utopia FM operates from it for a few weeks a year. Don't expect to get in on the average score of 160 points.

An interesting point about their Pharmacy course is the emphasis not only on practical and professional skills, but on legal and ethical aspects too. Again, the Business School's emphasis on vocational skills, as well as core academic skills, appeals to employers. This is a vocational uni. Academically they live in the real world up here, hardened by experience.

New courses include BSc Robotics, BSc Forensic Techniques and BA Criminology – a reflection perhaps of the preoccupations of students already living in they eye of this urban vortex?

There is a disability support team and an outstanding learning support programme for dyslexic students.

SOCIAL SCENE

STUDENTS' UNION Three main student haunts are the **Wearmouth Bar** at Chester Road campus, **Manor Quay** nightclub at St Peter's and the **Bonded Warehouse** across the river from St Peter's at Panns Bank.

An early 19th-century marine store and smithy, the Bonded Warehouse has a shop and bar downstairs and right across the first floor is this large, beamed bar with snooker table and big screen. Initial custom was 'a slow but steady stream,' then they started a series of comedy nights, which appears to have won them a decent audience. One or two eateries are opening up nearby, but the Bonded barman to whom I spoke doubted that the area would take off like Newcastle's Quayside. The Metro rapid transit system Sunderland Direct opens this year. There'll

be University station (at the city centre campus) and a station out here at St Peter's. Soon you'll be able to travel here direct from Newcastle.

The main nightspot remains **Manor Quay**, however. Regular clubnights are Wednesday: *Relax*; Friday: *Amnesia*; Saturday: *The Beat Goes On*; all of which sounds descriptive of normal student existence. Manor Quay incorporates **Roker Bar** and operates daily as watering hole, food bar, pool and games room. For footie nights *et al* it boasts 'the biggest screen in Sunderland'. With no residents in the near neighbourhood the 3 am chuck-out time on Mondays, Tuesdays and Thursdays causes no grief. The club is cool, with good size stage, balcony and bar. It's a major town venue and they sort it so that whatever's on at Manor Quay is not duplicated elsewhere. If it's indie at MQ it's dance music in town, etc.

Throughout the year poets and musicians (roots, jazz, classical) perform on campus. The Royal Shakespeare Company, Northern Play-

WHAT IT'S REALLY LIKE

UNIVERSITY:	
Social Life	★★★★
Campus scene	**Friendly, local**
Student Union services	**Good**
Politics	**Student issues**
	Activity low
Sport	**32 clubs. Skid**
	Snowbound,
	Gaelic Footie strong
National sporting position	**80th**
Sport facilities	**Improving**
Arts opportunities	**Film good; rest**
	'average'
Student magazine	**Degrees North**
Student newspaper	**Maclife**
Student radio	**Utopia fm**
Nightclub	**Manor Quay**
Bars	**Wearmouth,**
	Bonded Warehouse
Union ents	**Relax, Amnesia,**
	The Beat Goes On
Union clubs/societies	**51**
Most popular society	**People & Planet**
Smoking policy	**Bars OK**
Parking	**Adequate**
CITY	
Entertainment	★★
Scene	**Cheap fun**
Town/gown relations	**Poor**
Risk of violence	**Average**
Cost of living	**Low**
Student concessions	**Average**
Survival + 2 nights out	**£60 pw**
Part-time work campus/town	**Excellent/good**

wrights and Ballet Rambert have done workshops with the drama and dance elements of the Faculty of Arts, Design & Communication. Also on campus is the uni's **Screen on the River**, based in the 400-seater **Tom Cowie Theatre**, a focus for weekend film festivals, and sister cinema to Newcastle's little **Tyneside Cinema**, renowned for its arthouse fare.

There are nineteen societies, the most popular being People & Planet, and as many as thirty-two sports clubs. Joining the student radio station, Utopia fm and magazine, *Degrees North*, is a newspaper called *MACLIFE*.

SPORT Most popular clubs this year are Skid Snowboard, which came 2nd and 3rd (King's and Bugs respectively) in national competition, and Gaelic Football, which raised cheers in the North East championships. The Sports Centre has a two-storey fitness and cardiovascular suite, a 25-metre swimming pool with canoeing facilities, and a sports hall for badminton, football and basketball. Otherwise it's the city, which 'has a number of fitness clubs and sports centres – the Puma Tennis Centre, Nissan Sports Centre (brilliant football and basketball pitches), and Silksworth Sports Complex, with dry slope ski centre.

TOWN Masses of pubs around Chester Road. Popular among clubs are **Palace** (Monday), **Annabelle's** and *Panic Night* at **Pzazz** (Thursday). Wednesday, Friday and Saturday tends to be Manor Quay. Cost of living is low. Every university wants to play down problems with the town, but Sunderland cannot be classed as the safest of the cities we visit, though uni properties seem to be well protected.

PILLOW TALK

They guarantee all first-year students a single study bedroom in a university hall or house, whether or not you apply through the Clearing system. They offer self-contained flats and a small number of family houses and flats in halls. A Domestic Services Manager and a team of domestic staff manage the halls on a daily basis. All halls have 24-hour security and a team of resident tutors is on call during the evenings,

WHERE GRADUATES END UP	
20% Education,	Key Areas
10% Wholesale/Retail,	
10% Public Admin*,	
10% Health/Social Work,	
10% Manufacturing,	
6% Finance	
Chemical/Pharmaceutical*,	Niche Areas
Legal, Radio/TV,	
Sport, Telecom*	

*indicates Top 10 Graduate Provider

Approximate employed **94%**

throughout the night and at weekends. They also manage a range of private properties. Price range per week is £46.50 to £60.00 (for the 10% which are en suite). Rent for a small room in town is £32 per week. Halls are situated on both sides of the river, with the newly built Panns Bank and Scotia Quay being the pride of the university (close to Bonded Warehouse).

JOBS

The uni's strategic plan has a clear focus on 'student employability, entrepreneurship and creativity.' Government figures show that 94% of Sunderland full-time first degree students who graduated in 2000 were in employment or further study six months after completing their programmes. The uni's performance indicator is two per cent higher than the benchmark score for similar universities.

GETTING THERE

☞ By road: A1(M), A690 or A19, A690.
☞ By rail: Newcastle, 0:25; Leeds, 2:15; Edinburgh, 2:30, Manchester, 3:30, London King's Cross, 3:45.
☞ By air: Newcastle International Airport.
☞ By coach: London, 6:20; Bristol, 6:25.

UNIVERSITY OF SURREY

The University of Surrey
Guildford GU2 7XH

TEL 0800 980 3200 (freephone)
FAX 01483 689389
EMAIL information@surrey.ac.uk
WEB www.surrey.ac.uk

Surrey Students' Union
Guildford GU2 7XH

TEL 01483 259227
FAX 01483 534749
EMAIL info@ussu.ac.uk
WEB www.ussu.co.uk

VAG VIEW

Surrey, or UniS as it likes to be called, has roots in Battersea Poly. Its rise as a uni is a triumph of the career orientation of its courses and its teaching. Since receiving a Royal Charter in 1966, UniS has gone its own way, done its own thing, and with a great deal of success, making the whole business of higher education seem almost clinically straightforward. It is many students' first choice.

CAMPUS

UniS's self-contained, concrete, in-fill, landscaped campus lies just off the A3 in the ancient city of Guildford, adjacent to the cathedral, fifteen minutes walk from the city centre. Writes Madeleine Merchant: 'The campus contains most first-year residences, all the teaching buildings, lecture theatres, library, computer labs, a sports centre, a shop, a health centre, a counselling service, a post office, a NatWest bank, many cafés, restaurants, and bars, the Students' Union building, picnic areas and a lake. It is in an attractive setting with many trees and shrubs, on a hill in the shadow of Guildford Cathedral. Many students complain of being woken up on Sunday mornings by the cathedral bells! A train line runs around a third of the perimeter, and the trains can also be heard in some of the residences.

'Much of the area is covered by CCTV cameras, and it is generally well-lit. A current debate in Student Council is whether more CCTV cameras should be put in for greater safety, even if they may overlook some student residences. Unfortunately, the off-campus paths are not so safe, and there have been attacks on students. However, the university is planning to take responsibility of up-keep and maintenance from the council for some of these

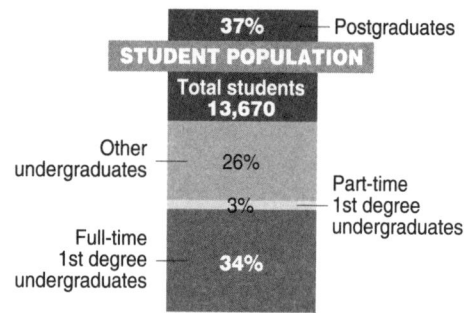

paths, and improve safety.'

See also University of Surrey Roehampton, *Satellite Campus*, below.

STUDENT PROFILE

'The University of Surrey may be a depressing collection of ugly concrete monstrosities,' writes Alistair Gerard, 'but it's not the buildings that make a university, it's the people, and I wouldn't have chosen to be anywhere else. Campus is a cosmopolitan enclave in the whole middle-class Caucasian experiment that is Guildford. Besides

UNIVERSITY/STUDENT PROFILE	
University since	**1966**
Situation/style	**Town campus**
Student population	**13,670**
Full-time undergraduates	**4,610**
- mature	**18%**
- overseas	**18%**
- male/female	**42/58**
- state sector intake	**84%**
- non-traditional student intake	**9%**
- drop-out rate	**8%**
- undergraduate applications	**Down 8%**
see Introduction for key to tables	

the obvious lean towards science and engineering bods at UniS, around a fifth of undergraduates are from overseas, nearly a quarter are mature students, and the state/independent ratio is about 4 to 1. Students are saved from the male dominance that can affect science unis by the nursing provision and Human Studies. Everyone is happy.'

Overseas applicants should note that the School of Biomedical & Life Sciences are lowering overseas tuition fees by £1,200 from the start of the 2002/2003 academic year.

ACADEMIA

The teaching assessment picture is good – 86% are Excellent (or 18+ out of 24). 'There's a good

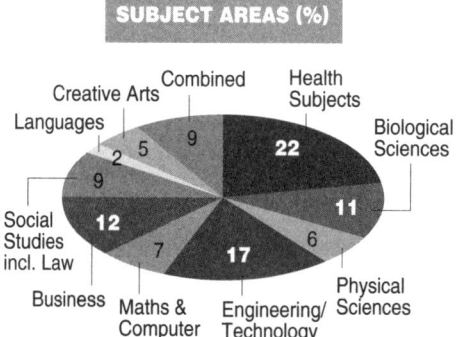

student/teacher ratio, many degree courses are modular, and communication, language and IT skills can be included as part of the degree or through additional study,' reports Craig Black. 'There are language areas offering interactive learning through a number of audio and visual methods, the IT facilities offer 24-hour access.'

In the Faculty of Engineering some courses have a European language, many point directly to a niche area of employment, such as offshore and maritime engineering; Electronic Engineering (which also includes Computing) was rated world class/Grade 5* in last year's research assessment. The Faculty of Science includes the School of Biomedical & Life Sciences which has caused such a stir as 'Subjects Allied to Medicine' in both the teaching assessments and the recent research assessment, again it was graded 5*; also the European Institute of Health & Medical Science (nursing and midwifery); finally, there are maths and computing courses in this faculty as well as in Engineering. In Human Studies besides the expected sociology, psychology, economics, law, we have the School of Management Studies for the Service Sector with courses like International Hospitality & Tourism Management and Retail Management, which severally translate into the hot graduate job areas, Hotel/Restaurant and Wholesale/Retail, listed in our *Employment* box (page 451). UniS come 6th nationally in the former area in our Employment Top 10s. From September 2002 the school will be moving into a new £11-million three-storey triangular building with central atrium, coffee lounge, computing facilities, a 400-seat lecture theatre, and a teaching restaurant and kitchen.

Finally, the Faculty of Human Studies introduces arts to the curriculum in the shape of the School of Performing Arts, which offers Music and Dance & Culture degrees.

Since receiving a Royal Charter in 1966, Surrey has gone its own way, done its own thing, and with a great deal of success, making the whole business of higher education seem almost clinically straightforward.

Intriguing curriculum niche areas are Sound Recording – Tonmeister; Physics with Satellite Technology. New courses mooted for 2002 entry are Biomedical Sciences, Business Management, Chiropractic, Law, Law & Spanish, Financial Mathematics, Mathematics with Music, Mathematics with Audio Technology, Sociology, Culture & New Media, Sociology & Social Research (the last two are both BScs).

Many courses are accredited by professional bodies and release the student from elements of further training. A new £10 million building

ACADEMIC EXCELLENCE	
TEACHING:	
(Rated Excellent or 17+ out of 24)	
Business & Management, Music	**Excellent**
Physics, Electronic Eng, Education, Economics	**23**
Psychology, Civil Engineering, Materials Science & Eng	**22**
Organismal Biosciences, Subjects Allied to Medicine, Food Science, Sociology, Molecular Biosciences, Maths	**21**
Dance	**20**
Nursing	**19**
Chemical Eng, Modern Langs	**18**
RESEARCH :	
*Top grades 5/5**	
Subjects Allied to Medicine, Electrical & Electronic Eng, Sociology	**Grade 5***
Psychology, Physics, Applied Maths, Statistics, Chemical Eng/Environmental Strategy, European Studies, Russian/Slavonic/East European	**Grade 5**

opened to the European Institute of Health & Medical Sciences this year. The institute provides health sciences, nursing and midwifery degrees in the Science faculty.

Work placements are salaried; often courses stretch to four years to accommodate them.

SOCIAL SCENE
STUDENTS' UNION Bars include **Union Bar**, **Hari's**, **Helyn Rose**, **Chancellor's**, Roots and Rushes. Regular clubnights are on Wednesday and Friday. On Friday is *FNO*, the biggest attraction in the area (total capacity is 1,600, licensed till 2) – dance in main venue, specialist music in smaller venue. Wednesday is Outrage – cheese in main venue, garage and R&B in smaller venue. Recent visitors include Seb Fontaine, Paul Oakenfold, Steve Lamacq, Ministry of Sound tour,Oliver Macgregor, DJ Touche and Cut la Roc. Then there are the big black tie balls.

Music and dance departments evolve their own series of concerts and the uni choir, orchestra, chamber orchestra and student Drama Society regularly perform. UniS also has a special

WHAT IT'S REALLY LIKE

UNIVERSITY:	
Social Life	★★★★
Campus scene	**Efficient, techy**
Student Union services	**Good**
Politics	**Low interest**
Sport	**40+ clubs; gymnastics big**
National team position	**49th**
Sport facilities	**Good**
Arts opportunities	**Dance, music good; drama avg, film, art poor**
Student newspaper	**Barefacts**
Student radio	**GU2**
Nightclub	**4-bar foum, 1,600 capacity**
Bars	**Union, Hari's, Helyn Rose, Bottle Bank, Chancellors**
Union ents	**F.N.O., Outrage**
Union clubs/societies	**100+**
Most popular societies	**Hellenic, Music**
Smoking policy	**Union, halls OK**
Parking	**Non-existent**
TOWN:	
Entertainment	★★-★
Scene	**Rich man's clubs/pubs**
Town/gown relations	**OK-good**
Risk of violence	**Off campus**
Cost of living	**Very high**
Student concessions	**Good**
Survival + 2 nights out	**£60 pw**
Part-time work campus/town	**Excellent/good**

year, they have a world-class trampolinist apparently, and the gymnastic team was sent to the world championships in China. Sports bursaries are available.

Writes Madeleine: 'There are many clubs, both competitive – e.g. hockey, waterpolo – and non-competitive: mountain climbing, hiking, etc. Everyone gets Wednesday afternoons free of lectures as these are set aside for BUSA matches. If you aren't interested in sports, the university offers free language courses. As in sport, all levels are catered for.'

TOWN Writes Alistair. 'London is only thirty-five minutes away by train. Ergo, Guildford is very expensive. With the introduction of tuition fees, this must now be a consideration. There are sociological implications, too. It's a notoriously blue pocket of middle-class conservatism. Guildford shuts at 11 pm, with the exception of its nightclubs, where prices reflect this. The people who live in Guildford have done their partying; they have moved to a gilt-edged ghetto to live in peace and tranquillity.'

Writes Madeleine: 'There is a mixture of the usual high street shops with student discounts, and the more expensive variety such as French Connection, Gap, House of Fraser etc, two theatres and a large Odeon, two or three nightclubs and many pubs and bars. At time of writing, **Wetherspoons** and **Yates** are actually cheaper for drinks than the Union, an issue that is being dealt with.

PILLOW TALK

All freshers are guaranteed accommodation in the uni's courts of residence flats. None is catered, 30% are en suite, the price per week ranges from £36.00 (duplex) to £67.50 (en suite). Millennium House is

relationship with Guildford School of Acting, validating its degrees in Acting and Stage Management. See web: www.gsa.drama.ac.uk. Tel: 01483 560 701; e-mail: enquiries@gsa.drama.co.uk.

There is a student radio station, GU2, newspaper *Bare Facts*, and occasionally *a* student magazine appears. There is also a film unit and many other societies (60+) within the Union: cultural, religious, political, course/interest-based. Generally, due to student apathy in this direction, political activity is low.

SPORT The Campusport Centre is the sports hall. The Varsity Centre is for field, squash and tennis, and pitches. Guildford's Spectrum Leisure Centre, home to ice hockey team, the Guildford Flames, provides facilities for swimming, ice skating and athletics, and the uni provides a bus linking Spectrum with other pick-ups in the city and the uni campus. Uni teams came 49th nationally last

AT A GLANCE

ACADEMIC FILE:	
Assessments	**22**
Excellent	**86%**
Average requirements	**260 points**
Students-staff ratio	**14:1**
First/2:1 degree pass rate	**56%**
ACCOMMODATION FILE:	
Guarantee to freshers	**100%**
Style	**Flats**
Catered	**None**
En-suite	**30%**
Price range pw	**£36-£67.50**
Town rent pw	**£58-£70**

the newest court, the three-storey building opened in 2001. It has 200 en-suite rooms arranged into flats of six rooms with a shared kitchen. All student rooms have telephones. Calls across campus and modem links to the academic network are free; all 3,000 phones have voice mailboxes. Rent in town is anything from £58.00.

JOBS

96% of traceable year 2000 graduates are reported to be in employment or further training. UniS has been ranked either first or second in the national university league table for low unemployment over the past six years. Characteristically, graduates get jobs for which they have been educated – they enter employment not only at graduate level but in occupations directly related to their degrees. This is not typical through length and breadth of the graduate nation.

'In the third year, most students work for companies in placements, and earn lots of money,' Madeleine reports, 'and from what I've heard, most of these come back in the fourth year with clear ideas about whether they really want to continue working in that field, and many have definite job offers for when they graduate.

'For temporary ways to earn money, Guildford shops and businesses usually have positions available, and the university runs a Job Shop. The union also employs many casual staff. Many student nurses supplement their income by working at the local hospital as "bank" health care assistants, and for agencies.'

SATELLITE CAMPUS

THE UNIVERSITY OF SURREY, ROEHAMPTON Whitelands College, West Hill, London SW15 3SN. Tel: 020 8392 3232. Fax: 020 8392 3470. E-mail: enquiries@roehampton.ac.uk. Web: www.roehamton.ac.uk.

The institute comprises four colleges, three of which (Digby, Froebel and Southlands) are cosily set together on the edge of Richmond deer park. A bolder sibling (Whitelands) is down the road in Southfields. Digby College contains a large ents venue and boasts a brand **Learning Resource Centre**, self-catering flats and a warm, welcoming atmosphere. Froebel College is dominated by the imposing, **Georgian Grove House**, its period feel making it popular with students and TV productions such as *Inspector Morse*. Southlands, was relocated from Wimbledon in 1997, and its brand new feel makes you want to eat your dinner off the lecture stands. It is clean, modern and the musical pulse of USR, with studios, a Steinway concert grand and a double-manual French harpsichord. Yowsa!

WHERE GRADUATES END UP	
22% Manufacturing*, 18% Health/Social Work, 8% Wholesale/Retail, 6% Finance, 5% Public Admin	Key Areas
Aeronautical Manufacture, Chemical/Pharmaceutical, Eng/Industrial Design*, Electron/Electric*, Market Research, Hotel/ Restaurant*, Artistic/ Literary, Publishing	Niche Areas

*indicates Top 10 Graduate Provider

Approximate employed **96%**

ACADEMIA Roehampton is renowned for its drama and QTS courses. However, its golden eggs are its combined degrees. These programmes allow for such intriguing hybrids as History and Dance and Calligraphy and Bookbinding. With the exception of Psychology & Counselling, and Teaching Studies, *all courses may be studied part-time*. Faculties include Arts & Humanities, Education, Sciences, Social Sciences.

SOCIAL Each of the four campuses has its own bar, although only the one at Whitelands is run by the SU. Food on site is provided famously by **Brenda's Café** (at Digby), while the fodder at Whitelands is damned with faint praise as 'better than school dinners'. For those keen on cooking (and yes, toast does count as cooking), the union runs a free bus service to nearby Asda on Sunday's.

Ents-wise the **Litten Tree** in Wandsworth knocks out cheap booze at a students' night on Tuesday, and the more up-market **Half Moon** in Putney also offers a good deal for the Roehamptonites. **Liquid**, 'Roehampton's favourite Student Night', also in Wandsworth, is the most popular club.

USR competes in the BUSA leagues, and a local rivalry with Kingston Uni adds spice to their rugby especially. Also popular are tennis, football and rowing on the Thames. Each college has its own teams, and the football battles between the Digby Lions and their 'natural prey', the Froebel Zebras, are legendary.

Societies tend to be transient things here. Large and long-standing socs are RIACAS, which promotes Afro-Caribbean and Asian culture, and the top Open Mic Soc. They hold massively popular clubnights at the Half Moon.

Information is spread by the monthly OURSU pamphlet, a sort of menu for socialites, and the more substantial and bi-monthly *Scream*, 'The George Michael of truth entering the Lavatory of reason,' (ahem).

PILLOW TALK

The cheapest self-catering flats sting you for around £65 weekly at Digby, rising to £80+ for all-inclusive packages. A limited number of rooms have en-suite facilities and Internet access.

GETTING THERE

☛ Surrey Uni by road: A3, signs to University.
☛ By coach: London, 1:00; Birmingham, 4:30.
☛ By rail: London Waterloo, 30 mins.
☛ By air: Gatwick and Heathrow.
☛ US Roehampton, Barnes British Rail station or No. 72 bus from Hammersmith Underground; No. 265 runs from Putney Bridge.
☛ Whitelands College, East Putney or Southfields Underground or Clapham Junction British Rail and No. 170 bus.

● ●

SURREY INSTITUTE OF ART & DESIGN

Surrey Institute of Art & Design
University College
Falkner Road
Farnham
Surrey GU9 7DS

TEL 01252 892609/10/11
FAX 01252 892624
EMAIL registry@surrart.ac.uk
WEB www.surrart.ac.uk

Surrey Institute Students' Union
Falkner Road
Farnham
Surrey GU9 7DS

TEL 01252 710263
FAX 01252 713591
EMAIL su@surrart.ac.uk
WEB www.dooyoo.co.uk/product/150868.html

VAG VIEW

*S*urrey, which has long had its own degree awarding powers and was awarded University College status recently, drives home a few key points to prospective students from their leafy, suburban locations, 32 miles apart, at Farnham (on a 16-acre campus) and at Epsom.

This is all art and design, but of a particularly focused nature: animation sits next to fashion journalism, interior design next to textiles. There are all sorts of packaging and promotion and marketing ideas in bed with serious three-dimensional design, etc.

Applicants must be totally committed.

INSTITUTE PROFILE	
University College since	**1999**
Situation/style	**Suburban campus/sites**
Student population	**2,760**
Full-time undergraduates	**2,590**
- mature	**26%**
- overseas	**16%**
- male/female	**42/58**
- state sector intake	**94%**
- drop-out rate (non-mature)	**10%**
ACCOMMODATION:	
Availability to freshers	**90%**
Style	**Halls, flats, houses**
Cost pw (no food)	**£33-£52**
Town rent pw Farnham/Epsom	**£65/£47**

DEGREE SUBJECTS:
Animation, Design Mgt, Fashion, Film, Fine Art, Graphic Design, Interior Design, Journalism, Packaging Design, Photography, Textiles, 3D Design (Ceramics, Glass, Metals)

One of the college's principal aims is to get students into work and they do this by integrating into their courses the processes and disciplines of market realities. The onus is on students of certain courses to 'produce' their own projects; finding sponsors for a film project becomes as important as finding locations. Skills students will need to negotiate themselves into a position to put their talent to work are part of the programme. Meanwhile the college tutors are constantly involved with the industries and professions and agencies on which their students livelihoods will depend. It is all an impressive proposal.

There are two halls at Farnham and a student village on the Farnham campus (flats). No accommodation at Epsom.

ACADEMIA

They achieved 21 points out of 24 in the teaching assessments for Art & Design, did less well (17 points) for Communications & Media, and took a respectable 3a grade in the research assessments. Degree courses include Animation, Design Management, Fashion, Film & Video, Fine Art, Graphic Design, Interior Design, Journalism, Packaging Design, Photography, textiles, 3D Design (ceramics, glass, metals).

SOCIAL SCENE

Ents are getting better. Leavers is the big ball, there are also Christmas and Freshers' balls. There's a bar at each site. Each week the main club night is Thursday with guest DJs. They also have regular comedy and karaoke nights, and there's a winter term trip to Amsterdam.

There are three film societies – 'A really popular night is Tuesday, when the Film & Video Society do their stuff,' I am told; 'it's £1 a ticket.' The Rock Society arranges trips to visit the Brixton Academy or take in metal nights at **Bojanglez** in Guildford, and a Drama Society is up and running at Farnham (there's no dance, but workshops run in the theatre in town); at Epsom there's the 400-seater **Playhouse Theatre** and a smaller one for jazz and comedy.

Student-recommended pubs at Farnham include **Blues Tavern** (live music, DJs, great

WHERE GRADUATES END UP	
23% Manufacturing*, 21% Wholesale/Retail*, 6% Computer	Key Areas
Radio/TV*, Advertising*, Architecture, Film/Video, Artistic/Literary*, Journalism, Library/ Archival*, Publishing*, Eng/Industrial Design	Niche Areas

*indicates Top 10 Graduate Provider

Approximate employed **93%**

atmosphere), **Hogshead** and **The Nelson** (great atmosphere and close to campus, though none compares to **The Glasshouse**), and **The Jolly Sailor** (gay pub), favoured by the LGB Society. At Epsom it's **The Litten Tree** (student night Monday; resident DJ), **Chicago Rock Café** (Thursdays till 1 am), Epsom **Playhouse** (bar with films, alternative comedy, jazz), and student friendly **Symonds Well** and **The Rising Sun;** occasional forays are made to handbag clubs **Volts** and **Options** in Kingston.

GETTING THERE

☛ By road to Farnham: A325 towards centre; turn left up The Hart. Epsom: A24 to centre, under the railway bridge; turn left at lights into Ashley Road.
☛ By train to Farnham: London Waterloo, 45 mins. Epsom: London Waterloo/Victoria, 30 mins.

UNIVERSITY OF SUSSEX

University of Sussex
Sussex House
Falmer
Brighton BN1 9RH

TEL 01273 678416
FAX 01273 678545
EMAIL
ug.admissions@sussex.ac.uk
WEB www.sussex.ac.uk

Sussex Students' Union
Falmer House
Falmer
Brighton BN1 9QF

TEL 01273 678555
FAX 01273 678875
EMAIL info@ussu.ac.uk
WEB www.ussu.co.uk

VAG VIEW

Sussex University first admitted students in October 1961. In its first decade or more, it was the place to be – home of '60s radicalism, fighter of causes, defender of the

student realm. Then all went quiet. Financial problems and a mouldering of relations between the uni and its students meant that 'any student triumphs occurred despite rather than because of the powers that be,' as a student put it.

Now, Sussex is back on top, but on a

different academic footing to the one that first brought it to prominence.

CAMPUS

The Sussex campus, its award-winning design by Sir Basil Spence, is an 18th-century park designated as an area of outstanding beauty, on the South Downs, five miles north east of Brighton.

'At times being on campus can feel a bit isolated and claustrophobic,' writes Keren Rosen, 'but it is fifteen minutes to Brighton by bus and you are never more than ten minutes walk from the fields of the South Downs. Escape is always possible.

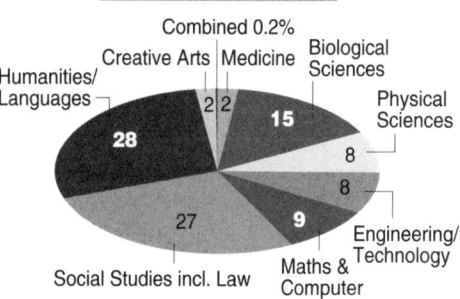

SUBJECT AREAS (%)

Combined 0.2%
Humanities/Languages — 28
Creative Arts 2
Medicine 2
Biological Sciences 15
Physical Sciences 8
8
Engineering/Technology 9
Maths & Computer
Social Studies incl. Law 27

UNIVERSITY/STUDENT PROFILE

University since	**1961**
Situation/style	**Campus**
Student population	**11,640**
Full-time undergraduates	**6,480**
- mature	**21%**
- overseas	**14%**
- male/female	**44/56**
- state sector intake	**83%**
- non-traditional student intake	**6%**
- drop-out rate	**9%**
- undergraduate applications	**Down 6%**
see Introduction for key to tables	

STUDENT PROFILE

'Owing to its strong international links, roughly a third of the student population comes from foreign parts and although the rest tend to come from London and the south of England, in general there is quite a nice mix of backgrounds,' continues Keren. 'There is also a large number of mature students studying at Sussex and although socially it is quite divided they definitely add a different perspective to study.' The ratio of state to independent entrants is roughly 4 to 1. There is likely to be an increase in local students as a deal

has been struck whereby Sussex, Brighton and University College Chichester guarantee to offer places to applicants from local sixthforms and further education colleges.

ACADEMIA

Academics in at the start-up were an impressive bunch – men like Asa Briggs, the famous historian, and David Daiches, the Cambridge professor who put down Sussex's English and American Studies markers on the world university map.

Briggs was put to work on Sussex's academic strategy and he came up with something original and far-seeing, a programme of study that facilitated interdisciplinary teaching and research. Sussex undergraduates would take a major subject and a cluster of contextual courses that would reveal hidden conceptual relationships between disciplines, thence new thought associations. Enhancing understanding in this way had revolutionary advantages. A different light may be shed on a subject through the lens of different disciplines; a student or researcher may begin to acknowledge the relative nature of what different disciplines regard as truth; hitherto unthought of avenues of exploration may be suggested and encouraged.

Sussex doesn't have the industrial links-ups of a UMIST. They are more tied up with what they refer to as 'the knowledge economy' than with industry, producing articulate, adaptable people, often capable of finding fulfilment in their own way, not slotting in to someone else's production line. This, they believe, is where the cross-faculty potential inherent in Briggs' ideal took Sussex students. 'Also, we get the feedback from employers that they like the fact that our students are taught in seminars and are used to getting up and giving presentations and are articulate and confident, that they think on their feet, are analytical.'

Nevertheless, there are those who maintain that Briggs' strategy was not always well applied in

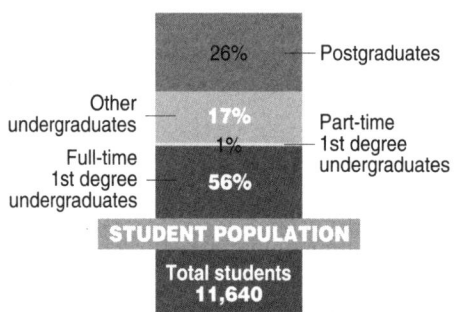

26% — Postgraduates

Other undergraduates — 17%
1%
Full-time 1st degree undergraduates — 56%

Part-time 1st degree undergraduates

STUDENT POPULATION

Total students
11,640

the curriculum, and the curriculum planners at Sussex today have decided to modify it, much to the apprehension of some students to whom we talked.

When we spoke to the planners, they made it clear that they did not intend to relieve the curriculum of the advantages of interdisciplinarity, rather to release the curriculum from the rigidity of the schools structure within which the different disciplines were allowed to interact: 'What we found – and it took quite a long time – was that the structures set up [these schools of study] were not fostering new interdisciplinarity... In fact they were actually inhibiting this.'

> *The campus is buzzing again. After a fallow period from the mid-1970s, Sussex is back on top.*

On the one hand, it seems, they want to suggest a whole host of cross-discipline courses that would not have been possible within the original schools structure, which must surely be welcomed. On the other, they are clearly driven to make this change to increase ubdergraduate applications, which is a different first principle altogether: 'Are we actually shooting ourselves in the foot because we have a very strong department of this and a very strong knowledge base of that and yet we are not putting them together in an academic degree? There are plenty of undergraduates out there who would like to be at Sussex studying History and English, yet we do not offer History and English.'

However, when we met they persisted in the point that the principle of interdisciplinarity would not only be preserved in the re-think, but enhanced: 'We want not only to have subject A and subject B [in a course], but to mount bridging courses that explicitly bring out the tensions or connections of A and B.'

The new syllabus and their students will eventually tell. All unis have principles on which their curriculum strategies are based – at Stirling, for example, a subject is given an application that will convert it into a career prospect. It would be sad, and out of character, if Sussex lost the important principle that inspired its schools in a Government-pressured drive for more students.

By and large the science side of Sussex was always less affected by the old schools system, the main exception being the creation of the School of Cognitive Sciences, and degrees such as BSc Artificial Intelligence with Euro/Management/North American Studies.

On the engineering side, not wanting to compete with the likes of UMIST, they have tended towards the exotic/esoteric, like Formula One racing. 'We have an automotive engineering degree for example, the leading edge engineering rather than another mechanical engineering degree or smokestack type of thing. We are looking to be a bit more specialist in what we provide – most Formula One are based in southern England.'

In the early 1990s the teaching of ten Sussex departments was rated merely Satisfactory (or 17/24), results which have depressed their overall Excellence rating (64%) ever since. At recent assessments they have dropped virtually no points at all. Top scoring are Philosophy, Sociology (both full marks), Politics, American Studies, Maths & Statistics, Media (all 23 out of 24 points), Linguistics, French, Physics, Biosciences (22).

The uni's performance in the recent research assessments was also good (see box, below), even if a Grade 5* did elude them. They came 31st overall, with unis like Newcastle, Dundee, Glasgow, Leeds close by. Note, especially, the position that life sciences enjoy both in the teaching and research assessments. It is an aspect of Sussex which is really moving ahead. 'It's a research based thing. We are strong on biological sciences, genome is flavour of the month at the moment.' And it has sparked the uni's biggest news this year – the new medical school to be formed with neighbouring Brighton University. 'It ties in with the new Genome Centre on our campus, and a £5.5 million

ACADEMIC EXCELLENCE

TEACHING :
(Rated Excellent or 17+ out of 24)

English, Music, Anthropology	**Excellent**
Philosophy, Sociology	24
Politics, American Studies,	23
Maths & Statistics, Media	
Linguistics, French,	22
Physics, Biosciences	
Electric & Electron Engineering,	21
Economics, Psychology	
History of Art	20

RESEARCH:
Top grades 5/5*

Psychology, Chemistry,	**Grade 5**
Biological Sciences, Physics,	
Applied Maths, Computer,	
General Eng, Anthropology,	
Science/Technology Policy	
Research, American Studies,	
English, History of Art/	
Architecture/Design,	
Philosophy, Music	

AT A GLANCE

ACADEMIC FILE:

Subjects assessed	**28**
Excellent	**64%**
Average requirements	**280 points**
Students-staff ratio	**17:1**
First/2:1 degree pass rate	**58%**

ACCOMMODATION FILE:

Guarantee to freshers	**95%**
Style	**Halls, houses, flats**
Approx price range pw	**£53**
City rent pw	**£45-£80**

teaching building will be erected – a 250-seater lecture theatre, eight seminar rooms, a café and computer suite.'

SOCIAL SCENE

One reason why Sussex students to whom we spoke were anxious about the curriculum change was that the interdisciplinary approach impacts not only on the inferences you draw in your studies, but on the social fabric of the place: 'In some universities, if say you are taking Geography, the only students you will sit next to will be other students studying geography,' said one. 'But here, because you are taking these interdisciplinary courses, you may be sitting next to someone whose major is Philosophy. You have a much wider circle of friends and acquaintances and colleagues and so on, which is why this is a genuinely friendly campus.'

Moving over to the Students' Union I ask whether it is still true that campus is a weekday place, too close to London to hold its students over the weekend. In fact, campus is largely a first-year affair, more 24/7 than it was in the '80s/'90s, but in your second year attention diverts to the city of Brighton.

Ents are good, despite union facility problems. Basically, there are two SU bars, **East Scope** (250 capacity) and **Park Village** (60), and then there's the **Grapevine** with plush armchairs You can expect up to ten events a week.

Media is a very active student area: the newspaper is *Badger*, the magazine is *Pulse*, the radio station is URF. All frequently win awards. Last year *Pulse* was runner up in the *Independent* awards as Magazine of the Year. What of the student politics? I ask. Is that really all yesterday's '60s-student glory? Apparently not, for today, it seems, the radicals are not only the students: 'Politics are as important today as they were in the late '60s,' I

was told, but it was the vice-chancellor who radicalised the anti-war protest during the bombing by America of Afghanistan. The first of a series of anti-war demos was instigated by a postgrad from Pakistan, whose exhortations in Library Square attracted barely a dozen listeners, but he turned out to be so eloquent on the subject of terrorism and Western imperialism that soon over a hundred had gathered. Demos then became a weekly feature and were followed by the v-c urging the sale of the uni's shares in the weapon manufacturer BAe Systems, which in turn led a Sussex University Coalition Against the War.

Later, students marched on the British naval centre at Arts D on campus, occupying the building to chants such as 'George Bush we know you. Your daddy was a killer too.'

Back in Brighton after talking to Sussex students at Falmer, we were handed flyers about a

WHAT IT'S REALLY LIKE

UNIVERSITY:

Social Life	★★★★
Campus scene	**First-year only holiday camp**
Student Union services	**Average**
Politics	**Increasingly left-wing/concerned**
Sport	**Less pro than Brighton**
National team position	**81st**
Sport facilities	**Good**
Arts opportunities	**Drama, film excellent; dance, art, music good**
Student newspaper	**Badger**
Student magazine	**Pulse**
Student radio	**URF**
Nightclub	**The Hot House**
Bars	**Falmer Bar, Grape Vine, East Slope, Park Village**
Union ents	**The safe option to Brighton city**
Union clubs/societies	**200**
Smoking policy	**None**
Parking	**Poor**

CITY:

Entertainment	★★★★★
Scene	**Exceptional**
Town/gown relations	**OK**
Risk of violence	**Low**
Cost of living	**High**
Student concessions	**Good**
Survival + 2 nights out	**£80 pw**
Part-time work campus/town	**Good**

teach-in on the war in Afghanistan outside the arts building on Grand Parade. Professors from Brighton, Sussex and York universities were on the bill.

SPORT It's sport-for-all at Sussex, not too keenly competitive – they came 81st in the national team ratings last year. There are two large sports halls, a fitness room with multigym and training facilities, four glass-backed squash courts, sauna, solarium, café and bar. Elsewhere on campus are the pitches, tennis courts, and five more squash courts.

TOWN 'The town centre is small enough to be covered in its entirety on foot, but it manages to squeeze in a huge amount of clubs, pubs, bars and shops to suit every taste,' writes Keren. 'The theatre and art scene has a real emphasis on individuality. As the gay capital of England, Brighton has a laid back, party atmosphere and students and locals live in peaceful harmony. Brightonians do have a tendency to be a little self-consciously cool, verging at times on the pretentious, but there are enough different types of people that it is possible to avoid that world completely if its not your thing.'

It's a great city, lots of free festivals. Right now, Sussex students tend to frequent **Paradox**, the **Event** and **Club Barcelona**. See *Student Brighton*, page 87, for more.

PILLOW TALK

As far as accommodation goes, the majority of first years get housed on campus or in one of the student houses in Brighton and this works on a first come, first served basis. The standard of accommodation is pretty high; it is all self-catering and varies between flats and rooms on corridors. A cluster-flat extension to Lewes Court at the back end of campus will provide 250 new places in 2003, and take residences overall up to 3,050.

JOBS

'We have an Innovation Centre, where a number of outfits up there were student-started. It is an incubation centre rather than a money-making business park.'

WHERE GRADUATES END UP

12% Finance,	Key Areas
10% Health/Social Work,	
9% Education,	
8% Wholesale/Retail,	
7% Manufacturing,	
7% Public Admin,	
6% Personnel,	
6% Computer	
Advertising, Radio/TV*,	Niche Areas
Defence, Journalism*,	
Business/Management,	
Legal, Library/Archival,	
Market Research,	
Property, Publishing	

*indicates Top 10 Graduate Provider

Approximate employed **96%**

Graduate employment rates are high, and what is interesting about the niche areas quoted in our box, above – publishing, radio/TV, journalism – is that graduates entering these industries came not from departments dedicated to turning out media types – Media Studies and the like – but from across the scholastic board, out of a combination of application no doubt encouraged through the curriculum and extra-curricular interest, which is exactly what you want from a university. Sussex is a small university, but it has more extra curricular clubs and societies (200) than virtually any other. There is a very strong student culture, and whether or not it comes with a hands-on, vocational degree, employers like to pick the fruits of that.

GETTING THERE

☛ By road: M23, A23, A27.
☛ By coach: London, 1:50.
☛ By rail: London Bridge/Victoria, 1:10; Portsmouth, 1:30; Birmingham New Street, 3:45; Leeds, 4:15; Manchester Piccadilly, 5:00.
☛ By air: Gatwick and Heathrow Airports.

UNIVERSITY OF WALES, SWANSEA

University of Wales, Swansea
Swansea SA2 8PP

TEL 01792 295111
FAX 01792 295110
EMAIL admissions@swan.ac.uk
WEB www.swan.ac.uk

Swansea Students' Union
Swansea SA2 8PP

TEL 01792 295466
FAX 01792 206029
EMAIL eugenoff@swan.ac.uk
WEB www.swansea-union.co.uk

VAG VIEW

Swansea isn't a university that people immediately consider, despite there being some excellent academic departments, especially in the engineering fields, incredible sport and great laid-back vibes. Perhaps it has something to do with its out-of-the-way location. If so, do yourself a favour, go see it.

'You can come here and never leave it,' a student said to me. 'It's a bit like a black hole.' How else to explain a mere 5% drop-out rate, despite a heavy non-traditional student bias at application? How else to explain why so many students stay on in the area after graduation?

CAMPUS

The campus is set in a glorious position with wide open Swansea Bay stretched out in front and parkland behind, just a couple of miles west of the town. Further west along the coast you come to the old fishing village of Mumbles (birthplace of Catherine Zeta Jones), its pubs, fish & chip and Indian restaurants a favourite trawl for students, and the Gower Peninsula, described by Dylan Thomas as 'one of the loveliest sea-coast stretches in the whole of Britain.' On a sunny day I didn't disagree, nor do Swansea's surfer dudes. 'It's all so easy, see; everything's in walking distance,' the same student opined. 'Students come to Swansea for that alone.' He was pointing at the surf.

Writes Maxine French: 'The Gower is a stretch of coastline incorporating bays such as Caswell, Port Eynon and Langland, the last a favourite spot for surfers and host recently to the Welsh leg of some mad, never-ending surf competition. During the summer term its almost compulsory to go to Caswell when the Geography Society holds its annual beach party. For those whose lives are not ruled by tide tables, the coast means the Mumbles,

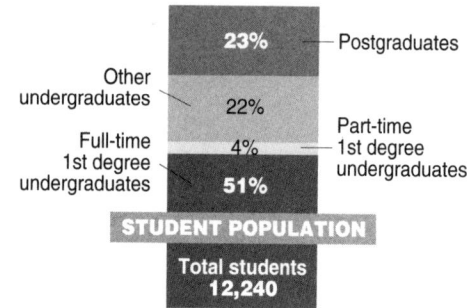

STUDENT POPULATION

Total students
12,240

renowned for the "Mile", strictly non-athletic, a pub crawl to end all pub crawls, something Dylan Thomas might have liked too.'

STUDENT PROFILE

This is one of the government's favoured 'elite access' universities. They take 89% of their students from the state sector (5% more than their benchmark). Nearly a quarter come from social classes IIIM, IV, V and 13% from so-called low-participation neighbourhoods – postcodes which don't traditionally turn out undergraduates. Swansea is thus doing well in attracting people to

UNIVERSITY/STUDENT PROFILE	
University since	**1920**
Situation/style	**Campus-by-the-sea**
Student population	**12,240**
Full-time undergraduate	**6,280**
- mature	**12%**
- overseas	**10%**
- male/female	**47/53**
- state sector intake	**89%**
- non-traditional student intake	**13%**
- drop-out rate	**5%**
- undergraduate applications	**Up 2%**
*see Introduction for key to tables	

university who up till now might not have thought of it. But you don't become one of the elite just for that. You have to have a very good teaching base and be able to keep your students for the duration – which involves a good student culture.

They have all of these at Swansea; and the campus is a very laid-back, friendly sort of place, more noticeably Welsh than Cardiff Uni; people are chatty, the scene a good deal less pressured than in some more cosmopolitan, civic universities. It does strike you that it would be an easy place to settle, and not simply for yhe duration of a three year degree course.

SUBJECT AREAS (%)

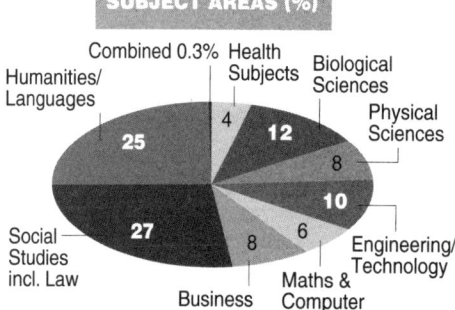

Combined 0.3%
Humanities/Languages 25
Health Subjects 4
Biological Sciences 12
Physical Sciences 8
Social Studies incl. Law 27
Business 8
Maths & Computer 6
Engineering/Technology 10

ACADEMIA

Entry requirements are actually highish, but there's a good chance of getting in anyway. 'Once they are here, people do well here,' a student said, 'but I guess it comes down to nothing else to do but work.' Performance in the teaching assessments has been good. Besides the obvious strength of engineering, languages are an important element in many courses; both teaching and research assessments show the department as especially strong.

ACADEMIC EXCELLENCE	
TEACHING :	
History, Computer Science, Geography, Psychology, Physics, Electrical & Electronic Engineering, Modern Langs (German, Italian, Spanish), Biosciences, Chemical Eng, Materials Eng, Civil Eng, Classics & Ancient History.	**Excellent**
RESEARCH:	
Top grades 5/5*	
Civil Engineering, Social Work	**Grade 5***
Physics, Pure Maths,	**Grade 5**
Celtic Studies, German/Dutch/ Scandinavian, Iberian/Latin American, Computer	

SOCIAL SCENE

There are 111 societies and clubs – the most active societies being RAG, Politics, Philosophy, Debating, Art, Roleplayers, Italian – a student newspaper (*Waterfront*) and radio station (X-Treme). They have a new Societies Centre to service it all. In the bars, **Divas** (600 capacity) and **Idols** (300; it's at Hendrefoelan Student Village) there's something going on most nights, but a number of student nights are by arrangement with clubs in town. Monday is *Essential Student Session* @ **Time** (cheesy) is one of these; there's also *Comedy Club* @ **Divas**. Tuesday is *Good Vibrations* (breaks, beats, hip hop) @ **Divas** and karaoke @ **Idols**. Wednesday is *The Eclectic Collection* (bit of lots, but a cheese-free zone); Thursday is karaoke; Friday is *Disco Inferno* – two rooms, different sounds – and *Love-Shack*. Saturday is again two rooms - *Smooth & Creamy* with DJ Angel Delight – and Saturday is *Session* @ Idols. Sunday they have big screen movies. Recent

WHAT IT'S REALLY LIKE	
UNIVERSITY:	
Social Life	★★★★
Campus scene	**Laid-back surfers**
Student Union services	**Good**
Politics	**NUS issues, average interest**
Sport	**46 clubs**
National team position	**47th**
Sport facilities	**Good**
Arts opportunities	**Drama, dance excellent, music, film, art good**
Student newspaper	**Waterfront**
Student radio	**X-Treme**
Nightclubs/bars	**Divas, Idols**
Union ents	**Good Vibrations, The Eclectic Collection, Disco Inferno, Love-Shack**
Union clubs/societies	**111**
Smoking policy	**Bars OK**
Parking	**Adequate**
TOWN:	
Entertainment	★★★
Scene	**Clubs, pubs, sea**
Town/gown relations	**Good**
Risk of violence	**Average**
Cost of living	**Average**
Student concessions	**Good**
Survival + 2 nights out	**£50 pw**
Part-time work campus/town	**Good**

visitors have been Space, Echobelly, Wheatus, The Proclaimers, Chesney Hawkes, Jason Donovon, Judge Jules, Liberty 37, Manlion, Howard Marks, Dodgy, the Webb Brothers, Black Legend. So, you can see that they put on the best kinda show!

There's an international Swansea Arts Festival every autumn. **The Glynn Vivian Gallery** in town, **The Swansea Arts Workshop** in the Maritime Quarter (the former docklands) and **The Taliesin Arts Centre** on campus, deliver year-round exhibitions and events. Taliesin was and is the poetic spirit of Wales, his story among the oldest of Welsh myths. Here is a constantly unfolding programme (for and by students and outsiders) of drama, dance, film and concerts from classical through jazz and rock. The building has a bar and a bookshop. For Swansea-based opera and comedy there's the **Pontardawe Arts Centre**; for comedy,

> *Here's another surfer's paradise. You can come here and never leave it; it's a bit like a black hole. It's all so easy, see.*

AT A GLANCE	
ACADEMIC FILE:	
Subjects assessed	**26**
Excellent	**46%**
Average requirements	**240 points**
Students-staff ratio	**18:1**
First/2:1 degree pass rate	**57%**
ACCOMMODATION FILE:	
Guarantee to freshers	**98%**
Style	**Halls, student village**
Approx price range pw	**£45-£67**
City rent pw	**£35-£45**

PILLOW TALK

'Swansea is small. Wherever you choose to live – in campus halls or in Clyne Halls or two miles away in the student village at Hendrefoelan – you'll find a community of really good friends,' writes Maxine. 'The same is true even in private accommodation at Brynmill, an area close by but considered by many (though probably not by its long-term residents) as a second student village. There is this sense that everyone is linked in some way, friends, friend of a friend and so on. Students here are generally very laid back, and not just the surfers.'

JOBS

They have a consistently good employment rate and take 2nd place in our Telecom Top 10.

rock, classical and musicals there's the **Penyrheol Theatre**, while **The Grand** delivers Welsh National Opera, Lily Savage, *The Pirates of Penzance*, Paul Merton and the *South Wales Evening Post Fashion Show* in quick succession (classify that!).

SPORT Interest in sport is huge. Rugby is bigger than huge; Robert Howley and Dafydd James are alumni. Football and netball teams are currently Welsh champions. A new Olympic-size swimming pool and Sports Village are currently under construction. There's a sports centre with hall, squash courts, weight training room, climbing wall and indoor swimming pool (a new Olympic-size pool is due for completion in 2001). Two sets of playing fields include a floodlit synthetic pitch, athletics track, field sport areas, six tennis courts, two netball courts, a rifle range and fishing lake.

There's also sailing, rowing (on the River Tawe), surfing and canoeing, and £700 annual sports scholarships, for which you should apply before you join up.

WHERE GRADUATES END UP	
10% Manufacturing,	Key Areas
10% Health/Social Work,	
9% Finance,	
9% Public Admin,	
9% Education,	
6% Wholesale/Retail	
Chemical/Pharmaceutical,	Niche Areas
Construction, Defence,	
Legal, Market Research,	
Sport, Telecom*	
*indicates Top 10 Graduate Provider	
Approximate employed	**96%**

GETTING THERE

☞ By road: M4/J42B.
☞ By coach: Cardiff, 1:10.
☞ By rail: London Paddington, 2:50; Bristol, 2:00; Cardiff, 0:50; Birmingham, 3:15; Manchester, 4:30.
☞ By air: Cardiff Airport.

SWANSEA INSTITUTE

Swansea Institute
Mount Pleasant
Swansea SA1 6ED

TEL 01792 481000
FAX 01792 481085
EMAIL (via website)
WEB www.sihe.ac.uk

VAG VIEW

*T*he institute operates five faculties out of three sites in Swansea town. Three-quarters of students are local and Welsh, about a quarter are part-time. There is accommodation for around 50% of freshers, who can live in hall for about £40 a week. Entry requirements are low.

Foundations on which they are building are the Excellent-rated Business and Art & Design faculties. In the same faculty as Business are the

Schools of Computing, Law and Leisure, and Tourism & Transport. Other faculties include Applied Design & Engineering and Humanities, Education & Healthcare. Degrees are awarded by the University of Wales and the University of the West of England, Bristol.

The Students' Union run a popular work link employment scheme for students. Ents are looking up, with club-nights three nights a week, and there's an inexpensive and varied town-life – hardened clubbers at **Escape**, funky divas at **Barons**, cheesy disco-babes at **Spoofers**.

Sport is competitive and they have recently built a fitness centre on the city centre site.

INSTITUTE PROFILE	
Founded	**1976**
Status	**HE College**
Degree awarding university	**Wales**
Situation/style	**Town campus**
Student population	**4,730**
Full-time undergraduates	**2,200**
ACCOMMODATION FILE:	
Availability to freshers	**50%**
Style	**Halls**
Cost pw (no food)	**£45**
Town rent pw	**£35-£40**

GETTING THERE

☛ By road: M4/J42B.

☛ By coach: Cardiff, 1:50.

☛ By rail: London Paddington, 2:50; Bristol, 2:00; Cardiff, 0:50; Birmingham, 3:15; Manchester, 4:30.

☛ By air: Cardiff Airport.

UNIVERSITY OF TEESSIDE

The University of Teesside
Middlesbrough
Tees Valley TS1 3BA

TEL 01642 384229
FAX 01642 384201
EMAIL reg@tees.ac.uk
WEB www.tees.ac.uk

Teesside Students' Union
Borough Road
Middlesbrough TS1 3BA

TEL 01642 342234
FAX 01642 342241
EMAIL st.union@utu.org.uk
WEB www.utu.org.uk

VAG VIEW

*T*eesside (two 'ss') is in Middlesbrough (one 'o'), which makes the soccer chant of 'Boro' strictly incorrect. But I wouldn't argue. They call themselves the Opportunity University, and sit high in the league table of universities that have worked hardest at widening access to higher education. What this means in their case is that entry requirements are not demanding, may well not include A levels, and that the undergraduate population, many of whom are mature, is largely drawn from the region.

Out-of-towners will cloud these facts with their own preconceptions about the university, as surely as one's first time view of the town is clouded by the Satanic vision of sulphurous chimneys off the A1.

CAMPUS

The campus is located within a few minutes walk of the centre of Middlesbrough, on the south bank

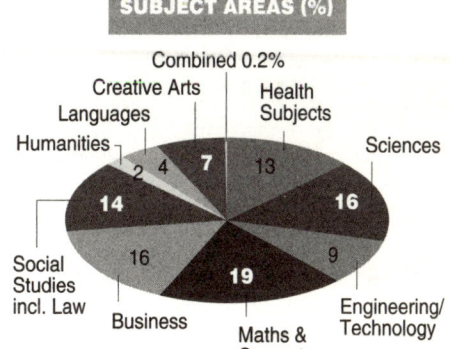

SUBJECT AREAS (%)

Combined 0.2%
Creative Arts
Languages
Humanities
Health Subjects
Sciences
2 4 7 13 16
14
16 19 9
Social Studies incl. Law
Business
Maths & Computer
Engineering/ Technology

of the River Tees, a short hop from the North Yorks Moors and Redcar and Saltburn beaches.

Students using the union building must run a gauntlet of pubs on Southfield Road: **The Dickens' Inn**, licensed till midnight, **The Star & Garter**, offering '£1-a-pint, £2-for-2' (to whom in their cups does that seem like an increasingly good deal?) and **The Fly & Firkin.** The architecture of the union

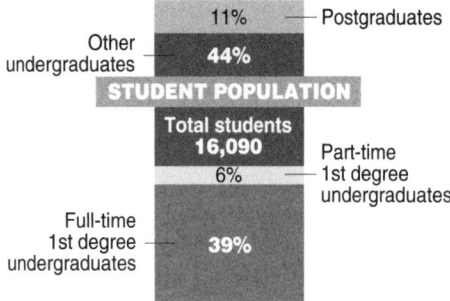

STUDENT POPULATION

- Postgraduates 11%
- Other undergraduates 44%
- Total students 16,090
- Part-time 1st degree undergraduates 6%
- Full-time 1st degree undergraduates 39%

and adjacent, £11-million, 5-storey Learning Resources Centre stuns – these delicately ribbed, green-tinted glass buildings glistening with seductive appeal.

STUDENT PROFILE

There's a large mature student intake and many come from non-traditional uni heartlands. Those who come here and stay – and there's a highish drop-out rate (11%) – have a job-seeker's attitude to academia, i.e. serious, which is just what is needed. Afterwards, many have a similar appetite for the hedonistic pleasures that union and town afford.

ACADEMIA

They have a reputation for business, for health, for engineering, for computing, and links with Cleveland and Durham constabularies underwrite the pioneering BSc in Criminology – see also law, crime scene science (forensic, etc) and fraud management.

The largest schools are Health & Social Care, followed by Computing & Mathematics. The first subject to be assessed Excellent was Computer Science and this has been a crucial focus of investment. The Innovation Centre incorporates the unique Virtual Reality Centre, with large-scale VR development and viewing facilities, including a

UNIVERSITY/STUDENT PROFILE

University since	**1970**
Situation/style	**Town campus**
Student population	**16,090**
Full-time undergraduates	**6,280**
- mature	**36%**
- overseas	**3%**
- male/female	**43/57**
- state sector intake	**98%**
- non-traditional student intake	**25%, high**
- drop-out rate	**13%**
- undergraduate applications	**Up 11%**
see Introduction for key to tables	

purpose-built Hemispherium (immersive VR experience) and VR cinema, as well as labs for the development of VR environments. Look at BScs in Interactive Entertainment Systems, in Virtual Reality and in Integrated Engineering.

Courses keep appearing that surprise, such as Creative Visualisation (a course for careers in TV and film animation, special effects or the computer games industry), or Information Society (an innovative social science/visual design mix for a career in the digital information service area or developing multimedia areas). Now they have

ACADEMIC EXCELLENCE

TEACHING:

(Rated Excellent or 17+ out of 24)

Computer Science	**Excellent**
Nursing	**23**
Art & Design Subjects Allied to Medicine	**22**
Electric & Electron Eng, Sport	**21**
Psychology	**20**
Civil Eng, Sociol & Criminology	**19**
Civil Engineering	**18**

RESEARCH :
Top grades 5/5*

History	**Grade 5**

introduced a range of 70/30, major/minor combinations in a variety of areas.

In the health area, both teaching assessments and employment statistics (see box above and on page 464) point to the success of departments dealing with nursing, midwifery, social work, occupational therapy, physiotherapy, radiography, etc. There is a new purpose-built Centuria Building for these health and social care students.

You may care, also, to peruse their sport & exercise provision (including Sport Therapy) and media production – there are some good four-year sandwich courses (i.e. with job placements).

Oh, and just to show that they can toe the traditional academic line as well as the next, in the national research assessments they just copped Grade 5* (that's world class) for History.

SOCIAL SCENE

On the first floor of the union there's the **Studio Café** and the students' own **Union Central**. This incorporates alcohol and coffee bars and a pool & games area in sight of a huge screen and stage, within a long, wood-panelled long room, furnished with cubicle seating arranged maze-like both to maximise capacity and permit a degree of privacy.

The high mature population was not obvious, and when I remark on this, students' union bod Michelle Berry informs me, 'I lived with students, 27, 28, 29 years old, who would be classified as mature, but they hung around with the traditional students and didn't look that different. We do try and concentrate on integration, encourage everyone to get along.'

No need for the usual uni pressure valve apparently, 'We actually don't have a Nightline here, and there doesn't seem to be the call for one. The university draws largely from round here and students know what to expect. The Advice Centre dealt with 8,500 enquiries last year, which is about one per student, but most were financial, and we promote the centre not as a place to which you go when something has gone wrong, but to make sure nothing does.'

On a Friday evening in **Union Central** the buzz is tangible. 'I've lived down south,' said Michelle, 'and I am not being biased, but the scene up here is great, one of the best in the North East. We've got far too many bars, people are just competing with each other, so it's great for students. We have the **Empire** [renowned for *Sugar Shack* – Jeremy Healy, Boy George, Paul Oakenfold and Sasha and Digweed hit the decks], it's one of the best known nightclubs in the country, if you look in dance mags. We've got **Tall Trees** in Yarm, which is internationally recognised [a huge club set in fantastic grounds with inimitable nights]. We have

> *They call themselves the Opportunity University, and sit high in the league table of universities that have worked hardest at widening access to higher education.*

our balls there. Then we have the **Millennium** [chart, retro, house, Brutus Gold's *Love Train* – capacity 2,000]. There are plenty of others, and the **Arena** is nationally known [*Cactus* and *Shagged* are two nights with an excellent reputation; student night is Monday]. Then there are the gay bars, **Strings**, **Annie's Bar**, **Cassidy's**, **Corner-house**.'

Gay bars in macho Teesside? 'It's fairly underground,' conceded Michelle, squirming at my stereotyping. 'It's all happened in the last few years. The students have done it. Bars are opening all the time – the **Crown** on the corner was the old Bingo hall, a **Yates's**, **Huster's**, **Rat & Parrot**, **Hogshead**, **Byzantia** – they're springing up everywhere.'

So what, I wonder, goes on here, at the union? **Club One** is their 1,000-capacity student nightclub, a huge space with specially treated dancefloor,

---

AT A GLANCE

ACADEMIC FILE:

Assessments	**20**
Excellent	**50%**
Average requirements	**180 points**
Students-staff ratio	**18:1**
First/2:1 degree pass rate	**45%**

ACCOMMODATION FILE:

Guarantee to freshers	**Uni residences exclusive to freshers**
Style	**Halls, flats, houses**
Catered	**None**
En-suite	**32%**
Price range pw	**£30.70-53.25**
City rent pw	**£25-£32.50**

WHAT IT'S REALLY LIKE

UNIVERSITY:

Social Life	★★★★
Campus scene	**Lively, local scene**
Student Union services	**Good**
Politics	**Student issues, activity low**
Sport	**Competitive**
National teamposition	**48th**
Sport facilities	**Poor**
Arts opportunities	**Dance, music excellent, rest OK**
Student magazine	**U2U**
Student newsletter	**Teesguide**
Nightclub	**Club One**
Bars	**Union Central**
Union ents	**Vegas, High Spirits, Connexion, Luv Bug**
Union clubs/societies	**56**
Most popular society	**Interlink**
Smoking policy	**Zonal**
Parking	**Poor**

TOWN:

Entertainment	★★★★
Scene	**Pubs, big-time clubs**
Town/gown relations	**Average**
Risk of violence	**Average**
Cost of living	**Low**
Student concessions	**Good**
Survival + 2 nights out	**£50-£60 pw**
Part-time work campus/town	**Excellent/good**

WHERE GRADUATES END UP

18% Health/Social Work, 12% Manufacturing, 11% Public Admin*, 11% Wholesale/Retail, 6% Finance, 7% Computer	Key Areas
Hotel/Restaurant*, Business/Management*, Chemical/Pharmaceutical, Construction, Defence, Eng/Industrial Design, Film/Video, Telecom	Niche Areas

*indicates Top 10 Graduate Provider

Approximate employed **91%**

8,000 watt sound system, DJ control bridge, raised seating areas and no-smoke chill-out room. On Friday, it's *Fruity*, on Saturday *Vegas*, *High Spirits*, *Connexion* and *Luv Bug* alternate. Recent visitors have been SPACE, Chesney Hawkes, Shed Seven, Near Say.

Nor is it all night-time reverie. There are nineteen societies and thirty-seven sports clubs. Student media includes a magazine, *U2U*, and a weekly newsletter, *Teesguide*. Most popular is the International Students Society with about 100 members. Then there are things like the Dilated Pupil Society, the dance music society which is very active now. Drama is doing a series of satirical sketches this Christmas; they do plays regularly. There's a singing society and they're doing a Christmas concert. There's a Cultural Studies society that organises exchange trips and so on, a film sci fi society. Our Law society is very successful in the courtroom battles with high profile universities in the North East, Durham, Newcastle, etc. Art comes via one of our franchise colleges, Cleveland College of Art & Design [see entry]. They set up the Burlam Road Society.'

CLEVELAND COLLEGE has three campuses, two in Middlesbrough, one in Hartlepool. It is a large art college with 2,000 students, about 10% of whom study for the Teesside degrees in Design Crafts for the Entertainment Industries, Fine Art, Photography, and Textiles. Tel: 01642 288888. E-mail admissions@ccad.ac.uk. Web: www.ccad.ac.uk

SPORT They have a fitness centre and a sports hall and are hoping to get their own pitches, soon.

PILLOW TALK

Places in campus residences are allocated exclusively to first year students. Apply early for any accommodation as there isn't enough to go round. There are houses, halls, flats and managed housing off campus. Five mixed halls of residence all have self-catering facilities; 32% of campus accommodation is en suite. Last year's prices ranged from £30.70 per week to £53.25. Town rent is an unusually precise £29-£32.50.

JOBS

Their ethos is clearly vocational with some interesting specialist niches (see *Academia*, see page 462). The 18% health industry employment figure is the single biggest employment area. The uni came 6th nationally for Business/Management, 8th for Hotel/Restaurant (there is a good degree in Tourism Management), and 6th for Public Administration. Law is also a good area. Computing and engineering degrees feed through with strength to areas such as Defence, Radio/TV, Telecom, Computing and Engineering/Industrial Design.

GETTING THERE

☞ By road: A19, or A1/M, A66.
☞ By rail: Newcastle, 1:15; Leeds, 1:45; Manchester Piccadilly, 2:45; Liverpool Lime Street, 3:45; London King's Cross, 3:30.
☞ By air: Teesside International Airport.
☞ By coach: Birmingham, 3:15; York, 1:15.

THAMES VALLEY UNIVERSITY

Thames Valley University
St Mary's Road
London W5 5RF

TEL 020 8579 5000
FAX 020 8231 1353
EMAIL learning.advice@tvu.ac.uk
WEB www.tvu.ac.uk

Thames Valley Students' Union
St Mary's Road
London W5 5RF

TEL 020 8231 2276
FAX 020 8231 2589
EMAIL matthew.pledger@tvu.ac.uk
WEB www.tvu.ac.uk

VAG VIEW

*F*ormerly West London Poly and incorporating the Ealing School of Art, where Pete Townshend (the Who), Ronnie Wood (the Stones) and Freddie Mercury (Queen)...erm...studied, TVU works with local colleges on access programmes, allowing successful completion of an access course as an alternative to usual entry requirements.

CAMPUS

TVU is based on four sites in Ealing (West London) and Slough. Shuttle buses run between the two campuses until late each night. There is no residential campus accommodation.

STUDENT PROFILE

Today, with most students from the locality, high ethnicity, many from overseas and many mature students, its boast of a diverse mix is certainly valid. 'The most positive point to be made about TVU concerns the diversity,' writes student Ian Draysey. 'Students of all ages come from all over the world and studying there has given me the opportunity to meet people I never would have otherwise. The majority of universities make similar claims, but in this case it's true, honest!'

ACADEMIA

On the face of it, TVU is a model of the government's policy to facilitate access for social groups without a tradition in higher education. In practice the strategy would seem to have failed because, while Thames Valley showed they had the political will, they lacked the special talents required to add real value, to raise standards. The drop-out rate is 21%, which is very high and suggests serious problems continue. In November

STUDENT POPULATION

- Postgraduates 10%
- Other undergraduates 58%
- Total students 16,100
- Part-time 1st degree undergraduates 9%
- Full-time 1st degree undergraduates 23%

SUBJECT AREAS (%)

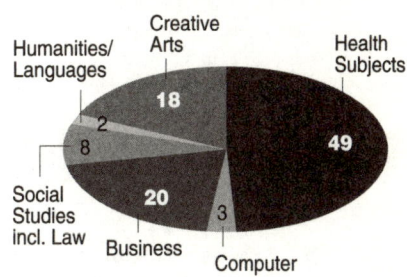

- Creative Arts 18
- Humanities/Languages 2
- 8
- Health Subjects 49
- Social Studies incl. Law 20
- Business 3
- Computer

1998 the Quality Assessment Agency found the university's 'structures and procedures for safeguarding quality and standards' fell below acceptable levels.

Their public humiliation at the hands of the QAA culminated in the resignation of the vice-chancellor. The forward strategy became to build on its core competences, namely Business & Management, Law, Music, Digital Arts, Hospitality & Catering, Tourism, and Nursing and Midwifery.

As it struggles to gain a foothold on a slippery

UNIVERSITY/STUDENT PROFILE	
University since	**1992**
Situation/style	**City/suburban campuses**
Student population	**16,100**
Full-time undergraduates	**3,720**
- mature	**75%**
- overseas	**22%**
- male/female	**34/66**
- state sector intake	**98%**
- non-traditional student intake	**13%**
- drop-out rate	**21%, high**
- undergraduate applications	**Down 8%**
see Introduction for key to tables	

ACADEMIC EXCELLENCE	
TEACHING:	
(Rated Excellent or 17+ out of 24)	
Sociology, Linguistics, Tourism	**22**
Psychology, Nursing, Health	**20**
Modern Languages	**18**
RESEARCH :	
*Top grades 5/5**	**None**

slope, it is all too easy to forget TVU's high points. Back in 1996, a jewel was the award of a prestigious Grade 5 (for Linguistics) in the research assessments – practically unheard of among new unis. But in last year's assessments there were no such highlights. In fact they came last of all the institutions that were involved.

They make much of their Learning Resource Centres as the fulcrum on which the learning of their non-traditional uni applicants will turn.

> *TVU is a model of the Government's policy to facilitate access for social groups without a tradition in higher education. In practice, the strategy would seem to have failed.*

LRCs, they say, are designed 'to open up and demystify education. Resource-based learning encourages students to learn at their own pace and to take responsibility for their own learning.' They want to encourage 'independent, but not isolated, learners.' In effect LRCs are simply research centres – libraries of books, audio-visual material, music scores, slides and media equipment: 270,000 items altogether. There is help at hand with literacy, numeracy and IT skills.

WHAT IT'S REALLY LIKE

UNIVERSITY:	
Social Life	★★
Campus scene	**London diversity, closed weekends**
Student Union services	**Average-poor**
Politics	**Student issues; interest low**
Sport	**Relaxed; few team sports**
National team position	**None**
Sport facilities	**Average**
Arts opportunities	**Music excellent; film, art average; drama, dance poor**
Student magazine	**Undergrad**
Student newspaper	**The Voice**
Student radio	**Tube**
Nightclub	**The Studio**
Bars	**The Studio Bar**
Union ents	**Some**
Union clubs/societies	**11**
Most popular society	**Tube Radio**
Smoking policy	**None**
Parking	**Adequate**
CITY:	
Entertainment	★★★★★
Scene	**London**
Town/gown relations	**Average**
Risk of violence	**Average**
Cost of living	**Very high**
Student concessions	**Good**
Survival + 2 nights out	**£80 pw**
Part-time work campus/town	**Average/excellent**

SOCIAL SCENE

STUDENTS' UNION The **Studio** opens Monday to Friday 11 am to 11 pm, the **Coffee Stop**, 8 am - 6 pm Monday to Thursday, 8 am - 4 pm on Fridays. At the Ealing campus, traditional pool table and juke-box scenario is supplemented by Bhangra music and Hindi films. Over half of TVU's undergraduates are Asian, a fact variously reflected in the substance if not the form of the entertainments provided – live bands, karaoke, DJs and drinking competitions. The uni's degrees in music (including Popular Music Performance) and its association with the London College of Music and Media (LCM2) provide additional musical input, and the fledgling Tube Radio, ambitiously aimed not just at students but at the wider community around Ealing, also benefits from LCM2's input and hardware.

The largest venue at TVU is **Artwood's**, with a capacity of 1,200. It has attempted to overcome its school hall demeanour with the installation of a bar to complement its livestock-bothering sound system, and has a good atmosphere when crowded.

Over at the Slough campus, the **Moon and Cucumber** bar, buffet bar, **Hamlyn Hall** and the smokeless **Studio Bar** offer alternative recreational facilities. Slough also houses a gym for those who'd rather build up their muscles than their beer guts.

They say that societies range from the Radio Society to the Asian Society and come under four categories, Cultural (Asian, Chinese), Religious (Christian Union, Islamic), Social (Radio, Music Industry), and Academic (Law, Psychology). Sport at TVU has swung away from the more team-oriented stance of many universities, with activities such as badminton, fencing and aerobics gaining more members than football. There was no team placement in last year's national uni leagues.

JOBS

A Careers & Employment Service offers materials and advice. TVU Temps looks after term-time jobs.

Graduates (17%) find their way into the health industry via courses in nursing, counselling, etc. The large number of hospitality and tourism courses achieved a very good score of 22 out of 24 points recently at the teaching assessments, and the success of this area feeds graduate employment, as may be seen from our *Employment* box, page 467 (Hotel/Restaurant). The Telecom strength comes not through engineering but via their law, business and information courses. A large

AT A GLANCE	
ACADEMIC FILE:	
Subjects assessed	**18**
Excellent	**39%**
Average A level requirements	**140 points**
Students-staff ratio	**31:1**
First/2:1 degree pass rate	**35%**
ACCOMMODATION FILE:	
Availability in college	**None**
Town/city rent pw	**£65-£90**

WHERE GRADUATES END UP	
17% Health/Social Work,	Key Areas
15% Wholesale/Retail*,	
8% Computer,	
7% Manufacturing,	
6% Finance,	
5% Education	
Advertising,	Niche Areas
Market Research*,	
Film/Video, Publishing,	
Radio/TV, Telecom*,	
Hotel/Restaurant	

*indicates Top 10 Graduate Provider

Approximate employed **89%**

number ending up in Wholesale/Retail also approached via TVU's business and information courses. Marketing/ advertising and media/radio broadcasting subjects are also clearly productive in the jobs market.

GETTING THERE

☛ Ealing: Ealing Broadway Underground (Central and District Lines).

☛ Slough: By road: M4/J6, A4. By rail: London Paddington, 25 mins.

TRINITY & ALL SAINTS COLLEGE

Trinity & All Saints College
Brownberrie Lane
Horsforth
Leeds LS18 5HD

TEL 0113 283 7123
FAX 0113 283 7321
EMAIL admission@tasc.ac.uk
WEB www.tasc.ac.uk

VAG VIEW

*T*rinity and All Saints is an independent Catholic foundation and college of the University of Leeds, situated on a 40-acre campus about six miles out of the city.

Given its foundation, TAS, as the college is known, assumes a particular responsibility for the education of teachers for Catholic schools. Recent introductions to the degree programme include Sport, Health, Exercise & Nutrition and Digital Media Technology & Culture. Sociology, Psychology and Sport/Health/Leisure (with Management, Media or Nutrition) all scored an excellent 20/24 points at the assessments. Modern Languages and Communication & Media Studies performed less well at 17, while the primary training was rated good by Ofsted.

There is a two-thirds majority of female undergrads, nine halls of residence, a union

COLLEGE PROFILE	
Founded	**1974**
Status	**Uni College**
Degree awarding university	**Leeds**
Situation/style	**City campus**
Student population	**2,640**
Full-time undergraduates	**2,030**
ACCOMMODATION:	
Availability to freshers	**90%**
Style	**Halls**
Cost pw	**£64-£73**
City rent pw	**£30-£65**

building, the Abbey Bar, Priory Bar and 500-capacity BASE nightclub. What were once merely karaoke and 'Morgan-on-the-organ' nights are now regularly blessed with Cheddar, a cheese/party night, Under Construction (house, garage) and Hard Beatz (R&B, hip hop). Recent live acts have been Pusher (Usher soundalike), David Craig

(Craig David Impersonator) and Bucks Fizz.

With media courses and a purpose-built *Media Centre, full of TV production, editing and sound recording equipment, extra-curricular media activities are blossoming. Besides the magazine,* News From The Base, *there is TASC Radio, now the most popular of seventeen union societies.*

See also Student Leeds, *page 260.*

GETTING THERE

☛ By road: From east, M62/J39, M1. From west, M62/J27, M621. From north, A1, A58. From northwest, A65, A650.

☛ By coach: London, 4:00; Edinburgh, 6:00; Bristol, 5:45.

☛ By rail: Newcastle, 1:45; London Euston, 2:30; Birmingham New Street, 2:20.

☛ By air: inland and international flights from Leeds/Bradford Airport.

TRINITY COLLEGE, CARMARTHEN

Trinity College, Carmarthen
Dyfed SA31 3EP

TEL 01267 676767
FAX 01267 676766
EMAIL registry@trinity-cm.ac.uk
WEB www.trinity-cm.ac.uk

VAG VIEW

*T*rinity is a teacher training college that has moved into degrees in subjects such as tourism, sport, archaeology, media, theatre, English, history, religion. Some 60% of its graduates still end up in Education.

Its Welshness and distinctive mix of the three Rs (religion, rugby and raucousness) make it a viable option for some.

The town of Carmarthen is a small community with a population of about 15,000. There are some sixty pubs, four nightclubs, a cinema and bingo hall. In general it's quite a picturesque town, but it can get a bit rough on Thursday and Saturday nights. The college, built in 1848, overlooks the town from its hill site. There are more women than men, a majority of Welsh. Students at Trinity are into the social side of life, although in recent years the college has attracted more mature students who tend to make more use of the library.

COLLEGE PROFILE	
Founded	**1848**
Status	**HE College**
Degree awarding university	**Wales**
Situation/style	**Rural campus**
Student population	**2,670**
Full-time undergraduates	**990**
ACCOMMODATION FILE:	
Availability to freshers	**80%**
Style	**Halls**
Cost pw (no food/food)	**£52-£68**
Town rent pw	**£40**

The Trinity lager louts are also heavily into sport. As well as the men's and now women's rugby there are male and female hockey, netball, men's football, a much defeated women's football team, and a selection of other sporting activities, ranging from Gaelic football to fencing. Considering the size of the college the sports facilities are pretty good – a floodlit Astroturf, swimming pool, two gyms, a weights room and a number of pitches just down the road.

GETTING THERE

☛ By road: M4, A48, A40 or A495, A40.
☛ By coach: Cardiff, 2:05.
☛ By rail: Cardiff, 1:30; Birmingham, 4:10.

UNIVERSITY OF ULSTER

University of Ulster
University House
Cromore Road
Coleraine
Co. Londonderry BT52 1SA

TEL 028 7034 4221
FAX 028 7032 4908
EMAIL online@ulster.ac.uk
WEB www.ulst.ac.uk

Ulster Students' Union
Cromore Road
Coleraine BT52 1SA
Northern Ireland

TEL 028 7036 5121
FAX 028 7032 4915
EMAIL su.president@ulst.ac.uk
WEB www.ulst.ac.uk/(surf)

VAG VIEW

*U*lster is the largest of the nine
universities on the island of Ireland.
*Spread across four sites (between seven and
eighty miles apart) it is an enormous place in
terms of students, 80% of whom are local.*

*The uni came out of a merger in 1984
between Ulster Poly (now the Jordanstown
campus) and the New University of Ulster
(which was the old university, if you follow).
Sites are at Belfast (art college), at
Newtownabbey, in the hills above Belfast (the
Jordanstown campus), at Coleraine (this is HQ,
far northwest of Belfast, near the Giant's
Causeway), and in Londonderry (Magee College
campus, founded in 1865), yet further west.*

*With the kind of communications problems
which the layout poses, it is apposite that they
have formed a wireless microwave network
capable of transmitting data of* Encyclopedia
Britannica *proportions in a second. The Centre
for Communications Engineering links them to
Queen's Uni and Nortel Networks, and is a
feature of their strategy for close working with
industry.*

UNIVERSITY/STUDENT PROFILE

University since	**1984**
Situation/style	**4 urban/rural campus sites**
Student population	**22,000**
Full-time undergraduates	**11,490**
- mature	**20%**
- overseas	**10%**
- male/female	**40/60**
- state sector intake	**100%**
- non-traditional student intake	**11%**
- drop-out rate	**11%**
- undergraduate applications	**Down 1%**

see Introduction for key to tables

STUDENT PROFILE

There's a high mature undergrad percentage and
an unusually high number of part-timers among
the predominantly local student body; university
strategy ensures that many, too, come from social
groups with no great tradition of higher education.
Together with social and educational progress
comes a high drop-out rate – 11% of non-mature
entrants.

BELFAST York Street, Belfast BT15 1ED. **Location:**
close to city centre. **Faculty HQs:** Art & Design.
Other faculty courses: Technology & Design.
Accommodation: none, but small number of
Belfast students may use Jordanstown. **Ents
facilities: Conor Hall** (400-capacity venue).
Sports facilities: 'What's sport?' said a student
when asked. Arts facilities: foyer exhibition area,
art shop, artist (writer, artist or musician) in
residence. **Arts opportunities:** 'Second to none,
vibrant, innovative, love it!' said our student
contact. **Media:** monthly magazine, *Ufouria*.

JORDANSTOWN Newtownabbey BT37 OQB.

AT A GLANCE

ACADEMIC FILE:	
Subjects assessed	**36**
Excellent	**67%**
Average requirements	**240 points**
Students-staff ratio	**18:1**
First/2:1 class degree pass rate	**64%**

ACCOMMODATION FILE:	
Guarantee to freshers	**100%**
Style	**Halls, flats, houses; not Belfast**
Approx price range pw	**£33-£36**
Approx off-campus rent pw	**£35**

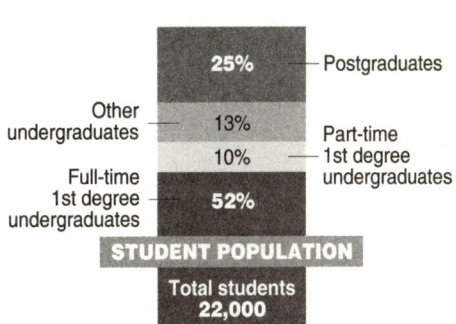

- Postgraduates **25%**
- Other undergraduates **13%** — Part-time
- **10%** — 1st degree undergraduates
- Full-time 1st degree undergraduates **52%**

STUDENT POPULATION

Total students
22,000

SUBJECT AREAS (%)

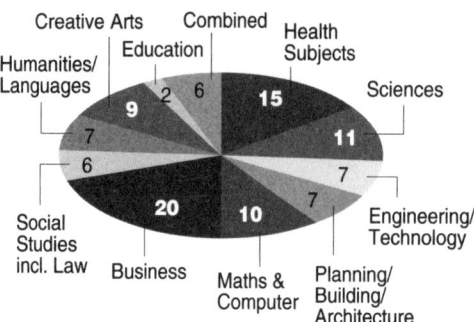

Creative Arts — 7
Combined — 2
Education — 6
Health Subjects — 15
Humanities/Languages — 9
Sciences — 11
Social Studies incl. Law — 6
Business — 20
Maths & Computer — 10
Planning/Building/Architecture — 7
Engineering/Technology — 7

Location: seven miles north of Belfast; largest site. **Faculty HQs:** Business & Management (including Government & Law, Law & Economics), Engineering (including Biomedical Eng), Informatics, Social & Health Sciences. Other faculty courses: Music, Modern Studies (social & cultural), Applied Biochemical Sciences, Clinical Science, Radiography. **Accommodation:** res. blocks, six-bedroom houses, flats & study-bedrooms in halls; self-catering. **Ents facilities: Students' Union Bar** (700 capacity), split level, two stages, tiered seating/standing; regular disco night is Monday. **Sports facilities:** two large sports halls, gym, fitness suite, six squash courts, eight-lane

ACADEMIC EXCELLENCE

TEACHING
(Rated Excellent or 17+ out of 24)

Music, Social Policy & Admin, Environmental Studies. Studies, Land & Property Mgt.	**Excellent**
Business & Management	**24**
Tourism, Philosophy, Psychology	**23**
American Studies, Drama, Maths, Nursing, Molecular Biosciences, Subjects Allied to Medicine	**22**
Communication & Media, Building, Organismal Biosciences	**21**
Electrical & Electronic Eng, French, General Engineering.	**20**
German, Civil Eng, Art/Design	**19**
Iberian	**18**

RESEARCH :
Top grades 5/5*

Celtic, Biomedical Science	**Grade 5***
Built Enviro, Law, Art/Design	**Grade 5**

WHAT IT'S REALLY LIKE

UNIVERSITY:	
Social Life	★★★
Campus scenes	**Local, lively, diverse**
Student Union services	**Average**
Politics	**High activity: Irish politics, student funding**
Sport	**Big at Coleraine & Jordanstown**
Sport facilities	**Good**
Arts opportunities	**Art excellent; drama, dance, film, music good**
Student magazine	**Ufouria**
Union ents	**13 pw**
Live venues	**Conor Hall** (Belfast), **Biko Hall** (Coleraine), **The Bunker** (Magee), **Arthur's** (Jordanstown)
Union clubs/societies	**100+**
Most popular society	**Irish Society**
Smoking policy	**Union OK**
Parking	**Adequate**

swimming pool and hydrotherapy pool, playing fields, synthetic training pitch, local water sports facility and River Lagan. **Arts facilities:** recital rooms, concert hall. Low key. **Media:** *Naked* is student newspaper.

COLERAINE (address above) **Location:** market town close to north coast, 35 miles from Derry. Admin HQ for Uni. **Faculty HQs:** Humanities, Science. Other faculty courses: Banking & Finance, Business/Computing, Business Studies/Japanese, Euro Business, Retail Management, Social Psychology, Psychol & Sociology, Nursing, Social & Admin Policy. **Accommodation:** recently refurbished res. blocks and new student houses. Most students prefer to live out in coastal resort towns Portrush and Portstewart. **Ents facilities: Biko Hall** (venue) and recently rebuilt **Uni-Bar**; 550 capacity. Regular disco night is Monday. **Sports facilities:** Biko Hall is sports hall by day, five squash courts, fitness suite, solarium and steam room, playing fields, floodlit football pitch, pavilion, tennis courts, water sports centre on River Bann. **Arts facilities:** the **Octagon** (500-seat recital room), the **Diamond** (1,200-seat concert hall, prestigious **Riverside Theatre**, third largest pro theatre in Ireland, venue for drama, rock and classical concerts, ballet, opera, etc.

MAGEE COLLEGE Northland Road, Londonderry BT48 7JL. **Location:** residential quarter of Derry,

Ireland's second largest city. **Faculty HQs:** None. **Courses:** Various from Faculties of Art & Design, Business & Management, Engineering, Humanities (including interesting Peace & Conflict Studies), Informatics, Social & Health Sciences. **Accommodation:** three halls of residence and student village (modern houses). **Ents facilities:** two bars, **The Terrapin** (known as 'the wee bar') and **The Bunker** (bar/nightclub, 400 capacity). **Ents:** bands and discos (Thursday); Derry wild with pubs. **Sports facilities:** sports hall, fitness suite and solarium; recent additions include sports pavilion, sand-carpet soccer pitch, synthetic training pitch; sailing at Fahan, rowing and canoeing on the Foyle. **Arts facilities:** the **Great Hall** (concerts).

GETTING THERE

☛ An hour by air from London, with at least 24 flights a day each way.

☛ Ulsterbus operates a fast and frequent service across Northern Ireland.

WHERE GRADUATES END UP	
19% Health/Social Work,	Key Areas
14% Wholesale/Retail,	
9% Manufacturing,	
9% Computer*,	
6% Public Admin,	
5% Finance,	
5% Education	
Accountancy,	Niche Areas
Aeronautical Manufacture,	
Chemical/Pharmaceutical,	
Eng/Industrial Design*,	
Legal, Library/Archival,	
Construction*	

*indicates Top 10 Graduate Provider

Approximate employed **91%**

UNIVERSITY COLLEGE, LONDON

University College, London
Gower Street
London WC1E 6BT

TEL 020 7679 3000
FAX 020 7679 3001
EMAIL (via website)
WEB www.ucl.ac.uk/admission

UCL Students' Union
25 Gordon Street
London WC1H 0AH

TEL 020 7387 3611
FAX 020 7383 3937
EMAIL mc.officer@ucl.ac.uk
WEB www.uclu.org

VAG VIEW

*T*he college was the original University of London, the first in England after Oxford and Cambridge, inspired by the first principle of Utilitarianism, 'the greatest happiness of the greatest number'. It was a pioneering move by a group of thinkers, John Stuart Mill among them, for an alternative approach to higher education, which, in 1826, meant the privileged education dished out by Oxford and Cambridge.

The idea was to open the doors of education to the rising middle-classes and to free the educational establishment from the doctrinal prejudices of the Anglican Church. Roman Catholics, Jews and Nonconformists were barred from an Oxbridge education in those days. To ensure freedom from dogma, it was decided not to have subjects

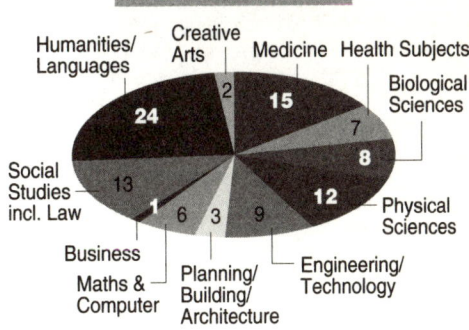

SUBJECT AREAS (%)

appertaining to religion taught at UCL.

UCL remains one of our foremost seats of learning, its research record formidable and its Slade School of Fine Art reckoned to be the best in its area. Its merger with the School of Slavonic & East European Studies and the

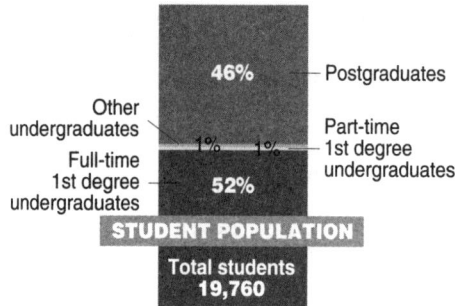

STUDENT POPULATION

46% — Postgraduates
Other undergraduates
1% 1% — Part-time 1st degree undergraduates
Full-time 1st degree undergraduates
52%

Total students
19,760

foundation of the Wolfson Institute for Biomedical Research would seem to shore up the academic infrastructure yet further.

CAMPUS

The location of UCL's main sites, just to the north of London's West End and hard by the University of London Students' Union building, provides students with amazing resource opportunity. What's more, most halls of residence are within walking distance.

STUDENT PROFILE

The heavy imbalance in favour of public school wallahs is quite ironic in the light of its history (see *Profile* box and *VAG View*). Today, they hardly fill the bill as 'Cockney College', the name given in the

UNIVERSITY/STUDENT PROFILE	
College of London Uni since	**1826**
Situation/style	**Civic**
Student population	**19,760**
Full-time undergraduates	**10,300**
- mature	**15%**
- overseas	**21%**
- male/female	**49/51**
- state sector intake	**58%, low**
- non-traditional student intake	**6%, low**
- drop-out rate	**6%**
- undergraduate applications	**Down 6%**
see Introduction for key to tables	

19th century by those who feared the consequences of UCL's open-access stance. Few universities take a smaller percentage of state sector pupils, and in fact UCL fail to meet any of their Government benchmarks set to encourage them to entice applications down the social order. However, judging by the recent concentration of activity in the areas of special needs and academic counselling (see *Academia*), UCL just might be tooling up to make a big change.

Worth noting, too, in this context is a new Intermediate Certificate Course in Science and Engineering, a foundation programme offered through a collaboration between UCL and the School of Oriental and African Studies (see separate entry) to students from countries where their school-leaving certificate does not qualify them for direct entry to university in the UK. Successful completion of the ICC for Science and Engineering will be recognised for entry to UCL's science and engineering undergraduate degree programmes.

Inter-collegiate rivalry has always existed between UCL and its counterpart King's College, London. Throughout its history this rivalry has centred around the stealing of mascots – Reggie at King's and Phineas at UCL. While modern policing methods have put a damper on these activities, students still manage the odd attack, one of the most embarrassing occurring against UCL. The real preserved head of Jeremy Bentham (an atheist behind the concept of UCL's foundation, whose preserved body sits in a case outside the Provost's office) was stolen from UCL and then suffered considerable damage at the hands, or one should say feet, of King's students. Nowadays a wax replica of the head sits on the body while the real head resides in the College safe! Phineas, on the other hand, remains intact and watches over students from an alarm armed glass case in the union bar which bears his name.

AT A GLANCE	
ACADEMIC FILE:	
Subjects assessed	**40**
Excellent	**90%**
Average requirements	**320 points**
Students-staff ratio	**9:1**
First/2:1 degree pass rate	**70%**
ACCOMMODATION FILE:	
Guarantee to freshers	**Deadline 31.5**
Style	**Halls, houses**
Catered	**36%**
En-suite	**11%**
Price range pw	**£48-£98**
City rent pw	**£70-£110**

ACADEMIA

UCL places great importance on its tutorial system. All students are allocated a personal tutor for consultation on academic or personal matters. Further support is offered by departmental and faculty tutors and two advisers specialising in women students. There's also a professional counselling service and a Students' Union Rights &

Advice Centre to see you through any problems academic, financial or emotional. Also, a new special educational needs IT suite was opened in December 2001, offering computers and related software and equipment. An IT trainer and a disabilities co-ordinator are at your disposal.

Academically the college is strong throughout its eight faculties, with teaching at the forefront of knowledge in many areas – the research base has strengthened considerably over the past twenty years; it now stands 7th best in the nation, according to the recent assessments, and over a third of the student body is now made up of postgraduates. Add to this the current £65 million development known as The Cruciform Project (making UCL globally recognised in the field of biomedicine) and you might be left feeling slightly daunted.

The merger in 1999 with SSEES (School of Slavonic and East European Studies, see *Satellite Campuses*, below) has expanded the range of languages degrees taught; degrees in new language combinations have since been developed, and at UCL they are actively encouraging students to add an international dimension to their degree programmes. A growing number of courses now include a year abroad in another European country, or in the US, and many more can provide an opportunity for students to spend some time abroad, for example as part of a Socrates exchange. A newly established Study Abroad Office advises students on the opportunities open to them, ensures that students going abroad are fully briefed, and also works to expand further UCL's links with overseas organisations.

A new integrated medical curriculum was introduced from September 2000, which consists of a six-year training, including an intercalated BSc. The curriculum combines not only the essential scientific basis and clinical training for medicine, but also continuous personal and professional development. UCL Hospitals have recently taken over the specialist Heart Hospital using £27.5 million of government money and more than doubling their cardiac capacity.

A degree in Biomedical Sciences was introduced from September 2001, which provides a broad experience of anatomy, cell biology, developmental biology, genetics, neuroscience, physiology, pharmacology and psychology in the first year, enabling students to pursue their developing special interests in the subsequent years. As you can see from the *Academic Excellence* box (which lists the subjects whose teaching gives UCL an overall 90% Excellent or 19+ out of 24 points score) the health provision is world class. The so-called 'Subjects Allied to Medicine' are, in

ACADEMIC EXCELLENCE

TEACHING :
(Rated Excellent or 17+ out of 24)

History, Law, Anthropology, Architecture, English, Geography, Geological Sciences	**Excellent**
Economics, History of Art, Organismal Biosciences, Subjects Allied to Medicine	24
German, Scandinavian Studies, Dentistry, Maths, Physics, Archaeology, Philosophy, Classics, Art & Design	23
Linguistics, Dutch, Electrical & Electronic Eng, Psychology, Molecular Biosciences, Anatomy, Library/Info, Politics, Psychology	22
Medicine, French	21
Italian, Chem & Biochem Eng	20
Pharmacology	
Iberian Studies, Civil Eng	19

RESEARCH
Top grades 5/5*

Hospital-based Clinical - Child Health/Neurology/ Ophthalmology, Pharmacology, Psychology, Chemistry, Chemical Eng, Geography, Law, Anthropology, Economics, English, German, Italian, Linguistics, Classics	**Grade 5***
Hospital-based Clinical - Royal Free, Clinical Dentistry, Anatomy, Other Subjects Allied to Medicine, Biochemistry, Biology, Physics, Earth Sciences, Pure Maths, Applied Maths, Statistics, Computer, Civi/ Environmental Eng, Electrical/ Electronic Eng, Mechanical, Aeronautical/Manufacturing Eng, European Studies, French, Dutch, Scandinavian, Archaeol, History, History of Art, Philosophy, Art and Design	**Grade 5**

UCL's case, BSc degrees in Speech Sciences and Communication for Intercalating Medical Students.

Four-year degrees with study abroad options are being developed in the Faculties of Engineering, Life Sciences, and Mathematical and Physical Sciences. In addition, the Law Faculty will, from 2003, be offering a new degree in English and French Law, LLB with Maîtrise, in which students spend two years at UCL and two years at the

Université Paris I (Sorbonne) gaining a dual qualification.

WHAT IT'S REALLY LIKE	
UNIVERSITY:	
Social Life	★★★★★
Campus scene	**Affluent south-east dominates**
Student Union services	**Good**
Politics	**Activity average: ethical, anti-war & internal**
Sport	**55 clubs. Jitsu strong this year**
National team position	**17th**
Sport facilities	**Good**
Arts opportunities	**Excellent**
Student magazine	**Pi Magazine**
Student radio	**Rare FM**
Student TV	**Bloomsbury TV**
Nightclub	**Windeyer**
Bars	**Easy J's. Gordons, 2econd Floor, Huntley, Phineas, SSEES**
Union ents	**Topdown, Jazz Jammin', Retribution, GTI, Easy Gays, Fives**
Union clubs/societies	**150**
Most popular societies	**Drama, Economics**
Smoking policy	**Union bars OK**
Parking	**None**
CITY:	
Entertainment	★★★★★
City scene	**Wild, expensive**
Town/gown relations	**OK**
Risk of violence	**Average**
Cost of living	**Very high**
Student concessions	**Abundant**
Survival + 2 nights out	**£60+ pw**
Part-time work campus/town	**Average/excellent**

SOCIAL SCENE

STUDENTS' UNION UCL obviously lacks the feel of a campus university, but not to its detriment. For social purposes, the Students' Union has four main sites, as well as other satellite areas. **Gordon Street** is part of the main college block and contains four bars, one with a dance area and each with some kind of catering outlet including the renowned **Easy J's** fast food set-up. The union offices, photocopy service, branch of Campus Travel, hairdresser and shop complete this main building.

Huntley Street, the medics hang-out, contains two bars and a large hall which houses games machines and pool tables and has a stage for student productions. The largest single venue is the comfortable **Windeyer** with a capacity of 550, large dance floor and a variety of catering.

Ents-wise, if it's Monday it's *Make Mine a 99*, a naughty 99p drinks promo, and *Topdown*, a bubblin' mix of funk, latin, soul and jazz, blended by DJs Rockit & Jonny Deckstrous – **Gordon's Bar** from 8.00pm. Tuesday sees *Jazz Jammin'*, again in Gordon's, an evening of improvised syncopation. Monthly in **Easy J's**, you'll find *Open Mic Night*, managed by the Live Music Society. Also monthly, *Retribution*, courtesy of the Rock Society – 'a mosh pit of rock, metal, industrial and goth packing an up-for-it crowd into Easy J's'. Wednesday attracts *Ministry of Comedy* at the union, and alternate Wednesdays in Huntley Street, and, of course, *SportsNite*, highly rated uncouth behaviour and general debauchery in the **2econd Floor** bar. Thursday's *Cocktails* runs across all three union sites – at Gordon's, at Easy J's, at **Phineas** (also Gordon Street,) and at the **Windeyer Bar** (46 Cleveland Street) and at Huntley Street – different venues, different sounds, different crowds. On Friday, jump aboard *GTI*, the weekend warm-up in Easy J's, splendid mix of chunky US house, funky UK progressive & disco flavours, a night of quality dance music, *GTI* runs every Friday from 7-11 pm and is free. Also *Easy Gays* – this year's new night in Easy J's. *Gay Gordons* became such a popular night not only with the LGB Society, so a bigger venue was organised: 'a fab selection of trashy toons keeps it naughty with tongues firmly in cheek.' Then finally comes Saturday's *Fives*. Now entering its third year, it's a fortnightly advance sell-out, entry at £5, drinks at 50p.

The union oversees more than 150 clubs and societies, based, for the most part, in a specially created, open plan area with computers, phones, photocopy and TV/video facilities. The union's many arts societies fill a gap in UCL's academic curriculum. Drama Soc performs to professional level at UCL's **Bloomsbury Theatre** and there's a smaller experimental **Garage Theatre** and a stage in Huntley Street. Student media is active with *Pi Magazine*, the student radio station, Rare fm, and student TV – Bloomsbury Television (BTV). The college has also just signed up the New London Orchestra to boost its musical culture. It will become a kind of orchestra-in-residence at the Bloomsbury Theatre.

Notwithstanding all this arts interest, probably the most active society remains Economics, which enjoys regular meetings with all 150 members in attendance, organises events, sponsorship, and other involvements. Political activity currently focuses on ethical issues, anti-war issues, and on issues concerning union structure and club/society regulations – they're campaigning for more space (the main union building was given to the students by the College on a temporary basis fifty years ago, and they're after more.

Academically the college is strong, its reputation world class. Aware that some might be left feeling slightly daunted, there's a surprise new focus on special needs and academic counselling

West is currently closed for renovation, but will reopen later this year. Two new residences are expected to come on stream in 2003.

SPORT There are fifty-five active sports clubs. Team sports took them to 17th place nationally in the BUSA leagues last year. The Jitsu Club took gold at the Atemi Nationals. Facilities include two large grounds (with bars), a gym, fitness centre (with multigyms, squash courts, Dojo, aerobics/dance hall, sunbeds & sauna) and a large sports hall. For those who want to swim, there is access to the University of London Union pool, next door to UCL.

TOWN London itself is a huge city and there is always the chance to do something a bit more expensive now and again. Obviously all this spending needs to be covered and most students get some kind of part-time work to supplement the loans. The union itself employs many casual staff and runs the Workstation, a job agency which emails registered students about short term jobs which are easy to fit around studies.

PILLOW TALK

Accommodation is guaranteed to all single, first-year undergraduates providing they firmly hold an offer of a place on a degree programme, apply for accommodation by the deadline (currently May 31 of year of entry), and have not previously been a degree student living in London.

There are two types of accommodation on offer: halls of residence (catered/breakfast and evening meal) and student houses (self-catering accommodation, some purpose built, others converted private houses). Altogether, 36% (out of a total of 3,800 places) are catered, while 11% are single, en-suite rooms. There are, in addition, a number of flats with private bathroom for couples, and self-contained flats for groups of two to eight students. Prices per week range from £48 to £98. Students pay, on average, £80-£90 weekly rent in London, though the price range varies greatly as to location and facilities.

UCL has a rolling programme of upgrading and renovating its accommodation. Newer residences have en-suite facilities and computer points networked to the UCL system. Campbell House

JOBS

96% of students who graduated in 2000 were in employment or undertaking further study or training six months after graduation.

SATELLITE CAMPUSES

ROYAL FREE HOSPITAL MEDICAL SCHOOL Tel 020 7794 0500. Merged with UCL to form the Royal Free & University College Medical School, it is situated in Hampstead, one of the safest, most aesthetically pleasing areas of London. 'The Free's biggest selling point has to be how friendly it is,' writes James Varley. 'The majority of first years say it's the big reason that swayed them, having got a feel for the place on their interview day.'

SCHOOL OF SLAVONIC & EAST EUROPEAN STUDIES Tel 020 7862 8520. SSEES (pronounced Cease), an enigmatic institution specialising in the study of Eastern Europe, 'It holds the academically acknowledged best lecturers in their fields,' says Gideon Dewhurst, 'and the largest East European library in Britain. Amongst our luminaries were Tomas Masaryk, professor here, then first President of Czechoslovakia, and Jonathan Ross, though apparently he now denies it and says he went to

---

WHERE GRADUATES END UP

**33% Health (incl Medicine)*,
8% Finance,
6% Manufacturing,
6% Computer,
5% Personnel,
5% Wholesale/Retail
Accountancy,** Niche Areas
**Business/Management,
Architecture, Film/Video,
Eng/Industrial Design,
Legal, Library/Archival*,
Market Research,
Advertising*, Publishing**

*indicates Top 10 Graduate Provider

Approximate employed **94%**

LSE (snob).' The atmosphere created by the tiny throng of students is a real pleasure, not cliquey, just bubbling with intelligence, fun and activity.

GETTING THERE
☛ UCL: Euston Square (Metropolitan, Circle, Hammersmith & City lines), Warren Street (Victoria, Northern), Euston (Victoria, Northern). Royal Free: Belsize Park Underground (Northern line) or overland railway, Hampstead Heath.

UNIVERSITY OF WALES COLLEGE OF MEDICINE

The University of Wales College of Medicine
Heath Park
Cardiff CF4 4XN

TEL 029 2074 2027
FAX 029 2074 4170
EMAIL (via website)
WEB www.uwcm.ac.uk

VAG VIEW

The college is situated on a 53-acre, '70s-built campus, a few miles north of Cardiff city. Nearly half the intake is Welsh. They welcome applications from students offering a European language as third subject, as there's an optional two-month research project abroad in the fourth year.

There is also a Pre-Med Foundation course for applicants with three Arts A levels or two Arts plus one Science A (though two of Chemistry, Biology or Physics must be offered at GCSE). Besides Medicine and Dentistry, degree courses are offered in Occupational Therapy, Physiotherapy, Diagnostic and Therapeutic Radiography – requirements range from BB-CCD – and in Nursing (CCC), hence a 66% female population.

Students in the first two years of the medical degree and the first year of their dental degree do some of their studies at Cardiff Uni, and can use social, accommodation and other facilities of the university. The college has its own **MedClub Bar**. *Friday is* Disco Night. *There are Tuesday and Thursday night bus trips to Cardiff nightclubs, enhanced at* **Reds**

COLLEGE PROFILE	
School of Uni of Wales since	**1931**
Situation/style	**City site**
Student population	**3,650**
Full-time undergraduates	**1,430**
ACCOMMODATION FILE:	
Availability to freshers	**100%**
Style	**Halls**
Cost pw (no food)	**£38**
City rent pw	**£38-£42**

with the new Stashcard, a student debit card just launched with nearby UWIC (see entry). Men's Rugby is most popular of around 30 clubs and societies (but the choir gets around too). Leech-y-Glen *is the magazine. Accommodation is both self-catering and full board, some in the college's own high-rise block on site.*

GETTING THERE
☛ By car: M4/J29, A48. Good bus service.
☛ By coach: London, 3:00; Manchester, 5:40; Exeter, 4:00
☛ By rail: London Paddington, 2:30; Birmingham New Street, 2:45; Manchester Piccadilly, 4:00.
☛ By air: Cardiff Airport.

WARRINGTON COLLEGIATE INSTITUTE

Warrington Collegiate Institute
Padgate Campus
Fearnhead
Warrington: Cheshire WA2 0DB

TEL 01925 494494
FAX 01925 494289
EMAIL registry.he@warr.ac.uk
WEB www.warr.ac.uk

VAG VIEW

*W*arrington is the birthplace of Chris Evans, the resting place of Bing Crosby, the home of Vladivar Vodka and a centre of excellence for Rugby League. Since the 1960s the town has developed massively into a major distribution centre and high-tech industry base The Padgate campus, the college's base, is a 55-acre site close to the town centre.

The college has faculty status within Manchester University, who validate its degrees. Entry requirements are lowish, averaging around 12 points at A level. The Business Management course may be taken neat or laced with Sports Studies, Leisure Studies, Performing Arts or Media Studies. There is also a broad-based Combined Studies BA Hons, which allows students one Business element along with a choice of modules from Media, Leisure, Performing Arts, Sport and Community Studies. There are two part-time Professional Studies BAs in either Education or Social Work. Work placements play a major role. For ents **The Bunker** is the venue, tribute bands to the fore. The student newspaper is called Shrapnel.

COLLEGE PROFILE

College of Manchester Uni since	**1993**
Situation/style	**Town campus**
Student population	**1,318**
Undergraduate population	**785**

ACCOMMODATION:

First year institutional	**98%**
Style	**Halls, houses**
Cost pw	**£30-£39**
Town rent pw	**£35-£50**

DEGREE SUBJECT AREAS:
Media (incl Music Production, Radio Production, Multimedia Journalism, TV Production), business, leisure, sport, performing arts, social work, education

---

There are good sporting facilities, rugby league is their main success story. Accommodation consists of single or shared study-bedrooms.

GETTING THERE
☛ By road: M6/J21 and M62/J10.
☛ By rail: either Padgate or Birchwood stations on the Liverpool to Manchester line (40 mins).

UNIVERSITY OF WARWICK

The University of Warwick
Senate House
Coventry CV4 7AL

TEL 02476 523723
FAX 02476 524649
EMAIL ugadmissions@warwick.ac.uk
WEB warwick.ac.uk

University of Warwick Students' Union
Gibbet Hill Road
Coventry CV4 7AL

TEL 02476 572777
FAX 02476 572759
EMAIL enquiries@sunion.warwick.ac.uk
WEB www.sunion.warwick.ac.uk

VAG VIEW

*W*arwick has exploded upon the university scene in the last ten years and there can be few who wouldn't want to have it on their UCAS list. 'I knew from the first time that I visited that it was the place for me,' writes Emma Burhouse. 'As far as I could see, it had the ideal balance of a good reputation, a sound education and an excellent social life...'

SUBJECT AREAS (%)

- Education
- Biological Sciences
- Creative Arts
- Medicine
- Physical Sciences
- Humanities/Languages — 22
- Engineering/Technology
- 1, 6, 1, 10, 6, 9
- Social Studies incl. Law — 21
- Business — 7
- Maths & Computer — 17

CAMPUS

Warwick, lovely little market town, big castle... And not a university within ten miles of the place.

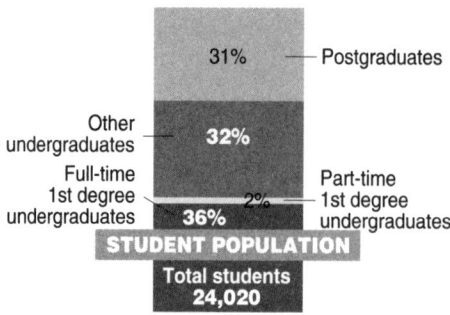

	31% — Postgraduates
Other undergraduates	32%
Full-time 1st degree undergraduates	2% — Part-time 1st degree undergraduates
	36%

STUDENT POPULATION

Total students 24,020

STUDENT PROFILE

'You get the usual independent school boys and girls, for whom going to a university is the first time they haven't had to wear a uniform,' and, as Andrew points out, 'an unusually high mix of international students, meaning that, although most of the British students are from a middle-class background, there is still plenty of variety propping up the bar with you. The English – there are few Scots and Welsh – generally have the bland accentless tone of the home counties. Regional individuality may be gently mocked, but is in fact both envied and welcomed. Students on the whole are genuinely friendly here, and if you can't make any friends then you probably don't deserve to.'

Says Emma: 'From my own experience, the ones who fit in best are those who are out for a laugh, enjoy drinking and are open-minded, basically your average student.'

Don't be fooled, the University of Warwick is not in Warwick, it's in Coventry. The reason it's called Warwick is that it was part-funded by Warwickshire County Council.

'Campus architecture is entirely uninspiring,' reports Simon McGee, 'but the greyness of the endless car parks and square buildings is fortunately balanced by hundreds of acres of surrounding grassland and forest.'

A second campus, ten minutes' walk away, houses the university's Education Institute and Westwood Halls of Residence. The point about Warwick is that like UEA, it is a campus apart from the town, and may seem to some a bit like living in a box.

'If you' re not paying attention, campus can feel a Doctor Seuss cartoon – you are surrounded by pointy concrete and sculptures straight off the set of *Blake Seven*. Some people take to campus life, and others quite frankly don't,' writes Andrew Losowsky.

'If your first priority is the ability to step straight from your lectures into a bustling shopping centre, then Warwick probably isn't for you. Students here have to get a bus in order to clap eyes on old people, babies, dogs. If, however, you enjoy a friendly community, like spending time with lots of students, then maybe you'll fit right in.'

UNIVERSITY/STUDENT PROFILE

University since	**1964**
Situation/style	**Campus**
Student population	**24,020**
Full-time undergraduates	**8,610**
- mature	**8%**
- overseas	**10%**
- male/female	**51/49**
- state sector intake	**76%**
- non-traditional student intake	**7%**
- drop-out rate	**3%, low**
- undergraduate applications	**Down 3%**

see Introduction for key to tables

ACADEMIC EXCELLENCE

TEACHING:

(Rated Excellent or 17+ out of 24)

History, Business & Management, Computer Science, English, Law.	**Excellent**
Sociology, Theatre Studies, Politics, Philosophy, Economics, Physics, Education	**24**
Classics, German, Film & TV, Organismal Biosciences, Molecular Biosciences	**23**
Maths	**22**
Italian, French, Engineering, History of Art, Psychology	**21**

RESEARCH:
Top grades 5/5*

Applied Maths, Statistics, Economics, Business, English, Drama/Dance/Performing Arts	**Grade 5***
Psychology, Biological Sciences, Chemistry, Physics, Pure Maths, Applied Maths, Computer, General Eng, Law, Politics, Social Work, Sociology, French, German/Dutch/Scandinavian, Italian, Classics, History, History of Art, Philosophy, Media Studies	**Grade 5**

ACADEMIA

It is a top-rated uni academically – 92% Excellence ratings or 20+ out of 24; and recently seven perfect scores – full marks for Politics and

International Studies, Philosophy, Economics, Sociology, Theatre Studies, Physics and Warwick's Education Departments (Institute of Education and Continuing Educ-ation). There's a fine research record, too – the uni came 6th in the recent assessments, only Oxbridge, Imperial, LSE and the Institute of Caner Research were ahead of them. Small wonder, perhaps, that 72% of graduates attain a first class degree or upper second. Many choose Warwick over Oxbridge and few look at it as second choice. Nottingham may at one time have had the edge with their Faculty of Medicine, but the new Warwick/Leicester medical school opened recently. A five-year course is based at Leicester, an accelerated four-year course for graduates with a degree in Biological Sciences is based at Warwick campus. Said Vice-Chancellor Sir Brian Follett: 'Warwick has always wanted a medical school. We need one to reflect the fact that we have become a large, research-led civic university. We need medicine in order to develop our biosciences research.'

STUDENTS' UNION

STUDENTS' UNION For most students the central point is the union, recently expanded to include a decent supermarket, post office, pharmacy, hairdresser, and a laid-back, chill-out spot for coffee or a glass of wine called Café Xanana. There are also three banks and the usual mix of STA, Endsleigh, and National Express, and facilities for the student societies, leaving the old building (Union South) to focus on bars, pool tables, food and ents.

In it you'll find three sandwich bars, a fast-food outlet and, most importantly, five bars: the main studenty bar, Cholo, plus the Cooler (nightclub), Grumpy Johns (main stage view and Sunday quiz night), Zippy's (smaller venue, home of the Comedy Superstore and many society events), and the Graduate (another smaller venue). Ents are well organised – Monday is *Top Banana* (cheese, free, plays to 2,500); Tuesday, *Heat* (music from around the world); Wednesday, *Score!* (music from '89 to '96); Thursday, *Mojo* (acid jazz, hip hop, breakbeat, latin, nig beat...) or *Pressure* (drum and bass); Friday is *The Function* (age-old, weekly dancefest) or *F2* (old skool and dance anthems) or *Junction* (dance music from '80s to today); and Saturday is *Quench* (uplifting trance/house). Recent visitors include PPK, Orango tour, Timmy

Mallet, Rainbow Road Show, Mr Scruff.

Strong in the student scene is not only ents but clubs & societies – there are an amazing 240 (70-odd sport), which must be a record, and they don't sustain them if interest flags. Encourag-ing them each year are their own society awards. For last year, Best New Soc was Free Spirits (cocktail appreciation), Most Improved Soc was the radio station, RaW, and Thai Soc. Nightline, the student-run helpline, won the

> Warwick has brilliant academic form, and a rich student culture. As the student said, 'It's ace, eventful and memorable. These are the best years of your life times ten.'

WHAT IT'S REALLY LIKE	
UNIVERSITY:	
Social Life	★★★★★
Campus scene	**Good mix, non-elitist, vibrant**
Student Union services	**Good-excellent**
Politics	**Activity high, whole spectrum**
Sport	**70+ clubs**
National team position	**34th**
Sport facilities	**Good**
Arts opportunities	**Drama, music, film, art excellent; dance good**
National drama awards	**Physical Theatre, Performance, Lighting**
Student magazine	**The Word**
Student newspaper	**The Boar**
Student radio	**RaW**
Nightclub	**Cooler**
Bars	**CHOLO, Grumpy Johns, Zippy's, The Graduate**
Union ents	**Top Banana, Score!, Mojo, Pressure, Junction, Quench, Heat, F2**
Union clubs/societies	**240**
Most popular society	**Cinema**
Smoking policy	**Union, halls OK**
Parking	**None**
TOWN/CITY:	
Entertainment	★★★
Scene	**Local homely**
Town/gown relations	**Average**
Risk of violence	**Average**
Cost of living	**Average**
Student concessions	**Average**
Survival + 2 nights out	**£50-£60 pw**
Part-time work campus/town	**Excellent/good**

AT A GLANCE

ACADEMIC FILE:

Subjects assessed	**25**
Excellent	**92%**
Average requirements	**320 points**
Students-staff ratio	**16:1**
First/2:1 degree pass rate	**72%**

ACCOMMODATION FILE:

Guarantee to freshers	**Deadline 31.8**
Style	**Halls, flats**
Catered	**Dining cards**
Price range pw	**£50-£80**
City rent pw	**£37**

Continuous Outstanding Achievement award.

Media is especially strong – magazine (*The Word*), newspaper (*The Boar*), student radio (RaW), which was Station of the Year two years ago in the Radio 1 awards. Strong, too, are arts activities – the **Warwick Arts Centre** is the biggest performing arts complex in the UK outside of London. It has a concert hall, theatre, cinema, and art gallery. Student theatrical societies do well in the Edinburgh Festival and took three awards at the NUS Drama Festival this year. RAG and Community Action (13 projects in Coventry and Leamington Spa) are popular and the non-party political union works hard on ethical, human rights and environmental campaigns, though recently effort has been focused on anti-war and education funding.

SPORT Facilities are excellent – athletics track, games fields, artificial pitch and recently completed, £1-million sports pavilion. The Sports Centre is free for students, and also hosts Bear Rock, a rather vicious looking climbing wall for eager lemmings to try and scale. Teams came 34th last year in the national BUSA league last year. They have an Olympic trampolinist, but perhaps the general tenor is more accurately given by Ultimate Frisbee being Sports Club of the Year for two years in succession.

TOWN 'Cov has a reputation for being dangerous,' writes Andrew, 'though in fact it's just like any other city. But even cities can be a shock after a year on campus, and few people spend time in Coventry. Which is a shame, as underneath the concrete nightmare is a friendly enough place, if you give it half a chance. Reasons to "brave" Cov practically quadrupled with the recent opening of **Skydome**, a huge multiplex with a sizeable gig venue, nine screen cinema, bars, restaurants and two outstanding clubs. It'll never quite beat the **NEC**, but a valiant effort nonetheless, and much closer to home. Most pubs in Cov are of the **Rat, Parrot and Firkin** ilk, but **The Golden Cross** and **The Hand and Heart** are worth a look for something different.

'As for Leam, it's a haven for trendy bars and homely pubs – don't miss **The Sozzled Sausage**, **Ocean** and **The Jug and Jester**. There is one naff club, **Mirage** – get strutting your stuff in that cage, boy! – and one half- decent one (**Sugar**), rated by Ministry mag as one of the best.'

PILLOW TALK

Uni accommodation is guaranteed if you accept a place by the end of August and they receive your accommodation application by the same date. 'Every effort is made to accommodate students admitted through the Clearing scheme,' the uni says, but places cannot be guaranteed.

There are halls and flats. Almost all halls are self-catering now – there are fifteen restaurants and fast-food outlets on campus – but there's still a sort of catering scheme at Westwood, a package which includes meals at the Westwood Restaurant and food outlets on campus.

From last year, a dining card has been available entitling students to spend £285 on meals each term. There's a 10% discount on cash prices.

Each hall has its own quirks (Jack Martin = plush and dull, Westwood = further away and friendly, Rootes = close and insane), but everyone gets thrown out in their second year to live in Coventry or Leamington. The university owns plenty of houses, but most people end up going to private estate agents.

Each place has its merits. Leam is cheap, Cov even more so, and most student houses get cable

WHERE GRADUATES END UP

13% Education,	Key Areas
12% Finance,	
11% Manufacturing,	
7% Public Admin,	
6% Wholesale/Retail	
Accountancy*,	Niche Areas
Business/Management,	
Aeronautical Manufacture,	
Construction, Defence,	
Electron/Electric, Market	
Research, Telecom	

*indicates Top 10 Graduate Provider

Approximate employed	**97%**

TV. By living in Coventry you sacrifice the more pleasant market town for the proximity of the city. If you can't handle a twenty-minute bus ride each day, then Leam is not an option.

JOBS

94% of year 2000 were known to be in employment or further study six months later; 6% had not responded to surveys. They came second nationally in the Accountancy employment table.

GETTING THERE

☛ By road: M1/J21, M69, A46; or M1/J17, M45, A45, or M40/J15, A46; or M5/J4a, M42/J6, A45.
☛ By rail: Birmingham New Street, 30 mins; Manchester Piccadilly, 2:30; Nottingham, 1:45; Bristol, 2:30; London Euston, 1:20.
☛ By air: Birmingham International Airport.
☛ By coach: London, 1:20; Leeds, 4:00.

WELSH COLLEGE OF MUSIC & DRAMA

Welsh College of Music & Drama
Castle Grounds
Cathays Park
Cardiff CF1 3ER

TEL 029 2234 2854
FAX 029 2223 1304
EMAIL info@wcmd.ac.uk
WEB www.wcmd.ac.uk

VAG VIEW

This is the Welsh conservatoire, the major centre in Wales for the training of musicians and drama professionals. Once housed in Cardiff Castle, it now occupies purpose-built premises nearby. The Grade 2 listed Castle Mews next to the college opened as the Anthony Hopkins Centre a year ago, providing new teaching, rehearsal and performance facilities. Acting-wise, a cross-disciplinary programme is the means to an organic development, rather than just a skills training. Music Department teaching involves the Welsh National Opera and the BBC National Orchestra of Wales. Performance is

COLLEGE PROFILE

Founded	**1949**
Status	**Conservatoire**
Situation/style	**City site**
Student population	**567**
Degree undergraduates	**413**
College accommodation	**None**
City rent pw	**£38-£42**

DEGREE COURSES:
Acting; Design; Stage Management, Music

central; every student has a personal tutor. No accommodation, but they'll help you find it. See Cardiff entry, page 117, for city/travel info.

UNIVERSITY OF WESTMINSTER

The University of Westminster
309 Regent Street
London W1B 2UW

TEL 020 7911 5000
FAX 020 7911 5858
EMAIL admissions@wmin.ac.uk
WEB www.wmin.ac.uk

Westminster Students' Union
32-38 Wells Street
London W1P 4DJ

TEL 020 7911 5000 x 2396
FAX 020 7911 5793
EMAIL gensec@WMIN.ac.uk
WEB www.uwsu.com

VAG VIEW

The uni comes out of The Royal Polytechnic Institution, established in 1838 by (among others) Sir George Cayley, the North Yorkshire squire who invented the first man-powered flying machine, inveigling his unwilling butler to fly it solo through Brompton Dale.

On the surface, Westminster might appear to suffer all sorts of drawbacks characteristic of a new university in the metropolis – split sites, low entry requirements/open access/high drop-

out rate, high vocational content in its courses/lower end of the employment spectrum at graduation. Drop-out rate aside, because of its challenging commitment to an impressive curriculum, Westminster, in point of fact, flies higher (particularly in certain directions) than ever Cayley could have dreamt it would.

CAMPUSES

REGENT CAMPUS (address above). **Faculties** on four neighbouring sites: *Regent Street* (Social & Behavioural Sciences, including Psychology, some Business courses), *Little Titchfield Street, Euston Centre* and *Wells Street* (Law and Languages). **Academic resources:** Self-Access Language Centre, libraries, IT suites. **Leisure facilities:** Sport and Fitness Centre with cardiovascular and resistance equipment, saunas, solaria and indoor games hall; **Deep End Café** (Regent Street).

CAVENDISH CAMPUS 115 New Cavendish Street, London W1M 8JS (use main phone number above). **Courses:** Biosciences, Engineering, Computing, Maths, Complementary Therapies (developed with the London School of Acupuncture & Traditional Chinese Medicine and the London College of Classical Homeopathy: the BSc degrees in Acupuncture and Homeopathy are unique). **Academic resources:** computing suites, science labs, library. **Leisure facilities:** bar and refectory. They are about to embark upon a new building here, which they promise will provide 'some of the best public IT facilities in the capital.'

MARYLEBONE CAMPUS 35 Marylebone Road, London NW1 5LS (use main tel. above). **Faculties:** Built Environment and Westminster Business School. **Academic resources:** library and laboratory. **Leisure facilities:** bar (designed by

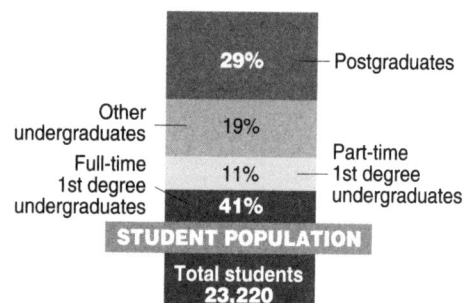

STUDENT POPULATION	
Postgraduates	29%
Other undergraduates	19%
Part-time 1st degree undergraduates	11%
Full-time 1st degree undergraduates	41%
Total students 23,220	

students on the Architecture BA) and **Café West**. They have just completed the first phase of a £10-million makeover of this campus.

HARROW CAMPUS Watford Road, Northwick Park, Harrow HA1 3TP. Tel: 020 7911 5936; Fax: 020 7911 5943. **Style:** well-designed, self-contained campus, close to horrendous looking hospital.

AT A GLANCE	
ACADEMIC FILE:	
Subjects assessed	**30**
Excellent	**73%**
Average requirements	**200 points**
Students-staff ratio	**13:1**
First/2:1 degree pass rate	**55%**
ACCOMMODATION FILE:	
Guarantee to freshers	**No guarantee**
Style	**Halls**
Catered	**1,277 places**
En-suite	**Harrow Hall**
Price range pw	**£65-£114**
London rent pw	**£70**

Faculties/courses: Media Design & Communications, Computer Science, Harrow Business School. **Academic resources:** Information Resources Centre, including library, computers (1,000 + campus-wide), AV aids for presentations; also TV, radio, photography and music studios. **Leisure facilities:** venue, open-air performance court, **The Undercroft Bar**, sports hall, fitness suite and playing fields close by.

UNIVERSITY/STUDENT PROFILE	
University since	**1992**
Situation/style	**City sites & campus**
Student population	**23,220**
Full-time undergraduates	**9,510**
- mature	**43%**
- overseas	**8%**
- male/female	**50/50**
- state sector intake	**92%**
- non-traditional student intake	**11%**
- drop-out rate	**15%, high**
- undergraduate applications	**Up 0.1%**
see Introduction for key to tables	

STUDENT PROFILE

In its student clientele, Westminster mirrors many other ex-polys. There's a sizeable mature, part-time, local and overseas population – they received a Queen's Award for Enterprise for their success in International Markets, and were the first post-1992 uni to have been so rewarded.

There's also a significant non-degree student population, and many students are the first in their families to experience university – 38% of non-mature entrants come from social groups IIIM, IV and V, and 11% from so-called low-participation neighbourhoods.

ACADEMIA

'If you want to study at a traditional university,' writes Calvin Holbrook, 'then don't come to Westminster. The courses here have a mainly hands-on approach that sets students up for the real world. Bookworms need not apply.' This may sound like a put-down, but is certainly not meant as one: 'As a university it's way ahead of its time. If you want to be on the cutting edge, come to Westminster,' Calvin also urges, and if we consider the uni's results at inspection and the employment

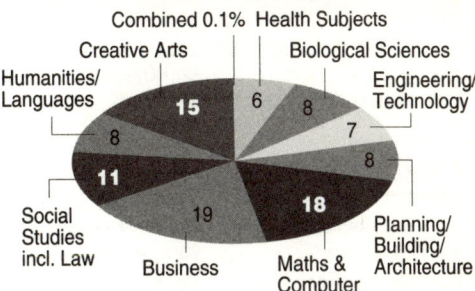

SUBJECT AREAS (%)

Combined 0.1% Health Subjects
Creative Arts Biological Sciences
Humanities/Languages — 15
Engineering/Technology
8 — 6 — 8 — 7
11 — 8
Social Studies incl. Law — 19 — 18 — Planning/Building/Architecture
Business Maths & Computer

ACADEMIC EXCELLENCE

TEACHING :
(Rated Excellent or 17+ out of 24)

Tourism, Psychology	**24**
French, Asian Studies, Media, Subjects Allied to Medicine	**23**
Building, International Relations	**22**
Electric/Electron Eng, Anatomy, Art & Design, Biosciences	**21**
Linguistics, German, Civil Eng, Business, Maths	**20**
Italian	**19**
Russian, Sociology, Iberian	**18**

RESEARCH :
Top grades 5/5*

Law, Asian Studies, Linguistics, Communication, Cultural & Media Studies	**Grade 5**

---

picture (see box, page 484) one cannot but agree.

In its vocational, modular course planning it has taken advice from the professions and industry, and translated it into a strategy underpinned by an expert language provision (its School of Professional Language Studies lays claim to the widest range of language teaching in the UK) and a 'mathematics for all' initiative. Westminster offers twenty-eight languages from beginner to postgraduate level. See its very high inspection scores for French and Asian Studies (23 points out of 24), while Iberian

Studies, German, Italian and Russian all did well.

There is success, too, in research, unprecedented for a new university: five departments made international waves – Law, Asian Studies, Linguistics, Communication, Cultural & Media Studies. Their media research facility imbues an undergraduate provision in which places to study TV, radio and print media could be filled thirty times over, literally. The Communication, Design & Media Faculty, out on the Harrow campus, is a £30-million project with fantastic facilities, industry-standard equipment. Harrow is the campus where students of Commercial Music, Fashion and Photography take their respective industries by storm, too.

Note an intriguing little niche – the BA in Medical Journalism, which medics with two years pre-clinical training can complete in a year. Also in the health area, there's an innovative programme of complementary therapies: Acupuncture and Homeopathy were the first named degrees of their kind in the UK.

Finally, if you are looking for something more down to earth you could do a lot worse than scan their property portfolio – from Architecture through Surveying, Construction, Estate Management and Urban & Housing Development, they would seem to have the whole thing tied up. Now go to the Employment box, page 484, and see how all these strengths translate directly into jobs.

Westminster have made vocational degrees an attractive proposition. Media & Communications out at Harrow is, inevitably, heavily oversubscribed, but there are other nuggets. Just don't expect your traditional formula.

SOCIAL SCENE

Out at Harrow, where there is a purpose-built, self-contained campus, Westminster has an opportunity to enrich the student-culture, to facilitate all sorts of student activities and involvements. They

WHAT IT'S REALLY LIKE

UNIVERSITY:

Social Life	★★★
Campus scene	**Diverse, non-traditional**
Student Union services	**Average**
Politics	**Interest low**
Sport	**14 clubs**
National sporting position	**None recorded**
Sport facilities	**Improving**
Arts opportunities	**Drama excellent; film, music good; dance, art poor**
Student newspaper	**The Smoke**
Nightclub	**Area 51**
Bars	**Dragon Bar, Undercroft Bar**
Union ents	**House, garage, dance, pop, hip hop, soul and swing**
Union clubs/societies	**46**
Most popular society	**Islamic**
Smoking policy	**Union & halls OK**
Parking	**Adequate**

CITY:

Entertainment	★★★★★
City scene	**Wild, expensive**
Town/gown relations	**Average-good**
Risk of violence	**Average**
Cost of living	**Very high**
Student concessions	**Good**
Survival + 2 nights out	**£70 pw**
Part-time work campus/town	**Average outatown**

WHERE GRADUATES END UP

11% Computer*,	Key areas
10% Wholesale/Retail,	
10% Manufacturing,	
8% Finance,	
7% Health/Social Work,	
5% Personnel	
Business/Management,	Niche Areas
Advertising, Film/Video,	
Architecture, Artistic/	
Literary*, Journalism,	
Legal, Library/Archival,	
Market Research,	
Eng/Industrial Design,	
Property*, Publishing*,	
Radio/TV*, Telecom	

*indicates Top 10 Graduate Provider

Approximate employed **91%**

flats in Marylebone Road, Highgate Village and Victoria, and the accommodation at Harrow is good, all en suite.

JOBS

Their whole ethos is workplace education, and it is clear from the box, below, that Westminster is succeeding by the most direct routes. They figure in five of our Top 10s, showing a concentration of efforts in Computing (where they were 2nd), Artistic/Literary Creation (the art side – graphic design, illustration, photographic/digital arts: also 2nd), Publishing (these are not just from the art side, but out of business, computer, information, even biological sciences – 5th), Radio/TV (2nd) and Property (2nd). See *Academia*, above for the course leads into some of these areas.

GETTING THERE

☛ To Regent Campus: Oxford Circus Underground (Bakerloo, Central and Victoria lines).
☛ To Cavendish Campus: Warren Street Underground (Northern and Victoria lines).
☛ To Marylebone Campus: Baker Street Underground (Bakerloo, Metropolitan, Hammersmith & City, Circle, Jubilee lines).
☛ By road to Harrow Campus: A404 accessible via M25, M1 or M40/A40; by Underground – Northwick Park (Metropolitan line).

don't do a bad job at it. Some of the best society activity comes out of course disciplines (media, music), but you can't help wondering whether, if they really got this aspect of student life together, they might whittle down the drop-out rate (15%), which has grown since our last edition.

Area 51 is the Harrow nightclub. From Kool Herc to Clint Boom, from So Solid Crew to Keith Harris & Orville, you can imbibe and enjoy till chuck-out time, which is as late as 2 am. There's also **The Undercroft**, open 9 am-11 pm, Monday to Friday, 5-11 pm on Saturday, 6-10.30 pm on Sunday. Drink promos, big screen footie, karaoke nights, quizzes, the Westminster gameshow – *Pull My Jugs*, a kinda pre-club for Area 51.

PILLOW TALK

There's no accommodation guarantee, but they'll bend over backwards to help you find somewhere to lay your weary head. There are halls, rooms or

WIMBLEDON SCHOOL OF ART

Wimbledon School of Art
Merton Hall Road
London SW19 3QA

TEL 020 8408 5000
FAX 020 8408 5050
EMAIL registry@wimbledon.ac.uk
WEB www.wimbledon.ac.uk

VAG VIEW

*T*he college has an impressive record of taking students through foundation courses to DipHE and BA (Hons) degrees in both the Theatre and Fine Arts Departments.

The three chief areas of study in the Theatre Department are Theatre Design (set and costume design), Costume Design, and Technical Arts (set and lighting design). The Department of Fine Art focuses on Painting, Sculpture or Printmaking.

Learning resources are good (a 28,000-volume Library and IT Centre). Wimbledon has the advantages of being within easy reach of lively Fulham and central London, there's a theatre with a good reputation, a beautiful common, and something of a village atmosphere. It is, however, expensive, which perhaps makes it just as well that the school is in fact in nearby Merton, more accessible price-wise. Accommodation is in a nearby house, owned by the school.

SCHOOL PROFILE

Founded	**1890**
Status	**Art School**
Degree awarding university	**Surrey**
Total student population	**825**
Degree undergraduates	**413**

ACCOMMODATION:
Availability to freshers	**17%**
Style	**House**
Cost pw (no food)	**£65**
City rent pw	**£65-£90**

DEGREE COURSES:
Theatre Design Costume (Design or Interpretation), Theatre Design Technical Arts (Design or Interpretation), Fine Art (Painting, Printmaking, Sculpture)

GETTING THERE
☛ By road: A3, Raynes Park/Bushy Road turn-off.
☛ By rail: Wimbledon Chase or Merton Park Overland.

UNIVERSITY OF WOLVERHAMPTON

The University of Wolverhampton
Wulfruna Street
Wolverhampton WV1 1SB

TEL 01902 321000
FAX 01902 323744
EMAIL enquiries@wlv.ac.uk
WEB www.wlv.ac.uk

Wolverhampton Students' Union
Wulfruna Street
Wolverhampton WV1 1LY

TEL 01902 322021
FAX 01902 322020
EMAIL ex1226@wlv.ac.uk
WEB www.wlv.ac.uk/su

VAG VIEW

*T*he university was spawned by the Wolverhampton Poly following its merger with three teacher training colleges and West Midlands College of Higher Education. Operating on campus sites in and around Wolverhampton and in Shropshire, they have recruiting associations with dozens of colleges, and were the first to attract entrants via a High Street shop. As many as 25,000 people a year visit the shop and more than 7% sign up.

CAMPUSES
This year there are big changes afoot. Dudley Campus has closed (June 2002), most of its operations are moving to Wolverhampton in a big new building programme. Walsall, meanwhile, is to become a centre of sporting excellence and will be greatly enhanced.

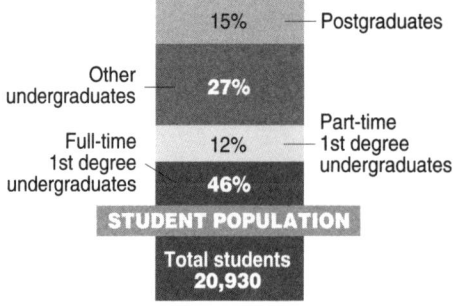

STUDENT POPULATION

Total students
20,930

STUDENT PROFILE

Wolverhampton has a unique student intake. As many as 47% of non-mature undergraduate entrants come from social classes IIIM, IV and V, which is 19% more than the average national influx from this lower end of the income bracket into university education. Nearly half of its undergraduate intake are mature students, a great number are part-timers, and the SU tells me that there is a high percentage of disabled students, too. (There are certainly a number of very good special needs degree courses.)

CITY CAMPUS (address, page 485) **Location:** a few minutes walk from rail or bus station. **Campus scene:** the busy centre of it all. **Courses:** Applied Sciences, Art & Design, Computing, Construction, Engineering, Health Sciences, Languages, Humanities and Social Sciences, including Law.

COMPTON PARK CAMPUS Compton Road West, Wolverhampton WV3 9DY. **Location:** mile or so west of main campus. **Courses:** Business Admin, Info Management, some Human Resourcing, Marketing, some Computing.

WALSALL CAMPUS Gorway Road, Walsall WS1 3BD. **Location:** six miles east of town centre. **Campus scene: known as** 'the concrete jungle', but strong community spirit. **Courses:** Education (incl. Sports Studies).

SHROPSHIRE (TELFORD) CAMPUS Priorslee Hall, Shifnal Road Telford TF2 9NT. **Location:** 12 miles northwest of town. **Campus scene:** the International Students' Association thrives; football is the big thing; they won the intra-mural five-a-side championship last year; 'e-mail is a way of life'. **Courses:** Business, Computer-aided Product Design.

UNIVERSITY/STUDENT PROFILE	
University since	**1992**
Situation/style	**City campus, town sites**
Student population	**20,930**
Full-time undergraduates	**9,650**
- mature	**37%**
- overseas	**13%**
- male/female	**46/56**
- state sector intake	**98%**
- non-traditional student intake	**23%, high**
- drop-out rate	**14%, high**
- undergraduate applications	**Up 6%**
see Introduction for key to tables	

Such cold statistics do little to express the busy and persistently cheerful student scene at Wolverhampton. 'If there is any university with ambition, giving clear signs that it wants to play with academia's big boys, then Wolverhampton surely is the one,' said sabbatical student Mark Wilson. 'It may take a few years, but there is no doubt that it will get there!'

ACADEMIA

'Wolverhampton. Wally Poly? You can get in with a Tesco discount card, can't you?' chimed another student contributor. 'We've all heard the jokes and most of us have felt that way when we got here.' So, what has the university got to offer to make three or four years here worthwhile?

Fundamental to its business-like ethos is the vocational education on offer – 'the best thing may be that they teach subjects which lead to jobs, engineering, film, computer programming and many more,' writes Mark. A close association with industry in this high density industrial area, as well as commerce and the professions, gives confidence in terms of graduate employment, and their employment record is good not only locally. A particular emphasis is on languages – students of all disciplines may study a language and the

SUBJECT AREAS (%)

Physical Sciences 2%

Biological Sciences

Health Subjects

Combined

Engineering/ Technology 2%

Planning/ Building/ Architecture 1%

21

6

6

7

9

15

2

13

15

Education

Creative Arts

Humanities

Business

Maths & Computer

Social Studies incl. Law

ACADEMIC EXCELLENCE

TEACHING :
(Rated Excellent or 17+ out of 24)

Philosophy	**24**
Education, Molecular &	**23**
Organismal Biosciences	
Russian, Subjects Allied to	**22**
Medicine	
Linguistics, American Studies,	**21**
Nursing, Art & Design,	
Psychology, Theology	
Iberian Studies, Sociology,	**20**
Building, General Eng, Maths,	
Civil Engineering, Mathematics	
French, Drama, Dance &	**19**
Cinematics, Media	

RESEARCH:
Top grades 5/5* **None**

teaching assessments have been good: Russian scored 22 points out of 24, Spanish 20, French 19, German 17.

Two niche areas in our *Employment* box (page 488) pick up on other valuable areas of the curriculum. Their success in the hotel/restaurant industry directs us to the excellent Business School, in particular to courses in Hospitality and Licensed Retail Management. Success in the creative arts/design and radio/TV industries directs us to their performance arts and media degrees, to the £2-million, Lottery-funded redevelopment of their **Arena Theatre**, and to the School of Art & Design's **Gallery** space, home to a range of courses, from Animation to Journalism & Editorial Design, from Computer-Aided Design to Sculpture, from Floorcoverings & Interior Textile Design to Painting.

Unassuming and blisteringly ambitious, there's a positive attitude at Wolverhampton that sits well with their mission to teach subjects which lead to jobs.

A £4.5-million Learning Centre opened in Wolverhampton recently – 967 study spaces, 130 IT spaces, 200,000 volumes – following the opening of a similar centre in Shropshire. Then there's the Virtual Reality Centre in the School of Engineering – look for up-and-coming courses in Auto Design, Computer-Aided Engineering/Product/ Industrial Designs, at engineering mixes with law and business.

Look, too, at the Sports Technology degree, geared to develop their national reputation in the sports industry. Then there are the health courses

– Complementary Therapies, Health Sciences, Midwifery, Public Health, Occupational Health, Registered Nurse, Rehabilitation Studies – a faculty which scored 23/24 points in the assessments and each year propels 10% of graduates into the industry.

'Do not feel disappointed if you are asked (sic) to come here,' Mark urges. 'The teaching is particularly good for the vocational courses on which we focus – lectures and seminars, but also film screenings, guest speakers, hands-on activities and group work with assessments. The uni is generally fun and relaxed, the facilities, all £60 million of them, are excellent, the entertainments are lively, the people are friendly. We are fortunate to have a 25,000-strong melting pot of cultures, skills, talents – sectors, like Lesbian, Gay & Bisexual (LGB), mature students or ethnic minorities, get people together and entertain them. Wolverhampton students enjoy a good night out, as is shown by attendances at our live shows, like recently Shanks & Bigfoot, the Radio 1 Rap Show, Bizarre Roadshow, Steve Lamacq, Emma B, Stevie Starr, Buffalo Souljah, the Tarantinos and Dave Pearce. It may take time to shake the wally poly sterotype, but the future is looking blinding from where I stand.'

SOCIAL SCENE
STUDENTS' UNION 'In the same year that they closed the union's most active campus at Dudley, the first Student Festival was put on...at Dudley,' writes Mark Wilson. Besides the fest, the year was made memorable by hundreds of students tripping off to Amsterdam, to an SU regional rally in Birmingham and the national anti-fees demo in London.

AT A GLANCE

ACADEMIC FILE:
Subjects assessed	**33**
Excellent	**67%**
Average requirements	**160 points**
Students-staff ratio	**20:1**
First/2:1 degree pass rate	**49%**

ACCOMMODATION FILE:
Guarantee to freshers	**80%**
Style	**Halls**
Approx price range pw	**£40-£52**
Town rent pw	**£30-£40**

WHAT IT'S REALLY LIKE

UNIVERSITY:

Social Life	★★★
Campus scene	**Local, lively**
Student Union services	**Average**
Politics	**Student issues**
Sport	**20+**
National team position	**98th**
Sport facilities	**Good**
Arts opportunities	**Music, art excellent; drama, dance good; film average**
Student magazine	**Cry Wolf**
Nightclub	**The JL Club**
Bars	**Fat Mick's, Poly Bar, Bertie's, Auntie Rita's**
Union ents	**Danger, Quid's In**
Union clubs/societies	**50**
Most popular societies	**Qur'an & Sunnah, Christian Union**
Smoking policy	**Union OK**
Parking	**Poor**
TOWN:	
Entertainment	★★★
Scene	**Pubs, diverse studenty clubs**
Town/gown relations	**OK-ish**
Risk of violence	**Average**
Cost of living	**Low**
Student concessions	**Good**
Survival + 2 nights out	**£45 pw**
Part-time work campus/town	**Good**

Now, the uni have announced that they are putting plans in place for a new SU, both in Wolverhampton and in Walsall. The latter will also soon be home to an NBL-standard basketball arena and the National Judo Centre of Excellence. 'Meanwhile,' says Mark, 'Wolves is buzzing, growing and generally full of "beautiful people"!'

There are various bar areas at the main campus, **Fat Micks** (dancefloor, food, pool tables, widescreen TV, 1,200 capacity, licensed till midnight), the **Poly Bar** (a pre-club comedy or light entertainment venue) and the JL club (nightclub and venue, capacity 600, licensed till 2 am Wednesday through Saturday). Changes are due in 2003. DANGER on Wednesdays plays cheesy classics, normally very popular and occasionally themed. *Quids In* on Friday is a mandatory night out! This year they also had *Sick Squid* on Mondays at **Atlantis** in town.

They claim around thirty societies. Christian Union apparently runs its own Alpha course.

Compton Park facilities include a bar, but for ents it's the main campus. At Walsall the bar's called **Berties** (capacity 300)– masses of drinks promos/sporting debauchery, pool competitions, comedy, specials, movies, theme nights; good number of clubs/pubs locally but not always friendly. At Dudley, there's a bar and discos, hypnotists, steel bands, traditional Irish music. At Telford the bar's called **Auntie Rita's** (capacity 250), ents are theme nights, quizzes, movie nights, barbecues.

SPORT There are sports hall, squash courts, fitness centre at Wolverhampton; sports hall, playing fields, running track, swimming pool, dance studio, tennis courts at Walsall (see also more to come, above), and at Telford, there's a gym; otherwise it's local facilities, which are good: sports centre, ski slope, windsurfing, etc.

TOWN Wolverhampton can be unnerving, but the SU supplies advice, information, attack alarms, and it's generally safe. Clubland is good for house, garage, rock, indie, bhangra, jungle techno, acid jazz, folk. Cinemas include **The Light House** (mainstream and foreign); **Wolverhampton Art Gallery** for one of finest collections of British and American Pop Art in the country. Arts facilities: uni's own **Arena Theatre** for alternative, touring and student drama and music; Wolverhampton's **Grand Theatre** for London shows.

Student tales of pub fights in Walsall and race attacks in Telford are nothing compared to what they once had in Dudley – a prize bull ran amok and was taken out by a police marksman.

JOBS

There is a vocational drift to everything on offer at Wolverhampton, and many of the academic strands already drawn out, above, can be seen

WHERE GRADUATES END UP

	Key Areas
13% Education,	
13% Wholesale/Retail,	
11% Health/Social Work,	
9% Manufacturing,	
8% Computer,	
7% Finance,	
6% Public Admin	
5% Personnel	
Film/Video, Advertising,	Niche Areas
Hotel/Restaurant, Artistic,	
Construction, Journalism,	
Radio/TV, Legal	
Approximate employed	**88%**

playing their part in graduate employment.

GETTING THERE
☛ By train: London Euston less than two hours;
☛ By road: M6/J10, M54/J2, M5/J2
☛ By coach: London,

UNIVERSITY COLLEGE WORCESTER

University College Worcester
Henwick Grove
Worcester WR2 6AJ

TEL 01905 855111
FAX 01905 855132
EMAIL (via website)
WEB www.worc.ac.uk

UC Worcester Students' Union
Henwick Grove
Worcester WR2 6AJ

TEL 01905 740800
FAX 01905 740801
EMAIL (via website)
WEB www.worcsu.com

VAG VIEW

*W*orcester began as a teacher training college in 1946. In the '70s it became a college of higher education. In 1995 it merged with a college of nursing and midwifery, and in February last year it was granted university college status. Now they are bidding for full university status, underlining the seriousness of it with a new research-led partnership with Birmingham University.

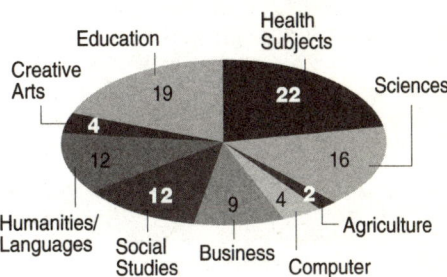

SUBJECT AREAS (%)

COLLEGE/STUDENT PROFILE	
University College since	**1999**
Situation/style	**City campus**
Total student population	**6,340**
Full-time undergraduates	**2,230**
- mature	**44%**
- overseas	**nil**
- male/female	**27/73**
- state sector intake	**96%**
- non-traditional student intake	**11%**
- drop-out rate	**7%**
- undergraduate applications	**Up 6%**
see Introduction for key to tables	

STUDENT PROFILE

The predominantly female intake is mainly regional. More than a third of undergraduates are mature and a fair proportion (31% of non-mature entrants) who are from families not traditionally given to sending their sons and daughters to uni. It would seem to be the kind of friendly, efficient higher-ed college every town and city should have.

ACADEMIA

Besides the BA QTS provision, they dispense their own degrees in health, social studies, media, arts, science, business and horticulture.

SOCIAL SCENE

'If UCW were embodied in one article of clothing it would be trainers,' suggests Emma Aves. 'Why? Because trainers are the foundation of an outfit, a requisite to get you from A to B in a comfortable and protective way. They offer style and design to suit your tastes, developing with the times without being the most ultra-advanced clothing concept. UCW may not be the most prestigious, grand or fashionable place to study, but the care and quality

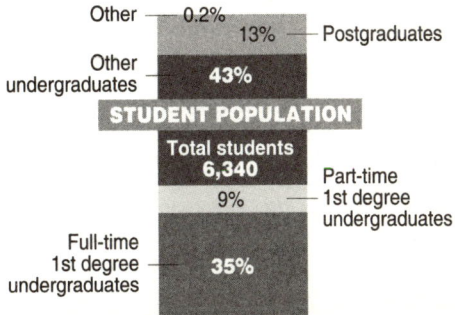

ACADEMIC EXCELLENCE

TEACHING:
(Rated Excellent or 17+ out of 24)
Sociology, Art & Design, **21**
Business
Psychology **20**

WHAT IT'S REALLY LIKE

COLLEGE:	
Social Life	★★
Campus scene	**Local, lively**
Politics	**Controlled**
Sport	**Competitive**
National team position	**79th**
Arts opportunities	**Drama excellent, film & art good, dance avg, music poor**
Daily student newspaper	**Tableslips**
Student magazine	**The Voice**
Nightclub/bar	**The Dive**
Union ents	**Happy hours, pre-clubs, Lush + 4 big balls**
Union clubs/societies	**37**
Smoking policy	**Bar OK**
Parking	**Adequate**
CITY:	
Entertainment	★★
Scene	**Cathedral, arts, cricket, pubs**
Risk of violence	**Low**
Cost of living	**Average**
Student concessions	**Excellent**
Survival + 2 nights out	**£50 pw**
Part-time work campus/town	**Excellent**

it offers students more than compensates for what it lacks in notoriety.

'UCW gains greatly from the sense of intimacy which its size brings, you feel truly part of the institution, one that supports you throughout your course. The onus is on you to balance your interests and ensure academic requirements are fulfilled, but a personal tutor system is available to all and helps to compensate for the formal nature of lectures.'

STUDENTS' UNION The union is now growing into its university college role, taking student support quite seriously. They have a Student Advice Bureau and well-equipped Employment Bureau, and are active in work-related skills training of

AT A GLANCE

ACADEMIC FILE:	
Subjects assessed	**9**
Excellent	**44%**
Average requirements	**180 points**
Students-staff ratio	**19:1**
First/2:1 degree pass rate	**45%**
ACCOMMODATION FILE:	
Guarantee to freshers	**90%**
Style	**Halls**
Approx price range pw	**£38-£48**
City rent pw	**£40-£45**

undergrads. Actions and awareness campaigns have included Carbon Monoxide, Meningitis, Sexual Health, Education & Welfare. It is indeed a happy place, with only a 7% drop-out rate (6% lower than benchmark), a grand sporting tradition – they came 79th in the national BUSA team ratings last year, which is above bigger unis like Sunderland, Sussex, Dundee, Liverpool John Moores – an effort supported by PE and Sports Studies courses.

There are decent ents in the **Dive Bar** (this year they have reverted it from Hangar back to its original name) – Monday's bingo, booze and karaoke; Tuesday, there's a quiz and sometimes big screen footie; Wednesday's *LUSH* – don't forget

your knee pads because you may be crawling home, Friday's *Gangster Night* – band, DJ and 12.00 am closing, while Saturday is just promo/happy hours – £1 doubles and £1 Carling from 7pm to 12.30am. Why the let-down? Because, as yet, most students are local and go home at weekends. It's the nut every would-be university must crack. Sunday's a film night.

'Entertainment at the Dive is safe, non-extreme, yet fun,' writes Emma. 'Fortunately, the town is close by and has bars ranging from Irish to rock, gay to trendy, and three popular yet cheesy nightclubs.

'Activities such as RAG and Student Community Action are enthusiastically attended in order to establish that we are here for more than personal gain. There is no pressure to take up recreational activities, but it is strongly advocated as a means of getting the most out of your time here. There are many clubs and societies, from traditional sports like football and netball to alternative pursuits like juggling or T'ai Chi.

PILLOW TALK

'Accommodation on campus ranges from ancient room-only halls to comfy, modern flats, but there are enough only for first years and international students. Never mind, there is a vast assortment of off-campus accommodation on which the accommodation service has basic information.'

JOBS

The college is highly focused on getting its graduates jobs, and so concentrate on certain areas that they figure in five of our Employment Top 10s.

GETTING THERE

☛ By road: M5/J7.
☛ By rail: Cheltenham Spa, 24 mins; Hereford, 40 mins.

WHERE GRADUATES END UP	
30% Education*,	Key Areas
14% Wholesale/Retail*,	
10% Health/Social Work,	
7% Personnel*,	
5% Finance,	
5% Manufacturing,	
5% Public Admin	
Sport*, Agric/Forestry*	Niche Area
Hotel/Restaurant	
*indicates Top 10 Graduate Provider	
Approximate employed **94%**	

WRITTLE COLLEGE

Writtle College
Lordship Road
Writtle
Chelmsford
Essex CM1 3RR

TEL 01245 424200
FAX 01245 420456
EMAIL postmaster@writtle.ac.uk
WEB www.writtle.ac.uk

VAG VIEW

*W*rittle, founded in 1893, lies just outside Chelmsford. Degree programmes range from Rural Environmental Management through European Horticulture to Equine Studies. On its 220-hectare country estate there is farmland running to 135 hectares, an arboretum with more than 1,000 trees, and grounds with 70,000 bulbs and numerous other plants.

Some £8 million has been spent on development. There is a sports hall and squash courts and playing fields – rugby, soccer, cricket, hockey, netball and Gaelic football are the most popular team sports. First-year accommodation is in one of their nine halls of residence. There's a lively ents programme – discos, balls, theme nights and quizzes.

COLLEGE PROFILE	
Founded	**1893**
Status	**F/HE College**
Degree awarding university	**Essex**
Situation/style	**Rural campus**
Total student population	**1,260**
Degree undergraduates	**670**
ACCOMMODATION:	
Availability to freshers	**80%**
Style	**Halls**
Cost pw (food)	**£65-£75**
Town rent pw	**£45**

GETTING THERE

☛ By road from the northwest: M11/J8, A1060; from the West, M11/J7, A414; from the southwest, M25/J28, A12; and A12 from the northeast.
☛ By coach: London, 1:40.
☛ By rail: Chelmsford is 35 minutes away from London Liverpool Street.

UNIVERSITY OF YORK

The University of York
Heslington
York YO1 5DD

TEL 01904 433533
FAX 01904 433538
EMAIL admissions@york.ac.uk
WEB www.york.ac.uk

York University Students' Union
Student Centre
Heslington
York YO1 5DD

TEL 01904 433723/4
FAX 01904 434664
EMAIL su@yorl.ac.uk
WEB www. yusu.co.uk

UNIVERSITY/STUDENT PROFILE	
University since	**1962**
Situation/style	**City campus**
Student population	**9,480**
Full-time undergraduates	**5,140**
- mature	**14%**
- overseas	**10%**
- male/female	**49/51**
- state sector intake	**80%**
- non-traditional student intake	**10%**
- drop-out rate	**6%**
- undergraduate applications	**Up 1%**
*see Introduction for key to tables	

VAG VIEW

Founded in 1963, York is a small university with a huge reputation for its teaching, and unusually for a top-of-the-range higher education institution, they manage to achieve a sound balance between state and public school entrants, and to offer their teaching to a wide socio-economic range – they'd been monitoring GNVQ students for years before the government began exerting pressure to do so. Also, UK students are drawn fairly equally from the Southeast, from the North and elsewhere.

York is very popular with its students, who are bright, fun-loving and notably unpretentious. They still would like a university ents venue, but have concluded that 'the university are too mean.'

CAMPUS

It's a purpose-built campus at Heslington, on the south-east edge of the city: 'Very suburban, not at all monumental. It could get on the garden register,' mused Elaine Harwood of English Heritage. Student Gemma Thomas disagrees, 'Overall, the campus is a very pleasant place to live and along with York itself, one of the safest places. Heslington Hall, a gorgeous manor house on the edge of campus, provides an antidote to some of the bleaker aspects. It possesses extensive gardens, part of which, the Quiet Place, a collection of gigantic topiary knobs, is perfect for late-night games of hide-and-seek, or whatever else springs to mind.' The York Quakers, who were among those responsible for raising £70,000 for the Georgian gazebo and garden known as the Quiet Place, will no doubt be pleased it is being put to such imaginative use. Thoughtfully designed as a peaceful student retreat, perhaps it will take over as perennial talking point from the campus ducks, which inhabit the campus-central lake, 'the largest plastic-lined lake in Europe... blaa, blaa.'

STUDENT PROFILE

'The most important point to consider before choosing York concerns your feelings about ducks,' writes Gemma. 'Do NOT come here if you are anything less than tolerant of them. They are everywhere. On the lake, crossing paths, dive-bombing students wending their way to early morning lectures (or not). Fetishists will tell you of their predilection for feeding the pitiful duck-loners who hang about dejectedly outside windows, while others take bets on the outcome of duck brawls.

'After ducks, students form the second most numerous campus species. No one type dominates, the balance between state and private sectors a surprise bonus in a university with this much prestige. York is a small, friendly, unpretentious university, which makes it incredibly easy to settle in. Also, student welfare is taken very seriously. Nightline, chaplains, a range of counselling services and equal opportunities are promoted heavily.'

ACADEMIA

There are Applied & Natural Sciences, Arts, Computer Science & Engineering, Mathematical Sciences, and the School of Politics, Economics &

SUBJECT AREAS (%)

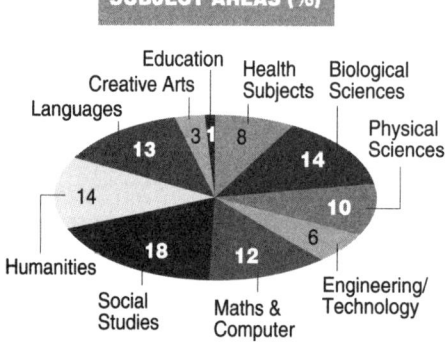

Education 3
Creative Arts
Languages
Health Subjects 1
Biological Sciences 8
Physical Sciences 14
13
14
10
18 12 6
Humanities
Social Studies
Maths & Computer
Engineering/ Technology

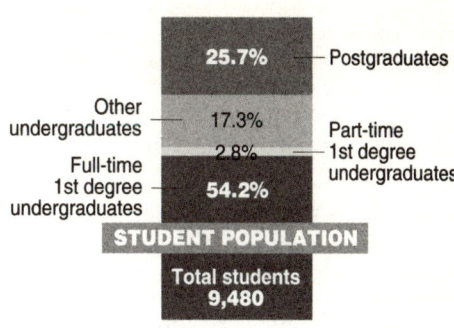

STUDENT POPULATION

- 25.7% — Postgraduates
- Other undergraduates 17.3%
- Part-time 1st degree undergraduates
- Full-time 1st degree undergraduates 2.8%
- 54.2%

Total students
9,480

ACADEMIC EXCELLENCE

TEACHING:
(Rated Excellent or 17+ out of 24)

History, Applied Social Work, Architecture (MA), Computing, English, Music, Social Policy	**Excellent**
Electric & Electron Engineering, Archaeology, Economics, Educ, Philosophy, Politics, Organismal Biosciences, Physics, Psychology	**24**
Sociology	**23**
Management, Languages, Maths	**22**
History of Art, Nursing	**21**

RESEARCH:
Top grades 5/5*

Psychology, Computer, English	**Grade 5***
Community-based Clinical, Nursing, Biological Sciences, Chemistry, Pure Maths, Applied Math, Economics, Politics, Social Policy, Social Work, Sociology, Linguistics, History, Philosophy, Music	**Grade 5**

Philosophy. Their teaching assessments have been exemplary – 96% Excellent or 21 points or more out of 24. There have been so many full marks recently that you can begin to see why the Russell Group wanted to do away with assessments, at least in this form. Electrical & Electronic Engineering, Archaeology, Economics, Education, Philosophy, Politics, Genetics, Physics and Psychology all scored 24. And the recent research exercise left them in 18th place with three Grade 5* – that's world class research – in English, Computing, and Psychology. Their Grade 5s in Community-based Clinical subjects, in Nursing and Biological Sciences suggests that the so-called HYMS – the Hull-York Medical School, which is due for launch in 2003 – is in safe hands.

SOCIAL SCENE

Famously, there is no union venue – concerts in **Central Hall** were banned after Bob Geldof trashed it back in the early '80s – though many students seem quite happy with life without one. Each college has its own Junior Common Room (JCR) Committee, who run about two events per week per college and two or three big events per year.

> *York is a small university with a gigantic reputation for teaching. It is not a hip place to be, but stuff goes on, activity levels beyond mere ents are high.*

The Students' Union organises up to five large-scale events per ten-week term – clubnights we hear about were cheesy Club D, House Trained (yes, house), Cooker (funk), Dust (skar & funk), and they do a battle of the bands. Since Shed Seven played here a few years ago (at Derwent College), they are beginning to be taken more seriously by the promoters, and claim recent visits by Ash, Scratch Perverts, Artful Dodger and Manchiled.

The point about York is the interest and activity levels beyond mere ents. 'Students get involved,' said Helen Woolnough. 'The university has an excellent academic reputation, but its students don't work themselves into the ground twenty-four hours a day and they certainly don't take themselves too seriously.'

Student media include University Radio York (URY), launched by John Peel thirty years ago and now with fm licence, and York Student Television (YSTV), plus two fortnightly newspapers, *Nouse* (pronounced 'Nooze' after the River Ouse, which flows through York, and of course 'news', which is what it dispenses) and *York Vision*, and now a magazine called *Re:Fresh*. Other publications appear occasionally – *Point Shirley*, a literary arts magazine; *PS...*, an arts review; *Havoc*, a miscellany of creative writing; *Matrix*, a women's issue paper; *Christis*, a Christian magazine, and *Mad Alice*, an on-line features magazine.

At the *Independent* awards *York Vision* was acclaimed Best Small Budget publication, and the student website was a runner-up in the *Guardian* awards. There is a tradition of political activity and a left-wing slant. Campus-based issues and wider student issues find a place (tuition fees, differential rents, the venue issue, security provision on campus, etc), but national and international issues are also very much on the agenda.

Among some ninety societies this year there are eight active drama societies with three venues, the intimate **Drama Barn**, the large and versatile **Wentworth College Audio Visual Studio** and the aforementioned Central Hall, which is huge.

SPORT For such a small uni they do all right at sport – the teams came 65th nationwide in the BUSA leagues last year. The Boat Club went to Henley Royal Regatta, the Lacrosse team went to the world championships, basketball is a bit a speciality and they have the best parachutists in the country apparently. There are forty acres of playing fields – rugby, football, hockey, cricket – floodlit artificial hockey pitch, all-weather (three floodlit) tennis

AT A GLANCE	
ACADEMIC FILE:	
Subjects assessed	**23**
Excellent	**96%**
Average requirements	**300 points**
Students-staff ratio	**14:1**
First/2:1 degree pass rate	**63%**
ACCOMMODATION FILE:	
Guarantee to freshers	**100%**
Style	**Halls, flats, houses**
Catered	**Pay-as-you-eat**
En-suite	**36%**
Approx price range pw	**£48-£61**
City rent pw	**£50**

WHAT IT'S REALLY LIKE	
UNIVERSITY:	
Social Life	★★★★
Campus scene	**Bright, friendly, small and unpretentious**
Student Union services	**Good**
Politics	**Activity high Student issues**
Sport	**50 clubs**
National team position	**65th**
Sport facilities	**Good**
Arts opportunities	**Drama, film excellent; dance, music, art avg**
National drama awards	**Craft/Imagination**
Student newspapers	**Nouse, York Vision**
Independent awards	**Best small-budget newspaper**
Student radio station	**URY station**
Student TV	**YSTV**
Nightclub	**College-based only**
Bars	**1 in every college**
Union ents	**Club D, House Trained, Cooker, Dust**
Union clubs/societies	**140**
Most popular societies	**Media, Drama**
Smoking policy	**Bars, halls OK**
Parking	**Non-existent**
CITY:	
Entertainment	★★★
City scene	**Tourist haven**
Town/gown relations	**Good**
Risk of violence	**Low**
Cost of living	**Average**
Student concessions	**Good**
Survival + 2 nights out	**£50 pw**
Part-time work campus/town	**Excellent/good**

courts, squash courts, a sports centre for archery, badminton (seven courts), basketball, climbing, cricket (five nets), fencing, five-a-side soccer, judo, karate, netball, sauna, table-tennis, tennis, trampoline, volleyball, a 400-metre, seven-lane athletics track. Rowing and sailing are on the Ouse about a mile from the University, golf at Fulford Golf Club, swimming at the Barbican Centre half a mile from campus. Gliding, hang-gliding, riding and other facilities also found locally.

TOWN York itself is one of our most beautiful cathedral cities, a magnet for tourists from all over the world owing to the wealth of Viking and Roman remains, as well as its Medieval resonances in the Minster, in streets like the Shambles (where buildings lean inwards and over you as if out of a fairytale), in street names like Whip-Ma-Whop-Ma-Gate, and in the snickleways which offer those in the know an alternative way to scuttle about. Then there are the waters of the Ouse, lapping over green-field banks or warehouse walls, redolent of the city's merchant past.

It is, however, far from being the clubbing capital of the North. The four clubs are **Icon & Diva** out at Clifton Moor Estate (free bussing implicit) and, in the city, **The Gallery**, **Toff's** and **Ziggy's**. 'The names say it all,' remarks Gemma. In truth York is a pub city. 'From the relaxed atmosphere of the Deramore in Heslington,' notes the union's excellent *Alternative Prospectus* (phone for one), 'to the vibrancy of O'Neill's, ideal as a starting place for a night of fun and frolics in the clubs...' If you are a hardened clubber, take our advice, take a 20-minute ride to Leeds (see *Student Leeds* and uni entries).

For theatre, there's the **Arts Centre** and the **Theatre Royal** (a good rep company), and the

Grand Opera has a full programme of touring companies and performances, both theatre and music. There's a multi-screen **Warner's** cinema out at Clifton Moor Estate (on the north side of the city), **Odeon** and independent **City Screen** in York, as well as **York Student Cinema** on campus.

PILLOW TALK

All freshers are guaranteed a place in uni accommodation – halls, flats and houses. None is catered – all pay-as-you-eat. Around 36% are en suite. Cost per week ranges from £48 to £61, most are in the £51-£56 area.

JOBS

Students from a university with good teaching and a rich student culture appeal strongly to employers. York is no exception. As the *Employment* box shows, a large number go into Commerce – financial activities, accountancy and business management (they came 6th in our Employment Top 10s Finance and 10th for Accountancy). But York graduates appeal widely.

GETTING THERE

☞ By road: A1237 ring road; Heslington is on the southeast side, 10 miles from A1/M1; 20 from M62.

☞ By coach: London, 4:30; Edinburgh, 5:15.
☞ By rail: Leeds, 20 mins; Sheffield, 1:15; Manchester, 1:30; London King's Cross, 2:00.
☞ By air: Nearest airport is Leeds.

WHERE GRADUATES END UP	
14% Manufacturing,	Key Areas
13% Finance*,	
9% Public Admin,	
8% Education,	
8% Health/Social Work,	
8% Computer,	
7% Hotel/Retail	
Accountancy*,	Niche Areas
Business/Management,	
Chemical/Pharmaceutical*,	
Advertising, Defence,	
Aeronautical Manufacture,	
Electron/Electric*,	
Library/Archival,	
Market Research,	
Publishing	

*indicates Top 10 Graduate Provider

Approximate employed **93%**

YORK ST JOHN

College of York St John
Lord Mayor's Walk
York YO31 7EX

TEL 01904 716771
FAX 01904 712512
EMAIL admission@ucrysj.ac.uk
WEB www.ucrysj.ac.uk

VAG VIEW

The college dropped the word 'Ripon' from its title this year, and from the start of the current academic year, the York campus is its sole base. The college's strategy has been driven by self-preservation in these competitive times. They reckoned they were wasting 20% of their budget – £1 million – on duplicating campus facilities. They can no longer guarantee campus residence to freshers.

COLLEGE PROFILE	
Founded	**1841**
Status	**HE College**
Degree awarding university	**Leeds**
Situation/style	**City campus**
Student population	**4,910**
Full-time undergraduates	**3,100**
ACCOMMODATION:	
Guarantee to freshers	**No guarantee**
Style	**College**
Catered	**21%**
En-suite	**146**
Approx price range pw	**£50-£65**
City rent pw	**£50**

CAMPUS

The college is situated close to York Minster on a very attractive, quadrangle campus, and on one or two other sites in this ancient city.

STUDENT PROFILE

There is a preponderance of females and mature students body, and they do well recruiting through the state sector (95%) and from a wide socio-economic spectrum. With degrees in counselling, welfare is to the fore and the Education & Welfare Committee is one of the strongest in the union.

ACADEMIA

Founded by the Anglican Church in 1841 as a teacher training college, York St John also offer degrees in performing arts (music, dance, drama), film & TV, social and cultural studies and social sciences, languages, humanities (including Theology and History), and environmental sciences, health sciences (including Occupational Therapy, a professional qualification), Leisure & Tourism Management, and Physical Education – a Sport & Exercise Science degree is in its first year.

Between 50% and 70% of the Film, TV, Literature & Theatre Studies degree is in production activity, its success visible in our *Employment* box data. Resources include two theatre studios, two TV studios and eight editing

ACADEMIC EXCELLENCE

TEACHING:
(Rated Excellent or 17+ out of 24)

Occupational Therapy	**22**
Art, Design & Technology,	**21**
Business & Management,	
Theology, Sports	
Film, TV, Lit & Theatre Studies,	**20**
Media & Performance Studies,	
Psychology	
Linguistics	**19**

suites. There is a four-week placement in the second year, an internship with a professional company in the third (as well as pro-linking projects) and plenty of opportunity for study abroad.

'Some of the performing arts, some of the therapies, counselling, linguistics, I have heard some very good reports about,' said one school careers teacher. 'We had someone with straight A grades, could have gone anywhere, but chose Ripon.'

There's to be a new Learning Centre for books, journals, media materials, archives and IT, space for individual study, bookable group rooms for project work/meetings, IT teaching rooms and a lecture theatre. Access 24/7 to the computers is to be made secure by CCTV and swipe-card control. There'll be 500 computer network points, most equipped with PCs but with access points to enable connection via lap top to World Wide Web/college intranet. The School of Sport is also getting a new building, lecture space, performance and laboratory space. Both buildings will be complete by Autumn 2003.

SOCIAL SCENE

An ents committee devises a programme of club-nights, discos, live music, balls in summer and at Christmas. There are squash courts and a swimming pool on campus.

PILLOW TALK

For many years nearly all first years who wanted to live in college accommodation have been able to do so, but no longer, now that they have drawn their horns in and moved back to York. There is a new en-suite development a walk of seven minutes from the main campus, however – the twenty-five flats provide 146 en-suite single study bedrooms, each flat with a shared kitchen. If you're unable to secure uni accommodation, they promise to help you find an alternative in private sector lodgings/houses and flats in York.

JOBS

Figures on graduates in the year 2000 show that 77% are in employment 6 months after graduation, 14% have moved on to further study. Education is the strong bias (28%), but hard on its heels comes health & social work (21%), and there is a strong showing in the area of Archival/Cultural jobs (galleries, museum, libraries, etc.), and Radio/TV. They claim that every undergraduate programme has employment skills integrated into it.

WHERE GRADUATES END UP

28% Education,	Key Areas
21% Health/Social Work	
10% Wholesale/Retail,	
5% Hotel/Restaurant	
Artistic/Literary,	Niche Areas
Library/Archival, Radio/TV:	
Approximate employed	**96%**

GETTING THERE

☛ By road: A1.
☛ By coach: London, 4:30; Edinburgh, 5:15.
☛ By rail: Leeds, 30 mins; Sheffield: 1:15; Manchester 1:30; London King's Cross, 2:00; Birmingham New Street, 3:00.